Why Do You Need this New Edition?

Renzetti/Curran/Maier:
Women, Men and Society, 6/e
If you are looking for
10 good reasons....

1. Thoroughly updated to reflect the latest developments and research in the study of gender and gender inequality.

2. Discussion on how girls are now being favored over boys in elementary schools; backlash against female's success in education. Detailed discussion of sexual harassment in elementary and secondary schools, and the influence of race/ethnicity and social class on sexual harassment.

3. The controversy surrounding assisted reproductive technology due to birth of eight children by Nadya Suleman (Octomom).

4. Comparison of happiness of partnered gays and lesbians to legally married heterosexuals, cohabitating heterosexuals, and single gays.

5. Discussion of the effects of the recession on employment of both men and women; while the economic recession hurts both men and women, men have been becoming unemployed more quickly than women.

6. Lilly Ledbetter Fair Pay Act of 2009.

7. The problems of cyberbullying and the widespread availability of internet pornography.

8. Violence against women as human rights violations; rape in countries divided by civil war such as the Democratic Republic of Congo, Darfur, ad the Republic of Burundi in Eastern Africa.

9. New data on the significant increase in women office holders and cabinet appointments; discussion of the politics of gender in the 2008 presidential election.

10. Discussion of data showing disproportionately high rates of sexual harassment and sexual assault of female military personnel; discussion of the official response to the problem.

Avitar Books

Sixth Edition

Women, Men, and Society

Claire M. Renzetti
University of Kentucky

Daniel J. Curran
University of Dayton

Shana L. Maier
Widener University

Boston   Columbus   Indianapolis   New York   San Francisco   Upper Saddle River
Amsterdam   Cape Town   Dubai   London   Madrid   Milan   Munich   Paris   Montréal   Toronto
Delhi   Mexico City   São Paulo   Sydney   Hong Kong   Seoul   Singapore   Taipei   Tokyo

Editorial Director: Craig Campanella
Editor in Chief: Dickson Musslewhite
Executive Editor: Karen Hanson
Editorial Project Manager: Carly Czech
Director of Marketing: Brandy Dawson
Senior Marketing Manager: Kelly May
Marketing Assistant: Diana Griffin
Digital Media Editor: Tom Scalzo
Digital Media Project Manager: Nikhil Bramhavar
Editorial Production Service: PreMediaGlobal
Senior Manufacturing and Operations Manager for Arts & Sciences: Mary Fischer

Operations Specialist: Alan Fischer
Senior Managing Editor: Maureen Richardson
Senior Project Manager: Denise Forlow
Art Director: Anne Nieglos
Cover Designer: Pat Smythe
Cover Image: Laurin Rinder/Fotolia
Full-Service Project Management/Composition: Revathi Viswanathan/PreMediaGlobal, Inc.
Printer/Bindery and Cover Printer: RR Donnelley
Text Font: Garamond 10/12

Credits appear on page 560, which constitutes an extension of the copyright page.

Library of Congress Cataloging-in-Publication Data
Renzetti, Claire M.
  Women, men, and society / Claire M. Renzetti, Daniel J. Curran, Shana L. Maier. — 6th ed.
    p. cm.
  Includes bibliographical references and index.
  ISBN-13: 978-0-205-45959-9
  ISBN-10: 0-205-45959-5
  1. Sex role—United States. 2. Sexism—United States. 3. Women—Socialization—United States.
  4. Women—United States—Social conditions. I. Curran, Daniel J. II. —Maier, Shana L. III. Title.

HQ1075.5.U6R46 2012
305.3—dc23

2011043103

10 9 8 7 6 5 4 3 2

ISBN-10: 0-205-45959-5
ISBN-13: 978-0-205-45959-9

In memory of Joseph P. and Clara M. Renzetti, and Daniel J. Curran, Sr.
and with thanks to Nancy Curran, and Karl and
Mary Patricia Maier

CONTENTS

PREFACE

Although this is a coauthored book, I took it upon myself to write the preface because I have been the one who has fielded the most questions about this new edition over the past eight years. The most common question initially was, "When is the book coming out?" But as the date shifted repeatedly and time wore on, the most common question became, "What's happened to you?" I was told a few stories that people had heard about my whereabouts and state of mind; some were amusing, others alarming. Of course, my life is always far more interesting in rumor than in fact. I will not bore you with a detailed chronicle of my life over the past eight years. Suffice it to say that several factors, including the prolonged illness and death of my mother, a weekly commute between Philadelphia and Dayton for three years, and two significant job changes and moves, drew my time, energy, and attention away from many of my ongoing projects. I apologize that my excuses are so mundane. If you prefer to believe any of the more exciting stories you've heard, I don't mind as long as you share them with me so I can enjoy the vicarious thrill. On a serious note, though, I wish to thank the many students and colleagues who have contacted me not only with questions, but also with feedback on the fifth edition and suggestions for revision. My coauthors and I appreciate hearing from you, and we have tried to address your concerns and incorporate innovative ideas. We hope you will continue to stay in touch with us as you use this edition of the book. Please email me at: claire.renzetti@uky.edu; or Dan and Shana at: Daniel.Curran@notes.udayton.edu and slmaier@mail.widener.edu, respectively.

One important—and pleasant—outcome of the long revision process is the addition of a third author, Shana Maier. Shana was one of my students at St. Joseph's University and is now an outstanding sociologist who brought her knowledge of contemporary gender research and her strong organizational skills and efficiency to this book. I am delighted to call Shana my friend, my colleague, *and* my coauthor, and I am looking forward to working with her on future projects.

What else is new in this edition? We have updated all the statistics and as many of the citations as possible. Although this might be taken for granted in any new edition of a textbook, it has become somewhat more challenging with the voluminous amount of electronic resources currently available. We have done our best to check the reliability of our sources and to use empirically based research as much as possible, so that the statistics we provide and the studies we discuss are accurate and useful to readers. We have also added several new text boxes that cover such timely and important topics as cyberbullying, the risk of intimate partner violence for women with disabilities, pornography on the internet and gender differences in the consequences of heavy or binge drinking on college campuses.

Popular features from previous editions that continue to appear in this edition include the photos, the key terms, the annotated suggested readings at the end of each chapter, and the glossary at the end of the book. Our major goals are the same in this edition as they have been in every incarnation of *Women, Men, and Society*. Our first goal is to assist students in connecting a central element of their personal lives—their gendered experiences—with the social and political world in which they live. To do so, we present a broad, but thorough sampling of the wealth of recent scholarship on gender and gender-related issues. Most of this research is sociological, but we also draw on the work of biologists, anthropologists, psychologists, economists, historians, and others. We have been blessed over the years with a tremendous proliferation of feminist scholarship, but like many blessings, this one is also in some ways a curse in that it is incredibly difficult to keep abreast of it all. We apologize if we have overlooked any significant studies, and we encourage you to send us your research reports and articles so that we may cite your work in future editions.

Our second goal is intertwined with the first. Specifically, we seek to persuade students to look beyond the boundaries of their own lives so they can understand the complexity and diversity of gendered experiences in terms of race and ethnicity, cultural context, social class, sexual orientation, age, and physical ability/disability. Although our primary focus is a critical assessment of gender inequality, we emphasize in every chapter the interdependence of multiple inequalities. We want students to understand how the constraints imposed on women and men by specific social constructions of gender may be tightened when combined with a devalued racial/ethnic status, sexual orientation, age, economic status, or physical trait or challenge. Moreover, while the book is written from a feminist perspective, we expose students to the diversity that makes up contemporary feminism, turning the analytic lens so that they see an issue from various feminist *perspectives*.

Third, we hope to accomplish these first two goals by presenting the material in a way students find stimulating, clear, and highly readable. Together, we have brought to this edition more than twenty-five years of textbook writing experience, and more than fifty years of experience teaching the sociology of gender, women's studies, feminist theories, marriage and family, and similar courses. During our years in the classroom, we have observed that students who take such courses often come from diverse academic backgrounds. Although most are juniors or seniors, many have had only one or two introductory-level social science courses. With this in mind, we have incorporated into the text a number of useful pedagogical tools. We have already mentioned the captioned photos in each chapter. In addition, we continue to boldface key terms or concepts in the chapter narratives so students can study them in the context in which they were introduced. The key terms are also grouped at the end of each chapter, where they appear with a brief definition, and at the end of the book, where they are alphabetized and defined in a glossary. We have also noted that the list of suggested readings at the end of each chapter is annotated. An electronic instructor's manual and test bank are available as well. Supplements can be accessed at the following URL http://www.pearsonhighered.com

With every book we write, we add more threads to the web of personal and professional relationships that enrich our lives and work. Among them are those who reviewed all or part of the fifth edition and this manuscript; generously shared journals, books, and reports; and offered constructive criticism and insightful comments. I am also grateful to L. Sue Williams, Kansas State University; Jill Harrison, University of Rhode Island; Stephen B. Groce, Western Kentucky University; Phyllis L. Baker, University of Northern Iowa; Margaret H. Williamson, University of Georgia; Jeanie Akamanti, Southern Illinois University; Lynn Smith-Lovin, Duke University. I also wish to express my appreciation to Carol Jordan, director of the Center for Research on Violence Against Women; Patrick Mooney, chair of the sociology department; and all of my colleagues in the CRVAW and the sociology department at the University of Kentucky. Thank you for making me feel so warmly welcomed and for providing me with a supportive environment in which to get my work done. A special word of thanks, too, to Raquel Bergen, St. Joseph's University, with whom I have worked on many projects, but also with whom I have shared many laughs, even during some very unfunny times. I cherish our friendship. Shana would also like to thank her colleagues at Widener University for their support, especially William E. Harver, Nancy Blank, Lauren Shermer, Dean Matthew Poslusny, Associate Dean James Vike, Mrs. Susan Murray, and Mrs. Linda Hoffecker.

We extend our sincere thanks as well to Amy Batchman, my editorial assistant for the journal, *Violence Against Women*. During the last few months of the revision process, we asked Amy to assist us with her top-notch editing skills. She did so with her usual good humor and efficiency, all the more extraordinary given that at the same time she was getting her organic farm, Radical Roots, up and running (check it out at http://www. localharvest.org/radical-roots-M42035). It is also noteworthy, especially given that this is a book on gender, that only 14 percent of principal operators of farms in the United States are women. At one point I asked Amy if I could have her cloned, to which she replied that many folks would probably look unfavorably on an organic farmer participating in cloning.

Karen Hanson, our editor at Pearson, is also an extraordinary individual in so many ways, but especially in her knowledge of the field and the market; in her patience with us, and me, in particular; and in her loyalty and friendship. Thank you, Karen, for never giving up on the book or on me. How is it possible that we have worked together for more than twenty-five years and, amazingly, we still look the same—at least I think we do and I will not entertain any dissenting opinions on that issue. Thank you, too, to Revathi Viswanathan, who shepherded the book through production. She remained poised and cheerful despite the pressure of a very tight schedule. It has been delightful to work with her.

The three of us are fortunate to have some very special people in our lives who share in our ups and downs throughout the course of a project and who sustain us with laughter, encouragement, and unconditional love. Shana, as the newest member of this writing team, gets to go first with these acknowledgments:

I (Shana) wish to thank my parents, Karl and Mary Patricia Maier, for their love and guidance. Without their sacrifices over the years, I would not be where I am today. I also thank the Winnington family for their encouragement and love. A very special acknowledgment is due to my son and angel, Gabriel Albert Maier Winnington. His hugs and laughter brighten my days and I am so very proud to be his mom. Last, but certainly not least, I thank my husband, Paul F. Winnington III, for his unwavering love, patience, and encouragement. I am extremely blessed to share my life with him.

We (Claire and Dan) thank our sons, Sean and Aidan, who never fail to remind us what our priorities are—or should be. When we wrote the first edition of this book, Sean was a year old and Aidan had not yet been born. Now in their twenties, the boys have grown into thoughtful, insightful young men who often challenge us to defend our positions on various issues, but still make us laugh and, every single day, make us proud.

NEW TO THIS EDITION

- The sixth edition is thoroughly revised and updated with the latest cutting-edge research in gender studies. New data are provided in all tables and graphs and within the chapter narratives as well.

- New research is discussed on such topics as gender crossing and multiple genders, gender differences in online communication, gender messages in children's cartoons, gay and lesbian evangelical Christians, and occupational sex segregation.
- Issues of global importance are discussed, including gender and education in developing countries, the sex imbalance in the populations of some developing countries, the gendered division of labor in the global marketplace, rape as weapon of war, and violence against women as human rights violations.
- Continuing the long-standing focus of looking at men's issues as well as women's issues, the authors discuss such topics as fathers' rights groups, the effects of the recession on employment of both men and women, the objectification of men and women in advertising, and the impact of adherence to traditional masculinity on men's health.
- High-interest, timely topics are covered, including same-sex marriage and civil unions, cyberbullying, the proliferation of internet pornography, the gendered impact of binge drinking on college campuses, and the significant increase in women office holders and cabinet appointments, as well as a discussion of the politics of gender in the 2008 presidential election.
- Continuing emphasis on intersecting inequalities, illustrating through a discussion of such issues as intimate partner violence against women with disabilities, and the repeal of "Don't Ask, Don't Tell," how gender intersects with other social locating variables including physical ability/disability and sexual orientation, as well as race and ethnicity, social class, and age to disadvantage – or privilege – particular groups of women and men.

Chapter 1

Studying Gender

An Overview

We describe ourselves in many different ways. One of the most fundamental ways is to say, "I am a man" or "I am a woman"—that is, to describe ourselves in terms of our sex. However, the information conveyed by these simple phrases goes beyond mere anatomical description. It also conjures up a configuration of personality traits and behavior patterns. Without ever having seen you, others are likely to draw conclusions about you—about the clothes you wear, the way you express yourself, and the various activities you pursue.

If you are a woman, for example, people would not be surprised to see you wearing slacks, but they might expect, and even be pleased, to see you in a dress. Most also expect you to be rather emotional and given to crying easily. They will think of you as nurturing; preoccupied with romance, personal relationships, and your appearance; and inept with things mechanical.

If you are a man, though, people will expect to see you wearing slacks, and they would be shocked, maybe even frightened, to see you in a dress. Most also expect you to be assertive and always in control of your emotions. They will think of you as ambitious and competitive; preoccupied with your studies, work, or sports; and mechanically inclined.

In other words, a biological given, **sex** (i.e., maleness or femaleness) is used as the basis for constructing a social category that we call **gender** (i.e., masculinity or femininity). It may be that few of the socially defined characteristics of your gender describe you accurately, but this is perhaps less important than the fact that people believe these assumptions to be true or appropriate and that they act on their beliefs, treating women and men differently, even as opposites. Many people use gender stereotypes to guide their interactions with others. A *stereotype* is an oversimplified summary description of a group of people. There are positive and negative stereotypes, and virtually every group in our society has been stereotyped at one time or another; women and men are not exceptions. **Gender stereotypes**, then, are simplistic descriptions of the supposedly "masculine male" or "feminine female." Most people conceive of these stereotypes in bipolar terms; that is, a normal male supposedly lacks any feminine traits, and a normal female lacks masculine traits (Deaux & Kite, 1987; Ridgeway & Correll, 2004; Risman, 2004). Thus, gender stereotypes are all-inclusive; every member of each sex is thought to share the characteristics that constitute their respective gender stereotypes. The reality, as we will learn throughout this book, is that many members of each sex do not conform to their stereotyped images. Sometimes this may be looked upon favorably by others, but often the nonconformist is labeled deviant, abnormal, or bad and is treated as such (Lucal, 1999).

Significantly, this kind of differentiation occurs not only on an interpersonal level between individuals, shaping women's and men's personalities, but also on a cultural level as people interact with one another in everyday life and, on an institutional level, where the distribution of a society's resources and rewards takes place. Every society prescribes traits, behaviors, and patterns of social interaction for its members on the basis of sex. Further, these prescriptions are embedded in the institutions of the society—in the workplace, government, education, religions, family forms, and so on. Taken together, these three interrelated levels form a society's **gender structure**. As Risman (2004, p. 433) explains, "The gender structure differentiates opportunities and constraints based on sex category and thus has consequences on three dimensions: (1) At the individual level, for the development of gendered selves; (2) during interaction as men and women face different cultural expectations when they fill identical structural positions; and (3) in institutional domains where explicit regulations regarding resource distribution and material goods are gender specific." Of special concern to us throughout this book will be the ways in which the gender structure functions as a system of *social stratification;* that is, the extent to which women and men, and the traits and behaviors respectively associated with them, are valued unequally in society.

Given that social institutions are imbued with the power to reward and punish—to bestow privileges as well as to impose obligations and restrictions—the gender structure has a profound impact on the lives and life chances of women and men. Consider, for example, that in most industrialized countries throughout the world, during the last two decades, women have entered the paid labor force in dramatic numbers, yet across countries, economic sectors, occupations, and educational levels, women's wages are significantly lower than men's wages, and women continue to shoulder primary responsibility for traditional household chores (United Nations, 2000). These startling observations reflect the fact that most women and men worldwide live in societies with patriarchal gender structures. A **patriarchy** is a type of gender structure in which men dominate women, and what is considered masculine is more highly valued than what is considered feminine. This example also shows that while changes on the individual level are important, they are not sufficient to produce gender equality; the cultural level (e.g., beliefs about "appropriate" work for women and men) and the institutional level (e.g., workplaces that are not family-friendly) matter just as much. However, as we will learn in this text, patriarchy is by no means universal. Thus, one of our tasks here will be to examine alternative, more egalitarian gender structures. We will also find that patriarchy does not benefit all groups of men equally, just as it disadvantages some groups of women more than others. We will also see that changes at the individual level *can* produce changes at the cultural and structural levels and vice versa. "That is, social structure shapes individuals, but simultaneously, individuals shape the social structure....We must pay attention both to how structure shapes individual choice and social interaction and how human agency creates, sustains, and modifies current structure" (Risman, 2004, p. 433).

Before we undertake our analysis of gender and gender structures, though, we should realize that not all sociologists agree on how to study gender or on what aspects of structures are most important to study. Why the disagreement? To understand it better, let's look at some of the research on gender and the various theoretical perspectives that have informed it.

SOCIOLOGICAL PERSPECTIVES ON GENDER

Broadly defined, **sociology** is the scientific study of human societies and cultures and of social behavior. Not all sociologists undertake this work in the same way, however. Rather, a single social phenomenon—gender, for instance—may be researched and explained differently by different sociologists. This may be a bit puzzling, since it is commonly assumed that all sociologists by virtue of being sociologists share the same perspective. Certainly, the traditional image of science itself is one of a cumulative enterprise. That is, each scientist, whatever his or her specific field, supposedly works to solve the problems that the members of the discipline have agreed are most important. Each scientist's work progressively builds on that of others until the answer or truth is attained. The fact of the matter is, though, that scientists, including sociologists, conduct their research within the framework of a particular *paradigm*.

What is a paradigm? A **paradigm** is a school of thought that guides the scientist in choosing the problems to be studied, in selecting the methods for studying them, and in explaining what is found. This implies that research carried out within a specific framework is, to some degree, predetermined. The paradigm, in focusing researchers' attention on certain issues, simultaneously blinds them to the significance of other issues and also colors their view of the social world. This is not to say that there is no objective social reality or that sociology is simply what our favorite paradigm tells us it is. Instead, we can see that sociological research, like all scientific research, is subjective as well as objective. This is an important point, and we will return to it shortly.

Sociology is a multiple-paradigm science; that is, it is made up of a number of different—and some would say, competing—paradigms (Ritzer, 1980). This observation solves our earlier puzzle of how a single social phenomenon can be researched and explained differently by different sociologists. At any given time, however, one paradigm tends to dominate the discipline. This does not mean that other paradigms are ignored, but rather that one paradigm seems to better explain current social conditions. Consequently, the majority of sociologists at that time will carry out their work within the framework of the dominant paradigm.

From the 1940s through the 1960s, the dominant paradigm in sociology was structural functionalism. The structural functionalist perspective was particularly influential in the study of gender, so it is important for us to examine it carefully.

Structural Functionalism

The **structural functionalist paradigm** depicts society as a stable, orderly system in which the majority of members share a common set of values, beliefs, and behavioral expectations that may be referred to collectively as *societal consensus*. The social system itself is composed of interrelated parts that operate together to keep the society balanced or, as a functionalist would say, in equilibrium. Each element of the society functions in some way to maintain social order. Change, then, must come about slowly, in an evolutionary way; rapid social change in any element would likely be disruptive and, therefore, dysfunctional for the system as a whole.

In their analysis of gender, structural functionalists begin with the observation that women and men are physically different. Of special significance are the facts that men tend to be bigger and stronger than women and that women bear and nurse children. According to functionalists, these biological differences have led to the emergence of different *gender roles*. More specifically, a social role, not unlike a theatrical role, includes a set of behavioral requirements expected of the person occupying the role. The concept of **gender roles** refers to the behaviors that are prescribed for a society's members, depending on their sex.

Functionalists maintain that for much of human history, women's reproductive role dictated that their gender role be a domestic one. Given that women bear and nurse children, it makes sense for them to remain at home to rear them. It then follows that if women are at home caring for children, they will assume other domestic duties as well.

In contrast, men's biology better suits them for the roles of economic provider and protector of the family. As one prominent functionalist theorist put it:

> In our opinion the fundamental explanation for the allocation of the roles between the biological sexes lies in the fact that the bearing and early nursing of children establishes a strong and presumptive primacy of the relation of mother to the small child and this in turn establishes a presumption that the man who is exempted from these biological functions should specialize in the alternative [occupational] direction. (Parsons, 1955, p. 23)

Structural functionalists point out that the work women do in the home is functional. In many ways, women reproduce society: by giving birth to new members, by teaching or socializing them to accept the culture's agreed-upon values and norms, and by providing men and children with affection and physical sustenance. However, some functionalists also devalued traditional women's work, referring to it as a "duty" and designating men as the instrumental leaders of their families.

EVALUATING STRUCTURAL FUNCTIONALISM   Let's evaluate the central themes of the structural functionalist perspective of gender. First, functionalists see gender differences as *natural* phenomena deriving from human biology. Portraying masculinity and femininity as natural, however, confuses gender with sex and suggests immutability. The implicit message is that efforts to change our definitions of masculinity and femininity will have little, if any, effect on human behavior. Women and men cannot help that they think and act the way they do; it's in their nature. Moreover, men and women are opposites, and efforts to alter this natural dichotomy will likely do more harm than good. Yet, the fact is that gender is quite amenable to change; what constitutes masculinity and femininity varies tremendously throughout history and across societies and cultures, among groups within a single society, and across varying social contexts. That is because gender as we defined it at the outset is a social creation, not a biological given. Even if biological factors play some part in producing gender differences, available evidence shows that biologically determined traits can be modified or completely overridden by environmental influences. We will discuss this point further throughout the text, but it is the primary focus of Chapters 2 and 3.

Another serious consequence of depicting gender differences as natural the way functionalists do is that such a position traditionally has been used to justify inequality and discrimination on the basis of sex. History offers abundant examples. In the fifth century B.C.E., for instance, the Chinese philosopher Confucius declared that while women are human beings, they are of a lower state than men (Peck, 1985). In 1873, Myra Bradwell was denied admission to the Illinois bar and the right to practice law on the ground that "the natural and proper timidity and delicacy which belong to the female sex evidently unfits it for many of the occupations of civil life" (quoted in Goldstein, 1979, p. 50). More recently, Dr. Lawrence Summers, while president of Harvard University, in an address on the progress of women in academia, stated that bias was only part of the reason for the small number of women in the sciences and engineering. According to Dr. Summers, a second reason is that women lack the high aptitude necessary to succeed in these fields (Healy & Rimer, 2005; see also Chapters 2 and 5.

It may well be the case that biological factors are responsible for many of the personality and behavior differences that we may observe between women and men. However, that does not mean that one sex or gender is better than the other or that members of one sex deserve a disproportionate share of society's resources and rewards because of their sex. In Chapter 2, we will more thoroughly evaluate claims regarding biologically based differences between the sexes; however, the problems of gender inequality and discrimination will occupy us throughout the text.

This brings us to another major theme in the structural functionalist perspective: the conception of gender in terms of roles. Although this position recognizes the importance of social learning in the development of gender, it also presents several problems. Stacey and Thorne (1985, p. 307) succinctly summarize them:

> The notion of "role" focuses attention more on individuals than on social structure, and implies that "the female role" and "the male role" are complementary (i.e., separate or different, but equal). The terms are depoliticizing; they strip experience from its historical and political context and neglect questions of power and conflict. It is significant that sociologists do not speak of "class roles" or "race roles."

A key concept in this critique is power. **Power** is the ability to impose one's will on others. The most powerful members of a society are usually those who control the largest share of societal resources, such as money, property, and the means of physical force. In hierarchically structured societies such as our own, these resources may be distributed unequally on the basis of characteristics over which individuals have no control, such as race and ethnicity, age, and *sex*. In overlooking the issue of power relations, then, the structural functionalist perspective neglects significant dimensions of gender: the structural causes of gender-based inequality and the consequences this inequality has for women and men in society.

This point of view also has serious implications with regard to social change. If we put too much emphasis on the process of individual learning, we may be tempted to assume that the solution to gender inequality lies simply in teaching people new social roles. Although much has been accomplished by individuals learning to reject the social constructions of gender that they find oppressive, we will see in the chapters that follow that far-reaching and effective social change requires a fundamental restructuring of society's basic institutions. A major weakness in the structural functionalist analysis of gender is its defense of the status quo.

A Paradigm Revolution

We noted earlier that structural functionalism was the dominant paradigm in sociology from the 1940s through most of the 1960s. Like most dominant paradigms, however, structural functionalism began to wear out; that is, it could no longer adequately explain social conditions or problems without being revised in some fundamental way (Harding, 1979). When this occurs, a *paradigm revolution* is likely. This means that members of a scientific discipline reject the dominant paradigm in favor of a competing paradigm that is better able to explain prevailing conditions (Kuhn, 1970). What prompted a paradigm revolution in sociology during the 1960s?

The popularity of structural functionalism during the years following World War II is understandable, given the conservative political climate of the time. The decade of the 1960s, however, was a period of widespread social protest and activism. Although opposition to the Vietnam War is usually viewed as the focal point of this unrest, other social problems mobilized various groups of people for collective action. At the heart of their concern was the widespread inequality that characterized American society. Some sociologists, for instance, documented the existence of pockets of poverty and malnutrition in the United States, a finding that showed that American affluence was not as widely shared as many people believed (Harrington, 1962). The African American civil rights movement vividly brought to the public's attention the fact that an entire segment of the U.S. population was systematically denied both full participation in society and equal access to society's resources and rewards simply on the basis of their race. And, as we will see shortly, the women's liberation movement, which also emerged at this time, raised public awareness of discrimination on the basis of sex.

Sociologists began to question the accuracy of depicting society as an orderly, harmonious social system. Many also rejected the notion of societal consensus and focused instead on how dominant ideologies developed out of the struggles between the haves and have-nots in a society. At the center of their analysis was the issue of power relations.

A number of different paradigms emerged out of the turmoil. Particularly important to the sociological study of gender was the development of the feminist paradigm. Although it has been argued that feminism has had less revolutionary effects on sociology than on other disciplines, its impact nonetheless has been far-reaching (Abbott, 1991; Acker, 2006; Baca Zinn, 1992; Chafetz, 1988; Kramarae & Spender, 1992; Lorber, 2006; Stacey & Thorne, 1985; Stanley, 1992). Today, there are more sociologists researching and teaching about gender than any other specialized area of the discipline, and the Sex and Gender section of the American Sociological Association has more members than any other section (Risman, 2003; see also Wharton, 2006).

A FEMINIST SOCIOLOGY OF GENDER

Table 1.1 summarizes the basic differences between the feminist paradigm and the structural functionalist paradigm, but we must begin this discussion with a caveat: Feminism is not a single, unified perspective. Rather, as Delmar (1986, p. 9) points out, it is more accurate to think in terms of a "plurality of feminisms." The diversity within feminism is a benchmark of the extent to which it has developed and matured. But before we discuss some of the diverse perspectives that make up feminist sociology, let's consider some principles that virtually all feminist-identified perspectives share.

The **feminist paradigm** acknowledges the importance of both nature and learning in the acquisition of gender. However, feminist sociologists stress that it is virtually impossible to separate out the precise influences of biology because, as we will see in Chapter 4, the learning process begins immediately after birth. The complex interrelation between biological and cultural factors is also emphasized. Our genes, they tell us, "do not make specific bits and pieces of a body; they code for a range of forms under an array of environmental conditions. Moreover, even when a trait has been built and set, environmental intervention may still modify [it]" (Gould, 1981, p. 156).

The feminist perspective, therefore, begins with the assumption that gender is essentially socially created, rather than innately determined. Feminists view gender, in part, as a set of social expectations that is reproduced and transmitted through a process of social learning. In this way, the expectations become fundamental components of our personalities. But feminists also recognize that a complete understanding of

TABLE 1.1	**Sociological Perspectives on Gender**	
Perspective	**Basic Assumptions and Central Principles**	**Key Concepts**
Structural Functionalism	Society is a stable, orderly system in which the majority of members share a common set of values, beliefs, and behavioral expectations (societal consensus).	Gender roles
	The social system is composed of interrelated parts that operate together to keep the society in equilibrium. Each element of the society functions in some way to maintain social order, so change must come about through a slow, evolutionary process.	
	Women and men are biologically different, and these biological differences, especially reproductive differences, have led to the emergence of different gender roles. These gender roles emerged early in human history and were institutionalized because they were adaptive and assisted in the survival of the species.	
	Women's and men's roles are opposite, but complementary. Because they are products of nature, social efforts to change them will be futile at best, but could also be harmful for society as a whole.	
Feminist Sociology	Gender is socially created, rather than innately determined. It is generated within the context of a particular social and economic structure and is reproduced and transmitted through a process of social learning.	Sexism, gender structure, patriarchy, sexual politics
	Gender is a central organizing factor in the social world and so must be included as a fundamental category of analysis in sociological research. Researchers should take an empathic stance toward their research and acknowledge their personal biases, but maintain scientific standards in their research.	
	The consequences of gender inequality are not identical for all groups of women and men. Therefore, research must analyze the interrelationships among multiple oppressions, including sexism, racism, classism, ageism, heterosexism, and ableism.	
	A major goal of sociological work should be the development of effective means to eradicate gender inequality and to change those aspects of our social constructions of gender that are harmful or destructive.	

gender requires more than an analysis of this learning process. They point out, in fact, that what we learn is itself a social product that is generated within the context of a particular political and economic structure. Consequently, feminist sociologists seek to answer research questions that set them apart from structural functionalists and other nonfeminist sociologists.

Feminists take issue with the inherent sex bias or sexism in traditional sociological research. **Sexism** is the differential valuing of one sex, in this case, men, over the other. Historically, sexism in sociology was in part the result of the relatively low numbers of women faculty and students at academic and research institutions. However, it also reflects a broader societal prejudice against women, which is embodied in the assumption that what women do, think, or say is unimportant or uninteresting (Lorber, 1993).

The influence of these factors on sociological research has been threefold:

1. Most sociological studies were conducted by men, using male subjects, although findings were generalized to all people.
2. Gender was considered an important category of analysis only in a limited number of sociological subfields, such as marriage and family, whereas in all others (e.g., sociology of work, complex organizations, or sociology of law), it was ignored.
3. When women were studied, their behavior and attitudes were analyzed in terms of a male standard of normalcy or rightness.

A few examples should make these points clearer.

Consider, for instance, the classic research in the subfield of urban sociology. In her review of this literature, Lyn Lofland (1975, p. 145) found that women were "part of the locale or neighborhood or area—described like other important aspects of the setting such as income, ecology, or demography—but are largely irrelevant to the analytic action." Thus, although urban sociologists claimed to be studying community, their focus was limited to empirical settings in which men were likely to be present (e.g., urban street corners or neighborhood taverns). They completely overlooked the areas of urban life where women were likely to be found (e.g., in playgrounds with their children or at grocery stores), although few of us would deny that these locales are also central components of human communities.[1]

Sociologist Dale Spender (1981) provided another example. Studies of sex and language have shown differences in women's and men's speech. Spender found in her review of this research that many studies were designed to discover deficiencies in women's speech. The underlying assumption of the research was that there must be something wrong with women's speech if it is different from men's speech. In other words, men's speech has been considered normative, so speech that is different has been assumed to be deficient (see Chapter 6).

In short, feminist sociologists have shown that "most of what we have formerly known as the study of society is only the male study of male society" (Millman & Kanter, 1975, p. viii). Feminists, in contrast, include gender as a fundamental category of analysis in their research and teaching because they view the understanding of gender relations as central to understanding other social relations. Gender, they maintain, is embedded in all social interactions and processes of everyday life as well as all social institutions (Lorber, 1994, 2005a). Unfortunately, as some observers point out, it is still "very difficult, if not impossible, to get mainstream sociology to use the concept of gender as a building block and organizational principle of social orders and social institutions, let alone gender as a social institution itself" (Lorber, 2006, p. 449). Consequently, while there are many more course offerings on gender in sociology departments, there has been little, if any, integration of gender or the examination of gendered processes "in courses such as those on the environment or on globalization" and many sociology textbooks reflect this lack of integration as well (Acker, 2006).

Nevertheless, for feminist sociologists, the recognition of gender as a central organizing factor of social life and social structure has important implications for the research process and its outcomes. For one thing, it means that although feminist researchers strive to uncover similarities and differences in women's and men's behaviors, attitudes, and experiences, they do not do this so they can estimate the value of one relative to the other. Rather, their goal is to develop a *holistic* view of how women and men, because of their different locations in the social structure, encounter differential opportunities and constraints, and resist or respond to their relative circumstances (Hess & Ferree, 1987; Offen, 1988).

We are speaking here of the differential consequences of particular social arrangements on the lives of women and men and of women and men as agents of social change. We will return to each of these issues momentarily. Notice first, however, that feminists do not exclude male experiences and perspectives from their research, but they do insist on the inclusion of female experiences and perspectives. Feminists

deliberately seek to make women's voices heard in sociological research, where previously they have been silenced or ignored. To do this, feminists reject the traditional model of science "as establishing mastery over subjects, as demanding the absence of feeling, and as enforcing separateness of the knower from the known, all under the guise of 'objectivity'" (Hess & Ferree, 1987, p. 13; see also Naples, 2003; Reinharz, 1992). Feminist researchers instead take an *empathic stance* toward their research subjects. Feminist researchers frequently use more inclusive research methods that allow subjects to express their feelings and to speak for themselves, rather than imposing the researchers' own ideas or categories of response on their respondents.

Feminist researchers are committed to including women in their studies, so they often go to locales where women are likely to gather, such as parks and playgrounds.

The experiential emphasis in feminist research has frequently drawn charges of bias from more traditional sociologists. However, feminists do not deny the partiality of their work; on the contrary, they acknowledge that it is intentional. Feminists recognize that sociological research is *dualistic:* It has both subjective and objective dimensions. On the one hand, no research is completely unbiased or value-free. No matter how objective sociologists may like to think they are, they cannot help but be influenced by values, personal preferences, life experiences, and aspects of the cultural setting in which they live. On the other hand, this does not mean that research is completely subjective either. While a researcher may be influenced by *values* (i.e., judgments or appraisals), her or his goal is the collection of *facts* (i.e., phenomena that can be observed or empirically verified). Feminists call for open acknowledgment by researchers of their assumptions, beliefs, sympathies, and biases. They question not only the possibility, but also the desirability, of a value-free sociology. While they reject the notion of value-free science, however, feminists do not reject "scientific standards" in their research (Reinharz, 1992).

The dualistic nature of sociological research makes it especially challenging, particularly for those of us interested in the study of gender. This is because of our intimate tie to what we are studying—after all, each of us is gendered. But this duality also makes gender research very promising. Just as our values affect what we choose to study and how we choose to study it, they can also guide us in deciding how the facts we gather can be put to practical use. As we will show shortly, the scientific knowledge that feminist sociologists acquire through the research process empowers many of us to act to change behaviors and conditions that are harmful or oppressive.

Let's return for a moment to the issue of consequences. Feminist sociologists are fundamentally concerned with the question of how specific social constructions of gender impinge on the lives of women and men. The feminist research we will review in this text documents the serious and far-reaching effects of sexism in our society and in others. Chapters 7 and 8, for example, discuss how sexist beliefs that devalue women's labor have served as justifications for paying women less than men and often as excuses for not paying them at all. This, in turn, is one of the major reasons women outnumber men among the ranks of the world's poor. Similarly, Chapter 12 shows that the notion that men should be stoic and unemotional has had profound consequences for their physical and mental health.

This latter example highlights an important point that was raised earlier but is worth repeating here. Specifically, although many people tend to think of feminism as applicable only to so-called "women's issues," feminists themselves see their paradigm as relevant to the experiences of women *and* men. Certainly, feminists' primary concern has been to study the position of women in society, largely because, as we have already noted, women and women's experiences have long been devalued or ignored in scientific research. Nevertheless, feminists have not left the social construction of masculinity unanalyzed. In studying men's lives, in fact, feminist researchers have found that, although virtually all men benefit from institutionalized patriarchal privilege, not all men actually have power in our society. As Bem (1993, p. 3) points out, "the term *male power* should thus be construed narrowly as the power historically held by rich, White, heterosexual men, for it is they who originally set up and now primarily sustain the cultural discourses and social institutions of this nation. It is thus not women alone who are disadvantaged by the organization of U.S. society but poor people, people of color, and sexual minorities as well" (see also Connell, 1995).

Feminists, therefore, also recognize that the consequences of sexism are not identical for all groups of women and men. Instead, the effects of gender inequality are made worse by other types of discrimination. Consider, for example, the likely dissimilarities in the lives of a White, middle-class, middle-aged, gay man and a poor, Latina teenager who is pregnant and unmarried. Both may think of themselves as oppressed, but their objective circumstances are very different. Feminist research, therefore, attempts to account for the gender-based experiences of many diverse groups of women and men in our society. It analyzes the inextricable links among *multiple* oppressions: sexism, racism, classism, ageism, heterosexism, and ableism (Calhoun, 2000; Crenshaw, 1994; King, 1988). An examination of these complex *intersecting inequalities*, or what others refer to as *multiple axes of oppression* (Risman, 2004), is a central theme of this text.

Finally, just as other sociological models, such as structural functionalism, have implications for social change, so does the feminist paradigm. Feminist sociologists, in fact, are advocates of social change. They seek to develop effective means to eradicate gender inequality and to change those aspects of our social constructions of gender and the gender structure that are harmful or destructive.

An important first step in this process is for people to develop a *group consciousness;* that is, they must begin to see that their problems are not personal ones, but rather are shared by others like them. Until a group consciousness develops, change is likely to be limited to the individual level. As one observer explained, "People tend to think that personal problems can be solved simply by working harder. Personal problems become political demands only when the inability to survive, or to attain a decent life, is seen as a consequence of social institutions and social inequality rather than personal failure, and the system is blamed" (Klein, 1984, p. 3). Once a group consciousness emerges and institutional arrangements are identified as the source of the problem, collective action can be taken to bring about structural

Feminists have drawn public attention to many social problems, including sexual violence against women.

change. A **social movement**—a group that has organized to promote a particular cause through collective action—may develop. Movement members take a stand for or against something and work together to get their position integrated into official public policy.

Feminist research serves to raise our consciousness about gender inequality, and it has spurred many people to work together for social change. This collective effort is usually referred to as the **feminist movement** or the **women's movement**. Throughout this text, we will examine the extent to which feminists have been successful in their efforts to reconstruct gender, to make gender relations more equitable, and to reconfigure the gender structure to make it more egalitarian. Now, though, let's return to the issue of diversity in feminism. Although feminists share similar views with regard to the themes we have discussed so far, they also comprise heterogeneous factions with different interests and perspectives. This diversity has given rise to different tactics or strategies within feminism to achieve various objectives. However, before we discuss contemporary feminist theories and movement strategies, we will first put feminism in historical perspective.

FEMINISM IN HISTORICAL PERSPECTIVE

The First Wave of Feminism

Most of us have grown up uneducated about women's history. If, in fact, we rely only on the information in standard history texts, we are left with the impression that the sole preoccupation and accomplishment of nineteenth- and early twentieth-century women was winning the right to vote. Not surprisingly, then, to some people, the word *feminist* is synonymous with *suffragist* when discussed in the context of the nineteenth century. However, feminist historians who have studied the *woman movement,* as it was called back then, emphasize that the singular focus on suffrage emerged only after a decades-long campaign that addressed numerous dimensions of gender inequality. Even then, many feminists objected to making suffrage the primary goal of the movement and continued to draw attention to other aspects of women's oppression (Cott, 1987; Delmar, 1986; Goldsmith, 1998). Early feminism, like contemporary feminism, was far more diverse than has been depicted in traditional historical accounts (see Box 1.1).

Historians have also discovered that feminist ideas predate the period that is typically identified as the "first wave" of feminism, from 1830 to 1920. For example, historian Marlene LeGates (2001) divides the history of feminism into three stages, the first of which she identifies as early Christianity and the Middle Ages and the second as the periods encompassing the Renaissance and the Reformation. During these two stages, LeGates argues, feminism primarily took the form of individual women rebelling against sexist gender norms. It is only in the third stage, during the eighteenth century, that a collective feminist *movement* developed. Similarly, historian Gerda Lerner (1993) analyzed historical documents dating back to the Middle Ages and discovered a tradition of women's protest against patriarchal oppression, although it is fragmentary largely because, as she points out, women's actions and writings were not systematically included in the historical record. Indeed, women were systematically *excluded* from history-making because men have had the power to define what is history and what is important. Consequently, most women who resisted gender inequality were unaware of similar efforts by other women who came before them. This, in turn, inhibited the development of a *feminist consciousness:* a recognition by women that they are treated unequally as a group and that their subordination is socially created and maintained by a system that can be replaced, through collective action, with a more equitable social structure. Thus, although examples of feminist resistance can be found throughout history, a feminist social movement did not emerge until near the turn of the nineteenth century (see also Norton, 1997).

During the late 1700s, a number of women began publicly calling for equal rights with men, especially equal educational opportunities. These women, such as Judith Sargent Murray and Mary Wollstonecraft, were from the middle and upper classes. The men of their social station were espousing a political philosophy of individualism and democracy, asserting that "all human beings had equal rights by nature ... and that everyone

BOX 1.1
Early Feminists

Although the first wave of feminism in the United States is often depicted as a single-minded social movement aimed at securing suffrage for women, the activities of nineteenth- and early twentieth-century feminists in this country demonstrate otherwise. They were involved in a wide range of political and social reforms, including public health and hygiene, "moral uplift," abolition, and public education. We offer a small sampling of brief biographies of some of these women to illustrate the diversity in their backgrounds, ideas, and goals.

- **Elizabeth Blackwell** (1821–1910) The first female physician in the United States, Blackwell rejected marriage in favor of a career in medicine. She was a practicing physician, though, for only a short time before she moved into hospital administration and from there into public health. She was instrumental in the enactment and implementation of a number of public sanitation reforms that substantially improved the health and living conditions of the poor, the working class, racial and ethnic minorities, and immigrants.

- **Charlotte Perkins Gilman** (1860–1935) As a professional writer, social critic, journalist, and public speaker, Gilman was one of the intellectual leaders of the first wave of feminism in the United States. She wrote and lectured on such topics as sex differences, social evolution, women and work, and child development. Although she preferred to be called a "sociologist" and not a "feminist," the influence of her work is evident in contemporary socialist feminist theory. At the turn of the century, she advocated changes in traditional practices of child care and housework to relieve the double burden of women who worked outside the home. She was less concerned with securing formal legal rights for women than she was with bringing about practical institutional changes to improve the everyday lives of poor and working-class women.

- **Margaret Sanger** (1879–1969) It is perhaps inappropriate to include Sanger here, since her work for women's rights to control their bodies spans more than five decades of the twentieth century. Nevertheless, her pioneering efforts during the early 1900s are especially significant because she carried them out at a time when contraceptive devices and even the dissemination of information about birth control had been outlawed and deemed immoral; Sanger was arrested and prosecuted several times for her activities. Nevertheless, she remained committed to this cause throughout her life because she recognized that gender equality was impossible if women could not prevent and control the timing of pregnancy and childbirth. While she is best known for her advocacy of reproductive freedom, Sanger also labored to improve employment and living conditions for the working class and was politically active for many socialist causes.

- **Maria W. Stewart** (1803–1879) Orphaned at the age of five, this Black woman was bonded as a servant to the home of a White clergyman and his family, where she stayed until she was fifteen. In 1832, she became the first Black woman born in the United States to deliver a public lecture. In a series of four lectures that she gave that year in Boston, she encouraged women domestics and laborers to educate themselves and to strengthen their talents, which she saw as being dulled by women's servitude and subordination. She also defended women's rights to speak in public. Later, she became a teacher, and in 1863 she opened her own school in Washington, DC.

- **Sojourner Truth** (1797–1883) Born a slave in New York, Sojourner Truth was sold several times during her childhood and suffered many indignities at the hands of her masters, including rape. When slavery was outlawed in New York, she began traveling as an itinerant preacher, and in her homilies she advocated abolition, protection and assistance for the poor, and equal rights for women. During the Civil War, she visited Union troops, and following the war, she worked for freedmen's resettlement and relief.

- **Ida B. Wells-Barnett** (1862–1931) The daughter of slaves, Wells-Barnett became a world-renown crusader against the horrific practice of lynching. In the late 1800s, over 100 African Americans a year were lynched, primarily in the rural South. Through her well-documented research and powerful writing as a journalist based in Chicago as well as through public speaking tours, Wells-Barnett led the campaign to end lynching. Tireless in her pursuit of social justice and the elimination of racism, she was also active in politics and helped educate women about elections both before and after they won the right to vote. Wells-Barnett ran for the Illinois Senate in 1930, but lost to a Black man. (The contemporary sociologist and social activist, Troy Duster, is Wells-Barnett's grandson.)
- **Frances Willard** (1839–1898) Founder and early president of the Women's Christian

Temperance Society (WCTU), Willard was active in a number of civic and moral reform movements, but is perhaps best known for her campaigning for strict laws regulating the sale and consumption of alcohol. One source of Willard's motivation in working tirelessly for temperance was her desire to protect women and children who were often abused by intoxicated husbands and fathers.

- **Victoria Claflin Woodhull** (1838–1927) One of the most flamboyant and controversial first wave feminists, Woodhull gained public notoriety for her advocacy of free love and her illicit relationships with wealthy men, including Cornelius Vanderbilt. However, Woodhull is also notable as the first woman to operate a Wall Street brokerage firm, the first American woman to address Congress, and the first American woman to run for president (even though women could not vote and Woodhull herself was below the constitutional age requirement).

Sources: Compiled from Gabriel, 1998; Gray, 1979; Hill, 1980; Hine & Thompson, 1997; Lerner, 1972; Rossi, 1973; Thompson, 1990.

should have an equal chance of free development as an individual" (Klein, 1984, p. 530). But none of this seemed to apply to women, nor, for that matter, to anyone other than White men. Even as middle-class women acquired more education during the 1800s, they found most professions legally closed to them. Their alternative to filling hours at home with knitting and needlework was philanthropy and, as historian Lois Banner (1986) has observed, there were plenty of charitable voluntary organizations for them to join, particularly in the northern states.

Of course, to the targets of these social reform groups—that is, African Americans and European immigrants, the poor, and the working class—the goal of equal rights for women must have seemed irrelevant at best. Black women were enslaved with Black men, both equal in a sense in their oppression, exploitation, and lack of any rights of citizenship. While upper- and middle-class women were demanding access to jobs and equality with men, working-class and poor women wanted protection and differential treatment from men (Klein, 1984). Poor women had no choice but to work outside the home for wages to help support their families. They typically earned $1 to $3 a week and labored in unsafe, unsanitary, and overcrowded factories (Banner, 1986). Certainly, it is not difficult to understand, then, why the early feminists failed to attract broad-based support for their demands. (As we shall soon see, racism and elitism still plague some segments of the women's movement and are, at least in part, responsible for some frag-mentation within contemporary feminism.)

Ironically, it was their experiences in antislavery organizations that attracted many White, middle- and upper-class women to feminism. Work in other social reform groups equipped these women with valuable organizational and administrative skills, but their focus tended to be local and their interests diverse. Abolitionism brought geographically dispersed women together and united them for a common cause. In addition, it has been argued that the ideology of abolitionism provided these women with a framework for understanding their own inequality relative to men. However, it is also likely that the way they were treated by supposedly liberal male abolitionists helped greatly to politicize them. In 1840, for example, at the first international antislav-ery conference in London, women delegates were prohibited from speaking publicly and were segregated from the men in a curtained-off section of the convention hall. Understandably, the women were outraged, and many, including Lucretia Mott and Elizabeth Cady Stanton, resolved to hold their own conferences in the United States— on women's rights as well as abolitionism (Banner, 1986; O'Neill, 1969; Simon & Danziger, 1991).

Over the next twenty years, many such conferences were held, the most famous one being at Seneca Falls, New York, on July 19 and 20, 1848. There, led by Mott and Stanton, about three hundred women and some sympathetic men—men originally were not to be admitted, but ended up chairing the meeting—adopted a Declaration of Sentiments, deliberately modeled on the Declaration of Independence, along with twelve resolutions. The latter were mostly general statements in support of the prin-ciple of equality between the sexes and in opposition to laws and customs that pre-served women's inferior status. All except one—specifically, *"Resolved,* That it is the duty of the women of this country to secure to themselves the sacred right to the elec-tive franchise"—were adopted unanimously. Those who opposed the call for women's enfranchisement expressed concern that such a radical demand would weaken public support for the more reasonable proposals and would possibly discredit the entire movement. Nevertheless, the resolution was finally accepted by the majority, and the Seneca Falls Convention became known as the official launch of the campaign for women's suffrage (Hole & Levine, 1984; O'Neill, 1969).

Still, it was not until after the Civil War that the drive for women's enfranchise-ment became paramount. In the prewar period, at women's rights conferences, before state legislatures, and in their own newspapers, feminists addressed a variety of issues such as dress reform, changes in divorce and custody laws, property rights, and the right to control their earnings. However, once the Civil War broke out in 1861, many feminists began to neglect the women's movement to devote their time and energy to the war effort. Although some, such as Susan B. Anthony, were openly pessi-mistic about this strategy, most assumed that the Republican administration would reward them for their wartime support by granting women the right to vote. They were wrong. In the aftermath of the war, Congress not only failed to grant women equal rights, but it also added a sex distinction to the Constitution by using the word "male" in the second section of the Fourteenth Amendment. The Fifteenth Amendment was passed with the specification that suffrage could not be denied on the basis of race, color, or previous condition of servitude; the word "sex" was excluded (Banner, 1986; Hole & Levine, 1984).

Disappointed and angry, feminists took up the fight for women's rights on a state-by-state basis, starting in Kansas. In 1867, Kansas voters were called on to decide two referendums, one to enfranchise Blacks and one to enfranchise women. State Republicans supported the former, but openly opposed the latter. The Democrats, hardly friends of feminism, allowed their racism to get the better of them and campaigned for women's suffrage with the hope of defeating the referendum for Blacks. Both measures lost at the polls, but the Kansas campaign caused serious divisions in the women's movement. Feminists, such as Stanton and Anthony, who had sided with the Democrats, alienated other feminists, who were appalled by their blatant hypocrisy and racism. Because of this as well as other disagreements over strategies and goals, some of these women formed their own organization, the American Woman Suffrage Association (AWSA), with the sole objective of enfranchising women and Blacks. Stanton and her supporters organized the rival National Woman Suffrage Association (NWSA), which, despite its name, lobbied for a variety of causes in addition to suffrage. Neither group enjoyed much popularity with the general public, but the NWSA had the greatest difficulty because some of its members advocated "free love" and Marxism, which gave the organization an anti-American, antifamily image (Cott, 1987; Goldsmith, 1998). By 1890, though, both groups merged into the National American Woman Suffrage Association (NAWSA) to pool all their resources to win women the right to vote. (Black men were enfranchised in 1870.)

Expediency characterized the movement by the turn of the century, and some feminists appeared willing to exploit virtually every prejudice and stereotype, no matter how harmful, if it helped garner support for their cause. While some argued that women deserved the vote because in a democracy all people should rule themselves, others maintained that women should vote because they would purify politics. Women, the latter claimed, would bring to the political process natural talents, such as nurturance, which made them not men's equals, but their moral superiors (Cott, 1987). In a similar vein, the suffragists capitalized on the growing anti-immigrant sentiment of middle-class, native-born Whites, as well as their longstanding racism against Blacks (Caraway, 1991; Simon & Danziger, 1991; "Suffragette's Racial Remark," 1996).

At the same time, however, there were some feminists, such as Charlotte Perkins Gilman, who successfully mobilized working-class women and men and new immigrants into suffrage organizations. According to historian Nancy Cott (1986, p. 53), "As never before, men and women in discreet ethnic or racial or ideological groups saw the advantage of doubling their voting numbers if women obtained suffrage" (see also Cott, 1987). Black women's organizations, such as the National Association of Colored Women's Clubs, the National Federation of Afro-American Women, and the Northeastern Federation of Colored Women's Clubs, established suffrage departments or committees and conducted classes on civics and the Constitution to prepare women for enfranchisement (Hine & Thompson, 1997). For Black women, suffrage was more than a women's rights issue; it was a means to address the often violent subversion of Black men's voting rights in the South (Cott, 1987; Yee, 1992). "[T]hey mobilized not only as a matter of gender justice but of race progress, despite [or perhaps because of] their awareness that White racist arguments were simultaneously being raised on behalf of women's suffrage" (Cott, 1986, p. 53). Black women were systematically excluded from most White suffrage organizations (Caraway, 1991; Simon & Danziger, 1991). Certainly, by the early 1900s, it was clear that "mainstream feminism" was not every woman's movement, but rather an explicitly White, middle-class women's movement.

During the 1890s, several Western states enfranchised women—for example, Wyoming in 1890, Colorado in 1893, and Utah and Idaho in 1896—but no other states were won until 1910. NAWSA and other groups, such as Alice Paul's National Women's Party (NWP), continued to stage petition drives, demonstrations, and other media events, but ironically, it took another war, World War I, to turn the political tide for women's enfranchisement. Most feminists supported President Wilson's position on the war and contributed to the war effort in many ways, but, unlike during the Civil War, suffrage organizations remained active during World War I and targeted senators who opposed suffrage for election defeat. Finally, in a special legislative session held in the spring of 1919, both the House and the Senate approved the Nineteenth Amendment, sending it to the states for the two-thirds ratification. Ratification took little more than a year; on August 26, 1920, twenty-six million American women won the right to vote.

What followed can best be described as anticlimactic. For one thing, suffrage did not have the impact that feminists had promised, which is not surprising given that it was sold as a panacea for virtually all of society's ills. Once the vote was won, women did not go to the polls as often as men, and, when they did go, they voted similarly to men (see Chapter 10). More importantly, the suffrage campaign cost feminism much of its active support since many women withdrew from the movement in the belief that equality had been won along with the right to vote. Young women in particular ignored the women's movement or rejected it outright, depicting feminists as lonely, unmarried women who needlessly antagonized men. In the politically conservative postwar era, social activism fell into disfavor and the "cult of Domesticity" was resurrected with a slightly new twist: The modern "emancipated" middle-class housewife was a "household manager" who mixed science and "aesthetic inspiration" to produce an efficient and tranquil home for her family. As O'Neill (1969, p. 313) concludes, "femininity, not feminism, was increasingly the watchword."

This does not mean that feminism disappeared completely. For example, Alice Paul, who has been described as "a dedicated, iron-willed 'superfeminist'," led a small following in the National Women's Party, which continued to lobby for women's rights in a number of arenas, but they focused primarily on the Equal Rights Amendment (Taylor, 1990, p. 287).[2] Other organizations, such as the National Federation of Business and Professional Women's Clubs, the National Association of Women Lawyers, and the American Medical Woman's Association, worked to get women elected to political office and appointed to policy-making positions in government. Thus, as Taylor (1990, p. 284) explains, the period following the ratification of the Nineteenth Amendment into the early 1960s was not a time of mass mobilization for the women's movement, but the movement was also by no means completely dormant (see also Cott, 1987). The early 1960s, however, became a period of mass mobilization for the movement, both in the United States and abroad (see Box 1.2); feminism was revitalized.

The Second Wave of Feminism

Several factors contributed to the resurgence of feminism in the early 1960s. One important impetus was the publication in 1963 of Betty Friedan's book, *The Feminine Mystique*. Friedan voiced the unhappiness and boredom of White, educated,

BOX 1.2
Feminism in Great Britain and Western Europe[3]

British and Western European feminists, like their counterparts in the United States, emerged out of particular social, political, and economic circumstances (Offen, 2000). The Enlightenment—with its emphasis on reason, progress, education, the fulfillment of the individual, and freedom from restrictions—has been identified as an important antecedent, although the major Enlightenment philosophers, such as Rousseau, were openly opposed to equal rights for women. Nevertheless, we can see the influence of Enlightenment ideals in the writings of early British and Western European feminists, such as Mary Wollstonecraft. In her 1792 treatise, *A Vindication of the Rights of Woman,* Wollstonecraft denounced traditional male authority and female subservience and called for equal educational opportunities for women as the means for their liberation and full development as individuals.

The French Revolution and the rise of liberalism also contributed to the emergence of nineteenth-century British and Western European feminism. Women were actively involved in the French Revolution, leading protests and forming political clubs, and writers like Olympe de Georges argued vehemently for full economic and political rights for women under the new government. (Unfortunately, de Georges was beheaded by Robespierre, and the Revolutionary Assembly outlawed all women's organizations.) The writing of John Stewart Mill in *The Subjection of Women* illustrates liberalism's emphasis on removing legal barriers to equal rights, although Mill was one of the few liberal male philosophers who took up the cause of women's rights. At the same time, socialists such as August Bebel and Frederich Engels developed their critiques of the subordination of women in the family under capitalism and exhorted women to join the socialist movement to secure their emancipation.

With these diverse origins, it is not surprising that early British and Western European feminists tackled a range of issues, including the protection of women and children from battery and sexual abuse, prevention of the exploitation of women through prostitution, divorce reform, revisions in property laws, increased employment opportunities, equal access to education, and, of course, the right to vote, but their concerns were broader than formal legal rights. "Europeans focused as much or more on elaborations of womanliness; they celebrated sexual difference rather than similarity within a framework of male/female complementarity; and instead of seeking unqualified admission to male-dominated society, they mounted a widespread critique of the society and its institutions" (Offen, 1988, p. 124). Still, British and Western European feminists exchanged ideas and experiences with their American sisters through participation in international feminist organizations, such as the International Council of Women, the International Women's Suffrage Alliance, and the Socialist Women's International (Cott, 1987; Lovenduski, 1986; Rupp & Taylor, 1999).

The success of British and European feminists' struggles depended to a large extent on specific conditions in the country in which they were waged (Chafetz, Dworkin, & Swanson, 1990). In most European countries, for instance, divorce laws were gradually liberalized during the nineteenth and early twentieth centuries, but in strongly Catholic-identified countries, divorce was prohibited until relatively recently. In Ireland, for example, divorce was prohibited until 1985, and many restrictions still remain. Most European nations enfranchised women during or shortly after World War I, although some had granted women full suffrage rights much earlier (e.g., Finland in 1906) and others much later (e.g., France in 1944) (Lovenduski, 1986; Rowbotham, 1997).

The upheaval of war in Europe and increasing political conservatism in its aftermath helped to suppress feminism in many

(continued)

BOX 1.2
Continued

countries and to drive it underground in others. During the 1960s and 1970s, however, Britain and Western Europe, like the United States, experienced a resurgence of feminism. Although a variety of factors undoubtedly contributed to this resurgence, it was due at least in part to widespread dissatisfaction among women regarding how little genuine equality they enjoyed despite several decades of formal legal rights that had been secured largely through the efforts of nineteenth-century feminists (Lovenduski, 1986; Rowbotham, 1997). This dissatisfaction has given rise to a multiplicity of feminist groups and organizations, which, like those in the United States, have diverse philosophies, strategies, and goals (Bashevkin, 1996; Bull et al., 2000; Margolis, 1993).

middle-class housewives. Isolated in suburban homes, which Friedan referred to as "comfortable concentration camps," these women found their personal growth stunted. After subordinating their own needs to those of their husbands and children, they were left with a profound sense of emptiness rather than fulfillment. This Friedan dubbed "the problem that has no name," but the real significance of *The Feminine Mystique* was Friedan's labeling this not an individual problem, but a *social* problem. The book quickly became a bestseller, but more importantly, it served as a springboard for developing analyses of **sexual politics**, that is, the examination of gender inequality as rooted not only in the public sphere, but also "in the 'privacy' of our kitchens and bedrooms," the intimate relationships between women and men (Stacey, 1986, p. 210). From such analyses has come the much-quoted feminist slogan, "The personal is political."

However, even before the publication of *The Feminine Mystique,* the federal government took action that drew attention to the problem of sex discrimination. In 1961, President John F. Kennedy appointed a Presidential Commission on the Status of Women at the urging of Esther Peterson, whom he later named as an assistant secretary of labor. Kramer (1986) reports that Peterson advocated the establishment of the commission to placate members of the NWP and the Federation of Business and Professional Women's Clubs, who were intensifying their lobbying efforts for the Equal Rights Amendment. In its final report, the commission focused primarily on the persistent and severe discrimination experienced by women in the labor force. The report subsequently provided the basis for the Equal Pay Act of 1963 (see Chapter 8), led to the appointment of two permanent federal committees on women's issues, and served as a model for the numerous state-level commissions that were established in its wake. The state commissions, in turn, became vehicles for gathering and distributing information on women's issues (Freeman, 1973; Kramer, 1986). The state commissions also helped give rise to the National Organization for Women (NOW), which was founded in 1966 by Betty Friedan and twenty-seven others who were representing state women's commissions at a national assembly in Washington. NOW became a model for a variety of other feminist groups, such as the National Women's Political Caucus, the Women's Equity Action League, the Congressional Caucus for Women's Issues, and the National Abortion and Reproductive Rights Action League (Barakso, 2004).

At about the same time that NOW was being formed, a second, more militant branch of feminism was emerging from different sources. More specifically, this feminism had its origins in the political left, centered largely on college campuses, and developed among women who were active in other social movements during the 1960s, such as the civil rights movement and the anti-Vietnam War movement. The leadership of these latter social movements was male-dominated, but large numbers of women participated, running the same risks and fighting for the same goals as the men (O'Neill, 1969). Nevertheless, these women often found themselves relegated to traditional female roles, as cooks, typists, and sexual partners. They were struck by the glaring contradiction between the ideology of equality and freedom espoused by radical men and the men's sexist treatment of women (Evans, 1979; Rosen, 2000; Shulman, 1980). By the late 1960s, these women had formed their own feminist organizations, less formally structured and more radical than NOW and similar groups. The focus was on developing a theoretical analysis of women's subordinate status as well as engaging in political activism to end gender oppression (Rosen, 2000).

Feminist groups at this time attracted many women who personally felt the sting of gender discrimination, including many lesbians. According to Pearlman (1987, p. 317), the feminist movement was central to lesbians' politicization as a group. "Feminism gave lesbianism a female-oriented political movement and a political understanding of the basis of their persecution.... Feminist political activity gave lesbians places to meet outside of the bars through consciousness raising groups, women's centers, and services such as rape crisis and women's health centers." A more open and supportive environment meant that lesbians could be visible and active. However, as lesbian feminists increased their participation in the women's movement and began to contribute their own critical analyses of heterosexual relations, some straight feminists grew more defensive and argued that a visible and vocal lesbian presence would hurt the movement by delegitimating it. This eventually led to a lesbian/straight split in the women's movement, with lesbian feminists forming their own organizations, such as Radicalesbians (Cruikshank, 1992; Faderman, 1991; Pearlman, 1987). Although in recent years this split has mended somewhat, there remains an uneasy alliance between lesbian and straight feminists within some segments of the women's movement.

Like the first wave of feminism, then, the second wave was hardly homogeneous. These differences and divisions have given rise to the many perspectives that make up feminism today, including, as Box 1.3 shows, a pro-feminist men's movement. Let's consider some of these perspectives now.

CONTEMPORARY FEMINISMS

Sociologist Judith Lorber (2005b) has developed a useful way of categorizing the diverse perspectives that make up contemporary feminism. She identifies three major categories of feminist theory: gender-reform feminisms, gender-resistance feminisms, and gender-rebellion feminisms.

According to Lorber, *gender-reform feminisms* emphasize the similarities rather than the differences between women and men. Their goal is for women to have the same opportunities as men to fully participate in all aspects of social life, reflecting personal choices, not society's sexist dictates. Lorber identifies four feminisms— liberal, Marxist, socialist, and postcolonial—as gender-reform feminisms. Liberal feminism focuses on securing the same legal rights for women that men enjoy, whereas Marxist and socialist feminisms see women's oppression as caused by economic dependence and thus emphasize increasing women's employment opportunities and bettering their wages and working conditions. Postcolonial feminism reflects the concerns of women in

BOX 1.3
Men, Masculinity, and Feminism

To many people, the terms *masculinity* and *feminism* are incompatible. After all, isn't it traditional masculinity that has oppressed women and against which feminists have rebelled? While it is true that men benefit most from patriarchal social arrangements, it is nevertheless also the case that there are many ways that gender stratification and norms of dominant masculinity—what some sociologists call *hegemonic masculinity* (see Connell & Messerschmidt, 2005)—are harmful to men. For example, men's higher rate of mortality from various diseases as well as from accidents and homicide (see Chapters 9 and 12) is linked to masculine gender norms. Moreover, as we have already pointed out, the social category "man" is as diverse as the social category "woman." Although all men benefit to some extent from the "patriarchal dividend," the distribution of societal resources—most importantly, wealth, prestige, and power—varies among men according to their race and ethnicity, social class, age, physical ability, and sexual orientation (Connell, 1995).

In the early 1970s, some men, mostly White, educated professionals in colleges and universities, began to meet in small informal groups to discuss their experiences as men, their interpersonal relationships, and their notions of masculinity and how these impinge, for better or for worse, on their lives. These men formed consciousness-raising groups that focused initially on how gender norms and stereotypes were limiting them (Messner, 1998; Segal, 1990). By the end of the 1970s, though, "men's liberation" had divided into two branches, each with very different emphases and goals. Harry Brod (1987), a leader in the field of men's studies, labels these two branches *male-identified* and *female-identified,* respectively.

The male-identified branch of the men's movement is composed largely of men's rights groups. According to supporters of this perspective, male privilege is an illusion; it is women who are advantaged in our society. They argue, in fact, that men are victimized by women: that is, women seduce men and then falsely accuse them of rape; men are routinely denied custody of their children following a divorce, or they are falsely accused by their ex-wives of sexually molesting their children, so they are denied access to their children. Yet, men are still expected to be protectors and economic providers for women and children. And in this view, feminism has simply made things worse for men, allowing women to "have their cake and eat it too" (Dragiewicz, 2011; Rosen et al., 2009).

The male-identified branch of the men's movement is clearly antifeminist. It includes some faith-based men's groups, such as the Promise Keepers and the Nation of Islam, as well as the mythopoetic men's groups that "foster a search for the inner primitive or 'wildman'" (Lorber, 2005b, p. 226). Each of these groups has unique characteristics and strategies, but they share a common objective: They exhort men to assume their "rightful" place as heads of society and heads of the household (Kimmel, 1995).

In contrast to the male-identified branch of the men's movement, the female-identified branch is explicitly pro-feminist. Pro-feminist men examine both men's relationships with women and men's relationships with one another in terms of dominance and subordination grounded not only in gender, but also in race and ethnicity, social class, sexual orientation, and other social-locating factors. They argue that changing the individual attitudes of men is not sufficient to address the "structural conditions of gender inequality or the power differences between men and women and among men" (Lorber, 2005b, p. 226). Instead, it is necessary to reconstruct social relations in society. Among the ways men can do this is to engage in *nonsexist* behavior and relinquish some of the privileges they enjoy at the expense of subordinate groups.

Pro-feminist men have developed men's studies programs and organized workshops and conferences on such topics as homophobia, the harmful effects of pornography on women and men, and the causes and consequences of men's physical and sexual violence against women. Their work has been critical in the struggle for gender equity. Given that in recent years, the male-identified men's rights groups have garnered considerable media attention and won significant victories, particularly in family courts (Rosen et al., 2009), a strong alliance between feminist women and men is necessary for continued progress toward social justice.

economically developing countries in the Caribbean, Latin America, Africa, and Asia. It analyzes the role of women in the global economy with the goal of improving women's health as well as their work and educational opportunities, especially in newly industrialized economies, through the mobilization of grassroots organizing (see Box 1.4).

Gender-resistance feminisms argue that formal legal rights alone cannot end gender inequality because male dominance is too ingrained into everyday social relations, including heterosexual sexual relations. These perspectives not only focus on how women's ideas and experiences are different from those of men, but also urge women to break away from male dominance by forming separate, women-only organizations and communities. Lorber calls these perspectives "gender resistant" because while this separatist strategy resists the gendered social order, it does nothing to change it. Lorber includes radical feminism, lesbian feminism, psychoanalytic feminism, and standpoint feminism in the gender-resistant category. Radical and lesbian feminisms focus on the sexual exploitation of women by men and especially on men's violence against women. Psychoanalytic feminism uses the ideas of Sigmund Freud to explain gender inequality in terms of sex differences in personality development, while standpoint feminism attempts to examine all aspects of life from a woman's unique standpoint.

Finally, *gender-rebellion feminisms,* Lorber notes, are sometimes called *third wave feminisms* because they represent a major break in the way sex and gender have been conceptualized by the perspectives that grew out of the first and second wave feminist movements. Gender-rebellion feminisms focus on the interrelationships among inequalities of gender, race and ethnicity, social class, and sexual orientation, and analyze gender inequality as one piece of a complex system of social stratification. Gender-rebellion feminisms include multicultural/multiracial feminism, men's feminism, social construction feminism, postmodern feminism, and third wave feminism. Multicultural/multiracial feminism highlights how one's various social locations within the stratification hierarchy—especially one's race/ethnicity and social class—privilege or disadvantage groups of women and men in different ways. Men's feminism also examines how a specific group of men— White, economically privileged, heterosexual men—dominate society to the disadvantage of women and other groups of men. Social construction feminism examines the ways that people construct varying identities and social labels through their everyday interactions with one another. Postmodern feminists conceptualize sex and gender as social scripts and then rewrite the parts and alter the props as they see fit for specific situations. Gender, for postmodern feminists, is fluid. Lorber refers to third wave feminists as the "daughters of feminism" and sees this as an emerging perspective among young women who emphasize empowerment of women and oppressed groups and who focus on human rights issues. We will have more to say about third wave feminism momentarily.

BOX 1.4
Feminism in Developing and Undeveloped Countries

Feminism in the economically undeveloped and developing countries of Africa, Asia, and Latin America is sometimes referred to as *Third World feminism,* reflecting the traditional designation assigned by sociologists and economists to impoverished countries of these regions.[4] Histories of feminist activism in these countries are relatively scarce, however. Although there is now a sizable body of scholarship on women's involvement in liberation movements in these countries, this work usually does not focus on feminist activism per se (Mohanty, 1991). For many people in low-income countries, the struggle for women's liberation has been inseparable from the one for national liberation from Western imperialism or for liberation from political dictatorships. And while writers have recently begun to document the history of women's activism on behalf of women *as women* in the developing and undeveloped world (see, for example, Jayawardena, 1986; Lobao, 1990), there is still much more known about contemporary feminism in these countries than about feminism historically.

In the impoverished countries of Africa, Asia, and Latin America, daily economic survival usually takes precedence over any attempts to win formal legal rights for women. Men in these countries are also oppressed by imperialism, racism, and social class inequality, so many women in these countries view the goals of Western feminism as separatist and ethnocentric. As Johnson-Odim (1991, p. 320) writes, "In 'underdeveloped' societies it is not just a question of internal redistribution of resources, but of their generation and control; not just equal opportunity between men and women, but the creation of opportunity itself; not only the position of women in society, the position of the societies in which Third World women find themselves" (see also Margolis, 1993; Moyo, 1996). Nevertheless, women in these societies experience oppression not only because they are citizens of countries oppressed by economic exploitation and racism, but also because they are women oppressed by patriarchy.

In other words, women in these countries experience a *double deprivation:* the deprivation of living in a poor country and the deprivation imposed because they are women.

Consider education, for example. Many governments, international development agencies, and indigenous women's rights groups in developing countries encourage parents to send their daughters as well as their sons to school. Few Western observers would object to this worthwhile goal, and recent statistics show that primary school enrollment of girls in countries in sub-Saharan Africa has increased in recent years. However, girls in developing countries confront obstacles to education that girls in industrialized Western countries do not. Most African girls, for instance, drop out of school by fifth or sixth grade, not just because parents pressure them to marry once they reach puberty, but also because of safety and hygienic reasons. Once the girls reach puberty, they experience problems such as sexual harassment by male students and teachers and fear traveling to and from school, which may be some distance from their homes. In addition, very few schools in sub-Saharan Africa, especially those outside major cities, have clean private toilets and water for washing hands. Menstruating girls are considered unclean in many cultures and cannot share toilets that boys use. Consequently, without a private toilet, sanitary hygiene products, and water, about one in ten African girls misses school when menstruating or drops out completely (LeFraniere, 2005).

Another example is reproductive freedom. In the Western world, as we have noted, reproductive freedom has been a central feminist goal. This has largely taken the form of freedom from childbearing. However, for women in low-income countries, reproductive freedom sometimes has a different meaning. In some countries, where women are exhorted to bear many children to populate a small labor force or to staff revolutionary armies, reproductive freedom often means access to contraception and abortion. But in other countries where women gain status and material security through childbearing, they also often encounter pressures from Western agencies, such as the World Bank and the International Monetary Fund, as well as from their own governments, to use contraceptives (some forms of which have not been approved for use in the West) or to undergo sterilization (Chesler, 1994). In these countries, reproductive freedom is the right to *have* children. In addition, in countries where women are weakened by pregnancies and births spaced too close together and where malnutrition and disease make it unlikely that most of their children will live into adolescence, reproductive freedom may simply mean the right to give birth to healthy babies whose lives may be sustained through adulthood (Bulbeck, 1988; United Nations, 2000; Wines, 2000). Reproductive freedom may also be more broadly defined to include both the right to decide *with whom* one will have children and the right to protect oneself from sexually transmitted diseases. It is women and girls in low-income countries, especially in Asia and Eastern Europe, who are the victims of sex tourism, the mail-order bride business, and the international prostitution trade (Lim, 1998; Miller & Jayasundara, 2001; see also Chapter 9).

These are some of the central concerns raised by feminists in developing and underdeveloped countries (Johnson-Odim, 1991). However, Mohanty (1991, p. 6) cautions that to locate these women solely in the contexts of underdevelopment, oppressive traditions, poverty, overpopulation, and similar problems is to mask the diversity among them and to collapse

the fluid and dynamic character of their everyday lives into "a few frozen 'indicators' of their well-being" (see also Mohanty, 2003; Moyo, 1996). Brah (1991) gives us some sense of this problem when she writes about her experiences of racism as an Asian woman living in Great Britain. She notes, though, that her membership in a dominant caste also affords her a position of power relative to lower-caste Asian women living in Britain. Consequently, she argues that feminist politics necessarily requires women in industrialized, developing, and undeveloped countries "to examine the ways in which their 'womanhoods' are both similarly and differently constructed within patriarchal, racial, and class relations of power" (Brah, 1991, p. 73; see also Basu, 1995; Mohanty, 2003; Ray, 2006). Tripp (2000) provides another example when she argues that while recognizing differences among women in other societies, Western feminists must be careful not to universalize their conception of difference—that is, Western feminists should not assume that their idea of "difference" applies to all societies or time periods. She points out, for instance, that "in countries such as Uganda, Sudan, Rwanda, or South Africa, where politicization of difference has resulted in civil war or violent conflict based on ethnic, racial, religious, or other differences, the challenge for women's movements has been to find ways to focus on commonalities among women and to minimize difference" (p. 649). Thus, feminists must not only acknowledge differences among women, they must understand that difference has various meanings cross-culturally as well as historically.

As extensive as Lorber's classification scheme is, it is not exhaustive. Within each of these branches or categories of feminism, there are still other divisions. And, of course, many of these perspectives are not mutually exclusive. Our brief discussion of divisions within feminism is, by necessity, overly simplistic—a presentation of *ideal types* or characterizations of the essential elements of each category that does not do justice to the multifaceted nature of a movement in which differences often are not so clear cut and factions frequently unite. Our intent here was merely to give readers a sense of the rich diversity of contemporary feminism, a diversity that we pointed out earlier has given the movement strength and resiliency.

However, diversity also has generated problems for feminism. One of the most serious problems is what one observer calls a "sclerosis of the movement" in which segments "have become separated from and hardened against each other. Instead of internal dialogue there is a naming of the parts: there are radical feminists, socialist feminists, Marxist feminists, lesbian separatists, women of color, and so on, each group with its own carefully preserved sense of identity. Each for itself is the only worthwhile feminism; others are ignored except to be criticized" (Delmar, 1986, p. 9). The "discourse of difference," in other words, has not always been accompanied by an "ethic of conflict or criticism" (Hirsch & Keller, 1990). The criticism and conflict that erupt around differences of perspectives and strategy have sometimes disintegrated into censorship or trashing of competing feminist viewpoints. There exists, then, a tension within feminism between the felt urgency to present concerns and grievances as a single, unified group of women and the need to give voice to the variations in concerns and grievances that exist among feminists on the basis of race and ethnicity, social class, sexual orientation, age, physical ability/disability, and a host of other factors. Consequently, what feminists must recognize, as Childers (1990, p. 70) points out, is that "practicing conflict is also practicing feminism." Or, to paraphrase Hirsch and Keller (1990, p. 380), although feminists may be invested in the possibility of speaking with a common voice, they must also give equal value to the integrity of diverse voices (see also Risman, 2003; Rupp & Taylor, 1999). This attention to the plurality of voices within feminism is becoming increasingly important for young women and women of color who bring their own concerns and strategies to the feminist movement.

The Future of Feminism: Young Women and Women of Color

During the 1980s and 1990s, media reports pronounced feminism dead. In light of our discussion thus far, they obviously were wrong. In fact, as we see in Box 1.4, feminism has grown into a global social movement. But what prompted the media to make such a claim?

Hall and Rodriguez (2003) identify several reasons the media and others sounded the death knell for feminism. For instance, a number of writers argued that some groups of women, including young women and women of color, seemed to be increasingly antifeminist. It also appeared that others felt the movement had become irrelevant or unnecessary, and still others adopted what Hall and Rodriguez call a "no but..." version of feminism whereby they are reluctant to label themselves feminist, even though they support various feminist goals, such as equal pay, sexual freedom, and reproductive choice (p. 878). However, in an analysis of major national opinion polls over the period 1980 to 1999, Hall and Rodriguez found no data that support the notion that feminism is dead or even dying. To the contrary, their analysis indicates that levels of support for feminism have either increased or remained stable over time. Moreover, young women and African American women appear *more* supportive of the women's movement than older women and White women. The opinion polls show that perceived relevance of the movement remained stable from 1980 to 1999, and the percentage of adults who identified themselves as feminists during this period increased.

Additional research tends to support Hall and Rodriguez's conclusion that the claim that we have entered the era of "postfeminism" is largely a myth (see, for example, Aronson, 2003; Peltola, Milkie, & Presser, 2004), although some researchers have found a reluctance among some groups to explicitly self-identify as feminists despite their strong support for feminism (see, for instance, Baumgardner & Richards, 2000; Boxer, 1997; McCabe, 2005). Although the media and others (Faludi, 1991; Goldner, 1994; Rosen, 2000) argue that this reluctance stems from negative images of feminists as "manhaters," Rhode (1997) points out that there may be other sources of resistance to the feminist label, such as the reluctance on the part of many Americans to see themselves "as victims or perpetrators of injustice; our desire for roles that provide power, status, security, and a comfortable way of life; and our anxiety about alternatives" (p. 227).

There is evidence of increased involvement of young women in feminism in recent years. Analysts tie this renewed feminist groundswell to a number of events, including attacks on abortion clinics and providers by antiabortion groups, widely publicized sexual harassment and sexual assault cases, the AIDS epidemic, and the repeal of affirmative action programs and policies in some states (De Witt, 1996; Manegold, 1993; White, 1999). Significantly, the result has been not only an increased individual commitment to feminism among many young women, but also a growing willingness to take collective action to bring about change, leading some observers to argue that these young women constitute a distinct "third wave" of feminist activism (Lorber, 2005b). Moreover, this third-wave feminism is rebellious in its celebration of sexuality, autonomy, and women's agency, exemplified best perhaps in the music, art, and dress of "grrl power" (Lorber, 2005b).

An important concern of many third-wave feminists is inclusion. Many groups of young feminists have adopted a multiracial/multicultural emphasis and attempt to address problems resulting from racism, social class inequality, and homophobia as well as sexism. The inclusiveness of third-wave feminism may prove to be the key to the continued viability of the feminist movement. If the movement is to remain strong and make up ground lost as a result of the conservative backlash of recent years, then the needs and experiences of diverse groups of women must not just be taken into account by the powers that be within feminism, they must reshape the focus and course of the movement itself (Baumgardner & Richards, 2000; Hurtado, 1996; King, 1988).

As we have already noted, research indicates that women of color are more likely than White women to identify themselves as feminists (Hall & Rodriguez, 2003; Hunter & Sellers, 1998). Historically, as we have seen, mainstream feminism has largely ignored the concerns of non-White women unless its own ends were also served by addressing them, and White feminists have not infrequently been racist. Women of color confront a double oppression in the forms of sexism *and* racism, oppressions that frequently generate a third burden: poverty. Their objective life experiences as people of color frequently lead them to conclude that they have more in common with men of color, who also have been victimized by racism, than White women who, despite sexism, enjoy numerous privileges because of their race (Brush, 1999; King, 1988; Roth, 2004). Women of color have confronted such problems as forced sterilization, inadequate and unaffordable housing, and the degradation of welfare. It is no wonder that they often (rightly) perceive White feminists as pursuing liberation defined as "access to those thrones traditionally occupied by White men—positions in kingdoms which support racism" (Hood, 1984, p. 192; see also Hooks, 1990; Hurtado, 1996; King, 1988; Roth, 2004; White, 1999).

Black third-wave feminists "want to take feminism out of the academy and away from an ideology of women as victims and men as oppressors. While not ignoring Black men's sexism, Black third-wave feminists bring them along in the fight against racism, AIDS, and poverty" (Lorber, 2005b, p. 298). Black third-wave feminists are infusing contemporary feminism with alternative ways of understanding gender oppression, understandings that are generated from their lived experiences as marginalized members of society. Sociologist Patricia Hill Collins (1986), one of the leading theorists of multiracial/multicultural feminism, has pointed out that members of marginalized groups—those who live in the dominant society, but are shunned as out groups—can provide unique insights from their vantage point as "outsiders within." "Most basically, research by and about marginalized women has destabilized what used to be considered universal categories of gender. Marginalized locations are well suited for grasping social relations that remained obscure from more privileged vantage points" (Baca Zinn & Dill, 1996, p. 328). Women of color are themselves a diverse group, composed of African Americans, Latinas, Asian Americans, and Native Americans, categories that also mask numerous differences in history, culture, and contemporary opportunities and barriers. This research is generating new data on women—and men—who occupy diverse social locations, not only in terms of their race and ethnicity, but also their social class, sexual orientation, age, and other factors. With these heretofore silenced voices raising new issues and injecting fresh perspectives, the future of feminism promises to be richly diverse indeed.

THE PERSPECTIVE OF THIS TEXT

We have discussed feminism at length because it is the paradigm that informs this book. We do not propose to resolve the debates that divide feminists of different perspectives. For the most part, we see these differences as beneficial to the development of the paradigm and the feminist movement. Instead, our goal in this text is to highlight and analyze these differences and debates in the context of available empirical research. In the chapters that follow, you will hear diverse feminist views as we examine gender relations within specific areas of social life.

Despite the diversity of perspectives that are labeled feminist, there are themes or principles shared by all feminists. We think that these themes, coupled with the diverse interests and emphases within feminism, broaden the usefulness of the paradigm. The fact that feminism is interdisciplinary—that feminist sociologists share their research with and learn from the work of feminist psychologists, biologists, historians, and others—further adds to the paradigm's ability to account for the many observed variations and similarities of gender. We second Kramarae and Spender's (1992, p. 6) point that

> Whatever the approaches used most frequently these days—postmodernism, French feminisms, deconstructionism, ecofeminism…—we should not overlook the role that feminist scholarship has played in shifting the criteria of knowledge making. Feminist scholarship has helped formulate a model which values plurality and commonality, which presupposes diversity as well as interconnectedness.

In short, the feminist paradigm, taken as a whole, offers a comprehensive and insightful framework for the analysis of gender and gender inequality.

Key Terms

feminist movement (women's movement) a social movement that spans more than a century of U.S. and European history and that is represented today in most countries of the developing world as well; it is composed of many diverse segments, each committed to eliminating gender oppression as well as other inequalities

feminist paradigm a school of thought that explains gender in terms of the political and socioeconomic structure in which it is constructed and emphasizes the importance of taking collective action to eradicate sexism in sociology as well as in society and to reconstruct gender so that it is neither a harmful nor an oppressive social category

gender   socially generated attitudes and behaviors, usually organized dichotomously as masculinity and femininity

gender roles   social roles that are prescribed for a society's members, depending on their sex

gender stereotypes   summary descriptions of masculinity and femininity that are over-simplified and generalized

gender structure   a system for differentially distributing opportunities and imposing constraints based on sex categories with consequences on three levels: the individual, the cultural, and the institutional

paradigm   a school of thought that guides a scientist in choosing the problems to be studied, in selecting the methods for studying them, and in explaining what is found

patriarchy   a sex/gender system in which men dominate women, and what is considered masculine is more highly valued than what is considered feminine

power   the ability to impose one's will on others

sex   the biologically determined physical distinctions between males and females

sexism   the differential valuing of one sex over the other

sexual politics   analysis of gender inequality as rooted not only in the public sphere, but also in the supposedly private sphere of the family and intimate male/female relationships

social movement   a group that has organized to promote a particular cause through social action

sociology   the scientific study of human societies and cultures and of social behavior

structural functionalist paradigm   a school of thought that explains gender as being derived from the biological differences between the sexes, especially differences in reproductive functions

Suggested Readings

Each chapter of this text will conclude with a list of books that we feel will enhance your understanding of the issues just discussed. We begin with several that provide a good introduction to the study of gender and to the theoretical perspectives that inform it, both in the United States and abroad.

Barakso, M. (2004). *Governing NOW: Activism in the National Organization for Women*. Ithaca, NY: Cornell University Press. A well-researched study of the development and strategies of one of the best-known feminist organizations in the United States, from its founding in 1966 to 2003.

Baumgardner, J., & Richards, A. (2000). *Manifesta: Young women, feminism, and the future*. Written by two "third wave" feminists, this book discusses the major concerns of young feminists and considers the future of feminism from their perspective.

Connell, R. W. (1995). *Masculinities*. Berkeley: University of California Press. A leader in the pro-feminist men's movement, Connell examines various kinds of masculinity and the construction of masculine identity by looking at work, exercise, illness, and sexual relationships among four different groups of men.

Lorber, J. (2005b). *Gender inequality: Feminist theories and politics*. Los Angeles: Roxbury. An excellent, highly readable discussion of the diversity of feminisms that includes not only each perspective's theoretical principles, but also its strategies for social change.

Mohanty, C. T. (2003). *Feminism without borders: Decolonizing theory, practicing solidarity*. Durham, NC: Duke University Press. A forceful argument for the need for multicultural feminist perspectives in the age of global capitalism.

Roth, B. (2004). *Separate roads to feminism: Black, Chicana, and White feminist movements in America's second wave*. New York: Cambridge University Press. An insightful analysis of the factors contributing to the development of feminist movements among diverse groups of women, with important lessons for the future of feminism.

Wharton, A. (Ed.) (2006). Symposium: "The missing feminist revolution in sociology" twenty years later: Looking back, looking ahead. *Social Problems*, *53*(4). A reassessment of feminism's

impact on the discipline of sociology, including commentary by Barrie Thorne and Judith Stacey who made the original assessment in 1985.

Notes

1. Sociologist Liz Stanley (1992) points out that urban sociology remains one of the subfields of the discipline that is most resistant to feminist critiques and suggestions for more inclusive sociological work. Abbott (1991) argues that the areas of greatest resistance are sociological theory, the study of social class, and political sociology. These three disciplinary subfields, she maintains, are high status and male-dominated. For a feminist analysis of gender and social theory, see Evans (2003). Especially relevant for urban sociologists, Domosh and Seager (2001) provide a feminist analysis of the gendering of cities and of gendered space.

2. The Equal Rights Amendment is simple and straightforward: "Equality of rights under the law shall not be abridged by the United States or by any State on account of sex." It was introduced in Congress in 1923, but received little support, even among some feminists, who argued that it would invalidate wages and hours laws and other legislation that gave women legal protections. In 1946, it passed the Senate by a close vote, 38 to 35, but a two-thirds majority was needed for adoption. Riders were added to the amendment in 1950 and 1953 to prevent it from overturning protective legislation. During the resurgence of the feminist movement starting in the 1960s, the amendment gained additional support, and, by 1970, it was endorsed by Lyndon Johnson and Richard Nixon. It was adopted in the House of Representatives that same year by a vote of 350 to 15 and was adopted 84 to 8 in the Senate in 1972. At that point it needed to be ratified by thirty-eight states to become part of the U.S. Constitution, and the Senate put a seven-year limit on the ratification process. Ratification at first seemed easy to achieve. Within the first three months, twenty-two states ratified the amendment, and by 1973 the total was thirty. However, the process slowed dramatically after that. The ratification

deadline was extended to 1982, but ultimately ratification of the ERA failed, three states short of the needed three-fourths majority. In 2003, efforts were made to get national legislation passed to restart the ratification process; a bill to this end was introduced by Democrats in both the Senate and the House. Legislation to pass the amendment has also been introduced in several states (Canedy, 2003). For an analysis of the ERA ratification process, see Berry (1986), Klatch (1988), and Mansbridge (1986).

3. Our focus on British and Western European feminism is not meant to diminish the struggles and achievements of feminists in other industrialized countries in other parts of the world, such as Eastern Europe, Japan, Australia, and New Zealand. For a comparison of feminist movements in some of these countries, see Buckley, 1997; Drakulic, 1991; Eisenstein, 1991; Funk & Mueller, 1993. Our goal here is simply to emphasize the international character of feminism; a complete cross-cultural examination of feminist movements is beyond the scope of this book.

4. The term "Third World" is often used in everyday speech and academic writing to refer to the poor, nonindustrialized countries of Africa, Asia, and Latin America. However, many sociologists object to this term for a number of reasons, one of the most important being that this term groups over one hundred highly diverse countries into a single category, masking not only significant variation in their relative wealth, but also important differences in culture and traditions that affect life conditions, including gender relations. Another objection is that the term "Third World" implies a hierarchy with the industrialized countries of Europe (the "First World") and North America, including the United States (the "Second" or "New" World), being superior to the developing countries of Asia and Africa.

Chapter 2

Biology, Sex, and Gender

The Interaction of Nature and Environment

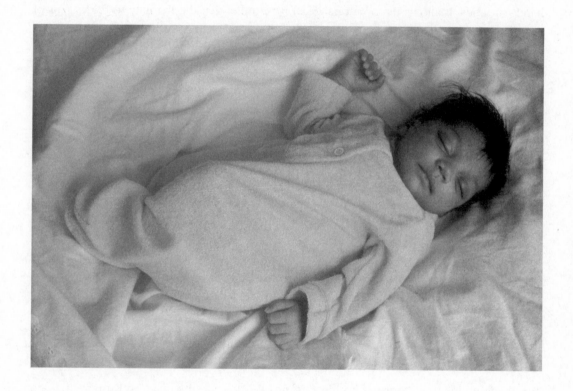

We all probably have childhood memories of meeting some of our parents' friends for the first time and of having to stand by with a tolerant smile while they chattered on about how much we resembled Mom or Dad or Aunt Tilly or Uncle Ned. Thinking about it for a moment, you can probably recall innumerable instances of being told you have your mother's eyes or your father's chin.

In recollecting these experiences, we are doing more than just reminiscing about the little indignities of childhood. Rather, we are beginning to get an inkling of the extent to which most people incorporate the idea of inheritance into their understanding of the world around them. Not only do we hear from others how much we physically resemble our kin, we often hear about the behavioral traits we have inherited as well. You may have been told, for instance, that you are stubborn like your father or outgoing like your mother. Of course, this kind of explanation for our actions and appearance can come in handy at times. It allows us to rationalize, for example, that the inability to find a pair of jeans that fit properly is because of the large bone structure passed on from our mother's side, rather than recent overindulgence in pepperoni pizza. Undoubtedly, the notion that genetics or, more generally, biology, is responsible for who we are socially, as well as physically, holds considerable appeal (see, for example, Burham & Phelan, 2000). Not surprisingly, it has been very popular as a way of explaining many of the differences we observe between men and women.

Documenting differences between women and men has long been a preoccupation of many scientists (see, for example, Caplan & Caplan, 1994; Turner & Sterk, 1994). Drawing these comparisons, however, often goes beyond simply cataloging difference; particular attitudes, aptitudes, and behaviors are imbued with differential value. One trait or behavior is typically, even if only implicitly, considered superior to the other—the "other" almost always being associated with the female. Moreover, like the general public, scientists have not infrequently explained sex differences solely in terms of "natural" or biological differences between women and men, without recognition of the interaction between the biological and social dimensions of life. Psychologist Carol Tavris (1992, p. 24) offers an explanation for this state of affairs:

> Views of women's "natural" differences from man justify a status quo that divides work, psychological qualities, and family responsibilities into "his" and "hers." Those who are dominant have an interest in maintaining their difference from others, attributing those differences to "the harsh dictates of nature," and obscuring the unequal arrangements that benefit them.

Tavris maintains that "there is nothing *essential*—that is, universal and unvarying—in the natures of women and men" (1992, p. 21; see also Lorber, 1993). And, as we will see shortly, the social may influence the biological as much as the biological influences the social.

In this chapter, we will examine some of the available scientific evidence on the impact of biology on gender. We will discuss how biological factors such as genetics, hormones, and the structure and organization of our brains may possibly influence gender and sexuality. To make sense of all this, however, we need some background of how we become male or female in the first place. Let's begin, therefore, by discussing the process of sexual differentiation—a process that begins not long after conception.

THE SEX CHROMOSOMES AND SEXUAL DIFFERENTIATION

Human development is extraordinarily complex. Consider the process of sexual differentiation, for example. Typically—although not always, as we'll see shortly—a person is born with forty-six chromosomes arranged in twenty-three pairs, one of each pair contributed by the individual's mother and one by his or her father. One pair of chromosomes is referred to as the **sex chromosomes** because it plays the primary role in determining whether a fertilized egg will develop into a male or a female fetus. The sex chromosomes of a genetically normal male consist of one X and one Y chromosome, while genetically normal females have two Xs. Thus, since the mother of a child always contributes an X to the sex chromosome pair, it is the father's genetic contribution that determines the child's sex.

It is not until the sixth week of embryonic development that the process of sexual differentiation begins. This means that from the moment of conception until the sixth week of their development, all embryos, be they XX or XY, are *sexually bipotential;* they are anatomically identical, each possessing the necessary parts to eventually develop as a male or a female. During the first six weeks, the embryo develops a gonad (called the "indifferent gonad" by scientists because it looks the same in XX and XY embryos) and two sets of ducts, one female (the Müllerian ducts) and one male (the Wolffian ducts). What happens during week six? Scientists are not entirely certain, but they have isolated a gene on the Y chromosome that appears to trigger a sequence of events, beginning in week six, that leads to the development of a fully recognizable male fetus. The gene, which scientists have labeled *SRY* (sex-determining region of the Y), seems to stimulate the transformation of the indifferent gonad into fetal testes. It is still unclear how SRY operates; it may, in fact, work in conjunction with other genes located on the Y chromosome that have not yet been isolated. Nevertheless, SRY seems to be a key component in the sexual differentiation of an embryo into a male (McLaren, 1990; Page et al., 1990; Sinclair et al., 1990).

Once developed, the fetal testes begin to synthesize a whole group of hormones called *androgens*. (Hormones are chemical substances secreted by organs to stimulate a variety of biological activities within the body.) Two of the most important androgens are *Müllerian inhibiting substance (MIS)* and *testosterone*. MIS causes the degeneration of the female duct system, while testosterone promotes the further growth of the male (Wolffian) duct system. The secretion of another hormone, *dihydrotestosterone (DHT)*, during week eight prompts the formation of the external genitals. The genital tubercle (another bipotential structure like the indifferent gonad) develops into a penis and the surrounding tissue becomes a scrotum. DHT also contributes to the "masculinization" of the male brain—a topic to which we will return later in the chapter (Hoyenga & Hoyenga, 1993).

What about the development of a female fetus? Traditionally, it was argued that the absence of a Y chromosome and the subsequent lack of testosterone production prompts the indifferent gonad of an XX embryo to transform into ovaries at about the twelfth week of gestation. In other words, female development was conceptualized in terms of a *lack* of the male or Y chromosome. More recent research, however, suggests a more balanced alternative hypothesis: A genetic parallel to male gonadal development exists for females and spurs the formation of ovaries (Angier, 1999a; Eicher & Washburn, 1986). Some scientists have theorized that estrogen (often referred to as one of the "female sex hormones") synthesized by the fetal ovaries may be responsible for the development of the female genitalia in much the same way that androgens are involved in male genital development (Fausto-Sterling, 1985). This hypothesis, though, is refuted by evidence that shows that the ovaries actually develop after the female external genitalia have begun to develop (Hoyenga & Hoyenga, 1993). Other scientists think that a genetic signal over-rides testosterone and initiates the development of ovaries (Angier, 1999a). Obviously, much more research is needed before the entire puzzle of sexual differentiation is solved.

Figure 2.1 summarizes the process of sexual differentiation in the human embryo. We know that males and females are identical in their development until the sixth

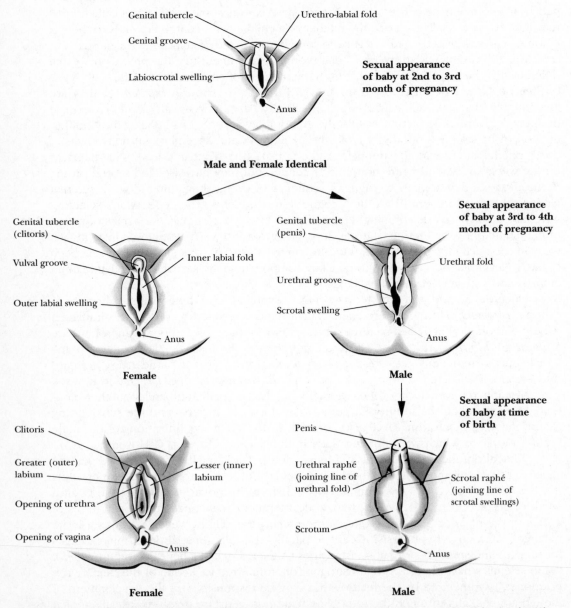

FIGURE 2.1   External Genital Differentiation in the Human Fetus.   *Source:* Money, J., & Ehrhardt, A.A. (1973). *Man and woman, boy and girl.* Baltimore, MD: Johns Hopkins University Press, Fig. 3,2, p. 44. Reprinted by permission of John Money.

week of gestation, when genetics, along with various hormones, come into play to help produce those physical differences between the sexes of which we are all very aware. However, several questions remain: Do chromosomes or hormones contribute in any way to the behavioral and personality differences we often observe between males and females? If so, to what extent? And given that these are biologically based differences, are they immutable? There are a variety of ways scientists have tried to answer these questions, and a discussion of their work will occupy us for the remainder of this chapter. Let's begin by taking a brief look at studies of individuals with genetic configurations other than XX or XY.

Chromosomes and Gender

Before an egg is even fertilized, events can occur during sperm production that later result in the birth of individuals with a complement of sex chromosomes other than XX or XY. During sperm production, the chromosomes divide and duplicate themselves in a two-stage process called *meiosis*. This usually produces two kinds of sperm—those that carry a Y chromosome and those that carry an X chromosome. (Remember: A woman always contributes an X chromosome to her offspring.) Sometimes, however, the sperm fail to divide properly, a problem called *nondisjunction*. If nondisjunction occurs during the first meiotic division (stage one), two kinds of sperm are produced: those with both an X and a Y and those with neither an X nor a Y. If one of these sperm fertilizes an egg, the offspring will be either XXY or XO. If nondisjunction occurs during the second meiotic division (stage two), three kinds of sperm are produced: XX, YY, and those with no sex chromosomes. Eggs fertilized by these sperm would produce offspring that are XXX, XYY, and XO, respectively. Figure 2.2 depicts typical male meiosis as well as nondisjunction. Do the chromosomal differences produced by nondisjunction have any effect on gendered behavior or personality traits?

Individuals who are XO have **Turner syndrome**. Because they do not have a Y chromosome, they do not develop as males. However, without a second X chromosome, they have no gonadal tissue and produce no sex hormones. They are reared as females because their external genitals appear to be female. Early research with Turner syndrome girls and women showed stereotypical femininity in their behavior and personalities (Baker, 1980; see also Money & Ehrhardt, 1972). These researchers report that compared with XX girls, XO girls liked to wear "frilly dresses" more, strongly preferred girls over boys as playmates, and played only with girls' toys (e.g., dolls) rather than boys' toys (e.g., trucks and building blocks). There is no unequivocal biological explanation for these findings. Instead, it may be that some parents of girls with Turner syndrome, determined to compensate for the missing X chromosome, intensified the feminine socialization of their daughters.

Women with Turner syndrome have very short stature and do not develop secondary sex characteristics at puberty, although growth hormone and estrogen are usually prescribed to increase their height and stimulate the development of secondary sex characteristics. Some studies of young women with Turner syndrome show that they have a relatively high incidence of social adjustment problems, such as immaturity, anxiety, and low self-esteem (Ross et al., 2000). To some extent, these difficulties stem from the young women's dissatisfaction with their appearance, but they are also products of teasing and ridicule from their peers (Rickert et al., 1996). The girls' social difficulties are lessened by strong social supports, such as parents who are open and willing to discuss the girls' concerns with them (Kagan-Krieger, 1999; Ross et al., 2000).[1]

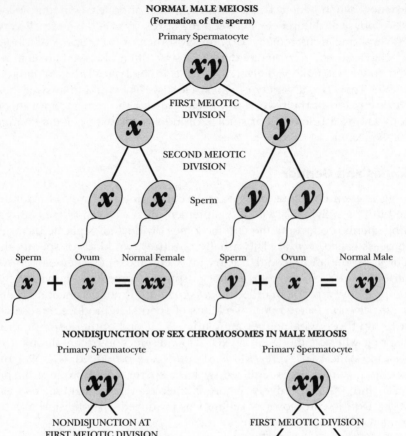

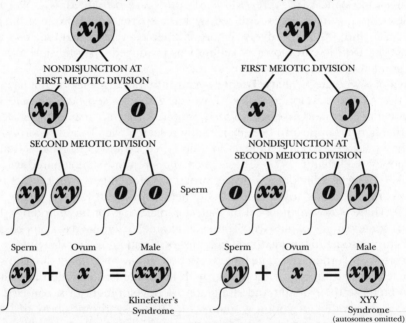

FIGURE 2.2   Normal Male Meiosis and Nondisjunction of Sex Chromosomes in Male Meiosis.   *Source:* Montagu, M.F.A. (1968, October). "Chromosomes and crime," *Psychology Today*, p. 47.

Women and men with an extra X chromosome (that is, those who are XXX and XXY, respectively) differ considerably. XXX women show few visible signs of abnormality, although they tend to be taller than XX women and have a higher incidence of learning disabilities (Hoyenga & Hoyenga, 1993). Men with the XXY chromosome combination, a condition known as **Klinefelter syndrome**, experience various physical problems. They have, for example, a high incidence of language-based learning difficulties. Boys and men with Klinefelter syndrome usually have small testes. At puberty, although they tend to grow taller than average, their voices do not deepen, their testes do not enlarge, and they do not produce sperm. In fact, Klinefelter syndrome is the most common genetic cause of male infertility (Lanfranco et al., 2004). Boys with Klinefelter syndrome may also experience some breast development at puberty, and many grow little or no pubic or facial hair. Early research with males with Klinefelter syndrome reported that they are at an increased risk for developing emotional and interpersonal problems and that they are uninterested in women, dating, or sex (Hoyenga & Hoynega, 1993). Recent research, however, shows that although males with Klinefelter syndrome may have an elevated risk of anxiety and depression—certainly understandable given that they live in a culture that places a high value on traditional masculinity and uses genital size as a marker of virility—they enjoy meeting people and place great importance on their relationships with family, friends, and romantic partners (Geschwind & Dykens, 2004).[2]

During the 1960s, scientists became interested in another chromosomal configuration known as *XYY syndrome.* Their interest was sparked by reports of an unusually high incidence of the configuration among institutionalized and incarcerated men. Some studies showed a frequency ten to twenty times greater than in the general population. Moreover, two infamous serial killers—Daniel Hugon in France and Richard Speck in the United States—reportedly had XYY syndrome.[3] By 1970, more than two hundred scientific articles and books had been written on XYY syndrome (Ellis, 1982).

Why would having an extra Y chromosome predispose men to behave violently? As we stated earlier, the presence of a Y chromosome is associated with the secretion of the hormone testosterone and, as we will discuss in greater detail shortly, testosterone has been linked with aggression. Consequently, it was hypothesized that an extra Y chromosome would lead to elevated testosterone levels, which, in turn, would increase the likelihood of aggressive, even violent, behavior. However, subsequent research failed to support the hypothesized relationship between the extra Y chromosome and violent behavior by men (Sarbin & Miller, 1970; Witkin et al., 1976). An extra Y chromosome does not appear to elevate testosterone levels.

The discussion of XYY syndrome highlights scientists' interest in how specific hormones may influence gender development and gendered behavior. This influence, some scientists maintain, begins even before a person is born. Let's look then at the research on prenatal hormones.

Prenatal Hormones and Gender

Earlier in the chapter we said that during the sixth week of pregnancy, the presence of a Y chromosome in a fetus causes the indifferent gonad to develop into testes, which produce a group of hormones called androgens that, in turn, promote the formation of male sexual organs and genitalia. What if somehow a female fetus gets exposed to androgens?

Will such a child exhibit behavior that is considered more masculine than feminine as she grows up? Or, suppose the cells of a male fetus are insensitive to the androgens it secretes. Will that child behave like a "typical" boy or like a girl? Events such as these actually do occur, and many researchers see them as providing a unique opportunity to gauge the effects of hormones on the development of gender.

The first situation we described is referred to as **congenital adrenal hyperplasia (CAH)**; it is also called *adrenogenital syndrome* (*AGS*). It occurs in 1 in 5,000 to 1 in 15,000 births and is caused by a malfunction in the mother's or the fetus's adrenal glands or from exposure of the mother to a substance that acts on the fetus like an androgen (Fausto-Sterling, 2000; Hines & Kaufman, 1994). Individuals with CAH are exposed to abnormally high levels of androgens prenatally, but if the condition is detected at birth, their androgen levels are usually regulated throughout their lives with regular doses of cortisol, another hormone (Fausto-Sterling, 2000). Both males and females may have AGS, but genetic females are more severely affected.[4] These are individuals whose genetic sex is female (XX) and who were exposed to androgens in the womb *after* their internal reproductive organs (ovaries, fallopian tubes, and uterus) had developed. Consequently, the androgens have a masculinizing effect on their external genitals (i.e., the clitoris is enlarged and may resemble a small penis, the labia may be fused, and the vagina may be closed). Because their internal reproductive organs are female and they are often fertile, surgery is typically used to redesign their external genitals so they are consistent with their genetic sex. CAH females also usually undergo hormone replacement therapy, so they experience female pubertal development (Fausto-Sterling, 2000; Hoyenga & Hoyenga, 1993).

Researchers have studied CAH girls to determine whether their excessive exposure to male hormones in utero affects their gender identities or behavior. Most of these studies involve interviews with fetally androgenized girls who are undergoing medical treatment for CAH or related health problems. The girls—and sometimes their parents—are questioned about such things as preferences in clothing, toys, and playmates as well as their future goals (i.e., desire to raise a family, desire to pursue a career). The studies that compare CAH girls with other girls similar in age and other social characteristics but without CAH have yielded inconsistent findings. Some research indicates that CAH girls are more likely to describe themselves, and to be described by others, as "tomboys" than are non-CAH girls. Some researchers also report that CAH girls are more likely to choose toys considered more appropriate for boys (e.g., trucks, building blocks), prefer boys as playmates, and prefer wearing shorts and slacks instead of skirts and dresses. Older CAH girls have been reported to express a greater interest in pursuing a career full-time instead of becoming full-time homemakers and mothers than non-CAH girls do (Berenbaum, 1999; Berenbaum & Hines, 1992; Dittman et al., 1990a, 1990b; Leveroni & Berenbaum, 1998). Some studies indicate that CAH girls also display higher energy levels and rougher or more aggressive behavior than non-CAH girls do. However, other scientists report that there is no evidence that shows CAH girls are more physically aggressive or assert more dominance than non-CAH girls do (Fausto-Sterling, 2000).

While at least one study of twelve CAH women who had originally been studied as adolescents showed that four had married and none had difficulty establishing relationships with men (Money & Matthews, 1982; see also Zucker et al., 1996), other studies suggest that CAH women begin dating and engaging in sexual relations later than non-CAH women (Dittman, Kappes, & Kappes, 1992; Hurtig & Rosenthal, 1987; Slijper et al.,

1992), and some report dreams or fantasies involving bisexual sexual relations (Ehrhardt & Meyer-Bahlburg, 1981). A delay in dating and sexual behavior, however, may be related to the extensive hormone replacement therapy most of these women undergo, and there is little evidence that their experiences of bisexual dreams or fantasies occur with greater frequency than those of non-CAH women who consider themselves heterosexual. Indeed, research indicates that women as a group are more flexible with regard to sexuality than men are (see Chapter 7). Before we discuss interpretations and difficulties of the CAH research, let's consider two other prenatal hormonal events that have been studied in terms of their potential effects on gender development.

Sometimes an XY fetus has a genetic problem that causes it to be unresponsive to the androgens its testes secrete, a condition known as **androgen insensitivity syndrome** (or **AIS**).[5] Individuals who are androgen-insensitive are sometimes referred to as "XY females" because even though they possess the sex chromosomes of males (XY), they are born with the external genitalia of females. They look like girls at birth, so they are typically raised as girls by their parents. In fact, their condition is sometimes not discovered until puberty when, because they have no uterus, they do not menstruate, although their internal testes will produce estrogen so they develop female secondary sex characteristics. But do their XY chromosomes predispose them to behave in a masculine manner? According to researchers, androgen insensitive individuals are as feminine (and sometimes more feminine) than XX females. In one study, for example, AIS girls expressed as pronounced an interest in dolls, dresses, housewifery, and motherhood as non-AIS girls who were identical to them in terms of age, race, social class, and IQ test scores (Angier, 1999a; Baker, 1980; Brooks-Gunn & Matthews, 1979; Frieze et al., 1978; Money & Ehrhardt, 1972). However, the methodological limitations of much of this research means that the findings should be viewed cautiously, a point to which we will return shortly.

Another condition, which involves partial rather than total androgen insensitivity, is **DHT deficiency syndrome**, also called *5-alpha-reductase deficiency*. In individuals with this condition, an enzyme (5-alpha-reductase) responsible for converting testosterone into dihydrotestosterone (DHT), is low or absent. Recall that DHT is the hormone that prompts the formation of external genitalia—the scrotum and the penis. Individuals low in DHT or who lack it completely are born with undescended testes and internal male accessory organs. Externally, they have female genitals that are partially masculinized (an enlarged clitoris that resembles a small penis and sometimes an incomplete scrotum that looks similar to the female labia). Because of the presence of normal testes, however, at puberty, when the testes begin to produce large amounts of testosterone, the external genitalia change: The penis grows, the scrotum descends, and the body becomes more muscular (Blum, 1997; Hoyenga & Hoyenga, 1993).

Imagine the havoc this condition must wreak on an individual's gender identity. However, some researchers who have studied these cases report that DHT-deficient individuals experience little difficulty in changing their sex and gender identities at puberty when their external genitalia become masculinized. Not surprisingly, other scientists have questioned this finding. For instance, in a cluster of small rural villages in the Dominican Republic as well as in the highlands of Papua New Guinea, the deficiency seems to occur with unusually high frequency. Imperato-McGinley and her colleagues (1982) studied eighteen males from a Dominican village who had the syndrome and reported that although they had been reared as girls, they easily switched their identities when their genitalia masculinized: At puberty, they became men. Imperato-McGinley's controversial explanation for this ease of transition is that their brains, having been exposed to prenatal testosterone, had been masculinized in utero, thus allowing them to quickly ignore or reject seven to twelve years of socialization as a female (see also Moir & Jessel, 1989).

A number of scientists have challenged this conclusion, as well as the research itself. For one thing, they have questioned the extent to which affected individuals were reared as "normal" females prior to puberty. There is considerable evidence that they were recognized as "different" or "special" at birth and treated accordingly (Herdt, 1994; Herdt & Davidson, 1988; Rubin, Reinisch, & Haskett, 1981). In fact, in the Dominican Republic, boys who have the condition are called *guevedoces* ("eggs" or testes at twelve) or *machi-hembra* (man-woman). In New Guinea, they are called *kwolu-aatmwol*, which translates as the transformation of a person into a "man thing." Research with DHT-deficient individuals in other societies indicates that not only are they treated differently than normal boys during childhood, but their attempts to change their sex and gender identities at puberty or in adulthood are sometimes not as smooth as Imperato-McGinley and others maintain (Herdt, 1994; Herdt & Davidson, 1988; Hoyenga & Hoyenga, 1993). Moreover, their transformation into men may have more to do with the strong preference for "maleness" and the greater power and privileges accorded to men in these societies than with the circulation of prenatal testosterone in utero (Fausto-Sterling, 2000; Herdt, 1994).

Genital Ambiguity: What Can It Teach Us about Gender?

We must be cautious in applying findings from research with very small, atypical groups of individuals to women and men generally (Rogers & Walsh, 1982). These studies are often plagued by serious methodological difficulties inherent in this type of research. For example, although researchers usually match subjects with a control group similar in various social characteristics, other important factors are sometimes ignored or are simply not controllable. Consider, for instance, that CAH females who have participated in studies were familiar with the researchers and were already comfortable with the clinical setting in which the research took place. It's possible that the results reflect a greater willingness on the part of CAH girls to talk about sex-atypical behavior and attitudes, rather than reflecting a genuine difference between CAH and non-CAH girls (Frieze et al., 1978). In addition, the researchers themselves are aware of which subjects have atypical chromosomal configurations or hormonal exposures or insensitivities and which do not. This knowledge might unconsciously bias their assessments of the attitudes and behavior of the patient-subjects (Fausto-Sterling, 1985; Longino & Doell, 1983).

Despite these problems, though, the research does offer us important lessons with regard to the relationship of chromosomes and hormones to gender. It suggests that the development of a masculine or feminine gender identity is quite independent of either the presence of a pair of XY

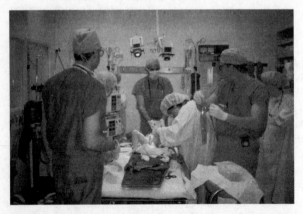

Surgery to "correct" genital ambiguity is often motivated by cultural norms rather than by health concerns.

or XX sex chromosomes or the production of particular hormones. More importantly, this research indicates that neither sex nor gender is dichotomous. When we speak of sex, we may be referring to chromosomal sex, hormonal sex, gonadal sex, or genital sex. Although for most individuals these are consistent with the category male or the category female, the research we have discussed so far shows vividly how they may sometimes be inconsistent, so that, difficult as it may be for us to do, we should stop thinking of sex as a unidimensional characteristic with dichotomous attributes. Similarly, gender—what we generally call masculinity and femininity—far from being an either/or phenomenon, includes a broad spectrum of attitudes, behaviors, and social expectations that we acquire during our lifetimes, through interactions with one another and experiences in various environments.

Suzanne Kessler (1996) has criticized physicians who rush to surgically "correct" genital ambiguity, pointing out that their decisions are influenced as much by cultural factors as by medical ones: They use medical technology to convert the non-normative (intersexuality) into the normative (one of two sexes/genders). "[G]enital ambiguity is 'corrected' not because it is threatening to the infant's life, but because it is threatening to the infant's culture" (Kessler, 1996, p. 362; see also Angier, 1997, 1999a; Preves, 2003; Turner, 1999; and Chapter 3). As we will learn in Chapter 3, in other societies, the fluidity of sex and gender is accepted as natural, and multiple genders are the norm: In some societies, there are three genders, in others, four. In some societies, individuals may choose to adopt the gender behavior ascribed to members of the opposite sex without fear of being stigmatized as abnormal or deviant. Besides the natural fluidity of gender, humans also add their own creativity to the process of social organization. This is not to say, however, that biology plays no role in shaping gender identity and behavior. To paraphrase science writer Deborah Blum (1997), it's not a question of *if* biology influences human behavior, but rather of *how* and *how much*. Let's continue to explore these questions by examining recent research on the structure and function of women's and men's brains.

THE CASE FOR HIS AND HER BRAINS

The notion that men and women have different brains is an old one. Nineteenth-century scientists maintained, for instance, that women were less intelligent than men because their brains are smaller. When it was pointed out that elephants, then, should be more intelligent than men, given the relative size of their brains, the argument was quickly modified. It was subsequently argued that the best estimate of intelligence could be obtained by dividing brain size by body weight. However, this hypothesis, too, was abandoned when it was discovered that according to this measure, women were more intelligent than men (Fausto-Sterling, 1985; Gould, 1980; Harrington, 1987). Today, there are few scientists who argue that size differences in men's and women's brains make one sex intellectually superior to the other (but for examples, see Lynn, 1994; and Rushton & Ankney, 1996). Still, an interest in how sex differences in the brain might contribute to differences in men's and women's behavior remains strong. The focus of research nowadays, though, is primarily on how our brains are organized. Indeed, it has been hypothesized that the differential organization of the brain is not only the source of behavioral differences between women and men, but it may also be responsible for the development of sexual orientation (see Box 2.1).

One of the difficulties in looking for sex differences in the brain is that much of the research uses the brains of animals, usually rats, not humans (see, for instance,

BOX 2.1
Biology and Sexual Orientation

In the August 30, 1991, issue of the prestigious journal *Science,* neuroscientist Simon LeVay reported the results of a study he conducted in which he examined the postmortem tissue of the brains of six women and sixteen men that he presumed had been heterosexual, and those of nineteen men who had been homosexual. LeVay found that one node of the anterior hypothalamus (an area of the brain that scientists speculate may play a part in sexual behavior) was three times larger in the heterosexual men than in the homosexual men, whose nodes were closer in size to the ones found in the heterosexual women's brains. Soon after LeVay's findings appeared in *Science,* major national newspapers and news magazines ran prominently placed articles with titles such as "Brain May Determine Sexuality; Node Seen as Key to Gay Orientation" (*Washington Post,* August 30, 1991); "Zone of the Brain Linked to Men's Sexual Orientation" (*New York Times,* August 30, 1991); and "Born or Bred?" (*Newsweek,* February 24, 1992). One year later, another study reported that the anterior fissure (a cord of nerves that is thought to facilitate communication between the two hemispheres of the brain) is larger in homosexual men than in either heterosexual men or women (Allen & Gorski, 1992). These findings, like LeVay's, not only triggered a storm of media attention, but also added fuel to a heated debate over whether sexual orientation is innate or learned.

On the one hand, there are those—including members of the gay community—who welcome such findings, arguing that they will reduce prejudice and discrimination against gays. If homosexuals cannot help what they do—if their sexual behavior is biologically programmed and not freely chosen—then they are not responsible for their sexual orientation and should therefore be granted the same basic rights as other minority groups (e.g., racial minorities) whose minority status is based on a biological trait (Herek, 1991). On the other hand, there are those—also including members of the gay community—who maintain that negative attitudes toward homosexuals are not likely to be changed by research findings indicating that homosexuality is biologically based. Rather, they maintain that such findings have the potential for doing more harm than good to gay people. They warn, for instance, that the research could be used to support a eugenics movement to eliminate homosexuality through genetic engineering, surgery, or some other interventionist strategy (Zicklin, 1992).

Members of the scientific community are also divided in their assessment of these studies. Some claim that the studies provide support for the hypothesis that sexual orientation is biologically determined, while others are more skeptical. Nearly everyone cautions that researchers simply do not yet fully understand how humans (or even other animals) develop sexual orientation. There are too many unanswered questions and the behavior involved is too complex to reduce to a cause-and-effect relationship with one minute area of the brain (Blum, 1997).

One hypothesis linking brain structures with sexual orientation suggests that a genetic mechanism (i.e., a gene or genes) triggers hormonal secretions prenatally that organize the brain in such a way that a person is later attracted to the opposite sex or the same sex (Blum, 1997). There is research showing a genetic link to sexual orientation (Bailey & Pillard, 1991; Bailey et al., 1993; Hamer et al., 1993; Hu et al., 1995). However, other researchers have been unable to replicate the findings of these studies as well as those of LeVay (Blum, 1997; Marshall, 1992; Risch, Wheeler, & Keats, 1993; Spanier, 1995). The research has also been criticized on methodological grounds. For example, lesbians have been largely left out of the research. When they are included, the findings are nonconfirming, although some scientists argue that this is because sexuality in females is governed by a different "genetic scenerio" than sexuality in males (Blum, 1997). A second methodological problem is that most of the studies are based on very small samples: LeVay, for instance, examined a total of forty-one brains; Allen and Gorski studied 193 brains, but only thirty-four came from known homosexual men. Furthermore, the relationship between brain and behavior is unclear; it is possible that the differences observed by LeVay and Allen and Gorski are caused by homosexuality rather than the reverse.

Despite these cautions and the tentative nature of the research that has generated them, many people have come to accept the findings as scientific "facts." Science—even rather shaky science—carries considerable weight in our society because it is considered "objective" and this ascribed objectivity often makes it a powerful political tool (see, for example, Gould, 1981; Hubbard & Wald, 1993). As the public debates show, the findings of the studies discussed here became politicized almost instantly. What remains to be seen are their political consequences for homosexual people. As one scientist observed, however, "in an ideal world...it shouldn't matter whether there's a biology to sexual preference or not; we should merely respect each other" (quoted in Blum, 1997, p. 135).

Vandenbergh, 2003). Are rat brains comparable to human brains? No one can say for sure, but researchers looking for sex differences in human brains that have been identified in rat brains are often unsuccessful (Blum, 1997). A second problem is that the human brain changes as people age and in response to experience and environmental conditions. For example, although men's brains are, on average, larger than women's brains, men lose brain tissue three times faster than women as they age, but it is unclear at this point why (Cowell et al., 1994). Nevertheless, new nerve growth can be stimulated in the brains of both elderly women and men by introducing new challenges into their environment (Blum, 1997), and there is considerable evidence that the human brain is quite malleable throughout the life course, a phenomenon known as *neuroplasticity* (Doidge, 2007).[6] A third, related problem is that scientists do not yet fully understand how the way specific parts of the brain are structured affects how they function. Interestingly, some scientists speculate that the relationship may actually be the opposite of what we might think: Instead of structure determining function, the way the brain works causes it to build or alter its structure (Blum, 1997). Keeping these issues in mind, then, let's consider the findings on sex differences in the brain.

As Figure 2.3 shows, the brain is divided into two halves or *hemispheres,* one on the right and one on the left. In the late 1960s, Dr. Roger Sperry and his colleagues, working with a group of patients suffering from severe epileptic seizures, discovered that each hemisphere appears to "specialize" in certain functions or tasks (Sperry, 1982). This specialization is referred to as hemispheric asymmetry or **brain lateralization**. The left hemisphere (which controls the right side of the body) is responsible for language and emotion processing, among other things, whereas the right hemisphere (which controls the left side of the body) handles visuospatial activity (Azim et al., 2005). In working with patients recovering from strokes, other researchers found that women tend to recover more quickly than men and to show less profound impairment from brain damage. It was hypothesized that the reason for this difference may be that men are more lateralized than women—that is, they are more dependent on one hemisphere of their brains to complete certain tasks, whereas women draw on both hemispheres (Gazzaniga, 1992).

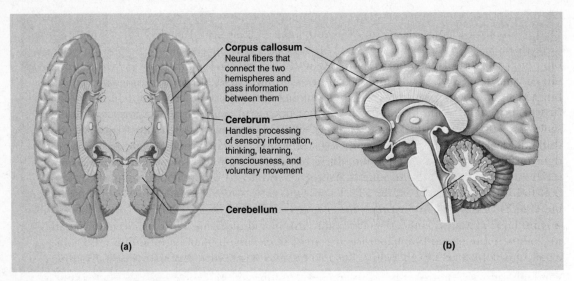

FIGURE 2.3   The Human Brain.

Subsequent research using sophisticated technology, such as magnetic resonance imaging (MRI), functional magnetic resonance imaging (fMRI), and magnetoencephalography (MEG), provides support for this hypothesis.[7] For example, in one study that asked subjects to complete a rhyming task, MRI images showed men's brains glowing in a small frontal center on the left side of their brains as they worked, whereas women's brains glowed on both sides in this area (Shaywitz et al., 1995). In another study comparing the electrical activity in men's and women's brains while they performed a series of word selection tests, most women had equal activity in both hemispheres, while most men had activity in just the left hemisphere (Blum, 1997). It has been reported that women have more gray matter in their brains than men do, but some neuroscientists dispute this, saying that women simply have a higher ratio of gray matter to white matter—1.35 in women's brains vs. 1.26 in men's brains—but that this difference is due to the fact that women have less white matter rather than more gray matter (Allen et al., 2004). The brain's gray matter is made up of the neurons that do most of the brain's thinking, whereas the white matter is the tissue that makes connections between neurons.

In practical terms—that is, in terms of men's and women's everyday lives and interactions—what do these findings mean? After all, as we have already pointed out, the existence of a difference does not necessarily mean differences in outcomes or in quality or value. There are a number of hypotheses, though, about how these sex differences in the brain may influence gender differences in behavior, including the performance of cognitive tasks. For example, some researchers speculate that observed sex differences in brain organization and functioning explain why males outperform females in spatial tasks that involve rotating objects in space, navigation, and map reading, while females outperform males in emotion recognition, social sensitivity, and verbal fluency. Another way to state this is that males are stronger at systemizing, whereas females are stronger at empathizing—a principle psychologists call *empathizing-systemizing* (or *E-S*) *theory* (Baron-Cohen et al., 2005; see also Chapter 5). Nevertheless, even neuropsychologists who emphasize gender differences in cognitive task performance concede that there is considerable overlap in the male and female distributions and that most differences are relatively small (Azim et al., 2005; Baron-Cohen et al., 2005; Hyde, 2005). Indeed, in a review of forty-six meta-analyses of gender differences studies, psychologist Janet Hyde (2005) found that males and females were more similar than different and that the gender differences that were observed varied substantially in magnitude at different ages and depended on the context in which the measurement occurred.

Regardless of the specific gender differences observed or the magnitude of these differences, the larger question looming in the minds of many concerns the source of the differences. Are sex differences in the brain present at birth the products of innate biology? Or, do they develop in response to males' and females' differing socialization experiences (see Chapter 4)? It may be, for instance, that women and men *learn* throughout their lives to process language and interpret spatial relationships differently, and their brains have adapted to these socialization experiences. Indeed, the discovery of a difference probably reveals as much about culture and experience as it does about biology, since the two spheres, as we have already noted, are not separate and distinct. Instead, it appears that their relationship is best conceptualized as an *interactive* feedback loop. As one scientist put it, "Everything is biologically determined at one level, but its expression is always an interaction with an environment" (Wallen, quoted in Blum, 1997, p. 279).

"MY HORMONES MADE ME DO IT"

One popular explanation of sex differences in brain organization and function is that they are due to hormonal exposure, specifically androgen exposure. For example, gender differences in performance of spatial tasks are observed in rats just as they are in humans, but the differences disappear if male rats are castrated or female rats are treated with testosterone neonatally (Baron-Cohen et al., 2005). Recall that during early fetal development of humans, the presence of a Y chromosome causes the indifferent gonad to develop into testes that produce the hormones called androgens, or the "male sex hormones." Scientists hypothesize that these hormones not only affect genital development during this time, but also brain development, essentially "hardwiring" sex differences in the brain that, in turn, cause gender differences in behavior. The increased production of these sex hormones, again at puberty, triggers the already hormonally organized brain, resulting in differences in the sexual behavior of males and females, as well as sex-specific behaviors such as mothering (Fausto-Sterling, 2000). As Fausto-Sterling (2000) points out, however, there is no direct evidence as yet that confirms this hypothesis.

Still, as we saw in our discussion of prenatal hormones and gender, the question of how the various sex hormones affect behavior that our culture has socially constructed as masculine and feminine is one that continues to fascinate many scientists. One case that drew widespread attention to this question was that of a boy initially studied by John Money at the Johns Hopkins University Gender Identity Clinic in Baltimore, Maryland in the early 1970s. The boy, who, along with an identical twin brother, was born a chromosomally and physically normal male but had his penis almost completely destroyed when he was eight months old as a doctor tried to repair the foreskin. Following the accident and in consultation with physicians, his parents decided in favor of sex reassignment; at seventeen months of age, the boy was surgically reconstructed as a girl and lifelong hormone replacement therapy was planned. Money and his colleagues reported in 1973 that the reassigned twin had been "successfully" socialized as a girl: She preferred to wear dresses rather than slacks, had feminine toy and play preferences, and, in contrast to her brother, was neat, clean, and enjoyed helping with housework.

In 1997, two other researchers, Milton Diamond and H. Keith Sigmundson, reported the findings of their follow-up study with the child. They found that at about the age of twelve, the child began to experience serious emotional problems because, even though she was receiving estrogen treatments that promoted breast development and other female secondary sex characteristics, she had a decidedly masculine appearance and was the brunt of much cruel teasing by her peers. Her parents had not told her about the accident nor about the fact that chromosomally she was male. Her early feminine behavior was simply an attempt to win social approval, but at fourteen, the child decided to stop living as a female and refused further hormonal treatments and genital surgery. When her father finally told her about her medical history, the teenager said she felt relieved. Eventually, she decided to undergo male hormone therapy and a mastectomy and had a penis surgically constructed. At the age of twenty-five, this person married a woman who already had children and, most recently, he was reported to be happy and well-adjusted as a man (Diamond & Sigmundson, 1997).

Certainly, caution is in order in interpreting the significance of this case, given that it is only a single incident—and one embedded in highly unusual circumstances at that. However, Diamond and Sigmundson's controversial explanation as to why this child could not be "successfully" socialized as a girl was that her brain had been exposed to the male hormone testosterone, making her ineradicably male. No matter how hard people worked at making her female, her brain knew otherwise (Diamond & Sigmundson, 1997). Other cases of sex reassignment of males following the accidental loss of the penis, though rare, have also found that most exhibit what may be considered strong "behavioral masculinity" and most are also sexually attracted to females (see, for example, Bradley et al., 1998). Testosterone, we know, does contribute to differences in the physical appearance of males and females. But does the secretion of testosterone also produce a male brain, which, in turn, generates those distinctive personality traits and behaviors that we, in our culture, associate with masculinity? Let's consider some of the research on the effects of testosterone on behavior and then turn our attention to a discussion of the effects of the "female" sex hormones.

Testosterone and Gender

If you were to ask others what they consider to be the most fundamental behavioral difference between males and females, most would likely say aggression—specifically, that males are more aggressive than females. Research on aggression, in fact, has yielded some of the most consistent findings of sex differences in behavior, from preschoolers to adults. One explanation for sex differences in aggression centers around the fact that males secrete higher levels of the hormone testosterone. (It is important to note here that both males and females produce the same sex hormones, but in different amounts. Males secrete more testosterone and other androgens, while females produce more estrogen and progesterone. All the steroid hormones are derivatives of cholesterol.)

The evidence linking testosterone to aggression has come primarily from animal studies. Typically, in these experiments, laboratory animals (rats, mice, or monkeys) are injected with testosterone. The usual outcomes are that, regardless of their sex, the animals show a significant increase in impatience, rough-and-tumble play, and fighting behavior. A variation on this theme is to castrate newborn animals, with the result that as they mature, they display little aggressive behavior.

Some people accept such findings as strong indicators that males are biologically programmed to be aggressive. However, there is reason to be cautious in interpreting these results. For one thing, there is tremendous variation in behavior across animal species. Female gerbils and hamsters, for instance, are just as aggressive as the males of their species, without being injected with hormones (Fausto-Sterling, 1985). Clearly, this variation points to the difficulty in generalizing about behavior from one species of rodents to another, let alone from rodents to human beings (Angier, 1992).

In research with humans, findings do indicate that high levels of circulating testosterone are correlated with edginess, competitiveness, and anger. This result holds for both men and women. For example, in a study of female athletes who had taken synthetic testosterone during training, research-ers found that the women were more easily irritated and more quickly angered than women who had not used testosterone (Van Goozen, Frijda, & Van De Poll, 1994). How-ever, scientists have not been able to pinpoint the relationship between testosterone and specific behaviors in humans for a number of reasons. One is that the hormone fluctuates dra-matically over the course of a day and in response to environmental stim-uli (Angier, 1999a; Blum, 1997). For instance, we noted that testosterone is correlated with competitiveness, with the traditional hypothesis being that high testosterone makes a person

Research shows that women can be just as aggressive as men in some situations and if their aggression is rewarded.

more competitive. But research shows that testosterone levels rise and fall *in response to* competitive challenges. In one study, researchers found that testosterone rises in male tennis players before a match, goes down as the match is being played, and then rises dramatically in players who win, but drops just as dramatically in those who lose (Booth et al., 1989; Mazur & Lamb, 1980). A similar pattern was found in chess players (Mazur, Booth, & Dabbs, 1992).

Such findings have led some scientists to hypothesize that it is not the relation-ship between testosterone and aggression that is significant, but rather the relationship between dominance/eminence and testosterone. *Dominance* "refers to an elevated social rank that is achieved by overcoming others in a competitive confrontation, and *eminence* is where the elevated social rank is earned through socially valued and approved accomplishment" (Kemper, 1990, pp. 27–28). Thus, Booth and his col-leagues (1989) discovered a rise in testosterone in male medical school graduates the day before graduation—that is, the day before they achieved an eminent status. This research not only reframes our understanding of the relationship between testosterone and aggression, but also illustrates how biology itself is affected by social factors (Kemper, 1990).

Finally, scientists have had difficulty specifying more precisely the relationship between testosterone and human aggression because testosterone is only one of several chemicals interacting in the body that affect human behavioral response. For example, *neurotransmitters* are chemical compounds found between nerve cells and send messages or signals from one neuron to another. Our bodies produce many different neurotransmitters, only about fifty of which have been studied extensively (Lefton, 2000). However, research on neurotransmitters shows that they have a direct impact on behavior, emotions, moods, and learning. Among the most important with regard to aggression are norepinephrine, a "watchdog" chemical that helps us respond to threats of danger; dopamine, a chemical involved in feelings of pleasure and reinforcement or reward; and serotonin, a chemical that regulates impulsivity and reactions to sensory information (Niehoff, 1999). However, similar to the research on hormones, much of the research on neurotransmitters has been done on animals, thereby raising caution about its generalizability to humans. In addition, the studies often produce contradictory findings, leading some researchers to speculate that the relationship between a particular neurotransmitter and a specific behavioral outcome is not one of direct cause and effect, but is rather a *reciprocal interaction effect,* where fluctuations in the neurotransmitter contribute to certain behaviors, but engaging in certain behaviors or having particular experiences also produces fluctuations in the neurotransmitter (Niehoff, 1999). Thus, specific behavioral outcomes associated with the production of a specific neurotransmitter may vary depending on an individual's unique social *and* biological history.

Such research indicates that human social behavior is highly governed by the situation or context in which it occurs, and that this, in turn, may override or alter the potential effects of various hormones and chemicals. Studies with women, for example, show that they can be just as aggressive as men in certain situations, such as when they are rewarded for behaving aggressively or when they think no one is watching them (Frieze et al., 1978; Hyde, 1984; Putallaz & Bierman, 2004). This research suggests that females may simply inhibit aggression because of social pressures to conform to a feminine or ladylike ideal; in the absence of such pressures, they may be as likely as males to express aggression. Cross-cultural research, in fact, indicates that women may behave as aggressively as men, but how they express aggression (for example, verbal versus physical aggression) may be structured by their culture's gender norms (Angier, 1999a; Bjokqvist, 1994; Crick & Grotpeter, 1995; Lepowsky, 1994). A related finding is that females are more likely than males to perceive aggressive behavior on their part as posing a danger to themselves and, therefore, they may inhibit aggression when the likelihood of retaliation is high (Bettencourt & Miller, 1996; Eagly, 1987; Eagly & Steffan, 1986). Moreover, for both males and females, aggressiveness decreases as age and education increase (Harris & Knight-Bohnhoff, 1996).

While testosterone and its impact on aggression has probably been the most widely studied hormonal gender difference, the "female" sex hormones have not escaped scientific—and popular—scrutiny. Let's consider, then, the effect of the "female" sex hormones on behavior.

Women, Hormones, and Behavior

We've all heard stories and jokes about changes in women's personality and behavior that result from the fluctuation of hormones in their bodies every month. The stereotype is of a woman out of control; she is depressed, enraged by the slightest perceived transgression, and overcome by the need to satisfy her cravings for sweets or salty foods—all signs that her menstrual period will start in a few days. The official name given to this malady is *premenstrual syndrome,* or PMS for short.

The notion that women's personalities and behaviors are dictated by their hormones is an old one. After all, as science writer Deborah Blum (1997, p. 189) reminds us, the word *androgen* comes from the Greek word for "man," while *estrogen* comes from the Greek word for "frenzy." Premenstrual syndrome, however, was not discussed in the medical literature until about sixty-five years ago. It captured the attention of the general public during the 1980s, largely as a result of media coverage of two British homicide trials. The first case in 1980 involved a thirty-seven-year-old woman who drove her car at full speed directly at her boyfriend, pinning him to a telephone pole and killing him. She was subsequently convicted of manslaughter instead of murder and was released on probation because of a mitigating factor in her case: At the time of the crime, her defense attorney argued, this woman was suffering from premenstrual syndrome, a condition that may cause those afflicted to behave violently. Also in 1980, a twenty-nine-year-old woman was convicted of killing a coworker at the London pub where she tended bar, but she too was sentenced to probation on the basis of the premenstrual syndrome defense. As a condition of probation, both women were required to receive monthly hormone injections to control their PMS symptoms (Glass, 1982; Parlee, 1982).

These cases undoubtedly reinforced the image of the premenstrual woman as under the influence of "raging hormones." Certainly, the treatment of PMS has become a thriving business, with PMS treatment clinics operating in the United States and numerous over-the-counter medications and self-help books being readily available (Brizendine, 2006; Chrisler & Levy, 1990; Kraemer & Kraemer, 1998; Markens, 1996). Moreover, the American Psychiatric Association added PMS to its *Diagnostic and Statistical Manual* (the *DSM*) under the name *premenstrual dysphoric disorder* and classifies it not as a gynecological problem but as an "unspecified mental disorder." But while PMS and other hormonally caused syndromes, such as postpartum depression syndrome, have been receiving a great deal of attention in recent years, the crucial question that remains unanswered is whether women really are transformed each month by fluctuations in their hormones. Let's consider the *scientific* evidence.

As we noted earlier, both men and women secrete the sex hormones, which, besides testosterone and other androgens, include estrogens (estrone, estradiol, and estiol) as well as progestins. Of the estrogens, men secrete only estradiol, whereas women produce all three estrogens. Of the three, estradiol has been the most extensively studied and, unlike testosterone, levels of this hormone in a woman's body do not fluctuate as much over the course of a day nor in response to environmental stimuli, such as competitive challenges. Instead, female hormone production is influenced by the monthly reproductive cycle as well as the cessation of reproductive capacity (menopause) during the life course.

A woman's monthly cycle is twenty-eight days, although for some women it is slightly longer, and for others, slightly shorter. During the first two weeks of the cycle, estradiol production increases as an egg matures in the ovaries. When ovulation occurs at the end of this period, progesterone production increases, which prompts another surge in estradiol. But if the egg is not fertilized, both progesterone and estradiol production drop and within a few days menstrual bleeding occurs. More than 85 percent of women report a number of physical changes about a week before their menstrual period begins. These include acne flair-ups, cramping, an increase or decrease in appetite, fluid retention, headaches, forgetfulness, and irritability, and for about 2 percent to 10 percent of women, the changes are severe (Kraemer & Kraemer, 1998). But do these changes constitute a *syndrome,* that is, a medically diagnosable physical and/or psychological abnormality?

One of the difficulties in answering this question is that much of the research on PMS is plagued by serious methodological difficulties. Indeed, Blume (1983) has argued that available data on PMS are "seriously flawed." For instance, the majority of studies have relied on subjects' self-reports in determining the onset of premenstrual symptoms (see, for example, Thys-Jacobs, Alvir, & Frataracangelo, 1995). However, this method is unreliable for several reasons. First, there is evidence that retrospective studies dependent on subjects' recall produce exaggerated results compared with prospective studies, which begin with a sample of women who subsequently chart their cycles over several months (Koeske, 1980; Sommer, 1983). Second, studies show that there is a tendency for women with random mood changes to selectively remember those changes happening during the premenstrual phase of the cycle or to label them PMS if they occurred during this phase of the cycle (Hardie, 1997; Widom & Ames, 1988). Third, women who perceive researchers as condescending toward them are reluctant to report information about how they feel and behave during their menstrual cycles (Culpepper, 1992). Fourth, several studies indicate that social and psychological factors have an influence on the experience of PMS symptoms. It has been argued, for example, that the attitudes toward menstruation prevalent in a particular culture, or even an individual family, may affect women's reactions to their monthly periods (Woods et al., 1982). In the United States, menstruation has long been viewed by many as a negative event in a woman's life—at best it is an inconvenience, at worst, a "curse." Women have also been led to believe that they are physically unattractive just prior to and during menstruation and that they should restrict their behavior during their periods. Although these negative attitudes have diminished somewhat in recent years, research indicates that they still are not uncommon. In one study, for instance, nearly a third of the male and female respondents felt that women need to restrict their physical activities while menstruating; more than half felt that women should not have sexual intercourse while menstruating; and one-quarter said that women look different when menstruating (Golub, 1992; see also Angier, 1999a; Jurgens & Powers, 1991; Markens, 1996).

Negative attitudes and expectations may influence women's experience of PMS symptoms. One researcher, for instance, asked a group of students to evaluate the behaviors of several hypothetical female patients. Included with each case was information about the patient's menstrual cycle. When the students thought that the patient was in the premenstrual phase of her cycle, they attributed any hostile, aggressive, or negative behaviors to biological causes; interestingly, they attributed positive behaviors during the same period to nonbiological factors (Koeske, 1980). In a second experiment, psychologist Diane Ruble (1977) told a group of female subjects that physical tests indicated that they were in the premenstrual phase of their cycles. In reality, all the women were in another cycle phase, but they began to report PMS symptoms (see also Hardie, 1997).

Given these findings, what actual behavioral or personality changes have been found to be related to the menstrual cycle, especially the premenstrual phase? The results of most studies are inconsistent. Some of the research on mood swings, for example, has found that women tend to feel less able to cope with everyday problems during the premenstrual phase of their cycles than during the ovulatory phase (Friedman et al., 1980). But others report that negative changes in mood, as well as physical changes, may have more to do with stressful external events (e.g., the triple burden of child care, housework, and work outside the home) than with the phase of the menstrual cycle (Golub, 1992; Hardie, 1997; Ripper, 1991). Interestingly, in two studies in which both men and women participated, men were equally likely to experience mood swings, problems at work, and physical discomfort (Hardie, 1997; Rossi & Rossi, 1977).

A few studies show improved task performance premenstrually, leading one researcher to suggest that perhaps we should study "premenstrual elation syndrome" (Parlee, 1983). There is no evidence to support the notion that women's academic or work performance declines during the premenstrual phase of their cycles. The majority of studies report no relationship between task performance and menstrual cycle at all (Chrisler, 1991; Morgan, Rapkin, & Goldman, 1996). Some researchers have observed a relationship between menstrual cycle phase and such psychophysiological functions as visual, auditory, and olfactory sensitivity; galvanic skin response; and spontaneous body movement (Angier, 1999a). "However, the variations among findings are such that one could select studies to support almost any hypothesis one chose" (Sommer, 1983, p. 82).

It does appear that many women experience some physical discomfort around the time of menstruation, but the majority appear to accept this as normal and do not see menstruation as debilitating (Golub, 1992). Ripper (1991) hypothesizes, in fact, that one of the reasons that researchers frequently find negative attitudes toward menstruation is that the questionnaires most often used in such studies only ask about negative effects. In her research using a questionnaire from which the bias toward negativity had been eliminated, she found that "The menstrual cycle did have an impact on most of the moods and perceptions of performance [of the women studied]; however, it is more accurate to describe this variation as positive, rather than negative" (Ripper, 1991, p. 25; see also Culpepper, 1992). Moreover, research suggests that for most women, the best way to reduce menstrual cramping and other premenstrual discomforts is not with drugs or hormone supplements that may have serious side effects, but by eating a low-fat vegetarian diet (Barnard et al., 2000).

We must be careful not to interpret these findings to mean that what women experience during their menstrual cycles is "all in their heads." Nor is it to say that biological factors are insignificant in women's menstrual experiences; the menstrual cycle is clearly rooted in biology (Blum, 1997). Instead, the point we are trying to make is that some caution should be exercised in pursuing a PMS "cure." Research on premenstrual syndrome has been conducted for more than seventy years, and scientists are still unsure of precisely what it is or what causes it. Meanwhile, women have been encouraged to seek treatment for PMS, using substances that are known to be detrimental to their health, while the structural factors that produce stress in their lives and may lead to depression—such as the difficulty of balancing work and family responsibilities—are ignored (Markens, 1996; see also Chapters 7, 8, and 12).

THE INTERACTION OF BIOLOGY AND CULTURE

The issues we have discussed in this chapter highlight the interaction between the social and the biological. However, it behooves us at this point to consider more precisely what we mean by *interaction*. Lynda Birke (1992, p. 74) has argued that feminist critiques of biological theories of gender have tended to conceptualize biology as something that comes first—"the biological base *onto* which experience and the effects of the environment are added during our development as individuals" (author's emphasis). Birke maintains that the difficulty with such a position is that it portrays development as progressing along a simple linear path: A person's biological beginnings impose constraints on what she or he can learn from the cultural environment, but the individual has no role or active part in her or his own development. Birke emphasizes, in contrast, that continuous and transformative change occurs throughout a person's lifetime and that the person's behavior can alter not only his or her environment, but also his or her biology and physiology. Certainly, much of the research we have reviewed in this chapter confirms this.

Birke urges feminist scientists to move beyond critiques that simply replace biological determinism with social constructionism that denies the body altogether. She urges instead the formulation of a transformative account of gender development, and we echo her call. Social constructionist critiques have been central in challenging the oppressive aspects of many biological determinist theories, but they have tended to reinforce the dichotomous view of biology versus environment, rather than transcending it. To focus on only the biological or the social is to tell, at best, just half the story. As Birke (1992, p. 76) points out, "our bodies are social, too, and our experiences of, and engagement with, a gendered world is as *embodied* persons. Surely those bodies, and their (often messy) processes, must be part of any continuing construction of gender?"

A **transformative account of gender development**—one that examines how culture and individual behavior may impact biology and physiology as well as vice versa—underlines the pitfalls of using biological principles to justify gender inequality and also overcomes a longstanding preoccupation with sex differences. As Janet Sayers (1987, p. 68) has observed, "Preoccupation with sexual difference and inequality has tended to be particularly intense at those times when prevailing differences between the sexes seem most likely to be eroded" (see also Fausto-Sterling, 2000; Markens, 1996). We may only speculate on the motives that underlie some scientists' tenacious attempts to establish a biological basis for behavioral and personality differences between women and men. The existence of difference, even if biologically caused, does not imply a hierarchical ordering, nor does it imply that one behavior or trait is inherently superior to another. That women and men are different in many ways is an observable fact; however, that either is discriminated against on the basis of these differences is a social injustice.

Key Terms

androgen insensitivity syndrome (AIS) a genetic defect that causes an XY fetus to be unresponsive to the androgens its testes secrete

brain lateralization the specialization of the right and left hemispheres of the brain for different tasks

congenital adrenal hyperplasia (CAH) or adrenogenital syndrome (AGS) a condition occurring prenatally that is caused by a malfunction in the mother's or the fetus's adrenal glands or from exposure of the mother to a substance that acts on the fetus like an androgen

DHT deficiency syndrome a condition in which an individual has no or abnormally low 5-alpha-reductase, an enzyme responsible for converting testosterone into dihydrotestosterone

Klinefelter syndrome a chromosomal condition in which an individual has three (XXY) sex chromosomes, rather than two (XX or XY)

sex chromosomes one of the twenty-three pairs of human chromosomes that plays a primary role in determining whether a fertilized egg will develop into a female or a male fetus

transformative account of gender development a theory of gender development that recognizes the truly interactive nature of biology and environment as well as individual agency in the creation of gender by examining how culture and individual behavior may impact biology and physiology and vice versa

Turner syndrome a chromosomal condition in which an individual has only one sex chromosome (an X), rather than two (XX or XY)

Suggested Readings

Brookey, R. A. (2002). *Reinventing the male homosexual: The rhetoric and power of the gay gene.* Bloomington: Indiana University Press. Brookey analyzes how the research on the biological causes of homosexuality may be used to deny homosexuals rights as much as it can be used to secure rights by the homosexual rights movement.

Fausto-Sterling, A. (2000). *Sexing the body: Gender politics and the construction of sexuality.* New York: Basic Books. This thoroughly researched historical analysis looks at how medical and scientific research on anatomy and physiology have been used for over a hundred years to fuel political debates about the origins and consequences of gender and sexuality.

Preves, S. E. (2003). *Intersex and identity: The contested self.* New Brunswick, NJ: Rutgers University Press. Through her sociological analysis of interviews with thirty-seven intersexed adults, Preves shows how sex has been medicalized, much to the detriment of intersexuals.

Roughgarden, J. (2004). *Evolution's rainbow: Diversity, gender, and sexuality in nature and people.* Berkeley: University of California Press. This book covers scientific research on gender and sexual diversity across various species, including humans, in language accessible to nonscientists.

Notes

1. The Turner Syndrome Society of the United States (http://www.turner-syndrome-us.org) has also been instrumental in providing support groups for XO girls and women, educational resources, and advocacy with the medical establishment.

2. Lanfranco et al. (2004) report that breast development and the lack of body and pubic hair in males with Klinefelter syndrome may be remedied with testosterone replacement therapy, although this treatment has no effect on infertility. Instead, one way that

infertility may now be handled by a man with Klinefelter syndrome is the extraction of sperm through a testicular biopsy, which is subsequently used to inseminate the man's partner through artificial means. This method has resulted in pregnancies and live births for female partners of men with Klinefelter syndrome (Lanfranco et al., 2004). Of course, couples may also opt for donor insemination. More information on Klinefelter syndrome and additional resources, including a list of support groups, is available from the Klinefelter Syndrome Organization (http://www.klinefeltersyndrome.org) and in the United Kingdom, from the Klinefelter Organisation (http://www.klinefelter.org.uk).

3. It was later discovered that Richard Speck, who brutally murdered nine student nurses in their dormitory rooms, was not, in fact, XYY.

4. Indeed, Hoyenga and Hoyenga (1993) note that were it not for illnesses that AGS males contract, they would most likely go undetected.

5. Kessler (1996) states that it is impossible to get accurate statistics on the incidence of conditions such as androgen insensitivity syndrome because unlike chromosomal conditions, hormonal conditions are not officially registered. In fact, the physicians she interviewed would not even guess at the incidence, although all agreed that such conditions are very rare. The condition recently received media attention when it was reported that "gender tests" of South African track star, Caster Semenya, showed that she has no ovaries or uterus, but internal testes. Some observers protested that Semenya should not be permitted to compete as a woman because her testes—and, therefore, her ability to secrete testosterone—give her an "unfair advantage" over other female athletes. Many physicians have responded, however, that Semenya's condition does not mean that she is a male masquerading as a female so as to more successfully compete; she is clearly a woman (Borenstein, 2009).

6. Additional research shows that for both women and men, being the victim of violence can alter the structure and functioning of the brain. The trauma of violent victimization can induce structural brain defects that in turn affect brain functioning by, for instance, reducing short-term memory and contributing to stress-related illnesses (Bremner, Randall, & Vermetten, 1997; McEwen, 2003; McGowen et al., 2009; Stein et al., 1997).

7. MRI is a procedure that produces high-resolution images of the living brain by measuring the waves that hydrogen atoms emit when they are activated by radio-frequency waves in a magnetic field (Pinel, 1997). Pinel (1997) also provides an excellent discussion of other technology that researchers and physicians use to study the brain, including computed tomography (CT scans), positron emission tomography (PET scans), and single photon emission computed tomography (SPECT scans). Both PET and SPECT allow researchers to not only pinpoint brain damage, but also trace brain activity in a snapshot fashion within seconds after it occurs. The neuroimaging technique fMRI maps changes in blood flow to various areas of the brain in response to specific stimuli, and MEG measures magnetic fields produced by electrical activity in the brain. See also Niehoff, 1999.

Chapter 3

Ancestors and Neighbors

Social Constructions of Gender at Other Times, in Other Places

None of us was alive six million years ago when humans as a species diverged from the apes, but all of us probably think we have a pretty good idea of what life was like for our prehistoric ancestors. For most of us, the quintessential symbol of prehistory is the caveman: a hairy, club-wielding cross between a man and an ape, who fiercely protected the home front and hunted wild animals to provide food for his dependents. Where do women fit into this scenario? "If women appear at all, they are at the edge of the picture, placid-looking, holding babies, squatting by the fire, stirring the contents of a pot" (Bleier, 1984, p. 116; see also Conkey, 1997; Conkey & Gero, 1991).

"The theory that humanity originated in the club-wielding man-ape, aggressive and masterful, is so widely accepted as scientific fact and vividly secure in our popular culture as to seem self-evident" (Bleier, 1984, p. 115). Yet, this theory has been challenged recently by scientists uncovering new data and reexamining existing data. In this chapter, we will discuss the *Man the Hunter* theory of human evolution more fully, and we will review some of the major scientific criticisms that have been leveled against it. Our discussion will be based on evidence from three sources:

1. the archeological record, which includes fossil remains;
2. primatology, especially studies of living nonhuman primates, such as chimpanzees and bonobos; and
3. anthropological studies of preindustrial societies, which scientists believe may be very similar to, if not replicas of, the earliest human communities.

To begin, then, let's turn to the archeological evidence.

BONES AND STONES: THE ARCHEOLOGICAL RECORD

Scientists confront a number of problems when attempting to reconstruct evolutionary history. For one thing, archeological finds are relatively sparse and fragmentary and, as Ruth Hubbard (1990, p. 67) points out, "behavior leaves no fossils." Scientists must rely on a few, very general clues—a jaw or skull (but often just pieces of them), some teeth, or chipped stones—as they try to solve the puzzle of how our early ancestors lived hundreds of thousands of years ago. The farther back in time we go, the less evidence we have and the more geographically spread out the puzzle is. For some periods, there is a "fossil gap," that is, there are no fossil remains for periods of a million years or more (Bleier, 1984; Gilchrist, 1999; Hubbard, 1979). Adding to the difficulty is the fact that only certain types of material, such as bone and stone, can be preserved. Organic materials, such as reeds and other plants as well as wood and bark, decay (Bleier, 1984; Ehrenberg, 1997). Consequently, "the fossil record available for study is not a representative sample of the human groups that have inhabited the earth," nor of the foods they ate nor of the tools they used. "Even armed with the maximum amount of information currently available for study...the amount of knowledge we do *not* possess is so vast that no one can claim a definitive theory of human origin and evolution" (Bleier, 1984, pp. 122–123, author's emphasis). Theories about the history and process of human evolution remain, as John Dupre (1990, p. 57) notes, at the level of "origin myths."

Despite these difficulties, however, archeologists and anthropologists have provided us with what by now has become a familiar account of prehistory focusing on Man the Hunter. According to this traditional reconstruction, some time between 12 and 28 million years ago, our ape ancestors were forced down out of the trees as the climate became dryer, causing their subtropical forest habitat to recede. One of their most important adaptations to life on the ground was **bipedalism**: the ability to walk upright on two feet. This freed their hands for reaching, grasping, and tearing objects; for carrying; and eventually, for using tools. However, bipedalism had other significant consequences as well. Standing and walking upright led to a narrowing of the pelvis so that the internal organs would be held in place. But as language developed, the size of the brain and, therefore, the head increased substantially relative to body size. To compensate for these anatomical changes, offspring were born at an earlier stage of development than had previously been the case, making them more dependent on their mother's care for survival. Obviously, females burdened with helpless infants could not roam very far in search of food, so the role of breadwinner was taken up by the males.

In assuming the responsibility of breadwinner, males faced a special challenge: the spread of indigestible grasses in their new savanna habitat made foraging for vegetation an unreliable food source. Gradually, hunting replaced foraging as the primary subsistence strategy, and meat became a central part of the early human diet. The most successful hunts were cooperative, so men banded together on hunting expeditions. This, in turn, led to the further evolution of their communication skills (in particular, language) and to the invention of the first tools (weapons for hunting and for defense). After a successful hunt, the men would share the kill and carry it back to their home bases where the women would prepare it for eating (Ehrenberg, 1997; Gough, 1975).

This sexual division of labor—women as caretakers of home and children, and men as breadwinners and protectors—was adaptive; those who conformed to it enjoyed a distinct advantage in the struggle for survival. In addition, these mutually exclusive female and male roles gave rise to particular personality traits; women grew to be empathic, nurturing, and dependent, whereas men were daring, unemotional, and aggressive. Over time, these adaptive characteristics were also naturally selected in the evolutionary process (Ardrey, 1966; Lovejoy, 1981; Tiger & Fox, 1971).[1]

It is hardly a coincidence that this depiction of prehistoric social life bears an uncanny resemblance to the traditional, middle-class nuclear family of Western societies. Anthropology, like most scientific disciplines, has been dominated by White, middle- and upper-middle-class men from Western industrialized countries, primarily the United States, Great Britain, and France (Kehoe, 1998). As we argued in Chapter 1, the values and beliefs of our society, as well as those of the specific groups to which we belong in that society, can strongly influence or bias our understanding of the world around us. Indeed, feminist anthropologists have identified two types of bias in the traditional Man the Hunter theory of human evolution: **ethnocentrism** and **androcentrism**.

To be ethnocentric means that one views one's own cultural beliefs and practices as superior to all others. Looking again at the Man the Hunter argument, we can see that it is ethnocentric in two ways. First, it inaccurately depicts contemporary Western gender relations as universal, both historically and cross-culturally. In other words, it makes it seem as if the behaviors and traits that are typically viewed as masculine or feminine in modern industrial societies like the United States are the same for men and women everywhere and that they have remained basically unchanged throughout human history. Second, and perhaps more importantly, this argument implies that the contemporary Western model of gender relations is the only correct or appropriate model because it is natural and adaptive (Conkey, 1997; Wylie, 1991). We will return to these criticisms shortly, but for now let's examine the second type of bias inherent in the Man the Hunter perspective.

Androcentric means male-centered. The Man the Hunter theory clearly emphasizes male behavior, with females being overlooked altogether or, at best, being portrayed as passive child bearers (Conkey, 1997; Ehrenberg, 1997; Tanner & Zihlman, 1976). Cooperation and sharing, competition and aggression, communication and the development of material technology are all seen as deriving from the exclusively male role of hunter, offering an incomplete and probably inaccurate picture of the diversity of gender roles and relations in various prehistoric societies (Ehrenberg, 1997; Gero, 1991).

Initially, feminist anthropologists attempted to correct the ethnocentrism and male bias characteristic of traditional anthropology by "finding women" in the archeological record (Di Leonardo, 1992; Gilchrist, 1999; Wylie, 1991). Largely by reexamining existing evidence, they developed alternative reconstructions of our prehistoric past that highlight the female role in human evolution. For example, Tanner and Zihlman (1976) argued that the traditional notion of apes being forced into the open savanna as forests receded was no longer tenable. Instead, they maintained that our ape ancestors moved away from the forests as their numbers grew, so as to avoid competition with the various species of monkeys and other animals living there. On the forest fringe, they found not just indigestible grasses, but a plentiful variety of foods, including nuts and seeds, fruits and berries, roots and tubers, eggs and insects, and several species of small animals, some of which burrowed underground. Successful exploitation of these resources, as well as the need for protection and defense in the open savanna habitat, required new survival strategies and adaptations. Bipedalism was one such adaptation, as it freed the hands for other tasks.

As this feminist reconstruction goes, bipedalism did result in other physiological changes, including the birth of offspring at an earlier stage of development. Rather than forcing mothers and children to become dependent on males, these changes spurred females to be more innovative in their quest for food and in the defense of their young against predators. The mothers' food-gathering task was made more difficult by additional physiological changes, especially the loss of body fur. This meant that infants had to be carried, since they could no longer cling to their mother's fur the way ape offspring do. Consequently, women had to invent something to carry their babies in so they could keep their hands free for collecting food. Moreover, they may have extended this innovation to food gathering itself, making carriers that permitted them to collect more food than could be eaten on the spot (Bleier, 1984; Slocum, 1975; Tanner & Zihlman, 1976).

The value of the initial feminist reconstructions, such as this one, is not that they are necessarily more accurate than those of traditional anthropology, but that they force us to consider alternative visions of prehistory. They suggest that perhaps the first material technology was not weapons for hunting, but rather slings or carriers for babies and food. They also suggest that females, far from being passive, dependent childbearers, may have been active technological innovators who provided food for themselves and their young and defended against predators (Ehrenberg, 1997). Instead of living in nuclear families, our prehistoric ancestors may have lived in mother-centered kin groups with flexible structures.

By reconceptualizing prehistory, this initial feminist research—which Wylie (1991) has referred to as "remedial"—encouraged feminist anthropologists to reexamine gender attributions in the archeological record. **Gender attribution** is the process of linking archeological data (e.g., tools and other artifacts) with males and females. Gender attributions rest on assumptions about what males and females did in prehistory, but these assumptions have often been colored by contemporary stereotypes of appropriate

BOX 3.1
Interpreting the Origin and Function of the "Venus" Figurines

The carved figurine that you see in this photo is one of many that have been discovered across Europe in an area stretching from southern France into Russia. Thought to be as much as 30,000 years old, they are often referred to as the "Venus" figurines. That label gives us a hint of how archeologists have traditionally interpreted the origin and meaning of the figurines. As Nelson (1997) found in her survey of introductory level archeology textbooks, the figurines are usually said to have been carved by men for sexual or reproductive purposes. For

What does this figurine tell you about the gender norms of Europeans who lived 30,000 years ago?

example, these archeologists emphasize the nakedness of the statuettes as well as their large breasts and broad hips. These traits they have assumed indicate early man's "obsessive need for women who would bear him lots of children" (quoted in Nelson, 1997, p. 70) or reflect his erotic desires for an "ample" woman to give

him pleasure. One writer even referred to the figurines as "Pleistocene pinup or centerfold girls" (quoted in Nelson, 1997, p. 69).

Looking at the Venus figure shown here, can you think of alternative origins or functions for such carvings? Isn't it possible that they could have been created by women, perhaps to teach girls about puberty or reproduction? Maybe they depict priestesses who were thought to perform ritual functions. Nelson (1997) further suggests that their nakedness may have nothing to do with sexuality or eroticism—after all, it is likely that men as well as women probably spent a good deal of their time unclothed or scantily dressed, especially when they were inside their caves or huts where fires warmed them. Today, in many parts of the world, especially in warm climates, women do not cover their breasts, and this partial nudity is not associated by them or the men of their society with eroticism.

Archeologists' traditional gender attributions of these figurines likely tell us more about the gender norms and stereotypes of the archeologists' culture than they do about sexuality and gender roles 30,000 years ago. This does not mean that the alternative attributions we have suggested are more accurate or correct. Rather, they simply remind us that we must be careful not to superimpose on the past the gender ideologies and stereotypes that are prevalent in contemporary society.

masculine and feminine behavior (see, for example, Box 3.1). Feminist reexaminations of the archeological record offered alternative gender attributions for various artifacts. For instance, the earliest archeological evidence for the hunting of animals with weapons is only 100,000 years old. (Bows and arrows appeared about 15,000 years ago.) Older tools—small hand-sized stones dating as far back as about 2.5 million years ago—might have been used for cutting and scraping meat, but would not have made good weapons for killing animals (Ehrenberg, 1997; Gero, 1991; Gilchrist, 1999; Longino & Doell, 1983). Moreover, archeological finds of early hominid teeth indicate that they were used primarily for grinding, most likely "to process gritty food from the ground, characteristic of much vegetable food" (Tanner & Zihlman, 1976, p. 598). This and other research (e.g., Gailey, 1987; Slocum, 1975) indicated that meat probably made up a fairly small portion of the early human diet. Gatherers, not hunters, therefore, likely made the major contribution to early humans' nutritional needs.

Nevertheless, feminist anthropologists themselves recognized some of the difficulties inherent in this "Woman the Gatherer" response to Man the Hunter theory. In its **gynecentrism** (that is, its "woman-centeredness"), the Woman the Gatherer reconstruction "simply reproduced or inverted the androcentric assumptions underlying the patently sexist research it was meant to challenge" (Wylie, 1991, pp. 39–40; see also Eller, 2000; Gilchrist, 1999). Feminist anthropologists began to consider what it means to "engender the past." Conkey and Gero's (1991) response to this question is worth quoting at length:

> Engendering the past becomes much more than "finding" men and women. It is trying to understand how gender "works" in all of its dimensions: as gender ideology, gender roles, gender relations, as well as a significant source of cultural meanings related to the construction of social lives....Larger questions...should lie at the heart of evolutionary studies...: has there always been a sexual division of labor? has there always been gender? what alternative forms of labor division might exist? how might such divisions of tasks, in fact, "create" gender?...Even if some version of *a* sexual division of labor *is* one of the entry points through which we engender our narratives of the past, this division of labor—as an object of knowledge—should not go unquestioned or unchallenged. (pp. 12, 14; authors' emphasis)

Feminist anthropologists who have undertaken research with these questions in mind have focused largely on interpersonal relations and household activities, rather than the traditional areas of trade, politics, and government. However, they emphasize that household production and social life cannot be separated from the "external" public domain because these activities are critical to the ability of a population to grow and sustain itself, and they also make possible the work that a state requires (Conkey & Gero, 1991; Gilchrist, 1999). These studies have found that in many early human societies, males and females often had overlapping experiences, and there is ample evidence that women participated in activities, such as flint-knapping and the creation of art, from which they were previously thought to have been excluded (Gero, 1991; Gilchrist, 1999; Handsman, 1991). The gendered division of labor has also featured in a recent theory explaining the extinction of Neanderthals, a population that lived in Europe for about 100,000 years. According to this theory, the skeletal remains of Neanderthals indicate that all members of the society—men, women and children—hunted large animals at close range, a survival strategy that did not produce a continuous food supply, but that was very dangerous and imperiled the reproductive core of the population. In contrast, the ancestors of modern humans, who lived from 45,000 to 10,000 years ago during the Upper Paleolithic period, had a gendered division of labor in which men primarily hunted large animals and women and children hunted or trapped small animals and gathered vegetation, a survival strategy that was safer and resulted in a more diverse and more reliable food supply, thus giving them an evolutionary advantage (Kuhn & Stiner, 2006). Again, because of the fragmentary nature of the archeological record, we may never have definitive evidence to establish the accuracy of any of these theories. But what is more significant perhaps is that feminist anthropologists have developed new ways of writing about the past that, unlike the traditional sterile accounts, convey more vivid images of our prehistoric ancestors, not only as gendered but also as purposeful human actors (Rautman, 2000; Spector, 1991).

Engendering the past has not only occurred in archeology, but also in other branches of anthropology, including primatology and ethnographic studies of contemporary nonindustrial societies. Let's examine some of this research now.

OUR PRIMATE RELATIVES

Because of the many gaps in the archeological record, scientists have sought additional sources of data to help them piece together our evolutionary past. Research on living, nonhuman primates—a field of study called **primatology**—has been especially useful in this regard. Recent studies have identified close biological similarities between humans and various species of monkeys and apes, particularly chimpanzees and bonobos. Recent DNA analyses, in fact, show that chimpanzees and bonobos are the primates most closely related to humans and that they differentiated about 5.5 million years ago, a relatively short time in evolutionary history (Angier, 1999a; de Waal, 2005; Zihlman, 1993). Therefore, observing what our closest living primate relatives do as they adapt to the various environments in which they live should tell us something about the social behavior of our ancestors and perhaps about contemporary human behavior as well.

Of course, this approach has its problems too. For one, "The women and men who have contributed to primate studies have carried with them the marks of their own histories and cultures. These marks are written into the texts of the lives of the monkeys and apes, but often in subtle and unexpected ways" (Haraway, 1989, p. 2). Second, primate species vary widely in the extent to which there are both anatomical and behavioral differences between the sexes. There are about two hundred species of primates, and in about 40 percent of these, females are dominant or equal to males (Wright, 1993). We will return to this point shortly, but for now suffice it to say that the tremendous variability among primate species makes it possible for one to cite examples of virtually any behavior one is looking for simply by choosing a particular animal (Dupre, 1990; Hubbard, 1990). Finally, "most scientists find it convenient to forget that present-day apes and monkeys have had as long an evolutionary past as we have had, since the time we went our separate ways millions of years ago" (Hubbard, 1979, p. 30). Nevertheless, keeping the limitations of these data in mind, many scientists, feminists included, maintain that much can be learned about human evolutionary history by studying present-day primates, especially our closest primate relatives, the chimps and bonobos.

Early primate studies were much in the tradition of the Man the Hunter theory (de Waal, 2005; Haraway, 1989). They characterized the primates ancestral to humans as killer apes, with the males of the species competing aggressively with one another for food and sexual access to females. Primate herds were said to be organized into *dominance hierarchies* with the largest male assuming the role of leader and being accorded special sexual privileges as well as top priority in the food distribution order (Ardrey, 1966; Lovejoy, 1981).

Wright (1993) maintains that the gender stereotypes that emerged from this early research were due to the fact that the studies were based on only cursory observations of certain types of primates. However, more recent and more thorough field studies of a diversity of primate species show tremendous variation in their social organization and in male/female behavior. We now know, for example, that most primate groups are **matrifocal**, that is, a system of group life and social organization centered around mothers or females generally. For instance, although chimpanzee communities are male-dominated and include a good deal of fighting and violence, females are not "supported" by males; females acquire their own food and food for their offspring (Angier, 1999a; Bleier, 1984). Male and female chimps participate in food acquisition activities and use tools for these tasks. In fact, female chimps learn to use sticks for "termite fishing" (i.e., extracting termites from mounds for snacks) about two years earlier than male chimps do, and it is their mothers who teach them how to do this (Lonsdorf et al., 2005). And despite chimps' relatively high levels of aggression, they also display a high level of sociability and cooperation (see, for example, Melis et al., 2006). Female chimpanzees have been observed removing stones from a male chimp's hands to avert a fight and trying to reconcile male chimps after a fight has occurred (de Waal, 2006).

Bonobos are sociable and cooperative, and live in peaceful female-centered communities.

Bonobo communities are female-focused and revolve not only around cooperation but also empathy, nurturance, and sexuality. "Among bonobos, there's no deadly warfare, little hunting, no male dominance, and enormous amounts of sex" (de Waal, 2005, p. 30). Female bonobos have sex with other females as well as with males. Moreover, female bonobos are the ones in the community who migrate; they leave home at puberty, while male bonobos stay with their mothers for care and protection. When there is aggression among bonobos, it is often females who fight and, if males are involved, they are typically the ones who end up injured.[2] Overall, however, bonobo daily life takes place in peaceful, female-centered communities and, significantly, bonobos are as closely related to humans as chimps are (de Waal, 2005).

What does all of this tell us about the evolution of human gender relations? Although we must remember the dangers of making generalizations about human behavior based on observations of even our closest primate relatives, studies of primate behavior and social organization may provide us with clues—albeit limited ones—about our ancestral roots. At the very least, such research calls into question gender stereotypes derived from early cursory studies of a small percentage of primate species and highlights the important roles females play in structuring primate societies (Angier, 1999a; Ward, 1996; Wright, 1993). It points to "the *range* of behavior our ancestors may have shown" (de Waal, 2005, p. 11, emphasis added). Certainly, such research forces us to consider the possibility that our prehuman ancestors, quite unlike so-called killer apes, lived in groups characterized by sociability and cooperation among males and females. Such gender relations are not unknown among contemporary human societies, as we will see next.

WOMEN AND MEN ELSEWHERE: ARE WESTERN CONSTRUCTIONS OF GENDER UNIVERSAL?

Earlier we discussed the ethnocentric bias of the Man the Hunter theory. This perspective portrays male dominance and female subordination as historical and cultural universals. It assumes that men everywhere and at all times have been women's superiors and that the work men do is more important or more highly valued than women's work. Not surprisingly, this theory was developed largely by Western male anthropologists who were viewing other societies through the tinted lenses of their own culture. Assuming male dominance, they often overlooked women's roles in the societies they were observing, or they relied on male informants for data on women (Gailey, 1987; Rogers, 1978; Ward, 1996). The question, then, bears re-asking: Are Western constructions of gender universal?

More than seventy-five years ago, the pioneering anthropologist Margaret Mead answered that question in the negative based on her field research among three societies in New Guinea. Mead observed cultures in which men were expected to be timid and nurturant, but women could be described as aggressive and competitive (Mead, 1935). Since Mead's work was published, more research has been done on cross-cultural variations in gender. Rather than lending support to the notion of the universality of Western constructions of gender or gender inequality, these studies reveal a rich assortment of patterns of gender relations throughout the world.

Every known society has a division of labor by sex (and also by age). However, what is considered men's work versus what is considered women's work varies dramatically from society to society. In some cultures, for instance, women build the houses; in others, this is men's work. In most societies, women do the cooking, but there are societies in which this is typically men's responsibility. There are very few societies in which women participate in metalworking, lumbering, and hunting large land and sea animals, although there are exceptions (Murdoch & Provost, 1973). For example, among the Agta of the Philippines, women hunt deer and wild pigs with knives and bows and arrows (Estioko-Griffin, 1986). In most cases, though, women's hunting activities do not involve the use of spears, bows and arrows, or heavy clubs (Harris, 1993). It has also been argued by some researchers that in virtually all societies men hold a monopoly on the use of physical violence (e.g., Harris, 1993; Konner, 1982), but others have reported on female warriors and soldiers (e.g., Sacks, 1979; see also Chapter 10). There is also considerable evidence that women may behave as aggressively as men, especially when competitiveness and verbal abusiveness are included as measures of aggression (e.g., Angier, 1999a; Björkqvist, 1994; Crick et al., 2004; Lepowsky, 1994; Putallaz & Bierman, 2004).

Are there societies that are *matriarchal* in the same way that other societies are patriarchal? In other words, are there societies in which women dominate men the way men dominate women in patriarchal societies and societies in which what is considered masculine is systematically devalued while what is feminine is revered? For the most part, the answer to these questions is no. But as anthropologist Peggy Reeves Sanday has pointed out, these questions themselves are ethnocentric and androcentric. "Defining a female-oriented social order as the mirror image of a male form is like saying that women's contribution to society and culture deserves a special label only if women act and rule like men" (Sanday, 2002, p. xi). Instead of a matriarchy akin to a patriarchy, anthropologists have documented numerous examples, both historical and contemporary, of matrifocal or *matricentric* (i.e., female-centered) societies. Rather than emphasizing female dominance, however, these societies tend to be gender-egalitarian, with social relationships based on *linkages* instead of rankings (Sanday, 2002; Ward & Edelstein, 2006).

Some of these societies are **horticultural societies**, in which the primary economic activity is farming using digging sticks, hoes, and similar technology (Blumberg, 2005; Sanday, 2002; Ward & Edelstein, 2006). Many, however, are foraging societies. Anthropologists have argued that foraging societies are probably most like the communities of our earliest human ancestors (Bonvillain, 1998; O'Kelly & Carney, 1986). This is not to say that contemporary foraging societies are exact replicas of prehistoric societies. These societies, like all others, have experienced numerous environmental and social changes throughout their histories, not the least of which came through contact with European and American colonizers during the past six hundred years (Bleier, 1984; Bonvillain, 1998; Etienne & Leacock, 1980; Leacock, 1993). Today, contact with Westerners continues to erode, if not destroy, the traditions of many foraging and horticultural societies in the name of "modernization." Foraging societies, though, are still the smallest (25 to 200 members) and least technologically developed of all human societies, so contemporary foraging peoples may offer us further clues as to how our early ancestors may have lived, while teaching us valuable lessons about the diversity of social constructions of gender today.

Gender Relations in Contemporary Foraging Societies

The **foraging society** is also referred to as the *hunting-gathering society* because its members meet their survival needs by hunting game (and often by fishing) and by gathering vegetation and other types of food in their surrounding environment. Just who performs each task, however, varies somewhat from society to society. The pattern most frequently observed is one in which men hunt large animals and go deep-sea fishing if possible, while women take primary responsibility for gathering and for hunting small animals as well as for food preparation, home building, and child care (Bonvillain, 1998; O'Kelly & Carney, 1986). In most societies, though, in spite of a clear division of labor by sex in principle, in practice there is actually considerable overlap in what men and women do, and there are "crossovers in role," as Gilmore (1990) refers to them, without shame or anxiety for women or men (see also Lepowsky, 1993). Food and other resources are reciprocally shared in what Ward and Edelstein (2006) call the "pot-luck principle"—that is, each member of the society contributes what she or he can to meet everyday survival needs because these needs can be met more effectively and efficiently through *collective* efforts rather than each individual working alone.

O'Kelly and Carney (1986, pp. 12–21) have identified six different patterns of the gendered division of labor among hunting and gathering societies:

1. men hunt, women process the catch;
2. men hunt, women gather;
3. men hunt, men and women gather;

4. men hunt and fish, women hunt and gather;

5. men and women independently hunt, fish, and gather;

6. men and women communally hunt and gather.

In the first type, which is common among Eskimo groups, meat and fish are the dietary staples, and men are the chief food providers. This puts women at a disadvantage relative to men; they are dependent on men for food as well as for goods obtained through trade with non-Eskimos. Consequently, men in these societies have more power and prestige than women, but this does not mean that women are powerless or that women's work is considered unimportant. Women gather vegetation and birds' eggs, fish, and, in inland areas, participate in caribou drives. Women in some communities also hunt animals and birds, and they fish (Bonvillain, 1998).[3] But women's most important responsibility is making the clothing and much of the equipment men need to hunt and fish. Without warm clothes and watertight boots, hunters (as well as all other residents) would quickly perish in this harsh environment (Bonvillain, 1998; O'Kelly & Carney, 1986). As a result, "the skills of women are as indispensable to survival as are those of men, and they are so perceived by men.... The question, 'Which is better (or more important), a good hunter or a good seamstress?' is meaningless in Eskimo; both are indispensable" (quoted in Sacks, 1979, pp. 89–90).

Despite the complementarity of gendered behaviors in hunting-gathering societies of this first type, they are the least egalitarian of all hunter-gatherers. Women who live in societies characterized by one of the five other previously listed patterns take a more direct and active role in food acquisition that, in turn, affords them more equal access to their societies' resources and rewards. Among the Ju/hoansi bush-living people of the Kalahari Desert, for example, women provide about 70 percent of the society's food through their gathering activities.[4] The Ju/hoansi division of labor conforms to the second type on our list, but the game hunted by men is a much less dependable food source than the plant and small animal food obtained by women. The women are respected for their specialized knowledge of the bush; "successful gathering over the years requires the ability to discriminate among hundreds of edible and inedible species of plants at various stages in their life cycle" (Draper, 1975, p. 83). In addition, women return from their gathering expeditions armed not only with food for the community, but also with valuable information for hunters, such as herd sightings and animal tracks.

The Ju/hoansi have a clear division of labor by sex, but it is not rigidly adhered to, and men and women sometimes do one another's chores. This is especially true of men, who frequently do "women's work" without any shame or embarrassment. Child care is viewed as the responsibility of both parents, and "as children grow up there are few experiences which set one sex apart from the other" (Draper, 1975, p. 89). In fact, child rearing practices are very relaxed and nonauthoritarian, reflecting Ju/hoansi social relations in general. Among the Ju/hoansi, aggressive behavior on the part of men or women is discouraged, and they rarely engage in organized armed conflict (Bonvillain, 1998; Draper, 1975; Harris, 1993; Shostak, 1981). As Harris (1993) notes, although Ju/hoansi boys are taught from early childhood how to kill large animals, they are not taught to kill other people.

Egalitarian gender relations like those of the Ju/hoansi are also characteristic of the other types of hunting-gathering societies remaining on our list. In these societies, one sex is not intrinsically valued over the other. Rather, an individual wins respect and influence within the community based on his *or her* contribution to the general well-being of the group (Bleier, 1984). The Aka (type 6 in the preceding list) who live in the tropical rain forests in the south of the Central African Republic and northern Congo, provide another example. Among the Aka, work is a collective enterprise, and few tasks are assigned exclusively to one sex. Women, men, and children share infant care; forage together for nuts, vegetation, and caterpillars; and hunt cooperatively. The Aka hunt with nets; women have the responsibility of tackling the animal caught in the net and killing it. Aka women and men are described as indulgent parents, but fathers are significantly more likely than mothers to hug, kiss, or soothe a fussy infant they are holding. Aka fathers reportedly hold their infants five times more often in a twenty-four-hour period than fathers in other cultures. The Agta of the Philippines also have this type of division of labor (type 6). As noted previously, Agta women and men hunt, using knives or bows and arrows. They fish with spears while swimming underwater, an activity that requires considerable skill and physical stamina. Although hunting and fishing supply most of the Agta's food, members of both sexes gather vegetation as well and share child care (Estioko-Griffin, 1986). As O'Kelly and Carney (1986, p. 13) observe, "This cooperative interdependence is associated with highly egalitarian gender roles."

As we have already noted, egalitarian gender relations are not limited to hunting and gathering societies, although they appear to be more common in these types of societies than in others. Lepowsky (1993, 1990) has conducted research among the people of Vanatinai, a small island southeast of mainland Papua New Guinea. In this horticultural society both women and men plant, tend, and harvest garden crops; men hunt animals with spears, while women hunt using traps. Women have more responsibility than men for child care, but men share this task quite willingly. Members of both sexes learn and practice magic; participate in warfare, peacemaking, and community decision making; and undertake sailing expeditions in search of ceremonial valuables. Sanday's (2002) findings from her extensive research among the Minangkabau of Western Sumatra, "the largest and most stable matrilineal society in the world today," are similar in documenting gender egalitarianism.

Several important points can be drawn from these cross-cultural data. First, it should be clear to us by now that contemporary Western constructions of gender are not universal. The research indicates that there is a wide range of gender relations cross-culturally and that in some societies, gender relations are highly egalitarian. Furthermore, if contemporary foraging societies do resemble the communities in which our earliest ancestors lived, they do not lend support to the reconstruction offered by the Man the Hunter theory. Instead, they reinforce archeological and primatological data that indicate that at least some of our early ancestors may have lived in groups characterized by cooperation and reciprocity and in which adults of both sexes actively contributed to group survival.

A second significant point that can be gleaned from these anthropological studies is that a gendered division of labor does not necessarily produce gender inequality. The key intervening variable appears to be the *value* that the members of a society attach to a particular role or task. In our own society, the work women do is typically viewed as less important than the work men do. But in the societies discussed here, women are seen as "essential partners" in the economy and in decision making, even though women and men may be responsible for different tasks or have different spheres of influence (Bonvillain, 1998; Gailey, 1987; Miller, 1993). As Sacks (1979, pp. 92–93) observes, "Many nonclass societies have no problem in seeing differentiation without having to translate it into differential worth."

A third point concerns women's capacity to bear children. We noted earlier in the chapter that some scholars maintain that women's reproductive role prevents them from fully participating in other activities, such as food acquisition. However, the anthropological studies reviewed in this section suggest that women are not automatically excluded from certain activities because they bear children. Nor are men automatically excluded from child rearing simply because they cannot bear children.

> It is important to see that, unlike breathing, for example, the biological capacity to reproduce does not necessarily mean that one *has* to reproduce or even be heterosexually active, nor does it dictate the social arrangements for child nurturance and rearing or determine how child rearing affects one's participation in other cultural activities. Whether or not we bear, nurse or mother children is just as much a function of cultural, social, political, economical, and, no more importantly, biological factors as whether we are poets or soccer players. (Bleier, 1984, p. 146, author's emphasis)

In preindustrial societies, like those we have discussed so far, child bearing and child rearing do not isolate mothers as they frequently do in societies like our own. "The tasks are absorbed by a broader range of people, and children are more incorporated into public activities....Moreover, motherhood (either through childbirth, adoption, or fosterage) often conveys an *increase* in status, giving women a greater say in matters than when they were not fully adult" (Gailey, 1987, pp. 45–46, author's emphasis). Women's ability to bear children is recognized as a valuable contribution to the survival of the group, equivalent in some societies to obtaining meat for food through hunting (Biesele, 1993).

It appears, then, that nonbiological factors—among them environmental resources, size of the group, the economy, and, of course, ideology—play at least as significant a part in determining what the members of a society define as appropriate "men's work" and "women's work" as biological factors do. Contrary to Sigmund Freud's assertion, anatomy is *not* destiny. This point is made even clearer when we consider examples of multiple genders.

Multiple Genders

Throughout this chapter so far, we have discussed gender as a dichotomous category. However, as we learned in Chapter 2, such a conceptualization of gender is at best misleading. Anthropological research also provides fascinating data that call into question the notion of gender as a dichotomy. Indeed, in some societies there are three genders, and in others, four. The *berdache* of some Asian, South Pacific, and North American Indian societies is an excellent example. *Berdaches* were individuals who adopt the gender behavior ascribed to members of the opposite sex. While women could become *berdaches,* most research has focused on men who chose to be *berdaches.*

Berdaches lived, worked, and dressed as members of the opposite sex, although they were often specialists in tasks associated with both sexes (Gailey, 1987; Martin & Voorhies, 1975; Roscoe, 1991; Ward & Edelstein, 2006; Whitehead, 1981; W. L. Williams, 1986). The Mohave, for instance, allowed men and women to cross genders. Boys who showed a preference for feminine toys and clothing would undergo an initiation ceremony at puberty during which they became *alyha*. As *alyha,* they adopted feminine names, painted their faces as women did, performed female tasks, and married men. When they married, *alyha* pretended to menstruate by cutting their upper thighs. They also simulated pregnancy. "Labor pains, induced by drinking a severely constipating drug, culminate in the birth of a fictitious stillborn child. Stillborn Mohave infants are customarily buried by the mother, so that an *alyha*'s failure to return to 'her' home with a living infant is explained in a culturally acceptable manner" (Martin & Voorhies, 1975, p. 97).

We'wha, a Zuni berdache, enjoyed high social status in his community.

A Mohave female who wished to pursue a masculine lifestyle underwent an initiation ceremony to become a *hwame*. *Hwame* dressed and lived much like men; they engaged in hunting, farming, and shamanism, although they were not permitted to assume leadership positions or participate in warfare. They did, though, assume paternal responsibility for children; some women, in fact, became *hwame* after they had children. Importantly, neither *hwame* nor *alyha* were considered abnormal or deviant within their cultures (Martin & Voorhies, 1975).

Anthropologist Will Roscoe (1991) has conducted extensive research on Zuni *berdaches,* called *lhamana* by this American Indian nation. Roscoe points out that although *berdaches* cross-dressed, it is inaccurate to label them transvestites or transsexuals as some researchers have done. This is because their cross-dressing was routine, public, and without erotic motives. Nor were *berdaches* necessarily homosexual as we think of this sexual orientation today. There were Zunis who were sexually oriented to the opposite sex, some who were sexually oriented to the same sex, and still others who were sexually oriented to *berdaches*. "Such an organization of gender geometrically increased options for individual identities and behaviors" (Roscoe, 1991, p. 146). Moreover, Roscoe emphasizes that there was no stigma attached to the *berdache* status; *berdaches* were not viewed negatively as deviants. Roscoe attributes this openness to the Zuni conception of gender acquisition, which maintained that gender is not something one is born with, but rather something that develops over the course of one's life. In fact, until about age six, gender was not seen as an important attribute of a child, and children of both sexes, rather than being called "boy" or "girl," were simply referred to as "child." According to Roscoe (1991):

> In Zuni philosophy, one's status as a man, woman, or berdache was a product of culture, the result of [socialization], while gender balance, the possibility of combining or temporarily adopting roles and experiences of more than one gender, was a desirable end for all Zunis. Berdaches were not branded as threats to a rigid gender ideology; rather, they were considered an affirmation of humanity's original, pre-gendered unity—representatives of a form of solidarity and wholeness that transcended the division of humans into men and women. (p. 146)[5]

Unfortunately, this positive evaluation of *berdaches* and broad conception of gender were virtually extinguished through contact with White society, especially Christian missionaries. Although *berdaches* certainly did not disappear, by the end of World War II, the common attitudes toward them in many, though not all, Native American communities were shame and often hostility. Native Americans with traits and interests that previously could have been expressed by becoming *berdaches* were forced to either deny their feelings or hide them. However, anthropologists have been documenting a rediscovery of *berdachism* among North American Indians, largely through the combined efforts of the Native American rights movement and the gay rights movement. Today, the term *Two-Spirit* is preferred over *berdache* because *berdache* is actually a Western word that, while commonly used, "may not accurately reflect patterns or values of gender variance in the contemporary communities of Native North Americans" (Ward & Edelstein, 2006, p. 182). Rather, *Two-Spirit* "better integrates the sexual, gendered, political, artistic, and spiritual meanings of crossing the [gender] borders" (Ward & Edelstein, 2006, p. 182; see also Gilley, 2006; Leland, 2006).

Other examples of such gender crossing can also be found in Tahitian culture (Gilmore, 1990), among the Omani Muslims (Wikan, 1984), and in rural northern Albania (Bilefsky, 2008). One well-documented group is the *hijras* of India (Jaffrey, 1996; Nanda, 1990). The *hijras* are men who dress and behave as women, although in somewhat exaggerated and "unfeminine" or immodest ways. Many undergo castration, which is viewed as a transition from one status to another—the person who performs the surgery, in fact, is called a midwife—and there are a variety of rituals associated with the periods before and after the surgery. *Hijras* live together in communities, and they are recognized as having special spiritual powers (Ward & Edelstein, 2006). They earn a living by collecting alms or offerings as well as by being paid for performing at and blessing special occasions, such as weddings and births, especially the births of male infants (Jaffrey, 1996).

Other researchers have identified societies in which gender is considered a process rather than a stable social category. Meigs (1990) and Gailey (1987) report that among the Hua of Papua New Guinea, gender is perceived as changing throughout an individual's life. The Hua bestow high status on masculine people, but view them as physically weak and vulnerable. Feminine people are regarded as invulnerable, but polluted. When children are born, they are all at least partially feminine because the Hua believe that women transfer some of their own femininity to their offspring. Thus, the more children a woman has, the more femininity she loses. After three births, she is no longer considered polluted. She may participate in the discussions and rituals of men and share their higher status and authority, but she must also observe their diet and sanitation customs since she has now become vulnerable.

Hua men, meanwhile, gradually lose their masculinity by imparting it to young boys during growth rituals. As this happens, they become regarded as physically invulnerable, but polluted. Consequently, old men work in the fields with young women and have little social authority. "Among the Hua, then, gender is only tangentially related to sex differences; it is mutable and flows from person to person. The process of engendering is lifelong, and through it males and females shed the gender they were born with and acquire the opposite characteristics" (Gailey, 1987, p. 36).

Each of these examples illustrates the fluidity of gender as well as the creativity that humans bring to the process of social organization. While "our society typecasts women and men from birth through death...other societies exist where gender differences are not extended beyond adult reproductive roles" (Gailey, 1987, p. 35).

GENDER, EVOLUTION, AND CULTURE

In this chapter, we examined evolutionary perspectives of gender. The traditional view—Man the Hunter theory—rests on the assumption that the gender inequality and asymmetry attached to masculinity and femininity in modern Western industrial societies are historical and cultural universals. This position maintains that contemporary Western constructions of gender evolved from a prehistoric past in which women were necessarily dependent on men for food and protection as a result of the burdens of pregnancy and motherhood. Women, then, were relegated to the "home," whereas men assumed the public roles of defender and food provider. They fulfilled the latter primarily by hunting together in groups, and it was through these hunting activities that the hallmarks of the human species—in particular, language and the invention of material technology—supposedly developed.

In contrast to Man the Hunter theory, we also discussed feminist perspectives of the evolution of gender. Feminist social scientists have sought new evidence and reexamined existing evidence from three main sources—the archeological record, primatology, and ethnographic studies of contemporary preindustrial societies. Standing alone, each of these data sources has serious drawbacks, but taken together they allow us to develop alternative reconstructions of our prehistoric past. Although initial feminist efforts to correct the androcentric bias in Man the Hunter theories resulted in reconstructions that were also sexist because of their gynecentrism, more recent research has revealed that at least some early human communities were probably cooperative and quite flexible in their social organization. Moreover, women, rather than being passive and dependent, were instead likely to have been active food providers as well as inventors and crafters of new material technology. Not unlike our closest primate relatives and probably very similar to members of contemporary foraging societies, our early human ancestors of both sexes were hunters and gatherers, although gathering may have been a more successful subsistence strategy.

In any event, the research reviewed in this chapter suggests that if we are to develop a more balanced account of the evolution of gender, we need to explore further the very strong possibility that both females and males were full and active participants in the struggle for survival. A presumption of gender inequality appears to be unfounded and misleading. Moreover, the existence of multiple genders in some societies underlines the point that sex and gender are distinct and sometimes independent categories. Gender is not an either/or category, but rather a fluid one that can best be conceptualized as multifaceted rather than dichotomous.

One question that remains unanswered is how did we get here from there? That is, if gender relations in some societies were (and still are) highly egalitarian, what factors gave rise to the pervasive gender inequality characteristic of societies like our own? Any answer remains speculative, but scientists who have addressed this question have identified a number of related factors, including population growth, increased environmental danger from ecological changes or warfare, the establishment of trade or exchange relations between societies, a change from a nomadic to a sedentary lifestyle, and technological advances allowing for the accumulation of a surplus of food and other goods (Bonvillain, 1998; Gailey, 1987; Harris, 1993; Lepowsky, 1990; Nelson, 1993; O'Kelly & Carney, 1986). Certainly, much more research is needed to clarify the relationship between each of these conditions and the emergence of gender inequality. However, the available evidence indicates that specific gender relations appear to arise largely in response to external circumstances—economic, political, and social—not biological imperatives. In succeeding chapters, we will focus on how particular gender relations are reinforced and perpetuated.

Key Terms

androcentrism   male-centered; the view that men are superior to other animals and to women

bipedalism   walking upright on two feet

ethnocentrism   the view that one set of cultural beliefs and practices is superior to all others

foraging societies   (hunting and gathering societies) small, technologically undeveloped societies whose members meet their survival needs by hunting and trapping animals, by fishing (if possible), and by gathering vegetation and other types of food in their surrounding environment; characterized by highly egalitarian gender relations

gender attribution   the process of linking archeological data with males and females

gynecentrism   female-centered; the view that females are superior to other animals and to men

horticultural society   a preindustrial society in which the primary economic activity is farming using digging sticks, hoes, and similar technology

matrifocal   a system of social organization and group life centered around mothers

primatology   the study of living, nonhuman primates

Suggested Readings

de Waal, F. (2005). *Our inner ape*. New York: Riverhead Books. A readable survey of the research on both chimps and bonobos by a leading primatologist who explains why the "killer ape" theory of human ancestry is misleading and how the gentle and conciliatory behavior of bonobos can teach us just as much about our evolutionary heritage.

Gilley, B. J. (2006). *Becoming Two-Spirit: Gay identity and social acceptance in Indian country*. Lincoln: University of Nebraska Press. A readable ethnography of contemporary Two-Spirit societies and their members, showing how Two-Spirits are reclaiming this aspect of their tribal ancestry and at the same time developing positive self-images and social relationships that affirm their gender and sexual identities.

Jaffrey, Z. (1996). *The invisibles: A tale of the eunuchs of India*. New York: Vintage. An ethnography of the *hijra* communities by an American author of Indian descent.

Rautman, A. E. (Ed.) (2000). *Reading the body: Representations and remains in the archeological record*. Philadelphia: University of Pennsylvania Press. A collection of papers written by archeologists and others, who reexamine various sets of artifacts, calling into question previous gender attributions and offering alternative interpretations.

Sanday, P. R. (2002). *Women at the center: Life in a modern matriarchy*. Ithaca, NY: Cornell University Press. Sanday reports on her field research among the Minangkabau of Indonesia that she conducted from 1981 to 1999.

Travis, C. B. (Ed.) (2003). *Evolution, gender, and rape*. Cambridge, MA: MIT Press. A collection of essays based on extensive research in a variety of disciplines that offers a thorough critique of the evolutionary psychological theory of rape.

Wood, J. C. (1999). *When men are women: Manhood among Gabra nomads of East Africa*. Madison: University of Wisconsin Press. A fascinating study of the fluidity of gender in a nomadic camel-herding society that devalues females and femininity but considers its highest-status men, the elder experts in ritual, to be women.

Notes

1. The idea that gender differences in emotions, as well as behaviors, developed millions of years ago and have been passed on genetically through generations because they were adaptive—that is, they enhanced survival and reproductive success—is central to the field of study known as *evolutionary psychology*. Evolutionary psychologists have used this idea to explain many complex human traits and behaviors, including sexual attraction and mate selection. One recent controversial application of the idea, for example, proposes that sexual coercion and rape have evolved as part of contemporary social life because those among our prehistoric male ancestors who were rejected by females as mates used these strategies to increase their reproductive success (Thornhill & Palmer, 2000). Evolutionary psychology is enjoying a resurgence in popularity, and evolutionary psychologists are even publishing self-help books based on Darwinian principles (see, for instance, Burnham & Phelan, 2000). However, this particular position on rape has been seriously criticized, even by some prominent evolutionary psychologists (see, for instance, Buller, 2005; Coyne & Berry, 2000; Goode, 2000a; Travis, 2003).

2. Recent research in the Congo, however, indicates that both female and male bonobos may occasionally engage in group hunts for other primates, such as smaller tree-dwelling monkeys (Surbeck & Hohmann, 2008).

3. Bonvillain (1998) reports that among some groups living in Arctic areas, fathers teach their daughters to hunt. The father may favor his daughter over his son, or he may simply have no sons. Further, Bonvillain (1998) notes that in families with only male or only female children, parents may teach the children skills associated with the other sex as well as those associated with their own. "These individuals," according to Bonvillain (1998, p. 26), "are valued as spouses because they have a double set of subsistence skills."

4. The Ju/hoansi (pronounced "ju-*twan*-si) were traditionally called the !Kung by anthropologists. However, Ju/hoansi, which means "real people," is the name they use in their language to refer to themselves (Bonvillain, 1998).

5. Compare the attitude of the Zuni with that of our own society toward individuals who make gender choices different from traditional norms of femininity or masculinity. See, for example, Lucal, 1999.

Chapter 4

Early Childhood Gender Socialization

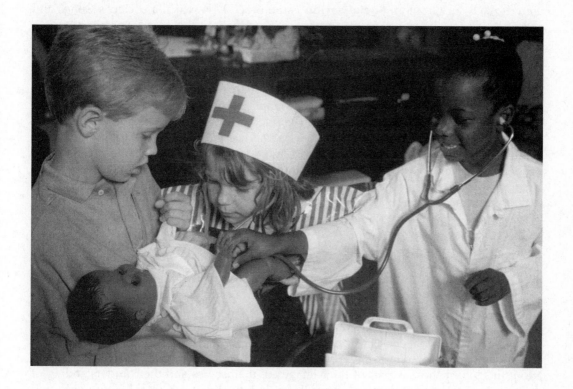

Peering at babies through the window of a hospital nursery, onlookers can usually tell with little difficulty which infants are girls and which are boys. This ability to discern the newborn's sex is not because of obvious physical differences between the female and male babies, but rather because hospital staff wrap the girls in pink blankets and the boys in blue or write the girls' names on pink cards and the boys' names on blue ones. Rhode (1997) reports that at the beginning of the twentieth century, girls were dressed in blue because that color was associated with delicacy, while boys wore pink because that color implied manliness. The specific colors, of course, are irrelevant. What is important are the traits the colors are supposed to signify. From the moment they are born, girls are considered dainty and boys strong—popular gender stereotypes that translate into expectations of children's behavior.

In this chapter, we will discuss how gendered expectations are transmitted to children through socialization. **Socialization** is the process by which a society's values and norms, including those pertaining to gender, are taught and learned. Socialization is a lifelong process that we will examine throughout the text, but in this chapter, we will concentrate on the socialization that occurs mostly in the early childhood years. Gender socialization is sometimes a conscious effort in that expectations are reinforced with explicit rewards and punishments. Boys in particular receive explicit negative sanctions for engaging in what is considered gender-inappropriate behavior. Gender socialization may also be more subtle, however, with gender messages relayed implicitly through the ways adults interact with one another as well as with children, through children's clothing, and through their books and toys. In addition, children socialize one another, explicitly and more subtly, through their interactions in peer groups. However, before we discuss the research on the content of early childhood gender socialization, let's look at the socialization *process*. To begin, we'll consider some of the theories that have been developed to explain *how* young children acquire their gender identities.

LEARNING GENDER

Research indicates that children as young as eighteen months old show preferences for gender-stereotyped toys. By the age of two, they are aware of their own and others' gender, and between two and three years of age, they begin to identify specific traits and behaviors in gender-stereotyped ways (Golombok & Fivush, 1994). Sex-typed behavior increases through the preschool years (Freeman, 2007; Golombok et al., 2008). Obviously, children are presented with gender messages very early in their lives, but how do they come to adopt this information as part of their images of themselves and their understanding of the world around them? In other words, how do little girls learn that they are girls, and how do little boys learn that they are boys? Perhaps more importantly, how do both learn that only boys do certain (masculine) things and only girls do other (feminine) things? A number of theories have been offered in response to such questions. We will discuss the three major categories of theories: psychoanalytic theories, social learning theories, and cognitive developmental theories.

Psychoanalytic Theories

Certainly, the most famous psychoanalytic theory of gender identity development was presented by the Austrian physician, Sigmund Freud (1856–1939). Freud's perspective is known as *identification theory*.

According to Freud, children pass through a series of stages in their personality development. During the first two stages, referred to respectively as the *oral* and *anal* stages, boys and girls are fairly similar in their behavior and experiences. For both boys and girls, their mother is the chief object of their emotions since she is their primary caregiver and gratifies most of their needs. It is around age four, however, that an important divergence occurs in the personality development of girls and boys. Then, children become aware both of their own genitals and of the fact that the genitals of boys and girls are different. This realization signals the start of the third stage of development, the *phallic* stage. It is during the phallic stage that **identification** takes place; that is, children begin to unconsciously model their behavior after that of their same-sex parent, thus learning how to behave in gender-appropriate ways. Significantly, identification does not occur for girls the same way it does for boys.

For boys, identification is motivated by what Freud called **castration anxiety**. At this age, a boy's love for his mother becomes more sexual, and he tends to view his father as his rival (the *Oedipus complex*). What quickly cures him of this jealousy is a glimpse of the female genitalia. Seeing the clitoris, the little boy assumes that all girls have been castrated for some reason, and he fears that a similar fate may befall him if he continues to compete with his father. Boys perceive the formidable size and power of their fathers and conclude that their fathers have the ability to castrate competitors. Consequently, instead of competing with his father, the little boy tries to be more like him and ends up, in a sense, with the best of both worlds: He gets to keep his penis *and* he can have a sexual relationship with his mother vicariously through his father. The boy, therefore, comes to identify with his father, incorporating his father's traits and behaviors, including those pertaining to gender, into his own social repertoire.

In contrast, a girl's identification with her mother is motivated by what Freud called **penis envy**. Penis envy develops in girls on first sight of the male genitals. Seeing the male's "far superior equipment" as Freud put it (1983/1933, p. 88), the little girl also thinks she has been castrated. She becomes overwhelmed by her sense of incompleteness, her jealousy of boys, and her disdain for her mother and all women since they share her "deformity." Instead, she shifts her love to her father, who does possess the coveted penis, and begins to identify with her mother as a means to win him. Eventually, the girl realizes that she can have a penis in two ways: briefly through intercourse and symbolically by having a baby, especially a baby boy. In other words, her wish for a penis leads her to love and desire men (initially in the person of her father), since they have a penis and can also provide a baby (Frieze et al., 1978). However, a female never fully overcomes the feelings of inferiority and envy, which leave indelible marks on her personality:

> Thus, we attribute a larger amount of narcissism to femininity, which also affects women's choice of object, so that to be loved is a stronger need for them than to love. The effect of penis envy has a share, further, in the physical vanity of women, since they are bound to value their charms more highly as a late compensation for their original sexual inferiority. Shame, which is considered to be a feminine characteristic par excellence but is far more a matter of convention than might be supposed, has as its purpose, we believe, concealment of genital deficiency.... The fact that women must be regarded as having little sense of justice is no doubt related to the predominance of envy in their mental life. (Freud, 1983/1933, pp. 90, 92)

Freud's work called attention to the importance of childhood experiences and forced the scientific community of his time to consider that children might have sexual feelings and that what happens during childhood can have a lasting impact on an individual's personality. But before you start looking askance at every four-year-old you meet, let us also point out that identification theory has received considerable criticism. For one thing, the theory maintains that identification is an unconscious process. As such, we have no objective means to verify it. Instead, we must rely on either the psychoanalyst's interpretation of an individual's behavior or the individual's memories of childhood. Even if we are willing to trust the memories of individuals, we are still left with the problem of observer bias. Because the methods of psychoanalysts are extremely subjective, we may question whether their interpretations of individuals' experiences are accurate or whether they simply reflect what the psychoanalyst expects to find in light of identification theory. Other than clinical reports of psychoanalysts themselves, there is little evidence of the existence of castration anxiety in boys or penis envy in girls (Frieze et al., 1978; Sherman, 1971).

Freud also portrayed the gendered behaviors acquired in early childhood as fixed and stable over time. In other words, the theory leaves little room for personal or social change. However, while it is certainly the case that gender is resilient, it is also true that learning continues throughout our lives and that we may modify our behavior and attitudes as we are exposed to new situations and models.

Finally, it is impossible to overlook the antifemale bias in Freudian identification theory. Females are defined as inadequate; they are jealous, passive, and masochistic. Freud defined women as "an inferior departure from the male standard" (Bem, 1993, p. 59). Femininity itself was seen as a pathology (Brennan, 1992). In short, identification theory asserts that women are clearly men's inferiors. At its best, the theory legitimates gender inequality; at its worst, it is misogynistic and harmful to women.[1]

In light of these serious weaknesses, it is not surprising that some of Freud's early supporters, as well as more contemporary theorists working within a psychoanalytic framework, have offered substantial revisions or reinterpretations of Freud's original argument. Karen Horney (1967), Erik Erikson (1968), and Melanie Klein (1975), for instance, felt that Freud's theory was too "phallocentric," although each theorist continued to focus on how innate differences between the sexes influenced their respective psychological development. Horney rejected the idea that penis envy played a central role in females' psychosexual development and offered the provocative suggestion that males harbor jealousy toward females for their unique ability to bear children, a phenomenon she referred to as *womb envy*. Erikson also claimed that women's reproductive capacity—the fact, as he put it, that women have an inner space in which to carry and nurture new life—causes them to develop a psychological commitment to caring for others. In contrast, men's reproductive organs are external and active, which in turn is reflected in the male psyche with its external focus and action orientation (Bem, 1993). And Klein argued that the primary relation in the development of gender identity was not the father-son or father-daughter relationship centering around the penis, but rather the mother-child relationship centering around the breast, especially in terms of the emotions and conflicts the breast evokes in children (e.g., goodness/plentitude, badness/destructiveness) (Chodorow, 1989, 1995).

Others utilizing a psychoanalytic perspective, including Clara Thompson (1964), Jacques Lacan (1977), and Juliet Mitchell (1974), have placed the notion of penis envy in a social context. That is, women are jealous of the male organ only in that it is a symbol of male power and privilege in a patriarchal society. From this point of view, then, women are actually envious of men's higher status and freedom.

Feminist theorist Nancy Chodorow (2004, 1989, 1978) also offers a revision of identification theory that places gender acquisition squarely in a social context. Her goal is to explain why females grow up to be the primary caretakers of children and why they develop stronger affective ties with children than males do. She suggests that identification is more difficult for boys since they must psychologically separate from their mothers and model themselves after a parent who is largely absent from home, their fathers. Consequently, boys become more emotionally detached and repressed than girls. Girls, in contrast, do not experience this psychological separation. Instead, mothers and daughters maintain an intense, ongoing relationship with one another. From this, daughters acquire the psychological capabilities for mothering, and "feminine personality comes to define itself in relation and connection to other people more than masculine personality does" (Chodorow, 1978, p. 44).

Chodorow's work is provocative, but like other psychoanalytic theories, it has been criticized as largely untestable and, therefore, lacking supporting evidence (Lorber et al., 1990). Chodorow has responded that her theory is empirically derived and is supported by clinical observations (Chodorow, 1995). She later responded, "[I]t is not the case that I explicitly brought in personal experience, or shifted voice, in making my theoretical arguments" (Chodorow, 2004).

But the reliability of clinical psychoanalytic data remains a concern; while Chodorow may interpret her patients' statements as supportive of identification theory, another clinician—even one who shares a feminist psychoanalytic perspective—may interpret the patients' statements differently. Moreover, her data are obtained from individuals who have sought her help in resolving problems, crises, and conflicts, so they may not be representative of the nonclinical population.

Chodorow's work has also been criticized as ethnocentric. As we read in Chapter 3, the sexual division of labor in which only women care for infants is not present in all societies, yet children in all societies acquire gender, whatever its specific content. Thus, the developmental sequence described by Chodorow seems to apply only to Western families and not all Western families at that (Lorber et al., 1981). Chodorow's model, for example, may describe best the process of gender acquisition in White, middle-class families, but as Joseph (1981) argues, it does not accurately reflect the experiences of most African American mothers and daughters. Similarly, Segura and Pierce (1993) maintain that certain features of Mexican American families, such as the presence of multiple mothering figures (grandmothers, godmothers, aunts), require extensions or modifications of Chodorow's model to account for racial, ethnic, and social class differences in gender acquisition.

Chodorow (1995) has responded to this criticism by calling on feminist psychoanalysts to conceptualize gender identity development in nonuniversal and less essentialist terms, taking into account the diversity in people's backgrounds and experiences, including race, ethnicity, social class, and sexual orientation. According to Chodorow, each individual participates in the construction of her or his gendered self through emotional reactions to experiences and even through fantasies, so that in a sense, each person's gender identity is unique. "I suggest," writes Chodorow, "that each person's sense of gender— her [or his] gender identity or gendered subjectivity—is an inextricable fusion or melding of personally created (emotionally and through unconscious fantasy) and cultural meaning" (1995, p. 517).

Chodorow's elaboration of feminist psychoanalytic theory is generating debate, some of which continues to focus on the issue of testability since the unconscious remains a central theme. However, psychoanalytic theories are not the only available explanations of gender acquisition. Let's consider other theoretical perspectives.

Social Learning Theories

Social learning theories are more straightforward than psychoanalytic theories in that they focus on observable events and their consequences rather than on unconscious motives and drives (Bandura, 1986). Although there are a number of social learning theories, they share several basic principles that derive from a particular school of thought in psychology known as *behaviorism*. You are probably somewhat familiar with at least one important idea of behaviorism, the notion of **reinforcement**: A behavior consistently followed by a reward will likely occur again, whereas a behavior followed by a punishment will rarely reoccur. So, for example, your dog will probably learn to play Frisbee with you if you give it a biscuit every time it runs to you with the plastic disk in its mouth. Conversely, the dog will stop urinating on your houseplants if you put it outside each time it squats or lifts a leg near the indoor foliage. According to behaviorists, this same principle of reinforcement applies to the way people learn, including the way they learn gender.

More specifically, social learning theory posits that children acquire their respective gender identities by being rewarded for gender-appropriate behavior and punished for gender-inappropriate behavior. Often the rewards and punishments are direct and take the form of praise or admonishment. For instance, while waiting in a check-out line, one of the authors overheard a little girl asking her father to buy her a plastic truck. Looking at her with obvious displeasure, he said, "That's for boys. You're not a boy, are you?" Without answering, the little girl put the toy back on the shelf. However, children also learn through indirect reinforcement. They may learn about the consequences of certain behaviors just by observing the actions of others (Burton & Meezan, 2004). Recent research has looked at the discrepancy between parents' reactions to their children's selection of cross-gender toys and children's prediction of how they think their parents would react to their selection of an inappropriate toy (Freeman, 2007). First, five-year-old and three-year-old boys and girls believed their opposite sex parent would be more accepting if they selected a toy appropriate for a child of the opposite sex (cross-gender toy). Second, although all parents stated they would not be upset if their daughter engaged in play stereotypically more appropriate for boys, less than half of the girls thought their parents would not be upset. The same was found for boys. Although most parents stated they would not be upset if their son engaged in play stereotypically more appropriate for girls (e.g., taking ballet lessons, playing with dolls), less than half of the boys thought their parents would approve and they thought their father was more likely than their mother to disapprove (Freeman, 2007).

In general, boys' behavior receives more scrutiny when it deviates from what is considered the masculine norm (Blakemore, 2003). Therefore, it should not be surprising that while boys and girls tend to pick same-sex heroes, girls are more likely than boys to pick opposite-sex heroes. Boys are socialized to avoid feminine behavior more than girls are socialized to avoid masculine behavior (Holub, Tisak & Mullins, 2008).

This raises a second important principle of social learning theories: Children learn not only through reinforcement, but also by imitating or **modeling** those around them. Of course, the two processes—reinforcement and modeling—go hand in hand. Children will be rewarded for imitating some behaviors and punished for imitating others. At the same time, children will most likely imitate those who positively reinforce their behavior. In fact, social learning theorists maintain that children most often model themselves after adults whom they perceive to be warm, friendly, and powerful (i.e., in control of resources or privileges that the child values). Moreover, these theorists predict that children will imitate individuals who are most like themselves (Bussey & Bandura, 1984). This has been supported by recent research that concluded that children tend to imitate same-sex models (Grace, David, & Ryan, 2008) and prefer objects favored by children of their same sex (Shutts, Banaji, & Spelke, 2009). Obviously, this includes same-sex parents, older siblings, and peers, but as we will see in Chapters 5 and 6, teachers and media personalities also serve as effective models for children.

The social learning perspective is appealing. Chances are that most of us have seen reinforcement in practice, and we know that children can be great imitators (sometimes to the embarrassment of their parents). However, the social learning approach is not without difficulties. First, studies of same-sex modeling indicate that children do not consistently imitate same-sex models more than opposite-sex models (Raskin & Israel, 1981). Rather, sex may be less important in eliciting modeling than other variables, especially the perceived power of the model (Jacklin, 1989). Girls are more likely to imitate male models than boys are to imitate female models, which may be because females are considered less powerful than males (see, for example, McGuffey & Rich, 1999). As Golombok and Fivush (1994) put it, boys have a lot to lose by emulating female models. Boys, though, are also actively discouraged from imitating girls (Barker, 2006). This finding suggests that children have some knowledge of gender apart from what they acquire through modeling. Finally, social learning theorists depict children as passive recipients of socialization messages: "Socialization is seen as a unilateral process with children shaped and molded by adults" (Corsaro & Eder, 1990, p. 198). There is evidence, though, that children actively seek out and evaluate information available in their social environment (Bem, 1983; Crouter et al., 2007; McGuffey & Rich, 1999).

One set of theories that attempts to address these criticisms is the cognitive developmental perspective, the third explanatory framework of gender learning that we will examine in this chapter.

Cognitive Developmental Theories

Cognitive developmental theories derive from the work of psychologists Jean Piaget and Lawrence Kohlberg, who studied the mental processes children use to understand their observations and experiences. The unifying principle of cognitive developmental theories is that children learn gender (and gender stereotypes) through their mental efforts to organize their social world. Think of a very young child who is literally new to the world. Life must certainly seem chaotic. Thus, one of the child's first developmental tasks is to try to make sense of all the information he or she receives through observations and interactions in the environment. According to cognitive developmental theorists, young children accomplish this by looking for patterns in the physical and social world. Children, they maintain, have a natural predilection for pattern seeking; "Once they discover those categories or regularities, they spontaneously construct a self and a set of social rules consistent with them" (Bem, 1993, p. 112).

The organizing categories that children develop are called **schema**. Sex is a very useful schema for young children. Why sex? The answer lies in the second major principle of the cognitive developmental perspective: Children's interpretations of their world are limited by their level of mental maturity. Early on in their lives (from about eighteen months to seven years of age, according to Piaget), children's thinking tends to be concrete; that is, they rely on simple and obvious cues. In our society (and most others), women and men look different: They dress differently, have different hairstyles, do different jobs. So sex is a relatively stable and easily differentiated category with a variety of obvious physical cues attached to it (Bem, 1993). Children first use the category to label themselves and to organize their own identities. They use gender category information to draw conclusions about ambiguous behavior (Giles & Heyman, 2004), and most children at age two use gendered language correctly (i.e., gendered nouns and pronouns) (Gelman, Taylor, & Nguyen, 2004; Zosuls et al., 2009). They then apply the schema to others in an effort to organize traits and behaviors into two classes, masculine or feminine, and they attach values to what they observe—either gender appropriate ("good") or gender inappropriate ("bad").

Cognitive developmental theory helps explain young children's strong preferences for sex-typed toys and activities and for same-sex friends, as well as why they express rigidly stereotyped ideas about gender (Cann & Palmer, 1986; Cowan & Hoffman, 1986). Two- to six-year-old children are in the early stage of development that Piaget called the *preoperational stage*. During this stage, children tend to see every regularity in their world as a kind of immutable moral law, and they are not yet capable of *conserving variance*—that is, they cannot understand that even if superficial aspects of an object change (e.g., the length of a man's hair), the basic identity of the object remains unchanged (e.g., the person is still a man even if his hair falls below his shoulders). Studies indicate that as children get older and their cognitive systems mature, they appear to become more flexible with regard to the activities that males and females pursue, at least until they reach adolescence (Bem, 1993; Golombok & Fivush, 1994; Ruble et al., 2007; Stoddart & Turiel, 1985; for a contrasting view, see Carter & McClosky, 1983). However, research has also found that change in gender attitudes depends on the youth's personal characteristics and parents' gender attitudes (Crouter et al., 2007). For example, second-born children were more likely than firstborn children to have a sharp decline in traditional attitudes about gender around the age of 10, followed by a sharp increase in traditional gender attitudes at around age 15. Girls and boys with parents with more traditional gender attitudes tended to also have traditional attitudes about gender after age 15 (Crouter et al., 2007).

Social learning theory maintains that children learn gender through modeling and reinforcement.

Critics of the cognitive developmental perspective have raised several concerns. One issue centers around the question of the age at which children develop their own gender identities. Cognitive developmental theorists place this development between the ages of three and five, but research indicates that it occurs sooner—as young as two years old (Cowan & Hoffman, 1986; Fagot & Leinbach, 1983). In addition, research indicates that not everyone uses sex and gender as fundamental organizing categories or schemas (Blakemore & Hill, 2008; Luyre, Zosuls, & Ruble, 2008; Skitka & Maslach, 1990). Females, for example, are more flexible in their views about cross-gender activities and behaviors (Blakemore & Hill, 2008; Leaper & Friedman, 2007; McGuffey & Rich, 1999). This is not surprising given that parents expect sons to conform to gender appropriate behavior more than daughters (Leaper, 2002). Thus, the process by which a child learns to use sex as an organizing schema and the intervening variables that may mediate this learning process need to be better understood.

Research indicates that gender role identity and concepts differ across ethnic and socioeconomic groups (Ruble, Martin, & Berenbaum, 2006; see also Leaper, 2002). Unfortunately, however, most of the research has been conducted with White, middle-class children from two-parent, heterosexual families, so little is known about how race and ethnicity, social class, family structure, and the sexual orientation of parents might affect the salience of sex and gender as organizing schema for diverse groups of young children. One study that includes Latino participants concludes that Latino parents socialize their daughters to behave in traditional gender-typed ways (Raffaelli & Ontai, 2004). Looking at racial/ethnic socialization, other research including African American youth finds that caregivers are more likely to engage in more socialization regarding African American history and ethnic pride with female adolescents than male adolescents (Brown, Linver, & Evans, 2010). In contrast, McHale et al. (2006) concluded that fathers are more likely to educate their sons than their daughters about African American culture to prepare them for discrimination and racism. Hill (2005) explores how race and class influence gender socialization and argues that gender socialization matters less for African Americans as they struggle to care for their children, keep them safe, and fight racial inequality. She reflects on African American mothers' fears for their sons as they negotiate discrimination and exposure to crime in poor neighborhoods.

In one study, unique because it looks at the simultaneous impact of race and social class on gender socialization, sociologist Shirley Hill (1999; Hill & Sprague, 1999) found that White parents more often than Black parents place a heavy emphasis on obedience and respect for their sons; this is especially true among poor White parents. In fact, Hill found that among working-class and lower-middle-class White parents, differential socialization of sons and daughters was much stronger than among working-class and lower-middle-class Black parents. However, differential socialization of sons and daughters was more common among upper-middle-class Black parents than upper-middle-class White parents. Hill's data indicate that race and class intersect in important ways to influence how parents construct gender and socialize their children in gendered ways. "Parents operate within their own specific economic and social constraints....In struggling within these constraints and expectations, they draw on the values they learned from their own families and communities, which are marked by race and class. In parenting, and probably in the rest of life, race, class, and gender dynamics intereact" (Hill & Sprague, 1999, p. 497; see also Hill, 2005). Clearly, more research like Hill's is needed for us to better understand how these interacting variables operate to produce different gender socialization experiences.

Another related criticism of cognitive developmental theory is that it downplays the critical role of culture in gender socialization by portraying gender learning as something children basically do themselves and by presenting the male-female dichotomy as having perceptual and emotional primacy for young children because it is natural and easily recognizable (Bem, 1993; Corsaro & Eder, 1990). We may agree that children actively seek to organize their social world, but that they use the concept of sex as a primary means for doing so probably has more to do with the gender-polarizing culture of the society in which they live than with their level of mental maturity. Moreover, the male-female dichotomy may have perceptual and emotional primacy for young children not because it is a *natural* division, but because members of the children's social world consistently interact with them on the underlying assumption that they are, in some unitary and bipolar way, male or female and, therefore, they teach them to organize their own identities and the world around them according to this same gender-polarizing schema (Davies, 1989). For example, research compared the different gender role messages mothers and fathers give to sons and daughters and found that mothers are more likely than fathers to provide both sons and daughters with feminine gender role messages (Horan, Houser, & Cowan, 2005). Clearly, parents play a role in gender socialization. There are other organizing categories available with obvious physical cues, but children use sex instead—not because it is natural, but because in the culture of their society, sexual distinctions are emphasized.

Psychologist Sandra Bem, whose work has made significant contributions to the cognitive developmental perspective (see, for example, Bem, 1983), has formulated an alternative perspective on gender acquisition that takes these criticisms into account. Let's briefly consider her ideas.

BEM'S ENCULTURATED LENS THEORY OF GENDER FORMATION   Bem (1993) begins with the observation that the culture of any society is composed of a set of hidden assumptions about how the members of that society should look, think, feel, and act. These assumptions are embedded in cultural discourses, social institutions, and individual psyches, so that in generation after generation, specific patterns of thought, behavior, and so on are invisibly, but systematically reproduced. Bem calls these assumptions lenses. Every culture contains a wide assortment of lenses; for example, one of the lenses of U.S. culture that Bem identifies is radical individualism—but she concentrates her analysis on the lenses of gender. There are three gender lenses in the United States and in most Western cultures: gender polarization, androcentrism, and biological essentialism. **Gender polarization** refers to the fact that not only are males and females in the society considered fundamentally different from one another, but also these differences constitute a central organizing principle for the social life of the society. Bem uses the term **androcentrism** to refer to both the notion that males are superior to females and the persistent idea that males and the male experience are the normative standard against which women are judged. And finally, **biological essentialism** is the lens that serves to rationalize and legitimate the first two by portraying them as the natural and inevitable products of the inherent biological differences between the sexes. Bem's chief concern is how these lenses operate to mold males and females into the sex-typed likenesses enshrined in our culture.

The process of gender acquisition, Bem tells us, is simply a special case of the process of *enculturation* or socialization in general. She discusses two processes that she considers critical to "successful" enculturation. First, the institutionalized social practices of a society preprogram individuals' daily experiences to fit the "default options" of that society's culture for that particular time and place. At the same time, individuals are constantly bombarded with implicit lessons—what Bem calls *metamessages*—about what is important, what is valued, and what differences between people are significant in that culture. It is through these two processes that the lenses of the culture are transmitted to the consciousness of the individual; the processes are so thorough and complete that, within a fairly short period of time, the individual who has become a "cultural native" cannot distinguish between reality and the way his or her culture construes reality.

One gets some sense of this melding of realities when visiting a society where the culture is different from one's own; "their" way of doing things seems wrong, even shocking. However, Bem (1993, p. 140) argues that a true native consciousness is acquired through enculturation during childhood because children "learn about their culture's way of construing reality without yet being aware that alternative construals are possible. In contrast to the adult visiting from another culture, the child growing up within a culture is thus like the proverbial fish who is unaware that its environment is wet. After all, what else could it be?"

The lens of gender polarization, Bem observes, begins to organize children's daily lives from the moment they are born. Recall the example that opened this chapter: Pink or blue name tags are attached to their bassinets in the hospital, and children are wrapped in pink or blue blankets. As we will discuss later in the chapter, this gender polarization continues throughout childhood through clothing, hair styles, bedroom decor, and toys. Is it any wonder that by the age of two, children are aware that there are "boy things" and "girl things"?

We may recognize in Bem's theory aspects of the social learning perspective as well as the cognitive developmental perspective. Gender socialization may be explicit, but Bem focuses more on the metamessages about gender—how gender polarization is taught implicitly through the way we organize our everyday lives and the lives of our children. (A metamessage about gender is sent, for instance, every time children observe that although their mother can drive a car, their father is the one who drives when their parents or the family go out together.) However, Bem does not see children (or adults) as passive receptors of culture. "[A] gendered personality is both a product and a process" (Bem, 1993, p. 152). Like other cognitive developmental theorists, she argues that the child is ripe to receive the cultural transmission because she or he is an active, pattern-seeking human being. By the time people become adults, it is not just the culture that imposes boundaries on their definitions of gender appropriateness, it is their own willingness to conform to these boundaries and evaluate themselves and others in terms of them. Moreover, what they have internalized as children is a social/cultural definition of sex, not a biological one, so that the cues children use for distinguishing between the sexes—a significant task in a gender-polarized society such as ours—are also social/cultural (e.g., hair style, clothing) rather than biological (genitals).

Bem also extends the cognitive developmental perspective by emphasizing that the lens of androcentrism is superimposed onto the lens of gender polarization. Children learn not only that males and females are different, but also that males are better than females and that what males do is the standard, while what females do is some deviation from that standard. The inclusion of the lens of androcentrism "dramatically alters the consequences of internalizing the gender lenses. Whereas before, the individual has been nothing more than a carrier of the culture's gender polarization, now the individual is a deeply implicated—if unwitting—collaborator in the social reproduction of male power" (Bem, 1993, p. 139).

The implications of Bem's theory for social change are fairly obvious. All societies must enculturate new members, but at least with respect to gender, we must alter the cultural lenses that are transmitted. This will involve nothing less than eradicating both androcentrism and gender polarization. Bem notes that some may argue that the former is currently underway because antidiscrimination laws have been enacted. However, she points out—and we will provide ample evidence of this throughout the text—that our society is so thoroughly organized from a male perspective that even policies and practices that appear to be gender-neutral are, on closer examination, strongly androcentric. "[A]ndrocentrism so saturates the whole society that even institutions that do not discriminate against women explicitly...must be treated as inherently suspect" (Bem, 1993, p. 190; see also Rhode, 1997).

At first glance, it may seem that eradicating gender polarization might be easier than eradicating androcentrism. However, Bem cautions that dismantling gender polarization involves more than simply allowing males and females greater freedom to be more masculine, feminine, androgynous, heterosexual, homosexual, bisexual, or whatever they would choose to be. Rather, it involves a total transformation of cultural consciousness so that such concepts are absent from both the culture and individual psyches. In addition, parents must provide their children with alternative lenses for organizing and comprehending information. She suggests that parents substitute an "individual differences" lens that emphasizes the "remarkable variability of individuals within groups" (Bem, 1983, p. 613).

Throughout her discussion, Bem (1993) presents a number of research studies that support parts of the theory, particularly the various effects of gender polarization (see, for instance, Bem, 1975, 1981; Bem & Lenney, 1976; Frable & Bem, 1985). Like Chodorow's (1995) revision of the psychoanalytic perspective, Bem's ideas are certainly provocative enough to generate extensive research, as well as debate. For one thing, providing children with alternative lenses for organizing and understanding information can be considerably more difficult than it sounds. Research indicates that even parents who deliberately try to socialize their children in nontraditional, non-gender-stereotyped ways often end up interacting differently with their sons and daughters and encouraging gender-typed play and behavior (Golombok & Fivush, 1994). Parents are more likely to encourage girls to show emotion and boys to show aggression (Chaplin, Cole, & Zahn-Waxler, 2005). As previously stated, mothers more so than fathers provide their children with feminine gender role messages (Horan et al., 2005).

Additional research shows that even when a person does not want to do gender (West & Zimmerman, 1987) or wants to do gender in ways not recognized in our society, other people will gender the person by categorizing her or him into one of the two acceptable genders based on the physical cues they read from the person (Lucal, 1999). But Bem's theory must also be empirically tested with diverse families—diverse in terms of race and ethnicity, social class, and family structure—because, like cognitive developmental theory, it seems to treat gender lenses in our society as monolithic when, in fact, they may differ across various social groups.

Table 4.1 summarizes Bem's theory and the other theories of gender socialization we have discussed. Let's turn our attention now to the ways in which parents socialize their young children with respect to gender.

TABLE 4.1	Theories of Gender Socialization	
Theory	**Key People**	**Central Principles**
Psychoanalytic Theories (e.g., identification theory)	Sigmund Freud, Karen Horney, Erik Erikson, Melanie Klein, Clara Thompson, Jacques Lacan, Juliet Mitchell, Nancy Chodorow	Children pass through a series of stages in their personality development. Until around age four, these developmental experiences are similar for girls and boys. At age four, however, children unconsciously begin to model their behavior after that of their same-sex parent, thus learning how to behave in gender-appropriate ways. For boys, the motivation for identification is castration anxiety, whereas for girls, it is penis envy.
		Modifications of this basic argument include the notion of womb envy as well as a focus on the mother-child relationship rather than the father-son or father-daughter relationship centering around the penis. This latter revision includes the view that gender acquisition revolves around the fact that boys must psychologically separate from their mothers, while girls do not experience this separation.
Social Learning Theories	Albert Bandura	Children acquire gender in two ways: through reinforcement (i.e., by being rewarded for gender-appropriate behavior and punished for gender-inappropriate behavior) and through modeling.
Cognitive Developmental Theories (e.g., gender schema theory, enculturated lens theory)	Jean Piaget, Lawrence Kohlberg, Sandra Bem	Children learn gender and gender stereotypes through their mental efforts to organize their social world. To make sense of sensory information, children develop categories or schema, which allow them to organize their observations and experiences according to patterns or regularities. Sex is one of their first schema because it is a relatively stable, easily differentiated category with obvious physical cues attached to it.
		In the enculturated lens theory of gender formation, which also incorporates elements of social learning theory, children are socialized to accept their society's gender lenses (i.e., assumptions about masculinity and femininity). This enculturation occurs through institutionalized social practices as well as implicit lessons or "metamessages" about values and significant differences, which organize children's daily lives from birth.

GROWING UP FEMININE OR MASCULINE

If you ask expectant parents whether they want their baby to be a boy or a girl, most will say they don't have a preference (Steinbacher & Gilroy, 1985). The dominance of this attitude, though, is relatively recent; from the 1930s to the 1980s, most Americans expressed a preference for boys as only children and, in larger families, preferred sons to outnumber daughters (Coombs, 1977; Williamson, 1976). More recent research has indicated that men are more likely to prefer sons than daughters (Kane, 2005). Moreover, in some parts of the world today, boys are still strongly favored over girls. In fact, as Box 4.1 shows, in some countries this preference has resulted in a population imbalance, with a disproportionate ratio of males to females.

BOX 4.1
Where Have All the Young Women Gone? Sex Preference and Gendercide

In Turkey, a boy is considered "the flame of the hearth, a girl its ashes" (Delaney, 2000, p. 124). This saying captures well the devaluation of female infants and children in many cultures throughout the world. Boys are more highly valued in some societies because they carry on the father's family name, whereas girls take their husband's family name when they marry. Some cultures require that certain rituals be performed only by males. For example, in Bali, sons see to it that when a parent dies the proper cremation ceremony takes place. This is a purification ritual that allows the parent's soul to separate from the body and become an ancestor. Sons are also responsible for maintaining household ancestor shrines (Diener, 2000). In such societies, it is commonly believed, despite educational efforts to counter the myth, that women are responsible for determining the sex of the children they bear. Women who bear at least one son have more stable marriages and are less likely to be divorced by their husbands. Thus, there is considerable pressure on women to bear sons.

In some societies, a woman who bears only daughters may be able to adopt a male child, such as one of her husband's nephews. In Bali, another possibility is for a woman's daughter to marry a man who is willing to sever ties to his own ancestral line and take part in a ceremony making him a member of his father-in-law's family so that he can then assume responsibility for his in-laws' cremation ceremonies and ancestral shrine (Diener, 2000). However, in some societies, the devaluation of girls results in neglect, abuse, and even infanticide and selective abortion.

Under normal circumstances, the birth rate of boys and girls in a society is roughly equal, but in countries where son preference has been exceptionally strong, the sex ratio is skewed toward males (Coale, 1991). This imbalance has been the case historically in these countries as well; female infants were often killed at birth. However, with the introduction of medical technology, including ultrasound and amniocentesis, female infanticide is being replaced in some societies by selective abortion of female fetuses (Burns, 1994; Gargan, 1991; Glenn, 2004; Margaret Sanger Center International, 2008). This is despite the fact that sex selective abortions are illegal in most countries and have been illegal in India and China since the mid-1990s. However, in countries where abortion is legal it is almost impossible to determine if the only reason the fetus is being aborted is because of sex (*Economist*, 2010a, 2010b). A Chinese publication quoted a man from a rural community who said, "Ultrasound is really worthwhile, even though my wife had to go through four abortions to get a son" (quoted in Kristof, 1991, p. C12). This sex selection is widening the sex imbalance in some countries' populations, leading observers to argue that couples are practicing systematic *gendercide* (Baculinao, 2004; Warren, 1985). Since the 1970s, in fact, the sex imbalance in China and India is large, and gendercide in these countries has been prevalent (Burns, 1994; Jeffery, Jeffery & Lyon, 1988; Kristof, 1991; Sharma, 2007; Shenon, 1994). In the early 1980s the ratio of boys to girls born in China was 108.5 to 100; it is now 120 to 100 (Baculinao, 2004; *Economist*, 2010a).

Also contributing to the sex imbalance of the population in some countries are cultural practices that put girls at a substantial health disadvantage relative to boys (Green & Taylor, 2010). In countries such as China, India, Papua New Guinea, and the Maldives, female infants and children historically died at a higher rate than male infants and children because they were fed less, exposed to the elements, or otherwise neglected. For example, in India, infant girls were fed uncooked rice to expedite their death (Bhaskar, 2008). Females seem to have a biological and genetic advantage over males in the first year of life, which results in lower infant mortality for girls. However, in some countries, discriminatory nutritional and health care practices against girls override any biological advantages girls enjoy, and they consequently experience excess mortality. For example, in India, the infant mortality rate for girls is 52.4 deaths per 1,000 live births, and the rate for boys is 49.3 deaths per 1,000 live births. In China, the infant mortality rate is 21.8 per 1,000 live births of girls and 18.9 per 1,000 live births of boys (World Factbook, 2009).

Most people think of gendercide as a problem of the undeveloped world, but some analysts predict that at least one form of gendercide, fetal sex selection, has become more prevalent in the United States and Europe, as more advanced medical technologies make fetal sex identifiable as early as the ninth week of pregnancy. Surveys indicate a growing willingness on the part of the medical community to use fetal diagnostic tools solely for identifying fetal sex. For example, in 1972, only 1 percent of U.S. physicians said they were willing to use fetal diagnostic technology solely to determine fetal sex, but within just three years, 25 percent stated they were willing to do so. Similarly, in an international survey conducted in 1988, 24 percent of geneticists in Britain, 47 percent in Canada, and 60 percent in Hungary said sex selection is morally acceptable (Kolker & Burke, 1992). Nevertheless, research conducted in the United Kingdom and the United States shows that the majority of the lay public believes nonmedical sex selection (for reasons other than to avoid chromosomally-linked genetic disorders) is unethical or objectionable (Kalfoglou, Scott, & Hudson, 2008; Scully, Shakespeare, & Banks, 2006).

The debate over sex selection continues. Some argue that personal reproductive decisions are the right of the parents (Dahl, 2007; Harris, 2004). Others point to the problems caused by sex selection such as demographic imbalance (Blyth, Frith, & Crawshaw, 2008; see also Strange, 2010 for a review of arguments for and against nonmedical sex selection). One problem may be the inability of men to find a spouse. Another problem includes the rise in cases of kidnapping and trafficking of women (Blyth et al., 2008). In January 2010 the Chinese Academy of Social Sciences claimed that within ten years young men would be unable to find a bride because of the lack of young women; in 2020 China will have an estimated 30 to 40 million more males than females aged nineteen and younger (cited in *Economist*, 2010b). But as one group of researchers stated, "A morally acceptable position is that children should be wanted and valued for their intrinsic worth as human beings and this value should not be conditional on their possession of specific characteristics" (Blyth et al., 2008, p. 43).

Even though American parents do not express a strong sex preference, research shows that parents do have different expectations of their babies and treat them differently, simply on the basis of sex. It has even been argued by some researchers that gender socialization actually may begin in utero by those parents who know the sex of their child before it is born. As Kolker and Burke (1992, pp. 12–13) explain, "The knowledge of sex implies more than chromosomal or anatomical differences. It implies gender, and with it images of personality and social role expectations." Such a hypothesis is difficult, if not impossible, to test, but what currently is known is that gender socialization gets underway almost immediately after a child is born. Research shows, for instance, that the vast majority of comments parents make about their babies immediately following birth concern the babies' sex (Woollett, White, & Lyon, 1982). Moreover, although there are few physiological or behavioral differences between males and females at birth, parents tend to respond differently to newborns on the basis of sex. For example, when asked to describe their babies shortly after birth, new parents frequently use gender stereotypes.

Infant boys are described as tall, large, athletic, serious, and having broad, wide hands. In contrast, infant girls are described as small and pretty, with fine, delicate features (Reid, 1994). Also, when an infant shows the same emotional response, infant girls are described as being more emotional than infant boys, and a girl's emotional response is interpreted as fear while a boy's emotional response is interpreted as anger (Plant et al., 2000). These findings are quite similar to those obtained in a study conducted twenty-five years earlier (Rubin, Provenzano, & Luria, 1974), indicating that there has been little change in parental gender stereotyping of newborns.

That parents associate their child's sex with specific personality and behavioral traits is further evidenced by the effort they put into ensuring that others identify their child's sex correctly. It's often difficult to determine whether a baby is a boy or a girl because there are no physical cues: Male and female infants overlap more than they differ in terms of weight, length, amount of hair, alertness, and activity level. Parents make their child's gender obvious through clothing, accessories, and hair style (Zosuls et al., 2009). Boys are typically dressed in dark or primary colors, such as red and blue. They wear overalls that are often decorated with sporting or military equipment, trucks and other vehicles, or superheros. Girls are typically dressed in pastels, especially pink and yellow. Their dresses and slacks sets are decorated with ruffles, bows, flowers, and hearts. Gender may be more significant for girls because of the distinct style of their clothing (i.e., ruffles) (Ruble, Lurye, & Zosuls, 2007). Parents also often put satiny headbands on their baby daughters (despite their lack of hair) and have their ears pierced. Disposable diapers are even different for girls and boys, not only in the way they are constructed, which arguably might have a rational basis to it, but also in the way they are decorated: Girls' diapers often have pink flowers on them or Dora the Explorer; boys' diapers are embellished with cars and trucks or Thomas the Tank Engine. Thus, clothing usually provides a reliable clue for sex labeling, although mistakes still occur, which often anger parents. As one new mother told us in frustration, "I dress her in pink and she always wears earrings, but people still look at her and say, 'Hey, big fella.' What else can I do?"

Clothing plays a significant part in gender socialization in two ways. First, as children become mobile, certain types of clothing encourage or discourage particular behaviors or activities. Girls in frilly dresses, for example, are discouraged from rough-and-tumble play, whereas boys' physical movement is rarely impeded by their clothing. Boys are expected to be more active than girls, and the styles of the clothing designed for them reflect this gender stereotype. Second, by informing others about the sex of the child, clothing sends implicit messages about how the child should be treated (Shakin, Shakin, & Sternglanz, 1985).

Clothing clearly serves as one of the most basic ways in which parents organize their children's world along gender-specific lines. But do parents' stereotyped perceptions of their babies translate into differential treatment of sons and daughters? If you ask parents whether they treat their children differently simply on the basis of sex, most would probably say "no." However, there is considerable evidence that what parents *say* they do and what they *actually* do are frequently not the same. Let's examine some of this research.

Parent-Child Interactions

The word *interaction* denotes an ongoing exchange between people. This meaning is important to keep in mind when discussing parent-child interactions, for the relationship is not one-way—something parents do to their children—but rather two-way, a give-and-take between the parent and the child. Parents sometimes raise this point themselves when they are questioned about the style and content of their interactions with their children. Parents report that male infants and toddlers are "fussier" than female infants and toddlers; boys, they say, are more active and anger more easily than girls. Girls are better behaved and more easy-going. So if we observe parents treating their sons and daughters differently, is it just because they are responding to biologically based sex differences in temperament? Perhaps, but research by psychologist Liz Connors (1996) indicates that girls may be better behaved than boys because their mothers expect them to be. In observing girls and boys three-and-a-half to fourteen months old, Connors found few differences in the children's behavior. However, she also found that the mothers of girls were more sensitive to their children, while the mothers of boys were more restrictive of their children. Connors reports that fourteen-month-old girls are more secure in their emotional attachment to their mothers than fourteen-month-old boys, and she attributes this difference to mothers' differential treatment of their children.

Additional research lends support to Connors's conclusion. For example, Fagot and her colleagues (1985) found that although thirteen- and fourteen-month-old children showed no sex differences in their attempts to communicate, adults tended to respond to boys when they "forced attention" by being aggressive or by crying, whining, and screaming, whereas similar attempts by girls were usually ignored. Instead, adults were responsive to girls when they used gestures or gentle touching or when they simply talked. Significantly, when Fagot and her colleagues observed these same children just eleven months later, they saw clear sex differences in their styles of communication; boys were more assertive, whereas girls were more talkative.

In studies with a related theme, researchers have found that parents communicate differently with sons and daughters. Parents use a greater number and variety of emotion words when talking with daughters than with sons. They also talk more about sadness with daughters, whereas they talk more about anger with sons (Adams et al., 1995; Fivush, 1991; Kuebli, Butler, & Fivush, 1995). One outcome of this differential interaction is that by the age of six, girls use a greater number of and more specialized emotion words than boys (Adams et al., 1995; Kuebli et al., 1995). Also, mothers of girls talked more to their daughters while mothers of boys gave more instructions to their sons (Clearfield & Nelson, 2006). Researchers have found that preschoolers whose mothers engaged in frequent emotion talk with them are better able to understand others' emotions (Denham, Zoller, & Couchoud, 1994), and by first grade, girls are better at monitoring emotion and social behavior than boys are (Davis, 1995). This early socialization also appears to influence how children express emotions. Research with preschool-age children found that while girls are more likely to display sadness, boys are more likely to display anger (Chaplin et al., 2005).

Research indicates that mothers are warmer toward daughters than fathers are (Shanahan et al., 2007). Mothers are also more attuned to the emotions of their daughters and fathers are more attuned to the emotions of their sons (Cassano, Perry-Parrish, & Zeman, 2007; Wong, McElwain, & Halberstadt, 2009). This may have important ramifications for boys considering that mothers are more likely than fathers to stay home to raise children. Fathers are less likely than mothers to provide children with physical and emotional care and are generally less involved in their children's lives (Moon & Hoffman, 2008; Ozgun & Honig, 2005). Even though more women work outside the home, they still have more responsibility for parenting than fathers do (Moon & Hoffman, 2008, see also Chapters 7 and 8).

Certainly, it is not unreasonable to speculate that through these early socialization experiences, parents are teaching their daughters to be more attentive to others' feelings and to interpersonal relationships, while they are teaching boys to be assertive, but unemotional except when expressing anger. Is it any wonder that among adults, women are better able than men to interpret people's facial expressions and are more concerned about maintaining social connections (Brody & Hall, 2008; Goleman, 1996; Schneider et al., 1994)? Researchers have also discovered that women are better able than men to recall and retrieve childhood memories of life events associated with both positive and negative emotional states but there are no gender differences in recall and retrieval for life events not associated with emotions (Davis, 1999).

Are there other ways in which parent-child interactions differ by sex of the child? Research indicates that parents tend to engage in rougher, more physical play with infant sons than with infant daughters (MacDonald & Parke, 1986). When looking specifically at aggression, socialization predisposes boys more than girls to aggression and violence (Pollack, 2006). This is even true for rather young children (Archer & Cote, 2005). One study found that at 17 months boys were more physically aggressive than girls; for every physically aggressive girl, there were five boys who displayed physically aggressive behavior on a frequent basis (Baillargeon et al., 2007).

The sex of the parent also appears to be significant. Fathers usually play more interactive games with infant and toddler sons and also encourage more visual, fine-motor, and locomotor exploration with them, whereas they promote vocal interaction with their daughters. At the same time, fathers of toddler daughters appear to encourage closer parent-child physical proximity than fathers of toddler sons (Bronstein, 1988). Both fathers and mothers are more likely to believe—and to act on the belief—that daughters need more help than sons (Burns, Mitchell, & Obradovich, 1989; Snow, Jacklin, & Maccoby, 1983). In these ways, parents may be providing early training for their sons to be independent and their daughters dependent. Research exploring the behavior of two-year-old children found that girls were more likely than boys to stick close to their mother. However, when children became distressed, boys were more likely than girls to move closer to their mother. The researchers conclude that this may be because girls were already closer to the mother before becoming distressed and boys sought comfort from their mother only when they became so distressed they could not handle the situation on their own (Buss, Brooker, & Leuty, 2008, p. 20).

Weitzman and her colleagues (1985) looked at how mothers communicate with their children. They included mothers who professed not to adhere to traditional gender stereotypes. Although the differential treatment of sons and daughters was less pronounced among these mothers, it was by no means absent. This is an important point because it speaks to the strength of gender bias in our culture, reminding us that gender stereotypes are such a taken-for-granted part of our everyday lives that we often discriminate on the basis of sex without intentionally trying. "Even when we don't think we are behaving in gender stereotyped ways, or are encouraging gender-typed behavior in our children, examination of our actual behavior indicates that we are" (Golombok & Fivush, 1994, p. 26; see also Lewis, Scully, & Condor, 1992; Weisner, Garnier, & Loucky, 1994).

Still, it is also important to keep in mind that, like the research we discussed earlier, these studies are based almost exclusively on White, middle-class, two-parent, heterosexual families. We must ask how the findings might be different if the samples were more diverse. There is evidence that for both male and female children, Black parents place great stress on the importance of hard work, independence, and self-reliance. Research finds that Black children are imbued with a sense of financial responsibility toward their families, as well as racial pride and strategies for dealing with racism (Barr & Neville, 2008; Brown, 2008; Hale-Benson, 1986; Murry & Brody, 2002; Murry et al., 2009; Poussaint & Comer, 1993; Scott, 1993). The nontraditional content of this gender socialization could contribute to less gender stereotyping among Black children (Reid & Trotter, 1993), although research indicates that the socialization experiences of young Black males and females are not identical or equal (Hale-Benson, 1986, Hill, 1999; Price-Bonham & Skeen, 1982).

Similarly, studies that have examined social class have found modest support for the hypothesis that gender-stereotyped interaction decreases as one moves up the social class hierarchy (Burns & Homel, 1989; Lackey, 1989; but for contradictory findings, see Bardwell, Cochran, & Walker, 1986). As we noted earlier, Shirley Hill's (1999) research examining both social class and racial and ethnic effects indicates that class and race/ethnicity interact in influencing parents' interactions with sons versus daughters. However, Hill cautions that the racial and ethnic differences we see in parents' gender socialization practices may be "an artifact of the way race corresponds to class in American society" (i.e., African Americans are disproportionately represented among the lower social classes) (Hill & Sprague, 1999, p. 496).

Finally, there is limited research on gender socialization in gay and lesbian families, although available studies indicate that children reared in such families are no different in their gender role behavior than children reared in heterosexual families (for a review, see Stacey & Biblarz, 2001). Research has found that lesbian parents have less traditional views of gender compared to heterosexual parents and were less likely to decorate their children's bedrooms with gender-typed décor or colors (Sutfin et al., 2007).

Clearly, much more research is needed to elucidate the rich diversity of parent-child interactions and their outcomes among not only gay and lesbian families, but also families of color and families of different social classes, as well as the intersections of sexual orientation, race and ethnicity, and social class.

Toys and Gender Socialization

Say the word "toys" in the company of children and you are likely to generate a good deal of excitement. Children will eagerly tell you about their favorite toy or about a "cool" new toy they'd like to have. Toys are, without a doubt, a major preoccupation of most children because, as any child will tell you, they're fun. However, toys not only entertain children, they also teach them particular skills and encourage them to explore through play a variety of roles they may one day occupy as adults. Are there significant differences in the toys girls and boys play with? If so, are these different types of toys training girls and boys for separate (and unequal) roles as adults?

More than thirty-five years ago, two researchers actually went into middle-class homes and examined the contents of children's rooms in an effort to answer these questions (Rheingold & Cook, 1975). Their comparison of boys' and girls' rooms is a study of contrasts. Girls' rooms reflected traditional conceptions of femininity, especially in terms of domesticity and motherhood. They contained an abundance of baby dolls and related items (e.g., doll houses) as well as miniature appliances (e.g., toy stoves). Few of these items were found in boys' rooms, where, instead, there were military toys and athletic equipment. Boys also had building and vehicular toys (e.g., blocks, trucks, and wagons). In fact, boys had more toys overall as well as more types of toys, including those considered educational. The only items girls were as likely to have as boys were musical instruments and books.

A decade later, another group of researchers (Stoneman Brody & MacKinnon, 1986) replicated Rheingold and Cook's study and obtained similar findings: Toys for girls still revolved around the themes of domesticity and motherhood, while toys for boys focused on action and adventure. A quick perusal of most toy websites reveals that little has changed in this regard in recent years either. The toys for sale online are often pictured with models, which can be taken as an indication of the gender appropriateness of the toy. On the websites we examined in January, 2010 (F.A.O. Schwarz, Fisher-Price, Toys R Us), most of the toys were obviously gender-linked.[2] We found, for instance, that little girls were most frequently shown with dolls or household appliances. The "dolls" boys were pictured with were referred to as "action figures" and included Batman, Transformers, X-Men, G.I. Joe, and characters from the *Star Wars* film series. On the Fisher-Price site, girls were shown driving the pink Barbie Cadillac Escalade, the pink Barbie Jammin' Jeep Wrangler, and the hot pink Barbie Ford Mustang. On the same site, boys were shown driving the Ford F-150 truck, the blue Jeep Wrangler Rubicon, the black Cadillac Escalade, and the "Jeep Hurricane with Monster Traction," claiming that "Hard surfaces, grass, and rugged terrain are no match for the Jeep® Hurricane!" There were also ATVs being sold. The Kawasaki "Brute Force" advertised as, "Experience the ultimate terrain traction!" was driven by boys, and the Nick Jr./Dora the Explorer ATV was driven by a girl. The few times when a boy and girl were pictured together, they were in a black Cadillac Escalade or a red Ford Mustang. In both pictures, the boy was the driver.

Fisher-Price also offers "role play" toys, and F.A.O Schwarz offers "pretend play" toys. Girls and boys were pictured with very gender-specific Fisher-Price toys: Girls were shown with a purse, a kitchen, a dollhouse, and a baby stroller; boys were pictured with a tool set, a workbench, a fire station, and a lawn mower. There were four items advertised for the Fisher-Price "Play My Way" line. Boys were pictured playing a doctor and using a "workshop" and girls were pictured using a kitchen and a baby care set. There were two pictures, however, that were not traditionally gendered on the Fisher-Price website: a boy was pictured pushing a shopping cart and a vacuum cleaner. F.A.O. Schwarz listed a total of thirty-three occupational pretend play costumes or props. Boys were shown dressed as doctors, Armed Forces pilots, airline pilots, astronauts, and firefighters. Although there were two girls shown dressed as doctors, one was wearing pink scrubs. When narrowing the occupational pretend play costumes or props by gender, we found that there were still thirty-two options listed for boys—the only costume removed was the pink scrubs. On the other hand, there were only eleven options listed for girls. The costumes or props for the following occupations were eliminated for girls: train engineer, construction worker, Armed Forces pilot, airline pilot, astronaut, firefighter, and jewel thief (although we are not quite sure why that is listed as an occupation). Only one police officer costume remained an option for girls, while the other seven options were eliminated.

Fisher-Price's website has a link to "kitchen sets and play food toys." There are three kitchen sets shown. Two are pictured with a girl and the other is pictured with a girl and boy. However, in the latter the girl is cooking and the boy is crawling through the archway of the kitchen. F.A.O. Schwarz's website also has a link to "kitchens." One kitchen set is shown with a girl, and one is shown with a boy and a girl.

Since many people now shop for toys online, it is not surprising that toy stores and manufacturers' websites are also gender specific. For example, Toys R Us and Mattel's websites have separate links for boys and girls. The link for girls displays Barbie dolls and products such as "Little Mommy" dolls, while the link for boys displays trucks and action figures.

Of course, it may be argued that toy catalogs and websites are directed primarily to parents, and parents usually claim that they buy gender-typed toys because that's what their children prefer. Research does show that children express gender-typed toy preferences as early as one year of age, but their toy "choices" may have been inspired even earlier by parental encouragement. For example, when adults were given the opportunity to interact with a three-month-old infant dressed in a yellow gender-neutral jumpsuit, they usually used a doll for play when they thought the infant was a girl, but chose a football and a plastic ring when they thought the infant was a boy (Seavy, Katz, & Zalk, 1975; see also Caldera, Huston, & O'Brien, 1989; Fisher-Thompson, Sausa, & Wright, 1995). Parental encouragement of gender-typed toy choices are further reinforced by television commercials, by the pictures on toy packaging, and by the way toy stores often arrange their stock in separate sections for boys and girls and by the suggestions of sales staff (Pike & Jennings, 2005; Shapiro, 1990).

In considering the toys we've described, it is not difficult to see that they foster different traits and abilities in children, depending on their sex. Toys for boys tend to encourage exploration, manipulation, invention, construction, competition, and aggression. They tend to be competitive, exciting, and violent (Blakemore & Centers, 2005). Research has also found that boys are more likely than girls to prefer toys that they can use to inflict physical aggression on some inanimate object (e.g., an action hero) (Benenson, Carder, & Geib-Cole, 2008). In contrast, girls' toys typically are perceived as attractive and relating to nurturance and domestic skill (Blakemore & Centers, 2005). Cherney and London (2006) found that boys report their favorite toys are ones they can manipulate, like blocks and Legos, while girls report their favorite toys are dolls, stuffed animals, and educational toys.

One of the most popular toys for girls continues to be Barbie, manufactured by Mattel, Inc., the world's largest toy-maker. In recent years, Barbie has been given limited nontraditional roles, including computer engineer, news anchor, and "newborn baby doctor." However, most Barbie dolls continue to portray gender stereotypes and provide messages for what should be important to girls. For example, there is the Barbie Wedding Day Sparkle Doll, the Barbie Fairy-Tastic Princess Doll, the Barbie Loves Hair Doll, and the Barbie Loves Nails doll.[3]

Disney products continue to be popular with children and the most successful line of products is the princess line, which produced $4 billion in global retail sales in 2007 (Disney Consumer Products, 2007). Disney Princess is a franchise of Walt Disney Company Franchise that features nine princesses. In 2010 a tenth princess, Rapunzel, was added to the line. Research has found that when girls engage in "princess play" they model behavior that is stereotypically appropriate for displays of femininity such as wearing makeup and trying to appear pretty (Blaise, 2005).

Racially and ethnically diverse Barbie dolls and Disney Princesses have historically been few. Although Mattel introduced Christie, the first African American Barbie, in the 1960s, most Barbie dolls are White. It was not until September 2009 that Mattel released a new line of African American Barbie dolls, So In Style™ dolls. Although Disney has featured Asian, Native American, and Middle Eastern princesses in earlier films (*Mulan, Pochantas, Aladdin*) it was not until 2009 that Disney featured its first African American female lead character in an animated feature film (Princess Tiana in *The Princess and the Frog)*. The film is about a young girl living in New Orleans who kisses a frog prince and turns into a frog herself. Despite the excitement over Disney's first African American princess, the film has been criticized for failing to feature an African American prince and showing the princess more as a frog and less as a woman (Gibbs, 2009).

One exception to the lack of diversity among dolls are the Bratz dolls, released by M.G.A. Entertainment in 2001. Most Bratz dolls appear to be non-White (Talbot, 2006), and the dolls are known for their ethnic diversity (Lamb & Brown, 2007). Others describe them as "ethnically indeterminate" (Hains, 2008, p. 201) or a "multiethnic crew" (American Psychological Association, 2007, p. 14). However, given the sexualized nature of these dolls, their ethnic diversity may have negative consequences rather than positive ones in terms of stereotypical images of young women of color. The dolls are dressed in provocative clothing such as miniskirts and fishnet stockings. As one writer described them, they look like "pole dancers on their way to work at a gentleman's club" (Talbot, 2006, p. 74).

In short, with few exceptions, toys for young children tend to strongly reinforce gender stereotypes. These toys—and the marketing and packaging for the toys—tell children that what they *may* do, as well as what they *can* do, is largely determined and *limited* by their sex. Apart from toys, what other items are significant in early childhood gender socialization? You may recall from the Rheingold and Cook (1975) study that books are one of only two items that boys and girls are equally likely to have. Let's take a brief look, then, at children's literature.

Gendered Images in Children's Literature

Traditionally, children's literature ignored females or portrayed males and females in a blatantly stereotyped fashion. For example, the popular Disney story *Cinderella* stressed the importance of physical beauty in attracting a mate, or the prince (Baker-Sperry, 2007). In the early 1970s, Lenore Weitzman and her colleagues (1972) found in an analysis of award-winning picture books for preschoolers that males were usually depicted as active adventurers and leaders, while females were shown as passive followers and helpers. Boys were typically rewarded for their accomplishments and for being smart; girls were rewarded for their good looks. Books that included adult characters showed men doing a wide range of jobs, but women were restricted largely to domestic roles. In about one-third of the books they studied, however, there were no female characters at all.

Fifteen years later, Williams et al. (1987) replicated the Weitzman study and noted significant improvements in the visibility of females. Of the books published in the early 1980s that they examined, only 12.5 percent had no females, while a third had females as central characters. Nevertheless, although males and females were about equal in their appearance in children's literature, the ways they were depicted remained largely unchanged. According to Williams et al. (1987, p. 155), "With respect to role portrayal and characterization, females do not appear to be so much stereotyped as simply colorless. No behavior was shared by a majority of females, while nearly all males were portrayed as independent, persistent, and active. Furthermore, differences in the way males and females are presented is entirely consistent with traditional culture."

In 1997, children's librarian Kathleen Odean reported that although over four thousand children's books are published each year, in the vast majority females are presented in supporting roles and very few female characters are brave, athletic, or independent. Out of the thousands of books available for children of all ages, from preschoolers to adolescents, she compiled a list of just six hundred that are about girls who go against feminine stereotypes: girls who take risks and face challenges without having to be rescued by a male, girls who solve problems rather than having the solutions given to them, and girls who make mistakes but learn from them. There are, she notes, few books about girls' sports teams, even though over 2 million girls play on such teams (see Chapter 12), and no animal fantasies analogous to the popular *Wind in the Willows* with female characters. One recent exception to the lack of independent female characters are books featuring Dora the Explorer, a bilingual Latina girl, who is the lead character on a popular animated program on Nickelodeon. Dora the Explorer is independent, adventurous, and may empower girls (Ryan, 2010).

Research continues to show that how men and women are portrayed in children's picture books has not drastically changed or become less stereotypical. Hamilton et al. (2006) examined how gender was constructed in two hundred children's picture books. They found that males were more likely than females to be the title characters, and female characters were less likely than male characters to work outside the home; female characters were more likely to be portrayed as nurturers. Anderson and Hamilton (2005) also specifically examined how fathers were portrayed in children's picture books. Results indicate that mothers were more likely than fathers to be portrayed in the books, and mothers were more likely than fathers to be portrayed as caring for children and having close, personal contact with them. An analysis of coloring books also found that gender stereotypes are prevalent in this medium (Fitzpatrick & McPherson, 2010).

One study indicates that at least for children's picture books, the race of the illustrator might make a difference in the amount of gender stereotyping depicted. Roger Clark and his colleagues (1993) analyzed children's picture books that received awards during the years 1987 through 1991 and compared those illustrated by White illustrators with those illustrated by African American illustrators. Among their findings were that while children's picture books contained more female central characters who are depicted as more independent,

Fathers typically play more interactive games with their sons than their daughters.

creative, and assertive than those in the past, the books illustrated by African American artists (and written by African American authors) gave female characters the greatest visibility and were significantly more likely to depict these females as competitive, persistent, nurturant, aggressive, emotional, and active. Clark, Lennon, and Morris (1993) argue that books illustrated by White artists reflect the liberal feminist emphasis on more egalitarian depictions of female and male characters, whereas those illustrated by African American artists reflect the aims of Black feminist theorists who emphasize women's greater involvement in an ethic of care and an ethic of personal accountability.

There is no doubt, then, that children's literature is less sexist than it was when Weitzman carried out her research, but for the most part, the changes have been modest. But modest though they may be, the question remains as to what impact less stereotyped books have on children's thinking about gender. In one study that tried to answer this question, the researcher found that nontraditional gender messages may be lost on young children. Bronwyn Davies (1989) read storybooks with feminist themes to groups of preschool boys and girls from various racial and ethnic and social class backgrounds. She found that the majority of children expressed a dislike for and an inability to identify with storybook characters who were acting in nontraditional roles or engaged in cross-gender activities. There were no differences across racial, ethnic, or social class lines. What did emerge as significant was parents' early efforts to socialize their children in nonsexist, non-gender-polarizing ways. Thus, the two children in the study whose parents did not support polarized gender socialization did not see anything wrong with characters engaged in cross-gendered behaviors and had less difficulty identifying with these characters—an encouraging finding that not only offers support for Bem's theory of gender acquisition that we discussed earlier, but also shows that non-stereotyped gender socialization is possible with concerted effort.

This finding is also especially important in light of research that shows that when characters are depicted as genderless or gender-neutral, adults typically label the characters in gender-specific ways. In 95 percent of these cases, the labeling is masculine (DeLoache, Cassidy, & Carpenter, 1987). The only pictures that seem to prompt feminine labels are those showing an adult helping a child, an interpretation consistent with the gender stereotypes that females need more help than males and that females are more attentive to children. Based on this research, then, it appears that "picturing characters in a gender-neutral way is actually counterproductive, since the adult 'reading' the picture book with the child is likely to produce an even more gender-biased presentation than the average children's book does" (DeLoache, Cassidy, & Carpenter, 1987, p. 176).

To summarize our discussion so far, we have seen that virtually every significant dimension of a young child's environment—his or her clothing, toys, and, to a lesser extent, books—is structured according to cultural expectations of appropriate gendered behavior. If, as the cognitive developmental theorists maintain, young children actively try to organize all the information they receive daily, their parents and other adults are clearly providing them with the means. Despite their claims, even most parents who see themselves as egalitarian tend to provide their children with different experiences and opportunities and to respond to them differently on the basis of sex. Consequently, the children cannot help but conclude that sex is an important social category. By the time they are ready for school, they have already learned to view the world in terms of a dichotomy: his and hers.

Parents are not the only socializers of young children, however. Research has also highlighted the importance of peers in early childhood socialization. To conclude this chapter, then, let's consider the ways young children help to socialize one another.

EARLY PEER GROUP SOCIALIZATION

As we noted previously, socialization is not a one-way process from adults to children. Rather, childhood socialization is a collective process in which "children creatively appropriate information from the adult world to produce their own unique peer cultures" (Corsaro & Eder, 1990, p. 200). Indeed, according to Beverly Fagot (1985), children's same-sex peers are the most powerful agents of socialization.

Children socialize one another through their everyday interactions in the home and at play. Research indicates, for example, that one of young children's first attempts at social differentiation is through increasing sex segregation. Observations of young children at play show that they voluntarily segregate themselves into same-sex groups. This may be because preschool age children perceive their same-sex peers to have more in common with them than opposite-sex peers (Tisak, Holub, & Tisak, 2007). This preference for play with same-sex peers emerges between the ages of two and three and grows stronger as children move from early to middle childhood (Feiring & Lewis, 1987; Serbin et al., 1991). Moreover, when compared with girls, boys tend to interact in larger groups, be more aggressive and competitive, and engage in more organized games and activities (Corsaro & Eder, 1990; Maccoby, 1988; Sheldon, 1990). Boys who are shy and do not actively engage with their peers are more likely than girls who are shy to report feeling lonely (Coplan, Closson, & Arbeau, 2007). It is less socially acceptable for boys than for girls to be shy or socially withdrawn (Rubin & Coplan, 2004).

Thorne (1993) is critical of much of this research for focusing solely on sex differences and ignoring sex similarities and cross-sex interaction. She gives a number of examples in which young children work cooperatively and amiably in sex-integrated groups (see also Goodenough, 1990). She also points out that children frequently engage in "borderwork"; that is, they attempt to cross over into the world of the other sex and participate in cross-gender activities. Nevertheless, there is considerable evidence that even very young children reward gender-appropriate behavior and show disapproval for cross-gender behavior in their peers (Fagot & Leinbach, 1983; Goodenough, 1990; Leaper & Friedman, 2007; C. L. Martin, 1989). In fact, research shows that preschoolers disapprove of gender-inappropriate behavior by their peers more so than by adults (Golombok & Fivush, 1994).

Both boys and girls who choose gender-appropriate toys are more liked by their peers and have a better chance of getting other children to play with them (C. L. Martin, 1989; Roopnarine, 1984). Fagot and Leinbach (1983) found that for boys, peers are often more powerful socializers than teachers. These researchers observed young children in day care, paying particular attention to messages teachers and peers gave about gender-typed behavior. When teachers and peers sent contradictory messages – for example, a teacher expressed approval of a behavior, while peers expressed disapproval – little boys paid more attention to their peers than to their teachers; teachers' exhortations had little impact on their behavior.

Clearly, young children actively participate in the socialization process. We will return to this topic in Chapter 5, when we discuss children's interactions with one another in school. Here, however, we can say that available data show that young children should be considered partners with parents and other caregivers in socialization, including gender socialization.

BY THE TIME A CHILD IS FIVE

In summary, during early childhood, boys and girls—at least those from White, middle-class, two-parent, heterosexual families—are socialized into separate and unequal genders. Little boys are taught independence, problem-solving abilities, assertiveness, and curiosity about their environment—skills that are highly valued in our society. In contrast, little girls are taught dependence, passivity, and domesticity—traits that our society devalues. Children themselves reinforce and respond to adults' socialization practices by socializing one another in peer groups.

May we conclude from all this that nonsexist socialization is impossible? Certainly not. Recall Davies's (1989) study showing that conscious efforts at nonsexist socialization by parents do have a positive impact on children's attitudes and behavior (see also Lorber, 1986). However, we must keep in mind that parents are not the only ones responsible for gender socialization. Indeed, as we will see in Chapters 5 and 6, schools and the media take up where parents leave off, and peers remain active socializers throughout our lives.

Key Terms

androcentrism   male-centered; the notion that males are superior to females and that males and the male experience are the normative standard against which females should be judged

biological essentialism   the idea that gender differences are the natural and inevitable products of the inherent biological differences between the sexes.

castration anxiety   Freud's notion that boys fear their fathers will castrate them because of their sexual attraction to their mothers

gender polarization   the assumption that males and females are fundamentally different from one another, and the practice of using these differences as a central organizing principle for the social life of the society

identification   a central concept of the Freudian-based theory of gender socialization; the process by which boys and girls begin to unconsciously model their behavior after that of their same-sex parent in their efforts to resolve their respective gender identity complexes

modeling   the process by which children imitate the behavior of their same-sex parent, especially if the parent rewards their imitations or is perceived by them to be warm, friendly, or powerful; a central concept of the social learning perspective of gender socialization

penis envy   Freud's notion of girls' jealousy of the male sexual organ

reinforcement   a central principle of social learning theories of gender socialization, which states that a behavior consistently followed by a reward will likely occur again, whereas a behavior followed by a punishment will rarely reoccur

schema   a central concept of the cognitive developmental perspective of gender socialization; a category used to organize and make sense of information and experiences

socialization   the process by which a society's values and norms, including those pertaining to gender, are taught and learned

Suggested Readings

Gipson, C. (2009). *Parenting practices of lesbian mothers: An examination of the socialization of children in planned lesbian-headed families*. Saarbrucken, Germany: VDM Verlag. This book looks at how lesbian parents socialize their children and prepare them to handle possible prejudice.

Hill, S. A. (2005). *Black intimacies: A gender perspective on families and relationships*. Lanham, MD: AltaMira Press. In the chapter on socializing Black children, Hill discusses how social class influences parents' gender and racial socialization of their children. She explores the different experiences of secure middle class, new middle class, and economically disadvantaged families.

Siegler, R. S., DeLoache, J. S., & Eisenberg, N. (2010). *How children develop, 3/e*. New York: Worth. This textbook covers a variety of topics about child development. One chapter is dedicated to gender development.

Notes

1. Nevertheless, see Chodorow, 1994, for a feminist defense of Freud. Chodorow acknowledges the weaknesses in Freud's theory and addresses feminist critiques of Freud as well as Freudian critiques of feminism. See especially Chapter 1, and also Chodorow, 1989, 2004.

2. Similar to our examination of toy catalogs in 1993, 1997, 2000, and 2003 we found that the 2009 and 2010 websites had racially and ethnically diverse models, but rarely showed children with disabilities.

3. In 1997, Mattel, the makers of Barbie, announced that the doll was being redesigned to have more realistic body proportions; ever since Barbie hit the toy market in 1959, she has had high-heeled feet to fit into the equivalent of 5-inch heels and proportions of 36-20-32 (that is, the bust of an adult woman, the waist of a child, and the hips of a teenager). The redesigned Barbie has a larger waist and a belly button. Research has found girls' body image changes after being exposed to Barbie dolls. Girls as young as 5 report lower body esteem and a greater desire for a thinner body after being exposed to Barbie dolls (Dittmar, Halliwell, & Ive, 2006).

Chapter 5

Schools and Gender

In a speech before a group of educators in 1980, Florence Howe, herself an educator, began by quoting from the writings of Frederick Douglass, the famous abolitionist. In the passage she selected, Douglass recalls his childhood as a slave on a Southern plantation and relays a conversation he overheard between the slave owner and the slave owner's wife. Said the slave owner to his wife, "If you teach that … nigger how to read, there would be no keeping him. It would forever unfit him to be a slave. He would at once become unmanageable, and of no value to his master. As to himself, it could do him no good, but a great deal of harm. It would make him discontented and unhappy" (quoted in Howe, 1984, p. 247). Howe selected this passage because it aptly illustrates what she calls the "power of education." Both Douglass and his master recognized that education may enable us to understand our social position and thus empower us to act to change it.

To this observation we must add another: Education is powerful in the sense that it may also serve to keep us in our respective places. More specifically, schools are officially charged with the responsibility of equipping students with the knowledge and skills they need to fill various roles in their society. This is accomplished primarily by requiring students to study subjects (e.g., reading, writing, mathematics, and history), known collectively as the **formal curriculum**. But schools also teach students particular social, political, and economic values. This instruction, too, may be done explicitly (by punishing students for being late, for instance), but just as often, these value messages are implicit in the curriculum materials used to teach traditional academic subjects. They constitute, in other words, a kind of **hidden curriculum** that operates alongside the more formal one. However, the subtle nature of the hidden curriculum in no way lessens its significance. Through it, students learn to view the world in particular ways. More importantly, they learn what they can expect for themselves in that world and, for certain groups of students, this may result in very low aspirations.

In this chapter, we will examine the kinds of messages both the formal and informal curricula send about gender, and we will assess their impact on the aspirations and achievements of male and female students. In addition, we will explore some of the recent efforts to transform the educational experience into a richer, more equal one for all students, male and female, from diverse backgrounds. Before we examine the current relationship between schools and gender, however, let's begin with a brief discussion of how this relationship has developed and changed over time.

AN HISTORICAL OVERVIEW OF WOMEN AND MEN IN EDUCATION

The word *school* comes from an ancient Greek word that means "leisure." This makes sense when we consider that until relatively recent times, only the very wealthy had enough free time on their hands to pursue what may be considered a formal education. Literacy was not a necessity for the average person; most people acquired the knowledge they needed to be productive citizens either on their own or from parents, other relatives, coworkers, or tradespeople. In the post-Revolutionary War period, formal education came to be seen as a means of instilling patriotism and "civic virtue" in citizens who would now be voting for political leaders. Keep in mind, however, that voting was restricted to White, male property holders, so formal education remained largely their privilege, too. However, even for these privileged few, education was still somewhat haphazard. The educated man—for formal education was not open to females until 1786—was schooled in the classics, moral philosophy, mathematics, and rhetoric, although he acquired this knowledge through private study, tutoring, and travel as well as in a classroom (Graham, 1978). Those who went to college were trained in self-discipline and moral piety as much as in academic subjects, for upon graduation they were to take their places among the White "ruling class" as ministers, lawyers, and other professionals (Howe, 1984).

Upper-class White women, when educated, were taught at home, but what they learned was far more restricted than the knowledge imparted to men. Women learned music and were given "a taste" of literature and a foreign language. Their education prepared them not to assume public leadership positions, but rather to better fulfill their "natural" roles in life as demure, witty, well-groomed partners for their elite husbands and as the first teachers of sons who would grow up to be voting citizens (Schwager, 1987). Even when schools for girls began to open in America—the first, the Young Ladies Academy, established in Philadelphia in 1786—the rationale behind them centered on women's domestic roles. The Young Ladies Academy, like most of the schools attended by wealthy young women and men, was private, although public schools did exist for White children of all social classes. However, the public schools at that time charged tuition, which put them out of reach for most families. It was also illegal to educate slaves, so most African American children, regardless of sex, were denied formal schooling of any kind (Hellinger & Judd, 1991; Howe, 1984).

With increasing industrialization in the United States during the nineteenth century, basic literacy and numeracy skills became more important. Such skills were not needed for the manual labor predominant in agricultural societies, but were necessary for many newly created industrial jobs, including operating machinery, marketing and selling products, and keeping track of inventory. Also, as work moved away from the home and into factories, so did responsibilities traditionally fulfilled by the family, including education. And as immigration from Europe increased, education came to be seen as a means of insuring that American values were not "corrupted" by foreign influences (Hellinger & Judd, 1991). In 1830, the first free public schools for girls and boys opened in Massachusetts, and by 1850, all the states had established government-supported elementary and secondary schools to educate White children of all social classes. Black children were excluded until after the Civil War, and even then, schools were racially segregated.

Mass public education produced two major consequences. The first was that White female literacy rates, at least in the northeastern part of the country, rose to match White male literacy rates. Unfortunately, Black literacy rates for both males and females remained substantially lower because of the tremendous barriers African Americans faced in obtaining an education (Schwager, 1987).

Second, the proliferation of elementary schools provided women with new career opportunities as teachers. In the early 1800s, men dominated teaching and looked on it as a good sideline occupation that provided extra income. The school year was relatively short and was structured around the farm calendar with classes held during the winter months when farm chores were light. However, with urbanization and growing demands for higher educational standards in an industrialized society, teaching became a full-time job, albeit one that carried a salary too low to support a family. As a result, educational administrators employed women as a cheap and efficient means to implement mass education (Strober & Lanford, 1986). Women were paid 40 percent less than their male counterparts on the (often false) assumption that they had only themselves to support (Schwager, 1987). Their "maternal instincts" made them naturally suited to work with young children, and if a disciplinary problem arose, they could enlist the aid of the school principal or superintendent, who invariably was a man. Valued, too, were their supposed docility and responsiveness to male authority since male-dominated school boards were handing down strict guidelines for instruction and a standardized curriculum (Strober & Lanford, 1986; Strober & Tyack, 1980).

Black women, such as Lucy C. Laney, Nannie Helen Burroughs, Charlotte Hawkins Brown, and Mary McLeod Bethune, founded schools for Black children. Teaching was a particularly attractive career choice for Black women. For economic reasons, most had to work outside the home, but their employment opportunities were often limited to domestic service (see Chapter 8). Teaching not only improved their status and standard of living, "but often shielded [Black] women from the sexual harassment that many of them confronted in White homes" (Giddings, 1984, p. 101).

Given these circumstances, it is not surprising that teaching had become a "female profession" before the turn of the twentieth century (Schwager, 1987). Most of the women who became teachers were trained in *normal schools* (precursors to teacher training colleges) or in female seminaries, such as the Troy Female Seminary established in 1821. It was not until 1832 that women were permitted to attend college with men. Oberlin College in Ohio was the first coeducational college in the United States; it was, incidentally, also the first White college to admit Black students. In 1862, Mary Jane Patterson became the first African American female to graduate from college when she completed her degree at Oberlin College (Harper, Patton, & Wooden, 2009). Lawrence College in Wisconsin followed suit in 1847, and by 1872, there were ninety-seven coeducational American colleges (Leach, 1980). Still, the more prestigious institutions, such as Harvard, Yale, and Princeton, continued to deny women admission on a number of grounds. It was widely believed, for example, that women were naturally less intelligent than men, so that their admission would lower academic standards. A second popular argument was that women were physically more delicate than men and that the rigors of higher education might disturb their uterine development to such an extent that they would become sterile or bear unhealthy babies. Others argued that women would distract men from their studies or that college would make women more like men: loud, coarse, and vulgar (Howe, 1984).[1]

Even at coeducational colleges, however, women and men had very different educational experiences. At liberal Oberlin, for instance, female students were expected to remain silent at public assemblies; in addition, they were required to care not only for themselves, but also for the male students by doing their laundry, cleaning their rooms, and serving them their meals (Flexner, 1971). Moreover, there, and at virtually every other coeducational college, women and men were channeled into different areas of study. Men specialized in fields such as engineering, the physical and natural sciences, business, law, and medicine. Women, in contrast, studied home economics, nursing, and, of course, elementary education (Howe, 1984). In fact, a teaching degree or certificate remained one of the few avenues of upward mobility for White, Black, and immigrant women well into the twentieth century (Giddings, 1984).

Nevertheless, some women did earn degrees in nontraditional or male-dominated fields, and many of them graduated from women's colleges. Wheaton College, in Norton, Massachusetts, was established in 1834 as the first women's college. In the late 1880s, the elite "Seven Sisters" colleges (Mount Holyoke, Vassar, Wellesley, Smith, Radcliffe, Bryn Mawr, and Barnard) were opened. What is perhaps most significant about these institutions is that they offered women the traditional men's curriculum in a highly supportive environment that fostered their ambitions and encouraged achievement. Consequently, "these institutions produced an exceptional generation of women during the 1890s who, nurtured by the collective female life of the women's college, emerged with aspirations to use their educations outside the confines of women's domestic sphere as it was narrowly defined in marriage" (Schwager, 1987, p. 362). Many of these women became leaders of the various social reform movements, including the suffrage movement that grew during the early 1900s. A substantial percentage pursued further training or entered the professions. Even midway through the twentieth century when, as we will soon see, the overall percentage of female Ph.D.s dropped considerably, the women's colleges continued to graduate exceptional female students who often went on to graduate and professional schools (Tidball, 1980).

Women and Men in Education during the Twentieth and Twenty-first Centuries

The emphasis on mass education did not diminish during the early decades of the twentieth century, fueled in large part by widespread concern over the influx of European immigrants into the United States. Special efforts were made to teach immigrants English and basic literacy skills, for according to many social reformers, education would help solve the social problems associated with immigrant life (e.g., poverty, alcoholism, and juvenile delinquency). This, along with continuing industrialization, promoted a steady rise in elementary and secondary school enrollments throughout the first half of the century.

Still, as Table 5.1 indicates, an education gap between males and females persisted, especially at the higher educational levels. To some extent, this was because of the popular belief that education was less important for females. Although Tyack and Hansot (1990) maintain that gender was rarely a major factor in the development of educational policy, there is evidence that in the often overcrowded public schools, administrators appeared quite willing to let girls drop out, since their departure would open more spaces for boys. In the 1930s, however, many states enacted laws that made school attendance until age sixteen mandatory. This, in turn, narrowed the gap at the secondary school level, but other factors operated to preserve it in colleges and graduate programs.

Looking again at Table 5.1, we see that, until the 1980s, women consistently comprised less than half the undergraduate student body in the United States, despite the fact that they make up slightly more than 50 percent of the country's population. Interestingly, in 1920, they did approach the 50 percent mark, but by 1930, their numbers had dwindled, and continued to fall until 1960. A similar pattern can be seen with regard to graduate school as measured by the percentage of doctoral degrees awarded to women. The percentage of female recipients of doctorates peaked in 1930, but then dropped considerably until 1970, when it began to rise once again. By 1990, women were the majority of those in graduate school (U.S. Department of Commerce, Bureau of the Census, 2008). In addition, we can see by looking at Table 5.1 that the percentage of doctorate degrees earned by women rose from 10 percent in 1960 to 50 percent in 2007, and between 1960 and 2007 the percentage of women earning master's degrees almost doubled.

How can we account for this kind of roller-coaster pattern in women's representation in higher education? As we mentioned previously, a number of factors appear to be

TABLE 5.1	The Education Gap between the Sexes, 1870–2007				
Year	Percentage of Population Enrolled in Elementary and Secondary School (M/F)	Females as Undergrads (%)	Females as Bachelor's Degree Recipients (%)[a]	Females as Master's Degree Recipients (%)	Females as Doctorates (%)
1870	49.8/46.9	21	15	n.a.	0
1880	59.2/56.5	32	19	n.a.	6
1890	54.7/53.8	35	17	n.a.	1
1900	50.1/50.9	35	19	n.a.	6
1910	59.1/59.4	39	25	n.a.	11
1920	64.1/64.5	47	34	n.a.	15
1930	70.2/69.7	43	40	n.a	18
1940	74.9/69.7	40	41	n.a.	13
1950	79.1/78.4	31	24	29.3	10
1960	84.9/83.8	36	35	32	10
1970	88.5/87.2	41	41	39.7	13
1980	95.5/95.5	52.3	47.3	49.3	29.8
1990	96.3/95.9	54.5	53.2	52.5	36.2
1997	96.9/96.8[b]	55.7	55.6	56.8	41.3
2007	50.9/49.1	57.2	57.4[c]	60.6[c]	50.1[c]

[a]Includes first professional degrees from 1870 to 1970.

[b]1995 data.

[c]2006–2007 data.

Sources: Commission on Professionals in Science and Technology, 1992; Graham, 1978; U.S. Department of Commerce, Bureau of the Census, 1976, 1985, 1991, 2000, and 2008; U.S. Department of Education, 2009.

involved. The early growth in female college and graduate school enrollments was probably due, at least in part, to the first feminist movement and the struggle for women's rights (see Chapter 1). In addition, with males off fighting World War I, colleges may have looked to (tuition-paying) females to take their places (Graham, 1978). The Great Depression of the 1930s dashed many young people's hopes of attending college, but it is likely that women more often sacrificed further schooling, given the old belief that education (particularly a college education) was less important for them. World War II sent men abroad again to fight, while women were recruited for wartime production jobs (see Chapter 8). After the war ended, an unprecedented number of men entered college, thanks to the GI bill. For women, though, the dominant postwar ideology idealized marriage and motherhood and promoted a standard of femininity by which women were judged according to how well they cared for their families, their homes, and their appearance. During the late forties and throughout the fifties, the number of women entering the professions declined substantially, while marriage and birth rates rose dramatically. The birth rate peaked in 1957; that same year, the average age for a first marriage for women was about twenty (Graham, 1978, p. 772).

Not all women bought into the postwar feminine ideal, and some pursued a college education with plans for a professional career. However, women who went to college during the forties, fifties, and even in the early sixties were often accused of pursuing a *Mrs.* instead of a *B.S.,* for the college campus came to be seen as the perfect setting for meeting a promising (i.e., upwardly mobile) mate. Sometimes, women dropped out of school to take jobs to help support their student-husbands. Today women may be more likely than men to attend college; women (and men) are postponing marriage and there is the growing expectation that women will work outside the home after they marry (Goldin, Katz, & Kuziemko, 2006).

The pattern we have observed so far appears applicable only with regard to the educational history of White women, however. When race is taken into account, a different historical overview emerges. According to Giddings (1984), for example, during the time that White women began to drop out of or not attend college, the number of Black women in college, especially in Black colleges, increased:

> By 1940, more Black women received B.A. degrees from Black colleges than Black men (3,244 and 2,463 respectively). By 1952–1953, the surge of Black women had increased significantly. They received 62.4 percent of all degrees from Black colleges when, in all colleges, the percentage of women graduates was 33.4 percent. The percentage of Black women graduates was in fact just a little below that of male graduates in all schools (66.6 percent) and substantially higher than that of Black men (35.6 percent). An important dimension of this was that a large proportion of these women were the first in their families to receive college degrees. (p. 245)

Also significant is the fact that many of these women went on to graduate school. By the early 1950s, the number of Black women with master's degrees exceeded the number of Black men with this level of education. However, Black male Ph.D.s and M.D.s still outnumbered their female counterparts by a considerable margin (Giddings, 1984). Interestingly, Smith (1982) reports that Black females' educational aspirations are higher than those of Black males until college, when they begin to decline. This is a point to which we will return shortly.

Since the 1970s, the percentage of women and minority undergraduates and graduate students has risen substantially. In 1970 there were 1.5 million fewer women than men enrolled in higher education, but by 2005 there were 2.6 million more women enrolled in higher education (Mortensen, 2008, p. A30). As we can see in Table 5.1, in 2007, women were over half of all undergraduate students, bachelor's degree recipients, and master's degree recipients. In addition, considerable attention has been given to the problems of sexism and racism at every level of schooling. Undoubtedly, the civil rights movement and the resurgence of the feminist movement during the 1960s and 1970s played a major part in bringing about these changes. With respect to sex discrimination, in particular, feminist lobbying efforts were instrumental in the passage of the Education Amendments Act of 1972 that contains the important provisions known as **Title IX**. Simply stated, Title IX forbids sex discrimination in any educational program or activity that receives federal funding. This law has resulted in a number of beneficial reforms in education, including gender equitable access to school athletic programs (see Chapter 12), standardized testing, and career advising and planning programs. Nevertheless, the educational experiences of males and females remain different and, more significantly, unequal. This is despite the recent argument that the remarkable gains in education made by females is at the expense of males. More specifically, a number of observers have argued that females are now being favored in school and that males are at a disadvantage (Connell & Gunzelmann, 2004; Conlin, 2003; Gunzelmann & Connell, 2006; Lewin, 2006; Warner, 2006).

Corbett, Hill, and St. Rose (2008) respond to the so-called educational "crisis" for boys by noting that "If girls' success comes at the expense of boys, one would expect to see boys' scores decline as girls' scores rise, but this has not been the case" (p. 2). The backlash against females' success in education was sparked by a report released by the American Council on Education in 2006 indicating that the gender gap in higher education was widening with women pulling far ahead of men (American Council on Education, 2006). However, in January 2010 the American Council on Education released another report indicating that the gender gap in higher education had reached a plateau or stabilized (American Council on Education, 2010).

In the remainder of this chapter, we will examine the various structural factors that serve to perpetuate inequality in education, from elementary school through graduate school, comparing the experiences of various groups of females and males. Meanwhile, Box 5.1 looks at gender inequality in education internationally.

EDUCATING GIRLS AND BOYS: THE ELEMENTARY AND MIDDLE SCHOOLS

Boys and girls may have rather different experiences in elementary and middle school. First, boys are more likely than girls to have their entry into kindergarten postponed (Malone et al., 2006). Second, boys are more likely than girls to be held back a grade or more while in elementary school (Entwisle, Alexander, & Olson 2007). Third, while boys tend to score higher on standardized tests, girls tend to have better grades (Duckworth & Seligman, 2006), even in math and science (Perkins et al., 2004). In addition, teachers may interact differently with boys and girls (Francis & Skelton, 2005).

When elementary schoolteachers are asked about the way they treat their students, they respond in the same way that parents do and state that they treat all their students fairly, regardless of their sex. Research indicates, however, that in practice, teachers typically interact differently (and often inequitably) with their male and female students. The interactions differ in at least two ways: the frequency of teacher-student interactions and the content of those interactions.

There is some disagreement with regard to the question of whether teachers interact more with male students than female students. Some research concludes that teachers favor girls (Sommers, 2000). There are studies that report no difference, but the majority of studies show that regardless of the sex of the teacher, male students interact more with their teachers than female students do (American Association of University Women [AAUW], 1992; Drudy & Chathain, 2002; Francis & Skelton, 2005). Other research has found that teachers are more likely to initiate conversations with boys (Voyles, Haller,

BOX 5.1
Gender and Education in Developing Countries

Access to education continues to be a problem for children in many countries. In 2007, 101 million children of primary school age were not enrolled in school. Of those children, 88 percent lived in Africa and Asia; 35 million lived in South Asia, 25.4 million lived in Central and South Africa, and 20.1 million lived in Eastern and Southern Africa (UNICEF, 2009b).

The gender gap in access to all levels of education has narrowed in most countries throughout the world since the 1980s, possibly in part because of efforts made by the United Nations and other worldwide organizations (Stromquist, 2006). In 2005, 94 girls started Grade 1 for every 100 boys, according to the global average. This is a slight improvement from 1999 (91 girls started grade 1 for every 100 boys) (UNESCO, 2008). Despite improvement, however, the gender gap in enrollment remains wide and continues to favor boys. Girls worldwide continue to face challenges gaining equal access to education (Herz & Sperling, 2004; UNICEF, 2009a), and the gaps are the widest in Africa, parts of Asia, and the Middle East. In sub-Saharan Africa, 54 percent of girls do not complete even a primary school education (Bruns, Mingat, & Rakotomalala, 2003). As one moves up through the grades, the gap grows. Only 17 percent of girls in Africa are enrolled in secondary school (UNESCO, 2003). In India, 83 girls are enrolled in secondary school for every 100 boys. In Pakistan, 76 girls are enrolled in secondary school for every 100 boys. In Yemen, 49 girls are enrolled in secondary school for every 100 boys. In Afghanistan, 34 girls are enrolled in secondary school for every 100 boys (World Bank, 2007). Only 17 percent of girls in Africa are enrolled in secondary school (UNESCO, 2003).

Children in rural areas have less access to school than children in urban areas; the primary school completion rate for girls in rural areas is three times lower than that for boys, and in urban areas it is twice as low (Herz & Sperling, 2004). In some countries in Asia and Africa, schools are sex-segregated, and there simply are no schools for girls that are reasonably close to their homes (Persell et al., 1999; United Nations, 2000). As we noted in Chapter 1, the distance girls must travel to and from school often raises serious safety and hygiene concerns.

The populations of Southern Asia and sub-Saharan Africa are "among the world's fastest growing, suggesting that the absolute number of illiterate women in these regions will continue to be enormous" (United Nations, 2000, p. 86). Illiteracy means lacking the ability to read or write in one's native language at a level sufficient to meet the demands of daily living. It is estimated that 876 million people throughout the world are illiterate and about two-thirds of them are women. In addition, girls who are denied education are more vulnerable to poverty, hunger, violence, abuse, exploitation, trafficking, HIV/AIDS and other diseases, and maternal mortality (UNICEF, 2006, p. 5).

Thus, despite improvements in school enrollments that have lowered illiteracy rates, especially among younger segments of the population (persons aged 15 to 24), illiteracy remains high in those countries where many girls and boys still do not go to school or drop out early (e.g., after fourth grade). Girls are more likely than boys to leave school early, citing as their main reasons that they did not like school, they did not pass their exams, their family could not afford the school fees, or they were needed at home to help their families (Persell et al., 1999; United Nations, 2000). For example, on average, a Pakistani girl receives only 2.5 years of schooling, while boys receive five years (Latif, 2009).

Girls who attend school may actually be discouraged from continuing their education by the gendered messages they receive in school curricula and textbooks (UNESCO, 2008). For example, textbooks used in India depict women engaging in gender-stereotypical behavior (e.g., in the kitchen, caring for home and children) (Ahmed, 2006), as do textbooks used in Brazil (Vianna & Unbehaum, 2006). Gender-biased texts coupled with the lack of female teachers in developing countries (UNICEF, 2006) is problematic, especially given norms in some Middle Eastern countries and Muslim societies that prohibit interaction between males and females. Students may not be exposed to gender equitable viewpoints, female role models, or women in any position of authority, thus discouraging them from persisting to school completion.

& Fossum, 2007), and even when boys do not voluntarily participate in class, teachers are more likely to solicit information from them than from girls (Sadker & Sadker, 1994; Sadker & Zittleman, 2009). Of course, the greater attention boys get from teachers may be due to the fact that boys are more demanding than girls. Boys, for instance, are more likely than girls to call out answers in class, thus directing a teacher's attention to them more often.

Apart from the frequency of teacher-student interactions, the content of teacher-student interactions may also differ, depending on the sex of the student. Teachers provided boys with more remediation; for instance, more often, they helped boys find and correct errors. In addition, they posed more academic challenges to boys, encouraging them to think through their answers to arrive at the best possible academic response (Sadker & Sadker, 1994; Sadker & Zittleman, 2009). Other research, however, has found that there is very little difference in boys' and girls' beliefs that both male and female teachers encouraged and challenged them (Carrington, Connell, & Lee, 2007).

At the same time, while some studies show that boys generally engage in more positive intellectual interactions with teachers, other researchers emphasize that boys also experience more negative interactions with teachers. Boys are more likely than girls to exhibit disruptive behavior (Downey & Vogt Yaun, 2005; Eamon & Altshuler, 2004) and less likely to be able to self-regulate their behavior (Matthews, Ponitz, & Morrison, 2009). In addition, male and female students believe that boys are more likely than girls to get in trouble with teachers and be treated more negatively than girls are (Myhill & Jones, 2006; Zittleman, 2007). Research has also found that boys are more likely than girls to be expelled from school (Gillium, 2005).

Just as teachers maintain that they are gender-blind, they also declare themselves color-blind (Schofield, 2010; Vaught & Castagno, 2008). When considering race, however, research has found that African American girls are disciplined less by teachers than African American boys are (Lopez, 2003). However, African American girls are reprimanded more than African American boys and girls of other races/ethnicities for calling out in class (Morris, 2007). When acting assertively in class, teachers see African American girls as abrasive, and they encourage them to be more "ladylike" (Morris, 2007). African Americans, mostly boys, are much more likely than White students to face expulsion (Witt, 2007).

Boys also receive lower marks than girls for deportment (e.g., conduct, effort, paying attention, completing assignments, classroom interest, cooperation, and compliance). Doris Entwisle and her colleagues (1997, 2007) argue that these negative conduct ratings for boys translate into lower academic marks, particularly in reading, even when male and female students have the same standardized test scores. While boys and girls may begin first grade with similar scores on reading tests, as they continue through elementary school, the gender gap widens with girls' scores exceeding boys' scores (Entwisle et al., 2007).

Not all teachers favor girls, but the academic performance of students is affected by teacher bias regardless of which sex is favored. Specifically, Entwisle, Alexander, & Olso (1997) found that "over the first year, gains on standardized tests and improvement in marks were both greater for children of the sex favored by the teacher's interest-participation ratings. . . . Other things being equal, children of one sex or the other did significantly better on standardized tests of reading and math according to whether the teacher favored members of their sex in terms of interest/participation in class" (pp. 129–130).

While teacher-student interactions are complicated by the factors of social class, gender, and race, these factors are important when considering educational expectations and achievement. Research has found that parents and teachers have lower expectations for future educational achievement of African American boys than girls (Wood, Kaplan, & McLoyd, 2007). Teachers, including high school teachers and counselors, appear to have lower expectations of students coming from lower socioeconomic backgrounds (Auwater & Aruguete, 2008; Thompson, Warren, & Carter, 2004; see also Persell, 2010). Low-income and racial minority boys do not do as well in school as middle-class and White boys (Kimmel, 2006; Reichert & Hawley, 2006). Other research supports that race, social class, and gender are important factors to consider when looking at academic achievement. For example, research has found that African American eighth grade female students score higher on tests than African American eighth grade male students. However, girls' achievement was influenced by their family's socioeconomic status, while peers, attitudes about education, and the school environment influenced boys' achievement (Greene & Mickelson, 2006). Clearly, social class and racial prejudices interact with sexism to have an especially pernicious effect on some students' educational experiences.

Gender and race may also affect diagnosis and treatment for disabling conditions. Boys significantly outnumber girls in referrals by teachers to special education programs (Gunzelmann & Connell, 2006; Hibel, Farkas, & Morgan, 2006). Boys are more likely to be diagnosed with reading disabilities, mental retardation (Rutter et al., 2004), and attention deficit disorders (Biederman & Faraone, 2005; Leslie et al., 2008; Rutter et al., 2004; Wheeler et al., 2008). However, research has found that girls are more likely than boys to be "declassified" or stop receiving special education services (Daley & Carlson, 2009). In trying to explain these gender differences, some analysts have argued that more boys than girls are born with disabling conditions. However, medical reports indicate that the sex distribution of learning disabilities and attention deficit disorder (ADHD) is nearly equal. Consequently, school personnel may not be accurately identifying learning problems; they may be misidentifying behavioral problems in boys AAUW, 1992). This may be because girls are quieter in school, so they are more easily overlooked. Boys are more likely to act out, so they are placed in special education programs that may not address their specific problems and needs (see, for example, Willcut & Pennington, 2000).

At the same time research indicates that African Americans are more likely to be referred to school-based services for ADHD (Bussing et al., 2005), and African American, Native American and Latino students are more likely to be labeled as needing special education services (Artiles, Trent, & Palmer, 2004; Hosp & Reschly, 2004). In 2006, American Indian students were most likely to be classified as having a learning disability, followed by African American and Hispanic students (U.S. Department of Education, 2009). Some researchers argue this is because of racial prejudice, but others argue that minority children are more likely than White children to be poor; they may lack adequate housing and food, which will inhibit their ability to concentrate in school, thereby leading to developmental delays and learning disabilities.

Students may also receive gender messages through traditional curricular materials available in elementary schools. We noted at the outset of this chapter that students learn not only the academic subjects of their school's formal curriculum, but also a set of values and expectations known as the hidden curriculum. We can see the hidden curriculum at work in the selective content of textbooks and other educational materials. For example, Chick (2006) finds that women are absent in elementary and high school social studies books. Studies conducted during the 1970s (see, for example, Weitzman & Rizzo, 1976) showed that, although the United States is a country with citizens of both sexes who share a rich and varied racial and ethnic heritage, racial minorities and women were conspicuously absent from elementary school textbooks and readers. During the 1980s and throughout the 1990s, researchers found some improvements. Clark, Allard, and Mahoney (2004) compared American history textbooks published in the 1960s, 1980s, and 1990s, and Clark and colleagues (2005) compared world history textbooks in the same decades and found that women are more likely to be included in books published in the 1990s. The gender bias in textbooks, then, appears to be decreasing, but slowly (Blumberg, 2008).

The presentation of women and racial and ethnic minorities in textbooks and curricula is usually limited to a few "famous women" or "famous Blacks"; or they are mentioned only in traditional contexts (slavery, the Civil War, and the civil rights movement for Blacks; the suffrage movement for women) or in terms of traditional roles (e.g., women who were married to famous men). One review of twenty-nine books appropriate for prekindergarten to third grade students found that the literature only included European American and African American ethnic groups (Boutte, Hopkins, & Waklatsi, 2008). The lack of racial diversity in texts and school curricula is problematic given that researchers posit that the identity of students of color is influenced by their experiences in school (Baron-Fritts, 2004; J. R. Davis, 2007).

Furthermore, Davis (1995) found that the material is sometimes belittling and at other times, inaccurate. In one text, for example, aviator Amelia Earhart is referred to as a stewardess; in other books, women's struggle for equal rights is discussed as the fight for equal rights for wives. Rarely is mention made of women's role in the westward expansion of the United States or in the Vietnam War (E. A. Davis, 1995). That there is a heterosexist bias in the texts goes without saying.

Most publishers also issue guidelines to textbook authors to assist them in avoiding sexist language, but the extent to which the guidelines are actually followed is uneven, and such guidelines do little to increase the representation of women and minorities in the texts nor to expand the content of the texts to include the perspectives of women and minorities on their own terms (AAUW, 1992; Sadker & Sadker, 1994). For example, there is evidence that children's readers have improved significantly with respect to the use of gender-neutral language and the inclusion of females. However, there continue to be imbalances in favor of males with regard to the rate of portrayal and types of roles assigned to males and females in the stories (e.g., girls need to be rescued more than boys; boys are more adventurous than girls; women work for men, but not vice versa) (Persell et al., 1999). As discussed in Chapter 4, research has found that female characters in children's picture books are less likely than male characters to work outside the home (Hamilton et al., 2006).

The organization of school activities also gives children messages about gender. For example, teachers continue to use various forms of *sex separation* in their classrooms: They may ask girls and boys to form separate lines, or they may organize teams for a spelling or math competition according to students' sex. Teachers also sometimes assign girls and boys different classroom chores; for instance, girls may be asked to dust or water the plants, whereas boys are asked to carry books, rearrange desks, or run equipment. Sociologist Barrie Thorne (1993), who has made extensive observations of elementary school classrooms, points out that teachers engage in contradictory practices: Sometimes they reinforce sex separation, but at other times they challenge or disrupt it. She notes that teachers more often mix boys and girls than separate them, but that separating girls and boys in lines or seating arrangements, as well as pitting them against one another in classroom contests, is not uncommon. Even preschool teachers segregate their classes by gender (Bigler, 2005). Moreover, this physical separation is reinforced by a verbal separation, in that teachers routinely use

On school playgrounds, children typically organize themselves into sex-segregated groups to engage in what they consider gender-appropriate activities.

gender labels as terms of address to the students and invariably put "boys" first in speaking to the children, as in "boys and girls." Thorne observed that girls and boys typically separate themselves in school lunchrooms and on school playgrounds—probably much more than they do in their home neighborhoods—and teachers and aides often ratify this division by seeing certain areas as "girls' territory" and other areas as "boys' territory." Thorne's research receives support from recent studies that also conclude that boys and girls self-segregate and select same-sex friends (see, for example, Mehta & Stough, 2009; Pelligrini et al., 2007).

Trivial though they may appear to be, these kinds of interactions have at least three interrelated consequences. First, sex separation in and of itself prevents boys and girls from working together cooperatively, thus denying children of both sexes valuable opportunities to learn about and sample one another's interests and activities. Second, sex separation makes working in same-sex groups more comfortable than working in mixed-sex groups—a feeling that children may carry with them into adulthood and that may become problematic when they enter the labor force (see Chapter 8). Third, sex separation reinforces gender stereotypes, especially if it involves differential work assignments (Sadker & Zittleman, 2009).

Thorne (1993) found that in a classroom activity with a central focus, such as the collective making of a map or taking turns reading aloud from a book, girls and boys participated together. Similar observations have prompted some educators to advocate that classroom activities be reorganized to facilitate *cooperative learning.* Cooperative learning involves students working together in small, mixed-sex, mixed-race/ethnic groups on a group project or toward a group goal (e.g., solving a problem, writing a report). The cooperative learning approach is designed to lessen classroom competition, maximize cooperation, foster group solidarity and interdependence, and promote understanding among members of diverse groups of children. Research indicates that cooperative learning does have a number of benefits. Moreover, students positively evaluate small-group learning (Florez & McCaslin, 2008). Additional research shows that African American males in elementary school benefit from cooperative learning (Wilson-Jones & Caston, 2004). Cooperative learning also appears to increase interracial/interethnic friendships as well as the popularity of immigrant students (Oortwijn et al., 2008).

Unfortunately, there is research indicating that small-group learning may be less successful in fostering positive relationships between boys and girls in school. Similar to what occurs on school playgrounds, the use of small, unstructured work groups in the classroom, especially if it is infrequent, gives boys, but not girls, leadership opportunities that can raise their self-esteem. Girls end up taking direction from boys, a pattern that reinforces gender stereotypes and lowers girls' self-esteem and their academic achievement (AAUW, 1992; however, for a different outcome see Strough & Diriwächter, 2000). More fundamental changes than simply providing mixed-group learning activities are necessary to bring gender equity to elementary school classrooms.

Finally, children receive messages about gender simply by the way adult jobs are distributed in their schools. First, one is much less likely to find a male teacher in the front of the room, especially in the earlier grades. While approximately one-quarter of all teachers are men, less than 10 percent of teachers in the elementary grades are men (Johnson, 2008; "The missing male teacher," 2009). In 2008, approximately 98 percent of preschool and kindergarten teachers and 81 percent of elementary and middle school teachers were women. This is not surprising given that teaching is associated with care and nurturance and is perceived to be "women's work"—that is, an unacceptable profession for men (Anliak & Beyazkurk, 2008; Johnson, 2008). Even while kindergarten students perceived both male and female teachers as able to fill most of the roles they associated with teachers (i.e., someone who plays, cares for, and teaches them), they identified male teachers as someone who participated in sports and physical games (Harris & Barnes, 2009). Furthermore, men who want to teach young children are met with suspicion and encouraged to avoid being alone with a child to avoid perceptions or accusations of inappropriate or indecent behavior (Johnson, 2008). The lack of male teachers in the earlier grades may be problematic for boys, however, given that boys report building closer relationships with male teachers (Harris & Barnes, 2009).

Women are also underrepresented in the upper management of school administrations. For example, in 2006, 54 percent of public elementary school principals and assistant principals were women (U.S. Department of Commerce, Bureau of the Census, 2010). Female principals, though, are more likely to be found in charge of "undesirable" schools—i.e., large urban or small rural schools where funding and under-resourcing are problems (Persell et al., 1999).

We have already mentioned that girls on average earn higher grades than boys throughout their elementary school years (AAUW, 1992; Duckworth & Seligman, 2006), and boys are more likely than girls to be retained one or more grades during elementary school (Entwisle et al., 2007). However, girls' achievement test scores, as well as their self-confidence, often decline as they progress through the educational system (AAUW, 1992; AAUW, 2008; Gilligan, Lyons, & Hanmer, 1990; Sadker & Sadker, 1994). Girls' decline in self-confidence and aspirations specifically for math begins to emerge in middle school (Linver & Davis-Kean, 2005). Let's examine girls' and boys' educational experiences in high school in order to better understand these findings.

EDUCATING TEENAGE GIRLS AND BOYS: THE SECONDARY SCHOOLS

Both parents and teenagers will attest that adolescence is one of the more stressful periods of the life cycle. As a teenager's body changes and matures, interests change as well, and the opinions of friends take on greater significance in the formation of self-concept. Young men and women both feel the need to be popular with their peers, but the means and measures of their success at this are somewhat different.

For teenage boys, the single most important source of prestige and popularity is athletic achievement. Related sources of social acceptance and self-esteem include physical and verbal fighting skills, dominance in peer groups, a good sense of humor, and a willingness to take risks and defy norms of politeness (Eder, 1995; Rose & Rudolph, 2006). The "non-jock" is at a serious disadvantage, socially and psychologically, in high school. It is the "jock" who conforms to the ideals of masculinity (Miller, 2009). Moreover, on the court or on the playing field, boys are taught a variety of stereotypically masculine skills and values: aggression (including sexual aggression and the objectification of women), endurance, competitiveness, stoic invulnerability, self-confidence, and teamwork (Cheng, 2008; Eder, 1995). Unfortunately, the jock identity has been associated with problem drinking (Miller et al., 2003) and interpersonal violence (Miller et al., 2006).

What about girls? For one thing, physical prowess and athletic ability are not girls' chief sources of prestige and popularity. Indeed, most teenage girls learn that to be strongly athletic is to be unfeminine and, as we will discuss in Chapter 12, school officials reinforce this message by under-resourcing girls' sports programs. Instead, what contributes most to a teenage girl's prestige and popularity is physical attractiveness. Girls' attractiveness may be enhanced when they wear stylish clothes and makeup, but too much makeup and too obvious an attempt to appear sexually alluring can result in negative labels, such as "whore" and "slut." Teenage girls must walk a fine line by demonstrating that they are sexually knowledgeable, but not sexually aggressive. Unlike boys, girls are supposed to be sexually passive, the objects of boys' sexual advances, but not sexual initiators themselves (Eder, 1995; Kiefer & Sanchez, 2007; Kim & Ward, 2004).

Obviously, both female and male teenagers who are not heterosexual face tremendous difficulties in high school and, as Box 5.2 shows, frequently experience isolation and ostracism from their peers as well as from adults. Also frequent targets of ridicule in high

BOX 5.2
The Middle and High School Experiences of Lesbian and Gay Youth

Adolescence is a period of tremendous physical and emotional change. It is a time when most young women and men begin to actively explore their sexuality and sexual identities. Historically, our schools have been woefully remiss in educating young people about sex, but they have been most neglectful with respect to lesbian and gay youth. Although surveys indicate willingness on the part of most teachers and school administrators to treat homosexual students in a nonjudgmental way and to attend school-sponsored workshops related to homosexual students, there remains among most an unwillingness to proactively address the special needs of homosexual students or to openly affirm their sexual identities (Sears, 1992). The majority of school personnel continue to assume the heterosexuality of their students and never raise the issue of sexual orientation. This may be in part because teachers are not trained or taught how to handle and address sexual issues. Education textbooks fail to include sexual orientation topics, and teacher training programs ignore lesbian, gay, bisexual, and transgender (LGBT) issues (Jennings & Sherwin, 2007; Macgillivray & Jennings, 2008).

With the exception of responding to especially blatant or heinous forms of harassment against homosexual students, most school personnel do not seriously confront the problem of **homophobia**—an unreasonable fear of or hostility toward homosexuals—in their classrooms or on school grounds (Logan, 2001; Wragg, 2005). Students may not feel encouraged to report harassment or bullying as they believe teachers will not address it (Rutter & Leech, 2006; Trotter, 2009). Because of recent incidents of extreme violence (e.g., the Columbine High School shooting), school administrators have become much less tolerant of bullying and harassment (Stein, 2003) than they were in the past. Despite these changes, homophobia remains a serious problem in schools. Sexual minority students are more likely than heterosexual students to be physically assaulted (Fineran, 2002) or sexually harassed (Fineran, 2002; Gruber & Fineran, 2008; Trotter, 2006; Williams

et al., 2005). A majority of students who identify as gay, lesbian, or bisexual report experiencing bullying (79 percent) or sexual harassment (71 percent), compared with 50 percent of heterosexual students who experienced bullying and 32 percent who experienced sexual harassment (Gruber & Fineran, 2008). A report published by the Massachusetts Department of Education (2007) states that students who identify as gay, lesbian, or bisexual are almost twice as likely as their heterosexual peers to have been bullied, almost three times as likely to have been threatened or injured with a weapon at school, over four times as likely to have experienced dating violence, and almost four times as likely to have experienced sexual contact against their will.

When comparing the experiences of middle school students to high school students, research finds that LGBT middle school students endure more harassment than LGBT high school students. The majority (90 percent) of LGBT middle school students report that they have heard the word "gay" used in a derogatory manner, and over half (63 percent) report that they have even heard staff members make homophobic statements (Gay, Lesbian and Straight Education Network [GLSEN], 2009).

Transgendered students are even more likely than lesbian, gay, or bisexual students to experience harassment (Greytak, Kosciw, & Diaz, 2009). One study found that of the 295 transgendered students surveyed, most (69 percent) felt unsafe at school because of their sexual orientation, and in the year prior to the survey, the vast majority (89 percent) had been verbally harassed and 28 percent had been physically assaulted because of their sexual orientation (Greytak et al., 2009).

Harassment and bullying are often detrimental to school achievement, attendance, and health (Dodds, Keogh, & Hickson, 2005; Greytak et al., 2009; Rivers, 2006). The Massachusetts Department of Education (2007) reports that students who identify as gay, lesbian, or bisexual are significantly more likely than their heterosexual peers to have skipped

(continued)

BOX 5.2
Continued

school because they felt unsafe, were less likely to receive good grades, and were more likely to carry a weapon or report involvement in a physical fight (see also GLSEN, 2009). Compared to heterosexual victims of bullying or sexual harassment, homosexual or bisexual students are more likely to suffer from poorer self-esteem, poorer physical and mental health, have more trauma symptoms (Gruber & Fineran, 2008), and are at an increased risk for committing or attempting suicide (Lock & Kleis, 1998; Poteat & Espelage, 2007).

In response to these disturbing statistics, organizations have been established throughout the United States to specifically meet the special needs of lesbian and gay youth (Harris, 1997; Woog, 1995). These include schools for gay, lesbian, and bisexual students or the children of gays, lesbians, and bisexuals. The first such school, the Harvey Milk School in New York, was founded in 1985, and in 2008 had about ninety-six students. Most organizations, however, do not provide direct schooling, but rather offer other services, such as counseling, tutoring, meals, and sometimes shelter for homosexual and bisexual youth who have been kicked out of their homes after coming out to (or being found out by) their parents. Some organizations also offer programs, such as peer trainings at local schools to help foster acceptance of homosexual and bisexual youth and to help prevent harassment and violence. A number of organizations lobby school boards and state departments of education to make school activities and curriculum more inclusive of gay and lesbian youth (Green, 1993; Harris, 1997; Woog, 1995). Resources for serving sexual minority youth are available from the Hetrick-Martin Institute (www.hmi.org) and the Gay, Lesbian, and Straight Education Network (www.glsen.org; for policies established in the United Kingdom, see Fiddy & Hamilton, 2004; Jennett, 2004; O'Loan et al., 2006). Efforts have also been made to create "friendlier" college campuses for LGBTQ (lesbian, gay, bisexual, transgendered, queer) students and faculty. Although it is only less than 8 percent of all accredited colleges and universities in the United States, the Human Rights Campaign has identified 567 colleges and universities that offer protection against discrimination, and 309 that provide health care benefits to same-sex domestic partners (Messinger, 2009). Given recent suicides by homosexual and transgendered students after anti-gay bullying, these schools and programs may literally be life savers for some students (see, for example, GLSEN, 2009; NPR, 2010).

school are students who have physical disabilities, those who are in special education programs (Eder, 1995), or who are obese (Farhat, Iannotti, & Simons-Morton, 2010; Fox & Farrow, 2009). Eder argues that the status hierarchies that emerge in high school are to some extent influenced by students' race and social class as well. In particular, when students of color are a numerical minority in a school environment, they are more easily socially isolated. Lower-class students are often regarded as deviant because of their clothing and appearance, although they may view wealthier students as "stuck-up." Social class intersects with gender in significant ways. For girls who are poor, opportunities to participate in activities that increase popularity are fewer because of their limited financial resources. Their families cannot afford name-brand clothes or summer cheerleading camp, for example (see Milner, 2004). For lower-class boys, however, athletics is a primary vehicle for overcoming the obstacles to popularity that poverty imposes (Eder, 1995; see also Chapter 12).

It is also in high school that young men and women are expected to formulate their career goals. Until the late 1960s, studies showed that high school boys had higher academic and career aspirations than high school girls. However, more recent research has found that young women have high aspirations for future careers (Goldin et al., 2006), although some girls decrease their occupational aspirations as they progress through school (Danzinger & Eden, 2007). Regardless of their aspirations, teenage girls still tend to underestimate their academic abilities (Chevalier et al., 2006).

In their studies of adolescent girls, for example, psychologist Carol Gilligan and her colleagues found that by age fifteen or sixteen, girls who had earlier exuded confidence became less outspoken and more doubtful about their abilities. Gilligan's initial research was with girls attending the Emma Willard School, an elite, private, single-sex school in New York (Gilligan et al., 1990). Gilligan and her colleagues then studied girls from poorer backgrounds in less privileged schools, including twenty-six racially and ethnically diverse teenage girls considered at high risk of dropping out of school and becoming unmarried mothers (Gilligan, Taylor, & Sullivan, 1995). These researchers' findings once again highlight the intersection of gender with race/ethnicity and social class.

Gilligan and her colleagues (1995) report that at adolescence, regardless of race/ethnicity or social class, girls increasingly find that their experiences are devalued or ignored in patriarchal culture. The desirable or idealized woman in this culture often does not match their experience or their sense of themselves. Their socialization experiences have taught them to see themselves *relationally* (i.e., in connection to others), so in order to maintain and preserve the relationships they value, adolescent girls learn to be silent and, in the process, lose their energy and vitality to succeed on their own terms. They come to "absent themselves in order to be with other people" (Gilligan et al., 1995, p. 5). Girls from privileged backgrounds change or moderate their voices so they are more "acceptable" to those who show interest in them (e.g., boys, teachers, parents). In this way, they don't jeopardize the relationships that promise them honor, riches, and marriage in the future. Poor girls, who are disproportionately racial and ethnic minorities, don't live under such constraints. Their experience, however, tells them that while they can speak, nobody really cares about what they have to say; they are irrelevant, invisible. When they do speak up, their "big mouths" frequently get them into trouble. These girls become socially and psychologically isolated, which Gilligan and her colleagues (1995) see as the precursors to problems such as dropping out of school and early single motherhood (see also Fordham, 1996).

Although Gilligan's theory has been criticized for various reasons (see, for instance, Gottschalk, 2007; Hirsch & Keller, 1990; Jorgensen, 2006) and her research uses small convenience samples, her work does offer a provocative counterpoint to earlier theorists who argued that females' self-confidence and self-efficacy decline during adolescence because women fear success. During the 1970s, for example, psychologist Matina Horner (1972) argued that her research, which showed that women tended to perform better on word-game tasks when they worked alone rather than in mixed-sex groups, indicated that women are uncomfortable competing with men. Horner hypothesized that women may deliberately, although perhaps unconsciously, underachieve because they fear the consequences that success in high-achievement situations might bring—specifically, that they will appear unfeminine and therefore be rejected socially.

There is evidence that girls tend to feel uneasy and embarrassed about academic success (Orenstein, 1994; Sherman, 1982), and some avoid subjects defined as masculine or minimize or hide their achievements because they fear rejection by their peers (Kramer, 1991; Monks & Van Boxtel, 1995; Noble, 1989; Renold & Allan, 2006; Skelton, Francis, & Read, 2010). There is also evidence that their concerns are not unfounded: Girls who behave in ways defined by their peers as gender-inappropriate are likely to be unpopular and ostracized (Eder, 1995; Luftig & Nichols, 1991; Renold & Allan, 2006; Skelton et al., 2010).[2] Boys who behave in gender-inappropriate ways are also ridiculed and ostracized by peers, but boys do not appear to lower their academic or career aspirations as a result. Why?

One answer is that girls face a number of obstacles imposed by others that inhibit the realization of their academic and occupational goals. These obstacles are sometimes collectively called the *invisible* or *glass ceiling* (see also Chapter 8). One element of the invisible ceiling is the widespread belief that girls are not as intellectually gifted as boys and therefore cannot be expected to do as well in school. Such beliefs are contradicted by data showing that girls' high school GPA's are slightly higher than boys' GPA's (Corbett et al., 2008), and girls are more likely than boys to take Advanced Placement exams and score a 3 or higher on them (Handwerk, Tognatta, & Coley, 2008). But research reveals that parents usually attribute boys' academic achievements to ability, whereas girls' achievements are attributed to effort or hard work (Raty et al., 2002). Also, parents believe girls are more persistent with their education than boys are (Kärkkäinen, Räty, & Kasanen, 2009). Female high school seniors do spend more time than male high school seniors studying and doing homework (Sax, 2009).

In addition, high school teachers, like their elementary school counterparts, tend to offer male students more encouragement, publicly praise their scholastic abilities, and be friendlier toward them than they are toward female students (Bush, 1987; Jones & Wheatley, 1990; Orenstein, 1994). However, research has also found that high school teachers believe girls work harder in school than boys do (Downey & Vogt Yuan, 2005). There is evidence that students internalize these beliefs, which, if one is female (and poor and non-White), could reasonably lead to lowered self-confidence and self-efficacy—not for fear of success, but for fear of failure (AAUW, 1992; Bush, 1987; Fordham, 1996; Gilligan et al., 1995; Orenstein, 1994).

Another element of the invisible ceiling imposed on girls in secondary schools can be found in curriculum materials that often send girls the message that they are unlikely to realize their ambitions. Reviews of high school textbooks, for instance, found both subtle and blatant gender biases, including language bias, gender stereotypes, omission of women, and neglect of scholarship by women (Blumberg, 2008; Clark et al., 2004; Clark et al., 2005; Davis, 1995). As in elementary school, research indicates that the type of curriculum materials used in the schools clearly has an impact on students' attitudes and behaviors. According to the authors of a review of more than one hundred studies of gender-fair curriculum materials, "Pupils who are exposed to sex-equitable materials are more likely than others to (1) have gender-balanced knowledge of people in society, (2) develop more flexible attitudes and more accurate sex-role knowledge, and (3) imitate role behaviors contained in the material" (Scott & Schau, 1985, p. 228). The gender bias common in high school curriculum materials is compounded by the lack of attention to racial and ethnic diversity and differences in sexual orientation. For example, Temple (2005) reviewed twenty high school textbooks on a variety of subjects and found that only 5 percent of the content of the books mentioned same-sex sexuality in any way, and most of the time it was portrayed negatively. Only 6 percent of lesbian, gay, bisexual, and transgender (LGBT) middle school students and 16 percent of LGBT high school students reported that LGBT-related topics were included in textbooks or other reading assigned by teachers (GLSEN, 2009).

School personnel may also contribute to making girls feel that they will be unable to fulfill their aspirations. Research exploring gender bias exhibited by school counselors is limited, but some studies indicate that school counselors provide less useful career information to girls. For example, in one survey, more than 70 percent of the six hundred female students questioned said that the career advice provided to them at school was either inadequate or not helpful (Miles, 1995). Studies also indicate that school personnel may channel male and female students into different (i.e., gender-stereotyped) fields and activities, with female students in particular being discouraged from pursuing such fields as mathematics, engineering, construction, information technology, and pharmaceuticals (AAUW, 1992; Creamer & Meszaros, 2009; Miles, 1995; see also Box 5.3).

Finally, although elementary school girls can identify with their teachers, who are almost always women, it becomes more difficult to do so in high school, where about 43.5 percent of the teachers are men (43 percent in public schools and 48 percent in private schools) (U.S. Department of Education, National Center for Education Statistics, 2007b).

Although there is no research that shows a clear cause-and-effect relationship, it is not unlikely that the rather discouraging nature of girls' high school experience, more than their fear of success, is what weakens their self-confidence and self-efficacy. Nevertheless, a high number of female high school graduates attend college. This may be due to the fact that more employers are requiring college degrees, the family expectations of women are changing, and women have more access to birth control (Goldin et al., 2006). In fact, as Table 5.1 shows, women now constitute a slight majority of college students. Although women are more likely than men to focus on the intellectual benefits of college (Sax, 2009), the education they receive often differs from that of their male peers in many important respects.

EDUCATING WOMEN AND MEN: COLLEGES AND GRADUATE SCHOOLS

"What's your major?" is certainly a question college students get asked a lot. The next time you are in a group and that question comes up, compare the responses of the male students with those of the female students. Chances are, you will discover an interesting sex-specific pattern, for as Table 5.2 shows, men and women continue to be concentrated in different fields of study. More male students pursue degrees in engineering, architecture, the physical sciences (e.g., astronomy, chemistry, physics), and business (e.g., banking and finance, economics). Female students are heavily concentrated in nursing, library science, social work, psychology, anthropology, sociology, and education. Even before they begin their college careers, females intend to major in different fields of study than males do. Research including high school valedictorians finds that girls are as likely as boys to intend to major in a science field (especially the biological and life sciences), more likely to intend to major in the humanities and social sciences, and less likely to intend to major in math, computer science, or engineering (York, 2008).

This imbalance persists and, in some cases, worsens at the graduate level. Again, looking at Table 5.2 we find that the graduate degrees of men and women tend to be concentrated in different fields. For example, men earn about 82 percent of the

BOX 5.3
Gender, Mathematics, and Computers

For many years, much has been made of the fact that boys score higher than girls do on the Scholastic Assessment Test (S.A.T., formerly the Scholastic Aptitude Test) and that the differences between boys' and girls' scores historically have been largest on the math portion of the exam. In 1998, the gender gap in S.A.T. scores narrowed somewhat, largely because the test had been revised following charges of gender bias. Nevertheless, the gender gap in math scores on the test remained (Arenson, 1998). Some data indicate that this trend continues; boys score better than girls on the math section of the S.A.T. (Corbett et al., 2008). Furthermore, data from the National Association of Education Progress (NAEP) show that boys perform better than girls in math and science courses (Mead, 2006). This gender gap occurs in countries other than the United States as well. Ma (2008) explored international differences in boys' and girls' achievements in science, reading, and math using Program for International Student Assessment data for forty-one countries including the United States. Significant gender gaps in math were found in twenty-nine countries with boys performing better than girls; in only five countries did girls perform better than boys.

Boys slightly outperform girls in math in earlier grades. According to 2007 National Assessment of Educational Progress (NAEP) data, fourth-grade boys did slightly better than girls in math, and the gap between girls' performance and boys' performance remained stable between 1990, 2005, and 2007 (Lee, Grigg, & Dion, 2007). According to the report, with the exception of geometry, fourth-grade boys scored higher on average than female students in all mathematics content areas. The trend continues for eighth-grade students. Eighth-grade boys did slightly better than girls in math, and the gap between girls' performance and boys' performance remained stable between 1990, 2005, and 2007 (Lee et al., 2007).

Some observers have argued that the gender gap in math is biologically or genetically caused—that males, for example, have a genetic predisposition to excel at math or

that the organization of their brains favors math achievement (see Chapter 2). Others maintain that boys and girls learn math differently (Geist & King, 2008; Gurian, Henley, & Trueman, 2002). And still others point to the fact that parents have lower expectations of their daughter's math ability (Simpkins, Davis-Kean, & Eccles, 2005). Despite widespread attention to such claims in the popular media, the scientific data to support them are sparse. There is evidence that boys do better at math because they have better spatial skills, but the research indicates that these better spatial skills may be as much, if not more, a product of experience than of biology. The development of spatial skills as well as problem-solving ability, for instance, is tied to participation in competitive sports, which boys do more than girls. These skills are also associated with greater independence from parents, exploratory play, and willingness to take risks—all activities more likely experienced by boys than by girls while growing up (Barnett & Rivers, 2004; Casey, Nuttall, & Pezais, 1997; Entwisle et al., 1997; Ramos & Lambating, 1996; see also Chapter 4).

In their classic study of gender and mathematics performance, Fennema and Sherman (1977) discovered that the major difference between males and females with regard to mathematics is not math ability per se, but rather the extent of exposure to mathematics. Throughout elementary school, when boys and girls take the same math classes, there is little, if any, difference in math achievement even though boys, as we have seen, score slightly higher on standardized tests. As the years progress, girls become less likely than boys to take any math courses beyond those required by their school for graduation (Persell et al., 1999). However, more recent research indicates that this trend may be changing. High school girls are taking more credits in math courses than boys are, and their GPA's in these classes are also higher (Catsambis, 2005; Gallagher & Kaufman, 2005; U.S. Department of Education, National Center for Education Statistics, 2007). Perhaps in the future, then, we will see the gender gap in math close.

TABLE 5.2   Percentage of Bachelor's, Master's, and Doctor's Degrees Conferred by U.S. Institutions of Higher Education to Women in Selected Fields, 2006–2007

Major Field of Study	% Bachelor's Degrees Conferred to Women	% Master's Degrees Conferred to Women	% Doctor's Degrees Conferred to Women
Accounting	57.1	54.2	45.7
Agriculture & Natural Resources	46.8	53.0	39.6
Anthropology	69.6	69.4	61.9
Architecture and Related Services	44.5	44.5	41.6
Astronomy	38.7	39.3	37.9
Banking & Financial Support Services	38.1	27.2	75.0
Biological & Physical Sciences	58.9	53.8	32.6
Business Administration & Management, General	49.8	41.8	41.3
Chemistry	49.4	46.7	37.2
Criminal Justice & Law Enforcement Administration	48.9	50.9	54.5
Economics	30.3	35.7	31.6
Education	78.7	77.3	67.5
Engineering	18.4	22.4	20.9
English Language & Literature, General	69.2	67.5	59.4
Health Professions & Related Clinical Sciences	85.9	80.5	73.2
History	41.3	46.0	40.1
International Relations & Affairs	60.6	53.2	41.7
Library Science	87.8	80.7	65.4
Mathematics	45.0	41.0	26.7
Nursing	89.8	91.0	93.7
Physics	21.1	23.8	17.7
Political Science & Government	46.0	45.2	41.9
Psychology	77.4	79.7	73.2
Social Work	89.1	87.3	77.8
Sociology	70.0	69.3	63.1
Visual & Performing Arts	61.6	57.1	54.2

Source: U.S. Department of Education, National Center for Education Statistics, 2006–2007 Integrated Postsecondary Education Data System (IPEDS), Fall, 2007. (This table was prepared June 2008.) Retrieved February 10, 2010, from http://nces.ed.gov/programs/digest/d08/tables/dt08_275.asp.

Ph.Ds in physics but less than 7 percent of the Ph.Ds in nursing. Conversely, women earn 78 percent of the doctorates in social work but just 21 percent of the doctorates in engineering.

An even more disturbing trend emerges at the highest graduate level: The number of female degree recipients declines. Consider that although women represent 57 percent of bachelor's (2006–2007) and 61 percent of all master's degree recipients (2006–07), they constitute 50 percent of all doctorate recipients. More importantly, the gender gap decreases at the Ph.D. level in several fields that have a higher concentration of women undergraduates. Education and health professions are good examples. As Table 5.2 shows, men receive 21 percent of the bachelor's degrees in education but about 33 percent of the doctorates. Similarly, in health professions, men are awarded about 14 percent of bachelor's degrees and 27 percent of doctorates.

If we consider race, we find that the overwhelming majority of bachelor's, master's, and doctorate degrees are awarded to Whites of both sexes (about 75 percent in 2006–2007; Table 5.3). Less than half of all African American students who start college at a four-year institution graduate in six years or less, which is more than 20 percentage points less than the graduation rate for White students (Carey, 2008). The higher up we go on the education ladder, the poorer the representation of non-White racial and ethnic groups. Nevertheless, these figures represent progress for people of color and women in higher education. In 1977, for example, people of color received only 10.5 percent of bachelor's degrees awarded, 11 percent of master's degrees, and 8.6 percent of doctorates; in 2006–2007, they received nearly 21 percent of bachelor's degrees, 17.5 percent of master's degrees, and 16.9 percent of doctorates (U.S. National Center for Education Statistics, 2008).

To some extent, progress for women and minorities in higher education resulted from affirmative action in college and university admissions. Some states, such as California, Texas, and Washington, repealed their affirmative action programs in the 1990s. Federal court rulings in 2000 upheld affirmative action admissions policies at the University of Michigan and the University of Washington Law School. The court in the University of Michigan case cited social science research demonstrating that a racially and ethnically diverse student body benefits *all* students. In particular, studies show that White students improve their reasoning skills on such campuses and also increase their likelihood of community involvement (Bok & Bowen, 1998; Steinberg, 2000). The affirmative action policy of the University of Michigan Law School was upheld by the U.S. Supreme Court in 2003 in the case of *Grutter* v. *Bollinger*, but the Supreme Court ruled in *Gratz* v. *Bollinger* (2003) that while race can be a factor in admission decisions, the undergraduate policy had to be revised. However, in 2007 the use of race and gender in public university admission decisions was banned in Michigan (Goodman, 2007). By 2009, affirmative action in higher education admission decisions had become illegal in all states (Moses, Yun, & Marin, 2009), and institutions wishing to increase minority student enrollment have been forced to develop alternative strategies to recruit and retain students of color and to promote campus diversity (Roach, 2008).

While more people of color are attending and graduating from colleges and universities and this trend is expected to continue (Hussar & Bailey, 2009), the outlook is not uniformly positive. Of special concern are Hispanic students who are more likely than White or Black students to drop out of high school. In 2007, 6 percent of Hispanic students dropped out of high school (grades 10 to 12), compared to 4.5 percent of Black students and 2.2 percent of White students (Cataldi et al., 2009; see also Snyder & Dillow, 2007). Furthermore, while more people of color are attending and graduating from colleges and universities, White students are still more likely than students of color to complete their degree requirements and receive their degrees at both the undergraduate and graduate levels (U.S. Department of Education, 2008a, 2009d).

Women, though, have made substantial gains at the highest educational levels. In 2009, for example, women received 52.3 percent of all doctoral degrees awarded; in 1980, they received 31.2 percent of doctorates awarded. When race and ethnicity are taken into account, we find that women of color have fared better than men of color. African American women, for instance, received 4.4 percent of all doctorates awarded in 2009, up from 1.7 percent in 1980, compared with African American men who received 2.2 percent of the doctorates awarded in 2009 and 2.1 percent in 1980. The percentage of doctorates awarded to women of color, in fact, increased for every racial and ethnic group between 1980 and 2009, whereas for men, the percentages were relatively stable or, in the case of American Indian/Alaskan Native men, decreased slightly from 0.3 in 1980 to 0.2 in 2009. Overall, however, the vast majority of doctorates continue to be awarded to White women and men (National Center for Education Statistics, 2010).

It is especially noteworthy that women have made some of their greatest gains in fields that have had the fewest female students, such as the physical sciences and engineering. Although still small, the number of doctorates earned by women in engineering increased significantly in recent years. For instance, in 2006–2007, 21 percent of doctorate degrees in engineering were awarded to women, while in 1996–1997, only 12 percent of doctorate degrees in engineering were awarded to women (U.S. Department of Education, 2008d). Nevertheless, some nagging questions remain: Why does sex segregation in particular fields persist, and why is there still an education gap between the sexes?

In addressing the first question, we must consider not only why women are largely absent from certain fields, but also why there are so few men in fields such as nursing, social work, and library science. We can say with some certainty that the scarcity of men in the female-dominated fields has less to do with discrimination against them than with their unwillingness to pursue careers in areas that typically have lower prestige and lower salaries than the male-dominated fields (Anliak & Beyazkurk, 2008). We have already noted that activities and topics deemed feminine are systematically devalued in our society. Until fields such as nursing and elementary education are considered as important as computer science or finance—and are rewarded with comparable salaries—it will remain difficult to attract men to major in them (see also Chapter 8). However, in solving the puzzle of women's relative absence from the more prestigious and higher paying male-dominated fields, the issue of discrimination is central.

It is widely thought that sex discrimination in education has virtually disappeared, thanks to Title IX. You may recall that Title IX is the provision of the 1972 Education Amendments Act that forbids discrimination in any educational program or activity that receives federal funding. However, Title IX has not eliminated sex discrimination in education. One important reason for the less than total success of Title IX is that, while the law abolished most overtly discriminatory policies and practices, it left more subtle forms of sex discrimination intact (Sandler & Hall, 1986). Sandler and Hall (1986, p. 3) refer to these subtle, everyday types of discrimination as **micro-inequities**. Micro-inequities single out, ignore, or in some way discount individuals and their work or ideas simply on the basis of an ascribed trait, such as sex. "Often the behaviors themselves are small, and individually might even be termed 'trivial' or minor annoyances, but when they happen again and again, they can have a major cumulative impact because they express under-lying limited expectations and a certain discomfort in dealing with women" (Sandler & Hall, 1986, p. 3).

Feeling ignored by professors in class could negatively influence women's aca-demic goals and confidence (Sax, 2008). Despite the fact that women earn higher grades than men in college, they tend to have lower confidence in their academic abilities and report higher levels of stress (Lederman, 2006; National Coalition for Women and Girls in Education, 2007; Sax, 2008). Female college students are more likely than male college students to report that they feel ignored, unwelcomed, or treated differently (Morris & Daniel, 2008) or experience a "chilly climate" (Sandler & Hall, 1986; Schulze & Tomal, 2006). Female students are also more likely than male students to report that other female students are given less value than male students (Schulze & Tomal, 2006).

Previous research found that inequities are more common in courses and fields of study traditionally dominated by men and that they intensify in graduate school (Angier, 2000; Sandler & Hall, 1986; Massachusetts Institute of Technology, 1999; Valian, 1999). For example, in recent research women in engineering and science graduate programs (Darisi et al., 2010) as well as computer science and computer engineering graduate programs (McGrath, Cohoon, Wu, & Chao, 2009) report disparaging remarks made by professors. In other studies, however, women in traditionally male-dominated majors (e.g., information technology, engineering) were less likely than women in tradition-ally female-dominated majors (e.g., nursing, education) to feel that they were ignored or treated differently. One hypothesized explanation of this finding relates to personal-ity differences; that is, women who pursue male-dominated fields of study may have developed personalities that make them less sensitive to and affected by being treated differently than male students (Morris & Daniel, 2008). If this is the case, an interesting question to explore in future research is whether such traits developed early in their lives, perhaps as a result of childhood socialization, and they therefore felt more comfort-able pursuing male-dominated fields when they grew up, or whether these traits emerge as a way to survive and prosper once they have entered male-dominated fields.

Subtle and blatant gender biases continue to be found in college textbooks. One content analysis of stories, pictures, and homework assignments in nineteen accounting textbooks published between 2003 and 2005 found that gender-role stereotypes persist. Specifically, women were less likely than men to be pictured in the textbook, women were more likely to be depicted as emotional (e.g., angry, upset), more likely to be depicted as caring for the home or children, and more likely to be depicted as having less power than men (Tietz, 2007). A review of twenty-three teacher education textbooks yielded similar findings. While texts are now more likely to include gender issues than they were in the past, only slightly more than 7 percent of the content in introduction and foundation textbooks was dedicated to gender issues (Zittleman & Sadker, 2002).

College textbooks also lack attention to racial and ethnic diversity. A review of thirty-one criminal justice and policing textbooks, for example, found that the rela-tionship between slavery and the early criminal justice system is typically overlooked (Turner, Giacopassi, & Vandiver, 2006). Wallace and Allen (2008) reviewed twenty-seven introduction to American government and politics textbooks and found that African

Americans are largely ignored and most books relegate their participation in America's political development to one chapter on the civil rights movement.

There are at least two other major barriers to equality for women in higher education: the lack of mentors and role models and the incidence of sexual harassment. Before we discuss each of these, it is important to note that college peer culture may interact with structural variables, as well as with students' views of school formed earlier in their lives, to diminish young women's ambitions. When young people go to college, they are often struck by the fact that they must study harder than they did in high school to achieve comparable grades (Eisenhart & Holland, 1992), and college students consistently report high levels of stress (American College Health Association, 2004). Moreover, research has indicated that while males and females do not differ in levels of perceived stress, males have more resources than females to deal with stress (Matheny, Roque-Tovar, & Curlette, 2008). Other research finds that women report more emotional distress than men do (Sax, Bryant, & Gilmartin, 2004). The annual national survey of college freshmen conducted by the Higher Education Research Institute at UCLA found that female students are more likely than male students to report feeling overwhelmed by all they had to do. In contrast, the survey found that male students were more likely to spend their time exercising or playing sports, which may help relieve stress (Sax & Harper, 2007).

Competing with study time, especially at residential colleges, is time for socializing with peers. Although a peer culture might help stimulate the development of high-achievement, career-related identities among college students—as we suspect it often does for male students—Eisenhart and Holland's (1992) research indicates that for women in college, the peer culture emphasizes involvement in romantic relationships and a concern with being physically attractive to men (see also Eisenhart & Finkel, 1999; Stombler & Martin, 1994). Women are more likely than men to be concerned with personal appearance and have negative body images (Muth & Cash, 2006). African American female college students were found to be as sexually exploited and caught up in romance as White female college students were, but the African American students placed less emphasis on the goal of "finding a man" in college and were also less likely to believe that a man would be their source of economic support in the future (see also Stombler & Padevic, 1994). White women were more likely than African American and Asian American women to report body dissatisfaction and disordered eating behaviors (Akan & Grillo, 2006; see also Chapter 12). Thus, peer culture must be added to young women's socialization experiences in college as well as at home as an important influence on their academic and career decisions.

Women Faculty and Administrators

Despite the gains that women have made in the percentage of advanced degrees awarded to them, their progress in university administration and faculty appointments has been somewhat mixed. In 2007, women held 53 percent of the administrative, managerial, or executive positions at U.S. colleges and universities, compared to 38 percent in 1987 and 46 percent in 1997 (U.S. Department of Education, 2008b); 78 percent of these women, however, were White (U.S. Department of Education, 2008c). The number of women college and university presidents has significantly increased over the past two decades; in 1986, 10 percent of college presidents were women, but in 2009, almost one-quarter

TABLE 5.3   Percentage of Bachelor's, Master's, and Doctor's Degrees Conferred by U.S. Institutions of Higher Education, by Race/Ethnicity and Sex, 2006–2007

	Racial/Ethnic Group & Sex*									
	White		Black		Hispanic		Asian/Pacific Islander		American Indian/Alaskan Native	
	Women	Men	Women	Men	Women	Men	Women	Men	Women	Men
Degree Conferred										
Bachelor's Degrees (Total = 1,524,092)	40.1	31.5	6.4	3.3	4.6	3.0	3.8	3.1	0.46	0.3
Master's Degrees (Total = 604,607)	41.0	25.0	7.4	3.0	3.7	2.0	3.3	2.7	0.38	0.2
Doctor's Degrees (Total = 60,616)	31.0	25.2	4.0	2.1	1.9	1.5	3.0	2.8	0.25	0.16

*Percentages do not add to 100 due to rounding and the exclusion of nonresident aliens.

Sources: U.S. National Center for Education Statistics, 2008, Bachelor's degrees conferred by degree-granting institutions, by race/ethnicity and sex of student: Selected years, 1976–77 through 2006–2007. Table 284. Retrieved February 13, 2010, from http://nces.ed.gov/programs/digest/d08/tables/dt08_284.asp.

(23 percent) of college/university presidents were women (American Council on Education, 2009b; Brown, 2009) and 40 percent of college/university chief academic officers were women (American Council on Education, 2009b). Four of the eight Ivy League schools were headed by women (Brown, 2009), a noteworthy achievement given that some Ivy League schools did not even admit women until relatively recently.

Among faculty, women represent approximately half of the instructors and lecturers on college campuses but only 27 percent of tenured faculty and 33 percent of full professors at four-year institutions (American Association of University Women, 2005). Women are also less likely to be full professors in most European countries (European Commission, 2006). It is important to recognize that while more women are now teaching college classes, they are not necessarily in full-time tenure track positions. While the total percent of women teaching at the college level increased from 41.2 percent in 1997 to 46.3 percent in 2007, their representation as full-time tenured or tenure track professors decreased during that period from 10.7 percent to 10.3 percent (American Federation of Teachers, 2009). There was a decrease in the percentage of full-time tenured or tenure-track positions for both women and men, but women's representation as full-time *non-tenure track* faculty, *part-time* faculty, and graduate assistants increased (American Federation of Teachers, 2009). These types of positions have far less security and lower pay than tenure-track and tenured positions. There are more women in tenure-track positions compared to women with tenure (West & Curtis, 2006), but men are more likely than women to be granted tenure (Gappa, Austin, & Trice, 2007; Parma, 2006; Samble, 2008).

Women faculty also tend to be concentrated in specific departments. For example, women professors are more prevalent in education and the humanities, while male professors are more prevalent in engineering and the natural sciences (U.S. Department of Education, National Center for Education Statistics, 2009e). Male professors are more prevalent in other science departments too, and in math departments as well (Freeman, 2004). Women are only 19 percent of tenure-track professors in math, 11 percent in physics, 10 percent in computer science, and 10 percent in electrical engineering (Sommers, 2008). Women are a much lower percentage of science and engineering full professors when one considers the percentage of women earning doctoral degrees in those fields (Burrelli, 2008).

In January 2005, then president of Harvard University, Lawrence Summers, commented on women's under representation in tenured positions in science and engineering at top universities and research institutions. His comments at the Conference on Diversifying the Science and Engineering Workforce, sponsored by the National Bureau on Economic Research, sparked much criticism and resulted in numerous newspaper and journal articles (for example, see Lawler, 2005; McDonnell, 2005; Traub, 2005). When discussing why women may have been underrepresented in tenured positions in science and engineering at top universities and research institutions, Summers hypothesized that it was due to "issues of intrinsic aptitude, and particularly of the variability of aptitude."[3] As we have seen in this chapter, however, the expectations and lack of support from parents, teachers and peers throughout the school years may dampen women's aspirations in these male-dominated fields more than lack of "natural" aptitude does.

Typically, in most fields, the higher the academic rank, the fewer the women. Looking at Table 5.4, we see that college and university faculties are dominated by male full

TABLE 5.4 Percent Distribution of Faculty by Academic Rank and Sex, Fall 2007		
	Sex	
Academic Rank	**Women**	**Men**
Professor	6.5	18.1
Associate Professor	8.1	12.3
Assistant Professor	11.3	12.6
Instructor	7.8	2.6
Lecturer	2.3	6.6
No Rank	5.7	6.4
All Combined	41.8	58.2

Source: U.S. National Center for Education Statistics, 2008. *Full-time instructional faculty in degree-granting institutions, by race/ethnicity, sex, and academic rank: Fall 2003, fall 2005, and fall 2007.* Table 249. Retrieved from http://nces.ed.gov/programs/digest/d08/tables/dt08_249.asp.

TABLE 5.5 Full-time Instructional Faculty at Institutions of Higher Education, by Sex and Race, Fall 2007

Racial/Ethnic Group	Sex (%)*	
	Women	Men
White	32.1	44.7
Black	2.9	2.5
Hispanic	1.6	1.9
Asian/Pacific Islander	2.8	4.9
American Indian/Alaskan Native	0.23	0.24
Nonresident Alien	1.5	3.0
Race/Ethnicity Unknown	0.74	.95

*Percentages do not add to 100 due to rounding.

Source: U.S. National Center for Education Statistics, 2008. *Full-time instructional faculty in degree-granting institutions, by race/ethnicity, sex, and academic rank: Fall 2003, fall 2005, and fall 2007.* Retrieved http://nces.ed.gov/programs/digest/d08/tables/dt08_249.asp.

professors, but just 6.5 percent of college and university faculty are female full professors. Women are employed by colleges and universities, but they are most likely to hold lower-ranking positions.

Table 5.5 shows that few college and university faculty are people of color. People of color are even more underrepresented among higher ranked faculty and in administrative positions. For example, in 2005 only 13 percent of full professors and 17 percent of college administrators were people of color, compared to 17.7 percent of associate professors, and 26.5 percent of assistant professors (American Council on Education, 2009a). In 2007, 70.7 percent of all full-time and part-time college faculty and instructional staff (including adjuncts and graduate assistants) were White (American Federation of Teachers, 2009). Women of color are most underrepresented in faculty appointments and administration, and overall appear to face additional challenges in academia as a result of both racism and sexism ("Barriers encountered by administrators of color," 2009; Berry & Mizelle, 2006; Diggs et al., 2009; Jackson & O'Callaghan, 2009).

Regardless of rank or tenure status, women faculty are paid less than men and, as Table 5.6 shows, the gap is widest at both the highest and lowest academic ranks. Indeed, although the number of faculty who are women has increased during the last few decades, male faculty typically earn more than female faculty members (American Association of University Professors, 2009; Barbezat & Hughes, 2006; Ryu, 2008; Samble, 2008; Toutkoushian, Bellas, & Moore, 2007). Even when female faculty members' experience, education, and research agendas are comparable to that of male faculty members, they still earn less (Toutkoushian & Conley, 2005).

Female faculty and administrators, like female students, confront innumerable inequities—some subtle, some overt—on the campuses where they work (Bagilhole, 1993; Massachusetts Institute of Technology, 1999; Sandler & Hall, 1986). They may find,

| TABLE 5.6 | Average Salary for Men and Women Faculty by Rank and Women's Salaries as a Percentage of Men's Salaries, 2008–2009 |

Academic Rank	Sex		Women's Salaries as a Percentage of Men's Salaries
	Women	Men	
Professor	$114,860	$126,214	91.0
Associate Professor	79,145	85,305	92.8
Assistant Professor	67,411	73,287	92.0
Instructor	46,726	49,135	95.1
Lecturer	51,023	57,930	88.1
No Rank	58,584	68,950	85.0

Source: AAUP. *On the brink: The annual report on the economic status of the profession.* March–April, 2009, p. 32. Retrieved www.aaup.org/NR/rdonlyres/B1AD6A4E-1365-410D-9D3E-4C15DB3D16C2/0/tab5.pdf.

for example, that some male colleagues feel free to address them as "honey" or "dear," or that students consistently address male faculty as "Dr." or "Professor" while they are "Miss" or "Mrs." (Miller & Chamberlain, 2000). At department or committee meetings, they may be expected to record the minutes or, as the "token woman," to provide the "women's point of view" as if one woman can speak for all. Their personal lives may be scrutinized (e.g., "Who takes care of her kids?"). It may be assumed married female faculty members do not need their position as much as men because they have a male partner to rely on for financial support (Hill & Warbelow, 2008). Furthermore, they may be reluctant to take family leave to have or care for children, may postpone having children until they are awarded tenure, may opt not to have children due to career constraints (Grappa, Austin, & Trice, 2007; Williams, 2006), have more difficulty balancing family and professional responsibilities (Probert, 2005), or choose not to pursue or continue a career in academia due to parenting responsibilities (Van Anders, 2004).

Perhaps most frustrating and damaging of all, their work may be devalued by both colleagues and students, even when it is equal or superior to that of a man (Kolodny, 1993; Miller & Chamberlain, 2000; M. Moore, 1997; Wennards & Wold, 1997). Female college students report that female professors are treated with less respect than male professors (Schulze & Tomal, 2006). Some research indicates that students believe male professors are more effective than female professors (Arbuckle & Williams, 2003), while other research finds that graduate students believe that professors of their same sex are more effective (Sprinkle, 2009).

Discrimination such as this effectively keeps women out of academia and prevents those already there from moving up. Once again, the problem is most acute in the academic disciplines traditionally dominated by men, but it has its greatest impact on women of color regardless of department. This is because women of color typically face double discrimination—discrimination on the basis of both race or ethnicity and sex—that is often perpetrated by White women as well as by men (Carty, 1992; Diggs et al., 2009; Nieves-Squires, 1991; Pollard, 1990; Sandler & Hall, 1986). This discrimination helps to account for the even greater absence of women of color from academe that we saw earlier.

A net result of the imbalance of university faculty is a lack of mentors for female students, students of color, and junior faculty. A **mentor** is a role model and more—usually an older, established member of a profession who shows young, new members "the ropes" by giving advice and providing valuable contacts with others in the field. However, since mentors tend to choose protegés who are most like themselves and since there are fewer women in the upper echelons of the academic hierarchy, female students and junior faculty may have fewer opportunities to establish mentoring relationships and thereby lose out on the benefits such relationships provide (Nevels, 1990; Turner & Thompson, 1993). This problem is especially acute for African American female students since women of color are underrepresented in academia (Johnson-Bailey, 2004; Patton, 2009; Patton & Harper, 2003). Some women have responded to the mentoring problem by establishing *peer* mentoring programs, in which women junior faculty as well as staff meet on a regular basis to provide one another with advice and support and to share ideas, information, and resources (Driscoll et al., 2009; Limbert, 1995; McCormack & West, 2006). Women's professional associations, such as Sociologists for Women in Society (SWS) have also established mentoring programs to connect senior and junior faculty and graduate students at different universities, which is valuable for women in departments and at institutions where there are few female faculty, especially female faculty of color (see http://www.socwomen.org).

Interestingly, some recent research has found that women generally report more frequent and positive interactions with their professors than men do (Sax, 2009, p. 5). While some research indicates that mentoring can indeed help address the gender inequality felt by female graduate students (Dua, 2007), other research finds that the professor's sex has little influence on the student's academic performance (Hoffman & Oreopoulos, 2009). Male students appear to have more academic success in courses taught by male professors, but the professor's sex seems to matter less for female students (Hoffman & Oreopoulos, 2009). This may be because research has also found few gender differences in what graduate students prefer in mentors. Both prefer mentors who provide them with guidance, advocate for their needs and interests, and are thoughtful and considerate (Bell-Ellison & Dedrick, 2008). However, women are more likely than men to say that having a mentor who believes in them is also important (Bell-Ellison & Dedrick, 2008; Levesque et al., 2005).

At the very least, the presence of senior female faculty and administrators communicates to students and other members of the campus community that women are as capable, productive, and serious professionally as their male counterparts. Research also indicates that the presence of female faculty on campus may benefit male as well as female students in a number of significant ways. For instance, one study (Statham, Richardson, & Cook, 1991) has shown that the teaching emphases of male and female faculty differ; female faculty focus more on the student as the locus of learning, whereas male faculty focus more on themselves. Female faculty also tend to use a more interactive style in the classroom, making greater efforts than male faculty to get students to participate in class. In fact, this study showed that female faculty report that their teaching satisfaction derives from "students relating to each other, developing their own ideas, and coming prepared to participate in class discussions," while male faculty tended to see students' class participation as either a requirement or a waste of class time (Statham et al., 1991, p. 126; see also Deats & Lenker, 1994; Maher & Tetrault, 1994; McCormick, 1994). Female faculty also interact more with students outside of class than male faculty do. They are more involved in campus "quality-of-life" programs (e.g., the women's center, rape crisis hotlines). They chat with students more and provide them with more counseling than do male faculty. Female faculty members may be more likely than male faculty members to be concerned with students' emotional development (Sax, 2008). Research has found that some departments chaired by women are more likely to have a formal mentoring policy for graduate students (Dua, 2008). In contrast, male faculty report negotiating more with students about their course grades (Kolodny, 1993; Statham et al., 1991). In short, what these data indicate is that female university faculty may utilize a kind of instructional and interactional style that is more conducive to learning and more beneficial to both male and female students.

This is not to say that male faculty cannot be mentors or role models for female students; in fact, they often are and as we have noted, the sex of a mentor matters less to female graduate students than specific mentor qualities. However, there is evidence that male faculty typically interact differently with male and female students; we have already discussed some of these findings. Male faculty sometimes feel uncomfortable with female students, or they may relate to them paternalistically rather than professionally (Angier, 2000; Limbert, 1995). Worse still, they may view their female students as potential sexual partners and use their positions of power and authority to coerce sexual favors. As we will see next, this is not an uncommon experience for college women.

Sexual Harassment

Sexual harassment involves any unwanted leers, comments, suggestions, or physical contact of a sexual nature, as well as unwelcome requests for sexual favors. There are actually two types of sexual harassment. If the harassment is directly tied to the granting or denial of a benefit or privilege, such as a course grade or the chance to work on an important research project, it is called *quid pro quo* harassment. The second type of harassment involves creating a *hostile environment* by, for example, telling sexual jokes, using sexual innuendo, spreading sexual rumors, or publicly displaying sexually explicit material.

According to a report published by the American Association of University Women, approximately two-thirds of college students experience some type of sexual harassment, and most cases involve a perpetrator who does not hold some authority over the victim (Hill & Silva, 2005). Therefore, most sexual harassment is perpetrated by peers. Peer sexual harassment is a problem not only on college and university campuses, but also in elementary and secondary schools as well (Brown, 2007; Craig & Pepler, 2003; Keddie, 2009; Miller, 2008; Shute, Owens, & Slee, 2008). For example, Leaper and Brown (2008) surveyed six hundred girls in middle, junior high, and high school and found that most (90 percent) reported sexual harassment. Over half (67 percent) reported receiving unwanted or inappropriate romantic attention by a male, 62 percent reported being called a nasty or demeaning name related to being a girl, 58 percent reported being teased about their appearance and 51 percent reported experiencing unwanted physical contact. Miller (2008) found that most (71 percent) young girls in her sample reported being the targets of inappropriate sexual comments. The common experience of sexual harassment is problematic especially given that research has found that sexual harassment negatively influences girls' adjustment and body image (Basow, 2009; Felix & McMahon, 2006; Goldstein et al., 2007).

Although only a small percentage of harassment victims experience quid pro quo harassment and most victims are harassed by peers, a substantial percentage experience unwanted touching and verbal harassment that make a hostile learning environment (Hill & Silva, 2005; Kalof et al., 2001; Loredo, Reid, & Deaux, 1995). Researchers have started to examine how race and ethnicity, social class, and sexual orientation intersect with gender in sexual harassment incidents to produce particular outcomes for victims as well as perpetrators or to influence the perception of the severity of the harassment (Buchanan et al., 2009; DeSouza, Solberg, & Elder, 2007; Rospenda, Richman, & Nawyn, 1998; Woods, Buchanan, & Settles, 2009; Yoon, Funk, Kropf, 2010). Leaper and Brown (2008) examined the influence of race/ethnicity and social class and found that girls from lower-class families report more sexual harassment, and Latinas and Asian American girls reported less sexual harassment than girls from other ethic backgrounds. Other research indicates that African American girls are more likely to experience sexual harassment than White girls are (Goldstein et al., 2007; see, however, Kalof et al., 2001 who found no differences between White and non-White students in terms of incidence of sexual harassment and types of harassment experienced).

Despite the widespread nature of sexual harassment, most incidents go unreported to school or campus authorities (Hill & Silva, 2005). To some extent, this is because students do not label what has happened to them as sexual harassment, they are afraid or embarrassed, they do not know who to report to, and they question their own behavior and culpability (Hill & Silva, 2005; Kalof et al., 2001). Many victims try to "manage" the problem (usually by simply avoiding the harasser whenever possible), or they tell only family members and friends about it (AAUW, 1993; Stanko, 1992). Neither of these tactics may be helpful, however. For example, attempts to avoid the harasser often are not easy; sometimes such efforts mean having to withdraw from a required course or other academic activity that may have been necessary or beneficial to the student's school achievement or career plans. In addition, family and friends sometimes blame the victim or, more often, simply advise her to ignore the harassment. There is evidence that minority women in particular may be reluctant to report sexual harassment for fear of losing educational rewards or because of cultural norms that discourage telling others about such behavior by men (Adams, 1997).

Research has found that when college students report sexual harassment to professors, they are more likely to provide them with factual information rather than taking action to help the student or provide emotional support (Bingham & Battey, 2005). Administrators may also downplay it and, despite the fears of overly harsh sanctions that are frequently voiced by faculty, harassers usually are dealt with informally, with the most common sanction being a verbal warning from a superior (Mitchell, 1997; Robertson, Dyer, & Campbell, 1988). Miller's research (2008) including high school girls yielded similar findings. These researchers reported that school administrators do not take peer sexual harassment seriously, and teachers tend to be unconcerned and fail to intervene. Few universities have dismissed perpetrators, especially tenured faculty members, in response to sexual harassment complaints (Carroll, 1993; Clark, 1997).

In 1992, the U.S. Supreme Court ruled that sexual harassment in school is a form of educational discrimination and that schools that fail to address the problem may be held liable for damages to victims. Some student victims have received monetary compensation as a result of this decision (see, for example, "Girl, 14, Wins Case" 1996; Walker, 2010).[4]

In 1998, the U.S. Supreme Court severely narrowed the circumstances under which schools may be held liable for sexual harassment of students by teachers. In a 5 to 4 decision, the Court ruled that students who are sexually harassed by a teacher may sue their school district for monetary damages only if they can demonstrate that school district officials knew about the harassment and deliberately did nothing to stop it (Biskupic, 1998). In 1999, the Court extended this standard to cases involving student-to-student sexual harassment. Ten years later, in 2009, the Supreme Court ruled that Title IX is not the exclusive means for suing school districts; individuals can also sue under federal law, referred to as a Section 1983 lawsuit, which gives citizens the right to sue anyone whom they feel violates their civil rights (Walsh, 2009).

Court decisions have certainly played a role in prompting most school districts as well as colleges and universities to enact policies that prohibit sexual harassment and establish formal procedures for handling complaints (Chamberlain, 1997; Hawkesworth, 1997). But universities have found that some of their attempts to regulate sexist and racist verbal harassment have not stood up well to court challenges. The courts have struck down a number of institutions' "speech codes," ruling that such regulations violate the First Amendment (Bernstein, 1993; "Free Speech on Campus", 2008). Some schools have also found that their handling of particular cases has led to angry charges of overreaction. For example, Essex (2009) reviewed an incident where a kindergarten student in Maryland was accused of sexual harassment after pinching the buttocks of a classmate; this accusation will remain on his school record until he goes to middle school. In another case, a preschooler was suspended for sexual harassment for hugging a teacher's aide and rubbing his face on her chest despite the fact that the student did not understand why hugging was inappropriate behavior (Essex, 2009).

In 1997, the Department of Education's Office of Civil Rights issued guidelines to assist educational institutions in defining, preventing, and responding to sexual harassment. According to the guidelines, it is acceptable for a professor to assign reading material that is sexually explicit and even derogatory of women, but it is unacceptable for a group of students to target a peer for sexual taunting or to write sexually explicit graffiti about her or him. The guidelines emphasize that education officials must take into account the alleged harasser's age, level of maturity, and relationship to the victim. In addition, the guidelines stress that in order for a behavior to constitute sexual harassment, it must be severe and repetitive; a single, inappropriate act is not considered sexual harassment (Lewin, 1997a). However, the guidelines have been criticized for being vague and allowing too much discretion in terms of how complaints of sexual harassment, especially peer sexual harassment, should be handled (see Walker, 2010).

As we have noted, only about 20 percent of sexual harassment cases involve a perpetrator who holds some formal authority or power over the victim (Hill & Silva, 2005). Research indicates that harassment of a subordinate by an authority figure (e.g., harassment of a student by a teacher) is judged by most observers to be more serious than peer harassment. However, women judge sexual harassment in general to be more problematic than men do, and women are less tolerant of it (Katz, Hannon, & Whitten, 1996; Loredo et al., 1995; Murnen & Smolak, 2000; Runtz & O'Donnell, 2006; Russell & Trigg, 2004). Perhaps this is because women are more likely than men to be victimized.[5]

Not all sexual harassment involves peers or a perpetrator who has formal authority over the victim. Researchers have also documented *contrapower sexual harassment,* which "occurs when the target of harassment possesses greater formal organizational power than the perpetrator" (Rospenda et al., 1998, p. 40). Contrapower sexual harassment occurs, for example, when a student sexually harasses a faculty member. Because the harasser is not in a position to grant or deny a benefit, it cannot be *quid pro quo* harassment. Contrapower sexual harassment is less likely than traditional harassment, when the perpetrator has more power than the victim, to be perceived as sexual harassment (Mohipp & Senn, 2008). According to Rospenda and her colleagues (1998), although contrapower sexual harassment has received less attention than peer and subordinate tar-get/superior perpetrator harassment, it nonetheless occurs at an alarming rate. Rospenda and her colleagues emphasize in their analysis of these cases that gender interacts with other social factors such as race, class, and sexual orientation, increasing the likelihood that members of particular groups will be targets and also affecting the outcome of the incidents (see also, Buchanan et al., 2009; DeSouza et al., 2007; Woods et al., 2009; Yoon et al., 2010). Not surprisingly, female professors are more likely than male professors to report feeling distressed or troubled by contrapower sexual harassment (DeSouza & Fansler, 2003; Lampman et al., 2009).

We will discuss the impact of sexual harassment on employees in Chapter 8. Here, however, let's examine the impact of sexual harassment on victims' educational experi-ence. Research findings indicate that sexual harassment has serious negative consequences for student victims, especially females. Female students who have been sexually harassed are more likely than male sexual harassment victims to report that the incidents frightened them or had a negative impact on their school work (Hill & Silva, 2005). Victims report psychological distress, depression, declines in their academic performance, discouragement about studying a particular field, lowered self-esteem, emotional disturbance, and increased substance abuse (Bagley, Bolitho, & Bertrand, 1997; Goldstein et al., 2007; Hill & Silva, 2005; Huerta et al., 2006). Although not necessarily of a sexual nature, victims of cyberbullying, like victims of sexual harassment, also report psychological distress (see Box 5.4).

At the very least, sexual harassment fosters tension-filled relationships rather than mentoring relationships between students and faculty or other authority figures. Students consciously avoid certain teachers, and some teachers, afraid that their interest may be misinterpreted, distance themselves from students, particularly female students. In short, sexual harassment creates an unpleasant and intimidating learning environment for stu-dents, especially female students, which, in turn, affects their performance, their personal and professional growth, and ultimately, their future careers.

STRUCTURING MORE POSITIVE LEARNING ENVIRONMENTS

It appears that girls are still shortchanged in their educational experiences, but the ques-tion of how to redress the inequities continues to be debated by educators. Some observers advocate sex-segregated schools or single-sex classes within mixed-sex schools as solutions. There is a growing movement toward single-sex public education because of the belief that since boys and girls may learn differently, separating them in the classroom may be ben-eficial to both (Cable & Spradlin, 2008; Chandler & Glod, 2008). According to the National Association for Single Sex Public Education, in February 2010 there were 540 public schools in the United States with single-sex educational opportunities, and approximately ninety of them were considered single-sex schools (see http://www.singlesexschools.org). South Carolina is one state that is offering more single-sex classes. In 2007, seventy schools in South Carolina offered single-sex classes, but by 2008, over two hundred schools had this option. Reports from this state indicate that single-sex classes have improved academic per-formance and decreased disciplinary problems for boys and girls, and most parents are satis-fied with single-sex classes (Rex & Chadwell, 2009).

Importantly, those who favor single-sex education are not promoting channeling girls and boys into "gender-appropriate" fields. To the contrary, their position is typi-cally that single-sex institutions and single-sex classes within mixed-sex schools make it

BOX 5.4
Cyberbullying

Undoubtedly, Internet use is widespread and adolescents and even young children are no exception. In fact, Internet use by teens continues to increase with the growth of mobile devices. In 2000, 73 percent of teens between the ages of 12 and 17 in the United States reported using the Internet; this rose to 87 percent in 2005 (Lenhart, Madden, & Hitlin, 2005), and 93 percent in 2009 (Lenhart, Purcell, Smith, & Zickuhr, 2010; see also Chapter 6). Not only are more teens using the Internet, they are also using it on a more consistent basis. In 2000 about 42 percent of teens reported using the Internet daily. This rose to 51 percent in 2005 (Lenhart et al., 2005) and 63 percent in 2009 (Lenhart et al., 2010). Very young children are also turning to the Internet for entertainment and communications. According to the Henry J. Kaiser Foundation, 17 percent of children under the age of six have sent an e-mail (Rideout, Vandewater, & Wartells, 2003). Similar numbers of girls and boys use the Internet (Lenhart et al., 2005).

Although many adolescents use the Internet on a regular basis for social networking, making purchases, getting news, or acquiring information about health or fitness (Lenhart et al., 2010), a relatively new disturbing trend is the use of the Internet to bully or harass (Patchin & Hinduja, 2006). Cyberbullying is defined as the "willful and repeated harm inflicted through the medium of electronic text" (Patchin & Hinduja, 2006, p. 152). It may include using electronic media to stalk, to make threats or degrading comments to someone, to spread rumors, or to distribute unflattering pictures or videos. Many adolescents also experience sexual harassment over the Internet (Katz, 2002). The term "cyberbullying" is not used when adults use the Internet or a medium of electronic text to harass.

Some studies have found no significant gender differences in perpetration of (Ybarra & Mitchell, 2004) or victimization by (Li, 2006) cyberbullying (see also Hinduja & Patchin, 2008b). But other studies have found that boys are more likely than girls to use cyberbullying (Calvete et al., 2010; Erdur-Baker, 2010; Li, 2006; Ybarra & Mitchell, 2007). For instance, of Li's (2006) sample of 264 middle school students, 22 percent of boys but less than 12 percent of girls admitted to being cyberbullies. Research on the gender gap in cyberbullying victimization offers mixed findings. Erdur-Baker (2010) concluded that boys are more likely than girls to be victims of cyberbullying while Ybarra, Mitchell, Wolak, and Finkelhor (2006) found that girls are more likely than boys to be targeted by Internet harassment. Burgess-Proctor, Hinduja, and Patchin (2010) found that many young women are victims of cyberbullying; 38 percent of their 3,141 Internet-using female respondents under age 18 reported being bullied online, and many reported being victims of online sexual harassment.

Not only does cyberbullying occur on a routine basis, the effects of cyberbullying are brought back into school (Trolley, Hanel, & Shields, 2006; Willard, 2007). This leaves teachers and school administrators in precarious positions. While intervention for victims is oftentimes necessary, school officials believe their intervention should be limited if the bullying does not occur in school. Furthermore, teachers and administrators are more likely to respond to bullying when they witness it and when it results in physical injury (Shariff, 2008). School officials may hesitate to involve law enforcement unless Internet bullying escalates. While bullying itself is not a crime, actions commonly involved in bullying are crimes (e.g., defamation of character, threats of physical harm, actual physical harm, harassment) (Hinduja & Patchin, 2008a; Shariff, 2008).

Researchers disagree over the likelihood of cyberbullying co-occurring with traditional bullying. Some studies have found that victims of online harassment are more likely than non-victims to also be victimized face-to-face by peers (see, for example, Ybarra et al., 2006). Others have found that many youth who are harassed online do not experience face-to-face bullying at school (see Ybarra, Diener-West, & Leaf, 2007).

(continued)

BOX 5.4
Continued

Erdur-Baker, (2010) found that 32 percent of the 276 adolescents included in research were victims of both cyberbullying and traditional, face-to-face bullying.

The effects of cyberbullying on victims are serious. Victims report feeling hurt, depressed, angry, and scared (Burgess-Proctor et al., 2010; Chait, 2008; Hinduja & Patchin, 2006). Other research finds that victims of Internet harassment and unwanted sexual solicitation who are between the ages of 10 and 15 are more likely than youth who have had little to no experience with this type of victimization to report using alcohol and marijuana (Ybarra, Espelage, & Mitchell, 2007). Some argue that cyberbullying has even more serious consequences for youth than face-to-face bullying does. It may be more constant or inescapable, and it can be done in a way so that others can witness the public humiliation (Willard, 2007). If someone is a victim of bullying at school, he or she can at least find some peace at home. This is not the case with cyberbullying. Also, while traditional bullying often requires that the bully have some degree of power, cyberbullying is available to youth who may not have power, be popular, or have the strength or build to physically bully another youth. The anonymity of cyberbullying may give power to those who otherwise lack power in school (Shariff, 2008). The recent suicides of young women and men—for example, Megan Meier in 2006, and Phoebe Prince and Tyler Clementi in 2010—highlight the tragic consequences of cyberbullying and have prompted many jurisdictions to enact legislation that specifically addresses cyberbullying (see http://www. cyberbullying.us).

easier for both young women and young men to pursue fields of study not traditionally dominated by members of their sex (Estrich, 1994; Pollard, 1999; Ruhlman, 1997; Sullivan, Joshi, & Leonard, 2010). Certainly, some parents have accepted this argument, since there has been a "resurgence of single-sex schools in the public sector" (Mael et al., 2005, p. ix). Is there empirical evidence, though, that single-sex schools are beneficial?

The available research is limited, and the findings are inconsistent. After reviewing the available research, Mael et al. (2005) concluded, "It is more common to come across studies that report no differences between SS [single-sex] and CE [coeducational] schooling than to find outcomes with support for the superiority of CE schooling" (p. 85). Similarly, a review of research conducted in the United States, Canada, Australia, New Zealand, Ireland, and the United Kingdom by Smithers and Robinson (2006) concluded that single-sex education is neither beneficial nor detrimental. Some studies of single-sex classes and schools for boys show that boys *behave* better in sex-segregated settings, but they perform better academically in coeducational settings (Pollard, 1999). Other research, however, finds that for both boys and girls, the move from coeducational classes to single-sex classes improves their academic achievement and their behavior (Hughes, 2006; Sax, 2005). Most studies also find that single-sex schooling improves test scores (see Mael et al., 2005 for a review). For instance, Piechura-Couture, Tichenor, & Heins (2007) compared scores on the Florida Comprehensive Assessment Test of boys and girls in single-sex classes to those of boys and girls in coeducational classes and found that those in the single-sex classes were more likely to score proficient on the test.

Much of the research indicates that girls who attend single-sex schools have, on average, higher levels of self-confidence and greater academic success throughout their school years, which eventually leads to higher status and higher paying jobs after graduation

(Dobrzynski, 1995; Pollard, 1999; Saltzman, 1996a). Research has also found that girls who graduate from single-sex high schools are more likely than girls who graduate from coeducational high schools to select gender-neutral majors in college (Billger, 2009; Karpiak et al., 2007), although they are no more likely than peers from coeducational high schools to graduate with gender-neutral majors (Karpiak, 2007). Women attending single-sex colleges feel more encouraged in classes than women attending coeducational colleges (Kinzie et al., 2007) and report more academic involvement (National Survey of Student Engagement, 2003).

Despite these findings, critics argue that the research does not convincingly demonstrate the benefits of single-sex education for girls, since it typically does not take into account other important factors in explaining results (Bracey, 2007; Smithers & Robinson, 2000). For example, many of the girls' schools that have been studied are small, with class sizes averaging 12 to 15 students resulting in a low teacher/student ratio, an important ingredient for positive academic outcomes. Thus, differences in academic success between girls in single-sex versus mixed-sex schools or classes may be due to this and other pedagogical variables rather than to gender composition per se (Smithers & Robinson, 2006; Wahl, 1999).

Opponents of single-sex education question whether single-sex education perpetuates gender stereotypes and sends a message of inequality (Cable & Spradlin, 2008). Opponents further point out that even if it helps some girls learn more and better, it does not adequately address the problem of gender inequality and discrimination that characterize the institutions of our society. It also does not prepare students for a "coeducational world" (Farell, 2007). They argue that our goal should be restructuring social institutions so that males and females can work together under equitable conditions with an equitable distribution of resources and rewards (AAUW, 1998; Wahl, 1999). Such restructuring was a major rationale for the enactment of Title IX. When it was enacted, Title IX stipulated that any sex segregation in public education had to be justified by compelling educational reasons.[6] However, the Supreme Court and the federal courts, in interpreting Title IX and the equal protection clause of the Fourteenth Amendment as it pertains to education, left open the possibility of single-sex public education as long as it serves to remedy past discrimination and break down

Researchers continue to debate the pros and cons of single-sex education versus coeducation, but a primary goal of any educational institution should be the equitable distribution of resources and rewards to all students.

rather than preserve traditional gender classifications (Brake, 1999; Logsdon, 2003). In 2006, the U.S. Department of Education changed the Title IX regulations to allow more flexibility in offering single-sex education in public schools. This applies to public elementary and secondary schools and nonvocational charter schools; it does not apply to public vocational schools (Kiselewich, 2008). Although some question the constitutionality of these changes (see English, 2009), others argue that the new regulations will "withstand judicial scrutiny" (Kiselewich, 2008, p. 217).

At the postsecondary level, the number of private, single-sex institutions has dramatically declined since the 1960s. By 1994, there were eighty-four private women's colleges in the United States (M. Allen, 1996); in 2010, there were only fifty-one (U.S. Department of Education, 2010). One reason for this change was the emphasis on equal educational opportunity, but financial concerns also played a part. In the 1980s and 1990s, the college-age population declined, forcing many single-sex institutions to become coeducational in the hopes of attracting more new students—and more revenue. However, it was a court ruling more than finances that caused the only two public men's colleges in the United States—the Virginia Military Academy (VMI) and the Citadel—to open their doors to women in 1996. The U.S. Supreme Court ruled in *United States* v. *Virginia* that the state of Virginia could not deny women the unique educational opportunities offered to men at VMI (Allen, 1996; Brake, 1999; Kiselewich, 2008).[7]

Although the debate over single-sex education has received considerable attention recently, there are other methods for balancing the educational experiences of the sexes. One method is to develop a gender-fair curriculum by integrating learning materials about women, as well as people of color and gays and lesbians, into the curricula of educational institutions. At the university level, this has been accomplished in part through women's studies programs. In recent years the number of women's studies programs has increased substantially (Stone-Mediatore, 2007).

One of the original goals of women's studies was to add women to the traditionally "womanless" curriculum (McIntosh, 1984). This resulted in numerous "special subject" courses or seminars—Women in History, Women in Literature, Women in Economics, and so on—not only in women's studies programs, but in other departments as well. Although this was an important step in increasing knowledge by and about women by making the invisible visible, these courses tended to focus on only those women who succeeded according to a male standard. Only "deserving" women were discussed—those women who behaved like men, who have done what men do. As a number of researchers have pointed out, such courses may actually have a negative impact on students, especially female students, because they may reinforce gender stereotypes and label women "failures" who cannot or will not behave like men (Goodstein, 1992; Koser, 1992).

Most women's studies and gender-based courses in other departments have moved well beyond this approach to one that considers how current knowledge bases, policies, and practices would be transformed if they were structured and organized from women's perspectives. This newer approach, for example, asks questions such as: How would the inclusion of women's unpaid labor in the home modify traditional analyses of the economy? and What are women's standpoints on various economic issues?

Of course, there are many different answers to such questions, since there are many different women's perspectives, which, as we noted in Chapter 1, are not only gendered, but also reflect the position holder's race, social class, sexual orientation, age, and physical ability/disability. Early evaluations of women's studies programs indicated that the challenge of diversity was one that was largely unmet in the majority of courses. For example, it was found that most courses did not include material from women of color and lesbians or used material on African American women to cover all racial issues (Cramer & Russo, 1992). However, women's studies courses are now more likely to include issues of race/ethnicity and sexuality than they were in the past (Elfman, 2009).

Feminist educators have also been working diligently to transform the traditional curriculum so that women's experiences and perspectives are not the material of just women's studies courses, but are taught as knowledge in their own right—as half the human experience studied in all courses. Unfortunately, both women's studies and curriculum revision or transformation projects have been threatened by policy makers, administrators, and faculty who see them as academically weak, narrow in focus, and politically biased (Ginsberg, 2008; Luebke & Reilly, 1994; J. R. Martin, 1994). Women and gender studies courses are also criticized for focusing too much on students' personal thoughts and experiences (see Stake, 2006), and, as explained by Elfman (2009), "[P]rograms and departments are still called upon by institutions to defend their right to exist" (p. 10).

There has been, however, a recent push to increase diversity education. Increasing attention to diversity in the classroom improves students' understanding and awareness of diversity in their everyday lives (Smith & Wolf-Wendel, 2005; see also Carr, 2007). Recent research indicates that courses are now more likely to include issues of gender (Blundell, 2009; Sciame-Giesecke, Roden, & Parkison, 2009). However, professors may be adding topics about diversity to their course content without addressing their own attitudes or students' attitudes about diversity issues, and diversity issues may be more likely to be included in social sciences or humanities courses rather than courses in all disciplines (Carr, 2007). Some faculty see the issue of gender (as well as race, class, sexual orientation, age, and disability) as unimportant or peripheral to what they teach (Garrison et al., 1992). This latter attitude is typified in the answers one of the authors received when she surveyed the faculty at an institution where she worked about whether they incorporated women's experiences and perspectives into their courses. The near-unanimous response was, "Only when they're relevant." When, we may ask, are the ideas and experiences of half of humanity not relevant?

There is evidence that women's studies courses and feminist education have a positive impact on students by diminishing stereotyped attitudes about women, increasing self-esteem, developing critical thinking skills, expanding students' sense of their options and goals in life, and helping students acquire a greater ability to understand their personal experiences in a broader social context (Howe, 1985; Luebke & Reilly, 1994; Stake, 2006). Nevertheless, a number of observers have expressed concerns about the future of women's studies programs. For instance, some argue that the renaming of women's studies as "gender studies" may serve to neutralize or dilute the emphasis on gender and sexual inequalities that constitutes the core of feminist analyses and reduce the political nature of the program (Berila et al., 2005; Cramer & Russo, 1992). Similarly, they argue that the establishment of men's studies programs by profeminist men can jeopardize the autonomy and strength of women's studies. Men's studies actually grew out of women's studies during the late 1970s and 1980s (Berila et al., 2005; Kimmel & Messner, 1998; Robinson, 1992). Leaders in the area of men's studies maintain that it is complementary to women's studies and informed by feminist scholarship (see, for example Kimmel, Hearn, & Connell, 2005; Schacht & Ewing, 2007; see also Chapter 1). Although male attitudes and behavior have been the almost exclusive focus of the academic canon historically—resulting, we might add, in no charges of narrowness from those who see women's studies as too narrow—the role of gender in shaping these attitudes and behaviors was not critically examined until the formation of men's studies. However, Cramer and Russo (1992, p. 106) warn that men's studies can be positive only when "truly feminist and committed to challenging male power, but too often it focuses on how sex differences limit all of us equally, rather than on sexual inequality and the social significance of men's subordination of women." In addition, although advocates claim that one of the goals of men's studies is to revise the traditional view of men's experience as homogeneous and to elucidate the diversity of men's lives (particularly in terms of race and ethnicity, social class, and sexual orientation), reviews charge that for the most part, men's studies has simply paid lip service to diversity (Robinson, 1992; for a different view, however, see Kimmel & Messner, 1998; Schrock & Schwalbe, 2009).

Courses in gay and lesbian studies have also emerged, partly in response to the failure of the traditional curriculum to examine the intersection of gender inequality and heterosexual privilege, and also in response to political and cultural events of the 1970s and 1980s (Escoffier, 1992; Zimmerman & McNaron, 1996; see also Mayo, 2010 on bringing minority sexuality into school curricula). For the most part, gay and lesbian studies courses have been housed in traditional academic departments or offered through research centers, such as the Lesbian/Gay Studies Center at Yale (established in 1986) and the City University of New York Center for Lesbian and Gay Studies (established in 1990). The City College of San Francisco was the first U.S. institution to establish a department of gay and lesbian studies in the United States (Collins, 1992). Several universities offer an undergraduate degree in lesbian, gay, bisexual and transgender studies, or gender/sexuality studies including Brown University, Amherst College, Carleton College, Hobart and William Smith Colleges, Indiana University, New York University, and Rice University (Beemyn, 2008). Many other colleges and universities offer minors, certificates, or concentrations in the field (Beemyn, 2008; "Gay studies thriving on U.S. campuses," 2007; "More universities offer gay studies classes," 2007). In 2009, Harvard University became the first university to endow a chair in lesbian, gay, bisexual, and transgender studies (Steinberg, 2009). Lesbian and gay studies programs can now be found throughout the world (see, for example, Hekma & van der Meer, 1992; Minton, 1992; Munt, 1996; Sayer, 1996). In 2005, for instance, Fudan University in Shanghai began to offer China's first undergraduate course in gay studies (Mooney, 2005).

While the number of gay and lesbian studies courses has increased in recent years, there is concern by some that divisions within gay and lesbian studies, particularly between lesbian feminists, bisexual theorists, and queer theorists (see Chapter 1; as well as Gammon & Isgro, 2006; Lovaas, Elia, & Yep, 2007) will undermine the strength and stability of some programs, making them easier targets for budget cuts. At the same time, there have been concerns that as lesbian and gay studies becomes institutionalized in academia, it may lose its ties to the lesbian and gay political movements (Minton, 1992). This has been a concern for women's studies advocates and feminist educators as well. These movements are sources of new ideas, diverse perspectives, and dynamic energy—all of which are vital in the continuing struggle against backlash and retrenchment.

GENDER, EDUCATION, AND EMPOWERMENT

In this chapter we have examined how the educational experiences of female and male students—from elementary school through graduate school—are different and, more importantly, often unequal. Although females constitute a majority of students and degree recipients, they continue to confront a number of structural barriers. We have seen, for example, that women are underrepresented in textbooks and course material. They are more likely to be interrupted and silenced in classroom discussions. They are channeled into relatively low-paying, low-prestige fields that have been devalued simply because they are female-dominated. They lack mentors and role models and, not infrequently, they are sexually harassed. This is not to say that males do not experience sexual harassment and are never subject to gender-based discrimination in education, especially in elementary school, but rather that when all dimensions of education are considered together, it is clearly girls and women who are disadvantaged.

We also discussed some of the means to remedy these inequities, such as increasing the number of feminist educators throughout the educational system; offering women's studies, feminist-based men's studies, and lesbian and gay studies programs; and initiating curriculum revision or transformation projects on an institution-wide basis. Given that we are not only citizens of a single country, but also a global community, the need for curriculum reform persists (Banks, 2009a, 2009b); an educational experience and curriculum that only take into account the experiences and needs of "mainstream Americans" have negative consequences for all students (Banks, 2009b, p. 234). It is only when men and women of diverse backgrounds are included that we may speak of education as an empowering agent of social change rather than as a preserver of the status quo.

Key Terms

formal curriculum   the set of subjects officially and explicitly taught to students in school

hidden curriculum   the value preferences children are taught in school that are not an explicit part of the formal curriculum, but rather are hidden or implicit in it

homophobia   an unreasonable fear of and hostility toward homosexuals

mentor   usually an older, established member of a profession who serves as a kind of sponsor for a younger, new member by providing advice and valuable contacts with others in the field

micro-inequities   subtle, everyday forms of discrimination that single out, ignore, or in some way discount individuals and their work or ideas simply on the basis of an ascribed trait, such as sex

sexual harassment   any unwanted leers, comments, suggestions, or physical contact of a sexual nature, as well as unwelcome requests for sexual favors

Title IX   the provisions of the Education Amendments Act of 1972 that forbid sex discrimination in any educational programs or activities that receive federal funding

Suggested Readings

Banks, B. J. (Ed.) (2007). *Gender and education: An encyclopedia*. Westport, CT: Praeger Publishers. This two-volume encyclopedia includes over one hundred entries on a variety of topics about gender and education from preschool to postsecondary school. Topics include gendered education policies, single-sex schools, harassment, gendered theories of education, and gender constructions of official and hidden curriculua.

Banks, J. A., & Banks, C.A.M. (Eds.) (2009b). *Multicultural education: Issues and perspectives* (7/e). Hoboken, NJ: John Wiley & Sons, Inc. This book has seventeen chapters written by two dozen authors covering a wide variety of topics pertaining to multicultural education The book not only explores the ways race/ethnicity, class and gender intersect to shape students' experiences but also discusses the importance of school reform.

Fennell, S., & Arnot, M. (2008). *Gender education and equality in a global context: Conceptual frameworks and policy perspectives*. New York: Routledge. This book explores the relationship between gender, education, and social change.

Morris, E. (2006). *An unexpected minority: White kids in an urban school*. New Brunswick, NJ: Rutgers University Press. The author of this insightful study explores attitudes about white identity and white privilege, including notions of hegemonic masculinity, in a Texas middle school where the majority of students are African American, Latino, and Asian American.

Pascoe, C. J. (2007). *Dude you're a fag: Masculinity and sexuality in high school.* Berkeley: University of California Press. This book is based on ethnographic research on how high school students construct and perform masculinity and

how boys engage in homophobic and sexist behavior to assert their masculinity.

Sadker, D., & Zittleman, K. R. (2009). *Still failing at fairness: How gender bias cheats girls and boys in school and what we can do about it.* New York: Charles Scribner. This book provides an update for the book published in 1994 by Sadker and Sadker. It explores how the classroom experience from elementary school to college differs for boys and girls.

Notes

1. Yale and Princeton did not admit women as undergraduate students until 1969. Harvard abandoned its practice of awarding separate degrees to Radcliffe graduates in 1963 and began awarding them Harvard degrees. However, the diplomas of male Harvard graduates had the signatures of the president of Harvard and the dean of the college, while the diplomas of female Harvard graduates were signed by the presidents of Harvard and Radcliffe. In 1999, Harvard and Radcliffe merged. Radcliffe became a Harvard Institute for Advanced Studies with a focus on women, gender, and society. Radcliffe no longer grants its own degrees, and its students are now Harvard students.

2. Studies show negative attitudes toward successful females as well as greater doubts about females' ability to succeed, especially in traditionally masculine tasks (Foschi, 1996; Heilman & Okimoto, 2007; Snipes, Oswald, & Caudill, 1998). Recent research also indicates that women may negatively view other women in stereotypically male jobs in order to improve their views of their own competence (Parks-Stamm, Heilman, & Hearns, 2008).

3. Summers's speech is available at http://bc.barnard.columbia.edu/~schapman/women/Summers.pdf.

4. University employees have also successfully fought sexual harassment. For example, in 2007, the University of Missouri at Kansas City agreed to pay $1.1 million to two employees (one graduate student and one psychology professor). The employees claimed that the lab they worked in was a "sexually hostile

work environment" and the university did nothing to remedy the problem. The university retained both alleged perpetrators (full professors); one victim continued to work at the university and the other victim successfully completed her graduate degree (Gravois, 2007). In a very different case, also settled in 2007, the University of Wisconsin agreed to pay $135,000 to a vice chancellor. After it was discovered that the vice chancellor was engaging in a consensual sexual relationship with a female graduate student and had also been accused of sexual harassment by two female employees, he was demoted. A university panel eventually decided that there was no just cause for disciplining the vice chancellor, but a letter stating his behavior toward women was unacceptable was still placed in his employment file by the provost (Wasley, 2007).

5. Available research shows that women are as sympathetic to male victims as they are to female victims, at least when the harassment is perpetrated by a member of the opposite sex (Kalof et al., 2001; Katz et al., 1996; Loredo et al., 1995). However, other research indicates that males who allege being victims of sexual harassment are believed less and liked less than females who allege victimization (Madera et al., 2007).

6. Private schools were always exempt from this Title IX provision.

7. In an attempt to avoid becoming coed, alumni and officials of VMI tried to raise $100 million to buy the school from the state of Virginia, but were unsuccessful.

Chapter 6

The Great Communicators: Language and the Media

Each year, American consumers spend a considerable amount of money on media including books, newspapers, magazines, CDs, DVDs, and digital downloads. Modern technology has changed the way many Americans receive media. For example, Digital Video Recorders (DVRs) and Video-on-Demand services allow people to record television programs in a digital format and watch them at their convenience, an activity referred to as "timeshifting." Also, Broadband Internet access provides high-speed connections, making it possible to watch television programs, movies, and videos through a computer. Smartphones or mobile phones with advanced operating systems allow people to watch television, movies, or videos anywhere. Ninety-eight percent of U.S. households have at least one television set, and many Americans (about 70 percent of adult Internet users) also stream television programs through their computers (Hope, 2010). In 2010, more than one-third (36.6 percent) of households had DVRs, 63.5 percent had Broadband Internet access, and 22 percent had Smartphones (Nielsen Company, 2010). As such technological gadgets are becoming the norm, it should not be surprising that Americans spend so much time consuming media. According to the Nielsen Company, the average American spends 35 hours and 34 minutes watching traditional TV, 2 hours and 9 minutes watching "timeshifted" TV, and 3 hours and 52 minutes using the Internet per week (Nielsen Company, 2010).

Obviously, the mass media are an important part of our everyday lives. Through them, we are both entertained and informed. In either case, however, we are mistaken if we think that the media are simply transmitting neutral or objective information and messages. Rather, as we will learn in this chapter, much of what is conveyed to us through the mass media is infused with particular values and norms, including many about gender. In other words, the media serve as gender socializers. Our focus in this chapter will be on what various media communicate about gender and how they communicate it. We will examine the gender images depicted in print media (newspapers and magazines) and an audiovisual medium (television), as well as a communication form common to both (advertisements). Although we will not discuss music, film, or theater, much of our analysis is applicable to those media, too.

Before we look at the content of specific media, however, it's important for us to examine the primary means by which media messages are conveyed—that is, through language. While "a picture paints a thousand words," the English language expresses our culture's underlying values and expectations about gender. Let's see how.

SEXISM AND LANGUAGE: WHAT'S IN A WORD?

"Sticks and stones may break my bones, but words will never hurt me!" How many times did you recite that chant as a child? In response to jeers or name-calling, we tried to tell our taunters that what they said had no effect on us. Yet, as we have grown older, we have come to realize that although words do not have the same sting as sticks and stones, they can indeed inflict as much harm. That is because words are symbols with meaning; they define, describe, and *evaluate* us and the world in which we live. The power of words lies in the fact that the members of a culture share those meanings and valuations. It is their common language that allows the members of a society to communicate and understand one another, and thus makes for order in society.

Language is a medium of socialization. Essentially, as a child learns the language of his or her culture, he or she is also learning how to think and behave as a member of

BOX 6.1
Sexism and Language

A. Connotations

governor—governess
master—mistress
patron—matron
sir—madam
bachelor—spinster

Word Pairs

brothers and sisters
husband and wife
boys and girls
hostess and host
queen and king
Eve and Adam

B. Generic He/Man

policeman
spokesman
manpower
Social Man
mankind
workman's compensation
"Man the oars!"
he, him, his

Source: Compiled from P. M. Smith, 1985; Strauss-Noll, 1984.

that culture. What gender socialization messages, then, are conveyed through our contemporary language? Let's consider some of them.

To begin, consider the first group of word pairs in Part A of Box 6.1. In each case, a word associated with men appears on the left and a word associated with women appears on the right. What does each word connote to you? The words associated with men have very different connotations than those associated with women, and the latter are uniformly negative or demeaning. The male words connote power, authority, or a positively valued status, while most of the female words have sexual connotations. Interestingly, many of these words originally had neutral connotations; *spinster*, for example, meant simply "tender of a spinning wheel." Over time, though, these words were debased, a process known as **semantic derogation**. "[L]exicographers have noted that once a word or term becomes associated with women, it often acquires semantic characteristics that are congruent with social stereotypes and evaluations of women as a group" (P. M. Smith, 1985, p. 48).

Reflecting on the words we have been discussing, what do their contemporary connotations tell us about the status of women in our society? In general, we see that women are associated with negative things and men with positive things. Additional examples are abundant. Linguist Alleen Pace Nilsen (1991, p. 267), for instance, points out that the word *shrew*, taken from the name of a small, but vicious, animal is defined in most dictionaries as "an ill-tempered scolding woman." The word *shrewd*, however, has the same root, but is defined as "marked by clever, discerning awareness." In the dictionary Nilsen analyzed, the meaning of *shrewd* was illustrated with the phrase "a shrewd businessman." Consider also *patron* and *matron*, both Middle English words for father and mother. Today, *patron* signifies a supporter, champion, or benefactor, such as a "patron of the arts." A *matron*, in contrast, is someone who supervises a public institution, such as a prison, or is simply an old woman.[1] And which would you rather be: an old *master* (someone who has achieved consummate ability in your field) or an old *mistress* (an elderly paramour) (Lakoff, 1991)? It is important to note that many of the most unflattering and derogatory words for women are reserved for old women (Nilsen, 1991). Ageism often combines with sexism to doubly disadvantage women in our society.

Another form of semantic derogation is illustrated by the second group of word pairs in Part A of Box 6.1. When you read each word pair, chances are that the word pairs in which the female term precedes the male term sound awkward or incorrect. The tradition of placing the female term after the male term further signifies women's secondary status and is hardly accidental. Eighteenth-century grammarians established the rule precisely to assert that "the supreme Being...is in all languages Masculine, in as much as the masculine Sex is the superior and more excellent" (quoted in Baron, 1986, p. 3). Thus, according to them, to place women before men was to violate the natural order. The masculine word also serves as the base from which compounds are made (e.g., from *king-queen* we get *kingdom*, but not *queendom*) (Nilsen, 1991). The exceptions to this usage rule are few (for instance, "ladies and gentlemen" and "bride and groom"), and most contemporary speakers of English perpetuate it—and its traditional connotation—in their everyday communications.

Semantic derogation is just one dimension of the larger problem of **linguistic sexism**. Linguistic sexism refers to ways in which a language devalues members of one sex, almost invariably women. In addition to derogating women, linguistic sexism involves defining women's "place" in society unequally and also ignoring women altogether. With respect to the former, for example, we may consider the commonly used titles of respect for men and women in our society. Men are addressed as *Mr.*, which reveals nothing about their relationship to women. But how are women typically addressed? The titles *Miss* and *Mrs.* define women in terms of their relationships to men. Even when a woman has earned a higher status title, such as *Dr.*, she is still likely to be addressed as *Miss* or *Mrs.* A couple we know, both Ph.Ds, often get mail from friends and relatives addressed to Dr. and Mrs. To a large extent, a woman's identity is subsumed by that of her husband, particularly if she adheres to the custom of adopting her husband's family name when she marries. She will find that she not only acquires a new surname, but also a new given name, since etiquette calls for her to be addressed as, for instance, Mrs. John Jones rather than Mrs. Mary Jones (Miller & Swift, 1991b; P. M. Smith, 1985). Since the 1970s, however, it has become more common for women to keep their maiden names upon marriage (Kopelman et al., 2009), but it is hard to ignore the connotation attached to the word "maiden" here.

Another way that our language ignores or excludes women is through the use of the supposedly generic *he* and *man*. Traditional rules of grammar hold that these two terms should be used to refer not only to males specifically, but also to human beings generally. Some have even argued that the use of the masculine generic has increased. However, empirical research raises serious doubts as to whether this he/man approach is really neutral or generic (e.g., Conkright, Flannagan, & Dykes, 2000; Gastil, 1990; Hamilton, 1988) and there is much more agreement now that the generic *he* is sexist (Curzan, 2009).

To understand the issue better, read the words in Part B of Box 6.1. What image comes to mind with each word? Do you visualize women, women and men together, or men alone? If you are like a majority of people, these words conjure up images only of men (Conkright et al., 2000; Silveira, 1980; Treichler & Frank, 1989a; Wilson & Ng, 1988). Of course, it could be argued that these words lack context; provided with a context, it would be easier to distinguish whether their referents are specifically masculine or simply generic.

Perhaps, but research indicates that context is rarely unambiguously generic and, consequently, the use of "he/man" language frequently results in "cognitive confusion" or misunderstanding. Lea Conkright and her colleagues (2000) found, for example, that children reading stories discerned the gender of the characters by the pronoun (*he* or *she*) used to refer to them, not by the activity in which the characters were engaged.

There are those who feel that this emphasis on language is trivial or misplaced. Some maintain, for example, that a focus on language obscures the more serious issues of gender inequality, such as the physical and economic oppression of women. [Blaubergs (1980) provides an excellent summary of this and other, less compelling arguments against changing sexist language.] But we should keep in mind that "one of the really important functions of language is to be constantly declaring to society the psychological place held by all of its members" (quoted in Martyna, 1980, p. 493; Treichler & Frank, 1989a). Given that women are denigrated, unequally defined, and often ignored by the English language, it serves not only to reflect their secondary status relative to men in our society, but also to reinforce it. Changing sexist language, then, is one of the most basic steps we can take toward increasing awareness of sexism and working to eliminate it.

How can sexist language be changed? Various simple, but effective, usage changes have been implemented by individuals and organizations. Substituting the title *Ms.* for *Miss* and *Mrs.* is one example.[2] Alternating the order of feminine and masculine nouns and pronouns is another (see Madson & Hessling, 1999). Perhaps most controversial has been the effort to eliminate the generic *he/man*. Instead of *he*, one may use *she/he*, or *he and she*, or simply *they* as a singular pronoun (Cheshire, 2008). Nouns with the supposedly generic *man* are also easily neutralized—for example, *police officer*, rather than *policeman*; *spokesperson*, rather than *spokesman*. *Humanity* and *humankind* are both sex-neutral substitutes for *man* and *mankind* (Baron, 1986; Frank, 1989; Treichler & Frank, 1989b). These kinds of changes are not difficult to make (see, for example, McMinn et al., 1991; McMinn, Williams, & McMinn, 1994).[3]

Because of the ease with which linguistic sexism can be overcome when the effort is genuinely made, we share Baron's (1986, p. 219) optimism "that if enough people become sensitized to sex-related language questions, such forms as generic *he* and *man* will give way no matter what arguments are advanced in their defense." Nevertheless, the way words and ideas are conveyed may be as important as the words and ideas themselves. Consequently, it is important that we also consider the issue of communication styles.

Do Women and Men Speak Different Languages?

Linguist Deborah Tannen (1990, 1994a, 1994b, 2010) argues that women and men are members of different speech communities. According to Tannen, women and men have different communication styles and different communication goals. Just as people from different cultures speak different dialects, women and men speak different *genderlects*. Women, maintains Tannen, speak and hear a language of intimacy and connection, whereas men speak and hear a language of status and independence. As a result, conversations between women and men are often like conversations between two people from different cultures and they produce a similar result: a great deal of misunderstanding (see also Shem & Surrey, 1998). But while Tannen's stories about miscommunications between women and men frequently bring smiles of recognition to people's faces, there are other researchers who question the extent to which women and men communicate differently (Smith, 2007). For example, some studies show few communication differences between women and men. Instead, they found that for both women and men, communication patterns and styles were influenced by a number of situational factors,

including the sex of the person with whom they were speaking, the context of the conversation, and the perceived status of both the speaker and the listener (Holmstrom, 2009; MacGeorge et al., 1999). Similarly, in a study of listeners' reactions to friends' self-disclosures, Leaper and colleagues (1995) found few differences between female and male listeners, with the exception that female listeners gave more "active understanding" responses (e.g., explicit acknowledgment of the speaker's feelings or opinions) when the speaker was a female friend (see also Ridgeway & Smith-Lovin, 1999). Findings such as these remind us that

Linguistic research indicates that women's communication styles tend to be more intimate than those of men, but factors besides gender influence these styles.

communication is an *interactive* process affected by a variety of factors, of which gender is only one.

Nevertheless, many researchers have observed that gender inequality characterizes much everyday communication, reflecting differences in men's and women's life experiences, social status, and power (Henley, Hamilton, & Thorne, 1985; Lakoff, 1990; Nichols, 1986). For example, in cross-sex conversations, researchers have found that men often do more of the talking, which is a direct result of the fact that in many situations (e.g., business meetings), they have more opportunity to express their opinions. Men also have more success than women in getting a conversation focused on topics they introduce. Moreover, when men speak, listeners of both sexes more actively attend to them than to women speakers (McConnell-Ginet, 1989; Ridgeway & Smith-Lovin, 1999). Research suggests that this may be due to the fact that men are more likely than women to use assertive speech (Leaper & Ayres, 2007), and men interrupt women more than women interrupt men (Leaper & Ayres, 2007). Women, though, are more likely than men to use intensifiers such as "really" and "very" (Mulac, 2006), and they are less likely than men to use profanity (Jay, 2009). The nonverbal communication of men in cross-sex interaction can also best be described as dominant. For instance, men control more space than women, and they touch and stare at women more. Women, in contrast, tend to avert their eyes when stared at by men, but they also smile and laugh more than men whether they are happy or not, a gesture that can be viewed as both social and submissive (McQuiston & Morris, 2009; Ridgeway & Smith-Lovin, 1999).

These findings fly in the face of the common stereotype that women are more talkative than men. Research on same-sex conversation, however, does show that in all-female groups, women talk more than men do in all-male groups. While men prefer to talk to one another about work, sports, or activities they have in common, women tend to prefer to talk to one another about more personal topics (Bischoping, 1993). In addition, studies of same-sex talk indicate that women's conversations are less individualistic and more dynamic than men's conversations, with women attempting to introduce topics and signaling active listening (nodding, making noise such as "*mmhmm*") (Helweg-Larsen et al., 2004; McConnell-Ginet, 1989; Ridgeway & Smith-Lovin, 1999). Interestingly, interruptions are frequent in women's conversations, but researchers have found that these interruptions are typically supportive rather than aggressive or hostile and often function to help the speaker put into words something she is having difficulty expressing (DeVault, 1986; Hayden, 1994; Ridgeway & Smith-Lovin, 1999).

Unfortunately, women's conversations have traditionally been negatively stereotyped and parodied. It is commonly believed, for example, that women devote the majority of their communications with one another to gossip and other frivolous matters, whereas men's communications with one another are more serious and, therefore, "important." Indeed, any negative traits and consequences of communication differences have been associated almost exclusively with women, in large part because men have had greater power to define acceptable standards of communication. In this way, women's communications have been considered not only different from men's, but also typically inferior.

Cross-cultural evidence indicates that this pattern is not normative in all societies. For example, Susan Rasmussen (2003), who researches gendered themes in public performances, analyzed the praise songs, dances and radio performances of Tuareg blacksmiths in West Africa. She found that in both rural and urban settings these stereotypically feminine forms of communication have become increasingly revered by the culture at large. Female smiths now perform alongside the male smiths, and their radio programs are designed with the specific intent to support their own agenda for gender and socioeconomic change. Rasmussen's research shows not only the cross-cultural variation in value ascribed to women's styles of communication, but also how ritual communication and media may be used to bring about cultural changes that empower women. Rasmussen's study also illustrates how self-perceptions, as well as others' perceptions of us, are shaped not only by direct interaction, but also by other communication media. We are, in fact, bombarded daily with media images of gender. Let's turn our attention, then, to the mass media in American society and their role as a gender socializer. First, though, Box 6.2 discusses another popular form of communication for which researchers are discovering gender differences.

GENDER AND THE MEDIA

Raise the question of media portrayals of men and women, and someone will invariably argue that the media only give the public what it expects, wants, or demands. This popular view is known in technical terms as the **reflection hypothesis**. Simply stated, the reflection hypothesis holds that media content mirrors the behaviors and relationships, and values and norms most prevalent in a society. There is certainly some truth to this position. After all, commercial sponsors (the media's most important paying customers) want to attract the largest audience possible, and providing what everyone wants or expects seems like a logical way to do this. However, media analysts also point out that, far from just passively reflecting culture, the media actively shape and create culture. How?

BOX 6.2
Gender Differences in Online Communication

With the increasing popularity of e-mail, blogging, message boards, and social networking sites (e.g., Facebook), it is hardly surprising that linguistic researchers have begun studying whether there are gender differences in online communication. Internet use is evenly divided between women (50 percent) and men (50 percent), with the total population having a rate of Internet access of approximately 79 percent (U.S. Department of Commerce, Bureau of the Census, 2010). Men and women are also equally likely to blog and use social networking websites. Men, though, are more likely than women to have their profile appear on LinkedIn, a business-oriented site typically used for professional networking, while women are more likely to have their profile appear on Facebook, which is primarily used for social networking (Lenhart, Purcell, Smith, & Zickuhr, 2010). But when they are online, do women and men communicate differently?

Several researchers report that women's and men's online communications mirror their in-person conversational styles. More specifically, these studies indicate that women's e-mail messages, whether to individuals or in online groups, are longer and more detailed than those of men. Women's messages also tend to have more emoticons and use more intensive adverbs (e.g., very, really); they are also more supportive and agreeable than men's messages. Men make stronger assertions and use profanity, insults, and sarcasm more than women do (Cohen, 2001; Thomson, Murachver, & Green, 2001). These differences have even shown up in studies of the use of the Internet for sex. Goodson and colleagues (2001), for example, found that although men (56.5 percent) were more likely than women (35.2 percent) to surf the Internet for sexually explicit materials, men were more likely to look at pornographic sites and masturbate, while women were more likely to engage in cyber sex with an online partner. Some researchers interpret such results as a further demonstration of women's tendency to use communication to build social connections and rapport with others in contrast to men's tendency to use communication more functionally or instrumentally. Gender differences also show up in studies of online medical support groups. For example, women were found to use an online cancer support group more than men, and were more likely to provide personal information, while men were more likely than women to use the site to obtain information (Andersen, Jeneson, & Ruland, 2007). Interestingly, however, Huffaker and Calvert (2005) studied gender differences in blog communication and concluded that men and women were equally as likely to use passive language. In attempting to explain their findings, the research speculated that women who blog hold less traditional gender roles than women who do not blog. Perhaps, but again this perspective assumes men's communication style to be normative and women's style as in need of explanation.

Some researchers argue that the distance that online communication puts between people allows some men to be more expressive and emotional than they would be in face-to-face communications (Cohen, 2001). But studies show that online communication styles may have more to do with the perceived sex of the message recipient than with the sex of the sender. In one study, for instance, Thomson and colleagues (2001) found that regardless of their own sex, participants in their experiment used a masculine style online if they thought their correspondent was male and a feminine style if they thought the correspondent was female. In other words, they adapted the gendered style of their communications to the perceived sex of the recipients. These researchers conclude that style of online communication is unstable and that each person selects from a range of styles depending on whom she or he is communicating with. Similarly, Lee (2003) found that men are more likely to use emoticons when instant messaging women rather than other men, while women use the same number of emoticons regardless of the gender of the message recipient. Other researchers point out that additional factors—including age, income, educational attainment, status, and the type of message (e.g., public vs. private, business vs. social)—likely intersect with gender to influence online communication styles (Cohen, 2001). No doubt this will continue to be fertile ground for future linguistic and communication studies.

Consider the network news. In a brief twenty-two minutes (accounting for commercials), these programs purport to highlight for us the most significant events that took place throughout the world on a given day. Obviously, decisions must be made by the program staff as to what gets reported, and that is precisely one of the ways the media shape our ideas and expectations. "The media select items for attention and provide rankings of what is and is not important—in other words they 'set an agenda' for public opinion....The way the media choose themes, structure the dialogue and control the debate—a process which involves crucial omissions—is a major aspect of their influence" (Baehr, 1980, p. 30; see also Phillips, 1998).

In addition to their role as definers of the important, the media are the chief sources of information for most people, as well as the focus of their leisure activity. There is considerable evidence indicating that many media consumers, particularly heavy television viewers, tend to uncritically accept media content as fact. Although there are intervening variables, such as the kinds of shows one watches and the behavior of the real-life role models in one's immediate environment, the media do appear to influence our worldview, including our personal aspirations and expectations for achievement, as well as our perceptions of others (L. Gross, 1991). Not surprisingly, therefore, feminist researchers have been especially concerned with media portrayals of gender. If these depictions are negative and sexist or if they distort the reality of contemporary gender relations, they may nevertheless be accepted as accurate by a large segment of the general public.

It has been argued that with respect to their treatment of women, the media are guilty of **symbolic annihilation** (Tuchman, Daniels, & Benet, 1978). That is, the media traditionally have ignored, trivialized, or condemned women. In the sections that follow, we will examine this charge more carefully. In addition, however, we will discuss the ways in which men have been exploited and denigrated by media portrayals. Although they typically fare better than women, men's media roles are also limited by stereotypes that are not always positive or flattering. Moreover, we will consider how symbolic annihilation occurs not only in terms of gender, but also in terms of race and ethnicity, social class, age, sexual orientation, and physical ability.

The Written Word: Gender Messages in Newspapers and Magazines

Researchers have found that regular reading of daily newspapers in the United States has declined significantly since the mid-1980s. In 2010, only one-quarter (26 percent) of Americans reported reading a newspaper in print form, a decline from 38 percent in 2006. However, the number of people getting their news online has increased over that same period from 9 percent in 2006 to 17 percent in 2010 (Pew Research Center, 2010). In 2009, *The Christian Science Monitor* became the first national newspaper to move to an online only format (Clifford, 2008).

When comparing men and women, men are more likely than women to regularly get news online or on a cell phone while women are more likely to turn to social networking sites (e.g., Twitter) for news (Pew Research Center, 2010). Researchers have also identified a gender gap in daily newspaper readership. In 1986, 65 percent of men and 61 percent of women were regular readers of daily newspapers; by 1997, 53 percent of men and just 49 percent of women said they read daily newspapers on a regular basis (Media Report to Women [MRTW], 1997a). In 2006, 44 percent of men and 38 percent of women were regular readers of daily newspapers (Pew Research Center, 2008). One of the main reasons for the overall decline in regular newspaper readership is that more people are turning to televised news and information programs and newsmagazine programs (e.g., *20/20* and *Dateline*) (MRTW, 1996a), as well as relying on the Internet as their sources of news (Pew Research Center, 2008). Nonetheless, women are still less likely than men to use online news sources (27 percent of women, 36 percent of men) (Pew Research Center, 2008). However, they are more likely than men to watch network morning shows (e.g., *Good Morning America*) as well as nightly network news and newsmagazine programs (Pew Research Center, 2008).

A number of explanations have been offered to account for the gender gap in newspaper readership. One researcher, for example, reports that the women who are least likely to read a newspaper every day are those who are young (between the ages of eighteen and thirty-four), unemployed, or who have children under the age of six. Readership is lower, then, among women who lack the time and financial resources that permit daily readership (MRTW, 1993a). But a second reason for the gender gap in newspaper reading is that newspapers often do not speak to women, or if they do, they do so in a denigrating or patronizing way (MRTW, 1998-B2).

Women and men certainly have different interests in news stories. Men are much more likely than women to closely follow sports news (74 percent of men, 26 percent of women), science and technology news (69 percent of men, 31 percent of women), and business and finance news (65 percent of men, 35 percent of women). In contrast, women are more likely than men to find news about religion, health, and entertainment interesting (Pew Research Center, 2008).

A quick perusal of just about any news daily gives one the impression that it is surely a man's world. News of women-centered activities and events or of particular women (with the exception of female heads of state, women who have died or been killed, and women notable for their association with famous men) is usually reported as *soft* news and relegated to a secondary, "non-news" section of the paper. For example, a two-week review of the *Washington Post* revealed that males dominate news coverage (MRTW, 2009). Topics identified as "feminist issues" that are commonly covered in newspapers across the country include abortion, workplace and educational equality, political election issues, and women's "safety issues" (Schreiber, 2010). Interestingly, one study found that during the period 1991 to 2004, the major newspapers tended to cover these topics in a reasonably balanced way, presenting both liberal and conservative women's perspectives. The single exception was the *New York Times,* which was found to cover "liberal" women's groups and perspectives 88.7 percent of the time.[4]

This research raises the question of how news about women is treated when it is reported as hard news. A 1980 study by Karen Foreit and her colleagues is enlightening on this point. These researchers found that in female-centered news stories, reporters were likely to mention an individual's sex (e.g., "the female attorney"), physical appearance (e.g., "the petite blonde"), and marital status or parenthood (e.g., "Dr. Smith is the wife of" or "the feisty grandmother"). Such details were rarely provided in male-centered stories. Descriptions such as these are sexist and objectifying and in the intervening years many newspapers have issued rules or guidelines to reduce sexism in reporting. Nevertheless, there remains no shortage of examples of sexist reporting today. For instance, when Senator Hillary Clinton ran for president, she was also often portrayed in a derogatory way as masculine. A columnist for the *New York Times*, for instance, referred to Clinton as "The Man" and described her as "the manliest candidate among the Democrats" (Media Matters, 2008). Feminists both here and abroad have long complained about media portrayals of themselves, as well as negative reporting of the women's movement. According to Faludi (1991), for example, the media depict feminists as a small, but vocal, radical fringe group that most members of the general public dislike. Feminists are divisive, and the women's movement is portrayed as the root cause for contemporary women's problems. Faludi presents numerous examples from newspapers and news magazines in which, she argues, the message reflects a backlash against feminism—that is, women who pursue true equality with men in our society will ultimately sacrifice true happiness.

In attempting to explain the symbolic annihilation of women by newspapers, many analysts have emphasized that most of the staff at the nation's daily newspapers are men. In 2009, women working full-time in daily newspapers totaled about 17,300 or 37 percent (American Society of Newspaper Editors, 2009).[5] Approximately 28 percent of television news directors are women (Papper, 2008) and approximately 15 percent of general managers of newsroom organizations are women (Papper, 2007). Women's under representation could contribute to their negative work experience. A survey of 715 U.S. newspaper journalists found that women are more likely than men to report exhaustion, less likely to report perceived organizational support, and more likely to report high job demands (Reinardy, 2009).

There does appear to be some effort being made, at least by mainstream newspapers throughout the country, to increase the diversity of newsroom staffs and newspaper management. It is impossible to determine how many lesbians and gay men work for newspapers in this country, since many remain closeted because of the intense stigma still attached to homosexuality. It is clear, though, that despite recent gains, racial and ethnic minorities, especially women of color, continue to be underrepresented on newsroom staffs, particularly in high-level positions. In 1978, racial and ethnic minorities made up just 3.95 percent of full-time newsroom employees (editors, reporters, copy editors, photographers). In 2010, the percent of minority journalists working at daily newspapers was 13.2 percent. Minorities accounted for 11.1 percent of all supervisors. In addition, women, particularly women of color, continue to be underrepresented in newsrooms. As noted previously, in 2010, only 37 percent of full-time workers for daily newspapers were women, and 34 percent of supervisors were women. Minority women accounted for 16.6 percent of female newsroom employees (American Society of Newspaper Editors, 2010).

The question remains, however, as to whether having more women—or people of color or gay men and lesbians—on newspaper staffs actually decreases sexism—or racism or homophobia—in the papers. Minority journalists may be compelled to ignore their racial identity to adapt to the norms of a White-dominated organization or to traditional journalistic norms (Husband, 2005; Nishikawa et al., 2009), and hiring minority journalists does not necessarily result in more stories covering issues of racial justice (Ankney & Procopio, 2003). For instance, from interviews with eighteen minority journalists working for a mainstream newspaper, Nishikawa et al. (2009) found that these journalists feel constrained by mainstream norms and actually avoid advocacy for people of color in their reporting.

Studies examining the relationship between the sex of reporter and sexist reporting or news coverage have produced contradictory findings. Studies, for instance, have found that although female journalists quote women as sources more frequently than male journalists do, they tend to define expertise the same way male journalists do and, consequently, seek out the same types of experts that male journalists do (Buresh, Gordon, & Bell, 1991; see also MRTW, 1996d, 1996e). One explanation of this phenomenon is that men still outnumber women in positions of authority. But, according to one sociologist of the media, it is also because women journalists' judgments about general news resemble those of men (Tuchman, 1979). For instance, a content analysis of the stories and sources published by a newspaper with an all female management team revealed that the content of the newspaper did not change significantly and the interests and activities of males remained dominant (Everbach, 2005).

GENDER AND MAGAZINES   Magazines are different from newspapers in many ways. Of particular interest to us is the fact that while newspapers seek a broad, general readership, magazines try to appeal to specific segments of the population. There are magazines that target specific racial and ethnic groups (e.g., *Latina, Ebony, Black Enterprise*). There are magazines that focus on particular interests or life experiences (e.g., *Popular Mechanics, Organic Gardening, Track and Field, Parents*). And there are women's magazines (e.g., *Redbook, Working Woman, O: The Oprah Magazine*), and men's magazines (e.g., *Esquire, Sports Illustrated, Penthouse*). Even within these two large groups, there are various subgroups that specialty magazines target as potential readers. Subscribers to *Ms.: The World of Women*, for instance, are likely to have very different attitudes and interests than subscribers to *Cosmopolitan*, although both groups are almost exclusively female, and both may see themselves as "liberated."[6]

Generally speaking, then, how do magazines expressly designed for women differ from those for men? Traditionally, women's magazines have promoted a "cult of femininity," that is, a definition of femininity as a narcissistic absorption with oneself—with one's physical appearance ("the business of becoming more beautiful"), with occupational success, and with success in affairs of the heart ("getting and keeping your man") (McCracken, 1993; Murphy, 1994). Although editors of many popular women's magazines say they think their readers today are more self-confident and accomplished and have a wider range of interests than readers of the past, researchers have found few substantial changes in most women's magazines.

For example, Kelley Massoni (2004) found that even though teen magazines for girls were claiming to be a source of entertainment and learning for "realized" young women, surveys of such magazines revealed messages more like "men are the norm as workers," "men hold the power," and that "fashion modeling is the pinnacle of women's work." Achieving the ideal still requires readers to buy particular clothes and cosmetics, to style their hair in particular ways, to say and do certain things in particular situations (in bed, on the job)—in short, to be *made over*, a theme (with instructions) found in nearly every issue of women's and girls' fashion magazines. The ultimate goal remains getting and keeping a man and achieving "beauty," even if the strategy is no longer romance or health, but rather aggressive sex appeal. Although some women's fashion and "service" magazines have done articles on formerly taboo subjects, such as lesbian relationships and bisexuality, they all remain firmly heterosexual in focus and exclude women who deviate from "normative, recognizable femininity" (McRobbie, 1996, p. 182; see also Eaton, 2007; Frith et al., 2005). Even magazines founded decades ago with a target audience of stay-at-home mothers (e.g., *Ladies Home Journal*) have increased their sexually explicit content and have initiated a sex column as a regular feature in the hope of attracting more readers (Kuczynski, 2000a).

We undertook our own unscientific analysis of women's and men's magazines to see how they are similar and different. We looked at issues of three of the most popular U.S. women's magazines: *Cosmopolitan* and *Glamour* (targeted primarily to young, urban, White women) and *Essence* (designed for young Black women). We also looked at *Latina*, a magazine for young Hispanic women. We found that in both *Cosmopolitan* and *Glamour* the dominant themes were sex, looking sexy, attracting men, and having relationships with men. For example, a recent cover of *Cosmopolitan* advertised articles on "secrets of male arousal," while a recent cover of *Glamour* advertised "10 sex and love thrills every woman should have." The advertisements in these magazines reinforced the dominant themes.[7] Nearly all of the ads in both magazines were for cosmetics, personal care products, and hair care, and the clear message was that these products would make a woman more beautiful and more physically appealing to men.

In contrast, the articles in both *Latina* and *Essence* were more diverse. *Latina* featured singer Shakira on the cover, with an article that discussed not only her success but also her activities as a philanthropist. Another issue featured actress Sara Ramirez ("Grey's Anatomy") on the cover, with an article that discussed her battle with depression. Other articles focused on hate crimes, ways to control spending, and students being bullied because of their Latino/Latina heritage. In *Essence*, feature articles covered actor and relationship expert Steve Harvey and actress Regina King. It's not that beauty, fashion, and interpersonal relationships were absent from *Latina* and *Essence*, but rather that they were less prominent; the magazines' coverage was more balanced with articles on jobs, reproductive health, and parenting in addition to several on fashion, hair styling, and relationships with men. The overwhelming majority of advertisements in *Essence* were for cosmetics, perfume, hair care, and personal care items, but the majority of the models shown were Black. Most of the ads in *Latina* were also for cosmetics, perfume, hair care, and personal care items, but these were more balanced with almost an equal number of ads for food products, clothing, cars, services, and other items (e.g., television programs). Although it was sometimes difficult to determine the race or ethnicity of the models in these ads, it appeared that most were women of color.

Men's magazines provide some interesting contrasts to women's periodicals. Most men's magazines can still be placed in one of three categories: finance/business/technology, sports/hobbies, and sex. Sex, which we have seen is by no means absent from women's magazines, is still typically discussed in women's periodicals in terms of interpersonal relationships, whereas men's sex-oriented magazines objectify and depersonalize sex. Men's magazines also offer instructions on achieving the attractive or valued body types. These ideals, however, are very different from those prescribed for women. Images of throbbing muscles, cold chiseled chins, and masculine poses and tasks all create a "branded masculinity" that may be as unhealthy and imbalanced as the images peddled in women's magazines (Alexander, 2003; see also Chapter 12).

Apart from these three types of magazines, however, what are the dominant themes in more general periodicals designed for men? To continue our unscientific analysis, we examined three men's magazines—*Esquire* ("Man at His Best") and *Gentleman's Quarterly*, which we felt were comparable to *Cosmopolitan* and *Glamour*; and *Black Men* ("For Strong, Protective, Caring Brothers"), which appeared comparable to *Essence*. Overall, the predominant theme in *Esquire*, *GQ*, and *Black Men* is living a leisurely lifestyle that is made possible by one's financial success. Articles about politics, music, art, film, sports, travel, and sophisticated or famous men are common to the three magazines. Conspicuous by their absence are articles about male/female relationships. The covers of *GQ* and *Esquire*, though, often feature a scantily clad female celebrity. For example, a 2008 cover showed Cameron Diaz wearing a revealing black bathing suit and high heels, and a 2010 cover showed singer Rhianna topless. A 2009 issue of *Esquire* featured actress Megan Fox wearing a trench coat and garter belt.

The low priority that men's magazines give to interpersonal relationships is reinforced by the advertisements that dominate their pages. Judging only by the ads, one might easily conclude that men—especially White men—spend the majority of their time driving around in their cars, drinking alcohol, and taking pictures with their digital cameras, much to the neglect of their personal hygiene. Apart from the clothing ads in *GQ*, the common ads in the magazines targeted at White men were for cars and alcohol.

Thus, periodicals intended for men generate their own gender images and ideals (see Barron & Kimmel 2000; Curry et al., 2002; Rajagopal & Gales, 2002). Normative masculinity according to these magazines does not include establishing a long-term relationship with a woman. Instead, the real man is free and adventurous. He is a risk taker who pursues his work and his hobbies—including, in this latter category, relationships with women—with vigor. He is concerned about his personal appearance, but not in an all-consuming sense as many women seem to be.[8] The magazines, of course, promise to help their readers achieve these goals, and, in this respect, they are not at all unlike the magazines for women.

Despite their continuing appeal, magazines like those we have been discussing have shown declines in sales (Clifford, 2010; Jackson et al., 2001; Smith, 2000). Media analysts report that consumers appear to be increasingly turning away from print media and utilizing more electronic, audiovisual media. Many analysts predict, in fact, that if access to the Internet and mobile technology continues to increase at its current rate, these forms of electronic media will replace television as the most popular form of electronic media For the time being, however, television remains extremely popular, even if it is viewed via the Internet. A critical question that arises, therefore, is whether the gender messages of television programming are any less sexist or exploitative than those we have found in the print media. Or do they simply reinforce the norms of femininity and masculinity promoted by the popular women's and men's magazines? These are questions that we will address next.

Television: The Ubiquitous Media Socializer

Television is without a doubt an important media socializer, given the number of televisions in the United States, as well as television's unique characteristics. Research documents the central place that television holds in the lives of most Americans. In 2008, 94.1 percent of U.S. citizens age 18 and older reported watching television (U.S. Department of Commerce, Bureau of the Census, 2010), and, as previously stated, the average American spends over 35 hours watching traditional television each week (Nielsen Company, 2010). Women watch television more than men do, and adults watch more than youth do (Nielsen Company, 2010). However, for children, watching television occupies more time than any other out-of-school activity; children watch, on average, 3.5 hours of television per day (American Academy of Child and Adolescent Psychiatry,

2006). In 2008, teenagers spent an average of three hours and 20 minutes a day watching television, a statistic that indicates they are watching more television than they have in the past (Nielsen Company, 2010).

Television also has special characteristics that add to its potency as an agent of socialization. For instance, it is available to just about everyone, and it does not even require viewers to leave the privacy of their homes, as movies and theater do. It requires no special skills, such as literacy, to watch, and everyone, regardless of sex, race, age, social class, sexual orientation, and often, geographic location, gets the same visual and verbal messages, although research shows that social factors such as sex and race, may influence how viewers interpret or relate to program content (Bjornstrom et al., 2010; Bulanda, 2004; Gruber & Thau, 2003). What sorts of socialization messages are television programs conveying?

One prominent message is that women are less important than men. Consider, for example, that there are fewer women than men on prime-time television (Lauzen, Dozier, & Horan, 2008; Signorielli, 2009b). Other studies show that women are less likely than men to play major characters, a phenomenon that has come to be called the "Smurfette Principle," after the children's cartoon story "The Smurfs," where, in a town of little blue elves, there were over ten male characters and only one female (Wade, 2010). Box 6.3 further explores the gender messages sent to children in cartoons and animated movies. Although the number of female characters on prime-time television has increased since the 1980s, women are still more likely than men to play minor roles. This, in turn, appears to have a significant impact on how viewers talk to each other about gender and the type of roles they discuss, an issue Jerome Sehulster (2006) explores in his writings about how television is discussed in everyday conversations.

Other factors combine with gender to send specific socialization messages through television. Consider, for example, that in general older people are underrepresented on television (Lauzen & Dozier, 2005; Robinson & Anderson, 2006). In addition, once characters reach sixty years of age, they are treated with less respect on television programs (Lauzen & Dozier, 2005). Women on television age faster than men, and the older they are, the more likely they are to be portrayed as unsuccessful or without clearly defined occupational roles, and their success and value are highly dependent upon how closely they conform to society's perscribed beauty standard (Shrikhande, 2003).

Female characters are typically thin and physically attractive. This may affect the way women viewing these images think about their own bodies. Want (2009) found that women exposed to television for even a very short time experienced decreased mood and self-esteem and had a lower opinion of their own bodies. Interestingly, Want found that when he spoke to the women before they were exposed to television about the tricks often employed to make actresses look thinner than they really are, the women did not experience negative mood changes as severely. Women on television are more likely than men to make or receive comments about their physical appearance and to be shown grooming or "preening." Female characters are more likely to wear sexy clothes and be shown scantily dressed (e.g., wearing just underwear), and they are more physically fit than male characters (see also Eisend & Moller, 2007; Lin & Yeh, 2009). In general, male television characters are given more leeway in terms of their appearance.

BOX 6.3
Gender Messages in Children's Television Cartoons and Animated Movies

The American Academy of Pediatrics (AAP) advises that children under the age of two should not watch television and has expressed concern over the amount of television viewed by children and adolescents. Specifically, the AAP points to the negative effects that television viewing can have on children such as increasing aggressive or violent behavior, poor body image, obesity, and decreasing school performance (American Academy of Pediatrics, 2001). Researchers have also found that early television viewing (i.e., viewing by children aged one to three) is associated with attention problems later (at age seven) (Christakis et al., 2004) and that boys who watch violent television shows between the ages of two and five are more likely to exhibit aggressive behavior between the ages of seven and ten (Christakis & Zimmerman, 2007).

Despite these warnings, children watch a considerable amount of television. In 2003, the Kaiser Family Foundation surveyed more than one thousand parents of children between the ages of six months and six years. Researchers found that the vast majority (91 percent) of children from younger than one to six years of age have watched television. Seventy-four percent of children between the ages of zero and two years have watched television, and the majority (59 percent) of children watch television and videos or DVDs (42 percent) in a typical day (Rideout, Vandewater, & Wartella, 2003). According to the Nielsen Company, children between the ages of two and five spend more than 32 hours a week on average watching television (McDonough, 2009). Forty-three percent of children between the ages of four and six and 68 percent of children eight and older actually have a television in their bedroom (Dubow, Huesmann, & Greenwood, 2007). Boys and girls watch the same amount of television (Rideout et al., 2003), and both report liking cartoons (Cherney & London, 2006).

Research on animated films and cartoons concludes that female characters are underrepresented (Anderson & Cavallaro, 2002; Baker & Raney, 2007; Fischer, 2010; Steinke et al., 2008). Leaper et al., (2002) found that female characters were less likely to be represented in traditional adventure cartoons and comedy cartoons. Because of the overrepresentation of male characters, young viewers may associate power with males (Leaper & Friedman, 2007).[9] Cartoons also provide the message that being physically attractive is important (Klein & Shiffman, 2006). Cartoon characters in television and film have gender-stereotyped roles (Leaper et al., 2002; Leaper & Friedman, 2007; Marshall & Sensoy, 2009). One cartoon that challenged gender stereotypes was *The Powerpuff Girls*, which ran from 1995 to 2006 on the Cartoon Network, and was "the first cartoon to feature little girls as superheroes on their own show" (Hager, 2008, p. 63). Typically, however, female characters are depicted as fearful and in need of the physical protection of male characters (Jhally, 2006; Leaper et al., 2002), while male characters are more likely than female characters to be shown acting physically aggressive (Luther & Legg, 2010). Studies indicate that children are receptive to the messages given them through television and movies, including animated programs and movies. This is especially concerning, however, given that most very young children cannot differentiate reality from fantasy (American Academy of Pediatrics, 2001).

This is not to say that the portrayal of women on television has not changed over the history of the medium. A number of researchers have documented important changes in the portrayal of women *and* men in recent years. For example, female prime-time characters today are more likely to work outside the home and to be strong and independent women who solve their own problems and achieve their goals (Dow & Condit, 2005).

There has also been a noticeable increase in the number of television heroines who are physically strong and supernaturally enhanced (e.g., *Buffy the Vampire Slayer*) (Dow & Condit, 2005). Husbands nowadays are more often depicted as idealized family men, who are sensitive to and supportive of their wives. These male characters are portrayed as quite willing to do more than an equal share of housework and child care. As we will learn in Chapter 7, this portrayal is clearly unrealistic given data on the amount of time men in "real life" spend on housework and child care.

But despite these changes in role portrayals, gender stereotypes are still prominent on television. Looking at 124 prime-time television shows aired on six networks during the 2005–2006 season, researchers found that female characters were more likely to enact interpersonal roles (e.g., family, romance), and men were more likely to enact work-related roles (e.g., showing desire for work-related success) (Lauzen et al., 2008). Men are more likely than women to be shown in professional roles, and women are more likely than men to be portrayed as not working outside the home (Signorielli, 2009b). Women are more likely than men to use sex or romantic charm to get what they want, and they are more likely to cry and whine. Men, in contrast, are more likely than women to use physical force (Eaton, 2007; Mackey, 2003; Patton-Owens, 2001; for a discussion of negative depictions of men on television, see Gates, 2000).

One of the most significant changes on prime-time programming since the 1970s has been the incorporation of women's rights and gender equality themes, often presented from what could be considered a feminist perspective (Dow & Condit, 2005). In addition, a number of prime-time programs and made-for-television movies have sensitively addressed such topics as sexual assault, spouse abuse, and incest. Nevertheless, strong or serious feminists are usually portrayed negatively, and feminism is portrayed as something both undesirable and irrational (Aronson, 2003; Purvis, 2004). Feminist politics are typically avoided, and political feminists are often punished for what is depicted as an unnecessary over-commitment to the feminist "party line."

Gender stereotypes frequently intersect with racial and ethnic stereotypes on television. Female or male, racial and ethnic minorities are less likely to be cast for television programs than Whites are (Signorielli, 2009a). Research that focused on major and supporting characters in ten weeklong samples of prime-time television shows between fall 1997 and fall 2006 found that most (55 percent) television programs had all White or mostly White characters (Signorielli, 2009b). While Latinos and Asians are underrepresented (Hunt, 2005; Signorielli, 2009a), Native Americans are not represented at all (Hunt, 2005). The newer networks—WB, UPN—have increased the number of African Americans on television by developing new series (primarily situation comedies) in which all the central characters are Black. Nevertheless, on the larger networks—ABC, CBS, NBC—only a handful of programs (mostly dramas) have racially and ethnically diverse casts. Most programs—particularly the sitcoms—remain "racially segregated" with a minor character of a race or ethnicity different from the core cast appearing only occasionally (Sanneh, 2001). Critics contend that major network programming that does include racial and ethnic minorities portrays them through White eyes and ignores racial conflicts (Fuller, 2005).

Other groups are invisible or negatively stereotyped in television programming as well. People with physical disabilities, for example, are just 1.9 percent of prime-time characters (Gerbner, 1998). Actors with disabilities, especially females, report challenges in finding employment or are restricted to disability-specific roles (Raynor & Hayward, 2009). Until recently, lesbian and gay characters were more likely to be found in made-for-television movies, particularly once the television industry began to address the problem of AIDS. However, the number of gay and lesbian characters on prime-time television has increased considerably in recent years. By 2010, there were several regular gay or lesbian characters on prime-time television programs, both on situation comedies and dramas. These characters are included on some of the most popular programs such as *Grey's Anatomy, Nurse Jackie, Glee*, and *Modern Family*. Not only are gay and lesbian characters more common on prime-time television, their portrayals are more positive, too (Hetsroni, 2007).

If we turn from prime-time entertainment programming to news programming, we find that some groups have made considerable progress in their presence on television. Indeed, the greatest move toward equality of the sexes in broadcasting has taken place in local television newsrooms. However, although more women are news reporters, gender segregation continues (Creedon & Cramer, 2007). By 2008, 28.3 percent of television news directors were women (Radio Television Digital News Association, 2008). All-male news desks are rare on local televised news programs, where the trend has been toward male-female anchor teams. Unfortunately, female coanchors often confront a double standard on the job. Higher standards of physical attractiveness and dress are sometimes set for them compared to their male colleagues, and they may be expected to look younger and act friendlier than male anchors (MRTW, 1999c). Consider, for example, the website "Zimbio," which lists "The 15 Hottest Female News Anchors" complete with pictures and comments (Zimbio, 2011).

In addition, recent research indicates that on local newscasts female reporters are more likely to report on human interest and health-related issues while male reporters are more likely to cover political stories (Desmond & Danilewicz, 2010). International research on gender and news also concludes that men are more likely to report on economic and political stories while women are more likely to report on social issues (Gallagher, 2005). When expert opinions are sought, men are more likely to be interviewed than women are (Desmond & Danilewicz, 2010).

Overall, women have also made progress on national network newscasts in recent years. Two of the three nightly news programs on the major networks—ABC, CBS, and NBC—have been anchored by women in recent years, including Katie Couric on *CBS's Evening News* and Diane Sawyer on *ABC's World News*. Research supports that news programs have become more diverse. For example, Ryan and Mapaye (2010) conducted a content analysis of all network news programs for one week in 2007 and compared the data to similar data collected twenty years prior in 1987. Their findings indicate that women are more likely than in the past to be seen as anchors and reporters. However, the data also indicate that the news women covered is more likely than in the past to be soft news, as discussed earlier in the chapter. Studies also show that male newscasters are perceived to be more credible than female newscasters (Brann & Himes, 2010).

Both minority men and women remain dramatically underrepresented on the network news, with only slight improvements in recent years. The California-based Tomas Rivera Policy Institute surveyed over one thousand Hispanics and over four hundred non-Hispanics on their opinions about minorities on television (Media Awareness Network, 2010). About 70 percent of Hispanics said that when they watch English-language news, stories on Hispanic men are most frequently about crime or immigration. Interestingly, non-Hispanics said that 56 percent of the news shows they watched portrayed Hispanics in a positive manner. No figures are available regarding the number of lesbian and gay newscasters; their heterosexuality seems to be assumed. In fact, it was not until May 2007 that the first gay newscaster, Jason Bellini of CBS News made his sexual orientation public (Hillis, 2007).

Off-camera, people of color have also fared poorly, although the trend is very slowly improving. Despite the fact that a 1998 federal court struck down a Federal Communications Commission requirement that television stations actively recruit, hire, and train minority job applicants (Holmes, 1998), ten years later in 2008 the percentage of minority television news directors reached an all-time high of 15.5 percent, up from 10.9 percent in 2006 (Benton Foundation, 2008).

Gender Messages in Advertisements: Does Sexism Sell?

- A soft drink commercial shows a couple on a date. The voiceover indicates that the young woman is wondering whether her date is financially successful, whether he loves his mother, and whether he'd like to have children some day. But when the camera pans to the young man, the voiceover indicates that the only thought repeatedly running through his mind is wanting to go to bed with his date—until, of course, the soft drink arrives at the table. Then his only thought is how much he wants the soft drink.
- A tortilla chip commercial shows three men enjoying a "boys' night in," relaxing and playing video games. When one of the men opens a bag of tortilla chips and bites a chip, a scantily clad female appears and suggestively jumps on him. When the other friend grabs the bag and eats a chip, two attractive women wearing nothing but towels appear.

These scenarios are quite familiar to us. They come, of course, from the contrived world of advertising, and, like most advertisements, they are selling us more than a specific product; they are peddling needs and desires. In the first example, the implicit message is that women value relationships and men are only interested in sex. In the second, men are told that regardless of what they look like or how socially inept they are, they too can attract beautiful women if they buy the advertised food. Just about everyone wants to be successful, physically attractive, and even sexy. What advertisers often do is play on these desires by implying that their products not only serve their intended purposes, but also offer bonuses as well. In this way, "advertisements portray an image that represents the interpretation of those cultural values which are profitable to propagate" (Courtney & Whipple, 1983, p. 192).

Advertisements portray images of gender that the advertising industry deems profitable. According to advertising analysts, for male consumers the message is typically to buy a particular product and get the "sweet young thing" associated with it, whereas for female consumers the message is to buy the product in order to be the sweet young thing (Cortese, 1999; Masse & Rosenblum, 1988; McCracken, 1993; Strate, 1992). The dominant philosophy of the advertising industry has traditionally been that "sexism sells" (Courtney & Whipple, 1983; Douglas, 2010; Drewniany, 1996; Lazier-Smith, 1989; Snyder, 1997). Also, sexism in advertising can be quite subtle. Consider, for example, the way models are posed. Women are often depicted in magazine advertisements in strange, child-like or subordinate poses, while men are presented in equally machismo settings and postures that play up their masculinity.

Gender stereotyping is prevalent in advertisements. What are some of the common gender stereotypes in print and television advertising? One set of stereotypes revolves around the occupations depicted. Although there has been minor improvement in recent years, occupational stereotyping by sex still pervades advertisements. Men hold positions of authority—they are the so-called experts—while women receive advice, usually from men, or are shown in traditional female occupations and roles (e.g., nurse, secretary, homemaker, mother), and this is especially true of advertisements in magazines for teenage girls (Massoni, 2004). Suppose we told you that we were about to show you ten advertisements featuring male models, and we asked you to guess what jobs they would most likely be doing. You would probably have little difficulty coming up with a long list of answers because men in advertisements are shown in a wide range of roles—from white-collar professionals such as scientists, physicians, and business executives, to blue-collar workers such as plumbers, electricians, and exterminators. Less often, they are shown in family roles as husbands and fathers. But what if we asked the same question using ads with female models? Chances are your list would be considerably shorter. Although nontraditional roles for women are appearing more often than in the past, women's traditional roles, especially homemaker and mother, continue to far outnumber nontraditional portrayals. Women are also less likely than men to be shown "on the job" in commercials. As Bradway (2010) explains, advertisements are one of the ways that occupational scripts are created for women. But how often do advertisements challenge these occupational scripts? Bradway (2010) found that in about 13 percent of the commercials she reviewed, women were shown in an occupation that is characteristically masculine, while only 3 percent of the commercials showed a man in a stereotypical female occupation.

In television commercials, women most often demonstrate household cleaning products, personal care items, and food, yet the announcers and background voices (known as voice-overs) in these ads are usually male. As recently as 2010, research showed that among the general American public, the male voice is still considered by many as "more forceful" (48 percent); 2 percent consider the female voice more forceful, although 50 percent said male and female voices are equally forceful (Dolliver, 2010). Correspondingly, when asked which voice was "more soothing," 46 percent of respondents in this study said the female voice, 8 percent the male voice, and 46 percent said they were both the same. The respondents indicated, though, that to them, the male and female voice-overs were equally "persuasive" (Dolliver, 2010).

At the same time, studies show that the sexually exploitative use of women in advertising has increased since 1970 (Cortese, 1999; Lanis & Covell, 1995). For example, a content analysis of almost two thousand ads in fifty-eight U.S. magazines revealed that on average one out of every two ads that showed women depicted them as sex objects (Stankiewicz & Rosselli, 2008). Women are exploited in advertisements when the female model has a purely decorative role; in other words, she has no clear relationship to the product and is shown simply because of her physical attractiveness and sex appeal. Typically, models are scantily dressed (e.g., in bathing suits or lingerie) and provocatively posed. Women are often shown in magazine advertisements in unnatural positions, and in child-like or subordinate poses, while men are shown in macho settings and posed in ways that play up their masculinity and dominance. While many consumers have come to expect these portrayals in personal care or cosmetics ads—indeed, they dominate such advertisements—they are also prevalent in nonappearance-related advertising (see Gill,

2008, p. 35, however, who argues that women in advertisements are now being represented as "independent" and "sexually powerful").

Researchers have found that the percentage of advertisements depicting men in decorative roles has also increased in recent years. As McGrath (2006) demonstrated, for at least the last forty years there has been a steady increase in the sexualization and objectification of men in advertising. And the body-types of men used have narrowed significantly, with the preference being for lean, muscular men (McGrath, 2006). Consider, for instance, the now famous Diet Coke commercial in which women at work in an office building time their daily break to coincide with the moment a handsome, athletic construction worker takes off his shirt. The women pop open their cans of Diet Coke to cool off from the sexual heat produced by watching the man "strip" (see Patterson, 1996, for other classic examples). It appears that the response of the advertising industry to complaints of sexism in ads using decorative female models has not been to eliminate such ads, but rather to demean men by portraying them as sex objects, too. This approach reflects the industry's confusion of gender equality with sexual permissiveness and exploitation.

The advertising industry is also increasingly using children, especially girls, in sexually exploitative ways, a trend referred to as the *Lolita syndrome* after a 1962 film that depicted a twelve-year-old girl seducing an elderly man. Such advertisements show the children in makeup and posed seductively, giving the impression that they are sexually available. According to critics, the trend has become so popular that adult models who have child-like bodies are often favored by advertisers (Karlyn-Bowe, 2004; Polyakov, 2010). The emphasis on youth in advertisements corresponds with the denigration of the elderly. Older models, male or female, are rare in advertisements for products other than health aids, vitamins, and insurance. But when older male models are used, they have a better chance than older female models of being portrayed as authority figures. Older female models usually play the roles of loving grandmother or perform some other home-bound task (Hiemstra, 2010). So while some observers report that older people have become more visible in television commercials (Vickers, 2007) and print advertisements (Robinson, Gustafson, & Popovich, 2008; Vickers, 2007), we must question the ageist ways they are depicted.

Other groups remain largely absent from advertising. Although African American models are now seen more often in advertisements, especially on television, other racial and ethnic groups, including Hispanic Americans, Asian Americans, and Native Americans are rarely seen (New Models, 2006). In a 2006 study of 3,419 print ads, 49 percent of the models were White women, 20 percent were African American women, 16 percent were Hispanic/Latina women, 10 percent were Asian women, 2 percent were East Indian women; for 4 percent race or ethnicity could not be determined (New Models, 2006). With the exception of the furniture store chain, Ikea, that ran a television ad about a gay male couple who decided to live together, advertisements that depict models in gay and lesbian relationships are even more rare. And how many advertisements—other than those for health care and charitable organizations—have you seen that use models with physical disabilities?

Despite industry claims that sexism sells, research provides only qualified support for this position. Advertisements that use women's sexuality to sell products to men appear to be appealing to and effective with that constituency. Ads emphasizing sex also often appeal to teenagers of both sexes. However, such ads are ineffective with a large segment of adult female consumers (deYoung & Crane, 1992; Grigsby, 1992; Lanis & Covell, 1995). Other studies have shown that while consumers in general do like to see attractive models of both sexes in advertisements, the use of nudity, seminudity, and sexual innuendo may inhibit consumers' ability to recall the products and the advertisements in which they appeared (Cortese, 1999; Courtney & Whipple, 1983).

It is estimated that the average American is exposed to between 850 and 3,000 advertisements each day (Texas A & M University, 2002; Union of Concerned Scientists, 2002), which is between 31,000 and 110,000 advertisements per year. The average youngster, while watching children's programming, now sees about 20,000 thirty-second television commercials each year (Herr, 2007). Print advertising is also increasing and can now be found on tiny stickers attached to fruits and vegetables, on bathroom stall doors and the walls over urinals, and on gasoline pumps (Cropper, 1998). Given the pervasive—some would say *invasive*—nature of advertisements, it makes sense to consider their potential effects on our attitudes and behavior. To conclude this chapter, then, let's look at the research on media effects.

IMAGES OF GENDER IN THE MEDIA: WHAT ARE THEIR EFFECTS?

Defenders of the media sometimes argue that while media portrayals are often sexist, their effects are benign. "That only happens on television," they say. "People don't really believe that stuff." There is evidence, though, that contradicts their argument; many people, it seems, do believe that stuff.[10]

The majority of research on media effects has focused on television largely because of its popularity, particularly with children, and because of its unique characteristics that we outlined earlier. A central issue has been the effects of violent television programming, an issue that we examine more closely in Box 6.4. With regard to violent behavior, television's impact hardly seems benign. Is there a similar relationship between television viewing and the perception of appropriate roles for women and men?

This research suggests that television viewing may affect an individual's self-evaluation as well as more general perceptions about gender. There are, though, several factors that mediate the effects of television on viewers' perceptions. One factor is the viewer's age. For example, the ability to correctly judge whether a program is fact or fiction increases with age; by about ten or eleven, most children can distinguish fact from fiction in television programming. However, judgments about the plausibility of a program's content (that is, whether the characters and their activities are similar to real life even if the program is fiction) are unrelated to viewer age. Instead, plausibility is related to viewing frequency: Heavy television viewers tend to judge programs as more realistic than light viewers do (Wright et al., 1995). Thus, a person who watches television a lot is more likely to consider the gender portrayals he or she sees as realistic. This does not mean that viewers just passively accept what they see and hear on television. Young women appear to be more critical of television than young men are, and their dissatisfaction stems from the lack of programs about "important and serious issues," as well as the lack of female characters in the programs (MRTW, 1995).

Some have argued that an observed relationship between television viewing and gender stereotyping does not necessarily mean that the television viewing causes the stereotyping. It may be that those who tend to stereotype also tend to watch more television (Courtney & Whipple, 1983), or more programming that confirms the stereotypes they already hold. There is research, for example, that shows that children tend to choose programs that conform to gender stereotypes they have already learned. In other words, the media reinforce gender stereotypes that children are taught both by their parents and

BOX 6.4
Violence and the Media

The debate about the effects of viewing violence is an old one among psychologists and sociologists, legislators and attorneys, representatives of the entertainment industry, and concerned parents. Occasionally, the debate is fueled by incidents involving viewers, especially young viewers, who act out what they have seen in a video game or film. For example, one of the Washington, DC snipers, Lee Boyd Malvo, was said to have been obsessed with the movie, *The Matrix* (BBC News, 2003). The popular video game *Grand Theft Auto* is said to have influenced a car theft ring (Cunningham, Engelstatter, & Ward, 2011). A number of films, including *Natural Born Killers* and *The Program,* have also been implicated in murders and other violent crimes (Mifflin, 1998).

Still, despite thousands of studies examining the question, "Does violent viewing *cause* violent behavior in viewers?" a precise answer remains elusive. Direct cause is extremely difficult to establish in the social sciences. There is a strong relationship between violent viewing and violent behavior, particularly among children and adolescents, but researchers—and representatives of the entertainment industry—are quick to point out that a *correlation* between two variables does not necessarily mean that one *causes* the other. In fact, some argue that there is no relationship between violent crime and media violence (see Ferguson et al., 2008).

There are three major theories about the relationship between violent viewing and violent behavior (Vivian, 1993). One emphasizes the *cathartic effect* of violent viewing. This perspective says that viewing violence can actually reduce the violent drives of viewers because watching allows viewers to fantasize about violence, thereby releasing the tensions that may lead to real-life aggression. It has also been argued that this catharsis may lead viewers to take positive rather than violent action to remedy a problem. For instance, Vivian (1993) reports that following the broadcast of the television movie, *The Burning Bed,*

in which a severely abused woman ultimately kills her batterer-husband by setting fire to his bed while he sleeps, domestic violence agency hotlines were flooded with calls from battered women seeking help.

Vivian also notes, however, that *The Burning Bed* appears to have inspired others to take violent action. One man set his estranged wife on fire and another severely beat his wife, both claiming they were motivated by the movie. Such acts of direct imitation are at the heart of a second theory that focuses on the *modeling effect* of violent viewing. Put simply, this perspective maintains that media violence teaches viewers to behave violently through imitation or modeling. Critics, though, point out that despite the sensationalism surrounding individual acts of direct imitation, they are very rare. Moreover, studies of social learning, as we found in Chapter 4, indicate that there are several intervening factors that play a role in determining whether a specific act will be modeled by others. These include the model's and the learner's relative age and sex, the model's objective status and her or his status in the eyes of the learner, and whether or not the model is rewarded or punished for engaging in the behavior in question.

These and other factors are analyzed by researchers who propose a third theory that emphasizes the *catalytic effect* of violent viewing. This position maintains that if certain conditions are present, viewing violence *may* prompt real-life violence. These researchers talk about violent viewing in terms of *probabilistic causation* rather than direct causation. The violent viewing "primes" the viewer for violent behavior and desensitizes the viewer to the violence and its effects. Thus, violent viewing increases the risk of violent behavior, just like smoking cigarettes increases the risk of developing cancer. If the violence is portrayed as realistic or exciting, if the violence succeeds in righting a wrong, if the program or film contains characters or situations that are similar to those the viewer actually knows or has

(continued)

BOX 6.4
Continued

experienced, and if the viewer's media exposure is heavy, the probability of the viewer behaving violently increases (Bok, 1998; Mifflin, 1998; Vivian, 1993).

Researchers—as well as parents and teachers—have been especially concerned with the effects of violent viewing on children and youth. Escobar-Chaves and Anderson (2008) found that adolescents' television viewing influenced their violent behavior. But research has also found that gender of the viewer is an important factor. Less television viewing by girls was found to be related to less aggressive behavior on their part; less television viewing by boys, though, was not related to their likelihood of aggression (Chowhan & Stewart, 2007). Others report that boys watch more violent programs than girls do, and they also engage in more aggressive and violent behavior (Dodge, Coie, & Lynam, 2006).

Studies indicate that younger children are especially susceptible to media messages because they have difficulty distinguishing between real and fictional images. Some researchers warn that high levels of television viewing by children can contribute not only to violence, but also substance abuse and sexual

exploitation, because these behaviors are often glamorized or depicted as "normal" (Bar-on, 2000). Other researchers clarify that the impact of violent media varies based on the number of hours exposed to violent media and parental supervision and control of children's media use.

Previous government attempts to regulate broadcast hours in order to prevent children from viewing programs or films with adult themes have been struck down by the courts as a violation of the First Amendment (see, for example, N. A. Lewis, 1993). In 1996, Congress passed a law requiring television manufacturers to equip all new televisions they produce with a V-chip that allows parents to block programs they consider inappropriate for children. However, most parents do not use the V-chip to block such programs (Fahri & Ahrens, 2007). In 2007, due to concern over the effect of television violence on children, the Federal Communications Commission (FCC) recommended that Congress enact legislation that would give government the ability to reduce violence in entertainment programming. Fist Amendment experts believe, however, that such regulation is unlikely to withstand court challenges even if it were passed (Fahri & Ahrens, 2007).

in school because children will select those media presentations that conform to what they have previously learned (Media Awareness Network, 2010).

Research on advertising has also generated interesting findings. In a now-classic study, Geis and her colleagues (1984) showed groups of students a series of television ads, some of which were gender-stereotyped and others that portrayed gender-role reversals. They then asked the students to write a short essay about how they pictured their lives ten years into the future. Women who saw the stereotyped ads tended to stereotype their futures; they emphasized homemaking and expressed few aspirations for achievement outside the home. In contrast, women who saw the role-reversed ads wrote essays similar to those of male subjects; their essays were achievement-oriented and had few homemaking themes. The researchers concluded that gender depictions in television advertising may be understood as gender prescriptions by female viewers and may affect their real-life aspirations (see also Baran & Blasko, 1984; but see Martin & Kennedy, 1996, for a somewhat different view regarding the effects of print advertisements, and Millard, 2009 for an analysis of an alternative advertising campaign).

Much research points to the detrimental effects of sexist media portrayals, but these studies are also significant because they indicate that gender-fair media images can have a positive impact. The media, especially television, are teaching tools; what is taught depends on what is shown. The evidence indicates when the media, and television in particular, provide "pro-social" content, they can effectively reduce gender stereotypes and other forms of prejudice. The positive effects of pro-social media content are strongest for young children (Condry, 1989;

Analysts continue to debate whether watching violent media and playing violent video games increases children's likelihood of perpetrating violence in "real life."

Mares, 1996). This suggests that one vehicle for reducing sexism is children's programming. The Federal Communications Commission has taken steps to improve the quality of children's programming; for example, the FCC requires television stations to provide three hours of educational programming to children each week. It remains to be seen whether such efforts are sufficient for achieving the task at hand.

LANGUAGE AND MEDIA AS SHAPERS OF GENDER

In this chapter we have examined the gender images communicated by the primary means by which we give and receive information: language and the mass media. Far from simply reflecting the values and norms of our culture, we have learned here how language and media shape and recreate culture. In this way, language and the media socialize us, and, with respect to gender, much of this socialization takes place through *symbolic annihilation*: symbolically ignoring, trivializing, or demeaning a particular group, which in this case has traditionally been women. We have found, for example, that language "tells a woman she is an afterthought, a linguistic variant, an 'et cetera'" (Butler & Paisley, 1980, p. 50). Newspapers convey a similar message, and magazines, television, and the advertisements that dominate both promote stereotypes of femininity and masculinity.

We have discussed evidence in this chapter indicating that such depictions do have a negative impact on men's and women's behaviors and self-concepts. But we have also reviewed research that shows that the media, particularly television, can be a powerful force in breaking down sexist stereotypes by sensitively and realistically portraying women and men in nontraditional roles. Some observers have argued that reducing sexism in the media will occur only if more women are hired for policy-making posts at newspapers, television stations, and advertising agencies. We, too, advocate a balanced representation of the sexes in these jobs, as well as a more diversified workforce in terms of race and ethnicity, age, sexual orientation, and physical ability. In addition, however, a concerned public must take action. At the very least, we must use nonsexist language in our own communication. Other strategies include letter-writing and email campaigns to newspapers and television stations and boycotts of products promoted in sexist advertisements. If language and the media help construct what comes to be defined as reality, we must act to ensure that the reality constructed is a nonsexist one.

Key Terms

linguistic sexism   ways in which language devalues members of one sex

reflection hypothesis   the belief that media content mirrors the behaviors, relationships, values, and norms most prevalent or dominant in a society

semantic derogation   the process by which the meaning or connotations of words are debased over time

symbolic annihilation   symbolically ignoring, trivializing, or condemning individuals or groups in the media

Suggested Readings

Cortese, A. J. (2007). *Provocateur: Images of women and minorities in advertising,* Third Edition. London: Rowman and Littlefield. An interesting and readable examination of how various aspects of advertisements, including body language and symbols, promote sexual exploitation of women and children, sexual violence, male dominance, and gender and racial/ethnic stereotypes.

Falk, E. (2010). *Women for president: Media bias in nine campaigns.* Chicago: University of Chicago Press. Updated to include Hillary Clinton's 2008 presidential campaign, Falk outlines the media biases present in presidential election races since the first woman ran for the office back in 1872.

Harp, D. (2007). *Desperately seeking women readers: U.S. newspapers and the construction of a female readership.* Lanham, MD: Lexington Books. Examines the newspaper industry's varying degree and type of inclusion of stories and issues involving women from the 1890s to the 2000s.

Postman, N. (2005). *Amusing ourselves to death: Public discourse in the age of show business.* New York: Penguin. An extensive discussion of how television and other social media are affecting the democratic process in the United States and our ability to think independently and critically.

Notes

1. It may be argued by some that a woman supporter of the arts could be called a *patroness* (which literally means "female father"). There are numerous other words like this: poetess, authoress, aviatrix, bachelorette. Miller and Swift (1991a) refer to these as "Adam-ribbisms." In each case, a neutral word is gendered in such a way that the base becomes male and the female is a diminutive. A similar effect is rendered when a gendered word is used to describe an otherwise neutral word. For instance, one often hears "woman judge" or, worse, "lady doctor," but rarely, if ever, "man judge" or "gentleman doctor." In fact, it has been argued that unless the jobholder's sex is identified as female with the adjective *woman,* most people simply assume the jobholder is a man. Thomson, Murachver, and Green (2001) studied the affect of gender-preferential language in e-mails and found that the gender of the author had little to do with the amount of gendered language used. In other words, men and women used gendered word choices equally in e-mails (see Box 6.2).

2. Zimmer (2009) reports the first use of the term *Ms.* as a replacement for *Miss* or *Mrs.* likely happened in a newspaper article in Springfield, Massachusetts in 1901. Lakoff (1990) notes that *Ms.* as a replacement for *Miss* or *Mrs.* has not been as widely accepted as its proponents had hoped, perhaps because it has been derogatorily labeled a "feminist word." It is most often used in place of *Miss,* and it is typically listed along with *Miss* and *Mrs.* as a form an individual may choose for her title of address if she wishes.

3. Interestingly, journalist Marlene Sanders reported in 1998 that whenever she used the word "newswoman," the spell check program on her computer suggested she change the word to "newsman." For the last edition of this text, we tried this with our spell check programs and had the same result. However, when we used "spokeswoman" and "policewoman," the programs offered no suggested changes. Trying the same test-words on our computers in 2011, we were relieved to find none of the three woman forms prompted a spelling change from our word processing programs.

4. An analysis of the sports sections in newspapers and magazines over the last three decades found that only about 10 percent of print media coverage goes to women's sporting news (Bernstein, 2002; see also Chapter 12).

5. According to statistics compiled by the International Women's Media Foundation (2008), the percentage of women working at daily newspapers increased slightly to 37.23 percent after two years of decline.

6. Indeed, *Cosmopolitan* has attempted to capitalize on its image of the "liberated" woman. Back in February 1997, for example, *Cosmo* celebrated "the *Cosmo* Girl—past, present, and future." Who is the *Cosmo* girl? In 1997, she was described as a woman who is both fun and fearless. In 2011, she was described as a woman who wants the magazine's editors to provide the most up-to-date and "hot" news and gossip about celebrities (Cosmo Girl, 2011).

7. McCracken (1993) points out that in addition to overt advertisements, magazines also contain covert advertisements, that is, advertisements camouflaged by the magazine's cover or stories. For instance, an article on how to prevent wrinkles in one's skin typically suggests or mentions various products one can use for this purpose. About 95 percent of the pages of women's magazines are devoted to overt advertising, but no estimate is available on how much space goes to covert advertising. Given the prominence of the ads, however, we must agree with McCracken that women's magazines should be considered "advertising magazines for women." See also Forde, 2002.

8. However, an analysis of the magazine, *Men's Health,* found that male readers are also encouraged to obsess about their body image and sexual attractiveness. The author of the study concluded that the magazine is "peddling a standard of male beauty as unforgiving and unrealistic as the female version sold by those dewy-eyed preteen waifs draped across the covers of *Glamour* and *Elle*" (quoted in MRTW, 1998b, p. 6). In 2010, issues of *Men's Health* featured articles on "looking great at any age" and "building huge arms in a hurry." The March 2011 "Style Special" section included tips on grooming and wardrobes. See Whitton (2001) and Alexander (2003).

9. When women do appear in children's television programs, they are still not depicted as strong, independent people. As Bradway (2010) explains, women are most often shown in a subordinate, supportive role.

10. Some writers claim that certain television crime dramas, such as *CSI* and *CSI: Miami,* have produced what they call a "CSI effect" in criminal jury trials. More specifically, they claim that jurors have become unwilling to convict defendants unless the prosecution can produce fairly sophisticated scientific evidence (e.g., DNA evidence) pointing to the defendant's guilt. Shelton, Barak, and Kim (2007) conducted the first empirical test of the CSI effect. They found that, indeed, study participants did hold high expectations for scientific evidence in criminal prosecutions, but that these expectations were not related to participants' viewing of particular television shows. Instead, they maintain jurors' demands for scientifically based evidence derives from a "tech effect," which is, like the hypothesized CSI effect, a product of changes in popular culture.

Chapter 7

Gender and Intimate Relationships

What do you think of when you hear the words "family" or "intimate relationship"? Maybe the image of someone you love dearly comes to mind. Or perhaps you remember a special event—or just everyday routines that when viewed nostalgically seem special—that you shared with relatives or close friends. Usually, when we think of families and intimate relationships, we think of people and places set apart, emotionally distinct from public life. The intimate environment of home is often thought of as a haven from the more public institutions of our society, such as the economy, the government, and the legal system. For many of us, home is a place where we "let down our hair"; we can be ourselves and still be accepted lovingly by those around us.

If we look carefully at our daily lives, we can easily see that reality is far different from this idealistic view of family life and intimate relationships. We know well from our personal experiences that what happens at home frequently affects our performance on the job and at school, and problems at work or school usually come home with us. For some people, too, home is hardly a protective haven. As we will discuss later in this chapter, domestic violence is a serious social problem in our society—one that disproportionately affects women and children—but is masked by the notion of family privacy.

On a structural level, too, we can see the intersection of the public and private realms of our lives, and this intersection is gendered. The word *family*, in fact, reveals much about the impact of gendered institutional arrangements on our private lives. *Family* derives from the Latin word *famulus*, which means "household servant or slave." Historically, a man's family—his wife, children, and slaves—along with his material possessions, were defined by law as his property, and it was his wife's and children's legal duty to serve him in exchange for his economic support of them. Although few of us think of the family in this way any more, the legal system still exercises considerable control over the family by defining the members' rights and obligations to one another, albeit in somewhat more liberal, but no less gendered, terms.

There are many other ways that the "private" world of the home is intertwined with the public world. For example, the type of jobs adult family members hold outside the home—or their lack of paid employment—affects the family's economic survival, where the family lives, how much time family members have to spend together, and what family members do for recreation (Thorne, 1992). As we will discuss in Chapter 8, the type of job a person is likely to hold, as well as that person's income, is related to gender. At the same time, families are in constant interaction with other institutions in society. For instance, poor families, especially poor women with children, must frequently interact with the state through social service agencies and the welfare system, whereas middle-class and wealthier families may utilize banks, stock brokerage firms, and similar organizations to handle their financial concerns (Thorne, 1992).

In this chapter, we will take a closer look at how the nonfamilial institutions and dominant norms of a society impinge on home life and intimate relationships, especially in terms of gender. At the same time, we'll examine how relations of production and reproduction in the home reinforce or undermine gender relations in society. These are by no means easy tasks, not only because the relationships between families and other institutions are complex, but also because much of our thinking about families is colored by our own familial experiences as well as by the culturally prescribed ideals of our society. In fact, sociology, as both a product and a reproducer of culture, has played a major role in the social construction of cultural images of families and intimate relationships.

To begin, let's look at what sociology has traditionally had to say about the family and then review feminists' critiques of this perspective.

SOCIOLOGY CONSTRUCTS *THE* FAMILY

Aulette (1994) identifies the sociologist Ernest Burgess as the founder of family sociology, but it was the work of Talcott Parsons that essentially shaped this subfield of the discipline from the 1940s to the 1960s.[1] As we discussed in Chapter 1, Parsons was a *structural functional* theorist, and he applied this perspective to his writings on families and home life, as well as gender. His focus was on the **isolated nuclear family**, composed of a husband, wife, and their dependent children. When we say this type of family is isolated, we mean, first, that family members live apart from other relatives (e.g., spouses' parents or siblings). Second, each family unit is isolated in that it is also financially independent of other relatives. Third, the family no longer performs many of its earlier functions—education, care of the sick, production of food and clothing—since these have largely been taken over by public institutions. Instead, the contemporary family has just two vital functions: "first, the primary socialization of children so that they can truly become members of the society in which they have been born; second, the stabilization of the adult personalities of the population of the society" (Parsons, 1955, p. 16).

In the isolated nuclear family, the two adults accomplish these tasks by following distinct and specialized roles: one expressive, the other instrumental. The **instrumental family role** includes leadership and decision-making responsibilities. It is filled by the spouse who is the economic provider for the family, traditionally the husband/father. The wife/mother assumes the **expressive family role**, which means that she does the housework, cares for the children, and sees to it that the emotional needs of family members are met. Although Parsons and other functionalists acknowledged that some married women, even a few with small children, were employed outside the home, they maintained that these women held jobs in the lowest occupational categories so as not to compete with or displace their husbands as chief "status-givers" and wage earners.

Of course, we might ask why this particular role differentiation came about. Why can't men sometimes be expressive and women sometimes be instrumental leaders? Recall from Chapters 1 and 3 that functionalists see these gender roles as rooted in the biological, especially the reproductive, differences between men and women. This role differentiation, they maintain, emerged among early humans as they adapted to physical as well as environmental changes. Because this role differentiation was functional, it was institutionalized over time.

Although much of the functionalist literature on the family was written in the 1950s, it warrants our examination for two reasons: first, because much of the sociological writing on families that followed bears its imprint, and second, because we still hear these ideas echoed today in the "family values" rhetoric of the political right wing. Not surprisingly, this perspective has also had its critics, including feminist sociologists. We noted in Chapter 3 that feminists have questioned functionalists' rendering of gender relations in prehistory, offering an alternative interpretation of the fossil record. Let's consider some other problems inherent in this depiction of the family.

EVALUATING THE FUNCTIONALIST PERSPECTIVE OF THE FAMILY

Critics of the functionalist perspective of the family question the extent to which the contemporary nuclear family is truly isolated from other kin. For one thing, functionalists juxtapose the contemporary family with the preindustrial family, implying that prior to industrialization, families enjoyed an extended structure—that is, grandparents, parents, children, and perhaps other relatives shared a common household. Although cross-cultural research indicates that such arrangements are common in many non-Western preindustrial societies, historical evidence shows that in preindustrial Western societies, extended families were rare, except perhaps among the aristocracy. A short life expectancy precluded the possibility of even a three-generation family for most people. Rather, it is more likely that "three-generation families actually developed as a consequence of industrialization rather than being destroyed by it" (Allan, 1985, p. 6). Moreover, research indicates that many contemporary families are not isolated from extended kin. For example, most senior citizens live near family members, including their adult children and grandchildren. Family members continue to turn first to kin for advice, emotional support, and financial help. Among non-White families, including African Americans, Hispanic Americans, and Asian Americans, and among the working class and the poor, researchers have found extensive kin and friendship networks in which resources are pooled so families can survive hard times (Jayakody & Chatters, 1997; Neighbors, 1997; Stacey, 1990).

Harsher criticism has been leveled at functionalists' rigid differentiation of roles between the sexes. In Chapter 1, we critiqued the role concept itself for depoliticizing the analysis of gender relations. However, there are other problematic aspects of depicting men's and women's roles as instrumental and expressive, respectively. First, this role differentiation erroneously separates public life—what functionalists and others see as the masculine world of work, government, and so on—from the private, feminine world of the family. As we noted at the outset of this chapter, the idea of home as a separate domain from the public world—an idea that sociologists call the **public/private split**—is simply false. In their everyday lives, families do not experience these spheres as separate; they experience the public and private interdependently.

Another major problem with functionalists' rigid role differentiation is that it portrays instrumental and expressive activities as being mutually exclusive and assumes their assignment on the basis of sex is natural. In other words, we are offered *the* male role and *the* female role, which are biologically based, and from this it follows that this arrangement is both normal and unchanging. We challenged this idea in earlier chapters, but we raise it again here because it extends to family forms and thus constructs *the* family as well. However, gender and family arrangements are not biologically given, but rather culturally prescribed and socially learned. Recall that in Chapter 3 we examined anthropological research that demonstrates the fluidity of gender and considerable anthropological data that show tremendous cross-cultural variation in family forms as well as in the division of labor within families. While every known society has a division of labor by sex (and also by age), what is considered men's work versus what is considered women's work varies dramatically from society to society.

We need not look to faraway societies for alternatives to the traditional isolated nuclear family. In the United States, there are many variations in family structure and composition. What are these different family forms? Let's consider them briefly.

Contemporary Families: Diversity and Change

The percentage of families in the United States with children living at home has declined in the past fifty years. According to the U.S. Census Bureau, the number of families with their own child living at home in 2008 decreased to less than half of all families (46 percent) compared with 52 percent in 1952 (U.S. Department of Commerce, Bureau of the Census, 2009b). One reason for the decrease in the percentage of family households with children under age 18 may be because more women are remaining childless. The percentage of women age 40 to 44 who were childless doubled in a thirty-year period. In 1976, 10 percent of women in that age group were childless while in 2006 20 percent of women in that age group were childless (U.S. Department of Commerce, Bureau of the Census, 2009b). Although motherhood is regarded by many as a source of meaning in life (Edin & Kefalas, 2007), research also indicates that women are more likely than men to have positive attitudes about childlessness (Koropeckyj-Cox & Pendell, 2007b). The number of childless or post-childrearing households has also increased, as more couples delay or forego having children and more couples live longer after their children grow up and leave home.

In addition, for two-parent families, the number in which both parents work outside the home has risen substantially. **Two-earner families** in which both adult partners are in the paid labor force have drastically increased and now make up the majority of married couple households with children. In 1970, 30 percent of married women with children under the age of 6 were in the paid labor force, while in 2008, 64 percent of women with children under 6 were in the paid labor force along with 60 percent of women with children under age 3, and 56 percent of women with children under one. In 2008, both mothers and fathers were employed in 62 percent of married-couple families with children (U.S. Department of Labor, Bureau of Labor Statistics, 2009b). It is certainly possible that more women with children would remain in the paid labor force but are unable to do so because of the cost of day care (Bayard et al., 2003; Pollitt, 2005).

It is also important to recognize how the recent economic downturn has influenced the family and men's and women's participation in the paid labor force. While the economic recession hurts both men and women, men have been becoming unemployed more quickly than women have (Rampell, 2010). Since the recession began in December 2007, men have lost 7.4 million jobs and women have lost 3.4 million jobs (Rampell, 2010, p. A10). In January 2010, 10 percent of adult men were unemployed, while 7.9 percent of adult women were unemployed (U.S. Department of Labor, Bureau of Labor Statistics, 2010). In the same month, women held just slightly over half (50.3 percent) of nonfarm jobs in the United States. Even while adjusting for regular seasonal factors (e.g., men are more likely to be employed in jobs that are influenced by the cold weather, such as construction work), women held 49.9 percent of all jobs (Rampell, 2010). Despite this shift, with women more likely than men to be the family breadwinners, the division of labor in the home has not changed. Even when women are breadwinners they continue to maintain more responsibility for child care and housework than men do. Although men often argue that they spend their time searching for employment which prevents them from doing more child care, unemployed men do not spend more time on child care duties than men who are employed (Rampell, 2009).

Recent research conducted by the Pew Research Center also shows that men are more likely now than in the past to be married to women who have more education and income than they do. Among U.S.-born men and women between the ages of 30 and 44, only 4 percent of women earned more than their husbands and 20 percent had more education in 1970. In 2007, 22 percent of women earned more than their husbands and 28 percent had more education (Fry & Cohn, 2010). Despite the increase in the number of women earning more than their husbands, marriage tends to be more financially beneficial overall for men than for women, a point we will discuss further later in this chapter and also in Chapter 8.

While the proportion of married couples with children has decreased in recent decades, there has been an increase in single-parent families. The number of **single-parent families**—families with children but only one adult who has financial responsibility for the household—has grown significantly faster than the number of married couple families. Most single-parent families are headed by women, as we will see shortly. The number of female-headed, single-parent families has grown much faster than the number of married couples with children since 1960 (Gerson, 2010; Schmitt, 2001; Teachman, Tedrow, & Crowder, 2000). Also growing is the number of unmarried heterosexual couples living together (Chandra et al., 2005; Schoen, Landale, & Daniels, 2007). In 2008, 66.9 million opposite-sex couples were living together; 6.8 million of them were not married (U.S. Department of Commerce, Bureau of the Census, 2009a).

Unmarried couples who live together are said to have formed **domestic partnerships**. Such domestic partnerships include not only heterosexual couples, but also gay and lesbian couples. The number of domestic partnerships reported by the Census Bureau is quite likely an underestimate, especially of gay and lesbian domestic partners, since concern about the consequences of homophobia inhibits many from publicly identifying as intimate partners. Some of these relationships may be hidden in the category "nonfamily households," a category that may include what Kath Weston (1991) calls **chosen families**, which are composed of people unrelated by ancestry, marriage, or adoption, but who are nonetheless considered members of the family. Weston studied the chosen families that gay men and lesbians formed with close friends and sometimes ex-lovers after they were shunned by their parents, siblings, and other relatives because of their sexual orientation. She found that chosen families meet many of the same needs for their members as other families do: intimacy, companionship, and financial support. Researchers report, in fact, that these traits are among the hallmarks of a successful family—that is, a family whose members manage the stresses and strains of life together and who resolve their conflicts fairly (Cox, 1993).

We will take a closer look at each of these types of families shortly. For now, however, our point is that diversity rather than uniformity is the best way to characterize family composition in the United States today. In fact, the family forms we have mentioned so far do not even cover all the family forms and kinship networks that researchers have recently identified. *Blended families*, for example, are increasingly common. Blended families form when a couple with children divorces and one or both partners remarry someone who also has children, or the new couples have children of their own, or both.

Similarly, sociologist Judith Stacey (1990) discovered what she calls *accordion households*. In her study of working-class families in California's Silicon Valley, she found households that expand and contract as the needs of various kin, including "ex-familia" (e.g., siblings or parents of divorced spouses), change over time. In accordion households, as kin are taken in and leave, resources are pooled and distributed both as a survival strategy and as a demonstration of caring and love (see also Herbert, 1999).

It appears, then, that the defining characteristics of a family are not official markers, such as marriage licenses, but rather emotional and financial ties. This definition is even being used increasingly by the courts in determining the rights and responsibilities of family members. For example, in a landmark case in 1989, the New York Court of Appeals ruled that a homosexual couple who had lived together for ten years could be considered a family under New York City's rent control regulations. The court reasoned that families are signified not only by signed marriage licenses, but also by long-term, exclusive relationships with the emotional and financial commitment of those involved (Gutis, 1989; see also Dunlap, 1994).

The diversity that characterizes families today is also characteristic of a related behavior, *sexual behavior*. Therefore, before we continue our discussion of diversity in families, let's look at several issues relating to sexuality and sexual behavior.

SEXUALITY, SEXUAL ORIENTATION, AND REPRODUCTIVE FREEDOM

Premarital sex is common among American adults as well as teenagers. Over 90 percent of men and 85 percent of women engage in sexual intercourse before marriage (Chandra et al., 2006). According to the Youth Risk Behavior Surveillance survey of 2006, approximately 47 percent of high school students in the United States reported being sexually active (Centers for Disease Control, 2006). By the age of 20, the vast majority (75 percent) have engaged in premarital sex (Finer, 2007). The median age that men and women first engage in premarital sex is 17.4 (Finer, 2007), but there are differences across racial and ethnic groups. African American high school students are more likely than White and Hispanic students to report having sex (67 percent compared to 44 percent and 52 percent, respectively) (CDC, 2008). Premarital sex is even common for those who consider themselves to be religious (Uecker, 2008). This may be surprising given the "pledging movement," which supports abstinence before marriage and encourages teens to promise or pledge that they will not engage in premarital sex. The first organization, True Love Waits, was founded by the Southern Baptist Convention in 1993. Some fundamentalist Christians have also reinstituted the practices of *courtship* and *betrothal*, in which a couple rejects dating and instead commits to marrying one another *before* they even begin to develop their relationship. They remain celibate until marriage, getting to know one another slowly, often over the course of many years and under the watchful eyes of parents, ministers, and like-minded peers (Goodstein, 2001).

Even teens who are virgins—that is, who have not engaged in vaginal intercourse— are often sexually active. In fact, studies of students in high school have found that students are more likely to engage in oral sex than vaginal intercourse. In addition, teens view oral sex as "not sex" and much less risky than vaginal intercourse in terms of health and emotional and social consequences (Halpern-Felscher et al., 2005). Although oral sex is "safer" than vaginal intercourse in the sense that one cannot get pregnant as a result and it is difficult to contract HIV/AIDS through oral sex (see Chapter 12), many teens mistakenly believe that one cannot contract other sexually transmitted diseases through oral sex. Unfortunately, physicians are reporting an increase in cases of pharyngeal gonorrhea (gonorrhea in the throat) among adolescent girls (Lewin, 2000).[2]

Boys' and girls' assessments of their sexual experiences differs. Researchers have found that adolescent girls and young women report more guilt and less pleasure than adolescent boys and young men after first intercourse. Young women are also less likely to find sexual intercourse satisfying and to express disappointment following first intercourse. A majority of young men (51 percent) say that their primary motivations for their first intercourse were status-seeking, curiosity, and feeling they were ready for the experience (compared with just 24 percent of young women), while most young women (48 percent) say their primary motivations for their first intercourse were affection for their partner and attaining approval (compared with 25 percent of young men) (Hyde & Jaffee, 2000; Little & Rankin, 2001). Less than half of adolescent women reported that they really wanted to have sexual intercourse the first time they did (Abma et al., 2004).

Certainly, attitudes toward premarital sex have become more liberal since the 1970s. For example, in 1972, 37 percent of respondents to a national survey said that premarital sex is "always wrong," compared with just 26 percent who gave that response in 1988. By the early 1990s, only 19.7 percent of respondents felt premarital sex is always wrong (Christopher & Sprecher, 2000; Kain, 1990; Michael et al., 1994). By 2009 the Gallup Poll showed that the majority of Americans (57 percent) believed premarital sex is morally acceptable (Gallup Poll, 2009).

Most teens report that while their friends think it is a good thing to remain a virgin, they also feel pressured to have sex, but girls experience this pressure less than boys (Kaiser Family Foundation, 2003). Some researchers question whether the sexual double standard is, for the most part, a thing of the past. The **sexual double standard** refers to the tradition in our society, and in many others, of permitting young men to engage in sexual activity—or at least ignoring, overlooking, or forgiving their sexual escapades— while simultaneously condemning or punishing the same behavior in girls. Despite the liberalization of attitudes toward premarital sex, however, a good deal of research indicates that the sexual double standard is alive and well. For instance, it is still common for young men to brag about their sexual conquests and win approval as "studs" for being sexually active. Although young women may engage in sexual activity more freely than in the past, they are still expected to do so within a committed relationship, a romance. Girls with multiple partners are often viewed negatively (Hyde & Jaffee, 2000; Kaiser Family Foundation, 2002; Marks, 2008) and girls who refrain from sexual activity are more likely than boys to report positive consequences (e.g., a good reputation) (Brady & Halpern-Felsher, 2008). In addition, female adolescents who are sexually active are more likely to suffer from depression and feel guilty about their behavior (Petre & MacFarlane, 2008; but see also Monahan & Lee, 2008).

We have focused our discussion so far on heterosexual sex. Research indicates that attitudes toward homosexuality have also become more liberal in recent years, although sexual prejudice is still common, as we will see next.

Sexualities

Accurate knowledge and genuine appreciation of sexual relationships other than heterosexual ones have been lacking at least in part because social science research itself has traditionally been heterosexist and homophobic. For example, until recently, it was unusual for anyone to propose an explanation of how or why one becomes heterosexual. Instead, homosexuality—as deviation from heterosexuality, or the "normal"— was what needed to be explained (Hyde & Jaffee, 2000). Moreover, we tend to think of sexual orientation the same way we think of sex and gender: in dichotomous terms (that is, one is *either* heterosexual *or* homosexual). Consequently, **bisexuality**—that is, being sexually and affectionally attracted to both women and men—was overlooked or dismissed by researchers. Bisexuals have often been regarded as heterosexuals who are just "experimenting" or "making due" when an opposite sex partner is not available or homosexuals who are afraid to admit or commit to that particular sexual orientation. However, research shows that bisexuality is a sexual orientation distinct from either heterosexuality or homosexuality (i.e., *monosexuality*) (Rust, 2000). Moreover, studies indicate that bisexuality may be more common than exclusively same-sex behavior (Rothblum, 2000; Rust, 2000).

Based on the 2002 National Survey of Family Growth conducted by the Centers for Disease Control and Prevention, among women between the ages of 18 and 44, 90 percent identify as heterosexual, 1.3 percent as homosexual, 2.8 percent as bisexual, and 3.8 percent as "other." Four percent of men identified as homosexual or bisexual (Mosher, Chandra, & Jones, 2005). However, it remains impossible to determine *precisely* how many homosexuals and bisexuals live in the United States today. For one thing, research shows that a sizable percentage of the population that self-identifies as heterosexual reports having engaged in sexual activities with someone of the same sex, and many self-identified homosexuals report having sex with someone of the opposite sex (Diamond & Savin-Williams, 2000; Laumann et al., 1994). And people may change their sexual behavior over the course of their lives, making it difficult at best to pin specific sexual orientation labels on them (Diamond & Savin-Williams, 2000; Michael et al., 1994). In fact, the longer the time period researchers ask about in their surveys, the less likely the respondent is to be exclusively homosexual or heterosexual (Rothblum, 2000; Rust, 2000).

Perhaps the greatest obstacle to accurately estimating and studying sexual minority groups is the stigma attached to any sexual orientation other than heterosexuality. As a result, many gay men and lesbians, in particular, hide or "closet" their sexual orientation from at least some people (such as researchers) or in certain situations (such as at work) (see, however, Butler, 2000).

Attitudes toward homosexuality have changed in recent years, becoming more positive. According to the Gallup Poll, in 2008 almost half (49 percent) of Americans believed gay or lesbian relations were morally acceptable (Gallup Poll, 2008), and over half (56 percent) believe that sexual orientation cannot be changed (CNN, 2007). However, negative attitudes toward homosexuality and homosexuals are still prevalent among older Americans, as well as those who are less educated, those with lower socioeconomic status, and those with a religious affiliation (Lemelle, 2004; Negy & Eisenman, 2005). Men also tend to be more sexually prejudiced than women (Andersen & Fetner, 2008; Herek, 2000; Herek & Capitanio, 1999; Loftus, 2001; Pew Research Center, 2006; Steffens & Wagner, 2004; Svallfors, 2006), and women are more likely than men to have positive attitudes toward same-sex marriage (Brumbaugh et al., 2008; Steffens & Wagner, 2004).

Largely as a result of social activism on the part of lesbians and gay men, more heterosexual Americans support some rights for homosexuals, including the right of gay and lesbian partners to receive health insurance and Social Security benefits and to inherit one another's property. Since the 1990s, an increasing number of municipal governments, universities, and large corporations (including Disney, Ford Motor Co., General Motors, and DaimlerChrysler Corp.) have extended to same-sex couples the benefits they offer to heterosexual couples. In June 2009, President Obama extended some partnership rights to federal workers in same-sex relationships (Rutenberg, 2009).

Many gay and lesbian rights activists argue that having the right to legally marry is one of the most important affirmations of intimate relationships (see, for example, E. Lewin, 1998). For instance, research exploring the impact of same-sex marriage on homosexual couples in Massachusetts who have been able to legally marry since 2004 found that while couples reported that marriage did not change their own perceptions of their relationship commitment, it changed others' perceptions positively and made family members more accepting of the relationship (Schecter et al., 2008). Some same-sex couples have commitment ceremonies because they cannot legally marry (Hull, 2006). Others, though, reject commitment ceremonies as pointless because they confer few, if any, legal rights on the couple (Reczek, Elliott, & Umberson, 2009). Box 7.1 discusses the controversy surrounding same-sex marriage and civil unions.

BOX 7.1
Same-sex Marriage and Civil Unions

Despite changing attitudes, same-sex marriage and civil unions remain controversial. In 2008, a Gallup Poll reported that 40 percent of Americans stated that same-sex marriage should be legally valid, up from 27 percent in 1996 when the Gallup Poll started asking Americans about same-sex marriage. The Pew Research Center reported in 2009 that just over half (54 percent) of those they surveyed opposed legalizing same-sex marriage (Masci, 2009). Support for same-sex marriage, though, varies across social groups. For example, African Americans express less support for marriage rights for same-sex couples than members of other racial and ethnic groups do (Sherkat, de Vries, & Creek, 2010).

The most common arguments against same-sex marriage is that it is "unnatural" (i.e., marriage is the union of a man and a woman for the purposes of procreation, which is impossible for same-sex couples) and that it weakens the institution of "traditional" marriage. Advocates of same-sex marriage argue, however, that prohibiting same sex-marriage denies citizens equal rights under the law (Olson, 2010).

Since 1995, forty-two states have passed laws or constitutional amendments that ban same-sex marriage (Olson, 2010; Pawelski et al., 2006). Only five states — Massachusetts (in 2004), Connecticut (in 2008), Iowa (in 2009), Vermont (in 2009), and New Hampshire (in 2010) — and the District of Columbia (in 2010) have legalized same-sex marriage. Other states, such as New Jersey, have come close to legalization, but ultimately have fallen short (Juarez, 2010). In California, when San Francisco began offering same-sex couples marriage licenses in 2004, over four thousand couples were married. But the California Supreme Court eventually overturned the licenses, and in 2008 Proposition 8 was approved by voters, overturning California's constitutional right to same-sex marriage. The California Supreme Court upheld the constitutionality of Proposition 8 (Masci, 2009). Unlike the United States, same-sex marriage is legal in many countries around the world.[3]

Ten states — California, Colorado, Hawaii, Maine, Maryland, Nevada, New Jersey, Oregon, Washington, and Wisconsin — recognize civil unions or same-sex domestic partnerships. Civil unions legally are not the same as marriage but carry all the legal rights, privileges, and burdens of marriage, including property rights, inheritance rights, and immunity from being compelled to testify in a court case against one's partner. In order to dissolve such a union, couples must go through a family court. However, as a result of the 1996 Defense of Marriage Act, the civil unions or same-sex marriages formed in states that recognize them may not have legal recognition in other states, and couples have no federal rights or protection.

Certainly, it is in the area of parental rights that lesbians and gay men continue to encounter the greatest hostility and resistance. Indeed, the right for all women and men to decide if and how they will become parents has mushroomed into one of the most hotly contested and divisive issues in the United States over the past four decades. Let's consider, then, the issue of reproductive freedom.

Reproductive Freedom

The term **reproductive freedom** refers to an individual's ability to freely choose whether or not to have a child. Most discussions of reproductive freedom center on an individual's desire *not* to have a child. We will start our discussion with this point, but as we will soon see, the issue of reproductive freedom is not unidimensional and includes concerns that arise as a result of the desire to *have* children.

CONTRACEPTION AND ABORTION   The desires to prevent pregnancy and to control family size are not new. Historical and archeological evidence provide abundant proof that contraceptive methods and abortive techniques have been known and widely practiced for thousands of years. In the United States, though, most methods of contraception, along with abortion, were made illegal by 1850. There are various explanations of why such legislation was enacted. One is that the new laws were the result of efforts by professionally trained physicians to take control of the provision of health care by displacing midwives who had performed and assisted with abortions as well as births (see Chapter 12). Another explanation is that the laws were an attempt by racist legislators and lobbyists to get White women to reproduce so that Whites would not be outnumbered by foreign immigrants and African Americans, whose populations were growing (Gordon, 1976; Luker, 1984; Mohr, 1978).

Whatever the reasons, it is women who have taken—some would say, have been forced to take—responsibility for birth control, so it is hardly surprising that they have led the social movements for planned parenthood and the legalization of contraception and abortion. Many women became active on these issues because they or someone close to them had experienced the stigma of illegitimacy or had suffered the painful, often tragic, consequences of illegal abortions. Minority women and poor women, in particular, frequently contributed to these causes with their health and their lives as the knowing or unwitting subjects in early medical research on the Pill, the IUD, and other contraceptive devices (see Chapter 12).

Abortion and certain forms of contraception remained illegal in this country until the 1970s, when the U.S. Supreme Court issued a series of rulings that made the decision to bear a child part of an individual's constitutionally protected right to privacy. The Court's landmark ruling in *Griswold* v. *Connecticut* (1971) served as a precedent for later cases. In *Griswold*, the Court invoked the right to privacy by invalidating laws that prohibit the use of contraceptives by married couples. One year later, the Court applied this principle in a case involving the distribution of contraceptives to unmarried adults (*Eisenstadt* v. *Baird*). Finally, in 1977, the Court ruled in *Carey* v. *Population Services International* that minors are protected by the same constitutional right to privacy. Therefore, the state cannot interfere in their decision not to bear children by denying them access to contraceptives.

Many young people now find it hard to believe that the distribution and use of contraceptives in the United States were illegal only about thirty years ago, and relatively few would like to see these decisions reversed. As Box 7.2 discusses, these legal changes have played an important role in reducing the rate of teen pregnancies and births in the United States. However, other Supreme Court rulings have generated more controversy, especially

BOX 7.2
Teen Pregnancy and Childbearing

Births to teens reached a record low in 1999, falling below 50 per 1,000 girls aged fifteen to nineteen for the first time since accurate statistics began to be recorded in 1940 (Rubin, 2001). In 2007, the rate of births to teens was 42 births per 1,000 girls aged fifteen to nineteen, but that rate actually alarmed many observers because it represented a 1 percent increase from the previous year (Hamilton, Martin, & Ventura, 2009). What is more, the United States continues to have nearly the highest rate of births to teen mothers among Western countries (Children's Defense Fund, 2005). What accounts for the relatively high rate of teen pregnancies in the United States? And what accounts for racial and ethnic disparities in teen pregnancies and births in this country? Researchers offer several answers to each of these questions.

The decline in teen pregnancies in the United States over recent years has been attributed to a decline in teens having sexual intercourse and also to the fact that those who are having intercourse are more likely to use contraception. Concerns not only about pregnancy, but also about contracting HIV/AIDS have motivated many teens to postpone intercourse, although as we noted earlier this does *not* mean that they are not sexually active. Those who are engaging in intercourse report more condom use than teens in the past, again to prevent pregnancy as well as the transmission of sexually transmitted diseases. More comprehensive sex education in the schools has certainly contributed to this greater awareness and changed behavior, too. Some schools even have condom distribution programs for their students. However, in an amendment to the Welfare Reform Act of 1996, Congress set aside funding only for sex education programs teaching abstinence as the only realistic method for avoiding disease and pregnancy. Unfortunately, there is little evidence that such programs are effective in delaying sexual intercourse among teens (Hampton, 2008; Kohler, Manhart, & Lafferty, 2007; Schemo, 2000).

Perhaps that is why the majority of parents—more than 80 percent according to the Kaiser Family Foundation (2000)—want their teens to learn not only about abstinence through their school sex education classes, but also about how to talk with a partner about birth control, how to use condoms, and how to use and where to get other types of contraception.

The disproportionately high rate of pregnancies and births to African American and Latina teens has been linked to the higher rates of poverty and lower levels of academic success among these populations. According to the Children's Defense Fund (1997), teens who are least likely to get pregnant and give birth are those who: (1) live in financially stable or affluent families; (2) are academically successful; and (3) have high aspirations with opportunities available to fulfill those aspirations (see also Gilligan, Taylor, & Sullivan, 1995; Luker, 1996). Edin and Kefalas (2007) found these factors also affected the likelihood of White teens getting pregnant and giving birth. In fact, in their study of poor White teens in Philadelphia the most powerful motivator for becoming a mother was the feeling among these young women that this was a role in which they could not only succeed, but rather they could excel. Since African Americans and Hispanics are more likely than Whites to be economically disadvantaged, one might expect this belief to be a strong motivator toward motherhood for them as well. Importantly, research shows that the programs most successful in reducing teen pregnancy are those that offer not only sex education, but also tutoring, SAT preparation, job skills, medical and dental care, sports, and creative arts—that is, programs that provide educational, employment, and personal enrichment opportunities (Lewin, 2001). Making contraceptives available, then, is not sufficient. Adolescents must be motivated to abstain from sex or to use contraceptives, and this motivation appears to be spurred by the availability of other opportunities for achieving status and self-esteem,

(continued)

BOX 7.2
Continued

instead of becoming a parent (Edin & Kefalas, 2007; Gilligan et al., 1995; Lewin, 2001; Luker, 1996).

Why the concern about teen pregnancy and childbearing? On a societal level, analysts have primarily focused on the economic consequences, such as increased medical expenses, lost tax revenue, and increased welfare payments. However, it is important to keep in mind that these costs derive from the devastating impact that pregnancy and childbearing have on the lives of teens themselves—especially teenage girls, on whom the burden of the pregnancy and childbearing falls disproportionately—and their children. For teen parents, and in particular, teen mothers, the consequences include

lowered chances of furthering their education, the financial burdens of raising a family, and few job opportunities. Babies born to teens are more likely than babies born to older women to be premature or low birth weight, largely because teen mothers are less likely than older mothers to receive adequate prenatal care (Children's Defense Fund, 2005; United Nations, 2000). These children are also more likely to grow up in poverty or near-poverty, to have various health problems, to have difficulty in school, to become enmeshed in the criminal justice system if they are boys, and to become teen mothers themselves if they are girls (Children's Defense Fund, 2005; Maynard 1996; but in contrast, see Shanok & Miller, 2007).

those dealing with abortion. In 1973, the Court ruled seven to two in the landmark case *Roe* v. *Wade* that women have a constitutionally protected right to choose abortion and that the state cannot unduly interfere with or prohibit that right. In this much misunderstood and hotly debated case, the Court actually made three rulings, one for each trimester of pregnancy. Specifically, the Court ruled that during the first trimester, the decision to abort is a strictly private one to be made by a woman in consultation with a physician; the state has no authority or compelling reason to interfere at this point. During the second trimester, abortion involves more health risks to women, so the state may impose some restrictions, but only to safeguard women's health. It is in the third trimester that the state's role is greatest; the Court ruled that the state may prohibit third-trimester abortions (except when an abortion is necessary to preserve a woman's life or health) because of the *viability* of the fetus—that is, the ability of the fetus to survive outside a woman's body. Importantly, though, in a companion case—*Doe* v. *Bolton*—the Court ruled that any restrictions imposed by the state must be reasonable and cannot inhibit a physician's duty to provide medical care according to his or her professional judgment. Thus, in *Doe* v. *Bolton*, the Court invalidated a number of state restrictions, including those that required two doctors to concur with the woman's decision to abort and a committee approval of the decision.

Since 1973, the Court has consistently reaffirmed the basic principles underlying *Roe* v. *Wade* and has refused to overturn that decision. Nevertheless, in subsequent cases, the Court has made rulings that have placed limits on abortion, making it more difficult for some women—especially teens, poor women, and women who live in rural areas—to obtain abortions. These restrictions include, for example, allowing states to require parental notification and consent when minors seek an abortion. Although the Alaska Supreme Court recently ruled that teenage girls do not need to obtain parental consent to get an abortion in Alaska ("Parents and Abortion," 2008), thirty-five states enforce parental consent or notification laws for minors; all but one of these states (Utah) allow a minor to get approval from the court to have an abortion without parental consent (Guttmacher

Institute, 2008a; Hatziavramidis, 2007). Other restrictions include providing women seeking abortions with counseling on alternatives such as adoption; imposing waiting periods on women seeking abortions; denying Medicaid funds to pay for abortions; and prohibiting abortions in public hospitals. In upholding these restrictions, the Court maintains that it is permitting the states to discourage women from obtaining abortions, although it will not allow the states to obstruct women's choice of abortion (Risen & Thomas, 1998).[4]

These restrictions, along with the increased use of contraceptives and a slight decrease in the number of women of childbearing age, have contributed to a drop in the rate and overall number of abortions performed in the United States. Between 1980 and 2005, the number of abortions per 1,000 women aged fifteen to forty-four declined more than 20 percent, falling from 25 per 1,000 women to 19.4 per 1,000 women in 2005, or 1.21 million abortions (Guttmacher Institute, 2008a). Half of all women having abortions are younger than 25; 37 percent are African American, 34 percent are White, and 22 percent are Hispanic (Guttmacher Institute, 2008a).

Another major factor contributing to this decline has been a decrease in the number of abortion providers. The Supreme Court has ruled that states can require that all abortions be performed by physicians (Carelli, 1997a). Between 2000 and 2005, the number of abortion providers declined by 2 percent (from 1,819 to 1,787) (Jones et al., 2008). Fewer obstetrics and gynecology residents are being trained to perform abortions, and since the mid-1980s there has been a decline in the number of hospitals providing abortion services. By 2005, in fact, 87% of counties in the United States had no abortion provider (Jones et al., 2008).

Another reason for the decline in abortion providers is the growing unwillingness of physicians to subject themselves to the threats and harassment of antiabortion activists (Henshaw, 1995; National Abortion Rights Action League [NARAL], 2000). Although the overall number of harassing incidents of abortion providers has decreased somewhat since the enactment of the federal Freedom of Access to Clinic Entrances (FACE) Act in 1994, physicians and clinic workers continue to report that they are targets of stalking, threats, and other forms of harassment and violence by radical antiabortion protestors. The activities of antiabortion groups have included putting glue in clinic locks, releasing noxious butyric acid inside clinics, picketing abortion providers' homes, harassing their children, and even firebombing clinics and shooting doctors and clinic workers (Clark, 1995; Henshaw, 1995; Navarro, 1996). In May, 2009, a doctor was shot and killed in Wichita, Kansas, by an abortion opponent. Dr. George Tiller ran a clinic that was one of the few in the United States that performed late-term abortions (Davey, 2009).

Public opinion polls show that most Americans personally dislike abortion and feel that it should be discouraged. According to a 2009 Gallup Poll, over half (51 percent) of Americans described themselves as pro-life, an increase from the previous year. A CNN/Opinion Research poll conducted in April 2009, however, found that slightly more people identified as pro-choice than pro-life (49 percent to 45 percent), and the majority (53 percent) believed that abortion should be legal "under certain circumstances" ("According to one poll," 2009). A much smaller percentage of the public supports late-term abortions and abortions performed using what is called the "partial birth" (dilation and extraction or "D & X") technique. Medical technology makes it possible for fetuses born at 23 to 24 weeks to survive (although only about 42 percent of fetuses born at 24 weeks actually do survive beyond the first year of life). However, late-term abortions (abortions performed more than 20 weeks into pregnancy) and abortions using the dilation and extraction method account for a tiny fraction of all abortions; 62 percent of abortions are done during the first 8 weeks of pregnancy, while only 5 percent are done at 16 weeks or later (CDC, 2009a).

In 2000, the U.S. federal government approved prescription use of the abortion pill RU-486 (also known as mifepristone) within the first 7 weeks of pregnancy. The availability of RU-486 allows women to have early abortions without going to abortion clinics. RU-486 has been available in many European countries for much longer. For example, it was approved in France in 1988, in Great Britain in 1991, and in Sweden in 1992. Research indicates that the availability of mifepristone in those countries did not lead to an increase in overall abortion rates (Jones & Henshaw, 2002). In the United States, the overall abortion rate has declined, while the rate of RU-486-induced abortions has increased (Stein, 2008). According to researchers at the Guttmacher Institute, medication abortions more than doubled since federal approval of the nonsurgical method in 2000 (RU-486), from 6 percent of all abortions that year to 13 percent in 2005, but the overall number of abortions decreased by 8 percent (Jones et al., 2008).

As we noted earlier, though, reproductive freedom is not only about abortion and contraception. Perhaps as controversial as abortion are some of the new reproductive technologies that are designed to assist women in becoming pregnant rather than preventing pregnancy.

REPRODUCTIVE TECHNOLOGIES   It is estimated that 7 percent of married women between the ages of 15 and 44 are infertile (Chandra et al., 2005). In addition, there are women, married and unmarried, who wish to have children but for whom pregnancy and childbirth pose severe health risks because of various physical disabilities (Asch, 1989). Postmenopausal women who want to have a child are unable to become pregnant by conventional means. Physically able single women and men may also wish to have children but not to marry or even enter into an intimate relationship to conceive a child. Furthermore, an increasing number of lesbian and gay couples are expressing a desire to become parents. For members of these groups, **reproductive technologies** (RTs) represent a potential solution to what was, less than four decades ago, an all but unsolvable problem.

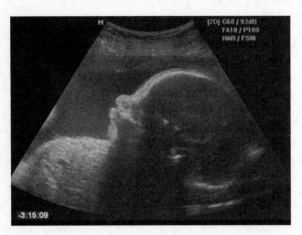

Reproductive technologies are is making it possible for many who previously could not have children to become parents.

After the birth of the first "test tube" baby in 1978, reproductive technology developed rapidly. Today, an array of options is available: in vitro ("test tube") fertilization (IVF), in which eggs are fertilized in a laboratory dish and then the embryos are implanted in the uterus; gamete intrafallopian transfer (GIFT), in which eggs and sperm are injected into the fallopian tubes with the goal that they will unite and produce embryos; zygote intrafallopian transfer (ZIFT), in which embryos fertilized in vitro are transplanted to the fallopian tubes; intracytoplasmic sperm injection (ICSI), in which doctors screen a man's sperm to find the strongest one and inject it into a woman's egg; egg donation, in which one woman's eggs are "harvested" and given to another woman; embryo donation, in which couples allow embryos they have not used to be "adopted" by other infertile couples and implanted in the female partners; and surrogacy, in which a woman, through in vitro fertilization, serves as the "gestational host" for another couple's baby, relinquishing the baby and all parental rights and responsibilities to that couple when the baby is born.

If all of this sounds complicated, be assured that the ethical and legal questions the RTs raise are far more complex than the procedures themselves. For instance, in vitro fertilization yields not one, but several embryos. Embryos not implanted are frozen for possible future use. Who decides the fate of these frozen embryos? What if one partner dies or a couple divorces? Who has "custody" of the frozen embryos (see, for example, Goldberg, 1999b; Gonzalez, 2009)? In surrogacy and egg and embryo donation cases, do surrogates and donors have any parental rights or responsibilities (see Becker, Bowman, & Torrey, 1994; Newman, 2000; Stolberg, 2001)? And what about the children born as a result of the RTs? Do the children have a right to know about their unconventional origins and who their true biological parents are? How do we even define *parent* in these circumstances (see Altman, 1998; Stolberg, 2001)?

While ethicists and legal scholars debate these and many other thorny issues posed by the new reproductive technologies, doctors, donors, and those seeking to have children are currently bound by relatively few regulations. The federal government for the most part has taken a hands-off approach toward regulating RTs, with the exception of issuing standards for fertility clinics in terms of their success rates (Cowan, 1992; Goldberg, 1999b).[5] However, the clinics have been criticized for using methods—such as implanting four, five, even ten embryos at a time into a woman's uterus—to drive up their success rates (Kolata, 1998). This practice gained added notoriety in 2009 when Nadya Suleman, using assisted reproductive technology, gave birth to eight children. Her fertility specialist, Michael Kamrava of the West Coast IVF Clinic in Beverly Hills, had implanted at least six embryos in Suleman's uterus but she delivered eight babies because two embryos split into two sets of identical twins. The controversy in this case, though, centered less on the number of children born than on the fact that Suleman, a single mother, already had six children at home and was not financially stable. Kamrava was subsequently expelled from the American Society for Reproductive Medicine ("Fertility group expels doctor of 'octomom,'" 2009).

Multiple implantations increase the chances of multiple fetuses (e.g., triplets, quadruplets, quintuplets, or even octuplets). In fact, multiple births occur in one in every three births resulting from RTs. These babies, though, are at greater risk of being premature, having low birth weight, and having serious disabilities. To avoid these problems, women found to be pregnant with multiple fetuses are often asked to undergo "fetal reduction"—that is, the selective abortion of one or more of the fetuses—a difficult, heart-wrenching decision for most women, even those who are pro-choice, especially when they went to extraordinary lengths to get pregnant in the first place (Altman, 1998; Kolata, 1998).

Clearly, the issues surrounding the new reproductive technologies pose some difficult dilemmas, not only for legislators, physicians, and ethicists, but also for the individuals who are using these technologies to have children. However, for many people who wish to have a baby but cannot, these issues are moot; they simply cannot *afford* any of the alternatives. None of the procedures is inexpensive, and they are rarely covered by insurance. The high price of the procedures makes them prohibitively expensive for many individuals and couples, even though their desire for a child is as strong as those who can afford the RTs. Surrogates and egg donors are paid for their services and are usually recruited through advertisements placed by fertility clinics or "donor brokers" (private entrepreneurs who are paid a finder's fee for locating donors). Surrogates and egg donors are typically younger and less financially secure than those who pay for these services, raising the possibility that women in need of income will be vulnerable to exploitation by wealthier couples seeking to have children (Shanley, 1993; but see also Hoffman, 1996). And then there is the issue of the "marketplace": Given the rising demand for eggs and reproductive services, as well as the rising costs, there is concern that our reproductive material, as well as babies themselves, are increasingly being seen as commodities to be bought and sold.

In short, social class plays a major role in determining who will and who will not bear children. It is sadly ironic that poor women and women of color are one-and-a-half times more likely to experience infertility, but because of the expense, are the least likely to be able to use any of the RTs we have discussed (Rothman, 1992). Although some feminists see the new reproductive technologies as potentially liberating for women by giving them greater control over the reproductive process, others are deeply concerned that such technologies turn children into products and may also give rise to a "breeder class" of women composed primarily of poor women who rent their bodies or sell their eggs to the wealthy (Goldberg, 1999a; Raymond, 1990; Shanley, 1993). The controversy is not likely to be resolved soon, even among feminists.

What is certain is that the new reproductive technologies are contributing to the growing diversity of family forms in this country. Let's discuss, then, various types of families and intimate relationships.

VARIETIES OF INTIMATE RELATIONSHIPS

Heterosexual Marriages

Although most of us think of marriage in romantic rather than legalistic terms, a marriage is a legally binding contractual agreement. Unlike most contractual agreements, though, the conditions of the marriage contract cannot be changed or negotiated by the two parties involved. Only the state has the right to set the terms of the marriage contract. In fact, the contracting parties in a marriage rarely even review the conditions of their agreement before entering into it.

Historically, a marriage contract specified an exchange relationship between husband and wife. A wife's obligations included housework and complying with her husband's requests for sex. In return, the husband was obliged to financially support his wife, although he could determine the level of financial support he considered appropriate. The law granted husbands all decision-making authority in the family (Lindgren & Taub, 1993).

Nowadays, when we think of marriages, we think of partnerships, not exchanges. However, as we have already noted, marriages are still subject to government regulation, which defines the rights and responsibilities of spouses and specifies who may marry in terms of age, sex, and health requirements. There is tremendous variation among the fifty states as to the specific conditions of their marriage contracts, but most share several underlying assumptions, which bear some resemblance to marriage contracts historically.

For example, some states continue to assume that the husband is the head of the family. Only in the 1970s did U.S. Supreme Court decisions begin to overturn state laws that impose the sex-based hierarchy in marriage.

Marital relations, then, are fundamentally power relations—usually the power of husbands over wives. As we saw in Chapter 1, power is essentially the ability to get others to do what we want them to do whether they want to do it or not. It is the ability to get one's own way. Again, however, many of us resist the idea of marriages as power struggles because we like to think that spouses are equal and if they disagree, they try to compromise. Does research support this view?

The answer to this question depends on how we measure power in marriage. Traditionally, sociologists measured marital power in terms of decision making. This strategy was developed in 1960 by Robert Blood and Donald Wolfe, who asked more than nine hundred wives who had the final say in such decisions as where to go on vacation, what car to buy, how much money to spend on food, where to live, and what doctor to consult. In general, their findings showed husbands to be more powerful than wives because they made most family decisions even though they usually talked matters over with their wives. Nevertheless, there were conditions under which this pattern varied. Blood and Wolfe found that the spouse who brought more "resources" to the marriage—for example, income, status, or education—was likely to be more powerful. Typically, this was the husband, but the greater a wife's resources, the more leverage she gained in decision making relative to her husband.

Although Blood and Wolfe's study was conducted more than fifty years ago, their findings have been substantiated by more recent research that has also found that, in most cases, the partner who earns more money tends to be the more powerful partner as measured by decision making. The more women earn relative to their husbands, the more power they accrue in the marriage; full-time homemakers, it seems, have little power (Blumstein & Schwartz, 1983). Nevertheless, there are also important exceptions. For instance, among couples who adhere to the belief that men should be the primary family breadwinners, husbands are more powerful regardless of either partner's earnings. The prevailing logic in such marriages is that if it is the man's role to be the family provider, then he should have the final say in most decisions (Thompson & Walker, 1989).

Pyke (1994) argues that a significant intervening variable in determining a couple's relative power in marriage is the *meaning* couples give to women's paid employment and unpaid household labor. For example, in her study of women in second marriages, Pyke found that some women, upon remarriage, moved out of the paid labor force into the role of full-time homemaker, but simultaneously increased their marital power. This is because during their first marriages, the women were employed in low-paying, low-status jobs, and the economic resources they brought to the marriage were devalued by their husbands. Their paid employment was not a source of marital power, but rather a source of exploitation and domination by their first husband. They viewed their withdrawal from the labor market on remarriage as a sign of their greater marital power and of the increased support of their new spouses. The value their second husband attached to their unpaid work in the home was evidenced in their husband's expressions of gratitude for this work and by power-sharing between the partners.

Such findings alert us to the fact that there is more to marital power than we can discern just by asking questions about family decision making. For one thing, not all decisions carry equal weight; some are more significant in their consequences than others

(Allan, 1985). In addition, power includes not only the authority to make decisions, but also the right to *delegate* responsibility for certain decisions to others (Blumstein & Schwartz, 1983). Finally, the old adage, "Actions speak louder than words" applies here. Some social practices are so taken-for-granted, so deeply embedded in ideology and family structure, that decisions do not have to be made about them; they are automatically carried out and rarely questioned (Allan, 1985). For example, even in marriages in which couples say they share power equally, researchers have found subtle, but important, power differences: Wives are more likely than husbands to worry about offending or upsetting their spouses, to accommodate to their spouse's needs and desires, and to adjust their schedule to their spouse's schedule (Kudson-Martin & Mahoney, 1998).

Perhaps, then, we can learn more about power in heterosexual marriages by observing who *does* what—that is, the division of household labor—and who benefits from it, rather than asking who decides what. Let's consider the division of household labor among heterosexual couples.

GENDER AND HOUSEWORK: WHO DOES WHAT?   When it comes to housework, research consistently shows that wives spend more time on these chores than husbands do. One review of more than two hundred scholarly articles and books on the subject found that although women have reduced and men have slightly increased their hourly contributions to routine household tasks, women still do at least twice as much housework as men do (Coltrane, 2000). Of course, this may not seem unfair if spouses are exchanging services according to the traditional marriage contract: She does the housework and he works in the paid labor force for their financial support. However, as we noted earlier in the chapter, this arrangement applies to only a small percentage of couples today. Most married women, like their husbands, are employed outside the home, and although husbands in two-earner families spend more time on housework than men who are sole breadwinners, they still do less than their wives. Husbands typically express a willingness to "help" their wives with the housework, but even among two-earner couples, the commonly held belief of both men and women is that housework is primarily "women's work" no matter what other demands wives have on their time (Coltrane, 2000; Shelton, 1992; Wilkie, 1993). Consequently, employed wives end up working what sociologist Arlie Hochschild (1989) calls the "second shift": They are wage earners for part of the day and then come home to still more, albeit unpaid, work.[6]

In fact, if you ask full-time homemakers what kind of work they do, they typically reply, "I don't work; I'm a housewife." What is so striking in such a response is that despite the fact that housework is socially and economically necessary work, it is not considered real work, not even by the women who have primary responsibility for doing it. One reason housework is not considered real work is that it is unspecialized, covering by some estimates more than eighty different tasks. It is also repetitive in that, in a sense, it is never fully finished: No sooner is a chore completed than it must be done again. This is because housework involves production for immediate consumption.

Another reason housework is not thought of as "real" work is that, unlike work in the paid labor force, there is no fixed work schedule for housework. Homemakers rarely get time off, not even holidays—who, for instance, cooks those large holiday meals? Housework also differs from what we usually think of as "real" work in that it is intertwined with love and feelings of care. It is also privatized. We see people leaving their houses *to go to work*; we see them in public on the job. But housework is done in isolation in the home, and much of it is done when other family members are elsewhere (e.g., in the labor force or at school). And of course, one of the main reasons housework is not considered "real" work is that it is *unpaid*. In a society such as ours, individuals' status—how much people are valued by others as well as by themselves—often is measured by how much money they make.

Usually, when complaints about doing housework are raised, someone quickly points out how much easier it is today than in the past; after all, contemporary homemakers have so many labor-saving appliances at their disposal. However, research indicates that today's homemaker spends about as much time on household chores as a homemaker in the late eighteenth century did (Cowan, 1984; Ogden, 1986). This is due in part to the fact that over the past two hundred years, as our standard of living has risen dramatically, so have our expectations of comfort and cleanliness at home. In addition, the average house is larger than it was two centuries ago, so there are more rooms to clean, and these rooms are filled with many more personal possessions. Our intent here is not to romanticize the past nor to suggest that homemakers would be better off if we turned back the clock. Rather, our point is that housework, despite technological advances and modern convenience, continues to be arduous and time-consuming work, and in most households, more of women's time than men's time is consumed by it.

Apart from the amount of time wives and husbands spend on housework, there are also differences in the kind of work they do around the house. Wives usually do most of the daily chores, such as cleaning and cooking. Men do less regular and less repetitive chores. So, for example, most wives prepare their families' meals, which must be done at least once or twice a day, every day. Husbands, though, usually mow the lawn and make minor repairs around the house, chores that need to be done only occasionally. Wives experience more time constraints because of the types of household chores they do, whereas husbands have more control over when they will do their chores (Hochschild, 1989; Shelton, 1992). Working the "second shift" means that wives have less leisure time. Wives also must balance home and employment responsibilities in ways that most husbands are not required to do. Husbands' relative freedom from housework lets them pursue employment opportunities, while wives may face restrictions on their employment opportunities because of their household responsibilities (Shelton, 1992; but for a different view, see Hochschild, 1997). However, the more income the woman contributes to the household and the more hours she works, the smaller her share of housework (Cunningham, 2007; Mannino & Deutsch, 2007; Portman & Van der Lippe, 2009). Even when women are breadwinners, they continue to shoulder the responsibility of caring for children and the home (Kalil, 2009; Rampell, 2009). Women's decrease in time spent on housework does not necessarily mean that men are picking up the extra household or child care duties. Women may just find ways to lessen their burden (e.g., hiring a cleaning service, picking up fast-food meals).

In addition, employed women, especially those who work long hours, experience more work-family conflict and more stress (see Blair-Loy, 2001; Moen & Yu, 2000; Stone, 2007). Moreover, there is a motherhood penalty for women in the public labor market as employers assume that women with children cannot efficiently balance work with motherhood (Correll, Benard, & Paik, 2007; Glauber, 2007; Winslow-Bowe, 2009 see also Chapter 8). The myth that women cannot balance a career with motherhood persists even though research that indicates that women are able to simultaneously value motherhood with involvement in the paid labor force despite the challenges and stress (see McQuillan et al., 2008).

There is also a wage penalty for mothers, In contrast, married men actually earn more when they become fathers. Research has found that for married African American men, fatherhood is associated with a 7 percent increase in wages and, for married White and Latino men, fatherhood is associated with a 9 percent increase in wages (Glauber, 2008, p. 17; see also Chapter 8). There is no wage increase for unmarried fathers (Glauber, 2008).

There is no denying that many couples today do strive to be more egalitarian, especially early on in their marriages, with a more equal division of labor between spouses. Men may also reduce their time in the paid labor market to spend time with their wives and children (Magnuson, 2008). However, even couples who wish to be egalitarian often find that their effort toward an equal division of labor breaks down when they become parents. Let's consider, then, the caregiving responsibilities of two-parent, heterosexual families.

CAREGIVING   Despite the widespread belief that the birth of a child brings marriage partners closer together, sociologists as well as marriage and family counselors have learned that the addition of children to a household increases stress and lowers marital satisfaction (Cox, 1985; Larson, 1988). This observation is not really so puzzling. Although new parents are typically excited about the birth of their baby, they are rarely prepared for the level of disruption that a baby causes in their lives. For example, their sleep is frequently interrupted and lessened. There is, by necessity, less spontaneity in the relationship and less time to pursue outside interests. Financial pressures increase, as do household chores, and as the couple becomes immersed in parental roles, the partner/lover roles get squeezed out (Cowan & Cowan, 1992, 1998).

Nevertheless, these stresses do not affect mothers and fathers equally. Although most men today are present at the birth of their children, they typically are significantly less involved than women in primary child care (e.g., bathing, changing clothes, feeding). They do spend more time on child care than they do on housework (Bianchi & Raley, 2005; Mannino & Deutsch, 2007). Nonetheless, although men's involvement in child care has increased during the past thirty years, especially in households in which both spouses are employed, women do more child care than their husbands (Arendell, 2000; Mannino & Deutsch, 2007).

In general, research shows that fathers tend to be least involved in primary child care when their children are infants. They become more involved when the children are around eighteen months old and walking and talking. Their greatest level of involvement occurs during the middle childhood period when the children are five to fifteen years of age. Even then, the time fathers spend with their children is more oriented to recreation or academics—playing, reading to them, teaching them something, coaching them—than to primary caregiving (Doucet, 2009; Thompson & Walker, 1989). Some research has indicated that African American fathers are more involved with child care than Latino or European American fathers (Shears, 2007). When fathers do participate in child care, they tend to spend more time with sons, both in the household and on outings, than they do with daughters (Gerstel & Gallagher, 2001). And not only do women do more of the primary child care, but they also do more of the "mental work" – e.g., worrying, seeking advice and information – involved in rearing children (Walzer, 1996).

Women who work outside of the home face more struggles balancing work with child care responsibilities than men do (Hammer et al., 2005). Mothers are more likely to adjust their work schedules to meet children's needs (Maume, 2008) and are also more burdened than fathers with facilitating children's organized "leisure activities" (extracurricular activities, sports) (Lareau & Weininger, 2008). However, research indicates that mothers report struggling less trying to balance work and family responsibilities when their husbands are more involved with child care and have more flexible work schedules (Fagan & Press, 2008).

Fathers also overestimate their involvement with their children. Mickelson (2008), for example, found that fathers reported spending almost 18 percent more time engaged in activities with their children than mothers reported that fathers did. In many households where husbands report that they and their wives share tasks equally, observations of husbands' behavior and their own words contradict them. Their wives usually must ask them to help and tell them specifically what to do (Deutsch, 1999; Walzer, 1996).

Some men say they would welcome greater involvement in the care of their children, but their chief responsibility as a husband/father is breadwinner, and the structure of work in our society makes it difficult, if not impossible, for them to do more at home (Arendell, 2000; Shelton, 1992; Snarey, 1993; Walzer, 1996; Weisner, Garnier, Loucky 1994; Wilkinson et al., 2009). As we will discuss in Chapter 8, the occupational structure of our society has traditionally operated under the assumption that men are the economic providers of families and women are the caretakers. Men are expected to invest time and energy in their jobs; women are expected to do so in their families. So even though the federal Family and Medical Leave Act now requires companies with more than fifty employees to provide women *and* men with up to twelve weeks unpaid family leave with no loss of seniority, many employers still say that male employees should not take family leave (Levine, 2000). Indeed, if one accepts the traditional gendered model of employment and parenting, there is no need for family leave, child care facilities, or equal pay for women and men.

Research has shown that men who hold white-collar professional, technical, and managerial positions are more likely than men in municipal and service jobs to be subjected to this sort of pressure. Men in lower-paid, blue-collar jobs have greater flexibility in their work schedules. Because of economic necessity, most of their wives also work outside the home, many in municipal and service jobs, too. These couples are less likely than white-collar professional couples to be able to afford paid child care, so the men have assumed a greater share of this responsibility. About 25 percent of fathers of children under age five, living in two-earner families, care for the children while their wives are working. Black and Hispanic preschoolers whose mothers were employed outside the home were more likely to be cared for by their grandparents than their fathers. Among preschoolers of employed non-Hispanic White mothers, about the same percentage were cared for by their fathers and their grandparents (29 percent) (U.S. Department of Commerce, Bureau of the Census, 2008g).

This gendered division of caregiving has advantages and disadvantages for both women and men. On one hand, women reap the benefits of developing close bonds with their children and of watching and contributing to their children's growth and development. These are experiences that most mothers find gratifying and emotionally fulfilling. At the same time, through their ties to their children and to their own parents and siblings, women are also *kinkeepers* in families; that is, they link the generations within the families and therefore are instrumental in preserving family cohesion. Kranichfeld (1987, p. 48) has identified this kinkeeping role as a source of family power in that as kinkeepers, "women do not just change the behavior of others, they shape whole generations of families" (see also Arendell, 2000; Collins, 1990; Stacey, 1990).

This almost exclusive responsibility for caregiving denies women much personal autonomy, however. Housework can at least be postponed but a child's needs must be met immediately. Child rearing, then, imposes severe limits on a mother's time and ability to pursue other interests, such as paid employment and leisure activities (Walzer, 1996). Fathers who have assumed an equal or near-equal role in child care have been quick to recognize these time constraints and the frustration they can entail (Deutsch, 1999; Lawlor, 1998).

The kinkeeper role can also be very stressful. For instance, women's midlife options may be constrained because their adult children need assistance with their own households or families or because elderly parents need care (Gerson, Alpert, & Richardson, 1984; Gerstel & Gallagher, 2001). An estimated 5.7 million children are living in a household with a grandparent present; 6.1 million grandparents have grandchildren under the age of eighteen living with them, 2.5 million grandparents are responsible for grandchildren's basic needs, and the vast majority of these caregivers are grandmothers (U.S. Department of Commerce, Bureau of the Census, 2007). This could be due to several reasons including poverty, parent's incarceration, parent's substance abuse, abandonment, or child abuse (Hayslip & Kaminski, 2005). Not surprisingly, assuming the primary caregiver role can be very stressful for grandparents, although social support may help relieve some of this stress (Gerard, Landry-Meyer, & Roe, 2006).

Similarly, four out of five disabled elderly living in the community rely on assistance from family members and others, but three of five rely exclusively on unpaid help, which typically is given by wives and adult daughters (Bogenschneider, 2000). Most adult female caregivers are employed outside the home; the majority are employed full-time (Montgomery & Datwyler, 1990). These women are attempting to balance careers, caring for their own children, and caring for elderly parents. According to the 2009 Caregiving in the U.S. study, almost two-thirds of surveyed caregivers have reported late to work or taken time off during the workday

An increasing number of adults are now caring for grandchildren or an elderly parent or both, and most of this responsibility falls on women who then have less time for their own pursuits.

because of caregiving issues (American Association of Retired Persons (AARP), 2009), an increase of about 8 percent from 2004. In addition, 10 percent of respondents to the 2009 survey stated that they needed to rearrange their work schedule or take a less demanding job to care for older adults. Also problematic is that the average age of the caregiver as well as the elderly parent has increased over the years. In 2004, the average caregiver was

46.4 and the average elderly care recipient was 66.5. In 2009, the average caregiver was 49.2 and the average recipient was 69.3. What has not changed however is the fact that most (66 percent) caregivers are women (American Association of Retired Persons [AARP], 2009).

In short, the research indicates that most men still escape many of the burdens of family care. They are relieved of the drudgery and the time constraints so that they may join the labor force to financially support their families. But if men have more freedom to give their time and energy to their jobs, the trade-off is social and emotional distance from their children. Research shows that children typically report feeling more closely attached to their mothers than their fathers and that mothers are usually more positive and supportive of their children than fathers are (Arendell, 2000). Although we are speaking here of intact two-parent families, there is a sense in which such families are "father absent." Both children and fathers are hurt by fathers' noninvolvement. Studies show that positive father involvement is beneficial to children and that fathers who spend time alone caring for their infant children remain more involved as parents in the ensuing years (Marsiglio et al., 2000; Orenstein & Van Straalen, 2001). The loss for fathers can perhaps best be found in the words of fathers who have taken responsibility for the care of their children. These men say that child care has made them more sensitive, less self-centered, and more complete as human beings (Coltrane, 1989; Deutsch, 1999; Lawlor, 1998; Levine, 1997; Snarey, 1993).

Single-Parent Families

The issue of shared parenting is irrelevant in single-parent families, where only one parent is present to meet all the children's needs. Most (87.5 percent) children living in single-parent households live with their mothers only: 84 percent of White children in single-parent families, 93 percent of African American children in single-parent families, and 92 percent of Latino children in single-parent families (U.S. Department of Commerce, Bureau of the Census, 2007).

Since the 1970s more U.S. children are being raised by single parents (Amato & Maynard, 2007). Part of the increase reflects the growing number of women who have children, but remain unmarried. In 1970, single mothers were 12 percent of families with children under 18; by 2002, they were 26 percent of families with children under 18 (Johnson & Favrault, 2004). In 2007, nearly four in ten U.S. births were to unmarried women, an increase of 4 percent from 2006. What is important to note, however, is that adult women age twenty and older account for much of this increase. In fact, the birth rate for teenage mothers has dramatically decreased over the past thirty years (see Box 7.2). In 1970, half of all births to unmarried women were to teenagers; in 2007, only 23 percent of all births to unmarried women were to teenagers. On the other hand, in 2007, over half (60 percent) of births to unmarried women were to women between the ages of twenty and twenty-nine and 17 percent were to women thirty or older (Ventura, 2009).

Both women and men may become single parents by being widowed, although the percentage of single-parent families in which the parent is widowed has declined since 1970. The most common way women and men become single parents is through divorce. Approximately half of couples divorce within eight years of pronouncing their wedding vows, and approximately one out of five adults has been divorced (Kreider, 2005).

Eleven percent of all people age fifteen and older are divorced (U.S. Department of Commerce, Bureau of the Census, 2009d). However, the divorce rate has remained relatively stable since 2000 and actually decreased slightly between 2007 and 2008 (3.6 per 1,000 to 3.5 per 1,000) (National Center for Health Statistics, 2009).

Before the Industrial Revolution, fathers were usually awarded legal custody of their children, not only because they had the economic means to support them but also because children were considered their father's property and the father was entitled to any products of their labor during their minority. As the Industrial Revolution progressed and production and education moved away from home, dominant ideas about childhood changed. Instead of being viewed as miniature adults, children came to be seen as helpless dependents in need of nurturing. Child rearing experts advised that mothers were better caregivers than fathers. By the turn of the twentieth century, the courts had adopted the *tender years presumption*—the idea that a young child needs to be with his or her mother—which produced a dramatic shift in custody decisions in favor of mothers and against fathers (Lindgren & Taub, 1993).

Today, nearly all state courts are forbidden from using gender-based presumptions in awarding custody. In most cases, mothers and fathers are granted equal rights in preserving their relationships with their children, and most judges favor joint custody arrangements. Such arrangements may involve *joint legal custody*, which gives parents equal decision-making authority in rearing their children, or *joint physical custody*, which means that children will reside with each parent on specified days, and both parents will have equal responsibility for the children's care and financial support. Such arrangements also typically spell out day care provisions, if needed, and specifications regarding children's education, health care, and any other matter significant to the parents or children (Bartlett, 2000). The guiding principle in determining custody arrangements is supposed to be in the "best interests of the child," and studies show that children adjust best to their parents' divorce when both parents remain actively involved in parenting following the marital break-up (Lamb, 1999). However, research indicates that such joint custody or co-parenting arrangements work well when the divorcing parents are able to maintain a high level of cooperation with one another and thus avoid involving their children in further conflicts (Ayoub, Deutsch, & Maraganore, 1999). In some states, there is a statutory presumption in favor of joint custody. Courts have even ordered joint custody in cases in which divorcing parents could not reach a custody agreement, mistakenly assuming that if joint custody is imposed, parents will be forced to cooperate with one another (Hardesty, 2002; Lindgren & Traub, 1993). In such cases, physical custody is usually awarded to the parent—typically, though not always, the mother—who is believed to be most willing to facilitate the continued parental involvement of the ex-spouse (Hardesty, 2002).

The number of single fathers has increased significantly in recent years (10 percent of single parents in 1970, 21 percent of single parents in 2010) (U.S. Department of Commerce, Bureau of the Census, 2010). Some observers attribute this increase to the success of fathers' rights groups in the United States and Canada, who have lobbied aggressively to change public and legal views of single fathers, particularly with regard to how child custody laws, child support laws, and visitation arrangements affect fathers (Crowley, 2006; Dragiewicz, 2011). Crowley (2006) conducted interviews with 158 members of fathers' rights groups in the United States and found that men (and some women) joined these groups for legal and emotional assistance while addressing their own child support and custody issues; 17 percent joined to try to change public policy and laws they believe are unfair to fathers. Some scholars argue that fathers' rights groups are an example of antifeminist backlash (Dragiewicz, 2011). Dragiewicz (2011), for example, points out that fathers' rights groups have opposed the Violence Against Women Act as well as anti-domestic violence efforts, since the amount of child support ordered by the court is contingent on the amount of time the child spends in the care of both parents. Allegations of domestic violence influence custody decisions, often resulting in mothers being awarded more custodial time with children, which in turn influences child support payments.

Although researchers have shown interest in fathers' rights groups, little research has been conducted with single fathers, especially fathers who live only with their children (approximately 7 percent of all single parents) (Hook & Chalasani, 2008; U.S. Department of Commerce, Bureau of the Census, 2011). The studies that have been done show that the single-parenting experiences of men and women differ in some ways. First, single fathers are less likely than single mothers to engage in various activities with their children, particularly with adolescent children (Hawkins, Amato, & King, 2006). Single fathers are more involved with their children than married fathers are, but they are less involved than single mothers are (Hawkins et al., 2006; Hook & Chalasani, 2008). Second, single fathers note that their social lives and careers become restricted by the demands of parenting and that they are often treated by others as less able or incompetent parents (Greif, 1985; Hanson, 1988; Teltsch, 1992). Research suggests that single fathers receive more support from friends, relatives, and neighbors than single mothers do because they are seen as needing it. As a result, single mothers often report feeling isolated (Kamerman & Kahn, 1988; Teltsch, 1992). Most single mothers, like single fathers, struggle to fulfill employment responsibilities without sacrificing the well-being of their children. Some of these women face career dilemmas that are similar to those of single fathers, but because women are less likely than men to have high-status, high-income jobs (see Chapter 8), their employment constraints are more often inflexible work schedules, inadequate salaries, and unaffordable or inadequate child care facilities. Simply finding a job may be difficult for a single mother, particularly if she has been out of the labor force for a number of years and has little work experience or has little education and few marketable skills. Not surprisingly, then, the biggest problem of most single mothers is money (Holden & Smock, 1991; Kurz, 1995; Seccombe, 2000).

Table 7.1 gives us a good indication of the financial problems of single-parent, female-headed families. Additional data indicate that in 2008 5.5 percent of married-couple families were living in poverty compared with 13.8 percent of male-headed families with no spouse present and 28.7 percent of female-headed families with no spouse present (U.S. Department of Commerce, Bureau of the Census, 2009c, 2008). A child living with only his or her mother is five times as likely to be poor as one living with both parents, while a child living with his or her father is two-and-a-half times as likely to be poor as one living with both parents (Children's Defense Fund, 2008; see also Stirling & Aldrich, 2008).

Researchers tell us that women, more than men, are hurt economically by divorce (Gadalla, 2009), and because they are most likely to have custody of their children, the children also suffer the economic consequences. One of the reasons women experience greater economic disadvantage following divorce is due to limited child support payments. In 2007, of the 6,375 custodial parents who were owed child support, 87 percent were mothers (U.S. Department of Commerce, Bureau of the Census, 2011). When women

TABLE 7.1	Median Family Income by Type of Family and Race/Ethnicity, 2008			
	Median Income ($)			
Type of Family	**All families**	**White, non-Hispanic**	**Black**	**Hispanic**
Married couple families	73,010	77,502	61,631	48,702
Male householder, wife absent	49,186	52,472	41,673	43,187
Female householder, husband absent	33,073	36,372	26,205	27,191

Source: U.S. Department of Commerce, Bureau of the Census, Current Population Survey, 2009. Annual Social and Economic Supplement. Retrieved February 18, 2010, http://www.census.gov/hhes/www/cpstables/032009/hhinc/new02_000.htm.

are awarded custody of children, they maintain responsibility for child care that can result in time lost from work and lost wages when children are sick or child care is unavailable. Furthermore, despite the increase in the percentage of women who earn more than their husbands, women generally receive lower wages than men, a point that we will examine at greater length in Chapter 8. Changes in social assistance programs, such as the 1996 Personal Responsibility and Work Opportunity Reconciliation Act (PRWORA), which transformed welfare from an income support program to a work and self-sufficiency program, have also contributed to the difficult economic circumstances of single mothers. Some single mothers who previously may have received cash assistance, food stamps, and housing subsidies following divorce, either are no longer eligible or are eligible for a limited period of time and then must transition to jobs, most of which do not pay enough to lift the women and their children out of poverty (Porter & Dupree, 2001). We will take up this issue again in Chapter 8.

It is important to recognize, however, that while divorced women often face financial difficulties, the extent of these difficulties is significantly affected by the family's financial status prior to the divorce. For instance, as we have pointed out, it is much more common today for both partners to work outside the home prior to divorce. In two-earner families—the majority of families today—women's income is critical to the family's well being, so that husbands in such families may end up experiencing a financial loss following divorce as well (McManus & DiPrete, 2001). Because of the recent economic recession, and the fact that men are losing jobs faster than women are, women are now slightly more likely than men to be the family's wage earner (Rampell, 2010). Furthermore, the wage gap between men and women has slightly narrowed (Oldham, 2008), and there has been an increase in the percentage of women who earn more than their husbands, although they remain a minority (Fry & Cohn, 2010; Raley, Mattingly, & Bianchi, 2006; see also Chapter 8). This is more likely the case for African American women than for White women (Winslow-Bowe, 2009).

Some analysts believe that both divorce and the lack of child support enforcement are major contributing factors to the *feminization of poverty*, that is, the high percentage of the total poverty population composed of women and their children (see Chapter 8). Within the poverty population are the *new poor*: people, many of whom are women, who were not born into poverty but who have been forced into it by recent events in their lives. According to researchers, a change in family composition, such as separation, divorce, marriage, remarriage, or becoming a parent, is the single most important factor affecting the economic well-being of families; the second most important factor is the labor market participation of family members, that is, who works outside the home (Holden & Smock, 1991; Kamerman & Kahn, 1988). Consequently, Bane (1986) refers to the poverty experienced by some recently divorced women and their children as *event-driven poverty.*

The feminization of poverty and the concept of the new poor are important for understanding the consequences of gender inequality in marriage and divorce. Nevertheless, these concepts have been criticized for being both color-blind and class-blind. There are important economic differences among female-headed households of different social classes, races, and ethnicities. Upper-middle-class and wealthy women who divorce may experience a drop in income and standard of living, but they are more likely than lower-middle-class, working-class, and already poor women to own property and other assets independent of their husbands and to have the skills and educational background to help them to continue to live comfortably. These women are more likely to be White than non-White. Consequently, the poverty experienced by non-White women and their children after divorce is more likely to be what Bane calls *reshuffled poverty.* In other words, poor families dissolve and the women and children form new, but still poor families. "Reshuffled poverty as opposed to event-caused poverty for [racial and ethnic minorities] challenges the assumption that changes in family structure have created ghetto poverty. This underscores the importance of considering the ways that race produces different paths to poverty" (Bane, 1986, p. 277).

Sociologists and others have traditionally equated female-headed families in general, and minority female-headed families in particular, with pathology (Smith, 1993). The female-headed family has been seen as a cause of not only poverty but also a variety of other social problems, including juvenile delinquency, drug abuse, and alcoholism. This view, which also informs much of the debate over welfare "reform," holds that in single-parent families, mothers are either too distracted with other concerns or, worse, too focused on their own needs and desires, to adequately tend to their children. Children in single-parent families are being reared in permissive homes where their physical and emotional needs are largely unmet. In contrast, according to this position, in traditional two-parent families, the needs of children always come first (see, for example, Popenoe, 1993). But such a view ignores the high levels of stress, conflict, violence, and other forms of dysfunction in many traditional two-parent families, a point to which we will return

Some analysts see female-headed families, especially those headed by women of color, as the cause of many social problems, but other researchers have shown that the Black female-headed family is a source of strength and resistance to oppression.

shortly (Cowan & Cowan, 1998; Silverstein & Auerbach, 1999). Moreover, research has failed to uncover anything inherently "pathological" or "abnormal" in the female-headed family structure. In fact, researchers have argued that the Black female-headed family has historically been a source of strength and resistance to oppression (Collins, 1990; Height,

1989; Jewell, 1988; Ladner, 1971; McAdoo, 1986). If we are going to understand and help solve the problems of single-parent families, then we have to take into account how gender inequality intersects with social class and racial and ethnic inequalities. The kinds and levels of stress experienced by single-parent families, and the families' methods and chances of success in dealing with them, are strongly influenced by these factors (Brewer, 1988; Jayakody & Chatters, 1997; McAdoo, 1986; Neighbors, 1997).

Intertwined with the financial consequences of divorce are the emotional consequences. Research findings, however, are mixed in terms of gender differences in emotional well-being during and after dissolution (Amato, 2000). Analyses of gender differences in the divorce experience, are complicated by several factors. First, a person's feelings are likely to vary depending on who initiated the divorce and the reasons underlying the divorce. Feelings also change during the divorce process (Amato, 2000). For example, research indicates that for a majority of women, the most difficult emotional period occurs prior to the couple's separation. During this time, many women try hard to hold the marriage together, whereas men show a much lower level of awareness of marital difficulties. Following separation and divorce, though, many studies show that women generally adjust better than men (Diedrick, 1991). Women report feeling more in control of their lives and greater independence (Altenhofen, Biringen, & Mergler, 2008).

A second problem in identifying gender differences in the divorce experience is that many studies use large aggregate samples, but the relative impact of divorce on the divorcing partners varies across subgroups of women and men. Research indicates that among those who experience the greatest difficulty in adjusting to divorce are women with dependent children, especially those with children under six years of age (Maudlin, 1991). These women tend to experience higher levels of depression than childless women or women with grown children, and this depression is often related to their financial circumstances.[7] In fact, one of the best predictors of the relative well-being of divorced wives and husbands is the economic independence of the individual spouses (Holden & Smock, 1991). It is not surprising, therefore, that divorced women who are middle-aged, with a professional career, and either childless or without dependent children exhibit the highest level of post-divorce well-being (Gross, 1992). Being able to balance work and family is related to postdivorce adjustment for mothers (Altenhofen et al., 2008).

Race and ethnicity also intersect with gender to influence individuals' adjustment during and after divorce. For example, Song (1991) points out that Asian American women who strongly identify with their traditional ethnic community experience serious difficulty adjusting to divorce. This difficulty is an outgrowth of traditional Asian gender norms that label adult women who are unattached to men as "social nonpersons." These women may receive little emotional and financial support from others because they are blamed for the failure of their marriages. They also often become socially dislocated from community activities and friendships because other married women see them as potential seducers of their husbands, and married men worry that the behavior of these women might encourage their wives to divorce. It is not surprising, then, that these women tend to experience severe depression and other forms of distress following divorce (Song, 1991). However, research findings do not show significant differences between White and African American women and men in terms of postdivorce emotional adjustment (Amato, 2000).

Although men almost always fare better than women economically following divorce, they often do not do as well emotionally or psychologically. One indication of this is the higher remarriage rate of divorced men compared with that of divorced women. Although women's best chances of improving their financial status after divorce is to remarry (Morrison & Ritualo, 2000), they are more reluctant to do so than divorced men are. The remarriage rates of both divorced men and women have declined since 1970, but divorced men are more likely to remarry than divorced women (Coleman, Ganong, & Fine, 2000; Teachman et al., 2000). In fact, of divorced people age 25 and older, 55 percent of men but only 44 percent of women remarry (Kreider, 2005). One reason for this difference is that because divorced men are less likely to have custody of their children, it is easier for them to participate in social activities where they may meet potential remarriage partners. It is also the case that because of traditional gender norms in our society, men have more to gain from remarriage than women do. For instance, given the typical division of household labor in heterosexual marriages, one benefit of remarriage for men should be obvious. As one divorced man stated in an interview, what he missed most about marriage was "having a wife to 'keep the social life running' and to tend to 'certain little touches' that make a house a home" (quoted in Gross, 1992, p. A14). It is also the case that husbands are more likely than wives to rely on their spouses as their sole confidants (see Chapter 12).

As Box 7.3 shows, many of the findings on adjustment to widowhood parallel those obtained in the divorce research. Let's turn now to a discussion of other types of families and intimate relationships.

Singles and Domestic Partnerships

When we think of singles, most of us probably think of young heterosexual women and men who have not yet married. However, the single population in the United States is far more diverse. In addition to never-married heterosexuals, the single population includes gay men and lesbians who are not involved in a committed relationship; women and men, heterosexual and homosexual, who are not married but living with an intimate partner in what is called a *domestic partnership*; and separated, divorced, and widowed women and men with or without dependent children. We have already discussed divorce, widowhood, and single parenting, so let's look now at heterosexual and homosexual never-married singles and domestic partners.

HETEROSEXUAL SINGLES AND DOMESTIC PARTNERS   There are several common stereotypes about never-married heterosexuals. One stereotype is the swinging bachelor who "plays the field" and cherishes his independence. Another is the unmarried woman or "old maid" who struggles with loneliness and is desperate to find a man to marry before her "biological clock" stops ticking. Of course, in this case like most others, real life is quite different from stereotypes.

For most heterosexual young adults, singlehood is a temporary status. The vast majority eventually marry, but they are delaying marriage longer than in the past (Goldstein & Kenney, 2001). In 1970, for example, the median age at first marriage was 20 for women and 22 for men (Schmitt, 2001); by 2008, it was 25.6 for women and 27.4 for men (U.S. Department of Commerce, Bureau of the Census, 2009b). The number of people aged fifteen and older who have never married has increased from 27 percent in 2000 to 31 percent in 2008 (U.S. Department of Commerce, Bureau of the Census, 2009d).

BOX 7.3
Gender Differences in Adjusting to Widowhood

It is not surprising that psychologists tell us that the death of one's spouse is one of life's most emotionally traumatic experiences. Being happily married contributes to higher levels of self-esteem, better health, and lower levels of psychological distress (Hawkins & Booth, 2005). Women and men adjust differently to widowhood. A crucial determinant of well-being for those who are widowed is the economic status of the individual spouses. Men are far less likely than women to experience financial difficulties during widowhood, primarily because men traditionally have had longer and more stable employment histories than women, earn more on average than women do, and are more likely than women to be employed in occupations that carry benefits such as pensions (Holden & Smock, 1991; see also Chapter 8). But not all women experience negative financial consequences from being widowed. Women who had low incomes before widowhood are likely to sink further into poverty after their husbands die. Since non-White couples are at greater risk of living in poverty, becoming a widow is more likely to have a detrimental economic impact on women of color (Davis et al., 1990; Holden & Smock, 1991).

As we will see in Chapter 12, men have higher mortality rates than women, even at middle age, so the majority of those widowed are women. In fact, 4 percent of men but 12 percent of women have been widowed, and widowed men are more likely to remarry (Kreider, 2005). For one thing, widowed men have a larger pool of potential partners available to them, especially since men often marry women who are several years younger than they are. Second, men who are widowed, like men who are divorced, have more to gain from remarriage in terms of having their daily household needs met (Bedard, 1992). Many women—especially those who have established careers, individual identities, and financial independence—do not find widowhood debilitating. This is not to say that they do not experience tremendous sorrow when their husbands die. Rather, it appears that widowed women adjust better to life alone than widowed men, particularly if they have been involved in activities outside the marriage and are financially secure (Janke, Nimrod, & Kleiber, 2008a, 2008b; Nemy, 1992).

Unfortunately, many married couples do not have adequate life insurance or personal savings to guarantee financial security in widowhood, and Social Security and other government assistance programs, though helpful, are not sufficient. Consequently, widowhood doubles the poverty rate of women and substantially lowers women's standard of living in most socioeconomic groups (Holden & Smock, 1991). Young widows without children often experience the greatest financial difficulties, since they typically have little financial protection. They are not eligible for Social Security, and although their husbands may have had pensions at work, they may not have worked long enough to be vested. Moreover, some pensions do not pay benefits to the widow until the year in which her deceased husband would have been eligible for retirement benefits. Most young couples have little or no savings, and few have mortgage insurance that pays for their home if one spouse dies. Even though younger women are more likely than older women to have income from their own jobs, their salaries may not be sufficient to meet all the expenses that were incurred during the marriage. Still, while young widows, like older widows, experience a significant decline in their standard of living immediately following their husbands' deaths, their long-term prospects for improved financial circumstances are better than those of older widows to a large extent because they are more likely than older widows to remarry (Coleman et al., 2000; Holden & Smock, 1991).

Singles delay and postpone marriage for several reasons, including more positive social attitudes toward singlehood; greater reluctance to marry given high divorce rates and growing awareness of domestic violence; and more widespread use of contraceptives, which means fewer marriages because of unwanted pregnancies. Another important reason young adults delay marriage is financial constraints (Bedard, 1992). The decision to marry includes expectations about partners' economic roles and contributions to the household. Consequently, many couples feel that they should reach a certain level of financial security—e.g., steady employment, a specific quality of housing—before they marry (Seltzer, 2000). Historically, researchers found that marriage, particularly among Whites, was more common when the men were steadily employed and as their levels of education and income increased, whereas it was less common when the women were steadily employed and as their levels of education and income increased (Teachman et al., 2000). But researchers have more recently found a reversal of this trend for women, regardless of race. Specifically, studies show that women with higher education and socioeconomic status are more likely than women with less than a college education and low socioeconomic status to marry (Goldstein & Kenney, 2001). This may be because both women and men who are employed and financially secure are seen as more attractive marriage partners because of the resources they can bring to the household (Goldstein & Kenney, 2001; Teachman et al., 2000).

Certainly, trying to find a suitable marriage partner is a major reason for delaying or forgoing marriage. Women and men who are physically or mentally disabled, for example, need intimacy and sexual gratification the same as other people, but their needs may go unfulfilled because others see them as unattractive or sexless (Hall, 1992; Kelly, 1995). A contracted pool of marriage partners is also given as one of the primary factors underlying the gap in marriage rates between White and African American women. African American women who are economically disadvantaged face particular difficulty finding marriage partners for several reasons. One reason is the high mortality rate of young African American men (see Chapter 12). The death rate of African American men aged fifteen to twenty-four is 194.6 per 100,000, whereas for White men the same age, the death rate is 101.2 per 100,000 (National Center for Health Statistics, 2000). The life expectancy of White males born in 2007 is 75.9 but it is only 70.0 for African American males (National Center for Health Statistics, 2010). A second reason is the disproportionate number of young African American men who are in prison. In 2008, African American males were incarcerated at a rate six-and-a-half times higher than that of White males -- 3,161 per 100,000 Black males compared to 487 per 100,000 White males (Sabol, West, & Cooper, 2009). A third reason fewer African American than White women marry is that African American men have poorer economic prospects, which as we have noted makes them less desirable partners (Lloyd & South, 1996; Teachman et al., 2000; Tucker & Mitchell-Kernan, 1995; W. J. Wilson, 1987).

Instead of marrying, some heterosexual singles choose a domestic partnership, which we defined earlier as a cohabiting relationship between intimate partners not married to each other. Domestic partnerships appear to be an increasingly appealing lifestyle choice. In 2008, there were 6.6 million unmarried heterosexual couples living together in the United States, an increase of more than 4 million since 1980 and more than 5 million since 1970 (U.S. Department of Commerce, Bureau of the Census, 2011). While this number represents only about 11 percent of all couples, the increase over the past four decades has been substantial.

Domestic partnerships are likely to be different for couples at different stages of life, but sociologists have identified several trends that characterize most domestic partnerships. First, cohabiting relationships are much less stable than marital relationships (Garrison, 2008). Most domestic partners either break up or marry; very few adopt cohabitation as a permanent lifestyle. Second, most heterosexual domestic partners are childless. Married couples maintain most (67 percent) households with children under eighteen. Of all households with children under eighteen, unmarried partners maintain 6.4 percent of them (Kreider & Elliott, 2009). Research has indicated several factors that make U.S. cohabiting households disadvantageous for children. These factors include lower income, poorer relationship quality, and a higher chance that the relationship will end compared to married couple households (Cavanaugh & Huston, 2006; Manning & Brown, 2006; Osborne & McLanahan, 2007).

The increase in domestic partnerships in recent decades reflects not only economic constraints experienced by young adults, especially racial and ethnic minorities, but also growing social acceptance of cohabitation and modified goals of young adults. As Seltzer (2000, p. 1249) reports, "Most young people expect to marry and believe it is important to have a good marriage and family life, but most do not believe that they must marry to live a good life." One factor that may influence this view among those who choose domestic partnerships over marriage, at least initially, is whether or not their parents divorced. Studies consistently show that those who live with a partner before marriage are more likely to have parents who divorced than those who do not (Black & Sprenkle, 1991; Seltzer, 2000).

Some local governments and employers allow heterosexual domestic partners to register their relationships, but many jurisdictions restrict such registration to same-sex couples only or to same-sex couples and some types of heterosexual couples (e.g., senior citizens) (Seltzer, 2000). Even in those jurisdictions that allow heterosexual domestic partners of all ages to register, most attorneys advise domestic partners to draw up contracts if they want legal protection in the event of a break-up. Some courts, however, have been reluctant to enforce such contracts because they see them as potentially undermining the institution of marriage, and court rulings regarding the legal rights of heterosexual domestic partners have been inconsistent.[8] Consequently, if a domestic partnership breaks up, one partner may lose out financially or a battle may ensue over the division of assets. If the relationship endures, other difficulties may arise. For instance, if one partner dies without a will, his or her property may be inherited by family members instead of the domestic partner (Rankin, 1987).

Although heterosexual domestic partners sometimes confront these problems, they at least have the option to legally marry. Most gay and lesbian partners do not have that option; for them, the dilemmas posed by domestic partnerships in general are often made worse by the social stigma attached to gay and lesbian relationships.

GAY AND LESBIAN SINGLES AND DOMESTIC PARTNERS   As we stated earlier, it may be impossible to know exactly how many homosexuals there are in the United States largely because the social stigma attached to homosexuality in our society causes many to hide their sexual orientation. According to the U.S. census, there were 564,743 unmarried same-sex households in 2008 (48 percent male-male couples, 52 percent female-female couples). Same-sex households represent .9 percent of all households (married opposite-sex households, unmarried opposite-sex households, unmarried same-sex households) (U.S. Department of Commerce, Bureau of the Census, 2011). We must continue to keep in mind, though, that accurate knowledge and genuine appreciation of gay and lesbian relationships are still goals rather than achievements largely because social science research has traditionally been heterosexist and homophobic. Much of what was written before the 1960s was written by heterosexuals and discussed from a psychoanalytic or psychiatric perspective, which until recently assumed that homosexuality is pathological and that homosexuals are "sick" or "abnormal" (Krieger, 1982). Research that is now being done on gay and lesbian relationships is often conducted by gay and lesbian social scientists, and the findings indicate that there is as much diversity among gay men and lesbians as there is among heterosexual men and women. In other words, there is no uniform "homosexual lifestyle."

Recent research also refutes many other common myths about gay and lesbian relationships. For example, it is widely believed that gays and lesbians are sexually promiscuous and unable or unwilling to form committed intimate relationships. However, studies show that like most heterosexual women and men, most lesbians and gays establish enduring intimate relationships. For example, surveys show that 40 percent to 60 percent of gay men and 45 percent to 80 percent of lesbians report being currently involved in steady romantic relationships. Such numbers are thought to be underestimates because most surveys use samples of relatively young respondents who may not have partnered yet with a steady companion (Patterson, 2000). Gays and lesbians report levels of relationship satisfaction that are as high as those of heterosexual men and women, and research shows that sexual orientation has no effect on relationship quality (Patterson, 2000). When partnered gays and lesbians were compared to legally married heterosexuals, cohabitating heterosexuals, and single gays and lesbians, results indicated that the partnered homosexuals reported less happiness than married heterosexuals, but were just as happy as cohabiting heterosexuals. Moreover, gay men and lesbians in relationships reported more happiness than gay men and lesbians who are single (Wienke & Hill, 2009). Other research indicates that homosexual couples are just as satisfied with their relationships as heterosexuals are (Peplau & Fingerhut, 2007).

However, just as there is no distinct homosexual lifestyle, there is also no distinct homosexual value orientation toward love relationships. Instead, what appears to be more important than sexual orientation is one's sex—being male or female—and one's background. "Women's goals in intimate partnerships are similar whether the partner is male or female. The same is true of men" (Peplau, 1986, p. 118). Women typically place a higher value on emotional expressiveness in their intimate relationships (see also Blum, 1997). In gay male relationships, but even more so in lesbian relationships, equality between partners is also highly valued (Patterson, 2000; Peplau, 1986). This is not to say that egalitarianism is always achieved in these relationships (see, for example, Caldwell & Peplau, 1984; Patterson, 2000; Renzetti, 1992), but a significantly higher percentage of lesbian and gay male couples report being treated as equals by their intimate partners than do heterosexual couples (Patterson, 2000).

Research indicates that gay men are less supportive of monogamy in their intimate relationships than are either lesbian or heterosexual couples, and gay men do have on average more partners than straight men (Christopher & Sprecher, 2000; Patterson, 2000).

However, the longevity of same-sex intimate relationships does not differ significantly from the longevity of heterosexual intimate relationships, particularly among couples who have been partnered for at least ten years. In such cases, the research shows that break-up rates are 6 percent for lesbian couples, 4 percent for gay couples, and 4 percent for married heterosexual couples. Break-up rates are higher for those partnered for less than two years—22 percent of lesbian couples, 16 percent of gay couples, and 17 percent of heterosexual cohabiting couples—although for married heterosexual couples the rate continues to be only 4 percent (Patterson, 2000). What this means, of course, is that marriage is an inhibitor to breaking up, but as we have already discussed, lesbian and gay couples are legally prohibited from marrying. Some researchers also feel that gay and lesbian relationships are held to a higher standard than heterosexual relationships. After all, about half of all heterosexual marriages end in divorce within eight years (Kreider, 2005).

Sociologist Kath Weston (1991) found in her research on gay and lesbian families that when gay and lesbian partners break up, they frequently maintain a close relationship with one another by making a transition from being lovers to being friends. Consequently, Weston argues, "one could make a good case that gay relationships endure longer on average than ties established through heterosexual marriage. If two people cease being lovers after six years but remain friends and family for another forty, they have indeed achieved a relationship of long standing" (p. 120). What is perhaps surprising to many observers is that gay and lesbian relationships can be so long-lasting, given how destructive the discrimination against them must be.

Earlier in this chapter, we pointed out that an increasing number of municipal governments, states, as well as universities and corporations are openly recognizing gay and lesbian domestic partnerships by allowing them to officially register and thereby obtain many of the rights and benefits of married couples (see Box 7.1) Besides lending legitimacy to the relationship, registration has practical consequences for lesbian and gay couples, including insurance coverage for partners, family leaves, family membership rates, and inheritance protection. The AIDS epidemic has heightened concern over the need for legal recognition of domestic partnerships. Many gay men have had their dying partners removed from their care by an estranged and angry parent; have been excluded from decisions regarding their partner's care or even where the partner will be buried; and, in the absence of a will, have seen their deceased partner's belongings inherited by estranged parents or siblings.

The landmark case of Sharon Kowalski and Karen Thompson drew attention to this issue. Kowalski and Thompson had exchanged rings and pledged to be life partners, but because they were not—could not be—legally married, they were, as Robson (1992) put it, legally strangers. When Kowalski was severely disabled in a car accident in 1983, her parents removed her from the home she shared with Thompson, put her in a nursing home, and barred Thompson from even visiting her. Thompson subsequently went to court asking to be made Kowalski's legal guardian. A lower court ruled in favor of the parents, but in 1991, an appeals court ruled that the medical testimony indicated that Kowalski was able to express a preference as to where and with whom she wanted to live, and she had consistently chosen to live at home with her partner. In addition, the appeals court stated that Kowalski and Thompson were a "family of affinity," a relationship that deserves to be respected.

The legal victories of gays and lesbians have been fewer in the areas of parenting and parental rights. To a large extent, negative attitudes toward gays and lesbians as parents stem from widespread myths about relationships between homosexuals and children. For example, many heterosexuals believe that gay men try to seduce young boys, but the data on child molesters show that about 90 percent are men who identify as heterosexual (Estes & Weiner, 2001; Greenfeld, 1996; Prentky, Knight, & Lee, 1997; Rind, 2001). Many heterosexuals also think that homosexuals try to "recruit" children to their "lifestyle" and that simply seeing homosexual couples leads children into immorality. Such beliefs have been used repeatedly to prevent lesbians and gay men from becoming foster or adoptive parents and to deny them custody or visitation rights to their own children. Nonetheless, more gay parents are raising children than in the past. Gay parents are raising 4 percent of all adopted children in the United States and 3 percent of all foster children ("Study on adoption and foster care by lesbians and gay men," 2009).[9]

Despite the persistent myths, research consistently shows that children raised by gay and lesbian parents are emotionally healthy and well-adjusted (Lambert, 2005; Patterson, 2000; Stacey & Biblarz, 2001). Such children appear to be no different than children of heterosexual parents in terms of their cognitive development and psychological well being. They do tend to be less gender-typed in their behavior. In addition, although the vast majority identify as heterosexual, children of lesbian and gay parents appear to be more accepting of diversity and open to homosexuality. They are more relaxed and more experimental than children who grow up in other households, but they are not at greater risk of experiencing confusion about their own sexual orientation (Golombok & Tasker, 1996; Stacey & Biblarz, 2001). Research even indicates that there may be special benefits to children of lesbian couples in particular. Studies show that lesbian parents often enjoy greater compatibility in terms of their child-rearing views and practices as well as a more equal division of caregiving responsibilities than either gay male parents or heterosexual parents. This may increase the emotional closeness between children and their parents and reduce parenting conflicts that can negatively affect children (Stacey & Biblarz, 2001). These findings underline a point that many lesbian and gay parents already know well: It is love that makes a family.

VIOLENCE IN FAMILIES AND INTIMATE RELATIONSHIPS

The image of the family as a haven from the harshness of the public world is tarnished by reports of widespread family violence. Approximately 1.3 million women and 835,000 men are physically assaulted by an intimate partner annually in the United States (Tjaden & Thoennes, 2009). An estimated 1,181 women and 329 men are victims of intimate partner homicide each year (U.S. Department of Justice, Bureau of Justice Statistics, 2007). Many victims, however, are reluctant to report the abuse. One national survey, for instance, found that about half of women assaulted by an intimate partner reported the assault to the police (Rennison & Welchans, 2000). Thus, the official statistics probably underestimate the problem. To conclude this chapter, we'll discuss three forms of violence in intimate relationships: partner abuse, child abuse, and elder abuse.

Partner Abuse in Heterosexual Relationships

Studies of married and cohabiting heterosexual couples have produced varying estimates of the incidence of intimate partner violence. A number of researchers report that women are as likely—some say women are slightly more likely—to assault their intimate partners as men are (Archer, 2000; Dutton, 2006; Dutton, Corvo, & Hamel, 2009; Dutton, Nicholls & Spidel, 2005; Fiebert, 1997; Straus, 2007). In other words, these findings suggest that far from being a one-sided attack, partner abuse is usually *mutual abuse*, an exchange of physical blows and psychological or verbal sparring between partners. Various men's rights advocates have seized such findings as evidence that women are as violent as men and that battered men need equal protection from abusive wives and girlfriends (see, for example, Dragiewicz, 2011; Usher, 2005).

However, several serious criticisms have been raised against this perspective. One criticism stems from research showing that men are more likely than women to underreport both the frequency and severity of the intimate partner violence they inflict (Crowell & Burgess, 1996; Dobash et al., 1998). But even if women report perpetrating as much violence against their intimate partners as men do, this does not mean that women's and men's abusive behavior is the same. For one thing, women's and men's motivations for using violence against an intimate partner appear to be different. Men are more likely to use violence against an intimate partner when they perceive themselves losing control of the relationship or when they interpret their partners' words or behavior as challenges to their authority. Women are more likely to use violence, especially severe physical violence, against an intimate partner in self-defense, when they believe they are in imminent danger of being attacked, or to fight back when being attacked (Barnett, Lee, & Thelan, 1997; Dobash et al., 1998; Rajan & McCloskey, 2007). Researchers who have studied women arrested for domestic violence have found that most were previously victimized by their partners (Abel, 1999; Dasgupta, 1999; S. L. Miller, 2001). When women are arrested with their partner (dual arrest) rather than arrested alone, they are more likely to need medical attention and show physical signs of injuries (Muftic, Bouffard, & Bouffard, 2007).

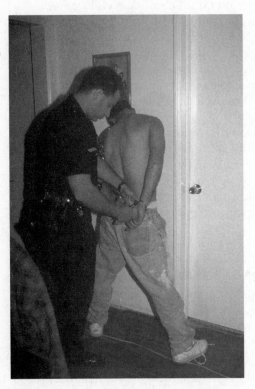

The federal Violence Against Women Act (VAWA) has improved the police response to intimate partner violence.

This last finding is related to a second important difference between men's and women's violence: its consequences. All studies that ask about injuries from intimate partner violence have found that male perpetrators are significantly more likely than female perpetrators to inflict a physical injury on their intimate partners (Archer, 2000). Moreover, injuries inflicted by men are more severe and more likely to require medical attention or hospitalization (Menard, Anderson, & Godboldt, 2009; Tjaden & Thoennes, 2000). Men are also more likely to kill their intimate partners than women are. In 2005, 329 men and 1,181 women were killed by an intimate partner. Although intimate homicides have declined in recent years, men were the major beneficiaries of this decrease. Between 1976 and 2005, intimate partner homicides of Black men decreased by 83 percent, and intimate partner homicides of White men decreased by 61 percent. In contrast, during the same period, intimate partner homicides of Black women decreased 52 percent, and intimate partner homicides of White women decreased by only 6 percent (Fox & Zawitz, 2007).

Clearly, then, intimate partner violence, like other behavior, is gendered. Women's and men's violence against their intimate partners differs in quality, and there are those that argue that it also differs in quantity. Patricia Tjaden and Nancy Thoennes (1998, 2000), for instance, conducted a national survey using a random sample of 8,000 men and 8,000 women and found that men are three times more likely than women to perpetrate intimate partner violence. Indeed, they conclude that violence against women is primarily intimate partner violence.

In trying to determine what causes partner abuse, some researchers have focused on the personal characteristics of batterers, asking, "What makes this person violent?" Answers to this question have ranged from evolutionary explanations to hormonal and neurological factors to personality traits and mental disorders. Other researchers have looked at socialization experiences, especially the experience of witnessing or being victimized by violence as a child. And still other researchers have examined institutional factors, including the influence of the media, religious traditions, and gender norms. What the research taken together suggests, however, is that partner abuse is not caused by any single factor, but by multiple factors, individual as well as structural (Crowell & Burgess, 1996; DeKeseredy & Schwartz, 2011).

Many people believe that alcohol and drug abuse cause intimate violence. Researchers have found a high incidence of alcohol and drug use associated with battering incidents (see, for example, Luthra & Gidycz, 2006), but the relationship between substance abuse and battering is complex and not yet well understood. For example, the likelihood of violent behavior increases with excessive alcohol and drug use, but it is not certain if this outcome is because alcohol and drugs lower inhibitions, cloud judgment, or have some other physiological effects on the brain and nervous system (Bennett & Bland, 2008; Crowell & Burgess, 1996). It is also sometimes the case that drinking and drug use do not *cause* battering, but instead are offered to *justify* or *excuse* such behavior: "I didn't know what I was doing; I was drunk" (Gelles, 1993). Most batterers, however, are not alcoholics or drug addicts (Bennett & Bland, 2008; Gelles, 1993).

Another common belief is that partner abuse only occurs among working-class and poor couples or among non-White couples. Research demonstrates, however, that domestic violence is far more widespread and cuts across social class as well as racial and ethnic boundaries. Nevertheless, research also shows that battering is not evenly distributed among social classes or racial or ethnic groups. Intimate partner violence is more frequent in low-income families (Brush, 2000; Renzetti, 2009; Tolman, 1999), although when race and ethnicity are taken into account, the results are less consistent. Although studies show that women of color are at greater risk of victimization than White women are (Caetano et al., 2005), this may be due to their overrepresentation among the economically disadvantaged (Benson et al., 2004). Low income and poverty, then, seem to place women at higher risk of violent victimization by an intimate partner. These factors also help keep abused women trapped in violent relationships (Renzetti, 2009; Renzetti & Larkin, 2009).

Some people are unsympathetic to abused women because they believe that women should leave a relationship as soon as it becomes abusive. "If it's so bad," they ask, "why does she stay?" Research indicates that abused women typically do leave their partners, sometimes more than once, but leaving is more difficult than most people think

(Allen, Larsen, & Walden, 2011; DeKeseredy & Schwartz, 2009; Miller, Iovanni, & Kelley, 2011). For one thing, they must have someplace to go. They may not have relatives or friends they can count on, and battered women's shelters may be full or unable to accommodate their needs (Dobash & Dobash, 1992; Donnelly, Cook, & Wilson, 1999; Zweig, Schlichter, & Burt, 2002). For many low-income battered women, leaving their abusive partners means becoming homeless (Browne & Bassuk, 1997). Second, these women must be able to support themselves and their children if they leave. In Chapter 8 we will discuss how various forms of employment and wage discrimination keep women in low-paying, low-status jobs. And we noted earlier in this chapter that many women experience a substantial drop in their standard of living when they separate from their husbands. Economic dependence, therefore, keeps some women trapped in violent family relationships. For some women, leaving an abusive partner means having to go on welfare (Brandwein, 1999), but as a result of changes to welfare laws in 1996, this social assistance program is not a reliable or stable source of financial security (Tolman & Raphael, 2001). Women who are quick to leave an abusive relationship tend to be gainfully employed or to have good chances for employment, possess above-average resources, and have relatives nearby who are willing and able to help them (Pagelow, 1981). It is also important to keep in mind that leaving an abuser does not guarantee that the abuse will stop. In fact, research shows that abuse often escalates when a woman tries to leave or after she has left (DeKeseredy, 1997; DeKeseredy & Schwartz, 2009; Fleury, Sullivan, & Bybee, 2000; Kurz, 1995). Women with disabilities may face additional challenges accessing services and leaving abusive relationships. Box 7.4 discusses the unique challenges and experiences faced by women with disabilities who are abused by intimate partners.

Partner abuse takes place in the context of a violent society. Some people consider violence a normal part of everyday life, and a sizable minority of the population believes that under certain circumstances, men are justified in hitting their wives or girlfriends (DeKeseredy & MacLeod, 1997). Not surprisingly, women express less acceptance of violence in marriage than men do (Merten & Williams, 2009), and women are more likely than men to label specific incidents of physical and sexual aggression perpetrated by an intimate partner as domestic violence (Nabors, Dietz, & Jasinski, 2006). Additional research has identified several factors that, along with gender, influence acceptance of relationship violence. For example, Forbes et al. (2006) found that high school males who are involved in sports are more accepting of dating violence. This may be because aggression in sports is normalized. But research also shows that it is not athletic involvement per se that encourages adolescent male athletes to be more accepting of relationship violence; rather, it is their adoption of a "need to win" attitude (Merten, 2008).

Many advocates for battered women have criticized the legal system for not treating domestic violence as a serious problem and not responding to it effectively. Research shows that the police and the courts do not respond consistently or effectively to the needs of battered women (DeJong, Burgess-Proctor, & Elis, 2008; Fleury, 2002; Ptacek, 1999). Since the late 1970s, however, important legal changes have occurred, including passage of the federal Violence Against Women Act (VAWA) in 1994. This legislation includes increased funding for battered women's shelters and programs, a mandate for harsher penalties for batterers, and a provision that makes crossing state lines in pursuit of a fleeing partner a federal offense. Research has found that VAWA has resulted in more aggressive criminal justice responses to violence against women and more contact between victims and criminal justice and legal authorities (Cho & Wilke, 2005). The impact of the law continues to be

BOX 7.4
Women with Disabilities who Experience Intimate Partner Violence

Research shows that, for women, having a disability increases rather than reduces the risk of intimate partner violence. Indeed, researchers have found that compared to women without disabilities, women with disabilities are more likely to experience physical and sexual abuse (Brownridge, 2006; Martin et al., 2006; Rajan, 2004; Smith, 2008). For example, Brownridge (2006) found that women with disabilities had a 40 percent greater chance of being abused by their partners in the five years prior to when the research was conducted than women without disabilities. In addition, women with disabilities tend to endure abuse for longer periods of time compared to women without disabilities (Brodwin, Orange, & Chen, 2004; Nosek et al., 2001).

Not only are women with disabilities at greater risk for intimate partner violence, they may also be less likely to report abuse or access services because of their dependence on the abuser (Copel, 2006). Research shows that women with disabilities are more likely than women without disabilities to be unemployed, which in turn may increase their dependence on an abusive partner (Brownridge, 2006). In addition, the poverty experienced by women with disabilities has worsened following welfare reform (Chouinard & Crooks, 2005).

Agencies providing services to abused women with disabilities must recognize their unique needs. For instance, services must be architecturally accessible and staff must be available who can competently assist women with specific disabilities, including women who are deaf (Elman, 2005; Powers, Hughes, & Lund, 2009). Women with disabilities, however, are not a homogenous group, and as Powers and her colleagues (2009) point out, more research is needed on the experiences of women of color with disabilities, as well as women with disabilities who identify as bisexual, homosexual, transgendered, or lesbian. Consider, for example, that women of color with disabilities may confront obstacles stemming from their disability as well as from racism when they seek help to address the abuse (Lightfoot & Williams, 2009).

assessed, but the hope is that it will help turn the tables on batterers who historically have been afforded more legal protection in our society than those they victimize.[10]

Partner Abuse in Gay and Lesbian Relationships

Much less is known about partner abuse in lesbian and gay relationships. For one thing, we cannot do studies using large, national samples of gay and lesbian couples because many gay men and lesbians are not open about their sexual orientation. Therefore, it is impossible to establish with much accuracy the incidence of violence in same-sex relationships. Some researchers argue that it occurs at about the same rate or at higher rates as violence in heterosexual relationships (Bernhard, 2000; Petermen & Dixon, 2003; Poorman, 2001; Seelau, Seelau, & Poorman, 2003; Stanley et al., 2006). However, these claims are based on studies of lesbians and gay men who volunteer for the research and who therefore may not be representative of the general lesbian and gay population. While we do not have very good estimates of the incidence of same-sex domestic violence, the limited research available shows that it does occur and, like heterosexual domestic violence, it is not a one-time situational event. Once it occurs, it is likely to reoccur and to grow more severe over time (Merrill & Wolfe, 2000; Renzetti, 1992).

Many people assume that it is easier for abused lesbians and gay men to leave their partners because they are not married. However, research shows that gay men and lesbians have a high level of closeness and attachment to their partners; they have difficulty leaving abusive partners because they have a deep personal commitment to them and to the relationship. A second problem in leaving is that many lesbians and gay men are involved in domestic partnerships in which they share housing with their partners and have made joint purchases. Leaving an abusive partner may result in a substantial financial loss that may or may not be recoverable through legal action should the abused partner choose to take such action. Most, though, do not feel comfortable turning to the courts for help (Cabral & Coffey, 1999; Fray-Witzer, 1999; Renzetti, 1992). Third, there are few shelters and services specifically for victims of same-sex domestic violence, and many lesbians and gay men do not feel welcome at shelters and services designed for heterosexual women (Hassouneh & Glass, 2008; Merrill & Wolfe, 2000; Renzetti, 1996). Consequently, for gay men in particular, the only alternative when leaving an abusive relationship is to go to a homeless shelter. While many abused heterosexual women turn to their relatives for help, this isn't an option for some abused lesbians and gay men because they have not come out to their relatives about their sexual orientation or they have severed ties with their relatives (Merrill & Wolfe, 2000; Renzetti, 1992). Fourth, victims of same-sex intimate partner violence may not report the crime because they fear that police will not help them or take them seriously. In many cases, police only take same-sex intimate partner violence seriously when it is severe and results in injuries (Pattavina et al., 2007). And finally, among gay men, HIV/AIDS increases abuse victims' reluctance to leave abusive partners. An abuse victim whose batterer has AIDS may feel tremendous guilt about leaving a dying partner with no one else to care for him. Conversely, an abuse victim who has AIDS may be so dependent on his batterer for financial support and physical assistance that he prefers to remain in the relationship rather than risk living alone (Letellier, 1996; Merrill & Wolfe, 2000). In short, lesbian and gay victims of domestic violence are inhibited from leaving abusive partners not only because of their personal circumstances but also because the homophobia that is prevalent in our society cuts them off from most alternatives.

Child Abuse

We often tell children to be wary of strangers, but the fact is that they are more likely to be harmed by someone they know, especially a family member. In 2007, approximately 3.2 million referrals of child abuse and neglect were made to child protective services (CPS) on behalf of about 5.8 million children (U.S. Department of Health and Human Services, 2009). Many observers maintain, though, that these figures are underestimates because they are based only on official reports and many cases never come to the attention of CPS. Definitions and reporting requirements also vary across states, and the ability to investigate and substantiate claims of child maltreatment often depends on the availability of staff and other resources (Children's Defense Fund, 2001; Jones & Finkelhor, 2009).

Official data show that most maltreated children are victims of neglect (about 59 percent), while nearly 11 percent are physically abused and about 8 percent are sexually abused (U.S. Department of Health and Human Services, 2009). There are differences across age groups, with the youngest children (aged 0–3 years) at greatest risk. Statistics also show varying rates of maltreatment across racial and ethnic groups: 9.1 victims per 1,000 White children, 10.3 victims per 1,000 Hispanic children, 14.2 victims per 1,000 American Indian children, and 16.7 victims per 1,000 African American children (U.S. Department of Health and Human Services, 2009). Children living in poor families also appear to be at greater risk of abuse and neglect than children living in more financially secure families. One of the strongest correlates of child abuse rates in a geographic area is the percentage of children in that area who are living in poverty (Jogerst, Dawson, & Schweitzer, 2000). This factor, then, may help to explain the differential rates of abuse and neglect by race and ethnicity, since racial and ethnic minorities are disproportionately represented among the poor.

Girls are slightly more likely than boys to be abused; girls are 52 percent of child abuse victims. However, when type of abuse is taken into account, there are important gender differences. Boys are more likely than girls to be physically abused and neglected. Girls are more likely to be sexually abused (Finkelhor et al., 2005; Peter, 2009), although research indicates that boys are less likely than girls to disclose child sexual abuse (Priebe & Svedin, 2008). Sexual exploitation of children may be perpetrated by strangers, but most victims know their abusers. The abuser is usually a relative, stepparent, family friend, neighbor, teacher, or coach (Estes & Weiner, 2001). Recent research indicates that male survivors of child sexual abuse experience intimacy problems, alienation, and anger (Kia-Keating, Sorsoli, & Grossman, 2009). Female survivors of child sexual abuse are more likely than other females to experience subsequent sexual or physical victimization, as well as intimate partner violence (Barnes et al., 2009).

About 80 percent of perpetrators of child maltreatment are the victim's parents; it is estimated that another 7 percent of perpetrators are other relatives of the victim (Jones & Finkelhor, 2009; U.S. Department of Health and Human Services, 2009) Children living in single-parent homes are at greater risk of maltreatment (Fuller, 2005). Most studies also show that mothers are more likely than fathers to abuse children (U.S. Department of Health and Human Services, 2009), although it is unclear whether this finding simply reflects the greater time that mothers spend with their children. It may also be caused in part by the greater social isolation of mothers that we discussed earlier. Parents who are socially isolated are more likely to abuse their children (Straus & Smith, 1990). But while mothers more often than biological fathers abuse their children, stepfathers and boyfriends of single mothers are also frequent abusers, especially sexual abusers (Estes & Weiner, 2001).

Severe child abuse and neglect may result in death. In 2007, there were about 1,760 child fatalities attributed to abuse and neglect (Child Welfare Information Gateway, 2009), and data indicate that the number of child maltreatment fatalities has risen in recent years (Jones & Finkelhor, 2009). Young children (aged 3 and younger) are thought to be at greatest risk. About 70 percent of child homicides are perpetrated by a victim's parents, and more than a quarter of these (27 percent) are perpetrated by the mother alone (Child Welfare Information Gateway, 2009).

Elder Abuse

Elder abuse refers to the physical, sexual, psychological, or financial maltreatment, neglect, or exploitation of a senior citizen by an adult caregiver. Obviously, such abuse can be inflicted by anyone entrusted with the care of an elderly person, such as nurses, physicians, home health aides, bankers, or lawyers. However, research shows that the typical abuser is a family member (Griffin, Williams, & Reed, 1998; Hildreth, Burke, & Glass, 2009; Kosberg, 1988; Mates, 1997; Pillemer & Finkelhor, 1988). Victims and perpetrators of elder abuse are more likely to be women (Teaster et al., 2006). However, males are more likely to sexually victimize the elderly (Ramsey-Klawsnick et al., 2008).

Similar to child abuse, it is difficult to estimate the incidence of elder abuse because underreporting is widespread. The abused elder may be physically or financially dependent on the abuser, or, in the case of elderly parents, there is a strong reluctance to have one's adult child arrested. In addition, budget cuts in Medicare programs have resulted in a decrease in staff to provide protective services for the elderly. And although all states have laws to protect the elderly from abuse, the laws vary in their criteria for protection (e.g., some exclude the able-bodied elderly), procedures for reporting and investigation, classification of abusive acts as criminal or civil violations, and remedies (Griffin et al., 1998).

Research on elder abuse has increased significantly since the 1980s, and more recent research has focused on the experiences of elder abuse across diverse social groups (see, for example, Paranjape et al., 2009 for a discussion of the association between intimate partner violence and poor health for older African American women). These studies indicate that those at greatest risk of being victimized are women who are aged seventy-five and older, infirm, and physically or financially dependent on others for meeting their basic daily needs (Decalmer, 1993; Kosberg, 1988; Pillemer & Finkelhor, 1988; Pillemer & Suitor, 1998). Women may have higher rates of victimization because they outnumber elderly men, but also because they are more vulnerable to sexual assault and they have lower social status than elderly men. Recent research also suggests that the financial strain experienced by older African Americans may put them at increased risk of abuse (Malley-Morrison, 2004; Paranjape et al., 2009).

Research on abusers shows that they are sometimes the elderly person's spouse, continuing a pattern of abuse in the marriage or taking revenge for previous abuse by the now-impaired partner (Kosberg, 1988; Pillemer & Finkelhor, 1988; Pillemer & Suitor, 1998). One study found that 3.5 percent of women aged sixty-five and older experienced domestic violence within the five years prior to the study (Bonomi et al., 2007). Older women's physical and health impairments may increase their vulnerability. In addition, they may be reluctant to leave abusive relationships because of traditional attitudes regarding gender roles and marriage (women should be wives and homemakers and submissive to their husbands) (Zink et al., 2006). Intimate partner violence against older women includes the types of abuse perpetrated against younger women (e.g., physical abuse, verbal abuse) but may also include neglect and giving improper doses of medication (Straka & Montminy, 2006).

Besides intimate partners, recent research indicates that oftentimes older people are abused by their adult children (AuCoin, 2005; Teaster et al., 2006). Some of these adult children were abused by their parents when they were growing up and learned that violence toward intimates is acceptable behavior. Some may be retaliating against their abusive parents (Decalmer, 1993; Kosberg, 1988; Paranjape et al., 2009). Often, though, the abusers are adult daughters who have brought severely impaired parents into their home to care for them. The daughters continue to care for their own families and often work outside the home as well. They typically receive little or no outside help in caring for their parents, and eventually the psychological and financial stress become so great that they use violence to control their parents or to express resentment about the situation (Decalmer, 1993; Jogerst et al., 2000; Mates, 1997; Steinmetz, 1993).

The vast majority of states and the District of Columbia have enacted laws making reporting of incidents of abuse or neglect of senior citizens mandatory. Some analysts, however, question the effectiveness of such laws because they address the problem *after* abuse occurs and they often impinge on the individual rights of the elderly whom they are supposed to protect. Also, the programs created by the laws are usually too under-funded to meet the needs of elderly victims (Callahan, 1988; Griffin et al., 1998; Kosberg, 1988). Many advocates for the elderly believe that the best approach is prevention by, for example, providing adult children with greater professional assistance and support in caring for their parents.

FAMILIES AND OTHER INTIMATES: THE IDEAL AND THE REAL REVISITED

Our discussion in this chapter highlights the disparity between traditional images of ideal intimate relationships and their reality in everyday life. We have discussed how the social construction of *The Family*—that is, the isolated nuclear family of husband/breadwinner, wife/homemaker, and dependent children—is not an accurate description of the majority of families in the United States today. Unfortunately, this idealization creates another false idea: that other family arrangements and relationships, including single-parent families and gay and lesbian relationships, are inherently deviant or abnormal.

Another myth generated by the idealization of the isolated nuclear family is the notion of the family as a private retreat from the harsh public world. We have learned that while the family is, for many of us, a place where we can be our "real" selves and still be loved, it is also a place at the center of gendered struggles. Within the family, the gender inequal-ity of the larger society is often replicated and preserved in a variety of ways: through the power imbalance between intimate partners, an inequitable division of household labor and caregiving responsibilities, the economic difficulties of female-headed households, and domestic violence. Many of these problems are made worse by racism, ageism, heterosex-ism, social class inequality, and discrimination on the basis of physical ability.

The idea of family privacy also overlooks the many ways in which other social institutions, such as government, impinge on intimate relationships. A recurring theme in this chapter has been the intersection of family life and employment. We have argued, in fact, that family relations cannot be understood in isolation from employment issues. In the next chapter, we turn to the topic of gender and the occupational work world, but because of the intersection of family life and work, many of the points we raised here will come up again.

Key Terms

bisexuality   sexual and affectionate attrac-tion to both women and men

chosen families   composed of people un-related by ancestry, marriage, or adoption, but who are nonetheless considered family members

domestic partnership   a cohabiting rela-tionship between intimate partners not mar-ried to each other

expressive family role   the role of house-keeper and caregiver in the family, a role held by the wife/mother in a traditional isolated nuclear family

instrumental family role   the role of pro-viding financial support for the family and making key decisions, a role held by the hus-band/father in the traditional isolated nuclear family

isolated nuclear family   a family in which the husband/father, wife/mother, and their dependent children establish a household geographically and financially separate from other kin, and the adults carry out distinct, specialized roles

public/private split   the idea that home is a separate domain from the public world

reproductive freedom   an individual's ability to freely choose whether or not to have a child

reproductive technologies   a variety of laboratory techniques that allow people who are infertile, physically unable to conceive or sustain a pregnancy, do not have a partner, or do not wish to enter into a committed relationship to become parents

sexual double standard   the tradition of permitting young men to engage in sexual activity while simultaneously condemning and punishing the same behavior by young women

single-parent family   a family with children but only one adult who has financial responsibility for the household

two-earner family   a family in which both adult partners are in the paid labor force

---

Suggested Readings

DeKeseredy, W. S., & Schwartz, M. D. (2009). *Dangerous exits: Escaping abusive relationships in rural America*. New Brunswick, NJ: Rutgers University Press. Based on interviews with women living in rural areas, this book documents the violence and terror these women experience, especially as they attempt to leave their intimate partners.

Finkelhor, D. (2008). *Child victimization: Violence, crime, and abuse in the lives of young people*. New York: Oxford University Press. A thorough examination of child victimization, including how the criminal justice system responds to the victimization of children and some of the challenges children and their families may encounter in their quest for assistance and justice.

Gerson, K. (2010). *The unfinished revolution: How a new generation is reshaping family, work, and gender in America*. New York: Oxford University Press. Gerson interviewed over one hundred women and men between the ages of eighteen and thirty-two to capture how the structure of their families changed. She focuses on the fluidity and flexibility of families and also finds that the young men and women whom she interviewed desire flexible and egalitarian partnerships in their own committed relationships.

Mezey, N. J. (2008). *New choices, new families: How lesbians decide about motherhood*. Baltimore: Johns Hopkins University Press. Mezey conducted focus-group interviews with thirty-five lesbians to explore why some choose motherhood while others do not.

Stone, P. (2007). *Opting out? Why women really quit careers and head home*. Berkeley: University of California Press. Stone explores the conflict women in high-status, demanding careers face when trying to balance the responsibilities of work with family demands, and how these conflicts influence their decisions to leave their jobs to stay home with their children.

Notes

1. Certainly Parsons was not the only significant family sociologist of this period, but he is considered by many to be the most preeminent. Aulette (1994, p. 11), for example, quotes D. H. Morgan, who wrote, "It would not be too much of an exaggeration to state that Parsons represents *the* modern theorist on the family" (original emphasis).

2. Research shows, however, that girls who lose their virginity at very young ages (eleven or twelve years old) often have much older male partners. The research also shows that these girls experience higher rates of serious problems, including substance abuse and suicide attempts, than girls with sexual partners closer to them in age (Leitenberg & Saltzman, 2000).

3. In 1989, Denmark became the first country in the world to legalize homosexual marital unions by extending to officially registered homosexual couples all but a few of the rights and responsibilities of legally married heterosexual couples. In 2000, the Netherlands passed laws allowing same-sex couples to marry and adopt children. Today, nearly all the Scandinavian countries as well as Holland, Switzerland, Belgium, Spain, Germany, and France recognize same-sex partnerships. In Italy such unions are recognized in certain localities.

4. According to the World Health Organization (2005), there are approximately 87 million unwanted pregnancies worldwide each year. More than half of these women (46 million) have abortions, and approximately 18 million will do so under unsafe circumstances. Almost all of these unsafe abortions occur in developing countries in South America and Africa. Women undergoing unsafe abortions tend to be young; two-thirds are between the ages of fifteen and thirty.

5. A particularly disturbing example of the consequences of not regulating RTs is the web site of a former fashion photographer who offers the eggs of pornographic models for sale to the highest bidder. While federal laws prohibit trafficking in human organs, the sale of eggs and sperm in this manner is legal (Goldberg, 1999a).

6. Cha and Thebaud (2009) examined how men's beliefs of the proper roles for men and women change when they share the breadwinner role with their spouse. They examined this change across twenty-seven countries that have varying labor market structures. Their findings show that men working in countries with more rigid labor markets (i.e., workers do not change jobs often because it is more difficult in those countries for employers to hire and fire employees) hold a stronger male breadwinner ideology.

7. The issue of how children fare following the break-up of their parents' marriage is hotly debated by researchers. There are those, such as psychologist Judith Wallerstein (Wallerstein, Lewis, & Blakeslee, 2000), who argue that divorce has long-term traumatic effects on children that manifest not only when they are young, but also well into adulthood. Others, however, fault Wallerstein's research on methodological grounds, pointing out that her sample is small and homogeneous and, therefore, not representative of the population of children of divorced parents. As a result, her work likely exaggerates the negative effects of divorce on children. Some studies show that children of divorced parents, compared with children of continuously married parents, experience a host of problems, including lower academic achievement, high rates of single parenthood, low self-esteem, and high rates of teen suicide (Amato, 2000; Nicholi, 1991). However, the statistical differences are small, and many of these studies do not make clear whether such problems emerged during the marriage or after the divorce (Amato, 2000; Furstenberg & Cherlin, 1991). Some researchers maintain that children living in homes with high levels of conflict between the parents suffer as many, if not more, negative consequences as children of divorced parents. In fact, divorce appears to have positive consequences for children of parents in high-conflict marriages (Amato, 2000).

8. In five states (Florida, Virginia, West Virginia, Michigan, Mississippi), cohabitation remains illegal, although such laws are rarely enforced. Laws prohibiting cohabitation were not repealed in North Dakota until 2007 and in North Carolina in 2006.

9. Arkansas and Utah prohibit adoption and foster parenting by same-sex couples, and Mississipppi prohibits same-sex couples but not single homosexuals from adopting children.

10. For a cost-benefit analysis of VAWA see Clark et al., 2002. In addition, Zweig and Burt (2003) have evaluated how VAWA has influenced collaborations among police, prosecutors, and service agencies in addressing the problem of violence against women.

Chapter 8

Gender, Employment, and the Economy

When we speak of a society's **economy**, we are referring to its system of managing and developing its resources, both human and material. The human resources of the economy constitute the **labor force**. Sociologists have long emphasized the significance of work in people's lives. At the most basic level, work is necessary to meet survival needs. Most work, though, is not done by individuals in isolation, but rather entails the coordination of the activities of a group. Work, in other words, is *social* as well as *economic,* and in the United States, as in other industrialized capitalist societies, the social organization of work is hierarchical. People do different jobs that are differentially valued and rewarded. Ideally, the value and rewards attached to a particular job should reflect its intrinsic characteristics—for example, the degree of skill required, the amount of effort expended, the level of responsibility involved, and the conditions under which it is performed. In practice, however, the value and rewards of a job often have more to do with the ascribed traits of workers—their race and ethnicity, for instance, and/or their sex.

Our focus in this chapter is on the different economic and employment experiences of women and men and the differential values and rewards that have been attached to their work. Both men and women have always worked, but the kinds of work opportunities available to them and the rewards they have received have typically depended less on their talents as individuals than on culturally prescribed and enforced notions of "women's work" and "men's work." These prescriptions vary from society to society, and they vary historically within a single society. We will begin our discussion here, then, with a brief historical overview of men's and women's labor force participation in the United States.

U.S. WORKING WOMEN AND MEN IN HISTORICAL PERSPECTIVE

Men's and women's participation in the wage labor force has been shaped by a number of factors, not the least of which have been changes in production and demographic changes. These, too, have influenced prevailing gender ideologies of men's and women's appropriate work roles.

Undeniably, one of the most important changes occurred during the nineteenth century when the American economy shifted from being predominantly agricultural to becoming industrialized, moving production off the farms and into factories. Interestingly, industrialization is frequently discussed only in terms of its effects on male workers, the common assumption being that women did not accompany men into the factories, but instead remained at home as family caretakers. This was true only in certain households, however. Overall, men entered the paid labor force in significantly greater numbers than women. At the same time, dominant middle-class ideology dictated that the so-called true woman stayed at home and supposedly did not work. But among particular groups of women—women in poor and working-class families, women rearing children alone, women of color, and immigrant women—few could afford to stay at home. The exigencies of survival required that they find paid employment, and the harsh reality of their work world stood sharply juxtaposed to the prosperous middle-class image of genteel womanhood (Cott, 1987; Glenn, 1992; Stansell, 1986).

In 1800, only about 5 percent of women worked outside the home, but by 1900, about 30 percent of women living in large U.S. cities were employed and a substantial number were factory workers (Dublin, 1994). In the New England textile mills, for instance, most of the labor force was female by 1850 (Dublin, 1994; Werthheimer, 1979).

In cities such as Boston and New York, women were heavily concentrated in the garment industry as seamstresses (Glenn, 1990; Stansell, 1986). Other women did piecework, such as folding books, rolling cigars, or making flowers for wealthier women's hats. They labored fourteen to eighteen hours a day under extraordinarily unsafe conditions for a daily wage of ten to eighteen cents. While for some even these wages gave them independence from their families, many others turned most or all of their wages over to their parents to help support the household (Dublin, 1994).

Of course, factory work was unpleasant and dangerous for male as well as female workers, but from the outset, men and women were largely segregated into different jobs, with the more skilled—and better paid—work open only to men. Widespread stereotypes about women's innate passivity and physical weakness as well as their greater tolerance for tedium legitimated offering women work that was usually the most boring and repetitive. And despite the fact that many women's wages were crucial to their family's welfare, the belief that women worked only temporarily until they married was used to justify their lower wage rates (Kessler-Harris, 1990; Reskin & Hartmann, 1986). Both labor organizers and male workers capitalized on the notion that paid work was "unladylike" and argued that no woman would have to work if men were provided a "family wage." Trade unions systematically excluded women or organized them into separate unions. Far fewer women than men were unionized. Even in unions with large numbers of female members, the union leadership was typically male, although several historical analyses show that in some unions women did gain valuable organizing and leadership experience (Gabin, 1990; Glenn, 1990). Nevertheless, until the 1930s, most unions were racially segregated as well as sex segregated (Gabin, 1990; Hine, 1989).

Jobs in manufacturing were available primarily to White women. Women of color, though more likely than White women to be in the paid labor force, historically have found their employment opportunities largely limited to agricultural work (e.g., fruit and vegetable harvesters), domestic work (e.g., housemaids), and laundry work (Amott & Matthaei, 1991). For instance, in 1890, 38.7 percent of Black female workers held agricultural jobs, 30.8 percent were domestics, 15.6 percent were laundresses, but only 2.8 percent worked in manufacturing. Three decades later, agriculture, domestic service, and laundries still employed 75 percent of Black female workers and, although more Black women were in manufacturing, they faced widespread segregation and discrimination in the factories: "White women were sometimes able to start work one hour later, and when amenities such as lunchrooms, fresh drinking water, and clean toilets were available, they were available primarily to White women" (Sidel, 1986, p. 60).

The experiences of Asian and Latina workers were similar to those of Black women with the important exception, of course, that Black women had also been enslaved in the United States (Romero, 1992; Zavella, 1987). It is true, too, that the dirtiest, most menial, and lowest-paying jobs went to minority men as well as minority women, but while minority men received considerably lower wages than White men, they were paid more than minority women (see, for example, Zavella, 1987). Historically, women of color have been the lowest-paid members of the labor force.

Ironically, the social disorganization that many groups experienced as a result of industrialization, urbanization, and immigration during the nineteenth century actually created new job opportunities for White middle-class women, especially those who had a college education. Extending their domestic roles to the larger society, they took up "civic housekeeping" and lobbied for a variety of social welfare reforms, including wages and hours laws, child labor prohibitions, improved housing for the poor, and public health measures. Some supported these causes by forming or joining voluntary organizations, but others made a career of it by entering the "female professions" of nursing, teaching, and social work (Cott, 1987; Evans, 1987). Such jobs were not considered a threat to genteel womanhood since women were expected to perform good works and care for others. Other gender stereotypes were used to justify hiring women for secretarial and other clerical positions when production expanded and the need for service workers grew. It was argued, for instance, that women's natural dexterity and compliant personalities made them ideally suited for office work (Kessler-Harris, 1982). The idea that women's work was temporary or secondary to men's remained intact and helped to keep jobs sex segregated and women's wages depressed.

Table 8.1 shows men's and women's labor force participation rates from 1900 to 2008. The early decennial statistics, however, mask some important changes in the labor force

TABLE 8.1 Labor Force Participation Rates by Sex, 1900–2008 (percent of population sixteen and older)[*]

Year	Male	Female
1900	53.7	20.0
1920	54.3	22.7
1930	53.2	23.6
1940	55.2	27.9
1945	61.6	35.8
1950	59.9	33.9
1955	60.4	35.7
1960	60.2	37.8
1965	59.7	39.3
1970	61.3	43.4
1975	78.4	46.4
1980	77.8	51.6
1985	76.3	54.5
1990	69.0	56.8
1995	87.4	71.5
2001	74.1	60.2
2008	73.0	59.5

[*]Prior to 1947, the Census Bureau included in these figures all persons fourteen years and older in the labor force.

Sources: Bartsch, 2009; Taeuber & Valdisera, 1986; U.S. Department of Commerce, Bureau of the Census, 1976, 1990, 2000; U.S. Department of Labor, 2002a.

during the first half of this century, especially during the Great Depression. You will notice in Table 8.1 that between 1920 and 1930, men's labor force participation rate declined slightly, whereas women's rose slightly. During the Depression, many married women entered the paid labor force to support their families when their husbands were out of work. Unfortunately, these women were often accused of stealing jobs from men, although "in reality, the pervasive sex segregation of the labor force meant that women and men rarely competed for the same jobs" (Evans, 1987, p. 46). In fact, the clerical and service jobs in which these women were concentrated have traditionally been less sensitive to economic downturns than male blue-collar jobs in manufacturing and the building trades (Reskin & Hartmann, 1986). Nevertheless, "numerous states, cities, and school boards passed laws prohibiting or limiting the employment of married women. And since cultural norms still ascribed the breadwinner's role to men, those women who lost paid jobs, or were unable to find paid work, found that relief programs for the unemployed consistently discriminated against them" (Evans, 1987, p. 47).

With the outbreak of World War II, the U.S. economy reversed itself, and the wartime production boom created jobs for millions of Americans, but especially for women. The enlistment of a large percentage of men into the military resulted in critical labor shortages and forced employers to recruit women to take men's places. Women entered the labor force in unprecedented numbers between 1940 and 1945, but, more importantly, they were given jobs previously held only by men—for example, welding, riveting, ship fitting, and tool making. Women of color, though still severely discriminated against, also had new job opportunities opened to them during the war, not only in blue-collar work, but in clerical fields and in nursing as well (Glenn, 1992). For the duration of the war, the federal government campaigned aggressively to recruit women for the labor force by appealing to their sense of patriotism; the government also urged employers to pay women the same wages men would have received and sponsored public day care centers, both of which were important practical incentives to women (Bergman, 1986; Gluck, 1987; Milkman, 1987).

Once the war ended, women were laid off to make room in the labor force for returning servicemen. Federal war programs, such as public child care facilities, were discontinued, and new government-issued propaganda told women to return to their "normal" roles as wives and mothers at home. Some women did quit their jobs, and marriage and birth rates soared in the early postwar years. But public opinion polls showed that as many as 80 percent of the women who held jobs during the war wished to keep them, and a substantial number simply moved into the traditionally female-dominated—and lower paying—service sector rather than leave the labor force (Evans, 1987; Kesselman, 1990; Milkman, 1987).

As we see in Table 8.1, women's labor force participation rate never returned to its prewar level. In fact, since 1950, even though men's labor force participation rate has fluctuated in response to dips in the economy and calls to service during military conflicts, women's labor force participation rate rose steadily at least up to 1995. The greatest increases, however, occurred after 1965. To some extent, this was due to an important demographic change: Women's life expectancy increased, and their fertility rate (even during the baby boom years) decreased compared with earlier generations. This meant that middle-class women who had been full-time homemakers could expect to spend fewer years rearing children, and, therefore, they had greater freedom to pursue other activities including paid employment, although in recent years this freedom has been tempered for some who have taken on the responsibility of caring for grandchildren or for aging parents in their homes (see Chapter 7).

Also, political and social changes were important, particularly those prompted by the feminist movement. The feminist movement called into question traditional notions of women's "proper place" and encouraged women to redefine their roles and seek paid employment. Moreover, feminist activists were instrumental in securing the passage of legislation, which we will discuss later in this chapter, that facilitated women's greater participation in the labor force.

The rising divorce rate since the 1960s, coupled with changes in divorce laws discussed in Chapter 7, also resulted in more women entering the labor force to support themselves and their children without the financial help of a spouse. Recent economic changes have played a major part, too. For one thing, economic recessions fueled women's labor force participation as two incomes became a necessity to make ends meet in many families (Smith, 1987). While the economic recession hurts both men and women, men have become unemployed more quickly than women have (Rampell, 2010). Recent reports also indicate that not only are men more likely than women to be unemployed, they are also more likely than women to be unemployed for a long period of time (52 weeks or more). According to a report issued by the U.S. Department of Labor in October 2010, 58 percent of those unemployed were men and 61 percent of those unemployed for 52 weeks or more were also men (U.S. Department of Labor, 2010c).

Like women who entered the paid labor force to support their families when their husbands were out of work during the Depression, many women today are finding themselves in the same predicament. For example, many women who left the paid labor market to raise children are now attempting to find employment because their husbands are unemployed, their salaries have been reduced, or family investments have dropped in value (Greenhouse, 2009). In fact, 40 percent of U.S. women returning to work are the primary family breadwinner (Banderas, 2009). As mentioned in Chapter 7, in January 2010, women held just slightly less than half (49.9 percent) of all jobs (Rampell, 2010).

One of the most dramatic increases in labor force participation, in fact, has been among married women with children under the age of six. As discussed in Chapter 7, in 1970, 30 percent of married women with children under the age of six were in the paid labor force. In 2007, 61.5 percent of married women with children under the age of six were in the paid labor force (U.S. Department of Commerce, U.S. Census Bureau, 2009c).

Today, the typical woman, like the typical man, is in the paid labor force and is working full time, year-round. However, there are significant differences between women's and men's employment experiences. One important difference is the kinds of jobs women and men typically do. Women and men remain largely segregated in different occupations, which are considered women's work and men's work, respectively. This segregation has serious consequences for both female and male workers, so let's examine it more closely.

SEX SEGREGATION IN THE WORKPLACE

Occupational sex segregation refers to the degree to which men and women are concentrated in occupations in which workers of one sex predominate. A commonly used measure of occupational sex segregation is the **dissimilarity index**, also called the **segregation index** or sometimes simply **D**. Its value is reported as a percentage that tells us the proportion of workers of one sex that would have to change to jobs in which members of their sex are underrepresented in order for the occupational distribution between the sexes to be fully balanced (Reskin & Hartmann, 1986).

Looking at the index of dissimilarity, we find that about fifteen years ago researchers indicated that the United States had a dissimilarity index of 38.4 (Jacobs & Lim, 1995). This means that about 38 percent of the female labor force in the United States would have had to change jobs in order to equalize their representation across occupations. Jacobs and Lim (1995) reported that while occupational sex segregation was stable during most of the twentieth century, it declined steadily after 1970. Nevertheless, by 2001, the dissimilarity index in the United States had stabilized at 31, meaning that about 31 percent of the female labor force in the United States would have had to change their jobs in order to equalize their representation across occupations (Gabriel & Schmitz, 2007). While this may be discouraging, it is important to realize that the dissimilarity index is even higher in other countries. For example, in 2005–2006, the dissimilarity index in Pakistan was 44.6 (Ahmed & Hyder, 2009). In Turkey, occupational sex segregation has actually increased since 1975 (Rich & Palaz, 2008). And Scandinavian countries also have high levels of occupational sex segregation (Estevez-Abe, 2006).

One major weakness of the index of dissimilarity is its sensitivity to types of occupational classifications. The broader the occupational categories, the lower the index tends to be (Jacobs & Lim, 1995; Reskin, 1993; Sokoloff, 1992). Thus, in one study of the United States, the dissimilarity index was 40 when ten broad occupational categories were used, but rose to 62.7 when 426 detailed occupational categories were examined (Jacobs, 1983). A second serious problem with the index of dissimilarity is that it masks both industry-wide and establishment sex segregation, a point to which we will return later (Carlson, 1992; Reskin, 1993).

Another way to gauge occupational sex segregation is simply to look at the percentage of workers of each sex that holds a specific job. Table 8.2 provides us with such information by showing the top occupations employing the largest numbers of men and women. One of the most striking features of this table is the lack of overlap in the jobs held by men and women. Men, we find, are concentrated in the skilled trades and operative jobs. Women, in contrast, are primarily in teaching, clerical, and other service occupations. For example, women are highly concentrated in office and administrative support occupations and personal care and service occupations (U.S. Department of Labor, Bureau of Labor Statistics, 2009a).

A second significant feature of Table 8.2 is the extent to which the jobs listed employ one sex relative to the other. Men also tend to be concentrated in supervisory positions, even in areas that otherwise are predominantly female, such as sales and clerical work. For example, about 29 percent of managers of office and administrative support workers are male, although 96.8 percent of secretaries and administrative assistants are female (U.S. Department of Labor, Bureau of Labor Statistics, 2009a).

This is not to say that there has been no improvement in occupational sex segregation over the years. As we noted previously, researchers found that occupational sex segregation was on the decline after 1970 (Jacobs & Lim, 1995; Reskin & Padevic, 1999), but progress slowed or stalled in the 1990s and 2000s (Cohen, Huffman, & Knauer, 2009; Cotter, Hermsen, & Vanneman, 2004; Hegewisch et al., 2010; Tomaskovic-Dewey et al., 2006). There is evidence of reduced occupational sex segregation in some occupations. Sales jobs, for instance, are relatively well balanced in terms of their sex distribution,

TABLE 8.2 Top Occupations for Men and Women, 2009	
Men	**% Occupation Male**
Logging worker	99.3
Carpenters	98.4
Construction and extraction workers	97.4
Firefighter	96.6
Pest control	96.5
Grounds maintenance worker	94.7
Mechanical engineer	94.1
Construction manager	94.1
Civil engineer	92.9
Computer hardware engineer	91.4
Women	**% Occupation Female**
Pre-K and kindergarten teacher	97.8
Dental assistant	97.6
Secretary and administrative assistant	96.8
Speech and language pathologist	95.8
Child care worker	95.0
Bookkeeper, accounting/auditing clerk	92.2
Registered nurse	92.0
Hairdresser, stylist, cosmetologist	90.4
Paralegal and legal assistant	85.9
Librarian	81.8

Source: U.S. Department of Labor, Bureau of Labor Statistics, 2009a.

and research indicates that women have been moving into managerial and professional occupations since the 1980s (Webb, 2009). At the same time, though, it appears that women have not been as successful entering various scientific, technical, and business occupations (Katz, Stern, & Fader, 2005), and despite women's strides toward leadership positions, they are underrepresented in positions of power (Kellerman & Rhode, 2007). For example, less than 3 percent of Fortune 500 CEOs are women (Scherer, 2010; Soares et al., 2010).

Studies of long-term trends in occupational sex segregation indicate that women have had modest success in moving into a small number of male-dominated occupations, especially in the professions, which do not appear in Table 8.2. This helped to

Sex segregation in the workplace has traditionally relegated women to lower-paying, lower-status jobs than those of men, such as pre-K and kindergarten teaching.

erode occupational sex segregation. However, men continue to find little incentive to enter traditionally female-dominated jobs (England, 2010).

While small numbers of women and men entered sex-atypical occupations, many more men and women entered sex-typical jobs. Therefore, as Jacobs and Lim (1995) point out, the increase in women's labor force participation has to an appreciable extent offset the decrease in occupational sex segregation. Thus, although occupational sex segregation overall has clearly declined, women's chances of sharing the same job as men has simultaneously declined. There is also evidence that workers who hold sex-atypical jobs leave them at a disproportionate rate (see, for example, Wright, 1996). In short, these factors have tempered the gains made in reducing occupational sex segregation.

Consequently, the labor market in the United States continues to be a **dual labor market**, characterized by one set of jobs employing almost exclusively men and another set of jobs, typically viewed as secondary, employing almost exclusively women. This conclusion may come as a surprise to some readers in light of the extensive media coverage that has been given to "the new professional women" and to women now holding nontraditional blue-collar jobs (e.g., carpenters, pipe fitters, miners). Certainly, we are not suggesting here that women have not made inroads into the high-status, high-paying professions as well as the skilled trades. To the contrary, available data indicate that they have. For instance, in 1962, the percentage of female physicians was 6 percent while in 2009, 32.2 percent of physicians and surgeons were women (Sidel, 1986; U.S. Department of Labor, Bureau of Labor Statistics, 2002a, 2009a).

But while there have been widely acclaimed improvements, occupational sex segregation remains a feature of the U.S. labor market and labor markets throughout most of the world (Cohen et al., 2009; Estevez-Abe, 2006; U.S. Department of Labor, Bureau of Labor Statistics, 2009a). Getting a precise reading of occupational sex segregation is complicated by several factors. First, the number of women in many occupations historically has been so low that to say it doubled, tripled, or even increased tenfold does not mean that large numbers of women now hold these jobs or that the jobs are no longer male-dominated. For example, in 1974, women were just 3 percent of lawyers; in 2001, women were 29 percent of lawyers but that translated into about 272,000 female lawyers in the United States (U.S. Department of Commerce, Bureau of the Census, 1993; U.S. Department of Labor, Bureau of Labor Statistics, 2002b). In 2009, women were still only 32 percent of lawyers (U.S. Department of Labor, Bureau of Labor Statistics, 2009a). Even though the number of women employed in skilled trades increased by almost 80 percent between 1960 and 1970, by 2001, women were only 1.7 percent of carpenters, 1.5 percent of auto mechanics, 1.8 percent of electricians, and 5.8 percent of painters (Eisenberg, 1998; Sidel, 1986; U.S. Department of Labor, Bureau of Labor Statistics, 2002b). Moreover, women's progress into such occupations has not shown much improvement in recent years (England, 2010). For example, in 2009, women were 1.6 percent of carpenters and 2.2 percent of electricians (U.S. Department of Labor, Bureau of Labor Statistics, 2009a).

A second factor that complicates the full picture of occupational sex segregation is the fact that in recent years, several female-dominated occupations grew even more female-dominated. For instance, women were 77.7 percent of bookkeepers in 1950 but 92.9 percent of bookkeepers and auditing clerks in 2009 (U.S. Department of Labor, Bureau of Labor Statistics, 2009a).

Occupational sex segregation is also complicated by differences across various groups of workers. For example, the ages of workers are significant. Young workers who are new to the full-time labor force show a moderately lower dissimilarity index than older workers. It is young women, in particular, who appear most likely to enter the male-dominated fields of engineering, science, management, and administration (Reskin & Hartmann, 1986; however, see also Wright, 1996). But this trend of increasing integration by young workers seemed to end in the late 1990s, so that by 2009, women between the ages of twenty-five and thirty-four were no more likely to be found in male-dominated occupations than women between the ages of thirty-five and forty-four (Hegewisch et al., 2010).

Education is also an intervening variable. Women's level of education is negatively correlated with level of occupational sex segregation (Hegewisch et al., 2010; Reskin, 1993; but see also Ashraf, 2007; Bellas & Coventry, 2001). However, recent research has found that progress toward gender integration has stalled for all workers, including the college-educated, since the 1990s (Hegewisch et al., 2010). Class is also an important factor. For example, England (2010) explains that "middle class jobs" have become more desegregated than "working class jobs" (i.e., nonprofessional service work) (p. 9).

Another factor to be considered is race and ethnicity. As Carlson (1992, p. 271) points out, "Sex and race *simultaneously* structure individuals' labor market experiences and their concrete material outcomes" (author's emphasis). Dramatic drops in the dissimilarity index were reported for women of color, especially for Latinas and Asian American women, during the 1970s, but gains eroded somewhat during the 1980s (Carlson, 1992), and that trend has continued in recent years for all racial/ethnic groups (Hegewisch et al., 2010). In 2009, the dissimilarity index was highest for Hispanic workers, followed by African American workers and Asian workers (Hegewisch et al., 2010). Unlike the experiences of White women, only a small part of the decline in occupational sex segregation for racial and ethnic minorities appears to be due to women of color moving into professional occupations (Reskin & Hartmann, 1986, p. 23; see also Glenn, 1992; Lewis & Nice, 1994; Reskin & Padevic, 1999).

Although there are important differences between specific racial and ethnic groups within the broader categories—for example, between Japanese Americans and Vietnamese Americans—a good deal of the occupational shifting among minority women workers has been from one female-dominated service job to another. For instance, Hispanic women's representation as sales and clerical workers exceed their representation in the population (EEOC, 2003). Black and Hispanic women have made substantially less progress than White women in moving into the professions traditionally dominated by White men. In 2009, for example, 34 percent of Black women and 25 percent of Hispanic women were employed in management, professional, and related jobs, compared to 41 percent of White women and 47 percent of Asian women (U.S. Department of Labor, Bureau of Labor Statistics, 2010).

Still, many minority men also have not fared well in the professions. In 2009, for example, 24 percent of Black men and 16 percent of Hispanic men were employed in management, professional, and related jobs, compared to 35 percent of White men and 50 percent of Asian men (U.S. Department of Labor, Bureau of Labor Statistics, 2010).

Besides workers' age, education, and race and ethnicity, another factor that complicates the analysis of occupational sex segregation is the trend toward **occupational resegregation**. As Reskin and Hartmann (1986, p. 31) explain, "Perhaps after reaching some 'tipping point' integrated occupations become resegregated with members of one sex replaced by members of the other" (see also Reskin & Roos, 1990). This often occurs when a shortage of male employees leads employers to seek out female employees. The shortage of male employees may be the result of rapid growth of the field, which causes a high demand for workers, but it is often the result of men deliberately leaving an occupation because they perceive it as declining in skill, prestige, and salary (Wright & Jacobs, 1995). We saw an example of this in Chapter 5 where we discussed the transition of teaching from a male-dominated to a female-dominated profession. Interestingly, the professionalization of teaching during the nineteenth century helped raise wage rates for teachers even though the profession was increasingly feminized. However, men benefited more from these wage increases than women did, especially as they assumed the higher status positions in school administration (Preston, 1995). A more recent example of an occupation that has experienced occupational resegregation is court reporting. Jacobsen (2007) maintains that this shift is due to the feminization of clerical work and the association between such work and court reporting. According to Irvine and Vermilya (2010), occupational resegregation has also been occurring in veterinary medicine (see also Lincoln, 2010).

Finally, any beneficial effects on workers from declines in occupational sex segregation may be undermined by other forms of workplace sex segregation, in particular industry sex segregation and establishment sex segregation. **Industry sex segregation** occurs when women and men hold the same job title in a particular field or industry, but actually perform different jobs. Women are typically concentrated in the lower-paying, lower-prestige specialties within the occupation. Tallichet (2006), for example, studied the integration of women into underground coal mining. Despite the hiring of more women in this occupation in the 1970s, Tallichet found that the majority are concentrated in laboring jobs, the lowest level of mining that usually involves mine maintenance. Similarly, Wright and Jacobs (1995) point out that when women are bakers, they tend to work in food stores while men dominate the more skilled positions in bakeries. Among real estate agents, women are less likely than men to be found in the more profitable arena of commercial real estate (Commercial Real Estate Women Network, 2005).

Establishment sex segregation occurs when women and men hold the same job title at an individual establishment or company, but actually do different jobs. Again, women's jobs are usually lower-paying and less prestigious. For instance, it is not uncommon for women to be working in family law or employment law, while men dominate the more lucrative specializations (Dinovitzer, Reichman, & Sterling, 2009). In the nursing field, when the field of nurse anesthesia changed from being female-dominated to male-dominated, it transformed to a high-status specialization (Lindsay, 2007). In a department store, men typically sell "big ticket" items like large appliances and computers, while women sell clothing, cosmetics, and housewares (Bellas & Coventry, 2001; Reskin, 1993).

In sum, although occupational sex segregation has declined in recent years, it has declined more for certain groups than for others; for the majority of workers, it remains a fact of everyday work life. Moreover, the gains that have been made are tempered by resegregation, industry-wide sex segregation, and establishment sex segregation. At this point, you are probably wondering why this is the case, especially since so much public attention has been given to policies such as affirmative action that were supposed to remedy employment discrimination. However, before we explore the reasons behind the persistence of occupational sex segregation, let's examine some of its most serious consequences.

CONSEQUENCES OF OCCUPATIONAL SEX SEGREGATION

One serious consequence of occupational sex segregation is that it limits employment opportunities. Occupational sex segregation limits the employment opportunities of both sexes, but as we have already noted, it disadvantages women workers most because what is typically labeled "women's work" has some very negative features associated with it. Many women's jobs—such as librarian and elementary or kindergarten teacher—are considered by many people to be boring and tedious jobs. Women's jobs are generally thought to have less autonomy than men's jobs and require less skill or intelligence. And, perhaps most important, women's jobs typically offer few rewards in the forms of compensation, mobility, union protection, benefits, or prestige. Occupational sex segregation keeps more women than men locked into such jobs (Doyal, 1990a; Reskin & Padevic, 1999; C. L. Williams, 1992, 1995).

One interesting way to examine how occupational sex segregation affects employment opportunities is to consider the experiences of workers who obtain employment in jobs nontraditional for their sex. In her classic study of women and men in corporate management, Rosabeth Moss Kanter (1977, p. 209) discussed this problem in terms of **tokenism**, the marginal status of a category of workers who are relatively few in number in the workplace. Tokens, according to Kanter, are "often treated as representatives of their category, as symbols rather than as individuals."

Kanter identified a number of serious consequences for token workers. For instance, because of their conspicuousness in the workplace, they are more closely scrutinized by others. This places intense pressure on them to perform successfully, creating a work situation that is highly stressful. In addition, tokens experience what Kanter calls *boundary heightening*; that is, dominant workers tend to exaggerate the differences between themselves and the tokens and to treat the tokens as outsiders. Thus, researchers have noted that women workers sometimes find themselves excluded from formal information networks that help them do their jobs, but more often they are shut out of informal social networks that may be just as crucial for their job performance and advancement. As male workers are well aware, important business is conducted not only in board rooms or at union meetings but also on golf courses and in local taverns. However, it is these sorts of informal social/business activities in which women workers are least likely to be included by their male coworkers or supervisors (Davies-Netzley, 1998; Mooney & Ryan, 2009; Scott, 1996).

Kanter makes the argument that tokenism is a problem of numbers and, therefore, the employment experiences of women in sex-atypical occupations should become more positive as more women enter such positions. However, some researchers argue that women's negative treatment in the workplace is not so much influenced by their presence as a numerical minority as it is by men's belief that women are inferior (Stichman, Hassell, & Archbold, 2010; C. L. Williams, 1995; Zimmer, 1988). For example, Stichman et al. (2010) interviewed female police officers working for a department where female officers constituted over 17 percent of the force. Despite exceeding what Kanter believes is the "tipping point" of 15 percent, these officers still felt underestimated by their peers. Research on female veterinarians also draws the same conclusion. Despite the feminization of the profession, female veterinarians continue to experience the effects of hegemonic masculinity in veterinary medicine (Irvine & Vermilya, 2010). In other words, "the crucial factor" that determines employment experiences "is the social status of the token's group—not their numerical rarity" (C. L. Williams, 1992, p. 263).

Although women and men in sex-atypical jobs encounter discrimination, its forms and consequences differ significantly depending on the job holder's sex. Sociologist Christine Williams's (1992, 1995) fascinating study of men in female-dominated occupations strongly supports this argument. Researchers who have studied women in sex-atypical occupations report that they are usually disadvantaged in hiring and promotions and that they encounter a "glass ceiling" as they attempt to navigate their way up the occupational hierarchy. The **glass ceiling** refers to the invisible barriers that limit workers'—typically women workers' and racial and ethnic minority workers'—upward occupational mobility. Some reports reveal that women's mobility to leadership positions has improved (Barreto et al., 2009). For example, three of the five Securities and Exchange Commission (SEC) commissioners are women (Scherer, 2010). However, one of Williams' most intriguing findings is that men in sex-atypical occupations often receive preferential treatment in hiring and, instead of encountering a glass ceiling, ride a *glass escalator* up the hierarchy of these professions. According to Williams (1995), men in sex-atypical jobs frequently encounter invisible and sometimes less subtle pressures to move up in their professions. These pressures may take quite positive forms, such as close mentoring and encouragement from supervisors (who, as we have already noted, are often men even though the field is female-dominated), but they may also be the result of prejudicial attitudes by those outside the profession, including the general public and clients, who question the masculinity of men in a traditionally female occupation. One male librarian whom Williams interviewed, for example, was transferred from the children's collection to the adult reference section of the library because some people complained about a man working with children. The underlying assumption here is that "only men who are child molesters or sexual perverts would be drawn to [this] specialty" (C. L. Williams, 1995, p. 13). But for this man, like many others in sex-atypical jobs, the prejudice worked to his advantage: He was transferred to a more prestigious department, to a job that carried more authority. More recent research supports Williams's findings. For instance, studies show that while men are underrepresented in the nursing profession, they are overrepresented in leadership positions (Brown, 2009; Porter-O'Grady, 2007).

What about men who are in sex-atypical jobs that have few, if any, opportunities for advancement? Henson and Krasas Rogers (2001) studied male temporary clerical workers and found that the strategies these men used to address the gendered nature of their work served to reinforce traditional masculine ideals and the subordination of women. For instance, many of the men renamed or reframed their work tasks, refusing to label them "secretarial" and instead describing them in more masculine terms, focusing on the technical competencies required. Many men in sex-atypical jobs had a "cover story" to offer, a socially acceptable explanation of why they were working in a female-dominated job (Henson & Krasas Rogers, 2001; Lupton, 2006; Simpson, 2005).

Christine Williams (1995) reports that the men she interviewed indicated that their supervisors were more likely to discriminate against female employees than against them. An important exception, however, was men who were openly gay; gay men did not receive the favorable treatment afforded their straight male colleagues. For instance, Williams relates the experience of a male nurse who worked in a hospital where one of the physicians preferred to staff the operating room exclusively with male nurses as long as they were not gay.[1] But recent research by Williams, Guiffre, and Dellinger (2009) found that homosexual workers even in gay-friendly workplaces must often conform to heterosexual standards to feel accepted. It is not uncommon, though, for men in sex atypical jobs to be thought to be gay by co-workers regardless of their actual sexual orientation (Burton & Misener, 2007).

Another difference between men's and women's experiences of tokenism that Williams (1992, 1995) discovered was that men reported feeling "in control" in a female-dominated work environment. Women in male-dominated work environments report feeling intimidated and controlled. Other research has found that women in male-dominated occupations, such as information technology, find ways to maintain their feminine gendered identity (Guerrier et al., 2009), and men in female-dominated occupations, such as nursing, find ways to maintain their masculinity (Snyder & Green, 2008). These differential experiences are further reflected in the incidence of sexual harassment in the workplace.

Sexual Harassment in the Workplace

You may recall that in Chapter 5 we defined sexual harassment as any unwanted leers, comments, suggestions, or physical contact of a sexual nature, as well as unwelcome requests for sexual favors. Men rarely experience sexual harassment in the workplace. For example, of the almost 13,000 reports of sexual harassment filed with the Equal Opportunity Employment Commission (EEOC) and state and local Fair Employment Practices Agencies (FEPA) in 2009, only 16 percent were filed by men EEOC 2010).[2] Women, on the other hand, routinely experience sexual harassment in the workplace (Ragins & Scandura, 1995; Bruce et al., 2003).

Women in all types of occupations, from mining (Tallichet, 2006) to law enforcement (Kauppinen & Patoluoto, 2005), experience sexual harassment on the job. Some researchers maintain that sexual harassment is especially pervasive in male-dominated jobs, regardless of whether the jobs are white-collar or blue-collar, because harassment may serve as a means for male workers to assert dominance and control over women who otherwise would be their equals (Berdahl, 2007; Gruber & Morgan, 2005; Stockdale, 2005; Tallichet, 2006), although women in these fields may remain silent about the pervasive sexual harassment they experience in order to keep peace with their coworkers

Sexual harassment, such as unwanted touching, has serious health consequences for women workers.

(Watts, 2007). Interestingly, some researchers have found that women with what may be considered more "masculine" personalities and who work in male-dominated occupations experience even more sexual harassment (Berdahl, 2007).

Temporary workers appear to be at high risk of sexual harassment (Crozier & Davidson, 2007; Rogers & Henson, 1997). Immigrant women who hold low-wage factory and agricultural jobs are also frequent victims of sexual harassment (Preston, 2008; Waugh, 2010). These women are particularly vulnerable because they often do not understand U.S. employment laws or their rights as workers, they may speak little or no English, and they have little or no job mobility (Kiel, 2000; Waugh, 2010).

Regardless of the types of jobs in which it occurs, the consequences of sexual harassment for female workers are serious and harmful. Harassed women report a number of physical responses to the harassment, including chronic neck and back pain, upset stomach, colitis and other gastrointestinal disorders, and eating and sleeping disorders. Harassed women also become nervous, irritable, depressed, and exhibit other symptoms of posttraumatic stress (Buchanan & Fitzgerald, 2008; Saltzman, 1996b; Stanko, 1985).

Despite the number of reports of sexual harassment, most women still do not make official complaints. Instead, many women quit their jobs in order to end the harassment, although given the extent of the problem, this is no guarantee that they will not encounter a similar situation at another work site. Women may also cope with sexual harassment by engaging in work withdrawal (e.g., absenteeism, tardiness) (Buchanan & Fitzgerald, 2008).

Employers have responded to sexual harassment claims in a variety of ways. There is evidence that employers prefer to handle complaints quietly, through private mediation (Fine, 1997), although research also shows that employers who take a visible, proactive approach to addressing sexual harassment are more successful in lowering the incidents of harassment than employers who just provide information about the problem to their employees (Gruber, 1998). Some employers have simply banned sexual relationships between coworkers, even if they are consensual, and a few require coworkers who wish to become intimate to sign "consensual relationship agreements" to protect against sexual harassment suits (Robinson & Gosselin, 1998). Nevertheless, in 1998, the U.S. Supreme Court ruled that even employers who have a sexual harassment policy in place can be held liable for a supervisor's sexual misconduct toward an employee if the victimized employee suffered a "tangible employment action" (e.g., being fired or demoted). If the victimized employee did not suffer a tangible employment action, the employer can successfully defend against liability by showing that they made reasonable efforts to prevent or promptly stop sexual harassment and that the employee unreasonably failed to take advantage of these efforts.

This decision by the Court has made it easier for employees to file—and win—sexual harassment suits. For example, in 1986 and in a subsequent decision in 1993, the Court ruled that sexual harassment so severe and pervasive as to alter the conditions of the victim's employment constitutes a form of sex discrimination. The Court broadened the definition of sexual harassment to include any action that creates a work environment that would be reasonably perceived as hostile and abusive. Moreover, the Court held in 1993 that workers do not have to prove that the harassment caused them severe psychological injury in order to win a suit for damages, and in 1998 the Court unanimously agreed that federal law protects people in the workplace from being harassed by coworkers or supervisors of the same sex.[3] In 2004, the Supreme Court ruled that an employee faced with a situation in which a "reasonable person" would have felt compelled to quit could bring suit even if she or he had not filed a report with the employer before resigning. However, employers could use the failure to report, along with evidence of the safeguards in place to prevent harassment, in their defense. If the employer could prove that the employee had not tried to prevent the harassment and that the safeguards in place would have prevented it if the employee had made use of them, then the employer cannot be held liable.

Sexual harassment is undoubtedly one of the most serious consequences of occupational sex segregation. However, there is one additional consequence that deserves special attention because of the harm it produces. This is the economic impact of sex segregation or what is perhaps better known as the *wage gap*.

THE MALE/FEMALE EARNINGS GAP

In their longitudinal analysis of the economic well-being of women and children, Corcoran, Duncan, and Hill (1984, pp. 233–234) quote a biblical verse in which God, speaking to Moses, said, "When a man makes a special vow to the Lord which requires your valuation of living persons, a male between twenty and sixty years old shall be valued at fifty silver shekels. If it is a female, she shall be valued at thirty shekels." As Corcoran and her colleagues subsequently note, this biblical custom of valuing women's labor at three-fifths that of a man appeared to have carried over into the contemporary work world. From 1960 to 1990, year-round female workers earned on average between 59 and 70 percent of what male workers earned. In other words, for every dollar a male worker made, a female worker made on average between 59 and 70 cents. For more than three decades, this ratio fluctuated within these boundaries (Taeuber & Valdisera, 1986; U.S. Department of Commerce, Bureau of the Census, 1991). In 1993, however, the earnings gap closed to 77 percent, a figure not worth celebrating, but an indication of progress.[4]

This progress has continued in recent years, although some of the factors contributing to it are less than positive. By 2008, the wage gap had narrowed to 80 percent, but at the same time mean wages for some occupations dominated by women had declined. For example, between 2002 and 2007, the mean hourly wage for office and administrative support positions decreased from $15.28 an hour to $15.00 an hour. The mean hourly wage for cashiers and customer service representatives also declined (Keller, 2009). Some observers attributed the slight changes in the wage gap to changes in welfare eligibility that sent many young, unskilled women into the labor force, a point to which we will return shortly, and others pointed out that much of the narrowing of the gap was the result not of women's wages rising, but of men's real wages falling so that they were closer to women's wages (Lewin, 1997c). A third contributing factor has been increases in the minimum wage. The federal minimum wage increased from $6.55 to $7.25 an hour in July 2009. Since more women than men are minimum wage workers, an increase in the minimum wage would help narrow the earnings gap, if only slightly. In 2009, 6 percent of women but only 4 percent of men earned wages at or below the minimum wage (U.S. Department of Labor, Bureau of Labor Statistics, 2010). Still, a fourth contributing factor was an increase in women entering traditionally male-dominated fields that pay more (England & Folbre, 2005).

As Table 8.3 shows, in 2008, the gender gap in wages was about 80 percent. These data also show that race and ethnicity are important intervening variables. We see first that the median weekly earnings of men and women of color are significantly lower than those of White men and women. Second, if we were to look only at the earnings gap by race and ethnicity, we would find that in 2008, African Americans earned about 79.4 percent of what Whites earned, while Hispanic Americans earned only 71.3 percent of what Whites earned. However, by making within-sex comparisons by race and ethnicity, we get a better picture of how race and ethnicity intersect with sex to depress wages. Using the data in Table 8.3, we can determine that in 2008, African American women earned 84.7 percent of what White women earned, whereas Hispanic American women earned just 76.6 percent of what White women earned. For African American and Hispanic American men, the wage gap relative to White men was 75.2 percent and 67.8 percent, respectively. Thus, although Hispanic American women have the lowest median

TABLE 8.3   Median Weekly Earnings of Full-Time Wage and Salary Workers by Race/Ethnicity and Sex, 2008

Race/Ethnicity & Sex	Median Weekly Earnings	Female/Male Wage Gap
Total	$722	
Male	798	
Female	638	79.9%
White	742	
Male	825	
Female	654	79.3%
African American	589	
Male	620	
Female	554	89.4%
Hispanic American	529	
Male	559	
Female	501	89.6%

Source: U.S. Department of Labor, Bureau of Labor Statistics, 2009b.

earnings of all groups, the earnings gap between their earnings and those of White women is actually narrower than the earnings gap between men of color and White men.

Of course, one's level of educational attainment affects one's earnings. However, men with the same level of education as women continue to earn higher wages. While women's progress in higher education has influenced the narrowing of the wage gap, women continue to major in fields that command lower salaries (Bobbitt-Zeher, 2007). In addition, the race/ethnicity earnings gap has actually widened over the years, despite a narrowing of the gap in educational attainment between African Americans and Whites (Neal, 2004). In fact, Grodsky and Pager (2001) discovered that the wage gap between African American and White men increased as one went *up* the occupational hierarchy in private sector employment. In other words, the higher the job status and pay—and, therefore, the higher the educational qualifications required to fill it—the greater the disparity in wages between African American and White men who held the same positions.

Another factor that has been found to be correlated with the male/female earnings gap is whether or not female employees have children. Research shows that female employees—but not male employees—who have children pay a *motherhood wage penalty* of 5 to 13 percent (Budig & England, 2001; Waldfogel, 1997). The cumulative earnings of working women without children in the United States are 64 percent of men's earnings, while the cumulative earnings of working mothers are 52 to 57 percent of men's earnings depending on the number of children they have (Sigle-Rushton & Waldfogel, 2007). However, as we discussed in Chapter 7, having children is associated with a wage increase for married men. For married African American men, fatherhood is associated with a 7 percent increase in wages, and for married White and Latino men, fatherhood is associated with a 9 percent increase in wages (Glauber, 2007).

After controlling for years of job experience—under the assumption that working mothers may accrue less employment experience because they take more time off from work for childbearing and rearing than working women without children—Budig and England (2001) still found a penalty of 5 percent per child. The penalty was higher for married women with children than unmarried women with children, and very little of the penalty could be explained away by low wages attached to "mother-friendly" jobs—i.e., jobs with flexible hours, few travel demands, no evening or weekend work hours, on-site day care, and the ability to make phone calls while working to check on children. Instead, they conclude that the penalty stems from either the effects of motherhood on worker productivity or discrimination by employers, issues to which we will return later in the chapter. The motherhood wage penalty may also vary by race/ethnicity. For example, Glauber (2007) found that regardless of their marital status, all White women with one or two children experienced a wage penalty, while Hispanic women did not experience any penalty and African American women only experienced a wage penalty if they had more than two children.

An individual's earnings are also affected by the type of work she or he does. As we have already noted, women and minorities continue to experience widespread occupational segregation. The jobs in which they predominate not only tend to be less prestigious than those dominated by White men, but also to pay less (England, 2010). Statistics also indicate that minorities and women are more likely than Whites and men to be hired as contingent workers, temporary employees, on-call workers, and day laborers. Contingent workers do not have continuous, ongoing employment, but rather work at a job for a fixed period of time, usually less than a year; their employment is contingent on employers' needs for their services. Temporary workers usually obtain employment through a temp agency; they typically work sporadically throughout the year and move from job site to job site as demand requires. Finally, as we have already noted, women are more likely than men to be employed in minimum wage jobs than in salaried occupations. In 2008, 49.6 percent of hourly wage workers were male; 1.9 percent earned the minimum wage or less. In contrast, 50.4 percent of hourly wage workers in 2008 were women and of these, 3.9 percent earned the minimum wage or less (U.S. Department of Commerce, Bureau of the Census, 2010).

The monetary rewards to the employers of these workers are obvious; not only do contingent, temporary, on-call, day labor, and minimum-wage employees receive lower wages than employees in traditional work arrangements and salaried occupations, but also they typically are not entitled to costly employment benefits such as medical and disability insurance, pensions, and paid vacations, and these workers are rarely unionized. Regardless of the economic benefits for employers, the effects on female and minority workers are overwhelmingly negative (Kalleberg et al., 1997; but for a different view, see McCall, 2001). Indeed, given these data, it is hardly surprising that women and racial and ethnic minorities are disproportionately represented among the poor.

The Earnings Gap, Poverty, and Welfare Policy

Approximately 8.6 percent of the White population in the United States is officially poor, whereas 11.8 percent of the Asian American population, 24.7 percent of the Black population, 23.2 percent of the Hispanic population, and 31.2 percent of the Native American population are officially living below the poverty line (U.S. Department of Commerce, Bureau of the Census, 2009e).[5] As we learned in Chapter 7, female-headed families are also disproportionately represented among the poverty population; 28.7 percent of female-headed households live below the poverty line. A child living with only his or her mother is five times more likely to be poor than a child living with both parents (Children's Defense Fund, 2008). When the race of female-headed households is taken into account the figures are even more concerning: 23.8 percent of White female-headed households, 39.8 percent of African American female-headed households, and 40.6 percent of Hispanic female-headed households live below the poverty line (DeNavas-Walt, Proctor, & Smith, 2008; Drake & Rank, 2009).

When we think of poverty, we often think of unemployment. Unemployment rates, like the other statistics we have examined, vary by sex and race and ethnicity, although race and ethnicity have a greater impact on unemployment than sex does.[6] In 2001, the overall unemployment rates of both men and women, aged twenty and over, were quite low (4.6 percent and 4.5 percent, respectively). However, by mid-2010, the unemployment rate had risen to 9.6 percent (9.8 percent for men, 8.0 percent for women). The unemployment rate was highest for African Americans: 8.7 percent of Whites, 7.2 percent of Asian Americans, and 12 percent of Hispanic Americans were unemployed, but 16.3 percent of African Americans were unemployed in 2010 (U.S. Department of Labor, Bureau of Labor Statistics, 2010b). What these unemployment rates also tell us is that the majority of those living in poverty, including the majority of women who head households, are working. Some work only part time year-round or sporadically throughout the year, but many work full-time. Of course, being unemployed significantly increases one's chances of falling into poverty, but employment does not necessarily lift an individual and her or his family above the poverty threshold. Consider, for example, that if one held a minimum wage job paying $7.25 per hour, even if one worked forty hours per week, fifty-two weeks a year, the income before deductions ($15,080) for Social Security and employment-related expenses (e.g., child care, transportation, clothing) was still significantly below the poverty threshold of $18,310 for a family of three in 2009. In her participant observation study of the working poor, Barbara Ehrenreich (2001) found that working full-time in unskilled service jobs paying $6 or $7 per hour did not give her sufficient income to pay for rent in low-income housing and still have enough to buy food, clothing, and transportation to and from work. She, and many of the people who worked with her, often held two jobs, but still found the income too low and housing costs too high to live much above the poverty line. For example, the household income for a family with one minimum wage worker is only 54 percent of the poverty line, or 107 percent of the poverty line for a family with two minimum wage workers (Manpower Demonstration Research Corporation, 2006).

Similarly, sociologists Kathryn Edin and Laura Lein (1997) found in their study of impoverished women that working mothers fared worse financially than mothers on welfare.

Even though work seemed to bring in about 42 percent more income than welfare benefits, the gain was significantly diminished by employment-related expenses. Moreover, about 40 percent of the working mothers Edin and Lein interviewed lacked health insurance, while the women on welfare received Medicaid (federally financed health insurance), so the working mothers were more likely than the welfare recipients to forgo necessary medical care (see also Edin & Kissane, 2010; Porter & Dupree, 2001).

While conducted over a decade ago, Edin and Lein's (1997) research is important because it debunks popular myths about welfare recipients and alerts us to the dangers inherent in the welfare "reforms" signed into law by President Clinton in 1996. One widespread myth about welfare recipients is that they can live quite well on the benefits they receive. Edin and Lein's study shows that welfare benefits are not sufficient to even make ends meet. For example, Edin and Lein found that only 7 percent of a welfare recipient's income is spent on unnecessary items such as movies, a meal out, cigarettes, or alcohol, and Black women and Latinas spend less on these items than White women do. Rather, the inadequacy of welfare means that most of these women must find additional sources

The current economic recession and home foreclosure crisis are increasing the number of homeless families in the U.S.

of income—legal or illegal—to meet their daily needs. It also means that most live in substandard housing and many cannot adequately feed and clothe their children. Indeed, Edin and Lein found that one in eight women in their study had kept their children home from school during the winter because they did not have sufficient clothing.

The number of single mothers in the labor force has increased dramatically since 1993. In fact, the percentage of single mothers in the labor force is now higher than the percentage of married mothers in the labor force (U.S. Department of Labor, Bureau of Labor Statistics, 2010). A substantial portion of this increase is undoubtedly the result of welfare "reform," known officially as the Personal Responsibility and Work Reconciliation Act (PRWRA), signed into law by President Clinton in 1996 (Seefeldt, 2008). The way out of poverty, according to the rationale behind the reform, is through work, but the only way welfare recipients will get jobs is if they are required to do so. Consequently, the PRWRA contains among its provisions a mandatory work requirement after two years of assistance, a cap of five years on the total time a family can receive assistance, permission for the states to deny additional benefits to women who have more children while on welfare, the elimination of the bonus welfare mothers receive for helping the government collect child support from absent fathers, and significant reductions in the food stamp program (McCrate & Smith, 1998; Porter & Dupree, 2001). These "reforms" reduced the number of people on welfare, from 12.2 million in 1996 to 5.3 million in 2002. However, it is not surprising given our current recession that the number of people on welfare is on the rise (Murray, 2009; Wolf, 2010). In fact, the number of people on welfare in December 2007 was 3.8 million people (Wolf, 2010).

In addition, the poverty rate declined somewhat in the late 1990s. The percentage of children living in poverty decreased from 20.5 percent in 1996 to 16.2 percent in 2002 (Pear, 2002). However, these changes occurred during a period of economic prosperity in the United States, when unskilled, low-wage jobs were relatively plentiful. The more recent outlook is bleak and entry-level employment has become more difficult to find (Loprest & Zedlewski, 2006).

GENDER, POVERTY, AND THE ELDERLY   While we have emphasized the intersection of sexism and racism in the generation and reproduction of poverty, it is also important to consider a third factor: age. Women are disproportionately represented among individuals living in poverty, but the statistics mask the fact that among these individuals, a large percentage are elderly women who live alone. The poverty rate of the elderly population declined significantly between the late 1960s and late 1990s—from 28.5 percent, or more than twice the rate of the general population in 1966, to 10.5 percent, somewhat less than the 12.7 percent rate for the general population, in 1998 (U.S. Department of Commerce, Bureau of the Census, 2000). Recent data indicate that the poverty rate for the elderly continues to decrease. The poverty rate declined for seniors age sixty-five and older from 3.7 million in 2008 to 3.4 million or 8.9 percent in 2009 (U.S. Department of Commerce, Bureau of the Census, 2010). However, improvement has been slower for elderly women (Carr, 2010; U.S. Department of Commerce, U.S. Census Bureau, 2000). Many elderly people who live alone are widows and, in contrast with the stereotype of the "old, rich widow," many elderly widows are poor (Gillen & Kim, 2009). In addition to gender and marital status, race and ethnicity are also significant factors. For example, the poverty rate for married White men age sixty-five and older is 3.1 percent, while the poverty rate for Black women living alone is 37.5 percent and the poverty rate for Hispanic women living alone is 40.5 percent (Carr, 2010).

One of the reasons there are more women than men among the elderly poor is simply that there are more elderly women than elderly men; women, on average, live longer than men (see Chapter 12). Moreover, the longer they live, the greater their chances are of depleting their savings and slipping below the poverty line (Feldstein, 1998). The economic difficulties of elderly women are also directly related to their employment patterns, the wages they earned during their work lives, and their job benefits. For example, women are less likely than men to be employed in jobs that have private pension plans (Christensen, 2002). In addition, women frequently interrupt their labor force participation because of caregiving responsibilities (see Chapter 7). Employment interruptions not only limit job opportunities, but also prevent women from accruing sufficient retirement benefits (Davis et al., 1990; Jacobsen & Levin, 1995). Adding to this problem is the "motherhood wage penalty" we discussed earlier. As a result of these factors, many older women, especially those who reentered the labor force relatively late due to divorce, are now forced to delay retirement for as long as they are able (Uchitelle, 2001). Although Supplemental Security Income (SSI) was designed to assist those not covered by Social Security or those for whom Social Security benefits are inadequate, the program has stringent eligibility requirements that disqualify many individuals even though they are poor.

Another segment of the poverty population is made up of the homeless. As Box 8.1 shows, the homeless population, like the poverty population as a whole, is diverse. Women's and men's experiences of homelessness, we learn, differ, as do those of single individuals and families.

At this point it is clear that the wage gap contributes to many pervasive and serious problems. A question that remains, however, is how the wage gap is related to occupational segregation. To answer this question, we need to examine explanations of the wage gap itself. In addressing this topic, we will concentrate primarily on the gender gap in wages, but we will also consider to some extent the racial/ethnic gap in wages.

Explaining the Wage Gap

Table 8.4 shows median weekly earnings of selected occupations in 2008. The table contains a broad range of jobs that require different levels of training, skill, effort, and responsibility, but one consistent observation that can be made is that female-dominated occupations usually pay significantly less than male-dominated occupations. Research documents a strong inverse relationship between the extent to which women are represented in a specific job and that job's median earnings (Blau & Kahn, 2007; England, Allison, & Wu, 2007). As women's share of an occupation increases, the pay of both men and women in that occupation decreases (Kay & Hagan, 1995; Reskin & Padevic, 1999).

Many employers, economists, and public policy makers acknowledge that "women's work" almost always pays less than "men's work," but they maintain that the reason particular jobs have become female-dominated is because large numbers of women have freely chosen to enter them. Central to their argument is the assumption that women's primary allegiance is to home and family; thus, they seek undemanding jobs that require little personal investment in training or skills acquisition so that they can better tend to their household responsibilities. In other words, women choose to invest less than men in employment outside the home so they get less in return. This explanation is called **human capital theory**.

BOX 8.1
Gender and Homelessness

In the minds of many of us with homes, myths rather than facts about homelessness predominate (Golden, 1992). So, the first question we need to address is: Who are the homeless?

Some estimates indicate that there are well over a million homeless people in Western Europe and North America (Fazel et al., 2008), and other estimates indicate that there are over 3 million people in the United States alone who experience homelessness in a given year (National Law Center on Homeless and Poverty, 2007). However, it is challenging to get an accurate estimate of the number of homeless people since most studies count people in shelters or on the streets, but ignore the homeless living with friends or relatives (National Coalition for the Homeless, 2009a).

Research indicates that the homelessness are far more diverse than one might suppose. It is commonly believed that the homelessness are unemployed single men and women who are alcoholics, drug addicts, or people with mental illnesses who were indiscriminately released from psychiatric hospitals. Homelessness is associated with mental health issues such as bipolar disorder and schizophrenia (Folsom et al., 2004). However, it is unclear whether substance abuse and symptoms of mental illness (e.g., hearing voices, "antisocial" behavior, hoarding) emerge before or after the individual becomes homeless—that is, whether these behaviors are adaptations to homelessness rather than causes of homelessness. Consider carefully for a moment what life on the streets or in public shelters might be like. The demoralization and disorientation that result from having to keep moving without having any place to go and having no structure to one's life are likely to psychologically weaken even the emotionally strong.

Research indicates that what all homeless people share in common is poverty. Since certain groups, such as racial and ethnic minorities, are disproportionately represented among the poor, they are also at greater risk of becoming homeless. African Americans are disproportionately represented in the homeless population (Folsom et al., 2005; Rossi, 1989). And while the vast majority of the homeless are not employed, most express a desire to work, but cannot because of a lack of jobs, a lack of training or education, poor interviewing skills, their homeless status, lack of appropriate clothing, lack of transportation, or health or disability problems (National Coalition for the Homeless, 2009b).

The fastest growing segment of the homeless population is families with children (Children's Defense Fund, 2005; National Coalition for the Homeless, 2009a). Due to the economic recession and the home foreclosure crisis, the number of homeless people has increased, including the number of homeless children (Glod, 2009; Goodman, 2009).

For many, homelessness is an extension of the high rate of poverty among female-headed families. Some research has found that homeless Hispanic women are more likely than homeless White or homeless African American women to be caring for children (Austin, Andersen, & Gelberg, 2008). A substantial number of women and children become homeless as a result of leaving an abusive husband/father. For abused women and children, living on the street may be a survival strategy (Browne & Bassuk, 1997; Golden, 1992). In fact, Jasinski and her colleagues (2010) report that homeless women are two to four times more likely to have been physically or sexually victimized as adults when compared to women of similar economic status who are not homeless. In addition, research has found that homeless White women are more likely than homeless women of other races/ethnicities to report childhood or recent physical or sexual assault (Austin et al., 2008). Other research supports the fact that many children become homeless when they leave home to escape witnessing violence between family members or their own physical, sexual, or emotional abuse by a family member (Johnson, Rew, & Sternglanz, 2006; Rosenthal, Mallett, & Myers, 2006).

Golden (1992) emphasizes the gender differences in the causes of homelessness among single women and men. She points out, for instance, that the deinstitutionalization movement of the 1970s made more women than men homeless, because more women than men were residents of psychiatric facilities during this period. Recent research has found that homeless women are more likely than women with homes to suffer from mental health problems such as depression, anxiety, schizophrenia, and post-traumatic stress disorder (Folsom et al., 2005). The primary reason for homelessness among women was the loss of relationships. The majority of women Golden (1992) met as a shelter volunteer had adhered to a traditional feminine role of financial dependency on someone else, usually a husband, boyfriend, or father. When, because of death or some other reason, these relationships dissolved, the women simply could not fend for themselves.

Although it certainly may not be said that life on the streets is easy for men, it is nevertheless the case that street life is more difficult for women. For one thing, it is more dangerous in certain ways. Women are more vulnerable to physical assault, and many homeless women report that rape and other sexual assaults are not uncommon (Golden, 1992; Goodman, Fels, & Glenn, 2006; Jasinski et al., 2010; Vanderstaay, 1992). And only women run the risk of becoming pregnant as a result of a forced or consensual sexual encounter.

Even the most routine aspects of daily living are more difficult for homeless women than for homeless men. This largely results from the virtual absence of privacy afforded the homeless and the fact that in our society women more than men are socialized to value privacy, especially when carrying out basic hygienic functions. Thus, relieving oneself in public is not only physically, but also psychologically more difficult for women. Cleaning oneself in a public washroom or showering with others in a public shelter have a similar psychological effect on homeless women. And, as Golden (1992, p. 160) notes, "Any woman can imagine the potential for agonizing humiliation in having one's period on the street."

While it is true that many of those with homes tend to blame the homeless for their own plight, homeless women are especially stigmatized, and much of this stigma is sexually charged (Golden, 1992). It is assumed, for example, that homeless women are promiscuous and immoral. If they have children, they are stereotyped as "welfare mothers" who freeload off the system and promiscuously reproduce. If they are alone, they do not escape the label of promiscuity—in fact, they are frequent targets of sexual harassment because of it—but it is also assumed that their problems would be solved if they could just find a "good man." Ironically, what is overlooked in these cases is the fact that it was their relationships with men that often initially propelled these women into homelessness.

In evaluating human capital theory, we will focus first on the issue of women's "choice" of occupations. It is certainly the case, as we learned in Chapter 7, that women bear primary responsibility for home and family care, but what is less clear is the extent to which this is voluntary. A major weakness in human capital theory is that it fails to distinguish between self-imposed job restrictions and structurally imposed ones. For instance, are unemployed mothers who cannot find affordable and reliable child care really making a "free choice" to stay out of the labor market? The decision to remain at home or to accept low-paying jobs because the hours or work arrangements better suit one's child care responsibilities is most often a response to a structurally imposed

TABLE 8.4   Median Weekly Earnings of Selected Male-Dominated and Female-Dominated Occupations, 2008

Occupation	Female (%)	Median Weekly Earnings ($)
Dental hygienist	97.3	976
Child care worker	94.3	396
Receptionist and information clerk	93.3	503
Registered nurse	90.0	1,022
Hairdresser, hairstylist, or cosmetologist	87.9	496
Bank teller	84.0	469
Librarian	81.6	878
Elementary and middle school teacher	81.0	890
Social worker	78.7	784
Telemarketer	64.0	457
Physician or surgeon	31.8	1,731
Mail carrier	29.9	908
Architect, except naval	23.3	1,128
Police officer or sheriff's patrol officer	15.0	893
Taxi driver or chauffeur	14.4	503
Chemical engineer	12.5	1,546
Firefighter	4.6	970
Aircraft pilot or flight engineer	4.3	1,390
Electrician	0.8	807
Roofer	0.7	558

Source: U.S. Department of Labor, Bureau of Labor Statistics, 2009b.

constraint on women's occupational opportunities—that is, our government's failure to enact a national child care policy (see Box 8.2).

In fact, as we have already seen, the majority of women with very young children do work outside the home. Moreover, some research shows that, contrary to the argument of human capital theorists, women's probability of working in a nontraditional occupation increases with the number of children they have. Although mothers of young children do try to avoid jobs with rotating shifts because of the child care difficulties they pose, having children has been positively correlated with women's efforts to leave female-dominated jobs for male-dominated ones (Reskin, 1993), possibly because they offer higher salaries. Still, some women do not seek work in male-dominated jobs because they perceive them to be less flexible (Frome et al., 2006).

BOX 8.2
The Child Care Dilemma

Work in the United States is organized under the assumption that workers are men who, if they have children, also have a wife at home to care for them (Arendell, 2000; Perry-Jenkins et al., 2000). As we have seen, however, this is not the case. The number of single-parent families in the United States has increased significantly during the last forty years, and women with preschool-aged children have been one of the fastest growing segments of the labor force. Nevertheless, the federal government and most employers have responded ineffectively at best to these demographic changes. The United States, unlike at least 146 other countries, has no official government policy mandating *paid* parental leave, and we are one of the few advanced industrialized countries that lacks a government-mandated child care system (United Nations, 2000; USA Today, 2005). One study of twenty-one high-income countries found that the United States ranked twenty out of twenty-one in terms of unpaid leave (Ray, Gornick, & Schmitt, 2010). Other than Australia, the United States was the only country that provided no paid leave for new parents. In addition, the only country that provided fewer weeks of job-protected leave than the United States was Switzerland; however, Switzerland provides financial support of 80 percent of a mother's usual earnings during that leave (Ray et al., 2010).

It was not until 1993 that the United States had any federal legislation mandating parental leave. Currently, the Family and Medical Leave Act requires employers with fifty or more employees to offer both women and men up to twelve weeks *unpaid* leave following the birth or adoption of a child or to care for a sick child or family member. Research on the impact of the Family and Medical Leave Act in the United States indicates that men are far less likely than women to take the leave, primarily for two reasons. The first is money. As we have already learned, there is a substantial wage gap between women and men; few families can afford to have fathers, who typically earn more than mothers, stay at home

on unpaid parental leave. Second, although employers are required to offer the leave to both male and female employees, studies show that men fear that their employers will view them as less dedicated to their careers and their companies if they take more than just a few days off following the birth of a child. The men worry that their employers may "punish" them for taking parental leave (Hansen, 2010). These perceptions are not unfounded, since studies also show that the majority of employers think that their male employees should take no parental leave (Levine, 2000).

The provisions of the Family and Medical Leave Act may also be unfeasible for many female workers as well, and again the reason is economic. Few single women who have babies can afford to take much unpaid time off from work. Among the working class and working poor, even in two-parent households, both partners' incomes are necessary for the economic survival of the family, thus making an unpaid leave for a woman, even in a low-paying job, financially unfeasible. Consequently, women in such circumstances, as well as workers in companies with fewer than fifty employees, must often return to work within days of their child's birth, arranging some form of child care for the infant.

It is not overstating the point to say that many working parents in the United States confront a child care crisis. With the welfare law now mandating that beneficiaries go to work, the number of children in need of care has increased. But affordable, reliable, and high-quality child care is difficult to find, and for low-income families, the problem is especially acute. Low-income families can apply for child care subsidies from their state governments, but most states have lengthy waiting lists for these subsidies. Also, many states are cutting state-run subsidized child care programs (Goodman, 2010). When families do receive child care assistance as they leave welfare, their employment success rate goes up dramatically. Twenty-eight percent of families who did not receive child care assistance within

(continued)

BOX 8.2
Continued

three months of leaving welfare returned to welfare, while only 19 percent of those who received child care assistance returned to welfare (Matthews, 2006).

Some corporations and businesses have opened their own child care centers in recognition of the importance of family concerns and as a means to attract and retain workers. Others provide child care referral services or a child care subsidy as a job benefit. Still others permit "flextime" (employees set their own work schedule as long as they work a requisite number of hours per day or week) and "flexplace" (employees work out of their homes at least part of the work day or week). Regardless of the advantages or disadvantages of any of these options, a more important point is that they remain exceptions. Most employers, as well as most employees, continue to view child care needs as a "private" rather than a business matter (Gerstel & Clawson, 2001). Moreover, these options are rarely available to low-income workers and the working poor. For instance, child care centers available at the worksite are not free, and their average cost typically puts them out of reach for all but the highest-paid employees (Gerstel & Clawson, 2001).

For many years, sociologists, child psychologists, pediatricians, and other experts debated the issue of whether day care is harmful to young children. After conducting literally hundreds of studies, their conclusion is really not surprising: The important question is not whether day care itself is good or bad; rather, the important issue is the quality of care provided. When caregiver-child ratios are low, children reap benefits: They have fewer behavior problems, are more proficient in language, engage in more complex play, and spend more time in learning activities. Especially important is the level of verbal interaction between caregivers and children; children who are provided with a high level of language stimulation during their first three years develop the verbal and cognitive skills they need to be schoolready (Children's Defense Fund, 2001). What is striking is the *lack* of day care providers who meet even minimal standards of care, let alone the high standards recommended by these studies.

The lack of affordable, reliable, and high-quality child care has led many observers in the United States to question, despite ideological claims to the contrary, whether we are a nation that truly cares about the well-being of our children. After all, other countries, such as France, whose taxes are higher, whose gross national product is lower, and whose government has cut spending over the years, nevertheless provide high-quality child care and preschool education that are heavily subsidized by the government (Greenhouse, 1993; Simons, 1997). Clearly, our nation's leaders and we as citizens must decide if our society is willing to provide at least adequate care for *all* of our children and, if so, we must make the commitment of public funds necessary to make that goal a reality.

Even if a woman prefers a male-dominated job, the choice to take such a job obviously is constrained by its availability. We use the term *availability* here to refer not only to a job opening, but also to the extent to which a job seeker perceives that she has a fair chance of being hired for the job, feeling welcome on the job, and succeeding in the job. Research shows that workers' decisions to take specific jobs reflect the occupational opportunities available to them. Historically, women have not been hired for jobs such as coal mining, construction, and shipbuilding, but evidence indicates that once employers began to open job opportunities in these fields, women responded by seeking such jobs (Denissen, 2010; Eisenberg, 1998; Reskin & Hartmann, 1986; Tallichet, 2006). However, the number of women already working in a particular job also has been shown to be important because such women serve as role models and mentors to other female job aspirants (Ferguson & Dunphy, 1992; Tahmincioglu, 2006; see also Chapter 5). If few or no women hold particular jobs, then women are likely to believe that these jobs are not really open to them, and they will rarely pursue them. The lack of women in an occupation or field sends a message to other women: You are unlikely to succeed here (Riger, 1988). Some researchers have found that males with mentors in male-dominated fields, such as the legal field, are more likely than women with mentors to benefit from higher salaries and perceive the work environment as fair (Fay & Wallace, 2009). But other researchers report that male mentors may be more beneficial to females than males. For example, Ramaswami and colleagues (2010) found that female lawyers with male mentors were more likely than male lawyers with male mentors to earn higher salaries and report higher job satisfaction.

Some women may choose not to enter certain occupations because they do not want to subject themselves to discrimination on the job and to a working environment that is hostile to women (Riger, 1988; Yount, 2005). Women in male-dominated jobs also sometimes struggle to find an appropriate workplace identity. For example, based on interviews with women who work in the building trades, Denissen (2010) concluded that women in traditional male jobs are "held accountable to contradictory expectations for a feminine presentation of self and a masculine performance of work" (p. 1051).

Research has documented male workers' efforts to exclude women from certain occupations by, for instance, deliberately excluding them from particular activities or even sabotaging their work (Tallichet, 2006). In addition, historical research has shown how the actions of some unions have successfully excluded women from certain occupations, although the research findings are mixed with regard to unions' positions on sex integration of particular jobs (see, for example, Cobble, 1991; Gabin, 1990). Some studies show that occupational sex segregation is low when unions are weak (Moller & Li, 2009), but Gerstel and Clawson (2001) caution that there is tremendous variation among unions, making it inappropriate to talk about a single union position on any particular work issue, such as family benefits. However, these researchers did find that strong unions with a high percentage of female members as well as a strong (female) union leader had higher levels of family benefits than weaker unions, unions with low female membership, and unions with a low proportion of female leaders (see also Schmitt, 2009).

Clearly the evidence we have discussed so far does not lend support to the human capital theory, but for the sake of argument, let's assume for the moment that the theory is correct: Women choose jobs that involve fewer skills, fewer time demands, and less training than the jobs men choose. To what extent does this explain the difference in women's and men's wages? The answer appears to be very little. As England et al. (2007) explain, "Predominantly female occupations pay less than 'male' occupations, even after adjusting for skills" (p. 1237). Moreover, in one test of human capital theory, Kay and Hagan (1995) found that participation variables (e.g., weeks worked per year, hours per week invested in work, and hours per week devoted to child care responsibilities) accounted for practically none of the sizable wage gap they observed between male and female lawyers. Large differences in patterns of job tenure between male and female workers also explained little of the wage gap. In fact, all of the factors they analyzed, taken together, accounted for less than a third of the wage gap between White men and

White women and only about a quarter of the wage gap between White men and Black women (see also Budig & England, 2001; England, 2005; Reskin & Padevic, 1999).

In addition, sex differences in education have little to do with the wage gap (Levanon, England, & Allison, 2009). In a study among U.S. college graduates from the 1990s, (Catherine Weinberger & Kuhn, 2005) observed that differences in pay between men and women remained the same over the length of their careers. That is to say, the wage discrimination did not change over time. It was initially present at the start of their careers and was not an accumulation of merit-based differences, but was instead discrimination-based. Consider, for example, that in 2007, the median income for a female college graduate was $36,167 while the median income for a male who only completed high school was only slightly less at $31,337 (U.S. Department of Commerce, Bureau of the Census, 2008).

Another difficulty inherent in human capital theory is the assumption that women's work automatically entails lower skill, effort, and responsibility than traditional men's work. It fails to account for the fact that female-dominated jobs that require basically the same (and sometimes more) skill, effort, and responsibility as male-dominated jobs still pay less. To understand this point, return to the figures in Table 8.4. Here we find, for instance, that a child care worker earns $512 less per week than a mail carrier and $162 less than a roofer. Additional examples are abundant. As Boraas and Rodgers (2003) point out, several factors compound this, such as education, race, and age, but by far the largest influencing factor, they found, was the number of women in an occupation. For example, in 1999, a woman working in a predominately female occupation earned 25.9 percent less than a woman working in a predominately male occupation (Boraas & Rodgers, 2003). Skills that are utilized in predominantly female occupations, such as teaching, nursing, and social work, are frequently not recognized as compensable skills in job evaluation systems, at least in part because they are viewed as an extension of women's unpaid work in the home. As we learned in Chapter 7, most people do not think of housework and child care as "real" work—as work that requires any special skill, formal education, or training. Indeed, women are supposed to be nurturers "by nature." The incorporation of such stereotypes into job evaluation programs has caused the systematic devaluing of jobs traditionally held by women, while jobs traditionally held by men have often been overvalued.

In sum, what we have found here is that occupational sex segregation and the wage gap have little to do with the preferences or free choices of individual workers. A competing explanation of these problems focuses less on the choices and behaviors of workers (the "supply side" of the labor market) and more on the choices and behaviors of employers (the "demand side" of the labor market), including the employers' tendency toward sex discrimination as well as other forms of discrimination. We turn now to an evaluation of this alternative perspective, but as Reskin (1993) cautions, it must be kept in mind that in the everyday operations of workplaces, both demand-side and supply-side factors likely interact with one another to produce particular employment outcomes.

THE WORK WORLD: IDEOLOGY AND THE ROLE OF LAW

A demand-side explanation for occupational sex segregation and the wage gap emphasizes how the actions of employers combine with structural aspects of the workplace to lessen the chances for sex integration and to widen sex differences in earnings. Among the factors considered crucial are the extent to which gender stereotypes come into play in hiring and promotion decisions as well as in the assignment of specific work tasks, in institutionalized recruitment and promotion procedures, and in pressures from regulatory agencies. Let's consider each of these.

Gender Stereotypes at Work

In our earlier discussion, we saw how beliefs about women's and men's "appropriate" roles historically helped give rise to a dual labor market. To review, the prevalent ideology was that a "proper lady" did not work unless she was unmarried or, if married, then childless. A wide range of occupations were open to men, but women entered a limited number of jobs that supposedly matched their "natural" talents and simply extended their family roles into the public arena. These, as we have noted, were occupations in the "helping professions" and in blue-collar and low-level service fields (e.g., clerical work, sewing, assembling, and canning). This ideology gave rise to a corollary set of beliefs: that women did not need to work; that they worked only briefly until they married or had children (things all women should do) and that if they worked after marriage or the birth of children, it was only to buy "extras" for the family or to "help out" financially.

In short, employers and employees alike, women as well as men, came to see women's employment as secondary to that of men and to view women workers as less serious about or less committed to their jobs. The fact that such ideas stood in stark contrast with the reality of many women's everyday lives did not make these beliefs any less powerful or any less widely held. To the majority, it appeared that women deserved to be relegated to the lower rungs of the job hierarchy and to be paid less than men. What is more, the ideology of "true womanhood" was never extended to women of color. As Glenn (1987, pp. 359–360) notes, "Racist ideology triumphed over sexist ideology. Women of color were not deemed truly women, exempting them from the protective cloaks of feminine frailty or womanly morality."

Many readers probably think these ideas are "old-fashioned" and no longer prevalent in the work world. "People just don't think like that anymore," our students frequently tell us. However, research indicates that sexist and racist ideologies have not disappeared from the workplace. This is particularly true when it comes to views on working mothers. For example, Kennelly (1999) found that White employers typify the woman worker in general as a mother, a role they associate with being frequently late or absent from work. She found that White employers associate Black workers generally with tardiness, low education and skill, laziness and belligerence. Black women, in particular, Kennelly found, were stereotyped by White employers as single mothers, a group they typified as unskilled and uneducated. Recent research that further explores the "motherhood" penalty at work refutes these stereotypes. While employers view mothers differently than fathers and employees without children, Kmec (2010) found that mothers are similar to fathers in exhibiting "pro work" behavior; mothers are actually more likely than fathers to report greater work intensity and job engagement, and mothers are similar to employees without children in their work behavior.

Nevertheless, there remains in the minds of many employers and the general public a strong belief that there are certain jobs for which women and men are naturally unsuited (Reskin, 1993; Tallichet, 2006; White & White, 2006). Studies show that employers still often make hiring decisions on the basis of their beliefs about the kinds of jobs women like (see also Box 8.3). It is commonly believed, for example, that

BOX 8.3
The Gendered Division of Labor in the Global Marketplace

We have seen that the division of labor in the United States is gendered with tasks sorted into "women's work" and "men's work." These gender stereotypes permeate the production process worldwide, intersecting with other inequalities based on race and ethnicity, social class, and geographic location. To better understand this point, we need to examine how production typically takes place nowadays in the global marketplace.

Many of the goods we take for granted—clothing, for example, or DVDs, mp3 players, and computers—are largely manufactured outside the United States, in developing countries in Asia and Latin America. But these countries form just one link in a *commodity chain*—that is, a network of tasks that includes product design, marketing, and sales, in addition to product assembly. Each of the tasks in the commodity chain may be carried out in a different country, separated by thousands of miles, since there is no need for the tasks to be performed in close geographic proximity. Indeed, the corporations that make these products are called *multinationals* because they extend production and marketing throughout the world community. Consider, for instance, the production of electronics components, which is dominated by large corporations such as Motorola and Matsushita (which manufactures the brand names Panasonic, Technics, and JVC). Components are designed and fabricated in the corporation's host country—in this case, the United States and Japan. The components are then assembled in a developing country, such as Malaysia, where workers may be supervised by managers from another country, such as Korea. Once assembled, the components are shipped to their major markets—primarily Western industrialized countries—for final testing, packaging, advertising, and distribution.

Notice in this example that the tasks that require technical expertise in fields such as engineering and marketing are carried out in economically developed countries, whereas the low-skill operations take place in poor, developing countries. There is a clear pecking order in the commodity chain, and the pecking order is differentiated not only by geographic location and the level of economic development of the country in which each task takes place, but also by the race/ethnicity, social class, and sex of the workers who perform each task. Design and fabrication, as well as marketing and distribution, are dominated by White men who are well paid for their efforts. Supervision of assembly is dominated by Asian and Latino men, depending on the country in which assembly takes place. Although not as well paid as the designers, fabricators, advertisers, and distributors, indigenous supervisors are paid significantly more than assemblers, who are primarily young women. These women often work ten hours a day, six days a week, in unsafe manufacturing plants, for a wage of about one to two dollars per day, which Powell and Skarbek (2004) found to be a level of income higher than most of their peers. It is still a hard case to make that this pay scale is fair, since the work is often dirty, dangerous, and repetitive, and the pay ranges from $0.13 per hour in Bangladesh to $2.38 in Costa Rica, clearly well below the minimum wage in the United States (Powell & Skarbek, 2004). And women *still* earn less than men, 63 percent of what the men earn, even at these extremely low wage levels (Marron, 2010).

In their effort to drive profits up and production costs down, the multinationals are clearly taking advantage of the fact that resources—human as well as material—are far cheaper in developing countries than in industrialized ones. They are also capitalizing on the lack of health and safety regulations in these countries, which further helps to depress production costs. However, if these were the only reasons for basing assembly operations in the developing world, why don't the multinationals hire more men as assemblers? The answer to this question reflects not only gender stereotypes, but also the greater economic vulnerability of women in developing countries. According to Marron (2010), the multinationals hire mostly women for assembly because they believe women have the small, nimble fingers as well as the patience to perform the tedious, repetitive task of electronics assembly. Also, because of women's devalued status in many countries, companies can pay them even less than indigenous men. Despite the low wages, however, the women workers are more productive than the men. They are also thought to be more docile and less likely to unionize, but just to be sure, the corporations keep them on short-term contracts; the prospect of losing the job because of labor unrest or changes in market demand is an ever-present threat.

Electronics is not the only industry to exploit the inequalities of international commodity chains. Consider, for example, the Nike Corporation. In Indonesia and Vietnam, thousands of women, typically under the age of twenty-five, labor ten-and-a-half hours a day, sixty-five hours a week, sewing Nike athletic shoes in manufacturing plants where exposure to carcinogens is 177 times higher than allowable by *local* standards and exposure to dust particles is eleven times higher than local standards (DeTienne & Lewis, 2005). The women earn about $2 a day. On such wages, most can only afford to live in bamboo or tin huts without running water. Many of the women are from rural areas, and they cannot afford to bring their children with them to the cities. Indeed, it is the prospect of earning a better living that draws them to the Nike factories in the first place. But their wages are not sufficient to allow them to return to their villages to visit their children more than once a year. Meanwhile, Nike's holdings in these countries are worth billions of dollars and Nike's president, Philip Knight, is the twenty-third richest person in America with an estimated worth of $11.3 billion ("*Forbes* Four Hundred," 2011).

We can expect these trends in the international division of labor to continue as more and more companies move their production processes to developing countries. Research indicates that woman-centered development strategies—for example, providing women with micro-loans and training them in skills so they can start their own small businesses—can play a major role in reducing poverty and related social problems such as hunger in developing nations (Odutolu et al., 2003). Nevertheless, international agencies, such as the World Bank and the International Monetary Fund, are encouraging developing countries to build their economies on export-oriented industrialization—a strategy, as we have seen here, that reproduces inequalities between countries as well as between the women and men who work in those countries (Babb, 2005; Temkin, 2004).

women like jobs that are clean and relatively easy. Consequently, employers considering applicants for a traditionally male job may justify their decision not to hire a woman on the grounds that she wouldn't like the job or wouldn't be happy in it because the work is dirty or difficult. However, such decisions are probably rationalizations, since research indicates that while women are more likely than men to emphasize the importance of clean working conditions (Ferriman, Lubinski, & Benbow, 2009), the jobs in which women are concentrated are no cleaner than male-dominated jobs (Jacobs & Steinberg, 1990). Clean working conditions and how easy the job is simply do not rank highly among women workers' concerns. Instead, women workers' primary concerns are equal pay for equal work, affordable health insurance, paid sick leave, flexibility in work schedules, and pension and retirement benefits (Ferriman et al., 2009; Reskin & Padevic, 1999).

When employers make employment decisions about an individual on the basis of characteristics thought to be typical of a group to which that individual belongs, the employers are engaging in what is called **statistical discrimination**. In other words, employers do not hire anyone who is a member of a group they think has low productivity. Statistical discrimination serves as a quick and inexpensive screening device (Oaxaca & Dickinson, 2006; Reskin & Hartmann, 1986). On the face of it, statistical discrimination may not seem unfair; it certainly does not appear to be inherently sex-biased. However, as Reskin and Hartmann (1986) and others (e.g., Pager & Karafin, 2009; Pager, Western, & Bonikowski, 2007) convincingly demonstrate, it is often premised on gender (and racial) stereotypes. For example, when making a choice between two job applicants with the same qualifications, one a young man and the other a young woman, employers still often favor hiring the young man, especially for a job requiring extensive training, because they think that many young women leave the labor force to have children. Notice, however, that their hiring decision is made irrespective of this individual applicant's child bearing or work intentions, of which the employer has no knowledge. Notice, too, that employers also assume that men have little interest in or responsibility for child rearing—believing that men who have children also have a spouse to care for them. Although such assumptions may reflect the family lives of most men, they nevertheless disregard individual circumstances and work against single fathers and men who prefer an equal or primary parenting role (see Box 8.2 and Chapter 7). As previously discussed, when married men have children, their wages increase (Glauber, 2007). Perhaps the difference is due to employers' beliefs that men in traditional families, as sole breadwinners, work longer and harder than men whose wives also work and with whom they may need to share some child care responsibilities.

Sexist workplace ideology also operates to preserve industry and establishment sex segregation. Because femaleness, as we noted previously, is a devalued trait in some workplaces, a concern over loss of prestige or status may prompt some firms or businesses to restrict their hiring of women (and racial minorities) either to "back office" jobs that have little contact with clientele (Glenn, 1992; Hartmann, 1987; Reskin & Padevic, 1999) or to a few "tokens" (Mooney & Ryan, 2009; Reskin & Hartmann, 1986). An example of this kind of thinking was provided by a colleague who works in a department of three men and three women at a small, private college. She recounted to us how one of her coworkers had objected to the hiring of another woman on the ground that the department would then be female-dominated and would consequently lose status within the institution.

There is evidence that some work-related gender stereotypes have weakened and that women who have entered male-dominated occupations have positively changed many workplaces (see, for example, Huffman, Cohen, & Pearlman, 2010; Lunneborg, 1990). Consequently, it is sometimes argued that sexist workplace ideology, although slow to change, will eventually break down as more women and men enter occupations nontraditional for their sex. However, there is also evidence that as particular gender stereotypes are refuted, new ones may develop to replace them (Reskin & Hartmann, 1986). Women, for example, sometimes feel they must adopt men's work styles in order to get ahead in their fields (see, for example, Roth, 2006). Ironically, traits or behaviors admired in workers of one sex may be negatively redefined when exhibited by workers of the opposite sex so as to make the latter fit a stereotyped image. Thus, a male worker may be complimented for being aggressive in his work, while a female worker exhibiting the same behavior is likely to be derided for being "too pushy." Moreover, women who reach high-level positions may find it difficult to mentor women in the lower ranks because of institutional barriers, such as their boss's disapproval of all-female mentoring groups or fears that if their protégés do poorly, it will reflect negatively on them (see Baumgartner & Schneider, 2010; Saltzman, 1996b).

In addition to gender stereotyping, other factors having to do with the economics of the labor market and the organization of the workplace contribute to an increase or decline in occupational sex segregation and the wage gap. As we noted earlier, for example, an increased demand for workers, such as during wartime or in a period of strong economic growth, can help to integrate traditionally segregated jobs. A rise in the demand for workers may also result from the rapid growth of a specific industry. Jacobs (1992) reported a reduction in overall occupational sex segregation during the two decades 1970 to 1990 simply as a result of the rapid growth of managerial jobs. A reduction in occupational sex segregation could also result from the fact that women are close to surpassing men in the paid labor force, not due to gender equality but out of necessity (Rampell, 2010). As we mentioned previously, the current economic recession has caused more women to enter the paid labor market (Rampell, 2010), and many women are attempting to find employment because their husbands are unemployed, their husbands' salaries have been reduced, or family investments have dropped significantly in value (Greenhouse, 2009).

Research also shows that even when chief executives of companies support diversity in hiring in order to reach a more diverse clientele, the individuals who actually make the hires and who evaluate current employees can act to preserve occupational segregation. Research indicates that although hiring managers say that personality traits (e.g.,, emotional stability, extraversion) and general intellectual ability (e.g., problem solving ability) are the most important factors in hiring (Tews, Stafford, & Tracey, 2010), those actually responsible for hiring feel most comfortable developing relationships and collaborating with employees similar to themselves. Indeed, one manager actually said, "When we find minorities and women who think like we do, we snatch them up" (quoted in Kilborn, 1995, p. A14).

Various strategies have been suggested for reducing occupational segregation and narrowing the wage gap. They include integrating lower-level positions first so there is a diverse pool from which to promote internally; waiving seniority requirements for promotion for women and minority job holders; expanding job postings throughout a workplace so that workers will be made aware of position openings in areas that may not be closely related to the ones in which they are currently working; setting up mentoring programs; recruiting nontraditional workers both from current employees as well as the external labor market; and improving training that would change existing gender stereotypes (Knox, 2008; Reskin, 1993; U.S. Department of Labor, 1997a; C. L. Williams, 1995; see also Eveline & Todd, 2010). However, while such strategies may prove effective, a number of analysts maintain that many employers lack sufficient motivation to implement change. Employers, they argue, must be *forced* to change discriminatory policies and procedures. One important impetus for such changes has come from legislation. During the past four decades, several laws have been enacted in an effort to remedy occupational segregation and its consequences, especially the wage gap. However, as we shall learn next, there sometimes has been a disparity between the written law and the law in action, producing uneven results.

Legislation for Equality in the Workplace

Until the 1960s, the legal system functioned largely to reinforce gender discrimination in the workplace, rather than to remedy it. For the most part, law and judicial actions simply codified widespread gender stereotypes about men's toughness and women's innate weaknesses, which as Justice Bradley argued in 1872, "unfits [women] for many of the occupations of civil life" (*Bradwell* v. *Illinois,* 1872). Legislators and judges maintained that women were a "special class" of citizens in need of protection: "That her physical structure and a proper discharge of her maternal functions—having in view not merely her own health, but the well-being of the race—justify legislation to protect her from the greed as well as the passion of man" (*Muller* v. *Oregon,* 1908). Consequently, most states enacted laws restricting women's working hours and the kind of work women could do. In many states, for instance, women were prohibited from working at night or from performing a work task that involved lifting more than a prescribed maximum weight. Other states forbade employers from hiring women for jobs ruled dangerous or morally corrupting (e.g., bartending). Initially, a variety of reform groups, including suffrage and feminist organizations, endorsed protective labor laws in the belief that they would benefit women workers, but as the decades passed, it became clear that such legislation usually served to severely restrict women's employment (Christensen, 1988).

In the 1960s, owing in part to the efforts of the feminist and civil rights movements, the federal government acted to outlaw sex discrimination in employment.[7] The first important piece of legislation in this regard is **Title VII of the 1964 Civil Rights Act**. Title VII forbids discrimination in hiring, benefits, and other personnel decisions (such as promotions or layoffs) on the basis of sex, race, color, national origin, or religion, by employers of fifteen or more employees.[8] There are, however, a few exceptions permitted by the law. For instance, an employer may hire an employee on the basis of sex (or religion or national origin, but never race or color) if the employer can demonstrate that this is a *bona fide occupational qualification* (BFOQ), that is, a qualification "reasonably necessary to the normal operation of that particular business or enterprise." However, since the courts have interpreted the BFOQ exception narrowly, there are few occupations to which it applies, such as mandatory retirement ages for bus drivers or airline pilots. According to guidelines issued with the law, sex is considered a bona fide occupational qualification in those instances where authenticity and genuineness are required, such as roles for actors and actresses (Pay Scale, 2010). Title VII has been implemented and enforced by the Equal Employment Opportunity Commission (EEOC), which can bring suit on behalf of an employee or class of employees who have been discriminated against by their employer.

A second important federal antidiscrimination policy is **Executive Order 11246**, better known as **Affirmative Action**, which was amended in 1968 to prohibit sex discrimination in addition to discrimination on the basis of race, color, national origin, and religion. Executive Order 11246 applies to employers who hold contracts with the federal government. It states that employers may be fined or their contracts may be terminated or they may be barred from future contracts if discrimination is found. But Executive Order 11246 goes beyond the mere prohibition of employment discrimination by requiring employers to take affirmative actions to recruit, train, and promote women and minorities. Since 1978, contractor compliance has been monitored by the Office of Federal Contract Compliance (OFCCP) in the Department of Labor. Besides this enforcement agency, the U.S. Department of Justice may also bring suit against discriminating employers, although it has rarely done so (Lindgren & Taub, 1993).

The impact of both Title VII and Executive Order 11246 is visible and far-reaching. Peruse the "want ads" of your local newspaper and you will see one result: Employers may no longer advertise sex-labeled or sex-specific jobs. Employers also may not use customer preference as a justification for sex discrimination. For instance, in *Diaz* v. *Pan American*

World Airways, Inc. (1971), the Fifth Circuit Court ruled that men could not be denied employment as flight attendants on the ground that passengers expect and prefer women in this job. In addition, employers may not: use sex-based seniority lists; administer discriminatory pre-employment selection tests; set different retirement ages for workers of each sex; impose double standards of employment, such as policies requiring only female employees to remain unmarried; penalize women workers who have children; or discriminate on the basis of pregnancy (Christensen, 1988; Lindgren & Taub, 1993). Under these regulations, the courts have also struck down most state protective labor laws and, as we have learned, ruled that sexual harassment is a form of employment discrimination.

It is difficult to reconcile the clear evidence of persistent discrimination that we have presented in this chapter with the prohibitions stipulated by these laws and court decisions. Why, more than forty-five years after the passage of this legislation, is occupational sex segregation still pervasive?

At least part of the answer rests with the limitations of the laws and the inconsistency with which they have been enforced. For one thing, Title VII and Executive Order 11246 define employment discrimination in limited, but complex, terms, leading judges to arrive at varying interpretations of both these regulations and appropriate affirmative measures to remedy past discrimination (Lieberman, 2002). Moreover, since the mid-1980s, the U.S. Supreme Court has handed down rulings that have substantially increased the burden on employees in proving they have been discriminated against. For example, previously in cases in which an employee accused an employer of directly discriminating against her or him, the employee only had to provide *prima facie evidence* of discrimination in an employment decision (e.g., hiring, promotion, dismissal) and then to demonstrate that the employer's argument that the decision was not discriminatory was not credible. Since 1993, however, employees have been required to provide *direct evidence* of discrimination (e.g., witnesses, or a letter or memo), which can be hard to come by, making it more difficult for employees to win their lawsuits (*St. Mary's Honor Center* v. *Hicks,* 1993).

Another factor influencing enforcement is changes in government and political climate. The Republican administrations since 1980 have opposed large lawsuits against employers filed by a whole class of employees, favoring instead cases in which individual victims could be identified. They also opposed affirmative action and took steps to dismantle it. One strategy for doing so was to significantly reduce the budgets and staff of the EEOC and OFCCP. Less money and fewer staff attorneys meant that fewer cases could be processed and the number of cases dismissed by the compliance agencies rose significantly during the 1980s. Lax law enforcement sends employers the message that the government will tolerate a high degree of occupational sex segregation (Reskin, 2000).

Thus, while Title VII and Executive Order 11246 have made visible dents in our society's discriminatory work structure, the effects of these policies have been limited for at least two reasons. First, the inherent weaknesses and complexities of the laws themselves give judges considerable discretion, which frequently produces negative or contradictory outcomes for female and minority workers. Second, these policies, like all public policies, are vulnerable to political change. The future of Title VII and especially affirmative action depends to a large extent on rulings by the U.S. Supreme Court.

The wage gap has also been attacked directly by legislation that outlaws discriminatory pay policies. Perhaps the best known and most frequently used law of this type is the **Equal Pay Act of 1963**. The Equal Pay Act prohibits employers from paying employees of one sex more than employees of the opposite sex when these employees are engaged in work that requires equal skill, effort, and responsibility and that is performed under similar working conditions. This prohibition extends to other forms of discrimination in compensation, such as overtime. However, pay need not be equal if the difference is based on employees' relative seniority, merit, the quantity or quality of their production, or "any other factor other than sex" such as the profitability of their work (Christensen, 1988; Lindgren & Taub, 1993). Thus, for example, the Equal Pay Act may not prevent wage discrimination for women in leadership or managerial positions (Eisenberg, 2010, p. 19). Female CEOs in private firms earn 46 percent less than males even when controlling for age and education (Cole & Mehran, 2008). Since the Equal Pay Act requires that jobs require equal skill, effort, and responsibility, it is challenging for women in high positions to prove they are not receiving pay equal to that of their male counterparts, since these positions tend to be less standardized (Eisenberg, 2010).

The courts have ruled that the work performed by employees of different sexes does not have to be identical to require equal pay; it needs to be only *substantially equal*. The courts have also ruled that employers may not justify unequal pay for their male and female workers by creating artificial job classifications that do not substantially differ in content (England, 1992). A major difficulty with the Equal Pay Act, however, is that it does not address the problem of sex-segregated employment, which, we have argued, is a root cause of the wage gap. The benefits of a law designed to provide equal pay for equal work are limited, therefore, if, as we have found, men and women are largely segregated into different jobs and predominantly female jobs are systematically devalued (Bayard et al., 2003).

It is for this reason that women workers and others have increasingly called for **comparable worth**, that is, equal pay for different jobs of similar value in terms of factors such as skill, effort, responsibility, and working conditions. Comparable worth has been more popular in other countries, such as Australia, Great Britain, and Canada, than in the United States. In the 1980s, a number of comparable worth cases were brought on behalf of women workers in this country, but in general, the courts have not looked favorably on comparable worth as a means to remedy gender inequities in pay (England, 1992). Their reluctance is the result of two reasons: They do not wish "to punish employers who rely on the market in setting wages and who are not individually responsible for societal discrimination" and they do not wish "to become involved in trying to evaluate the worth of different jobs," which has proven to be a very difficult task (Christensen, 1988, p. 340; see also. deLange, 2007).

One recent legislative development intended to promote greater gender equity in pay is the Lily Leadbetter Fair Pay Act, which President Obama signed into law in January, 2009. This law supersedes a 2007 Supreme Court decision (*Ledbetter* v. *Goodyear Tire & Rubber Co*) supporting the Title VII requirement that plaintiffs file suit within 180 days after an alleged unlawful employment practice happened. The Ledbetter Act amends Title VII so that the time limit for filing suit begins each time an employer issues a paycheck (Feder & Levine, 2010). It is too early, of course, to gauge the impact of the Ledbetter Act on gender equity in employment.

The Intersection of Home and the Work World

A major theme of this chapter and the preceding chapter has been the interrelationship between family life and the work world. Men and women possess different levels of power in the family with women typically being the less powerful partners. In Chapter 7, we learned that differences in power between intimate partners are related to differences in their income and other resources. The work women do in the home is unremunerated and, therefore, not even regarded as "real" work. As we saw in this chapter, however, women's jobs in the labor force are often seen as an extension of their work at home. Women's work is devalued and remunerated at a substantially lower rate than men's work.

Since employed women continue to bear primary responsibility for housework and child care, they shoulder a double work load compared with employed men, but receive fewer rewards. The unavailability of adequate and affordable child care, we have learned, is a major obstacle to employment for many women. But regardless of their objective circumstances, the widespread belief among employers and coworkers that women are physically and emotionally incapable of performing certain jobs serves to justify discrimination against them in hiring, promotion, and other employment-related opportunities and also constrains men from assuming equal caregiving responsibilities within families. The evidence discussed in this chapter shows that persistent stereotypes about women's and men's "appropriate" roles reinforce and perpetuate workplace sex segregation and its attendant consequences, including the male/female earnings gap. The prevailing assumption seems to remain that the public world of work is men's domain, whereas the private world of home belongs to women. If women are in the labor force, their employment is secondary to that of men. From our discussions in this chapter and Chapter 7, we know that these assumptions are patently false. We know, too, that both women and men suffer negative consequences from blind adherence to them.

Legislation, such as Title VII, Executive Order 11246, the Equal Pay Act, and the Lilly Ledbetter Fair Pay Act of 2009, is designed to protect workers of both sexes and racial and ethnic minorities from discriminatory employment practices. Although the legislation has fallen far short of equalizing the job opportunities and salaries available to female and male workers, and among workers of different racial and ethnic groups, there is evidence that when the laws are stringently enforced, they can help to lessen employment inequities. Still, this legislation was not designed to alter the gendered division of unpaid household labor. Since we know that this is directly tied to sex-based employment discrimination, we cannot expect women or men to be free to choose the work that best suits them as individuals unless the simultaneous elimination of both of these inequities becomes a central goal of our nation's public policy.

Key Terms

Affirmative Action (Executive Order 11246) forbids federal contractors from discriminating in personnel decisions on the basis of sex, as well as race, color, national origin, and religion, and requires employers to take affirmative measures to recruit, train, and hire women and minorities; since 1978, implemented and enforced by the OFCCP

comparable worth the policy of paying workers equally when they perform different jobs that have similar value in terms of such factors as skill, effort, responsibility, and working conditions

dissimilarity index (segregation index, D) a measure of occupational sex segregation, reported in percent, that indicates the proportion of workers of one sex that would have to change to jobs in which members of their sex were underrepresented to achieve a balanced occupational distribution between the sexes

dual labor market a labor market characterized by one set of jobs employing almost exclusively men and another set of jobs, typically lower paying and with lower prestige, employing almost exclusively women

economy   the system for the management and development of a society's human and material resources

Equal Pay Act of 1963   forbids employers from paying employees of one sex more than employees of the opposite sex when these employees are engaged in work that requires equal skill, effort, and responsibility and is performed under similar working conditions, although exceptions, such as unequal pay based on seniority, merit, the quality or quantity of production, or any other factor besides sex, are allowed

establishment sex segregation   a form of occupational sex segregation in which women and men hold the same job title at an individual establishment or company, but actually do different jobs

glass ceiling   invisible barriers that limit women workers' and minority workers' upward occupational mobility

human capital theory   explains occupational sex segregation in terms of women's free choice to work in jobs that make few demands on workers and require low personal investment in training or skills acquisition based on the assumption that women's primary responsibility is in the home

industry sex segregation   a form of occupational sex segregation in which women and men hold the same job title in a particular field or industry, but actually perform different jobs

labor force   the human resources of the economy

occupational resegregation   sex-integrated occupations become resegregated with members of one sex replaced by members of the opposite sex as the predominant workers

occupational sex segregation   the degree to which men and women are concentrated in occupations that employ workers of predominantly one sex

statistical discrimination   employers do not hire anyone who is a member of a group they think has low productivity, regardless of an individual applicant's qualifications or intentions

Title VII of the 1964 Civil Rights Act forbids discrimination in employment on the basis of sex, race, color, national origin, or religion, by employers of fifteen or more employees, although exceptions, such as the BFOQ, are allowed; implemented and enforced by the EEOC

tokenism   the marginal status of a category of workers who are relatively few in number in the workplace

Suggested Readings

Dobbins, F. (2009). *Inventing equal opportunity.* Princeton, NJ: Princeton University Press. An examination of racism and sexism in employment practices as well as policies intended to eliminate sexual harassment and create more equal, family-friendly work environments.

Hochschild, A., & Machung, A. (2003). *The second shift.* New York: Penguin. One of the first books to offer a sociological analysis of the causes and consequences of women's double work load in two-earner households.

Jasinski, J. L., Wesely, J. K., Wright, J. D., & Mustaine, E. E. (2010). *Hard lives, mean streets: Violence in the lives of homeless women.* Boston: Northeastern University Press. Through interviews with more than 700 women, Jasinski and her colleagues examine how violence contributes to homelessness among women, the interactions of homeless women with the criminal justice system, and policy changes that must be made to reduce homelessness, especially among women.

Seefeldt, K. S. (2008). *Working after welfare: How women balance jobs and family in the wake of welfare reform.* Kalamazoo, Michigan: W.E. Upjohn Institute for Employment Research. This book discusses the variety of struggles faced by single women who left welfare to work outside their homes. It is rich in data but also provides a personal glimpse into the lives of women struggling to balance work with family responsibilities.

Notes

1. The heterosexual men Williams interviewed also related some negative experiences of gender discrimination associated with gender stereotypes of masculinity, although these were rare. For example, male social workers and nurses reported that they were usually expected to handle aggressive or violent clients and patients. Similarly, a male librarian found himself transferred to the city's main library so he could double as a security guard. A male nurse also reported that during fire drills at the hospital where he worked, male nurses were required to go to the scene of the fire with the maintenance and housekeeping staff, presumably to help fight the fire, while female nurses were required to remain on the patient floors, closing doors, and clearing the hallways (C. L. Williams, 1995).

2. In 2010, a male Los Angeles police deputy was awarded $350,000 after suing his male supervisor whom he alleged had sexually harassed him (Contra Costa Times, 2010).

3. Prior to the Court's decision in this case, *Oncale* v. *Sundowner Offshore Services,* most lower federal courts simply rejected same-sex harassment claims, arguing that Congress never intended same-sex harassment to be included as grounds for damages under civil rights law. Those courts that agreed to hear same-sex harassment claims usually limited them to cases involving heterosexual employees who filed complaints against homosexual coworkers (Greenhouse, 1998).

4. Our calculations of the earnings gap, unless otherwise noted, are based on *weekly* median earnings of full-time workers. The size of the gap varies depending on the type of wages one examines; the widest gap is found in annual wages because these figures usually include factors such as overtime and, therefore, reflect the differences in the total annual hours worked by women and men. We are grateful to Jane Hood for pointing out this variation to us.

5. The official government measure of poverty, known as the poverty line, is the amount of money an individual or family needs to purchase a minimally nutritional diet multiplied by three because it is assumed that the poor spend about one-third of their income on food. However, the measure has been widely criticized on a number of grounds, including the fact that the average family spends not one-third, but rather one-fifth of its income on food. In addition, the current poverty measure does not take into account the value of in-kind benefits, the impact of taxes, nor the cost of work-related expenses such as child care. Consequently, critics argue that the official measure severely undercounts the poor (Tenny & Zahradnik, 2001).

6. The unemployment rate is officially defined as the percentage of the working-age population that is currently out of work, but actively looking for a job. This measure, though, undercounts the unemployed because it excludes "discouraged workers," that is, individuals who have given up hope of finding a job because they believe none is available or because they lack marketable skills. Discouraged workers are a subset of another group not counted in the unemployment rate, "persons marginally attached to the labor force." The marginally attached are people who want work, are available for work, and have looked for a job in the past year, but have not sought work in the past month. At the start of 2011, the Department of Labor estimated that about 1.8 million people were marginally attached to the labor force, and more than 1.0 million were discouraged workers.

7. Our discussion of these laws is, by necessity, simplistic. For a more detailed and thorough discussion, see Baer and Goldstein (2006) and Bartlett and Rhode (2010).

8. Notice that sexual orientation is not a protected category under Title VII. In 1998, President Clinton signed an executive order to protect gay and lesbian *federal* employees from job discrimination. Although some states (for example, California, Connecticut, Hawaii, Massachusetts, Minnesota, Nevada, New Hampshire, New Jersey, Oregon, Rhode Island, Vermont, and Wisconsin) and some cities have added sexual orientation to the protected categories under their antidiscrimination laws, the U.S. Congress has resisted extending the protection of Title VII to homosexuals (see also Kramer, 2009).

Chapter 9

Gender, Crime, and Justice

Equality before the law is a constitutional guarantee in the United States. Yet, we know from our discussions so far that the laws of our land have allowed—indeed, even prescribed—discriminatory treatment of different groups of citizens. Women, for example, were historically defined by law as men's property and were systematically denied their civil rights, including the right to vote. In fact, in 1894, the U.S. Supreme Court ruled that women were not "persons" under the law. The case, *In re Lockwood*, was heard on appeal from the state of Virginia, where Belva A. Lockwood had been denied a license to practice as an attorney even though state law permitted any "person" licensed as an attorney in any other state to practice in Virginia. The Supreme Court upheld a lower court opinion that the word "person" meant "male." Consequently, "from 1894 until 1971 states could maintain that women were not legally 'persons' by virtue of this single Supreme Court decision" (Hoff-Wilson, 1987, p. 8; Sachs & Wilson, 1978).

Most of the court cases we discuss in this text fall within the realm of civil law, that is, the body of law that focuses on settling private disputes, such as divorces, contracts and private property issues, and conflicts in the workplace. In this chapter, however, we will focus on gender and *criminal law*. Criminal law encompasses behaviors that supposedly imperil the general welfare of the society and, consequently, it is the state that prosecutes the offender, not the individual citizen who has been harmed by the offending behavior. In other words, the violation of a criminal law is viewed, in theory at least, as a transgression against society as well as against an individual citizen.

What is defined in law as criminal, though, does not necessarily represent the interests of all segments of society. Rather, criminal law typically represents the interests of lawmakers. Historically, those who have had the power to make laws in the United States have been wealthy White men (see Chapter 10). Not surprisingly, therefore, the experiences of women and men in the criminal justice system tend to be different. Compounding these sex differences are differences in race, social class, age, and sexual orientation.

This chapter begins with a discussion of men and women as offenders. First, we will examine men's and women's relative crime rates. In addition, we will address their differential processing through the criminal justice system: from arrest to prosecution to conviction to sentencing to imprisonment. In studying the administration of justice, we will also have the opportunity to discuss issues pertaining to men's and women's roles as criminal justice professionals. Finally, we will conclude the chapter by examining differences in the criminal victimization of men and women, with special attention given to sexual assault and other violent crimes against women.

WOMEN AND MEN AS OFFENDERS

Among the questions most often addressed by criminologists, two in particular seem most relevant to our present discussion: Who commits crime? and why? Traditionally, a common response to the first question has been men, especially young men. Indeed, a careful survey of criminological research conducted prior to the mid-1970s would probably lead you to conclude that women are rarely criminal. The little attention that was given to female offenders was largely limited to three contexts: (1) comparisons to underscore women's low crime rates relative to those of men; (2) studies of prostitution; and (3) analyses of the depravity of violent women, the rationale being that since "normal" women are passive, the few women who do commit violent crimes must be "sick" (Stanko, 2001). Clearly, in the minds of criminologists and the general public, "criminal" was equated with "male."

In 1975, however, this perception began to change, owing largely to the publication of two books—Freda Adler's *Sisters in Crime* and Rita James Simon's *Women and Crime*—each of which received widespread attention in both the academic and popular presses. A central theme in both books is that women's crime had begun to change both in its nature and in the number of offenses committed. In fact, according to Adler, the United States at that time was in the midst of a female crime wave. Although men were still committing a greater absolute number of offenses, the female crime rate was increasing more than the male crime rate. Thus, for example, Adler presented statistics from the F.B.I. *Uniform Crime Reports* (UCR) that show that between 1960 and 1972, women's arrest rates for robbery increased 277 percent compared with a 169 percent increase for men. Statistics on juvenile offenders revealed similar changes. What is more, Adler argued, females were not only engaged in more crime than previously, but also their criminal activity had assumed a more serious and violent character: Women were committing crimes that traditionally had been committed by men. In this respect, Simon's work closely resembles Adler's, with the exception that Simon saw the increase in women's crime limited primarily to property offenses rather than violent crimes against persons. Still, she maintained that women were committing more crimes generally characterized as masculine, particularly white-collar and occupationally related offenses such as fraud and embezzlement.

These claims did not cause the greatest stir, however. Indeed, what received the most attention, especially from the popular media, were Adler's and Simon's explanations of their findings. Specifically, both argued that the changes they uncovered in the rate and character of female crime were logical outcomes of the women's liberation movement. As Adler (1975, p. 10) phrased it, "Is it any wonder that once women were armed with male opportunities they should strive for status, criminal as well as civil, through established male hierarchical channels?" Simon's position was a bit more complex. She argued that violent crimes by women had actually decreased because of feminism. "As women feel more liberated physically, emotionally, and legally, and less subjected to male power, their frustrations and anger decrease ... [which results] in a decline in their desire to kill the usual objects of their anger or frustration: their husbands, lovers, and other men upon whom they are dependent, but insecure about" (Simon, 1975, p. 40). The down side, however, is that the feminist movement, by encouraging women's participation in the paid labor force, had also contributed to the rise of female property crime. "As women increase their participation in the labor force their opportunity to commit certain types of crime [e.g., white-collar and occupational crimes] also increases" (Simon, 1975, p. 40). Because of its emphasis on the women's movement, Adler's and Simon's perspective has become known as the **emancipation theory** (also called the **liberation theory**) of female crime.

Actually, this argument is not totally new. As Chesney-Lind and Eliason (2006) point out, during the first wave of feminism, criminologists and others warned that the emancipation of women would increase crime and immorality among women and girls. However, the greatest value of Adler's and Simon's work is that it forced a contemporary reassessment of the relationship between gender and participation in criminal activity.

In critiquing Adler and Simon, subsequent analyses shed light on the extent to which female crime had actually changed and the degree to which the women's movement may have contributed to such a change. Let's consider some of these criticisms and, in doing so, examine what more recent studies tell us about the relationship between gender and crime.

One problem with both Adler's and Simon's work was their reliance on official crime statistics. These statistics represent only those crimes known to the police, which, it is estimated, are about half of all violent crimes committed and about 39 percent of all property crimes committed (Truman, 2011). A substantial amount of crime goes undetected or is not reported by victims. And even when a crime is reported, the police exercise considerable discretion in deciding which complaints warrant their attention and which should be ignored, so not even all reported crimes are passed along to the F.B.I. But a more serious problem stems from the way Adler, in particular, used the UCR data. In comparing male and female rates of increase for specific crimes, she didn't control for the large difference in the absolute base numbers from which the rates of increase were calculated. If one base figure is small, even a slight rise will exaggerate the rate change. Conversely, a sizable increase in a large base figure is likely to appear as only a minor change (Smart, 1982; Terry, 1978). Take arrests for homicide, for example. Between 1965 and 1970, years included in Adler's analysis, the number of arrests of women for homicide increased almost 79 percent; during the same period, the number of homicide arrests for men increased 73 percent. However, in absolute terms, the number of homicides committed by women rose from 1,293 to 1,645, whereas for men, the figures were 6,533 and 8,858, respectively. If we look only at percent changes without taking into account these major absolute base differences, we end up with a very distorted picture of men's and women's involvement in crime.

A more accurate measure of changes in men's and women's criminal activity is to calculate sex-specific arrest rates, that is, the number of men arrested for a crime per 100,000 of the male population and the number of women arrested for the same crime per 100,000 of the female population. The sex differential in arrest rates can then be determined by calculating women's share of all arrests, male and female, for a specific offense. Researchers who have used this method to analyze the sex differential in arrest rates in recent years have found that there has been neither a dramatic widening nor a dramatic narrowing of the gender gap in arrests, with the important exception of certain types of property crimes (burglary and larceny-theft) and drug offenses (Chesney-Lind, 1997; Schwartz et al., 2009; Snyder & Sickmund, 2006; Steffensmeier, 2001). As Table 9.1 indicates, between 1999 and 2008, women's arrests for property crimes increased by only 0.8 percent. Their arrest rate for violent crime *decreased* by 10 percent. To examine if the gender gap in violent offending has changed dramatically over time, Rennison (2009) took a different approach. Instead of looking at arrest data, she looked at victimization data. Rennison also concluded that there is no real change in women's violent offending rates and that any narrowing of the gap between violent offending for males and females is attributable to the fact that males' violent offending decreased more than females' violent offending did. Thus, the research findings do not support the argument that progress toward equality and independence for women has led to a convergence in offending rates between men and women (Rennison, 2009).

TABLE 9.1 Arrest Trends by Sex (Adults), 1999–2008						
	Males			**Females**		
Offense Charged	*1999*	*2008*	*Percent Change*	*1999*	*2008*	*Percent Change*
Total[1]	**6,279,139**	**6,083,494**	**–3.1**	**1,778,501**	**1,985,133**	**+11.6**
Murder and nonnegligent manslaughter	6,636	6,292	–5.2	831	780	–6.1
Forcible rape	15,452	12,474	–19.3	179	148	–17.3
Robbery	54,658	64,844	+18.6	6,261	8,615	+37.6
Aggravated assault	228,525	202,645	–11.3	55,814	54,400	–2.5
Burglary	149,875	157,341	+5.0	23,106	29,055	+25.7
Larceny-theft	461,632	431,212	-6.6	254,629	308,011	+21.0
Motor vehicle theft	60,540	43,801	–27.6	11,331	9,344	–17.5
Arson	8,317	7,116	–14.4	1,373	1,291	–6.0
Total violent crime[2]	305,271	286,255	–6.2	63,085	63,943	+1.4
Total property crime[2]	680,364	639,470	–6.0	290,439	347,701	+19.7
Other assaults	564,655	560,226	-.8	169,665	196,577	+15.9
Forgery and counterfeiting	38,570	31,947	–17.2	24,253	19,631	–19.1
Fraud	114,020	80,973	–29.0	96,234	65,637	–31.8
Embezzlement	5,768	6,575	+14.0	5,634	7,039	+24.9
Stolen property: buying, receiving, possessing	56,110	53,172	–5.2	10,350	14,116	+36.4
Vandalism	135,146	137,165	+1.5	24,317	28,213	+16.0
Weapons: carrying, possessing, etc.	87,790	93,112	+6.1	7,492	7,480	–0.2
Prostitution and commercialized vice	19,762	12,133	–38.6	25,240	25,164	–0.3
Sex offenses (except forcible rape and prostitution)	48,800	40,876	–16.2	3,670	3,769	+2.7
Drug abuse violations	711,384	784,531	+10.3	155,256	185,201	+19.3
Gambling	4,481	2,227	–50.3	800	350	–56.3
Drunkenness	370,924	347,399	–6.3	55,670	66,883	+20.1

TABLE 9.1 (Continued)

Offense Charged	Males			Females		
	1999	*2008*	*Percent Change*	*1999*	*2008*	*Percent Change*
Total[1]	6,279,139	6,083,494	−3.1	1,778,501	1,985,133	+11.6
Disorderly conduct	262,713	243,865	−7.2	82,332	89,530	+8.7
All other offenses (except traffic)	1,687,374	1,724,690	+2.2	444,312	517,358	+16.4

[1]Some crime categories have been omitted from this table.

[2]These crimes are collectively known as the Index Offenses. Violent Index Offenses are: murder, forcible rape, robbery, and aggravated assault. Property Index Offenses are: burglary, larceny-theft, motor vehicle theft, and arson.

Source: Federal Bureau of Investigation, 2009, Table 33.

Box 9.1 discusses the complex relationship between drugs and crime that is further complicated when gender, race/ethnicity, social class, and age are taken into account. Let's take a closer look, though, at research that has tested the emancipation theory of female crime. Do these studies show that women's crime is the same as men's crime—that, for instance, the property crimes women are committing are occupationally related offenses? And do they show that female offenders are "liberated" women?

BOX 9.1
Drugs, Crime, and Gender

The arrest of women for drug offenses increased more than 59 percent between 1991 and 2000, leading some observers to conclude that the "war on drugs" was actually a war on women, particularly women of color (Bush-Baskette, 1998). This upward trajectory of drug arrests for women continued over the past ten years, although it has not been as dramatic. Between 1999 and 2008, women's arrests for drug offenses increased by 19 percent compared with 10 percent for men (Federal Bureau of Investigation, 2009). However, despite this increase, men still comprise the vast majority of arrests for drug offenses (82 percent in 2008).

Certainly, the war on drugs has emphasized making more arrests and imposing harsher punishments. Underlying this strategy is the assumption that taking drug offenders off the streets will dramatically lower the overall crime rate, since drug users and addicts regularly commit other crimes either because the drugs lower their inhibitions and distort their judgment or because they are desperate for money to feed their habit. This view is reinforced by reports by prisoners that they committed the crime for which they are serving time to get money for drugs. In 2004, 17 percent of state prisoners and 18 percent of federal inmates said they committed their current offense to obtain money for drugs (U.S. Department of Justice, Bureau of Justice Statistics, 2006). Drug use is also a significant factor in crimes committed by juvenile

(continued)

BOX 9.1
Continued

females. Analyzing data from focus groups of girls involved in the juvenile justice system, Garcia and Lane (2009) concluded that drug use was the key factor that led girls into trouble.

While the link between drug abuse and crime is well documented, the examination of the gendered relationship between drug abuse and crime cannot be overlooked. James Inciardi and his colleagues' (1993) early research on women's use of crack cocaine found that involvement in both drugs and crime seem to begin at around the same time, usually during adolescence. Most adolescents eventually "age-out" of drug use and criminal activity, but for those who continue, escalation of both activities is likely. While increased crime to finance the drug use and simply to survive is one outcome, the relationship can also occur in the opposite direction—that is, a lucrative criminal career can make it financially easier to buy drugs, thus increasing drug use. "Over time, any single heroin or cocaine addict experiences many of these drug/crime interactions, leading to a sometimes chaotic existence. Anything that changes one factor—drug use or crime—will have an impact on the other" (Inciardi, Lockwood, & Pottieger, 1993, p. 112; see also Mancuso & Miller, 2001; Raphael, 2004, 2007).

More recently, Griffin and Rodriguez (2008) looked at how the strategies to acquire marijuana and crack differ by gender. While men were more likely than women to obtain both marijuana and crack, acquisition strategies varied. Women were less likely than men to obtain marijuana directly, but were more likely than men to purchase marijuana from regular sources. On the other hand, women were no more likely than men to obtain crack directly, and gender did not have an effect on the likelihood of obtaining crack as a gift or on credit. When marijuana was not paid for with cash, women were more likely to receive it as a gift, while men were more likely to use credit. Women were more likely than men to use cash to purchase both marijuana and crack in their own neighborhoods.

In comparing male and female street addicts, researchers have found that in many ways they are similar. The greater their drug use, the more likely they are to be involved in other types of crime. They may commit a wide variety of offenses, but typically they engage in property crime and drug dealing, for which the probability of arrest is very low. Baskin and Sommers (1997) argue that female drug users are increasingly committing violent crimes, such as robbery, largely because conditions in impoverished inner-city neighborhoods encourage violence by both men and women. However, other researchers have not found a significant increase in violence among female drug users, although these women are frequently violent crime victims. Male drug users, it appears, are more likely to commit and to be victims of violent crime (Inciardi et al., 1993; Mahan, 1996; Mancuso & Miller, 2001). The research also shows that men who sell drugs are more likely than women to be "big-time dealers," perhaps increasing their risk of being involved in drug-related violence. Women who sell drugs are typically "small-time dealers," with each transaction averaging $10 or less. Because the financial payoff is so low, women dealers may make more transactions per day than men dealers, thus increasing their probability of being arrested (Mancuso & Miller, 2001).

Another significant gender difference in the drugs/crime relationship is that prostitution is often tied to drug use by women. It appears that many female drug users engaged in prostitution at least sporadically before they became heavy users, as a way to earn money to support themselves and their children. However, heavy drug use prompts many women to engage in prostitution to earn money for drugs, or they may exchange sex for drugs (Inciardi et al., 1993; Mancuso & Miller, 2001; Raphael, 2004). It is also the case that a female addict is more highly stigmatized than a male addict and is expected to prostitute herself. Most importantly, the exchange of sex for drugs routinely puts women at risk for violent victimization (see Shannon et al., 2008; Wechsberg et al., 2003).

Answers to these questions come from at least two sources. First, studies of female offenders reveal that they are reluctant at best to identify themselves as feminists. In fact, Adler's (1975) own work indicated that female offenders often expressed a strong dislike of the women's movement and not infrequently considered feminists "kooks." Research also indicates that while many female offenders express traditional ideas about gender roles, they have often had to live their lives independent of men and may present themselves to others as "tough" or "bad," a protective strategy in response to their vulnerability to or actual experiences of victimization (J. Miller, 2001).

Second, as we saw in Chapter 8, although women's labor force participation has risen dramatically over the past thirty years, women remain segregated in low-prestige, low-paying clerical, sales, and service occupations. The influx of women into these types of jobs affords them greater opportunities to embezzle, defraud, and forge, but only small, not large sums. It is the low level of financial gain attached to these offenses, as well as characteristics of the offenders themselves, that have led researchers to maintain that to label them "white-collar" crimes is misleading. For instance, in her study of male and female white-collar offenders, Daly (1989a) found that the number of women involved in corporate crime (e.g., insider trading, advertising fraud) was low. Moreover, while the men had committed both serious and petty crimes, almost all of the women's crimes were petty offenses. The financial gains of the male offenders were ten times greater than the financial gains of the female offenders.

The types of offenses committed as well as the financial outcomes of these crimes were related to the relative employment status of men and women. While more than half of the male offenders held professional or managerial positions, most of the female offenders who had been employed were bank tellers and clerical workers. A higher percentage of the female offenders, though, had no ties to the paid labor force; they were involved in offenses that were not occupational, but instead included such activities as defrauding banks through loans or credit cards or defrauding the government by obtaining benefits to which they were not legally entitled. The motives of the female and male offenders also differed, with the former more frequently citing family responsibilities rather than personal excesses or corporate profit-making as the underlying reasons for their behavior. Consequently, Daly (1989a, p. 790) concludes that, "The women's socioeconomic profile, coupled with the nature of their crimes, makes one wonder if 'white-collar' aptly describes them or their illegalities" (see also English, 1993). Certainly, they do not appear to be "liberated" women in any sense of the term.[1]

Additional research indicates that a large share of female property crimes is accounted for by shoplifting. Other property crimes for which women are typically arrested are consumer-based currency crimes, including passing bad checks, using forged or stolen credit cards, nonpayment of services, and benefits fraud (Steffensmeier, 2001). In other words, women are not committing more violent, masculine, or serious offenses; they are committing crimes that they have traditionally committed. The women who are arrested for these property offenses, as well as for drug offenses, are not liberated women in the paid labor force, but rather poor women who are economically marginalized. Research indicates that the typical female offender is young, nonwhite, poor, a high school dropout, and a single mother (Chesney-Lind, 1997; Steffensmeier, 2001). As we learned in Chapter 8, economic discrimination against women has the greatest impact on young, single, women of color, and welfare "reforms" are actually making the financial circumstances of many of these women and their children worse instead of better. Feminist criminologists maintain that it is these factors that propel women into crime, especially petty property crime and, increasingly, drug offenses.

In sum, the claims of the emancipation or liberation theorists seem overstated at best. Women have not made significant gains on male rates of crime, nor are they "acting like men" when they offend. Returning to Table 9.1, we see that crime remains, for the most part, a male enterprise, virtually untouched by feminism and the women's movement. About 75.5 percent of those arrested in the United States in 2008 were males; males accounted for 82 percent of those arrested for violent crimes and 65 percent of those arrested for property crimes (Federal Bureau of Investigation, 2009b). Recent research indicates that, particularly in urban areas of the United States, official arrest statistics for the past several decades have been dominated by fifteen- to twenty-nine-year-old non-white males. The debate continues as to why this has been so, and we will address it in the next section.

Given that women, poor and nonpoor alike, are fairly law-abiding and that when they do offend, their crimes are relatively minor, one might expect that those women who are apprehended and processed through the criminal justice system would be treated relatively leniently. This position is known as the **chivalry hypothesis (paternalism hypothesis)**. To evaluate its accuracy, we need to turn our attention to the administration of justice in the United States.[2]

WITH JUSTICE FOR ALL?

Criminologists point out that crime and criminals are, to a large extent, socially and legally produced or constructed. Edwin Schur (1984) explains:

> The production of "criminals" involves the creation of crime definitions by legislation, and the application of those definitions to particular persons through the various stages of criminal justice processing. At every stage decisions are being made by ordinary, fallible, and sometimes biased human beings. (p. 224)

Thus, in assessing the differential treatment of male and female offenders, we first need to examine some of the relevant characteristics of those charged with administering justice.

The Administration of Justice

One of the most salient features of the criminal justice system in the United States is male dominance. Historically, the overwhelming majority of police, attorneys, judges, corrections officers, and other law enforcement personnel have been White men. Table 9.2 shows the percentage of women represented in local law enforcement.Traditionally, a variety of reasons were offered to justify the exclusion of women from careers in law and law enforcement. It was said, for instance, that women were too weak and timid to enforce the law or to serve as corrections officers. Others maintained that women were too emotional and sentimental—easy "push-overs." Still others claimed that women were too "good" or righteous for such work. Of course, there were those who used similar arguments to promote women's involvement in law enforcement, the legal professions, and prison reform. It was argued, for example, that women would have a

TABLE 9.2 Full-Time Sworn Personnel in Local Police Departments by Size of the Population Served, Race/Ethnicity, & Sex, 2003*									
		Percent of Full-Time Sworn Personnel							
		White		*Black*		*Hispanic*		*Other***	
Population Served	*Total*	*M*	*F*	*M*	*F*	*M*	*F*	*M*	*F*
All sizes	**100**	**69.4**	**7.0**	**9.0**	**2.7**	**7.8**	**1.3**	**2.5**	**0.3**
1 million or more	100	53.2	7.9	11.3	5.4	15.7	3.6	2.6	0.2
500,000–999,999	100	54.1	7.8	18.0	6.4	6.8	1.0	5.4	0.6
250,000–499,999	100	57.7	8.9	15.3	4.1	10.0	1.3	2.4	0.3
100,000–249,999	100	68.2	7.8	9.8	2.1	8.2	0.9	2.8	0.2
50,000–99,999	100	76.6	6.7	6.3	1.1	6.2	0.8	2.2	0.1
25,000–49,999	100	80.8	6.7	4.9	0.9	5.0	0.5	1.0	0.2
10,000–24,999	100	84.6	5.8	4.0	0.4	2.8	0.2	1.9	0.2
2,500–9,999	100	84.5	5.3	3.7	0.5	3.2	0.2	2.3	0.3
< 2,500	100	83.8	4.7	5.1	0.6	3.2	0.2	2.2	0.3

*Percentages may not add to 100 due to rounding.

**Includes Asians, Native Hawaiians, Pacific Islanders, American Indians, Alaska Natives, and any other race.

Source: U.S. Department of Justice, Bureau of Justice Statistics (2006). *Local Police Departments, 2003*, NCJ 210118, p. 7.

civilizing influence on the courtroom and the prison because of their "higher morality" and their innate need to help relieve the suffering of others. Interestingly, this notion of female morality and sentiment is still with us in scholarly as well as popular literature (Gilligan, 1982; Kerber et al., 1986). As Martin and Jurik (1996) point out, however, constructing women as different is problematic for several reasons. For instance, feminine virtues may be equated with incompetence if a job is defined in terms of traditional masculinity; such images ignore diversity among women, and if it turns out that women do not exhibit these supposed differences on the job, then there is no longer a valid reason to hire and promote them (see also Worden, 1993 for an excellent discussion of this debate).

Within police training academies, law enforcement agencies, and correctional facilities, assumptions about the supposed innate differences between women and men may be used to justify policies and practices that prevent the full integration of women into criminal justice and law-related occupations. Male coworkers and supervisors alike often consider women to be physically and psychologically weaker than men, as manipulative and untrustworthy, as requiring and requesting special treatment, and as either "good" (supportive wives and mothers) or "bad" (seductresses and sex objects). Although Title VII successfully prohibited the exclusion of women from law enforcement and other occupations (see Chapter 8), ideas such as these continue to manifest themselves in behaviors that are nonetheless discriminatory against women and create at best an uncomfortable and at worst a hostile work environment for them. These behaviors include sexual harassment and other forms of harassment, differential assignment of duties, closer scrutinization of the work and appearance of women, and exclusion of women from informal activities (Burke & Mikkelsen, 2005; Heidensohn, 1992; Martin & Jurik, 1996; Morash & Haarr, 1995).

Consider police work, for example. Although women have constituted an increasing number of police recruits since the 1970s, they may be marginalized in training at many police academies (Pike, 1992). Instructors frequently use sexist (and typically sexual) humor to "liven up" the classes. They also commonly refer to female recruits as "girls," "gals," and "ladies," while the male recruits are "men" and "guys." They tell recruits that female victims and suspects are more troublesome than male victims and suspects. Female victims are portrayed as helpless, but also unpredictable—they may turn on an officer. Special care must be taken with female suspects; for instance, they may act seductively in an encounter and then become violent, or they may unjustifiably claim they were molested during a search, although, recruits are told, male suspects do not seem to mind being searched by female officers.

Not surprisingly, these attitudes and behaviors carry over into police departments. As we see in Table 9.2, the number of female police officers in the United States remains small, but these figures represent significant increases since the 1970s. The largest increases, in fact, have been among White female recruits followed by African American female recruits, particularly during the 1990s. Recent research has also looked at the experiences of African American male police officers. One study of 123 African American leaders in police departments indicated a high level of acceptance by their white colleagues (Thompson, 2006). Other research, however, indicates that minority officers experience more problems on the force than white officers do. For example, they are more likely than white officers to have formal complaints filed against them by their supervisors and colleagues, although officers' race does not appear to influence determination of guilt or the penalty applied (Rojek & Decker, 2009).

Belknap (2001) credits the increase in female police officers since the 1970s to affirmative action programs, Title VII lawsuits brought by women officers and recruits, legal limitations on the use of violence and force by officers, and the adoption of formal procedures for allocating assignments and promotions. In addition, the adoption of *community policing* in many jurisdictions throughout the country may have also helped to improve the status of women in policing. Unlike the traditional policing orientation, which emphasizes "crime-fighting" as opposed to community service, community policing focuses on community service and requires officers to develop cooperative relationships with neighborhood residents. Proactive problem solving and relational skills (traditionally identified as feminine) are more important in community policing than toughness and physical aggression (traditionally identified as masculine) (Horne, 2006; S. L. Miller, 1999). This is interesting given that results of a survey of 531 female police officers reveal that their primary motivation for entering law enforcement was the desire to help people (Seklecki & Paynich, 2007). Nevertheless, it is still unclear to what extent police departments have truly embraced community policing and reoriented the police role as opposed to simply paying lip service to community policing principles (see, for example, Websdale, 2002).

Researchers have identified other serious problems that continue to disadvantage women in law enforcement. First, female officers often face hurdles at work when they become pregnant. Cowan and Bochantin (2009), for example, interviewed fifteen female police officers about balancing their policing career with pregnancy and motherhood. Their findings reveal that pregnancy and motherhood jeopardize women's law enforcement careers and are viewed negatively by their department, where motherhood skills tend to be devalued. Women talked about their struggles balancing parenting responsibilities with policing responsibilities. In addition, the belief in male superiority is still strong in many police departments. There may be double standards of behavior for women and men and different criteria for evaluation (Pelkey & DeGrange, 1996). When a female officer makes a mistake, for example, the consequences may be exaggerated. Department members also continue to make references to women's physical size and strength and to question the impact of these physical qualities on the effectiveness of female officers. Moreover, female officers face a double bind: If they conform to the men's conceptions of "good" women, they will be viewed as too weak to do a competent job, but if they behave like the men, they will be labeled "bitches" and "dykes" (see also Haarr, 2005; Johnston, 1995; Worden, 1993).[3]

This point raises one final way that male officers attempt to assert their superiority: by sexualizing the workplace. Sexual teasing, jokes, and innuendo are routine in police departments. Research conducted in Florida reveals that the most common forms of sexual harassment include crude or offensive remarks and unwanted sexual attention (Collins, 2006). Many female officers do not report harassment because they see that the women who do report experience retaliation by other officers and may informally be forced to resign (Horne, 2006). However, there are several recent examples of female officers filing and winning sexual harassment suits against their departments. In 2006, for example, Suzanne Barth, a female officer in Mokena, Illinois, was awarded almost $2.2 million in a sexual harassment lawsuit ("Female Police Officer Wins," 2006; see also Lee, 2009). What such cases demonstrate is that sexual harassment remains a serious problem in policing, and it occurs not only in local and state departments, but in federal agencies, such as the F.B.I. as well.[4]

Despite the prevalent stereotypes about female police officers, there is little evidence that they differ from their male colleagues in their attitudes toward either police work or citizens. Experience, measured in years spent on the force, appears to be more important than an officer's sex in affecting her or his attitudes (Worden, 1993). In general, research indicates there are few gender differences in sources of stress among officers, but women's stress levels increase when they have to deal with sexism, racism, heterosexism, ageism, or other forms of discrimination against themselves or others (Antoniou, 2009; Haarr & Morash, 1999; McCarty, Zhao, & Garland 2007; Morash, Haarr, & Kwak, 2006). Recent research also indicates that female officers are more prone to depression and suicidal thoughts than male officers are. However, being married reduces suicidal ideation among depressed female officers (Violanti et al., 2009).

The heightened stress that some female officers experience does not appear to interfere with their ability to perform their duties effectively. Research has found, for example, that female officers are more likely than male officers to follow legal restrictions in situations involving weapons (Eterno, 2006). Studies also show that female officers tend to have a less aggressive style of policing than do their male counterparts (Belknap, 2001), have better communication skills (Horne, 2006), are less likely to use force (Schuck & Rabe-Hemp, 2005), and write better reports (Seklecki & Paynich, 2007). However, the style used by an officer, female or male, is influenced by many factors, including the sex, race or ethnicity, and demeanor of suspects (Martin & Jurik, 1996).

As Morash and Greene (1986) have pointed out, much of the research evaluating female officers' performance has been sexist in that it has focused on how well the women measure up to the men. In other words, male officers' performance was the standard by which female officers were evaluated, regardless of whether the traits or behaviors identified were relevant to effective policing. Martin and Jurik (1996), however, note that

> Effective police officers of both genders are flexible, able to use both the crime fighter script (associated with masculinity) and the service script (associated with femininity), according to situation demands....Ineffective officers may either too rigidly rely on their formal authority, and enact only the crime-fighting aspects of their role, or alternatively emphasize only the community service script and fail to maintain control of interactions when they are challenged. (pp. 92–93)

Research indicates that female correctional officers in prisons and jails have experiences similar to those of women in police work (Lawrence & Mahan, 1998; McMahon, 1999: Pogrebin & Poole, 1997; Zupan, 1992). As with other law enforcement occupations, the number of female correctional officers has increased since the 1970s and, although women have a much briefer employment history at all-male facilities than at all-female facilities, their numbers in men's prisons have gone up in recent years. Still, women make up only 13.5 percent of correctional officers in the federal system (U.S. Department of Justice, 2004). In the state prison system, about 28 percent of staff is female, although many of these positions do not involve the direct supervision of inmates (Belknap, 2001; Martin & Jurik, 1996; U.S. Department of Justice, 2003).

A number of factors contributed to the increase in female correctional officers in recent years, including affirmative action programs, successful Title VII lawsuits brought by women seeking positions as correctional officers at all-male facilities, a decline in job applications by men, and the belief by policy makers that the addition of women staff would have a "calming effect" on inmates and would promote more humane treatment (Martin & Jurik, 1996; Zupan, 1992).[5] These factors have also contributed to the high representation of women of color among correctional officers; depending on the facility, women of color may make up from one-quarter to nearly one-half of the corrections staff (Belknap 1991; Maghan & McLeish-Blackwell, 1991).

Nevertheless, the increased presence of women in corrections has not led to their full integration in the workplace. Female correctional officers confront resistance and harassment from male administrators, coworkers, and inmates (Belknap, 2007; Britton, 2003; Martin & Jurik, 1996).[6] Training and work assignments favor male correctional officers, and performance evaluations, which are supposedly based on objective criteria, disadvantage women for promotion (Britton, 2003; Lawrence & Mahan, 1998; Martin & Jurik, 1996). Researchers, for example, have found that performance evaluations tend to focus on skills traditionally considered masculine (security functions), while ignoring skills traditionally considered feminine (communication and conflict diffusion skills) (Jurik, 1985; Zimmer, 1987). Moreover, there is no evidence that female correctional officers cannot perform security functions as well as male correctional officers. For instance, Lawrence and Mahan (1998) found that although male guards often report that they feel their safety is endangered when they work with female guards, prison records of prisoner assaults of guards showed that female officers were no more likely than male guards to be assaulted (see also Hogan et al., 2005).

Lawrence and Mahan (1998) also found that female correctional officers viewed the prison as less dangerous than the male correctional officers did. In fact, similar to police officers, female and male correctional officers show few differences in their attitudes toward their work and toward inmates. Female correctional personnel appear to value rules and structure more than their male coworkers do, and they experience more job-related stress; both of these findings are likely related to the pressure, criticism, and harassment they receive from their male colleagues (Jurik & Halemba, 1984; Lawrence & Johnson, 1991; Tewksbury & Collins, 2006). Female correctional officers are also more pessimistic about their chances for career advancements and promotions (McMahon, 1999).

Women in more prestigious positions, female attorneys and judges, for instance, also experience discriminatory treatment. Recent research, in fact, demonstrates that even though women outnumber men as law school students, sexism remains a pervasive bias in our nation's law firms and courtrooms (American Bar Association, 2001; Epstein, 1998; Padevic & Orcutt, 1997). For example, in 2008, women represented 88 percent of all paralegals but only 34 percent of lawyers (U.S. Department of Labor, 2009). Research conducted in the 1990s indicated that colleagues and judges subjected female attorneys to disparaging and offensive remarks and behaviors both inside and outside the courtroom, which could have made female lawyers' work stressful and lowered their credibility in the eyes of clients and the courts, jeopardizing their courtroom success (MacCorquodale & Jensen, 1993). However, the treatment of female lawyers has improved, and blatant gender bias is now rare, possibly due to programs that educate judges on gender fairness (Samborn, 2002). Nevertheless, women of color continue to face challenges as lawyers because of their race as well as their sex. The American Bar Association Commission on Women in the Profession, for instance, reports that women of color employed by private law firms are more likely than White men employed by private law firms to experience demeaning comments or harassment (49 percent compared to 3 percent) (American Bar Association, 2006). In 2008, an American Bar Association report on follow-up interviews with twenty-eight women of color who were partners in national law firms found that these women faced gender and racial biases when they became the first partner of color or female partner of color in their firms (American Bar Association, 2008).

There are far fewer female judges than female attorneys. Women were not permitted to stand for election to judgeships in most states until 1920, when the Nineteenth Amendment was passed (see Chapter 10). Once they were able to hold judgeships, however, most were elected or appointed to seats in family or juvenile courts. A woman was not appointed to the federal bench until 1949, and by 1976, there were still only nineteen female federal judges (Abrahamson, 1998). In 2009, 212 women held federal judgeships, more than one quarter of the federal judiciary (Sherman, 2009). There have been four women on the U.S. Supreme Court, three of whom are still serving: Sandra Day O'Connor (1981–2006), Ruth Bader Ginsburg (since 1993), Sonia Sotomayor (since 2009), and Elena Kagan (since 2010). The National Association of Women Judges (2010) reports that 4,521 of the 17,108 state judges (about 26 percent) are women. Women are 31 percent of judges in state courts of last resort, 31 percent of judges in state intermediate appellate courts, 24 percent of judges in state courts with general jurisdiction, and 30 percent of judges in state courts with limited jurisdiction.

Research on gender and judging is limited. Most studies show no gender differences in how judges evaluate evidence and determine sentences (see, for example, Abbate, 2000; Fox & Van Sickel, 2000; Westergren, 2004). Other research indicates that women bring a unique perspective to the bench—a gendered voice, although these studies have focused on family law, not criminal law. For example, Martin and Pyle (2005) looked at unanimous decisions in state high courts in the area of divorce law. They concluded that the judge's gender predicted support for female litigants in cases concerning divorce, child support, child custody, and property settlement. Similarly, Miller and Maier (2008) interviewed thirteen female family court judges about the role they believed gender plays in their decision-making and legal reasoning. Although judges in this study acknowledged that their gender influenced their legal reasoning, they maintained that male and female judges reach the same legal decision regardless of their gender.

It is clear from our discussion so far that sexism, as well as racism and heterosexism, are widespread in the criminal justice system. But to what extent do such attitudes affect the disposition of cases? For example, does sexism disadvantage male offenders by affording their female counterparts greater leniency before the law? Or are male offenders advantaged by sexism in the criminal justice system? As a preliminary response, we can say that the sex of the offender does appear to play a part in the disposition of a case. However, a number of other factors interact with sex in producing specific outcomes. These include the offender's age and race or ethnicity as well as the offense with which he or she is charged and the number of previous criminal convictions. We can understand this better by comparing conviction rates and sentencing patterns for male and female offenders.

Do the Punishments Fit the Crimes?

More than thirty years ago, criminologist Clayton Hartjen (1978, p. 108) observed that "although a suspect's behavior is of primary importance in determining his or her chances of being arrested, in most cases the decision to arrest a person is based on factors that have little to do with the degree of a person's behavioral criminality.... It is not so much what a person does as what kind of person he [or she] is (or is seen by the police to be) that affects official labeling." Hartjen's argument can be extended to other stages of criminal justice processing that follow arrest, including the arraignment (at which time a plea is entered by the defendant), the trial (either by a judge—which is known as a bench trial—or by a jury), and sentencing. This treatment of defendants occurs because official actors within the criminal justice system—that is, the police, attorneys, and judges—exercise considerable discretion in deciding how particular cases, and, therefore, particular defendants, will be handled. This discretion may lead to widespread disparities in the treatment of offenders, which have less to do with the offenders' behavior than with their membership in specific groups, such as their social class, race and ethnicity, and sex.

Consider, for instance, the practice of *plea negotiation*, better known as *plea bargaining*. In a plea bargain, the prosecutor and the defense attorney work out an agreement whereby the defendant will plead guilty in exchange for some prosecutorial or judicial concession, usually a reduced charge (and, therefore, a reduced sentence), the reduction of multiple charges, or a recommendation of leniency by the prosecutor (which also has the effect of reducing the severity of the potential sentence). In 2008, 96.3 percent of criminal convictions in U.S. District Courts were the result of guilty pleas (U.S. Department of Justice, Bureau of Justice Statistics, 2009). In 2004 (the most recent year for which data were available), 95 percent of felony convictions in state courts were guilty pleas (U.S. Department of Justice, Bureau of Justice Statistics, 2004). Research indicates that plea bargaining may operate differently for different groups of offenders

(Sentencing Project, 2008). Some have argued that defendants who are poor and racial and ethnic minorities (who are disproportionately represented among the poor) experience greater pressure to enter a guilty plea because the public defenders assigned to them wish to dispose of as many cases in their overwhelming caseloads as quickly as possible (Mann, 1993).[7] More recent research, however, has found that African American defendants are less likely to plead guilty and are more likely to go to trial (Frenzel & Ball, 2007; Kellough & Wortley, 2002). African American defendants' refusal to plea bargain and their desire for a trial, particularly a jury trial, could result from their distrust of the criminal justice system and hope that a jury of their peers will be more fair.

Legal "reforms," enacted as part of the federal government's and state and local jurisdictions' renewed efforts to "get tough" on crime, have ruled out the possibility of plea bargaining for certain offenses and have also had a disparate impact on racial and ethnic minorities as well as women. Research shows that policies such as mandatory sentences for drug offenses and "three strikes and you're out" laws (i.e., a mandatory life sentence following a third felony conviction) resulted in an increase in the number of women and racial and ethnic minorities sentenced to prison. Between 1986 and 2006, the number of women incarcerated in state prisons for drug offenses increased more than threefold (Spohn & Brennan, forthcoming). In 2006, 28.7 percent of women in state prisons were incarcerated for drug offenses compared with 18.9 percent of men incarcerated in state prisons (Spohn & Brennan, forthcoming). But the most dramatic increase in incarceration was experienced by Black women. During the 1980s, the number of Black women incarcerated in state and federal prisons increased by 278 percent, while the number of incarcerated Black men increased 186 percent; the overall prison population increased 168 percent. In fact, during that period, the increase for Black females was largest among all groups—Black, White, and Hispanic females and males (Bush-Baskette, 1998). More recently, the growth in the prison population has slowed, and it is expected to decrease significantly over the next several years, due largely to government budget crises. Although this decline has benefited African American women and men, they remain considerably more likely to be incarcerated than white and Hispanic women and men, a point to which we will return later in the chapter (Sabol, West, & Cooper, 2009).

For many years, researchers have documented differences in criminal sentencing based not only on offenders' sex and race or ethnicity, but also on their age, marital status, and a host of other nonlegal factors. This leads to **sentencing disparity**, the imposition of different sentences on offenders convicted of similar crimes. It is not difficult to understand why sentencing disparity is problematic; it results in unfair and inappropriate sentences that may be disproportionate to the severity of the crime or the offender's criminal history and are based instead on irrelevant factors, such as the offender's sex and race or ethnicity.

Early studies of sentencing disparities between male and female offenders reported that women were given preferential treatment by the courts and were less likely than men to receive prison sentences for their crimes (Faine & Bohlander, 1976; Nagel & Weitzman, 1972). However, as Chesney-Lind (1986) points out, the difficulty with much of this early research is that it did not control for the less serious nature of most women's crimes. One study that took into account such factors as type of offense and prior convictions showed that offense severity and prior record have the largest effects on sentencing for both male and female offenders and that when men and women appear in court under similar circumstances—that is, charged with similar crimes and coming from similar backgrounds—they are treated alike (Steffensmeier, Kramer, & Streifel, 1993). But other researchers dispute this finding (Spohn & Brennan, forthcoming). For example, some researchers have argued that the perceived *respectability* of the offender—male or female—in terms of conformity to traditional gender norms influences sentencing. According to Miethe and Moore (1986), married, employed men with no prior offense record—that is, men who conform to the gender prescription of "respectable" masculinity—are sentenced more leniently than single, unemployed men with previous arrests or convictions. This is especially true for men of color. For instance, Spohn and Holleran (2000) found that young, unemployed Black and Hispanic offenders are significantly more likely than middle-aged, employed White male offenders to be sentenced to prison (see also Doerner & Demuth, 2010; Steffensmeier, Ulmer, & Kramer, 1998). Recent research supports that White felony drug offenders received lesser sentences than Black or Hispanic felony drug offenders (Brennan & Spohn, 2008), but age alone does not appear to affect sentencing (Wu & Spohn, 2009).

Women who conform to a traditional model of femininity—for instance, economic dependence on a man, no evidence of drug or alcohol use, no evidence of sexual deviance—may receive lighter sentences than women deemed less "respectable" by the courts.[8] Daly (1994) refers to this pattern of bias in judicial decision making as *familial-based justice.* She reports that defendants with family ties, especially those who are the primary caregivers of children, are treated more leniently by the courts than nonfamilied defendants. Based on interviews with court officials, she concluded that the protection of families and children, not the protection of women, influences much judicial decision making. These findings help to explain why most incarcerated women are not only Black, but also young, poor, unmarried mothers, who are in prison for petty property crimes or drug offenses, usually drug possession rather than drug trafficking (Bush-Baskette, 1998; Chesney-Lind, 1997; Mancuso & Miller, 2001). However, Stacey and Spohn (2006) found that at least in federal courts, there are no differences in sentences imposed on female offenders with children and those without children. Spohn (1998) found, though, that women who have dependent children and are repeat drug offenders are as likely as men to be incarcerated by judges in state courts.

Another manifestation of "get tough" "lock 'em up" crime control policies is the imposition of longer sentences. Again, however, race and sex intersect to produce differential outcomes. Researchers have found that not only are non-White women more likely to be sentenced to prison, but the actual time served is longer for non-White women than for White women. Steffensmeier and Demuth (2006) examined the effects of gender and race on sentencing. They concluded that females and Whites are sentenced more leniently than males, Hispanics, and African Americans. However, when comparing the combined effects of race/ethnicity and gender, they found that race and ethnicity influence sentence length for male but not for female offenders. In other words, female offenders, regardless of race, receive shorter sentences than males. Black and Hispanic males receive more punitive sentences than white males (see also Brennan, 2009; but see Crawford, 2000; Crawford, Chiricos, & Kleck, 1998; and Crow & Kunselman, 2009 for findings from studies in Florida that show that women of color receive harsher sentences than white women and are perceived to be more dangerous.).

Finally, the "get tough" approach to crime control, which emphasizes punishment over rehabilitation, has also resulted in a greater willingness to sentence offenders to death. Between 1930 and 2007, 4,958 people were executed in the United States. Of the

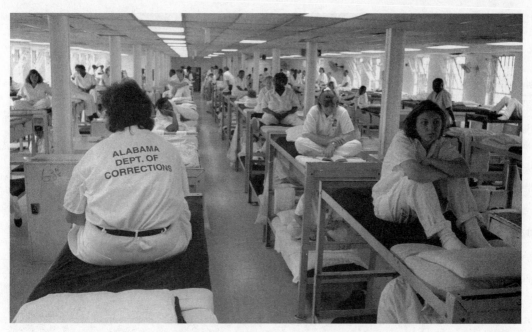

Although women make up only a small percentage of the U.S. prison population, their incarceration rates increased significantly after the 1970s.

1,099 prisoners executed since 1977, 43 percent were non-White, a figure disproportionate to their representation in the general population; only 33 percent of the U.S. population is non-White (U.S. Department of Commerce, Bureau of the Census, 2007a). In 2010, of the 3,261 offenders on death row in the United States, only 62 (less than 2 percent) were women (Death Penalty Information Center, 2011). Since the death penalty was reinstated in 1977, 12 women have been executed (Death Penalty Information Center, 2011).

As Spohn and Brennan (forthcoming) point out, comparisons of death penalty sentencing by sex are meaningless because there are simply too few women convicted of death-eligible crimes. Instead, they report on research that examines the effect of the *victim's sex* in death penalty cases. These studies (e.g., Holcomb, Williams, & Demuth, 2004; Williams, Demuth, & Holcomb, 2007) indicate that the sex and race of the victim matter in such cases. Offenders who are convicted of killing white females are significantly more likely than those who killed white males or black females and black males to be sentenced to death.

Thus, although there appears to be a widespread belief that women are treated chivalrously by the courts—being allowed, at times, to get away with murder (see, for example, Mansnerus, 1997)—the empirical research we have reviewed here does not support such a view. Rather, studies indicate that multiple legal and extra-legal factors, especially the race of the offender and the race and sex of the victim, intersect with the sex of the offender to influence sentencing outcomes.

GENDER AND JUVENILE OFFENDERS   Our focus so far has been on adult offenders, but research indicates that the age of the offender is also an important variable. Let's briefly consider how age intersects with sex as well as race and ethnicity to produce differential justice system involvement for juvenile offenders.

TABLE 9.3 Arrest Trends by Sex (Juveniles under 18), 1999–2008						
	Males			**Females**		
Offense Charged	**1999**	**2008**	**Percent Change**	**1999**	**2008**	**Percent Change**
Total[1]	**1,007,838**	**819,807**	**−18.7**	**381,243**	**351,558**	**−7.8**
Murder and nonnegligent manslaughter	673	625	−7.1	62	45	−27.4
Forcible rape	2,487	1,824	−26.7	52	24	−53.8
Robbery	14,283	17,737	+24.2	1,390	1,914	+37.7
Aggravated assault	31,107	24,333	−21.8	8,832	7,317	−17.2
Burglary	52,009	43,702	−16.0	6,897	6,713	−2.7
Larceny-theft	148,181	105,099	−29.1	80,799	84,160	+4.2
Motor vehicle theft	21,344	10,774	−49.5	4,455	2,136	−52.1
Arson	4,733	3,583	−24.3	619	1,291	−22.1
Total violent crime[2]	48,550	44,519	−8.3	10,336	9,300	−10.0
Total property crime[2]	226,267	163,158	−27.9	92,770	93,491	+0.8
Other assaults	93,177	87,815	−5.8	40,573	45,527	+12.2
Stolen property: buying, receiving, possessing	14,269	10,178	−28.7	2,095	2,429	+15.9
Vandalism	60,183	54,680	−9.1	8,273	8,482	+2.5
Weapons: carrying, possessing, etc.	20,957	20,420	−2.6	2,083	2,068	−0.7
Prostitution and commercialized vice	315	206	−34.6	390	643	+64.9
Sex offenses (except forcible rape and prostitution)	8,897	7,151	−19.6	719	698	−2.9
Drug abuse violations	93,229	85,601	−8.2	16,655	16,376	−1.7
Driving under the influence	10,228	6,772	−33.8	2,033	2,171	+6.8
Liquor laws	63,176	44,707	−29.2	28,036	26,231	−6.4
Drunkenness	10,902	7,854	−28.0	2,689	2,450	−8.9
Disorderly conduct	66,044	62,816	−4.9	26,559	31,342	+18.0
Vagrancy	1,119	776	−30.7	247	197	−20.2
All other offenses (except traffic)	185,631	149,326	−19.6	62,654	52,253	−16.6

TABLE 9.3 (Continued)	Males			Females		
Offense Charged	*1999*	*2008*	*Percent Change*	*1999*	*2008*	*Percent Change*
Total[1]	1,007,838	819,807	–18.7	381,243	351,558	–7.8
Curfew and loitering law violations	56,843	40,275	–29.1	25,370	19,935	–21.4
Runaways	37,359	26,923	–27.9	54,048	34,363	–36.4

[1]Some crime categories have been omitted from this table.

[2]These crimes are collectively known as the Index Offenses. Violent Index Offenses are: murder, forcible rape, robbery, and aggravated assault. Property Index Offenses are: burglary, larceny-theft, motor vehicle theft, and arson.

Source: Federal Bureau of Investigation, 2008, Table 33.

Table 9.3 shows arrest trends for juveniles from 1999 to 2008. Girls, we can see, are more likely than boys to be charged with **status offenses**, that is, behavior which if engaged in by an adult would not be considered a violation of the law. These include, for example, running away from home, incorrigibility, truancy, being a "juvenile in need of supervision" (JINS), and being in danger of becoming "morally depraved." Girls face harsher punishments than boys do for status offenses and are more closely monitored by the juvenile justice system (Flynn, Hanks, & Gurley, 2007; Garcia & Lane, 2009). However, as Brown and her colleagues (2007) point out, often these charges represent parents' attempts to adhere to and enforce the sexual double standard (see Chapter 7). Parents are significantly more likely to bring a daughter to court for her behavior than to bring a son for his (Brown, Chesney-Lind, & Stein, 2007; Chesney-Lind, 2001). Research shows that parents of adolescents at high risk for delinquent behavior— for example, they live in economically marginalized, high-crime neighborhoods and have siblings who have been adjudicated delinquent—impose more restrictions on their daughters than on their sons. Boys have greater freedom to engage in activities outside the home, especially at night, whereas girls are often expected to help raise younger children in the household and their out-of-home activities are more closely monitored, particularly at night (Bottcher, 1995). Not surprisingly, then, boys typically engage in more delinquent behavior than girls and their offenses are more serious (Flynn et al., 2007).

Research also reveals that many young women charged as runaways are often attempting to escape from physically and sexually abusive homes (Siegel & Williams, 2003). Studies of young people entering the juvenile justice system show that girls are more likely than boys to have been abused and to have entered the juvenile justice system because of status offenses, while boys' entry was more often precipitated by involvement in more delinquent offenses (Flynn et al., 2007). Unfortunately, because of the juvenile courts' commitment to preserving parental authority, they frequently have forced these girls to return to their abusers, routinely ignoring girls' complaints about abuse (Arnold, 1990;

Chesney-Lind, 1997; Davis, 1993). Ironically, then, "statutes that were originally placed in law to 'protect' young people have, in the case of some girls, criminalized their survival strategies" (Chesney-Lind, 1997, p. 28; see also Siegel & Williams, 2003).

Females charged with status offenses are more harshly treated at every step of criminal justice processing and are more likely than males to be institutionalized for status offenses (Chesney-Lind, 2001; Chesney-Lind & Shelden, 1992; Poe-Yamagata & Butts, 1996). Sentencing reforms to address these disparities have been enacted, but their effectiveness is questionable. For instance, one federal policy, the Juvenile Justice and Delinquency Prevention Act of 1974, required states receiving funds for delinquency prevention programs to divert status offenders away from juvenile correctional facilities. Since girls are more likely to be charged with status offenses, this policy at least initially helped to reduce their incarceration rates (Teilmann & Landry, 1981). However, in 1980, those rates again began to climb as a "get tough" attitude took hold with respect to juvenile offenders just as it did for adult offenders. In many jurisdictions, attempts were made to close what many viewed as loopholes permitted by the 1974 act by reclassifying many status offenses as criminal offenses. Research indicates that this reclassification impacted more negatively on girls than on boys (Curran, 1984; Feld, 2009). Similarly, legal mandates that remove female status offenders from secure juvenile facilities—a practice that is undoubtedly beneficial to them—does not necessarily result in freedom from incarceration (Feinman, 1992). In fact, Chesney-Lind (1997, p. 75) argues that this "reform" has actually created a "two-track juvenile justice system—one track for girls of color and another for white girls." White girls are significantly more likely to be recommended for "treatment" (e.g., placement in a mental health facility), whereas girls of color are more likely to be recommended for a "detention-oriented" placement. Moreover, when institutional placements are examined, White girls are more likely to be placed in private facilities, while girls of color are more likely to be placed in public facilities (see also Bartollas, 1993).

More recently there has been concern about the fact that while arrests of juveniles for nearly all types of offenses have declined, girls' arrest rates have not declined as much as boys' arrest rates have. Looking at Table 9.3 we see that between 1999 and 2008, the overall arrest rate of male juveniles declined more than twice as much as the overall arrest rate of female juveniles (Tracy, Kempf-Leonard, & Abramoske-James, 2009; see also Puzzanchera, 2009). Moreover, despite the decline in overall arrests, there have been substantial increases in girls' arrests for specific crimes; girls' arrests for robbery, prostitution and commercialized vice, buying and receiving stolen property, and disorderly conduct have increased most significantly. And even though boys are nearly three times more likely than girls to be arrested, arrests of girls for crimes such as simple assault and larceny have increased while boys' arrests for these crimes have decreased (Feld, 2009; Puzzanchera, 2009). Girls are more likely to be arrested for simple or aggravated assault than they are for drug abuse violations (Snyder & Sickmund, 2006; Tracy et al., 2009).

The media have given considerable attention to girls' violence, sounding the alarm about ultra-violent "mean girls" (Kluger, 2006; Sanders, 2005). Research, however, does not support the media image. If we look again at Table 9.3, we see that in 2008 females accounted for only 18 percent of violent crimes committed by juveniles. In addition, although girls' arrests for violent crimes have failed to decline as much as boys' arrests have (or in some cases have increased), it does not appear accurate to characterize girls as becoming more violent (Chesney-Lind & Belknap, 2004; Steffensmeier et al., 2005).

We need to consider base numbers of arrests as we did with adult offenders. Returning to Table 9.3, we see, for instance, that while girls' arrests for violent crime increased by 1.4 percent between 1999 and 2008, in raw numbers this amounts to 858 additional arrests. Moreover, girls' increased arrest rate for violent offenses may be a result of changes in policy. Steffensmeier et al. (2005) examined boys' and girls' arrest records and concluded that the increase in arrests of girls for violent crimes was primarily due to the fact that police, in their "get tough" on crime approach, have become more likely to charge less serious actions as assaults and this change affects girls more than boys.

There is increased attention to girls' use of violent behavior in self-defense. Jones's (2009) ethnographic research explores the violence perpetrated by young girls. Adolescent girls living in the inner-city encounter a myriad of violence in their daily lives and may turn to violence and retaliation simply to survive and maintain respect (see also J. Miller, 2008). Other researchers have found a relationship between girls' victimization experiences and their subsequent involvement in crime. For instance, Widom and Maxfield (2001) reported a significant increase in violent crime among girls who had been neglected and abused compared with girls who were not neglected and abused, but this relationship did not hold for boys. Similarly, Siegel and Williams (2003) found that girls who were sexually abused were three times more likely than girls who were not sexually abused to run away from home and subsequently be arrested for violent offenses. Importantly, childhood abuse is also associated with women's, but not men's, violent offending as adults (English, Widom, & Brandford, 2001).

An additional concern has been girls' involvement in gangs. Research shows differences in girls' and boys' gang involvement. For instance, female gang members tend to be younger than male gang members. Nevertheless, the risk factors associated with gang involvement are similar for girls and boys: for example, living in disadvantaged neighborhoods; fighting with peers; and less parental availability, attachment, and involvement (Bell, 2009). Girls may also become involved in gangs for protection or as a survival strategy. As Jody Miller's (2001) ethnographic research on the gendered nature of gangs shows, female gang members realized that their gang involvement may put them at higher risk for various forms of victimization, but it also provided them with protection. They felt that they were not as much at risk for random violence and violence in the home by being a gang member; disturbingly, their potential victimization was, to them, more predictable.

To sum up our discussion so far, it appears that a number of extralegal factors routinely come into play in the administration of justice. These include offenders' sex, race/ ethnicity, age, and perceived respectability. "Taken together, [the] research findings suggest that the criminal justice system has been involved in the enforcement of traditional [and racialized] sex-role expectations as well as, and sometimes in place of, the law" (Chesney-Lind, 1986, p. 92). Let's turn our attention now to an examination of how these factors carry over from sentencing into corrections.

Gender and Corrections

The United States has one of the largest correctional populations in the world. In 2008, over 7.3 million adult Americans were under some sort of correctional supervision: They were on probation, in jail or prison, or on parole (U.S. Department of Justice, Bureau of Justice Statistics, 2008). In 2008, 1.6 million adult Americans were in federal or state prison; this is one out of every 198 adult U.S. residents, giving the U.S. the dubious distinction of incarcerating more of its adult citizens than any other democratic nation (U.S. Department of Justice, Bureau of Justice Statistics, 2009). As we have already noted, incarceration rates rose during the 1980s and 1990s, due largely to mandatory sentencing policies. However, since 2000, the incarceration rate has grown more slowly: an average of 1.8 percent per year vs. an average of 6.5 percent during the 1990s (Sabol et al., 2009).

Historically, women have constituted only a small fraction of U.S. prison and jail populations. For example, at the turn of the century, women were just 4 percent of the prison population in the United States; in 1970, they made up only 3 percent of this population. But the "lock 'em up" mentality of the 1980s and 1990s swelled the total U.S. prison population and women's representation in it even though women's involvement in serious crime did not increase significantly (Owen, 2001; see Tables 9.4 and 9.5). The number of women incarcerated or on probation has risen dramatically in recent years. Between 1995 and 2007, the total number of incarcerated women rose by 67 percent, and the number of women on probation rose by 52 percent (U.S. Department of Justice, Bureau of Justice Statistics, 2008). Nevertheless, men continue to be incarcerated at a much higher rate than women. In 2008, males were incarcerated at a rate 15 times higher than females (Sabol et al., 2009). Women are just 7 percent of the U.S. prison population (Sabol et al., 2009) and approximately 23 percent of those on probation (U.S. Department of Justice, Bureau of Justice Statistics, 2008). Fifteen percent of the approximately 93,000 juveniles held in residential placement facilities in 2006 were girls (Office of Juvenile Justice and Delinquency Prevention, 2006). Looking again at Tables 9.4 and 9.5, we see that women of color are disproportionately represented among incarcerated women.

Traditionally, the small numbers of incarcerated women have been offered as a rationale for paying little attention to them in both research and policy making. At the same time, the physical plant of women's prisons appeared less harsh than facilities that housed men and, therefore, less "problematic." The rapid rise in the number of female prisoners and jail inmates, however, brought more attention not only to the problems of incarceration in general, but also to the special problems faced by incarcerated women. For example, although some women's prisons are relatively more physically attractive than men's facilities and less secure—with minimum, medium, and maximum security inmates housed together—living conditions are not necessarily less harsh, less regimented, or less degrading (Owen, 2001).

TABLE 9.4 Adult Prisoners Under State or Federal Jurisdiction, 2000, 2006, & 2007, by Sex, Race, & Hispanic Origin

| | Numbers of Prisoners | | | | | |
| | White | | Black | | Hispanic/Latino | |
	Male	*Female*	*Male*	*Female*	*Male*	*Female*
2000	401,900	33,600	532,400	32,200	242,600	13,100
2006	478,800	49,200	535,100	28,600	291,000	17,500
2007	471,400	50,500	556,900	29,300	301,200	17,600

Source: West, H. C., & Sabol, W. J. (2008). *Prisoners in 2007*. U.S. Department of Justice, Bureau of Justice Statistics. NCJ 224280. Table 5, p. 3.

TABLE 9.5 Estimated Rate of Sentenced Prisoners Under State or Federal Jurisdiction, per 100,000 U.S. Residents, by Sex, Race, and Hispanic Origin, 2000, 2007, 2008

	Rate of Imprisonment					
	White		*Black*		*Hispanic/Latino*	
	Male	*Female*	*Male*	*Female*	*Male*	*Female*
2000	449	34	3,457	205	1,220	60
2007	481	50	3,138	150	1,259	79
2008	487	50	3,161	149	1,220	75

Source: Sabol, W. J., West, H. C., & Cooper, M. (2009). *Prisoners in 2008*. U.S. Department of Justice, Bureau of Justice Statistics. NCJ 228417.

Another difference between women's prisons and men's prisons is the availability of educational and vocational programming. Historically, these programs have been grossly underfunded in women's prisons, the rationale being that large numbers of programs for small numbers of women would not be cost-efficient. Traditionally, these programs reinforced gender stereotypes and conformity to the turn-of-the-century philosophy that the rehabilitative goal of women's prisons should be to teach "fallen women" how to be good wives and mothers. Consequently, these programs emphasized domestic "skills" over marketable job skills. Research indicates that women are more responsive to prison programs than men are, but women still have fewer opportunities to participate in such programs. Moreover, prison programs continue to ill-equip women for the contemporary work world and for successfully meeting the challenge of economic survival for themselves or as primary providers for their families. Unlike vocational programs in men's prisons, which at least focus on skilled trades such as carpentry, electronics, plumbing, and construction, most vocational programs in women's prisons train inmates for clerical work, cosmetology, and garment manufacturing (Moyer, 1991; Sharp, 2002; Simon & Landis, 1991).

Several lawsuits that challenged sex discrimination in prison vocational and education programs did successfully broaden offerings in some prisons to include such courses as electronics, general business education, computer programming, commercial art, and food service. Despite these rulings, however, observers note that factors such as overcrowding, resistance by administrators, and the punishment ideology prevalent among legislators and other officials have prevented implementation of more diverse vocational and educational offerings in many women's prisons (Belknap, 2007; Sharp, 2002). The recent economic recession is expected to negatively affect prison programming as well, since states have less money to spend on what some consider "unnecessary" or "frivolously indulgent" programs.

Also inadequate in women's prisons are medical care and treatment programs. This is especially problematic given that women are more likely than men to have health issues or be infected with HIV or AIDS. More than half (53 percent) of female jail inmates reported having a medical problem, compared to 35 percent of male inmates (Maruschak, 2006). More female inmates in state and federal prisons (1.9 percent) than male inmates (1.5 percent) were infected with HIV or AIDS in 2008 (Maruschak & Beavers, 2009). However, Pollock-Byrne (1990) makes the important point that simply offering female inmates the same medical services as those offered to male inmates is an inappropriate solution to this problem, since the health care needs of women are different from those of men. Women, for instance, need gynecological and, not infrequently, obstetrical care while in prison. An estimated 5 percent of females entering prison are pregnant and the probability that these pregnancies are high-risk is greater due to lack of prenatal care (Lewis, 2006; Sharp, 2002). There are also a large number of women and men in prison with mental health issues. In 2006, there were three times more men and women with mental illnesses in prisons than in mental health hospitals in the United States (Human Rights Watch, 2006). Incarcerated women are more likely than incarcerated men to have some type of mental illness (e.g., depression, PTSD, anxiety disorders) (James & Glaze, 2006; Lewis, 2006; Sharp, 2002). Since the mental health needs of female inmates are different from those of men, their treatment should also be different. Research suggests women's treatment should focus more on issues of self-esteem, relationship difficulties, and challenges that result from their parental responsibilities (Salisbury, Van Voorhis, & Spiropoulos, 2009). Research also supports the provision of mental health services for incarcerated girls, since those with more emotional and behavioral problems are more likely to re-offend (Tille & Rose, 2007).

Despite the facts that a large percentage of women are imprisoned because of drug offenses (Lewis, 2006) and that women are more likely than men to be incarcerated for drug or property offenses than for violent crimes (Harrison & Beck, 2006), the drug treatment programs typically offered to female inmates are inadequate and ineffective (Sharp, 2002). This is problematic since research indicates that women who complete drug treatment programs in prison are more likely to remain arrest-free for the first 18 months following their release (Robbins, Martin, & Surratt, 2009). Women's programs are often modeled on men's treatment programs even though, as we will see in Chapter 12, women abuse drugs and alcohol for reasons different from those of men. Moreover, the treatment of other medical complaints in prison can actually make women's drug problems worse. For instance, two of the most common medical complaints of female inmates are anxiety and depression, and they are frequently treated with psychotropic drugs such as tranquilizers (Greenfeld & Snell, 1999; Ross, 2000). Such drugs are overprescribed for non-incarcerated women who seek medical help for these problems (see Chapter 12), but when this treatment is applied to incarcerated women, the majority of whom already have substance abuse problems, the result may be *transaddiction*—that is, addiction to different drugs (prescription drugs rather than street drugs) but addiction nonetheless. Once released from prison, the addiction may be fed with both prescription and illicit drugs, sometimes with fatal consequences. According to one study, in fact, "drug overdose, usually involving heroin in combination with prescription drugs, is the most common cause of death among women who leave prison" (Davies & Cook, 1999, p. 285).

Few institutions offer programs that effectively address the problems associated with physical and sexual abuse, despite the prevalence of abuse in the lives of incarcerated women. Many incarcerated women and girls had been abused by a male relative or intimate partner (Belknap & Holsinger, 2006; Davidson & Chesney-Lind, 2009; DeHart, 2008; Goodkind, Ng, & Sari, 2006; Raphael, 2007). McDaniels-Wilson and Belknap (2008) found that 70 percent of their sample of 391 adult incarcerated women reported a history of rape, and half reported child sexual victimization. Many report that their previous victimization contributed to their offending (Belknap & Holsinger, 2006; DeHart, 2008; English et al., 2001). Other research indicates that child abuse contributes to depression, anxiety, and substance abuse, which increases women's risk for incarceration.

The abuse women experienced prior to incarceration may continue while they are in jail or prison. Investigations have documented widespread physical and sexual abuse of female inmates by male employees, including guards, at federal and state prisons as well as at local detention centers. Despite the fact that the number of female correctional officers has grown in recent years, most female inmates continue to be guarded by men, and some of these men use their authority to sexually exploit women prisoners. The abuse includes beatings, rape, and sexual coercion (e.g., withholding or bestowing privileges or goods to compel inmates to engage in sexual acts). Apart from blatant sexual abuse, the women also report repeated violations of their privacy, with guards entering rooms unannounced or strip searches being conducted in the presence of male guards, an especially traumatic experience for a woman with a history of sexual abuse (Buchanan, 2005; Chesney-Lind, 1997; Holmes, 1996; Pleming, 2001; Sharp, 2002; "U.S. Bureau of Prisons," 1998).[9]

Finally, the separation of inmates from their families presents acute problems for women. In 2004, about 51 percent of male inmates in state prisons had children less than eighteen years of age, and 62 percent of female inmates in state prisons had children under eighteen years of age. Among male inmates with children under eighteen, 36 percent report having lived with them before being incarcerated. In contrast, more than half of female state prison inmates (55 percent) with children under eighteen lived with them before going to prison. As we learned in Chapter 7, few children live with their fathers only. If a man with children is sent to prison, it is likely that the mother of the children will retain custody of them and provide them with care; 88 percent of imprisoned men with children under eighteen report that the children are living with their mother. When a woman with children is sent to prison, however, it is often the case that the children's father played a small role in the children's lives and that their mother was their sole caregiver and provider. Consequently, rather than living with their father (37 percent), children of imprisoned mothers usually live with a grandparent (45 percent) or other relative (23 percent); about 11 percent are placed in foster homes or institutional care (Glaze & Maruschak, 2008).

The amount of time imprisoned mothers are permitted to visit with their children varies widely from institution to institution. A small number allow visitation seven days a week (Simon & Landis, 1991). Among these is the Bedford Hills Correctional Facility in New York, which established the first state prison nursery program that allows imprisoned mothers to care for their infants within the correctional facility until the infants are one year old or for eighteen months if the mother is to be paroled within that period. This program also provides incarcerated mothers with parenting classes and supplies child care for the infants while the mothers go to prison jobs or prison classes to earn high school diplomas (Harris, 1993; see also Snyder-Joy & Carlo, 1998). Currently nine states have prison nursery programs in operation or under development. These programs are for children who are born to mothers while in custody; to qualify, the mother's conviction cannot be for a violent crime, nor can she have a past history of child abuse or neglect. The length of time the infant is permitted to stay in the program varies from thirty days (South Dakota Women's Prison) to three years (Washington Correctional Center for Women), but the average is twelve to eighteen months (Women's Prison Association, 2009).

In contrast, most facilities allow visitation once a week, while a few allow it only once or twice a month. The length of the visits in these institutions also varies, but most institutions report that they do not have rooms equipped for the visits of very young children (e.g., high chairs, cribs) or even rooms to talk privately or perhaps to listen to music with older children (Simon & Landis, 1991). While a majority of institutions report that they have furlough programs that allow incarcerated mothers to visit with their children at home or in halfway houses, Simon and Landis (1991) found that most of these have stringent eligibility requirements. Nevertheless, research shows that female inmates maintain closer contact with their children than male inmates do. Only 12 percent of female state prison inmates report that they have no contact with their children, whereas 21 percent of male state prison inmates say they never have contact with their children. Most of these contacts are by mail and telephone, not only because prison regulations limit personal visits, but also because 62 percent of state inmates (and 84 percent of federal inmates, regardless of sex), are imprisoned more than one hundred miles from their homes, making visits difficult for many family members (Mumola, 2000).

Apart from the economic consequences of imprisoning women who are the sole economic providers for and caregivers of their children, incarceration also has serious psychological consequences for both the women and the children. "For most mothers in prison, being separated from their children is the most painful part of their prison term" (Owen, 2001, p. 250; see also Barnacle, 1999; Foster & Lewis, forthcoming). The separation lowers the mothers' self-esteem and generates feelings of emptiness, helplessness, anger, bitterness, and guilt, as well as fears about the children's safety, of losing the children, or of being rejected by them (Baunach, 1992; Foster & Lewis, forthcoming; Snyder-Joy & Carlo, 1998). The children, depending on their age, experience a sense of failure and a range of feelings of traumatic loss and abandonment, anger, guilt, and fear for their mother's safety (Huie, 1994; Snyder-Joy & Carlo, 1998).

In sum, the picture with respect to law enforcement, sentencing, and corrections is a complex one. "Get-tough" crime control policies have generated a rhetoric of equality—if you commit the crime, you do the time, no matter who you are—but in practice, as we have seen, a multilayered standard of justice continues to operate. Does a multilayered standard of justice also come into play with respect to the treatment of male and female crime victims? We'll explore answers to this question in the next section.

CRIMINAL VICTIMIZATION: GENDER, POWER, AND VIOLENCE

Concern about becoming a crime victim is a common fear among the general population in the United States. There is, of course, a difference between fear of crime and the actual chances of becoming a crime victim. Looking at Table 9.6, we see data from the National Crime Victimization Survey (NCVS) showing rates of violent criminal victimization by sex. The NCVS is the second largest ongoing survey conducted by the federal government; it questions a random sample of American households about their criminal victimization experiences. Historically, men have been at greater risk for nearly all types of criminal victimization, and the data in Table 9.6 indicate that this remains the case, although analysts are concerned that men's and women's victimization rates are converging (Truman, 2011). If race is taken into account, we find that men of color have the highest victimization rates, and if we consider age, we find that those between the ages of sixteen and nineteen are at greater risk of criminal victimization. Social class matters as well; lower-income households are significantly more likely to be victimized than higher-income households (Truman, 2011). Being non-white, young, and poor significantly increases one's likelihood of criminal victimization. Box 9.2 discusses hate crime perpetration and victimization, which further underlines the need to examine the effects of intersecting inequalities.

BOX 9.2
Hate Crimes

Hate crimes, which are also called *bias crimes,* are crimes in which the offender's actions are motivated by hatred, bias, or prejudice, based on the actual or perceived race, ethnicity, national origin, religion, or sexual orientation of the victim. Hate crimes often take the form of slurs and vandalism, but not infrequently they involve violent physical attacks against individuals. For example, in 2008, over 2,200 incidents of hate crimes reported to the police (31 percent of all hate crimes) involved simple or aggravated assault (Federal Bureau of Investigation, 2008).The majority of hate crime perpetrators are young, white, heterosexual men. Researchers who have studied hate crime hypothesize, based on the characteristics of common perpetrators and victims as well as the characteristics of the crimes (e.g., language used by perpetrators, the group nature of perpetration, the use of alcohol by perpetrators) that offenders use these crimes as a way of accomplishing a particular type of masculinity, *hegemonic masculinity*—that is, white, Christian, able-bodied, heterosexual masculinity (Bufkin, 1999; Perry, 2001).

Not everyone is at equal risk for hate crime victimization, however. The FBI reports that over half (51 percent) of all incidents reported in 2008 were racially motivated and 12.5 percent were motivated by ethnicity or national origin (Federal Bureau of Investigation, 2008). Gay men and lesbians, too, are frequent targets of hate crimes. In 2008, 18 percent of reported hate crimes were motivated by sexual orientation (Federal Bureau of Investigation, 2008).

In the official definition of hate crime codified in the United States as the federal Hate Crime Statistics Act of 1990, actions motivated by the *sex* of the victim were not included. In other words, specific acts or threats against women that are intended to intimidate, harass, induce fear, coerce, or punish them because of the perpetrators' misogynistic feelings or hostility toward them *as women* were not counted as hate crimes and, therefore, were outside the bounds of redress provided in hate crimes statutes (Hodge, 2011). An important change occurred in October 2009 when President Barack Obama signed the Matthew Shepard and James Byrd Jr. Hate Crimes Prevention Act. Both Shepard and Byrd were killed in 1998, Shepard for his homosexuality and Byrd for his race. This act expanded the 1990 hate crime law to include crimes motivated by the victim's real or perceived gender, gender identity, sexual orientation, and disability (Barsotti, 2009; "Congress approves and President signs first federal law affirmatively to protect LGBT individuals", 2009).

The recognition of gender-based hate crime in the 2009 law is especially significant in light of recent and past incidents of gender-based violence. Consider, for example, the shooting deaths of four female students and a female teacher in a schoolyard in Jonesboro, Arkansas, in March, 1998, by a thirteen-year-old boy and his eleven-year-old friend. Although in the immediate aftermath of the shooting, the media focused on the problem of school violence, the motive for the killings offered by the thirteen-year-old was that he was angry at a girl who had broken up with him, and he wanted revenge against her and other girls like her (Morello & Katel, 1998). In other words, four girls and one woman were killed and another nine girls and a woman were injured in that Jonesboro schoolyard *because they were female.* A similar incident occurred in Montreal in 1991, when fourteen female engineering students were shot to death in a university classroom by a man who left a note proclaiming his hatred of women and his desire to "kill the feminists." In August 2009, George Sodini went to an LA Fitness health club in western Pennsylvania, walked into an aerobics class, and shot and killed three women and wounded nine others before killing himself. Based on Sodini's blog posts, detectives concluded that his act was at least

(continued)

BOX 9.2
Continued

partially gender-motivated. Sodini had been repeatedly rejected by women and sought revenge (Goldman, 2009; Roth, 2009).

Obviously, not all crimes involving female victims can be considered hate crimes. It is important to point out that in those instances when it is clear that women were victimized because of their sex, the advantage of having the category of sex included in hate crime laws is that offenders are more severely punished for their actions. This is because offenses prosecuted as hate crimes carry additional penalties above those normally prescribed for a specific offense. However, recent research with prosecutors in Texas, where gender-based violence was included in the state hate crime law before the federal law was passed in 2009, found that prosecutors believe crimes against women are motivated by power rather than hate and found that prosecuting offenders for gender-motivated hate crimes is difficult and problematic (McPhail & Dinitto, 2005; see also Hodge, 2011).

Although the NCVS is considered to be a fairly good indicator of the extent of criminal victimization in the United States and is the most widely utilized source of victimization statistics, there are several factors that make it problematic when considering the gendered nature of criminal victimization. For example, it was not until 1989 that the NCVS began to phase in questions to more accurately estimate the incidence of rape and violence perpetrated by intimates and other family members (Bachman, 2000). Still, many victims of such crimes—who are disproportionately women—may be missed by the NCVS. Rennison (2001c) points out that since the NCVS samples households, it does not include the victimization experiences of the homeless or those living in communal settings, such as battered women's shelters. In addition, although women report more crimes to survey interviewers than to the police—recall that about half of all violent crimes and only 39 percent of all property crimes are reported to the police (Truman, 2011)—they have particular difficulty reporting certain crimes, such as rape, to anyone. Research indicates that most rape victims do not report to the police (Ullman et al., 2008). Consequently, analysts estimate that official victimization data represent only 10 to 30 percent of the rapes that actually occur (Gordon & Rigor, 1991; Greenfeld, 1997).

TABLE 9.6   Rates of Violent Victimization, by Sex, 2010

	Average Annual Violent Victimization Rates (per 1,000 persons age 12 or older)					
	All	**Rape/Sexual Assault**	**Robbery**	**All Assault**	**Aggravated Assault**	**Simple Assault**
Male	15.7	0.1*	2.4	13.1	3.4	9.7
Female	14.2	1.3	1.4	11.5	2.3	9.2

*Based upon ten or fewer sample cases.

Source: Truman, J.L. (2011). *Criminal victimization, 2010*. U.S. Department of Justice, Bureau of Justice Statistics. NCJ 2277770. Table 9, p. 11.

There are other ways, too, that women's criminal victimization is hidden. For instance, Gerber and Weeks (1992) maintain that women have always been the victims of corporate crime—indeed, in cases such as the Dalkon Shield contraceptive device and silicone breast implants, women have been the only victims of such crimes—but most criminologists have overlooked the role of gender in their analyses of corporate criminality (for exceptions, see Baker, 2001; Rynbrandt & Kramer, 1995). Similarly, many criminologists who have studied homicide have focused largely on male victims as well as offenders, often including women only in discussions of "crimes of passion." While the Department of Labor (2009b) reports that women account for only 7 percent of on-the-job deaths, 26 percent of women who die on the job are murder victims; homicide virtually ties with highway accidents (28 percent) as the leading cause of on-the-job death for women. In contrast, the most common causes of on-the-job death for men are highway accidents (22 percent) and falls (14 percent). An analysis of homicides in the workplace over the period 1993–1999 shows that most are committed by strangers. However, in workplace homicides involving intimates, husbands were forty times more likely to kill their wives than wives were to kill their husbands (Duhart, 2001).

Considering these data, women's greater fear of crime becomes more understandable. As Stanko (2001) emphasizes, women's greater fear of crime stems both from their greater physical vulnerability and from the fact that their victimization is more likely to be hidden, overlooked, or trivialized relative to men's victimization. Contributing to women's fear are popularized images of crime and criminals. Regardless of their age, social class, race or ethnicity, most women believe the typical criminal is a poor, uneducated, young Black man, who is mentally ill or addicted to drugs. Women fear what they see as the randomness of violent crime: Their common fear is of a psychotic stranger coming out of nowhere to attack them when they are simply going about the routine business of their everyday lives (Madriz, 1997). As Madriz (1997, p. 342) notes, "female fear is fear of male violence." Yet, all the available data show that women are most likely to be victimized not by a stranger, but by someone they know. Nearly two thirds (64 percent) of the violent victimizations reported by women are perpetrated by someone they know (i.e., an intimate, other relative, friend, or acquaintance) compared with 22 percent perpetrated by strangers. In contrast, men are more likely to be victimized by a stranger than by someone they know. Forty percent of the violent victimizations reported by men are perpetrated by someone they know compared with 48 percent perpetrated by strangers (Truman, 2011). Let's explore this finding in greater detail by looking at the crime of rape.

Rape

Researchers have found that rape is the crime women fear the most (Ferraro, 1995; Fisher & Sloan, 2003; Gordon & Riger, 1991; Hilinski, 2009; Lane, Gover, & Dahod, 2009; Warr, 1985). The fear of rape derives not only from the fact that rape is a serious crime but also because it is a crime associated with other serious offenses, such as robbery and homicide, and with gratuitous violence in addition to the rape itself (Gordon & Riger, 1991; Madriz, 1997). The fear of contracting AIDS through rape also adds to women's fear of this crime (Center for Women Policy Studies, 1991a).[10]

According to both UCR and NCVS statistics, the number of rapes and sexual assaults, like the total violent crime rate, has decreased somewhat over the past decade.

According to the National Crime Victimization Survey, the rate of rape and sexual assault decreased by 53 percent between 1999 and 2008 (Rand, 2009). The FBI reported that in 2008 the estimated number of forcible rapes was the lowest it had been in twenty years (Federal Bureau of Investigation, 2009).[11] It is difficult to determine, however, whether the decline represents a real decrease in the number of rapes committed or is the result of police investigative practices or a lowered willingness on the part of victims to report the crime. For example, in Philadelphia, it was discovered that between 1981 and 1998, officers in the Sex Crimes Unit of the police department were "dumping" about one-third of the rapes reported to them into a case category called "investigation of the person" that resulted in little or no investigation. During the first six months of 1999, when the police were under severe pressure to end the "dumping" practice, the number of reported rapes on the official record increased by 17 percent (Fazlollah, Matza, & McCoy, 1999a). Still, sexual assault is one of the violent crimes victims are *least* likely to report to the police (Fisher et al., 2003; Ullman et al., 2008; Washington, 2001). Moreover, rape also has a relatively low arrest and conviction rate. About 40 percent of all reported rapes result in an arrest (Federal Bureau of Investigation, 2009), but only about 18 percent result in convictions (U.S Department of Justice, Bureau of Justice Statistics, 2010). Of those convicted, about 66 percent receive prison sentences; the average prison sentence is slightly less than ten years, but most offenders actually serve less than five years (Greenfeld, 1997). One cannot help but ask what factors give rise to such startling statistics.

Rape legally occurs when a person uses force or the threat of force to have some form of sexual intercourse (vaginal, oral, or anal) with another person. This rather straightforward definition might lead us to conclude that the prosecution of rape cases is fairly simple, especially given current medical technology and modern evidence collection techniques. However, although at first it may appear that rape can be thought of in dichotomous terms (that is, a specific encounter is or is not a rape), research indicates that what is defined as rape differs widely among various groups, including victims and perpetrators (Bondurant, 2001; Harned, 2005; Littleton, Breitkopf, & Berenson, 2008; Schwartz & Leggett, 1999; Sudderth, 1998; Washington, 2001). Unfortunately, the crime of rape is still prevalently viewed in our society in terms of a collection of myths about both rapists and rape victims. These include the notions that some women enjoy "being taken" by force; that women initially say "no" to men's sexual advances to appear "respectable" and must be "persuaded" to give in; that many women provoke men by teasing them and therefore these women get what they deserve; and that most "real" rapes are committed by strangers who attack lone women on isolated streets or in dark alleys. Many victims of rape do not label their experience as rape (Fisher et al., 2003; Harned, 2005; Littleton et al., 2008). They instead may call it a "miscommunication" (Littleton et al., 2008). Weiss (2009) reviewed 944 victim narratives from the National Crime Victimization Survey and found that one in five women who revealed their sexual victimization also excused or justified the perpetrator's actions. Specifically, they excused the man's behavior by asserting that male sexual aggression is natural or that he was not responsible for his actions due to drug or alcohol use. Furthermore, victims did not identify their experience as a "real" rape when they did not suffer serious injuries and blamed themselves for their victimization if they believed they had engaged in behavior that put them at risk for victimization (e.g., drinking alcohol). Factors that contribute to not labeling the incident as rape include: lack of physical force by the assailant, lack of resistance by the victim, and drinking by the victim and the assailant prior to the incident (Littleton et al., 2006;

Weiss, 2009). Moreover, when rape victims disclose to others, they face negative reactions and are stigmatized (Ullman et al., 2007). Therefore, it should not surprise us that most rape victims do not disclose their victimization to anyone (Ullman et al., 2008). To understand this better, let's examine several rape myths more closely.

One common rape myth is that rape victims have often done something to invite or precipitate the assault. Therefore, if they report the crime, rape victims must demonstrate that they are "real" or "worthy" victims (Caringella, 2009; Weiss, 2009). To do so successfully and thus have the complaint acted on by the criminal justice system, victims must report the assault promptly. A delay in reporting increases the probability the complaint will be *unfounded*; that is, the police officially declare that they do not believe the crime occurred or they consider it unprosecutable. Victims must also show emotional as well as physical trauma; an absence of cuts, bruises, and other injuries can cast doubt on the victim's credibility. And, most importantly, victims must convince authorities that they were in no way responsible for the crime (Caringella, 2009). This last condition is an especially difficult one to fulfill since even the slightest deviation from "respectable behavior" may be taken as evidence of the victim's culpability. For example, victims are held more responsible if they are dressed provocatively (Whatley, 2005) or were voluntarily intoxicated at the time of the rape (Gidycz, McNamara, & Edwards, 2006; see also Angelone, Mitchell, & Pilafova, 2007).

The suspicion of victim culpability affects male rape victims as well. First, there is the myth that men cannot be raped (Graham, 2006). Men who are raped by women are simply dismissed as not being victimized (Davies, Pollard, & Archer, 2006), and men who are raped by other men are perceived to be gay (Sivakumaran, 2005). In either case, they are not deemed "worthy" victims. Men appear to be even less likely than women to report that they have been raped—after all, men are supposed to be able to defend themselves. Few report to the police, seek medical attention or reach out for psychological help (Light & Monk-Turner, 2008). If male victims are in fact gay, reporting the assault may do more harm than good. Gays are rarely deemed "worthy" rape victims by virtue of their choice of a "deviant" lifestyle, and reporting could lead to harassment by the authorities and others (see, for instance, Ernst, Green, & Ferguson 2000; Todahl et al., 2009). Less than 5 percent of rape victims, however, are men (Rand, 2008). The victim precipitation myth also appears to render some groups of women, such as prostitutes and drug addicts, "unrapeable" in a sense. Rape complaints brought by prostitutes and addicts are routinely dismissed by police, and there are few services available for these victims (Zweig, Schlichter, & Burt, 2002). In a study including 891 police officers, 44 percent stated that they would be unlikely to believe a prostitute who claimed she or he was raped (Page, 2008).

Historically, the myths that women enjoy forced sex, that they really mean "yes" when they say "no," and that they often falsely accuse men of rape out of shame or revenge, led to strict rules of evidence in rape cases that essentially placed the burden of proof on the victim (Caringella, 2009). For instance, the victim's testimony had to be supported by other witnesses, and the state had to establish that she had tried sufficiently to resist her assailant. Today, many of these requirements have been revised or abolished both in the United States and abroad (Caringella, 2009). But despite legal reforms, judges, juries, and others to whom victims may go for help still seem reluctant to believe rape victims or to convict and punish accused rapists, and a victim's behavior, credibility, and resistance remain key factors in prosecution decisions (Caringella, 2009).

In the majority of rape cases, the central issue is not whether the complainant and the accused engaged in sexual intercourse, but rather whether the complainant *consented* to the act. As most prosecutors know quite well, it is the victim's consent that is most difficult to disprove, particularly in cases in which she and the accused know one another. A case involving a victim who knows or is familiar with her assailant is known as **acquaintance rape**. NCVS statistics show that about 73 percent of rapes are acquaintance rapes (Truman, 2011). The National Violence Against Women Survey also reveals that of the more than 300,000 women raped in the United States each year, most are raped by an acquaintance (Tjaden & Thoennes, 2006).[12] Yet the vast majority of acquaintance rapes go unreported; women and girls raped by acquaintances are significantly less likely to report the crime than women raped by strangers (Neville & Pugh, 1997; Sudderth, 1998; Washington, 2001; however, see Stermac, Del Bove, & Addison, 2001), and are more likely to excuse or justify the perpetrator's behavior (Weiss, 2009).

Acquaintance rapes are especially common on college campuses. Despite the claim that the term "date rape" is being widely misapplied to cases involving boyfriends verbally coercing their girlfriends or to intercourse that occurs because the woman is intoxicated and becomes "sexually confused" (e.g., Roiphe, 1992), empirical research indicates that the incidence of acquaintance or date rape on college campuses is hardly trivial. In a now-classic study involving an extensive three-year survey of college students, for example, Koss and her colleagues (1987) found that one in eight female college students reported being victimized during the preceding twelve-month period; 84 percent of those who had been victims of completed rapes knew their assailants. Other researchers have obtained comparable findings although some put the estimate lower and argue that it is influenced by how questions about sexual assault are phrased (see Cook, Gidycz, Koss, & Murphy, 2011; Fisher, 2009; Fisher, Cullen, & Thenen, 2001; Krebs et al., 2011; Schwartz & DeKeseredy, 1997). Research also shows that repeated sexual victimization is a problem for women in college (Daigle, Fisher, & Cullen, 2008).

College women have been found to be at especially high risk for sexual victimization for several reasons. The widespread availability and use of alcohol and drugs on college campuses increases women's risk of being raped (Gidycz et al., 2006; Messman-Moore et al., 2008). Minow and Einolf (2009) also concluded that sorority women are more likely to be victims of attempted and completed rape while in college compared to non-sorority women. While this may be partly because sorority women usually consume more alcohol, other factors may also be involved. Messman-Moore, Ward, and Brown (2009) found that college women with posttraumatic stress disorder (PTSD) caused by child abuse and traumatic experiences in early adulthood who had turned to substance use to cope were at higher risk for sexual victimization.

Acquaintance rape is so prevalent that some researchers argue that even if women do not go out alone at night and even if they stay away from certain parts of town, they are not necessarily well protected from the danger of being sexually assaulted (Gordon & Riger, 1991; Stanko, 2001). More than 33 percent of rapes take place in or at the victim's home, and 18.6 percent occur at, in, or near the home of one of the victim's friends, relatives, or neighbors (U.S. Department of Justice, Bureau of Justice Statistics, 2006).

One form of sexual assault that almost always occurs in the victim's home is **marital rape**, the sexual assault of a woman by her husband. Historically, a husband could not be charged with raping his wife even if he used physical violence to force her to have sex with him or even if they were legally separated. For the most part, this was because a wife was legally regarded as the property of her husband; certainly no man could be prosecuted for a personal decision to use his property as he saw fit. It was not until 1977 that the Oregon state legislature repealed the marital exemption to its rape statute. Two years later, James K. Chretien became the first person in the United States to be convicted of marital rape (Reid, 1987).

Research indicates that marital rape often accompanies other forms of family violence and typically involves a history of repeated sexual assaults by the husband (Basile, 2008; Campbell & Soeken, 1999; Mahoney, 1999; Stermac et al., 2001). Accurate statistics on the incidence of marital rape are, not surprisingly, difficult to obtain. The most commonly cited statistic is that rape occurs in 9 to 14 percent of all U.S. marriages (Bergen, 1996). It is important to emphasize that what we are discussing here is not a situation in which one spouse wishes to have sex and the other does not, but gives in out of love or to please (see, however, Basile, 1999). Marital rape is a brutal physical assault that may have a graver impact on a victim than stranger rape, given that the assailant is a person whom she knows and, at least at one time, loved and trusted (Bergen, 1996; Campbell & Soeken, 1999).

Although all states now have criminal statutes prohibiting forced sex between a husband and wife, as of 2005 thirty states exempted husbands from prosecution for rape under certain circumstances, largely because of lingering doubts about the ability to prove nonconsent in a marital relationship (Bergen, 2006). In some states, for instance, a woman may charge her husband with rape only if he used a weapon to force her to have sex. In a few states, a woman may charge her husband with rape only if they are not living together. Other states require that the partners be legally separated or have filed for divorce. In a few states, exemption from prosecution for rape extends to unmarried cohabiting partners as well as married couples (Bergen, 2006).

Many wives are reluctant to file rape charges against their husbands, especially if rape is part of an ongoing pattern of domestic violence. These women are fearful of retaliation by their husbands (see Chapter 7). Many women are also ashamed and do not want to make the problem public (Bergen, 1996; however, see Stermac et al., 2001). Failure to disclose is not surprising given that research indicates that many officers do not believe victims of marital rape. In a sample of 891 police officers from two southeastern states, 19 percent revealed that they would be unlikely to believe a woman who claimed her husband raped her (Page, 2008). Furthermore, as explained by Caringella (2009), prosecution of marital rape is "miniscule" (p. 201).

Over the last two decades, the treatment of rape victims by the criminal justice system and other service providers, such as medical personnel, has improved considerably. Most police officers, for example, now receive special training to sensitize them to the trauma of victims, although judges are much less likely than police to receive such training (Caringella, 2009; Kocieniewski, 1995). There are also many victim support and advocate services available throughout the country (see, however, Zweig et al., 2002). These are positive developments that should be applauded, but at the same time, they continue to focus attention on rape as primarily a "woman's problem," not as a problem of men's violence against women. When rapists are discussed, they are usually depicted as psychologically disturbed individuals who need special medical treatment (Madriz, 1997). Interestingly, however, researchers have been unable to uncover evidence of widespread psychological disturbance in rapists. Rapists are more likely than any other type of offender to have been physically or sexually abused as a child, but apart from this finding, psychological tests do not consistently discriminate between rapists and nonrapists (Greenfeld, 1997; Scully & Marolla, 1985). In fact, as Herman (1988, pp. 702–703) points out, "The most striking characteristic of sex offenders, from a diagnostic standpoint, is their apparent normality. Most do not qualify for any psychiatric diagnosis." An emphasis on the psychopathology of rapists preserves the common image of the rapist as a "monster," a "crazed animal"; after all, nice guys don't rape. Such images divert attention from both the cultural context and the power relations in which rape occurs (Madriz, 1997; Stanko, 2001).

So, if most rapists are not mentally ill, why do they rape? First, research indicates that alcohol use is positively correlated with rape (Davis et al., 2008). However, societal norms may be even more relevant. We think that an answer to the question of why rapists rape lies within the culture and social structure of a society. Consider, for instance, anthropological studies of societies that may be characterized as virtually "rape-free" (Lepowsky, 1994; Reiss, 1986; Sanday, 1981, 1996a; Sutlive, 1991). The most striking feature of these societies is their relatively egalitarian gender relations. Neither sex is viewed as more important or as more highly valued than the other, and both are considered powerful, although in different spheres of activity. Moreover, women in these societies are not socially and economically dependent on men; they control resources and act as autonomous decision makers. Finally, in most rape-free societies, nurturance and nonaggression are valued traits in individuals, and women typically are highly regarded not for their sexuality, but for their wisdom and skills.

Compare these societies with our own—one of the most "rape-prone" industrialized societies in the world. The contrasts are glaring. First of all, we live in an extraordinarily violent society. Not only is the rape rate exceptionally high, but the United States also has the highest homicide rate relative to other industrialized countries. Yet we know that violence is not condoned for everyone; it is expected of, even encouraged among men, not women. This is just one dimension of unequal gender relations in our society. Men control greater resources and, therefore, are more powerful than women. Not infrequently, they use violence to further expand their power. One of the few "bargaining chips" women have in our society is their sexuality, and male violence can deprive them of personal control over even that. As one convicted rapist told an interviewer:

> Rape is a man's right. If a woman doesn't want to give it, the man should take it. Women have no right to say no. Women are made to have sex. It's all they are good for. Some women would rather take a beating, but they always give in; it's what they are for. (quoted in Scully & Marolla, 1985, p. 261)

This quote also reveals the "conquest mentality" toward sex that is part of American culture in general, but which is particularly prominent in male peer group subcultures (Schwartz & DeKeseredy, 1997). Sex is something men get or take from women. Sometimes force is necessary to get women to "put out." It appears, then, that in the United States there is a very fine line between "normal" masculine sexual behavior and rape. Indeed, the rapist quoted here, like most rapists, did not think he had done anything wrong (Lisak & Miller, 2002; Lisak & Roth, 1988). But his attitude is not so unusual; consider, for example, the fact that large-scale studies of high school and college students have found a surprising number of young men and women who believe that under some circumstances—e.g., when a woman engages in some sexual activity, but then refuses to go further—it is all right for a man to force a woman to have sex (Schwartz & DeKeseredy, 1997; Yescavage, 1999). Such findings demonstrate the extent to which sexual violence against women is an acceptable part of our culture. Schwartz and DeKeseredy (1997) and others (Bleecker & Murnen, 2005; Boeringer, 1999; Forbes et al., 2006; Murnen & Kohlman, 2007; Sanday, 1996a) have found that among all-male social networks, especially those such as fraternities where heavy drinking is normative, as well as men's athletic teams, certain women, particularly those who are intoxicated, are considered "legitimate sexual targets." Such attitudes and behaviors are given tacit approval on campus because of the low probability that the complaints of victims deemed unworthy will be taken seriously and that assailants will be harshly punished (Benedict, 1997; Schwartz & DeKeseredy, 1997).

Finally, the words of the rapist we have quoted reflect the degree to which women are sexually objectified in our society. Unlike women in rape-free societies, women in the United States and many other countries are viewed as sex objects, and female sexuality itself is treated as a commodity. Clearly the most common form of objectified, commoditized female sexuality is pornography. Let's briefly discuss pornography and its relationship to violence against women.

Pornography

In 1969, the President's Commission on the Causes and Prevention of Violence concluded in its report that media portrayals of violence can induce individuals to behave violently. In 1971, the Presidential Commission on Obscenity and Pornography concluded in its report that there is no causal relationship between exposure to pornography and subsequent sexual violence against women. Pornography, it said, is basically harmless. In 1986, the Attorney General's Commission on Pornography (also known as the Meese Commission) brought the issue full circle by concluding that violent pornography is causally related to both sexual violence and discrimination against women.

The inconsistency that characterizes these official reports reflects the general confusion that historically has clouded debates about pornography and its effects. Before we take up this issue, let's first define what we mean by *pornography,* since there are conflicting definitions of what is pornographic. Certainly, few people would be willing to argue that any pictured nude or any description of a sexual act is pornographic, but where does one draw the line? As Supreme Court Justice William Douglas once noted in an obscenity trial, "What may be trash to me may be prized by others" (quoted in MacKinnon, 1986, p. 69).

Still, we can discern important objective differences between pornography and what may be called *erotica.* Gloria Steinem (1978) makes this distinction by pointing out that:

> "Pornography" begins with a root [*porne*] meaning "prostitution" or "female captives," thus letting us know that the subject is not mutual love, or love at all, but domination and violence against women. (Though, of course, homosexual pornography may imitate this violence by putting a man in the "feminine" role of victim.) It ends with a root [*graphos*] meaning "writing about" or "description of" which puts still more distance between subject and object, and replaces a spontaneous yearning for closeness with objectification and a voyeur. (p. 54)

In contrast, Steinem tells us, *erotica* is derived from the root *eros* meaning "sensual love" that implies the mutual choice and pleasure of the sexual partners. We can see, then, at least two distinct features of pornography. First, it depersonalizes sex and objectifies women. Second, and more importantly, pornography is not even about sex, per se, but rather the degradation of women and often children through sex. In fact, the sex depicted in pornography is secondary to the violence, humiliation, and dominance it portrays (see also Bridges & Jensen, 2010; Jensen, 2007). To be sure, not all pornography is violent, but the objective of all pornography is the objectification and control of women—male dominance of the female body for the purpose of sexually arousing the male consumer—and often violence is one of the ways pornography accomplishes this goal (Dines, Jensen, & Russo, 1998; Jensen, 2007).

Researchers have not been able to conclusively establish a direct causal link between viewing pornography and violence against women. Langevin and Curnoe (2004) found that very few sex offenders reported using pornography directly prior to committing an offense. However, there is substantial evidence that pornography, especially violent pornography, is a factor that at least *contributes to* violence against women (see Kingston et al., 2009).

At its most extreme, violent pornography takes the form of "snuff" and "slasher" films in which women are tortured, disfigured, murdered, or dismembered for sexual pleasure (Russell, 1993). However, a common theme in all forms of violent pornography is rape. "[N]ot only is rape presented as part of normal male/female relations, but the woman, despite her terror, is always depicted as sexually aroused to the point of cooperation. In the end, she is ashamed but physically gratified" (Scully & Marolla, 1985, p. 253; see also Jensen, 2007).

Vega and Malamuth (2007) found that high pornography consumption was significantly associated with sexual aggression among male college students. In laboratory studies, researchers have found that exposure to violent pornography increases men's sexual arousal and rape fantasies, lessens their sensitivity to rape and rape victims, increases their acceptance of rape myths, and, most importantly, increases their self-reported possibility of raping (Allen, D'alessio, & Brezgel, 1995; Weaver, 1992).[13] Two recent meta-analytic studies of experimental and nonexperimental research suggested that viewing pornography, particularly violent pornography, is related to having attitudes that support violence against women (Kingston et al., 2009).

Experimental research, though, has been criticized for a number of reasons, not the least of which is that it is "unnatural" or "artificial" (Jensen, 2007; Malamuth, Addison, & Koss, 2000; Seto, Maric, & Barbaree, 2001). However, research that relies on women's and men's accounts of their use of pornography and "real life" sexual violence shows a strong relationship between the two. Women who have been sexually abused frequently report that their abusers directed them to act out scenes the men had seen or read about in pornography, sometimes mentioning specific films (see Dines et al., 1998, for a detailed summary of this research; see also Bergen, 1996). Research with men, including sex offenders, shows that pornography helps shape a male-dominant view of sexuality, contributes to a user's difficulty in distinguishing between fantasy and reality, and is often used to initiate victims and break down their resistance to particular types of sexual activity. As Jensen (in Dines et al., 1998, p. 119) describes it, pornography provides "a training manual for abusers" (see also Jensen, 2007; Norris & Kerr, 1991; Scully & Marolla, 1985).

Despite these findings, it is often argued that regulating or outlawing pornography infringes on the First Amendment right of free speech, and some observers fear that such regulations could be used to legitimate government censorship of any sexually explicit material including information on contraception, "safe sex," and so on. Government efforts to censor art exhibitions are frequently cited as examples. The First Amendment argument has prevailed in law; antipornography laws that were passed in Indianapolis, Minneapolis, Los Angeles, Cambridge (Massachusetts), and Bellingham (Washington) were overturned by the courts on the ground that they violated First Amendment free speech guarantees. But to those who worry about encroachment on the First Amendment, antipornography activists ask if they would maintain the same position if the material in question was violently racist or anti-Semitic. As Russell (1993) argues:

> Indeed, there would be a public outcry—and rightly so—if there were special nonpornographic movie houses where viewers could see whites beating up people of color, or Christians beating up Jews, and where the victims were portrayed as enjoying or deserving such treatment. But if it's called pornography and women are the victims, then it is considered sex and those who object that it is harmful to women are regarded as prudes. (p. 11)[14]

It is unlikely that the debate over pornography will be resolved soon. Feminists themselves are divided over the questions of whether pornography is harmful and should be outlawed (see Berger, Searles, & Cottle, 1991; Dines et al., 1998). There are those, for example, who maintain that pornography, even in portraying sadomasochism, is potentially liberating for women in that through it, women may become less puritanical and sexually passive and more open or aggressive about their sexual desires. This argument has not been lost on the porn industry, which has attempted to market more products, primarily films, to women. However, research indicates that only about 2 percent of pornographic films are rented by women alone; 71 percent are rented by men alone and 19 percent by men with women (Egan, 2000). Men are also more likely than women to view online pornography (Wetzstein, 2009). As Box 9.3 shows, the Internet has become a highly profitable international marketplace for pornography.

Institutionalized Violence against Women: Custom or Crime?

The historical accounts left by colonists and missionaries along with the ethnographies of anthropologists testify to the extent to which violence against women has been an institutionalized component of the cultures of many societies throughout the world (see also Box 9.4). From the tenth to the twentieth centuries, for example, the Chinese engaged in the practice of binding the feet of young girls. This was accomplished by bending all of the toes on each foot (except the big toes) under and into the sole, then wrapping the toes and the heel as tightly together as possible with a piece of cloth. Every two weeks or so the wrapped feet were squeezed into progressively smaller shoes until they were shrunk to the desirable size of just three inches. Typically, the feet would bleed and become infected, circulation was cut off, and eventually one or more toes might fall off. Needless to say, the process was extremely painful and countless women were crippled by it. Yet, they endured and perpetuated the custom—usually from mother to daughter— for one thousand years in the belief that it made them beautiful, and beauty ensured a good and lasting marriage (Dworkin, 1983). The last assembly line of the last factory that made shoes for bound feet stopped in 1999 (Ko, 2005).

It was the case that men did not look favorably on natural-footed women. For one thing, they felt that tiny feet were feminine, and binding helped differentiate women from men (Ko, 2005). In addition, the immobile woman was a status symbol, "a testimony to

BOX 9.3
Pornography on the Internet

The Internet is a revolutionary communications tool. Using the Internet, you can send a message that can reach literally millions of people throughout the world in a matter of seconds. On the World Wide Web, with its sophisticated multimedia technology, you can go shopping for specific items, send and receive photographs or even video and audio clips, and move from one computer site to another just by clicking the mouse on a "hot link." You can do all these things in the privacy of your own home, conveniently, anonymously, and relatively inexpensively. Indeed, pornography played a crucial role in the development of the Internet. (Jensen, 2007, p. 82)

Jesnen (2007) is referring here to the fact that video streaming technology used widely on the Internet was developed for pornography sites (Barss, 2010). In light of the features Jensen describes and the more important fact that the Internet is largely unregulated, it is not surprising that the Internet is fast becoming the primary international marketplace for the sale and consumption of pornography. It is estimated that there are over 4 million pornography sites on the Internet (DeKeseredy, forthcoming) and that they are accessed by about 21 million people in the United States alone at least once a month (Egan, 2000). The Internet has become an easy way for minors to access pornography. Sabina, Wolak, and Finkelhor (2008), for instance, surveyed 563 college students and found that 93 percent of men and 62 percent of women were exposed to Internet pornography before turning eighteen (see also Paul & Shin, 2008).

Internet pornography is a very lucrative enterprise. Recent estimates indicate that Internet child pornography alone generates over $3 billion a year in revenue (Lucers, 2007). Pornography is the single most searched-for item on the Internet and also the most profitable (Eberstadt, 2009, p. 4), reportedly more profitable, in fact, than the combined revenues of Microsoft, Google, Amazon, eBay, Yahoo!, Apple, Netflix, and Earthlink (Zebisias, 2008). In addition, more "homemade" or "do-it-yourself" pornography is available on the Internet for free (Bridges & Jensen, 2010).

With the help of a search engine, an Internet user can find pornography to suit just about any taste, from bestiality to sadomasochism to pedophilia. What is more, the Internet user can meet and chat with others who share these interests, a fact that some observers find troubling. The Internet allows people with socially unacceptable interests, such as pedophiles, to find acceptability, which in turn validates and reinforces their feelings and behavior. In fact, the Internet is becoming the most prevalent means for people with such interests to share pornography and even recruit partners, including children, for sexual activity (DeKeseredy, forthcoming; Fox, 1998).

A number of software makers and commercial online service providers offer filters to screen or block offensive transmissions and access to pornographic sites on the Internet, products that parents, in particular, are welcoming. But attempts to legislate broader restrictions have met with strong opposition and claims of First Amendment infringement. No one owns the Internet, and currently, no one controls the communications that come across it. Although law enforcement agencies have begun to initiate "cyberstings" to catch pedophiles transmitting child pornography and arranging in-person meetings with children, even this area of law is still largely undefined. Defense attorneys and civil libertarians charge that such policing techniques constitute entrapment, which is an illegal form of law enforcement, while prosecutors, the F.B.I., and Congress see it as an effective way to catch sexual predators and prevent crimes against children. The courts are continuously challenged to clarify existing laws and develop new laws in response to the changing nature of the distribution of pornography on the Internet, particularly child pornography ("Child pornography, the Internet, and the challenge of updating statutory terms," 2009). In the meantime, there is little doubt that the production and consumption of pornography via the Internet will continue to flourish.

BOX 9.4
Violence Against Women as Human Rights Violations

Historically, the physical and psychological abuse of women, though widespread in many societies throughout the world, has not been considered a human rights problem. There has been, in fact, a high level of official and social tolerance of violence against women, with most governments and official agencies viewing the problem as an individual matter or simply as a consequence of being female (Chapman, 1990). Moreover, officials have not only excused or ignored such violence, they also have participated in it. The rape and sexual abuse of female political prisoners while in official custody has been documented by human rights advocates (Amnesty International, 1991; Chapman, 1990; "Women in INS custody," 2001). Indeed, rape is a common weapon of war (Borer, 2009; Diken & Lausten, 2005; "Rape as a war crime," 2009), and according to a 2005 United Nations report, it has been perpetrated in countries such as Haiti, Bosnia, Cambodia, and East Timor not only by warring factions, but also by UN peacekeeping forces (Bowcott, 2005).

Violence against women as a human rights issue began to command greater public attention when, in 1993, media in the United States and Europe began to report on the systematic rape, sexual enslavement, torture, and murder of Bosnian Muslim women and children by Serbian military forces in the former Yugoslavia. According to a report by a team of European Community investigators, it was estimated that 20,000 Muslim women were raped by Serb soldiers during the campaign against Muslim communities in the former Yugoslavia (Madden, 2009; Riding, 1993).

Rape served as a central element in the Serbian "ethnic cleansing" campaign: Bosnian men were murdered, while the women were raped with the goal of impregnating them to produce offspring with the "desirable" genetic material. At the same time, the rapes were intended to demoralize and terrorize the Muslim communities and to drive Muslims from their home regions. According to the European Community investigative team, rapes were often carried out in especially sadistic ways with the intent of inflicting the greatest humiliation on the victims. The investigators collected evidence that indicated that many Muslim women and children died during or after their rapes (Madden, 2009; Nikolic-Ristanovic, 1999; Riding, 1993).

Reports such as these rightfully produced widespread calls in the United States and abroad for international sanctions against the Serbian military and for efforts to bring the perpetrators to trial as war criminals. It is important to note, however, that systematic violence against women is not unique to the former Yugoslavia (see Farr, 1990), nor is it a new strategy. Nearly four decades ago, Susan Brownmiller (1975) showed that throughout history, sexual abuse of "enemy" women has been a common state-supported warfare tactic. This abuse has most frequently involved rape, but it also has taken other forms, such as sexual enslavement. In 1993, for instance, the Japanese government issued a report in which it admitted that during World War II, it was involved in coercing women into prostitution to sexually service Imperial Army soldiers. Although in reality the women were sex slaves, they were euphemistically called "comfort women." It is estimated that from 100,000 to 300,000 women were enslaved. Most were from South Korea, but some were from Indonesia, China, Taiwan, the Philippines, and the Netherlands (McGregor & Lawnham, 1993).

Rape is also prevalent in countries divided by civil war such as the Democratic Republic of Congo in Africa, ("Clinton pledges aid to Congolese rape victims," 2009). Estimates are that between 200,000 to 400,000 women have been raped since the war began in 2006 (Truscott, 2008; "What you can do about the war in Congo," 2009), and despite the peace agreement signed in January 2008, the sexual terrorism of women continued (Truscott, 2008).

The crisis is similar in other parts of Africa as well (see Borer, 2009; Farr, 2009). In Darfur, in the Sudan, rape is commonly used as a weapon of war, and soldiers routinely rape

(continued)

BOX 9.4
Continued

women in front of their families and members of their village (Van Zeijl, 2007). Tens of thousands of women have been raped and killed by an Arab Muslim militia known as the Janjawid since the war began in 2003 (Alvy, 2004). Rape of women also continues in the Republic of Burundi in East Africa even though the thirteen year civil war there ended (Sussman, 2008). Rape of prisoners and civilians has also been reported in Iraq ("Sex Abuse," 2009).

In 2000, the United Nations Security Council (UNSC) adopted Resolution 1325, which urges governments to include women in decision-making processes related to preventing and resolving conflicts and to take action to prevent sexual violence against women during conflicts, in the post-conflict period, and in refugee camps and camps for displaced persons. Since 2000, the UNSC has adopted additional resolutions (e.g., 1820, 1888, 1889) to enhance the provisions of UNSC Resolution 1325. Unfortunately, however, governments' support for these resolutions has been largely symbolic in many countries given that there are no mechanisms for accountability nor sanctions for noncompliance (Kuehnast, Oudraat, & Hernes, 2011). Consequently, violence against women, especially during intrastate conflicts and wars, continues with impugnity.

the wealth and privilege of the man who could afford to keep her" (Dworkin, 1983, p. 181). To escalate their status, some women even bound their own feet or their daughters' feet (Ko, 2005). Aspirations to higher status, however, prompted the lower classes to copy the tradition that originated with the nobility. And finally, but perhaps most importantly, footbinding ensured chastity, fidelity, and the legitimacy of children in a society in which women literally could not "run around." It was believed that women were naturally lustful and lascivious; footbinding kept them morally in check (Dworkin, 1983).

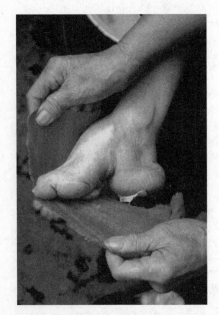

For ten centuries, the Chinese bound the feet of young girls, which rendered the girls largely immobile throughout their lives.

A similar rationale was offered for *suttee* or widow burning, a custom practiced in India for approximately four hundred years until it was officially outlawed in 1829. Suttee was a sacrificial ritual in which a widow climbed the funeral pyre of her deceased husband and either set herself or was set on fire. Although the practice was supposed to be voluntary, records indicate that extreme measures were taken to prevent escape in case the widow changed her mind, such as "scaffolds constructed to tilt toward the fire pit, piles designed so that exits were blocked and the roof collapsed on the woman's head, tying her, weighting her down with firewood and bamboo poles. If all else failed and the woman escaped from the burning pile, she was often dragged back by force, sometimes by her own son" (Stein, 1978, p. 255). Since polygamy was also practiced and marriages between child-brides and men of fifty or older were not uncommon, some wives, still in their teens, were burnt alive with dead husbands they had rarely seen since their wedding day (Daly, 1983; Stein, 1978).

It appears that most women did not have to be coerced into suttee, especially in light of their alternatives. "Since their religion forbade remarriage [of widows] and at the same time taught that the husband's death was the fault of the widow (because of her sins in a previous incarnation if not in this one), everyone was free to despise and mistreat her for the rest of her life" (Daly, 1983, p. 190). Religious law required that unburnt widows live a life of extreme poverty, shaving their heads, wearing drab clothes, eating just one bland meal a day, performing the most menial tasks, never sleeping on a bed, and never leaving their houses except to go to the temple. Obviously, death might have seemed more appealing to many. Certainly, relatives and in-laws preferred it. Since it was widely believed that women were by nature lascivious, the widow was viewed as a possible source of embarrassment to her family and in-laws who feared she would become sexually involved with other men and perhaps even get pregnant. (The practice of a deceased husband's male relatives forcing his young widow to have sex with them was historically so common that the Hindi word for widow became synonymous with prostitute.) But suttee also had an economic motive: It ensured that the widow would make no claim to her husband's estate and his family would not have to support her. Thus, the Indian widow had to decide between a miserable life of poverty and harassment or an honorable but excruciatingly painful death that elevated her status in the community. For most, such a choice was no choice at all.

Although, as we have noted, suttee was outlawed in the early 1800s, there is evidence that the cultural view of widows has not changed much in some regions of India. Widows are still expected to abide by the old religious customs, living alone and in abject poverty, often homeless. In some areas, widows live at Hindu temples where they adopt the surname *Dasi,* which means *servant,* to demonstrate their religious devotion. Many spend eight hours a day—four hours in the morning and four in the evening—reciting religious chants to earn the equivalent of five cents along with a ration of rice or lentils. Some of these women were widowed when they were just fourteen years old and sought refuge in the temples to avoid a life of servitude to their in-laws (Burns, 1998; Damon, 2007).

A related problem in contemporary India is *dowry harassment* and murder, also known as bride-burning. Despite the Dowry Prohibition Act, made law in 1961, the practice of a bride's parents providing dowry for their daughter remains widespread. To try to address the problem of dowry harassment and murder, the Protection of Women from Domestic Violence Act was passed in 2005. This law defines domestic violence as acts "that harass, harm, injure or endanger the aggrieved person with a view to coerce her or any other person related to her to meet any unlawful demand for any dowry or other property or valuable security" (Niazi, 2008, p. 99).

Daughters, though, are still considered an economic burden by many in India, so parents often try to marry them off at a young age and the promise of a dowry is seen as an incentive. However, expectations of the value of dowries have become inflated in recent years, and the groom's family, with whom the bride customarily lives, is sometimes so dissatisfied that they harass the new wife. The harassment may be only verbal, but frequently it is also physical. The abuse may drive the bride to suicide, but more commonly her husband or his family murder her, typically by dousing her with kerosene and setting her on fire (Ahmed-Ghosh, 2004; Waters, 1999). Accurate statistics on the number of dowry murders and attempted murders in India are difficult to come by, since these cases may be mislabeled "cooking accidents," but estimates put the figure at between two thousand and five thousand deaths per year (Ahmed-Ghosh, 2004; Bumiller, 1990; Singh & Unnithan, 1999; Stone & James, 1995; Vindhya, 2000). Some analysts report that cases of bride burning and dowry-related violence against women may actually be on the rise in India (Vaishalli, 2009). In 2006, 2,276 female suicides were reported as a result of dowry disputes (Niazi, 2008), although it is unclear whether this count is due to better enforcement of the law or an actual increase in incidents (see Schuler, Bates, & Islam, 2008, for a discussion of dowry-related violence in Bangladesh).

Another practice that has generated considerable controversy in recent years is *honor killing,* in which male members of a family kill a female relative whom they believe has acted inappropriately, thereby shaming or dishonoring the family. Often, it is an adolescent who does the killing because, as a minor, he will be treated leniently if legal action is taken. However, in many countries where honor killing is practiced, the shameful behavior of the girl or woman is considered a valid legal justification for her murder and no action or a greatly reduced sentence is imposed on the killer. Female family members frequently collude in the murder, accepting the stringent norms regarding appropriate feminine behavior and appropriate punishment for any transgressions. And there is a wide range of behavior that constitutes a transgression, including marital infidelity, premarital sex, divorcing one's husband, refusing to marry the man one's family has chosen as one's spouse, flirting, and going out alone with a man or a boy who is not one's relative. Rape victims may also be subject to honor killing or may be expected to kill themselves. There are documented cases in which the mere suspicion of inappropriate behavior triggered an honor killing; for example, a woman was killed after her husband dreamed she had been unfaithful. The women are not tried or even given an opportunity to prove their innocence, they have little if any legal protection, and only rarely are there shelters available to which they can try to escape and hide if they fear for their lives (Araji & Carlson, 2001; Baker, Gregware, & Cassidy, 1999; Sev'er & Yurdakul, 2001; United Nations, 2000). However, there are no reliable statistics on honor killing in countries such as Iraq, Afghanistan, and Pakistan, where it appears to occur most frequently (Susman & Ahmed, 2009).

Also in the international spotlight in recent years is the practice of *female genital mutilation* (FGM), the removal of all or part of a woman's genitals. Female genital mutilation actually takes several forms, the mildest being *Sunna,* in which the hood of the clitoris is cut analogous to the practice of male circumcision. Infibulation, the most extreme form of FGM, involves the removal of the clitoris, labia minora, and most of the labia majora, after which the vagina is stitched closed save for a tiny opening to allow for the passage of urine and menstrual blood. A third form is excision, whereby the clitoris as well as all or part of the labia minora are removed.

It is estimated that 100 to 140 million girls and women worldwide have experienced female genital mutilation (World Health Organization, 2008). FGM is practiced in at least twenty-six countries in Africa (Ball, 2008), as well as countries in Asia and the Middle East (Johansen, Bathija, & Khanna, 2009). In East and West Africa, the percentage of women who have had their genitals cut range from 5 percent to 97 percent, depending on the country (Mitike & Deressa, 2009; United Nations, 2000). While the practice of FGM is prevalent in Africa and the Middle East, it may be "exported" to other countries through migration. For example, it is estimated that sixty-six thousand immigrant and refugee women living in England and Wales have experienced FGM (Comery, 2009). The practice has been illegal in the United Kingdom since the Prohibition of Female Circumcision Act became law in 1985 (Lavender, 2009). In 2003, penalties for carrying out FGM increased to fourteen years of imprisonment, a fine, or both, and passage of the Female

Genital Mutilation Act made it a criminal offense to take a UK citizen or permanent resident outside the country for the procedure (Griffith & Tengnah, 2009).

In the Western world, publicity regarding FGM has triggered angry protests by feminists who have denounced the tradition as oppressive and barbaric, and who have insisted that governments immediately outlaw the practice (Walker & Parmar, 1993). However, only a few African governments, such as Kenya and Egypt, have passed laws prohibiting FGM, and even in those countries, there is evidence that the laws are weakly enforced at best or the practice is now done secretively rather than accompanied by the traditional village fanfare (Azzi, 2009; "Female genital mutilation common in Egypt despite ban," 2008; Lacey, 2002). In Canada, the threat of FGM in one's home country is grounds for granting those fleeing the practice refugee status. In the United States, the courts have been less sympathetic, although some have granted asylum to women seeking to escape the practice (Crossette, 1995; Love, 2009).

Given the way the operation is usually done and the serious medical problems that frequently result, the shock and indignation of Westerners is understandable. More specifically, the circumcision, excision, or infibulation is performed on young girls—sometimes as infants, but usually between the ages of six and fourteen—by an elder village woman or traditional birth attendant using various nonsurgical instruments such as a razor, a knife, a flattened nail, or a piece of broken glass. Anesthetics may not be available. Once the operation is completed, dirt, ashes, herbs, or animal droppings may be applied to the wound in the belief that they will stop the bleeding and aid in healing. Not surprisingly, complications are common and include shock, hemorrhage, septicemia, and tetanus, which can result in the girl's death. At the very least, those who have undergone the procedure are unlikely to ever experience sexual pleasure; in fact, FGM typically makes sexual intercourse quite painful and increases the likelihood of maternal and infant mortality (Johansen et al., 2009; Morris, 2008; Rayner, 1997; Wilson, 2002).

A small, but growing group of African women and men have been working to eliminate the practice in their own countries (Lacey, 2002; MacFarquhar, 1996; Walker & Parmar, 1993). However, they are encountering resistance from both women and men, who strongly object to having Western values imposed on them and who regard laws against FGM as tactics to destroy their culture (French, 1997; Graham, 1986; Lacey, 2002; MacFarquhar, 1996).

The primary purpose of female genital mutilation is to protect a girl from sexual temptations and thereby preserve her marriageability. Among most practicing societies, there exist firmly entrenched beliefs about the insatiable nature of female sexual desire. The uncut are considered "dirty" and unmarriageable, making them unfit to fulfill what are considered in their societies to be women's two most valued roles: wife and mother (MacFarquhar, 1996; Wilson, 2002). Many parents say that if they fail to have their daughters cut, no respectable men will associate with the girls (Crossette, 1995; MacFarquhar, 1996). No wonder, then, that the majority of parents in practicing societies state that they will carry on the tradition with their daughters and circumvent the law banning FGM in the United States.

In sum, female genital mutilation, like foot-binding, suttee, bride-burning, and honor killing, is a practice of institutionalized violence against women that many observers, particularly those in the West, have labeled criminal. Yet efforts to outlaw it have had limited success. Women themselves perpetuate the tradition of FGM, which to most Westerners appears irrational, but what we must consider is women's status in practicing societies. Female genital mutilation is one of the few means by which these women exercise power and achieve recognition. It is hardly surprising that women would cling to one of their only avenues of power and status, regardless of how damaging it may be. It may be argued, in fact, that their behavior is no less rational than that of Western women who very frequently seek harmful surgical procedures, such as breast implantation, or follow unhealthy diets for the sake of "beauty" (Wilson, 2002; see also Chapter 12).

If our goal, then, is the elimination of violence against women, laws banning particular practices must be simultaneously accompanied by policies and programs to implement and ensure gender equality. In the final analysis, violence against women, whatever its form, is a direct outgrowth of the devaluation of women.

Power, Crime, and Justice

We have seen here that in societies that have accepted or condoned violence against women, whatever its form—rape, pornography, foot-binding, suttee, honor killing, or genital mutilation—women are viewed as innately inferior to men and are deprived of valued resources. Indeed, women may even participate in their own victimization as a means to exercise some power in their lives and to acquire a higher status.

Powerlessness, we have also suggested, may help to explain crime rates and the differential treatment of offenders by the criminal justice system. It is the relatively powerless—young, economically marginalized women and men of color—who are disproportionately represented in the official crime statistics and who receive the harshest treatment within the criminal justice system. They, too, are most likely to be victimized by crime.

We have emphasized in this chapter that the content of laws and the way they are enforced have a lot to do with the values and interests of the powerful. The vast majority of lawmakers and law enforcement personnel are White men. In the next chapter, we will explore this issue further by examining politics, government, and the military.

Key Terms

acquaintance rape   an incident of sexual assault in which the victim knows or is familiar with the assailant

chivalry hypothesis (paternalism hypothesis)   the belief that female offenders are afforded greater leniency before the law than their male counterparts

emancipation theory (liberation theory) the theory that female crime is increasing and/ or becoming more masculine in character as a result of feminism or the women's movement

marital rape   the sexual assault of a woman by her husband

rape   when a person uses force or the threat of force to have some form of sexual intercourse (vaginal, oral, or anal) with another person

sentencing disparity   widely varying sentences imposed on offenders convicted of similar crimes, usually based on nonlegal factors, such as the offender's sex or race or ethnicity, or other inappropriate considerations

status offenses   behavior considered illegal if engaged in by a juvenile, but legal if engaged in by an adult

Suggested Readings

Caringella, S. (2008). *Addressing rape reform in law and practice*. New York: Columbia University Press. A careful and thorough analysis of how legal reforms intended to improve the treatment of victims and the prosecution of rapists have been limited in their positive outcomes due to how they have been implemented.

Jensen, R. (2007). *Getting off: Pornography and the end of masculinity*. Cambridge, MA: South End Press. Jensen explores how mainstream pornography, although normalized in American society, degrades women. He urges men to end their participation in the sex industry and join in the battle to end violence against women.

Jones, N. (2009). *Between good and ghetto*. New Brunswick, NJ: Rutgers University Press. Jones looks at how African American women living in the inner city handle the crime and violence they experience. The book explores how these women, living in neighborhoods where crime is common, survive and protect themselves.

Miller, J. (2008). *Getting played: African American girls, urban inequality, and gendered violence*. New York: New York University Press. Although the subtitle mentions only girls, Miller's book draws on interviews with seventy-five boys and girls. It sheds light on how important it is to consider gender, race, and class when looking at violence in urban neighborhoods.

Raphael, J. (2007). *Freeing Tammy: Women, drugs, and incarceration*. Boston: Northeastern University Press. In recounting the life history of one woman, Tammara Johnson, Raphael illuminates the relationship between women's victimization and offending, the gendered aspects of drug offending, and the detrimental effects of incarceration on women whose lives are characterized by trauma.

Renzetti, C. M., Eldeson, J. L., & Bergen, R. K. (Eds.) (2010). *Sourcebook on violence against women, 2nd ed.* Thousand Oaks, CA: Sage. A thorough review of the current research on various forms of violence against women, as well as methods for studying them, theories for explaining them, and strategies for preventing them and intervening on behalf of victims.

Notes

1. Women are also not well represented in blue-collar occupations such as truck driver, warehouse or dock worker, or delivery person, jobs that would provide them with opportunities for grand larceny, drug dealing, or the fencing of stolen merchandise (Steffensmeier, 1982).

2. The chivalry hypothesis has also been offered as an explanation for increases in female arrest rates. Specifically, proponents of this position contend that historically police, attorneys, and judges have been reluctant to process women through the criminal justice system. Those women who were prosecuted were supposedly treated leniently or "chivalrously." However, the recent emphasis on gender equality in society could not help but penetrate the criminal justice system, with the result that male and female offenders would more likely be treated similarly. Thus, a rise in female arrest rates is simply an artifact of the increased willingness among criminal justice personnel to apprehend and prosecute women.

3. Despite reports that lesbians and gay men are finding greater acceptance in some police precincts in a few large cities (see, for example, Blumenthal, 1993; Egan, 1992), homophobia remains a characteristic of many police departments (Colvin, 2009; Lyons et al., 2007). In addition, although there is evidence of less racism among White male officers toward minority male officers, minority female officers report experiences of both racism and sexism. The impact of these experiences is more complex than what is conveyed by the term "double jeopardy," since these women confront racism on the part of White male and female officers and sexism on the part of White and non-White male officers (see del Carmen, 2007; Haarr & Morash, 1999; Martin & Jurik, 1996). Women

of color are also less likely to hold high-ranking positions (Martin & Jurik, 2007).

4. The FBI only began to hire women as agents in 1972. Only 18.5 percent of FBI agents were women in 2004 (U.S. Department of Justice, 2006).

5. Some researchers argue that the 1977 Supreme Court ruling in *Dothard* v. *Rawlinson* ironically jeopardized women's employment progress in male correctional facilities. In *Dothard,* the Court struck down minimum height and weight requirements for guards in men's prisons, but also ruled (without supporting proof) that women could be barred from some prison jobs, such as those requiring direct contact with male inmates in maximum security prisons (Zupan, 1992). Another issue that is still unsolved in the courts is balancing prisoners' right to privacy with officers' right to employment. Suits have been brought on behalf of male prisoners claiming that the presence of female guards in certain areas, such as the showers, violates the male prisoners' privacy. Analyses of these cases show that some courts have allowed discrimination against women in terms of job assignments so as to protect male prisoners' privacy (Maschke, 1996). Belknap (2001, p. 386) makes an important observation on this issue: "It is significant that most of the focus of this problem has centered around women working in men's prisons, despite the history (including recent documentations) of the stronger likelihood for male officers to violate women prisoners' privacy than for women officers to violate men prisoners' privacy." We will take up this issue again when we discuss gender differences in incarceration experiences.

6. Martin and Jurik (1996) note that Black inmates sometimes show especially strong resentment toward Black women correctional officers because they see them as damaging racial unity and contributing to the emasculation of Black men. Rader (2005) also found that many female correctional officers express negative perceptions of other female correctional officers, ironically reinforcing the "ultra-masculine" culture of prisons and police departments.

7. Research has revealed what has come to be called the *jury trial penalty*. This refers to the fact that defendants who insist on a jury trial, if found guilty, are sentenced more harshly than defendants who plead guilty and thus avert a jury trial (see, for example, Spohn, 1990; Ulmer & Bradley, 2006).

8. The female prostitute, of course, represents in many ways the antithesis of respectable femininity. She is seen as independent and promiscuous, so, not surprisingly, she is the victim of routine harassment within the criminal justice system. But her customers, although guilty of breaking the law, are rarely prosecuted (Sanchez, 2001). Unfortunately, there are very little data available on male prostitution, to a large extent because researchers have focused on prostitution as an exclusively female crime (for exceptions, see Luckenbill, 1986; McNamara, 1994). However, given that male prostitutes violate our culture's gender prescriptions for men, they, too, may be treated more harshly than the average male offender.

9. Importantly, a U.S. Court of Appeals in 1993 ruled in the case of *Jordan* v. *Gardner* that although body searches of female prisoners by male guards does not violate the prisoners' Fourth Amendment right to privacy, such searches do violate the prisoners' Eighth Amendment right to freedom from cruel and unusual punishment in light of the high percentage of female prisoners with histories of physical and sexual abuse. The Court argued that such searches could worsen any psychological problems the prisoners already had as a result of earlier abuse (Belknap, 2001). However, it is not known what impact this decision has had nationwide in curbing body searches of female prisoners by male guards.

10. The statistical probability of contracting HIV/AIDS as a result of rape is unknown at this time. According to the Center for Women Policy Studies (1991, p. 6), "in cases of sexual violence, research seems to assume that a rape survivor may already be infected with HIV, thus emphasizing the survivor's sexual history and deemphasizing the crime of rape." There is currently a debate over mandatory HIV testing of convicted rapists, with test results being provided to both rapists and their victims. In 1997, the Supreme Court of New Jersey ruled that a rape victim

can demand that the rapist be tested for HIV/AIDS and the results be given to the victim. Congress enacted federal legislation requiring states to enact mandatory testing programs for sex offenders at the request of their victims in order to qualify for federal funds. However, because the federal government has not given specific guidelines on mandatory testing, laws vary from state to state (Fishbein, 2000). Some states only require testing after conviction while others require testing after formal charges are made. However, we must also note that some criminologists are critical of characterizing women's fear of crime as solely or even primarily fear of rape. Stanko (2001), for instance, argues that equating women's fear of crime with fear of rape causes us to overlook or minimize the many other types of victimization women experience in their daily lives, including sexual harassment on the street and at work, and domestic violence. Madriz (1997) was also critical of equating women's fear of crime with fear of rape because she saw this as homogenizing women's fear. According to Madriz, how much fear women feel and what they fear are influenced by their personal experiences as well as various social locating factors which, besides gender, include race

and ethnicity, social class, age, sexual orientation, and physical ability/disability.

11. The FBI has historically defined rape as the "carnal knowledge of a female forcibly and against her will," a definition that is narrower than the one used by many police departments in the United States and that grossly undercounts the number of rapes and sexual assaults committed in this country each year. In 2011, a panel of experts from outside the FBI unanimously voted to broaden the federal agency's definition of rape by deleting the requirement that the assault be "forcible," removing the designation of victims as females, and including rape by a blood relative and other types of sexual assault in addition to vaginal-penile rape.

12. Studies of male rape victims show that the majority—for instance, 66 percent in one study (Ernst, Green, & Ferguson, 2000)—also knew their assailants.

13. Krafka et al. (1997) also found a lowered sensitivity toward rape victims among women who viewed sexually explicit, violently graphic films.

14. Dines (1998), however, shows how hard-core pornography demonizes Black men by frequently depicting them as rapists, especially of White women.

Chapter 10

Gender, Politics, Government, and the Military

In the spring of 1776, Abigail Adams wrote to her husband John: "I long to hear that you have declared an independency—and by the way in the new Code of Laws which I suppose it will be necessary for you to make I desire you would Remember the Ladies, and be more generous and favourable to them than your ancestors." But his response revealed that the designers of the new republic had no intention of putting the sexes on an equal political footing. "As to your extraordinary Code of Laws," John Adams wrote back to his wife, "I cannot but laugh....Depend upon it, We know better than to repeal our Masculine systems" (quoted in Rossi, 1973, pp. 10–11).

That Adams' sentiments were shared by his fellow revolutionaries is clear from their declaration that all men are created equal, although at the same time they considered some men (White property holders) more equal than others (Blacks, Native Americans, the propertyless). Of course, it has been argued that the Founding Fathers used the masculine noun in the generic sense, but the fact is that when the Constitution was ratified, women lost rights instead of gaining them. For instance, prior to ratification, women were permitted to vote in some areas, including Massachusetts and New Jersey, a right that was lost in the former state in 1780 and in the latter in 1807 (Simon & Danziger, 1991). As we saw in Chapter 1, ratification of the Constitution did not enfranchise women in the states; female citizens did not win the constitutional right to vote until 1920.

In this chapter, we will focus on some of the similarities and differences in women's and men's political roles and behavior historically and in contemporary society, primarily in the United States, but also elsewhere. As sociologists have repeatedly pointed out, when we speak about *politics,* we are essentially speaking about power—the power to distribute scarce resources, to institutionalize particular values, and to legitimately use force or violence. To the extent that men and women have different degrees of political power, they will have unequal input into political decision making and, consequently, their interests and experiences may be unequally represented in law and public policy. What is the political power differential between the sexes today? We will address that question on one level by assessing men's and women's relative success in winning public office and securing political appointments. In addition, we will examine the roles of men and women in defense and national security by discussing the issue of gender and military service. To begin our discussion, however, we will first take a look at differences in men's and women's political attitudes and participation or what has become known in government circles as the *gender gap.*

THE GENDER GAP: POLITICAL ATTITUDES AND ACTIVITIES

There are few certainties for political candidates on election day, but from 1920, when women were granted full voting rights, until around 1980, there were two things they could count on: Fewer women than men would vote, and those women who did vote would vote similarly to men. Between 1920 and 1960, men's rate of voting exceeded women's rate by a considerable margin, although there was a gradual increase in women's voting rates over the four decades. During the 1960s, there was a sharp increase in women's voting rates, and, by 1980, the margin of difference between women's and men's voting rates was less than 1 percent, with more women than men going to the polls (Center for American Women and Politics [CAWP], 2005). Lake and Breglio (1992) attribute this change to the rise in women's level of educational attainment during this period as well as the rapid increase in the number of women working outside the home.

Nevertheless, although more women were going to the polls during the 1960s and 1970s, their voting behavior continued to parallel that of men.[1]

In the 1980 presidential election, however, two significant changes occurred: More women than men cast ballots, and women voted significantly differently than men. Although 51 percent of the votes cast went to Ronald Reagan, we see in Table 10.1 that he got just 47 percent of women's votes compared with 55 percent of men's votes. This 8 percentage-point gap between women's and men's votes was the largest gap recorded since 1952 when such statistics began to be collected. (John Anderson, the third candidate in the 1980 presidential election received equal support from women and men, garnering just 7 percent of their votes.)

Political analysts were uncertain as to whether such differences were merely a fluke or represented a genuine shift in women's and men's voting patterns. Subsequent elections confirmed the existence of what has come to be known as the **gender gap**: differences in voting patterns and political attitudes of women and men. Looking again at Table 10.1, we see that in the 1984 presidential election, there also was a gender gap in voting, but it was smaller than in 1980—6 percentage points. In 1988, following the spring primaries, there was an unprecedented gender gap of 20 percent, with significantly more women than men favoring Michael Dukakis over George Bush. By November, however, Bush had successfully narrowed the gap to just 7 percent. In the 1992 presidential election, the gender gap remained and appeared not only in differences between men's and women's support for Bill Clinton, but also their support for the

	TABLE 10.1 The Gender Gap in Presidential Elections, 1952–2008		
Election Year	**Candidate Elected**	**Percent of Women Who Supported This Candidate**	**Percent of Men Who Supported This Candidate**
1952	Eisenhower	58	53
1956	Eisenhower	61	55
1960	Kennedy	49	52
1964	Johnson	62	60
1968	Nixon	43	43
1972	Nixon	62	63
1976	Carter	50	50
1980	Reagan	47	55
1984	Reagan	56	62
1988	Bush	50	57
1992	Clinton	46	41
1996	Clinton	54	43
2000	Bush	43	53
2004	Bush	48	55
2008	Obama	56	49

Sources: "Who Voted," 2000; CAWP, 1987, 2004, 2008a.

third candidate, Ross Perot. While women and men supported Bush in relatively equal proportions (37 percent and 38 percent, respectively), Clinton received 5 percent more of his votes from women, and Perot received 4 percent more of his votes from men. In the 1996 election, the gender gap was wider than it has ever been: 11 percentage points (54 percent of women voted for Clinton, while only 43 percent of men did). In 2000, the gender gap remained wide; 53 percent of men voted for Bush, while just 43 percent of women did. (The third party candidate, Ralph Nader, received 3 percent of men's votes and 2 percent of women's votes.) In 2004, the gender gap narrowed again, but nevertheless remained substantial at 7 percent. The gender gap in 2008 was also 7 percent: 56 percent of women voted for Barak Obama compared to 49 percent of men.

In considering the gender gap, particularly in the 1980, 1984, 1988, 2000, and 2004 presidential elections, you may be wondering why the Republican candidates won, if more women than men were voting and more women than men supported the Democratic candidate. Lake and Breglio (1992) explain:

> The gender gap represents an important change in our political system, but has a direct impact on the outcome of an election only when the differences between men's and women's perceptions, priorities, and agendas are so pervasive and significant that they translate into a margin of support for a particular candidate among voters of one sex that more than offsets the margin of support the opposing candidate enjoys among voters of the other sex. (p. 199)

While this has occurred in several U.S. congressional elections since 1980, as well as a number of state senate and gubernatorial elections during the same period, it did not occur in a presidential election until 1996.

It is also the case that the gender gap is far more complex than it at first appears to be. The gender gap involves more than voting behavior; there are particular perspectives on political issues that underlie individuals' votes. Research consistently shows that at the heart of the gender gap are issues of economics, social welfare, foreign policy, and, to a lesser extent, environmental protection and public safety. Women, for example, feel—and rightfully so—more economically vulnerable than men (see Chapters 7 and 8). Women more than men express concern about health care (especially long-term care), child care, education, poverty, and homelessness. In contrast, men more than women express concern about the federal deficit, taxes, energy, defense, and foreign policy (CAWP, 1997). Since the 1980s, women have expressed greater pessimism about the economic condition of the country and showed greater favor toward increased government activity in the form of programs to help families, even if such programs require increased taxes (Bushey, 2008; CAWP, 1997; Goldberg, 1996b; Lake & Breglio, 1992; Sciolino, 1996; USA Today, 2008; see also Gidengil, 1995). Political analysts saw economic differences as underlying the gender gap in presidential elections as well. In 2000, for instance, polls showed Al Gore significantly favored by unmarried women, with or without children, while George W. Bush was ahead among married mothers and fathers as well as married men without children. Mr. Gore's constituents were more economically vulnerable than Mr. Bush's constituents (Seelye, 2000). Similarly, John Kerry's supporters in 2004 were nearly twice as likely as George Bush's supporters to be among the economically marginalized. The higher a person's family income, the greater the likelihood of that person voting for Bush in 2004 (Connelly, 2004). Polls indicated that in the 2008 campaign, the downward turn in the economy contributed more to women's than men's support for Barak Obama (Bushey, 2008).

A strong and consistent gender gap also emerges with respect to issues of war and peace. This difference in the political opinions of women and men can be traced as far back as World War I. Women more than men considered the entry of the United States into both world wars to be mistakes and also voiced greater opposition to the Korean and Vietnam Wars (Abzug, 1984; Baxter & Lansing, 1983). Similarly, in the wake of the 1983 terrorist attack in Beirut that killed more than two hundred U.S. Marines, considerably more women (62 percent) than men (34 percent) favored the withdrawal of U.S. troops from Lebanon (Abzug, 1984). Following the U.S. invasion of Grenada, Ronald Reagan's popularity increased significantly, but only among men, 68 percent of whom approved of the military action compared with only 45 percent of women (Raines, 1983). In the war in the Persian Gulf, more women than men favored a negotiated settlement over military action, and fewer women than men felt that the loss of life—both military and civilian—was worth the victory (Dowd, 1990; Lake & Breglio, 1992). However, women were nearly as likely as men to favor a military response following the terrorist attacks of September 11, 2001. This may be because these attacks took place on U.S. soil and killed thousands of innocent civilians. A majority of women and men supported President Bush's decision to invade Iraq in 2003, but women's support was weaker than that of men (60 percent vs. 80 percent, respectively) (Benedetto, 2003). Women are significantly more likely than men to support the decision to refuse to fight in a war that one considers morally wrong (54 percent vs. 41 percent, respectively) (CAWP, 1997).

But while women favor peaceful solutions over military ones to international conflicts and prefer domestic social spending over military spending, they express greater distrust of other nations than men do and worry about how international relations might pose risks for the future security of the country. This concern is especially strong among women with children (Goldberg, 1996b; see, however, Leonhardt, 2006). The concern carries over into issues of public safety, with women more than men expressing concern about crime and drugs (U.S. Department of Justice, 2010; see also Chapter 9). Although support for the death penalty is high among both women and men—61 percent and 69 percent, respectively, in favor of the death penalty for persons convicted of murder—there is nevertheless a gender gap on this issue. Women (55 percent) are also more likely than men (32 percent) to favor strict gun control laws (U.S. Department of Justice, 2010).

Despite sex differences in these areas, on other topics, men's and women's political opinions are more likely to converge. For example, women and men share similar views on protecting the environment. And interestingly, women's and men's opinions on women's rights issues are more similar than one might predict, although there are important areas of difference. For example, while a majority of both women and men support a woman's right to an abortion under at least some circumstances (U.S. Department of Justice, 2010; see Chapter 7), more women than men report that the position of a political candidate on this issue would affect their vote. This holds for both pro-choice and antiabortion women (Lake & Breglio, 1992; Sciolino, 1996).

Nevertheless, we should be cautious when making comparisons between women as a group and men as a group, for women and men, we have learned, are not homogeneous categories and frequently there are greater differences among groups of women and groups of men than between women and men. Other factors besides sex influence political attitudes and behavior. These factors include race and ethnicity, social class, age, marital status, sexual orientation, education, employment status, religiosity, and geographic location. Consider, for instance, the 2008 presidential election. While Obama fared better among women than among men overall, there were significant voting differences across groups of women and men by race and ethnicity. As Table 10.2 shows, 46 percent of White women compared with 41 percent of White men voted for Mr. Obama, indicating a fairly wide gender gap among White voters. But the gender gap was narrower among Hispanic voters and nearly disappeared among Black voters.

Sexual orientation has also been significant in recent elections. In 1992, for the first time in U.S. history, lesbians and gay men were a visible and vocal political constituency. Lesbian and gay political organizations carried out successful voter registration drives and raised millions of dollars in campaign funds, not only for Bill Clinton, but also for U.S. congressional and state and local politicians whom they supported. This political involvement has continued in subsequent elections with 92 percent of lesbian, gay, bisexual, and transgendered respondents to a recent survey saying they are registered to vote and 52 percent saying they vote in all elections. Although most lesbian, gay, bisexual, and transgendered voters describe themselves as politically moderate, they tend to vote Democratic (Gill Foundation, 2001). Nevertheless, about one-quarter of gay and lesbian voters supported George Bush in the 2000 and 2004 elections. Despite the Bush administration's open support for a constitutional amendment banning marriage between same-sex partners, gay and lesbian Republicans continued to stand by their party, claiming they are not "single-issue" voters (Healy, 2005). Indeed, Mary Cheney (2006), daughter of former Vice President Dick Cheney and a lesbian, has argued that while she would like to have her relationship with her long-term partner legally recognized as a marriage, it would be selfish for her to focus only on this one issue when the federal government's priorities should be national security and the war on terrorism. Religious and political conservatives within the Republican party, however, strongly oppose civil rights for gays and lesbians and have warned Republican office holders not to "court the homosexual lobby" (Stolberg, 2003; see also Chapter 7).

The gender gap has sometimes been explained as an expression of fundamental— some would even argue inherent—differences between the sexes: women's greater focus

TABLE 10.2 Voters in the 2008 Presidential Election		
	Percent* Who Voted for Obama	
Voters	**Women**	**Men**
All voters	56	49
Race/ethnicity		
White	46	41
African American	96	95
Hispanic American	68	64

*Percentages may not add to 100 due to rounding.
Source: CWAP, 2008a, p. 4.

on caring, community, and connectedness; men's greater focus on competition and individual rights (Gidengil, 1995; Lake & Breglio, 1992; McGlen et al., 2011). However, the differences among various groups of women—for instance, differences between full-time homemakers and women in the labor force, between White women and women of color, between lesbians and straight women—indicate that differences in voting and political attitudes reflect the life circumstances of different groups of citizens. Constituencies vote in response to candidates' expressed positions on issues salient to their lives. Nevertheless, gender stereotypes die hard, and the notion that women's political views will be more moralistic or humanitarian than men's views is also typically applied to candidates seeking political office. We will turn our attention to public officeholders shortly. First, though, it is important that we consider whether the gender gap is found in political activities other than voting.

Gender and Political Activities

There are many other forms of political activity besides voting. According to political scientist Lester Millbrath (1965), there are basically three levels of political activism. The lowest level, **spectator activities**, include wearing campaign buttons or putting a bumper sticker on your car. Millbrath also considers voting a spectator activity because it requires minimal effort. In the middle are **transitional activities**, such as writing to public officials, making campaign contributions, and attending rallies or meetings. The highest level of political activity, what Millbrath calls **gladiator activities**, include working on a political campaign, taking an active role in a political party, or running for public office. Gladiator activities require maximum effort and commitment.

Contrary to the popular myth that men are more interested and active in politics, there are actually few differences between the sexes in their level of political activism. As Table 10.3 shows, both women and men are fairly uninvolved in politics. Historically, women have been slightly less likely than men to engage in the spectator activities of wearing buttons and displaying bumper stickers, and men have also been more involved in transitional activities, especially contributing money to political campaigns (McGlen et al., 2011). To a large extent, the gender difference in campaign contributions has been due to the fact that women have had significantly less discretionary income than men, but in recent years women's campaign contributions have increased substantially. For example, as we see in Table 10.3, in the 2004 presidential election, the most recent election for which data are available, women were as likely as men to make a campaign contribution (National Election Surveys, 2006). We will return to this issue shortly.

It has also been the case that much of women's transitional political activism has been overlooked or devalued by researchers. Much of this activism has taken place at the grassroots community level by local groups of working-class women and women of color, who may identify with conservative or liberal political causes (Fowler et al., 2004; Naples, 1998). For instance, women have been at the forefront of political activism for school curricular reforms, with some women working to make the curriculum more conservative (e.g., teaching creationism or "intelligent design") and others working against such changes or in favor of a more inclusive curriculum (e.g., the study of the gay and lesbian civil rights movement). Women have organized and led protests, rent strikes, tenant unions, school boycotts, and petition drives. African American women, in particular, have

TABLE 10.3 Gender Differences in Political Activities, 2004		
	% of Americans Who Engaged in the Activity	
Political Activity	**Women**	**Men**
Cared about who won the presidential election	86	84
Read newspaper articles about political campaigns	65	69
Read magazine articles about political campaigns	26	30
Listened to campaign radio programs	45	57
Watched television programs about political campaigns	86	86
Wore a button or put a bumper sticker on one's car	19	19
Attended a political meeting or event in support of a specific candidate	7	7
Gave money to a political campaign	13	13
Tried to influence how others would vote	45	51
Worked for a party or a candidate	3	3

Source: National Election Surveys, 2006.

provided "most of the time and energy behind dozens of local African American political causes" and "the muscle for many day-to-day African American political efforts" (Fowler et al., 2004, p. 278). However, because the study of political activism traditionally has been limited to lobbying, elections, and office-holding, these significant and sometimes successful political challenges have gone unnoticed by many scholars (Bookman & Morgen, 1988; McGlen et al., 2002).

Indeed, a good deal of scholarly political research has focused on what Millbrath identified as the highest level of political activism, gladiator activities. Here the data are also mixed. Women, as Epstein (1983, p. 290) observed, have long served as political "foot soldiers": canvassing for votes door-to-door or by phone, stuffing envelopes, distributing campaign literature, and so on. "Informal reports and research on party activists indicate it is women who do the daily work of keeping the political parties functioning (McGlen et al., 2002, p. 89). However, although women are well

Women have traditionally been the "footsoldiers" of the political parties, but it has only been in the past twenty years that their election to political office has increased substantially.

represented among campaign staff and volunteers, men have traditionally dominated party conventions. Male dominance at the conventions is noteworthy because:

> it is at party conventions that formal decisions are made about the major presidential candidates and the party platform, which spells out the party's positions on public issues. At conventions various factions come together to discuss common problems and to indulge in the bargaining and compromising that create the coalitions that comprise our national parties. At conventions party leaders interact with rank-and-file members to learn about concerns and potential troublespots in the coming election. For many party workers, a convention is viewed as a reward for years of faithful service. (Lynn, 1984, pp. 409–410)

Until 1972, neither major party had ever had more than 17 percent female delegates at their national conventions. In 1972, however, the Democrats instituted affirmative action regulations that helped to dramatically increase the representation of female delegates to 40 percent. Although their numbers dropped in 1976, women finally achieved equal representation at the 1980 Democratic National Convention. Convention rules adopted by the Democratic National Committee state that each state's delegation must proportionately represent the racial and ethnic composition of the state and must include 50 percent women. In contrast, the Republicans, who have never adopted affirmative action rules for their conventions—opposition to affirmative action is included in the Republican Party platform—have typically had delegations with a majority of male members. For example, in 2004, the most recent year for which data are available, 43 percent of the delegates to the Republication National Convention were female. Only 15 percent of the Republican delegates were non-White, compared with 32 percent of the Democratic delegates in 2004 (Seelye & Connelly, 2004).

GENDER AND PUBLIC OFFICE

Women and men, it seems, have a similar interest in politics if we use their voting rates and political activism as indicators. Yet, historically, men have had a virtual monopoly on public officeholding throughout the world. There are 193 sovereign states in the world; in 2008, just sixteen had female heads of government (e.g., president, prime minister, chancellor). Throughout the world, women are underrepresented at all levels of political decision making. In countries with parliamentary governments—that is, 189 countries—women held 18.4 percent of the seats in 2008. Of the 189 parliaments, 76 are bicameral, resulting in 265 positions of Presiding Officer of Parliament or one of its houses; only thirty-one women held this position in 2008 (11.7 percent). While the current number of women parliamentarians represents a more than 600 percent increase since 1945, the number of parliaments has also grown (from 26 to 189). As Table 10.4 shows, women's highest representation in parliamentary government is in the Nordic countries, where they hold 41.4 percent of the seats. Women fare worst in the Arab states, where they hold just 9.7 percent of the seats (Inter-Parliamentary Union, 2008a, 2008b). Not surprisingly, women have had the greatest success in countries that have adopted proportional representation (PR) systems or quotas based on gender. In countries with PR systems, women on average held 20.7 percent of parliamentary seats in 2007, compared with

| | TABLE 10.4   Seats Held by Women in Parliamentary Governments, Regional Averages |

Region	Single House or Lower House	Upper House or Senate	Both Houses combined
Nordic countries	41.1%	—	—
Americas	21.7%	20.1%	21.4%
Europe: OSCE member countries (including Nordic countries)	21.1%	19.9%	20.9%
Europe: OSCE member countries (excluding Nordic countries)	19.2%	19.9%	19.3%
Asia	18.3%	16.5%	18.1%
Sub-Saharan Africa	17.9%	20.6%	18.2%
Pacific	12.9%	31.8%	14.9%
Arab States	9.7%	7.0%	9.1%

Source: Inter-Parliamentary Union, 2008b.

an average of 13.3 percent in non-PR system countries. Constitutional or electoral law quotas have been adopted in forty-three countries, and women's average representation was 21.9 percent in 2008 compared with an average of 15.3 percent in all other countries (UNIFEM, 2008). The United Nations World Development Fund for Women estimates that if current trends continue, parity between the sexes—i.e., neither sex holds more than 60 percent of the seats—will not be reached in developing countries until 2047 (UNIFEM, 2008). In 2008, Rwanda was the only country in the world with a parliamentary government in which women held an equal number of seats (forty of eighty) (Inter-Parliamentary Union, 2008c).

How well does the United States compare with other countries in terms of women's representation in national government? In 2008, the Inter-Parliamentary Union (2008c), published a progress report regarding women's representation in the national governing bodies of 188 countries. The United States ranked seventy-first. The U.S. standing reflects the fact that despite the progress women have made in the political arena at all levels—federal, state, and local—since the 1990s, they remain grossly underrepresented, especially in the federal government. Before we examine the numbers more closely, however, let's discuss some of the factors that historically contributed to the disparity between the sexes in public officeholding.

One explanation for the gender gap in officeholding is differential socialization of boys and girls. This argument holds that dispositions toward politics are formed in childhood when boys are told they can grow up to be president some day; the best girls can hope for is to grow up to marry a man who may one day be a president. Consequently, children learn that politics is a masculine activity, and this is reflected in their adult behavior: Women are less likely to run for public office.

This explanation has some appeal because, as we found in Chapter 4, early childhood socialization does have a powerful impact on the development of sex-typed attitudes and behaviors. Early research, however, found no sex differences in the political views of school-age children (Epstein, 1983). We would also expect to find less similarity in men's and women's interest in politics if differential socialization were at work. Nevertheless, at least one recent national survey of nearly 3,800 women and men who could be considered eligible candidates for public office because of their qualifications indicates that gender socialization does exercise some influence on women's and men's respective decisions to enter a political race (Lawless & Fox, 2005). Moreover, this study—the Citizen Political Ambition Study—found these gender differences to be stronger among young women and men (under the age of forty) than among those over the age of sixty. As Lawless and Fox (2005) point out, "For most people, choosing to run for office is not a spontaneous decision; rather, it is the culmination of a long, personal evolution that stretches back into early family life" (p. 154). Their findings show that during childhood, the women in the study were less likely than the men to have talked with their parents about politics and to be encouraged by their parents to run for office. Adding to the effects of childhood socialization is the availability of role models for young aspiring politicians. Young women have fewer role models than their male counterparts, although this is changing as more women each election year enter political races. The availability of role models and mentors is important; many female officeholders state that they were inspired by and assisted in their political careers by other women CAWP, 1984). It is too early to determine the effects of the 2008 general election, but hopefully Hillary Clinton's bid for the Democratic presidential nomination and Sarah Palin's vice presidential candidacy will encourage young women with political aspirations to run for office.

A second explanation for the small number of women officeholders is that women have greater difficulty meeting the demands of public life given their domestic responsibilities. Like most married employed women, female politicians who are married shoulder a double work load; their spouses, if they are married, do not usually assume primary responsibility for housekeeping or child care. Particularly at the national level, the demands of public office take an extraordinary toll on the amount of time an officeholder can spend with her or his family. It is not surprising, therefore, that women typically enter politics at a later age than men (after their children are grown) and that female political elites are more likely than men to be single, widowed, or divorced, although they may still have children (Lawless & Fox, 2005; Stolberg, 2003; Thomas et al., 2002). This does not mean that men do not experience conflict between their political careers and their family lives. Recent research indicates that they do and that the tension may be high. However, men are more likely to pursue their political ambitions despite the conflicts, and married men are more likely to have a spouse who handles most of the daily household and child care responsibilities. In one study of state legislators, for example, 73 percent of male officeholders said their spouses were full-time homemakers, whereas only 27 percent of female officeholders reported that their spouses did not work outside the home (Thomas et al., 2002). Women who are conflicted between their political careers and their family lives are more likely than men to try to manage the conflict by delaying their political careers or by giving up one role for the other, at least temporarily (Fox & Lawless, 2008; Thomas et al., 2002).

A third, although increasingly less frequent explanation is that men outnumber women in elected office because most women lack the necessary qualifications and credentials. It is certainly true that most female officeholders prior to World War II had inherited their seats and simply served out the terms of their deceased husbands or fathers. Even if they were elected, they usually had less education than the men, and because the legal and business professions were largely closed to them, they came to politics via different occupational backgrounds, typically teaching and social work. In recent years, however, this has changed. Female and male officeholders today have comparable educational backgrounds, and the number of women in public office who are lawyers and businesspeople has also risen along with those with previous elective experience. These facts make the "qualifications and credentials argument" less tenable today than in the past. Still, eligible women candidates who have worked in traditionally sexist professional environments, such as law and business (see Chapters 8 and 9), typically believe that they need to be *more* qualified than men to compete successfully in the political arena (Fox & Lawless, 2008).

A fourth argument, not unrelated to the second and third we have just discussed, is that women may be relatively scarce in public office because of prejudice and discrimination against them that may occur on two levels: among the electorate and within political office. Studies of sexism among the electorate indicate that, in general, sexism has declined in recent years (J. Clark, 1991; Moran & Taylor, 2008). For instance, in one national opinion poll taken during the 2008 presidential campaign, an overwhelming majority of voters—88 percent (nearly 100 percent of Democrats, 90 percent of independents, and 76 percent of Republicans)—said they were glad to see a woman as a serious contender for president. In addition, 63 percent said they hoped to see a woman president in their lifetime, although slightly fewer (60 percent) felt the country is ready for a female president. In contrast, 68 percent said the country was ready for a Black president (CBS News, 2008; see, however, Falk & Kenski, 2006, who found that among voters, political partisanship is more influential than a candidate's gender).

The public has clearly grown more accustomed to women running for political office and no longer considers it "unusual" or "unladylike." In an increasing number of political races, in fact, voters must choose between two female candidates, and voters tend to rely on the party affiliation of candidates and the issues as voting cues (Falk & Kenski, 2006; Matland & King, 2002). However, research indicates that sex continues to be an important factor in many elections, since the electorate often views the skills and qualifications of female and male candidates differently, and gender stereotypes still influence some voters' images of political candidates. The extent to which these stereotypes work against women candidates depends on a number of factors. One relevant factor is the type of issues that are most pressing on public awareness during a specific election campaign. For example, if voters are concerned about social issues, such as education, health care, homelessness, welfare policy, and reproductive freedom, women candidates may have an advantage over men because voters tend to perceive women as being better at responding to such problems. On the other hand, voters tend to see male candidates as being better able to lead the country during a national crisis (Bystrom et al., 2004). According to one study, the public views women as more honest and intelligent than men. Nevertheless, only 6 percent of respondents in this study felt that women are better political leaders than men; 21 percent said that men are better political leaders than women, and 69 percent said women and men are equally good as political leaders (Morin & Taylor, 2008).

The importance of a candidate's gender also varies with the office. In general, the higher the political office, the less likely voters are to consider women qualified to hold that office (see, for example, Bystrom et al., 2004, although the impact of the 2008 presidential race on such attitudes remains to be seen). And gender also intersects with political party in influencing voters' perceptions. Republican voters have historically been less supportive of female candidates and tend to see female candidates as more liberal than male candidates, making it more difficult for female Republican candidates to get elected (Matland & King, 2002; Morin & Taylor, 2008). But Sarah Palin's candidacy in 2008 as well as Michele Bachman's bid for the 2012 presidential nomination—and Republicans' enthusiastic support of her—may indicate a change in this pattern (see also Stout & Kline, 2011).

Of course, the media play a major role in shaping voters' perceptions of political candidates. Research shows that female and male candidates are covered differently by the media (see also Chapter 6). For instance, studies of elections during the 1980s showed that newspaper coverage of female candidates tended to emphasize their "feminine traits" and to raise questions about their viability as candidates (Kahn & Goldenberg, 1991). In a more recent review of newspaper coverage of candidates in the 1998, 2000, and 2002 elections, Bystrom and colleagues (2004) found that the amount of coverage male and female candidates received was nearly identical and that the slant of the coverage (positive vs. negative) was also relatively equal between men and women. Nevertheless, Bystrom et al. reported that in articles about women candidates, newspapers were more likely to highlight their gender than in articles about men candidates, and articles about women candidates were significantly more likely to mention their appearance and their marital status. During the 2008 Democratic presidential primaries, the media, particularly correspondents and commentators on the cable television networks, were frequently accused of sexist reporting. One study charted the media coverage of Barack Obama and Hillary Clinton on the three major broadcast networks (ABC, CBS, and NBC). The researchers found that beginning in December 2007, 90 percent of the comments about Obama were positive compared with 61 percent about Clinton. By June, when Clinton suspended her campaign, the study showed positive coverage of the two candidates to be more similar: 48 percent positive for Obama and 45 percent positive for Clinton (Seelye & Bosman, 2008).

Prejudice and discrimination against female candidates can be found at a second level as well: within the political parties. Historically, sexism within the political parties has been well documented (Niven, 1998; Witt, Paget, & Matthews, 1994). Today, the overwhelming majority of party leaders are men, some of whom continue to subscribe to traditional gender stereotypes, thinking that male candidates have a better chance of winning and will make better politicians than women (Niven, 1998). It is estimated that this bias reduces the number of women nominated for state legislative seats by about one-third (Lawless & Fox, 2005; Niven, 1998).[2] Party leaders, elected officials, and political activists are important as "electoral gatekeepers," especially at the state level. They groom eligible candidates for political races and their encouragement can be a critical factor in determining whether or not a potential candidate will run. Lawless and Fox's (2005) research indicates that men are 34 percent more likely than women to be recruited to run for office by a party official, an elected official, or a political activist.

Other serious obstacles for women seeking public office are incumbency and access to campaign funds. An **incumbent** is a person who holds political office and is seeking another term. Incumbents have several advantages during an election, not the least of which are high public visibility, recognition among voters, and the opportunity to campaign throughout their term in office. Because fewer women are in office, when they do run, it is more often as challengers rather than as incumbents and, not surprisingly, they lose more frequently when running against an incumbent than for an open seat. In 2004, for example, five of the ten women who ran for the U.S. Senate won election; all five were incumbents themselves. Of the 141 women who sought election in 2004 to the U.S. House of Representatives, 65 won. Fifty-seven of these women were incumbents and seven won open seats; only one of the sixty-four women who challenged incumbents won a House seat (CAWP, 2004b).

Incumbent or not, all political candidates need money to run a campaign, and the more prestigious the office they seek, the more money they need. Traditionally, political campaigns have been financed through personal wealth subsidized by party funds. Since women and minorities have had fewer financial resources than White men, when they ran for office, their campaigns often did not have sufficient funds to be successful. And today, even more than in the past, money is essential to winning elections. Consider, for example, that in 2008, in 93 percent of campaigns for seats in the U.S. House of Representatives and 94 percent of campaigns for U.S. Senate seats, the candidate who spent the most money won. The average amount spent on a U.S. senatorial campaign by a winning candidate in 2008 was almost $6.5 million and on a winning House campaign it was nearly $1.1 million (U.S. Department of Commerce, Bureau of the Census, 2011; "Money wins presidency," 2008).

Where do such enormous sums come from? Certainly, most candidates for public office, especially at the national level, continue to be individuals with considerable personal wealth, but the lion's share of campaign funds today comes from private corporations and groups representing special interests. In fact, some special-interest groups dedicate themselves to fundraising and distributing contributions to the political campaigns of candidates who support the group's cause. These special interest groups are called **political action committees** or **PACs**. There are more than 4,200 PACs in the United States today, representing corporations (the largest category, and includes such corporations as General Motors, Exelon, and Longheed Martin), particular industries and professions (e.g., the American Medical Association, the American Bar Association), and specific issues (e.g., pro- or antiabortion, pro- or anti-gun control). PACs contribute millions of dollars to campaigns, making them a powerful force on the political scene. In 2007–2008, for example, PACs contributed $78.2 million to candidates for the U.S. Senate and $300.4 million to candidates running for the U.S. House of Representatives (U.S. Department of Commerce, Bureau of the Census, 2011).

Historically, however, female and minority candidates have received a relatively small percentage of these funds, with PAC representatives arguing that the reason was these candidates frequently did not solicit them ("Seeking Corporate PAC Money," 1986). This may have been true to some extent, given that many PACs are parts of large corporations and professional associations in fields in which the percentage of women and minorities has been small, and women and minorities historically were not members of the interlocking professional, social, and political networks through which large campaign contributions were frequently generated (Scott, 1994). Nevertheless, even when contributions have been solicited, the funds received tended to be smaller on average than those given to White male candidates (Carroll, 1985). During the 1990s, however, even this dimension of the political arena began to change dramatically. For one thing, women's organizations successfully mobilized their memberships to support female or feminist candidates, not only "with their feet" by working on campaigns and voting, but also with their pocketbooks. In addition, women, racial and ethnic minorities, and lesbians and gay men established formal and informal political coalitions as well as their own PACs, such as the Future PAC (Women Building for the Future, the national African American women's PAC), the Women's Campaign Fund, and Emily's List, which is widely considered to be one of the most powerful women's PACs and ranked sixth in the 2008 election for both receipts and disbursements (McGlen et al., 2011).[3] By 2008, there were forty-seven PACs and donor networks (not including issue-focused PACs) that gave money primarily to female candidates or that had a predominantly female donor base (CAWP, 2010). Similarly, the gay and lesbian Victory Fund has raised hundreds of thousands of dollars in support of gay and lesbian political candidates. Research now shows that once incumbency is taken into account, there are no significant gender differences in campaign fundraising ability among candidates (Burrell, 2008; Fox & Lawless, 2008). Not surprisingly, then, women, racial and ethnic minorities, and gay men and lesbians are making successful bids for public office. Let's discuss now the relative numbers of women and men in specific elected and appointed offices and, when possible, look at race and ethnicity and sexual orientation as well.

Women and Men in State and Local Government

Table 10.5 shows the number of women holding selected state and local offices. Clearly, men continue to dominate state and local government as they constitute the vast majority of officeholders in every category. Still, it is at the state level that women have made their greatest political gains in recent years.

TABLE 10.5   Women in State and Local Government, Selected Offices, 2011

Public Office	Number of Women Officeholders
Governor	6
Lt. Governor	11 (of 42)
Secretary of State	11
Attorney General	7
State Treasurer or Chief Financial Officer	7
State Auditor or Comptroller	11
Chief State Education Official	5
Commissioner of Insurance	2
Commissioner of Labor	1
Corporation Commissioner	3
Public Service Commissioner	4
Public Utilities Commissioner	1
State Legislator	1,740 (23.6%)
Mayor (cities with populations over 30,000; n = 1,167 cities)	203 (17.4%)

Source: CAWP, 2011a, 2011b, 2011c.

Most important perhaps is the number of female state legislators. Although men continue to hold more than 76 percent of all state legislative seats, the number of women legislators has increased more than fivefold since 1971, from just 4 percent to over 23.6 percent in 2011. In four states, women hold a third or more of the state legislative seats: Colorado (41.0 percent), Vermont (38.3 percent), Arizona (34.4 percent), Hawaii (34.2 percent) and Washington (32.0 percent) (CAWP, 2011b).

Racial and ethnic minorities have made significant inroads at the state and local levels, too. For example, in 2008, there were 283 Hispanic state executives and legislators, up from 129 in 1985 (U.S. Department of Commerce, Bureau of the Census, 2011). The number of African American statewide elected officials has also grown significantly over the past four decades (Philpot & Walton, 2007). Nevertheless, women of color remain seriously underrepresented in state elected offices. Of the 71 women serving in state elective executive offices in 2011, eleven were women of color: four African American women, four Latinas, two Native Americans, and one Asian American. In 2011, women of color were just 4.7 percent of state legislators and 20 percent of female state legislators. African American women served in the legislatures of forty states; they were 3.6 percent of all state legislators, 13.8 percent of female state legislators, and 69.4 percent of minority female state legislators. Latinas served in the legislatures of twenty states, holding a total of sixty-three seats and constituting 3.3 percent of female state legislators. Asian American women served in ten states, held thirty-five seats, and were 2.0 percent of female legislators. Native American women served in seven states, but held just eight seats total, thus constituting only 0.4 percent of female legislators. Respectively, Hispanic, Asian American, and Native American women are 0.9 percent, 0.5 percent, and 0.1 percent of all state legislators nationwide (CAWP, 2011d).

Despite these low numbers, it is important to remember that they signify *gains* for racial and ethnic minorities, especially for women of color, in state elective offices over the past four decades. Lesbians and gay men appear to have had less success at the state level, although they have made inroads in local elections. Tony Miller became the first openly gay candidate to run for statewide elective office in 1994, seeking the position of California secretary of state. The Victory Fund of the Gay and Lesbian Leadership Institute provides a listing of out elected officials (see www.glli.org).

Women and Men in the Federal Government

Looking at Table 10.6, we see the number of women in the U.S. Congress from 1949 to 2011. What is most striking about the figures in this table is not so much the small number of women—most of you would probably predict that—but rather the slow rate of improvement in these numbers over a six-decade period. Until 1993, it could hardly be said that there was a strong pattern of growth in the number of female elected officials at the federal level, particularly in the Senate. Although women have served in Congress since 1916, when Jeannette Rankin was elected to the House of Representatives, 45 percent of congresswomen prior to 1949 came to office through *widow's succession*, that is, they were appointed or elected to finish the terms of their husbands who were congressmen, but who died or became too ill to serve. Women who entered congressional office this way were sometimes reelected after their husband's term expired. For female

TABLE 10.6	Women in the U.S. Congress, 1949–2011		
Year	Congress	Senate	House*
1949	81st	1	9
1951	82nd	1	10
1953	83rd	3	12
1955	84th	1	17
1957	85th	1	15
1959	86th	2	17
1961	87th	2	18
1963	88th	2	12
1965	89th	2	11
1967	90th	1	11
1969	91st	1	10
1971	92nd	2	13
1973	93rd	0	16
1975	94th	0	19
1977	95th	2	20
1979	96th	1	16
1981	97th	2	21
1983	98th	2	22
1985	99th	2	23
1987	100th	2	24
1989	101st	2	28
1991	102nd	2	28
1993	103rd	7	47
1995	104th	9	48
1997	105th	9	53
1999	106th	9	55
2001	107th	13	60
2003	108th	14	59
2005	109th	14	67
2007	110th	16	70
2009	111th	17	73
2011	112th	17	73

* The tally for the 105th Congress does not include two Democratic delegates to the House from the Virgin Islands and Washington, DC, nor does it include Susan Molinari (R-NY) who resigned in August, 1997. However, it does include three representatives who joined Congress in 1998 as a result of special elections: Lois Capps (D-CA), Mary Bono (R-CA), and Barbara Lee (R-CA). The tallies for the 106th–112th Congresses also do not include the 2 female delegates to the House from the Virgin Islands and Washington, DC.

Source: CAWP, 20011c.

senators especially, this was the primary means of holding an office; it was not until 1983 (the 98th Congress) that two women served in the Senate simultaneously without either of them having gotten their seats through widow's succession (Lynn, 1984). In the 1992 elections—dubbed the "Year of the Woman" by some political analysts—women made significant progress in congressional officeholding. A record number of women were nominated for congressional seats in 1992: 11 for the Senate, 5 of whom won; and 108 for the House of Representatives, 48 of whom won. It was in this election that for the first time both senatorial seats for a state were held by women: Barbara Boxer and Diane Feinstein, both Democrats, were elected in California. In fact, California has elected more women to Congress than any other state.[4] There is now more female representation in Congress than ever before, and there is no reason to believe that the number of congresswomen will not continue to grow in the future. But despite the fact that women are 51.6 percent of the voting population, they are still just 17 percent of U.S. senators and 16.8 percent of U.S. representatives (CAWP, 2011c).

When race and ethnicity are taken into account, we find that women and men of color remain underrepresented in Congress. In the 110th Congress (2007), for instance, there were forty-two African Americans, twenty-three Hispanic Americans, and four Asian Americans serving in the U.S. House of Representatives; there was one African American, three Hispanic Americans, and one Asian American in the U.S. Senate (U.S. Department of Commerce, Bureau of the Census, 2011). In 1992, Carol Moseley Braun (a Democrat from Illinois) became the first African American female senator; however, she lost her bid for reelection in 1998[5]. By 2011, only forty-two women of color had ever served in Congress (CAWP, 2011e). In 2011, in the House of Representatives there were twenty-four women of color holding 4.5 percent of the Congressional seats: thirteen African American women, four Asian American woman, and seven Latinas.[6]

What happens to women after they get to Congress? In the past, women senators and representatives rarely held leadership positions. By 1993, there were only two women in high-ranking leadership positions (Senator Barbara Mikulski, a Democrat from Maryland, assistant floor leader; and Congresswoman Barbara Kennelly, a Democrat from Connecticut, chief deputy majority whip) and none chairing standing congressional committees. In fact, until 1995 (104th Congress) only six women had ever chaired standing congressional committees, and they all served before 1977. In 2009, seven women senators and ten congresswomen had leadership positions in the 111th Congress. What is more, in 2007, Nancy Pelosi (D-CA) became the first woman Speaker of the House; in 2011, she was minority leader (CAWP, 2001f). Women, though, most often hold secondary positions, and serve on less prestigious committees. As McGlen and colleagues (2011) note, "Most prestigious committees have but token positions for women" (p. 108).

One of the reasons for women's exclusion from some positions and committees is their lack of seniority. For example, most analysts agree that it takes a minimum of five terms in the House before election or appointment to a powerful position is likely; floor leaders typically serve eighteen years before securing that spot (Gertzog, 1984; Lynn, 1984; McGlen et al., 2011). Such findings, then, underline the importance of female incumbents seeking and winning reelection to consecutive terms; otherwise, although more women may fill congressional seats, their junior status will continue to cause them to be underrepresented in high-level positions.

We know that every chief executive of the United States has been male, as has every vice president. There has never been a female candidate for president from either of the major political parties, although former Senator Patricia Schroeder sought the Democratic nomination in 1988 as did former Senator Hillary Clinton in 2008. It was not until 1984 that a woman was nominated by a major party for the office of vice president, and that has occurred only once since then, when Sarah Palin became John McCain's running mate in 2008. However, in considering the executive branch of the federal government, we must keep in mind that those elected to office also have the privilege of making a variety of high-ranking appointments. Presidential appointments, particularly for women and minorities, are critical for three major reasons:

1. They provide young professionals with valuable career experience.
2. They set an example for private employers to follow in hiring personnel.
3. They offer opportunities for input into policy making from individuals with diverse backgrounds and interests.

There are 290 top government positions for which the president makes appointments, subject to Senate confirmation, with cabinet appointments being the most prized. The first female presidential appointee was Frances Perkins who was appointed in 1933 by Franklin D. Roosevelt to head the Department of Labor. Since then, forty women have been appointed to cabinet posts by nine presidents; twenty-three have been appointed by Democratic presidents and seventeen by Republican presidents. Nearly all of these, however, have occurred since the 1980s. For instance, during Bill Clinton's two terms in office, he appointed thirteen women to cabinet-level posts. Clinton was the first president to appoint women to any of the "big four" cabinet posts (i.e., Defense, State, Justice, and Treasury). He appointed Janet Reno as Attorney General (1993-2001) and Madeleine Albright as Secretary of State (1997-2001) (McGlen et al., 2011). Clinton also appointed the first openly gay man and lesbian to high-ranking federal positions: Bruce A. Lehman, Assistant Secretary of Commerce and Commissioner of Patents and Trademarks, and Roberta Achetenberg, Assistant Secretary of Housing and Urban Development. George W. Bush appointed five women to his cabinet. His appointments also included two African Americans, two Latinos, and one Asian American to his cabinet. Importantly, he appointed Condoleezza Rice, an African American woman, to one of the highest cabinet posts—National Security Advisor—a position never before held by a woman or an African American. Mr. Bush, in fact, was applauded for the gender and racial diversity of his appointments. Barak Obama appointed four women to his cabinet, including one, Hillary Clinton, to a big four post, Secretary of State (CAWP, 2011g).

Among the most important appointments the president may make are those to the U.S. Supreme Court, because the impact of these appointments stretches well beyond the president's own administration, given that the justices hold life terms. Ronald Reagan nominated the first woman to the Supreme Court, Sandra Day O'Connor, in 1981. Historically, the all-male Court had done much to uphold and little to remedy sex discrimination. Well into the 1960s, the justices' decisions in sex discrimination cases reflected the opinion of Chief Justice Waite, who, in the 1875 case of *Minor* v. *Happersett*, declared that women, like children, are "a special category of citizens," in need of both discipline and protection. It was not until 1973 that the Court ruled that much of the discrimination against women was nothing more than "romantic paternalism" that, "in practical effect, put women not on a pedestal, but in a cage" (*Frontiero* v. *Richardson*). Nevertheless, as we have noted in other chapters, the Supreme Court did not subsequently strike down all forms of sex discrimination. With O'Connor's appointment, many feminists were hopeful that a woman on the Court would preserve the hard-won legal support of gender equality secured in earlier cases. However, O'Connor's record in this area was mixed. Although she typically supported equality in the area of employment, her opinions with respect to affirmative action were uneven. In addition, she did not act consistently to protect women's abortion rights; indeed, in her opinion in *Webster* v. *Reproductive Health Services* (1989), she explicitly called on the Court to reconsider its ruling in *Roe* v. *Wade* (see Chapter 7).

George H.W. Bush made two appointments to the Supreme Court. In 1990, it was rumored that he would nominate Edith H. Jones to replace retiring Justice William Brennan, who had been considered by many to be the leading liberal voice on the Court. Instead, Mr. Bush chose David H. Souter, a White man. In 1991, Mr. Bush nominated Clarence Thomas, a Black man, to the Supreme Court. Justice Thomas's appointment, however, was not considered a victory for either racial and ethnic minorities or women because of his conservative record on affirmative action and the charges of sexual harassment leveled against him by Professor Anita Hill during his confirmation hearings.

In 1993, Ruth Bader Ginsburg, nominated by President Clinton, became the second female justice on the U.S. Supreme Court. Justice Ginsburg, who replaced retired Justice Byron R. White, had a strong record in support of gender equality and abortion rights. In 1994, a second Clinton nominee, Stephen G. Breyer, a White man whose lower court decisions were supportive of civil rights and reproductive freedom, replaced Justice Harry Blackmun on the Supreme Court. George W. Bush also made two appointments to the high court, both white men: Samuel Alito and John G. Roberts, Jr. (who succeeded William Rehnquist as Chief Justice). Barak Obama tripled women's representation on the Supreme Court with his appointments of Sonia Sotomayor, a Latina, and Elena Kagan.

The justices have not done much to increase diversity in employment within the Court itself. Of the nine justices sitting on the Court in 2006, only Justice Breyer had consistently hired the same number of female law clerks as male clerks. However, the majority of his clerks have been White. About 46 percent of the clerks for Justices O'Connor and Ginsburg have been women, but most have also been White. Justice Stevens, who was on the bench from 1975 until 2010, hired about 28 percent female clerks and, with Justice Thomas, had the best record of hiring non-White clerks, 14 percent. Justice Scalia has the worst diversity record; between 2000 and 2006 he hired only two female clerks (7 percent) and all his clerks were White (Greenhouse, 2006).

It is important to keep in mind that the presence of a White woman or a person of color in a government post does not necessarily mean that women's or minorities' interests will be consistently and fairly represented or that gender and racial and ethnic

The composition of the U.S. Supreme Court is now more diverse than ever before, although the justices themselves have done little to increase the sex and racial or ethnic diversity of their staff.

equality will always be promoted. As we have already noted, and as politicians such as Sarah Palin, Michele Bachman, and Herman Cain illustrate, one's gender and one's race do not predetermine one's political perspective or interests.

Still, research indicates that women in elected offices usually have a positive impact on the passage of women's rights legislation and are more likely than male legislators to give top priority to issues of particular concern to women (McGlen et al., 2011). According to Lovenduski (1986, p. 243), it appears that "a certain 'critical mass' of women"—and we would add, *feminist* women—"must exist to enable the development of a group identity and the resistance of socialization into male norms of behavior." This is also essential for breaking down gender stereotypes. However, the more sex segregated an institution is, the more difficult this is to achieve, as we will see next in our discussion of the military.

WOMEN AND MEN IN THE MILITARY

We noted earlier that women tend to express greater opposition to military intervention than men, and, in general, they are thought to be more pacifistic. Clearly, this is not true for all women nor has it ever been. Historical and cross-cultural research shows, in fact, that women have often supported militarism and have even engaged in combat and other military activities. Archeologists, for example, have discovered graves in Kazakhstan near the Russian border containing the remains of women warriors who apparently defended their kin, land, and herds of animals while riding horseback, shooting with bows and arrows and wielding daggers (Davis-Kimball, 1997). During the nineteenth century, in the West African nation of Dahomey (now Benin), the king had an all-female fighting force of between four thousand and ten thousand soldiers as part of his standing army (Sacks, 1979). Israeli women fought in combat during the 1930s and 1940s, although their combat roles were not officially recognized. During World War II, Soviet women assumed combat roles as machine gunners and snipers, fighting with men in artillery and tank crews. Recent research also indicates that the involvement of German women in the Holocaust was far more substantial than was originally thought (Kershner, 2010) During the 1980s, twenty thousand Eritrean women fought with men, driving tanks and firing heavy artillery, as members of the rebel army that liberated Eritrea from Ethiopian rule in 1991 (McKinley, 1996; for other recent examples, see DePauw, 2000; MacDonald, 1992). In December 1986, Denmark became the first NATO country to allow women to join combat forces, with the exception of those on aircraft. Today, women in Canada, Britain, Norway, and Israel may assume jobs in every area of their country's armed forces, with few exceptions.[7]

In the United States, there are accounts of women who disguised themselves as men and fought at the front beside their husbands or brothers: Deborah Sampson, for instance, during the American Revolution; Lucy Brewer in the War of 1812; and Loretta Velasquez in the Civil War (Rustad, 1982). Although women have been officially prohibited from direct combat duty in the U.S. armed forces, they were employed during World War II as test pilots who flew bombers and pursuit planes, in espionage, and as saboteurs behind enemy lines. According to one researcher:

> The role of females was not trivial, and it certainly was in no way token. Indeed, this female role subjected women to risks of death or torture exactly parallel to those for males.... The meager evidence we have from the performance of women in espionage and sabotage suggests that women can be as

brave and as coldly homicidal as men, whenever their patriotism calls for it.
(Quester, 1982, pp. 226, 229; see also Yellin, 2004)

For the most part, however, these American women were an exceptional few. War-making has historically been a male activity in the United States, and the military a male-dominated institution. This is not to deny the widespread involvement of men historically and in contemporary society in antiwar movements and peace activities. Throughout U.S. history, men have been pacifists and conscientious objectors, but as we noted earlier, in general, men tend to be much more favorably disposed to military solutions to international conflicts than women are. As Cooke and Woollacott (1993) argue, war and the military are gendered and their gender is masculine; things that are feminine are derided in the military and consciously eliminated (see also Kuehnast, Oudraat, & Hernes, 2011). Gender integration of the armed forces in the United States was strongly resisted on the ground that women just don't have what it takes to be effective soldiers; they are too weak. For instance, General Josiah Bunting III, superintendent of the Virginia Military Institute (VMI), which refused to admit women until ordered to do so by the U.S. Supreme Court in 1996, warned prospective female applicants to VMI that military training is not for the "faint of heart." "We teach what are called the vigorous virtues—determination, self-reliance, self-control, and courage," said Bunting. "This is achieved through the application of mental stress, physical rigor, minute regulations of behavior, pressures, hazards, and psychological bonding"—conditions that Bunting felt few, if any, women could endure (quoted in Allen, 1996, p. 18).

When American women were first recruited for military service during World War I, they were limited to nursing and clerical jobs that did not carry full military status and therefore none of the benefits to which male military personnel were entitled. During the Second World War, the Women's Army Corps (WAC) was established and granted women full military status with benefits throughout the war and for six months afterward. Other military corps for women were also begun and included the Women's Reserve of the Navy (WAVES) and the Women's Air Force Service Pilots (WASPS). Still, women's roles were strictly limited, and the war department continued to adhere to a policy of recruiting men, no matter how uneducated, unskilled, or incompetent, before accepting women. Despite the fact that, especially as nurses and pilots, these women frequently faced dangerous and life-threatening conditions in war zones—some were wounded or killed—they were often derided by servicemen, civilians, and the press. Reporters seemed most interested in what the women were wearing, right down to whether they were issued girdles, whereas the general public and servicemen typically viewed them as whores or lesbians in search of partners (Rustad, 1982; Yellin, 2004).

Until the late 1960s, women served as a reserve army in the truest sense for the military. Recruited as a cheap source of labor when manpower was low, they were dismissed as soon as men were available to replace them. Shortly after World War II, for instance, 98 percent of the Women's Army Corps was discharged, but because women had not been given the same civilian reemployment rights as men, they had greater difficulty finding work, and many were forced to take jobs well below their skill levels. For example, women who had been pilots during wartime found at the war's end that the only jobs they could obtain in the airline industry were as flight attendants or typists (Rustad, 1982; Yellin, 2004). In addition, as Willentz (1991) has observed, the Veterans Administration was a system established by men for men, with the needs of female veterans largely overlooked (see also Palmer, 1993).

At the same time, women who joined the military had to meet higher enlistment standards than men; however, they were given fewer privileges and career opportunities and were subject to stricter regulations. For example, the 1948 Women's Armed Services Integration Act, while establishing a permanent place for women in the military, reserved 98 percent of the positions for men and placed a cap on the term of service and the number of women who could be promoted to the rank of full colonel or Navy captain: One. No woman could become a general or an admiral. As part of their training, women were instructed in how to maintain a "ladylike" appearance, how to apply makeup, and how to get in and out of cars in their tight-fitting uniform skirts. Unlike male military personnel, they had to remain childless—pregnancy was grounds for discharge—and, if married, they had to prove that they were their husbands' primary source of financial support in order to receive dependents' benefits (Stiehm, 1985; Yellin, 2004).

In the late 1960s and throughout the 1970s, a series of events took place that greatly expanded both the number and the roles of female military personnel. First, in 1967, Congress passed Public Law 90-30, which removed the limits on the number of enlisted women and the number of promotions for women officers. In addition, the women's movement was actively promoting the equal integration of women into all areas of life and, with the passage of the Equal Rights Amendment by Congress in 1972, many thought that this would extend to female military personnel as well. Also in 1972, congressional hearings were held on the role of women in the military, and the report that followed encouraged the Defense Department to recruit and utilize women on a more equal basis with men. In 1973, the military draft was replaced by the all-volunteer force, causing worried military planners to turn to the recruitment of women as a means to keep enlistments up. Adding to this were several court cases, such as *Frontiero* v. *Richardson* (1973), in which the Supreme Court, in fairly strong language that we have already quoted, overturned the military's policy of awarding dependents' benefits to female personnel using different standards from those applied to male personnel. Later in a federal court, the Navy's policy of barring women from sea duty was also struck down (*Owens* v. *Brown*, 1978). By 1976, ROTC was accepting women, as were the military academies, and Air Force women joined those in the Army and Navy in having flight schools open to them. Perhaps the most important change, though, occurred one year earlier in 1975, when the Defense Department lifted its ban on parenting for female personnel and made discharge for pregnancy available on a voluntary basis (Stiehm, 1985).

In light of this dramatic turn of events, it is hardly surprising that the number of women who entered our military rose substantially during the 1970s. Between 1972 and 1976, the number of military women tripled; by 1980, it had increased almost fivefold. Most of the increase occurred in the enlisted ranks, which, by 1980, accounted for 87 percent of female military personnel. However, like most men who enlisted, these women rarely stayed for more than one tour of duty, and, in 1980, there were actually fewer women in the higher enlisted ranks (E-8 and above) than in 1972 (Stiehm, 1985).

During the Carter administration, there appeared to be a strong commitment to recruit women for the military, and the president even favored requiring women to register for the military draft when registration was reinstated. Interestingly, despite Ronald Reagan's more "hawkish" attitudes and his support of military buildup, he took a more conservative stance toward women in the military and, shortly after his election, the Defense Department scaled down their recruitment of female enlistees (Quester, 1982).

Following the end of the Cold War and the fall of socialism in the former Soviet Union and Eastern Europe, the Pentagon began to reduce the size of its active-duty troops and closed a number of military bases. Consequently, there was a substantial decrease in active-duty military personnel at all levels during the 1990s. However, a second reason for the shrinkage was that enlistments also declined during the 1990s due in part to the relatively low pay offered by the military and the exceptionally low unemployment rate in the civilian labor market.

The terrorist attacks in the United States on September 11, 2011 were powerful motivators for military enlistment for both men and women. Enthusiasm waned somewhat, though, as the wars in Afghanistan and Iraq intensified. Still, these wars and other conflicts in which the U.S. became involved increased the need for military personnel, and the armed forces began to actively recruit women (Quenqua, 2008) as well as racial and ethnic minorities (Alvarez, 2006). Signing bonuses were added as well as other incentives. These efforts have proven fairly successful. In 2011, for example, women were 14.5 percent of active duty military personnel: 15.9 percent of officers and 14.2 percent of enlisted personnel (U.S. Department of Defense, 2011). And although whites are still a majority of military personnel (64.2 percent), 19.1 percent of active duty military personnel are African American, 9.0 percent are Hispanic, 4.1 percent are Asian American, 1.2 percent are Native American, and 0.2 percent identify as multi-racial (Military Family Resource Center, 2004).

The number of women of color, in particular, has grown dramatically, a fact that has led to some concern that women and minorities, especially women of color, are entering the military in greater numbers not because they freely choose to, but because they are the most economically vulnerable segments of the population, with limited alternative opportunities open to them. The military may be especially appealing to members of these groups because it provides benefits they may have difficulty getting in the society at large, including a steady income, health insurance, education, and job training (Enloe, 1987; Wilkerson, 1991b). However, recent research that examines income and educational background of military recruits does not indicate a greater likelihood for enlistees to come from low-income neighborhoods or to have low educational attainment (Watkins & Sherk, 2008).

With the growth in the proportion of women in the military, the jobs available to them have expanded as well. From the 1970s until 1994, the U.S. military utilized what was called the *risk rule* to determine the military jobs from which women would be barred. For the most part, these were ground combat and combat support jobs that entailed a substantial risk of being killed in action or captured as a prisoner of war. In 1993, then Secretary of Defense Les Aspin, on behalf of the Clinton administration, issued a directive ordering the armed services to permit women to fly aircraft in combat. In 1994, the Air Force and the Navy announced they had female pilots who were combat-ready. Also in 1994, the Army and Marine Corps opened combat support jobs to women, but continued to exclude them from direct combat, such as armor, infantry, and field artillery on the grounds that they lacked the physical strength needed for these jobs, and their presence would disrupt morale (Schmitt, 1994a). Nevertheless, it is estimated that about 90 percent of military posts are now open to women. It was in 1999 during the war in Kosovo that American women flew bombing missions for the first time. More than 10,000 women also now serve as sailors aboard navy warships, and in 2010 the Navy lifted its ban on women serving aboard submarines. The exclusion of women from combat roles has historically had important consequences for female military personnel, since such positions command substantially higher salaries on average than support positions do. They are also critical for promotion to the highest military ranks; in fact, it has been argued that combat exclusion has been women's greatest impediment in achieving promotions, what some have called the "brass ceiling" (Enloe, 1987; Jelinek, 2011; Sciolino, 1990; Swarns, 2008).

Many analysts have argued that the difference between many combat roles and combat support roles is more a matter of semantics than a reflection of the actual danger attached to the positions. For example, before women were permitted to fly combat aircraft, they regularly piloted the tanker aircraft that refuel fighters, making them targets for enemy fire (Lamar, 1988). Women also actively participated in the U.S. invasion of Panama, and, for the first time, a female Army captain commanded U.S. soldiers in combat. In 1990 and 1991, women accounted for more than 10 percent of the military troops deployed in the Persian Gulf crisis. Ironically, in this case, U.S. female military personnel risked their lives (five, in fact, were killed, and two were taken prisoners of war) in defense of a country in which women are afforded few civil rights—where, in fact, they are still considered men's property. But it was women's involvement in the Gulf War that prompted General Charles C. Krulak, Commandant of the Marine Corps, to order in 1995 that training of male and female marines be equalized and to order in 1997 that female marines participate in the seventeen-day combat training program previously required only of male marines (Janofsky, 1997).[8] Women are currently deployed in Iraq and Afghanistan; they are about 11.6 percent of U.S. troops serving in these countries. They have also been among the U.S. casualties in these conflicts; at the start of 2011, 110 U.S. female soldiers had been killed in Iraq (about 2.6 percent of U.S. casualties) and 24 had died in Afghanistan (1.7 percent of U.S. casualties) (Jelinek, 2011). In 2011, the Defense Department Advisory Committee on Women in the Services, recognizing that many female soldiers are already drawn into combat action, recommended that the combat prohibition on military women be lifted, a position that Defense Secretary Robert Gates strongly supported (Jelinek, 2011).

Female soldiers are more likely than male soldiers to be married to someone who is also serving in the military (Bethea, 2007). The deployment of female military personnel to Iraq and Afghanistan has drawn attention to another concern stemming from the increasing number of dual military career couples and single parents on active military duty. With the start of the wars in Iraq and Afghanistan, many couples received deployment orders, typically to different locales, but raising the possibility that both spouses could be killed in combat and their children orphaned. Although no branch of the armed forces deploys mothers of children less than four months of age, parents of very young children are fighting in Iraq and Afghanistan or are in harm's way elsewhere in the world. As a result, the military now requires single parents and dual military career parents to file a family care plan specifying their child care arrangements in the event that both spouses are deployed (Bethea, 2007; Stern, 2001).

Although many within the military and among the general public have praised the Defense Department's greater openness to women in recent years, other observers caution that simply permitting women to hold more military jobs does nothing to address the rampant sexism that continues to plague the military (see also Box 10.1). One of the most serious manifestations of this problem is widespread sexual harassment and abuse of female military personnel. Charges of sexual abuse have increased in all branches of the U.S. military and have prompted investigations at the military academies as well as the Citidel, where 20 percent of female cadets reported having been sexually assaulted in 2005 ("Fifth of Citadel females," 2006; see also Komarow, 2005; Moss, 2003). Research has shown that over 75 percent of women in the military have personally experienced sexual harassment. In one study, more than 50 percent of women veterans reported experiences of unwanted physical contact, about 25 percent report having been assaulted at some point during their military careers, and 19 percent said they had been raped. Moreover, this research indicated that the effects of victimization are long-lasting,

BOX 10.1
Homosexuals in the U.S. Military

On September 20, 2011, the United States government began to allow gays and lesbians to serve openly in the military. Since 1994, the federal government had followed a policy known as "Don't Ask, Don't Tell," that permitted lesbians and gay men to serve in the military as long as they were not open about their sexual orientation and did not engage in homosexual acts. A homosexual act was defined broadly as human contact to satisfy sexual desires between members of the same sex as well as any bodily contact that a reasonable person would see as demonstrating a propensity toward homosexual behavior (such as holding hands with a person of the same sex). Under this policy, men and women who joined the military were no longer asked if they were homosexuals nor were they supposed to be discharged from the military if they admitted to being homosexual. The "Don't Ask, Don't Tell" policy, however, was criticized by many as ineffective in preventing discrimination against and harassment of gay and lesbian servicemen and servicewomen. For example, if military personnel admitted to being homosexual they were still subject to investigation by military officials to determine if they were engaging in homosexual acts. Consequently, "Don't Ask, Don't Tell" basically forced homosexual military personnel to lie about their sexual orientation in order to serve their country.

The repeal of the "Don't Ask, Don't Tell" policy has been applauded by many, including senior military officials and Defense Secretary Robert Gates. But few observers believe that harassment of and discrimination against gays and lesbians in the military will suddenly come to an end. As one gay officer described it, the repeal creates "visible inequalities" for homosexuals in the military (Willon, 2011). For instance, while gay and lesbian military personnel no longer need to hide their intimate relationships, their partners are not eligible for any of the benefits to which the intimate partners of straight military personnel are entitled, including family support services, healthcare, housing, and even shopping privileges at military base commissaries (Willon, 2011). And awareness of the gender-based violence female military personnel have experienced has made gays and lesbians in the military worry that the repeal of "Don't Ask, Don't Tell" makes them easier targets for homophobic hate crimes. Such crimes certainly occurred under "Don't Ask, Don't Tell," even though homosexual military personnel were forced to be closeted. For example, in 1999, an army private, Pfc. Barry Wichell, was murdered by two fellow soldiers in his barracks because they thought he was gay. Soon after the murder, the results of a Pentagon survey of 71,570 military personnel documented a continuing climate of hostility toward gays and lesbians in the military. Eighty percent of survey respondents said they had heard derogatory remarks made about homosexuals, and 37 percent reported having witnessed or experienced an incident of harassment based on sexual orientation (Milloy, 2000). The number of reported anti-homosexual harassment incidents in the military increased from 871 in 2000 to 1,075 in 2001 (Marquis, 2002). Indeed, some observers argued that the controversy generated over the "Don't Ask, Don't Tell" policy actually caused a backlash against homosexuals in the military by focusing attention on them (Marquis, 2002; Shenon, 1997). The effects of the repeal in this regard remain to be seen, although the Pentagon and Defense Department are optimistic given that they report spending months preparing for the repeal by updating regulations and revising training.

with women feeling shame and embarrassment and experiencing symptoms of post-traumatic stress decades after the harassment occurred (Sadler et al., 2001). Most military women who are victimized, however, do not file formal complaints against their harassers because they believe that doing so will jeopardize their careers, causing them to be labeled "troublemakers," which may lead to careful scrutiny of their private lives (Becker, 2001; Moss, 2003). Even when incidents are reported, however, they may not lead to extensive investigation or charges filed against alleged perpetrators. In fact, recent studies have found that trials for accused military assailants are relatively rare and convictions are even more unusual ("Trials rare after charges of sex assault at Annapolis," 2006; see also Becker, 2001; General Accounting Office, 2011; Myers, 2009).

It has been argued that "the changing nature of warfare, which is based on technology rather than brute force, does not justify the exclusion of women" from any aspect of military duty (Rustad, 1982, p. 230). But in light of widespread reports of sexual harassment of women in the military and given the onerous tasks that military personnel are often called on to perform, especially during wartime, some observers wonder whether women's increased participation in the military is a positive development. Should we really want women to fully participate with men in all aspects of the military, including waging war? This question spotlights a feminist dilemma concerning women's and men's involvement in the military. As Rustad (1982, p. 5) phrased it, "Does the inclusion of women in martial roles mean greater opportunities or does it mean only that women will have the same rights as males to perform strenuous, dangerous, and obnoxious tasks?" There are those who maintain that if women want full equality with men, then they must accept the fact that this status entails obligations, including defending their country, as well as privileges. In fact, some people feel that this may be the only way for women to prove that they deserve equality. But opponents of these views emphasize that feminism's goal is not to turn women into men, but rather to establish a new value system in which nurturing instead of aggression is rewarded for both women and men. As political scientist Cynthia Enloe (1993, 2000) argues, an increase in the number of women in the military should not be viewed as a feminist victory. Women in the military are pressured to fit in, to become "one of the boys," which in turn legitimates rather than changes the masculinization of the military (see also Callahan, 2009).

Although it is unlikely that this debate will be settled soon, there are at least two important points that should be kept in mind. The first is that there are some women who wish to participate on an equal footing with men in the military, just as there are men who would welcome the combat exemption that historically was afforded to women. Inasmuch as feminism encourages individuals to exercise control over their lives, one feminist approach to the dilemma is to lobby the government to allow both women and men the right to choose whether they will serve in the military as well as in what capacity they wish to serve.

At the same time, however, feminism does not mean adherence to total relativism. That is, feminists do not need to see every life choice as positive or beneficial simply because some individuals favor it. It is possible to oppose militarism, but also hold that while the military establishment remains a central institution in our society, those women and men who participate in it should have equal roles. While we work to change the masculinization of the military, to end mandatory registration for military service, and to prevent military solutions to international conflicts, we should not make a choice "between our daughters and our sons," a choice that "robs women as well as men. In the long and short run, it injures us all" (quoted in Rustad, 1982, p. 4).

THE POLITICS OF GENDER

The purpose of this chapter was to examine the different political roles and attitudes of men and women primarily in the United States, but in other parts of the world, too. We have seen that women have been neglected in most discussions of government and politics. Denied the right to vote until 1920 and denied equal protection of the laws until the 1970s, American women have long been excluded from the practice of politics on the grounds that they were too stupid, too frail, too emotional, and too irrational.

As we have seen in this chapter, this situation is finally beginning to change. Once it was documented that women are as interested and active in politics as men are and, more significantly, that they are more inclined than men to vote, political analysts and campaign strategists began to sit up and take notice of female constituents and candidates. Differences in the political opinions of men and women received more careful study, and a gender gap on certain issues—economics, social welfare, and foreign policy, in particular—was revealed. Currently, more women are running for and being elected to public office, and more are obtaining political appointments than ever before. Along with White heterosexual women, women and men of color and lesbians and gay men are increasing their numbers in public officeholding and making themselves known as powerful political constituencies. Nevertheless, the percentage of women in general in government decision making and in the military remains small. Even more underrepresented in government are women and men of color and lesbians and gay men. Indeed, it could take many decades longer for parity among these groups to be achieved.

Historically, the exclusion of women as well as other oppressed groups from elected or appointed political and military leadership roles was justified on the ground of Divine will—that it was part of God's plan, in other words, and not "in the nature of things" for members of these groups to have authority over White, heterosexual men. Indeed, in the United States, despite the constitutionally established separation of church and state, sociologists have long recognized that religion and politics are highly interactive. In this chapter we have examined the role of government in perpetuating and often justifying inequality. In the next chapter, we will consider religion's role.

Key Terms

gender gap   differences in the voting patterns and political attitudes of women and men

gladiator activities   the highest level of political activism in Millbrath's typology; includes working on a political campaign, taking an active role in a political party, or running for public office

incumbent   an individual who holds political office and seeks another term

political action committees (PACs)   special-interest groups that dedicate themselves to fundraising and distributing contributions to the political campaigns of candidates who support their cause

spectator activities   the lowest level of political activism in Millbrath's typology; include voting, wearing a campaign button, or displaying a political bumper sticker

transitional activities   the mid-range of political activism in Millbrath's typology; includes writing to public officials, making campaign contributions, and attending rallies or political meetings

Suggested Readings

Boxer, B., Whitney, C., Collins, S., Mikulski, B., Feinstein, D., Snowe, O. J., Hutchinson, K. B., Murray, P., Landrieu, M., & Lincoln, B. L. (2001). *Nine and counting: The women of the Senate.* New York: Harper Trade. The nine women who served in the U.S. Senate during the 106th Congress tell their personal stories. Despite differences in age, political party, and years of involvement in politics, readers will find interesting similarities in these women's professional experiences.

Kuehnast, K., Oudraat, C.D., & Hernes, H. (Eds.) (2011). *Women and war: Power and protection in the 21st century*. Washington, DC: U.S. Institute of Peace Press. A groundbreaking collection of essays that bring women's voices and perspectives into areas from which they have historically been excluded: international relations, foreign policy, and national security.

O'Connor, S. D. (2002). *Lazy B: Growing up on a cattle ranch in the American southwest*. The fascinating autobiography of the first woman appointed to the U.S. Supreme Court. Despite the title, readers will learn a great deal about the barriers professional women faced in the 1940s and 50s—and even more recently.

Yellin, E. (2004). *Our mothers' war: American women at home and at the front during World War II*. New York: Free Press. A historical account of women's involvement in the second world war, both in the military and civilian life.

Notes

1. It is important to note that much of the information available on women's political behavior and opinions dates only to the early 1950s. It was not until 1952 that polltakers began to analyze political opinion data by sex. To gauge women's political activities and opinions, historians and political scientists have relied on other data sources, such as the archives of women's organizations.

2. Women in other countries also report that the prejudice of party leaders, the majority of whom are men, is a significant obstacle for women seeking political office. Of the 418 political parties in eighty-six countries surveyed by the Inter-Parliamentary Union (1997), only 10.8 percent of party leaders were women and only one-third of the positions in the parties' governing bodies were held by women (see also United Nations, 2000).

3. In 1990, Emily's list had only 3,500 members, but membership nearly tripled in just two years. Emily's List supports primarily pro-choice Democratic candidates.

4. In 2011, there were still four states that had never elected a woman to the U.S. Congress: Delaware, Iowa, Mississippi, and Vermont (CAWP, 2011e). Worldwide, by 1997, only nine of the 173 countries with legislatures had no female representatives (Inter-Parliamentary Union, 1997).

5. In 1992, a record number of minority candidates won elections to the U.S. Senate and House. According to political analysts, a major factor in their success was a provision in the Voting Rights Act that required congressional redistricting in the states to more accurately reflect the racial composition of those districts. In 1993, however, the U.S. Supreme Court ruled in a 5–4 decision that such redistricting may be unconstitutional gerrymandering if in effect it denies White voters equal protection of the law (*Shaw* v. *Reno*). The ruling affected redistricting plans nationwide (see, for example, Hicks, 1998).

6. In addition, two women of color served as delegates to the House of Representatives in 2011, one representing the Virgin Islands and the other representing the District of Columbia (CAWP, 2011e).

7. Norway has permitted women in nearly all military roles—except as para-rangers and marine commandos—since 1985. Britain prohibits female military personnel from driving tanks, serving in frontline infantry divisions, serving on submarines, and serving as mine clearance divers. Only four countries besides the United States, in fact, allow female military personnel to serve on submarines: Norway, Australia, Canada, and Spain (CBC News Online, 2006).

8. Until 2002, female military personnel stationed in Saudi Arabia were required to cover their bodies in long black robes and wear head scarves when they went off base. An Air Force Lt. Colonel, Martha McSally, filed a lawsuit to have the requirement rescinded on grounds that it unconstitutionally forced American women to conform to the religious and social customs of others. The Pentagon changed the dress code from being mandatory to being "strongly encouraged." However, it kept in effect both a ban on women driving off base and a requirement that female military personnel be accompanied by a male escort when they leave base. The government did not impose similar restrictions on female diplomats in Saudi Arabia (Sciolino, 2002).

Chapter 11

Gender and Spirituality

There is no doubt that religion or religious teachings play an important part in most people's lives. Consider, for example, that in the United States alone, there are currently more than thirteen hundred different religious denominations, sects, and cults; 83 percent of the population claims to be affiliated with a specific religion, 56 percent say that religion is very important in their lives, 39 percent attend services at least once a week, 58 percent pray at least once a day, and 71 percent believe in God with "absolute certainty" (Pew Forum on Religion and Public Life, hereafter Pew Forum, 2009; see also Dillon & Wink, 2007). Western religious beliefs differ significantly from those held by people in other parts of the world, but regardless of the specific content of religious teachings, religion appears to be a cultural universal. Every known society has some form of religion; archeologists have found what they think are religious artifacts dating back to the earliest cave-dwelling humans.

Why is religion so appealing? The answer lies in the fact that all religions, despite the tremendous variation among them, respond to particular human needs. First, virtually everyone seeks to understand the purpose of their existence as well as events in their lives and environments that seem unexplainable. Religion offers some answers to these puzzles, thus giving meaning to human existence and easing somewhat the psychological discomfort caused by life's uncertainties. Second, religion provides its followers with a sense of belonging, for it is not usually practiced alone, but rather, as the social theorist Emile Durkheim put it, in a "community of believers." And finally, religion lends order to social life by imposing a set of behavioral standards on its adherents. These include both prescriptions and proscriptions for how the faithful are to conduct themselves and relate to others. Importantly, however, religions typically establish different rules and often different rituals for men and women. These differences will be our main focus in this chapter.

Obviously, given the sheer number of religions, it's impossible for us to examine the gendered teachings of all of them. Instead, we will limit our discussion to three of the major religious traditions in the world today: Judaism, Christianity, and Islam. Throughout our discussion, we will find that historically, despite women's often greater religious devotion, the major religious traditions have been overwhelmingly patriarchal, according men higher spiritual status and privileges and frequently legitimating the subordination of women, as well as sexual minorities, various racial and ethnic groups, and members of other religions. Although religion has contributed to the oppression of women and other minorities, religious principles have also inspired many to work for social change as well as spiritual liberation. Therefore, this chapter would not be complete without a look at the efforts of both religious feminists and nonfeminists to influence not only religious attitudes and practices, but also social policies and social structure. Let's begin with a general discussion of the relationship between gender and religion.

GENDER AND RELIGIOSITY

Sociologists use the term **religiosity** to describe an individual or a group's intensity of commitment to a religious belief system. We noted at the outset of this chapter that 83 percent of people in the United States report a formal religious affiliation (Pew Forum, 2009). However, church membership as well as one's level of commitment to a professed religion (i.e., one's religiosity) varies across social groups. Looking at Table 11.1, for example, we find that most people, regardless of sex or race, hold some religious identification. Additional research shows that nearly one in five men claim to have no religious affiliation, but only 14 percent of women are religiously unaffiliated (Pew Forum, 2009). As Table 11.1 shows, though, race and ethnicity separate the religiously affiliated more than sex or age do. Indeed, on nearly all measures, African Americans express higher religiosity than White or Hispanic Americans, although Hispanic Americans also report greater religiosity than white Americans (Pew Forum, 2009).

Religious identification is just one of the ways religiosity can be measured, and some sociologists believe it is not the best way, since simply identifying with a particular religion does not necessarily mean that a person *practices* the religion. Table 11.2 shows differences between women and men on several other measures of religiosity commonly used by sociologists. Here we see that more women than men believe in God with

TABLE 11.1   Religious Identification by Sex, Race/Ethnicity, and Age, United States

	Age (%)				Sex (%)		Ethnicity (%)				
	18–29	30–49	50–64	65+	Male	Female	White	Black	Asian	Other/Mixed	Hispanic
National Total	20	39	25	16	48	52	71	11	3	3	12
Evangelical Churches	17	39	26	19	47	53	81	6	2	4	7
Mainline Churches	14	36	28	23	46	54	91	2	1	3	3
Historically Black Churches	24	36	24	15	40	60	2	92	0	1	4
Catholics	18	41	24	16	46	54	65	2	2	2	29
Mormons	24	42	19	15	44	56	86	3	1	3	7
Orthodox	18	38	27	17	46	54	87	6	2	3	1
Jehovah's Witnesses	21	39	25	14	40	60	48	22	0	5	24
Other Christians	6	35	27	22	46	54	77	11	0	8	4
Jews	20	29	29	22	52	48	95	1	0	2	3
Muslims	29	48	18	5	54	46	37	24	20	15	4
Buddhists	23	40	30	7	53	47	53	4	32	5	6
Hindus	18	58	19	5	61	39	5	1	88	4	2
Other Faiths	26	37	27	10	54	46	80	2	1	13	5
Unaffiliated	31	40	20	8	59	41	73	8	4	4	11

Source: The Pew Forum (2007). *The Pew Forum on Religion & Public Life: U.S. Religious Landscape Survey*. Retrieved from http://religions.pewforum.org/comparisons#.

TABLE 11.2 Gender Differences in Religiousness		
Item	**Women (percent)**	**Men (percent)**
Are affiliated with a religion	86	79
Have absolutely certain belief in a God or universal spirit	77	65
Pray at least daily	66	49
Say religion is very important in their lives	63	49
Have absolutely certain belief in a personal God	58	45
Attend worship services at least weekly	44	34

Source: Pew Forum on Religion and Public Life, 2009.

absolute certainty, say religion is important in their lives, pray at least daily, and attend services at least once a week (Pew Forum, 2009). Other studies show that, throughout their lives, women are consistently more religious than men (Dillon & Wink, 2007; Gallup, 2000; Miller & Hoffman, 1995). Additional research indicates that when race and ethnicity are also taken into account, women of color have especially high levels of religiosity. In the most recent U.S. Religious Landscape Survey (Pew Forum, 2009), 84 percent of black women stated that religion is very important in their lives and 59 percent attend services at least once a week. In fact, "no other group of men or women from any other racial or ethnic background exhibits comparably high levels of religious observance (Pew Forum, 2009, p. 2; see also Collier-Thomas, 2010; Gallup & Castelli, 1989; Gilkes, 1985; Grant, 1986; Lowen, 2011).

Several theories have been offered to explain sex differences in religiosity. One explanation, for instance, maintains that women are more submissive, passive, obedient, and nurturing than men, and these traits are related to high levels of religiosity. Proponents of this theory, however, disagree on at least two major points. One area of disagreement is whether these traits are "natural" or learned (see Chapter 4). A second area of dispute is the nature of the relationship between these personality traits and religiosity: Do these "feminine" traits precede a high level of religiosity and thus, perhaps, cause it, or does religiosity induce people to be more submissive, passive, obedient, and nurturing, regardless of sex? There is research that indicates that men who exhibit these characteristics are, like women, more religious than those who do not exhibit these characteristics, but this research still does not answer the temporal question of which comes first, the personality traits or the high level of religiosity (Sullins, 2006; Thompson, 1991).

A second theory of sex differences in religiosity has focused on the division of labor, specifically women's primary responsibility for family well-being and child care. One version of this theory argues that religious activities such as church attendance, are considered an extension of household responsibilities and, therefore, are more likely engaged in by women. A second version of this theory maintains that women simply have more time for religious activities. However, studies that have tested each version of this theory have obtained inconsistent findings (Civettini & Roth, 2008; Cornwall, 1989; Roth & Kroll, 2007). Clearly, more research is needed not only to clarify sex differences in religiosity, but also to pinpoint the source of these differences (see Miller & Hoffman, 1995; Roth & Kroll, 2007).

BOX 11.1
Imaging God

What does God look like? How you answer this question depends to a large extent on the dominant culture of your society. Most Western Christians and Jews image God as a White male. To envision God as Black or a female seems silly to some, heretical to others. Despite the fact that Jesus was a Middle Easterner and, therefore, probably dark-skinned with dark hair and eyes, he is typically depicted in the United States and other Western societies as White and often blond. Attempts to portray him otherwise are usually met with fierce opposition. In 1996, for example, when the director of a six hundred-year-old religious play to be staged in Canada announced that the part of God would be played by a woman, religious leaders denounced it as "paganism" (McDonald, 1996). So hostile are many White Christians to the idea of a Black Jesus that when, in 1997, a Catholic performing arts center in New Jersey announced that a Black man would portray Jesus in the annual Easter play, the center was flooded with complaints. Ironically, the same actor was also appearing as Lucifer in a play at a nearby theater, and he noted that no one had objected to a Black man playing the devil (McQuiston, 1997). And in 1998, the play "Corpus Christi," which portrays a Christ-like gay hero, provoked so much hate mail that theaters installed metal detectors to screen for weapon-carrying ticket holders (Brantley, 1998).

In many African American churches, we do find statues and portraits of God and Jesus as Black men. A number of denominations have also revised their prayer books and scripture readings to be more gender-inclusive, referring to God not only as Father, but also as "All-Holy Maker" and "She Who Dwells Within" (Cone, 2000; McDonald, 1996). Some women have also begun to pray to God personified as female, and they report a number of positive psychological effects, including spiritual growth, a stronger sense of religious belonging, and improved self-confidence (Christ, 2006; Houts, 2010; Lummis, 1999; McDonald, 1996; Sausy, 1991; Steinfels, 1994). Interestingly, while a majority (42 percent) of people believe God is male, more women (46 percent) than men (37 percent) believe this. Only 1 percent of people (both men and women) believe God is female. Thirty-eight percent (43 percent of men and 33 percent of women) believe God is neither male nor female, while 11 percent (9 percent of men and 12 percent of women) believe God is both male and female (Taylor, 2003).

Although women as a group show higher levels of religiosity than men, there is evidence that at least on some measures, such as church attendance, women's level of religiosity has been declining in recent years (Dinham, 2009; McDonald, 1996). Some analysts believe that this decline reflects in part the growing number of women who say they are alienated from mainstream religions because these religions are male-dominated and image God as male. One of our goals in this chapter is to evaluate this charge, and we begin in Box 11.1 by considering various images of God. As the box shows, most people in Western religions image God as male. There is evidence, though, that in previous historical periods and in other cultures, images of God were feminine or androgynous. Let's briefly examine some of this evidence.

GODDESSES AND WITCHES

Astarte, Anat, Anahita, Asherah, Attoret, Attar, and Au are names few of us recognize today, but each name was intimately familiar to worshippers thousands of years ago. These are a few of the names in different languages and dialects for the Great Goddess, known also as the Queen of Heaven and the Divine Ancestress. Archeologists have discovered relics of worship to her among the cultural remains of peoples as disparate as the ancient Babylonians and pre-Christian Celts, at sites as distant as northern Iraq and southern France, and dating as far back as 25,000 B.C.E. (Carmody, 1989; Gadon, 1989; Odegaard, 2005; Stone, 1976). For example, at sites of what are thought to be "the earliest human-made dwellings on earth" belonging to the Aurignaican mammoth hunters (Upper Paleolithic period), archeologists have found stone, clay, and bone figurines of women they think were the idols of "a great mother cult" (Stone, 1976, p. 13; see Chapter 3). Similarly, among the ruins of later cultures, such as the Catal Huyak who, around 6000 B.C.E., inhabited part of what is now Turkey, excavators have recovered sculptures of women depicted in various life stages and forms, leading them to conclude that one of the principal deities was a goddess who was associated with creativity, fertility, death, and regeneration (Carmody, 1989; Stone, 1976; see Box 3.1). Of course, we must be cautious in interpreting archeological finds, since the artifacts themselves do not prove that there were widespread and flourishing goddess cultures. However, it is the case that representations of goddesses are abundant in sites throughout the world, especially in some of the best preserved Old European caves (Carmody, 1989; Nelson, 2004).

The goddesses we have described so far were associated with fertility and were typically invoked as mother. Researchers who have studied goddess-worshipping societies point out that this demonstrates the high value placed on motherhood in these societies. Even in societies that also worshipped male gods, researchers tell us that female gods were believed to wield as much and often more power than male gods and were ascribed roles and traits, such as wisdom and courage, that only later were typed masculine. "Pre-Christian Celts, for example, worshipped Cerridwen as the Goddess of Intelligence and Knowledge. The Greek Demeter and the Egyptian Isis were lawgivers, wise dispensers of good counsel, and justice. Egypt also celebrated Maat, the Goddess of Cosmic Order, while Mesopotamia's Ishtar was the Prophetess, the Lady of Vision and Directoress of the People" (Carmody, 1989, p. 20; see also Connelly, 2007; Lipson & Brinkley, 2004). In India, Ireland, and Sumer, goddesses were credited with the invention of the alphabet, language, and writing (Carmody, 1989).

Thus, evidence of goddess worship is abundant and convincing, although its significance has been disputed (see, for example, Eller, 2000). It is also unclear why and how male or father-centered religions came to displace it. To explain this change, some theorists draw on the factors that may have originally given rise to matriarchal religions. Matriarchal religions are thought to have emerged out of early humans' concern for survival as well as their desire to explain the generation of life and the phenomenon of death. Significantly, these early peoples did not understand the relationship between sexual intercourse and childbearing and therefore assumed that women were the sole possessors of creative life forces. Women, then, were revered not only as producers of future generations, but also as the primal ancestor. What is more, since women alone were considered parents, children took the maternal name and traced descent along the mother's line. Although these theorists caution us not to romanticize or glorify this period as a golden matriarchal age, there is evidence that the status of women in these early human communities was high (Gimbutas, 1989; Parramore, 2008; Stone, 1976; see Chapter 3).

Researchers speculate that as the male role in reproduction came to be better understood, the appeal of matriarchal religions diminished. Once it was certain that the reproductive process could not take place without the help of a man, the status of the father became significant. But as male generative power increased in value, women's status declined. Women came to be seen merely as the carriers and caretakers of future generations, whereas men provided the generative "seed," making them the true sources of life.

Another explanation of how patriarchal religions supplanted matriarchal ones begins with the observation that female-centered religions were just one of many religious orientations adhered to in ancient societies. Besides monotheistic matriarchal religions, there were polytheistic religions that worshipped male and female deities; other monotheistic religions that worshipped a male deity; and even religions that worshipped the "sacred androgyne," a deity that was simultaneously female and male (Besserman, 2007; Carlin, 2010; Carmody, 1989). It has been argued that the displacement of most of these religious traditions by one that favored the worship of a single male god may have been the result of ongoing political battles among various societies—for example, disputes over land or over who should rightfully rule, as well as military conquests aimed at empire building. The victors in these struggles would, in all likelihood, impose their own standards and traditions—including religious ones—on the vanquished (Christ, 1983; Gimbutas, 1989). Proponents of this theory believe that the goddess cultures were usually pacifistic, which could have made them especially vulnerable to aggression from other societies (Carmody, 1989; Forth, 2009; Gimbutas, 1989).

Regardless of whether both or neither of these theories is correct, it is perhaps more significant that attempts to eradicate the worship of female gods have never been completely successful. For example, researchers have identified a number of female-dominant religions in contemporary societies, including the Umbanda of Brazil, the Zar cult of northern Africa and the Middle East, and the Sande secret societies of Sierra Leone (Ruether, 2010a; Sered, 1994). Hinduism, the third largest religion in the world today in terms of membership, includes worship of female deities as well as deities who change their sex or are transvestites. In fact, Hindu mythology depicts homosexuality and transsexuality in a positive rather than a negative light (Jaffrey, 1996; Bonvillain, 1998). Research also indicates that throughout history, many other groups continued to pay homage to a variety of female deities and spirits, although they were frequently forced to practice their rites and rituals secretly because of violent persecutions by those of the dominant faith (Connelly, 2007; Gimbutas, 1989). During early Christian times, for example, several groups claimed to be the disciples of Christ and wrote their own gospels of Christ's teachings. Among these were the gnostic Christian sects whose practices and beliefs were rich in female symbolism (Christ, 1983; Louth, 2009; Patterson, 2007). Some gnostic groups described God as a divine Dyad: the Primal Father and the Mother of All Things. Others spoke of the Holy Spirit as Mother, or as Wisdom, the female element in God. Women in the gnostic sects also held positions of authority; they were preachers and prophets and even ordained priests (Buckley, 1994; Pagels, 1979; Patterson, 2007). However, other, more patriarchal sects, led by those who eventually established themselves as the Church Fathers, suppressed the gnostics and branded them heretics. Although researchers emphasize that the gnostics were not declared heretical simply because of the high status they accorded women, the practical effect of their suppression was the exclusion of much female symbolism and leadership from what became the recognized Christian Church (Christ, 1983; Patterson, 2007).

Scholars have argued, too, that witchcraft was a carryover of the beliefs and traditions of the Great Goddess religions (Ginzburg, 1991; Pizza & Lewis, 2009). Although today most people associate witchcraft with evil spells and devil worship, the meaning of the word *witch,* "wise one," hints at the truer character of this practice. **Witchcraft** includes naturalistic practices that have religious significance, such as folk magic and medicine, as well as knowledge of farming, ceramics, metallurgy, and astrology. It was popular among plain, rural folk whose survival depended on good crops and healthy livestock. Because of women's long and close association with nature, fertility, and health, most witches were women. Their careful study of nature "enabled them to tame sheep and cattle, to breed wheat and corn from grasses and weeds, to forge ceramics from mud and metal from rock, and to track the movements of the moon, stars and sun" (Starhawk, 1979, p. 261). Appropriately, then, it was the witches who led the annual planting and harvesting celebrations. They also practiced folk magic and medicine, using herbs to cure the sick and relieve pain. Not surprisingly, many people sought their help and looked to them for comfort, especially during the painful process of childbirth. Many women associated with naturalistic healing were also midwives (Ehrenreich & English, 1973; Murphy-Geiss, Rosenfeld, & Foley, 2010; Starhawk, 1979; see Chapter 12).

It appears that witchcraft peacefully coexisted with the established Christian churches for quite some time. Many people, it seems, elected to observe the traditions of both, and there is evidence that country priests were sometimes reprimanded by their superiors for participating in the seasonal "pagan" festivals (Starhawk, 1979). Nevertheless, witchcraft clearly posed a threat to Church authority. Carol Christ (1983) explains:

> The wise woman was summoned at the crises of the life cycle before the priest; she delivered the baby, while the priest was called later to perform the baptism. She was the first called upon to cure illness or treat the dying, while the priest was called in after other remedies had failed, to administer the last rites. Moreover, if the wise woman had knowledge of herbs which could aid or prevent conception or cause abortion, she had a power over the life process which clearly was superior to that of the priest, and which according to official theology made her a rival of God himself. If, moreover, she appealed to pagan deities, some of them probably female, in the performance of divinations or blessings and spells used to promote healing and ward off evil, then it is not difficult to see why she was persecuted by an insecure misogynist Church which could not tolerate rival power, especially the power of women. (pp. 93–94)

Indeed, by the late fifteenth century, the Church had officially declared war on witches. The two Dominican theologians who were put in charge of routing out and prosecuting the witches, Heinrich Kramer and James Sprenger, actively promoted the notion of witchcraft as a satanic cult. They maintained that women were more attracted to witchcraft because they were less intelligent, more impressionable, and more lascivious than men (Christ, 1983).[1] Tragically, in their zeal to rid the world of witches, Catholic and Protestant authorities tortured and killed between one-half million and 9 million people during the fifteenth to eighteenth centuries, about 80 percent of whom were women (Barstow, 1992; Nelson, 1979; Starhawk, 1979).

As we have noted, the worship of female deities continues today in various societies throughout the world. In addition, however, many feminists have revived or developed woman-centered spiritual traditions as part of their effort to make religion more responsive and relevant to female experience. Before we discuss feminist spirituality, however, let's examine the traditional teachings on gender espoused by the predominant patriarchal religions that we identified at the opening of this chapter.

TRADITIONAL RELIGIOUS TEACHINGS ON GENDER

In trying to summarize the gendered teachings of even three major religious traditions, we immediately confront a number of problems. For one thing, although many denominations and sects share a few basic tenets—for instance, all Christians believe Jesus was the Son of God—they tend to diverge considerably when it comes to more specific religious principles and practices, including those that concern appropriate roles for women and men. For instance, the Southern Baptist Convention, the largest Protestant denomination in the United States, takes a conservative stance regarding the proper role of women in religious and social life. In 1998, the Southern Baptist Convention amended its official statement of beliefs for the first time in thirty-five years to state that a wife is of equal worth with her husband before God, but she should "submit graciously" to her husband, assuming her "God-given responsibility to respect her husband and to serve as his 'helper'" (Southern Baptist Convention, "The Baptist Faith and Message," Article XVIII).[2] In contrast, Quaker women have been called the "mothers of feminism," because of their social activism and the leadership roles they have historically held in their religious denomination (Apetrei, 2010; Bacon, 1986). Despite these clear differences, members of both groups are undeniably Christians. Similarly, the rules governing male and female behavior among Orthodox Jews are very different from those adhered to by Reform Jews, as we will see shortly.

We should also keep in mind that the beliefs, attitudes, and practices of individuals who claim membership in a particular religion often are quite diverse. Research, for example, shows that it is inaccurate to assume that all Catholics accept and respond to the official teachings of their church in the same way; Catholics, like those who identify with other religious traditions, are a heterogeneous group (D'Antonio, 2011; Princeton Religion Research Center, 1996; Steinfels, 1996; Tausch et al., 2007).

Our brief discussion in this chapter, therefore, is intended merely as an overview of the general attitudes toward men and women expressed in the teachings of three very broad religious traditions. We cannot address all the fine distinctions among the many sects and denominations that identify with a particular tradition, but we will try to show within each tradition some gradations in attitudes—conservative, moderate, and liberal—with respect to three main topics: (1) appropriate behavior and rituals for the male and female faithful; (2) the regulation of sexuality; and (3) the relative positions of men and women as church leaders or authorities.

Another problem arises, however, in interpreting scriptures and religious teachings. We will find that a single passage of sacred text may be translated or edited to legitimate gender oppression or to promote gender equality. As Virginia Sapiro (1986, p. 191) found, "The same Bible has proven to some people that women and men are equal and should take full leadership roles in religions and society, and it has proven to others that women are inferior, periodically unclean, dangerous, and subordinate to men" (see also Naude, 2004). These contradictions are especially significant given that religious leaders cite scripture or other sacred texts as the source of their authority and as the foundation of church doctrine. Thus, in evaluating a particular religious teaching and the official rationale behind it, we must also consider alternative interpretations of the sacred writings on which church leaders claim it is based. These reinterpretations are often the products of feminist religious scholarship.

With these qualifiers in mind, then, let's examine the gendered teachings of Judaism, Christianity, and Islam.

Judaism

Jewish history spans more than thirty-five hundred years. Throughout much of this period, Jewish women and men have been governed by a set of laws (*halakhah*) spelled out for them in the Talmud. The Talmud, thought to have been compiled around C.E. 200, records the oral interpretations of scripture by ancient rabbis and forms the crux of religious authority for traditional Judaism. However, in response to changing social conditions and political upheavals, such as diaspora and countless persecutions, Jewish leaders over the years have modified and reinterpreted Jewish law. In fact, as Paula Hyman (1979, p. 112) points out, "Much of the strength of the Jewish tradition has derived from its flexibility and responsiveness to the successive challenges of the environments in which it has been destined to live" (see also Adler, 1997; Burstein, 2007).

Contemporary Judaism is largely congregational. That is, "public rituals [are] practiced in local synagogues whose congregations selected a mode of worship and expressed their preference for certain Jewish theological interpretations" (Pratt, 1980, pp. 207–208; see also Kaplan, 2009). There are three major types of congregations: Orthodox, Conservative, and Reform.[3] Orthodox Jews most strictly adhere to the traditional teachings of the Talmud, and we will begin our discussion with them. Then we will see how the teachings and practices of the Conservative and Reform congregations differ.

Orthodox men and women have separate and very clearly defined rights and obligations under Jewish law. Orthodoxy requires that men preserve and carry on Jewish tradition through communal worship and daily prayer at specified times, and especially through religious study. Traditionally, the scholarly and spiritual realms have been reserved for men. Women, in contrast, are exempt from these religious duties (*mitzvot*) on the ground that fulfilling them would interfere with their primary roles as wives, mothers, and homemakers. Women, then, control the domestic realm, where they tend to the needs of their husbands and children. It is essentially because of his wife's household labor that the Orthodox man is free to pursue religious study and to fulfill his other *mitzvot*. Women must also see to it that their children, especially their sons, receive sound religious training. Orthodox women have their own *mitzvot* to fulfill, including separating bread dough in preparation for the Sabbath, lighting the Sabbath and holiday candles, assuring that the dietary laws are followed, and observing the rules of modesty (*tznoit*) and family purity (Carmody, 1989; El-Or, 1993).

Significantly, most Orthodox Jews do not see this separation of roles as the relegation of women to an inherently unequal or inferior status. Rather, Orthodoxy maintains that in preserving the moral purity of their households, women engage in a form of religious expression comparable to that of men, and for this, they are honored and respected both within the tradition and by their husbands and children (Kaufman, 1991). Nevertheless, critics have countered that women's exemptions in effect exclude them from public ritual—"the real heartland of Judaism"—and, therefore, from full participation in the religious community (Goldstein, 2009; Onishi, 1997; Umansky, 1985). Not surprisingly, women are not permitted to be ordained Orthodox rabbis. Besides their exemption from particular *mitzvot,* Orthodox women may not read the Torah during worship or in prayer groups. A woman may not lead a prayer service, and only men can be counted in a *minyan,* the quorum of ten needed to hold a prayer service. Women are not permitted to sing in the Orthodox synagogue, because "the ancient rabbis considered the female voice to be profane" (Pratt, 1980, p. 211), although recently exceptions have been made (see, for example, *Jewish Week*, 2010). *Mehitzah* mandates a seating division between men and women in synagogues; Orthodox women are often seated in the back of the synagogue or in balconies, although this arrangement is considered an improvement over earlier practices whereby women were forced to sit behind a curtain, in a separate room, or even outside the building (Keele, 2010; Neuberger, 1983). In some Orthodox congregations today, women and men simply sit on opposite sides of the synagogue.

Non-Orthodox feminist Jews have been especially critical of the laws governing male-female relations within the Orthodox family. Both women and men are permitted to acquire and inherit property, but wives may not bequeath their property while they are married without their husband's consent. Women may not formally initiate marriage, although once wed they are entitled to adequate support from their husbands (Shapiro, 2010). Perhaps the most disabling laws for women, however, are those regulating divorce and remarriage. Within Orthodoxy, divorce is unilateral: Only a husband may divorce his wife, not vice versa. A woman may institute divorce proceedings by charging her husband with "matrimonial offenses" before the religious court, which, in turn, can pressure the husband to grant his wife a *get* (a religious divorce). However, until the husband grants the *get,* the Orthodox woman is not free to remarry according to Jewish law, even if she has obtained a civil divorce.

Similar restrictions apply to the woman whose husband is "missing, presumed dead." According to Jewish law, an *agunah* (the "forsaken wife") cannot remarry unless a witness testifies to her husband's actual death. Under strict Jewish codes, such a witness must be a male Jew, but it has not been uncommon, especially during wartime and persecutions, for rabbis to make exceptions and accept the testimony of others, such as women, minors, and even non-Jews. Still, if the woman could not muster evidence of any sort, she remained married in the eyes of Orthodox authorities.

Despite these restrictions, however, Jewish law recognizes the rights of both women and men to sexual fulfillment in marriage. Religious scholars, in fact, often contrast what they consider to be a more positive attitude toward sexuality in Judaism with the more negative Christian view that we will discuss shortly. But others have argued that it is in the area of sexuality that the second-class status of women within orthodox Judaism is most pronounced and they typically cite dress codes and the laws of family purity to illustrate this point. For example, regardless of the temperature, Orthodox women are expected to wear long skirts, stockings, sleeves below the elbow, and, if they are married, hats or head scarves. The laws of family purity include the rules of bodily cleanliness that revolve around a woman's menstrual cycle. For a twelve-day period each month, the Orthodox woman is considered impure. During this time, anything the *niddah* (menstruating woman) touches also becomes impure. Consequently, she must be physically segregated from men, and contact with her is permitted only after she has stopped menstruating for seven days and has been ritually purified in a *mikveh* (a special bath) (Keele, 2010; Sontag, 2001).

Orthodox scholars and authorities justify the dress codes and purity laws on a number of grounds: For example, they promote modesty, they protect women's safety and health, they "spiritualize" sexual relations, and they help to "renew a marriage through a

kind of monthly honeymoon" (Webber, 1983, p. 144; see also Keele, 2010). Less sympathetic observers have characterized them as the products of patriarchal religious leaders'
fears and hatred of female sexuality. However, it may surprise you to learn that what
appears to be repressive religious law to non-Orthodox and feminist observers is considered quite liberating in a sense by many Orthodox Jewish women. In her fascinating
study of newly Orthodox Jewish women (or *ba'alot teshuvah*), for example, Kaufman
(1991, p. 8) found that these women valued the family purity laws as well as other halakic prescriptions because such rituals "put them in touch with their own bodies, in control
of their own sexuality, and in a position to value the so-called feminine virtues of nurturance, mutuality, family, and motherhood." Most of the women Kaufman interviewed were
young and well-educated with middle-class, non-Orthodox backgrounds. Prior to their
conversion to Orthodoxy, some had been married, but all had experienced what might
be called the downside of sexual freedom: frequent, casual, uncommitted sexual relationships with men. In Orthodoxy, they told Kaufman, they regained control over their sexuality, they felt an enhanced status as women and as mothers, and they considered the men
in their lives more respectful, supportive, and committed to their relationships.

To some readers, the Orthodox women in Kaufman's (1991) study certainly sound
like feminists. One of her most significant findings was that although the women said
they rejected feminism as antifamily, the way they described their Orthodox lives had a
great deal in common with many of the values espoused by radical feminists. Particularly
interesting are Kaufman's analyses of sex-segregated living under Orthodoxy and of the
mikveh as establishing a "women's community" and rituals that compose a "women's
culture." While Kaufman makes clear that the women who participated in her study defi-
nitely were not radical feminists, her research highlights the importance of attempting to
understand a group's behavior and experiences from the members' own perspective.

In contrast with the women in Kaufman's (1991) study, some Orthodox Jewish
women, especially those who are well-educated and have studied Torah, are less satis-
fied with various *halakic* proscriptions on women's religious participation and have tried
to change them. Most of these women say that their reason for seeking change has nothing to do with gender equality or feminism, but rather with a personal need to enrich
their religious experiences and thus deepen their spirituality. Among the recent changes
are the presence of women lawyers in Orthodox religious courts and women officers on
Orthodox synagogue boards. Some Orthodox women have formed women-only *davening*
(prayer) groups, which, though not technically a *minyan*, bring women together to worship, to sing, and to read the Torah and the rabbinical commentaries in an effort to develop
their own understanding of them (Goodstein, 2000a). Such groups, however, have received
strong negative reactions from many Orthodox rabbis and other members of the congregation. Although women's prayer groups are not in themselves a violation of Orthodox law,
the public reading of Torah by the women is (Onishi, 1997). At times, women's attempts
to pray as men do have been met by violence. For example, in the past women who have
tried to pray at the holy Western Wall in Jerusalem have been physically attacked and
had chairs and benches thrown at them (Shapiro, 1997; see also Onishi, 1997). In 2000,
however, the Israeli Supreme Court ruled that women had the right to hold traditional
services in the area of the wall reserved for them (Greenberg, 2000). As Kaufman (1991,
p. 68) points out, "The inviolability of the Jewish code of law mitigates against the possibility of women challenging a legal system developed, defined, and continuously refined by
males. Moreover, if women are not encouraged or given the opportunities to study the very

texts...from which interpretations of those laws derive, there is no opportunity for them to challenge those laws in a manner the community will perceive as authentic or legitimate, or to develop female leadership" (see also Adler, 1997; Keele, 2010; Roskies, 2010).

Both Reform and Conservative Judaism have opened rabbinical ordination to women.

There are signs, though, that at least in the United States some Orthodox congregations are becoming more gender-inclusive. A few Orthodox synagogues, for instance, recently hired women to assist the rabbis as paid interns, positions previously reserved for young men studying for the rabbinate. While the women perform some of the rabbi's duties, their roles remain fairly limited. Nevertheless, many Orthodox leaders have criticized the hiring of female interns and warn that opening more religious roles to women could eventually lead to a schism in Orthodox Judaism (Goodstein, 1998, 2000a).

Reform Judaism stands in stark contrast to Orthodox Judaism. Reform Judaism was begun in the mid-1800s to make Judaism more "up-to-date." Reform Jews reject the authority of the Talmud and also the Judaic principle that God will send a Messiah to lead the Jews back to the promised land (Johnstone, 1988). They focus on the importance of developing a personal standard of ethics rather than following rabbinic laws. A hallmark of Reform Judaism is its emphasis on gender equality. As early as 1845, Reform Judaism recognized the need for equal and integrated roles for women and men and, by the turn of the century, it had made significant strides toward this goal (Neuberger, 1983; Prell and Weinberg, 2007). The *mehitzah* (seating division) was abolished; women were permitted to sing in synagogue choirs and to be counted in a *minyan*; girls were included in religious education programs and confirmed along with boys; and the prayer book eliminated many of the blatantly sexist prayers, including men's daily thanksgiving that God had not made them women (Goodstein, 2007). The Reform Movement also established many social service and educational organizations in which women and men worked together. Women were even admitted to the rabbinical seminary, although when a woman first sought to become a Reform rabbi in 1922, authorities sternly rejected her (Briggs, 1987; Prell, 2007).

It was not until 1972 that Reform Judaism opened rabbinical ordination to women. Today, there are approximately 830 women rabbis in the United States, and the majority are in Reform congregations. Moreover, in 1990, Reform Judaism's Central Conference of American Rabbis voted to accept sexually active gay men and lesbians into the rabbinate (Goldman, 1990a), and, in 2000, the conference voted to support Reform rabbis who officiate gay and lesbian marriages, saying that same-sex unions are worthy of affirmation and may be officially blessed (Niebuhr, 2000a). Although the resolution states that rabbis are not required to officiate at gay and lesbian weddings if they do not want to, observers note that an increasing number of Reform rabbis are willing to officiate at such ceremonies and recognize them as legitimate Jewish marriages.[4]

The third Jewish denomination, Conservative Judaism, was deliberately established as a middle-of-the-road alternative to Orthodoxy and Reform Judaism. Conservative

Judaism originated in the United States in the 1880s, but gained members in the 1920s and 1930s as it appealed to European Jewish immigrants who had become "Americanized" and wished to "modernize" their worship (such as by praying in English), but did not want to abandon all their religious traditions (Cummings, 1986; B. Martin, 1978). It is understandable, then, that Conservative Judaism has moved more slowly than Reformism toward equality between the sexes.

Early on, Conservatism permitted women and men to sit together during worship, and women were encouraged to participate in the religious education of children and in the care and upkeep of the synagogue itself. Nevertheless, women were excluded from some of the most important parts of worship, including handling and reading the Torah (Pratt, 1980; Umansky, 1985). In 1973, these prohibitions were lifted, and, by the mid-1980s, women were permitted in the Conservative rabbinate (Cummings, 1986; Umansky, 1985). An even more significant step was taken in 1990 when the leadership of the Cantors Assembly, the professional organization of four hundred Conservative Jewish cantors, voted to admit women. Cantors chant liturgy on behalf of the congregation during religious services and so are considered to play a more central role in worship than rabbis, whose job it is to teach and preach (Goldman, 1990b).

Conservative Judaism did not allow the ordination of lesbians and gay men as rabbis until 2006 when the first official decision to allow homosexual rabbis was passed by a representative committee of Conservative rabbis within the Conservative Rabbinical Assemby (Cooperman, 2006). At the same time, however, this body also gave individual synagogues the right to decide whether to accept a gay or lesbian rabbi as the leader of their congregation (Goodstein, 2006). While Conservative Jewish authorities welcome lesbians and gay men as individual members of Conservative congregations, they leave the decisions of whether to hire homosexuals as teachers or youth leaders and whether to bless the celebration of same-sex commitment ceremonies up to individual rabbis in each Conservative synagogue (Goodstein, 2006).

Within Conservative and Reform Judaism, as in other religious congregations, there are many believers who identify themselves as feminists and attempt to integrate their feminist values into their religious practices. For example, Jewish feminists have rediscovered and begun to teach others about the biblical heroines among the Israelites. These include Deborah, who was not only a ruler, judge, priestess, and prophetess, but also a military commander who led the Israelites to victory in a major battle against the Canaanites (Pogrebin, 1992; Weissman, 2010). Jewish feminists are revising old rituals and developing new ones that emphasize the shared humanity and equal participation of women and men. For example, to mark Passover, women now hold Seders where they tell not only the story of Moses leading the Jews out of Egypt, but also the story of his sister Miriam, who saved his life by hiding him in the bullrushes. Some women have revived the ancient holiday of *Rosh Chodesh*, which celebrates the new moon each month (Cohen, 2005; McDonald, 1996). Also important are rituals to solemnize significant stages in a girl's life just as those in boys' lives are solemnized: for example, celebrating a daughter's birth with a special blessing, giving gifts on the occasion of a girl's "redemption," and celebrating the transition from childhood to womanhood through *bat mitzvah* (Carmody, 1989; Fuchs, 2010; Pogrebin, 1992).[5]

We will return to a discussion of feminist religious ritual at the conclusion of this chapter. Now, though, let's look at the gendered teachings of two other major religious traditions: Christianity and Islam.

Christianity

It is not uncommon for Christian church leaders and theologians to cite the teachings of St. Paul when delineating the proper roles of Christian women and men. In one frequently quoted passage, for example, Paul instructs the Christians of Ephesus:

> Let the wives be subject to their husbands as to the Lord; because a husband is head of the wife, just as Christ is head of the Church, being himself savior of the body. But just as the Church is subject to Christ, so also let wives be to their husbands in all things. (Ephesians 5:22–24)

Elsewhere, Paul explains why women must cover their heads at religious gatherings, but men need not:

> A man indeed ought not to cover his head, because he is the image and glory of God. But woman is the glory of man. For man is not from woman, but woman from man. For man was not created for woman, but woman for man. (I Corinthians, 11:7–9; the latter two lines appear to be references to the Genesis creation story)

The sexism in Paul's writings, although hotly debated, is perhaps less important than the fact that they have been repeatedly used by church fathers and Christian theologians to legitimate and even promote the subordination of women. Recall, for example, the amended statement of beliefs of the Southern Baptist Convention that we quoted earlier.[6]

There is considerable evidence that the leadership of the early Christian movement was shared by men and women. Both served as missionaries spreading the "good news of salvation." Both sheltered the persecuted, studied and interpreted scriptures, and prophesied (Carmody, 1989; Kostenberger, 2008; Lummis, 1999; McNamara, 1996; Schussler Fiorenza, 1979). Within the first hundred years, however, an all-male hierarchical structure was firmly in place. Somewhere along the line, it seems, the example and teachings of their first leader, Jesus, were forgotten or ignored. Feminist biblical scholars and theologians emphasize that there is no evidence that Jesus was in any way sexist. Instead, there is considerable evidence that he rejected the sexist norms of the society in which he lived by, for example, holding men and women to the same standard of morality and by not deriding women's nature or their abilities. It appears, in fact, that he related to women as he related to men: as individuals who needed his help, as colleagues, and as friends (Carmody, 1989; Kostenberger, 2008; McNamara, 1996; Patterson, 2007).

The rationale for the decision of male church authorities later to exclude women from leadership roles remains open to speculation. We have already discussed their efforts to suppress gnosticism, which could have been related to it. Soon we will examine some of the more recent arguments in favor of continuing this exclusion. What is clear at this point, however, is the effect of their choice: Women were relegated to a second-class citizenship within Christianity, a status that persists in many Christian denominations to this day.

Within the Christian tradition, both men and women have been characterized in contradictory ways. Men are supposed to be rational, authoritative, and in control, yet they are depicted as weak-willed when confronted with women's feminine charms. Indeed, women have often been portrayed as temptresses—"the devil's gateway" according to one church father—who cause men to sin much the same way Eve supposedly led Adam into the original sin in the Garden of Eden. At the same time, though, the virgin, pure of heart and body, has been extolled by Christianity, as has the good (i.e., docile, modest, and long-suffering) mother. Both are exemplified by Mary, the mother of Jesus, who is said to have been both virgin and mother simultaneously (Kostenberger, 2008; McNamara, 1996).

Such images hint at the Christian church's traditional teachings on sexuality. Historically, sex was discussed as an activity to be avoided if possible, except for the purpose of procreation. Celibacy was regarded by many as a better way of life. For instance, "John Chrysostom, a very influential Eastern father, urged virginity because marriage was only for procreating, the world was already filled [he was writing about C.E. 382], and marriage therefore tended to function as a concession to sin" (Carmody, 1989, p. 171; see also Van Dam, 2008). Similarly, according to Augustine, a highly influential father of the Western church, sexual intercourse was the means by which original sin was transmitted across generations. The Protestant reformers, such as Luther and Calvin, were more temperate in their views of sex. While restricting sex to married couples, they recognized both husbands' and wives' needs for the "medicine for venereal desire," but they warned against "overindulgence" and reminded their followers that women could only attain salvation through childbearing (Carmody, 1989; Roberts, 2007).

Today, Christian teachings on sexuality remain mixed. Virtually all sects and denominations continue to frown on nonmarital sex, although groups within various churches have recommended a more open-minded discussion of sexuality, including homosexuality. For instance, among "mainline" Protestant denominations (considered less theologically conservative than fundamentalist Christian denominations), the Episcopal Church, the United Church of Christ, and the Evangelical Lutheran Church of America permit gay and lesbian clergy members, including those in committed relationships, and they bless same-sex unions, although they do not consider them the same as marriages. The United Methodist Church allows gay and lesbian clergy only if they are celibate, but the Presbyterian Church (U.S.A.) continues to prohibit the ordination of homosexual clergy (Dallas & Heche, 2011; Luo & Capecchi, 2009, Streufert, 2010). Many Christian denominations, though, continue to not only prohibit gays and lesbians from ordained ministry and refuse to recognize same-sex unions, but go further by denouncing homosexuals as, at best, incompatible with Christianity, and at worst, "sinful," "perverse," an "abomination" (Banerjee, 2006a; Russell, 2008). As Box 11.2 shows, such discrimination has led some gay and lesbian evangelical Christians to form their own congregations and religious groups.

Even though a few Protestant churches appear open to reconsidering their official teachings on sexuality, the Catholic Church represents a denomination that has remained steadfastly resistant to change in this area. The Catholic Church, in fact, speaks as one of the most conservative denominations in this regard. It recently reiterated its strong disapproval of homosexuality, calling it a serious "disorder" (see, for example, Adamczyk & Pitt, 2009; Nigro, 2001). Although the Catholic Church has said that parents of homosexuals should love their children, it has also argued that discrimination against homosexuals in the area of adoption, foster care placement, military service, and employment as teachers and coaches is not unjust, and it has directed its bishops to actively oppose any legislation that promotes public acceptance of homosexuality and homosexual relationships (Steinfels, 1992; U.S. Conference of Catholic Bishops, 2010; B. Williams, 1987).

BOX 11.2
Gay *and* Evangelical

There is little doubt that many prominent conservative evangelical Christians are openly hostile, even hateful, toward gay men and lesbians, despite how contradictory such hostility and hatred appear to be to the teachings of Jesus Christ, whom they claim to follow. But suppose one is homosexual, but also an evangelical Christian? Where does one find a spiritual home? Congregations that are accepting of gays and lesbians are likely too theologically liberal for gay and lesbian evangelical Christians, but congregations that share their conservative, fundamentalist theology typically reject openly gay and lesbian members.

The answer for some gay and lesbian evangelical Christians is not to abandon their religious tradition or to find a more liberal congregation that is perhaps a different denomination than the one to which they prefer to belong. Instead, some gay and lesbian evangelical Christians establish their own organizations and religious groups, so they may practice the faith that is important to them, but at the same time remain true to their sexual identity. Such organizations include Evangelicals Concerned, founded in 1975 and currently with branches in various U.S. cities such as New York, Denver, and Seattle, and Soulforce, founded in 1993. There are also Web sites, including Christian-lesbians.com and gaychristian.net; there is even an Internet dating site for gay Christians. And some gay and lesbian Christians hold prayer and Bible study meetings in their own homes (Banerjee, 2006b). The Unity Fellowship Church Movement was founded in Los Angeles in 1982 and now has twelve churches nationwide; it is the only Christian denomination specifically for gay, lesbian, bisexual, and transgender people of color, whom some refer to as a "minority among minorities" (Newman, 2005).

Although most evangelical Christians, even those who are not openly hostile to homosexuals, maintain that one cannot be both an evangelical Christian and a practicing homosexual because the Bible unequivocally condemns homosexuality, homosexual evangelical Christians, not surprisingly, disagree. They, too, cite scripture to support their position that gays and lesbians should be not only accepted, but also welcomed into evangelical Christian churches. They point out, for example, that the Bible should be read as a historical document and understood in the context of the period in which it was written. As such, it does not address long-term committed same-sex relationships or even homosexuality as we know it today (Banerjee, 2006b).

Gay and lesbian evangelical Christians emphasize the critical need for more ministries that reach out to the LGBT community, not to chastise them or try to "convert" them to heterosexuality, but rather to embrace them as fellow Christ-followers. They point out the struggle that LGBT evangelicals have in reconciling their faith and their sexual orientation, especially when many religious leaders are referring to them as "adhorent, immoral, detestable" (Merritt, 2009). Such diatribes have led some gays and lesbians to live a double life in order to remain in their churches to practice the faith they cherish, while others have contemplated or committed suicide, ashamed of their "sinfulness" (Banerjee, 2006b). It is hoped that an increasing number of LGBT evangelical Christian ministries will prevent such tragedies in the future.

In addition to its condemnation of homosexual relationships, the Catholic Church also prohibits the use of artificial contraception and its opposition to abortion is well known. But the Vatican has also voiced objections to artificial insemination and in vitro fertilization, holding that it is "the right of every person to be conceived and to be born within marriage and from marriage" (Congregation for the Doctrine of the Faith, 1987, p. 703; see also Fisher, 2006). Medical intervention is acceptable only when it assists "the conjugal act," not when it replaces it (see, for example, Riding, 1992; Shea, 2003). The Church has also opposed stem cell medical research because such research requires the destruction of human embryos and is, therefore, in the Church's eyes, the willful destruction of human lives (O'Brien, 2011).

The Catholic Church has stood firm in its opposition to the ordination of women to the priesthood, with the Pope saying that the issue is not even open to debate among the faithful (Egan, 2008; Hooper, 2010). Church authorities argue that priests act in the name of Jesus and represent him physically; therefore, they must be men. They also point out that Jesus called twelve men to be his apostles, not twelve women, nor twelve men and women. Proponents of women's ordination to the priesthood counter with evidence that, in fact, many of the disciples of Jesus were women who held central leadership roles in the early Christian church. Junia, for example, is referred to in Romans 16:7 not only as an apostle, but as "outstanding among the apostles," and Phoebe was a missionary coworker with St. Paul (Bieringer, 2010; Egan, 2008). In fact, a commission of biblical scholars appointed by the Pope more than two decades ago concluded that there is no scriptural prohibition of the ordination of women (Steinfels, 1995a). Many U.S. Catholics apparently agree; a 2010 *New York Times* poll found that 59 percent of U.S. Catholics favor the ordination of women to the priesthood, and 39 percent of people who have left the Catholic Church have done so over the way the church treats women (Hanna et al., 2011; see also D'Antonio, 2011; Egan, 2008).

The issue of the ordination of women to the priesthood is without a doubt one of the most divisive issues in the Catholic Church today. Nevertheless, women's ministerial roles within the Catholic Church are increasing, largely as a result of a growing shortage of priests. Between 1980 and 2005, the number of priests in the United States declined by 26 percent, while, at the same time, the number of Catholics increased 29 percent. Over 3,200 Catholic parishes in the United States have no resident priests; many of these parishes are in rural and inner-city areas. Currently, about 80 percent of those doing professional ministry in U.S. Catholic parishes are laypersons and over 75 percent of them are women (Egan, 2008; Goodstein, 2005).

It has become increasingly difficult to recruit young men to the Catholic priesthood. About 75 percent of priests are 60 or older and of the remainder, the majority are at least 50 years old (Goodstein, 2009a). In 1968, about 16,000 men entered Catholic seminaries annually to become priests, but by 2006, the number of new seminarians each year had declined to less than two thousand with about half of them leaving before taking their final vows (Fitzpatrick, 2006; Goodstein, 2009a). Among the top reasons given for the decline in priests is the prohibition against priests marrying and the vow of celibacy they are required to take, neither of which the Catholic Church has been willing to change. Adding to this is the sexual abuse scandal involving Catholic priests. The scandal, which first came to public attention in 2002 in Boston, has since affected nearly every Catholic diocese in the United States as well as many abroad. Between 1950 and 2004, it is estimated that over nine thousand children and adolescents, most of them boys, were molested by priests; by 2004, about 4 percent of all Catholic priests had been accused of molestation (U.S. Conference of Catholic Bishops, 2004). Throughout much of this fifty-four-year period, the Church's response to the accusations was to send the accused priests for counseling and then to reassign them to a different parish. Not surprisingly, the priests typically reoffended in their new parishes.[7] Since 2004, the Church's response has been to remove accused priests from active ministry and, if the evidence is sufficient, to defrock them. At the same time, victims have successfully sued the dioceses and have been awarded cash settlements.

Unlike the Catholic Church, virtually all the Protestant churches now ordain women to their ministries (Niebuhr, 2000c; Weaver, 1995). In 1989, the Episcopal Church consecrated its first female bishop, Barbara C. Harris, despite strong opposition from some Episcopal Church leaders, and, in 1996, the World Methodist Council chose Frances Alguire as its first female and lay leader. The number of women priests and ministers in Protestant denominations has grown steadily since the early 1970s, and the number of women enrolled in seminaries and divinity schools has also increased. In fact, women make up a higher proportion of seminary students than their representation among clergy positions in congregations would suggest: 30 percent nationally and up to 50 percent in some denominations (Adams, 2007).

Nevertheless, women ministers still confront sexism in their churches and denominations. They often experience discrimination in access to leadership positions, ministerial assignments and responsibilities, and salary, even if they have higher degrees and more seminary training than most male ministers (Briggs, 1987; Jacquet, 1988; Lummis, 1999; Zoba & Lee, 1996). According to recent research, women and men usually obtain similar positions in the first few years after ordination, but within twenty years of ordination, 70 percent of men are leading medium or large congregations, whereas only about 37 percent of women are leading medium to large congregations (Carroll & McMillan, 2006). In fact, according to some observers, it is easier for a woman to get elected as a bishop than to lead a large congregation where the average Sunday attendance is 350 people or more. They explain that churchgoers continue to have difficulty seeing women as religious authority figures and express a strong preference for a pastor who is a young married man with children (Banerjee, 2006c). Even in mainline Protestant churches that have been ordaining women for many years, women make up only about 3 percent of pastors leading large congregations. Many of the conservative evangelical denominations, such as the Southern Baptist Convention, do not permit women to be pastors.[8] These gender disparities have led some observers to argue that women clergy encounter a "stained glass ceiling" within their churches. Although some women clergy are breaking through this ceiling (see, for example, Adams, 2007), most are finding that it is thicker, more opaque, and less permeable than the glass ceiling encountered by lay working women (Adams, 2007; Banerjee, 2006c; see Chapter 8).

The inequality that has historically characterized most Christian denominations leads one to wonder how church leaders can reconcile this discrimination with their professed concern for social justice. It has also caused many believers to question the relevance of organized Christianity to their own lives and to the contemporary world (Keller et al., 2006; McDonald, 1996; Vision, 2020, 2011; Welch, 1985; Wynn, 2005). Consequently, some have abandoned the Christian faith altogether or at least have stopped practicing their religion in any formal sense (see, for example, D'Antonio, 2011; Hanna et al., 2011; Hout & Greeley, 1987). But, as we have noted, other church members have chosen to stay and work for change from within their religious institutions by challenging church teachings and "depatriarchalizing" religious language, symbols, and ritual. This latter group, of course, includes Christian feminists (Lummis, 1999).

One of the most significant innovations of Christian feminism has been the establishment of the **Women-Church movement**, a coalition of feminist faith-sharing groups, which, although ecumenical, is composed largely of Roman Catholic women. Women-Church offers a feminist critique of traditional Christianity while providing members with alternative, woman-centered rituals and forms of worship (Anderson & Hopkins, 1991; Farrell, 1992; Hunt, 1991; McPhillips, 1993; Stein, 2004). For example, there are liturgies for the celebration of stages or milestones in a woman's life. And, like all religions, Women-Church practices rites of repentance and forgiveness, but Women-Church members also pray that patriarchal church members will repent from the sins they commit against women (Ruether, 1988, 2010b).

In addition to the woman-centered aspects of its rituals, Women-Church appeals to many Christian feminists because of its nonhierarchical organization and its emphasis on identifying with and serving all oppressed people in a "discipleship of equals" (Haardt, 2004; Hunt, 1991; McPhillips, 1993; Schussler Fiorenza, 1983). Nevertheless, Women-Church has been criticized from within for being predominantly White and middle class and for failing to incorporate religious forms of worship valued by women of color (Alexander, 2009; Collier-Thomas, 2010; Erikson, 1992; Hunt, 1991). Women-Church has also disappointed some early supporters who feel that it has not had as great an effect on traditional religious traditions and hierarchy as they had hoped it would (Erikson, 1992).

We will come back to the topic of feminist spirituality shortly. First, let's examine the gendered teachings and practices of one other world religion, Islam.

Islam

Islam, which means submission to Allah (God), is the second largest religion in the world in terms of membership—Christianity is the largest—but it is the world's fastest-growing religion, adding twenty-five million new members each year; it is projected that by 2050 it will grow by more than 87 percent (Marty & Appleby, 1992; World Christian Database, 2009). More than 1.3 million Muslims live in the United States (U.S. Department of Commerce, Bureau of the Census, 2011). Islam was founded by the prophet Muhammad. Muhammad was born in Mecca (now the capital of Saudi Arabia), but fled to Medina around C.E. 622. There he gathered followers and established himself as a powerful religious leader before returning to conquer Mecca in C.E. 630.

Muhammad is said to have received over the course of his lifetime a series of revelations from Allah, which he in turn passed on to his followers in the form of rules of behavior. These are compiled in the **Qur'an** (Koran) that Muslims accept literally as the word of God. Muhammad's teachings and those of his immediate successors are recorded in the *Hadith*, which, along with the Qur'an, serves as the basis for *shari a* (Islamic law). Taken together, these sources constitute a religious framework that governs every aspect of Muslims' daily lives, including interactions between women and men. Indeed, 80 percent of the Qur'an is devoted to prescriptive and proscriptive verses concerning proper relations between the sexes (Engineer, 1992; Haddad, 1985; Mattson & Loeffelholz, 2008).

It is clear that Islam radically altered male-female relations, although whether for better or for worse is a point still disputed by religious scholars. It appears that in the days of Muhammad, a variety of sociosexual arrangements coexisted. Some groups were decidedly patriarchal, valuing males above females (female infanticide was common) and allowing men as many wives as they could buy or steal regardless of the women's consent or the men's ability to support them (Ali, 2006; Barazangi, 2004; Carmody, 1989). Within other groups, however, women enjoyed considerable independence and practiced polyandry (had more than one husband). By the seventh century, there was movement away from gender equality among even some of these groups, particularly the ones in Mecca, as commercial expansion provided increasing contacts with northern societies whose religions (Judaism and Christianity) were already strongly patriarchal. Islam, some scholars maintain, consolidated this trend toward patriarchy, although Muhammad did not totally divest women of their rights (Ahmed, 1986; Ali, 2006; Barazangi, 2004; Engineer, 1992; Hekmat, 1997).

Muhammad declared that a woman's consent had to be obtained before a marriage and that she be paid the brideprice instead of her father. He also recognized women's conjugal rights, their rights to ownership of their jewelry and earnings, their right to initiate divorce, and their right to inheritance (although their share was half that of male heirs). Women, like men, were expected to adhere to the Five Pillars of Islam, which include prayer five times a day and fasting during the holy month called *Ramadan*, and they worshipped with men in the mosques (Engineer, 1992, 2004; Hekmat, 1997; Roald, 2001).

Muhammad permitted men to have more than one wife, imposing a generous limit of four as long as they could be supported. He opposed female infanticide, but gave men unconditional custody rights to their children (boys at age two, girls at age seven). Moreover, despite the Qur'an's verses on the centrality of justice and the equal worth of all human beings, it declares men to be women's "guardians" and "a degree above" them (Ahmed, 1986, pp. 678–679; see also Al-Hashimi, 2010). A wife's duties include obedience to her husband (Al-Hashimi, 2010; Higgins, 1985). According to the Qur'an, "Men are in charge of women because God has made one to excel over the other and because they spend their wealth" [referring to men's financial support of women] (quoted in Haddad, 1985, p. 294). Unfortunately, Muhammad's successors took these words to heart and used them to justify the suspension of many rights the prophet had allowed women, so that "by the second and third centuries of Islam, 'the seclusion and degradation of women had progressed beyond anything known in the first decades of Islam'" (Ahmed, 1986, p. 690; see also Al-Hashimi, 2010; Hekmat, 1997).

Today, many Islamic leaders maintain that men and women hold equal status, although they are quick to emphasize that this equality does not derive from sharing the same privileges and responsibilities, but rather from the *complementarity* of their roles. "In this world view men and women are equal before God, but they have somewhat different physical, mental, and emotional qualities, somewhat different responsibilities in the family and society, and therefore somewhat different rights and prerogatives" (Higgins, 1985, p. 491; see also Al-Hashimi, 2010).

In Islamic societies today, men are the undisputed head of both the sacred and secular realms, including the household. Theirs is the public sphere where they conduct religious and worldly affairs and assume a variety of roles with few restrictions. In orthodox Islamic societies, women are largely confined to the private sphere, the home, but even there they are not in charge. Their duties are to serve their husbands, to keep house, to bear many children, and to instruct the children in the ways of Islam. "Not only is [the Muslim woman] created to be pregnant [she is an "envelope for conception" according to one Islamic leader], but more specifically all her roles are defined by her relations to the men in her life" (Haddad, 1985, p. 286; see also Al-Hashimi, 2010). Prior to marriage, the Muslim woman is under the control of her father, brothers, and other male relatives. Her marriage is arranged for her, usually by these men, and she may be married while in her early teens to a man she has never met or has met only briefly in the presence of her male relatives, since Islamic law forbids any public contact between unmarried women and men (Islam Principles, 2008; Kinzer, 1997; Klinkhammer, 2010).

Islamic law imposes a number of restrictions on men's behavior—for example, they may not drink alcohol or gamble, and they must dress modestly—but men are given considerably more freedom than women are. Because men are thought to have a voracious sexual appetite and so are susceptible to corruption if their interactions with women are unregulated, extraordinary measures (by Western standards at least) are taken to prevent women from tempting men, making women responsible for controlling or managing men's sexuality (Read & Bartowski, 2000). Men and women are segregated, not only in the mosques, but in most areas of social life, including at home, where, if finances allow, men and women have different rooms for relaxing, watching television, and socializing with friends and relatives of the same sex. Women adhere to *purdah*, the practice in traditional Islamic societies of severely restricting women's access to public life by secluding them in their homes and permitting them to venture out only in cases of emergency or out of necessity.

In Islamic societies, such as Saudi Arabia, women are prohibited from traveling alone and must be accompanied by their fathers, brothers, or a close male relative, unless they have written permission from one of these individuals that states they may travel alone (Hekmat, 1997; Kingslave, 2011; Zoepf, 2008). When a Muslim woman appears in public, she must dress modestly, that is, veiled (in some societies with only a headscarf or *hijab*, which fits snugly around the face and covers the hair, ears, and neck, while in other societies the entire head and face are covered) and clothed in a loose-fitting garment (variously referred to as a *chador* or *abaya*) that covers her body completely so that no skin is exposed. Although the reasons for veiling are today disputed among some Muslims, it has been argued that, originally, such restrictions were imposed only on Muhammad's wives, but after his death they were extended to all Muslim women, a practice that continues in most Islamic societies today (Meneley, 2008; Sciolino, 1997). Official penalties for violating the dress code can be very serious, depending on the offense and the society in which it took place. Punishments range from reprimands to jail time to beatings (Sciolino, 1997).[9]

Of course, in all but the most traditional Islamic societies today, there are many women who go to school or work outside the home. Nevertheless, every effort is made to insure that they do not mingle with the opposite sex—that they are, in effect, invisible to men. There are female physicians, for instance, but they treat only female patients, just as female teachers instruct only female students. If a male teacher must instruct female students, he does so from behind a screen where he stations himself before the women enter the classroom (Al-Munajjid, 2011; Darrow, 1985; Sciolino, 1997). In Saudi Arabia, all banks have women's branches where only female tellers and lending officers work and attend to an all-female clientele, and there are women-only gyms, boutiques, travel agencies, sections of cafes and restaurants, and a women-only shopping mall (Goodwin, 1994; Sachs, 2000a; Zoepf, 2008). Women are also excluded from or segregated in the mosques; they may be required to pray in separate rows behind the men or in other rooms where they listen to a broadcast of the imam's sermon. They are also excluded from most religious rituals, although most women make regular visits to the sanctuaries of Islamic saints where men, though permitted, rarely go (Goodwin, 1994; Joseph et al., 2005; Mernissi, 1977). Muslim women in the United States, however, often take a more active role in their mosques, developing educational programs for children and raising money for missionary work (Elliott, 2005; Joseph & Najmabadi, 2005; Lummis, 1999), but they are not permitted to lead prayer and in about 65 percent of U.S. mosques, they pray behind partitions or in rooms separately from men (Elliott, 2005).

The level of orthodoxy practiced by Muslims does vary by country as well as by sect. Furthermore, Islamic countries and Muslim women and men have not been untouched by feminism, although for many it is a feminism developed in the context of deeply valued religious beliefs and does not mirror Western feminism (Artyk, 2008; Barlas, 2004; Cooke, 2000; Fernea, 1998; Mir-Hosseini, 1999; Moghissi, 1999; Tavernise, 2009). Small groups of Muslim women have organized to obtain more rights and freedom, including more job opportunities, the right to study the Qur'an and lead prayer at the mosque, and especially, greater equality under family law (Barlas, 2004; Elliott, 2005). In most Islamic societies, for example, women may be beaten by their husbands without legal recourse. Muslim women usually do not have the right to initiate divorce, although their husbands may divorce them simply by repudiating them, and fathers typically receive sole custody of their children after a divorce (Esposito & DeLong-Bas, 2001; Hekmat, 1997; Mydans, 1996; Sciolino, 1997). Under Islamic law, a woman who wishes to divorce her husband must prove to the court that he beats her, he is a drug addict, he is sterile, or he does not support the family. However, even in such cases, judges often discount the women's complaints. In addition, in cases when a divorce is granted, the husband may appeal the decree indefinitely, and many do so for ten years or more as a way to punish or control their wives (Sachs, 2000b).

Despite efforts by Islamic feminists to improve women's status and opportunities, the revolutions that have occurred recently in many Islamic countries have typically meant a return to orthodox practices after an interlude of modernization (Artyk, 2008; Moghissi, 1999). Interestingly, while some women and men, especially the young and well-educated, have expressed their displeasure over this renewed orthodoxy, there has not been widespread resistance among the majority of the countries' populations. Many women, in fact, have donned the veil and *chador* or *abaya* with a willingness that puzzles many Western observers. Ironically, however, it appears that they are motivated by many of the same factors that prompted the women in Kaufman's (1991) study that we discussed earlier to convert to Orthodox Judaism. More specifically, many Muslim women explain their openness to orthodoxy in terms of institutional protection. A veiled woman is recognized by all as religiously devout and off limits to men. She may go about her business without fear of being molested or harassed; she feels safe (El-Guindi, 1999; Read & Bartowski, 2000; Zoepf, 2006).

It is also the case that for some women, donning the veil and *chador* or *abaya* is a political statement, an expression not just of religious devotion, but of militancy, rebellion, and protest against oppressive political regimes, secularism, and Western imperialism in their countries (Afshar, 1993; Ahmed, 1992; Artyk, 2008; El Guindi, 1999; Kinzer, 1998; Read & Bartowski, 2000). To these women, the enemy is not male oppression, but rather outside forces that threaten to destroy the Islamic way of life. Through their devotion to Islam, as evidenced by their adherence to its laws and customs, some Muslim women see themselves on the front lines of the revolution (Artyk, 2008; Zoepf, 2006; however, see also Gole, 1996; Moghissi, 1999; Ruitenberg, 2006).

In some ways, then, the conservative politicization of Islamic women gives them more in common with Orthodox Jewish women and conservative American Christian women than would at first be thought (Gerami, 1996). Each of these groups embraces religious **fundamentalism**, a religious orientation that denounces secular modernity and attempts to restore traditional spirituality through selective retrieval of doctrines, beliefs, and practices from a sacred past (Antoun, 2008; Marty, 1992). These groups have a particular vision of how their society should be structured and women's distinct place within that structure—a vision shaped by their religious beliefs. Jewish, Christian, and Islamic fundamentalists integrate their religious beliefs into political activity in an effort to make their vision a reality. Let's consider this issue further by discussing the intersection of religious and political activism.

RELIGION, POLITICS, AND SOCIAL CHANGE

As we noted at the conclusion of Chapter 10, theoretically at least, the church and the government in the United States are supposed to constitute separate spheres of influence. Yet, sociologists have long recognized that the ideology of the separation of church and state is largely a myth. In practice, the affairs of the state and the interests of organized religion are closely and intricately intertwined. Historians tell us, for example, that Christian fundamentalists or "evangelicals" as they are sometimes called, were active in the American Revolution, the abolitionist movement, the campaign for prison reform in the late 1700s, and a number of other political causes and social reforms (Balmer, 1999; Marsden, 2006).

Today, evangelicals remain politically active. Many observers associate evangelical Christian political and social activism with what has been called the religious "right." It is estimated that the religious right has more than forty million members, which, although small relative to the total U.S. population, is still a sizable number. The religious right in the United States is made up largely of fundamentalist Christians.

Fundamentalist Christians interpret the Bible literally, taking it to be truly God's word. The Bible, to fundamentalists, not only teaches religious doctrine and moral principles, but also renders an accurate account of history and science (Ammerman, 1991; Mazza, 2009). A true believer unquestioningly accepts what is written in the Bible as Truth (Marty & Appleby, 1992; Mazza, 2009). At the same time, fundamentalist Christians believe that a person can only attain eternal salvation by living in accordance with the teachings of the Bible and thus developing a personal relationship with Jesus Christ. They also believe that it is their responsibility to "save" or "rescue" others by evangelizing— that is, zealously preaching God's word—through books, television and radio broadcasts, the Internet, door-to-door canvassing, and political lobbying (Ammerman, 1991; Stone, 2007). Fundamentalist church leaders exhort their congregations to be "soldiers of Christ" by combating the erosion of Christian values in the secular world. At the core of this erosion are feminism, the homosexual rights movement, and other liberal political and social movements (Gallagher & Smith, 1999; Klatch, 1988; Niebuhr, 2000c).

Not surprisingly, therefore, the fundamentalist Christian churches, along with other conservative Christian groups such as the predominantly Catholic Right to Life Movement, have been at the forefront of political opposition to feminist-supported policies and programs that they see as eroding morality and as antithetical to "family values." For instance, they lobbied aggressively and successfully against the Equal Rights Amendment, and they spearheaded campaigns to remove feminist and other types of "objectionable" books and materials from school libraries and classrooms. Since 1973, they have lobbied Congress for a Human Life Amendment that would overturn *Roe* v. *Wade*, once again outlawing abortion. They have also spearheaded congressional lobbying for passage of the Defense of Marriage Act (see Chapter 7). They believe that feminists, gays and lesbians, and other "political liberals" undermine the Christian family by promoting lifestyles and values inimical to "God's plan" for men and women. More specifically, they define marriage as a sacred union that can only be entered by a man and a woman. They adhere strongly to the belief that a man's role is to provide for and protect his family. In contrast, God's plan for women puts them at home caring for their husbands and children, and just as men are subordinate to God, so are women subordinate to men (Abbott, 2006; Gallagher & Smith, 1999).

The religious right has shown itself to be well-organized, persuasive, and resilient, having withstood a number of sexual and financial scandals involving church leaders. But not all evangelical Christian social activists support causes associated with the religious right. In fact, research shows a great deal of diversity among people who identify themselves as evangelical Christians, some of whom are actively involved in what are considered progressive social movements (Smith, 1996; see also Box 11.2). International Justice Mission, for example, is an evangelical Christian organization, headquartered in Washington, DC, that fights human trafficking throughout the world and promotes the notion of "right to life" to include improving the quality of life for people already born, but living as modern-day slaves.

Indeed, for some groups of people, religiously based social movements and religious teachings have been sources of inspiration and strength in their struggles to overcome discrimination and to secure equal rights and opportunities (Stanczak, 2006). One such group, for example, is made up of Christian members of religious orders and lay women and men who have made liberation theology part of their core religious belief system. *Liberation theology* merges the religious teachings and social functions of the Christian church with a critical analysis of the historical and contemporary experience of human suffering. It originated in Latin America during the 1960s when Catholic clergy there declared that the inhumane treatment of millions of people was not a product of fate, but a willful act of the powerful against the powerless. And because such behavior goes against the teachings of Christ, it should be addressed not simply through prayer, but through social activism (Batstone, 1994; Rowland, 2007). In Latin America, adherents to liberation theology have sometimes paid a high price for their commitment: Many have "disappeared" or been killed by government authorities, including the nuns and priests who have led the movement. Nevertheless, the violence has not stopped liberation theology from spreading beyond Latin America to other oppressed communities in the world, including those in the United States where the needs of poor women and men, especially immigrants, are addressed through neighborhood and community ministries that provide various social services such as legal aid (Hondagneu-Sotelo, 2008).

The Black churches have also produced many prominent and influential political leaders and social activists, such as the late Rev. Martin Luther King, Jr., and the late Rev. Leon Sullivan. A number of Black politicians were first ministers in Black churches: the Rev. Jesse Jackson, for instance. The Black churches, in particular, have provided an organizational center within the Black community where members can develop programs of action to overcome racial oppression; the Rev. King's strategy of nonviolent civil disobedience and direct action is an example (Lincoln & Mamiya, 1990).

Even before the Rev. King's leadership, however, the Black churches were centers of social and political activism for women of color. As we noted earlier, for example, women have been the majority of members of many Black churches (Collier-Thomas, 2010; Gilkes, 1985; Grant, 1986; Keller et al., 2006; Lummis, 1999). As historian Evelyn Brooks Higginbotham (1993) has documented, African American churchwomen's activities have long been a means by which they nurtured the survival of their communities, articulated a group consciousness, and organized resistance to oppression. Hunt (1991, p. 32) refers to their "holy boldness" as religious agents in their community churches, and Natividad (1992) even attributes the contemporary predominance of African American women in politics relative to other women of color to their long-term experiences as community and church leaders (see also Lindley, 1996; Prestage, 1991; Stanley, 2004).

Historically, women have been the majority of members of many Black churches, but they are underrepresented in leadership roles in their congregations.

Despite their membership numbers, their level of church participation and their strong support of their churches, Black women have encountered sexism and considerable resistance from Black male church leaders as they assume leadership roles within the church. Among Black female clergy, there appears to be some optimism that this situation will improve over the next several decades. For one thing, more Black women say they are called to careers in ministry. The number of Black women in seminaries nearly doubled during the first half of the 1990s. In the United States, just 8.2 percent of students enrolled in theological schools are Black, but 49 percent of Black students are women (Association of Theological Schools, 2010).

Minority churchwomen have been reluctant to identify their activities and concerns as feminist, since they generally see feminism as a White, middle-class women's movement (Briggs, 1987; Collier-Thomas, 2010; see also Chapter 1). Nevertheless, feminist theologians of color have often joined with White feminist theologians in critiquing the sexism and heterosexism of the dominant religious traditions and in working to depatriarchalize these religions. To conclude our discussion, then, let's look at some of their efforts.

CHALLENGES TO RELIGIOUS PATRIARCHY: FEMINIST SPIRITUALITY

It is really inaccurate to speak of **feminist spirituality** in the singular or to depict it as a unified religious movement, for within it one hears a plurality of voices professing different beliefs and advocating different strategies for change and reconstruction. Yet there are some common themes that feminist spiritualists share. Perhaps the most important theme that runs throughout feminist spirituality is the rejection of the *dualism* of patriarchal religions. That is, the major patriarchal religious traditions separate God and the world, the sacred and the profane, spirit and body (or nature), viewing them as distinct and placing human beings in tension between them. According to feminists, "This [dualistic model] is a model for domination, because [it divides reality] into two levels, one superior and one inferior" (Christ & Plaskow, 1979, p. 5; see also Erikson, 1993; Wilson, 2010). In contrast, feminists emphasize the unity of spirit and nature and see *experience* as the source of spirituality. Experience includes the events of the life cycle (e.g., menarche, coupling or marriage, parenthood, menopause, and so on) as well as developing an awareness of one's location in the social structure: recognizing oppression, confronting it, and acting to bring about liberation (Alcoff, 2011; Anderson & Hopkins, 1991; Eller, 1991; McPhillips, 1993; Ruether, 1988). One of the goals of feminist spirituality is to *resacralize* (define as sacred) the ordinary, what has been defined as profane by patriarchal religious traditions (Du, 2002; McPhillips, 1993). It is over the issue of how to implement this principle, however, that feminist spiritualists part company with one another.

There are those who feel that the Judeo-Christian traditions and other patriarchal religions are so hopelessly mired in sexism that they have abandoned these religions altogether. Instead, some feminists have turned to nature (see Box 11.3), others are reviving the practice of witchcraft, and still others are rediscovering the ancient prebiblical goddess traditions (Connelly, 2007; Reid-Bowen, 2007). In fact, these ancient spiritual traditions are becoming so popular that the travel industry has begun offering pilgrimages to the shrines of ancient goddesses, and *Publisher's Weekly,* which monitors the publishing industry, reports that books on women's spirituality make up one of the fastest-growing segments of the market (McDonald, 1996).

While some feminist spiritualists advocate a complete break with men and all that is male-identified (e.g., Braude, 2001; Daly, 1978, 1984), many welcome both women and men into their traditions on the ground that patriarchal religions may oppress members of both sexes, for example, through heterosexism, racism, and class bias. From this perspective, women's experiences may provide the foundation for a feminist spirituality; however, simply substituting female religious supremacy for male religious supremacy offers little potential for liberation for members of either sex (Anderson & Hopkins, 1991; Erikson, 1992; Seidler, 2009).

As we have noted throughout this chapter, however, not all feminists are completely disenchanted with the Judeo-Christian and Islamic traditions. Some, often called "reformers," have chosen instead to challenge patriarchal religious forms and to reclaim Judeo-Christian and Islamic history, language, symbols, and ritual as their own (Abu-Lughod, 2002; Crossette, 1996; McDonald, 1996; Vatuk, 2008). To them, Judaism, Christianity, and Islam contain "the seeds of [their] own renewal" and, more importantly, "these feminists believe that the church [and synagogue and mosque are] *worth* renewing" (Weidman, 1984, p. 2, author's emphasis).

The first challenge that feminist reformers face is to *rename* the elements of their religions so that they speak to women as well as to men (Chopp, 1989; Ra Mer Christensen et al., 2009). At the most basic level, this means divesting God-talk and religious symbolism of its he/man qualities by, for example, depicting the deity as both female and male, referring to God as She or Mother, or using gender-inclusive or gender-neutral language such as Mother and Father or simply Holy One.

Once God is no longer imaged solely as male, the next step is to rediscover women's contributions to religious heritage by critically rereading scriptures and sacred texts and examining other available evidence. From such careful study, for instance, we now know of the wealth of feminine imagery in the Old Testament and of the many ancient Hebrew heroines, wisewomen, and religious leaders; we have already mentioned Deborah, but there was also Vashti, Esther, Huldah, and Beruriah to name just a few examples (Haley Barton & Hybels, 2007; Pogrebin, 1992; Zaeske, 2000). We also noted Jesus' female disciples and their central leadership roles in the early Christian church. Feminist Islamic scholars have also begun reinterpreting sacred texts, arguing on the basis of their research that the Qur'an does not dictate a patriarchal society; rather, it has been interpretations of the Qur'an by patriarchal men that have produced such dictates (Artyk, 2008; Crossette, 1996; Haley Barton, 2007).

In addition to renaming and rediscovering, feminist reformers are restructuring religious ritual so that it is relevant to women as well as men. Jewish feminists, in particular, have been active in developing women's services and ceremonies for the Sabbath, Haggadah, Rosh Hodesh, Passover, and other holidays (Adler, 1997; Brozan, 1990; Lefkovitz & Shapiro, 2005; Pogrebin, 1992). Christian feminists have written women's prayers, organized women's prayer groups, and told women's stories and perspectives from church pulpits (Haley Barton & Hybels, 2007; Byrne, 1991). In some cases, their

BOX 11.3
Ecofeminism

Ecofeminism emerged during the 1970s as a branch of feminism that celebrates what its adherents see as innate personality traits of women—caring, nurturance, gentleness—and women's close association with nature. As Irene Diamond (1992, p. 371) explains, it is "an ethic and politics which sees a connection between the domination of women and the domination of nature" (see also Eller, 1991; Mies & Shiva, 1993; Page, 2008). Ecofeminism is an earth-based spirituality movement that draws heavily on goddess imagery and ritual, which is not surprising given that, as we learned earlier, goddess worship celebrated many aspects of female biology, but especially women's sexuality and reproductive capacities. There is an emphasis on healing, ecological balance, an equality of all living beings (human and nonhuman), and regeneration (Griffin, 1995; Page, 2008).

Ecofeminism combines its spiritual emphases with direct political action to bring about a more harmonious, ecologically balanced society. Because of women's biology—as reproducers and nurturers—they are seen as closer to the earth. Similarly, because women have been exploited and denigrated, they more fully understand the exploitation and denigration of the biosphere. And they understand the exploitation and denigration of people in economically undeveloped societies because of Western imperialism and Western economic development models (Mies & Shiva, 1993; Spencer & Nichols 2010). Consequently, it is women who are best suited to lead the ecology movement and to develop a nonhierarchical society based on respect for all living things. To be effective leaders, however, women must get back in touch with their bodies and discover the full power of their natural femaleness. Hence, the return to goddess spirituality.

It is hardly surprising that ecofeminism is a controversial movement, even among feminists. While it has been praised for highlighting the dangers of environmental exploitation, it has been criticized for biologizing traditional Western femininity and glorifying the notion of a universal female nature. A number of feminist theorists see a serious danger in ecofeminists' emphasis on women's biologically based differences from men. As one feminist critic (Biehl, 1990, pp. 9, 11) explains:

When sociobiological justifications of androcentrism build reproductive differences into elaborate theories of "female nature," feminists have traditionally shown that they unjustly shore up sexist institutions and ideologies.... When ecofeminists root women's personality traits in reproductive and sexual biology, they tend to give acceptance to those male-created images that define women as primarily biological beings.... Indeed, ecofeminism's healthy impulse to claim women's biology has in many cases become an acceptance of the same constricting stereotypes of "women's nature" that have long been used to oppress them.

Despite these objections to ecofeminism—and they are by no means insignificant—most feminists agree that this movement makes important contributions to both feminist spirituality and the political liberation of the oppressed. First, it provides women with another option for religious expression, one that accords them dignity and a special revered status. At the same time, and perhaps more importantly, it extends this dignity and status to the oppressed in developing countries. Consequently, it has succeeded in forging ties between Western feminists and people in developing societies—something mainstream feminism has long failed to do (see Chapter 1).

efforts have resulted in changes in mainstream religious practices, such as the adoption of gender-neutral language in church services (see, for example, Canadian Bishops' Pastoral Team, 1989; Dunlap-Berg, 2010; McDonald, 1996). Muslim women, too, have challenged patriarchal traditions in their faith by leading Islamic prayer services (Elliott, 2005).

Like those who have broken with the patriarchal religious traditions, religious reformers disagree on the issue of whether feminist spirituality should be a women-only enterprise or a joint venture that includes members of both sexes. There are some who maintain that women need separate places and methods for worship, at least until they have fully reclaimed their religious heritage and have reestablished a position of equal status and authority within the mainstream religions. Others are concerned that feminist spirituality is dominated by White heterosexual women, while the diverse traditions and spiritual needs of women and men of color along with lesbians and gay men are being overlooked. Consequently, there are those (e.g., Isasi-Diaz, 1991; Mollenkott, 1991) who are calling on members of these groups to rediscover or to construct new religious traditions and rituals that better express the spirituality of their life experiences. Still others, however, argue that separatism itself gives rise to and perpetuates inequality and that the goal of feminist spirituality should be the building of a nonhierarchical human fellowship that unites groups historically excluded from mainstream churches because of their sex, race or ethnicity, social class, or sexual orientation (Mikjel Rio & Smedal, 2009; Zappone, 1991; see also Box 11.2).

Of course, it may be that this issue is unresolvable, but we do hope that through the struggle to come to grips with it, people will develop better ways to fulfill what appears to be a basic human need, religious expression. What we must keep in mind, however, is that a resurging religious fundamentalism threatens to negate even the most modest steps that have been taken toward gender equality and gay and lesbian rights. Despite the appeal that orthodoxy has for some women, it is nevertheless the case that religious fundamentalists vehemently oppose liberal trends, especially in gender relations and equal rights for sexual minorities, and fundamentalist groups have become more active politically in order to get their position represented in civil as well as religious law. Increasingly, feminism and gay and lesbian rights groups are being held up as devils to be defeated, rather than as movements for liberation. In Israel, religious leaders are arguing that orthodoxy is a unifying force central to national security. In the Islamic world, women's liberation is described as a Western imperialist plot to weaken Islamic nations and eventually overthrow them. In the United States, Christian fundamentalist leaders have urged their followers to "rid the nation of the disease-ridden homosexual lifestyle" (quoted in Liston, 1998, p. A2). Perhaps the underlying message in all of this is that more can be gained by feminist spiritualists working together—women and men, homosexuals and heterosexuals, all races and ethnicities and social classes—than by each group going its separate way.

Key Terms

ecofeminism   an earth-based feminist spirituality movement that celebrates women's close association with nature and sees a connection between the domination of women and the domination of nature

feminist spirituality   a religious movement comprising diverse segments with differing beliefs and strategies for change, but unified in rejecting the dualism characteristic of traditional patriarchal religions; dualism is replaced with the theme of the unification of spirit and nature and the principle that human experience is the source of spirituality

fundamentalism   a religious orientation that denounces secular modernity and attempts to restore traditional spirituality through selective retrieval of doctrines, beliefs, and practices from a sacred past

liberation theology   a religious orientation that merges the religious teachings and social functions of the Christian church with a critical analysis of the historical and contemporary experience of human suffering.

Qur'an   (or Quran, variation of Koran) the book of sacred writings accepted by Muslims as revelations made to Muhammad by Allah;

understood by Muslims to be literally the word of God

religiosity   an individual's or a group's intensity of commitment to a religious belief system

Talmud   the foundation of religious authority for traditional Judaism

witchcraft   naturalistic practices with religious significance usually engaged in by women; includes folk magic and medicine as well as knowledge of farming, ceramics, metallurgy, and astrology

Women-Church movement   a coalition of feminist faith-sharing groups, which offers a feminist critique of traditional Christianity while providing members with alternative, woman-centered rituals and forms of worship

Suggested Readings

Coleman, I. (2010). *Paradise beneath her feet: Women and reform in the Middle East.* New York: Random House. An analysis of how grassroots efforts by Muslim women in several Middle Eastern countries have produced incremental, yet significant changes that improve women's lives socially, politically, and spiritually.

Collier-Thomas, B. (2010). *Jesus, jobs, and justice: African American women and religion.* New York: Alfred A. Knopf. The author traces the church-based social activism of Black women historically and in contemporary U.S. society, demonstrating their commitment and successes in the face of numerous obstacles, including resistance and discrimination by Black male clergy.

Connelly, J. B. (2007). *Portrait of a priestess: Women and ritual in ancient Greece.* Princeton, NJ: Princeton University Press. A fascinating historical analysis that concludes that in ancient Greece,

women derived status and power from their participation in religious practices and ritual.

Dillon, M., & Wink, P. (2007). *In the course of a lifetime: Tracing religious belief, practice, and change.* Berkeley: University of California Press. Based on a sixty-year study of two hundred mostly Protestant and Catholic women and men, this book documents changes in the religiosity of the study participants over the course of their lives and in response to major life events.

Sullivan, R. (2005). *Visual habits: Nuns, feminism, and American postwar popular culture.* Ontario, Canada: University of Toronto Press. Sullivan considers the confluence of three waves of monumental societal change that occurred in the United States during the 1950s and 1960s—i.e., the Second Vatican Council, the second wave of feminism, and the sexual revolution—and she explores the role that nuns had in these changes, as well as how their traditional religious roles were affected by the changes occurring around them.

Notes

1. Men did not completely escape persecution for witchcraft, however. Even brother Dominicans were not immune from prosecution. For example, Giordano Bruno, a Dominican philosopher, was burned alive in 1600 because he used magic and gnosticism to defend Copernicus's theory of the solar system.

2. In 1999, the Baptist General Convention of Texas, the largest state organization within the national Southern Baptist Convention, voted overwhelmingly to reject the "submit graciously" policy. However, it continues to generate controversy nationally, such as in 2007 when presidential candidate Mike Huckabee signed his name to a full-page ad in *USA Today* that said, "a wife is to submit graciously to the leadership of her husband" (Lowen, 2007).

3. A fourth congregation, Reconstructionist Judaism, was established in the 1960s. Reconstructionist Judaism rejects all the doctrines of traditional Judaism, including the Torah and Talmud; stories in the Bible are considered myths. Instead, Reconstructionist Jews emphasize humanistic values and the cultural heritage of Judaism. Reconstructionist Judaism is highly egalitarian and allows the fullest participation of women; about 19 percent of female rabbis are in Reconstructionist congregations.

4. While there appears to be an increasing willingness among Reform and Conservative rabbis to officiate at same-sex unions, there remains a reluctance to officiate at interfaith marriages. One survey of rabbis, for instance, found that none in the Orthodox or Conservative traditions had officiated at interfaith marriages, although 11 percent of Orthodox rabbis and 32 percent of Conservative rabbis said that they had referred interfaith couples to other rabbis who would marry them. Significantly more Reform and Reconstructionist rabbis had married interfaith couples: 36 percent of Reform rabbis and 62 percent of Reconstructionist rabbis had officiated at interfaith weddings; 69 percent of Reform rabbis and 100 percent of Reconstructionist rabbis said they also referred interfaith couples to other rabbis who would marry them (Niebuhr, 1997). Among Jewish congregants, however, there has been widespread acceptance of interfaith marriages. In one recent survey, for example, 69 percent of Jewish respondents said that Jews had an obligation to urge Jews to marry Jews, but only 12 percent strongly disapproved of interfaith marriages and 80 percent said they felt such marriages are inevitable in an open society (Niebuhr, 2000b). There are indications, though, that a more concerted effort is now being made in Reform congregations to encourage non-Jewish spouses to convert to Judaism (Luo, 2006). These data remind us of a story a friend recently told us. Our friend, who is a Jewish lesbian, introduced her new lover, who happened to be Catholic, to her mother: "What," our friend's mother asked, "you couldn't find a nice Jewish girl?"

5. For a compelling analysis of divisions within Jewish feminism in Israel, see Motzafi-Haller (2001). Motzafi-Haller also draws some interesting parallels between the dominant feminist movement in Israel and the White, mainstream women's movement in the United States, which we discussed in Chapter 1.

6. Research indicates, however, that while many conservative religious sects, such as Protestant evangelicals, continue to profess "symbolic traditionalism," their everyday lives may be characterized by "pragmatic egalitarianism." More specifically, Gallagher and Smith (1999) found in their study of Christian evangelicals that more than 90 percent emphasized men's family headship as biblically prescribed and respect and deference to husbands/fathers as earned rewards for men's family responsibilities. Nevertheless, in most of these families, wives were employed and made decisions jointly with their husbands, an arrangement the respondents did not see as conflicting with men's ultimate authority in the home.

7. Many advocates of women's ordination are especially angry over the Church's response to the sexual abuse crisis, pointing to the leniency in the way sexually abusive priests—and the bishops who covered up their crimes for many years—have been treated. In contrast, they say, the very small number of women, ordained as Catholic priests in ceremonies the church deems illicit and refuses to recognize, have been excommunicated, even though they are ministering to the sick, the elderly, the poor, and other oppressed groups (Berggren, 2006). The Catholic Church does have women religious who are not priests; they are nuns. Historically, nuns were expected by church leaders to be silent and obedient helpmates of the bishops (McNamara, 1996; Sullivan, 2005; Weaver, 1995). At the same time, however,

religious sisters played an active role in secular society, especially in Catholic schools and hospitals (Briggs, 1987; Ebaugh, 1993; Keller et al., 2006; Lummis, 1999; McNamara, 1996; Sullivan, 2005). Since the mid-1960s, largely because of widening roles for laypeople within the church, but also as a result of a growing feminist consciousness, the number of women joining religious orders has dropped dramatically. There are only about 72,000 Catholic nuns today, compared with 180,000 in 1965; 91 percent are at least sixty years old (Goodstein, 2009). The women entering convents nowadays are, like the men entering seminaries, older on average than in previous decades. Many of these women have had professional careers and hold college and graduate degrees, and some are feminists who support the ordination of women and challenge the sexism of the Church from within the organization itself— a point to which we will return momentarily (Beckwith, 2000; Ebaugh, 1993; Egan, 1999; Steinfels, 1995b; Wallace, 1992; Weaver, 1995).

8. In 2007, a prominent Southern Baptist seminary denied a female professor tenure on the ground that the Bible does not permit women to instruct men or to have authority over them ("Professor says," 2007).

9. Women who violate the rules of modest dress or who engage in immodest activity are also punished by male relatives and even by angry citizens, who may mock or insult them, or who may go so far as to beat them or kill them. As we discussed in Chapter 9, "honor killings," as they are called, still occur in some Islamic societies, where male relatives stone or stab to death a woman who has dishonored her family by, for instance, committing adultery, engaging in premarital sex, or simply just socializing with a man in public. Women who are raped are also in danger of being imprisoned or killed, although they are expected to kill themselves for having "engaged in sex outside of marriage" unless the victim can produce four male witnesses who will testify on her behalf that she was indeed raped (Kristof, 2005). See Awwad (2001); Baker, Gregware, and Cassidy (1999); and Sev'er and Yurdakul (2001) for analyses of honor killings.

Chapter 12

Gender and Health

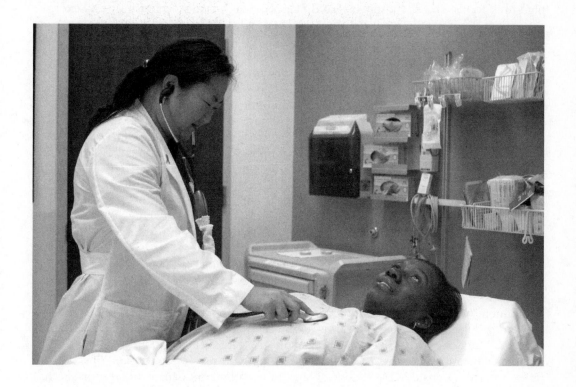

Health care and, in particular, access to health care, have been top priorities on the national agenda since the 1980s. As health care costs rose at an average annual rate higher than any other category on the Consumer Price Index (CPI), access to health care was limited for large segments of the U.S. population. In 2001, 14.2 percent of the U.S. population (39.1 million people) were medically uninsured (Centers for Disease Control and Prevention [CDC], 2002; U.S. Department of Commerce, Bureau of the Census, 1997) but by 2009, the percentage of uninsured persons had risen to 15.3 percent (46 million people) (CDC, 2010).

At the same time that access to health care was shrinking for specific segments of the population, there was increasing interest in how diet and lifestyle choices contribute to health. In response to reports that diet, exercise, and other aspects of an individual's lifestyle affect her or his health, many Americans quit smoking, began eating low-fat, high-fiber foods, and spent millions of dollars on health club memberships and exercise equipment. Importantly, however, the individuals who make up the first group we have discussed—the uninsured—have little in common with those who make up the second group. About 8.2 percent of the uninsured are children under the age of eighteen, the majority of whom live with an unemployed parent or a parent who is working part time or full time in a job that provides no medical benefits (CDC, 2010). In fact, 88.2 percent of medically uninsured children live with at least one parent who is working (Insure Kids Now, 2011). About 25 percent of the uninsured have an annual family income below the poverty line and are disproportionately Hispanic, as Hispanics represent 14 percent of U.S. residents but comprise 30 percent of the uninsured (U.S. Department of Health and Human Services, 2005). In contrast, the "health club set" is predominantly White with middle-class or higher average annual incomes (60 percent earn more than $45,000 per year) and is between the ages of twenty-five and forty-four (My Wellness, 2000).

In short, although research has established direct links between diet, lifestyle, and health, what we eat and how we live is less of a choice for some people than for others. In fact, researchers have found that even as there has been a push for all Americans to get more exercise, improve their eating habits, and cut down on smoking and drinking, the difference in life expectancies between poor and affluent Americans has increased, with affluent individuals living longer. For example, in 1982, people in the affluent economic class could expect to live 2.8 years longer than those in the less affluent group (75.8 versus 73 years); however, by 2000, the difference in life expectancy had increased to 4.5 years (79.2 versus 74.7 years) (Pear, 2008). In other words, a person's health and access to health care, along with his or her diet and lifestyle, are influenced to a considerable extent by a number of factors over which he or she has little control: most importantly, social class, race and ethnicity, age, and, as we will learn in this chapter, sex.

In this chapter, we will consider how sex and gender relations affect health status and how they interact with other factors—social class, race and ethnicity, age, sexual orientation—to shape not only health status, but also the physician-patient relationship and treatment by the health care system. It is important to keep in mind, though, that when we talk about health, we're talking about more than simply the absence of illness. Health is, as the World Health Organization (1960, p. 1) has told us, multidimensional. It is "a complete state of physical, mental, and social well-being." Let's begin our discussion by looking first at physical health; then, later in the chapter we will take up the issue of mental health.

GENDER AND MORTALITY

One of the most consistent sex differences that can be observed across contemporary industrialized societies is that women, on average, live longer than men. Looking at Table 12.1, we see first that the United States ranks low relative to many other

Country	Female Life Expectancy (in years)	Male Life Expectancy (in years)
Japan	86.0	79.2
France	84.4	77.5
Spain	84.3	77.8
Italy	83.8*	77.9*
Australia	83.7	79.0
Finland	83.1	76.0
Sweden	83.0	78.9
Austria	82.9	77.3
Iceland	82.9	78.3
Norway	82.9	77.1
Germany	82.7	77.4
Republic of Korea	82.7	76.1
Belgium	82.6	77.1
Canada	82.6*	77.8
Netherlands	82.3	78.0
Luxembourg	82.2	76.7
New Zealand	82.2	78.2
Portugal	82.2	75.9
Ireland	82.1	77.4
Greece	82.0	77.0
United Kingdom	81.0*	76.8*
Denmark	80.6	76.2
United States	80.4	75.4
Czech Republic	80.2	73.8
Poland	79.7	71.0
Slovak Republic	78.1	70.5
Mexico	77.4	72.6
Hungary	77.3	69.2
Turkey	75.6	71.1

TABLE 12.1 Life Expectancy at Birth, by Sex for Selected Countries, 2007

*2004 data

Source: National Center for Health Statistics (2010). *Health, United States, 2010*, p. 132.

countries in terms of both female and male life expectancy (Clark, 2011). (**Life expectancy** refers to the average number of years an individual may be expected to live from a given age or from birth.) The United States is in twenty-third place in terms of female life expectancy and ranks twenty-second in male life expectancy. (The U.S. rankings have declined since the 1980s.) However, in all of the countries listed, women have a longer life expectancy than men. Of the countries listed, the gap is narrowest in New Zealand, but even there the difference is four years.

As Table 12.2 shows, even though life expectancy for both sexes has improved over the decades, women's advantage increased significantly from the turn of the century until 1975. In the United States, for example, there was only a two-year difference in female and male life expectancies in 1900. By 1970, the life expectancy gap between the sexes had widened to 7.7 years. Since 1975, the sex gap in life expectancy has narrowed, although it remained significant at five years in 2007.

We also see in Table 12.2 a consistent racial disparity in life expectancy. Whites enjoy almost a five-year advantage over Blacks in terms of life expectancy. In fact, the life expectancy of Black males in 2007 was only slightly better than the life expectancy of White males in 1975. Similarly, the life expectancy of Black females in 2007 was little better than the life expectancy of White females in 1970. The gender gap in life expectancy has not narrowed as much for Blacks as it has for Whites, indicating that race is a more

TABLE 12.2	Life Expectancy at Birth, by Sex and Race, 1900–2007					
	All Races		**White**		**Black***	
Year	**Male**	**Female**	**Male**	**Female**	**Male**	**Female**
1900	46.3	48.3	46.6	48.7	32.5	33.5
1920	53.6	54.6	54.4	55.6	45.5	45.2
1930	58.1	61.6	59.7	63.5	47.3	49.2
1940	60.8	65.2	62.1	66.6	51.5	54.9
1950	65.6	71.1	66.5	72.2	58.9	62.7
1960	66.6	73.1	67.4	74.1	60.7	65.9
1970	67.1	74.7	68.0	75.6	60.0	68.3
1975	68.8	76.6	69.5	77.3	62.4	71.3
1980	70.0	77.4	70.7	78.1	63.8	72.5
1985	71.1	78.2	71.8	78.7	65.0	73.4
1990	71.8	78.8	72.7	79.4	64.5	73.6
1995	72.5	78.9	73.4	79.6	65.2	73.9
2000	74.1	79.3	74.7	79.9	68.2	75.1
2005	74.9	79.9	75.4	80.4	69.3	76.1
2007	75.4	80.4	75.9	80.8	70.0	76.8

*Data for the years 1920, 1930, and 1940 include other non-White populations in addition to the Black population.

Sources: National Center for Health Statistics. (2010). *Health, United States, 2010*, p. 134.

significant factor than sex in the life expectancies of African Americans. Nevertheless, a significant sex difference in life expectancy persists regardless of race.[1]

A number of theories have been offered to account for the sex differential in life expectancy. At least part of the difference appears to be caused by biological factors. Genetics, for instance, play a role. As we learned in Chapter 2, humans have twenty-three pairs of chromosomes, one of which determines sex. If an individual is male, his sex chromosomes are XY; a female has two X chromosomes. Scientists know that the X chromosome carries more genetic information than the Y, including some defects that can lead to physical abnormalities, but instead of making females more vulnerable to X-linked disorders, this seems to give them a genetic advantage. A female typically needs two defective X chromosomes for most genetically linked disorders to manifest themselves; otherwise, one healthy X chromosome can override the abnormal one. On the other hand, a male who has a defective X chromosome will have the genetically linked disease because that is the only X chromosome he has. This is thought to account for the higher number of miscarriages of male fetuses and the greater ratio of male to female neonatal deaths (106:100) and infant deaths (Jehan et al., 2009; Stillion, 1995). Hormonal differences between the sexes also contribute to the life expectancy gap. In particular, the female sex hormones, the estrogens, appear to give women some protection against heart disease, the number one cause of death in the United States (Paranjape et al., 2005; Waldron, 1995).

Marital status is also related to life expectancy, at least for men. In one study, for instance, researchers found that after controlling for crucial intervening variables, such as income, education, smoking, drinking, and obesity, men between the ages of forty-five and sixty-five who lived alone or with someone other than a spouse were twice as likely to die within ten years as men of the same age who lived with spouses. This relationship did not hold for women; women were more negatively affected by low income than by lack of a spouse (Davis et al., 1990; see also Felder, 2006; Hu & Goldman, 1990). Although researchers are not certain why marriage appears to be so important to the health of men, studies show that men rely almost totally on their spouses for social support. Not surprisingly, then, married men express a higher level of well-being than their nonmarried peers. There appears to be no difference, however, in the level of contentment expressed by married versus nonmarried women. Women have wider social support networks than men. When a woman's husband dies, she typically retains the social support of relatives and friends (Helgeson, 1995; Newman & Newman, 2008; see also Chapter 7). Moreover, research shows that when spouses become seriously ill, wives are more likely than husbands to nurture their spouses through the illness. Men are significantly more likely than women to divorce seriously ill spouses (M. S. James, 2001).

We will return to the relationship between marital status and well-being later in this chapter. Importantly, though, this relationship may be an indicator of another major component of the gender gap in life expectancy: behavior differences between the sexes. More specifically, we can observe a relationship between life expectancy and conformity to traditional gender stereotypes. To understand this better, let's examine male and female mortality rates for particular causes. (A **mortality rate** is simply the number of deaths in proportion to a given population.) Table 12.3 provides sex- and race-specific mortality rates for the leading causes of death for each group. Let's look at some of these more closely.

TABLE 12.3 Leading Causes of Death by Race & Sex, 2007 (as a percentage of total deaths for each group)

Cause of Death	White Male	White Female	Black Male	Black Female	Hispanic Male	Hispanic Female	American Indian/ Alaska Native Male	American Indian/ Alaska Native Female	Asian/ Pacific Islander Male	Asian/ Pacific Islander Female
Diseases of the heart	26.1%	25.2%	24.1%	25.2%	20.7%	22.3%	19.3%	17.4%	24.0%	22.3%
Malignant neoplasms (cancer)	24.6	22.1	22.3	21.9	19.1	22.0	17.1	18.8	26.8	27.2
Cerebrovascular diseases (including stroke)	4.4	6.7	5.1	6.7	4.4	6.3	3.4	4.9	6.6	9.2
Diabetes	2.8	2.6	3.7	4.9	4.2	5.4	4.8	6.3	3.6	4.1
Kidney disease	1.8	1.8	2.5	3.3	*	2.2	*	2.6	2.0	1.9
Septicemia	*	1.4	*	2.5	*	*	*	2.0	1.3	*
Chronic liver disease & cirrhosis	*	*	*	*	3.7	*	5.3	4.5	*	*
Chronic lower respiratory diseases	5.5	5.9	2.8	2.6	2.5	2.7	3.8	4.8	3.3	2.5
Influenza & pneumonia	2.0	2.4	*	*	*	2.3	1.9	2.0	3.0	2.9
HIV/AIDS	*	*	2.8	*	*	*	*	*	*	*
Alzheimer's disease	2.0	4.6	*	2.5	*	2.8	*	*	*	2.3
Unintentional injuries (accidents)	*	3.6	6.2	3.0	1.2	4.8	14.3	8.8	5.8	3.8
Suicide	2.4	*	*	*	2.7	*	3.9	*	2.6	*
Homicide	*	*	5.1	*	3.9	*	2.1	*	*	*

*This is not one of the top ten causes of death for this group.

Heart Disease

The male death rate from heart disease is about 84 percent higher than the female death rate from heart disease. In fact, the greatest single contributor to men's higher mortality rate overall is coronary heart disease, which includes heart attacks (American Heart Association, 2011; Waldron, 1995). What accounts for this particular sex disparity in mortality? Scientists have found a number of behavioral and cultural factors that are contributors.

First, more men than women smoke, and men are more likely than women to be heavy smokers. Cigarette smoking has been shown to cause and worsen heart disease. It is estimated that sex differences in smoking account for about one-third of the sex differences in heart disease mortality (Population Reference Bureau, 2011; Waldron, 1995). However, the gender gap in smoking began to narrow, starting in the 1940s, as more women took up smoking, and more men than women have quit smoking. In 1965, for example, 51.2 percent of men, aged eighteen and older, smoked, compared with 33.7 percent of women, aged eighteen and older. By 1998, about half as many men were smoking (25.9 percent), while 22.1 percent of women were smokers (National Center for Health Statistics, 2000). And by 2008, 20.7 percent of men were smoking, while 16.2 percent of women were smokers (Kaiser Family Foundation, 2008). Because there is a lag time between when a person begins smoking and the appearance of detrimental effects of smoking on the person's health, including heart disease mortality, the impact of women's increased smoking during the 1940s, 1950s, and 1960s has only recently shown itself in a narrowing of the gender gap in heart disease mortality. In fact, although heart disease mortality has decreased for both women and men over the last decade, the male decrease has been higher than the female decrease (American Heart Association, 2011; Thun et al., 1995; Waldron, 1995).

However, while cigarette smoking obviously plays a major role in the gender gap in heart disease mortality, other factors also contribute since the difference is substantial even among nonsmokers. Another factor that some researchers believe contributes to the gender gap in heart disease mortality is men's greater likelihood to adopt the Coronary Prone Behavior Pattern, or what many call the *Type A personality*. Research indicates that Type A individuals are more than twice as likely as laid-back Type B personalities to suffer heart attacks, regardless of whether or not they smoke. Interestingly, the characteristics of Type A closely parallel those typical of traditional masculinity: competitive, impatient, ambitious, aggressive, and unemotional (Helgeson, 1995; Mitaishvili, 2006; Park, 2010). Recent studies have shown that individuals who are highly anger-prone, be they men or women, are at significantly greater risk of having a heart attack than individuals who do not anger easily (Rutledge et al., 2001; Williams et al., 2000). Moreover, men who spend all of their time working and refuse to take a vacation are also at elevated risk of developing coronary heart disease (Gump & Matthews, 2000). Not surprisingly, researchers have found that coronary patients who display strong or extreme masculinity in a negative sense do more poorly healthwise than other coronary patients (Barrett-Connor, 2007; Emslie, 2009; Helgeson, 1995).

Another configuration of personality traits recently associated with coronary heart disease is what researchers are calling the *Type D personality* (Haupt, 2010; Lesperance & Frasure-Smith, 1996; Park, 2010). Traditionally described as the "strong, silent type," the Type D personality has difficulty expressing negative emotions. They typically keep their feelings hidden and see talking about their worries as a sign of weakness. Research shows that this personality type is more common among men than women and is consistent with traditional masculinity. Men are less likely than women to disclose their needs and feelings of vulnerability (Haupt, 2010; Helgeson, 1995; Park, 2010). In contrast, women typically react to stress by turning to their children and friends for support—what researchers call the "tend-and-befriend" response (Taylor et al., 2000; see Box 12.1). The research indicates that Type D personalities have an increased risk of heart attacks and have poorer recovery rates following a heart attack (Haupt, 2010; Lesperance & Frasure-Smith, 1996).

The findings with regard to Type A and Type D personalities are useful because they show the detrimental impact that adhering to a traditional masculine gender role can have on men's health. However, more research is needed with diverse groups of study subjects to more fully understand the relationship between gender roles and heart disease, especially since much previous research was based largely on samples of White men and was sometimes influenced by stereotypes. For example, early reports depicted heart disease as a health problem of executives, a middle- and upper-class disease, or, as some referred to it, a "disease of affluence." Those most likely to be stricken were said to be hardworking, successful professional men—men striving to "keep up with the Joneses" and to get ahead. Blue-collar workers and housewives were thought to be less susceptible, supposedly because they were less pressured, although it was predicted that women's rates of coronary heart disease would rise as more women entered professional fields (Ehrenreich, 1983; Ezzat et al., 2005; House, 1986; Wood, 2005).

However, assumptions like these ignore the serious stressors that blue-collar workers confront: for example, long hours, little or no control over work, low pay, and job insecurity. This may partially account for the higher coronary heart disease mortality rate among African American men who, as a group, are underrepresented among white-collar professionals and overrepresented among unskilled laborers. Many female-dominated jobs, especially in the service sector, may also be considered highly stressful for these same reasons (Bekker, Nijssen, & Hens, 2001; LaCroix & Haynes, 1987). Female heart attack patients report having experienced more stressful life events than male heart attack patients (Agency for Healthcare Research and Quality, 2010; Helgeson, 1990). Several studies have shown a strong correlation between living in neighborhoods with high concentrations of female-headed households and heart disease mortality among women (Cubbin, Hadden, & Winkleby, 2001; LeClere, Rogers, & Peters, 1998). Obviously, poverty may be the underlying contributing factor here, since such neighborhoods have significantly lower median incomes than neighborhoods dominated by male-headed households (see Chapter 7). However, the researchers found that for older women, the relationship holds even when poverty is taken into account. This finding indicates that such neighborhoods may be more stressful environments for older women, perhaps because there are fewer social supports for them, given that younger single mothers must devote most, if not all, of their time attending to the immediate needs of their families.

It has also been argued that the traditional homemaker role can be highly stressful (Doyal, 1990a; Harding, 2009). Interestingly, while employed women face the doubly stressful burden of job responsibilities coupled with home and family care, they do not appear to be more likely than full-time homemakers to develop coronary heart disease. In fact, some studies indicate that just the opposite may be the case. In general, women employed outside the home appear to be healthier than nonemployed women, even when employed women must fulfill multiple roles, such as worker, parent, spouse, and homemaker. Again, more research is needed on diverse groups of women, comparing women employed in low-status, low-income jobs with women in high-prestige, well-paying jobs, since there is evidence that role *quality* may be more important for well-being than role occupancy per se (Barnett & Baruch, 1987; Harding, 2009; Messias et al., 1997). For instance, several studies show that employed mothers are healthier than women who are full-time moms, but that the health benefit is greatest for working mothers who have access to high-quality child care, flexible work options, a sense of control over their work, and the support of their partners (Duxbury, Higgins, & Lee, 1994; Houston Barrett & Stuchell, 2007; Roxburgh, 1997). The last factor in this list indicates that more research is also needed on sex differences in social support networks within families, among coworkers, and on relationships between supervisors and their employees. The socioeconomic benefits of working outside the home and sex differences in access to and use of health care services among employed and unemployed women and men also need further study.

Although the female mortality rate from heart disease is lower than the male mortality rate from heart disease, diseases of the heart are still the primary causes of death for women. In fact, when age is taken into account, more women than men die from heart disease and related disorders. In addition, 42 percent of women who have heart attacks die within one year, compared to 24 percent of men (Women's Heart Foundation, 2010). Although heart attacks are rare for premenopausal women under the age of fifty, the heart attack rate for postmenopausal women climbs quickly, soon equaling the heart attack rate for men over fifty years old. It appears that women actually develop heart disease at a rate similar to that of men, but six to ten years later in life and that the symptomatic manifestation of heart disease in women may follow a different pattern than that in men (*American Heart Journal*, 2011; Henig, 1993; Weidner, Kopp, & Kristenson, 2002; Women's Heart Foundation, 2010). Women also are more likely than men to experience a condition known as *insulin resistance*, also sometimes called *Syndrome X*, a health problem in which the body makes sufficient insulin, but is unable to use it properly. Insulin resistance is thought to be responsible for as much as 60 percent of heart disease in women, but only 25 percent in men. However, it is difficult to detect because it does not show up in routine blood tests usually done during medical check-ups (Agency for Healthcare Research and Quality, 2003; ReavEn, Fox, & Strom, 2000).

Despite all that we do know about gender differences in heart disease, many medical researchers argue that far less is known about heart disease in women than in men. The major reason for this discrepancy is that until quite recently, studies of heart disease focused exclusively on male subjects, thus perhaps erroneously generalizing from the findings on one sex to both sexes and reinforcing the false notion that women are unlikely to suffer from heart disease and its effects (Women's Heart Foundation, 2010; Nechas & Foley, 1994). Another source of gender differences in relation to heart disease is the fact that women often receive treatment later than men. Women take longer to report the physical alarms they experience, and once they have notified their physician, their treatment takes longer (Orrange, 2011). In addition, women seem to report their husband's heart attacks more quickly than their own and likewise seek treatment for their spouse more diligently (Worell, 2001).

African American men's and women's mortality rates from heart disease are considerably higher than those of White men and women, although the rate for African American women is still far below that of African American men. African Americans are twenty times more likely than Whites to suffer from high blood pressure, a condition that contributes to heart disease (Connecticut Health Foundation, 2007; see, however, Gillum, Mussolino, & Madans, 1997). Research has linked elevated blood pressure in African Americans to the stress of dealing with racial discrimination in everyday life. In fact, one study found that stress induced by racial discrimination has as much or more of an impact on blood pressure as smoking, lack of exercise, and a high-fat, high-sodium diet (Atlanta Medical Center, 2011; Kreiger & Sidney, 1996; see also Armstead et al., 1989; Klag et al., 1991). Once African Americans are diagnosed with heart disease, they are 40 percent less likely than Whites to undergo bypass surgery or angioplasty, a statistic that some researchers also attribute to racism: Most cardiologists are White, and they may have difficulty communicating effectively with Black patients, making it harder for the patients to trust them (Haney, 1996a; Savitt, 2001). However, another recent study found that Black patients who had a heart attack were 60 percent less likely than White heart attack patients to undergo a potentially life-saving procedure called cardiac catheterization, regardless of the race of their physician (Krumholz, 2001).

We will discuss the patient-physician relationship in greater detail shortly, but first let's consider the gender gap in mortality for other causes of death.

Cancer

Men's death rate due to cancer is 40 percent higher than women's cancer death rate (National Center for Health Statistics, 2000). Again, men's smoking habits contribute to this difference. As we noted earlier, historically, more men than women have smoked, and men's smoking habits are riskier than women's (e.g., they smoke more of each cigarette they light) (Quit SA, 2008; Waldron, 1995). However, we have also noted that more men than women have quit smoking in recent years. In addition, as with coronary heart disease, the gender gap in mortality for lung, trachea, and bronchus cancers is narrowing because we are beginning to see the ill effects of smoking on women who took up the habit decades ago. From the 1950s through the 1990s, for example, women's mortality from lung, trachea, and bronchus cancers increased nearly 700 percent, from 3.9 per 100,000 in 1950 to 26.9 per 100,000 in 1998. Men's lung, trachea, and bronchus cancer mortality rose from 18.4 per 100,000 in 1950 to 58.5 per 100,000 in 1990. After 1990, men's lung, trachea, and bronchus mortality rate began to decline, reaching 49.5 per 100,000 in 1998 (National Center for Health Statistics, 2000). In 2007, 158,760 Americans died from lung, trachea, and bronchus cancer (88,372 men and 70,080 women); the median age of diagnosis was 71 (Legacy, 2010). There has been no increase in the lung cancer mortality rate of nonsmokers, strong evidence of the major role smoking plays in the development of lung disease (Thun et al., 2006).

Adding to the risk of developing cancer are industrial hazards, especially the inhalation of particular dusts such as asbestos, and exposure to toxic fumes and chemicals. Men are more likely to experience toxic workplace exposures—another byproduct of occupational sex segregation (Bevc et al., 2007; Waldron, 1995; World Bank, 2009). However, certain female-dominated jobs—such as micro-chip and electronic component assembly that is more than 90 percent female, a majority of whom are women of color—involve extensive exposure to toxic chemicals (Fox, 1991; Garcia-Alonso et al., 2009). Yet, less is known about occupationally related cancers and female mortality, since most research involving women's health and the workplace has focused on reproductive health. There are, however, a variety of ways that the work environment can affect a person's health, so let's take a closer look at occupational health hazards.

Occupational Hazards to Male and Female Workers

There's a certain irony in the phrase, "to work for a living," given that many workplaces are quite hazardous, even deadly. Historically, a recognition of this led to the enactment of laws prohibiting the employment of women in particular occupations. The stated rationale for such measures was not simply that women are "the weaker sex," but also that their child-bearing function warranted them special protection so as to ensure the health and viability of future generations. In practice, "protective" legislation has had two major effects: (1) legitimation of employment discrimination against women; and (2) neglect of the potential risks posed by workplace hazards to male workers' health, including their reproductive health.

The Pregnancy Discrimination Act of 1981 forbids employment discrimination against women workers solely on the basis of pregnancy. If a hazard can be shown to affect a fetus through either the mother or the father, then excluding only women from the workplace is illegal. It is estimated that over fourteen million U.S. workers each year are exposed to known or suspected reproductive hazards in the workplace. Not surprisingly, then, reproductive disorders are among the ten most frequent work-related injuries and illnesses in the United States. However, little is known about the effects of most workplace toxins and other occupational hazards on the reproductive health of either sex, and male workers in particular have been virtually ignored (Blakeslee, 1991; Paul, Daniels, & Rosofsky, 1989). Recently researchers in several disciplines have begun to call for more research in this area, especially since over 87,000 chemical substances are registered for commercial use in the United States (Bhatt, 2000; Till, Koren, & Rovet, 2008; Woodruff et al., 2008). It is clear that workplace toxins can affect the female reproductive system in many different ways, particularly during pregnancy, but it is also plausible that these toxins could damage sperm or be transmitted through semen, causing visible congenital malformations as well as the possibility of childhood or adult cancer in the offspring (Quigley et al., 2009).

Unfortunately, many researchers, employers, and policy makers traditionally operated under the assumption that women are more important than men in the reproductive process. Until 1991, most employers simply excluded women from certain hazardous jobs or employed only infertile or surgically sterilized women in such jobs (Newburger, 1998; Samuels, 1995; L. A. Williams, 1988). In other words, employers have typically addressed the problem by removing women from the workplace instead of rendering the workplace safe for both female and male workers (Kolb, 2008; Paul et al., 1989; Samuels, 1995). This is no solution at all, for the fact of the matter is that environmental and occupational exposures adversely affect both female and male reproduction (Chalupka, 2010). Nevertheless, it is still the case that only women are encouraged to take precautionary action to prevent toxic exposures harmful to reproduction (Chalupka & Chalupka, 2010). "Toxic chemicals do not discriminate—they affect both female and male hearts, muscles, livers, and kidneys—and both female and male reproductive systems....Men, women, and their offspring, are all at risk from toxic exposures; we do not know whether these risks are sufficiently different to justify the selection of one of them as needing more protection than the other" (Bellin & Rubenstein, 1983, pp. 87, 97).

We suspect that protection of women and their offspring was less a motivating factor in the adoption of exclusionary policies than employers' concern with corporate liability and the advantages they accrued from a sex-segregated labor force (see Chapter 8). For one thing, exclusion from the workplace does not necessarily protect women or children from exposure to toxins. Men may transport residues home on their hair, skin, and clothes, with women being exposed through their daily unpaid activities as housewives and children being exposed if they hug, kiss, or play with their fathers. The residues may also get into furniture, rugs, and bedding (Armour, 2000; Rosenberg, 1984).[2] Take-home contamination has been documented for at least forty industries, including construction and medical research, and between 1980 and 2000, there were more than 1,000 cases of home contamination (Armour, 2000).[3]

Second, exclusionary policies were common in male-dominated industries, but not in equally hazardous female-dominated occupations (Doyal, 1990a; Goldhaber, Poland, & Hialt, 1988; Hoeksma, 2005). We know from our discussion in Chapter 8 that women, especially women of color, have always worked at dangerous jobs. In fact, racial discrimination in the workplace has meant that Black workers of both sexes are at significantly greater risk of suffering an occupational injury or illness than White workers. For example, historically, approximately 89 percent of Black steel workers worked at the coke ovens compared with about 32 percent of White steel workers; the coke ovens were the most dangerous work site in the steel industry (Newburger, 1998; Staples, 1995; see also Fox, 1991).[4]

In 1991, sex-biased workplace exclusionary policies were successfully challenged when the U.S. Supreme Court reversed a lower court's decision that women could be barred from jobs that might potentially harm a fetus. The case, *United Automobile Workers* v. *Johnson Controls*, involved a battery company that prohibited fertile women, pregnant or not, from working at jobs that entailed exposure to lead. The company argued that the exclusionary policy was not discriminatory because it is in the public's interest to protect the health of unborn children. However, the Supreme Court maintained that although employment late in pregnancy may sometimes pose a risk to the fetus, it is up to the woman to decide whether or not she will continue to work. Employers, ruled the Court, may not force a woman to choose between having a job and having a baby. Not surprisingly, most employers have complied with this decision, not by making the workplace safer for the reproductive health of employees of both sexes, but rather by simply leaving it up to workers themselves to decide whether or not to risk working in an unsafe, unhealthy work environment. Such a choice is really no choice at all for most workers in toxic work environments, since they have few other job options.

Exposures to workplace toxins, however, are not the only hazards women and men face on the job. Accidents and homicides also claim workers' lives, although not surprisingly, male and female workers face different levels of risk. For example, although men make up 54 percent of the labor force, they account for 93 percent of workers who die from job-related injuries (U.S. Department of Labor, 2005). (Most of these men die accidentally—for example, in vehicle accidents, from falls, and in fires or explosions.) While women are far less likely than men to die in a work-related incident, the major causes of work-related death for women are vehicle accidents and homicides (see Chapter 9). Twenty-six percent of women who die on the job are murder victims (U.S. Department of Labor, 2009b). These deaths are largely a result of women being concentrated in retail trade and food service, where workers engage in cash transactions or have valuables on hand; most of these homicides are associated with robberies or robbery attempts. About 17 percent of female homicide victims killed at work were murdered by husbands, ex-husbands, boyfriends, and ex-boyfriends, the end product of a history of domestic violence (U.S. Department of Labor, 2005, 2009b).

Women and men also have significantly different rates of death from non-job-related accidents and homicides, a point that we will take up next.

Other Causes of Death

In considering the other causes of death listed in Table 12.3, we find that these, too, are associated with behavioral differ-

Men are significantly more likely than women to be involved in fatal auto accidents in which the driver was under the influence of alcohol.

ences between the sexes. For example, men are involved in nearly twice as many fatal car accidents in which the driver was intoxicated (Century Council, 2010; Waldron, 1995). As we will discuss later in this chapter, men are significantly more likely than women to drink excessively. Even when not drinking, though, men drive more recklessly than women. Despite the unflattering stereotype of "the woman driver," women have fewer accidents than men, even when we control for sex differences in the number of miles driven. Men are about 2.5 times more likely to be behind the wheel of a fatal crash than women (Insurance Institute for Highway Safety, 2010). Women have also shown greater improvements in driving-related safety habits (e.g., wearing seat belts) than men have; women wear seatbelts 27 percent more often than men (Insurance Institute for Highway Safety, 2010). Females, of course, are socialized to act safely, to seek help, and to avoid risks. Males, in contrast, are encouraged at an early age to be adventurous, independent, and unafraid of taking risks (see Chapter 4). Consequently, they, more often than females, are involved in the kinds of dangerous situations that may lead to accidental death (National Vital Statistics System, 2010; Staples, 1995; Stillion, 1995).

Masculinity, we also know, is equated in many people's minds with aggressiveness. Men are expected, even encouraged, to behave violently, and this in turn is reflected in their higher suicide rate and their higher death rate due to homicide (National Vital Statistics Systems, 2010; Stillion, 1995). Although women make twice as many suicide attempts as men, they are less likely to succeed in killing themselves. Moreover, the gender gap in suicide has increased slightly in recent years (Cutright, 2001; Moller-Leimkuhler, 2003; Waldron, 1995). Some analysts have interpreted these findings to mean that most women who attempt suicide do not really wish to kill themselves, but rather to seek help, while more men actually kill themselves because they have difficulty seeking help or because they are simply more determined to kill themselves (Moller-Leimkuhler, 2003; Stillion, 1995). Others, however, have hypothesized that men are more successful in committing suicide because of the methods they use to accomplish the task. Women and men attempt suicide using items from their environment with which they are most familiar and to which they have easiest access. "Masculine" items, such as guns, tend to be more lethal than "feminine" items, such as pills (Kushner, 1985; Schimelpfening, 2009).

The mortality rates from homicide are particularly illuminating for they are products of the intersection of sexism, racism, and social class inequality. In general, men are nearly four times more likely than women to be murdered or to die from "legal intervention" (National Center for Health Statistics, 2010). In 2010, about 62 percent of homicides involved both a male victim and a male perpetrator. By comparison, 27 percent of homicides in the same year involved a female victim and a male perpetrator (Federal Bureau of Investigation, 2010). Race, though, is a more important variable than sex. Although Black females are far less likely than Black males to be murdered, they have a higher rate of victimization than either White males or White females. Most of the excess of male mortality caused by homicide, however, is accounted for by Black male victimization. Indeed, homicide and firearm-related injuries are the leading causes of death for young Black males aged fifteen to twenty-four (National Center for Health Statistics, 2010). The high homicide rate of Black males reflects to a large extent their residential concentration in urban, high-crime neighborhoods and their disadvantaged economic position (Geronimus, Bound, & Colen, 2011; Lee, 1989; Staples, 1995). To paraphrase one observer, there appears to be incestuous relationships between racism, sexism, poverty, crime, and ill health (Holloman, 1983).

Acquired Immune Deficiency Syndrome (AIDS)

The Centers for Disease Control (CDC) reported the first cases of AIDS in the United States in June, 1981. At the end of 2006, an estimated 1.1 million persons in the United States were living with HIV infection (CDC, 2009). Importantly, since 1992, while the number of diagnoses has decreased, the estimated prevalence has continued to increase (CDC, 2009). The diagnosis rate fell significantly around 1992, but has since nearly leveled off at 40,000 new cases diagnosed each year since 1998 (CDC, 2009). According to the CDC, as many as 50 percent of Americans infected with HIV either do not know they have it or do not seek care. That percentage translates into 180,000 to 280,000 people who are infected but do not know it. However, as with the other diseases we have discussed, not everyone is at equal risk of becoming infected with the human immunodeficiency virus (HIV, the virus that causes AIDS). Risk of HIV infection is influenced by sexual orientation, race and ethnicity, and gender.

There are only a few ways that HIV is transmitted. HIV is carried through blood, semen, and vaginal secretions, so one of the most common ways for the disease to be transmitted is by sexual contact with an infected person. The riskiest form of sexual contact is anal intercourse because it frequently causes tears in the rectal lining and blood vessels, allowing the virus to pass from the semen of the infected partner into the blood of the other partner. Gay and bisexual men have accounted for about 56 percent of total AIDS cases reported each year, but the percentage of people with AIDS who are gay or bisexual men has varied in recent years. In 1985, for example, 66.8 percent of people with AIDS were gay and bisexual men, but by 1995, the percentage had dropped to 40.9; in 2009, the percentage had risen again to about 43 percent, still well below the 1985 percentage (CDC, 2010; National Center for Health Statistics, 2000). Experts attribute this decline to successful education campaigns in the gay community about AIDS prevention. One exception to this decline is young gay Black men, whose rate of infection, at least in major urban centers of the United States, has risen in recent years. One reason for this disparity may be a greater stigma attached to homosexuality in the African American community, which may prevent young Black gay men from acknowledging their sexual orientation and practicing safe sex (Altman, 2001).

A second common way of contracting HIV is by using contaminated needles to inject drugs. The disease can be transmitted if a drug user injects himself or herself with a used needle that has traces of blood containing HIV. People with AIDS who are injection drug users increased from 17.2 percent in 1985 to over 27 percent in 1998; in 2009, they were 24.9 percent of people with AIDS and 14.4 percent of new cases (CDC, 2009; National Center for Health Statistics, 2000). Research indicates that impoverished racial and ethnic minorities are more likely than Whites to be injection drug users, so their risk of infection is greater. In 2007, for instance, 19.7 percent of Whites with AIDS had contracted the disease through injection drug use, compared with 53.4 percent of African Americans and 25 percent of Hispanics (Avert, 2011). AIDS is already a leading cause of death among African Americans aged twenty-five to forty-four. It is expected that by 2025 more than half of all people with AIDS will be African American; an African American will be nine times more likely to be diagnosed with AIDS than someone who is not African American (Human Sciences Research Council, 2003; Rimer, 1996). Efforts to curb HIV transmission among injection drug users by establishing needle exchange programs have not been widely supported by federal, state, and local governments because some people believe that such programs encourage illegal drug use, even though research has demonstrated that such programs do reduce the transmission of HIV and do not increase the rate of drug use (Vlahov, 2001).

Vaginal intercourse, although less risky than anal intercourse and injection drug use, is also a means of HIV transmission (see Box 12.1). About 64 percent of those who have contracted HIV through heterosexual sex are women, and the majority of them through unprotected vaginal intercourse with an infected partner (Avert, 2011). Between 1985 and 1998, the percentage of people with AIDS who were women more than tripled, increasing from 6.5 percent to 22.8 percent (National Center for Health Statistics, 2000). Once again, however, race and ethnicity intersect with gender to affect risk. African American and Hispanic American women are especially at risk, since so many more African American and Hispanic American men are infected than White men. African American women, for instance, make up 60 percent of all women infected with HIV (Avert, 2011).

The risk of HIV infection is also high for poor women, a disproportionate number of whom are women of color. For some poor women, sex is a source of income (Osmond et al., 1993; Ramesh et al., 2008). Health experts are also concerned that the use of illegal drugs and the rising incidence of other sexually transmitted diseases in poor urban areas contribute to HIV infection. Female drug users often engage in unprotected sex in exchange for money or drugs (Logan & Leukefeld, 2000; Inciardi et al., 1993; Sterk, Elifson, & German, 2000). And the presence of other sexually transmitted diseases, such as syphilis, can facilitate HIV transmission. The second most frequent means of HIV infection among women is injection drug use: 32.1 percent of women with AIDS in 2007 were infected as a result of injecting drugs (Avert, 2011).

The number of people infected with HIV continues to grow, but the number of AIDS deaths declined in 1997 for the first time since the epidemic began. The decline indicates that people who become infected with HIV are not developing AIDS as quickly

BOX 12.1
Violence Against Women and Risk of HIV/AIDS Transmission

We have learned that one of the easiest and most effective ways of preventing HIV/AIDS transmission is the use of condoms during sexual activity. Nevertheless, some groups are less able to negotiate condom use than others. One such group is women involved in abusive intimate relationships. In fact, researchers report that intimate partner violence (IPV) and HIV/AIDS infection are two linked threats to women's health (Enriquez et al., 2009). In Chapter 9, we saw that while it is widely believed that women are usually sexually assaulted by strangers, the fact is that most women are sexually assaulted by men they know, including their intimate partners. In a national study using a large random sample, researchers found that 4.5 percent of the women reported they had been physically forced by an intimate partner to have sex (Tjaden & Thoennes, 2000). Another study of college women found that 31 percent said they had been sexually assaulted by their boyfriends while they were in high school (Smith et al., 2002; see also Salazar et al., 2009). Sexual assault is not an uncommon occurrence in abusive intimate relationships.

Men typically control the use of condoms in intimate relationships. Studies indicate that although condom use is low in steady intimate relationships, it is further reduced in abusive intimate relationships, even though abusive men are more likely to have sex with multiple partners, thus raising the risk of transmitting HIV/AIDS as well as other sexually transmitted diseases (STDs) (Coker, 2007; Roberts et al., 2005; Salazar et al., 2009). Purdie and her colleagues (2010) studied abusive men who had forced their intimate partners to have sex without a condom and compared them with abusive men who had not done this. They found that abusive men who forced sex without a condom were more likely than other abusive men to have been somewhat more physically assaultive toward their partners. They also had more positive attitudes toward casual sex and had sex more often. (But both groups of men appeared to be equally motivated in forcing sex by their desire to exert sexual dominance over women.) Moreover, Purdie et al. (2010) report that forced sex without a condom was quite common among the men in their sample; about 50 percent of the men who had forced their intimate partners to have sex forced them to do so without a condom.

Women in abusive intimate relationships may be reluctant to insist that their intimate partners use condoms during sex because they fear their partners will react with greater anger and aggression in a situation that already involves unwanted or forced sex. The findings of Purdie et al. (2010) indicate that this fear is not unfounded, given that the men in their study who forced sex without a condom were more likely to have physically injured their intimate partners. This research has important implications for HIV/AIDS and STD prevention and treatment programs as well as for IPV prevention and intervention programming. Both types of efforts must address the links between these health hazards. Studies indicate that women in groups at high risk for both HIV and STD infection and for IPV victimization (e.g., low-income women, substance-using women, and women with mental health problems) are receptive to interventions that teach self-protective strategies that increase their ability to more successfully negotiate safer sex practices. Of course, primary responsibility for prevention should focus on men with programming that targets norms supportive of men's violence against and sexual dominance of women as well as the idea of condom use (or nonuse) as a man's prerogative or as a power issue in a relationship (Enriquez et al., 2009; Solomon et al., 2009).

as in the past and that people with AIDS are living longer. Most experts credit new HIV treatments, particularly drugs called protease inhibitors (Altman, 1997; Villarosa, 2001). It remains to be seen whether the drugs will lower AIDS mortality in the long term, since they are very expensive—well beyond the financial reach of the people who are most at risk of contracting HIV.

People with HIV and AIDS are severely stigmatized. To a large extent, the social stigma stems from people's misunderstandings about HIV transmission. Despite efforts to educate the general public, the level of misinformation is still high, and widespread myths and stereotypes often lead to prejudice and discrimination against people with HIV/AIDS (Anderson et al., 2008; Herek & Glunt, 1997; Thi et al., 2008). Meanwhile, people with AIDS and those close to them must cope with not only the physical devastation wrought by the disease, but also in many cases the psychological trauma of devastated social networks and increased social isolation (see, for example, Smith & Christakis, 2008; Turner, Pearlin, & Mullan, 1998; Weitz, 1991). Certainly, public anxiety about diseases such as HIV and AIDS is understandable, but discrimination against and isolation of people with AIDS and their families is an unacceptable response to this health crisis.

Women, Men, and Morbidity

We have seen that, on average, women outlive men by almost six years. Despite their longer life expectancy and lower mortality rates, women have higher **morbidity rates**— i.e., rates of illness—than men. Women have higher rates of illness from acute conditions and nonfatal chronic conditions, and they are slightly more likely to report their health as fair to poor. They make more physician visits each year, and they have twice the number of surgical procedures performed on them as men do (Doyal, 1990b; Hootman, 2001; McDonald & Hertz, 2009; Waldron, 1995). Cleary (1987, p. 55) reports that "Those differences are largest during women's reproductive years (ages seventeen to forty-four) but even when reproductive conditions are excluded, there is a residual gender difference in short-term disability."

The higher morbidity of women may be related to their longer life expectancy. The older one is, the more likely one is to suffer from a chronic illness that restricts one's activities. Women comprise 57 percent of the population over 65 and 67 percent of those 85 and older (U.S. Department of Commerce, Bureau of the Census, 2011). Low income adds to the health problems of the elderly, particularly elderly women (K. Davis et al., 1990; Fox et al., 2010). As we saw in Chapter 8, elderly women, especially women of color, are significantly more likely than elderly men to live below the poverty line. There is a direct relationship between poverty and ill health (Brady, 2004; Engelhardt, 2004; Gornick et al., 1996; Schweder, 1997; Syme & Berkman, 1997). Studies, in fact, found a strong relationship between women's experiences of gender inequality, including lower incomes and greater financial hardship, and poor health (Ross & Bird, 1994; World Health Organization, 2011). Moreover, official measures of poverty miss a considerable number of the elderly poor who are housed in public institutions and nursing homes. Almost 68 percent of nursing home residents are female (U.S. Department of Commerce, Bureau of the Census, 2011).

A second explanation of women's higher morbidity is that it is simply an artifact of their greater use of medical services. That is, men may experience as many or more symptoms as women, but they ignore them. Such behavior is again compatible with traditional gender norms: Men are stoic and physically strong, while women are frail and need assistance (Helgeson, 1995; Lamm, 2008). There is some evidence to support this hypothesis. For example, although women delay as long as men before getting medical attention for some disorders, men tend to underestimate the extent of their illness more than women do, and they utilize preventive services less often (Commonwealth Fund, 2000; Waldron, 1995). As we noted earlier, some men obtain treatment because their wives or daughters seek it out for them by making their physician appointments or calling 911 in a medical emergency. In addition, the medical community itself is not free of these gender stereotypes and may serve to reinforce them. Historical research, in fact, indicates that physicians have frequently equated normal femininity with the sick role (Ehrenreich & English, 1986; Eisler & Hersen, 2000). To understand this better, though, we need to look at the differences in the ways women and men are treated by the health care system.

SEXISM IN HEALTH CARE

Medical practitioners in the United States subscribe, for the most part, to a *functional model* of health, which sees the human body as analogous to a machine. Illness temporarily disrupts the normal functioning of this "machine," preventing its owner from fulfilling his or her usual responsibilities. Although more emphasis has been placed on preventative medicine in the United States in recent years, most medical practice continues to be curative medicine, which specializes in the scientific repair (i.e., diagnosis, treatment, and cure) of the malfunctioning human machine. "Once 'fixed' the person can be returned to the community" (Rothman, 1984, p. 72).

Sociologist Barbara Katz Rothman (1984) argues that the functional model of health has traditionally made women more than men susceptible to "illness labeling" by the medical establishment. This is because historically, women in general have not been considered contributing members of society—"as people doing important things"—since their primary roles were performed outside the public sphere, in the home. "[W]omen were more easily *defined* as sick when they were not seen as functional social members" (Rothman, 1984, p. 72, author's emphasis). This was particularly significant during the nineteenth and early twentieth centuries when physicians were competing with other healers for patients. The "nonfunctional" woman was a status symbol as well as a symbol of femininity. This image, though, was class- and race-specific; only middle- and upper-class White women (physicians' best-paying customers) were viewed as delicate and frail. Poor and working-class women, immigrant women, and women of color were thought to be more robust; it was argued that their less civilized nature made them strong and able to withstand pain. Of course, these women could hardly afford to be sick, even if their wealthy mistresses and employers had permitted it (Ehrenreich & English, 1986; Eisler & Hersen, 2000; Rothman, 1984).

At the same time, many women of that period did display symptoms of physical weakness, for example, fatigue, shortness of breath, fainting spells, and chest and abdominal pains. These symptoms, though, were probably the consequences of stylishness:

> A fashionable woman's corset exerted, on the average, twenty-one pounds of pressure on her internal organs, and extremes of up to eighty-five pounds had been measured. Add to this the fact that a well-dressed woman wore an average of thirty-seven pounds of street clothing in the winter months, of which nineteen pounds were suspended from her tortured waist. (Ehrenreich & English, 1986, p. 285)

Physicians at the time, however, overlooked the effects of clothing styles on women's health and took these symptoms instead as further evidence of women's inferior constitutions. It was obvious to them that women needed special care, and they responded with the medical specialties of obstetrics and gynecology. Essentially, these specialties medicalized the natural biological events in women's lives: menstruation, pregnancy and childbirth, lactation, and menopause.

There is substantial evidence that early on, physicians' services were often more detrimental than beneficial to women's health. Medical intervention in childbirth is an example. Prior to the nineteenth century, the birth of a child was looked on as a family event, not a medical one. Women gave birth in the presence of female friends, relatives, and midwives who took a noninterventionist approach, letting nature take its course. For the most part, their role was supportive, trying to ease the labor of the birthing woman by making her as comfortable as possible. But when competition for patients began to intensify during the nineteenth century, physicians, who were virtually all men, began to deride midwives as uneducated "quacks." Physicians claimed to have scientific expertise in the area of childbirth. Only they had access to the specialized knowledge and medical instruments that would make childbirth safer, easier, and quicker. Eager for relief from the birthing trauma, women who could afford it increasingly gave birth with a physician, rather than a midwife, in attendance. The physician, having made his claims, felt pressured to "perform," especially if witnesses were present. "The doctor could not appear to be indifferent or inattentive or useless. He had to establish his identity by doing something, preferably something to make the patient feel better" (Wertz & Wertz, 1986, p. 140). However, these were the days before asepsis (the germ theory of disease—that germs cause disease—wasn't proven until 1876), anesthesia, and other important medical developments. Medical schools in the early 1800s offered only a few courses and no clinical experience (Ehrenreich & English, 1986; Porter et al., 2008; Starr, 1982). Doctors' interventions were typically crude and harmful: for instance, bloodletting until the laboring patient fainted, the application of leeches to relieve abdominal and vaginal pain, the use of chloride of mercury to purge the intestines, and the administration of emetics to induce vomiting (Ehrenreich & English, 1986; Wertz & Wertz, 1986).

Given these techniques, it is hardly surprising that births attended by physicians had higher maternal and infant mortality rates than those attended by midwives for most of the 1800s (Developmental Psychology Netletter, 2011; Rothman, 1984). Nevertheless, the physicians succeeded in convincing state legislators—men with socioeconomic backgrounds similar to their own—that midwifery and other types of "unscientific" medicine (e.g., herbal medicine) were dangerous. After 1910, the states enacted strict licensing laws that, in effect, drove midwives, herbalists, and other healers out of the business of birthing babies and the practice of medicine (Nechas & Foley, 1994; Starr, 1982). Between 1900 and 1957, the number of practicing midwives in the United States declined dramatically from about three thousand to two (Barker-Benfield, 1976; Frontier Nursing Service, 2011).

Today, obstetricians and gynecologists retain their virtual monopoly on women's health care. Women, in fact, are encouraged to obtain their general medical care from these specialists. Note that there are no comparable medical specialties devoted to "men's diseases" or men's reproductive health, but about 64 percent of obstetricians/gynecologists are men. The overwhelming majority are also White (American Medical Association, 2000).

Advances in medical science and technology have clearly benefited women and saved many lives; deaths from breast cancer, for example, have declined steadily since 1985, owing in large part to widespread availability of mammograms that aid early detection. But many analysts still question how much medical intervention into women's normal biological functioning is really necessary. Consider again medical intervention into pregnancy and childbirth. During pregnancy, women normally gain weight, retain fluids, and experience nausea. Doctors have sometimes responded to these changes by prescribing special diets and medications. These may prove helpful for some women, but there are well-documented and tragic examples of how various drugs, such as thalidomide and Bendectin, have produced severe fetal deformities and illness. The drug diethylstilbestrol (DES), a synthetic estrogen, was once widely prescribed to prevent miscarriages, but was taken off the market when it was found to cause cancer in the daughters of women who had taken it (Newbold, 2006; Rothman, 1984).

Studies also show that doctors may intervene in pregnancy for the sake of convenience—their own and the mother's—as well as to reduce their chances of facing malpractice claims (Davis-Floyd, 1992; Nakamura, 2010). For example, the rate of caesarian deliveries in the United States doubled between 1975, when it was just 10.4 births per 100 live births and 1997, when the rate of caesarean deliveries was 20.8 per 100 live births. The Centers for Disease Control maintain that a rate of 15 caesarean births per 100 is more medically appropriate (U.S. Department of Commerce, Bureau of the Census, 2000). In 2007, the rate of caesarian deliveries skyrocketed to 31.8 percent, meaning that almost one out of every three mothers now give birth by cesarean section and that the caesarian rate is more than double the recommended rate (Childbirth Connection, 2011). Most caesarians are scheduled, rather than emergency deliveries, and the Centers for Disease Control maintain that about 36 percent of caesarean deliveries are medically unnecessary (Angelle, 2010; CDC, 1993). The federal government and health insurers have become more concerned about the high rate of caesarian deliveries because they raise health care costs; caesarians are almost twice as expensive as vaginal deliveries. The majority of caesarian deliveries are performed in for-profit hospitals on women covered by private medical insurance (CDC, 1993; Porterfield, 2006).

The medicalization of pregnancy and childbirth is just one example of often unnecessary medical intervention into normal biological events in a woman's life; there are numerous others. Menopause, for instance, is still viewed as problematic by many physicians who treat it as a hormone deficiency. Synthetic estrogens are frequently prescribed to help women overcome the side effects of menopause, such as hot flashes, depression, irritability, and vaginal inelasticity. Hormone replacement therapy seems to have beneficial effects for some women, including protection from heart disease, but there are also negative effects as well, especially among long-term users, such as an increased risk of breast cancer (Grady, 2002). Moreover, these treatments are often touted in ageist as well as sexist terms, promising women eternal femininity and youthfulness (Greer, 1992; Side Effects of Hormone Replacement Therapy, 2011).

However, it is poor women and women of color who have suffered most at the hands of the medical establishment. Historically, these women have been treated by physicians as little more than training and research material. In fact, gynecological surgery was developed by physicians who first practiced their techniques on Black and immigrant women. It has been documented, for example, that J. Marion Sims, the "father of gynecology" and one of the early presidents of the American Medical Association, kept a number of Black female slaves for the sole purpose of surgical experimentation. "He operated [without anesthesia] on one of them thirty times in four years.... After moving to New York, Sims continued his experimentation on indigent Irish women in the wards of New York Women's Hospital" (Ehrenreich & English, 1986, p. 291).

Researchers have also documented widespread sterilization abuse of poor women and women of color because of racial, ethnic, and social class discrimination (Ruzek, 1987; Volscho, 2010). Davis (1981), for instance, found that as recently as 1972, 100,000 to 200,000 sterilizations took place that year under the auspices of federal programs. The majority of these sterilizations involved poor minority women who allegedly underwent the surgery voluntarily, although there is evidence that many were misled or coerced. "Women were sterilized without consent, or consent was obtained on the basis of false or misleading information—commonly, that the operation was reversible or that it was free of problems and side effects. Information was given in language women did not understand; women were threatened with loss of welfare or medical benefits if they did not consent; consent was solicited during labor; and abortion was conditioned upon consent to sterilization" (Committee for Abortion Rights and Against Sterilization Abuse, 1988, pp. 27–28). In 1979, the federal government issued regulations to prevent involuntary sterilizations, but some analysts maintain that poor women are still coerced into sterilization in other, more subtle ways. One way, for instance, is the virtual elimination of federal funding for abortions. "The federal government assumes 90 percent of the cost of most sterilizations under Medicaid at the same time that it pays for only a minuscule number of abortions. This funding disparity amounts to a government policy of population control targeted at poor people and people of color" (Committee for Abortion Rights and Against Sterilization Abuse, 1988, p. 28; see also Bartz & Greenberg, 2009; Sonfield et al., 2008). Not surprisingly, statistics continue to show that Black women are significantly more likely to be surgically sterilized than White and Hispanic women are (Beal, 2008).[5]

Sexism is not unique to obstetrics and gynecology; research shows that sexism can be found in virtually all medical specialties. For instance, one study found that male physicians better understand and communicate more effectively with male patients than female patients. In this study, the researchers found that female patients were more than twice as likely as male patients to have the motivation for their office visit misunderstood by their male physicians (Boland et al., 1998; see also Hall & Roter, 2002). Cardiology provides another example. Cardiology is male-dominated in terms of both physicians and patients. We have already noted the widespread belief that women are at low risk for heart disease and its consequences, including heart attacks. Recent studies show that most physicians do not respond as quickly to female patients' symptoms of heart disease as they do to male patients' symptoms. For example, recent studies found that women with heart disease are not receiving aggressive treatment for dangerously high cholesterol levels, although 80 percent of the female patients studied could have achieved safe cholesterol levels if their doctors had prescribed the appropriate drugs—drugs that are routinely prescribed for men with heart disease (Blomkans et al., 2005; Schrott et al., 1997; Stenvinkel et al., 2002). Women must often prove that there is a genuine problem with their hearts by being significantly sicker (e.g., having a heart attack or congestive heart failure) in order for their complaints to be acted on aggressively by a physician (Albarran, Clarke, & Crawford, 2007; Nechas & Foley, 1994). This in large part helps to explain why women are less likely than men to survive heart bypass surgery. By the time they undergo the operation, they are usually much sicker and slightly older than the male patients (Kahn et al., 1990; Norton, 2005). Additional studies show, in fact, that when women go to emergency rooms with complaints about chest pains, they wait twice as long as men to see a doctor and twice as long for an electrocardiogram, and they are 50 percent less likely to be given medications that inhibit further damage to the heart and other parts of the body following a heart attack (Henig, 1993; Pope, 1999; Rathore et al., 2000a). After a heart attack, women make more visits to their doctors, but they receive fewer diagnostic tests and medical procedures during this period than male patients do (Schwartz, Fisher, & Wright, 1997; Women's Heart Foundation, 2010). Women are also less likely than men to receive the most sophisticated type of pacemaker, even when differences in their cardiac conditions are controlled for (Schuppel, Buchele, & Koenig, 1998; Women's Heart Foundation, 2010).

In short, research documents a legacy of negative and stereotypic attitudes among physicians toward women, especially poor women, women of color, and elderly women. Women's health concerns not infrequently are trivialized or misunderstood. This, in turn, leads to less than humane treatment and less effective health care for women (Nechas & Foley, 1994; Ward et al., 2008; Weitz, 2009). As Box 12.2 shows, lesbians and gay men also receive less humane and effective treatment because of heterosexism in health care.

Many medical students arrive at medical school with particular prejudices, and these prejudices—sexism, racism, ageism, classism, and heterosexism—are reinforced during medical training (see, for example, Rathore et al., 2000b). The role models available to medical students—medical school faculty and practicing physicians—are often individuals who themselves have been steeped in this tradition, and it may appear in their teaching as well as their interactions with students, colleagues, and patients. Nechas and Foley (1994), for example, found that sexual remarks, jokes, and innuendo were common in medical schools. Other studies have found that nearly half of female physicians surveyed (47.7 percent of 4,501 female physicians) reported having been harassed by male colleagues and teachers simply because they are women. For instance, they were called "honey" in front of patients or other medical personnel, or they were told that medicine was not an appropriate field for women. In one study, 36.9 percent of female physicians reported experiences of sexual harassment by male colleagues and teachers, including lewd remarks, groping, and kissing (Frank, Brogran, & Schiffman, 1998; see also Conley, 1998; Kagan, 2008; Palmore, Branch, & Harris, 2005). Female physicians also report frequent harassment by male patients, who make suggestive remarks and gestures, expose themselves in sexually suggestive ways, and touch them inappropriately (Kagan, 2008; Palmore, Branch, & Harris, 2005; Phillips & Schneider, 1993). However, patients may also be harassed and sexually abused by physicians: In one survey of six hundred emergency room physicians in Canada, for instance, researchers found that 9 percent knew a colleague who had had sex with a patient, while 6 percent admitted they themselves had had sex with a patient (Ovens & Permaul-Woods, 1997; see also Goldie, Schwartz, & Morrison, 2004). However, another study conducted in the United States found that 40 percent of physicians who had been charged with sexual misconduct continue to practice medicine ("Sex Offender MDs Still Practicing," 1997; Vitals, 2010).

The traditional doctor-patient relationship itself appears to be unhealthy, especially for women seeking medical care. It has been argued, though, that this relationship will gradually change as more women enter the medical profession, since they will be better able to communicate with female patients and they have a better understanding of the female body (Carvajal, 2011; Chen, 2010; Fee, 1983; Klass, 1988). Others are skeptical of this argument and call for more radical changes in health care delivery. Before we

BOX 12.2
Heterosexist Health Care

When choosing a physician, what characteristics do you look for? Most likely, you consider the physician's credentials: medical school attended, board certification, years practicing, perhaps even awards and honors. You may also ask around to see what kind of reputation the physician has. But if you are a lesbian or gay man, one of the most important characteristics to you as a patient is that the physician feels comfortable with homosexuals and is knowledgeable about the special health needs of gay men, lesbians, bisexuals, and transgendered people. Research indicates that homosexuals often do not disclose their sexual orientation to health care providers because they fear rejection, ridicule, and disrespect (Klitzman & Greenberg, 2002; Tiemann, Kennedy, & Haga, 1998; White & Dull, 1998; Wilkes, 2008). Many believe their care will be negatively affected if providers are aware of their sexual orientation (Johnson et al., 1981; Petroll & Mosack, 2011). However, by not disclosing their sexual orientation, gay men, lesbians, bisexuals, and transgendered people run the risk of not getting appropriate care or not being screened for conditions that are especially prevalent among these groups (Columbia University & the Gay and Lesbian Medical Association, 2000). For instance, lesbians have higher rates of breast cancer than heterosexual women. Although doctors are unsure why this is the case, it may be because childless women have higher rates of breast cancer than women who have had children; lesbians are significantly less likely than heterosexual women to have had children. In any event, this elevated risk of breast cancer should prompt physicians to prescribe mammograms for lesbians at younger ages and more frequently than they do for heterosexual women.

Studies show, however, that about 40 percent of physicians are uncomfortable caring for gay, lesbian, bisexual, and transgendered patients. Heterosexual physicians assume their patients are straight; some exhibit homophobia when they learn otherwise. Consider, for example, the lesbian who went to a neurologist because she was having severe headaches and occasional memory loss. While taking this woman's medical history, the physician questioned why she did not use contraception. When she replied that she was a lesbian, the neurologist reassessed all her symptoms in light of this information and decided she should have psychological testing and an evaluation by a clinical psychologist. Her physical problem was redefined as a psychological disorder stemming from her sexual orientation. Another lesbian who disclosed her sexual orientation to her allergy specialist was told that her lesbianism might be caused by her allergies and that perhaps a series of injections would "cure" her (Tiemann et al., 1998). Other gay men, lesbians, bisexuals, and transgendered people report that although their health care providers don't explicitly state their disapproval or discomfort with their patients' sexual orientation, their behavior betrays their feelings: They are startled, become nervous, and can no longer maintain eye contact, preferring to look at the floor or past the patient. The providers may also stop talking with the patient or not engage in extensive questioning, which in turn, could result in misdiagnoses or inadequate treatment (Petroll & Mosack, 2011; Stevens, 1998).

There are no comprehensive data available on how many physicians are themselves gay, lesbian, bisexual, or transgendered, or who they are and where they are located, apart from a few directories. Understandably, many if not most LGBT physicians may not wish to publicize their sexual orientation. And although such information might be helpful to GLBT patients when choosing a physician, it does not address the widespread problem of heterosexism among health care professionals, the majority of whom appear to be straight.

consider these alternatives, let's take a closer look at the roles and experiences of women and men in the health care professions, especially in light of what we have already learned about the gender-based and sexual harassment of female physicians.

The Patriarchal Hierarchy of Health Care Work

In Chapter 7, we discussed how functionalist sociologists, such as Talcott Parsons, differentiate between male and female roles as instrumental and expressive, respectively. Within the traditional patriarchal family, men are the instrumental leaders of the household and command greater power in decision making, primarily because they are the breadwinners. Women, in contrast, are housekeepers and nurturers. Interestingly, critics of traditional medical practice in the United States draw parallels between patriarchal relations in the family and the male-female relations dominant in the delivery of health care. "The doctor/father runs a family composed of the nurse (wife and mother) and the patient (the child). The doctor possesses the scientific and technical skills and the nurse performs the caring and comforting duties" (Fee, 1983, p. 24; see also Ehrenreich & English, 1986).

Historically, the sex distribution of workers across specific health care fields makes this parallel even sharper. Health care has been an area of high female employment because many health care jobs were viewed as an extension of women's roles in the home. Women have been concentrated in the "helping," "nurturing," and housekeeping jobs in health care. They are the majority of registered nurses, nurses aides, nutritionists, and dieticians (U.S. Department of Labor, 2010). These positions have lower prestige and lower incomes than male-dominated health professions, such as physician. The least prestigious and lowest paying jobs are filled largely by minority workers (Brox, 2011).

We have already seen how male physicians drove female health care providers, such as midwives, out of practice early in this century.[6] In addition, women and racial and ethnic minorities historically were excluded from medical schools or discouraged from entering or completing medical training, either through blatant or, more recently, subtle forms of discrimination (Ehrenreich & English, 1986; Nechas & Foley, 1994). Since 1971, however, the number of female and minority medical school students and graduates has increased significantly (see Table 12.4). In 1971, for example, women were just 10.9 percent of medical school students; by 1980, their numbers had more than doubled to 28.9 percent, and by 2010, women were 47.4 percent of the total (Association of American Medical Colleges, 2011). In 1975, women were just 13.4 percent of medical school graduates, whereas in 2002, they were 44.2 percent of medical school graduates and, in 2010, 48.3 percent of the total graduates (Association of American Medical Colleges, 2011, 2000). As Table 12.4 shows, racial and ethnic minorities have also increased their representation among medical school students and graduates, although what the table does not show is that in 1997 there was an 11 percent drop in minority medical school enrollments. Most experts attribute this decline to federal court decisions and state referenda that ended affirmative action programs in medical school admissions, discouraging some minorities from applying and causing school administrators to be overly cautious in admissions decisions so as to avoid a "reverse discrimination" lawsuit ("Minority Enrollment Drops," 1997).[7] By 2010, the proportion of minority medical school students had once again increased, although with the exception of Asian Americans, they are still underrepresented (Dunham, 2010).

TABLE 12.4   Medical School Enrollments and Graduates by Sex and Race, Selected Years

Percent of first-year students enrolled in medical school who were:	1980–1981	2002–2003	2009–2010
Women	28.9	46.4	47.4
White (non-Hispanic)	82.9	62.6	60.1
Black (non-Hispanic)	7.9	7.4	7.0
Hispanic	4.8	6.6	8.2
Asian	3.3	20.1	22.0
American Indian	0.4	0.7	0.8
Percent of total students enrolled in medical school who were:	**1980–1981**	**2002–2003**	**2009–2010**
Women	28.9	46.4	47.4
White (non-Hispanic)	82.9	62.6	60.1
Black (non-Hispanic)	7.9	7.4	7.0
Hispanic	4.8	6.6	8.2
Asian	3.3	20.1	22.0
American Indian	0.4	0.7	0.8
Percent of medical school graduates (M.D.'s) who were:	**1980–1981**	**2002–2003**	**2009–2010**
Women	na	44.2	48.3
White (non-Hispanic)	na	64.1	63.4
Black (non-Hispanic)	na	6.9	6.8
Hispanic	na	6.1	7.5
Asian	na	19.4	20.8
American Indian	na	0.8	.08

Sources: Digest of Education Statistics, 2000; National Center for Health Statistics, 2000, pp. 312–314; Association of American Medical Colleges, 2011.

Although the greater presence of women and people of color in medical school classes is certainly a welcome trend, some observers question the extent to which these groups will be able to change the sexism and other inequalities that seem entrenched in our health care system. Some of this skepticism stems from the fact that female and minority medical students receive their training in the same sexist, racist, class-biased, and homophobic system of medical education that White males do. As we have already noted, they have fewer role models. The representation of women among medical school faculty has improved significantly since 1975, from 15.1 percent to 34 percent in 2009 (Association of American Medical Colleges, 2011). But while the number of minority faculty has increased considerably since 1975, the percentage of medical school faculty who are racial and ethnic minorities is still just 20.7 percent (Association of American Medical Colleges, 2011).

Moreover, both women and racial and ethnic minorities are concentrated in the junior academic ranks and are less likely than their White male colleagues to be promoted to the senior ranks or to hold administrative positions such as department chair or dean (Association of American Medical College, 2011; Nonnemaker, 2000; Palepu et al., 1998).

We have already discussed the widespread gender discrimination, including sexual harassment, that female physicians experience. A rather discouraging finding of the Frank, Brogran, and Schiffman study (1998; see also Carr et al., 2003) was that young women were the most likely to have these negative experiences, an indication that despite the greater presence of women in the medical profession, their situation is not significantly improving. Moreover, this study found that women in the male-dominated (and highest-paying) specialties, such as surgery, were more likely than other women to report harassment and discrimination. This finding helps to explain why these specialties remain male-dominated (Manning, 1998; Stratton et al., 2005). Not surprisingly, women are concentrated in general medicine, pediatrics, and other lower-paying specialties (American Medical Association, 2002).[8]

Recent research indicates that female physicians appear to care for female patients better than male physicians do. For example, female physicians have been found to perform more Pap tests on their patients and to order significantly more mammograms. This is especially true when the practices of younger female and male physicians are compared (Franks & Clancy, 1993; Lurie et al., 1993; Schmid, Cronauer, & Cousin, 2010). Nevertheless, some observers continue to express concern that as long as medical students are socialized into a physician role that is paternalistic and authoritarian, the detrimental aspects of the physician-patient relationship, particularly for female and non-White patients, are not likely to improve. From this perspective, the solution to the inequities in health care is not simply to put more women and people of color in positions of power within the current medical system, but rather to change the system itself. As we will see next, this goal is a cornerstone of the feminist health care movement.

Feminist Health Care

The feminist health care movement emerged during the 1960s as an outgrowth of the broader feminist struggle against sexism and gender inequality (see Chapter 1). Women meeting in small consciousness-raising groups began to relate their individual medical experiences, which contained some common themes: "[the doctor-patient relationship] was all too often characterized by condescension and contempt on the part of the doctor, and feelings of humiliation on the part of the patient" (Marieskind & Ehrenreich, 1975, p. 39). Out of these discussions grew the realization that women needed to develop their own standards of health and normalcy by studying women's bodies, including their own. By 1975, these early efforts had produced more than 1,200 feminist health care groups in the United States alone.

The feminist health care movement combines self-help with political practice (Newman, 2007; Withorn, 1986). According to health education specialist Sheryl Ruzek (1987, p. 188), feminist health activists "educate themselves and other women about health issues, provide alternative services, and work to influence public policies affecting women's health." They accomplish these goals in diverse ways. With regard to education, for instance, feminists have produced a large and impressive body of literature covering diverse health and medical issues in a nontechnical, highly readable style and format.

One of the first, and perhaps the best known, example is the Boston Women's Health Collective's book *Our Bodies, Ourselves*, published in 1973 and revised in 1992, 2005, and 2011. A walk through the health section of any mainstream bookstore today will demonstrate the wide array of feminist health care publications currently available.

Feminist health activists have also organized "know-your-body courses," in which women not only learn about their bodies—thereby demystifying them—but also learn how to provide themselves with basic care through, for example, breast self-exams and pelvic self-exams. In the way of alternative medical care, women have opened their own clinics to provide a variety of services, such as gynecological care, pregnancy testing, counseling, and abortion services. There are two distinctive features of feminist clinics: (1) "the bulk of a patient's encounter, from initial intake to the final counseling, is with women like herself"; and (2) "the woman is not the object of care but an active participant" (Marieskind & Ehrenreich, 1975, p. 39).

Finally, in terms of influencing public policy, feminist health activists have formed organizations, such as the National Women's Health Network (see http://www.nwhn. org), which has more than twenty thousand members. Such groups lobby local, national, and international decision makers regarding policies affecting women's health throughout the world.

The feminist health care movement has not been free of problems. For one thing, women's clinics often face severe staffing shortages and funding difficulties. Such clinics are among the first to lose during government budget cuts (Gold, 2010; Withorn, 1986). Not surprisingly, the clinics can usually provide only limited services, typically just obstetrical and gynecological care. In addition, the movement in general has sometimes been criticized for not posing a more serious challenge to the medical establishment. "Many health activists believe that it is virtually impossible to create a truly humane health care system for women in a capitalist society. Yet none of the strategies used directly attack the underlying economic organization of society" (Ruzek, 1987, p. 195). Most still focus on individual treatment, rather than institutional change. And there is the added danger that an emphasis on self-care may simply serve to relieve the state of any responsibility for ensuring the health of its citizens, female and male (Lipsky, 2010; Ruzek, 1987; Withorn, 1986). Some critics maintain that many women's health centers have been co-opted by mainstream medical practices and hospitals, which see the centers as a marketing ploy to attract female health care consumers. Indeed, these critics argue that the financial difficulties faced by most independent women's health centers left them no choice but to partner with hospitals, with the result that "the promise of a fundamental shift in the philosophy and organization of private sector care for women…largely disappeared" by the mid-1990s (Zimmerman & Hill, 1999, p. 506).

Despite these difficulties, the feminist health care movement is to be applauded for providing many women with safer, more affordable, and more affirming medical services. Equally important has been the movement's central role in identifying and publicizing the inadequacies and inequities of our traditional health care system. Although the movement's focus has been on women, its analysis of the problems inherent in traditional health care delivery has also been beneficial to men, especially poor, working-class, and minority men who not infrequently are also subjected to inhumane and condescending treatment at the hands of an elitist medical establishment. Evidence of the movement's success can also be found in U.S. medical schools that have adopted some of its ideas. For example, many medical schools now have genital teaching associate programs to teach aspiring physicians how to do a pelvic exam. Similar to the early "know-the-female-body" courses, genital teaching associate programs hire women to teach medical students how to more sensitively perform a pelvic examination. The focus of these programs is on developing interpersonal skills as much as medical techniques (Kelly, 1998; McMurray et al., 2000).

Another contribution of the feminist health care movement has been to give women "a sense of pride and strength in their bodies" (Marieskind & Ehrenreich, 1975, p. 38; see also Skarderud, 2007). Let's continue to explore this issue by discussing gender, physical fitness, and athletic participation.

GENDER, SPORT, AND FITNESS

Knowing the particular strengths and weaknesses of one's body, feeling fit and energized, being comfortable with and appreciative of one's body are all empowering. What is more, developing one's physical potential instills a sense of achievement that encourages an individual to undertake other types of challenges (Lenskyj, 1986; Mellor et al., 2010; Skarderud, 2007). A recognition of this underlies the much quoted phrase, "sports builds character." Unfortunately, the missing, but nevertheless understood adjective here has long been *masculine* character. Consider, for instance, the 1971 case of *Hollander* v. *Connecticut Conference, Inc.*, in which a female student was barred from competing on her high school's boys' cross country team, even though she had qualified, because the state interscholastic athletic conference prohibited coed sports. In deciding in favor of the athletic conference, the judge stated, "Athletic competition builds character in our boys. We do not need that kind of character in our girls, the women of tomorrow" (quoted in Lawrence, 1987, p. 222).

The judge's statement reflects the traditional belief that athletics is a masculine pursuit incompatible with our cultural standards of feminine beauty and female heterosexual attractiveness. In one sense, this is true; the ways in which sporting and fitness activities are typically organized and played out represent the antithesis of our culture's definition of femininity. The main ingredients of sport in our society are competition and domination, self-control and toughness, and violence and aggression. From their earliest encounters with sports, males are taught to develop a "killer instinct" on the playing field or court. Sport, they learn, is confrontation with an opponent; it entails a certain degree of sweat, exhaustion, and, most importantly, pain to be satisfying. Winning, of course, is "everything." Men and boys who don't play this way—who do not exhibit "forceful masculinity" in athletics—are ridiculed for playing "like girls" (Messner, 2007; White, Young, & McTeer, 1995; Young, 2005).

Females have not been excluded from sport and physical fitness activities altogether, but their participation historically was limited. They were encouraged to assume a supportive role as cheerleaders rather than as direct participants. Those who participated directly were channeled into "feminine sports," such as swimming and diving, skating, gymnastics, and aerobic dancing. Those women who seriously pursued sports often did so under great stress, being labeled "mannish" and "unfeminine" or inept by others (Blinde & Taub, 1992; Jarrat, 1990; McDonagh & Pappano, 2007; Nelson, 1992; Young, 2005). For instance, one study showed that in the minds of many people, a serious female athlete must be a lesbian, and this labeling, in turn, continues to control the number of women in sports and the behavior of female athletes. "Women athletes are seen as something less than 'real women' because they do not exemplify traditional female qualities (e.g., dependency, weakness, passivity)" (Blinde & Taub, 1992, p. 163; see also Caggiano, 2010; Cashmore, 1996). The exception, according to some observers, is the Black female athlete who, in the Black community, may be viewed as strong and competent in sports but not unwomanly (Carter, 2010; Hart, 1980).

Another common and equally sexist representation of female athletes is media coverage and advertising that sexualizes and objectifies these women, instead of presenting them as the strong and physically talented individuals they are (Bernstein, 2002; Messner, 2002, 2007). An example of this is Danica Patrick, a professional NASCAR driver who has achieved many distinctions, including Rookie of the Year for both the 2005 Indianapolis 500 and the 2005 IndyCar Series season. In 2008, she became the first woman to win an Indy car race and she placed third in the 2009 Indianapolis 500, which was both a personal best and the highest finish by a woman in the event's history. Despite these accomplishments Patrick is perhaps equally well known for her sexually provocative advertisements, such as those for the Internet domain registrar and web hosting company, Go Daddy. Often photographed prone and wearing minimal clothing, she is clearly not represented as a strong, talented, self-fulfilled woman. In 2007, Patrick was voted "sexiest athlete" on the Victoria's Secret "What is Sexy" list, while in 2008, rather ironically and disconcertingly, she won the "Kids Choice Award" for favorite female athlete.

In the early 1970s, a number of developments began to transform both women's and men's participation in sport and fitness activities. Perhaps the most important event was passage in 1972 of Title IX of the Education Amendments Act. You may recall from Chapter 5 that Title IX prohibits sex discrimination in educational programs, including sports, that receive federal funding. In effect, Title IX forced most U.S. educational institutions to broaden their athletic programs for girls and women and to spend more money on girls' and women's sports. The effects have been significant: For example, at U.S. colleges and universities, the percentage of female varsity athletes rose from 16 percent in 1971 to 40 percent in 1998; money spent on athletic scholarships to women at the highly competitive National Collegiate Athletic Association (NCAA) Division I schools increased from 20 percent in 1977 to about 40 percent in 1998. Today, more female athletes are participating in college sports than ever before (Asher, 1999; "Conference Report," 1997; Women's Sports Foundation, 2011).

But while there have clearly been significant improvements in women's athletics since the early 1970s, inequities remain. For instance, the average Division I NCAA-member school increased spending on women's sports by 67.2 percent between 2004 and 2009, from $4.3 million to $6.4 million. During the same period, spending on men's sports increased by 69 percent, from $12.5 million to $18.1 million (NCAA, 2010). Men's sports receive 67 percent of the funds budgeted for athletics, and 70 percent of the money spent on recruiting is spent recruiting male athletes ("Suit Unfairly Attacks," 2002). In 2010, the NCAA reported that the median salary for a men's head basketball coach was $911,000, while a women's head basketball coach was earning a median salary of $308,000. These large disparities in salaries paid to coaches of men's and women's teams, respectively, exist across most sports (Asher, 1999; Kamphoff, 2010; NCAA, 2010; see also Theberge, 1993 for a discussion of sex disparities among coaches in Canada).

A similar pattern can be found throughout the sports world. Since the 1970s, women have made tremendous gains in athletic participation. In 1994, for instance, 328 young women played on their high school's boys' varsity football team. Although they were a minuscule 0.03 percent of all high school football players, they significantly increased girls' representation in this sport; today more girls slowly continue to enter the sport (Bloom, 1995; Queens of the Gridiron, 2011). However, as recently as August 2008, Kacy Stuart, the kicker in the Georgia Football League, was dismissed from her private school team for "being a girl" (ESPN High School, 2008). At the amateur level, ice hockey has been growing in popularity among women. Between 1988 and 1998, the number of women registered with USA Hockey, the national organization that governs amateur hockey, increased from about 5,500 to over 20,000. This number was expected to grow even more because of the gold medal win by the U.S. women's ice hockey team at the 1998 Winter Olympics (Kannapell, 1998; Lapointe, 1998, but see also Theberge, 2000). As predicted, by the close of 2009, 465,975 women were registered ice hockey players in the United States, second in number only to Canadian women, who had 499,695 registered players (International Ice Hockey Federation [IIHF], 2009). Women are also playing more at the professional level; the WNBA (Women's National Basketball Association) has twelve teams, and the Women's United Soccer Association had eight teams during the three years the league was open, from 2001 to 2003 (Structure of Women's Soccer Leagues, 2011). Since 2003, women's soccer teams in the United States have been members of the USL, the United Soccer League, a worldwide organization. As of 2011, there were eight U.S. teams (Structure of Women's Soccer Leagues, 2011). In 1997, two women were hired as referees in the men's NBA (National Basketball Association) (Wise, 1997), and currently the NBA has one active female referee. The National Basketball Development League (D League, as it is often called) has one female head coach, Nancy Lieberman, who coaches the Texas Legends. Women have also increased their representation in executive positions. For instance, in 2010, 20 percent of the NBA's top management team was female.

Still, most people continue to devalue women's involvement in sports, regarding women as less serious athletes than men and questioning female athletes' physical and psychological strength and stamina. Consider, for example, that veteran players in the WNBA are paid an average salary of $35,000 for the entire three-month summer season, an amount less than what most NBA starters are paid *per* game (Navarro, 2001). The average annual salary of a player in the NBA in 2009 was $5.84 million (Graham, 2010).

Of course, many people would argue that men's sports produce greater revenues than women's sports, and they would be right, at least at the professional level. At the college level, the data indicate that this is true only at some schools. For instance, more than 50 percent of NCAA Division I-A and Division I-AA football teams do not bring in enough revenue to be self-supporting, let alone subsidize other sports ("Suit Unfairly Attacks," 2002). However, the revenue argument also overlooks the fact that our culture trivializes women's sports and women athletes, while promoting sport as the epitome of masculinity and proof of the physical basis of gender difference (Cashmore, 1996; Crothers & Lockhart, 2000; Scranton & Flintoff, 2002; White et al., 1995). We can see this in the way the media report on men's and women's sports. First, women athletes and women's sporting events are underreported, except during the Olympic Games or other major competitions (Greer, Harden, & Horman, 2009; Kian et al., 2009; Messner, Duncan, & Jensen, 1993). For example, Messner and his colleagues (1993) found that men's sports get 92 percent of televised sports news coverage in the United States, whereas women's sports get just 5 percent of such coverage; the remaining coverage is mixed or gender-neutral. Second, the media's sports reporting also emphasizes a certain type of "orthodox masculinity," particularly toughness and courage in the face of physical risk (Messner, 2007, 1992; White et al., 1995). Women athletes not only do little to sell this kind of masculinity, but they also pose a serious challenge to it. Third, as we have already noted, when women are highlighted in the media, it is often as sex objects or as victims. For example, over the past sixty years only about 4 percent of all *Sports Illustrated* covers have portrayed women, excluding the notorious "swimsuit issues" (Chandler, 2010; see also Ryan, 1994). On one occasion, the women were not athletes, but rather the widows of two professional baseball players who had been killed in a boating accident. Three other women who were athletes were featured as victims rather than victors: Monica Seles, the professional tennis player, was shown with a knife protruding from her back after she had been stabbed by a spectator at a match; Mary Pierce, another tennis player, was featured in a special report on her father's abuse of her; and Nancy Kerrigan, the Olympic figure skater, was featured after she had been attacked by associates of a rival skater. There are now, however, a wide variety of sports magazines designed specifically for female audiences, including *Athletic Women Magazine, Women's Sports Report*, and *Women's Adventure*. One analysis of women's sports magazines reported that they focus more on health and fitness than on sport per se, but many do profile competitive sportswomen (Fink & Kensicki, 2002; MRTW, 1998b; see also Messner, 1993, 2007, O'Reilly & Cahn, 2007).

Despite the continued gender stereotyping of athletes, considerable research has emerged from the fields of sports medicine and sports psychology that debunks many of the myths about the physical and emotional consequences of athletics for men and women. One of the first myths that was refuted, for instance, was the notion of "no pain, no gain" in exercise. Sports medicine specialists were quick to point out that by ignoring the signals their bodies send them through pain, athletes were likely to injure themselves, sometimes permanently (men are more likely to subscribe to this tenet than women are) (Hammerschmidt, 2009; Smith, Weber, & Gale, 2008; White et al., 1995). Sports medicine researchers also demonstrated that participation in sports and vigorous exercise do not "androgenize" women's muscles nor do they harm the female reproductive system (Cashmore, 1996; Hammerschmidt, 2009). To the contrary, exercise may lessen menstrual discomfort and ease childbirth (Brubaker & Dillaway, 2009). Third, the notion that men are naturally better athletes than women because of biological differences in their physical size and strength is also being called into question, especially for certain sports. Recent analyses, for example, show that in track, although men's running times have been improving since the turn of the century, women's running times have been improving at more than double the men's rate, so that if such trends continue, women's and men's track performances will be comparable in the near future (Cashmore, 1996; Fletcher, 2007; Whipp & Ward, 1992).

Meanwhile, sports psychologists have found that while physical exercise and participation in sports can increase self-confidence as well as reduce the likelihood of developing various chronic illnesses such as coronary heart disease, a focus on winning at all costs can produce unhealthy outcomes, including serious illness and injury, as well as a sense of failure, especially in men, since so few ever reach the top of the athletic hierarchy (Hanton, Neil, & Mellalieu, 2008; Klein, 1995; Mellalieu et al., 2009; White et al., 1995).[9] Sports sociologist Harry Edwards has highlighted the disproportionate impact these negative outcomes have had on young Black men, since they are typically channeled into sports but rarely have a "social safety net" to protect them if they "fail." Indeed, Edwards and others have played a major part in uncovering both the exploitation of African American athletes and the racism that continues to permeate organized sports. As one writer expressed it, "In sports, as in the plantation system of the Old South, the overseers are white and the workers are black" (Runfola, 1980, p. 83; see also Majors, 2001; Messner, 1987).

There is evidence that although most female athletes are highly competitive, females in general tend to approach sports differently than males in general. Studies, for example, indicate that women and girls tend to be more flexible and cooperative players of team sports and have a greater concern for the fairness of the game rather than "winning at all costs" (Deboer, 2004; Gilligan, 1982; Jarratt, 1990; Nelson, 1992). In a sense, then, women and girls actually have been freer to approach sports in the way that at least theoretically they are supposed to be approached—in the spirit of play and for the purpose of personal enjoyment and enrichment.

The growth in fitness activities and sports participation has not been lost on entrepreneurs. Selling everything from clothing to exercise equipment to "power" foods, they recognize the growing national interest in exercise and sports as big business, a business that yields more than $24.2 billion a year (IBIS World, 2011). Interestingly, however, their marketing strategy is often not significantly different for male and female consumers. Research shows that many of the fitness products and programs are being touted to women *and* men with promises of youthfulness, thinness, and sex appeal rather than health, well-being, and physical agility (Epstein & Fitzgerald, 2009). Nevertheless, as we will discuss in the final section of this chapter, the commercial tendency to imbue women and, increasingly, men, with insecurity about their bodies and appearance often results in serious psychological as well as physical harm.

GENDER AND MENTAL HEALTH AND ILLNESS

Up to this point, we have been discussing physical health and illness, but let's take some time to explore gender issues in mental health and illness. Gender provides a strong link between physical and mental health since physicians have tended to view women's physical complaints as psychosomatic, that is, as "all in their heads." Research shows that physicians often see women's use of medical services as one of the ways women typically cope with psychological problems. Consequently, physicians commonly prescribe psychotropic drugs for women who visit them with complaints of physical ailments. According to the Department of Health and Human Services (2010), more than 17 million women reported using prescription medication for treatment of a mental or emotional condition in 2009. This represents 14.8 percent of all women in the United States over the age of 18, which is nearly double the rate of use among men. Women receive about 66 percent of psychoactive drug prescriptions. These prescriptions are typically written by internists, general practitioners, and obstetricians/gynecologists rather than psychiatrists.

Historically, it was also common for physicians to assume that "malfunctions" in women's reproductive systems caused psychological disturbances. Around the turn of the twentieth century, for instance, physicians maintained that ovarian dysfunctions caused "personality disorders" in women—specifically, troublesomeness, eating like a ploughman, masturbation, attempted suicide, erotic tendencies, persecution mania, simple "cussedness," and dysmenorrhea. The "cure" physicians devised was ovariotomy (i.e., removal of the ovaries, or "female castration"). Ehrenreich and English (1986) report that:

> In 1906 a leading gynecological surgeon estimated that there were 150,000 women in the United States who had lost their ovaries under the knife. Some doctors boasted that they had removed from fifteen hundred to two thousand ovaries apiece....Patients were often brought in by their husbands who complained of their unruly behavior...The operation was judged successful if the woman was restored to a placid contentment with her domestic functions. (p. 290)

Drugs, such as synthetic hormones that have been linked to cancer and mood altering drugs including Serafem (the antidepressant Prozac) have superseded surgery as "treatment."

These examples highlight some of the difficulties we need to consider when discussing mental health and illness: the problems of definition, identification, and appropriate treatment. Psychiatrists themselves disagree as to what does and what does not constitute mental illness. At one extreme are those who claim that most mental disorders are objective conditions that have identifiable organic or genetic causes. At the other extreme are those who argue that mental illness is a political and moral label, not a medical one, and that mental institutions are not hospitals but rather facilities to control those singled out as deviant.

Although most mental health specialists hold a position somewhere in between these two extremes, the disagreement itself makes it obvious that the identification of mental illness is a difficult enterprise at best. Just how difficult it is was demonstrated by D. L. Rosenhan and his colleagues in a classic experiment conducted in 1973. Rosenhan and seven associates were admitted to several different mental hospitals by claiming they were hearing voices. Their symptom, though, was contrived, as were the names and occupations they gave; however, they made no other changes in their life histories or regular behavior. Each of these pseudopatients expected to be identified quickly as an imposter by hospital personnel, but none was. Instead, the hospital staffs reinterpreted their normal behavior and previous life experiences to coincide with the mental illness diagnosis. They spent an average of nineteen days in the hospital, with all but one diagnosed schizophrenic.

The Rosenhan experiment illustrates that what is identified as mental illness "may be in the culturally filtered eye of the beholder rather than in the malfunction of the physiology or psyche of the person whose behavior is being judged" (Little, 1983, p. 345). Because mental health practitioners, like other human beings, are not immune from social conditioning and therefore cannot be completely objective, we may expect their clinical judgments to reflect, at least in part, aspects of the culture to which they belong. Throughout this text, we have identified a variety of cultural stereotypes regarding gender, sexual orientation, race and ethnicity, age, and social class. How do such stereotypes influence clinical assessments of mental health and illness? Let's consider this question now.

The Double Standard of Mental Health

Over forty years ago, a group of social scientists asked seventy-nine mental health professionals (forty-six men and thirty-three women) to describe "a healthy, mature, socially competent (a) adult, sex unspecified, (b) man, or (c) woman" (Broverman et al., 1970, p. 1). What they discovered was that the characteristics of mental health in the responses differed according to the sex of the person being described. More importantly, however, they found that traits considered healthy for an adult *person* were almost identical to those judged healthy for *men,* including independence, a sense of adventure, and asser-tiveness. In contrast, the healthy, mature, socially competent adult woman was described as submissive, dependent, excitable in minor crises, and conceited about her appearance. As Broverman et al. (1970, p. 5) concluded, "This constellation seems a most unusual way of describing any mature, healthy individual."

Since 1970, this study has been replicated a number of times under a variety of cir-cumstances and with different subjects (Brooks-Gunn & Fisch, 1980; Hansen & Reekie, 1990; Philips & Gilroy, 1985; Schroering, 2003; Wise & Rafferty, 1982). These replica-tions have yielded results that support Broverman et al.'s original findings. What we see here, then, is that stereotypical masculine behavior is assumed by many clinicians to be the norm or the ideal standard of mental health. This, in turn, puts women in a double bind. On one hand, if they choose to behave as a healthy, mature adult, they risk being labeled abnormal (i.e., masculine women). On the other hand, women who follow the cultural script for the healthy, mature woman may find themselves unhappy, dissatisfied, and psychologically troubled (Gilbert & Scher, 1999; Tavris, 1992). And for readers who think the traditional view of the "healthy" woman is a thing of the past, consider that Joan Schroering (2003) found it to be a commonly held view among many of the mental health professionals she surveyed in 2003.

Robertson and Fitzgerald's (1990) research demonstrates how this stereotype may also work against men who choose to deviate from traditional norms of masculin-ity. Robertson and Fitzgerald showed one of two versions of a videotaped conversation between a male patient (in reality, an actor) and his therapist to forty-seven other thera-pists. In one of the tapes, the patient stated he was an engineer with a wife at home who cared for their children. In the other tape, he indicated that his wife was an engineer and he stayed home with the children. Therapists who viewed the first tape attributed the man's problems to job or marital pressures or to biological causes. However, those who saw the second tape typically diagnosed the man as severely depressed and attributed the depression to his adoption of the domestic role, even though he reported to his ther-apist in the tape that his staying at home had worked out well for the family. In addition, these therapists tended to focus on the man's adoption of the domestic role as something to be treated through therapy, and some appeared hostile toward the patient, question-ing his notion of what it means to be a man. In short, this study indicates that men who choose not to adhere to the traditionally prescribed masculine role are at risk of being labeled mentally ill (see also Addis & Mahalik, 2003; Gilbert & Scher, 1999; Hansen & Reekie, 1990; Martindale, 2011; Tavris, 1992).

Besides sex, an individual's race or ethnicity may influence whether he or she is labeled mentally ill as well as the particular disorder that is diagnosed. Loring and Powell (1988), for example, found that mental health professionals were more likely to diag-nose Blacks than Whites as violent, even though the cases they were evaluating were identical in all other respects (see also Borowsky et al., 2000; Fulani, 1988; Littlewood & Lipsedge, 1989; Satcher, 2001). However, more recently Kales and Mellow (2006) found that the race of an individual did not seem to affect the diagnosis of depression among the elderly, indicating that age may intersect with race and gender to affect diagnoses.

Finally, it is also the case that definitions of mental illness and standards of mental health change over time as a behavior gains greater acceptance by the general public or as a result of successful lobbying on the part of a particular group. For instance, in its 1980 revi-sion of the *Diagnostic and Statistical Manual of Mental Disorders*—the official psychiatric classification scheme—the American Psychiatric Association (APA) voted to delete homosexuality from the listing. Prior to this time, homosexuality was officially considered a mental illness and was sometimes "treated" with aversion therapy (e.g., the injection of drugs to induce vomiting while the "patient" looked at homosexual erotica) and electroshock therapy. The demedicalization of homosexuality in 1980 was chiefly the result of tireless campaigning and political confrontation between gay rights activists, such as the National Gay and Lesbian Task Force, and the APA (Busfield, 1986, see also Oliver, 2009).

In the sections that follow, we will discuss several mental disorders that have a higher incidence among members of one sex than the other. We'll pay particular attention to how traditional gender relations may foster these disorders and how gender stereotypes may affect clinicians' diagnoses and treatments of patients. In addition, we will consider how other factors, including a patient's race and ethnicity, age, social class, and sexual orientation, may influence diagnoses and clinical outcomes.

GENDER AND DEPRESSION   Each of us, at one time or another, has felt depressed. In everyday usage, depression refers to feeling down, "blue," or sad. Depression as a clinical syndrome, however, is more severe and prolonged. **Clinical depression** entails persistent feelings of discontent or displeasure accompanied by at least four of eight symptoms (poor appetite or weight loss, insomnia or increased sleep, psychomotor agitation or retardation, loss of interest in usual activities, loss of energy or fatigue, feelings of worthlessness, diminished concentration, and suicidal ideation) that are present daily for at least two weeks without evidence of any other disorder (Beck & Alford, 2009).

Women have consistently higher rates of depression than men, according to studies of both clinical populations and the general public. It is estimated that during the course of their lives, 15 percent of men, but 24 percent of women in the United States experience clinical depression; more than twice as many women as men experience a major depressive episode each year (Mazure, Keita, & Blehar, 2002). Globally, it is estimated that by 2020 the most prevalent mental disorder, unipolar depression, will be twice as common in women than men (World Health Organization [WHO], 2011). What is more, this sex difference begins to emerge as early as puberty (Allgood-Merten, Lewinsohn, & Hops, 1990; Gurian, 2011; Rudolph & Hammen, 1999). Before adolescence, equal numbers of boys and girls are diagnosed as depressed, about 10 to 15 percent (Gurian, 2011). However, after the age of thirteen the rates of depression diverge dramatically, when nearly twice as many girls as boys are diagnosed depressed, a proportion which, as discussed above, persists into adulthood (Gurian, 2011).

The incidence of depression among men and women, however, also varies by race and ethnicity, social class, and marital status. Women of color and poor women who head households (among whom racial minorities are disproportionately represented) have the highest rates of depression of any group (Landrine & Klonoff, 1997; Mazure et al., 2002; National Institute of Mental Health, 2008; Yang & Lee, 2009). Cannon and her colleagues (1989) report, though, that the interaction of race and social mobility affects rates of depression among middle-class women. In their study of two hundred female professionals and managers employed full time, they found that Black women who had been raised in middle-class households and White women who had been raised in working-class households had the highest levels of depressive symptoms. Their study also shows that single women and women with children are more likely to be depressed than married women or childless women.

However, other researchers have found that married women are more susceptible to depression than both never-married women and married men. Interestingly, the reverse is true for men: Never-married men are more likely to suffer depression than married men. According to the American Psychological Association (1985, p. 8), "marriage is associated with a 71 percent reduction in illness for minority men, 63 percent for white men, 28 percent for white women, and 8 percent for minority women" (see also Gutierrez-Lobos et al., 2000). Also of special interest is the observation that among divorced women and men, the former experienced more depression during the marriage whereas the latter grew depressed during the marital separation (Rothblum, 1982; see also Helgeson, 1994; Law & Sbarra, 2009; Chapter 7).

A number of theories have been developed to explain these differences. One is that the difference is merely a statistical artifact of women's greater likelihood to seek help for their problems. There is evidence of bias among psychiatrists, especially male psychiatrists, toward diagnosing depression in women (Borowsky et al., 2000; Loring & Powell, 1988), and there is also evidence of men's unwillingness to seek professional help for depression since such behavior is considered "unmanly" (Addis & Mahalik, 2003; Real, 1997). It is also possible that because men's suicide attempts are successful twice as often as women's there are more mentally ill women who remain alive and therefore contribute to the overall tally of depressed females (All About Depression, 2011). These findings, though, leave unexplained the higher rate of depression reported by women in general community surveys in which respondents, regardless of sex, have not usually sought help (Cleary, 1987; Joiner & Blalock, 1995; Landrine & Klonoff, 1997; Schimelpfening, 2008). It also cannot explain the variation in depression by age, race and ethnicity, social class, and marital status.

A second argument focuses on hormonal differences between the sexes, but studies looking at hormonal causes have not produced consistent or conclusive findings (Mazure et al., 2002). There is a strong relationship between postpartum hormonal changes and depression (see Chapter 2), but this can account for only a small portion of the rate variation between the sexes, and it also does not explain the variation between White women and women of color and between poor women and more affluent women.

It seems more likely that social factors are responsible for the differences in depression rates that we have observed. There are two major psychological explanations: the *learned helplessness hypothesis* and the *social status hypothesis*. According to the learned helplessness hypothesis, females are socialized to respond passively to stress, but males are taught to respond assertively. Consequently, when confronted with a stressful life event, men are more likely to take some kind of action, whereas women tend to become depressed. At first glance, this argument is appealing, but if we look at it closely, we see that it amounts to little more than victim blaming. "Many women find their situation depressing because real social discrimination [not faulty socialization] makes it difficult for them to achieve by direct action and self-assertion, further contributing to their psychological distress" (Weissman, 1980, p. 102; see also Barry et al., 2008; Miller & Kirsch, 1987; National Institute of Mental Health, 2011). For instance, research indicates that an important contributing factor to women's increased risk of clinical depression is their greater vulnerability to physical and sexual abuse. According to Nechas and Foley (1994), if one controls for the incidence of physical and sexual abuse among depressed women, the rates of depression for women and men are equalized (see also Mazure et al., 2002). The learned helplessness hypothesis overlooks the fact that most women *do* take direct action to address the source of their depression, although in many instances their efforts are unsuccessful because of their limited resources (Bargai et al., 2007; Davies, Lyon, & Monti-Catania, 1998). There is a substantial body of research, for instance, showing that women who experience abuse in their intimate relationships are active help seekers, who turn to multiple sources, informal and professional, for help in ending the abuse (Barrett & St. Pierre, 2011; Flicker et al., 2011; Moe, 2007). Thus, it appears that the social and economic conditions under which particular groups of women live, not certain inherent or learned feminine traits put them at greater risk for clinical depression and that their agency in addressing these conditions is often overlooked or devalued.

Although mental health professionals often attribute women's higher rates of depression to "learned helplessness," research shows that the best predictor of women's depressive symptoms is personal experiences of sex discrimination.

This is precisely the premise of the social status hypothesis, which also emphasizes that the traditional roles afforded women (i.e., homemaker, mother) offer limited sources of personal satisfaction compared with the diversity of jobs available to men (U.S. Department of Labor, Bureau of Labor Statistics, 2011; Doyal, 1990b). Given their double burden of housework and paid work, one would expect employed women to experience greater psychological distress than full-time homemakers, but interestingly, research shows that just the opposite is usually the case (Ericson, 2008; Thoits, 1987). Moreover, women who have high-income, high-status jobs also have high levels of psychological well-being and few symptoms of psychological distress, irrespective of marital status. A recent study found, for instance, that most women who hold high-paying, high-status jobs, regardless of marital or parenting status, report that their jobs afford them emotional as well as tangible rewards that benefit their interpersonal relationships and well-being (Rose, 2010; see also Golding, 1988; Horwitz, 1982). If we consider the stress and disadvantages imposed by poverty, sexism, and racial and ethnic discrimination, the depression so prevalent among low-income women and women of color is easy to understand. In fact, one recent study found that the single best predictor of women's depressive symptoms was their personal experiences of sex discrimination and, since women of color were found to have more discriminatory experiences than White women, it was not surprising that sex discrimination had an even greater negative impact on their psychological well-being (Landrine & Klonoff, 1997; see also Brown et al., 2000; Mazure et al., 2002).

These findings are not unrelated to those regarding the lower incidence of depression in married men compared with never-married men. Research suggests first of all that married men usually have someone available in whom to confide: their wives (Helgeson, 1995). Married men are nine times less likely to be diagnosed with clinical depression than their single counterparts, but the risk of suicide doubles for men who have been divorced or separated from their wives (Stewart, 2011). Women, who are socially expected to give others emotional support, typically display a willingness to listen to their husbands' problems and try to help. Interestingly, husbands are not inclined to reciprocate when their wives are troubled (Lott, 1987; Strazdins & Broom, 2004). Recall the study cited earlier in this chapter showing that men are significantly more likely than women to divorce their spouses if the spouses become ill (James, 2001). In addition, as we learned in Chapter 7, men's traditional roles as husbands and fathers place relatively fewer demands on them in the home and permit them considerable control over the demands that are made of them. In contrast, women's traditional roles as wives and mothers afford them fewer options, thereby combining high demands with little control, an inherently stressful situation that obviously could foster depression (Barnett & Baruch, 1987; Strazdins, 2004). In short, a person's level of psychological well-being within a marriage is strongly affected by his or her marital power (Steil & Turetsky, 1987; Strazdins, 2004; see also Chapter 7).

SUBSTANCE ABUSE   Some researchers, we have said, claim that in reacting to stress, women tend to be passive, whereas men typically take some sort of action. Although research does not support such claims, it is the case that in the extreme, males may respond to stress by "acting out," for example, by fighting or becoming abusive, and by abusing alcohol or drugs. Men have consistently higher rates of problem drinking and illicit drug use than women do.

With respect to alcohol use, men outnumber women among heavy drinkers, regardless of race or ethnicity. In general, men are twice as likely as women to be heavy drinkers (Mancuso & Miller, 2001). Men do more public drinking than women, so they are less likely to drink alone. They also engage in more "binge drinking" or episodic heavy drinking (CDC, 2010; Ettorre, 1997; Wechsler et al., 1995).

According to Morrissey (1986, p. 159), "The availability of and accessibility of alcohol to specific groups is symbolic of the positions of those groups in a hierarchy." She notes that at the turn of the century, the sociologist Thorstein Veblen observed that the taboo against women drinking was one of the ways men in the United States symbolically demonstrated their higher status. In other words, drinking for men historically has been a kind of status symbol, and male dominance in society afforded men greater access to alcohol, which, in turn, increased their likelihood of developing drinking problems.

Alcohol consumption certainly appears to be compatible with stereotyped masculinity (Chavez et al., 2011; Lemle, 1984). Researchers have found, for instance, that males who exhibit exaggerated masculinity ("hyper-masculinity") are more likely to be substance (i.e., alcohol and drug) abusers (Bartolucci, Zeichner, & Miller, 2009; Mosher & Sirkin, 1984).[10] Males also receive greater indirect social support for drinking. In general, there continues to be stronger social disapproval of heavy drinking by women than by men (Chawla et al., 2009). According to Ettorre (1997, p. 14), the gender norms regarding drinking can be summed up in the phrases, "real men drink," but "nice girls don't." Parents monitor daughters' behavior more than sons' behavior, thus giving sons more opportunities to drink (Barnes, Farrell, & Dintcheff, 1997; Schinke, Cole, & Fang, 2009). Wives are more tolerant of their husbands drinking than vice versa. About 90 percent of wives remain with alcoholic husbands compared with just 10 percent of husbands who stay with alcoholic wives (American Psychological Association, 1985; O'Farrell, Harrison, & Cutter, 2006). However, a study of twenty-nine men married to alcoholic wives reported the unexpected finding that these husbands approached their situation more often by using engaging rather than withdrawing behaviors (Philpott & Christie, 2008).

Since the 1970s, some observers have worried that the push for gender equality would lead to a breakdown in traditional gender norms regarding drinking, thus leading more women to drink more heavily (that is, to behave like men). Others were concerned that as more women moved into the labor force, especially into male-dominated positions, they would experience greater stress that might lead to increased drinking. Such concerns have been fueled by liquor advertisements designed to appeal to "liberated women" (Morrissey, 1986; Smith & Foxcraft, 2009). There is, however, no empirical support for these concerns, which together are often referred to as the *convergence hypothesis*. For one thing, findings with regard to the gender gap have been somewhat inconsistent over the past thirty years. During the 1990s research suggested that the gender gap in heavy drinking was widening because there had been a decrease in heavy drinking by both women and men, but the decline was greater for women than men (Waldron, 1995). However, research published in 2007 indicated the opposite: the gender gap in alcohol consumption is closing because men and women are over-consuming alcohol at similar rates (Keyes, Grant, & Hasin, 2007). Nevertheless, data indicate that underage drinking declined for both sexes in recent years (2002–2008) (Students Against Drunk Driving [SADD], 2011). Second, although employed women are less likely than unemployed women to be total abstainers, this does not mean that they engage in more stress-related drinking. Their drinking habits may simply reflect their greater opportunity to drink socially or their greater exposure to alcohol in both work-related and social settings (Biener, 1987; Jacobsen, 2007). Success-oriented women appear the least likely to become substance abusers in reaction to stress (Blum & Roman, 1997; Moore et al., 2007; Snell, Belk, & Hawkins, 1987). As one writer put it, "If female drinking problems are increasing, it is most likely not because women's liberation has arrived but because it has not" (Sandmair, 1980, p. 242). Indeed, heavy drinking by women seems to be preceded by depression, and, as we have already noted, poor women, especially those with young children, are at high risk of developing clinical depression (Dixit & Crum, 2000; Mazure et al., 2002). Moreover, men are still nearly twice as likely to report alcohol problems that interfere with work. A study of working men and women, for instance, found that 11.6 percent of the men and 6 percent of the women reported drinking *at work* to an extent that interfered with their competence (Jacobsen, 2007).

Of course, as with the other health-related behaviors we have discussed, sex is not the only important variable to consider. Research shows that a number of factors affect the sex-alcohol use relationship. As Box 12.3 shows, age is a relevant variable. Another important factor is sexual orientation. Although women are less likely than men to be heavy drinkers, studies indicate that lesbians are significantly more likely than heterosexual women to engage in heavy drinking, have drinking problems, or become alcoholic. Alcoholism is also considered a serious problem among gay men (Cochran et al., 2000). Although the reasons for this greater risk are not well understood, it is thought to be due at least in part to the fact that because bars historically have been relatively safe havens for lesbians and gay men, they assumed a central role in gays' and lesbians' social lives and leisure activities. A recent study looked more deeply into the relationship between sexual orientation and drinking at bars in the San Francisco Bay Area (Trocki & Drabble, 2008). There was no difference in drinking levels among heterosexual and gay men at the bars. However, among women, lesbians drank more than heterosexual women, and bisexual women drank significantly more than average (Trocki & Drabble, 2008). Homophobia and oppression of homosexuals, which generate feelings of alienation and isolation, are likely major contributing factors to high drinking levels among lesbians and gay men; these feelings are associated with increased alcohol consumption (Ettorre, 1997; Nicoloff & Stiglitz, 1987; Trocki & Drabble, 2008). However, estimating the incidence of problem drinking among lesbians and gay men is difficult; lesbians and gay men as well as problem drinkers (homosexual and heterosexual) are stigmatized in our society, so members of both groups sometimes closet themselves.

Race and ethnicity are also important factors to consider when looking at the sex-alcohol relationship. Research shows that Black women and men, for example, are more likely than White women and men to be abstainers from alcohol. Among people of color who drink, alcohol abuse rates are higher for men than women and for Whites than people of color (National Institute on Alcohol Abuse and Alcoholism [NIAAA], 2011). The overall male rate of alcohol abuse is 6.93 percent; for White men, the rate is 7.45 percent; for Black men, 5.71 percent; and for Hispanic/Latino men, 6.21 percent. The overall female rate is 2.55 percent; for White women, it is 2.92 percent; for Black women, 1.41 percent; and for Hispanic/Latina women, 1.65 percent (NIAAA, 2011). Among American Indians and Alaskan Natives, however, rates of alcohol abuse are significantly higher than for other minority groups; this is the case for women as well as men. Returning to Table 12.3, for example, we find that chronic liver disease and cirrohsis of the liver are leading causes of death for American Indian/Alaskan Native men *and* women, indicating the seriousness of alcohol abuse among this population. The only other group for whom these diseases are a leading cause of death is Hispanic men, but their death rate is lower than that of both Native American men and women.

Social class and age also intersect with race and sex in influencing drinking patterns. For instance, if we use education as an indicator of social class, we find that Black men with less than a high school education drink three times as much as White males with the same educational background. As a general rule, the higher the men's educational attainment, the lower their rates of drinking, regardless of race (but see Box 12.3). However, highly educated Black men who drink are more likely to develop a serious drinking problem than similarly educated White men who drink. It has been hypothesized that this may be due less to the fact that they are actually more likely to become alcoholic than it is to the fact that as high-status minorities, their behavior is more closely scrutinized and, therefore, any deviance is more easily detected. Finally, it has been found that heavy drinking by Black males increases as they grow older, in particular from young adulthood to middle age, whereas the reverse pattern is true for White males (see Box 12.3). This difference may be the result of White males' greater probability of increasing economic stability as they age compared with the cumulative effect of Black males' experiences of discrimination and economic marginalization (Bachman et al., 1997; Barr et al., 1993; Gilbert & Collins, 1997; Kerr et al., 2009).

Once again, therefore, it appears that the social-structural conditions in which particular groups of women and men live affect the likelihood that they will develop drinking problems. It is important to note, though, that with regard to sex, there are physiological factors that also must be taken into account. More specifically, when women drink heavily, they suffer greater impairment than men who are heavy drinkers. Recent medical research has shown that females have less of a particular stomach enzyme that helps the digestion of alcohol before it passes into the bloodstream. Consequently, more alcohol goes into women's bloodstreams than into men's, even if women drink the same amount as men relative to body size. More importantly, heavy drinking further inhibits the

BOX 12.3
Gender Differences in the Consequences of Heavy or Binge Drinking on College Campuses

Drinking has long been an accepted part of college life. Business owners in communities where college campuses are located usually view college students as a significant clientele for their establishments that include bars, clubs, and restaurants that serve alcohol. National studies show that four out of five college students drink alcohol. Most are not heavy, episodic, or binge drinkers—defined as those who consume four (women) or five (men) alcoholic drinks in a row—but at least 40 percent report recent (i.e., within the two weeks prior to being surveyed) binge drinking (Dowdall, 2008; Wechsler & Nelson, 2001). First-year students appear particularly susceptible to binge drinking as they adjust to the freedom that the college environment offers them and the absence of parental monitoring of their behavior (Wechsler & Nelson, 2001).

Many studies do not show significant differences in rates of binge drinking among male and female college students. But research does show significant gender differences in the consequences associated with heavy or binge drinking. Male binge drinkers, for example, are more likely than non-binge drinkers to damage property and get into trouble with the police. They are also more likely to die from alcohol-related causes (Dowdall, 2008). Male binge drinkers are at greater risk of engaging in assault and fighting and being physically injured while drunk (Rothman & Silverman, 2007). Female binge drinkers, though, are at very high risk of being *sexually* assaulted. Studies show that in 30 to 70 percent of sexual assaults of female college students, the victim was under the influence of alcohol (Abbey et al., 2001; Parks & Fals-Stewart, 2004). Many of these sexual assaults are *incapacitated rapes*, that is, rapes that occur when the victim is too intoxicated to give consent (Kilpatrick et al., 2007). College women are at significantly greater risk of incapacitated rape than forcible rape (Brown et al., 2009; Kilpatrick et al., 2007; Mohler-Kuo et al., 2004).

Heavy or binge drinking has a negative impact not only on students who engage in it, but also on the entire campus and the surrounding community. Binge drinkers create problems for other students, and, again, these problems are gendered. Male students are more likely to report being pushed, hit, or assaulted, while female students are more likely to report unwanted sexual advances and attempted or completed sexual assaults (Dowdall, 2008). Consequently, sociologist George Dowdall (2008), who has studied college alcohol consumption and its consequences, urges universities and local communities to collaborate on strategies to reduce heavy episodic or binge drinking among students. These prevention and intervention efforts should focus not only on individual students who drink, but also on the entire student body to engage the larger community. Such programs should include education about state and university alcohol policies, the sanctions for violating these laws and policies, and the health and safety risks of alcohol consumption. Stronger restrictions should be placed on advertising and on events on or around campus that promote alcohol consumption, since research has shown that such policies lower college binge drinking rates. Other observers also advocate programs that educate parents about how to talk with their children about binge drinking and its inherent dangers *before* the children leave for college (Ichiyama et al., 2009). Ultimately, a significant step in addressing the problem of college binge drinking and the serious consequences it entails is to change the university's culture related to alcohol consumption and to *enforce* the laws and policies in place to regulate it. According to Dowdall (2008), different campuses have different "drinking cultures," and these are related to, among other factors, the prominence of athletes as well as fraternities and sororities on the campus—all of which are associated with increased heavy or binge drinking. Dowdall's research makes clear that these factors should be as important in selecting a college as the availability of specific majors or the prominence of the faculty.

production of the enzyme, so that alcoholic men lose some of their ability to digest alcohol but alcoholic women lose this ability completely because their stomachs have virtually none of the enzyme. As a result, women are more susceptible to liver damage and other physical problems if they become alcoholic (Freeza et al., 1990; Rehm et al., 2009).

Despite such findings, the fact that more males than females develop drinking problems has led to the view that alcoholism is a "male disease." Consequently, alcoholism treatment programs typically have been designed by men for men (Ettore, 1997; Grella, 1999). Moreover, women alcoholics suffer greater stigmatization than do male alcoholics at least in part because excessive drinking violates traditional gender norms for women. Not surprisingly, then, women alcoholics express greater reluctance than male alcoholics about entering treatment programs. The most frequent reason underlying this reluctance—2.3 men enter into treatment for every 1 woman—is fear of the adverse consequences of being officially labeled alcoholic, such as losing custody of their children (All Treatment, 2011; Blume, 1997; Ettorre, 1997).

Just as alcohol has been more readily available to men, so too have men had greater access to illicit drugs. Men, in fact, control the illicit drug trade in the United States and abroad, which is not surprising given their greater involvement in virtually all forms of criminal activity (see Chapter 9). Men use illicit drugs more than women do, and they are more likely to be regular or habitual users. In 2009, the National Survey on Drug Use and Health found that 10.8 percent of males and 6.6 percent of females used illicit drugs, and men were more likely than women to use several different drugs at one time (Substance Abuse and Mental Health Services Administration [SAMHSA], 2010). As is the case with alcohol consumption, there is no evidence that male and female patterns of drug use are converging, although since the 1980s among twelve- to seventeen-year-olds, there has only been a 1 to 2 percentage-points sex difference in marijuana and cocaine use. Men, however, are involved in over 60 percent of all cocaine-related emergency room episodes, a figure that has shown little variation since 1985 (National Center for Health Statistics, 2000). Nevertheless, women's use of cocaine, especially during pregnancy, has received a good deal of publicity in recent years (Babcock, 2008; Inciardi et al., 1993), which some observers attribute to the application of a sexual double standard.

> Women's cocaine use is seen as more alarming than men's because it is connected to both old ideas about women's drug use (but not men's) being a source of sexual corruption and newer ideas about women's work-force participation leading to new pressures and temptations for women—including drug use—because they are taking on male role characteristics. (Inciardi et al., 1993, pp. 38–39)

Thus, although there are no empirical data to support these claims, women's drug use, like their alcohol use, is more negatively stereotyped and more highly stigmatized than similar behavior by men.

This is further reflected in traditional analyses that have depicted female drug abusers as showing greater psychological maladjustment than their male counterparts; that is, they are considered sicker than male drug abusers. Recent research, however, fails to support this claim. Female and male drug abusers score similarly on tests of psychological adjustment and report similar routes to their introduction to drug use. Both males and females were typically introduced to drugs by a relative (including a parent or stepparent or a sibling) or by their peers, and 80 percent of the time the drug was given as a gift (Chesney-Lind, 1997; Raphael, 2004, 2007; Wood et al., 2008). Both men and women are usually introduced to drugs by men: their fathers or stepfathers, uncles, brothers, and, for women, boyfriends (Chesney-Lind, 1997; Inciardi et al., 1993; Raphael, 2004, 2007; Wood et al., 2008). Once they have been initiated into illicit drug use, though, men's and women's reasons for continued use differ. Men are more likely to continue to use drugs for thrills or pleasure; women are more likely to continue to use drugs as a kind of self-medication. For example, women who abuse drugs are more likely than male abusers to have a long history of physical and sexual abuse (Kendler et al., 2000; see also Coffey et al., 2002). For women, then, drugs are often used "as a coping mechanism for dealing with situational factors, life events, or general psychological distress" (Inciardi et al., 1993, p. 25; see also Chesney-Lind, 1997; Fullilove, Lown, & Fullilove, 1992; McCabe, Teter, & Boyd, 2006; Raphael, 2004, 2007).

These findings make clear that drug treatment programs for women must be designed to address women substance abusers' unique needs and concerns, but this is rarely the case. Instead, the typical response to women drug abusers has been increasingly harsh punishment rather than treatment. This approach can be seen in state legislative efforts to criminalize pregnant drug users (for delivering drugs to a minor through the umbilical cord or for child abuse under the assumption that the fetus is a person). Similarly federal and state legislators have proposed to protect children from drug-abusing parents by using drug testing. However, the focus of such laws are not on *parents* but rather on *mothers,* since it is the mothers' and not the fathers' drug test results and previous drug convictions that are scrutinized (Mancuso & Miller, 2001). Those who oppose such legislation point out that besides the constitutional issues it raises, it also overlooks the lack of drug treatment programs for women, especially pregnant women. The women who are targeted by the laws are typically poor, have long-term substance abuse histories, and have had little or no drug treatment made available to them. Sixty-seven percent of drug treatment programs, even those designed specifically for women, do not accept pregnant women, women who receive Medicaid (the federal government's health insurance program for the poor), or crack-addicted pregnant women who receive Medicaid (Kumpfer, 2011; Mahan, 1996; Mancuso & Miller, 2001; Pearson & Thoennes, 1996).

Research indicates that women who enter treatment often encounter opposition and less support from their families and friends than men who enter treatment. Although female addicts may initially get help from extended family, such as shelter for themselves and their children or financial support, they experience increasing isolation as their addiction worsens (Chesney-Lind, 1997; Grella, 1999). They often end up alone. According to one researcher, only one woman in ten leaves her addicted male partner, whereas nine out of ten men leave addicted female partners (Drug Addiction Treatment, 2011). In one study that asked addicts who among their family and friends would help them end their drug habits, the most common response for female addicts was no one; 50 percent more female addicts than male addicts reported that they had no friends or family members to provide them with that kind of support (Inciardi et al., 1993; see also Arevalo, Prado, & Amaro, 2007).

Significantly, the same reason that underlies women's dependence on illicit drugs—responding to a history of abuse as well as the depressed circumstances of their lives—also appears to be responsible for their dependence on prescription drugs. The one form of drug addiction more common among women than men involves the use of prescription drugs (Lowinson, Ruiz, & Millman, 2005). Women have relatively easy access to prescription drugs. We noted earlier that doctors often prescribe mood-altering psychotropic drugs to women. The most frequently prescribed drugs are antidepressants, minor tranquilizers, and sedatives, such as benzodiazepines. In fact, research indicates that primary care physicians are increasingly responding to patients' complaints of non-specific distress by prescribing an antidepressant drug. This has resulted in a higher rate of prescriptions for antidepressants than the estimated prevalence rate of depression in the general community (Coyne, 2001). Such drugs can be highly addictive even when taken in normal therapeutic doses, and since 2007, antidepressants have been the most prescribed class of drugs in the United States (Cohen, 2007; Ettorre, 1997). About half of all American women use psychotropic drugs; they are 70 percent of habitual tranquilizer users and 72 percent of antidepressant drug users (Cohen, 2007; see also Inciardi et al., 1993).

One final note: Women are more likely than men to suffer *cross-addictions*—that is, simultaneous addiction to both alcohol and drugs (Ettorre, 1997; Haver et al., 2009; Nechas & Foley, 1994). This appears to be due to women's greater likelihood to report alcohol-related problems to their physicians, who then may prescribe tranquilizers or antidepressants to help the women "cope" better and, therefore, stop drinking. Unfortunately, this frequently exacerbates the problem and may result in an overdose due to the combination of tranquilizers and alcohol, another tragic consequence of sexist health care.

EATING DISORDERS   In considering eating disorders, it is useful to think in terms of a continuum (Buckroyd & Rother, 2008; Cassell & Gleaves, 2006; Wooley & Wooley, 1980). At one end is *obesity*; an individual is obese if he or she is 25 percent above the average weight for someone of his or her age and height. Americans in general have been gaining weight over the past four decades. By 1996, there were more overweight than normal or underweight men and women in the population. Among adults, obesity increased from 13 percent to 32 percent between the 1960s and 2004 (Wang & Beydoun, 2007). It is predicted that by 2015, 75 percent of adults will be overweight and 41 percent of these will be obese (Wang & Beydoun, 2007). But while more men (59.4 percent) than women (49.9 percent) are overweight, more women (28.1 percent) than men (19.9 percent) are obese (National Center for Health Statistics, 2000). Moreover, poor women and African American women (whom we know are disproportionately represented among the poor) are more likely than more affluent and White women to be obese. Poor women are seven times more likely than nonpoor women to be obese, while 60 percent more African American women than White women are obese (Barboza, 2000; Freedman, 1986; Gortmaker et al., 1993; National Center for Health Statistics, 2000).

The obese are usually blamed for their condition. It is assumed that they lack self-control, are lazy, and engage in overeating. However, research indicates that often the obese eat no more than those who are thin; sometimes, they eat much less. It appears that for many, obesity is caused by factors over which they have little or no control: heredity, metabolism, and nutrition (which helps to account for the social class dimension of the problem) (Barry et al., 2009; Peters et al., 2007; Popkin et al., 1996; Rosin, 2008; Wadden et al., 1997). Nevertheless, tremendous pressure is put on the obese to lose weight. For example, they are discriminated against in the job market, made the brunt of jokes by the media and others, and judged by the general public to be sloppy, stupid, and ugly (Attie & Brooks-Gunn, 1987; Goldberg, 2000; Hunte & Williams, 2009), and there is evidence that discrimination agains the obese has become more prevalent in recent years (Andreyeva, Puhl, & Brownell, 2008). Women suffer more negative consequences from being obese than men do (Puhl et al., 2008). According to one recent study, for example, obese women are more likely than obese men to lose socioeconomic status independently of their family's social status and income; they are also 20 percent less likely than non-obese women to marry. In contrast, the negative impact of obesity on men's socioeconomic status and chances of marrying are much smaller (Gortmaker et al., 1993). Another recent study found that obese men and women are both less likely to enter into an intimate cohabitating relationship than their non-obese peers, but only obese women are less likely to marry than their non-obese peers (Mukhopadhyay, 2008). This does not mean that men are not stigmatized for deviating from cultural norms of male physical attractiveness, but for men, short stature has a greater negative impact than obesity (Gortmaker et al., 1993; Sargent & Branchflower, 1994; Weeden & Sabini, 2005).

The findings of these studies are also important in understanding why the vast majority of people with other eating disorders are women. In the United States, fat is equated with ugliness, whereas thinness is associated with beauty and high social status. (Consider, for instance, the often-quoted adage, "You can never be too rich or too thin.") It also appears that our cultural standard has idealized an increasingly thinner body since the 1920s (Attie & Brooks-Gunn, 1987; Brumberg, 1997; *Coventry Journalism Review*, 2008; Silverstein et al., 1986). This is true for men as well as women, but men, as we have already seen, are given considerably more leeway with regard to their weight. Moreover, women are frequently judged less by what they do than by how they look.

Not surprising, therefore, is the fact that women tend to evaluate their self-worth in terms of their appearance. Unfortunately, their estimates of themselves are often unrealistically negative. Women consistently express dissatisfaction with their bodies, and most frequently they couch this dissatisfaction in terms of weight. They are more likely than men to see being overweight as a character flaw and to blame themselves and their personal lack of self-discipline for their weight gain ("Men, Women, and Battles of the Bulges," 2000). In fact, one national survey found that women's dissatisfaction with their bodies has intensified in recent years. This study showed that 48 percent of women between the ages of eighteen and seventy had negative global body evaluations in 1995 compared with 30 percent in 1985. Most of these women were dissatisfied with their middle or lower torso, their weight, and their muscle tone (Cash & Henry, 1995; see also Grogan, 2007). While this study surveyed *adult* women, other studies show that adolescent girls express even greater dissatisfaction with their bodies (Brumberg, 1997; Dunkley, Wertheim, & Paxton, 2001; Stice, 2002; Strauss, 1999). Young women, in particular, hold inaccurate perceptions about their bodies, especially their body weight. For example, they typically overestimate their weight, whereas young men tend to underestimate theirs. Mintz and Betz (1986) found in their study of college students that the majority of women felt that, on average, they were ten pounds overweight, whereas the majority of men considered themselves an average of three pounds underweight. Overweight men in this study perceived themselves to be thinner than they actually were, whereas the only women who judged themselves as being of normal weight were really slightly underweight. This finding was replicated by the American College Health Association in 2005 (as described in Nevid, 2008; see also McCauley, Mintz, & Glenn, 1988). Significantly, more women than men, the research tells us, are obsessed with the desire to be thin (Hesse-Biber, 1989; however, see Luciano, 2001).

Today, more men are undergoing treatments to make themselves look younger and more physically attractive.

This cultural and personal obsession with weight can lead to eating disorders. One is *chronic dieting*. Seventy-eight percent of women and 64 percent of men report that they are dieting to lose weight or keep from gaining weight (Kolata, 2000). Although some physicians and nutritionists argue that such vigilance is good given that the majority of adults in our society are overweight, chronic dieting can have severe physical and psychological consequences (Wang & Beydoun, 2007). Chronic dieters try dozens of different diet plans—many of which are dangerously unhealthy—over the course of many years, sometimes beginning when they are as young as ten or eleven years old. Ironically, the dieting may have the opposite effect of what they desire, since restricting food intake can lower one's metabolic rate, which, in turn, requires that dieters eat even less to sustain further weight loss. This is why after a dieter stops following some diets, she (or he) often regains lost pounds quickly, prompting the start of another diet (Jakicic et al., 2008; Sullivan & Cameron, 2009). Thus, a vicious cycle ensues, with chronic dieters perpetually dissatisfied with their appearance and, in extreme cases, being thin becomes more important than other aspects of the self and other activities (Jackicic et al., 2008).

Some people turn to eating as a way to handle stress. Women are more likely than men to do this (Ettorre, 1992; Heilbronn et al., 2006), perhaps because food shopping and preparation have been women's responsibilities and because women's magazines highlight food by presenting tempting recipes and advertisements juxtaposed with articles touting the importance of a slim figure and smooth thighs (Silverstein et al., 1986). However, since women also tend to be preoccupied by the fear of weight gain, some may develop the disorder known as **bulimia**. Bulimics engage in binge eating, consuming large quantities of food (usually "junk" food) in a short period of time. Afterwards, fearful that they will gain weight, they purge themselves of the food by fasting, taking laxatives (sometimes a dozen or two dozen a day), exercising excessively, and, most commonly, by inducing vomiting.[11]

Bulimia is difficult to detect because bulimics usually do not show extreme weight loss. Bulimia, though, causes serious psychological and physical damage. The binge-purge cycle may take on the character of an addiction, like alcoholism (Ettorre, 1992; Wilson, 2010). Frequently, the gastrointestinal tract is damaged due to the overuse of laxatives, and the esophagus is harmed by the effects of repeated vomiting. It is estimated that approximately 5.1 percent of women in college suffer from bulimia (Pale Reflections, 2011).

Finally, at the other extreme end of the eating disorders continuum, opposite obesity, is **anorexia**. Anorectics have a compulsive fear of becoming fat; they literally starve themselves to prevent weight gain or to lose more weight. Anorectics—an estimated 90 to 95 percent of whom are women—have an exceptionally distorted body image, feeling or considering themselves to be fat even when they are emaciated. An individual is considered anorectic if she (or he) loses 25 percent of original body weight and at the same time refuses to eat (Zandian et al., 2007; Zerbe, 1993).

Until quite recently, most research on anorexia focused on young, White hetero-sexual women in their teens and twenties, from middle-class or wealthy families, since it was assumed that it is this group who is most likely to become anorectic. However, studies using more diverse samples are now finding this eating disorder among working-class women, women of color, and lesbians (Root, 1990; Rosen et al., 1988; Stewart et al., 2008; Thompson, 1994) and among some groups of men (Carlat, Camargo, & Herzog, 1997; Cazzuffi et al., 2010; Raevuori et al., 2008; Striegel-Moore, Silberstein, & Rodin, 1986). It is unclear whether these changes represent a true increase in anorexia among these populations or whether the widespread stereotype of the anorectic as a young, wealthy, White heterosexual woman prevented clinicians from seeing anorexia in members of these groups. Research has shown that internalization of and identification with the dominant White culture's ideals of attractiveness are related to eating disorders among women of color (Botta, 2006; Regan & Petrie, 1998; Schooler et al., 2004). Studies now indicate that although rates of diagnosed anorexia are still higher among middle-class and wealthy White women, diagnoses of anorexia and related eating disorders are increasing among young, Black, Hispanic, Asian American, Native American, and immigrant women in rural and low-income areas (Baker, 1999; Pike et al., 2001; Rosen et al., 1988; Snow & Harris, 1989; Thompson, 1996). Also, it is reported that up to 15 percent of gay or bisexual men are, or have been, anorexic (Carlat et al., 1997; Feldman & Myer, 2007; Gettleman & Thompson, 1993; Jones, 2010). The Alliance for Eating Disorders reports that approximately 1 million boys and men in the United States are anorectic or bulimic (Pale Reflections, 2011).

Researchers and clinicians have found that anorectics often have difficulty express-ing their personal needs and desires and may feel they have little, if any, control over their lives. Their weight becomes the one thing they can control. Controlling their appearance is also a way to please others (Rumney, 2009; Zerbe, 1993). It is not difficult to see how this theory could apply to anyone with low self-esteem—not only White women, but also women of color and lesbians and gay men. But in trying to explain why so many anorectics are women, regardless of race and ethnicity, social class, or sexual orientation, clinicians have often resorted to the psychoanalytic literature claiming that female ano-rectics want to deny their womanhood by making their bodies masculine (i.e., noncurva-cious), that they are striking out against their mothers, or that they are confused about their sexuality. An alternative perspective sees anorectic women as actually embracing an exaggerated image of womanhood. "Anorectics are seeking beauty through body trans-formation (just as most 'healthy' women do). The goal is not to reject womanliness but to enact it by becoming thinner and lovelier than anyone else" (Freedman, 1986, p. 156, see also Nordbo et al., 2008).

Although cases of anorexia have been documented for at least a century, serious research on the disorder has only been underway for about fifty years. Anorexia was first described in 1684, but it was not identified as a distinct disorder until 1870. The media did not begin mentioning anorexia until the 1970s. Not surprisingly, then, there are no definitive findings with regard to causal factors, psychoanalytic or otherwise. Of course, a complex disorder such as anorexia is likely caused by multiple, intersecting factors. What concerns us here is that in studying anorexia and other eating disorders, clinicians and researchers have often focused on the pathologies of individuals rather than on the cultural and social environment in which they live. It is important not to lose sight of the fact that the predominance of eating disorders among women is a sociopolitical issue as well as a clinical one. To fully understand anorexia and other eating disorders, therefore, we need to examine not only women's personal backgrounds, but also our society's cultural constructions of femininity and the female body, as well as the various cultural meanings we associate with food and appetite. Some feminist researchers, for example, have argued that anorexia is not really about being thin, but about controlling female appetites, which include sexual desires as well as a desire for food. Others hypothesize that anorexia may be a way for women not to reject being female but rather to reject the stifling constraints of domesticity and traditional feminine roles. Unfortunately, however, anorexia produces effects that are the opposite of empowerment and independence: The physical weakness and frailty induced by anorexia eventually require the women to be cared for and their activities to be monitored by others (Bordo, 1993, Morgan, Barry, & Morgan, 2008; Morley, 2010).

Becky Thompson (1996) has suggested that anorexia and eating disorders are "survival strategies" for some women, coping responses to trauma (see also Hall, 1998). She argues that some women, including poor women, lesbians, and women of color, may use food and eating as a way to numb pain and cope with violations of their body. This is a hypothesis worthy of further investigation given that researchers have found an elevated risk of developing eating disorders among adolescents who have been sexually abused (Carter et al., 2006; Wanderlich et al., 2000). There is also research suggesting that anorectics are attempting to desexualize themselves as a self-protective strategy (Legrand, 2010).

As previously discussed, rates of obesity are skyrocketing in the United States. Rather ironically, as one segment of the population grows numerically and in terms of weight, an equally unhealthy portion of the population struggles to reduce its weight. Worldwide it is estimated that 70 million people suffer from the eating disorders of anorexia and bulimia, with about 7 million of those individuals living in the United States (Pale Reflections, 2011). This is a serious problem, given that eating disorders have the highest mortality rate of any mental illness (South Carolina Department of Mental Health, 2011).

While feminists have moved the analysis of anorexia and other eating disorders beyond a singular focus on weight loss, they still recognize the cultural obsession with thinness as an important contributing factor to these problems. The desirability of a slender body, though, is just one of our society's beauty norms. In Box 12.4, we take a closer look at beauty norms to see their differential impact not only by sex, but by race and ethnicity as well.

While men are increasingly buying products and undergoing treatments to make themselves look younger and more physically attractive, it is important to keep in mind that, unlike women, they are not consistently encouraged by their parents, peers, or the media to be obsessed with their appearance nor do they usually consider their bodies a material resource. And while more men are becoming conscious of their body image, attractiveness norms for men are hardly as arbitrary, capricious, or *dangerous* as those for women. For example, more than 70,000 women are thought to be seriously ill with infections, autoimmune reactions, and cancer from leaky breast implants alone, and the FDA estimates that one in four women with implants will experience some leakage (Rynbrandt & Kramer, 1995; Zuckerman, 2005). In contrast, few men die trying to be handsome.

BOX 12.4
Beauty Norms

What is beauty, and who is beautiful? Although it has been claimed that standards of beauty transcend culture (see, for example, Perrett, May, & Yoshikawa, 1994; Social Issues Research Centre, 2011), most research indicates that beauty norms vary historically as well as cross-culturally (Kwan, 2009; Millard, 2009; Rooks, 1996; Wolf, 1991). For example, in Niger, women are considered beautiful if they are fat. There are beauty contests before which women gorge themselves on food since the heaviest woman is always the winner. A thin woman is considered undesirable; her thinness is taken as a sign that her father or her husband is not taking care of her (Onishi, 2001). This example also illustrates that normative standards of beauty are gendered, and, in our society as in Niger and much of the rest of the world, women, more so than men, are valued by others and derive their self-worth from how well they match up to their culture's idealized image of the beautiful woman.

What does the beautiful woman in our society look like? As we have already discussed, she is thin. However, since the mid-1980s, the idealized female body also became curvier; the beautiful woman is thin, but has large breasts. And, of course, beauty is equated with youth; as a woman grows old in our society, she does not grow more beautiful. Consider the supermodels of recent years. They possess what has been dubbed the "waif-look": the look of the child-woman who is infantile and unthreatening, but alluring and, therefore, sexually appealing to many men in an age when most women are striving to be strong, independent adults (Kaye, 1993; Morin, 2010). The appeal of the child-woman can also be seen in the growth of beauty pageants for children, where girls six years old and younger are dressed in gowns and showgirl costumes; made up with eye shadow, blush, and lipstick; and encouraged to pose and perform with coquettish style. As one observer put it, this billion-dollar-a-year industry blurs "the lines between what is cute and what is sensual" (quoted in DeWitt, 1997, p. 4E). That line is further blurred by the marketing of sexy lingerie to girls between the ages of seven and fourteen (Reddy, 2001).

In our society, where women have long been held to unrealistic standards of beauty—whatever the specific characteristics of the ideal happened to be at the time—young, physically attractive women have been prized by men of all ages. A beautiful young woman many years younger than her male partner increases *his* prestige in the eyes of others; consider, for instance, that young, attractive women married to older men are often referred to as "trophy brides." Men, then, appear to benefit from the beauty norms imposed on women in our society, but what are the effects of these norms on women? As we have already noted, since body image is strongly linked to self-esteem, rigid unattainable beauty norms cultivate in women and girls anxiety about and dissatisfaction with their appearance, starting at an early age (Allgood-Merton et al., 1990; Kwan, 2009; Millard, 2009; Morin, 2010; Strauss, 1999; Whitaker et al., 1990). They also induce women to engage in unhealthy—and sometimes even life-threatening—practices, in order to try to attain the unrealistic ideal. Such practices include not only constant dieting, which may lead to more serious eating disorders, as we have discussed, but also to plastic surgery, typically to enlarge breasts, reduce or straighten noses, and remove wrinkles or body fat. Breast augmentation surgery, for example, is the most common type of cosmetic surgery performed in the United States, with the vast majority of women undergoing the procedure for nonmedical reasons, usually because they want bigger breasts. The second most common procedure is liposuction, in which a tube is inserted into the body through a tiny incision, usually in the thighs and abdomen, and fat is literally sucked out (Ihrai, 2010; Rynbrandt & Kramer, 1995). In 2002, the Federal Drug Administration (FDA) announced approval of Botox as a treatment for skin wrinkling. Botox is a diluted form of the neurotoxin that causes

(continued)

BOX 12.4
Continued

botulism. It is injected into the facial muscles and paralyzes them, causing wrinkles to disappear. Of course, such procedures are available only to those who can afford them since they are not covered by insurance if they are for cosmetic purposes only. Botox injections, for instance, cost between $300 and $1,000, but their effects last only three to four months and must be repeated (Kuczynski, 2002). It is also the case that many cosmetic procedures have negative effects, but this does not appear to deter women from having them. For example, leaking silicone from breast implants has been associated with serious illnesses and disfigurement. However, while the number of breast augmentation procedures declined during the early 1990s when these problems were first revealed, they were on the rise again by 1998. Between 2000 and 2010, there was a 39 percent increase in the number of breast augmentation surgeries performed in the United States (American Society of Plastic Surgeons, 2011).

Women of color are especially disadvantaged by the dominant culture's beauty norms, for a central component of idealized beauty is whiteness. Despite the positive impact of the "Black is beautiful movement" of the late 1960s, a number of analysts have observed a return to racist beauty standards within the African American community in recent years. As Sandler (1992) points out, historically, in this country, light-skinned Black people, especially Black women, have enjoyed greater status than dark-skinned Black people, a consequence associated with the greater status accorded the "house" versus the "field negro" (see also Samuels, 2010). In her interviews with African Americans, Sandler (1992) found that light-skinned Black people were considered privileged within the Black as well as the White communities. Light-skinned women were preferred as partners by Black men, regardless of the darkness of the color of the men's skin. Light-skinned Black women were preferred not only because of their skin color, but also because they often have narrower noses and

"good hair," that is, hair that is not "nappy" (see also Lester, 2000; Rooks, 1996). Lester (2000) and Younai (2011) document the negative impact racist beauty norms have on women of color as well as the lengths to which some non-White women will go to more closely resemble the idealized image of White beauty. Creams for lightening the skin and chemical treatments to straighten hair are two common "beauty techniques" Black women use, but cosmetic surgery to "Caucasianize" the nose (narrow the nostrils and build the bridge) has grown in popularity among middle-class Black women. Asian women, both in the United States and abroad, are also turning to cosmetic surgery to make themselves look more "Caucasian." In the United States and in Asia, they may have surgery to "Caucasianize" their eyelids; a long, expensive, and painful, but popular procedure in China is surgery to lengthen one's legs so as to become taller ("Surgery That's Painful," 2002). And remember the women from Niger? Many of them are ingesting cattle steroids and animal vitamins to increase their appetites and bulk up (Onishi, 2001). What all of these women have in common, despite the differences in the procedures they use or the outcomes they seek, is their motivation: approval and admiration from men.

It is the case that men are also increasingly using plastic surgery and other methods to better conform to our society's idealized image of male physical attractiveness (Luciano, 2001). This image emphasizes musculature of the body, and a growing number of men are using cosmetic surgery to enhance their calves, chests, and buttocks with silicone implants. Youthfulness is also an important dimension of male physical attractiveness, so more men are now having face-lifts, Botox injections, and hair implant surgery, as well as liposuction to reduce stomach, chest, and breast fat. According to the American Society of Plastic Surgeons (2011), men are fueling the increase in cosmetic surgery; in 2010, face-lifts for men increased 14 percent and liposuction increased 7 percent.

Sexism and Mental Health Services

We noted at the outset of our discussion of mental health and illness that diagnosis and, therefore, treatment of psychological problems are often highly subjective processes. Clinicians, like everyone else, bring to their work particular biases that derive from their personal backgrounds and characteristics as well as from their training in a specific institutional system. We have discussed that clinicians tend to use a masculine model of mental health. That this persists today is not surprising, given that the mental health professions, like medicine in general, are hierarchically structured, and men predominate at the top of the hierarchy. For example, only about a third of psychiatrists are women (American Medical Association, 2000). What are some of the other important features of traditional mental health care, and what are their implications for the treatment of female and male patients?

Critics of traditional mental health care have given special attention to what they see as its emphasis on conformity to dominant cultural standards and its corresponding intolerance of diversity or uniqueness (Ballou & Gabalac, 1985; L. Brown, 1994; Strickland, 2000). More specifically, mental health practitioners, while claiming to be objective medical experts, often function simply as upholders of the status quo. Their judgment of what constitutes mental health is conformity to dominant (i.e., White, middle-class, heterosexual, male) expectations, although, for many individuals, these are oppressive. Conversely, any departure from these norms can be interpreted as a symptom of pathology or mental disorder. The traditional clinician, then, sees the source or cause of a problem as existing within the patient; the goal is to change the patient rather than the external conditions that may be affecting the patient. Treatment is considered successful when the patient "adjusts" to (i.e., uncritically accepts and conforms to) her or his circumstances. This can be accomplished with a variety of techniques, such as psychoanalysis, behavior modification, or drug therapy.

Critics acknowledge that this model is more progressive and humane than many treatment models popular in the past. It also seems to be a beneficial approach to the most severe cases of mental illness. According to the critics, however, it is not an appropriate treatment model for the majority of patients who seek therapy or mental health care (Ballou & Gabalac, 1985; Satcher, 2001). Consider, for example, traditional clinical evaluations of homosexuals. Many gays and lesbians enter therapy because of low self-esteem and depression. Mental health practitioners may assess these troubles as resulting from homosexuality itself, rather than from societal discrimination against homosexuals. Among mental health professionals who hold this view, the first sign of "healthy adjustment" is for the patient to acknowledge his or her sexual orientation as the problem or "disorder" to be treated.[12]

Even more disturbing is the high incidence of sexual abuse of patients by their therapists. Research reveals that about 12 percent of male therapists and 3 percent of female therapists have been involved in at least one "incident of intimacy" with a patient (Pope, Levenson, & Schover, 2001); 80 percent of male therapists who have had intimate involvements have done so with more than one patient. In one study, half of the 1,320 clinical psychologists surveyed reported that they had treated patients who had had sexual relations with a previous therapist. These patients frequently experience emotional problems similar to those of incest victims. About 10 percent of these patients are so severely affected that they must be hospitalized; 1 percent commit suicide

(Dolan, 2011; Sonne & Pope, 1991). In about 90 percent of cases of sexual abuse by therapists, the patient/victim is a woman (Gilbert & Scher, 1999).[13] Sometimes, though, victimized patients are children, and more than 50 percent of child patient/victims are girls. Although the American Psychological Association considers sex between a therapist and client unethical, researchers have found that neither threats of malpractice nor felony convictions have been effective in deterring therapists from having sex with their patients (Citizens Commission on Human Rights, 2001). However, more victimized patients are choosing to sue their therapists, and the courts have ruled that consent of a patient to sexual relations is not an acceptable defense for therapists (Drukteinis, 2011; Gilbert & Scher, 1999; Pope, Sonne, and Holroyd, 1993).[14]

Feminist Therapy

More females than males make use of mental health services, and so the biases and problems inherent in the traditional system are especially detrimental to them. Recognizing this, some practitioners have sought to reform mental health care delivery through the adoption of *gender-aware* or *nonsexist counseling*. "Nonsexist counseling seeks to treat clients as human beings and actively to refute sex ascription in theory and in practice, that is, in options offered to the clients and in the values espoused by the therapist" (Ballou & Gabalac, 1985, p. 30; see also Trailer, Csiernik, & Didham, 2006). While nonsexist counseling clearly has advantages over the traditional model, some practitioners see it as only the first step in a series of necessary changes. These practitioners are striving to remodel mental health care along feminist lines. Let's briefly examine their work.

Feminist therapy is part of the broader feminist health care movement. Although there are actually a number of feminist therapies, we can identify several principles common among them that form the foundation of this approach to mental health care.

First, feminist therapists establish egalitarian relationships with their clients (Trailer et al., 2006; Gilbert & Scher, 1999). Rather than being someone to whom something is done by an expert, the client takes an active part in therapy, and the therapist engages in self-disclosure with the client. The therapy, then, is viewed as a shared learning process. A corollary to this is that the feminist therapist accepts the client's knowledge and personal experiences as valid, rather than interpreting them as defensive strategies. In other words, to the feminist therapist, the client may be the best authority on her or his problem.

A second related principle is that feminist therapy assumes that external conditions, not individual interpersonal ones, generate most psychological difficulties, particularly those experienced by women and other marginalized groups (L. Brown, 1994; see also Association for Humanist Psychology, 2001; Ponterotto et al., 2001). "The therapist facilitates the client's ability to understand, both generally and personally, the existence and impact of cultural conditioning and biased social/economic/cultural structures.... The goal is to build skills for coping and creating, to develop astute social analysis, and sophisticated consideration of the potential consequences of change" (Ballou & Gabalac, 1985, pp. 31, 33; see also Trailer et al., 2006). A fundamental part of this process is the analysis of gender relations (Association for Humanist Psychology, 2001; Burstow, 1992; Gilbert & Scher, 1999).

Finally, feminist therapists are committed to working for broader social changes that benefit not only their individual clients, but all women and oppressed groups

(Association for Humanist Psychology, 2001; L. Brown, 1994). For instance, they may lobby for adequate and affordable day care; for safe, sanitary, and low-cost housing; and for shelters for battered women and the sexually abused. In short, feminist therapists are advocates for social change that will empower the disadvantaged and provide them with social and economic autonomy—factors these therapists recognize as essential for mental health.

Although a goal of feminist therapy clearly is to assist members of oppressed groups, especially women, there is little empirical evidence so far that demonstrates its success in this regard. Future research should address this issue by determining to what extent feminist therapy is available to those most disadvantaged by the current social structure: poor women and women of color and their children (for steps in this direction, see L. Brown, 1994; Burstow, 1992; Ponterotto et al., 2001).

TOWARD A HEALTHY FUTURE

The data discussed in this chapter are disturbing. Taken together, they indicate, to paraphrase Harrison (1984), that traditional constructions of gender are hazardous to our health.

With regard to physical health, traditional masculinity appears to put men at greater risk for a variety of physical conditions, such as heart disease and stroke, various forms of cancer, and chronic liver disease. Their greater likelihood to smoke, drink alcohol, and engage in violence renders them more susceptible not only to these diseases, but also to accidents, homicide, successful suicide, and alcohol and drug abuse. In fact, it seems that the more a man conforms to traditional masculinity, the greater the risk to his health.

The same appears to be true with regard to women who firmly adhere to traditional femininity. For them, however, the greatest threat appears to be to their mental health. Those who embrace the traditional feminine role are more prone to depression and other psychological problems. Moreover, although women tend to live longer than men, there are indications that their quality of life may be poorer. This is evidenced by mental health statistics as well as their higher morbidity and greater likelihood of institutionalization.

With few exceptions, people of color and the economically disadvantaged have poorer health than White, middle-, and upper-class men and women. They also receive the poorest quality health care from a system that is sexist, racist, heterosexist, ageist, and class-biased. As we discussed in this chapter, this system of physical and mental health care has not infrequently done more harm than good, particularly to women, people of color, gay men and lesbians, and the poor, both historically and currently.

In response to the inadequacies and abuses of traditional health care, feminists have begun to offer alternative services. These have as their core principles: a nonhierarchical structure; an egalitarian and mutually educational relationship between patient and provider; a recognition of external (i.e., structural rather than personal) causes for individuals' physical and psychological troubles; and a commitment to advocacy and action to bring about social change. Although the feminist model of physical and mental health care is not without problems of its own, it does hold the promise of transforming our traditional medical services into "forces committed to undoing damage [and] achieving and maintaining health" (Ballou & Gabalac, 1985, p. 169).

A collaboration formed especially to achieve this purpose is the National Center for Medical-Legal Partnership (2011), whose goal is to help vulnerable individuals and families get and stay healthy. To do so we as a society, in conjunction with new organizations such as this one, need to broaden health care beyond the boundaries of curative medicine to identify and change the root causes of illness woven throughout our society and culture. For as the Indian philosopher Jiddu Krishnamurti (1986) wrote in his book, *The Future of Humanity,* "It is no measure of good health to be well adjusted to a profoundly sick society."

Key Terms

anorexia   an eating disorder in which an individual, because of an obsessive fear of becoming overweight, literally starves; characterized by a distorted body image, a 25 percent loss of body weight, and a refusal to eat; 90 to 95 percent of anorectics are females

bulimia   an abnormal and constant craving for food, also known as binge-purge syndrome, in which the individual consumes large quantities of food in short periods of time followed by fasting, the use of laxatives, or induced vomiting to purge the food and prevent weight gain

clinical depression   severe and persistent feelings of discontent or displeasure accompanied

by at least four of eight symptoms (poor appetite or weight loss, insomnia or increased sleep, psychomotor agitation or retardation, loss of interest in usual activities, loss of energy or fatigue, feelings of worthlessness, diminished concentration, and suicidal ideation) that are present daily for at least two weeks without evidence of any other disorder

life expectancy   the average number of years of life remaining to an individual at a given age

morbidity rate   the illness rate of a given population

mortality rate   the number of deaths in proportion to a given population

Suggested Readings

Bird, C. E., & Rieker, P. (2008). *Gender and health: The effects of constrained choices and social policies.* New York: Cambridge University Press. An accessible and interesting read in which the authors provide an overview of critical health issues (e.g., why women live longer than men, but suffer more chronic illness and disability; the effects of family roles; the influence of public policy) as well as an introduction to the theory of constrained choices.

Dowdall, G. W. (2008). *College drinking: Reframing a social problem.* Santa Barbara, CA: Praeger. A thorough and careful synthesis of the empirical research on heavy and binge drinking among college populations with special attention to gender differences, including the differential gendered consequences of this behavior.

Luciano, L. (2001). *Looking good: Male body image in modern America.* New York: Hill and Wang.

An interesting look at men's growing insecurity about their physical appearance and how marketers are capitalizing on it.

Raphael, J. (2004). *Listening to Olivia: Violence, poverty, and prostitution.* Boston: Northeastern University Press. Raphael explores the causes and consequences of substance abuse among poor women of color by telling the compelling story of one woman, Olivia, while also contextualizing her experiences in the research literature on gender and substance use, violence and prostitution.

Young, I.M. (2004). *On female body experience: "Throwing like a girl" and other essays.* New York: Oxford University Press. A provocative collection of essays on topics such as menstruation, breasts, pregnancy, old age, and feminine body language. Young's analyses focus on the effects of modern western culture on a woman's relationship with her body.

Notes

1. Life expectancy also varies significantly by the region of the country in which a person lives. In fact, scientists have found greater regional variation in life expectancy throughout the United States than in any other high-income industrialized country. In some parts of the United States, such as rural South Dakota, which is heavily populated by Native Americans, as well as in some inner-city areas, male life expectancy is more than fifteen years less than the average male life expectancy for the country as a whole. In fact, male life expectancy in these areas is as low as male life expectancy in some developing countries ("Surprises in a Study," 1997). In 2011, Mississippi was the state with the lowest overall life expectancy: 73.6 years on average (World Health Organization, 2011).

2. Housework itself is hazardous, involving exposure to toxins through skin absorption and inhalation, but it is rarely mentioned in discussions of occupational health and safety because it is not recognized as "real" work (Messias et al., 1997; Office of Waste Management, 2005; see also Chapter 7).

3. Researchers have also discovered another form of "take-home contamination." Husbands who are unfaithful to their wives may increase their wives' chances of developing cervical cancer. Researchers found that women whose husbands frequented prostitutes or who had many sexual partners were five to eleven times more likely to develop cervical cancer than women whose husbands were monogamous (Bosch et al., 1996; see also Papa et al., 2009).

4. Staples (1995) also reports that over 75 percent of hazardous waste sites are located in predominantly Black communities, a factor that likely contributes to the high cancer mortality rate of Black Americans. Members of all ethnic minorities are 50 percent more likely than whites to live in communities with hazardous waste sites (Bullard, 2007).

5. Minority men have also been subjected to abuses by the medical establishment. One especially egregious example is the "Tuskegee Study of Untreated Syphilis in the Negro Male," conducted from 1932 to 1972 in rural Alabama. In this study, more than four hundred Black men diagnosed with syphilis were denied treatment for the disease so that researchers from the U.S. Public Health Service could observe the disease's effects on Black men over the course of their lifetimes. The study was conducted without the informed consent of the research subjects and resulted in not only intense pain and suffering for the men, but also for their wives and children, who also sometimes became infected. In 1997, President Clinton formally apologized to the remaining survivors and to the families of the deceased for the federal government's sponsorship of the study. For a thorough discussion of what has come to be called the "Tuskegee Experiment," see Jones, 1993.

6. In medically underserved areas as well as in large practices with a high managed care case load, the use of nurse practitioners to handle some of the physician's routine duties is growing. In fact, some nurse practitioners are opening their own practices in direct competition with physicians. Although some physicians welcome the help, others see independent nurse practitioners as a threat to their practices and, therefore, their incomes (Flanagan, 2011; Freudenheim, 1997). It remains to be seen whether the increase in independent nurse practitioners will result in a professional "turf battle" like the one physicians waged against midwives, herbalists, and other healers in the nineteenth century.

7. Interestingly, one study shows that medical school graduates who were admitted to medical school with special consideration for race or ethnicity have the same graduation rate, get similar residency evaluations, choose their specialties in about the same percentages, and follow essentially equivalent career paths as graduates who were regularly admitted (Davidson & Lewis, 1997).

8. Importantly, surveys show that female physicians earn on average 14 percent less than male physicians, even after controlling for age, training, and practice characteristics (Ness et al., 2000). The income gap is found in all specialties and ranges from a $20,000 difference between male and female family

practitioners, to a $159,000 difference between male and female physicians who practice invasive cardiology (Angier, 1999b).

9. Messner (1987) notes, for instance, that only 6 to 7 percent of high school football players play in college and of those who do, about 8 percent are drafted into the pros, but only 2 percent eventually sign a professional contract. The odds are similar for basketball players. Moreover, even for those who reach the top, success may be short-lived: the average NFL career is four years, and the average NBA career is 3.4 years.

10. Interestingly, Wechsler and his colleagues (1995) found that female college students who adopted the masculine "animal house" values of fraternity members (e.g., viewing parties as a very important part of college life) were as likely as male college students to be heavy or binge drinkers. Moreover, Wechsler et al. found that male college athletes were more likely than nonathletes to be binge drinkers. We discuss these issues further in Box 12.3.

11. Bulimia is distinct from another eating disorder known as *binge eating disorder* that is estimated to affect about 2 percent of the population. Individuals with binge eating disorder have recurrent episodes of rapid, excessive food consumption over a brief period of time, but do not try to purge their bodies of the food like bulimics do. They also do not diet when not binging as bulimics do. They, therefore, tend to be overweight, even obese, rather than thin. However, clinicians disagree over whether binge eating disorder is simply overeating in response to stress or a distinct psychological disorder. Currently, binge eating disorder is considered a "provisional diagnosis" in the *Diagnostic and Statistical Manual,* until further study confirms it as a distinct disorder (Goode, 2000b). One study found a relationship between a chemical malfunction in the brain and bulimia (Smith, Fairburn, & Cowen, 1999), but it is not known whether a related biological problem triggers binge eating or overeating generally.

12. Some psychologists, such as Robert L. Spitzer, have recently claimed that homosexuals can be "treated" using "sexual reorientation therapy" or what is commonly called "reparative therapy," the goal of which is to get a person to change his or her sexual orientation from homosexual to heterosexual. Supported by social and religious conservative groups who oppose homosexuality, "reparative therapy" is not condoned by the American Psychiatric Association (APA). The APA has issued statements emphasizing the lack of scientific evidence showing that "reparative therapy" is beneficial and the availability of evidence showing that it can cause depression, anxiety, and self-destructive behavior in patients who undergo it.

13. Recent research also shows a high rate of sexual contact between psychologists and their students, again with significant gender differences. In a national survey of 1,000 psychologists, 16.5 percent of women, but just 3 percent of men reported having had sexual contact with a psychology educator when they were students; 19 percent of men, but just 8 percent of women reported having had sexual contact with students when they themselves were psychology educators (Pope, Sonne, & Holroyd, 2001).

14. Such cases are not unlike those involving Catholic priests who have sexually abused children and adolescents in their parishes. Whether the abuse is perpetrated by a psychologist or a clergyman, it is nevertheless a traumatic violation of trust by a person in authority against a relatively powerless and highly vulnerable victim. In cases involving priests, church authorities who were made aware of the problem usually responded by simply transferring the perpetrators to other parishes, where they continued to victimize others. It was not until 2002 that the problem was given widespread and serious public attention after many victims came forward with allegations of abuse against specific priests. In these cases, however, it appears that most of the victims were young boys (see Chapter 11).

GLOSSARY

acquaintance rape   an incident of sexual assault in which the victim knows or is familiar with the assailant

Affirmative Action (Executive Order 11246)   forbids federal contractors from discriminating in personnel decisions on the basis of sex, as well as race, color, national origin, and religion, and requires employers to take affirmative measures to recruit, train, and hire women and minorities; since 1978, implemented and enforced by the OFCCP

androcentrism   male-centered; the notion that males are superior to other animals and to females and that males and the male experience are the normative standard against which females should be judged

androgen-insensitivity syndrome (AIS)   a genetic defect that causes an XY fetus to be unresponsive to the androgens its testes secrete

anorexia   an eating disorder in which an individual, because of an obsessive fear of becoming overweight, literally starves; characterized by a distorted body image, a 25 percent loss of body weight, and a refusal to eat; 90 to 95 percent of anorectics are females

bipedalism   walking upright on two feet

bisexuality   sexual and affectionate attraction to both women and men

brain lateralization   the specialization of the right and left hemispheres of the brain for different tasks

bulimia   an abnormal and constant craving for food, also known as binge-purge syndrome, in which the individual consumes large quantities of food in short periods of time followed by fasting, the use of laxatives, or induced vomiting to purge the food and prevent weight gain

castration anxiety   Freud's notion that boys fear their fathers will castrate them because of their sexual attraction to their mothers

chivalry hypothesis (paternalism hypothesis) the belief that female offenders are afforded greater leniency before the law than their male counterparts

chosen families   composed of people unrelated by ancestry, marriage, or adoption, but who are nonetheless considered family members

clinical depression   severe and persistent feelings of discontent or displeasure accompanied by at least four of eight symptoms (poor appetite or weight loss, insomnia or increased sleep, psychomotor agitation or retardation, loss of interest in usual activities, loss of energy or fatigue, feelings of worthlessness, diminished concentration, and suicidal ideation) that are present daily for at least two weeks without evidence of any other disorder

comparable worth   the policy of paying workers equally when they perform different jobs that have similar value in terms of such factors as skill, effort, responsibility, and working conditions

congenital adrenal hyperplasia (CAH)   or adrenogenital syndrome (AGS) a condition occurring prenatally that is caused by a malfunction in the mother's or the fetus's adrenal glands or from exposure of the mother to a substance that acts on the fetus like an androgen

DHT deficiency syndrome   a condition in which an individual has no or abnormally low 5-alpha-reductase, an enzyme responsible for converting testosterone into dihydrotestosterone

dissimilarity index (segregation index, D)   a measure of occupational sex segregation, reported in percent, that indicates the proportion of workers of one sex that would have to change to jobs in which members of their sex were underrepresented to achieve a balanced occupational distribution between the sexes

domestic partnership   a cohabiting relationship between intimate partners not married to each other

dual labor market   a labor market characterized by one set of jobs employing almost exclusively men and another set of jobs, typically lower paying with lower prestige, employing almost exclusively women

ecofeminism   an earth-based feminist spirituality movement that celebrates women's close association with nature and sees a connection between the domination of women and the domination of nature

economy the system for the management and development of a society's human and material resources

emancipation theory (liberation theory) the theory that female crime is increasing and/or becoming more masculine in character as a result of feminism or the women's movement

Equal Pay Act of 1963 forbids employers from paying employees of one sex more than employees of the opposite sex when these employees are engaged in work that requires equal skill, effort, and responsibility and is performed under similar working conditions, although exceptions, such as unequal pay based on seniority, merit, the quality or quantity of production, or any other factor besides sex, are allowed

establishment sex segregation a form of occupational sex segregation in which women and men hold the same job title at an individual establishment or company, but actually do different jobs

ethnocentrism the view that one set of cultural beliefs and practices is superior to all others

expressive family role the role of housekeeper and caregiver in the family, a role held by the wife/mother in a traditional isolated nuclear family

feminist movement (women's movement) a social movement that spans more than a century of U.S. and European history and that is represented today in most countries of the developing world as well; it is composed of many diverse segments, each committed to eliminating gender oppression as well as other inequalities.

feminist paradigm a school of thought that explains gender in terms of the political and socioeconomic structure in which it is constructed and emphasizes the importance of taking collective action to eradicate sexism in sociology as well as in society, and to reconstruct gender so that it is neither a harmful nor an oppressive social category

feminist spirituality a religious movement comprising diverse segments with differing beliefs and strategies for change, but unified in rejecting the dualism characteristic of traditional patriarchal religions; dualism is replaced with the theme of the unification of spirit and nature and the principle that human experience is the source of spirituality

foraging societies (hunting and gathering societies) small, technologically undeveloped societies whose members meet their survival needs by hunting and trapping animals, by fishing (if possible), and by gathering vegetation and other types of food in their surrounding environment; characterized by highly egalitarian gender relations

formal curriculum the set of subjects officially and explicitly taught to students in school

fundamentalism a religious orientation that denounces secular modernity and attempts to restore traditional spirituality through selective retrieval of doctrines, beliefs, and practices from a sacred past

gender socially generated attitudes and behaviors, usually organized dichotomously as masculinity and femininity

gender attribution the process of linking archeological data with males and females

gender gap differences in the voting patterns and political attitudes of women and men

gender polarization the assumption that males and females are fundamentally different from one another, and the practice of using these differences as a central organizing principle for the social life of the society

gender roles social roles that are prescribed for a society's members, depending on their sex

gender stereotypes summary descriptions of masculinity and femininity that are oversimplified and generalized

gender structure a system for differentially distributing opportunities and imposing constraints based on sex categories with consequences on three levels: the individual, the cultural, and the institutional

gladiator activities the highest level of political activism in Millbrath's typology; include working on a political campaign, taking an active role in a political party, or running for public office

glass ceiling invisible barriers that limit women workers' and minority workers' upward occupational mobility

gynecentrism female-centered; the view that females are superior to other animals and to males

hidden curriculum the value preferences children are taught in school that are not an explicit part of the formal curriculum, but rather are hidden or implicit in it

homophobia an unreasonable fear of and hostility toward homosexuals

horticultural society a preindustrial society in which the primary economic activity is farming using digging sticks, hoes, and similar technology

human capital theory explains occupational sex segregation in terms of women's free choice to work in jobs that make few demands on workers and require low personal investment in training or skills acquisition based on the assumption that women's primary responsibility is in the home

identification a central concept of the Freudian-based theory of gender socialization; the process by which boys and girls begin to unconsciously model their behavior after that of their same-sex parent in their efforts to resolve their respective gender identity complexes

incumbent an individual who holds political office and seeks another term

industry sex segregation a form of occupational sex segregation in which women and men hold the same job title in a particular field or industry, but actually perform different jobs

instrumental family role the role of providing financial support for the family and making key decisions, a role held by the husband/father in the traditional isolated nuclear family

isolated nuclear family a family in which the husband/father, wife/mother, and their dependent children establish a household geographically and financially separate from other kin and the adults carry out distinct, specialized roles

Klinefelter syndrome a chromosomal condition in which an individual has three (XXY) sex chromosomes, rather than two (XX or XY)

labor force the human resources of the economy

liberation theology a religious orientation that merges the religious teachings and social functions of the Christian church with a critical analysis of the historical and contemporary experience of human suffering

life expectancy the average number of years of life remaining to an individual at a given age

linguistic sexism ways in which language devalues members of one sex

marital rape the sexual assault of a woman by her husband

matrifocal a system of social organization and group life centered around mothers

mentor usually an older, established member of a profession who serves as a kind of sponsor for a younger, new member by providing advice and valuable contacts with others in the field

micro-inequities subtle, everyday forms of discrimination that single out, ignore, or in some way discount individuals and their work or ideas simply on the basis of an ascribed trait, such as sex

modeling the process by which children imitate the behavior of their same-sex parent, especially if the parent rewards their imitations or is perceived by them to be warm, friendly, or powerful; a central concept of the social learning perspective of gender socialization

morbidity rate the illness rate of a given population

mortality rate the number of deaths in proportion to a given population

occupational resegregation sex-integrated occupations become resegregated with members of one sex replaced by members of the opposite sex as the predominant workers

occupational sex segregation the degree to which men and women are concentrated in occupations that employ workers of predominantly one sex

paradigm a school of thought that guides a scientist in choosing the problems to be studied, in selecting the methods for studying them, and in explaining what is found

patriarchy a sex/gender system in which men dominate women, and what is considered masculine is more highly valued than what is considered feminine

penis envy Freud's notion of girls' jealousy of the male sexual organ

political action committee (PAC) a special interest group dedicated to fundraising and distributing contributions to the political campaigns of candidates who support their cause

power the ability to impose one's will on others

primatology the study of living, nonhuman primates

public/private split the idea that home is a separate domain from the public world

Qur'an (or Quran, variation of Koran) the book of sacred writings accepted by Muslims as revelations made to Muhammad by Allah; understood by Muslims to be literally the word of God

rape when a person uses force or the threat of force to have some form of sexual intercourse (vaginal, oral, or anal) with another person

reflection hypothesis the belief that media content mirrors the behaviors, relationships, values, and norms most prevalent or dominant in a society

reinforcement a central principle of social learning theories of gender socialization, which states that a behavior consistently followed by a reward will likely occur again, whereas a behavior followed by a punishment will rarely reoccur

religiosity an individual's or a group's intensity of commitment to a religious belief system

reproductive freedom an individual's ability to freely choose whether or not to have a child

reproductive technologies a variety of laboratory techniques that allow people who are infertile, physically unable to conceive or sustain a pregnancy, do not have a partner, or do not wish to enter into a committed relationship to become parents

schema a central concept of the cognitive developmental perspective of gender socialization; a category used to organize and make sense of information and experiences

semantic derogation the process by which the meaning or connotations of words are debased over time

sentencing disparity widely varying sentences imposed on offenders convicted of similar crimes, usually based on nonlegal factors, such as the offender's sex or race or ethnicity, or other inappropriate considerations

sex the biologically determined physical distinctions between males and females

sex chromosomes one of the twenty-three pairs of human chromosomes that plays a primary role in determining whether a fertilized egg will develop into a female or a male fetus

sexism the differential valuing of one sex over the other

sexual double standard the tradition of permitting young men to engage in sexual activity while simultaneously condemning and punishing the same behavior by young women

sexual harassment any unwanted leers, comments, suggestions, or physical contact of a sexual nature, as well as unwelcome requests for sexual favors

sexual politics analysis of gender inequality as rooted not only in the public sphere, but also in the supposedly private sphere of the family and intimate male/female relationships

single-parent family a family with children but only one adult who has financial responsibility for the household

social movement a group that has organized to promote a particular cause through social action

socialization the process by which a society's values and norms, including those pertaining to gender, are taught and learned

sociology the scientific study of human societies and cultures, and of social behavior

spectator activities the lowest level of political activism in Millbrath's typology; include voting, wearing a campaign button, or displaying a political bumper sticker

statistical discrimination employers do not hire anyone who is a member of a group they think has low productivity, regardless of an individual applicant's qualifications or intentions

status offenses behavior considered illegal if engaged in by a juvenile, but legal if engaged in by an adult

structural functionalist paradigm a school of thought that explains gender as being derived from the biological differences between the sexes, especially differences in reproductive functions

symbolic annihilation symbolically ignoring, trivializing, or condemning individuals or groups in the media

Talmud the foundation of religious authority for traditional Judaism

Title IX the provisions of the Education Amendments Act of 1972 that forbid sex discrimination in any educational programs or activities that receive federal funding

Title VII of the 1964 Civil Rights Act forbids discrimination in employment on the basis of sex, race, color, national origin, or religion, by employers of fifteen or more employees, although exceptions, such as the BFOQ, are allowed; implemented and enforced by the EEOC

tokenism the marginal status of a category of workers who are relatively few in number in the workplace

transformative account of gender development a theory of gender development that recognizes the truly interactive nature of biology and environment as well as individual agency in the creation of gender by examining how culture and individual behavior may impact biology and physiology and vice versa

transitional activities the mid-range of political activism in Millbrath's typology; include writing to public officials, making campaign contributions, and attending rallies or political meetings

Turner syndrome a chromosomal condition in which an individual has only one sex chromosome (an X), rather than a pair (XX or XY)

two-earner family a family in which both adult partners are in the paid labor force

witchcraft naturalistic practices with religious significance usually engaged in by women; includes folk magic and medicine as well as knowledge of farming, ceramics, metallurgy, and astrology

Women-Church movement a coalition of feminist faith-sharing groups, which offers a feminist critique of traditional Christianity while providing members with alternative, woman-centered rituals and forms of worship

REFERENCES

Abbate, L. (2000). *Approaching the bench: Women justices of the Supreme Court of Texas*. Paper presented at the Southwest Political Science Association Annual Meeting, March 2000 in Galveston, TX.

Abbey, A. et al. (2001). Attitudinal, experiential, and situational predictors of sexual assault perpetration. *Journal of Interpersonal Violence, 16*, 784–807.

Abbott, J. (2006). *Religion and gender in the news: The case of Promise Keepers, feminists, and the "Stand in the Gap" rally*. Retrieved from: http://www.uttyler.edu/meidenmuller/religiouspersuasion/msworlddocuments/PK%20%20Abbottt.pdf

Abbott, P. (1991). Feminist perspectives in sociology: The challenge to "mainstream" orthodoxy. In J. Aaron & S. Walby (Eds.),*Out of the margins: Women's studies in the nineties* (pp. 181–190). London: Falmer Press.

Abel, E. M. (1999, July). *Comparing women in batterer intervention programs with male batterers and female victims*. Paper presented at the Sixth International Family Violence Research Conference, Durham, NH.

Abma, J. C., Martinez, J. M., Mosher, W. D., & Dawson, B. S. (2004). Teenagers in the United States: Sexual activity, contraceptive use, and childbearing, 2002. *Vital and Health Statistics, 23*(24), 1–87.

Abrahamson, S. S. (1998). Do women judges really make a difference? The American experience. In S. Shetreet (Ed.), *Women in law* (pp. 75–82). London: Kluwer Law International.

Abu-Lughod, L. (2002). Do Muslim women really need saving? Anthropological reflections on cultural relativism and its others. *American Anthropologist, 104*, 783–790.

Abzug, B. (1984). *Gender gap*. Boston: Houghton Mifflin.

"According to one poll, majority is 'pro-life.'" (2009, June 16). *Christian Century, 126*, p. 13.

Acker, J. (2006). Introduction: "The missing feminist revolution" symposium. *Social Problems, 53*, 444–447.

Adamczyk, A., & Pitt, C. (2009). Shaping attitudes about homosexuality: The role of religion and cultural context. *Social Science Research, 38*, 338–351.

Adams, J. (2007). Stained glass makes the ceiling visible: Organizational opposition to women in congregational leadership. *Gender & Society, 21*, 80–105.

Adams, J. H. (1997). Sexual harassment and Black women: A historical perspective. In W. O'Donahue (Ed.), *Sexual harassment: Theory, research, and treatment*. Boston: Allyn and Bacon.

Adams, K. L., & Ware, N. C. (1989). Sexism and the English language: The linguistic implications of being a woman. In J. Freeman (Ed.), *Women: A feminist perspective* (pp. 470–484). Mountain View, CA: Mayfield.

Adams, S., Kuebli, J., Boyle, P. A., & Fivush, R. (1995). Gender differences in parent-child conversations about past emotions: A longitudinal investigation. *Sex Roles, 33*, 309–323.

Addis, M., & Mahalik, J. (2003). Men, masculinity, and the contexts of help seeking. *American Psychologist, 58*(1), 5–14.

Adebayo, B. (2008). Gender gaps in college enrollment and degree attainment: An exploratory analysis. *College Student Journal, 42*, 1, 232–237.

Adler, F. (1975). *Sisters in crime*. New York: McGraw-Hill.

Adler, R. (1997). *Engendering Judaism*. New York: Jewish Publication Society.

Afshar, H. (Ed.) (1993). *Women in the Middle East*. New York: St. Martin's Press.

Agency for Healthcare Research and Quality, (2003). *Results of systematic review of research on diagnosis and treatment of coronary heart disease in women*. Retrieved from http://www.ahrq.gov/clinic/tp/chdwomtp.htm#Report

Agency for Healthcare Research and Quality. (2010). *Cardiovascular disease and other chronic conditions in women: Recent findings*. Retrieved from http://www.ahrq.gov/research/womheart.htm

Ahmed, A. M., & Hyder, A. (2009). Sticky floors and occupational segregation: Evidence from Pakistan. *Pakistan Development Review*. Retrieved November 10, 2010, http://www.pide.org.pk/psde24/pdf/27.pdf

Ahmed, F. B. (2006, February). Male bias in school texts. *Tribune Online Edition*. Chandigarh, India. http://www.tribuneindia.com

Ahmed, L. (1986). Women and the advent of Islam. *Signs, 11*, 665–691.

Ahmed, L. (1992). *Women and gender in Islam*. New Haven: Yale University Press.

Ahmed-Ghosh, H. (2004). Chattels of society: Domestic violence in India. *Violence Against Women, 10*, 94–118.

Akan, B. E., & Grillo, C. M. (2006). Sociocultural influences on eating attitudes and behaviors, body image, and psychological functioning: A comparison of African-American, Asian-American, and Caucasian college women. *International Journal of Eating Disorders, 18*(2), 181–187.

Albarran, J., Clarke, B., & Crawford, J. (2007). 'It was not chest pain really, I can't explain it!' An exploratory study on the nature of symptoms experienced by women during their myocardial infarction. *Journal of Clinical Nursing, 16*(7), 1292–1301.

Alcoff, L. (2011). *Feminism, sexuality and the return of religion*. Bloomington: Indiana University Press.

Alexander, E. (2009). "Woman's place is in the tea room": White middle-class American women as entrepreneurs and customers. *Journal of American Culture, 32*, 126–136.

Alexander, S. (2003). Stylish hard bodies: Branded masculinity in "Men's Health" magazine. *Sociological Perspectives, 46*(4), 535–554.

Al-Hashimi, A. (2010). *The ideal Muslim woman and her husband*. Retrieved from: http://www.wefound.org/texts/Ideal_Muslims_files/herhusband.htm

Ali, K. (2006). Sexual ethics and Islam: Feminist reflections on Qur'an, hadith, and jurisprudence. *American Journal of Islamic Social Sciences, 24*(4), 100–103.

All About Depression. (2011). *Suicide and depression*. Retrieved from http://www.allaboutdepression.com/gen_04.html

All Treatment. (2011). *Treatment programs for men*. Retrieved from http://www.alltreatment.com/science-of-addiction/treatment-programs-for-men

Allan, G. (1985). *Family life*. New York: Basil Blackwell.

Allen, D. (1997, Winter). Women are creating their own communications systems. *Media Report to Women*, p. 9.

Allen, J. J. B., Urry, H. L., Hitt, S. K., & Coan, J. A. (2004). The stability of resting frontal electroencephalographic asymmetry in depression. *Psychophysiology, 41*, 269–280.

Allen, L. S., & Gorski, R. A. (1992). Sexual orientation and the size of the anterior commissure in the human brain. *Proceedings of the National Academy of Sciences, 89*, 7199–7202.

Allen, M. (1996, September 22). Defiant V.M.I. to admit women, but they will face tough rules. *New York Times*, pp. 1, 18.

Allen, M., D'alessio, D., & Brezgel, K. (1995). A meta-analysis summarizing the effects of pornography II. *Human Communication Research, 22*, 258–283.

Allen, N. E., Larsen, S. E., & Walden, A. L. (2011). An overview of community-based services for battered women. In C.M. Renzetti, J.L. Edelson, & R.K. Bergen (Eds.), *Sourcebook on violence against women, 2nd edition* (pp. 245–264). Thousand Oaks, CA: Sage.

Allgood-Merten, B., Lewinsohn, P. M., & Hops, H. (1990). Sex differences and adolescent depression. *Journal of Abnormal Psychology, 99*, 55–63.

Al-Munajjid, S. (2011). *Islam questions and answers*. Retrieved from: http://www.islam-qa.com/en/ref/83032

Altenhofen, S., Biringen, Z., & Mergler, R. (2008). Significant family dynamics related to postdivorce adjustment in parents and children. *Journal of Divorce and Remarriage, 49*(1/2), 25–40.

Altman, L. K. (1997, February 28). U.S. reporting sharp decrease in AIDS deaths. *New York Times*, pp. A1, 24.

Altman, L. K. (1998, April 29). Health panel seeks sweeping changes in fertility therapy. *New York Times*, pp. A1, 22.

Altman, L. K. (2001, February 6). Swift rise in HIV cases for gay Blacks. *New York Times*, pp. A1, A16.

Alvarez, L. (2006, February 9). Army effort to enlist Hispanics draws recruits, and criticism. *New York Times*, pp. A1, A22.

Alvy, L. (2004). Violence against women in Sudan reveals common weapon of war. National Organization for Women. Retrieved December 4, 2009, http://www.now.org/issues/global/120304sudan.html.

Amato, P. R. (2000). The consequences of divorce for adults and children. *Journal of Marriage and the Family, 62*.

Amato, P. R., & Maynard, R. A. (2007). Decreasing nonmarital births and strengthening marriage to reduce poverty. *Future of Children, 17*, 2. Retrieved September 29, 2009, http://www.futureofchildren.org

American Academy of Child and Adolescent Psychiatry. (2006). Children & watching TV. *Facts for Families*. Washington, DC.

American Academy of Pediatrics. (2001). Children, adolescents, and television. *Pediatrics, 107*(2), 423–425.

American Association of Retired Persons. (2009). *Caregiving in the U.S.* Retrieved December 16, 2009, from http://assets.aarp.org/rgcenter/il/caregiving_09_es.pdf

American Association of University Professors (AAUP). (2009). *On the brink: The annual report on the economic status of the profession.* Retrieved from: http://www.aaup.org

American Association of University Professors. (2009). *On the brink: The annual report on the economic status of the profession, 2008–09.* Retrieved March 19, 2010, www.aaup.org/AAUP/comm/rep/Z/ecstatreport08-09/default.htm

American Association of University Women. (2009). 2008–09 report on the economic status of the profession. Retrieved March 17, 2010, from http://www.aaup.org/NR/rdonlyres/0A07ADBE-930F-461E-9140-C74F24122949/0/zreport.pdf

American Association of University Women (AAUW). (1992). *How schools shortchange girls.* Washington, DC: Author.

American Association of University Women (AAUW). (1993). *Hostile hallways: The AAUW survey on sexual harassment in America's schools.* Washington, DC: Author.

American Association of University Women (AAUW). (1998). *Separated by sex: A critical look at single-sex education for girls.* Washington, DC: Author.

American Association of University Women. (2001). *Latinas in school.* Washington, DC: Author.

American Association of University Women. (2005). *Tenure Statistics.* Retrieved March 26, 2010, from http://www.aauw.org/laf/library/tenure.cfm

American Association of University Women. (2008). *Where the girls are: The facts about gender equity in education.* Washington, DC: AAUW.

American Bar Association, Commission on Women in the Profession. (2006). *Visible Invisibility: Women of Color in Law Firms.* Chicago, IL: Author.

American Bar Association, Commission on Women in the Profession. (2008). *From visible invisibility to visibly successful: Success strategies for law firms and women of color.* Chicago: Author.

American Bar Association. (2001). *The unfinished agenda: Women and the legal profession.* Chicago: Author.

American College Health Association. (2004). *National College Health Assessment: Reference Group Executive Summary.* Baltimore: Author.

American Council on Education (2006). *Gender equity in higher education.* Washington, DC: Author.

American Council on Education. (2010). *Gender equity in higher education.* Washington, DC: Author.

American Council on Education. (2009a). *Minorities in higher education 2008: Twenty-third status report.* Washington, DC: Author.

American Council on Education. (2009b). *The CAO census: A national profile of chief academic officers.* Washington, DC: Author.

American Federation of Teachers. (2009). *American academic: The state of the higher education workforce 1997–2007.* Washington, DC: American Federation of Teachers. Retrieved March 19, 2010, http://archive.aft.org/pubs-reports/higher_ed/AmerAcad_report_97-07.pdf

American Heart Association (2011). *Heart attack and angina statistics.* Retrieved from http://www.americanheart.org/presenter.jhtml?identifier=4591

American Heart Journal. (2011). *Severe heart attack no more deadly to women than men.* Retrieved from http://doctor.ndtv.com/storypage/ndtv/id/5051/Severe_heart_attack_no_more_deadly_to_women_than_men.html?pfrom=home-DoctorNDTV

American Medical Association. (2000). *AAMC women in U.S. academic medicine, statistics 2000.* Available online: http://www.ama.org

American Medical Association. (2002). *Physician characteristics and distribution in the U.S.* Available online: http://www.ama.org

American Psychological Association, Task Force on the Sexualization of Girls. (2007). *Report of the APA task force on the sexualization of girls.* Washington, DC: American Psychological Association.

American Psychological Association. (1985). *Developing a national agenda to address women's mental health needs.* Washington, DC: Author.

American Society of Newspaper Editors. (2009). U.S. newsroom employment declines. Retrieved September 27, 2010, http://www.asne.org/article_view/smid/370/articleid/6.aspx

American Society of Newspaper Editors. (2010). Decline in newsroom jobs slows. Retrieved from: http://www.asne.org/article_view/articleid/763/delcine-in-newsroom-jobs.slows.aspx

American Society of Plastic Surgeons. (2011). Breast implant statistics. Retrieved from: http://www.thebreastsite.com/breast-surgery/breast-implants-statistics.aspx

Ammerman, N. (1987). *Bible believers: Fundamentalists in the modern world*. New Brunswick, NJ: Rutgers University Press.

Ammerman, N. T. (1991). North American Protestant fundamentalism. In M. E. Marty & R. S. Appleby (Eds.) *Fundamentalisms observed* (pp. 1–65). Chicago: University of Chicago Press.

Amnesty International. (1991). *Women on the front lines*. New York: Amnesty International.

Amott T. L., & Matthaei, J. A. (1991). *Race, gender and work*. Boston: South End Press.

AndersAnderson, C., Berkowitz, L., Donnerstein, E., Huesmann, L., Johnson, J., Linz, D., Malamuth, N., & Wartella, E. (2003). The influence of media violence on youth, *Psychological Science in the Public Interest, 4* (3) 81–110.

Andersen, R., & Fetner, T. (2008). Economic inequality and intolerance: Attitudes toward homosexuality in 35 democracies. *American Journal of Political Science, 52*(4), 942–958.

Andersen, T., Jeneson, A., & Ruland, C.M. (2007). Gender differences in online messages among cancer patients. In K.A. Kuhn, J.R. Warren, & T. Leong (Eds.), *Proceedings of the 12th World Congress on Health*, Amsterdam, Holland. Available online: http://www/search.informit.com.au/documentSummary.dn.789962856210151:res=IELHSS

Anderson, D. A., & Hamilton, M. (2005). Gender role stereotyping of parents in children's picture books: Theinvisible father. *Sex Roles, 52*, 3/4, 145–151.

Anderson, K. J., & Cavallaro, D. (2002). Parents or pop culture? Children's heroes and role models. *Childhood Education, 78*(3), 161–169.

Anderson, M. et al. (2008). HIV/AIDS-related stigma and discrimination: Accounts of HIV-positive Caribbean people in the United Kingdom. *Social Science and Medicine, 67*, 790–798.

Anderson, S. R., & Hopkins, P. (1991). *The feminine face of God*. New York: Bantam.

Andreyeva, T., Puhl, R. M., & Brownell, K. D. (2008). Changes in perceived weight discrimination among Americans, 1995–1996 through 2004–2006. *Obesity, 16*, 1129–1134.

Angelle, A. (2010). *Modern medicine: Unnecessary c-sections on the rise*. Retrieved from http://www.myhealthnewsdaily.com/unnecessary-c-sections-on-the-rise-0768/

Angelone, D. J., Mitchell, D., & Pilafova. (2007). Club drug use and intentionality in perceptions of rape victims. *Sex Roles, 57*, 283–292.

Angier, N. (1992, September 1). Hyenas' hormonal flow puts females in charge. *New York Times*, pp. C1, C10.

Angier, N. (1997, March 14). Sexual identity not pliable after all, report says. *New York Times*, pp. A1, A18.

Angier, N. (1999a). *Woman: An intimate geography*. New York: Anchor.

Angier, N. (1999b, January 12). Among doctors, pay for women still lags. *New York Times*, p. F7.

Angier, N. (2000, February 15). For women in astronomy, a glass ceiling in the sky. *New York Times*, p. F5.

Ankney, R. N., & Procopio, D. A. (2003). Corporate culture, minority hiring, and newspaper coverage of Affirmative Action. *Howard Journal of Communications, 14*, 159–176.

Anliak, S., & Beyazkurk, D. S. (2008). Career perspectives of male students in early childhood education. Educational Studies, 34(4), 309–317.

Antoniou, A. S. (2009). Occupation-specific precursors of stress among Greek police officers: The roles of rank and gender. *International Journal of Police and Science Management, 11*, 3, 334–344.

Antoun, R. (2008). *Understanding fundamentalism: Christian, Islamic, and Jewish movements*. Lanham, MD: Rowman & Littlefield.

Apetrei, S. (2010). *Women, feminism, and religion in early enlightenment England*. Cambridge: Cambridge University Press.

Araji, S. K., & Carlson, J. (2001). Family violence including crimes of honor in Jordan: Correlates and perceptions of seriousness. *Violence Against Women, 7*, 586–621.

Arbuckle, J., & Williams, B. D. (2003). Students' perceptions of expressiveness: Age and gender effects on teacher evaluations. *Sex Roles, 49*, 507–516.

Archer, J. (2000). Sex differences in aggression between heterosexual partners: A meta-analytic review. *Psychological Bulletin, 126*, 651–680.

Archer, J., & Cote, S. (2005). Sex differences in aggressive behavior: A developmental and evolutionary perspective. In R. E. Tremblay, W. W. Hartup, & J. Archer (Eds.), *Developmental *origins of aggression* (pp. 425–443). New York: Guilford Press.

Ardrey, R. (1966). *African genesis.* London: William Collins.

Arendell, T. (2000). Conceiving and investigating motherhood: The decade's scholarship. *Journal of Marriage and the Family, 62*, 1192–1207.

Arenson, K. W. (1998, January 14). A revamped student test reduces the gap between sexes. *New York Times*, p. B7.

Arevalo, S., Prado, G., & Amaro, H. (2007). Spirituality, sense of coherence, and coping responses in women receiving treatment for alcohol and drug addiction. *Evaluation and Program Planning, 31*(1), 113–123.

Armour, S. (2000, October 5). Workers unwittingly take home toxins. *USA Today*, pp. 1A, 4A, 6A.

Armstead, C. A., Lawler, K. A., Gordon, G., Cross, J., & Gibbons, J. (1989). Relationship of social stressors to blood pressure responses and anger expression in Black college students. *Health Psychology, 8*, 541–556.

Arnold, R. A. (1990). Processes of victimization and criminalization of Black women. *Social Justice, 17*, 153–165.

Arnow, P. (2004). New York Times bylines sideline women, female reporters found mainly on inside pages, back sections. *FAIR—Fairness and Accuracy in Reporting*. Retrieved February 23, 2011, www.arnow.org/clipextra.html

Aronson, P. (2003). Feminists or "postfeminists"?: Young women's attitudes toward feminism and gender relations. *Gender & Society, 17*(6), 903–922.

Arriaga & S. Oskamp (Eds.), *Violence in intimate relationships* (pp. 17–44). Thousand Oaks, CA: Sage.

Artiles, A. J., Trent, S. C, & Palmer, J. (2004). Culturally diverse students in special education: Legacies and prospects. In J. A. Banks & C. M. Banks (Eds.), *Handbook of research on multicultural education* (2nd ed.) (pp. 716–735). San Francisco: Josey-Bass.

Artyk, N. (2008, December 16). Muslim feminists confront a world of obstacles. *Women's enews*. Retrieved from: http://www.womensenews.org/article.cfm/dyn/aid/3848

Asher, M. (1999, May 16). Survey: Women are gaining, but athletic inequities remain. *Washington Post*, p. D12.

Ashraf, M. (2007). Factors affecting female employment in male-dominated occupations: Evidence from the 1990 and 2000 Census data. *Contemporary Economic Policy, 25*, 119–130.

Association for Humanistic Psychology. (2001). *Feminist therapy*. Retrieved from: http://www.ahpweb.org/rowan_bibliography/chapter16.html

Association of American Medical Colleges. (2001). *U.S. medical school faculty*. Available online: http://www.aamc.org

Association of American Medical Colleges. (2011). *Enrollment, graduates, and MD/PhD data*. Retrieved from https://www.aamc.org/data/facts/85910/enrollmentgraduate/

Association of American Medical Colleges. (2011). *Women in U.S. academic medicine: Statistics and benchmarking report, 2009–2010*. Washington, DC: Author.

Association of Theological Schools. (2010). *The Commission on Accrediting*. Retrieved from: http://www.ats.edu/Resources/Publications/Documents/AnnualDataTables/2009-10AnnualDataTables.pdf

Athanases, S.Z., & Comas, T.A. (2008). The performance of homophobia in early adolescents' everyday speech. *Journal of LGBT Youth, 5*, 2, 9–32.

Atlanta Medical Center. (2011). *What's race got to do with high blood pressure?* Retrieved from http://www.atlantamedcenter.com/en-US/ourServices/communityServices/Pages/What%E2%80%99s%20Race%20Got%20to%20Do%20with%20High%20Blood%20Pressure.aspx

Attie, I., & Brooks-Gunn, J. (1987). Weight concerns as chronic stressors in women. In R. C. Barnett, L. Biener, & G. K. Baruch (Eds.), *Gender and stress* (pp. 218–254). New York: Free Press.

AuCoin, K. (2005). Family violence against older adults. Family violence in Canada: A statistical profile, 2005. *Statistics Canada*, Catalogue No. 85-224-XIE. Available from http://www.statcan.gc.ca/pub/85-224-Z/85-224-X2005000-ENG/pdf

Aulette, J. R. (1994). *Changing families*. Belmont, CA: Wadsworth.

Austin, E. L., Andersen, R., & Gelberg, L. (2008). Ethnic differences in the correlates of mental distress among homeless women. *Women's Health Issues, 18*, 26–34.

Austin, J., Fabeo, T., Gunther, A., & McGinnis, K. (2006). *Sexual violence in the Texas prison system*. Austin, TX: FJA Institute.

Auwarter, A. E., & Aruguete, M. S. (2008). Effects of student gender and socioeconomic status on teacher perceptions. *Journal of Educational Research, 101*, 243–246.

Avert. (2011). Averting HIV and AIDS, United States, by race and age. Retrieved from: http://www.avert.org/usa-race-age.htm

Awwad, A. (2001). Gossip, scandal, shame and honor killing: A case for social constructionism and hegemonic discourse. *Social Thought and Research, 24,* 39–59.

Ayoub, C. C., Deutsch, R. M., & Maraganore, A. (1999). Emotional distress in children of high-conflict divorce: The impact of marital conflict and violence. *Family and Conciliation Courts Review, 37,* 297–314.

Azim, E., Mobbs, D., Booil, J., Menon, V., & Reiss, A.L. (2005). Sex differences in brain activation elicited by humor. *Proceedings of the National Academy of Science, 102,* 16496–16501.

Azzi, I. (2009, Summer). Progress on FGM in Africa. *Herizons,* p. 7.

Babb, S. (2005). The social consequences of structural adjustment: Recent evidence and current debates. *Annual Review of Sociology, 31,* 199–222.

Babcock, M. (2008). Substance-using mothers: Bias in culture and research. *Journal of Addictions Nursing, 19*(2) 87–91.

Baca Zinn, M. (1992). Reframing the revisions: Inclusive thinking for family sociology. In C. Kramarae & D. Spender (Eds.), *The knowledge explosion: Generations of feminist scholarship* (pp. 473–479). New York: Teachers College Press.

Baca Zinn, M., & Dill, B. T. (1996). Theorizing difference from multiracial feminism. *Feminist Studies, 22,* 321–331.

Bachman, J. G., Wadsworth, K. N., O'Malley, P. M., Johnston, L. D., & Schulenberg, J. E. (1997). *Smoking, drinking and drug use in young adulthood: The impacts of new freedoms and new responsibilities.* Mahwah, NJ: Lawrence Erlbaum.

Bachman, R. (2000). A comparison of annual incidence rates and contextual characteristics of intimate-partner violence against women from the National Crime Victimization Survey (NCVS) and the National Violence Against Women Survey (NVAWS). *Violence Against Women, 6,* 839–867.

Bacon, M. H. (1986). *Mothers of feminism.* San Francisco: Harper and Row.

Baculinao, E. (2004). China grapples with legacy of its "missing girls": Disturbing demographic imbalance spurs drive to change age-old practices. *MSNBC News.* Retrieved April 29, 2010, http://www.msnbc.msn.com/id/5953508

Baehr, H. (1980). The "liberated woman" in television drama. *Women's Studies International Quarterly, 3,* 29–39.

Baer, J., & Goldstein, L. F. (2006). *The constitutional and legal rights of women: Cases in law and social change.* New York: Oxford University Press.

Bagilhole, B. (1993). How to keep a good woman down: An investigation of the role of institutional factors in the process of discrimination against women academics. *British Journal of Sociology of Education, 14,* 26–274.

Bagley, C., Bolitho, F., & Bertrand, L. (1997). Sexual assault in school, mental health and suicidal behaviors in adolescent women in Canada. *Adolescence, 32,* 341–366.

Bailey, J. M., & Pillard, R. C. (1991). A genetic study of male sexual orientation. *Archives of General Psychiatry, 48,* 1089–1096.

Bailey, J. M., Pillard, R. C., Neale, M. C., & Agyei, Y. (1993). Heritable factors influence sexual orientation in women. *Archives of General Psychiatry, 50,* 217–223.

Baillargeon, R. H., Zoccolillo, M., Keenan, K., Cote, S., Persusse, D., & Wu, H., et al. (2007). Gender differences in physical aggression: A prospective population-based survey of children before and after 2 years of age. *Developmental Psychology, 43,* 13–26.

Baker, B. (1999). Eating disorder increasing among minority, poorer, and younger girls. *Clinical Psychiatry News, 27*(10), p. 33.

Baker, K., & Raney, A. A. (2007). Equally super?: Gender-role stereotyping of superheroes children's animated programs. *Mass Communication & Society, 10,* 1, 25–41.

Baker, L. (2001). Control and the Dalkon shield. *Violence Against Women, 7,* 1303–1317.

Baker, N. V., Gregware, P. R., & Cassidy, M. A. (1999). Family killing fields. *Violence Against Women, 7,* 164–184.

Baker, S. W. (1980). Biological influences on human sex and gender. *Signs, 6,* 80–96.

Baker-Sperry, L. (2007). The production of ʹing through peer interaction: Children ʹ Disney's *Cinderella. Sex Roles, 56,* 717-

Ball, J. D. (2005). Does violence beget vʹ Is it potato or potata? Tomato ʹ should we call the whole thirʹ *Justice Studies, 18,* 183–196.

Ball, J. D. (2009). Intergenerʹ of abuse of incarcerateʹ

measurement of abuse. *Journal of Family Issues, 30*, 3, 371–390.

Ball, T. (2008). Female genital mutilation. *Nursing Standard, 23*(5), 43–47.

Ballou, M., & Gabalac, N. W. (1985). *A feminist position on mental health*. Springfield, IL: Charles C. Thomas.

Balmer, R. (1999). *Mine eyes have seen the glory: Evangelical subculture in America*. New York: Oxford University Press.

Banderas, J. (2009). Moms increasingly going back to work in recession. *Fox News*. Retrieved from: http://www.foxnews.com/us/2009/10/29/moms-increasingly-going-work-recession/

Bandura, A. (1986). *The social foundations of thought and action: A social cognitive theory*. Englewood Cliffs, NJ: Prentice-Hall.

Bane, M. J. (1986). Household composition and poverty. In S. H. Danzinger & D. H. Weinberg (Eds.), *Fighting poverty: What works and what doesn't* (pp. 209–231). Cambridge, MA: Harvard University Press.

Banerjee, N. (2006a, December 13). Pastors' disclosures may stir empathy, some evangelicals say. *New York Times*, p. A26.

Banerjee, N. (2006b, December 12). Gay and seeking a place among evangelicals. *New York Times*, pp. A1, A18.

Banerjee, N. (2006c, August 26). Clergywomen find hard path to bigger pulpit. *New York Times*, pp. A1, A11.

Banks, B. J. (2007). *Gender and education: An encyclopedia*. Westport, CT: Praeger Publishers.

Banks, J. A. (2009b). Approaches to multicultural curriculum reform. In J. A. Banks & C.M. Banks (Eds.), *Multicultural education: Issues and perspectives, 7th ed.* (pp. 233–256). Hoboken, NJ: John Wiley & Sons, Inc.

Banks, J. A. (2009a). Multicultural education: Characteristics and goals. In J.A. Banks & C. M. Banks (Eds.), *Multicultural education: Issues and perspectives, 7th ed.* (pp. 3–32). Hoboken, NJ: John Wilely & Sons, Inc.

Banner, L. (1984). *Women in modern America: A brief history*. San Diego: Harcourt, Brace, Jovanovich.

Banner, L. (1986). Act one. *Wilson Quarterly, 10*, 90–98.

Banyard, V. L., Cross, C., & Modecki, K. L. (2006). Interpersonal violence in adolescence: Ecological correlates of self-reported perpetration. *Journal of Interpersonal Violence, 21*, 10, 1314–1332.

Barakso, M. (2004). *Governing NOW: Activism in the National Organization for Women*. Ithaca, NY: Cornell University Press.

Baran, S. J., &. Blasko, V. J. (1984). Social perceptions and the by-products of advertising. *Journal of Communication, 34*, 12–20.

Barazangi, N. (2004). *Women's identity and the Qur'an: A new reading*. Gainesville: University of Florida Press.

Barbezat, D. A., & Hughes, J. W. (2006). Salary structure effects and the gender pay gap in academia. *Research in Higher Education, 46*(6), 621–640.

Barboza, D. (2000, December 26). Rampant obesity, a debilitating reality for the urban poor. *New York Times*, p. F5.

Bardwell, J. R., Cochran, S. W., & Walker, S. (1986). Relationship of parental education, race, and gender to sex role stereotyping in five-year-old kindergartners. *Sex Roles, 15*, 275–281.

Bargai, N., Ben-Shakhar, G., & Shalev, A. (2007). Posttraumatic stress disorder and depression in battered women: The mediating role of learning helplessness. *Journal of Family Violence, 22*(5) 267–275.

Barker, G. (2006, September). *Engaging boys and men to empower girls: Reflections from practice and evidence of impact*. United Nations Division for the Advancement of women (DAW), Expert group meeting, Florence, Italy. Retrieved from: http://www.un.org/womenwatch/daw/egm/elim-disc-vio-girlchild/ExpertPapers/EP.3%20%20%20Barker.pdf

Barker-Benfield, G. J. (1976). *The horrors of the half-known life*. New York: Harper and Row.

Barlas, A. (2004). *The Qur'an, sexual equality, and feminism*. Retrieved from: http://www.asmabarlas.com/TALKS/20040112_UToronto.pdf

Barnacle, H. (1999). Ali's visit. In S. Cook & S. Davies (Eds.), *Harsh punishment: International experiences of women's imprisonment* (pp. 47–49). Boston: Northeastern University Press.

Barnard, N. D., Scialli, A. R., Hurlock, D., & Bertron, P. (2000). Diet and sex-hormone binding globulin, dysmenorrhea, and premenstrual symptoms. *Obstetrics and Gynecology, 95*, 245–250.

Barnes, G. M., Farrell, M. P., & Dintcheff, B. A. (1997). Family socialization effects on alcohol abuse and related problem behaviors among female and male adolescents. In R. W. Wilsnack & S. C. Wilsnack (Eds.), *Gender and alcohol* (pp. 156–175). New Brunswick, NJ: Rutgers Center of Alcohol Studies.

Barnes, J. E., Noll, J. G., Putnam, F. W., & Trickett, P. K. (2009). Sexual and physical revictimization among victims of severe childhood sexual abuse. *Child Abuse & Neglect, 33,* 412–420.

Barnett, B. M. (1993). Invisible Southern Black women leaders in the Civil Rights movement: The triple constraints of gender, race, and class. *Gender & Society, 7,* 162–182.

Barnett, O. W., Lee, C. Y., & Thelan, R. (1997). Gender differences in attributions of self-defense and control in interpartner aggression. *Violence Against Women, 3,* 462–481.

Barnett, R. C, & Rivers, C. (2004). The persistence of gender myths in math. *Education Week, 24*(7), 39.

Barnett, R. C., & Baruch, G. K. (1987). Social roles, gender, and psychological stress. In R. C. Barnett, L. Biener, & G. K. Baruch (Eds.), *Gender and stress* (pp. 122–143). New York: Free Press.

Baron, D. (1986). *Grammar and gender.* New Haven: Yale University Press.

Bar-on, M. E. (2000). The effects of television on child health: Implications and recommendations. *Archives of Disease in Childhood, 83,* 289–292.

Baron-Cohen, S., Knickmeyer, R., & Belmonte, M. (2005). Sex differences in the brain: Implications for explaining autism. *Science, 310,* 819–823.

Baron-Fritts, A. (2004). Alter(ing) identities: On becoming the other. *Black Scholar, 34*(1), 34.

Barr, K.E.M., Farrell, M. P., Barnes, G. M., & Welte, J. W. (1993). Race, class, and gender differences in substance abuse: Evidence of middle-class/underclass polarization among Black males. *Social Problems, 40,* 314–327.

Barr, S. C., & Neville, H. A. (2008). Examination of the link between parental racial socialization messages and racial ideology among Black college students. *Journal of Black Psychology, 32*(2), 131–155.

Barreto, M., Ryan, M. K., & Schmitt, M. T. (Eds.). (2009). *The glass ceiling in the 21st century: Understanding barriers to gender equality.* Washington, DC: American Psychological Association.

Barrett, B. J., & St. Pierre, M. (2011). Variations in women's help-seeking in response to intimate partner violence: Findings from a Canadian population-based study. *Violence Against Women, 17,* 47–70.

Barrett-Connor, E. (2007). Commentary: Masculinity, femininity and heart disease. *International Journal of Epidemiology,* (36), 621–622.

Barriers encountered by administrators of color in higher and postsecondary education. (2009). ASHE Higher Education Report, 35(3), 31–46.

Barron, M. & Kimmel, M. (2000). Sexual violence in three pornographic media: Toward a sociological explanation. *Journal of Sex Research, 37,* 2, 343–354.

Barry, C., Brescoll, V., Brownell, K., & Schlesinger, M. (2009). Obesity metaphors: How beliefs about the causes of obesity affect support for public policy. *Milbank Quarterly, 87*(1), 7–47.

Barry, L., Allore, H., Zhenachao, G., Bruce, M., & Gill, T. (2008). Higher burden of depression among older women: The effect of onset, persistence and morality over time. *Archives of General Psychiatry, 65*(2), 172–178.

Barsotti, N. (2009). U.S. passes new hate crime law: Should Canada do the same? *Xtra West, 423,* 7–8.

Barss, P. (2010). *The erotic engine: How pornography has powered mass communication from Gutenberg to Google.* Toronto: Random House.

Barstow, A. L. (1992). *Witchcraze.* New York: Harper Collins.

Bartlett, K. T. (2000). Improving the law relating to postdivorce arrangements for children. In R. Thompson & P. R. Amato (Eds.), *The postdivorce family: Children, parenting, and society* (pp. 71–102). Thousand Oaks, CA: Sage.

Bartlett, K. T., & Rhode, D. L. (2010). *Gender, law and policy.* New York: Wolters Kluwer Law and Business.

Bartollas, C. (1993). Little girls grown up: The perils of institutionalization. In C. Culliver (Ed.), *Female criminality: The state of the art* (pp. 469–482). New York: Garland.

Bartolucci, A., Zeichner, A., & Miller, J. (2009). Alcohol consumption and perceived sexual coercion: Effects of gender and personality determinants. *Substance Use and Misuse, 44*(9–10) 1399–1414(16).

Bartsch, K. J. (2009). The employment projections for 2008–2018. *Monthly Labor Review, 132,* 11, 3–10.

Bartz, D., & Greenberg, J. (2008). Sterilization in the United States. *Obstetrics & Gynecology, 1*(1), 23–32.

Bashevkin, S. (1996). Tough times in review: The British women's movement during the Thatcher years. *Comparative Political Studies, 28,* 525–552.

Basile, K. C. (1999). Rape by acquiescence: The ways in which women "give in" to unwanted sex with their husbands. *Violence Against Women, 5,* 1036–1058.

Basile, K. C. (2008). Histories of violent victimization among women who reported unwanted sex in marriages and intimate relationships. *Violence Against Women, 14*(1), 29–52.

Baskin, D. R., & Sommers, I. B. (1997). *Casualties of community disorder: Female violent offenders.* Boulder, CO: Westview.

Baskin-Sommers, A., & Sommers, I. (2006). The co-occurrence of substance use and high-risk behaviors. *Journal of Adolescent Health, 38*, 5, 609–611.

Basow, S. (2009). Women in education: Students and professors worldwide. In M.A. Paludi (Ed.), *Feminism and women's rights worldwide* (pp. 43–62). Santa Barbara, CA: ABC-CLIO.

Basu, A. (Ed.) (1995). *The challenge of local feminisms: Women's movements in global perspective.* Boulder, CO: Westview.

Batstone, D. B. (1994). Liberation theology in Latin America. In D. J. Curran & C. M. Renzetti (Eds.), *Contemporary societies: Problems and prospects* (pp. 333–344). Englewood Cliffs, NJ: Prentice Hall.

Baumgardner, J., & Richards, A. (2000). *Manifesta: Young women, feminism, and the future.* New York: Farrar, Straus, and Giroux.

Baumgartner, M. S., & Schneider, D. E. (2010). Perceptions of women in management: A thematic analysis of rzing the glass ceiling. *Journal of Career Development, 37*, 559–576.

Baunach, P. J. (1992). Critical problems of women in prison. In I. L. Moyer (Ed.), *The changing roles of women in the criminal justice system* (pp. 99–112). Prospect Heights, IL: Waveland.

Baxter, S., & Lansing, M. (1983). *Women and politics* (revised edition). Ann Arbor: University of Michigan Press.

Bayard, K., Hellerstein, J., Neumark, D., & Troske, K. (2003). New evidence on sex segregation and sex differences in wages from matched employee-employer data. *Journal of Labor Economics, 21*, 4, 887–922.

BBC News. (2003). Profile: Lee Boyd Malvo. Retrieved from: http://www.news.bbc.co.uk/go/pr/fr/-/2/hi/americas/3178504.stm

Beal, F. (2008). Double jeopardy: To be black and female. *Meridians: Feminism, Race, Transnationalism, 8*(2), 166–176.

Beck, A. J., & Karberg, J. C. (2001). *Prison and jail inmates at midyear 2000.* Washington, DC: U.S. Department of Justice, Bureau of Justice Statistics.

Beck, A., & Alford, B. (2009). *Depression: Causes and treatments.* Philadelphia: University of Pennsylvania Press.

Beck, A. J., & Harrison, J. M. (2007). *Sexual victimization in state and federal prisons reported by inmates, 2007.* (Reports No. NCJ 2194414). Washington, D.C.: U.S. Department of Justice.

Becker, E. (2001). Women in the military say silence on harassment protects careers. *New York Times*, pp. A1, A26.

Becker, M., Bowman, C. G., & Torrey, M. (1994). *Feminist jurisprudence.* Minneapolis: West.

Beckwith, K. (2000). Beyond compare? Women's movements in comparative perspective. *Journal of Political Research, 37*, 431–468.

Beckwith, K. (2000). Beyond compare? Women's movements in comparative perspective. *Journal of Political Research, 37*, 431–468.

Bedard, M. E. (1992). *Breaking with tradition.* Dix Hills, NY: General Hall.

Beemyn, B. G. (2008). Colleges and universities. *GLBTQ Social Sciences*, 1–4.

Bekker, M., Nijssen, A., & Hens, G. (2001). Stress prevention training: Sex differences in types of stressors, coping, and training effects. *Stress and Health, 17*, 207–218.

Belknap, J. (1991). Women in conflict: An analysis of women correctional officers. *Women and Criminal Justice, 2*, 89–116.

Belknap, J. (2001). *The invisible woman.* Belmont, CA: Wadsworth.

Belknap, J. (2007). *The invisible woman: Gender, crime, and justice* (3/e). Belmont, CA: Thompson Wadsworth.

Belknap, J., & Holsinger, K. (2006). The gendered nature of risk factors for delinquency. *Feminist Criminology, 1*(1), 48–71.

Bell, K. E. (2009). Gender and gangs: A quantitative comparison. *Crime & Delinquency, 55*(3), 363–387.

Bellas, M. L., & Coventry, B. T. (2001). Salesmen, saleswomen, or sales workers? Determinants of the sex composition of sales occupations. *Sociological Forum, 16*, 73–98.

Bell-Ellison, B. A., & Dedrick, R. F. (2008). What do doctoral students value in their ideal mentor? *Research in Higher Education, 49*, 555–567.

Bellin, J. S., & Rubenstein, R. (1983). Genes and gender in the workplace. In M. Fooden, S. Gordon, & B. Hughley (Eds.), *Genes and gender IV: The second X and women's health* (pp. 87–100). New York: Gordian Press.

Bem, S. L. (1975). Sex role adaptability: One consequence of psychological androgeny. *Journal of Personality and Social Psychology, 31*, 634–643.

Bem, S. L. (1981). Gender schema theory: A cognitive account of sex typing. *Psychological Review, 88*, 354–364.

Bem, S. L. (1983). Gender schema theory and its implications for child development: Raising gender-aschematic children in a gender-schematic society. *Signs, 8*, 598–616.

Bem, S. L. (1993). *The lenses of gender: Transforming the debate on sexual inequality*. New Haven: Yale University Press.

Bem, S. L., & Lenney, E. (1976). Sex typing and the avoidance of cross-sex behavior. *Journal of Personality and Social Psychology, 33*, 48–54.

Benedetto, R. (2003, March 24). Poll shows steady support for war. *USA Today*, p. 1A.

Benedict, J. (1997). *Public heroes, private felons: Athletes and crimes against women*. Boston: Northeastern University Press.

Benenson, J. F., Carder, H. P., & Geib-Cole, S. J. (2008). The development of boys' preferential pleasure in physical aggression. *Aggressive Behavior, 34*, 154–166.

Bennett, L., & Bland, P. (2008). *Substance abuse and intimate partner violence*. Harrisburg, PA: VAWnet. Retrieved from: http://www.vawnet.org

Benson, M. L., Wooldregde, J., Thistletheaite, A. B., & Fox, G. L. (2004). The correlation between race and domestic violence is confounded with community context. *Social Problems, 51*, 326–342.

Benton Foundation. (2008). *Women, minorities advance in local news*. Retrieved from http://benton.org/node/15394

Berdahl, J. L. (2007). Harassment based on sex: Protecting social status in the context of gender hierarchy. *Academy of Management Review, 32*, 641–658.

Berenbaum, S. A. (1999). Effects of early androgens on sex-typed activities and interests in adolescents with congenital adrenal hyperplasia. *Hormones and Behavior, 35*, 102–110.

Berenbaum, S. A., & Hines, M. (1992). Early androgens are related to childhood sex-typed toy preferences. *Psychological Science, 3*, 203–206.

Berenbaum, S. A., & Resnick, S. M. (1997). Early androgen effects on aggression in children and adults with congenital adrenal hyperplasia. *Psychoneuroendocrinology, 22*, 505–515.

Bergen, R. K. (1996). *Wife rape: Understanding the response of survivors and service providers*. Thousand Oaks, CA: Sage.

Bergen, R. K. (2006). Marital rape: New research and directions. *National Online Resource Center on Violence Against Women*. Retrieved October 27, 2009, from http://new.vawnet.org/Assoc_Files_VAWnet/AR_MaritalRapeRevised.pdf

Berger, R. J., Searles, P., & Cottle, C. E. (1991). *Feminism and pornography*. New York: Praeger.

Berggren, K. (2006, January 27). Some women seeking ordination won't wait for church's OK. *National Catholic Reporter*, pp. 5–6.

Berggren, K. (2006, January 27). Some women seeking ordination won't wait for church's okay. *National Catholic Reporter*, pp. 5–6.

Bergman, B. R. (1986). *The economic emergence of women*. New York: Basic.

Berila, B., Keller, J., Krone, C., Laker, J., & Mayer, O. (2005). His story/her story: A dialogue about including men and masculinities in the Women's Studies curriculum. *Feminist Teacher, 16*, 1, 34–52.

Bernhard, L. A. (2000). Physical and sexual violence experienced by lesbian and heterosexual women. *Violence Against Women, 6*, 68–79.

Bernstein, A. (2002). Is it time for a victory lap?: Changes in the media coverage of women in sport. *International Review for the Sociology of Sport, 37*, 3–4, 415–428.

Bernstein, R. (1993, May 30). Cap, gown and gag: The struggle for control. *New York Times*, p. E3.

Berry, M. F. (1986). *Why ERA failed: Politics, women's rights, and the amending process of the constitution*. Bloomington: Indiana University Press.

Berry, T. R., & Mizelle, N. (Eds.) (2006). *From oppression to grace: Women of color and their dilemmas within the academy*. Sterling, VA: Stylus Publishing.

Besserman, P. (2007). The female face of God. *Neohelicon, 34*(1), 125–135.

Bethea, M. C. (2007). *The long war and the forgotten families: Dual-military couples*. Unpublished Master's thesis, U.S. Army War College, Carlisle Barracks, PA.

Bettencourt, B. A., & Miller, N. (1996). Gender differences in aggression as a function of provocation: A meta-analysis. *Psychological Bulletin, 119*, 422–447.

Bevc, C., Marshall, B., & Picou, J. (2005). Environmental justice and toxic exposure: Toward a spatial model of physical health and psychological well-being. *Social Science Research, 36,* 48–67.

Bhaskar, V. (2008). Parental sex selection and gender balance. *CEPR Discussion Papers.* Retrieved April 30, 2010, http://www.ucl.ac.uk/~uctpvbh/sexratio-econ-12june-08.pdf

Bhatt, R. (2000). Environmental influence on reproductive health. *International Journal of Gynecology & Obstetrics, 70*(1), 69–75.

Bianchi, S. M., & Raley, S. B. (2005). The time allocation in families. In S. M. Bianchi, L. M. Casper, & B. R. King (Eds.), *Work, family, health, and well-being* (pp. 21–42). Mahwah, NJ: Erlbaum.

Bianchi, S., Subaiya, K., & Kahn, J. R. (1999). The gender gap in the economic well-being of nonresident fathers and custodial mothers. *Demography, 36,* 173–184.

Biederman, J., & Faraone, V. (2005). Attention-deficit hyperactivity disorder. *Lancet, 366,* 237–248.

Biehl, J. (1990). *Rethinking ecofeminist politics.* Boston: South End Press.

Biener, L. (1987). Gender differences in the use of substances for coping. In R. C. Barnett, L. Biener, & G. K. Baruch (Eds.), *Gender and stress* (pp. 330–349). New York: Free Press.

Bieringer, R. (2010). *Women and leadership in Romans 16: The leading roles of Phoebe, Prisca, and Junia in early Christianity.* Retreived from: http://eapi.admu.edu.ph/eapr007/RBieringer.htm

Biesele, M. (1993). *Women like meat: The folklore and foraging ideology of the Kalahari Ju/'hoan.* Johannesburg, South Africa: Witwatersand University Press.

Bigler, R. S. (2005). "Good morning, boys and girls." *Teaching Tolerance, 28,* 22–23.

Bilefsky, D. (2008, June 25). Albanian custom fades: Woman as family man. *New York Times.* Retrieved from: http://www.nytimes.com/2008/06/25/world/europe/25virgins=html?scp=7&sq=Bilefesky&st=nyt

Billger, S. M. (2009). On reconstructing school segregation: The efficacy and equity of single-sex schooling. *Economics of Education Review, 28,* 393–402.

Bingham, S. G., & Battey, K. M. (2005). Communication of social support to sexual harassment victims: Professors' responses to a student's narrative of unwanted sexual attention. *Communication Studies, 56*(2), 131–155.

Birke, L. (1992). Transforming biology. In H. Crowley & S. Himmelweit (Eds.), *Knowing women: Feminism and knowledge* (pp. 66–77). Cambridge: Polity Press.

Bischoping, K. (1993). Gender differences in conversational topics, 1922–1990. *Sex Roles, 28,* 1–18.

Biskupic, J. (1998, June 23). High court limits schools' liability on harassment. *Washington Post,* p. A1.

Bjorkqvist, K. (1994). Sex differences in physical, verbal, and indirect aggression: A review of recent research. *Sex Roles, 30,* 177–188.

Bjornstrom, E., Kaufman, R., Peterson, R., & Slater, M. (2010). Race and ethnic representations of lawbreakers and victims in crime news: A national study of television coverage. *Social Problems, 57*(2), 269–293.

Blackburn, A. G., Mullings, J. L., & Marquart, J. (2008). Sexual assault in prison and beyond: Toward an understanding of lifetime sexual assault among incarcerated women. *The Prison Journal, 88,* 3, 351–377.

Blair-Loy, M. (2001). Cultural constructions of family schemas: The case of women finance executives. *Gender & Society, 15,* 687–709.

Blaise, M. (2005). *Playing it straight: Uncovering gender discourses in the early childhood classroom.* New York: Routledge.

Blake, C. F. (1994). Foot-binding in Neo-Confucian China and the appropriation of female labor. *Signs, 19,* 676–712.

Blakemore, J. E. O. (2003). Children's beliefs about violating gender norms: Boys shouldn't look like girls, and girls shouldn't act like boys. *Sex Roles, 48,* 411–419.

Blakemore, J. E. O., & Centers, R. E. (2005). Characteristics of boys' and girls' toys. *Sex Roles, 53*(9/10), 619–633.

Blakemore, J. E. O., & Hill, C. A. (2008). The child gender socialization scale: A measure to compare traditional and feminist parents. *Sex Roles, 58,* 192–207.

Blakeslee, S. (1991, January 1). Research on birth defects turns to flaws in sperm. *New York Times,* pp. 1, 36.

Blau, F., Ferber, M., & Winkler, A. (2006). *The economics of women, men, and work (5/e).* Upper Saddle River, NJ: Prentice Hall.

Blau, F. D., & Kahn, F. D. (2007). The gender pay gap: have women gone as far as they can? *Academy of Management Perspectives, 21,* 7–23.

Blaubergs, M. S. (1980). An analysis of classic arguments against changing sexist language. *Women's Studies International Quarterly, 3,* 135–147.

Bleeker, E. T. & Murnen, S. K. (2005). Fraternity membership, the display of sexually degrading images of women, and rape myth acceptance. *Sex Roles, 53,* 487–493.

Bleier, R. (1984). *Science and gender.* New York: Pergamon Press.

Blinde, E. M., & Taub, D. E. (1992). Homophobia and women's sport: The disempowerment of athletes. *Sociological Focus, 25,* 151–166.

Blomkalns, A., Chen, A., Hochman, J., Peterson, E., Trynosky, K., Diercks, D., Brogan, G., Boden, W., Roe, M., Ohman, E., Gibler, W., & Newby, L. (2005). Gender disparities in the diagnosis and treatment of non-ST-segment elevation acute coronary syndromes. *Journal of the American College of Cardiology, 45,* 832–837.

Blood, R. O., & Wolfe, D. M. (1960). *Husbands and wives.* New York: Free Press.

Bloom, M. (1995, September 27). A show-stopper puts her best foot forward. *New York Times,* pp. B9, 14.

Blum, D. (1997). *Sex on the brain.* New York: Viking.

Blum, T. C., & Roman, P. M. (1997). Employment and drinking. In R. W. Wilsnack & S. C. Wilsnack (Eds.), *Gender and alcohol* (pp. 379–394). New Brunswick, NJ: Rutgers Center of Alcohol Studies.

Blumberg, R. L. (2008). The invisible obstacle to educational equality: Gender bias in textbooks. *Prospects, 38,* 345–361.

Blumberg, R. L. (2008). The invisible obstacle to educational equality: Gender bias in textbooks. *Prospects, 38,* 345–361.

Blumberg, R. L. (2005, August). *Women's economic empowerment as the "magic potion" of development.* Paper presented at the annual meeting of the American Sociological Association, Philadelphia, PA.

Blume, E. (1983). Methodological difficulties plague PMS research. *Journal of the American Medical Association, 249,* 2864–2866.

Blume, S. B. (1997). Women and alcohol: Issues in social policy. In R. W. Wilsnack & S. C. Wilsnack (Eds.), *Gender and alcohol* (pp. 462–490). New Brunswick, NJ: Rutgers Center of Alcohol Studies.

Blumenthal, R. (1993, February 21). Gay officers find acceptance on New York's force. *New York Times,* pp. 1, 30.

Blumstein, P., & Schwartz, P. (1983). *American couples.* New York: William Morrow.

Blundell, S. (2009). Gender and the classics curriculum: A survey. *Arts and Humanities in Higher Education, 8*(2), 136–159.

Blyth, E., Frith, L., & Crawshaw, M. (2008) Ethical objections to sex selection for nonmedical reasons. *Reproductive BioMedicine Online, 16,* (Supplement 1), 41–45.

Bobbitt-Zehr, D. (2007). The gender income gap and the role of education. *Sociology of Education, 80,* 1–22.

Boeringer, S. B. (1999). Associations of rape-supportive attitudes with fraternal and athletic participation. *Violence Against Women, 5,* 81–90.

Bogenschneider, K. (2000). Has family policy come of age? A decade of review of the state of U.S. family policy in the 1990s. *Journal of Marriage and the Family, 62,* 1136–1159.

Boivin, M., & Tremblay, R. E. (2007). Gender differences in physical aggression: A prospective population-based survey of children before and after 2 years of age *Developmental Psychology, 43,* 1, 13–26.

Bok, D., & Bowen, W. G. (1998). *The shape of the river: Long-term consequences of considering race in college and university admissions.*

Bok, S. (1998). *Mayhem: Violence as public entertainment.* Reading, MA: Addison-Wesley.

Boland, B. J., Scheitel, S. M., Wollan, P. C., Silverstein, M. D. (1998). Patient-physician agreement on reasons for ambulatory general medical examinations. *Mayo Clinic Proceedings, 73,* 109–117.

Bondurant, B. (2001). University women's acknowledgment of rape: Individual, situations, and social factors. *Violence Against Women, 7,* 294–314.

Bonomi, A., Anderson, M., Reid, R., Carrell, D., Fishman, P., Rivara, F., & Thompson, R. (2007). Intimate partner violence in older women. *Gerontologist, 47*(1), 34–41.

Bonvillain, N. (1998). *Women and men: Cultural constructs of gender.* Englewood Cliffs, NJ: Prentice Hall.

Bookman, A., & Morgen, S. (Eds.) (1988). *Women and the politics of empowerment.* Philadelphia: Temple University Press.

Booth, A., Shelley, G., Mazur, A. Tharp, G., and Kittock, R. (1989). Testosterone and winning and losing in human competition. *Hormones and Behavior, 23,* 556–571.

Boraas, S., & Rodgers, W. (2003). How does gender play a role in the earnings gap? An update. *Monthly Labor Review,* U.S. Department of Labor.

Retrieved March 8, 2011, http://bls.gov/opub/mlr/2003/03/art2full.pdf

Bordo, S. (1993). *Unbearable weight: Feminism, Western culture, and the body*. Berkeley: University of California Press.

Borenstein, S. (2009, September 13). The birth defect people don't talk about. *Associated Press*. Retrieved from: http://sports.yahoo.com/top/news

Borer, T. A. (2009). Gendered war and gendered peace: Truth commissions and postconflict gender violence: Lessons from South Africa. *Violence Against Women, 15*(10), 1169–1193.

Borowsky, S. J., Rubenstein, L. V., Meredith, L. S., Camp, P., Jackson-Triche, M., & Wells, K. B. (2000). Who is at risk of nondetection of mental health problems in primary care? *Journal of General Internal Medicine, 15*, 381–388.

Bosch, F.X. (1996). Male sexual behavior and human papillomavirus DNA: Key risk factors for cervical cancer in Spain. *Journal of the National Cancer Institute, 88*, 1060–1067.

Boston Women's Health Book Collective. (2011). *Our bodies, ourselves*. New York: Touchstone.

Botta, R. (2006). The mirror of television: A comparison of black and white adolescents' body image. *Journal of Communication, 50*, 144–159.

Bottcher, J. (1995). Gender as social control: A qualitative study of incarcerated youths and their siblings in Greater Sacramento. *Justice Quarterly, 12*, 33–58.

Boutte, G. S., Hopkins, R., & Waklatsi, T. (2008). Perspectives, voices, and worldviews in frequently read children's books. *Early Education & Development, 19*(6), 941–962.

Bowcott, O. (2005, March 2005). *Report reveals shame of UN peacekeepers*. Guardian. Retrieved December 4, 2009, http://www.guardian.co.uk/world/2005/mar/25/unitednations 0,3604,1445537,00.html

Boxer, B., Whitney, C., Collins, S., Mikulski, B., Feinstein, D., Snowe, O. J., Hutchinson, K. B., Murray, P., Landrieu, M., & Lincoln, B. L. (2001). *Nine and counting: The women of the Senate*. New York: Harper Trade.

Boxer, S. (1997, December 14). One casualty of the women's movement: Feminism. *New York Time*, p. WK3.

Boyer, C. B., Sebro, N. S., Wibbelsman, C., & Shafer, M. A. (2006). Acquisition of sexually transmitted infections in adolescents attending an urban, general HMO teen clinic. *Journal of Adolescent Health, 39*, 2, 287–290.

Bracey, G. W. (2007). The success of single-sex education is still unproven. *Education Digest, 72*(6), 22–26.

Bradley, S. J., Oliver, G. D., Chernick, A. B., & Zucker, K. J. (1998). Experiment of nature: Ablatio penis at 2 months, sex reassignment at 7 months, and a psychosexual follow-up in young adulthood. *Pediatrics, 102*. Retrieved from: http://pediatrics.aappublications.org/content/102/1/e9.full.html

Bradway, J. (2010). *Stereotypical gender roles portrayed in children's television commercials*. Retrieved from http://people.wcsu.edu/mccarneyh/acad/bradway.html

Brady, D. (2004). Reconsidering the divergence between elderly, child, and overall poverty. *Research on Aging 33*(2), 487–510.

Brady, S. S., & Halpern-Felsher, B. L. (2008). Social and emotional consequences of refraining from sexual activity among sexually experienced and inexperienced youths in California. *American Journal of Public Health, 98*(1), 162–168.

Brah, A. (1991). Questions of difference and international feminism. In J. Aaron & S. Walby (Eds.), *Out of the margins: Women's studies in the nineties* (pp. 168–176). London: Falmer Press.

Brake, D. L. (1999, October). A legal framework for single-sex education. *Women's Educational Equity Act (WEEA) Digest*, pp. 3–7.

Brandwein, R. (Ed.) (1999). *The ties that bind: Family violence, women, and welfare*. Thousand Oaks, CA: Sage.

Brann, M., & Himes, K. L. (2010). Perceived credibility of male versus female television newscasters. *Communication Research Reports, 27*(3), 243–252.

Brantley, B. (1998, October 14). Nice young man and disciples appeal for tolerance. *New York Times*, pp. E1, E9.

Braude, A. (2001). *Radical spirits: Spritualism and women's rights in nineteenth century America*. Bloomington: Indiana University Press.

Bremner, J. D., Randall, P., & Vermetten, E. (1997). Magnetic resonance imaging-based measurement of hippocampal volume in posttraumatic stress disorder related to childhood physical and sexual abuse—A preliminary report. *Biological Psychiatry, 41*, 23–32.

Brennan, P. K., & Spohn, C. (2008). Race/ethnicity and sentencing outcomes among drug offenders in North Carolina. *Journal of Contemporary Criminal Justice, 24*(4), 371–398.

Brennan, P. K. (2009). The joint effects of offender race/ethnicity and sex on sentencing outcomes. In M.D. Krohn, A.J. Lizotte, & G.P. Hall (Eds.), *Handbook on crime and deviance* (pp. 319–347). New York: Springer.

Brennan, T. (1992). *The interpretation of the flesh: Freud and femininity.* London: Routledge.

Brewer, R. M. (1988). Black women in poverty: Some comments on female-headed families. *Signs, 13,* 331–339.

Bridges, A., & Jensen, R. (2010). Pornography. In Renzetti, C. M., Eldeson, J. L., & Bergen, R. K. (Eds.). *Sourcebook on violence against women.* Thousand Oaks, CA: Sage.

Briggs, S. (1987). Women and religion. In B. B. Hess & M. M. Ferree (Eds.), *Analyzing gender* (pp. 381–407). Newbury Park, CA: Sage.

Britton, D. (2003). *At work in the iron cage: The prisons as gendered organizations.* New York: New York University Press.

Britton, D. M. (1997). Gendered organizational logic: Policy and practice in men's and women's prisons. *Gender & Society, 11,* 796–818.

Brizendine, L. (2006). *The female brain.* New York: Morgan Road Books.

Brod, H. (1987). The case for men's studies. In H. Brod (Ed.), *The making of masculinities* (pp. 39–62). Boston: Allyn and Bacon.

Brodwin, M. G., Orange, L. M., & Chen, R. K. (2004). Societal attitudes toward sexuality regarding people who have disabilities. *Directions in Rehabilitation Counseling, 15*(4), 45–52.

Brody, L. R., & Hall, J. A. (2008). Gender and emotion in context. In M. Lewis, J. M. Haviland-Jones, & L. F. Barrett (Eds.), *Handbook of Emotions. 3/e* (pp. 395–408). New York: Guildford Publications.

Bronstein, P. (1988). Father-child interaction. In P. Bronstein & C. P. Cowan (Eds.), *Fatherhood today: Men's changing role in the family* (pp. 107–124). New York: John Wiley.

Brookey, R. A. (2002). *Reinventing the male homosexual: The rhetoric and power of the gay gene.* Bloomington: Indiana University Press.

Brooks-Gunn, J., & Fisch, M. (1980). Psychological androgyny and college students' judgments of mental health. *Sex Roles, 6,* 575–580.

Brooks-Gunn, J., & Matthews, W. S. (1979). *He and she.* Englewood Cliffs, NJ: Prentice-Hall.

Broverman, I. K., Broverman, D. M., Clarkson, F. E., Rosenkrantz, P. S., & Vogel, S. R. (1970). Sex-role stereotypes and clinical judgments of mental health. *Journal of Clinical and Counseling Psychology, 34,* 1–7.

Brown, C. S. (2007). It's not easy being a girl in a man's world: The daily experience of sexual harassment by adolescent girls. Newsletter of the UCLA Center for the Study of Women. Retrieved June 9, 2010, http://escholarship.org/uc/item/5zw9f1nn

Brown, D. L. (2008). African American resiliency: Examining racial socialization and social support as protective factors. *Journal of Black Psychology, 34*(1), 32–48.

Brown, H. (2009). Women college presidents' tough test. *Forbes.* Retrieved April 25, 2010, http://www.forbes.com/2009/10/06/female-college-presidents-forbes-woman-power-women-tenure.html

Brown, J. (1997). Working toward freedom from violence: The process of change in battered women. *Violence Against Women, 3,* 5–26.

Brown, L. (1994). *Subversive dialogues: Theory in feminist therapy.* New York: Basic Books.

Brown, L. (1994). *Subversive dialogues: Theory in feminist therapy.* New York: Basic Books.

Brown, L. M., Chesney-Lind, M., & Stein, N. (2007). Patriarchy matters: Toward a gendered theory of teen violence and victimization. *Violence Against Women, 3*(12), 1249–1273.

Brown, T. L., Linver, M. R., & Evans, M. (2010). The role of gender in the racial and ethnic socialization of African American adolescents. *Youth & Society, 41*(3), 357–381.

Brown, T. N., Williams, D. R., Jackson, J. S., Neighbors, H. W., Torres, M., Sellers, S. L., & Brown, K. T. (2000). "Being Black and feeling blue": The mental health consequences of racial discrimination. *Race & Society, 2,* 117–131.

Browne, A., & Bassuk, S. S. (1997). Intimate violence in the lives of homeless and poor housed women. *American Journal of Orthopsychiatry, 67,* 261–278.

Brownmiller, S. (1975). *Against our will.* New York: Simon and Schuster.

Brownridge, D. A. (2006). Partners violence against women with disabilities: Prevalence, risk, and explanations. *Violence Against Women, 12*(9), 805–822.

Brox, D. (2011). Healthcare careers are fostering diversity. *New York Times.* Retrieved from http://career-advice.nytimes.monster.com/job-search/company-industry-research/health-care-careers-are-fostering-diversity-hot-jobs/article.aspx

Brozan, N. (1990, April 9). Telling the seder's story in the voice of a woman. *New York Times*, p. B4.

Brubaker, S., & Dillaway, H. (2009). Medicalization, natural childbirth, and birthing experiences. *Sociology Compass, 3*(1) 31–48.

Bruce, T., Vogt, D., Street, A. E., & Stafford, J. (2003, October). *Sexual harassment and attitudes toward women in the military*. Poster presented at the annual meeting of the International Society for Traumatic Stress Studies, Chicago, IL.

Brumbaugh, S. M., Nock, S. L., Wright, J. D. (2008). Attitudes toward gay marriage in states undergoing marriage law transformation. *Journal of Marriage and the Family, 70*, 345–359.

Brumberg, J. (1997). *The body project: An intimate history of American girls*. New York: Random House.

Bruns, B., Mingat, A., & Rakotomalala, R. (2003). *Achieving universal primary education by 2015: A chance for every child*. Washington, DC: World Bank.

Brush, L. D. (2000). Battering, traumatic stress, and welfare-to-work transition. *Violence Against Women, 6*, 1039–1065.

Brush, P. S. (1999). The influence of social movements on articulations of race and gender in Black women's autobiographies. *Gender & Society, 13*, 120–137.

Buchanan, K. S. (2005). Beyond modesty: Privacy in prison and the risk of sexual abuse. *Marquette Law Review, 88*(4), 751–813.

Buchanan, N. T., & Fitzgerald, L. F. (2008). Effects of racial and sexual harassment on work and the psychological well-being of African American women. *Journal of Occupational Health Psychology, 13*(2), 137–151.

Buchanan, N. T., Bergman, M. E., Bruce, T. A., Woods, K. C., & Lichty, L. L. (2009). Unique and joint effects of sexual and racial harassment on college students' well-being. *Basic & Applied Social Psychology, 31*(3), 267–285.

Buckley, J. (1994). Libertines or not: Fruit, bread, semen and other body fluids in gnosticism. *Journal of Early Christian Studies, 2*, 15–31.

Buckley, S. (1997). *Broken silence: Voices of Japanese feminism*. Berkeley: University of California Press.

Buckroyd, J., & Rother, S. (2008). *Psychological reponses to eating disorders and obesity: Recent and innovative work*. Hoboken, NJ: Wiley-Interscience.

Budig, M. J., & England, P. (2001). The wage penalty for motherhood. *American Sociological Review, 66*, 204–225.

Bufkin, J. (1999). Bias crime as gendered behavior. *Social Justice, 26*, 155–176.

Bulanda, R. (2004). Paternal involvement with children: The influence of gender ideologies. *Journal of Marriage and Family, 66*(1), 40–45.

Bulbeck, C. (1988). *One world women's movement*. London: Pluto Press.

Bull, A. C., Diamond, H., & Marsh, R. (Eds.) (2000). *Feminism and women's movements in contemporary Europe*. Basingstoke, UK: Macmillan.

Bullard, R. (2007). *Wasted people: Environmental racism, a 20-year saga*. Retrieved from: http://cagreening.blogspot.com/2007/04/environmental-racism.html

Buller, D. J. (2005). *Adapting minds: Evolutionary psychology and the persistent quest for human nature*. Cambridge, MA: MIT Press.

Bulman, E. (1998, March 20). UN: Unsafe abortions kill thousands. *Atlanta Constitution*, p. 1.

Bumiller, E. (1990). *May you be the mother of a hundred sons: A journey among the women of India*. New York: Random House.

Bureau of Labor Statistics (2011). *Household data, annual averages: Employed persons by detailed occupation, sex, race and Hispanic or Latino ethnicity*. Retrieved from http://www.bls.gov/cps/cpsaat11.pdf

Buresh, B., Gordon, S., & Bell, N. (1991). Who counts in news coverage of health care? *Nursing Outlook, 39*, 204–208.

Burgess, A. W., Ramsey-Klawsnik, H., & Gregorian, S. B. (2008). Comparing routes of reporting in elder sexual abuse cases. *Journal of Elder Abuse & Neglect, 20*, 4, 336- 352.

Burgess-Proctor, A., Patchin, J.W., & Hinduja, S. (2010). Cyberbullying and online harassment: Reconceptualizing the victimization of adolescent girls. In V. Garcia & J. Clifford (Eds.), *Female crime victims: Reality reconsidered* (pp. 162–176). Upper Saddle River, NJ: Prentice Hall.

Burham, T., & Phelan, J. (2000). *Mean genes: From sex to money to food: Taming our primal instincts*. New York: Perseus.

Burke, R. J., & Mikkelsen, A. (2005). Gender issues in policing: Do they matter? *Women in Management Review, 20*, 133–143.

Burns, A. L., Mitchell, G., & Obradovich, S. (1989). Of sex roles and strollers: Female and male attention to toddlers at the zoo. *Sex Roles, 20*, 309–315.

Burns, A., & Homel, R. (1989). Gender division of tasks by parents and their children. *Psychology of Women Quarterly, 13*, 113–125.

Burns, J. F. (1994, August 27). India fights abortion of female fetuses. *New York Times*, p. A3.

Burns, J. F. (1998, March 29). Once widowed in India, twice scorned. *New York Times*, pp. 1–12.

Burrell, B. (2008). Political parties, fundraising, and sex. In B. Reingold (Ed.), *Legislative women: Getting elected, getting ahead*. Boulder, CO: Lynne Reinner Publishers.

Burrelli, J. (2008). Thirty-three years of women in S & E faculty positions. *National Science Foundation*, 1–10.

Burstein, P. (2007). Jewish educational and economic success in the United States: A search for explanations. *Sociological Perspectives, 50*, 209–228.

Burstow, B. (1992). *Radical feminist therapy: Working in the context of violence*. Newbury Park, CA: Sage.

Burton, D. L., & Meezan, W. (2004). Revisiting recent research on social learning theory as an etiological proposition for sexually abusive male adolescents. *Journal of Evidence-Based Social Work, 1*(1), 41–48.

Burton, D. A., & Misener, T. R. (2007). Are you man enough to be a nurse? Challenging male nurse media portrayals and stereotypes. In C. E. O'Lynn & R. E. Tranbarger (Eds.), *Men in nursing: History, challenges, and opportunities* (pp. 255–269). New Yokr: Springer.

Busfield, J. (1986). *Managing madness*. London: Hutchinson.

Bush, D. M. (1987). *The impact of family and school on adolescent girls' aspirations and expectations: The public-private split and the reproduction of gender inequality*. Paper presented at the Annual Meeting of the American Sociological Association, Chicago, IL.

Bush-Baskette, S. R. (1998). The war on drugs as a war against Black women. In S. L. Miller (Ed.), *Crime control and women* (pp. 113–129). Thousand Oaks, CA: Sage.

Bushey, C. (2008, November 1). Economy stretches gender gap in Obama's favor. Retrieved from http://www.womensenews.org/article.cfm/dyn/aid/3800

Buss, K. A., Brooker, R. J., & Leuty, M. (2008). Girls most of the time, boys some of the time: Gender differences in toddlers' use of maternal proximity and comfort seeking. *Infancy, 13*, 1, 1–29.

Bussey, K., & Bandura, A. (1984). Influence of gender constancy and social power on sex-linked modeling. *Journal of Personality and Social Psychology, 47*, 1292–1302.

Bussing, R., Zima, B. T., Mason, D., Hou, W., Garvan, C. W., & Forness, S. (2005). Use and persistence of pharmacotherapy for elementary school students with Attention-Deficit/Hyperactivity Disorder. *Journal of Child & Adolescent Psychopharmacology, 15*(1), 78–87.

Butler, A. C. (2000). Trends in same-gender partnering, 1988–1998. *Journal of Sex Research, 37*, 333–343.

Butler, M., & Paisley, W. (1980). *Women and the mass media: Sourcebook for research and action*. New York: Human Sciences Press.

Byrd, P. M., & Davis, J. L. (2009). Violent behavior in female inmates: Possible predictors. *Journal of Interpersonal Violence, 24*, 2, 379–392.

Byrne, L. (Ed.) (1991). *The hidden tradition: Women's spiritual writings rediscovered*. New York: Crossroad.

Bystrom, D. G., Banwart, M. C., Kaid, L. L., & Robertson, T. A. (Eds.) (2004). *Gender and candidate communication*. New York: Taylor and Francis.

Cable, K. E., & Spradlin, T. E. (2008). Single-sex education in the 21st century. *Education Policy Brief, 6*(9), 1–11. Bloomington, IN: Center for Evaluation & Education Policy.

Cabral, A., & Coffey, D. (1999). Creating courtroom accessibility. In B. Leventhal & S. E. Lundy (Eds.), *Same-sex domestic violence* (pp. 57–69). Thousand Oaks, CA: Sage.

Caetano, R., Field, C. A., Ramisetty-Mikler, S., & McGrath, C. (2005). The 5-year course of intimate partner violence among White, Black, and Hispanic couples in the United States. *Journal of Interpersonal Violence, 20*, 1039–1057.

Caggiano, J. (2010). Girls don't just wanna have fun: Moving past Title IX's contact sports exception. *University of Pittsburgh Law Review 72*, 119.

Caldera, Y. M., Huston, A. C., & O'Brien, M. (1989). Social interactions and play patterns of parents and toddlers with feminine, masculine, and neutral toys. *Child Development, 60*, 70–76.

Caldwell, M. A., & Peplau, L. A. (1984). The balance of power in lesbian relationships. *Sex Roles, 10*, 587–599.

Calhoun, C. (2000). *Feminism, the family, and the politics of the closet: Lesbian and gay displacement*. New York: Oxford University Press.

Callahan, J. J. (1988). Elder abuse: Some questions for policymakers. *Gerontologist, 28*, 453–458.

Callahan, J. L. (2009). Manifestations of power and control: Training as a catalyst for scandal at the United States Air Force Academy. *Violence Against Women, 15*, 1149–1168.

Calvete, E., Orue, I, Estevez, A., Villardon, L., & Padilla, P. (2008). Cyberbullying in adolescents: Modalities and aggressors' profile. *Computers in Human Behavior, 26*, 1128–1135.

Campbell, J. C., & Soeken, K. L. (1999). Forced sex and intimate partner violence: Effects on women's risk and women's health. *Violence Against Women, 5*, 1017–1035.

Canadian Bishops' Pastoral Team. (1989, September 21). Inclusive language: Overcoming discrimination. *Origins, 21*(1), 259–260.

Canedy, D. (2003, May 4). Advocates of equal rights amendment resume their fight. *New York Times*, p. 41.

Cann, A., & Palmer, S. (1986). Children's assumptions about the generalizability of sex-typed abilities. *Sex Roles, 15*, 551–557.

Cannon, L. W., Higginbotham, E., & Guy, R. F. (1989). *Depression among women: Exploring the effects of race, class and gender*. Center for Research on Women, Memphis State University, Memphis, TN.

Caplan, P. J., & Caplan, J. B. (1994). *Thinking critically about research on sex and gender*. Reading, MA: Addison-Wesley.

Caraway, N. (1991). *Segregated sisterhood: Racism and the politics of American feminism*. Knoxville: University of Tennessee Press.

Carelli, R. (1997a, June 16). *Supreme Court upholds abortion ban*. Washington, DC: Associated Press. (Internet).

Carey, K. (2008). *Graduation rate watch: Making minority student success a priority*. Washington, DC: Education Sector.

Caringella, S. (2008). *Addressing rape reform in law and practice*. New York: Columbia University Press.

Carlat, D. J., Camargo, C. A., Jr., & Herzog, D. B. (1997). Eating disorders in males: A report on 135 patients. *American Journal of Psychiatry, 154*, 1127–1132.

Carlin, N. (2010). God's gender confusion: Some polymorphously perverse pastoral theology. *Pastoral Psychology, 59*, 109–124.

Carlson, S. M. (1992). Trends in race/sex occupational inequality: Conceptual and measurement issues. *Social Problems, 39*, 268–290.

Carmody, D. L. (1989). *Women and world religions*. Nashville: Abingdon.

Carr, D. (2010). Golden years? Poverty among older Americans. *Contexts, 9*, 62–63.

Carr, J. F. (2007). Diversity and disciplinary practices. In J. Branche, J. Mullennix, & E. Cohn (Eds.), *Diversity across the curriculum: A guide for faculty in higher education* (pp. 30–37). Bolton, MA: Anker.

Carr, P., Szalacha, Barnett, R., Caswell, C., & Inui, T. (2003). A "ton of feathers": Gender discrimination in academic medical careers and how to manage it. *Journal of Women's Health, 12*, 1009–1018.

Carrigan, T., Connell, B., & Lee, J. (1987). Toward a new sociology of masculinity. In H. Brod (Ed.), *The making of masculinities* (pp. 63–100). Boston: Allen and Unwin.

Carroll, C. M. (1993). Sexual harassment on campus: Enhancing awareness and promoting change. *Educational Record, 74*(1), 2126.

Carroll, J. W., & McMillan, B. R. (2006). *God's potters: Pastoral leadership and the shaping of congregations*. Grand Rapids, MI: William B. Erdmans Publishing.

Carroll, S. J. (1985). *Women as candidates in American politics*. Bloomington: Indiana University Press.

Carter, A. (2010). Perspectives of mentoring: The black feminist student-athlete. *Sport Management Review, 13*, 382–394.

Carter, D. B., & McClosky, L. A. (1983). Peers and the maintenance of sex-typed behavior: The development of children's conceptions of cross-gender behavior in their peers. *Social Cognition, 4*, 294–314.

Carter, J., Bewell, C., Blackmore, E., & Woodside, D. (2006). The impact of childhood sexual abuse in anorexia nervosa. *Child Abuse and Neglect, 30*, 257–269.

Carty, L. (1992). Black Women in academia: A statement from the periphery. In H. Bannerji, L. Carty, K. Dehli, S. Heald, & K. McKenna (Eds.), *Unsettling relations: The university as a site of feminist struggles* (pp. 13–44). Boston: South End Press.

Carvajal, D. (2011, March 8). The changing face of medical care. *New York Times*. Retrieved from: http://www.nytimes.com/2011/03/08/world/europe/08iht-ffdocs08.html?_r=1

Casanueva, C., Martin, S. L., & Runyan, D. K. (2009). Repeated reports for child maltreatment among intimate partner violence victims: Findings from the National Survey of Child and Adolescent Well-being. *Child Abuse & Neglect, 33,* 84–93.

Casey, M. B., Nuttall, R. L., & Pezais, E. (1997). Mediators of gender differences in mathematics college entrance test scores: A comparison of spatial skills with internalized beliefs and anxieties. *Developmental Psychology, 33,* 669–680.

Cash, T. F., & Henry, P. E. (1995). Women's body images: The results of a national survey in the U.S.A. *Sex Roles, 33,* 19–28.

Cashmore, E. (1996). *Making sense of sports.* London: Routledge.

Cassano, M., Perry-Parrish, C., & Zeman, J. (2007). Influence of gender on parental socialization of children's sadness regulation. *Social Development, 16,* 210–231.

Cassell, D., & Gleaves, D. (2006). *The encyclopedia of obesity and eating disorders.* New York: Infobase Publishing.

Cataldi, E. F., Laird, J., Ramani, A. K., & Chapman, C. (2009, September). *High school dropout and completion rates in the United States: 2007.* Washington, D.C.: U.S. Department of Education, National Center for Education Statistics.

Catsambis, S. (2005). The gender gap in mathematics: Merely a step function? In A. M. Gallagher & J. C. kaufman (Eds.), *Mind the gap: Gender differences in mathematics* (pp. 220–245). Cambridge: Cambridge University Press.

Cavanagh, S. E., & Huston, A. C. (2006). Family instability and children's early problem behavior. *Social Forces, 85*(1), 551–581.

Cazzuffi, A. et al. (2010). Young men with anorexia nervosa. *Journal of the Royal Society of Medicine Short Reports, 1*(5), 39.

CBC News Online. (2006, May 30). Women in the military – International. Retrieved from: http://www.cbc.ca/news/background/military-international/

CBS News (2008, March 19). CBS poll: Gender matters more than race. http://www.cbsnews.com/stories/2008/03/19/opinion/polls

Center for American Women and Politics (CAWP) (1984, June). *Women's routes to elective office.* New Brunswick, NJ: Author.

Center for American Women and Politics (CAWP) (2004b). *Women candidates for Congress 1974–2004.* Available online: http://www.cawp.rutgers.edu

Center for American Women and Politics (CAWP). (1987, April). *Fact sheet: The gender gap in Presidential elections, 1952–1984.* New Brunswick, NJ: Author.

Center for American Women and Politics (CAWP). (1993, April). *Women in the U.S. Congress, 1993.* New Brunswick, NJ: Author.

Center for American Women and Politics (CAWP). (1997). *The gender gap: Attitudes on public policy issues.* Available online: http://www.cawp.rutgers.edu

Center for American Women and Politics (CAWP). (1998d, January). *Women in the U. S. Senate, 1922–1998.* New Brunswick, NJ: Author.

Center for American Women and Politics (CAWP). (2002a). *Women in elective office, 2002.* Available online: http://www.cawp.rutgers.edu

Center for American Women and Politics (CAWP). (2002b). *Women of color in elective office, 2002.* Available online: http:www.cawp.rutgers.edu

Center for American Women and Politics (CAWP). (2002d). *Women in U.S. Congress, 2002— Leadership roles and committee chairs.* Available online: http://www.cawp.rutgers. edu

Center for American Women and Politics (CAWP). (2004a). *Women's routes to elective office.* New Brunswick, NJ: Author.

Center for American Women and Politics (CAWP). (2005). *Fact sheet: Sex differences in voter turnout.* Available online: http://www.cawp.rutgers.edu

Center for American Women and Politics (CAWP). (2008a). *Gender gap evident in 2008 election; women unlike men show clear preference for Obama over McCain.* Available online: http://www.cawp.rutgers.edu

Center for American Women and Politics (CAWP). (2010). *Women's PACs and donor networks: A contact list.* Available online: http:www.cawp.rutgers. edu

Center for American Women and Politics (CAWP). (2011a). *Statewide elective executive women 2011.* Available online: http://www.cawp.rutgers.edu

Center for American Women and Politics (CAWP). (2011b). *Women in state legislatures 2011.* Available online: http://www.cawp.rutgers.edu

Center for American Women and Politics (CAWP). (2011c). *Women mayors in U.S. cities 2011.* Available online: http://www.cawp.rutgers.edu

Center for American Women and Politics (CAWP). (2011d). *Women of color in elective office 2011.* Available online: http://www.cawp.rutgers.edu

Center for American Women and Politics. (CAWP). (2011e). *Women in the U.S. Congress 2011.* Available online: http://www.cawp.rutgers.edu

Center for American Women and Politics. (CAWP). (2011f). *Women in Congress: Leadership roles and committee chairs*. Available online: http://www.cawp.rutgers.edu

Center for American Women and Politics. (CAWP). (2011g). *Women appointed to presidential cabinets*. Available online: http://www.cawp.rutgers.edu

Center for Women Policy Studies. (1991). *More harm than help: The ramifications of mandatory HIV testing for rapists*. Washington, DC: Author.

Centers for Disease Control (CDC). (1993, April 23). Rates of caesarian delivery—United States, 1991. *Morbidity and Mortality Weekly Report 42*, 285–289.

Centers for Disease Control (CDC). (2000). *Abortion surveillance—United States*. Available online: http://www.cdc.gov/mmwr/PDF/ss/554911.pdf

Centers for Disease Control (CDC). (2002). *Early release of selected estimates of NHIS data from quarter 3 of the 2001 National Health Interview Survey*. Available online: http://www.cdc.gov

Centers for Disease Control (CDC). (2009). *HIV surveillance report: Diagnoses of HIV infection and AIDS in the United States and dependent areas, 2009*. Retrieved from http://www.cdc.gov/hiv/topics/surveillance/basic.htm#hivest

Centers for Disease Control and Prevention. (2005). *Fertility, Family Planning, and Reproductive Health of U.S. Women: Data from the 2002 National Survey of Family Growth. Morbidity & Mortality Weekly Report, 55* (SS-5), 1–108.

Centers for Disease Control and Prevention. (2006). Youth risk behavior surveillance- United States, 2005. *Morbidity & Mortality Weekly Report, 55* (SS-5), 1–108.

Centers for Disease Control and Prevention. (2008). Youth risk behavior surveillance- United States, 2007. *Morbidity and Mortality Weekly Report, 57*, SS-4.

Centers for Disease Control and Prevention. (2008b). *Youth risk behavior surveillance system- United States, 2007. Morbidity & Mortality Weekly Report, 55* (SS-4).

Centers for Disease Control and Prevention. (2009, July). *Sexual and reproductive health of persons aged 10–24 years– United States, 2002–2007, 58*, SS-6. Retrieved October 27, 2009, from http://www.cdc.gov/mmwr

Centers for Disease Control and Prevention. (2009, May). Increase in unmarried childbearing also seen in other countries. Retrieved September 29, 2009, from http://www.cdc.gov/nchs/pressroom/09release/unmarriedbirths.htm

Centers for Disease Control and Prevention. (2009a). *Abortion Surveillance- United States, 2006. Morbidity & Mortality Weekly Report, 5* (SS-8). Retrieved December 15, 2009, from http://www.cdc.gov/mmwr/PDF/ss/ss5808.pdf

Centers for Disease Control. (2010). *Behavioral risk factor surveillance system prevalence data*. Retrieved from http://www.cdc.gov/brfss/

Century Council. (2010). *Drunk driving research*. Retrieved from http://www.centurycouncil.org/learn-the-facts/drunk-driving-research#891

Cha, Y., & Thebaud, S. (2009). Labor markets, breadwinning, and beliefs: How economic context shapes men's gender ideology. *Gender & Society, 23*(2), 215–243.

Chafetz, J. S. (1988). *Feminist sociology: An overview of contemporary theories*. Itasca, IL: F. E. Peacock.

Chafetz, J. S., Dworkin, A. G., & Swanson, S. (1990). Social change and social activism: First-wave women's movements around the world. In G. West & R. L. Blumberg (Eds.), *Women and social protest* (pp. 302–320). New York: Oxford University Press.

Chait, J. (2008). *Cyerbullying statistics*. Retrieved June 14, 2010 from http://www.safety.lovetoknow.com/Cyber_Bullying_Statistics

Chalupka, S., & Chalupka, A. (2010). The impact of environmental and occupational exposures on reproductive health. *Journal of Obstetric, Gynecologic & Neonatal Nursing, 39*(1), 84–102.

Chamberlain, E. M. (1997). Courtroom to classroom: There is more to sexual harassment. *NWSA Journal, 9*, 136–154.

Chandler, M. A., & Glod, M. (June 15, 2008). More schools trying separation of the sexes. *Washington Post* (p. A 1). Retrieved March 24, 2010, http://www.washingtonpost.com/wp-dyn/content/article/2008/06/14/AR2008061401869.html

Chandler, R. (2010). *Does Lindsey Vonn SI cover objectivity women?* Retrieved from http://offthebench.nbcsports.com/2010/02/05/does-lindsay-vonn-si-cover-objectify-women/

Chandra, A., Martinez, G. M., Mosher, W. D., Abma, J. C., & Jones, J. (2005). Fertility, family planning, and reproductive health of U.S. women: data from the 2002 National Survey of Family Growth. *Vital Health Statistics, 25*, 1–160.

Chaplin, T. M., Cole, P., & Zahn-Waxler, C. (2005). Parental socialization of emotion expression: Gender differences and relations to child adjustment. *Emotions, 5,* 80–88.

Chapman, J. R. (1990). Violence against women as a violation of human rights. *Social Justice 17,* 54–70.

Charles, K., & Stephens, M. (2004). Job displacement, disability, and divorce. *Journal of Labor Economics, 22,* 489–522.

Chavez, P., Nelson, D., Naimi, T., & Brewer, R. (2011). Impact of a new gender-specific definition for binge drinking on prevalence estimates for women. *American Journal of Preventive Medicine, 40,* 468–471.

Chawla, N., Neighbors, C, Logan, D., Lewis, M., & Fossos, N. (2009). Perceived approval of friends and parents as mediators of the relationship between self-determination and drinking. *Journal of Studies on Alcohol and Drugs, 70,* 92–100.

Chen, P., (2010). Do women make better doctors? *New York Times.* Retrieved from http://www.nytimes.com/2010/05/06/health/06chen.html

Cheney, M. (2006). *Now it's my turn: A daughter's chronicle of political life.* New York: Threshold Editions.

Cheng, C. (2008). Marginalized masculinities and hegemonic masculinity: An introduction. *Journal of Men's Studies, 7*(3), 295–315.

Cherney, I. D., & London, K. (2006). Gender-linked differences in the toys, television shows, computer games, and outdoor activities of 5- to 13-year-old children. *Sex Roles, 54,* 717–726.

Cheshire, J. (2008). Still a gender-biased language? *English Today, 24*(1), 7–10.

Chesler, E. (1994, February 6). No, the first priority is stop coercing women. *New York Times Magazine,* pp. 31, 33.

Chesney-Lind, M. (1986). Women and crime: The female offender. *Signs, 12,* 78–96.

Chesney-Lind, M. (1997). *The female offender.* Thousand Oaks, CA: Sage.

Chesney-Lind, M. (2001). "Out of sight, out of mind": Girls in the juvenile justice system. In C. M. Renzetti & L. Goodstein (Eds.), *Women, crime and criminal justice* (pp. 27–43). Los Angeles: Roxbury.

Chesney-Lind, M., & Belknap, J. (2004). Trends in delinquent girls' aggression and violent behavior: A review of the evidence. In M. Putallaz & K. L. Bierman (Eds.), *Aggression, antisocial behavior, and violence among girls: A developmental perspective* (pp. 203–220). New York: Guilford Press.

Chesney-Lind, M., & Eliason, M. (2006). From invisible to incorrigible: The demonization of marginalized women and girls. *Crime, Media, Culture, 2*(1), 29–47.

Chesney-Lind, M., & Shelden, R. G. (1992). *Girls delinquency and juvenile justice.* Pacific Grove, CA: Brooks/Cole.

Chevalier, A., Gibbons, S., Thorpe, A., Snell, M., & Hoskins, S. (2009). Students' academic self-perception. *Economics of Education Review, 28,* 6, 716–727.

Chibbaro, L. (2009, July 31). New law benefits children of same-sex couples. *Washington Blade, 40,* 31, p. 8.

Chick, K. (2006). Gender balance in K-12 American history textbooks. *Social Studies Research and Practice, 1*(3) 284–290.

Child pornography, the Internet, and the challenge of updating statutory terms. (2009). *Harvard Law Review, 122*(8), 2206–2227.

Child pornography, the Internet, and the challenge of updating statutory terms. (2009). *Harvard Law Review, 122,* 8, 2206–2227.

Child Trends. (2006). *Facts at a glance.* Washington, D.C.: Author.

Child Welfare Information Gateway. (2009, April). Child abuse and neglect fatalities: Statistics and Interventions. Washington, DC: U.S. Department of Health and Human Services, Children's Bureau/Administration on Children, Youth and Families. Retrieved October 19, 2009, from http://www.childwelfare.gov/pubs/factsheets/fatality/cfm

Childbirth Connection (2011). *Cesarean section: Why does the national U.S. cesarean section rate keep going up?* Retrieved from http://www.childbirthconnection.org/article.asp?ck=10456

Childers, M. (1990). A conversation about race and class. In M. Hirsch & E. F. Keller (Eds.), *Conflicts in feminism* (pp.60–81). New York: Routledge.

Children's Defense Fund. (1997). *The state of America's children—Yearbook 1997.* Washington, DC: Author.

Children's Defense Fund. (2001). *The state of America's children, 2001.* Washington, DC: Author.

Children's Defense Fund. (2005). *Youth development: Poverty and the pipeline to prison.* Washington, DC: Author.

Children's Defense Fund. (2008). *Child poverty in America.* Washington, DC: Author. Retrieved from http://www.childrensdefense.org/child-research-data-publications/data/Child_Poverty_in_America__August_2008_ID8341.pdf

Children's Defense Fund. (2009). *The state of America's children, 2009*. Washington, DC: Author.

Cho, H., & Wilke, D. J. (2005). How has the Violence Against Women Act affected the response of the criminal justice system to domestic violence? *Journal of Sociology & Social Welfare, 32*(4), 125–139.

Chodorow, N. (1978). *The reproduction of mothering*. Berkeley: University of California Press.

Chodorow, N. (1989). *Feminism and psychoanalytic theory*. New Haven: Yale University Press.

Chodorow, N. (1995). Gender as a personal and cultural construction. *Signs, 20*, 516–544.

Chodorow, N. J. (1994). *Femininities, masculinities, sexualities: Freud and beyond*. Lexington: University of Kentucky Press.

Chodorow, N. J. (2004). Psychoanalysis and women: A personal thirty-five-year retrospect. *Annual of Psychoanalysis, 34*, 101–129.

Chopp, R. S. (1989). *The power to speak: Feminism, language, and God*. New York: Crossroad/ Continuum.

Chouinard, V., & Crooks, V. A. (2005). "Because *they* have all the power and I have none": State restructuring of income and employment supports and disabled women's lives in Ontario, Canada. *Disability & Society, 20*(1), 19–32.

Chowhan, J., & Stewart, J. M. (2007). Television and the behavior of adolescents: Does socioeconomic status moderate the link? *Social Sciences & Medicine, 65*, 1324–1336.

Chrisler, J. C. (1991). The effect of premenstrual symptoms on creative thinking. In D. L. Taylor & N. F. Woods (Eds.), *Menstruation, health, and illness* (pp. 73–83). New York: Hemisphere.

Chrisler, J. C., &. Levy, K. B. (1990). The media construct a menstrual monster: A content analysis of PMS articles in the popular press. *Women and Health, 16*, 89–104.

Christ, C. P. (1983). Heretics and outsiders: The struggle over female power in western religion. In L. Richardson & V. Taylor (Eds.), *Feminist frontiers* (pp. 87–94). Reading, MA: Addison-Wesley.

Christ, C. P., & Plaskow, J. (1979). Introduction: Womanspirit rising. In C. P. Christ & J. Plaskow (Eds.), *Womanspirit rising* (pp. 118). San Francisco: Harper and Row.

Christ, C. P. (2006). *Why women need the goddess*. Retrieved from: http://www.goddessariadne.org/ whywomenneedthegoddess.htm

Christakis, D. A., & Zimmerman, F. J. (2007). Violent television viewing during preschool is associated with antisocial behavior during school age. *Pediatrics, 120*, 993–999.

Christakis, D. A., Zimmerman, F. J., DiGiuseppe, D. L., & McCarty, C. A. (2004). Early television exposure and subsequent attentional problems in children. *Pediatrics, 113*(4), 708–713.

Christensen, A. S. (1988). Sex discrimination and the law. In A. H. Stromberg & S. Harkess (Eds.), *Women working* (pp. 329–347). Mountain View, CA: Mayfield.

Christensen, R. (2002). Value of benefits constant in a changing world: Findings from the EBRI/MGA Value of Benefits Survey. *EBRI Notes*, pp. 1–3.

Christopher, F. S., & Sprecher, S. (2000). Sexuality in marriage, dating, and other relationships: A decade review. *Journal of Marriage and the Family, 62*, 999–1017.

Citizens Commission on Human Rights. (2001). *Website tracking system of mental health criminals*. Available online: http://www.psychcrime. org

Civettini, N., & Glass, J. (2008). The impact of religious conservatism on men's work and family involvement. *Gender & Society, 22*, 172–193.

Clark, C. S. (1995, April 7). Abortion clinic protests. *CQ Researcher*, pp. 299–308.

Clark, J. (1991). Getting there: Women in political office. *The Annals of the American Academy of Political and Social Science, 515*, 63–76.

Clark, J. (2011). *Which country's people have the longest life expectancy and why?* Retrieved from http:// health.howstuffworks.com/diseases-conditions/ death-dying/life-expectancy.htm

Clark, K. A., Biddle, A. K., & Martin, S. L. (2002). A cost-benefit analysis of the Violence Against Women Act of 1994. *Violence Against Women, 8*, 417–428.

Clark, M. M. (1997). The Silva case at the University of New Hampshire. *NWSA Journal, 9*, 77–93.

Clark, R., Allard, J., & Mahoney, T. (2004). How much of the sky? Women in American high school history textbooks from the 1960s, 1980s and 1990s. *Social Education, 68*, 57–63

Clark, R., Ayton, K., Frechette, N., & Keller, P. J. (2005). Women of the world, re-write! Women in American world history high school textbooks from the 1960s, 1980s and 1990s. *Social Education, 69*, 41–46.

Clark, R., Lennon, R. & Morris, L. (1993). Of Caldecotts and kings: Gendered images in recent American children's books by Black and non-Black illustrators. *Sex Roles, 7*, 227–245.

Classen, C. C., Palesh, O. G., & Aggarwal, R. (2005). Sexual revictimization: A review of the empirical literature. *Trauma, Violence, & Abuse, 6*, 103–129.

Clearfield, M. W., & Nelson, N. M. (2006). Sex differences in mothers' speech and play behavior with 6-, 9-, and 14-month-old infants. *Sex Roles, 54*(1/2), 127–137.

Cleary, P. D. (1987). Gender differences in stress-related disorders. In R. C. Barnett, L. Biener, & G. K. Baruch (Eds.), *Gender and stress* (pp. 39–72). New York: Free Press.

Clifford, S. (2008). *Christian Science Paper to End Daily Print Edition.* Retrieved March 8, 2011, http://www.nytimes.com/2008/10/29/business/media/29paper.html?_r=1&adxnnl=1&adxnnlx=1299366098-hK/h9sn4kCOqYI1DFmlqFQ

Clifford, S. (2010, February 8). Magazines' newsstand sales fall 9.1 percent. *New York Times.* Retrieved from: http://www.mediacoer.blogs.nytimes.com/2010/02/08/magazines-newsstand-sales-fall-91-percent/

"Clinton pledges to aid Congolese rape victims." (2009, October). *Contemporary Sexuality, 43*(10), p. 8.

CNN. (2007). Poll majority: Gays' orientation can't change. Retrieved October 1, 2009, from http://www.cnn.com/2007/US/06/27/poll.gay/index.html

Coale, A. J. (1991). Excess female mortality and the balance of the sexes in the population: An estimate of the number of "missing females." *Population and Development Review, 17*, 517–523.

Cobble, D. S. (1991). *Dishing it out: Waitresses and their unions in the twentieth century.* Urbana: University of Illinois Press.

Cochran S. D., &. Mays, V. M. (1988). Issues in the perception of AIDS risk and risk reduction activities by Black and Hispanic/Latina women. *American Psychologist, 43*, 949–957.

Cochran, S., Keenan, C., Schober, C., & Mays, V. (2000). Estimates of alcohol use and clinical treatment needs among homosexually active men and women in the U.S. population. *Journal of Consulting and Clinical Psychology, 68*, 1062–1071.

Coffey, S. F., Saladin, M. E., Drobes, D. J., Brady, K. T., Dansky, B. S., & Kilpatrick, D. G. (2002). Trauma and substance cue reactivity in individuals with comorbind posttraumatic stress disorder and cocaine or alcohol dependence. *Drug and Alcohol Dependence, 65*, 115–128.

Cohen, D. N. (2005, April 16). Feminist seders now their own tradition. *New York Times*, p. A10.

Cohen, E. (2007). *CNN health: CDC antidepressants most prescribed drugs in the U.S.* Retrieved from http://articles.cnn.com/2007-07-09/health/antidepressants_1_antidepressants-high-blood-pressure-drugs-psychotropic-drugs?_s=PM:HEALTH

Cohen, J. (2001, May 17). He-mails, she-mails: Where sender meets gender. *New York Times*, pp. G1, G9.

Cohen, P. N., Huffman, M. L., & Knauer, S. (2009). Stalled progress? Gender segregation and wage inequality among managers, 1980–2000. *Work and Occupations, 36*(4), 318–342.

Coker, A.L. (2007). Does physical intimate partner violence affect sexual health? *Trauma, Violence and Abuse, 8*, 149–177.

Cole, R., & Mehran, H. (2008). What can we learn from privately held firms about executive compensation? MRPA Paper, #4710. University Library of Munich, Germany. Retrieved from: http://www.mpra.ub.uni-muechen.de/4710/1/MPRA_paper_4710.pdf

Coleman, I. (2010). *Paradise beneath her feet: Women and reform in the Middle East.* New York: Random House.

Coleman, M., Ganong, L., & Fine, M. (2000). Reinvestigating marriage: Another decade of progress. *Journal of Marriage and the Family, 62*, 1288–1307.

Collier-Thomas, B. (2010). *Jesus, jobs, and justice: African American women and religion.* New York: Knopf.

Collins, J. (1992). Matters of fact: Establishing a gay and lesbian studies department. In H. L. Minton (Ed.), *Gay and lesbian studies* (pp. 109–123). New York: Haworth.

Collins, P. H. (1986). Learning from the outsider within: The sociological significance of Black feminist thought. *Social Problems, 33*, S14–S32.

Collins, P. H. (1990). *Black feminist thought.* Cambridge, MA: Unwin and Hyman.

Collins, S. C. (2006). Portrait in blue: A demographic and behavioral profile of police sexual harassers. *Women & Criminal Justice, 18*(1/2), 79–106.

Coltrane, S. (1989). Household labor and the routine production of gender. *Social Problems, 36*, 473–490.

Coltrane, S. (2000). Research on household labor: Modeling and measuring the social embeddedness of routine family work. *Journal of Marriage and the Family, 62*, 1208–1233.

Columbia University & the Gay and Lesbian Medical Association. (2000). *Healthy people 2010*. New York: Authors.

Colvin, R. (2009). Shared perceptions among lesbian and gay police officers: Barriers and opportunities in the law enforcement work environment. *Police Quarterly, 12*(1), 86–101.

Comery, J. (2009). This is what I do. *Children and Young People Now*, p. 24. Retrieved November 30, 2009 from http://www.cypnow.co.uk

Commercial Real Estate Women Network. (2005). *Women in commercial real estate, 2005*. Lawrence, KS: Author.

Commission on Professional in Science and Technology. (1992). *Professional women and minorities*. Washington, DC: Author.

Committee for Abortion Rights and Against Sterilization Abuse. (1988). *Women under attack: Victories, backlash, and the fight for reproductive freedom*. Boston: South End Press.

Commonwealth Fund. (2000). *Out of touch: American men and the health care system*. New York: Author.

Condry, J. C. (1989). *The psychology of television*. Hillsdale, NJ: Lawrence Erlbaum Associates.

Cone, J. (2000). *Risks of faith: The emergence of a Black theology of liberation, 1968–1998*. Boston: Beacon Press.

Conference report. (1997, March 28). *Philadelphia Daily News*, p. 128.

Congregation for the Doctrine of the Faith. (1987). Instruction on respect for human life in its origin and on the dignity of procreation. *Origins, 16*, 698–711.

"Congress approves and President signs first federal law affirmatively to protect LGBT individuals." (2009). *Gay Law Notes*, p. 195.

Conkey, M. W. (1997). Men and women in pre-history: An archeological challenge. In C. B. Brettell & C. F. Sargent (Eds.), *Gender in cross-cultural perspective* (pp. 57–66). Englewood Cliffs, NJ: Prentice Hall.

Conkey, M. W., & Gero, J. M. (1991). Tensions, pluralities and engendering archeology: An introduction to women and pre-history. In J. M. Gero & M. W. Conkey (Eds.), *Exploring archeology* (pp. 3–30). New York: Basil Blackwell.

Conkright, L., Flannagan, D., & Dykes, J. (2000). Effects of pronoun type and gender role consistency on children's recall and interpretation of stories. *Sex Roles, 43*, 481–497.

Conley, F. K. (1998). *Walking out on the boys*. New York: Farrar, Straus & Giroux.

Conlin, M. (2003). The new gender gap. *Business Week*, 74–82.

Connecticut Health Foundation. (2007). Percentage of adults 18+ with high blood pressure, by race and ethnicity, for groups with >50 respondents, Connecticut BRFSS Survey, 2004–2007, *Connecticut Department of Public Health, Behavioral Risk Factor Surveillance Systems Survey*.

Connell, C. M., Vanderploeg, J. J., Katz, K. H., Caron, C., Saunders, L., & Tebes, J. K. (2009). Maltreatment following reunification: Predictors of subsequent Child Protective Services contact after children return home. *Child Abuse & Neglect, 33*, 218–228.

Connell, J. D., & Gunzelmann, B. (2004). The new gender gap: Why are so many boys floundering while so many girls are soaring? *Instructor*, 14–17.

Connell, R. W. (1995). *Masculinities*. Berkeley: University of California Press.

Connell, R. W., & Messerschmidt, J.W. (2005). Hegemonic masculinity: Rethinking the concept. *Gender & Society, 19*, 829–859.

Connelly, J. B. (2007). *Portrait of a priestess: Women and ritual in ancient Greece*. Princeton, NJ: Princeton University Press.

Connelly, M. (2004, November 7). How Americans voted: A political portrait. *New York Times*, p. 4WK.

Connors, L. (1996). *Gender of infant differences in attachment: Associations with temperament and caregiving experiences*. Paper presented at the annual conference of the British Psychological Society, Oxford, England.

Contra Costa Times. (2010, April 8). Male deputy awarded $350K in sexual harassment suit. Retrieved from: http://www.contracostatimes.com/california/ci_14836836

Cook, R. J., & Dickens, B. M. (2009). Reproductive and sexual health rights: From reproductive choice to reproductive justice. *International Journal of Gynecology and Obstetrics, 106*, 106–109.

Cook, S. L., Gidycz, C. A., Koss, M. P., & Murphy, M. (2011). Emerging issues in the measurement of rape victimization. *Violence Against Women, 17*, 201–218.

Cooke, M. (2000). Multiple critique: Islamic feminist rhetorical strategies. *Nepantla: Views from the South, 1*(1), 91–110.

Cooke, M., & Woollacott, A. (Eds.) (1993). *Gendering war talk*. Princeton, NJ: Princeton University Press.

Coombs, L. C. (1977). Preferences for sex of children among U.S. couples. *Family Planning Perspectives, 9*, 259–265.

Cooperman, A. (2006, June 12). Conservative rabbis allow ordained gays, same-sex unions. *Washington Post*. Retrieved from: http://www.washington-post.com/wp-dyn/content/article/2006/12/06/AR200612061247.html

Copel, L. C. (2006). Partner abuse in physically disabled women: A proposed model for understanding intimate partner violence. *Perspectives in Psychiatric Care, 42*, 114–129.

Coplan, R. J., Closson, L. M., & Arbeau, K. A. (2007). Gender differences in the behavioral associates of loneliness and social dissatisfaction in kindergarten. *Journal of Child Psychology and Psychiatry, 48*, 10, 988–995.

Corbett, C., Hill, C., & St. Rose, A. (2008). *Where the girls are: The facts about gender equity in education*. Washington, DC: AAUW Educational Foundation.

Corcoran, M., Duncan, G. J., & Hill, M. S. (1984). The economic fortunes of women and children: Lessons from the Panel Study of Income Dynamics. *Signs, 10*, 232–248.

Cornwall, M. (1989). Faith development of men and women over the life span. In S. J. Bahr & E. T. Peterson (Eds.), *Aging and the family* (pp. 115–139). Lexington, MA: Lexington Books.

Correll, S. J., Bennard, S., & Paik, I. (2007). Getting a job: Is there a motherhood penalty? *American Journal of Sociology, 112*, 1297–1338.

Corsaro, W. A., & Eder, D. (1990). Children's peer cultures. In W. R. Scott (Ed.), *Annual review of sociology, Volume 16* (pp. 197–220). Palo Alto, CA: Annual Reviews, Inc.

Cortese, A. J. (1999). *Provocateur: Images of women and minorities in advertising*. London: Rowman and Littlefield.

Cosmo Girl. (2011). *Cosmo girl celebrity gossip and latest news, Seventeen magazine*. Retrieved from http://www.seventeen.com/cosmogirl/

Cott, N. F. (1986). Feminist theory and feminist movements: The past before us. In J. Mitchell & A. Oakley (Eds.), *What is feminism? A reexamination* (pp. 49–62). New York: Pantheon.

Cott, N. F. (1987). *The grounding of modern feminism*. New Haven: Yale University Press.

Cotter, D. A., Hermsen, J. M., & Vanneman, R. (2004). *Gender inequality at work*. New York: Russell Sage Foundation.

Courtney, A. E., & Whipple, T. W. (1983). *Sex stereotyping in advertising*. Lexington, MA: Lexington Books.

Coventry Journalism Review. (2008). How journalism's portrayal of the thin ideal contributes to anorexia. Retrieved from: http://cjr08.wordpress.com/2008/06/05/how-journalisms-portrayal-of-the-thin-ideal-contributed-to-anorexia/

Cowan, C. P., & Cowan, P. A. (1992). *When partners become parents*. New York: Basic Books.

Cowan, G., & Hoffman, C. D. (1986). Gender stereotyping in young children: Evidence to support a concept learning approach. *Sex Roles, 14*, 211–224.

Cowan, P., & Cowan, C. P. (1998). New families: Modern couples as new pioneers. In M. A. Mason, A. Skolnick, & S. D. Sugarman (Eds.), *All our families* (pp. 169–192). New York: Oxford University Press.

Cowan, R. S. (1984). *More work for mother*. New York: Basic Books.

Cowan, R. L., & Bochantin, J. E. (2009). Pregnancy and motherhood on the Thin Blue Line: Female police officers' perspectives on motherhood in a highly masculinized work environment. *Women and Language, 32*, 1, 22–30.

Cowell, P. E., Turetsky, B. I., Gur, R. C., Grossman, R. I., Shtasel, D. L., & Gur, R. E. (1994). Sex differences in aging of the human frontal and temporal lobes. *Journal of Neuroscience, 14*, 4748–4755.

Cox, F. D. (1993). *Human intimacy: Marriage, the family and its meaning*. Minneapolis: West.

Cox, M. J. (1985). Progress and continued challenges in understanding the transition to parenthood. *Journal of Family Issues, 6*, 395–408.

Coyne, J. A., & Berry, A. (2000, March 9). Rape as adaptation: Is this contentious hypothesis advocacy, not science? *Nature*, p. 121.

Coyne, J. C. (2001). Depression in primary care: Depressing news, exciting research opportunities. *APS Observer*. Available online: http://www.psychologicalscience.org/observer/0201/

Craig, W. M., & Pepler, D. J. (2003). Identifying and targeting risk for involvement in bullying and victimization. *Canadian Journal of Psychiatry, 48*, 577–582.

Cramer, P., & Russo, A. (1992). Toward a multicentered women's studies in the 1990s. In C. Kramarae & D. Spender (Eds.), *The knowledge explosion* (pp. 99–117). New York: Teachers College Press.

Crawford, C. (2000). Gender, race, and habitual offender sentencing in Florida. *Criminology, 38*, 263–280.

Crawford, C., Chiricos, T., & Kleck, G. (1998). Race, racial threat, and sentencing of habitual offenders. *Criminology, 36*, 481–511.

Creamer, E., & Meszaros, P. (2009). Gender differences in factors that promote an interest in IT among high school and early and late college students. AMCIS 2009 Proceedings. Paper 333. Available http://aisel.aisnet.org/amcis2009/333

Creedon, P., & Cramer, J. (2007). Our conclusion: Gender values remain, inequity resurges, and globalization brings new challenges. In P. Creedon & J. Cramer, (Eds.), *Women in mass communication*(pp. 275–283). Thousand Oaks, CA: Sage.

Crenshaw, K. W. (1994). Mapping the margins: Intersectionality, identity politics, and violence against women of color. In M. A. Fineman & R. Myktiuk (Eds.), *The public nature of private violence* (pp. 93–118). New York: Routledge.

Crick, N. R., & Grotpeter, J. K. (1995). Relational aggression, gender, and social-psychological adjustment. *Child Development, 66*, 710–722.

Crick, N. R., Ostrov, J. M., Appleyard, K., Jansen, E. A., & Casas, J. F. (2004). Relational aggession in early childhood: "You can't come to my birthday party unless . . ." In M. Putallaz & K. L. Bierman (Eds.), *Aggression, antisocial behavior, and violence among girls: A developmental perspective*. New York: Guildford Press.

Cropper, C. M. (1998, February 26). Fruit to walls to floor, ads are on the march. *New York Times*, pp. A1, D8.

Crosnoe, R., Riegle-Crumb, & Muller, C. (2007). Gender, self-perception, and academic problems in high school. *Social Problems, 54*, 1, 118–138.

Crossette, B. (1995, December 10). Female genital mutilation by immigrants is becoming cause for concern in the U.S. *New York Times*, p. 18.

Crossette, B. (1996, May 12). Muslim women's movement gaining strength. *New York Times*, p. 3.

Crothers, L., & Lockhart, C. (2000). *Culture and politics, a reader*: Chapter nine: "The symbolic annihilation of women by the mass media." Palgrave Macmillan.

Crouter, A. C., Whiteman, S. D., McHale, S. M., & Osgood, D. W. (2007). Development of gender attitude traditionality across middle childhood and adolescence. *Child Development, 78*, 3, 911–926.

Crow, M. S., & Kunselman, J. C. (2009). Sentencing female drug offenders: Reexamining racial and ethnic disparities. *Women & Criminal Justice, 9*(3), 191–216.

Crowell, N. A., & Burgess, A. W. (1996). *Understanding violence against women*. Washington, DC: National Academy Press.

Crowley, J. E. (2006). Organizational responses to the fatherhood crisis: The case of fathers' rights groups in the United States. *Marriage & Family Review, 39*(1/2), 99–120.

Crozier, E. S., & Davidson, M. J. (2007, May). *Challenges faced by male clerical temporary workers: Examining implications for the individual and for management pratices*. EURAM Conference, Paris, France.

Cruikshank, M. (1992). *The gay and lesbian liberation movement*. New York: Routledge, Chapman and Hall.

Cruz, R. (2001). A victory for affirmative action. Coalition to defender affirmative action, integration, and immigrant rights and fight for equality by any means necessary. Retrieved February 18, 2010, from http://www.bamn.com/to.asp?/doc/2001/010615-opinion-victory-otrib.txt

Cubbin, C., Hadden, W., & Winkleby, M. (2001). Neighborhood context and cardiovascular disease risk factors: The contribution of material deprivation. *Ethnicity and Disease, 11*(4), 687–700.

Culpepper, E. E. (1992). Menstruation consciousness raising: A personal and pedagogical process. In A. J. Dan & L. L. Lewis (Eds.), *Menstrual health and women's lives* (pp. 274–284). Urbana: University of Illinois Press.

Cummings, J. (1986, August 3). Woman in conservative rabbi post. *New York Times*, p. 24.

Cunningham, M. (2007). Influences of women's employment on the gendered division of household labor over the life course: Evidence from a 31-year panel study. *Journal of Family Issues, 28*(3), 422–444.

Cunningham, S., Engelstatter, B., & Ward, M. R. (2011). Understanding the effects of violent video games on violent crime. Retrieved from: http://www.ssrn.com/abstract=1804959

Curran, D. J. (1984). The myth of the "new" female delinquent. *Crime and Delinquency, 30*, 386–399.

Curry, T., Arriagada. P., & Cornwell, B. (2002). Images of sport in popular nonsport magazines: Power and performance versus pleasure and participation. *Sociological Perspectives, 45*, 397–413.

Curzan, A. (2009). Says who? Teaching and questioning the rules of grammar. *PMLA, 124*, 3, 870–879.

Cutright, P. (2001). The relative gender gap in suicide: Societal integration, the culture of suicide, and period effects in 20 developed countries, 1955–1994. *Social Science Research 30*(1), 76–99.

Cyr, M., McDuff, P., & Wright, J. (2006). Prevalence and predictors of dating violence among female victims of child sexual abuse. *Journal of Interpersonal Violence, 21*, 1000–1017.

D'Antonio, W. V. (2011, October 28). Catholics in America: Persistence and change. *National Catholic Reporter*, pp. 1A–28A.

Dahl, E. (2007). The 10 most common objections to sex-selection and why they are far from being conclusive: a Western perspective. *Reproductive BioMedicine Online 14*, 158–161.

Daigle, L. E., Fisher, B. S., & Cullen, F. T. (2008). The violent and sexual victimization of college women: Is repeat victimization a problem? *Journal of Interpersonal Violence, 23*(9), 1296–1313.

Daley, T. C., & Carlson, E. (2009). Predictors of change in eligibility status among preschoolers in special education, *Exceptional Children, 75*(4), 412–426.

Dallas, J., & Heche, N. (2011). *The complete Christian guide to understanding homosexuality: A Biblical and compassionate response to same-sex attraction.* Irvine, CA: Harvest House Publishers.

Daly, K. (1989a). Gender varieties in white-collar crime. *Criminology, 27*, 769–793.

Daly, K. (1989b). Neither conflict nor labeling nor paternalism will suffice: Intersections of race, ethnicity, gender, and family in criminal court decisions. *Crime and Delinquency, 35*, 136–168.

Daly, K. (1994). *Gender, crime, and punishment.* New Haven, CT: Yale University Press.

Daly, M. (1978). *Gyn/Ecology.* Boston: Beacon Press.

Daly, M. (1983). Indian suttee: The ultimate consummation of marriage. In L. Richardson & V. Taylor (Eds.), *Feminist frontiers* (pp. 189–190). Reading, MA: Addison-Wesley.

Daly, M. (1984). *Pure lust.* Boston: Beacon Press.

Damasio, A. R., Grabowski, T. J., Bechara, A., Damasio, H., Ponto, L. L., Parvisi, J., & Hichwa, R. D. (2000). Subcortical and cortical brain activity during the feeling of self-generated emotions. *Nature Neuroscience, 3*, 1049–1056.

Damon, A. (2007, July 5). Shunned from society, widows flock to city to die. CNN World. Retrieved from: http://articles.cnn.com/2007-07-05/world/damon.india.widows_1_widows-vrindavan-india?_s=PM:WORLD

Danzinger, N., & Eden, Y. (2007). Gender-related differences in the occupational aspirations and career-style preferences of accounting students: A cross-sectional comparison between academic school years. *Career Development International, 12*(2), 129–149.

Dao, J. (2001, April 25). A sexual harassment scandal confronts the Marines. *New York Times,* p. A15.

Darisi, T., Davidson, V. J., Korabik, K., & Desmarais, S. (2010). Commitment to graduate studies and careers in science and engineering: Examining women's and men's experiences. *International Journal of Gender, Science, and Technology, 2*(1), 47–64.

Darrow, W. R. (1985). Woman's place and the place of women in the Iranian revolution. In Y. Y. Haddad & E. B. Findly (Eds.),*Women, religion and social change* (pp. 307–320). Albany: State University of New York Press.

Dasgupta, S. (1999). Just like men? A critical view of violence by women. In M. F. Shepard & E. L. Pence (Eds.), *Coordinating community responses to domestic violence: Lessons from Duluth and beyond* (pp. 195–222). Thousand Oaks, CA: Sage.

Davey, M. (2009, June 10). Kansas abortion clinic operated by doctor who was killed closes permanently. *New York Times,* p. A 16.

Davidson, J. T., & Chesney-Lind, M. (2009). Discounting women: Context matters in risk and need assessment. *Critical Criminology, 17*, 221–245.

Davidson, R. C., & Lewis, E. L. (1997). Affirmative action and other special consideration admissions at the University of California, Davis, School of Medicine. *Journal of the American Medical Association, 278*, 1153–1158.

Davies, B. (1989). *Frogs and snails and feminist tales.* Sydney: Allen and Unwin.

Davies, J., Lyon, E., & Monti-Catania, D. (1998). *Safety planning with battered women.* Thousand Oaks, CA: Sage.

Davies, M., Pollard, P., & Archer, J. (2006). Effects of perpetrator gender and victim sexuality on blame toward male victims of sexual assault. *The Journal of Social Psychology, 146*, 275–291.

Davies, S., & Cook, S. (1999). The sex of crime and punishment. In S. Cook & S. Davies (Eds.), *Harsh punishment: International experiences of women's imprisonment* (pp. 53–78). Boston: Northeastern University Press.

Davies-Netzley, S. A. (1998). Women above the glass ceiling: Perceptions on corporate mobility and strategies for success. *Gender & Society, 12,* 339–355.

Davis, A. (1981). *Women, race and class.* New York: Random House.

Davis, C. P. (2007). At-risk girls and delinquency: Career pathways. *Crime & Delinquency, 53*(3), 408–435.

Davis, E. A. (1995). *Sex bias in United States history textbooks.* Paper presented at the annual meeting of the Eastern Sociological Society, Philadelphia, PA.

Davis, J. R. (2007). Making a difference: How teachers can positively affect racial identity and acceptance in America. *Social Studies, 98*(5), 209–214.

Davis, K., Grant, P., & Rowland, D. (1990, Summer). Alone and poor: The plight of elderly women. *Generations, 14,* 43–47.

Davis, K. C., Schraufnagel, T. J., George, W. H., & Norris, J. (2008). The use of alcohol and condoms during sexual assault. *American Journal of Men's Health, 2,* 3, 281–290.

Davis, M., Neuhaus, J. M.. Moritz, D. J., & Segal, M. R. (1990). *Living arrangement influences survival of middle-aged men.* Paper presented at the Annual Meeting of the American Public Health Association, Santa Barbara, CA.

Davis, N. J. (1993, Summer). Female youth homelessness—systematic gender control. *Socio-Legal Bulletin,* pp. 22–31.

Davis, P. J. (1999). Gender differences in autobiographical memory for childhood emotional experiences. *Journal of Personality and Social Psychology, 76,* 498–510.

Davis, T. L. (1995). Gender differences in masking negative emotions: Ability or motivation? *Developmental Psychology, 31,* 660–667.

Davis-Floyd, R. E. (1992). *Birth as an American rite of passage.* Berkeley: University of California Press.

Davis-Kimball, J. (1997). Warrior women of the Eurasian steppes. *Archeology, 50,* 44–48.

De Pauw, L. G. (2000). *Battle cries and lullabies: Women in war from prehistory to the present.* Norman, OK: Oklahoma University Press.

De Waal, F. (2005). *Our inner ape.* New York: Riverhead Books.

De Waal, F. (2006). Morally evolved: Primate social instincts, human morality, and the rise and fall of "veneer theory." In S. Macedo & J. Ober (Eds.), *Primates and philosphers: How morally evolved?* (pp. 1–50). Princeton, NJ: Princeton University Press.

de Young, S., & Crane, F. G. (1992). Females' attitudes toward the portrayal of women in advertising: A Canadian study. *International Journal of Advertising, 11,* 249–255.

Death Penalty Information Center. (2011). *Race of death row inmates executed since 1976.* Retrieved from: http://www.deathpenaltyinfo. org/race-death-row-inmates-executed-1976

Deats, S. M., & Lenker, L. T. (1994). *Gender and academe: Feminist pedagogy and politics.* Lanham, MD: Rowman and Littlefield.

Deaux, K., & Kite, M. E. (1987). Thinking about gender. In B. B. Hess & M. M. Ferree (Eds.), *Analyzing gender* (pp. 92–117). Newbury Park, CA: Sage.

Deboer, K. (2004). *Gender and competition: How men and women approach work and play differently.* Monterey, CA: Coaches Choice Books.

Decalmer, P. (1993). Clinical presentation. In P. Decalmer & F. Glendenning (Eds.), *The mistreatment of elderly people* (pp. 35–61). Newbury Park, CA: Sage.

DeHart, D. D. (2008). Pathways to prison: Impact of victimization in the lives of incarcerated women. *Violence Against Women, 14*(12), 1362–1381.

DeJong, C., Burgess-Proctor, A., & Elis, L. (2008). Police officer perceptions of intimate partner violence: An analysis of observational data. *Violence and Victims, 23,* 6, 683–696.

DeKeseredy, W. S. (Ed.). (1997). Post-separation woman abuse. A special issue of *Violence Against Women, 3*(6).

DeKeseredy, W. S., & McLeod, L. (1997). *Woman abuse: A sociological story.* Toronto: Harcourt Brace Canada.

DeKeseredy, W.S. (forthcoming). Pornography.com and the abuse of women. In C.M. Renzetti & R.K. Bergen (Eds.), *Understanding diversity: Celebrating difference, challenging inequality.* Boston: Allyn and Bacon

DeKeseredy, W. S., & Schwartz, M. D. (2009). *Dangerous exits: Escaping abusive relationships in rural America.* New Brunswick, NJ: Rutgers University Press.

DeKeseredy, W. S., & Schwartz, M. D. (2011). Theoretical and definitional issues in violence against women. In C.M. Renzetti, J. L. Edleson, & R. K. Bergen (Eds.), *Sourcebook on violence against women, 2nd edition* (pp. 3–20). Thousand Oaks, CA: Sage.

Del Carmen, A. (2007). Minority women in policing in Texas: An attitudinal analysis. *Criminal Justice*

Studies, 20, 3, 281–294. Denavas-Walt, C., Proctor, B. D., & Smith, J. C. (2008). *Income, poverty, and health insurance coverage in the United States: 2007.* Washington, DC: U.S. Department of Commerce, Bureau of the Census.

Delaney, C. (2000). Making babies in a Turkish village. In J. S. DeLoache & A. Gottlieb (Eds.), *A world full of babies: Imagined childcare guides for seven societies* (pp. 117–144). New York: Cambridge University Press.

Delmar, R. (1986). What is feminism? In J. Mitchell & A. Oakley (Eds.), *What is feminism? A re-examination* (pp. 8–33). New York: Pantheon.

DeLoache, J. S., Cassidy, D. J., & Carpenter, C. J. (1987). The three bears are all boys: Mothers' gender labeling of neutral picture book characters. *Sex Roles, 17,* 163–178.

DeNavas-Walt, C., Proctor, B. D., & Smith, J. C. (2008). *Income, poverty, and health insurance coverage in the United States, 2007.* Washington, DC: U.S. Department of Commerce, Bureau of the Census.

Denham, S. A., Zoller, D., & Couchoud, E. A. (1994). Socialization of preschoolers' emotional understanding. *Developmental Psychology, 30,* 928–938.

Denissen, A. M. (2010). The right tools for the job: Constructing gender meanings and identities in the male-dominated building trades. *Human Resources, 63,* 1051–1069.

Department of Health and Human Services, (2010). *Women's health USA 2010, mental health care utilization.* Retrieved from http://mchb.hrsa.gov/whusa10/hsu/pages/311mhcu.html

Desmond, R., & Danilewicz, A. (2010). Women are on, but not in, the news: Gender roles in local television news. *Sex Roles, 62,* 11/12, 822–829.

DeSouza, E. R., Solberg, J., & Elder, C. (2007). A cross-cultural perspective on judgments of woman-to-woman sexual harassment: Does sexual orientation matter? *Sex Roles, 56*(7/8), 457–471.

DeSouza, E., & Fansler, G. A. (2003). Contrapower sexual harassment: A survey of students and faculty members. *Sex Roles, 48,* 529–542.

DeTienne, K., & Lewis, L. (2005). The pragmatic and ethical barriers to corporate social responsibility disclosure: The Nike Case. *Journal of Business Ethics, 60*(4), 359–376.

Deutsch, F. M. (1999). *Halving it all: How equally shared parenting works.* Cambridge: Harvard University Press.

DeVault, M. L. (1986). *Talking and listening from women's standpoint: Feminist strategies for analyzing interview data.* Paper presented at the annual meeting of the Society for Symbolic Interaction, New York, NY.

Developmental Psychology Netletter. (2011). *The history of birth.* Retrieved from http://www.mesacc.edu/dept/d46/psy/dev/Spring02/prenatal/history.html

DeWitt, K. (1996, February 5). New cause helps feminists appeal to younger women. *New York Times,* p. A10.

Dey, J. G., & Hill, C. (2007). *Behind the pay gap.* Washington, D.C.: AAUW Educational Foundation.

Di Leonardo, M. (1992). The female world of cards and holidays: Women, families and the work of kinship. In B. Thorne (Ed.), *The family: Some feminist questions* (pp. 246–261). Boston: Northeastern University Press.

Diamond, I. (1992). Ecofeminist politics: The promise of common ground. In C. Kramarae & D. Spender (Eds.), *The knowledge explosion: Generations of feminist scholarship* (pp. 371–378). New York: Teachers College Press.

Diamond, L. M., & Savin-Williams, R. C. (2000). Explaining diversity in the development of same-sex sexuality among young women. *Journal of Social Issues, 56,* 297–313.

Diamond, M., & Sigmundson, K. H. (1997). Sex reassignment at birth: Long-term review and clinical implications. *Archives of Pediatrics and Adolescent Medicine, 151,* 298–305.

Diedrick, P. (1991). Gender differences in adjustment to divorce. In S. S. Volgy (Ed.), *Women and divorce, men and divorce* (pp. 33–45). New York: Haworth.

Diener, M. (2000). Gift from the gods: A Balinese guide to early child rearing. In J. S. DeLoache & A. Gottlieb (Eds.), *A world full of babies: Imagined childcare guides for seven societies* (pp. 91–116). New York: Cambridge University Press.

Diggs, G., Garrison-Wade, D., Estrada, D., & Galindo, R. (2009). Smiling Faces and Colored Spaces: The Experiences of Faculty of Color Pursing tenure in the Academy. *Urban Review, 41,* 4, 312–333.

Diken, B., & Lausten, C. (2005). Becoming abject: Rape as a weapon of war. *Body & Society, 11,* 111–128.

Dillaway, H., & Pare, E. (2008). Locating mothers: How cultural debates about stay-at-home versus working mothers define women and home. *Journal of Family Issues, 29,* 4, 437–464.

Dillon, M., & Wink, P. (2007). *In the course of a lifetime: Tracing relgious belief, practice, and change*. Berkeley: University of California Press.

Dines, G. (1998). King Kong and the White woman: *Hustler* magazine and the demonization of Black masculinity. *Violence Against Women, 4*, 291–307.

Dines, G., Jensen, R., & Russo, A. (1998). *Pornography: The production and consumption of inequality*. New York: Routledge.

Dinham, A., Furbey, R., & Lowndes, V. (2009). *Faith in the public realm: Controversies, policies and practices*. Bristol UK: Policy Press.

Dinovitzer, R., Reichman, N., & Sterling, S. (2009). The differential valuation of women's work: A new look at the gender gap in lawyers' income. *Social Forces, 88*, 819–854.

Disney Consumer Products. (2007). Disney Princess. Retrieved December 27, 2009 from https://www.disneyconsumerproducts.com/Home/display.jsp?contentId=dcp_home_ourfranchises_disney_princess_us&forPrint=false&language=en&preview=false&imageShow=0&pressRoom=US&translationOf=null&region=0&ccPK=null

Dittman, R. W., Kappes, M. E., & Kappes, M. H. (1992). Sexual behavior in adolescent and adult females with congenital adrenal hyperplasia. *Psychoneuroendocrinology, 17*, 153–170.

Dittman, R. W., Kappes, M. H., Kappes, M. E., Borger, D., Meyer-Bahlburg, H. F. L., Stenger, H., Willig, R. H., & Wallis, H. (1990a). Congenital hyperplasia I: Gender-related behavior and attitudes in female patients and sisters. *Psychoneuroendocrinology, 15*, 401–420.

Dittman, R. W., Kappes, M. H., Kappes, M. E., Borger, D., Meyer-Bahlburg, H. F. L., Stenger, H., Willig, R. H., & Wallis, H. (1990b). Congenital hyperplasia II: Gender-related behavior and attitudes in female salt-wasting and simple-virilizing patients. *Psychoneuroendocrinology, 15*, 421–434.

Dittmar, H., Halliwell, E., & Ive, S. (2006). Does Barbie make girls want to be thin? The effect of experimental exposure to images of dolls on the body image of 5- to 8-year-old girls. *Developmental Psychology, 42*(2), 283–292.

Dixit, A. R., & Crum, R. M. (2000). Prospective study of depression and the risk of heavy alcohol use in women. *American Journal of Psychiatry, 157*, 751–758.

Dobash, R. E., & Dobash, R. P. (1992). *Women, violence and social change*. London: Routledge.

Dobash, R. P., Dobash, R. E., Cavanagh, K., & Lewis, R. (1998). Separate and intersecting realities: A comparison of men's and women's accounts of violence against women. *Violence Against Women, 4*, 382–414.

Dobbins, F. (2009). *Inventing equal opportunity*. Princeton: Princeton University Press.

Dobrzynski, J. H. (1995, October 29). How to succeed? Go to Wellesley. *New York Times*, pp. 1, 9.

Dodds, C., Keogh, P., & Hickson, F. (2005). *It makes me sick: Heterosexism, homophobia and the health of gay Men and bisexual men*. London: Sigma Research.

Dodge, K. A., Coie, J. D., & Lynam, D. (2006). In N. Eisenberg, W. Damon, & R. M. Lerner (Eds.), *Handbook of child psychology, 6th ed. Social, emotional, and Personality development, vol. 3*. (pp. 719–788). Hoboken, NJ: John Wiley & Sons.

Doerner, J. K., & Demuth, S. (2010). The independent and joint effects of race/ethnicity, gender, and age on sentencing outcomes in U.S. federal courts. *Justice Quarterly, 27*, 1–27.

Doidge, N. (2007). *The brain that changes itself*. New York: Penguin Books.

Dolan, M. (2011). *Therapist-patient sex violates trust*. Retrieved from: http://www.civilrightslawfirms.com/feed-item/therapist-patient-sex-violates-trust

Dolliver, M. (2010). *How people react to male vs. female voiceovers*. Retrieved from http://www.adweek.com/aw/content_display/news/agency/e3ie0341f942810261f54e20d17078f7923

Domosh, M., & Seager, J. (2001). *Putting women in place: Feminist geographers make sense of the world*. New York: Guilford Publications.

Donnelly, D. A., Cook, K. J., & Wilson, L. A. (1999). Provision and exclusion: The dual face of services to battered women in three deep south states. *Violence Against Women, 5*, 710–741.

Doucet, A. (2009). Dad and baby in the first year: Gendered responsibilities and embodiment. *Annals of the American Academy of Political and Social Science, 624*, 79–98.

Douglas, S. J. (2010). *The rise of enlightened sexism*. NY: St. Martin's Press.

Dow, B. J. (1996). *Prime-time feminism*. Philadelphia: University of Pennsylvania Press.

Dow, B. J., & Condit, C. M. (2005). The state of the art in feminist scholarship in communication. *Journal of Communication, 55*, 448–478.

Dowd, M. (1990, November 20). Americans more wary of Gulf policy, poll finds. *New York Times*, p. A12.

Dowdall, G. W. (2008). *College drinking: Reframing a social problem*. Santa Barbara, CA: Praeger.

Downey, D. B., & Vogt Yuan, A. S. (2005). Sex differences in school performance during high school: Puzzling patterns and possible explanations. *Sociology Quarterly, 46*(2), 299–321.

Doyal, L. (1990a). Waged work and women's well being. *Women's Studies International Forum, 13*, 587–604.

Doyal, L. (1990b). Hazards of hearth and home. *Women's Studies International Forum, 13*, 501–517.

Dragiewicz, M. (2011). *Equality with a vengeance: Men's rights groups, battered women, and antifeminist backlash*. Boston: Northeastern University Press.

Drake, B., & Rank, M. R. (2009). The racial divide among American children in poverty: Reassessing the important of neighborhood. *Children and Youth Services Review, 31*, 1264–1271.

Drakulic, S. (1991). *How we survived communism and even laughed*. New York: W. W. Norton.

Draper, P. (1975). !Kung women: Constrasts in sexual egalitarianism in foraging and sedentary contexts. In R. R. Reiter (Ed.), *Toward an anthropology of women* (pp. 77–109). New York: Monthly Review Press.

Drewniany, B. (1996). Super Bowl commercials: The best a man can get (or is it?). In P. M. Lester (Ed.), *Images that injure* (pp. 87–92). Westport, CT: Praeger.

Driscoll, L. G., Parkes, K. A., Tilley-Lubbs, G. A., Brill, J. M., & Pitts Bannister, V. R. (2009). Navigating the lonely sea: Peer mentoring and collaboration among aspiring women scholars. *Mentoring & Tutoring: Partnership in Learning, 17*(1), 5–21.

Drudy, S., & Chathain, M. U. (2002). Gender effects in classroom interaction: Data collection, self-analysis and reflection. *Evaluation and Research in Education, 16*, 34–50.

Drug Addiction Treatment (2011). *When the time comes to walk away*. Retrieved from http://www.drugaddictiontreatment.com/drug-addiction-treatments/addiction-recovery/when-the-time-comes-to-walk-away/

Drukteinis, A. (2011). Strict liability for psychotherapist-patient sex. Retrieved from: http://www.psychlaw.com/LibraryFiles/Liability.html

Du, S. (2002). *"Chopsticks only work in pairs": Gender unity and gender equality among the Lahu of southwest China*. New York: Columbia University Press.

Dua, P. (2007). Feminist mentoring and female graduate success: challenging gender inequality in higher education. *Sociology Compass, 1*, 594–612.

Dua, P. (2008). The impact of gender characteristics on mentoring in graduate departments of sociology. *American Sociologist, 39*(4), 307–323.

Dublin, T. (1994). *Transforming women's work*. Ithaca, NY: Cornell University Press.

Dubow, E. F., Huesmann, R. L., & Greenwood, D. (2007). Media and youth socialization: Underlying processes and moderators of effects. In Joan E. Grusec & Paul D. Hastings (Eds.), *Handbook of socialization: Theory and research* (pp. 404–430). New York: Guildford Press.

Duckworth A. L., & Seligman M. E. P. (2006). Self-discipline gives girls the edge: Gender in self-discipline, grades, and achievement test scores. *Journal of Educational Psychology, 98*(1), 198–208.

Duhart, D. T. (2001). *Violence in the workplace, 1993–99*. Washington, DC: U.S. Department of Justice, Bureau of Justice Statistics.

Dunham, K. (2010). A healthy trend at medical schools. *Boston Globe*. Retrieved from http://www.boston.com/jobs/news/articles/2010/12/05/minorty_enrollment_rises_at_medical_schools/

Dunkle, M. C. (1987). Women in intercollegiate sports. In S. E. Rix (Ed.), *The American woman, 1987–88* (pp. 228–231). New York: W. W. Norton.

Dunkley, T., Wertheim, E., & Paxton, S. (2001). Examination of a model of multiple sociocultural influences on adolescent girls' body dissatisfaction and dietary restraint. *Adolescence, 36*, 265–279.

Dunlap, D. W. (1994, November 17). End of co-op dispute hailed as victory for gay couples. *New York Times*, p. B3.

Dunlap, D. W. (1996, January 21). Gay images, once kept out, are out big time. *New York Times*, pp. 29, 32.

Dunlap-Berg, B. (2010). Gender-inclusive language challenges church. Retreived from: http://www.umc.org/site/apps/nlnet/content3.aspx?c=IwL4KnNlLtH&b=2789393&ct=8116523

Dupre, J. (1990). Global versus local perspectives on sexual difference. In D. L. Rhode (Ed.), *Theoretical perspectives on sexual difference* (pp. 47–62). New Haven, CT: Yale University Press.

Durant, R., Champion, H., Wolfson, M., Morrow, O., McCoy, T., D'Agostino, R. B., et al. (2007). Date fighting experiences among college students: Are they associated with other health-risk behaviors? *Journal of American College Health, 55*, 5, 291–296.

Dutton, D. G. (2006). *Rethinking domestic violence*. Vancouver, Canada: University of British Columbia Press.

Dutton, D. G., Corvo, K. N., & Hamel, J. (2009). The gender paradigm in domestic violence research and practice part II: The information website of the American Bar Association. *Aggression & Violent Behavior, 14*(1), 30–38.

Dutton, D. G., Nicholls, T., & Spidel, A. (2005) Female perpetrators of intimate violence. *Journal of Offender Rehabilitation, 41*(4), 1–32.

Duxbury, L., Higgins, C., & Lee, C. (1994). Work-family conflict: A comparison of gender, family type, and perceived control. *Journal of Family Issues, 15*, 449–466.

Dworkin, A. (1983). Gynocide: Chinese footbinding. In L. Richardson & V. Taylor (Eds.), *Feminist frontiers* (pp. 178–186). Reading, MA: Addison-Wesley.

Eagly A. H. (1987). *Sex differences in social behavior: A social-role interpretation*. Hillsdale, NJ: Lawrence Erlbaum Associates.

Eagly, A. H., & Steffan, V. J. (1986). Gender and aggressive behavior: A meta-analytic review of the social psychological literature. *Psychological Bulletin, 100*, 309–330.

Eamon, M. K., & Altshuler, S. J. (2004). Can we predict disruptive school behavior? *Children & Schools, 26*(1), 23–37.

Eaton, A. W. (2007). Sensible antiporn feminism. *Ethics, 117*, 674–715.

Ebaugh, H. R. (1993). Patriarchal bargains and latent avenues of social mobility: Nuns in the Roman Catholic Church. *Gender & Society, 7*, 400–414.

Eberstadt, M. (2009). Is pornography the new tobacco? *Policy Review, 154*, 3–18.

Economist. (2010a). Gendercide: Killed, aborted or neglected, at least 100m girls have disappeared—and the number is rising. *Economist, 394*, 8672, p. 13.

Economist. (2010b). The worldwide war on baby girls. *Economist, 394*, 8672, 77–80.

Eder, D. (1995). *School talk*. New Brunswick, NJ: Rutgers University Press.

Edin, K., & Kefalas, M. (2005). *Promises I can keep: Why poor women put motherhood before marriage*. Berkeley: University of California Press.

Edin, K., & Kissane, R. J. (2010). Poverty and the American family: A decade in review. *Journal of Marriage and Family, 72*, 460–479.

Edin, K., & Lein, L. (1997). *Making ends meet*. New York: Russell Sage Foundation.

Edin, K., Tach, L., & Mincy, R. (2009). Claiming fatherhood: Race and the dynamics of parental involvement among unmarried men. *The Annals of the American Academy of Political and Social Science, 621*, 149–177.

Egan, R. J. (2008, April 11). Why not? Scripture, history and women's ordination. *Commonweal*, pp. 17–27.

Egan, T. (1992, October 4). Police chief becomes target in anti-gay battle. *New York Times*, p. 22.

Egan, T. (2000, October 23). Technology sent Wall Street in to market for pornography. *New York Times*, pp. A1, A20.

Ehrenberg, M. (1997). The role of women in human evolution. In C. B. Brettell & C. F. Sargent (Eds.), *Gender in cross-cultural perspective* (pp. 15–19). Englewood Cliffs, NJ: Prentice Hall.

Ehrenreich, B. (1983). *The hearts of men: American dreams and the flight from commitment*. New York: Anchor-Doubleday.

Ehrenreich, B. (2001). *Nickel and dimed: On (not) getting by in America*. New York: Metropolitan Books/Henry Holt.

Ehrenreich, B., & English, D. (1973). *Witches, nurses, and midwives: A history of women healers*. Old Westbury, NY: Feminist Press.

Ehrenreich, B., & English, D. (1986). The sexual politics of sickness. In P. Conrad & R. Kern (Eds.), *The sociology of health and illness* (pp. 281–296). New York: St. Martin's Press.

Ehrenreich, B., & English, D. (2010). *Witches, Midwives & Nurses* (Second Edition*)*, New York Feminist Press.

Eicher, E. M., & Washburn, L. L. (1986). Genetic control of primary sex determination in mice. *Annual Review of Genetics, 20*, 327–360.

Eisenberg, D. T. (2010). Shattering the Equal Pay Act's glass ceiling. *Southern Methodist University Law Review, 63*, 2–64.

Eisenberg, S. (1998). *We'll call you if we need you: Experiences of women working construction*. Ithaca, NY: Cornell University Press.

Eisend, M., Moller, J. (2007). The Influence of TV Viewing on Consumers' Body Images and Related Consumption Behavior, *Marketing Letters, 18*, 1, 101–116.

Eisenhart, M. A., & Finkel, E. (1998). *Women's science: Learning and succeeding from the margins*. Chicago: University of Chicago Press.

Eisenhart, M. A., & Holland, D. C. (1992). Gender constructs and career commitment: The influence of peer culture on women in college. In

T. L. Whitehead & B. V. Reid (Eds.), *Gender constructs and social issues* (pp. 142–180). Urbana: University of Illinois Press.

Eisenstein, H. (1991). *Gender shock*. Boston: Beacon Press.

Eisler, R., & Hersen, M. (2000). *Handbook of gender, culture and health*. London: Psychology Press.

Elfman, L. (2009). A "second wave of feminism." *Diverse: Issues in Higher Education, 26*(2), 10–11.

El-Guindi, F. (1999). *Veil: Modesty, privacy, and resistance*. New York: Berg.

Eller, C. (1991). Revitalizing the patriarchy: The sacred history of the feminist spirituality movement. *History of Religion, 30*, 279–295.

Eller, C. (2000). *The myth of matriarchal prehistory*. Boston: Beacon Press.

Elliott, A. (2005, March 19). Challenging tradition: Woman leads Muslim prayer service in New York. *New York Times*, p. A12.

Ellis, L. (1982). Genetics and criminal behavior. *Criminology, 20*, 43–66.

Elman, A. (2005). Confronting the sexual abuse of women with disabilities. VawNethttp://new. vawnet.org/Assoc_Files_VAWNET/AR_SVDisability

El-Or, T. (1993). The length of the slits and the spread of luxury: Reconstructing the subordination of ultra-orthodox Jewish women through the patriarchy of men scholars. *Sex Roles, 29*, 585–598.

Emslie, C., & Hunt, K. (2009). Men, masculinities and heart disease: A systematic review of the qualitative literature. *Current Sociology, 59*(2), 155–191.

Engelhardt, G. (2004). *Social security and the evolution of elderly poverty*. Retrieved from http://www.nber.org/papers/w10466

Engineer, A. A. (1992). *The rights of women in Islam*. New York: St. Martin's Press.

Engineer, A. A. (2004). *The rights of women in Islam*. New Delhi: Sterling Publishers.

England, P. (1992). *Comparable worth: Theories and evidence*. New York: Aldine de Gruyter.

England, P. (2005). Gender inequality in labor markets: The role of motherhood and segregation. *International Studies in Gender, State and Society, 12*, 264–288.

England, P. (2010). The gender revolution: Uneven and stalled. *Gender & Society, 24*, 149–166.

England, P., & Folbre, N. (2005). Gender and economic sociology. In N. J. Smelser and R. Swedberg (Eds.)., *The handbook of economic sociology* (pp. 627–649). New York: Russell Sage Foundation.

England, P., Allison, P., & Wu, Y. (2007). Does bad pay cause occupations to feminize, does feminization reduce pay, and how can we tell with longitudinal data? *Social Science Research, 36*, 1237–1256.

English, A. (2009). *Restoring equal opportunity in education: An analysis of arguments for and against the Bush administration single-sex education regulations*. Washington, DC: Institute for Women's Policy Research. Retrieved May 5, 2010, http://www.iwpr.org/pdf/singlesexC368.pdf

English, D. J., Widom, C. S., & Brandfield, C. (2001). *Childhood victimization and delinquency, adult criminality, and violent criminal behavior: A replication and extension: Final report*. Washington, DC: U.S. Department of Justice, National Institute of Justice.

English, K. (1993). Self-reported crime rates of women prisoners. *Journal of Quantitative Criminology, 9*, 357–382.

Enloe, C. (2000). *Manuevers: The international politics of militarizing women's lives*. Berkeley: University of California Press.

Enloe, C. H. (1987). Feminist thinking about war, militarism, and peace. In B. B. Hess & M. M. Ferree (Eds.), *Analyzing gender* (pp. 536–548). Newbury Park, CA: Sage.

Enloe, C. H. (1993). *The morning after*. Berkeley: University of California Press.

Enriquez, M. et al. (2010). Development and feasibility of an HIV and IPV intervention among low-income mothers receiving services in a Missouri day care center. *Violence Against Women, 16*, 560–578.

Entwisle D. R., Alexander K. L., & Olson, L. S. (2007). Early schooling: the handicap of being poor and male. *Sociology of Education, 80*(2), 114–38.

Entwisle, D. R., Alexander, K. L., & Olson, L. S. (1994). The gender gap in math: Its possible origins in neighborhood effects. *American Sociological Review, 59*, 822–838.

Entwisle, D. R., Alexander, K. L., & Olson, L. S. (1997). *Children, schools and inequality*. Boulder, CO: Westview.

Epstein, C. F. (1983). Women and power: The roles of women in politics in the United States. In L. Richardson & V. Taylor (Eds.), *Feminist frontiers* (pp. 288–304). Reading, MA: Addison-Wesley.

Epstein, C. F. (1998). Reaching for the top: "The glass ceiling" and women in law. In S. Shetreet

(Ed.), *Women in law* (pp. 105–130). London: Kluwer Law International.

Epstein, S., & Fitzgerald, R. (2009) *Toxic beauty: How cosmetics and personal care products endanger your health...and what you can do about it*. Dallas, Texas: BenBella Books, Inc.

Equal Employment Opportunity Commission (EEOC). (2010). *Sexual harassment charges: EEOC & FEPAs Combined FY 1997-FY 2009*. Retrieved September 8, 2010, http://www.eeoc.gov/eeoc/statistics/enforcement/sexual_harassment.cfm

Erdur-Baker, O. (2010). Cyberbullying and its correlation with traditional bullying, gender and frequent and risky usage of internet-mediated communication tools. *New Media & Society*, 109–125.

Ericson, T. (2008). *Equalization of paid working hours in the dual-earner household: Does it increase women's double burden?* Retrieved from https://gupea.ub.gu.se/dspace/handle/2077/9678

Erikson, E. H. (1968). *Identity: Youth and crisis*. New York: Norton.

Erikson, V. L. (1992). Back to the basics: Feminist social theory, Durkheim and religion. *Journal of Feminist Studies in Religion, 8*, 35–46.

Erikson, V. L. (1993). *Where silence speaks: Feminism, social theory and religion*. Minneapolis: Fortress Press.

Ernst, A. A., Green, E., & Ferguson, M. T. (2000). The utility of anoscopy and colposcopy in the evaluation of male sexual assault victims. *Annals of Emergency Medicine, 36*, 432–437.

Escobar-Chaves, S. L., & Anderson, C. A. (2008). Media and risky behaviors. *Future of Children, 18*, 147–180.

Escoffier, J. (1992). Generations and paradigms: Mainstreams in lesbian and gay studies. In H. L. Minton (Ed.), *Gay and lesbian studies* (pp. 7–26). New York: Haworth Press.

ESPN High School. (2008). *Report: Kicker dismissed by Georgia team for being a girl*. Retrieved from http://sports.espn.go.com/ncaa/highschool/news/story?id=3560929

Esposito, J., & DeLong-Bas, N. (2001). *Women in Muslim family law*. Syracuse, NY: Syracuse University Press.

Essex, N. (2009). Student-on-student harassment and zero tolerance—Achieving a delicate balance. *ERS Spectrum, 27*(1), 1–6.

Estes, R. J., & Weiner, N. A. (2001). *The commercial sexual exploitation of children in the U.S., Canada, and Mexico*. Available online: http://www.ssw.upenn.edu/~restes/CSEC_Files/Complete_CSEC_010918.pdf

Estevez-Abe, M. (2006). Gendering the varieties of capitalism: A study of occupational sex segregation by sex in advanced industrial societies. *World Politics, 59*, 142–175.

Estioko-Griffin, A. (1986). Daughters of the forest. *Natural History, 95*, 5.

Estrich, S. (1994, May 22). For girls' schools and women's colleges, separate is better. *New York Times Magazine*, pp. 38–39.

Eterno, J. A. (2006). Gender and policing: Do women accept legal restrictions more than their male counterparts? *Women & Criminal Justice, 18*, 1/2, 49–78.

Etienne, M., & Leacock, E. (Eds.) (1980). *Women and colonization*. New York: Praeger.

Ettorre, E. (1992). *Women and substance abuse*. New Brunswick, NJ: Rutgers University Press.

Ettorre, E. (1997). *Women and alcohol: A private pleasure or a public problem?* London: Women's Press.

European Commission. (2006). *She figures, women and science, statistics and indicators*. Brussels: European Commission.

Evans, M. (2003). *Gender and social theory*. Buckingham, UK: Open University Press.

Evans, S. M. (1979). *Personal politics: The roots of women's liberation in the Civil Rights movement and the new left*. New York: Knopf.

Evans, S. M. (1987). Women in twentieth century America: An overview. In S. E. Rix (Ed.), *The American woman in 1987–88* (pp. 33–66). New York: W. W. Norton.

Eveline, J., & Todd, P. (2009). Gender mainstreaming: The answer to the gender wage gap? *Gender, Work and Organizations, 16*, 536–558.

Everbach, T. (2005). The "masculine" content of a female-managed newspaper. *Media Report to Women, 33*, 14–22.

Ezzati, M., Vander Hoorn, S., Lawes, C., Leach, R., James, W., Lopez, A., Rodgers, A., & Murray, C. (2005). Rethinking the "diseases of affluence" paradigm: Global patterns of nutritional risks in relation to economic development. *PLoS Medicine, 2*(5), 0404–0412.

Faderman, L. (1991). *Odd girls and twilight lovers*. New York: Columbia University Press.

Fagan, J., & Press, J. (2008). Father influences on employed mothers' work-family balance. *Journal of Family Issues, 29*(9), 1136–1160.

Fagot, B. I. (1985). Beyond the reinforcement principle: Another step toward understanding sex role development. *Developmental Psychology, 21,* 1097–1104.

Fagot, B. I., & Leinbach, M. D. (1983). Play styles in early childhood: Social consequences for boys and girls. In M. B. Liss (Ed.), *Social and cognitive skills: Sex roles and children's play* (pp. 93–116). New York: Academic Press.

Fagot, B. I., & Leinbach, M. D. (1989). The young child's gender schema: Environmental input, internal organization. *Child Development, 60,* 663–672.

Fagot, B. I., Hagan, R., Leinbach, M. D., & Kronsberg, S. (1985). Differential reactions to assertive and communicative acts of toddler boys and girls. *Child Development, 56,* 1499–1505.

Fagot, B. I., Hagan, R., Leinbach, M. D., & Kronsberg, S. (1985). Differential reactions to assertive and communicative acts of toddler boys and girls. *Child Development, 56,* 1499–1505.

Fahri, P., & Ahrens, F. (2007). FCC seeks to reign in violent TV shows. *Washington Post.* Retrieved from: http://www.washgintonpost.com/wp-dyn/content/article/2007/11/11/AR2007111101514.html

Faine, J. R., & Bohlander, E. (1976). *Sentencing the female offender: The impact of legal and extra-legal considerations.* Paper presented at the annual meeting of the American Society of Criminology, Tucson, AZ.

Falk, E. (2010). *Women for president: Media bias in nine campaigns.* Chicago: University of Chicago Press.

Falk, E., & Kenski, K. (2006). Sexism versus partisanship: A new look at whether America is ready for a woman president. *Sex Roles, 54,* 413–428.

Faludi, S. (1991). *Backlash: The undeclared war against American women.* New York: Anchor Books.

Farhat, T., Iannotti, R., Simons-Morton, B. (2010). Overweight, obesity, youth, and health-risk behavior. *American Journal of Preventive Medicine, 38*(3), 258–267.

Farr, K. (2009). Extreme war rape in today's Civil-War-Torn states: A contextual and comparative analysis. *Gender Issues, 26,* 1–41.

Farrell, J. (June 12, 2007). Class divide: Single-sex schoolrooms take off. Some wary of growing trend, but advocates' fervor is catching. Retrieved March 12, 2010 from http://www.courant.com/news/education/hcsamesexclass0612.artjun12,0,5709964.story?coll=hc-headlines-education

Farrell, S. A. (1992). *Women-church: A contradiction or the perfect feminist organization?* Paper

presented at the annual meeting of the American Sociological Association, Pittsburgh, PA.

Fausto-Sterling, A. (1985). *Myths of gender.* New York: Basic Books.

Fausto-Sterling, A. (2000). *Sexing the body: Gender politics and the construction of sexuality.* New York: Basic Books.

Fay, F. M., & Wallace, J. E. (2009). Mentors as social capital: Gender, mentors, and career rewards in law practice. *Sociological Inquiry, 79,* 418–452.

Fazel, S., Khosla, V., Doll, H., & Geddes, J. (2008). The prevalence of mental di. sorders among the homeless in Western countries: Ssytematic review and meta-regression analysis. *PLoS Medicine, 5,* 1670–1681.

Fazlollah, M., Matza, M., & McCoy, C. R. (1999a, December 2). Rape cases in city rise as reporting changes. *Philadelphia Inquirer,* pp. A1, A23.

Fazlollah, M., Matza, M., & McCoy, C. R. (1999b, December 19). The rape squad files, Part 1: A 7-year-old "knew who did it."*Philadelphia Inquirer,* pp. 1–2.

Feder, J., & Levine, L. (2010). *Pay equity legislation.* Washington, DC: Congressional Research Service.

Federal Bureau of Investigation. (2007). *Crime in the United States, 2007* and *Supplemental Homicide Reports.* Retrieved November 16, 2009, http://www.ojp.usdoj.gov/bjs/dcf/duc.htm

Federal Bureau of Investigation. (2008). *2008 Hate Crime Statistics.* Retrieved December 2, 2009 from http://www.fbi.gov/ucr/hc2008/incidents.html

Federal Bureau of Investigation. (2009). *Crime in the United States, 2008.* Retrieved November 19, 2009, http://www.fbi.gov/ucr/cius2008/index.html

Federal Bureau of Investigation. (2009a). *Crime in the United States, 2008.* Table 42. Arrests by Sex. Retrieved from: http://www.fbi.gov/ucr/cius2008/data/table_42.html

Federal Bureau of Investigation. (2009b). *2008 arrests in the United States.* Retrieved from: http://www.fbi.gov/ucr/cius2008/arrests/index.html

Federal Bureau of Investigaton. (2010). *Expanded homicide data, Table 6.* Retrieved from: http://www.fbi.gov/about-us/cjis/ucr/crime-in-the-US/2010/crime-in-the-US-2010/tables/10shrtb/06.xls

Federal Election Commission. (2008, January 17). FEC records slight increase in the number of PACs. Retrieved from: http://www.fec.gov/press/press2008/20080117paccount.shtml

Fee, E. (1983). Women and health care: A comparison of theories. In E. Fee (Ed.), *Women and health: The politics of sex in medicine* (pp. 17–34). Farmdale, NY: Baywood.

Feinman, C. (1992). Criminal codes, criminal justice and female offenders. In I. L. Moyer (Ed.), *The changing roles of women in the criminal justice system* (pp. 57–68). Prospect Heights, IL: Waveland Press.

Feiring, C., & Lewis, M. (1987). The child's social network: Sex differences from three to six years. *Sex Roles, 17*, 621–636.

Feld, B. C. (2009). Violent girls or relabeled status offenders? An alternative interpretation of the data. *Crime & Delinquency, 55*, 2, 241–265.

Felder, S. (2006). The gender longevity gap: Explaining the difference between singles and couples, *Journal of Population Economics, 19*(3), 543–557.

Feldman, M. B., & Meyer, I. H. (2007). Eating disorders in diverse lesbian, gay, and bisexual populations. *International Journal of Eating Disorders, 40*, 218–226.

Feldstein, K. (1998, April 13). Social Security's gender gap. *New York Times*, p. A27.

Felix, E. D., & McMahon, S. D. (2006). Gender and multiple forms of peer victimization: How do they influence adolescent psychosocial adjustment? *Violence and Victims, 21*, 707–724.

"Female genital mutilation common in Egypt despite ban." (2008). *New Scientist, 199*, 2674, p. 4.

"Female police officer wins harassment case." (2006, June 3). Associated Press. Retrieved November 18, 2009, from http://cbs2chicago.com/topstories/Suzanne.Barth.police.2.328885.html

Fennell, S., & Arnot, M. (2008). *Gender education and equality in a global context: Conceptual frameworks and policy perspectives*. New York: Routledge.

Fennema, E., & Sherman, J. (1977). Sex-related differences in mathematics achievement, spatial ability, and affective factors. *American Educational Research Journal, 14*, 51–71.

Ferguson, C. J., Cruz, A. M., Martinez, D., Rueda, S. M., Ferguson, D. E., & Negy, C. (2008). Personality, Parental, and Media Influences on Aggressive Personality and Violent Crime in Young Adults. *Journal of Aggression, Maltreatment, & Trauma, 17*(4), 395–414.

Ferguson, T., & Dunphy, J. S. (1992). *Answers to the mommy track*. Far Hills, NJ: New Horizon Press.

Fernea, E. W. (1998). *In search of Islamic feminism*. New York: Doubleday.

Ferraro, K. F. (1995). *Fear of crime: Interpreting victimization risk*. Albany: State University of New York Press.

Ferriman, K., Lubinski, D., & Benbow, C.P. (2009). Work preferences, life values, and personal views of top math/science graduate students and the profoundly gifted: Developmental changes and sex differences during emerging adulthood and parenthood. *Journal of Personality and Social Psychology, 97*, 517–532.

Ferro, C., Cermele, J., & Saltzman, A. (2008). Current perceptions of marital rape: Some good and not-so-good news. *Journal of Interpersonal Violence, 23*, 6, 764–779.

"Fertility group expels doctor of 'octomom.'" (2009). *USA Today*, p. 9D.

Fiddy, A., & Hamilton, C. (2004). *Bullying: A guide to the law*. Colchester, UK: Children's Legal Centre.

Fiebert, M. S. (1997). Annotated bibliography: References examining assaults by women on their spouses/partners. In B. M. Dank & R. Refinette (Eds.), *Sexual harassment and sexual consent* (Vol. 1, pp. 273–276). New Brunswick, NJ: Transaction.

Fifth of Citadel females report being sexually assaulted. (2006, August 24). *Dayton Daily News*, p. A24.

Fine, S. (1997, September 15). Sexual harassment policies softening. *Globe and Mail*.

Finer, L. B. (2007). Trends in premarital sex in the United States, 1954–2003. *Public Health Reports, 122*(1), 73–78.

Fineran, S. (2002). Sexual minority students and peer sexual harassment in high school. *Journal of School Social Work, 11*, 50–69.

Fink, J. S., & Kensicki, L. J. (2002). An imperceptible difference: Visual and textual construction of femininity in Sports Illustrated and Sports Illustrated for Women. *Mass Communication and Society, 5*, 317–339.

Finkelhor, D. (2008). *Child victimization: Violence, crime, and abuse in the lives of young people*. New York: Oxford University Press.

Finkelhor, D., & Jones, L. (2006). Why have child maltreatment and child victimization declined? *Journal of Social Issues, 62*, 4, 685–716.

Finkelhor, D., Ormrod, R., Turner, H., & Hamby, S. L. (2005). The victimization of children and youth: A comprehensive, national survey. *Child Maltreatment, 10*(1), 5–25.

Finkelhor, D., Ormrod, R. K., & Turner, H. A. (2009). Lifetime assessment of poly-victimization in a national sample of children and youth. *Child Abuse & Neglect, 33*, 403–411.

Fischer, A. R. (2007). Parental relationship quality and masculine gender-role strain in young men: Mediating effects of personality. *The Counseling Psychologist, 35*, 2, 328–358.

Fischer, S. (2010). *Powerful or pretty: A content analysis of gender images in children's animated films*. Unpublished Master's thesis, Auburn University, Auburn, AL.

Fishbein, S. B. (2000). Pre-conviction mandatory HIV testing: Rape, AIDS and the Fourth Amendment. *Hofstra Law Review, 28*, 835–867.

Fisher, B. S., & Sloan, J. J., III. (2003). Unraveling the fear of victimization among college women: Is the "shadow of sexual assault hypothesis" supported? *Justice Quarterly, 20*, 633–659.

Fisher, B. S., Cullen, F. T., & Thenen, M. G. (2001). *The sexual victimization of college women*. Available online: http://www.ncjrs.org/pdffiles1/nij/182369.pdf

Fisher, B. S., Daigle, L. E., Cullen, F. T., & Turner, M. G. (2003). Reporting sexual victimization to the police and others: Results from a national-level study of college women. *Criminal Justice and Behavior, 30*, 6–38.

Fisher, B.S. (2009). The effects of survey question wording on rape estimates: Evidence from a quasi-experimental design. *Violence Against Women, 15*, 133–147.

Fisher, I. (2006, May 2). Ideals clash as Vatican rethinks ban on condoms. *New York Times*, pp. A1, A10.

Fisher-Thompson, D., Sausa, A. D., & Wright, T. F. (1995). Toy selection for children: Personality and toy request influences. *Sex Roles, 33*, 239–255.

Fitpatrick, C. (2006, March 4). Lay ministry a Catholic compromise. *Dayton Daily News*, p. E3.

Fitzpatrick, M. J., & McPherson, B. J. (2010). Coloring within the lines: Gender stereotypes in contemporary coloring books. *Sex Roles, 62*(1/2), 127–137.

Fivush, R. (1991). Gender and emotion in mother-child conversations about the past. *Journal of Narrative and Life History, 1*, 325–341.

Flanagan, L. (2011). Family practice management: Nurse practitioners: Growing competition for family physicians? Retrieved from: http://www.aafp.org/fpm/981000fm/nurse.html

Fletcher, I. (2007). The acute effects of combined static and dynamic stretch protocols on fifty meter sprint performance in track-and-field athletes. *Journal of Strength and Conditioning Research, 21*(3).

Fleury, R. E. (2002). Missing voices: Patterns of battered women's satisfaction with the criminal legal system. *Violence Against Women, 8*, 181–205.

Fleury, R. E., Sullivan, C. M., & Bybee, D. I. (2000). When ending the relationship does not end the violence: Women's experiences of violence by former partners. *Violence Against Women, 6*, 1363–1383.

Flexner, E. (1971). *Century of struggle*. Cambridge, MA: Belknap.

Flicker, S. M. et al. (2011). Concommitant forms of abuse and help-seeking behavior among white, African American, and Latina women who experience intimate partner violence. *Violence Against Women, 17*, 1067–1085.

Florez, I. R., & McCaslin, M. (2008). Student perceptions of small-group learning. *Teachers College Record, 110*, 2438–2451.

Flynn, N. T., Hanks, R. S., & Garley, L. (2007). Stirred, shaken, or blended? Gender differences in processing and treatment of juvenile offenders. *Women & Criminal Justice, 18*(4), 17–36.

Foerstel, K., & Foerstel, H. N. (1996). *Climbing the hill: Gender conflict in Congress*. Westport, CT: Praeger.

Folsom, D. et al. (2005). Prevalence and risk factors for homelessness and utilization of mental health services among 10,340 patients with serious mental illness in a large public mental health system. *American Journal of Psychiatry, 162*, 370–376.

Fomby, P., & Cherlin, A. J., (2007). Family instability and child well-being. *American Sociological Review, 72*, 181–204.

Foran, H. M., & O'Leary, D. K. (2008). Problem drinking, jealousy, and anger control: Variables predicting physical aggression against a partner. *Journal of Family Violence, 23*, 141–148.

Forbes 400. (2011). The Forbes 400: The richest people in America, Retrieved February 28, 2011, http://www.forbes.com/wealth/forbes-400/list http://0-web.ebscohost.com.libcat.widener.edu/ehost/- bib14up

Forbes, G. B., Adams-Curtis, L. E., Pakalka, A. H., & White, K. B. (2006). Dating aggression, sexual coercion, and aggression-supporting attitudes among college men as a function of participation in aggressive high school sports. *Violence Against Women, 12*(5), 441–455.

Forde, K. (2002). Celluloid dreams: The marketing of Cutex in America, 1916–1935. *Journal of Design History, 15*(3), 175–189.

Fordham, S. (1996). *Blacked out: Dilemmas of race, identity, and success at Capital High*. Chicago: University of Chicago Press.

Foreit, K. G., Agor, T., Byers, J., Larue, J., Lokey, H., Palazzini, M., et al. (1980). Sex bias in the newspaper treatment of male-centered and female-centered news stories. *Sex Roles, 6*, 475–480.

Forth, C. (2009). *Imagining our ancient future*. Chicago: University of Chicago Press.

Foschi, M. (1996). Double standards in the evaluation of men and women. *Social Psychology Quarterly, 59*, 237–254.

Foster, H., & Lewis, J. (forthcoming). Race/ethnicity and living arrangements of children of incarcerated mothers: Comparative patterns and maternal experiences. In C.M. Renzetti & R.K. Bergen (Eds.), *Understanding diversity: Celebrating difference, challenging inequality*. Boston: Allyn and Bacon.

Fox, C. L., & Farrow, C. V. (2009). Global and physical self-esteem and body dissatisfaction as mediators of the relationship between weight status and being a victim of bullying. *Journal of Adolescence, 32*(5), 1287–1301.

Fox, J. A., & Zawitz, M. W. (2007). *Homicide trends in the United States, 2007*. Washington, DC: Bureau of Justice Statistics.

Fox, M. F. (2008). Gender, family characteristics, and publication productivity among scientists. *Social Studies of Science, 35*, 1, 131–150.

Fox, R., & Van Sickel, R. (2000). Gender dynamics and judicial behavior in criminal trial courts: An exploratory study. *Justice System Journal, 21*(3), 261–277.

Fox, R. L., & Lawless, J. L. (2008). *Why are women still not running for public office?* Washington, DC: Brookings Institution.

Fox, S. 1991 *Toxic work*. Philadelphia: Temple University Press.

Fox, T. G. (1998, July 12). Policing the net. *Hartford Courant*.

Frable, D. E. S., & Bem, S. L. (1985). If you're gender-schematic, all members of the opposite sex look alike. *Journal of Personality and Social Psychology, 49*, 459–468.

Francis, B. (2009). The role of The Boffin as abject Other in gendered performances of school achievement. *Sociological Review, 57*(4), 645–669.

Francis, B., & Skelton, C. (2005). *Reassessing gender and achievement: Questioning contemporary key debates*. London: Routledge.

Frank, E., Brogran, D., & Schiffman, M. (1998). Prevalence and correlates of harassment among U.S. women physicians. *Archives of Internal Medicine, 158*, 352–362.

Frank, F. W. (1989). Language planning, language reform, and language change: A review of guidelines for nonsexist usage. In F. W. Frank & P. A. Treichler (Eds.), *Language, gender, and professional writing: Theoretical approaches and guidelines for nonsexist usage* (pp. 105–133). New York: Modern Language Association of America.

Franks, P., & Clancy, C. M. (1993). Physician gender bias in clinical decisionmaking: Screening for cancer in primary care. *Medical Care, 31*, 213–218.

Fray-Witzer, E. (1999). Twice abused: Same-sex domestic violence and the law. In B. Leventhal & S. E. Lundy (Eds.), *Same-sex domestic violence* (pp. 19–41). Thousand Oaks, CA: Sage.

Free speech on campus. (2008). *Washington Times*, p. A26.

Freedman, R. (1986). *Beauty bound*. Lexington, MA: Lexington Books.

Freeman, C. E. (2004). *Trends in Educational Equity of Girls & Women: 2004*. National Center for Education Statistics Working Paper 2005–016. U.S, Department of Education, National Center for Education Statistics, Washington, DC: GPO.

Freeman, J. (1973). The origins of the women's liberation movement. *American Journal of Sociology, 78*, 792–811.

Freeman, N. K. (2007). Preschoolers' perceptions of gender appropriate toys and their parents' belief about genderized behaviors: Miscommunication, mixed messages, or hidden truths? *Early Childhood Education Journal, 34*(5), 357–366.

Freeza, H., Padova, C. D., Pozzato, G., Terpin, M., Baraona, E., & Lieber, C. S. (1990). High blood alcohol levels in women: The role of decreased gastric alcohol dehydrogenase activity and first-pass metabolism. *New England Journal of Medicine, 322*, 95–99.

French, H. W. (1997, February 2). Africa's culture war: Old customs, new values. *New York Times*, pp. E1, 4.

Frenzel, E. D., & Ball, J. D. (2007). Effects of individual characteristics on plea negotiations under sentencing guidelines. *Journal of Ethnicity in Criminal Justice, 5*, 4, 59–82.

Freud, S. (1983/1933). Femininity. In M. W. Zak & P. A. Motts (Eds.) *Women and the politics of culture* (pp. 80–92). New York: Longman.

Freudenheim, M. (1997, November 2). Nurses treading on doctors' turf. *New York Times*, p. WK7.

Friedan, B. (1963). *The feminine mystique*. New York: W. W. Norton.

Friedman, R. C., Hurt, S. W., Aronoff, M. S., & Clarkin, J. (1980). Behavior and the menstrual cycle. *Signs, 5*, 719–738.

Frieze, I. H., Parsons, J. E., Johnson, P. B., Ruble, D. N., & Zellman, G. L. (1978). *Women and sex roles*. New York: W. W. Norton.

Frith, K., Shaw, P., & Cheng, Hong. (2005). The construction of beauty: A cross-cultural analysis of women's magazine advertising. *Journal of Communication, 55*, 1, 56–70.

Froh, J. J., Yurkewicz, C., & Kashdan, T. B. (2009). Gratitude and subjective well-being in early adolescence: Examining gender differences. *Journal of Adolescence, 32*, 633–650.

Frome, P. M., Alfred, C. J., Eccles, J. S., & Barber, B. L. (2006). Why don't they want a male-dominated job? An investigation of young women who changed their occupational aspirations. *Educational Research and Evaluation, 12*, 359–372.

Frontier Nursing Service, Inc. (2011). *History of frontier school midwifery and family nursing*. Retrieved from http://www.frontiernursing.org/History/History-FSMFN.shtm

Fry, R., & Cohn, D. (2010). *Women, men, and the new economics of marriage*. Washington, DC: Pew Research Center. Retrieved February 18, 2010, http://pewsocialtrends.org/assets/pdf/new-economics-of-marriage.pdf

Fulani, L. (Ed.) (1988). *The psychopathology of everyday racism and sexism*. New York: Haworth.

Fuller, L. (2005). WLBT News in the Deregulation ERA: Modern racism or representative picture? *Journal of Black Studies, 42*(2), 262–292.

Fuller, T. L. (2005). Child safety at reunification: A case-control study of maltreatment reoccurrence following return home from substitute care. *Children and Youth Services Review, 27*, 1293–1306.

Fullilove, M., Lown, A., & Fullilove, R. (1992). Crack hos and skeezers: Traumatic experiences of women crack users. *Journal of Sex Research, 29*, 275–287.

Funk, N., & Mueller, M. (Eds.) (1993). *Gender politics and post-communism*. New York: Routledge.

Furstenberg, F. F., & Cherlin, A. (1991). *Divided families*. Cambridge: Harvard University Press.

Gabin, N. F. (1990). *Feminism in the labor market: Women and the United Auto Workers, 1935–1975*. Ithaca, NY: Cornell University Press.

Gabriel, M. (1998). *Notorious Victoria*. Chapel Hill, NC: Algonquin Books of Chapel Hill.

Gabriel, P. E., & Schmitz, S. (2007, June). Gender differences in occupational distributions among workers. *Monthly Labor Review*, 19–24.

Gadalla, T. M. (2009). Impact of marital dissolution on men's and women's incomes: A longitudinal study. *Journal of Divorce & Remarriage, 50*, 55–65.

Gadon, E. M. (1989). *The once and future goddess*. New York: Harper and Row.

Gailey, C. W. (1987). Evolutionary perspectives on gender hierarchy. In B. B. Hess & M. M. Ferree (Eds.), *Analyzing gender* (pp. 32–67). Newbury Park, CA: Sage.

Gallagher, A. M., & Kaufman, J. C. (2005). Gender differences in mathematics: What we know and what we need to know. In A. M. Gallagher & J. C. Kaufman (Eds.), *Mind the gap: Gender differences in mathematics* (pp. 316–332).

Gallagher, M. (2005). *Who makes the news?: Global Media Monitoring Project 2005*. World Association for Christian Communication.

Gallagher, S. K., & Smith, C. (1999). Symbolic traditionalism and pragmatic egalitarianism: Contemporary evangelicals, families, and gender. *Gender & Society, 13*, 211–233.

Gallup Poll. (2008, June). Americans evenly divided on morality of homosexuality. Retrieved September 30, 2009, from http://www.gallup.com/poll/108115/Americans-Evenly-Divided-Morality-Homosexuality.aspx

Gallup Poll. (2009, May). Republicans move to the right on several moral issues. Retrieved December 14, 2009, from http://www.gallup.com/poll/118546/Republicans-Veer-Right-Several-Moral-Issues.aspx

Gallup, G., & Castelli, J. (1989). *The people's religion*. New York: Macmillan.

Gammon, M. A., & Isgro, K. L. (2006). Troubling the canon: Bisexuality and queer theory. *Journal of Homosexuality, 52*(1/2), 159–184.

Gappa, J. M., Austin, A. E., & Trice, A. G. (2007). *Rethinking faculty work: Higher education's strategic imperative*. San Francisco: Jossey-Bass.

Garcia, C. A., & Lane, J. (2009). What a girl wants, what a girl needs: Findings from a gender-specific focus group study. *Crime & Delinquency*. Available online.

Garcia-Alonso, J., Greenway, G., Jardege, J., & Haswell, S. (2008). A prototype microfluic chip using flourescent yeast for detection of toxic compounds, *Biosensors and Bioelectronics, 24*(5), 1508–1511.

Gardner, M. (2006, October 30). The truth behind women "opting out." *Christian Science Monitor*. Retrieved October 19, 2009 from http://news.yahoo.com/s/csm/20061030/ts_csm

Gargan, E. A. (1991, December 13). Ultrasound skews India's birth ratio. *New York Times*, p. A13.

Garrison, C. G., McClelland, A., Dambrot, F., &. Casey, K. A. (1992). Gender balancing and the criminal justice curriculum and classroom. *Journal of Criminal Justice Education, 3*, 203–222.

Garrison, M. (2008). Nonmarital cohabitation: Social revolution and legal regulation. *Family Law Quarterly, 42*(3), 309–331.

Gastil, J. (1990). Generic pronouns and sexist language: The oxymoronic character of masculine generics. *Sex Roles, 23*, 629–643.

Gates, A. (2000, April 9). Men on TV: Dumb as posts and proud of it. *New York Times*, pp. 1, 35.

"Gay studies thriving on U.S. campuses." (2007). *New York Blade, 11*, 36, p. 7.

Gazzaniga, M. (1992). *Nature's mind*. New York: Basic Books.

Geis, F. L., Brown, V., Jennings (Walstedt), J., & Porter, N. (1984). TV commercials as achievement scripts for women. *Sex Roles, 10*, 513–525.

Geist, E. A., & King, M. (2008). Different, not better: Gender differences in mathematics learning and achievement. *Journal of Instructional Psychology, 35*(1), 43–52.

Gelles, R. J. (1993). Alcohol and drugs are associated with violence—They are not its cause. In R. J. Gelles & D. R. Loseke (Eds.), *Current controversies on domestic violence* (pp. 182–196). Newbury Park, CA: Sage.

Gelman, S. A., Taylor, M. G., & Nguyen, S. (2004). Mother-child conversations about gender: Understanding the acquisition of essentialist beliefs. *Monographs of the society for Research in Child Development, 69*, 1.

General Accounting Office. (2011). *Military justice: Oversight and better collaboration needed for sexual assault investigations and adjudications*. Washington, DC: Author.

Gerami, S. (1996). *Women and fundamentalism: Islam and Christianity*. New York: Garland.

Gerard, J. M., Landry-Meyer, L., & Roe, J. G. (2006). Grandparents raising grandchildren: The role of social support in coping with caregiver challenges. *International Journal of Aging and Human Development, 62*, 359–383.

Gerber, J., & Weeks, S. L. (1992). Women as victims of corporate crime: A call for research on a neglected topic. *Deviant Behavior, 13*, 325–347.

Gerbner, G. (1998). *Casting the American scene: A look at the characters on prime time and day time television from 1994–1997, The 1998 Screen Actors Guild Report: A cultural indicators project report*. Retrieved from http://www.media-awareness.ca/english/resources/research_documents/reports/diversity/upload/Casting-the-American-Scene-Report-pdf.pdf

Gero, J. M. (1991). Genderlithics: Women's roles in stone tool production. In J. M. Gero & M. W. Conkey (Eds.), *Engendering archeology* (pp. 163–193). New York: Basil Blackwell.

Geronimus, A., Bound, J., & Colen, C. (2011). Excess black mortality in the United States and in selected black and white high-poverty areas, 1980–2000. *American Journal of Public Health 101*(4), 720–729.

Gerson, K. (2010). *The unfinished revolution: How a new generation is reshaping family, work, and gender in America*. New York: Oxford University Press.

Gerson, M., Alpert, J. L., & Richardson, M. S. (1984). Mothering: The view from psychological research. *Signs, 9*, 434–453.

Gerstel, N., & Clawson, D. (2001). Unions' responses to family concerns. *Social Problems, 48*, 277–297.

Gerstel, N., & Gallagher, S. K. (2001). Men's caregiving: Gender and the contingent character of care. *Gender & Society, 15*, 197–217.

Gertzog, I. N. (1984). *Congressional women*. New York: Praeger.

Gerwitz, A. H., & Edleson, J. L. (2007). Young children's exposure to intimate partner violence: Towards a developmental risk and resilience framework for research and intervention. *Journal of Family Violence, 22*, 151–163.

Geschwind, D. H., & Dykens, E. (2004). Neurobehavioral and psychosocial issues in Klinefelter syndrome. *Learning Disabilities Research & Practice, 19*, 166–173.

Gettelman, T. E., & Thompson, J. K. (1993). Actual differences and stereotypical perceptions in body image and eating disturbance: A comparison of male and female heterosexual and homosexual samples. *Sex Roles, 29*, 545–562.

Gibbs, A. S. (2009, December/2010, January). Disney's Princess Tiana: A brown-skinned beauty finally gets her prince. *Ebony*, 62–63.

Giddings, P. (1984). *When and where I enter*. New York: William Morrow.

Gidengil, E. (1995). Economic man—social woman? The case of the gender gap in support for the Canada–United States Free Trade Agreement. *Comparative Political Studies, 28*, 384–408.

Gidycz, C. A., McNamara, J. R., & Edwards, K. M. (2006). Women's risk perception and sexual victimization: A review of the literature. *Aggression and Violent Behavior, 11*, 441–456.

Gilbert, L. A., & Scher, M. (1999). *Gender and sex in counseling and psychotherapy*. Boston: Allyn and Bacon.

Gilbert, M. J., & Collins, R. L. (1997). Ethnic variation in women's and men's drinking. In R. W. Wilsnack & S. C. Wilsnack (Eds.), *Gender and alcohol* (pp. 357–378). New Brunswick, NJ: Rutgers Center of Alcohol Studies.

Gilchrist, R. (1999). *Gender and archeology: Contesting the past*. New York: Routledge.

Giles, J. W., & Heyman, G. D. (2004). When to cry over spilled milk: Young children's use of category information to guide inference about ambiguous behavior. *Journal of Cognition and Development, 5*, 359–382.

Gilkes, C. T. (1985). Together and in harness: Women's traditions in the sanctified church. *Signs, 10*, 678–699.

Gill Foundation. (2001). *Out of the closet and into the voting booth: Lesbian, gay, bisexual and transgender voters in 2000*. Denver: Author.

Gill, R. (2008). Empowerment/sexism: Figuring female agency in contemporary advertising. *Feminism and Psychology, 18*, 35–60.

Gillen, M., & Kim, H. (2009). Older women and poverty transition: Consequences of income source changes from widowhood. *Journal of Applied Gerontology, 28*, 320–341.

Gilley, B. J. (2006). *Becoming Two-spirit: Gay identity and social acceptance in Indian country*. Lincoln: University of Nebraska Press.

Gilligan, C. (1982). *In a different voice: Psychological theory and women's development*. Cambridge, MA: Harvard University Press.

Gilligan, C., Lyons, N. P., & Hanmer, T. J. (Eds.) (1990). *Making connections: The relational worlds of adolescent girls at Emma Willard School*. Cambridge, MA: Harvard University Press.

Gilligan, C., Taylor, J. M., & Sullivan, A. (1995). *Between voice and silence: Women and girls, race and relationship*. Cambridge, MA: Harvard University Press.

Gillium, W. S. (2005). Pre kindergarteners left behind: Expulsion rates in state pre kindergartener systems. FCD policy brief series No. 3.

Gillum, R. F., Mussolino, M. E., & Madans, J. H. (1997). Coronary heart disease incidence and survival in African-American women and men. *Annals of Internal Medicine, 127*, 111–118.

Gilmore, D. O. (1990). *Manhood in the making*. New Haven, CT: Yale University Press.

Gimbutas, M. (1989). *The language of the goddess*. New York: Harper and Row.

Ginsberg, A. E. (Ed.) (2008). *The evolution of American women's studies: Reflections on triumphs, controversies and change*. New York: Palgrave Macmillan.

Ginzburg, C. (1991). *Ecstacies: Deciphering the witches' sabbath*. New York: Penguin.

Gipson, C. (2009). *Parenting practices of lesbian mothers: An examination of the socialization of children in planned lesbian-headed households*. Saarbrucken, Germany: VDM Verlag.

Girl, 14, wins case charging sex harassment. (1996, October 4). *New York Times*, p. A16.

Glass, R. (1982, January 24). Some fear abuses in premenstrual tension decisions. *Philadelphia Inquirer*, p. 8C.

Glauber, R. (2007). Marriage and the motherhood wage penalty among African Americans, Hispanics, and whites. *Journal of Marriage and Family, 69*(4), 951–961.

Glauber, R. (2008). Race and gender in families and at work: The fatherhood wage premium. *Gender & Society, 22*, 8–30.

Glaze, L. E., & Maruschak, L. M. (2008). *Parents in prison and their minor children*. Washington, DC: U.S. Department of Justice, Bureau of Justice Statistics. Available http://www.ojp.usdoj.gov/bjs/pub/pdf/pptmc.pdf

Glenn, D. (2004, April 30). A dangerous surplus of sons? *Chronicle of Higher Education*. Retrieved April 29, 2010, http://chronicle.com/article/A-Dangerous-Surplus-of-Sons-/8794/

Glenn, E. N. (1987). Gender and the family. In B. B. Hess & M. M. Ferree (Eds.), *Analyzing gender* (pp. 348–380). Newbury Park, CA: Sage.

Glenn, E. N. (1992). From servitude to service work: Historical continuities in the racial division of paid reproductive labor. *Signs, 18*, 1–43.

Glenn, S. A. (1990). *Daughter of the shtel: Life and labor in the immigrant generation*. Ithaca, NY: Cornell University Press.

Glod, M. (2009). Schools face sharp rise in homeless students. *Washington Post*. Retrieved from: http://www.washingtonpost.com/wp-dyn/

content/article/2009/02/07/AR2009020702015.
html?dis=ST2009020702072

GLSEN. (2009). *The experiences of lesbian, gay, bisexual and transgender middle school students* (GLSEN Research Brief). New York: Gay, Lesbian and Straight Education Network.

GLSEN. (2009, April 9). 11-year-old hangs himself after enduring daily anti-gay bullying. Retrieved from: http://www.glsenorg/cgi-ben/iowa/all/news/record2400.html

Gluck, S. B. (1987). *Rosie the riveter revisited*. New York: Twayne.

Gold, M. (1983). Sexism in gynecologic practices. In M. Fooden, S. Gordon, & B. Hughley (Eds.), *Genes and gender IV: The second X and women's health* (pp. 133–142). New York: Gordian.

Gold, R. (2010). Recession taking its toll: Family planning safety net stretched thin as service demand increases. *Guttmacher Policy Review, 13*(1), 8–12.

Goldberg, C. (1996b, October 5). Political battle of the sexes is sharper than ever: Suburbs' soccer moms, fleeing the G.O.P., are much sought. *New York Times*, pp. 1, 24.

Goldberg, C. (1999a, October 23). On web, models auction their eggs to bidders for beautiful children. *New York Times*, p. A11.

Goldberg, C. (1999b, November 5). Massachusetts case is latest to ask court to decide fate of frozen embryos. *New York Times*, p. A20.

Goldberg, C. (2000, November 5). Citing intolerance, obese people take steps to press cause. *New York Times*, pp. 1, 36.

Golden, S. (1992). *The women outside: Meanings and myths of homelessness*. Berkeley: University of California Press.

Goldhaber, M. K., Poland, M. R., &. Hialt, R. A. (1988). The risk of miscarriage and birth defects among women who use visual display terminals during pregnancy. *American Journal of Industrial Medicine, 13*, 695–706.

Goldie, J., Schwartz, L., & Morrison, J. (2004). Sex and the surgery: Students' attitudes and potential behaviour as they pass through a modern medical curriculum. *Journal of Medical Ethics, 30*(5), 480–486.

Goldin, C., Katz, L. F., & Kuziemko, I. (2006). The homecoming of American college women: The reversal of the college gender gap. *Journal of Economic Perspectives, 20*(4), 133–156.

Golding, J. M. (1988). Gender differences in depressive symptoms: Statistical considerations. *Psychology of Women Quarterly, 12*, 61–74.

Goldman, A. L. (1990a, June 26). Reform Judaism votes to accept active homosexuals in rabbinate. *New York Times*, pp. A1, A21.

Goldman, A. L. (1990b, September 19). A bar to women as cantors is lifted. *New York Times*, p. B2.

Goldman, R. (2009). George Sodini, alleged gym shooter "likely psychotic": Suspected shooter fits classic profile of neglected loner seeking attention. *ABC News*. Retrieved February 24, 2010, http://abcnews.go.com/US/story?id=8258525&page=1

Goldner, M. (1994). *Accounting for race and class variation in the disjuncture between feminist identity and feminist beliefs: The place of negative labels and social movements*. Paper presented at the annual meeting of the American Sociological Association, Los Angeles, CA.

Goldsmith, B. (1998). *Other powers*. New York: Alfred A. Knopf.

Goldstein, E. (2009). *New Jewish feminism: Probing the past, forging the future*. Woodstock, VT: Jewish Lights Publishing.

Goldstein, J. R., & Kenney, C. T. (2001). Marriage delayed or marriage foregone? New cohort forecasts of first marriage for U.S. women. *American Sociological Review, 66*, 506–519.

Goldstein, L. F. (1979). *The constitutional rights of women*. New York: Longman.

Goldstein, S. E., Malanchuk, O., Davis-Kean, P. E. & Eccles, J. S. (2007). Risk factors of sexual harassment by peers: A longitudinal investigation of African American and European American adolescents. *Journal of Research on Adolescence, 17*(2), 285–300.

Goldstein, S. E., Malanchuk, O., Davis-Kean, P. E., & Eccles, J. S. (2007). Risk factors of sexual harassment by peers: A longitudinal investigation of African American and European American adolescents. *Journal of Adolescence, 17*, 285–310.

Gole, N. (1996). *The forbidden modern: Civilization and veiling*. Ann Arbor: University of Michigan Press.

Goleman, D. (1996). *Emotional intelligence*. New York: Bantam Books.

Golombok, S., & Fivush, R. (1994). *Gender development*. New York: Cambridge University Press.

Golombok, S., & Tasker, F. (1996). Do parents influence the sexual orientation of their children? *Developmental Psychology, 32*, 3–11.

Golombok, S., Rust, J., Zervoulis, K., Croudace, T., Golding, J., & Hines, M. (2008). Developmental trajectories of sex-typed behavior in boys and girls: A longitudinal general population study of children aged 2.5–8 years. *Child Development, 79*(5), 1583–1593.

Golub, S. (1992). *Periods: From menarche to menopause.* Newbury Park, CA: Sage.

Gonzalez, M. C. (2009). Frozen embryos, divorce, and needed legislation: On the horizon or has it arrived? *Florida Bar Journal, 83*(4), 39–42.

Goode, E. (2000a, March 14). Human nature: Born or made? *New York Times,* pp. F1, F9.

Goode, E. (2000b, October 24). Watching volunteers, experts seek clues to eating disorders. *New York Times,* pp. A1, A6.

Goodenough, R. G. (1990). Situational stress and sexist behavior among young children. In P. R. Sanday & R. G. Goodenough (Eds.), *Beyond the second sex* (pp. 225–252). Philadelphia: University of Pennsylvania Press.

Goodkind, S., Ng, I., & Sarri, R. C. (2006). The impact of sexual abuse in the lives of young women involved or at risk of involvement with the juvenile justice system. *Violence Against Women, 12*(5), 456–77.

Goodman, C. C. (2007). Family dynamics in three-generation families. *Journal of Family Issues, 28*(3), 355–379.

Goodman, D. N. (2007). University of Michigan drops Affirmative Action for now school will continue its legal fight against a ban on the practice, however. *The Washington Post.* Retrieved February 18, 2010, http://www.washingtonpost.com/wp-dyn/content/article/2007/01/10/AR2007011002095.html

Goodman, L. A., Fels, K., & Glenn, C. (2006). *No safe place: Sexual assault in the lives of homeless women.* National Online Resource Center on Violence Against Women. Retrieved from: http://snow.vawnet.org/applied-research-papers/summary.php?doc_id=558&find_type=web_desc_AR

Goodman, P. S. (2010). Cuts to child care subsidy thwart more job seekers. *New York Times.* Retrieved from: http://www.nytimes.com/2010/05/24/business/economy/24childcare.html?_r=1&emc=eta1

Goodman, P.S. (2009). Foreclosures force ex-homeowners to turn to shelters. *New York Times.* Retrieved from: http://www.nytimes.com/2009/10/19/business/economy/19foreclosed.html

Goodson, P., McCormick, D., & Evans, A. (2001). Searching for sexually explicit materials on the internet: An exploratory study of college students' behavior and attitudes. *Archives of Sexual Behavior, 30*, 101–118.

Goodstein, L. (1992). Feminist perspectives and the criminal justice curriculum. *Journal of Criminal Justice Education, 3*, 165–182.

Goodstein, L. (1998, February 6). Unusual, but not unorthodox: Causing a stir, 2 synagogues hire women to assist rabbis. *New York Times,* pp. B1, 4.

Goodstein, L. (2000a, December 21). Women taking active role to study Orthodox Judaism. *New York Times,* A1, A29.

Goodstein, L. (2001, September 9). New Christian take on the old dating ritual. *New York Times,* pp. 1, 38.

Goodstein, L. (2005, October 15). Priests urged to recruit young men for the pulpit. *New York Times,* p. A12.

Goodstein, L. (2006, December 7). Conservative Jews allow gay rabbis and unions. *New York Times,* p. A24.

Goodstein, L. (2007, September 3). In new prayer book, signs of broad change. *New York Times,* p. A8.

Goodstein, L. (2009, August 11). New nuns and priests seen opting for tradition. *New York Times,* p. A12.

Goodstein, L. (2009a, August 11). New nuns and priests seen opting for tradition. *New York Times,* p. A12.

Goodstein, L. (2009b, July 1). U.S. nuns facing Vatican scrutiny. Retrieved from: http://www.nytimes.com/2009/07/02/us/02nuns.html?scp=10&sq=Catholic&st=nyt

Goodwin, J. (1994). *Price of honor.* Boston: Little, Brown.

Gordon, L. (1976). *Woman's body, Woman's right.* New York: Grossman Publishers.

Gordon, M. R. (1990, January 4). Woman leads G.I.'s in Panama combat. *New York Times,* p. A12.

Gordon, M. T., & Riger, S. (1991). *The female fear: The social cost of rape.* Urbana: University of Illinois Press.

Gorgan, E. (2009). *Body Image Takes a Hit After Viewing Thin Women on TV, Softpedia,* Retrieved from http://news.softpedia.com/news/Body-Image-Takes-a-Hit-After-Viewing-Thin-Women-on-TV-119497.shtml

Gornick, M. E., Eggers, P. W., Reilly, T. W., Mentneck, R. M., Fitterman, L. K., Kucken, L. E., & Vladeck, B. C. (1996). Effects of race and income on mortality and use of services among Medicare beneficiaries. *New England Journal of Medicine, 335*, 791–799.

Gortmaker, S. L., Must, A., Perrin, J. M., Sobol, A. M., & Dietz, W. H. (1993). Social and economic consequences of overweight in adolescence and young adulthood. *New England Journal of Medicine, 329*, 1008–1012.

Gottschalk, L. J. (2007). Carol Gilligan-psychologist, feminist, educator, philosopher: A research guide. *Behavioral & Social Sciences Librarian, 26*(1), 65–90.

Gough, K. (1975). The origin of the family. In R. R. Reiter (Ed.), *Toward an anthropology of women* (pp. 51–76). New York: Monthly Review Press.

Gould, S. J. (1980). *The panda's thumb.* New York: W. W. Norton.

Gould, S. J. (1981). *The mismeasure of man.* New York: W. W. Norton.

Grace, D. M., David, B. J., & Ryan, M. K. (2008). Investigating preschoolers' categorical thinking about gender through imitation, attention, and the use of self-categories. *Child Development, 79*(6), 1928–1941.

Grady, D. (2002). A 60-year-old woman trying to discontinue hormone replacement therapy. *Journal of the American Medical Association, 287*, 2130–2137.

Graham, E. (1986, June). African women fight clitoris cutting. *Off Our Backs*, p. 18–19.

Graham, I. (2010). *The average salaries of NBA players.* Retrieved from http://www.ehow.com/about_6506243_average-salaries-nba-players.html

Graham, P. A. (1978). Expansion and exclusion: A history of women in American higher education. *Signs, 3*, 759–773.

Graham, R. (2006). Male rape and the careful construction of the male victim. *Social and Legal Studies, 15*, 187–208.

Grant, J. (1986). Black women and the church. In J. B. Cole (Ed.), *All American women* (pp. 359–369). New York: Free Press.

Gravois, J. (2007). U. of Missouri at Kansas City settles sexual-harassment lawsuit for $1.1-million. *Chronicle of Higher Education, 53*, 47.

Gray, M. (1979). *Margaret Sanger.* New York: Richard Marek Publishers.

Greeley, A. M. (1990). *The Catholic myth.* New York: Charles Scribner's Sons.

Green, J. (1993, June 13). Out and organized. *New York Times*, pp. V1, V7.

Green, L., & Taylor, J. (2010). Exploring the relationship between gender and child health: A comparative analysis of high and low economic resource countries. In Featherstone, B., Hooper, C., Scourfield, J., & Taylor, J. (Eds.), *Gender and child welfare in society* (pp. 27–60). West Sussex, UK: John Wiley & Sons Ltd.

Greenberg, J. (2000, May 25). Israeli high court rules for women's services at Western Wall. *New York Times*, p. A6.

Greene, A. D. & Mickelson, R. A. (2006). Connecting pieces of the puzzle: Gender differences in Black middle school students' achievement. *Journal of Negro Education, 75*, 34–48.

Greenfeld, L. A. (1996). *Child victimizers: Violent offenders and their victims.* Washington, DC: U. S. Department of Justice, Bureau of Justice Statistics.

Greenfeld, L. A. (1998). *Violence by intimates.* Washington, DC: U.S. Department of Justice, Bureau of Justice Statistics.

Greenfeld, L. A., & Snell, T. L. (1999). *Women offenders.* Washington, DC: U.S. Department of Justice, Bureau of Justice Statistics.

Greenfeld, L. A. (1997). *Sex offenders and offenses.* Washington, DC: U.S. Department of Justice, Bureau of Justice Statistics.

Greenhouse, L. (1998, March 5). High court widens workplace claims in sex harassment. *New York Times*, pp. A1, 18.

Greenhouse, L. (2006, August 30). Women suddenly scarce among justices' clerks. *New York Times*, pp. A!, A16.

Greenhouse, S. (1993, November 14). If the French can do it, why can't we? *New York Times Magazine*, pp. 59–62.

Greenhouse, S. (2009). Recession drives women back to the workforce. *New York Times*. Retrieved November 10, 2010, http://www.nytimes.com/2009/09/19/business/19women.html?pagewanted=2&_r=1

Greer, G. (1992). *The change.* New York: Alfred A. Knopf.

Greer, J., Hardin, M., & Horman, C. (2009). *"Naturally" less exciting? Visual production of men's and women's track and field coverage during the 2004 Olympics.* Retrieved from http://www.allbusiness.com/sports-recreation/amateur-sports-olympics-summer/12387901-1.html

Greif, G. L. (1985). *Single fathers.* Lexington, MA: Lexington Books.

Grella, C. (1999). Women in residential drug treatment: Differences by program type and pregnancy. *Journal of Health Care for the Poor and Underserved, 10*(2) 216–229.

Greytak, E. A., Kosciw, J. G., & Diaz, E. M. (2009). *Harsh realities: The experiences of transgender youth in our nation's schools*. New York: The Gay, Lesbian and Straight Education Network.

Griffin, L. W., Williams, O. J., & Reed, J. G. (1998). Abuse of African American elders. In R. K. Bergen (Ed.), *Issues in intimate violence* (pp. 267–284). Thousand Oaks, CA: Sage.

Griffin, M. L., & Rodriguez, N. (2008). The gendered nature of drug acquisition behavior within marijuana and crack drug markets. *Crime & Delinquency*. Available online.

Griffin, S. (1995). *The eros of everyday life*. New York: Doubleday.

Griffith, R., & Tengnah, C. (2009). The Female Genital Mutilation Act 2003: An overview for district nurses. *British Journal of Community Nursing, 14*(2), 86–89.

Grigsby, J. S. (1992, November). Women change places. *American Demographics*, pp. 46–50.

Grodsky, E., & Pager, D. (2001). The structure of disadvantage: Individual and occupational determinants of the Black-White wage gap. *American Sociological Review, 66*, 542–567.

Grogan, S. (2007). *Body image: Understanding body dissatisfaction in men, women and children*. New York: Taylor and Francis.

Gross, J. (1992, December 7). Divorced, middle-aged and happy: Women, especially, adjust to the 90s. *New York Times*, p. A14.

Gross, J. (1994, January 4). Gay candidate making history in a state race. *New York Times*, p. A6.

Gross, L. (1991). Out of the mainstream: Sexual minorities and the mass media. *Journal of Homosexuality, 21*, 19–46.

Gruber, E., & Thau, H. (2003). Sexually related content on television and adolescents of color: Media theory, physiological development, and psychological impact. *The Journal of Negro Education, 72*(4), 438–456.

Gruber, J. E. (1998). The impact of male work environments and organizational policies on women's experiences of sexual harassment. *Gender & Society, 12*, 301–320.

Gruber, J. E., & Fineran, S. (2008). Comparing the impact of bullying and sexual harassment victimization on the mental and physical health of adolescents. *Sex Roles, 59*, 1–13.

Gruber, J.E., & Morgan, P. (Eds.). *In the company of men: Male dominance and sexual harassment*. Boston: Northeastern University Press.

Guerrier, Y., Evans, C., Glover, J., & Wilson, C. (2009). "Technical, but not very . . ." Constructing gendered identities in IT-related employment. *Work, Employment and Society, 23*, 494–511.

Gump, B. B., & Matthews, K. (2000). Are vacations good for your health? The 9-year mortality experience after the multiple risk factor intervention trial. *Psychosomatic Medicine, 62*, 608–612.

Gunzelmann, B., & Connell, D. (2006). How are the boys doing? The new gender gap: Social, psychological, neuro-biological, and educational perspectives. *Educational Horizons, 84*(2), 94–101.

Gurian, A. (2011). *Depression in adolescence: Does gender matter?* Retrieved from http://www.aboutourkids.org/articles/depression_in_adolescence_does_gender_matter

Gurian, A. (2011). Depression in adolescence: Does gender matter? New York: New York University Child Study Center. Retrieved from: http://www.aboutourkids.org/articles/depression_in_adolescence_does_gender_matter

Gurian, M., Henley, P., & Trueman, T. (2002). *Boys and girls learn differently: A guide for teachers and parents*. San Francisco: Jossey-Bass.

Gutierrez-Lobos, K., Wolfl, G., Scherer, M., Anderer, P. & Schmidl-Mohl, B. (2000). The gender gap in depression reconsidered: The influence of marital and employment status on the female/male ratio of treated incidence rates. *Social Psychiatry Psychiatrics Epidemiology, 35*(5) 202–210.

Gutis, P. S. (1989, August 31). What is a family? Traditional limits are being redrawn. *New York Times*, pp. C1, C6.

Guttmacher Institute. (2008a, July). Facts on induced abortion. Washington, DC: Guttmacher Institute. Retrieved October 27, 2009, from http://www.guttmacher.org

Haardt, M. (2004). A sense of belonging: On the challenging complexity of women and church. *International Journal for the Study of the Christian Church*, 4, 249–261.

Haarr, R. (2005). Factors affecting the decision of police recruits to "dropout" of police work. *Police Quarterly, 8*, 431–453.

Haarr, R. N., & Morash, M. (1999). Gender, race, and strategies of coping with occupational stress in policing. *Justice Quarterly, 16*, 303–336.

Haddad, Y. Y. (1985). Islam, women and revolution in twentieth-century Arab thought. In Y. Y. Haddad & E. B. Findly (Eds.),*Women, religion and social change*. (pp. 275–306). Albany: State University of New York Press.

Hager, L. (2008). "Saving the World Before Bedtime": The Powerpuff Girls, citizenship, and the little girl superhero. *Children's Literature Association Quarterly*, 62–78.

Hains, R. C. (2008). Bratz. In *Girl culture: An encyclopedia*, C. A. Mitchell & J. Reid-Walsh. (Eds.) (pp. 200–202). Westport, CT: Greenwood Press.

Hale-Benson, J. E. (1986). *Black children: Their roots, culture and learning styles* (rev. ed.). Provo, UT: Brigham Young University Press.

Haley Barton, R., & Hybels, L. (2007). *Longing for more: A woman's path to tranformation in Christ*. Downers Grove, IL: InterVarsity Press.

Hall, E. J., & Rodriguez, M. S. (2003). The myth of postfeminism. *Gender & Society, 17*, 878–902.

Hall, J., & Roter, D. (2002). Do patients talk differently to male and female physicians? A meta-analytic review. *Patient Education and Counseling, 48*(3), 217–224.

Hall, L. (1992). Beauty quests—A double disservice: Beguiled, beseeched, bombarded—Challenging the concept of beauty. In D. Dreidger & S. Gray (Eds.), *Imprinting our image: An international anthology by women with disabilities* (pp. 134–139). Toronto: gynergy books.

Hall, R. M., &. Sandler, B. R. (1985). A chilly climate in the classroom. In A. G. Sargent (Ed.), *Beyond sex roles* (pp. 503–510). New York: West.

Halpern-Felsher, B. L., Cornell, J. L., Kropp, R. Y., & Tschann, J. M. (2005). Oral versus vaginal sex among adolescents: Perceptions, attitudes and behavior. *Pediatrics, 115*, 4, 845–851.

Hamer, D. H., Hu, S., Magnuson, V. L., & Pattatucii, A.M.L. (1993). A linkage between DNA markers on the *X* chromosome and male sexual orientation. *Science, 261*, 321–327.

Hamilton, B. E., Martin, J. A., & Ventura, S. J. (2009, March). Births: Preliminary data for 2007. *National Vital Statistics Reports, 57*, 12. Hyattsville, MD: National Center for Health Statistics.

Hamilton, M. C. (1988). Using masculine generics: Does generic "he" increase male bias in the user's imagery? *Sex Roles, 19*, 785–799.

Hamilton, M., Anderson, D., Broaddus, M., & Young, K. (2006). Gender stereotyping and under-representation of female characters in 200 popular children's picture books: A twenty-first century update. *Sex Roles, 55*, 757–765.

Hammer, L. B., Cullen, J. C., Neal, M. B., Sinclair, R. R., & Shafiro, M. V. (2005). The longitudinal effects of work-family conflict and positive spillover on depressive symptoms among dual-earner couples. *Journal of Occupational Health, 10*, 138–154.

Hammerschmidt, A. (2009). No pain, no gain: An R & D model with endogenous absorptive capacity. *Journal of Institutional and Theoretical Economics JITE, 165*(5) 418–437.

Hampton, T. (2008). Abstinence-only programs under fire. *Journal of the American Medical Association, 299*, 2013–2015.

Handsman, R. G. (1991). Whose art was found at Lepinski Vir? Gender relations and power in archeology. In J. M. Gero & M. W. Conkey (Eds.), *Engendering archeology* (pp. 329–365). New York: Basil Blackwell.

Handwerk, P., Tognatta, N., & Coley, R. J. (2008). *Access to success: Patterns of advanced placement participation in U.S. high schools*. Princeton, NJ: Educational Testing Service.

Haney, D. Q. (1996a, March 28). Heart disease worse for Blacks. *Chattanooga Times*, p. F4.

Hanna, E., DiFranco, E., Meehan, B., & Sotelo, N. (2011). Catholics protest nationwide during Holy Week in support of women priests. Retrieved from: http://cta-usa.org/media/Media-Savannah-PressRelease-Apr11.pdf

Hansen, F. J., & Reekie, L. (1990). Sex differences in clinical judgments of male and female therapists. *Sex Roles, 23*, 51–64.

Hansen, J. (2010). Ladies, forget maternity leave. *Sunday Telegraph*. Retrieved February 27, 2011, http://www.dailytelegraph.com.au/news/ladies-forget-maternity-leave/story-e6freuy9–1225926011850

Hanson, S. M. H. (1988). Divorced fathers with custody. In P. Bronstein & C. P. Cowan (Eds.), *Fatherhood today: Men's changing role in the family* (pp. 166–194). New York: John Wiley.

Hanton, S., Neil, R., & Mellalieu, S. (2008). Recent developments in competitive anxiety direction and competition stress research. *International Review of Sport and Exercise Psychology, 1*, 45–57.

Haraway, D. (1989). *Primate visions*. New York: Routledge.

Hardesty, J. L. (2002). Separation assault in the context of postdivorce parenting. *Violence Against Women, 8*, 597–625.

Hardie, E. A. (1997). Prevelance and predictors of cyclic and noncyclic affective change. *Psychology of Women Quarterly, 21*, 299–314.

Harding, N. (2009). *Who is under more pressure: The breadwinner or the homemaker? Nick Harding and his wife do the stress test*. Retrieved from http://www.dailymail.co.uk/femail/article-1153566/

Who-pressure-breadwinner-homemaker-Nick-Harding-wife-stress-test-.html

Harding, S. G. (1979). Is the equality of opportunity principle democratic? *Philosophical Forum, 10*, 206–223.

Hargreaves, M., Homer, M., & Swinnerton, B. (2008). A comparison of performance and attitudes in mathematics amongst the "gifted". Are boys better at mathematics or do they just think they are? *Assessment in Education: Principles, Policy & Practice, 15*, 1, 19–38.

Harned, M. (2005). Understanding women's labeling of unwanted sexual experiences with dating partners: A qualitative analysis. *Violence Against Women, 11*, 374–413.

Harp, D. (2007). *Desperately seeking women readers: U.S. newspapers and the construction of a female readership*. Lanham, MD: Lexington Books.

Harper, S. R.; Patton, L. D., & Wooden, O. S. (2009). Access and equity for African American students in higher education: A critical race historical analysis of policy efforts. *Journal of Higher Education, 80*, 4, 389–414.

Harrington, A. (1987). *Medicine, mind, and the double brain*. Princeton, NJ: Princeton University Press.

Harrington, M. (1962). *The other America*. New York: Macmillan.

Harris, J. (1993, March 28). The babies of Bedford. *New York Times Magazine*, p. 26.

Harris, J. (2004). *On cloning: Thinking in action*. London: Routledge.

Harris, K., & Barnes, S. (2009). Male teacher, female teacher: Exploring children's perspectives of teachers' roles in kindergartens. *Early Child Development and Care, 179*, 2, 167–181.

Harris, M. (1993). The evolution of human gender hierarchies: A trial formulation. In B. D. Miller (Ed.), *Sex and gender hierarchies* (pp. 57–80). New York: Cambridge University Press.

Harris, M. B. (Ed.) (1997). *School experiences of gay and lesbian youth: The invisible minority*. New York: Harrington Park Press.

Harris, M. B., & Knight-Bohnhoff, K. (1996). Gender and aggression II: Personal aggressiveness. *Sex Roles, 35*, 27–41.

Harrison, J. B. (1984). Warning: The male sex role may be dangerous to your health. In J. M. Swanson & K. A. Forrest (Eds.), *Men's reproductive health.* (pp. 11–27). New York: Springer.

Harrison, P. M., & Beck, J. A. (2006). *Prisoners in 2005*. Washington, DC: U.S. Department of Justice, Bureau of Justice Statistics.

Hart, M. M. (1980). Sport: Women sit in the back of the bus. In D. F. Sabo & R. Runfola (Eds.), *Jock: Sports and male identity* (pp. 205–211). Englewood Cliffs, NJ: Prentice-Hall.

Hartjen, C. A. (1978). *Crime and criminalization*. New York: Holt, Rinehart and Winston.

Hartmann, H. I.,. Roos, P. A., & Treiman, D. J. (1985). An agenda for basic research on comparable worth. In H. I. Hartmann (Ed.), *Comparable worth: New directions for research* (pp. 3–33). Washington, DC: National Academy Press.

Hartmann, H. I. (1987). Internal labor markets and gender: A case study of promotion. In C. Brown & A. Pechman (Eds.), *Gender in the workplace* (pp. 59–106). Washington, DC: Brooking Institute.

Hassouneh, D., & Glass, N. (2008). The influence of gender role stereotyping on women's experiences of female same-sex intimate partner violence. *Violence Against Women, 14*(3), 310–325.

Hatziavramidis, K. (2007). Parental involvement laws for abortion in the United States and the United Nations conventions on the rights of the child: Can international law secure the right to choose for minors? *Texas Journal of Women and the Law, 16*, 185, 202–203.

Haupt, A. (2010). *'Type D' personality: How distress affects your health*. Retrieved from http://health.usnews.com/health-news/family-health/heart/articles/2010/09/14/type-d-personality-how-distress-affects-your-health

Haver, B., Gjestad, R., Lindberg, S., & Franck, J. (2009). Mortality risk up to 25 years after treatment among 420 Swedish women with alcohol addiction. *Addiction, 104*(3) 413–419.

Hawkesworth, M. (1997). Challenging the received wisdom and the status quo: Creating and implementing sexual harassment policy. *NWSA Journal, 9*, 94–117.

Hawkins, D. N., & Booth, A. (2005). Unhappily ever after: Effects of long-term, low-quality marriages on well-being. *Social Forces, 84*, 451–471.

Hawkins, D. N., Amato, P. R., & King, V. (2006). Parent-adolescent involvement: The relative influence of parent gender and residence. *Journal of Marriage and Family, 68*, 125–136.

Hayden, S. (1994). Interruptions and the construction of reality. In L. H. Turner & H. M. Sterk (Eds.), *Differences that make a difference* (pp. 99–106). Westport, CT: Bergin and Garvey.

Hayslip, B., & Kaminski, P. L. (2005). Grandparents raising their grandchildren: A review of the literature and suggestions for practice. *Gerontologist, 45*, 262–269.

Healy, P., & Rimer, S. (2005, February 18). Furor lingers as Harvard chief gives details of talk on women. *New York Times*, pp. A1, A16.

Healy, P. D. (2005, April 17). Gay Republicans soldier on, one skirmish at a time. *New York Times*, p. WK3.

Hegewisch, A., Liepman, H., Hayes, J., & Hartmann, H.I. (2010). *Separate and not equal? Gender segregation in the labor market and the gender wage gap*. Washington, DC: Institute for Women's Policy Research.

Heidensohn, F. (1992). *Women in control? The role of women in law enforcement*. New York: Oxford University Press.

Height, D. (1989, July 24–31). Family and community: Self-help—A Black tradition. *Nation, 249*, 136–138.

Heilbronn, L. et al. (2006). Effect of 6-month calorie restriction on biomarkers of longevity, metabolic adaptation, and oxidative stress in overweight individuals. *Journal of the American Medical Association, 295*, d1539–1548.

Heilbrun, K., Dematteo, D., Fretz, R., Erickson, J., Yasuhara, K., & Anumbra, N. (2008). How "specific" are gender-specific rehabilitation needs? An empirical analysis. *Criminal Justice and Behavior, 35*, 1382–1397.

Heilman, M. E., & Okimoto, T. G. (2007). Why are women penalized for success at male tasks?: The implied communality deficit. *Journal of Applied Psychology, 92*(1), 81–92.

Hekma, G., & van der Meer, T. (1992). Gay and lesbian studies in the Netherlands. In H. L. Minton (Ed.), *Gay and lesbian studies* (pp. 125–136). New York: Haworth Press.

Hekmat, A. (1997). *Women and the Koran*. Amherst, NY: Prometheus Books.

Helgeson, V. S. (1990). The role of masculinity in a prognostic predictor of heart attack severity. *Sex Roles, 22*, 755–774.

Helgeson, V. S. (1994). Long-distance romantic relationships: Sex differences in adjustment and breakup. *Personality and Social Psychology Bulletin, 20*, 254–265.

Helgeson, V. S. (1995). Masculinity, men's roles, and coronary heart disease. In D. Sabo & D. F. Gordon (Eds.), *Men's health and illness* (pp. 68–104). Thousand Oaks, CA: Sage.

Hellinger, D., & Judd, D. R. (1991). *The democratic facade*. Pacific Grove, CA: Brooks/Cole.

Helweg-Larsen, M., Cunningham, S., Carrico, A., & Pergram, A. (2004). To nod or not to nod: An observational study of nonverbal communication and status in female and male college students. *Psychology of Women Quarterly, 28*, 358–361.

Henig, R. M. (1993, October 3). Are women's hearts different? *New York Times Magazine*, pp. 58–61, 68–69, 82, 86.

Henley, N., Hamilton, M., & Thorne, B. (1985). Womanspeak and manspeak: Sex differences and sexism in communication. In A. G. Sargent (Ed.), *Beyond sex roles* (pp. 168–185). New York: West.

Henshaw, S. K. (1995). Factors hindering access to abortion services. *Family Planning Perspectives, 27*, 54–59, 87.

Henson, K. D., & Krasas Rogers, J. (2001). "Why Marcia you've changed!" Male clerical temporary workers doing masculinity in a feminized occupation. *Gender & Society, 15*, 218–238.

Herbert, W. (1999, November 29). Making stepfamilies work. *U.S. News & World Report*. Available online: http://www.usnews.com

Herdt, G. H., & Davidson, J. (1988). The Sambra 'Turnim-man': Sociocultural and clinical aspects of gender formation in male pseudohermaphrodites with 5 alpha-reductase deficiency in Papua New Guinea. *Archives of Sexual Behavior, 17*, 33–56.

Herdt, G. H. (1994). *Third sex, third gender: Beyond sexual dimorphism in culture and history*. New York: Zone Books.

Herek, G. M. (1991). Myths about sexual orientation: A lawyer's guide to social science research. *Law and Sexuality, 1*, 133–172.

Herek, G. M. (2000). The psychology of sexual prejudice. *Current Directions in Psychological Science, 9*, 19–22.

Herek, G. M., & Capitanio, J. P. (1999). Sex differences in how heterosexuals think about lesbians and gay men: Evidence from survey context effects. *Journal of Sex Research, 36*, 348–360.

Herek, G. M., & Glunt, E. K. (1997). An epidemic of stigma: Public reaction to AIDS. In P. Conrad (Ed.), *The sociology of health and illness* (pp. 125–132). New York: St. Martin's Press.

Herman, J. L. (1988). Considering sex offenders: A model of addiction. *Signs, 13*, 695–724.

Herr, N. (2007). *Television & health, internet resources to accompany the sourcebook for teaching science*. Retrieved from http://www.csun.edu/science/health/docs/tv&health.html

Herz, B., & Sperling, G.B.(2004). *What works in girls' education:* Evidence and policies from the developing world. New York: Council on Foreign Relations.

Hess, B. B., & Ferree, M. M. (1987). Introduction. In B. B. Hess & M. M. Ferree (Eds.), *Analyzing gender* (pp. 9–30). Newbury Park, CA: Sage.

Hesse-Biber, S. (1989). Eating patterns and disorders in a college population: Are college women's eating problems a new phenomenon? *Sex Roles, 20,* 71–89.

Hetsroni, A. (2007). Three decades of sexual content on prime-time network programming: A longitudinal meta-analytic review. *Journal of Communication, 57*(2), 318–348.

Hibel, J., Farkas, C., & Morgan, P. (2006). *Who is placed into special education?* (Working Paper No. 06- 05). University Park: Pennsylvania State University Population Institute.

Hickey, E. (2003). *Encyclopedia of Murder and Violent Crime.* Thousand Oaks, California: Sage Publications.

Hicks, J. P. (1998, February 9). Road gets tougher for political pioneer. *New York Times,* p. B3.

Hiemstra, R., Goodman, M., Middlemiss M. A., Vosko, R., & Ziegler, N., (2010). How older persons are portrayed in television advertising: Implications for educators, *Educational Gerontology,* 9 111–122.

Higgenbotham, E. B. (1993). *Righteous discontent.* Cambridge, MA: Harvard University Press.

Higgins, P. J. (1985). Women in the Islamic Republic of Iran: Legal, social, and ideological changes. *Signs, 10,* 477–494.

Hildreth, C. J., Burke, A. E., & Glass, R. M. (2009). Elder abuse. *Journal of the American Medical Association, 302,* 588.

Hilinski, C. M. (2009). Fear of crime among college students: A test of the shadow of sexual assault hypothesis. *American Journal of Criminal Justice, 34,* 84–102.

Hill, C., & Silva, E. (2005). *Drawing the line: Sexual harassment on campus.* Washington, DC: AAUW Educational Foundation.

Hill, C., & Warbelow, S. (2008). Tenure denied: Cases of sex discrimination in academia. *American Academic, 4,* 65–104.

Hill, M. A. (1980). *Charlotte Perkins Gilman: The making of a radical feminist, 1860–1896.* Philadelphia: Temple University Press.

Hill, S. A. (1999). *African American children: Socialization and development in families.* Thousand Oaks, CA: Sage.

Hill, S. A., & Sprague, J. S. (1999). Parenting in Black and White families: The interaction of gender with race and class. *Gender & Society, 13,* 480–502.

Hill, S. A. (2005). *Black intimacies: A gender perspective on families and relationships.* Lanham, MD: AltaMira Press.

Hillis, J. (2007). *Gay newsmen—A clearer picture, after Elton: The pop culture site that plays for your team.* Retrieved from http://www.afterelton.com/TV/2007/5/gaytvnewsmen?page=0,2

Hinduja, S., & Patchin, J. W. (2008a). *Bullying beyond the schoolyard: Preventing and responding to cyberbullying.* Thousand Oaks, CA: Corwin Press.

Hinduja, S., & Patchin, J. W. (2008b). Cyberbullying: An explanatory analysis of factors related to offending and victimization. *Deviant Behavior, 29,* 129–156.

Hine, D. C. (1989). *Black women in white: Racial conflict and cooperation in the nursing profession, 1890–1950.* Bloomington: Indiana University Press.

Hine, D. C., & Thompson, K. (Eds.) (1997). *A shining thread of hope: The history of Black women in America.* New York: Broadway Books.

Hines, M., & Kaufman, F. R. (1994). Androgen and the development of human sex-typical behavior: Rough-and-tumble play and sex of preferred playmates in children with congenital adrenal hyperplasia (CAH). *Child Development, 65,* 1042–1053.

Hirsch, M., & Keller, E. F. (1990). Conclusion: Practicing conflict in feminist theory. In M. Hirsch & E. F. Keller (Eds.), *Conflicts in feminism* (pp. 370–385). New York: Routledge.

Hochschild, A. R. (1989). *The second shift.* New York: Viking.

Hochschild, A. R. (1997). *The time bind: When work becomes home and home becomes work.* New York: Henry Holt and Company.

Hochschild, A., & Machung, A. (2003). *The second shift.* New York: Penguin.

Hodge, J. (2011). *Gendered hate: Exploring gender in hate crime law.* Boston: Northeastern University Press.

Hoeksma, N. (2005). *Regulating risk: Reproductive toxins in the workplace in the post-Johnson Controls era.* Retrieved from: http://heinonline.org/HOL/LandingPage?collection=journals&handle=hein.journals/scws14&div=15&id=&page=

Hoffman, F., & Oreopoulos, P. (2009). A professor like me: The influence of instructor gender on college achievement. *The Journal of Human Resources, 44*, 2, 479–494.

Hoffman, J. (1996, January 8). Egg donations meet a need and raise ethical questions. *New York Times*, pp. 1, 10.

Hoff-Wilson, J. (1987). The unfinished revolution: Changing legal status of U.S. women. *Signs, 13*, 7–36.

Hogan, N. L. et al. (2005). Is there a difference? Exploring male and female correctional officers' definition of and response to conflict situations. *Women and Criminal Justice, 15*, 143–165.

Holcomb, J. E., Williams, M. R., Demuth, S. (2004). White female victims and death penalty disparity research. *Justice Quarterly, 21*, 877–902.

Holden, C. (1987). Why do women live longer than men? *Science, 238*, 158–160.

Holden, K. C., & Smock, P. J. (1991). The economic costs of marital dissolution: Why do women bear a disproportionate cost? *Annual Review of Sociology, 17*, 51–78.

Hole, J., & Levine, E. (1984). The first feminists. In J. Freeman (Ed.), *Women: A feminist perspective* (pp. 533–542). Palo Alto, CA: Mayfield.

Holloman, J. L. S. (1983). Access to health care. In President's commission for the study of ethical problems in medicine and biomedical research. *Securing Access to Health Care* (pp. 79–106). Washington, DC: U.S. Government Printing Office.

Holmes, S. A. (1996, December 27). With more women in prison, sexual abuse by guards becomes a troubling trend. *New York Times*, p. A18.

Holmes, S. A. (1998, April 15). FCC requirement on minority hiring is voided by court. *New York Times*, pp. A1, 22.

Holmstrom, A. J. (2009). Sex and Gender Similarities and Differences in Communication Values in Same-Sex and Cross-Sex Friendships. *Communication Quarterly, 57*(2), 224–238.

Holub, S. C., Tisak, M. S., & Mullins, D. (2008). Gender differences in children's hero attributions: Personal hero choices and evaluations of typical male and female heroes. *Sex Roles, 58*, 567–578.

Hondagneu-Sotelo, P. (2008). *God's heart has no borders: How religious activists are working for immigrant rights*. Berkeley: University of California Press.

Hood, E. F. (1984). Black women, White women: Separate paths to liberation. In A. M. Jaggar & P. S. Rothenberg (Eds.), *Feminist frameworks* (pp. 189–201). New York: McGraw-Hill.

Hook, J. L., & Chalasani, S. (2008). Gendered expectations? Reconsidering single fathers' childcare time. *Journal of Marriage and Family, 70*, 978–990.

Hooks, b. (1990). A conversation about race and class. In M. Hirsch & E. F. Keller (Eds.), *Conflicts in feminism* (pp. 60–81). New York: Routledge.

Hooper, J. (2010). *Vatican makes attempted ordination of women a grave crime*. Retrieved from: http://www.guardian.co.uk/world/2010/jul/15/vatican-attempted-ordination-women-grave-crime

Hootman, J. M. (2001). Prevalence of disabilities and associated health conditions among adults—United States, 1999. *Morbidity and Mortality Weekly Report, 50*, 120–125.

Hope, D. (2010). The vast majority of Americans watch videos online. *Christian Science Monitor*. Retrieved September 13, 2010, http://www.csmonitor.com/Science/2010/0603/The-vast-majority-of-Americans-watch-videos-online

Horan, S. M., Houser, M. L, & Cowan, R. L. (2005). Are children communicated with equally? An investigation of parent-child sex composition and gender role communication differences. *Communication Research Reports, 24*(4), 361–372.

Horne, P. (2006). Policewomen: Their first century and new era. *Police Chief, 73*, 1–10.

Horner, M. S. (1972). Toward an understanding of achievement-related conflicts in women. *Journal of Social Issues, 28*, 157–175.

Horney, K. (1967). *Feminine psychology*. New York: Norton.

Horwitz, A. V. (1982). Sex-role expectations, power, and psychological distress. *Sex Roles, 8*, 607–623.

Hosp, J. L., & Reschly, D. J. (2004). Disproportionate representation of minority students in special education: Academic, demographic, and economic predictors. *Exceptional Children, 70*, 185–199.

House, J. S. (1986). Occupational stress and coronary heart disease: A review and theoretical integration. In P. Conrad & R. Kern (Eds.), *The sociology of health and illness* (pp. 64–72). New York: St. Martin's Press.

Houston Barrett, R., & Stuchell, S. (2007). *Current research: Mother who work*. Retrieved from http://www.aamftca.org/main/pdf/mother-swhowork.pdf

Houts, M. (2010). *Feminine images for God: What does the Bible say?* Retrieved from: http://clubs.calvin.edu/chimes/970418/o1041897.htm

Houts, M., &. Greeley, A. M. (1987). The center doesn't hold: Church attendance in the United States, 1940–1984. *American Sociological Review, 52,* 325–345.

Howe, F. (1984). *Myths of coeducation.* Bloomington: University of Indiana Press.

Howe, K. (1985). The psychological impact of a women's studies course. *Women's Studies Quarterly, 13,* 23–24.

Hoyenga, K. B., & Hoyenga, K. T. (1993). *Gender-related differences.* Boston: Allyn and Bacon.

http://www.uis.unesco.org/template/pdf/EducGeneral/UISFactsheet_2008_No%201_EN.pdf

Hu, S., Pattatucci, A. M. L., Patterson, C., Li, L., Fulker, D. W., Cherny, S. S., Kruglyak, L., & Hamer, D. H. (1995). Linkage between sexual orientation and chromosome *Xq*28 in males but not in females. *Nature Genetics, 11,* 248–256.

Hu, Y., & Goldman, N. (1990). Mortality differentials by marital status: An international comparison. *Demography, 27,* 233–250.

Hubbard, R. (1979). Have only men evolved? In R. Hubbard, M. S. Henifin, & B. Fried (Eds.), *Women look at biology looking at women* (pp. 7–36). Cambridge, MA: Schenkman.

Hubbard, R. (1990). The political nature of human nature. In D. L. Rhode (Ed.), *Theoretical perspectives on sexual difference* (pp. 63–73). New Haven, CT: Yale University Press.

Hubbard, R., & Wald, E. (1993). *Exploding the gene myth.* Boston: Beacon Press.

Huerta, M., Cortina, L. M., Pang, J. S., Torges, C. M., & Magley, V. J. (2006). Sex and power in the academy: Modeling sexual harassment in the lives of college women. *Personality and Social Psychology Bulletin, 32*(5), 616–628.

Huffaker, D., & Calvert, S. L. (2005). Gender, identity, and language use in teenage blogs. *Journal of Computer-mediated Communication, 10,* 00. Doi:10.1111/j.1083-6101.2005.tb00238.x.

Huffman, M. L., Cohen, P. N., & Pearlman, J. (2010). Engendering change: Organizational dynamics and workplace gender desegregation., 1975–2005. *Administrative Science Quarterly, 55,* 255–277.

Hughes, T. A. (2006). The advantages of single-sex education. *National Forum of Educational Administration and Supervision Journal, 23*(2), 5–14.

Huie, V. A. (1994). Mom's in prison: Where are the kids? In D. J. Curran & C. M. Renzetti (Eds.), *Contemporary societies: Problems and prospects* (pp. 481–484). Englewood Cliffs, NJ: Prentice Hall.

Hull, K. E. (2006). *Same-sex marriage: The cultural politics of love and law.* Cambridge, UK: Cambridge University Press.

Human Rights Watch. (2006). *U.S.: Number of mentally ill in prison quadrupled.* Retrieved October 19, 2009, from http://hrw.org/english/docs/2006/09/09/usdom14137_txt.htm

Human Sciences Research Council, (2003). HIV/AIDS epidemic is projected to slow down: New projections paint more positive trends. Retrieved from http://www.hsrc.ac.za/Media_Release-180.phtml

Hunt, D. (2005). Black content, white control. In D. M. Hunt (Ed.), *Channeling blackness: Studies on television and race in America.* (pp. 267–302). New York: Oxford University Press.

Hunt, M. E. (1991). The challenge of 'both/and' theology. In M. A. May (Ed.), *Women and church* (pp. 28–33). New York: Friendship Press.

Hunte, H. E. R., & Williams, D. R. (2009). The association between perceived discrimination and obesity in a population-based multiracial and multiethnic adult sample. *American Journal of Public Health, 99,* 1285–1292.

Hunter, A. G., & Sellers, S. L. (1998). Feminist attitudes among African American women and men. *Gender & Society, 12,* 81–99.

Hurtado, A. (1996). *The color of privilege.* Ann Arbor: University of Michigan Press.

Hurtig, A. L., & Rosenthal, I. M. (1987). Psychological findings in early treated cases of female pseudohermaphroditism caused by virilizing congenital adrenal hyperplasia. *Archives of Sexual Behavior, 16,* 209–223.

Husband, C. (2005). Minority ethnic media as communities of practice: Professionalism and identity politics in interaction. *Journal of Ethnic and Migration Studies, 31,* 461–479.

Hussar, W. J., & Bailey, T. M. (2009, September). *Projections of education statistics to 2018.* U.S. Department of Education, National Center for Education Statistics.

Hyde, J. S. (1984). How large are gender differences in aggression? A developmental meta-analysis. *Developmental Psychology, 20,* 722–736.

Hyde, J. S., & Jaffee, S. R. (2000). Becoming a heterosexual adult: The experiences of young women. *Journal of Social Issues, 56,* 283–296.

Hyde, J. S. (2005). The gender similarities hypothesis. *American Psychologist, 60,* 581–592.

Hyman, P. (1979). The other half: Women in the Jewish tradition. In E. Koltun (Ed.), *The Jewish woman* (pp. 105–113). New York: Schocken Press.

IBIS World (2011). *Gym, health & fitness clubs, U.S. industry report*. Retrieved from http://www.ibisworld.com/industry/default.aspx?indid=1655

Ichiyama, M. A. et al. (2009). A randomized trial of a parent-based intervention on drinking behavior among incoming college freshmen. *Journal of Studies on Alcohol and Drugs, Supp. 16*, 67–76.

Ihrai, T., Krishna, C., Claude, N., & Sarfati, I. (2010). The fat trap: A simple method for harvesting large amounts of adipose tissue during liposuction. *Plastic and Reconstructive Surgery, 126*(4), 206.

Imperato-McGinley, J., Peterson, R. E., Gautier, T., Looper, G., Danner, R., Arthur, A., Morris, P. L., Sweeney, W. J., & Schackleton, C. (1982). Hormonal evolution of a large kindred with complete androgen insensitivity: Evidence for secondary 5 alpha-reductase deficiency. *Journal of Clinical Endrocrinology Metabolism, 54*, 15–22.

Inciardi, J. A. (1993). *Criminal justice*. Orlando: Harcourt, Brace, Jovanovich.

Inciardi, J. A., Lockwood, D., & Pottieger, A. E. (1993). *Women and crack-cocaine*. New York: Macmillan.

Insurance Institute for Highway Safety. (2010). *Breaking down the numbers*. Retrieved from http://www.carinsurance.com/Articles/why-men-get-gypped.aspx

Insure Kids Now. (2011). *Facts and Figures*. Retrieved from http://www.insurekidsnow.gov/facts/index.html

International Ice Hockey Federation (IIHF) (2009). *Members*. Retrieved from http://en.wikipedia.org/wiki/Ice_hockey#cite_note-50

International Women's Media Foundation (IWMF) (2008). *North American Newsroom Employment Census, IWMF's Stats and Studies.*, Retrieved from http://www.iwmf.org/archive/articletype/articleview/articleid/456/stats-and-studies.aspx

Inter-Parliamentary Union (2008a). *Women speakers of national parliaments: History and the present*. Available online: http://www.ipu.org/wmn-e/speakers/htm

Inter-Parliamentary Union (2008b). *Women in national parliaments: World and regional averages*. Available online: http://www.ipu.org/wmn-e/world.htm

Inter-Parliamentary Union (2008c). *Women in national parliaments: World classification*. Available online: http://www.ipu.org/wmn-e/classif.htm

Inter-Parliamentary Union. (1997). *Men and women in politics: Democracy in the making*. Geneva: Author.

Irvine, L., & Vermilya, J. R. (2010). Gender work in a feminized profession: The case of veterinary medicine. *Gender & Society, 24*, 56–82.

Isasi-Diaz, A. M. (1991). Hispanic women in the Roman Catholic Church. In M. A. May (Ed.), *Women and church* (pp. 13–17). Grand Rapids, MI: Wm. B. Eerdmans Publishing Co.

Islam Principles. (2008). *Muslim guidance articles: Equality between men and women in Islam*. Retrieved from: http://muslimguidance.com/islam-principles/equality-between-men-and-women-in-islam.html

Jacklin, C. N. (1989). Female and male: Issues of gender. *American Psychologist, 44*, 127–133.

Jackson, J. F. L., & O'Callaghan, E. M. (2009). Ethnic and racial administrative diversity: Understanding work life realities in higher education. *ASHE (Association for Study of Higher Education), 35*(3), 1–95.

Jackson, K., & Bond, B. (2007). Gaming Magazines and the drive for muscularity in preadolescent boys: A longitudinal examination. *Body Image, 4*, 3, 269–277.

Jackson, P., Stevenson, N., & Brooks, K. (2001). *Making sense of men's magazines*. Cambridge: Polity Press.

Jackson, S., & Gee, S. (2005). 'Look Janet', 'No you look John': Constructions of gender in early school reader illustrations across 50 years. *Gender and Education, 17*(2), 115–128.

Jacobs, J. A. (1983). *The sex segregation of occupations and women's career patterns*. Unpublished doctoral dissertation, Harvard University.

Jacobs, J. A. (1992). Women's entry into management: Trends in earnings, authority, and values among salaried managers. *Administration Science Quarterly, 37*, 282–301.

Jacobs, J. A., & Lim, S. T. (1995). Trends in occupational and industrial sex segregation in 56 countries, 1960–1980. In J. A. Jabobs (Ed.), *Gender inequality at work* (pp. 259–293). Thousand Oaks, CA: Sage.

Jacobs, J. A., & Steinberg, R. J. (1990). Compensating differentials and the male-female wage gap: Evidence from the New York State comparable worth study. *Social Forces, 69*, 439–468.

Jacobs, J. A., & Gerson, K. (2004). *The time divide: Work, family, and gender inequality*. Cambridge, MA: Harvard University Press.

Jacobsen, J. (2007). *The economics of gender*. Hoboken, New Jersey: Wiley.

Jacobsen, J. P., & Levin, L. M. (1995, September). Effects of intermittent labor force attachment on women's earnings. *Monthly Labor Review*, pp. 14–19.

Jacobsen, J. P. (2007). Occupational segregation and the tipping phenomenon: The contrary case of court reporting in the USA.*Gender, Work and Organizations, 14*, 130–161.

Jacquet, C. H. (Ed.) (1988). *Women ministers in 1986 and 1987: A ten year view*. New York: Office of Research and Evaluation, National Council of Churches.

Jaffrey, Z. (1996). *The invisibles: A tale of the eunuchs of India*. New York: Vintage.

James, D. J., & Glaze, L. E. (2006). *Mental health problems of prison and jail inmates*. Washington, DC: Bureau of Justice Statistics. Available online: http://ojjp.usdoj.gov/bjs/pub/pdf/mhppji.pdf

James, M. S. (2001, May 12). Men more likely to divorce ill spouses. Available online: http://www.ABCNews.com

Janke, M. A., Nimrod, G., & Kleiber, D. A. (2008a). Leisure activity and depressive symptoms of widowed and married women in later life. *Journal of Leisure Research, 40*, 2, 250–266.

Janke, M. A., Nimrod, G., & Kleiber, D. A. (2008b). Leisure patterns and health among recently widowed adults. *Activities, adaptation, and aging, 32*, 1, 19–39.

Janofsky, M. (1997, April 1). Women in the Marines join the firing line. *New York Times*, p. A10.

Jarratt, E. H. (1990). Feminist issues in sport. *Women's Studies International Forum, 13*, 491–499.

Jasinski, J. L., Wesely, J. K., Wright, J. D., & Mustaine, E. E. (2010). *Hard lives, mean streets: Violence in the lives of homeless women*. Boston: Northeastern University Press.

Jay, T. (2009). Do offensive words harm people? *Psychology, Public Policy, and Law, 15*(2), 81–101.

Jayakody, R., & Chatters, L. M. (1997). Differences among African American single mothers: Marital status, living arrangements, and family support. In R. J. Taylor, J. S. Jackson, & L. M. Chatters (Eds.), *Family life in Black America* (pp. 167–184). Thousand Oaks, CA: Sage.

Jayawardena, K. (1986). *Feminism and nationalism in the third world*. London: Zed Press.

Jeffery, P., Jeffery, R., & Lyon, A. (1988). *Labor pains and labor power: Women and childbearing in India*. London: Zed Books.

Jehan, I., Harris, H., Salat, S., Zeb, A., Mobeen, N., Pasha, O., McClure, E., Moore, J., Wright, L., & Goldenberg, R. (2009). Neonatal mortality, risk factors and causes: A prospective population-based cohort study in urban Pakistan. *Bulletin of the World Health Organization, 87*, 130–138.

Jelinek, P. (2011, January 14). Military commission: Life ban, allow women in combat. Retrieved from: http://www.msnbc.msn.com/id/41083172/ns/us_news-life/t/military-commission-lift-ban-allow-women-combat/#.Tr8aeXFGyXU

Jennett, M. (2004). *Stand up for us: Challenging homophobia in schools*. London: NHS Health Development Agency.

Jennings, T., & Sherwin, G. (2007, April). Sexual orientation curriculum in elementary teacher preparation: Programs, content and priorities from across the United States. Paper presented at the annual meeting of the American Educational Research Association, Chicago, IL.

Jensen, R. (2007). *Getting off: Pornography and the end of masculinity*. Cambridge, MA: South End Press.

Jewell, K. S. (1988). *Survival of the Black family: The institutional impact of U.S. social policy*. New York: Praeger.

Jewish Week. (2010). Riverdale Orthodox shul to have woman lead kabbalat Shabbat tonight. Retrieved from: http://www.thejewishweek.com/news/breaking_news/riverdale_orthodox_shul_have_woman_lead_kabbalat_shabbat_tonight

Jhally, S. (2006). Advertising, gender, and sex: What's wrong with a little objectification? In S. Jhally (Ed.), *The spectacle of accumulation: essays in culture, media, & politics* (pp. 163–176). New York: Peter Lang.

Jogerst, G. J., Dawson, J. D., & Schweitzer, L. A. (2000). Community characteristics associated with elder abuse. *Journal of the American Geriatrics Society, 48*, 513–518.

Johansen, R. E. B., Bathija, H., & Khanna, J. (2009). Work of the World Health Organization on female genital mutilation: Ongoing research and policy discussions. *Finnish Journal of Ethnicity and Migration, 3*(2), 83–89.

Johnson, R. J., Rew, L.., & Sternglanz, R. W. (2006). Ther relationship between childhood sexual abuse and sexual health practices of homeless adolescents. *Adolescence, 41*, 221–234.

Johnson, R. W., & Favrault, M. M. (2004). *Economic status in later life among women raised children outside of marriage*. Washington, DC: Urban Institute.

Johnson, S. P. (2008). The status of male teachers in public education today. *Education Policy Brief*, Bloomington, IN: Center for Evaluation & Education Policy.

Johnson, S., Guenther, S., Laube, D., & Keettle, W. (1981). Factors influencing lesbian gynecologic care: A preliminary study. *American Journal of Obstetrics and Gynecology, 140*, 20–28.

Johnson-Bailey, J. (2004). Hitting and climbing the proverbial wall: Participation and retention issues for Black graduate women. *Race, Ethnicity and Education, 7*, 331–349.

Johnson-Odim, C. (1991). Common themes, different contexts: Third world women and feminism. In C. T. Mohanty, A. Russo, & L. Torres (Eds.), *Third world women and the politics of feminism* (pp. 314–327). Bloomington: Indiana University Press.

Johnston, D. (1995, September 20). F.B.I. hitting snag in talks about bias. *New York Times*, p. A18.

Johnstone, R. L. (1988). *Religion in society*. Englewood Cliffs, NJ: Prentice-Hall.

Joiner, T. E., & Blalock, J. A. (1995). Gender differences in depression: The role of anxiety and generalized negative affect. *Sex Roles, 33*, 91–108.

Jones, J. H. (1993). *Bad blood: The Tuskegee experiment*. New York: Free Press.

Jones, L., & Finkelhor, D. (2009). *Updated trends in child maltreatment, 2007*. Crimes Against Children Research Center. Retrieved November 2, 2009 from http://www.unh.edu/ccrc/pdf/Updated%20Trends%20in%20Child%20Maltreatment%202007.pdf

Jones, M. G., & Wheatley, J. (1990). Gender differences in teacher-student interactions in science classrooms. *Journal of Research in Science Teaching, 27*, 861–874.

Jones, N. (2009). *Between good and ghetto*. New Brunswick, NJ: Rutgers University Press.

Jones, R. K., & Henshaw, S. K. (2002). Mifepristone for early medical abortion: Experiences in France, Great Britain and Sweden. *Perspectives on Sexual and Reproductive Health, 34*, 3. Washington, D.C.: Guttmacher Institute. Retrieved from: http://www.guttmacher.org/pubs/journals/3415402.html

Jones, R. K., Zolna, M. R., Henshaw, S. K., & Finer, L. B. (2008). *Abortion in the United States: Incidence and access to services, 2005*. *Perspectives on Sexual and Reproductive Health, 40*, 1. Washington, DC: Guttmacher Institute. Retrieved from: http://www.guttmacher.org/pubs/journals/4000608.pdf

Jones, W. (2010). Eating disorders in men: A review of the literature. *Journal of Public Mental Health, 9*(2), 23–31.

Jorgensen, G. (2006). Kohlberg and Gilligan: Duet or dual? *Journal of Moral Education, 35*, 179–196.

Joseph, G. (1981). Black mothers and daughters. In G. Joseph & J. Lewis (Eds.), *Common differences: Conflicts in Black and White feminist perspectives* (pp. 75–126). New York: Anchor.

Joseph, S., & Najmabadi, A. (2005). *Encyclopedia of women and Islamic cultures: Family, law and politics*. Leiden, The Netherlands: Brill.

Juarez, V. (2010). New Jersey Senate defeats same-sex marriage bill. CNN. Retrieved February 22, 2010, http://www.cnn.com/2010/POLITICS/01/07/new.jersey.same.sex.marriage/index.html

Jurgens, J. J., & Powers, B. A. (1991). An exploratory study of the menstrual euphemisms, beliefs, and taboos of Head Start mothers. In D. L. Taylor & N. F. Woods (Eds.), *Menstruation, health, and illness* (pp. 35–40). New York: Hemisphere.

Jurik, N. C. (1985). An officer and a lady: Organizational barriers to women working as correctional officers in men's prisons. *Social Problems, 32*, 375–388.

Jurik, N. C., & Halemba, G. J. (1984). Gender, working conditions and the job satisfaction of women in a non-traditional occupation: Female correctional officers in men's prisons. *Sociological Quarterly, 25*, 551–566.

Kackicic, J., Marcus, B., Lang, W., & Janney, C. (2008). Effect of exercise on 24-month weight loss maintenance in overweight women. *Archives of Internal Medicine, 168*, 1550–1559.

Kagan, S. (2008). Ageism in cancer care. *Seminars in Oncology Nursing, 24*(4), 246–253.

Kagan-Krieger, S. (1998). Brief report: Women with Turner syndrome: A maturational and developmental perspective. *Journal of Adult Development, 5*, 125–135.

Kahn, K. F., &. Goldenberg, E. N. (1991). The media: Obstacle or ally of feminists? *Annals of the American Academy of Political and Social Science, 515*, 104–113.

Kahn, S. S., Nessim, S., Gray, R., Czer, L. S., Chaux, A., & Matloff, J. (1990). Increased mortality of women in coronary bypass surgery: Evidence for referral bias. *Annals of Internal Medicine, 112*, 561–567.

Kain, E. (1990). *The myth of family decline*. Lexington, MA: Lexington Books.

Kaiser Family Foundation. (2000). *Sex education in America: A view from inside the nation's classrooms*. Available at: http://www.kff.org

Kaiser Family Foundation. (2002). *Sex Smarts Survey: Gender roles*. Menlo Park, CA: Henry J. Kaiser Family Foundation. Available at: http://www.kff.org/entpartnerships/upload/Gender-Rolls-Summary.pdf

Kaiser Family Foundation. (2003). *The first time*. Menlo Park, CA: Henry J. Kaiser Family Foundation. Available at: http://www.kff.org/entpartnerships/upload/Virginity-and-the-First-Time-Summary-of-Findings.pdf

Kaiser Family Foundation. (2008). *Percent of adults who smoke by sex, 2008*. Retrieved from: http://www.statehealthfacts.org/comparetable.jsp?ind=81&cat=2

Kales, H., & Mellow, A. (2006). Race and depression: Does race affect the diagnosis and treatment of late-life depression? *Geriatrics, 61*(5) 18–21.

Kalfoglou, A. L., Scott, J., & Hudson, K. (2008). Attitudes about preconception sex selection: A focus group study with Americans. *Human Reproduction, 23*(12), 2731–2736.

Kalil, A. (2009). Joblessness, family relations and children's development. *Family Matters, 83*, 15–22.

Kalleberg, A., Rasell, E., Hudson, K., Webster, D., Reskin, B., Cassirer, N., & Appelbaum, E. (1997). *Nonstandard work, substandard jobs: Flexible work arrangements in the U.S.* Washington, DC: Economic Policy Institute.

Kalof, L., Eby, K. K., Matheson, J. L., & Kroska, R. J. (2001). The influence of race and gender on student self-reports of sexual harassment by college professors. *Gender & Society, 15*, 282–302.

Kamerman, S. B., & Kahn, A. J. (1988). *Mothers alone*. Dover, MA: Auburn House Publishing Co.

Kamp Dush, C., & Amato, P. (2005). Consequences of relationship status and quality for subjective well-being. *Journal of Social and Personal Relationships, 22*, 607–627.

Kamphoff, C. (2010). Bargaining with patriarchy: Former female coaches' experiences and their decision to leave collegiate coaching. *Research Quarterly for Exercise and Sport, 81*(3), 360–372.

Kane, E. W. (2005). Gendered anticipation: Parents' preferences for sons and daughters. annual meeting of the American Sociological Association, Philadelphia, PA.

Kannapell, A. (1998, February 17). Heading slowly into the ice age. *New York Times*, pp. B1, 6.

Kanter, R. M. (1977). *Men and women of the corporation*. New York: Basic.

Kaplan, D. (2009). *Contemporary American Judaism: Transformation and renewal*. New York: Columbia University Press.

Kärkkäinen, R., Räty, H., & Kasanen, K. (2009). Parents' perceptions of their child's resilience and competencies. *European Journal of Psychology of Education, 24*, 405–419.

Karlyn-Rowe, K., (2004). Too close for comfort: "American Beauty" and the incest motif, *Cinema Journal, 44*(1) 69–93.

Karpiak, C.P., Buchanan, J. P., Hosey, M., & Smith, A. (2007). University students from single-sex and coeducational high schools: Differences in majors and attitudes at a Catholic university. *Psychology of Women Quarterly, 31*, 282–289.

Katz, D. (2002). *Preventing and addressing: Sexual harassment*. New York: Downslope Industries, Inc.

Katz, M. B., Stern, M. J., & Fader, J. J. (2005). Women and the paradox of economic inequality in the twentieth century. *Journal of Social History, 39*, 65–88.

Katz, R. C., Hannon, R., & Whitten, L. (1996). Effects of gender and situation on the perception of sexual harassment. *Sex Roles, 34*, 35–42.

Kaufman, D. R. (1991). *Rachel's daughters: Newly orthodox Jewish women*. New Brunswick: Rutgers University Press.

Kauppinen, K., & Patoluoto, S. (2005). Sexual harassment and violence toward policewomen in Finland. In J. E. Gruber & P. Morgan (Eds.), *In the company of men: Male dominance and sexual harassment* (pp. 195–214). Boston: Northeastern University Press.

Kay, F. M., & Hagan, J. (1995). The persistent glass ceiling: Gendered inequalities in the earnings of lawyers. *British Journal of Sociology, 46*, 279–310.

Kaye, E. (1993, June 6). So weak, so powerful. *New York Times*, pp. V1, V10.

Keddie, A. (2009). Some of those girls can be real drama queens: Issues of gender, sexual harassment and schooling. *Sex Education, 9*(1), 1–16.

Keele, L. *Hidden worship: The religious rituals of Orthodox Jewish women*. Retrieved from: http://www.utoronto.ca/wjudaism/contemporary/articles/a_keele1.html

Kefalas, M. (2002, August). *Labor of love: Views on childbearing and motherhood among low-income, White single mothers*. Paper presented at the annual meeting of the Society for the Study of Social Problems, Chicago, IL.

Kehoe, A. B. (1998). *The land of prehistory: A critical history of American archeology*. New York: Routledge.

Keller, R. (2009). How shifting occupational composition has affected the real wage. *Monthly Labor Review, 132*, 26–38.

Keller, R., Radford, R., & Cantlon, M. (Eds.) (2006). *Encyclopedia of women and religion in North America*. Bloomington: Indiana University Press.

Kellerman, B., & Rhode, D. L. (Eds.) (2007). *Women and leadership*. San Francisco: Jossey-Bass.

Kellough, G., & Wortley, S. (2002). Remand for the plea: Bail decisions and plea bargaining as commensurate decisions. *British Journal of Criminology, 42*(1), 186–210.

Kelly, E. S. (1998, June 2). Teaching doctors sensitivity on the most sensitive of exams. *New York Times*, p. F7.

Kelly, G. F. (1995). *Sexuality today*. Dubuque, IA: Brown and Benchmark.

Kemper, T. D. (1990). *Social structure and testosterone*. New Brunswick: Rutgers University Press.

Kendler, K. S., Bulik, C. M., Silberg, J., Hettema, J. M., Myers, J., & Prescott, C. A. (2000). Childhood sexual abuse and adult psychiatric substance use disorders in women: An epidemiological and cotwin control analysis. *Archives of General Psychiatry, 57*, 953–959.

Kennelly, I. (1999). "That single mother element": How White employers typify Black women. *Gender & Society, 13*, 168–192.

Kerber, L. K. et al. (1986). On *In a different voice*: An interdisciplinary forum. *Signs, 11*, 304–333.

Kerr, W., Patterson, D., & Greenfield, T. (2009). Differences in the measured alcohol content of drinks between white and Hispanic men and women in a US national sample. *Addiction, 104*(9) 1503–1511.

Kershner, I. (2010, July 18). Women's role in Holocaust may exceed old notions. *New York Times*, p. 8.

Kessleman, A. (1990). *Fleeting opportunities: Women shipyard wokers in Portland and Vancouver duing World War II and reconversion*. Albany: State University of New York Press.

Kessler, S. J. (1996). The medical construction of gender: Case management of intersexed infants. In B. Laslett, S. G. Kohlstedt, H. Longino, & E. Hammonds (Eds.), *Gender and scientific authority* (pp. 340–363). Chicago: University of Chicago Press.

Kessler-Harris, A. (1982). *Out to work: A history of wage-earning women in the United States*. New York: Oxford University Press.

Kessler-Harris, A. (1990). *A woman's wage: Historical meanings and social consequences*. Lexington: University Press of Kentucky.

Keyes, K., Grant, B., & Hasin, D. (2007). Evidence for a closing gender gap in alcohol use, abuse, and dependence in the United States population. *Drug and Alcohol Dependence, 93*(1–2) 21–29.

Kia-Keating, M., Sorsoli, L., & Grossman, F. (2009). Relationship challenges and recovery process in male survivors of childhood sexual abuse. *Journal of Interpersonal Violence, 25*, 4, 666–683.

Kian, E., Mondello, M., & Vincent, J. (2009). ESPN-The women's sports network? A content analysis of internet coverage of March Madness. *Journal of Broadcasting & Electronic Media, 53*(3), 477–495.

Kiefer, A. K., & Sanchez, D. T. (2007). Scripting sexual passivity: A gender role perspective. *Personal Relationships, 14*, 269–290.

Kilborn, P. T. (1995, March 17). White males and the manager class. *New York Times*, p. A14.

Kilborn, P. T. (1997, March 12). 5 women say sex charges in army case were coerced. *New York Times*, p. A14.

Kilpatrick, D. G. et al. (2007). *Drug-facilitated, incapacitated, and forcible rape: A national study*. Washington, DC: U.S. Department of Justice, National Institute of Justice.

Kim, J. L., & Ward, L. M. (2004). Pleasure reading: Associations between young women's sexual attitudes and their reading of contemporary women's magazines. *Psychology of Women Quarterly, 28*, 48–58.

Kimmel, M. (1995). *Manhood in America*. New York: Free Press.

Kimmel, M. (2006). What about the boys? What the current debates tell us—and don't tell us—about boys in school. In E. Disch (Ed.), *Reconstructing gender: A multicultural anthology (4/e)*. (pp. 361–375). New York: McGraw-Hill.

Kimmel, M. S., & Messner, M. A. (Eds.) (1998). *Men's lives*. Boston: Allyn and Bacon.

Kimmel, M., Hearn, J., & Connell, R.W. (2005). *Handbook of studies on men and masculinities*. Thousand Oaks, CA: Rowman & Littlefield.

King, D. R. (1988). Multiple jeopardy, multiple consciousness: The context of a Black feminist ideology. *Signs, 14*, 42–72.

Kingslave. (2011). *Islam – Are women allowed to travel alone?* Retrieved from: http://islamgreatreligion.wordpress.com/2009/06/22/are-women-allowed-to-travel-alone/

Kingston, D. A., Malamuth, N. M., Federoff, P., & Marshall, W. L. (2009). The importance of individual differences in pornography use: Theoretical perspectives and implications for treating sexual offenders. *Journal of Sex Research, 46(2/3)*, 216–232.

Kinzer, S. (1997, May 27). Beating the system, with bribes and the big lie. *New York Times*, p. A4.

Kinzer, S. (1998, March 17). A woman, her scarf and a storm over secularism. *New York Times*, p. A4.

Kinzie, J., Thomas, A. D., Palmer, M. M., Umbach, P. D., & Kuh, G. D. (2007). Women students at coeducational and women's colleges: How do their experiences compare? *Journal of College Student Development, 48*, 145–165.

Kinzie, M. B., & Joseph, D. R. D. (2008). Gender differences in game activity preferences of middle school children: Implication for educational game design. *Education Tech Research Development, 56*, 643–663.

Kirschstein, R. L. (1996). Women physicians—Good news and bad news. *New England Journal of Medicine, 334*, 982–983.

Kiselewich, R. A. (2008). In defense of the 2006 Title IX regulations for single-sex public education: How separate can be equal. *Boston College Law Review, 49*, 217–261.

Klag, M. J., Whelton, P. K., Corech, J., Grim, C. E., & Kuller, L. H. (1991). The association of skin color with blood pressure in U.S. Blacks with low socioeconomic status. *Journal of the American Medical Association, 264*, 599–602.

Klass, P. (1988, April 10). Are women better doctors? *New York Times Magazine*, pp. 32–35, 46–48, 96–97.

Klatch, R. (1988). Coalition and conflict among women of the new right. *Signs, 13*, 671–694.

Klein, A. M. (1995). Life's too short to die small. In D. Sabo & D. F. Gordon (Eds.), *Men's health and illness* (pp. 105–120). Thousand Oaks, CA: Sage.

Klein, E. (1984). *Gender politics*. Cambridge, MA: Harvard University Press.

Klein, H., & Shiffman, K. S. (2006). Messages about physical attractiveness in animated cartoons. *Body Image, 3*, 353–363.

Klein, M. (1975). *Envy and gratitude and other works, 1946–1963*. New York: Delta.

Klinkhammer, G. (2010). *Women, Islam and modernity: Single women and sexuality*. Retrieved from:

http://www.google.com/url?sa=t&source=web&cd=3&ved=0CCkOFjAC&url=http%3A%2F%2F222.equinoxjournals.com%2FCIS%2Fdownload%2F4721%2F6390&rct=j&q=no%20public%20contact%20between%20unmarried%20women%20and%20men%20islam&ei=weq_TYT0LObb0QGsqYmlBQ&usg=AFQjCNGrKVx1Y1pFcRbV01SngRR7AyCwdQ

Klitzman, R., & Greenberg, J. (2002). Patterns of communication between gay and lesbian patients and their health care providers. *Journal of Homosexuality, 42*, 65–75.

Kluger, J. (2006). Taming wild girls. *Time, 167*(18), 54–55.

Kmec, J. A. (2010). Are motherhood penalties and fatherhood bonuses warranted? Comparing pro-work behaviors and conditions of mothers, fathers, and non-parents. *Social Science Research, 40*, 444–459.

Knox, A. (2008). Gender desegregation and equal employment opportunity in Australian luxury hotels. Are we there yet? *Asia Pacific Journal of Human Resources, 48*, 153–172.

Ko, D. (2005). *Cinderella's sisters: A revisionist history of footbinding*. Berkeley: University of California Press.

Kocieniewski, D. (1995, October 14). Judge ordered victim, 15, to re-enact sexual abuse in court. *New York Times*, pp. 21, 22.

Koeske, R. (1980). Theoretical perspectives on menstrual cycle research. In A. Dan, E. Graham, & C. P. Beecher (Eds.), *The menstrual cycle* (pp. 8–24). New York: Springer.

Kohler, P. K., Manhart, L. E., & Lafferty, W. E. (2007). Abstinence-only and comprehensive sex education and the initiation of sexual activity and teen pregnancy. *Journal of Adolescent Health, 42*, 344–351.

Kolata, G. (1998, March 10). Harrowing choices accompany advancements in fertility. *New York Times*, p. F3.

Kolata, G. (2000, October 18). No days off are allowed, experts on weight argue. *New York Times*, pp. A1, A20.

Kolb, R. (2008). *Encyclopedia of business ethics and society*. Thousand Oaks, CA: Sage.

Kolker, A., & Burke, B. M. (1992). *Sex preference and sex selection: Attitudes of prenatal diagnosis clients*. Paper presented at the annual meeting of the American Sociological Association, Pittsburgh, PA.

Kolodny, A. (1993). Raising standards while lowering anxieties: Rethinking the promotion and tenure process. *Concerns: Women's Caucus for the Modern Languages, 23*, 16–40.

Komarow, S. (2005, August 25). Abuse found in military schools. *USA Today*. Retrieved from: http://www.usatoday.com/news/nation/2005–08–25-academies-women_x.htm?csp=24&RM_Exc;ude=Juno&POE=click-refer

Konner, M. (1982). *The tangled wing: Biological constraints on the human spirit*. New York: Harper Colophon Books.

Kopelman, R. E., Shea-Van Fossen, R. J., Paraskevas, E., Lawter, L., & Protas, D. J. (2009). The bride is keeping her name: A 35-year retrospective analysis of trends and correlates. Social Behavior and Personality: An International Journal, 37(5), 687–700.

Koropeckyj-Cox, T., & Pendell, G. (2007a). Attitudes about childlessness in the United States: Correlates of positive, neutral, and negative responses. *Journal of Family Issues, 22*(4), 477–496.

Koropeckyj-Cox, T., & Pendell, G. (2007b). The gender gap in attitudes about childlessness in the United States. *Journal of Marriage and the Family, 69*, 899–913.

Kosberg, J. I. (1988). Preventing elder abuse: Identification of high-risk factors prior to placement decisions. *Gerontologist, 28*, 43–50.

Kosciw, J. G., Greytak, E. A., Diaz, E. M., & Bartkiewicz, M. J. (2010). *The 2009 National School Climate Survey: The experiences of lesbian, gay, bisexual and transgender youth in our nation's schools*. Washington, DC: Gay, Lesbian and Straight Education Network.

Koser, N. W. (1992). Feminist pedagogy in criminology. *Journal of Criminal Justice Education, 2*, 81–94.

Koss, M., Gidycz, C., & Wisniewski, N. (1987). The scope of rape: Incidence and prevalence of sexual aggression in a sample of higher education students. *Journal of Consulting and Clinical Psychology, 55*, 162–170.

Kostenberger, M. (2008). *Jesus and the feminists: Who do they say that he is?* Wheaton, IL: Crossway.

Kraemer, G. R., & Kraemer, R. R. (1998). Premenstrual syndrome: Diagnosis and treatment experiences. *Journal of Women's Health, 7*, 893–905.

Kraemer, G. R., & Kraemer, R. R. (1998). Premenstrual syndrome: Diagnosis and treatment experiences. *Journal of Women's Health, 7*, 893–907.

Krafka, C., Linz, D., Donnerstein, E., & Penrod, S. (1997). Women's reactions to sexually aggressive mass media depictions. *Violence Against Women, 3*, 149–181.

Kramarae, C., & Spender, D. (1992). Exploding knowledge. In C. Kramarae & D. Spender (Eds.), *The knowledge explosion: Generations of feminist scholarship* (pp. 1–24). New York: Teachers College Press.

Kramer, L. R. (1991). The social construction of ability perceptions: An ethnographic study of gifted adolescent girls. *Journal of Early Adolescence, 11*, 340–362.

Kramer, R. (1986). The third wave. *Wilson Quarterly, 10*, 110–129.

Kramer, Z. A. (2009). Heterosexuality and Title VII. *Northwestern University Law Review, 103*(1), 205–247.

Kranichfeld, M. L. (1987). Rethinking family power. *Journal of Family Issues, 8*, 42–56.

Krebs, C. P. et al. (2011). Comparing sexual assault prevalence estimates obtained with direct and indirect questioning techniques. *Violence Against Women, 17*, 219–235.

Kreider, R. M. (2005). *Number, timing, and duration of marriages and divorces, 2001*. Current Population Reports, P70–97. Washington, D.C.: U.S. Census Bureau.

Kreider, R. M., & Elliott, D. B. (2009). *America's Families and Living Arrangements: 2007*. Current Population Reports, P20–561. Washington, DC: U.S. Bureau of the Census. Retrieved from: http://www.census.gov/population/www/socdemo/hh-fam/p20–561.pdf

Kreiger, N., & Sidney, S. (1996). Racial discrimination and blood pressure: The CARDIA study of young Black and White adults. *American Journal of Public Health, 86*, 1370–1378.

Krieger, S. (1982). Lesbian identity and community: Recent social science literature. *Signs, 8*, 91–108.

Krishnamurti, J. (1986). *The future of humanity*. New York: Harper Collins.

Kristof, N. D. (1991, November 5). Stark data on women: 100 million are missing. *New York Times*, pp. C1, C12.

Kristof, N. D. (2005, August 3). A Pakistani rape – and love story. *Dayton Daily News*, p. A9.

Krumholz, H. (2001). Racial differences in the use of cardiac catheterization. *New England Journal of Medicine, 345*, 839.

Kuczynski, A. (2000a, February 28). Old-line women's magazines turn to sex to spice up their sales. *New York Times*, pp. C1, C15.

Kuczynski, A. (2002, February 7). In quest for wrinkle-free future, frown becomes thing of the past. *New York Times*, pp. A1, A26.

Kudson-Martin, C., & Mahoney, A. R. (1998). Language processes in the construction of equality in marriages. *Family Relations, 47*, 81–91.

Kuebli, J., Butler, S. A., & Fivush, R. (1995). Mother-child talk about past emotions: Relations of maternal language and child gender over time. *Cognition and Emotion, 9*, 265–283.

Kuehnast, K., Oudraat, C., & Hernes, H. (Eds.) (2011). *Women and war: Power and protection in the 21st century*. Washington, DC: United States Institute of Peace Press.

Kuhn, S. L., & Stiner, M. C. (2006). What's a mother to do? The division of labor among neadertals and modern humans in Eurasia. *Current Anthropology, 47*, 953–980.

Kuhn, T. S. (1970). *The structure of scientific revolutions*. Chicago: University of Chicago Press.

Kumpfer, K. (2011). *Treatment programs for drug-abusing women*. Retrieved from http://www.princeton.edu/futureofchildren/publications/journals/article/index.xml?journalid=69&articleid=500&sectionid=3402

Kurz, D. (1995). *For richer, for poorer: Mothers confront divorce*. New York: Routledge.

Kushner, H. I. (1985). Women and suicide in historical perspective. *Signs, 10*, 537–552.

Kwan, S. (2009). Beauty work: Individual ad institutional rewards, the reproduction of gender, and questions of agency. *Sociology Compass, 3*(1), 49–71.

La Franiere, S. (2005, December 23). Another school barrier for African girls: No toilet. *New York Times*, pp. A1, A10.

Lacan, J. (1977). *Ecrits: A selection*. London: Tavistock.

Lacey, M. (2002, January 6). In Kenyan family, ritual for girls still divides. *New York Times*, p. 4.

Lackey, P. N. (1989). Adults' attitudes about assignments of household chores to male and female children. *Sex Roles, 20*, 271–281.

LaCroix, A. Z., & Haynes, S. G. (1987). Gender differences in the health effects of workplace roles. In R. C. Barnett, L. Biener, & G. K. Baruch (Eds.), *Gender and stress* (pp. 96–121). New York: Free Press.

Ladner, J. (1971). *Tomorrow's tomorrow*. Garden City, NY: Doubleday.

Lake, C. C., & Breglio, V. J. (1992). Different voices, different views: The politics of gender. In P.

Ries & A. J. Stone (Eds.), *The American woman, 1992–93* (pp. 178–201). New York: W. W. Norton.

Lakoff, R. (1990). *Talking power: The politics of language in our lives*. New York: Basic Books.

Lakoff, R. (1991). You are what you say. In E. Ashton-Jones & G. A. Olson (Eds.), *The gender reader* (pp. 292–298). Boston: Allyn and Bacon.

Lamar, J. V. (1988, February 15). Redefining a woman's place. *Time*, p. 27.

Lamb, M. E. (1999). Noncustodial fathers and their impact on children of divorce. In R. A. Thompson & P. R. Amato (Eds.), *The postdivorce family: Children, parenting, and society* (pp. 105–125). Thousand Oaks, CA: Sage.

Lamb, S., & Brown, L. M. (2007). *Packaging girlhood: Rescuing our daughters from marketers' schemes*. New York: St. Martin's Griffin.

Lambert, S. (2005). Gay and lesbian families: What we know and where to go from here. *The Family Journal: Counseling and Therapy for Couples and Families, 75*(1), 43–51.

Lamm, S. (2008). *When booking a doctor's visit, gender plays a role*. Retrieved from http://today.msnbc.msn.com/id/23816393/ns/today-today_health/

Lampman, C., Phelps, A., Bancroft, S., & Beneke, M. (2009). Contrapower sexual harassment in academia: A survey of faculty experience with student incivility, bullying, and sexual attention. *Sex Roles, 60*, 331–346.

Landrine, H., & Klonoff, E. A. (1997). *Discrimination against women: Prevalence, consequences, remedies*. Thousand Oaks, CA: Sage.

Lane, J., Gover, A. R., & Dahod, S. (2009). Fear of violent crime among men and women on campus: The impact of perceived risk and fear of sexual assault. *Violence and Victims, 24*, 172–192.

Lanfranco, K., Kamischke, A., Zitzmann, M., & Nieschlag, E. (2004). Klinefelter's syndrome. *Lancet, 364*, 273–283.

Langevin, R., & Curnoe, S. (2004). The use of pornography during the commission of sexual offenses. *International Journal of Offender Therapy and Comparative Criminology, 48*, 572–586.

Lanis, K., & Covell, K. (1995). Images of women in advertisements: Effects on attitudes related to sexual aggression. *Sex Roles*, 639–649.

Lapointe, J. (1998, February 18). U.S. women first at gold in ice thriller. *New York Times*, pp. A1, C2.

Lareau, A., & Weininger, E. B. (2008). Time, work, and family life: Reconceptualizing gendered patterns through the case of children's organized activities. *Sociological Forum, 2*(3), 419–454.

Larson, J. H. (1988). The marriage quiz: College students' beliefs in selected myths about marriage. *Family Relations, 37*, 3–11.

Latif, A. (2009). A critical analysis of school enrollment and literacy rates of girls and women in Pakistan. *Educational Studies, 45*, 424–439.

Laumann, E. O., Gagnon, J. H., Michael, R. T., & Michaels, S. (1994). *The social organization of sexuality.* Chicago: University of Chicago Press.

Lauzen, M. M., Dozier, D. M., & Horan, N. (2008). Constructing gender stereotypes through social roles in prime-time television. *Journal of Broadcasting & Electronic Media, 52*, 200–214.

Lauzen, M. M., & Dozier, D. M. (2005). Maintaining the double standard: Portrayals of age and gender in popular films. *Sex Roles, 52*, 437–446.

Lavender, R. (2009). Female genital mutilation in a globalized age. *British Journal of Midwifery, 17*(6), 348–353.

Law, R., & Sbarra, D. (2009). The effects of church attendance and marital status on the longitudinal trajectories of depressed mood among older adults. *Journal of Aging Health, 21*, 803–823.

Lawler, A. (2005). Summers' comments draw attention to gender, racial gaps. *Science, 307*, 492–493.

Lawless, J. L., & Fox, R. L. (2005). *It takes a candidate: Why women don't run for office.* New York: Cambridge University Press.

Lawlor, J. (1998, April 26). For many blue-collar fathers, child care is shift work, too. *New York Times*, p. BU11.

Lawrence, R., & Johnson, D. (1991). *Women in corrections: The prospects for equality.* Paper presented at the annual meeting of the American Society of Criminology, San Francisco, CA.

Lawrence, R., & Mahan, S. (1998). Women corrections officers in men's prisons: Acceptance and perceived job performance. *Women and Criminal Justice, 9*, 63–86.

Lawrence, R., & Johnson, D. (1991). *Women in corrections: The prospects for equality.* Paper presented at the Annual Meeting of the American Society of Criminology, San Francisco, CA.

Lawrence, W. (1987). Women and sports. In S. E. Rix (Ed.), *The American woman, 1987–88* (pp. 222–226). New York: W. W. Norton.

Lazier-Smith, L. (1989). A new "genderation" of images of women. In P. J. Creedon (Ed.), *Women in mass communication* (pp. 247–260). Newbury Park, CA: Sage.

Leach, W. (1980). *True love and perfect union: The feminist reform of sex and society.* New York: Basic Books.

Leacock, E. (1993). Women in Samoan history: A further critique of Derek Freeman. In B. D. Miller (Ed.), *Sex and gender hierarchies* (pp. 351–365). New York: Cambridge University Press.

Leaper, C. (2002). Parenting girls and boys. In M. H. Bornstein, *Handbook of parenting: Vol. 1. Children and parenting*, 2nd ed., (pp. 189–225). Mahwah, NJ: Erlbaum.

Leaper, C., & Ayres, M. M. (2007). A meta-analytic review of gender variations in adults' language use: Talkativeness, affiliative speech, and assertive speech. *Personality and Social Psychology Review, 11*(4), 328–363.

Leaper, C., & Brown, C. S. (2008). Perceived experiences with sexism among adolescent girls. *Child Development, 79*(3), 685–704.

Leaper, C., & Friedman, C. K. (2007). The socialization of gender. In J. E. Grusec and P. D. Hastings (Eds.), *Handbook of Socialization: Theory and Research* (pp. 561–587). New York: Guilford Publications.

Leaper, C., Breed, L., Hoffman, L., & Perlman, C. A. (2002).Variations in the gender-stereotyped content of children's television cartoons across genres. *Journal of Applied Social Psychology, 32*, 1653–1662.

Leaper, C., Carson, M., Baker, C., Holliday, H., & Meyers, S. (1995). Self-disclosure and listener verbal support in same-gender and cross-gender friends. *Sex Roles, 33*, 387–404.

LeClere, F. B., Rogers, R. G., & Peters, K. (1998). Neighborhood social context and racial differences in women's heart disease mortality. *Journal of Health and Social Behavior, 39*, 91–107.

Lederman, D. (2006). Clues about the gender gap. *Inside Higher Ed.* Retrieved April 22, 2010, http://www.insidehighered.com/news/2007/01/15/freshmen

Lee, C. (2003). *How does instant messaging affect interaction between the genders?* Stanford, CA: Mercury Projext for Instant Messaging Studies, Stanford University.

Lee, F. R. (1989, July 17). Doctors see gap in Blacks' health having a link to low self-esteem. *New York Times*, p. A11.

Lee, H. K. (2009). Police face 7 sex discrimination lawsuits. *San Francisco Chronicle*, p. D4.

Lee, J., Grigg, W., & Dion, G. (2007). *The Nation's Report Card: Mathematics 2007.* National

Center for Education Statistics (NCES), Institute of Education Sciences, U.S. Department of Education, Washington, DC. Retrieved February 17, 2010, http://nces.ed.gov/nationsreportcard/pdf/main2007/2007494.pdf

Lefkovitz, L., & Shapiro, R. (2005). Ritualwellorg—Loading the virtual canon, or: The politics and aesthetics of jewish women's spirituality. *Nahsim: A Journal of Jewish Women's Studies, 9,* 101–125.

Lefton, L. A. (2000). *Psychology.* Boston: Allyn and Bacon.

Legacy. (2010). *Lung cancer and smoking.* Retrieved from http://www.legacyforhealth.org/PDFPublications/Lung_Cancer_and_Smoking.pdf

LeGates, M. (2001). In their time: A history of feminism in western society. New York: Taylor and Francis.

Legrand, D. (2010). Myself with no body? Body, bodily-consciousness, and self-consciousness. *Hadbook of Phenomenology and Cognitive Science, 10,* 180–200.

Leitenberg, H., & Saltzman, H. (2000). A statewide survey of age at first intercourse for adolescent females and age of their male partners: Relation to other risk behaviors and statutory rape implications. *Archives of Sexual Behavior, 29,* 203–215.

Leland, J. (2006, October 8). A spirit of belonging, inside and out. *New York Times.* Retrieved from: http://www.nytimes.com/2006/10/08/fashion/08SPIRIT.html?scp=14&sq=Leland&st=nyt

Lemelle, A. J. (2004). African American attitudes toward gay males: Faith-based initiatives and implications for HIV/AIDS services. *Journal of African American Studies, 7,* 59–74.

Lemle, R. (1984). *Alcohol and masculinity: A review and reformulation of sex role, dependency, and power theories of alcoholism.* Paper presented at the annual meeting of the American Psychological Association, Toronto, Canada.

Lenhart, A., Madden, M., & Hitlin, P. (2005). *Teens and technology.* Washington, DC: Pew Internet and American Life Project. Retrieved June 11, 2010 from http://www.pewinternet.org/~/media/Files/Reports/2005/PIP_Teens_Tech_July2005web.pdf

Lenhart, A., Purcell, K., Smith, A., & Zickuhr, K. (2010). *Social media and mobile internet use among teens and young adults.* Washington, DC: Pew Internet and American Life Project. Retrieved June 11, 2010 from http://www.pewinternet.org/~/media/Files/Reports/2010/PIP_Social_Media_and_Young_Adults_Rerpot.pdf

Lenskyj, H. (1986). *Out of bounds.* Toronto: Women's Press.

Lentz, B. F., & Laband, D. N. (1995). *Sex discrimination in the legal profession.* Westport, CT: Quorum Books.

Leonhardt, D. (2006, February 19). Children, the littlest politicians. *New York Times,* p. WK14.

Lepowsky, M. (1990). Gender in an egalitarian society: A case study from the Coral Sea. In P. R. Sanday & R. G. Goodenough (Eds.), *Beyond the second sex* (pp. 169–224). Philadelphia: University of Pennsylvania Press.

Lepowsky, M. (1993). *Fruit of the motherland: Gender in an egalitarian society.* New York: Columbia University Press.

Lepowsky, M. (1994). Women, men and aggression in an egalitarian society. *Sex Roles, 30,* 199–211.

Lerner, G. (1993). *The creation of feminist consciousness.* New York: Oxford University Press.

Lerner, G. (Ed.) (1972). *Black women in White America.* New York: Vintage.

Leslie, L. K., Lambros, K. M., Aarons, G. A., Haine, R. A., & Hough, R. L. (2008). School-based service use by youth with ADHD in public-sector settings. *Journal of Emotional & Behavioral Disorders, 16*(3), 163–177.

Lesperance, F., & Frasure-Smith, N. (1996). Negative emotions and coronary heart disease: Getting to the heart of the matter. *Lancet, 347,* 414–415.

Lester, N. (2000). Nappy edges and goldy locks: African American daughters and the politics of hair. *The Lion and the Unicorn, 24*(2), 201–224.

Letellier, P. (1996). Twin epidemics: Domestic violence and HIV infection among gay and bisexual men. In C. M. Renzetti & C. H. Miley (Eds.), *Violence in gay and lesbian domestic partnerships* (pp. 69–82). New York: Haworth.

Levanon, A., England, P., & Allison, P. (2009). Occupational feminization and pay: Assessing causal dynamics using 1950–2000 Census data. *Social Forces, 88,* 865–891.

LeVay, S. (1991). A difference in hypothalamic structure between heterosexual and homosexual men. *Science, 253,* 1034–1037.

Leveroni, C. L., & Berenbaum, S. A. (1998). Early androgen effects on interest in infants: Evidence from children with congenital adrenal hyperplasia. *Developmental Neuropsychology, 14,* 321–340.

Levesque, L. L., O'Neill, R. M., Nelson, T., & Dumas, C. (2005). Sex differences in the perceived importance of mentoring functions. *Career Development International, 10*, 429–443.

Levin, D. E., & Kilbourne, J. (2008). *So sexy so soon: The new sexualized childhood and what parents can do to protect their kids.* New York: Ballantine Books.

Levine, J. (1997). *Working fathers.* Reading, MA: Addison-Wesley.

Levine, S. B. (2000). *Father courage: What happens when men put family first.* New York: Harcourt.

Lewin, E. (1998). *Recognizing ourselves: Ceremonies of lesbian and gay commitment.* New York: Columbia University Press.

Lewin, T. (1997a, March 15). New guidelines on sexual harassment tell schools when a kiss is just a peck. *New York Times*, p. 8.

Lewin, T. (1997c, September 15). Women losing ground to men in widening income difference. *New York Times*, pp. A1, 12.

Lewin, T. (2000, December 19). Survey shows sex practices of boys. *New York Times*, p. A22.

Lewin, T. (2001, May 30). Program finds success in reducing teenage pregnancy. *New York Times*, p. A16.

Lewin, T. (2006). The new gender divide: At colleges women are leaving men in the dust. *New York Times.* Retrieved June 7, 2010, http://www.nytimes.com/2006/07/09/education/09college.html?ei=5088&en=cd9efba2e9595dec&ex=1310097600&partner=rssnyt&emc=rss&pagewanted=print

Lewis, C. (2006). Treating incarcerated women: Gender matters. *Psychiatric Clinics of North America, 29*, 773–789.

Lewis, C., Scully, D., & Condor, S. (1992). Sex stereotyping of infants: A re-examination. *Journal of Reproductive and Infant Psychology, 10*, 53–63.

Lewis, G. B., & Nice, D. (1994). Race, sex, and occupational segregation in state and local governments. *American Review of Public Administration, 24*, 393–410.

Lewis, N. A. (1993, November 24). U.S. restrictions on adult-TV fare are struck down. *New York Times*, pp. A1, A20.

Li, Q. (2006). Cyberbullying in schools: A research of gender differences. *School Psychology International, 27*, 157–170.

Lieberman, R. (2002). Ideas, institutions, and political order: Explaining political change. *American Political Science Review, 96*, 697–712.

Light, D., & Monk-Turner, E. (2009). Circumstances surrounding male sexual assault and rape: Findings from the National Violence Against Women survey. *Journal of Interpersonal Violence, 24*, 1849–1858.

Lightfoot, E., & Williams, O. (2009). The intersection of disability, diversity, and domestic violence: Results of national focus groups. *Journal of Aggression, Maltreatment & Trauma, 18*(2), 133–152.

Lim, L. L. (1998). The economic and social bases of prostitution in Southeast Asia. In L. L. Lim (Ed.), *The sex sector* (pp. 1–28). Geneva: International Labour Organization.

Limbert, C. A. (1995). Chrysalis, a peer mentoring group for faculty and staff women. *NWSA Journal, 7*, 86–99.

Lin, C., & Yeh, J. (2009). Comparing Society's Awareness of Women: Media-Portrayed Idealized Images and Physical Attractiveness, *Journal of Business Ethics, 90*, 61–79.

Lincoln, A. E. (2010). The shifting supply of men and women to occupations: Feminization of veterinary education. *Social Forces, 88*, 1969–1998.

Lincoln, C. E., & Mamiya, L. H. (1990). *The Black church in the African American experience.* Durham, NC: University of North Carolina Press.

Lindeqvist, K. (1996). Fighting repressive tolerance: Lesbian studies in Sweden. In B. Zimmerman & T. A. H. McNaron (Eds.), *The new lesbian studies* (pp. 229–233). New York: Feminist Press.

Lindgren, J. R., & Taub, N. (1993). *The law of sex discrimination.* Minneapolis: West.

Lindley, S. H. (1996). *"You have stept out of your place": A history of women and religion in America.* Louisville, KY: Westminster John Knox Press.

Lindsay, S. (2007). Gender differences in rural and urban practice location among mid-level health care providers. *Journal of Rural Health, 23*, 72–76.

Linver, M. R., & Davis-Kean, P. (2005). The slippery slope: What predicts math grades in middle and high school? Directions for Child and Adolescent Development, 110, 49–64.

Lipsky, M. (2010). *Street-level bureaucracy: Dilemmas of the individual in public service.* New York: Russell Sage Foundation.

Lipson, C., & Binkley, R. (2004). *Rhetoric before and beyond the Greeks: It all comes down to Maat.* Albany: State University of New York Press.

Lisak, D., & Miller, P. M. (2002). Repeat rape and multiple offending among undetected rapists. *Violence and Victims, 17*, 73–84.

Lisak, D., & Roth, S. (1988). Motivational factors in nonincarcerated sexually aggressive men. *Journal of Personality and Social Psychology, 55*, 795–802.

Liston, B. (1998, May 31). Abortion foes threaten to turn tactics on gay event. *Boston Globe*, p. A2.

Little, C. B. (1983). *Understanding deviance and control: Theory, research and public policy*. Itasca, IL: F. E. Peacock.

Little, C. B., & Rankin, A. (2001). Why do they start it? Explaining reported early-teen sexual activity. *Sociological Forum, 16*, 703–729.

Littleton, H., Breitkopf, C. R., Berenson, A. (2008). Beyond the campus: Unacknowledged rape among low-income women. *Violence Against Women, 14*, 269–286.

Littlewood, R., & Lipsedge, M. (1989). *Aliens and alienists: Ethnic minorities and psychiatry*. London: Unwin Hyman.

Lloyd, K. M., & South, S. J. (1996). Contextual influences on young men's transition to first marriage. *Social Forces, 74*, 1097–1119.

Lobao, L. (1990). Women in revolutionary movements: Changing patterns in Latin American guerrilla struggle. In G. West & R. L. Blumberg (Eds.), *Women and social protest* (pp. 180–204). New York: Oxford University Press.

Lock, J., & Kleis, B. N. (1998). A primer on homophobia for the child and adolescent psychiatrist. *Journal of the American Academy of Child and Adolescent Psychiatry, 37*, 671–672.

Lofland, L. H. (1975). The "thereness" of women: A selective review of urban sociology. In M. Millman & R. M. Kanter (Eds.), *Another voice* (pp. 144–170). New York: Anchor/Doubleday.

Loftus, J. (2001). America's liberalization in attitudes toward homosexuality, 1973 to 1998. *American Sociological Review, 66*, 762–782.

Logan, J. (2001). Sexuality, child care and social work education. *Social Work Education, 20*, 563–575.

Logan, T. K, & Leukefeld, C. (2000). Sexual and drug use behaviors among female crack users: A multisite sample, *Drug Alcohol Depend 58*(3), 237–245.

Logsdon, E. C. (2003). "No child left behind" and the promotion of single-sex public education in primary and secondary schools: Shattering the glass ceilings perpetuated by coeducation. *Journal of Law Education, 32*(2), 291–296.

Longino, H., & Doell, R. (1983). Body, bias, and behavior: A comparative analysis of reasoning in two areas of biological science. *Signs, 9*, 206–227.

Lonsdorf, E. V. (2005). Sex differences in the development of termite-fishing skills in the wild chimpanzees, *Pan troglodytes schweinfurthii*, of Gombe National Park, Tanzania. *Animal Behavior, 70*, 673–683.

Lopez, N. (2003). *Hopeful girls, troubled boys*. New York: Routledge.

Loprest, P., & Zedlewski, S. (2006). *The changing role of welfare in the lives of low-income families with children*. Occasional paper 73. Washington, DC: Urban Institute.

Lorber, J. (1994). *Paradoxes of gender*. New Haven, CT: Yale University Press.

Lorber, J. (1986). Dismantling Noah's ark. *Sex Roles, 14*, 567–580.

Lorber, J. (1993). Believing is seeing: Biology as ideology. *Gender & Society, 7*, 568–581.

Lorber, J. (2005a). *Breaking the bowls: Degendering and feminist change*. New York: W.W. Norton.

Lorber, J. (2005b). *Gender inequality: Feminist theories and politics*. Los Angeles: Roxbury.

Lorber, J. (2006). Shifting paradigms and challenging categories. *Social Problems, 53*, 448–453.

Lorber, J., Coser, R. L., Rossi, A. S., & Chodorow, N. (1981). On the Reproduction of Mothering: A methodological debate. *Signs, 6*, 482–514.

Loredo, C., Reid, A., & Deaux, K. (1995). Judgments and definitions of sexual harassment by high school students. *Sex Roles, 32*, 29–45.

Loring, M., & Powell, B. (1988). Gender, race and DSM-III: A study of psychiatric behavior. *Journal of Health and Social Behavior, 29*, 1–22.

Lott, B. (1987). *Women's lives: Themes and variations in gender learning*. Monterey, CA: Brooks/Cole Publishing Company.

Louth, A. (2009). From Clement to origen: The social and historical context of the church fathers. *Heythrop Journal, 50*, 313–314.

Lovaas, K. E., Elia, J. P., & Yep, G. A. (2007). Shifting ground(s): Surveying the contested terrain of LGBT studies and queer theory. *Journal of Homosexuality, 52*, 1/2, 1–18.

Love, A. A. (1998, June 9). Wage gap between the sexes narrowing. *Atlanta Constitution*, p. 1.

Love, C. A. (2008). Unrepeatable harms: Female genital mutilation and involuntary sterilization in U.S. Asylum Law. *Columbia Human Rights Law Review, 40*, 1, 173–230.

Lovejoy, O. (1981). The origins of man. *Science, 211*, 341–350.

Lovenduski, J. (1986). *Women and European politics*. Amherst: University of Massachusetts Press.

Lowen, L. (2011). The role of African American women in the Black church: Women outnumber men in the pews, yet are rarely seen in the pulpit. Retrieved from: http://womensissues.about.com/od/communityconnections/a/blackwomenchurc.htm

Lowinson, J., Ruiz, P., & Millman, R (2005). *Substance abuse: A comprehensive textbook*. United States: Wolters Kluwer Health.

Lucal, B. (1999). What it means to be gendered me: Life on the boundaries of a dichotomous gender system. *Gender & Society, 13*, 781–797.

Luciano, L. (2001). *Looking good: Male body image in modern America*. New York: Hill and Wang.

Luckenbill, D. F. (1986). Deviant career mobility: The case of male prostitutes. *Social Problems, 33*, 283–296.

Luders, W. (2007). Child pornography web sites: Techniques used to evade law enforcement. *FBI Law Enforcement Bulletin, 76*(7), 17–21.

Luebke, B. F., & Reilly, M. E. (1994). *Women's studies graduates: The first generation*. New York: Teachers College Press.

Luftig, R. L., & Nichols, M. L. (1991). An assessment of the social status and perceived personality and school traits of gifted students by non-gifted peers. *Roeper Review, 13*, 148–152.

Luker, K. (1984). *Abortion and the politics of motherhood*. Berkeley: University of California Press.

Luker, K. (1996). *Dubious conceptions: The politics of teen pregnancy*. Cambridge: Harvard University Press.

Lummis, A. T. (1999). Gender and religion. In J. S. Chafetz (Ed.), *Handbook on the sociology of gender* (pp. 601–618). New York: Kluwer.

Lunneborg, P. W. (1990). *Women changing work*. New York: Bergen and Garvey.

Luo, M. (2006, February 12). Reform Jews hope to unmix mixed marriages. *New York Times*, pp. 1, 20.

Luo, M., & Capecchi, C. (2009, August 22). Lutheran group eases limits on gay clergy. *New York Times*, pp. A8, A9.

Lupton, B. (2006). Explaining men's entry into female-concentrated occupations: Issues of masculinity and social class. *Gender, Work and Organizations, 13*, 103–128.

Lurie, N., Slater, J., McGovern, P., Ekstrum, J., Quam, L., & Margolis, K. (1993). Preventive care for women: Does the sex of the physician make a difference? *New England Journal of Medicine, 329*, 478–482.

Luther, C. A., & Legg, R. (2010). Gender differences in depictions of social and physical aggression in children's television cartoons in the U.S. *Journal of Children and Media, 4*(2), 191–205.

Luthra, J., & Gidycz, C. A. (2006). Dating violence among college men and women: Evaluation of a theoretical model. *Journal of Interpersonal Violence, 21* 713–721.

Luyre, L. E., Zosuls, K. M., & Ruble, D. N. (2008). Gender identity and adjustment: Understanding the impact of individual and normative differences in sex typing. *New Directions in Child Adolescent Development, 120*, 31–46.

Lynn, N. B. (1984). Women and politics: The real majority. In J. Freeman (Ed.), *Women: A feminist perspective* (pp. 402–422). Palo Alto, CA: Mayfield.

Lynn, R. (1994). Sex differences in intelligence and brain size: A paradox resolved. *Personal and Individual Differences, 17*, 257–271.

Lyons, P. M., DeValve, P. M., Garner, M. J., & Randall, L. (2008). Texas police chiefs' attitudes toward gay and lesbian police officers. *Police Quarterly, 11*(1), 102–117.

Ma, X. (2008). Within-School Gender Gaps in Reading, Mathematics, and Science Literacy. *Comparative Education Review, 52*(3), 437–460.

MacCabe, J. (2005). What's in a label? The relationship between feminist self-identificaton and "feminist" attitudes among U.S. women and men. *Gender & Society, 19*, 480–505.

Maccoby, E. (1988). Gender as a social category. *Developmental Psychology, 24*, 755–765.

MacCorquordale, P., & Jensen, G. (1993). Women in law: Partners or tokens? *Gender & Society, 7*, 582–593.

MacDonald, E. (1992). *Shoot the women first*. New York: Random House.

MacDonald, K., & Parke, R. D. (1986). Parent-child physical play: The effects of sex and age on children and parents. *Sex Roles, 15*, 367–378.

MacFarquhar, N. (1996). Mutilation of Egyptian girls: Despite ban, it goes on. *New York Times*, p. A3.

MacGeorge, E. L., Graves, A. R., Feng, B., Gillihan, S. J., & Burleson, B. R. (2004). The myth of gender cultures: Similarities outweigh differences in men's and women's provision of and responses to supportive communication. *Sex Roles, 50*, 143–175.

Macgillivray, I. K., & Jennings, T. (2008). A content analysis exploring lesbian, gay, bisexual and transgender topics in foundations of education textbooks. *Journal of Teacher Education, 59*(2), 170–189.

Mackey, M. (2003). Television and the teenage literate: Discourses of "Felicity." *College English, 65*(4), 389–410.

MacKinnon, C. (1986). Pornography: Not a moral issue. *Women's Studies International Forum, 9*, 63–78.

Madden, J. (2009). Captain Dragan raped me: Muslim women. *Australian*, p. 1.

Madera, J. M., Podratz, K. E., King, E. B., & Hebl, M. R. (2007). Schematic responses to sexual harassment complainants: The influence of gender and physical attractiveness. *Sex Roles, 56*, 223–230.

Madriz, E. I. (1997). Images of criminals and victims: A study of women's fear and social control. *Gender & Society, 11*, 342–356.

Madson, L., & Hessling, R. (1999). Does alternating between masculine and feminine pronouns eliminate perceived gender bias in text? *Sex Roles, 41*, 559–575.

Mael, F., Alonso, A., Gibson, D., Rogers, K., & Smith, M. (2005). Single-sex versus coeducational schooling: A systematic review. U.S. Department of Education: Office of Planning, Evaluation, and Policy Development. Washington, D.C.: Author. Retrieved May 5, 2010, http://www2.ed.gov/rschstat/eval/other/single-sex/single-sex.pdf

Maghan, J., & McLeish-Blackwell, L. (1991). Black women in correctional employment. In J. B. Morton (Ed.), *Change, challenge, and choices: Women's role in modern corrections* (pp. 82–99). Laurel, MD: American Correctional Association.

Magnuson, E. (2008). Rejecting the American dream: Men creating alternative life goals. *Journal of Contemporary Ethnography, 37*(3), 255–290.

Mahan, S. (1996). *Crack cocaine, crime, and women: Legal, social, and treatment issues.* Thousand Oaks, CA: Sage.

Maher, F. A., & Tetrault, M. K. T. (1994). *The feminist classroom.* New York: Basic Books.

Mahoney, P. (1999). High rape chronicity and low rates of help-seeking among wife rape survivors in a nonclinical sample: Implications for research and practice. *Violence Against Women, 5*, 993–1016.

Majors, R. (2001). *The masculinities reader.* Hoboken, NJ: Wiley.

Malamuth, N. M., Addison, T., & Koss, M. (2000). Pornography and sexual aggression: Are there reliable effects and can we understand them? *Annual Review of Sex Research, 11*, 26–91.

Malley-Morrison, K. (2004). *International perspectives on family violence and abuse.* Mahwah, NJ: Lawrence Erlbaum.

Malone, L. M., West, J., Denton, K. F., & Park, J. (2006). *The Early Reading and Mathematics Achievement of Children Who Repeated Kindergarten or Who Began School a Year Late.* Washington, DC: National Center Education Statistics.

Mancuso, R. F., & Miller, B. A. (2001). Crime and punishment in the lives of women alcohol and other drug (AOD) users: Exploring the gender, lifestyle, and legal issues. In C. M. Renzetti & L. Goodstein (Eds.), *Women, crime and criminal justice* (pp. 77–92). Los Angeles: Roxbury.

Mandel, R. B., & Dodson, D. L. (1992). Do women officeholders make a difference? In P. Ries & A. J. Stone (Eds.), *The American woman, 1992–93* (pp. 149–177). New York: W. W. Norton.

Manegold, C. S. (1993, May 9). Among Blacks, new voices emerge. *New York Times*, pp. 25, 32.

Mann, C. R. (1993). *Unequal justice: A question of color.* Bloomington: Indiana University Press.

Manning, A. (1998, February 23). Operating with sexism. *USA Today*, p. 1D.

Manning, W. D., & Brown, S. L. (2006). Children's economic well-being in married and cohabiting families. *Journal of Marriage and Family, 68*, 345–362.

Mannino, A. A., & Deutsch, F. M. (2007). Changing the division of household labor: A negotiated process between partners. *Sex Roles, 56*, 309–324.

Manpower Demonstration Research Corporation. (2006). *Low-wage workers and poverty: making work pay.* Retrieved from: http://www.mdrc.org/area_fact_29.html

Mansbridge, J. J. (1986). *Why we lost the ERA.* Chicago: University of Chicago Press.

Mansnerus, L. (1997, November 16). Sometimes the punishment fits the gender. *New York Times*, p. WK1.

Marcussen, K. (2005). Explaining differences in mental health between married and cohabitating individuals. *Social Psychology Quarterly, 68*, 239–257.

Mares, M. (1996). *Positive effects of television on social behavior: A meta-analysis.* Paper presented at the Annenberg Washington Conference on Children and Television, Washington, DC.

Margaret Sanger Center International at Planned Parenthood of New York City. (2008). *Doing* gender the "rights" way: A guide to promote gender equality in sexual and reproductive health programs. Retrieved April 29, 2010, http://www.plannedparenthood.org/nyc/files/NYC/GENDER_THE_RIGHTS_WAY5.pdf

Margolis, D. R. (1993). Women's movements around the world: Cross-cultural comparisons. *Gender & Society, 7*, 379–399.

Marieskind, H. I., & Ehrenreich, B. (1975). Toward socialist medicine: The women's health movement. *Social Policy, 6*, 34–42.

Markens, S. (1996). The problematic of "experience": A political and cultural critique of PMS. *Gender & Society, 10*, 42–58.

Marks, M. J. (2008). Evaluations of sexually active men and women under divided attention: A social cognitive approach to the sexual double standard. *Basic and Applied Social Psychology, 30*, 84–91.

Marquis, C. (2002, March 14). Discharges of gay troops rise, and so do bias incidents. *New York Times*, p. A22.

Marron, D. (2010). Gender arbitrage by multinationals. Donald Marron: Musings on Economics, Finance, and Life. Retrieved February 27, 2011. http://dmarron.com/2010/10/26/gender-arbitrage-by-multinationals/

Marsden, G. M. (2006). *Fundamentalism and American culture*. New York: Oxford University Press.

Marshall, E. (1992). Sex of the brain. *Science, 257*, 620–621.

Marshall, E., & Sensoy, O. (2009). The same old hocus-pocus: Pedagogies of gender and sexuality. *Shrek 2. Discourse: Studies in Cultural Politics of Education, 30*(2), 151–164.

Marsiglio, W., Amato, P., Day, R. D., & Lamb, M. E. (2000). Scholarship on fatherhood in the 1990s and beyond. *Journal of Marriage and the Family, 62*, 1173–1191.

Martin, B. (1978). Conservative Judaism and reconstructionism. In B. Martin (Ed.), *Movements and issues in American Judaism* (pp. 103–157). Westport, CT: Greenwood Press.

Martin, C. L. (1989). Children's use of gender-related information in making social judgments. *Developmental Psychology, 25*, 80–88.

Martin, J. R. (1994). *Changing the educational landscape*. New York: Routledge.

Martin, M. C., & Kennedy, P. F. (1996). The measurement of social comparison to advertising models: A gender gap revealed. In J. Curran, D. Morley, & V. Walkerdine (Eds.), *Cultural studies and communications* (pp. 104–124). London: Arnold.

Martin, M. K., & Voorhies, B. (1975). *Female of the species*. New York: Columbia University Press.

Martin, S. E., & Jurik, N. C. (1996). *Doing justice, doing gender*. Thousand Oaks, CA: Sage.

Martin, S., Ray, N., Sotres-Alvarez, D., Kupper, L., Moracco, K., Dickens, P., Scandlin, D. et al. (2006). Physical and sexual assault of women with disabilities. *Violence Against Women, 12*, 823–837.

Martin, S. E., & Jurik, N. (2007). *Doing justice, doing gender* (2/e). Thousand Oaks, CA: Sage.

Martin, S. E., & Pyle, B. (2005). State high courts and divorce: The impact of judicial gender. *University of Toledo Law Review, 36*(4), 923–948.

Martindale, G. (2011). *What it means to be masculine*. Retrieved from http://www.stateuniversity.com/blog/permalink/What-It-Means-To-Be-Masculine.html

Marty, M. E. (1992). Fundamentals of fundamentalism. In L. Kaplan (Ed.), *Fundamentalism in comparative perspective* (pp. 15–23). Amherst, MA: University of Massachusetts Press.

Marty, M. E., & Appleby, R. S. (1992). *The glory and the power*. Boston: Beacon Press.

Martyna, W. (1980). Beyond the "he/man" approach: The case for nonsexist language. *Signs, 5*, 482–493.

Maruschak, L. M. (2006). Medical problems of jail inmates. Washington, DC: Bureau of Justice Statistics. Available at http://www.ojp.usdoj.gov/bjs/pub/pdf/mpji.pdf

Maschke, K. (1996). Gender in the prison setting: The privacy-equal employment dilemma. *Women and Criminal Justice, 7*, 23–42.

Masci, D. (2009). A contentious debate: Same-sex marriage in the U.S. Washington, DC: Pew Research Center. Retrieved February 19, 2010, www.pewforum.org/docs/?DocId=422

Massachusetts Department of Education (2007). 2005 Youth Risk Behavior Survey. Malden, MA: Massachusetts Department of Education. Retrieved March 1, 2010, http://www.doe.mass.edu/cnp/hprograms/yrbs/05/ch5.doc

Massachusetts Institute of Technology (MIT). (1999). *A study on the status of women faculty at MIT*. Available online: http://web.mit.edu/fnl/women/fnlwomen.htm

Masse, M. A., & Rosenblum, K. (1988). Male and female created they them: The depiction of gender in the advertising of traditional women's and men's magazines. *Women's Studies International Forum, 11*, 127–144.

Massoni, K. (2004). Modeling work: Occupational messages in Seventeen Magazine. *Gender and Society, 18*(1), 47–65.

Mates, R. (1997, April 4). Financial abuse of elderly hits close to home. *Toronto Globe and Mail*, p. 1.

Matheny, K. B., Roque-Tovar, B. E., & Curlette, W. L. (2008). Perceived stress, coping resources, and life satisfaction among U. S. and Mexican college students: A cross-cultural study. *Anales de psicologia, 24*(1), 49–57.

Matland, R. E., & King, D. C. (2002). Women as candidates in Congressional elections. In C. S. Rosenthal (Ed.), *Women transforming Congress* (pp. 119–145). Norman: Oklahoma State University.

Matthews, H. (2006). *Child care assistance helps families work: A review of the effects of subsidy receipt on employment*. Washington, DC: Center for Law and Social Policy.

Matthews, J., Ponitz, C., & Morrison, F. (2009). Early Gender Differences in Self-Regulation and Academic Achievement, *Journal of Educational Psychology, 101*, 689–704.

Mattson, I., & Loeffelholz, F. (2007). *The story of the Qur'an: It's history and place in Muslim life*. Paris, France: Lavoisier.

Matza, M., Fazlollah, M., & McCoy, C. R. (1999, December 20). The rape squad files, Part 2: Jogger took initiative to seek attacker. *Philadelphia Inquirer*, pp. 3–4.

Mauldin, T. (1991). Economic consequences of divorce or separation among women in poverty. In S. S. Volgy (Ed.), *Women and divorce, men and divorce* (pp. 163–177). New York: Haworth.

Maume, D. J. (2008). Gender differences in providing urgent childcare among dual-earner parents. *Social Forces, 81*(1), 273–297.

Maynard, R. (1996). *Kids having kids*. Washington, DC: Urban Institute.

Mayo, C. (2010). Queer lessons: Sexual and gender minorities in multicultural education. In Banks, J. A. & Banks, C. A. M. (Eds.) (2010). *Multicultural Education: Issues and Perspectives* (7/e) (pp. 209–227). Hoboken, NJ: John Wiley & Sons, Inc.

Mazur, A., & Lamb, T. A. (1980). Testosterone, status, and mood in human males. *Hormones and Behavior, 14*, 236–246.

Mazur, A., Booth, A., & Dabbs, J. M., Jr. (1992). Testosterone and chess competition. *Social Psychology Quarterly, 55*, 70–77.

Mazure, C. M., Keita, G. P., & Blehar, M. C. (2002). *Summit on women and depression: Proceedings and recommendations*. Washington, DC: American Psychological Association.

Mazza, M. (2009). *This fierce geometry: Uses of the Judeo-Christian Bible in the anti-abolitionist and anti-gay rhetoric of the United States*. Retrieved from: http://challenger.library.pitt.edu/ETD/available/etd-04232009-104526/

McAdoo, H. P. (1986). Societal stress: The Black family. In J. B. Cole (Ed.), *All American women* (pp. 187–197). New York: Free Press.

McCabe, S., Teter, C., & Boyd, C. (2006). Medical use, illicit use, and diversion of abusable prescription drugs. *Journal of American College Health, 54*(5) 269–278.

McCall, L. (2001). Sources of racial wage inequality in metropolitan labor markets: Racial, ethnic, and gender differences. *American Sociological Review, 66*, 520–541.

McCarty, W. P., Zhao, J., & Garland, B. E. (2007). Occupational stress and burnout between male and female police officers: Are there any gender differences? *Policing: An International Journal of Police Strategies and Management, 30*(4), 672–691.

McCaulay, M., Mintz, L., & Glenn, A. A. (1988). Body image, self-esteem, and depression-proneness: Closing the gender gap. *Sex Roles, 18*, 381–391.

McConnell-Ginet, S. (1989). The sexual (re)production of meaning: A discourse-based theory. In F. W. Frank & P. A. Treichler (Eds.), *Language, gender, and professional writing: Theoretical approaches and guidelines for nonsexist usage* (pp. 35–50). New York: Modern Language Association of America.

McCormack, C., & West, D. (2006). Facilitated group mentoring develops key career competencies for university women: A case study. *Mentoring & Tutoring: Partnership in Learning, 14*, 4, 409–431.

McCormick, T. M. (1994). *Creating the nonsexist classroom*. New York: Teachers College Press.

McCoy, C. R., Fazlollah, M., & Matza, M. (1999, December 21). The rape squad files, Part 3: Police doubted teen was groped. *Philadelphia Inquirer*, pp. 5–6.

McCracken, E. (1993). *Decoding women's magazines*. New York: St. Martin's Press.

McCrate, E., & Smith, J. (1998). When work doesn't work: The failure of current welfare reform. *Gender & Society, 12*, 61–80.

McDaniels-Wilson, C., & Belknap, J. (2008). The extensive sexual violation and sexual abuse histories of incarcerated women. *Violence Against Women, 14*(10), 1090–1197.

McDonagh, E., & Pappano, L. (2007). *Playing with the boys: Why separate is not equal in sports.* New York: Oxford University Press.

McDonald, M. (1996, April 8). Is God a woman? *MacLean's Magazine.*

McDonald, M., & Hertz, R. (2009). Prevalence, awareness, and management of hypertension, dyslipidemia, and diabetes among United States adults aged 65 and older. *Journals of Gerontology: Series A 64A*(2), 256–263.

McDonnell, F. (2005). Why so few choose physics: An alternative explanation for the leaky pipeline. *American Journal of Physics, 73*(7), 583–586.

McDonough, P. (2009). TV viewing among kids at an eight-year high. The Nielsen Company. Retrieved May 19, 2010, http://blog.nielsen.com/nielsenwire/media_entertainment/tv-viewing-among-kids-at-an-eight-year-high/

McEwen, B. S. (2003). Mood disorders ad allostatic load. *Biological Psychiatry, 54*, 200–207.

McGlen, N. E., O'Connor, K., van Assendelft, L., & Gunther-Canada, W. (2011). *Women, politics and American society.* Boston: Longman.

McGlen, N. E., O'Connor, K., Van Assendelft, L., & Gunther-Canada, W. (2002). *Women, politics and American society.* Boston: Longman.

McGowan, M. R., Ladd, L., & Strom, R. D. (2006). Online assessment of the grandmother experience in raising grandchildren. *Educational Gerontology, 32*(8), 669–684.

McGowan, P. O., Sasaki, A., Allesio, A. C., Dymov, S., Lebonte, B., Szyf, M., et al. (2009). Epigenetic regulation of the glucocorticoid receptor in human brain associates with childhood abuse. *Nature Neuroscience, 12*, 342–348.

McGrath Cohoon, J., Wu, Z., & Chao, J. (2009). Sexism: Toxic to women's persistence in CSE doctoral programs. *ACM SIGCSE Bulletin, 41*(1), 158–162.

McGrath, E., Keita, G. P., Strickland, B. R., &. Russo, N. F. (1990). *Women and depression.* Washington, DC: American Psychological Association.

McGrath, M. (2006). *The "new" male consumer: Appearance management product advertising and the male physical ideal in men's interest magazines from 1965–2005,* Retrieved from http://etd.lib.fsu.edu/theses/available/etd-11012006–135408/

McGregor, R., & Lawnham, P. (1993, August 5). Japan apologizes to sex slaves. *Australian,* p. 8.

McGuffey, C. S., & Rich, B. L. (1999). Playing in the gender transgression zone: Race, class, and hegemonic masculinity in middle childhood. *Gender & Society, 13*, 608–627.

McHale, S. M., Crouter, A. C., Kim, J., Burton, L., Davis, K., Dotterer, A. M., et al. (2006). Mothers' and fathers' racial socialization in African American families: Implications for youth. *Child Development, 77*, 1387–1402.

McIntosh, P. (1984). *Interactive phases of curricular revision: A feminist perspective.* Wellesley Working Papers Series, No. 124. Wellesley, MA: Wellesley College Center for Research on Women.

McKinley, J. C. (1996, May 4). In peace, warrior women rank low. *New York Times,* p. 4.

McLaren, A. (1990). What makes a man a man? *Nature, 346,* 216–217.

McMahon, M. (1999). *Women on guard: Discrimination and harassment in corrections.* Toronto: University of Toronto Press.

McManus, P. A., & DiPrete, T. A. (2001). Losers and winners: The financial consequences of divorce for men. *American Sociological Review, 66,* 246–268.

McMinn, M. R., Troyer, P. K., Hannum, L. E., & Foster, J. D. (1991). Teaching nonsexist language to college students. *Journal of Experimental Education, 59*, 153–161.

McMinn, M. R., Williams, P. E., & McMinn, L. C. (1994). Assessing recognition of sexist language: Development and use of the Gender-Specific Language Scale. *Sex Roles, 31*, 741–755.

McMurry, J., Linzer, M., Konrad, T., Douglas, J., Shugerman, R., & Nelson, K. (2000). The work lives of women physicians: Results from the physician work life study. *Society of General Internal Medicine, 15*, 372–380.

McNamara, J. A. K. (1996). *Sisters in arms.* Cambridge, MA: Harvard University Press.

McNamara, R. P. (1994). *The Times Square hustler: Male prostitution in New York City.* Westport, CT: Praeger.

McPhail, B. A., & Dinitto, D. M. (2005). Prosecutorial perspectives on gender-bias hate crimes. *Violence Against Women, 11*(9), 1162–1185.

McPhillips, K. (1993). Women-church and the reclamation of sacredness. *Journal of Feminist Studies in Religion, 9*, 113–118.

McQuillan, J., Greil, A. L., Shreffler, K. M., & Tichenor, V. (2008). The importance of motherhood among women in the contemporary United States. *Gender & Society, 22*(4), 477–496.

McQuiston, D. H., & Morris, K. A. (2009). Gender differences in communication: Implications for salespeople. *Journal of Selling & Major Account Management, 9,* 54–64.

McQuiston, J. T. (1997, March 16). Caller objects to integration of lead role in Passion play, but threat report is denied. *New York Times,* p. B6.

McRobbie, A. (1996). *More!:* New sexualities in girls' and women's magazines. In J. Curran, D. Morley, & V. Walkerdine (Eds.), *Cultural studies and communications* (pp. 172–194). London: Arnold.

Mead, M. (1935). *Sex and temperament in three primitive societies.* New York: Dell.

Mead, S. (2006). *The evidence suggests otherwise: The truth about boys and girls.* Washington, DC: Education Science.

Media Awareness Network (2010). *Study conducted by Tomas Rivera Policy Institute, September 22, 1998.* Retrieved From http://www.media-awareness. ca/english/resources/research_documents/statistics/ minority_representation/minority_representation. cfm

Media Matters. (2008). Report: Maureen Dowd repeatedly uses gender to mock Democrats. Retrieved October 20, 2010, www.mediamatters. org/research/200806100002

Media Report to Women (MRTW). (1993a, Spring). *Newspaper gender gap widening says Newspaper Association of America.* p. 5.

Media Report to Women (MRTW). (1995, Fall). *And one more poll: The kids speak up about TV and its shortcomings.* pp. 8–9.

Media Report to Women (MRTW). (1996a, Summer). *Women utilize fewer media for '96 campaign news.* pp. 1–2.

Media Report to Women (MRTW). (1996d, Spring). *Women politicians said to attract different coverage than men.* pp. 5–8.

Media Report to Women (MRTW). (1996e, Summer). *Women, men and media roundtable assesses backlash in news coverage.* pp. 5–6.

Media Report to Women (MRTW). (1997a, Spring). *Briefs: Only 51% of adults read daily newspapers at least four times a week.* p. 9.

Media Report to Women (MRTW). (1998b, Spring). *Men's magazines now following women's magazines' formula.* p. 6.

Media Report to Women (MRTW). (1998-B2, Fall). *Women's pages: Some are being reintroduced to attract readers,* p. 7.

Media Report to Women (MRTW). (1999c, Winter). *Beauty more important than brains for women TV anchors, study shows,* p. 20.

Media Report to Women (MRTW). (2009, Winter). Departing *Washington Post* ombudsman discusses dearth of females in news coverage. Retrieved from: http://www.mediareporttowomen. com/issues/371.htm

Mehta, C. M., & Strough, J. (2009). Sex segregation in friendships and normative contexts across the lifespan. *Developmental Review, 29,* 201–220.

Meigs, A. (1990). Multiple gender ideologies and statuses. In P. R. Sanday & R. G. Goodenough (Eds.), *Beyond the second sex* (pp. 99–112). Philadelphia: University of Pennsylvania Press.

Melis, A. P., Hare, B., & Tomasello, M. (2006). Chimpanzees recruit the best collaborators. *Science, 311,* 1297–1300.

Mellalieu, S., Neil, R., Hanton, S., & Fletcher, D. (2009). Competition stress in sport performers: Stressors experienced in the competition environment. *Journal of Sports Sciences, 27*(7) 729–744.

Mellor, D., Fuller-Tyszkiewicz, M., McCabe, M., (2010). Body image and self-esteem across age and gender: A short-term longitudinal study. *Sex Roles, 63*(9–10), 672–681.

Men, women, and battles of the bulges. (2000, September 12). *New York Times,* p. F8.

Menard, K. S., Anderson, A. L., & Godboldt, S. M. (2009). Gender differences in intimate partner recidivism: A 5-year follow-up. *Criminal Justice and Behavior, 36,* 1, 61–76.

Meneley, A. (2008). Fashions and fundamentalism in fin-de-siecle Yemen: Chador Barbie and Islamic socks. *Cultural Anthropology, 22*214–243.

Mernissi, F. (1977). Women, saints, and sanctuaries. *Signs, 3,* 101–112.

Merrill, G. S., & Wolfe, V. A. (2000). Battered gay men: An exploration of abuse, help seeking, and why they stay. *Journal of Homsexuality, 39,* 1–30.

Merritt, J. (2009, April 20). An evangelical's plea: "Love the sinner." *USA Today,* p. 11A.

Merten, M. J. (2008). Acceptability of dating violence among late adolescents: The role of sports participation, competitive attitudes, and selected dynamics of relationship violence. *Adolescence, 43*(169), 31–56.

Merten, M. J., & Williams, A. L. (2009). Acceptability of marital violence among college men and women: Does gender and current relationship status matter? College Student Journal, 43(3), 843–851.

Messias, D. K. H., Im, E., Page, A., Regev, H., Spiers, J., Yoder, J. D., & Meleis, A. I. (1997). Defining and redefining work: Implications for women's health. *Gender & Society, 11*, 296–323.

Messinger, L. (2009). Creating LGBTQ-friendly campuses. *Academe, 95*(5), 39–42.

Messman-Moore, T. L., Coates, A. A., Gaffey, K. J., & Johnson, C. F. (2008). Sexuality, substance use, and susceptibility to victimization: Risk for rape and sexual coercion in a prospective study of college women. *Journal of Interpersonal Violence, 23*(12), 1730–1746.

Messman-Moore, T. L., Ward, R. M., & Brown, A. L. (2009). Substance use and PTSD symptoms impact the likelihood of rape and revictimization in college women. *Journal of Interpersonal Violence, 24*, 3, 499–521.

Messner, M. (1987). The meaning of success: The athletic experience and the development of male identity. In H. Brod (Ed.), *The making of masculinities* (pp. 193–210). Boston: Allen and Unwin.

Messner, M. (1992). Boyhood, organized sports, and the construction of masculinity. In M. Kimmel & M. Messner (Eds.), *Men's lives* (pp. 161–176). New York: Macmillan.

Messner, M. A. (1998). The limits of "the male sex role": An analysis of the men's liberation and men's rights movements' discourse. *Gender & Society, 12*, 255–276.

Messner, M. A., Duncan, M. C., & Jensen, K. (1993). Separating the men from the girls: The gendered language of televised sports. *Gender & Society, 7*, 121–137.

Messner, M. A. (2002). *Taking the field: Women, men and sports*. Minneapolis: University of Minnesota Press.

Messner, M. A. (2007). *Out of play: Critical essays on gender and sport*. Albany: State University of New York Press.

Mezey, N. J. (2008). *New choices, new families: How lesbians decide about motherhood*. Baltimore: Johns Hopkins University Press.

Miami judge rules against Florida gay adoption ban. (2008, December). *Gay & Lesbian Times*, 1093, 14–15.

Michael, R. T., Gagnon, J. H., Laumann, E. O., & Kolata, G. (1994). *Sex in America: A definitive study*. Boston: Little, Brown.

Mickelson, K. S. (2008). He said, she said: Comparing mother and father reports of father involvement. *Journal of Marriage and Family, 70*, 613–624.

Mies, M., & Shiva, V. (1993). *Ecofeminism*. London: Fernwood Publications/Zed Books.

Miethe, T. D., & Moore, C. A. (1986). Racial differences in criminal processing: The consequences of model selection on conclusions about differential treatment. *Sociological Quarterly, 27*, 217–237.

Mifflin, L. (1998, April 17). Increase seen in number of violent TV programs. *New York Times*, p. A16.

Mikjel Rio, K., & Smedal, O. (2009). *Hierarchy: Persistence and transformation in social formations*. New York: Berghahn Books.

Miles, T. (1995, April 25). Girls complain of "poor" school careers advice. *PA News* (Internet).

Military Family Resource Center. (2004). *2003 demographic profile of the military community*. Washington, DC: U.S. Department of Defense.

Milkman, R. (1987). *Gender at work: The dynamics of job segregation by sex during World War II*. Berkeley: University of California Press.

Millard, J. (2009). Performing beauty: Dove's "Real Beauty" campaign. *Symbolic Interaction, 32*(2), 146–168.

Millbrath, L. W. (1965). *Political participation*. Chicago: Rand McNally.

Miller, A. S., & Hoffman, J. P. (1995). Risk and religion: An explanation of gender differences in religiosity. *Journal for the the Scientific Study of Religion, 34*, 63–75.

Miller, B. D. (1993). The anthropology of sex and gender hierarchies. In B. D. Miller (Ed.), *Sex and gender hierarchies* (pp. 3–31). New York: Cambridge University Press.

Miller, C., & Swift, K. (1991a). One small step for genkind. In E. Ashton-Jones & G. A. Olson (Eds.), *The gender reader* (pp. 247–258). Boston: Allyn and Bacon.

Miller, C., & Swift, K. (1991b). Women and names. In E. Ashton-Jones & G. A. Olson (Eds.), *The gender reader* (pp. 272–286). Boston: Allyn and Bacon.

Miller, J. (1992, December 27). Women regain a kind of security in Islam's embrace. *New York Times*, p. E6.

Miller, J. (2001). *One of the guys: Girls, gangs, and gender*. New York: Oxford University Press.

Miller, J. (2008). *Getting played: African American girls, urban inequality, and gendered violence*. New York: NYU Press.

Miller, J., & Chamberlin, M. (2000). Women are teachers, men are professors: A study of student perceptions. *Teaching Sociology, 28*, 283–298.

Miller, J., & Jayasundara, D. (2001). Prostitution, the sex industry, and sex tourism. In C. M. Renzetti, J. L. Edleson, & R. K. Bergen (Eds.), *Sourcebook on violence against women* (pp. 459–480). Thousand Oaks, CA: Sage.

Miller, K. E. (2009). Sport-related identities and the "toxic jock." *Journal of Sport Behavior, 32*(1), 69–91.

Miller, K. E., Hoffinan, J. H., Bames, G M., Farrell, M. R, Sabo, D. F., & Melnick, M. J. (2003). Jocks, gender, race, and adolescent problem drinking. *Journal of Drug Education, 33*, 445–462.

Miller, K. E., Hoffinan, J. H., Bames, G. M., Farrell, M. R., Sabo, D. F., & Melnick, M. J. (2003). Jocks, gender, race, and adolescent problem drinking. *Journal of Drug Education, 33*, 445–462.

Miller, K. E., Melnick, M. J., Farrell, M. P., Sabo, D. F., & Bames, G M. (2006). Jocks, gender, binge drinking, and adolescent violence. *Journal of Interpersonal Violence, 21*, 105–120.

Miller, S. L. (1999). *Gender and community policing: Walking the talk.* Boston: Northeastern University Press.

Miller, S. L. (2001). The paradox of women arrested for domestic violence: Criminal justice professionals and service providers respond. *Violence Against Women, 7*, 1339–1376.

Miller, S. L., & Maier, S. L. (2008). Moving beyond numbers: What female judges say about different judicial voices. *Women, Politics, and Public Policy, 29*(4), 527–559.

Miller, S. M., & Kirsch, N. (1987). Sex differences in cognitive coping with stress. In R. C. Barnett & G. K. Baruch (Eds.), *Gender and stress* (pp. 278–302). New York: Free Press.

Miller, S. L. (2005). *Victims as offenders: The paradox of women's violence in relationships.* New Brunswick, NJ: Rutgers University Press.

Miller, S. L., Iovani, L., & Kelley, K. D. (2011). Violence against women and the criminal justice response. In C.M. Renzetti, J.L. Edleson, & R.K. Bergen (Eds.), *Sourcebook on violence against women, 2nd edition* (pp. 267–285). Thousand Oaks, CA: Sage.

Millman, M., & Kanter, R. M. (Eds.) (1975). *Another voice.* New York: Anchor.

Milloy, R. E. (2000, March 26). Survey on gays rings true to some in military. *New York Times*, p. 24.

Milner, M. (2004). *Freaks, geeks, and cool kids: American teenagers, schools, and the culture of consumption.* New York: Routledge.

Minority enrollment drops. (1997, November 2). *Atlanta Constitution.*

Minow, J. C., & Einolf, C. J. (2009). Sorority participation and sexual assault risk. *Violence Against Women, 15*(7), 835–851.

Minton, H. L. (1992). The emergence of gay and lesbian studies. In H. L. Minton (Ed.), *Gay and lesbian studies* (pp. 1–6). New York: Haworth Press.

Mintz, L. B., & Betz, N. E. (1986). Sex differences in the nature, realism, and correlates of body image. *Sex Roles, 15*, 185–195.

Mir-Hosseini, Z. (1999). *Islam and gender: The religious debate in contemporary Iran.* Princeton, NJ: Princeton University Press.

Missing male teacher. (2009, September). *USA Today Magazine*, 138, 2772, p. 6.

Mitaishvili, N. (2006). Personality type and coronary heart disease. *Georgian Med News*, (134), 58–60.

Mitchell, F. (1997). Keeping it all in the family: Sexual harassment policies and informal resolution in small colleges. *NWSA Journal, 9*, 118–125.

Mitchell, J. (1974). *Psychoanalysis and feminism.* New York: Random House.

Mitike, G., & Deressa, W. (2009). Prevalence and associated factors of female genital mutilation among Somali refugees in eastern Ethiopia: A cross-sectional study. *BMC Public Health, 9*, 264. Retrieved November 30, 2009, from http://www.biomedcentral.com/1471-2458/9/264

Moe, A. M. (2007).Silenced voices and structured survival: Battered women's help-seeking. *Violence Against Women, 13*, 676–699.

Moen, P., & Yu, Y. (2000). Effective work/life strategies: Working couples, working conditions, gender, and life quality. *Social Problems, 47*, 291–321.

Moghissi, H. (1999). *Feminism and Islamic fundamentalism: The limits of postmodern analysis.* London: Zed Books.

Mohanty, C. T. (1991). Cartographies of struggle: Third World women and the politics of feminism. In C. T. Mohanty, A. Russo, & L. Torres (Eds.), *Third World women and the politics of feminism* (pp. 1–47). Bloomington: Indiana University Press.

Mohanty, C. T. (2003). *Feminism without borders: Decolonizing theory, practicing solidarity.* Durham, NC: Duke University Press.

Mohipp, C., & Senn, C. Y. (2008). Graduate students' perceptions of contrapower sexual harassment. *Journal of Interpersonal Violence, 23*(9), 1258–1276.

Mohler-Kuo, M., Dowdall, G. W., Koss, M. P., & Wechsler, H. (2004). Correlates of rape while intoxicated in a national sample of college women. *Journal of Studies on Alcohol, 65*, 37–45.

Mohr, J. (1978). *Abortion in America*. New York: Oxford University Press.

Moir, A., & Jessel, D. (1989). *Brain sex*. London: Carol Publishing Group.

Mollenkott, V. R. (1991). Heterosexism: A challenge to ecumenical solidarity. In M. A. May (Ed.), *Women and church* (pp. 38–42). Grand Rapids, MI: Wm. B. Eerdmans Publishing Co.

Moller, S., & Li, H. (2009). Parties, unions, policies and occupational sex segregation in the United States. *Social Forces, 87*, 1529–1560.

Moller-Leimkuhler, A. (2003). The gender gap in suicide and premature death or: Why are men so vulnerable? *European Archives of Psychiatry and Clinical Neuroscience 253*(1), 1–8.

Monahan, K. C., & Lee, J. M. (2008). Adolescent sexual activity: Links between relational context and depressive symptoms. *Journal of Youth & Adolescence, 37*(8), 917–927.

Money wins presidency and 9 of 10 Congressional races in priciest U.S. election ever. (2008, November 5). Retrieved from: http://www.opensecrets.org/news/2008/11/money-wins-white-house-and.html

Money, J., & Ehrhardt, A. A. (1972). *Man and woman, boy and girl*. Baltimore: Johns Hopkins University Press.

Money, J., & Matthews, D. (1982). Prenatal exposure to virilizing progestins: An adult follow-up study on twelve young women. *Archives of Sexual Behavior, 11*, 73–83.

Monks, F., & Van Boxtel, H. (1995). Gifted adolescents: A developmental perspective. In J. Freeman (Ed.), *The psychology of gifted children* (pp. 275–295). New York: Wiley.

Montgomery, R. J. V., & Datwyler, M. M. (1990, Summer). Women and men in the caregiving role. *Generations 14*, pp. 34–38.

Moon, M., & Hoffman, C. D. (2008). Mothers' and fathers' differential expectancies and behaviors: Parent X child gender effects. *Journal of Genetic Psychology, 164*(3), 261–279.

Mooney, P. (2005). Gay-studies course is a first in China. *Chronicle of Higher Education, 52*(3), p. A39.

Mooney, S., & Ryan, I. (2009). A woman's place in hotel management: Upstairs or downstairs? *Gender in Management, 24*, 195–210.

Moore, M. (1997). Student resistance to course content: Reactions to the gender of the messenger. *Teaching Sociology, 25*, 128–133.

Moore, S., Sikora, P., Grunberg, L., & Greenberg, E. (2007). Work stress and alcohol use: Examining the tension-reduction model as a function of worker's parent's alcohol use. *Addictive Behaviors, 32*(12), 3114–3121.

Morash, M., & Greene, J. R. (1986). Evaluating women on patrol: A critique of contemporary wisdom. *Evaluation Review, 10*, 230–255.

Morash, M., & Haarr, R. (1995). Gender, workplace problems, and stress in policing. *Justice Quarterly, 12*, 113–140.

Morash, M., Haarr, R., & Kwak, D. H. (2006). Multilevel influences on police stress. *Journal of Contemporary Criminal Justice, 22*(1), 26–43.

More universities offer gay studies classes. (2007). *Gay Chicago Magazine*, 31(39), 20–21.

Morello, C., & Katel, P. (1998, March 20). Warning signals were simply seen as boyhood bravado. *USA Today*, pp. 1A–2A.

Morgan, H., Barry, R., & Morgan, H. (2008). Myoedema in anorexia nervosa: A useful clinical sign. *European Eating Disorders Review, 16*, 352–354.

Morgan, M., Rapkin, A. J., & Goldman, L. (1996). Cognitive functioning in premenstrual syndrome. *Obstetrics and Gynecology, 88*, 961–966.

Morin, D. (2010). It's your duty to be beautiful: The media's increasing demand for thinness in correlation with the eating disorder phenomena. Retrieved from: http://www.milligan.edu/academics/writing/pdfs/Morin.pdf

Morin, R., & Taylor, P. (2008). *Revisting the mommy wars: Politics, gender and parenthood*. Pew Research Center. Available online: http://pewsocialtrends.org/pubs/709/politics-gender-parenthood

Morley, J. (2010). Anorexia, weight loss, and frailty. *Journal of the American Medical Directors Association, 11*, 268–274.

Morris, E. W. (2007). "Ladies" or "loudies"? Perceptions and experiences of Black girls in classrooms. *Youth & Society, 38*(4), 490–515.

Morris, E. W. (2006). *An unexpected minority: White kids in an urban school*. New Brunswick, NJ: Rutgers University Press.

Morris, L. K., & Daniel, L. G. (2008). Perceptions of a chilly climate: Differences in traditional and nontraditional majors for women. *Research in Higher Education, 49*, 256–273.

Morris, N. H. (2008). Female genital mutilation. *AvMA Medical & Legal Journal, 14*(5), 189–192.

Morrison, D. R., & Ritualo, A. (2000). Routes to children's economic recovery after divorce: Are cohabitation and remarriage equivalent? *American Sociological Review, 65*, 560–580.

Morrissey, E. (1986). Power and control through discourse: The case of drinking and drinking problems among women. *Contemporary Crises, 10*, 157–179.

Mortensen, T. G. (2008). Where the boys were. *Chronicle of Higher Education, 54*(39), A30.

Moses, M. S., Yun, J. T., & Marin, P. (2009). Affirmative action's fate: Are 20 more years enough? *Education Policy Analysis Archives, 17*(17), 1–34.

Mosher, D. L., & Sirkin, M. (1984). Measuring a macho personality constellation. *Journal of Research in Personality, 18*, 150–163.

Mosher, W. D., Chandra, A., & Jones, J. (2005). Sexual behavior and selected health measures: Men and women 15–44 years of age, United States, 2002. *Advance data from vital and health statistics*, 362, 1–33. Washington, DC: U.S. Department of Health and Human Services, National Center for Health Statistics.

Moss, M. (2003, March 26). General's crackdown faulted in rapes. *New York Times*, p. A10.

Motzafi-Haller, P. (2001). Scholarship, identity, and power: Mizrahi women in Israel. *Signs, 26*, 697–734.

Moyer, I. L. (1991). *Women's prisons: Issues and controversies*. Paper presented at the annual meeting of the American Society of Criminology, San Francisco, CA.

Moyo, M. (1996, November 21). Gender equality polarizing women. Bulawayo, Zimbabwe: PanAfrican News Agency. (Internet).

Muftic, L. R., Bouffard, J. A., & Bouffard, L. A. (2007). An exploratory study of women arrested for intimate partner violence: Violent women or violent resistance? *Journal of Interpersonal Violence, 22*(6), 753–774.

Mukhopadhyay, S. (2008). Do women value marriage more? The effect of obesity on cohabitation and marriage in the USA. *Review of Economics of the Household, 6*, 111–126.

Mulac, A. (2006). The gender-linked language effect: Do gender differences really make a difference? In K. Dindia & D. J. Canary (Eds.), *Sex differences and similarities in communication* (pp. 211–231). Mahwah, NJ: Lawrence Erlbaum.

Mullally, S. (2007). The UN, minority rights and gender equality: Setting limits to collective claims. *International Journal on Minority and Group Rights, 14*, 263–283.

Mumola, C. J. (2000). *Incarcerated parents and their children*. Washington, DC: U.S. Department of Justice, Bureau of Justice Statistics.

Munt, S. R. (1996). Beyond backlash: Lesbian studies in the United Kingdom. In B. Zimmerman & T. A. H. McNaron (Eds.), *The new lesbian studies* (pp. 234–239). New York: Feminist Press.

Murdoch, G. P., & Provost, C. (1973). Factors in the division of labor by sex: A cross-cultural analysis. *Ethnology, 12*, 203–225.

Murnen, S. K., & Kohlman, M. H. (2007). Athletic participation, fraternity membership, and sexual aggression among college men: A meta-analytic review. *Sex Roles, 57*, 145–157.

Murnen, S. K., & Smolak, L. (2000). The experience of sexual harassment among grade-school students: Early socialization of female subordination? *Sex Roles, 43*, 1–17.

Murphy, B. O. (1994). Women's magazines: Confusing differences. In L. H. Turner & H. M. Sterk (Eds.), *Differences that make a difference* (pp. 119–128). Westport, CT: Bergin and Garvey.

Murphy-Geiss, G., Rosenfield, D., & Foley, L. (2010). Midwifery as established sect: An expanded application of the Church-sect continuum. *Community, Work, & Family, 13*, 101–122.

Murray, S. (2009). Numbers on welfare see sharp increase. *Wall Street Journal*, p. A1.

Murry, V. M., & Brody, G. H. (2002). Racial socialization processes in single-mother families: Linking maternal racial identity, parenting, and racial socialization in rural, single-mother families with child self-worth and self-regulation. In H. P. McAdoo (Ed.). *Black children: Social, educational, and parental environments* (pp. 97–115). Thousand Oaks, CA: Sage.

Murry, V. M., Berkel, C., Brody, G. H., Miller, S. J., & Chen, Y. (2009). Linking parental socialization to interpersonal protective processes, academic self-presentation, and expectations among rural African American youth. *Cultural Diversity and Ethnic Minority Psychology, 15*, 1–10.

Muth, J. L., & Cash, T. F. (2006). Body-image attitudes: What difference does gender make? *Journal of Applied Social Psychology, 27*(16), 1438–1452.

My Wellness. (2000). *In a 2000 survey of American adults, the National Sporting Goods Association found...* Retrieved from http://www.mywellness. com/default.asp?ipag=24&IDart=32

Mydans, S. (1996, October 10). Blame men, not Allah, Islamic feminists say. *New York Times*, p. A4.

Myers, S. L. (2009, December 28). Another peril in war zones: Sexual abuse by fellow G.I.'s. *New York Times*, pp. A1, A10.

Myhill, D., & Jones, S. (2006). "She doesn't shout at no girls": Pupils' perceptions of gender equity in the classroom. *Cambridge Journal of Education, 36*, 99–113

Nabors, E. L., Dietz, T. L., & Jasinski, J. (2006). Domestic violence beliefs and perceptions among college students. *Violence & Victims, 21*, 779–799.

Nagel, S., & Weitzman, L. J. (1972). The double standard of American justice. *Society, 9*, 171–198.

Nakamura, Y. (2010). Nursing intervention to enhance acceptance of pregnancy in first time mothers: Focusing on the comfortable experiences of pregnant women. *Japan Journal of Nursing Science 7*(1), 29–36.

Nanda, S. (1990). *Neither man nor woman: The Hijras of India*. Belmont, CA: Wadsworth.

Naples, N. A. (1998). *Grassroots warriors: Activist mothering, community work, and the war on poverty*. New York: Routledge.

Naples, N. A. (2003). *Feminism and method*. New York: Routledge.

National Abortion Rights Action League (NARAL). (2000). *Who decides? A state-by-state review of abortion and reproductive rights*. Available online: http://www.naral.org/mediaresources/ publications/2000/whod.html

National Association of Women Judges. (2009). *The American Bench – Judges of the Nation 2009 Edition*. Sacramento, CA: Forster-Long, LLC. Retrieved from: http://www.nawj.org/us_state_ court_statistics_2009.asp

National Association of Women Judges. (2010). *2010 representation of United States state court: Women judges*. Retrieved from: http://www. nawj.org/us_state court_statistics_2010.asp

National Center for Elder Abuse. (2006). Fact sheet: Abuse of adults aged 60+ 2004 survey of adult protective services. Washington, D.C.: National Center on Elder Abuse. Retrieved from: http:// www.elderabusecenter.org

National Center for Health Statistics. (2000). *Health, United States, 2000*. Hyattsville, MD: Author.

National Center for Health Statistics. (2004). *Health, United States, 2004*. Table 27. Life expectancy at birth, at 65 years of age, and at 75 years of age, according to race and sex: United States, selected years 1900–2002. Hyattsville, MD: National Center for Health Statistics.

National Center for Health Statistics. (2009). *National marriage and divorce rate trends*. Hyattsville, MD: National Center for Health Statistics.

National Center for Health Statistics. (2010). *Health United States, 2010*. Retrieved from: http://www. cdc.nchs/data/hus/hus10.pdf

National Center for Juvenile Justice. (2008, October 24). Juvenile arrest rates by offense, sex, and race. Available at http://ojjdp.ncjrs.org/ojstatbb/ crime/excel/jar_2007.els

National Center for Medical-Legal Partnership. (2011). Raising the bar for health. Retrieved from: http://www.medical-legalpartnership.org

National Coalition for the Homeless. (2009a). *How many people experience homelessness?* Retreived from: http://www.nationalhomeless.org/ factsheets/How_Many.pdf

National Coalition for the Homeless. (2009b). *Who is homeless?* Retrieved from: http://www.nation-alhomeless.org/factsheets/Whois.pdf

National Coalition for the Homeless. (2010). *Foreclosure to homelessness: 2009*. Retreived from: http://www.nationalhomeless.org/advocacy/ ForeclosuretoHomelessness0609.pdf

National Coalition for Women and Girls in Education. (2007). *Title IX at 35*. Washington, DC: Author.

National Collegiate Athletics Association (NCAA). (2010). College sports statistics and records. Retrieved from: http://www.ncaa.org/wps/wcm/ connect/public/ncaa/resources/stats

National Election Surveys (2006). Political involvement and participation in politics. Retrieved from: http://www.electionstudies.org

National Institute of Mental Health (2008). *Health place: America's mental health channel, suicide facts, suicide statistics*. Retrieved from http:// www.healthyplace.com/depression/suicide/ suicide-facts-suicide-statistics/menu-id-68/

National Institute of Mental Health (2011). *Psych central: Women and depression*. Retrieved from http://psychcentral.com/lib/2007/ women-and-depression/

National Institute on Alcohol Abuse and Alcoholism (NIAAA) (2011). *Twelve-month prevalence and population estimates of DSM-IV alcohol abuse by age, sex, and race-ethnicity: United States, 2001– 2002*. Retrieved from http://www.niaaa.nih.

gov/Resources/DatabaseResources/QuickFacts/AlcoholDependence/abusdep1.htm

National Law Center on Homelessness and Poverty. (2004). *Homelessness in the United States and the human right to housing*. Retrieved from: http://www.nlchp.org/Pubs/index.cfm?FA=7&TAB=2

National Survey of Student Engagement. (2003). *Converting data into action: Expanding the boundaries of institutional improvement*. Bloomington: Indiana University Center for Postsecondary Research.

National Vital Statistics System. (2007). *Death rates for 113 selected causes, by 10-year age groups, Hispanic origin, race for non-Hispanic population, and sex: United States, 2002–2003, 2005–2006*. Retrieved from http://www.cdc.gov/nchs/nvss/mortality/gmwkh250r.htm

Natividad, I. (1992). Women of color and the campaign trail. In P. Ries & A. J. Stone (Eds.), *The American woman, 1992–93* (pp. 127–148). New York: W. W. Norton.

Naude, J. (2004). An overview of recent developments in translation studies with special reference to the implications for Bible translation. *Acta Theologica, 34*, 101–112.

Navarro, M. (1996, April 4). Abortion clinics report drop in harassing incidents. *New York Times*, p. B14.

Navarro, M. (2001, February 13). Women in sports cultivating new playing fields. *New York Times*, pp. A1, D4.

Neal, D. (2004). The measured black-white gap among women is too small. *Journal of Political Economy, 112*, 1–28.

Nechas, E., & Foley, D. (1994). *Unequal treatment*. New York: Simon and Schuster.

Neff, J. L., & Waite, D. E. (2007). Male versus female substance abuse patterns among incarcerated juvenile offenders: Comparing strain and social learning variables. *Justice Quarterly, 24*, 106–132.

Negy, C., & Eisenman, R. (2005). A comparison of African American and White college students' affective and attitudinal reactions to lesbian, gay, and bisexual individuals: An exploration studies. *Journal of Sex Research, 42*, 291–298.

Neighbors, H. W. (1997). Husbands, wives, family, and friends: Sources of stress, sources of support. In R. J. Taylor, J. S. Jackson, & L. M. Chatters (Eds.), *Family life in Black America* (pp. 277–292). Thousand Oaks, CA: Sage.

Nelson, M. (1979). Why witches were women. In J. Freeman (Ed.), *Women: A feminist perspective* (2nd ed.) (pp. 451–468). Palo Alto, CA: Mayfield.

Nelson, M. B. (1992). *Are we winning yet?* New York: Random House.

Nelson, S. M. (1993). Gender hierarchy and the queens of Silla. In B. D. Miller (Ed.), *Sex and gender hierarchies* (pp. 297–315). New York: Cambridge University Press.

Nelson, S. M. (1997). Diversity in Upper Paleolithic "venus" figurines and archeological mythology. In C. B. Brettell & C. F. Sargent (Eds.), *Gender in cross-cultural perspective* (pp. 67–74). Englewood Cliffs, NJ: Prentice Hall.

Nelson, S. M. (2004). *Gender in archeology: Analyzing power and prestige*. Lnaham, MD: Rowman Altamira Press.

Nemy, E. (1992, June 18). "What? Me marry?" Widows say no. *New York Times*, p. C1, C8.

Ness, R. B. et al. (2000). Salary equity among male and female internists in Pennsylvania. *Annals of Internal Medicine, 133*, 104–110.

Neuberger, J. (1983). Women in Judaism: The fact and the fiction. In P. Holden (Ed.), *Women's religious experience: Cross-cultural perspectives* (pp. 132–142). London: Croom Helm.

Nevels, L. (1990). *Mentoring relationships and women*. Paper presented at the annual meeting of the Mid-Atlantic Association of Student Officers of Housing, Women's Issues Group, Glasboro, NJ.

Nevid, J. (2008). *Psychology: Concepts and applications*. Independence, KY: Cengage Brain.

Neville, H. A., & Pugh, A. O. (1997). General and culture-specific factors influencing African American women's reporting patterns and perceived social support following sexual assault: An exploratory investigation. *Violence Against Women, 3*, 361–381.

New Models. (2006). *Age, sex and race in modeling: New model*, Retrieved from http://www.new-models.com/race.html

Newbold, R. (2006). Adverse effects of the model environmental estrogen diethylstilbestrol are transmitted to subsequent generations. *Endocrinology, 147*(6), s11-s17.

Newburger, C. (1998). *Workplace toxins and African Americans*. Retrieved from http://academic.udayton.edu/health/01status/98newbur.htm

Newman, A. (2000, October 27). Visiting rights denied in embryo mix-up case. *New York Times*, p. B3.

Newman, A. (2005, September 16). Serving gays who serve God. *New York Times*, p. A21.

Newman, A. (2007). *Life support for feminist care?* Retrieved from http://www.rhrealitycheck.

org/blog/2007/01/09/life-support-for-feminist-health-care-part-ii

Newman, B., & Newman, P. (2008). *Development Through Life: A Psychosocial Approach.* Belmont, CA: Wadsworth Cengage Learning.

Niazi, S. (2008). India: State of dowry deaths. *Pakistan Journal of Women's Studies, 15*(1), 99–100.

Nicholi, A. M. (1991). The impact of family dissolution on the emotional health of children and adolescents. In B. J. Christensen (Ed.), *When families fail . . . The social costs* (pp. 27–41). New York: University Press of America.

Nichols, P. C. (1986). Women in their speech communities. In S. McConnell-Ginet, R. Borker, & N. Furman (Eds.), *Women and language in literature and society* (pp. 140–149). New York: Greenwood.

Nicoloff, L. K., & Stiglitz, E. A. (1987). Lesbian alcoholism: Etiology, treatment, and recovery. In Boston Lesbian Psychologies Collective (Eds.), *Lesbian psychologies* (pp. 283–293). Urbana: University of Illinois Press.

Niebuhr, G. (1997, October 12). Rabbis still resist interfaith marriage, study shows. *New York Times*, p. 28.

Niebuhr, G. (2000a, March 30). Reform rabbis back blessing of gay unions. *New York Times*, pp. A1, A20.

Niebuhr, G. (2000b, October 31). Marriage issue splits Jews, poll finds. *New York Times*, p. A25.

Niebuhr, G. (2000c, May 19). Southern Baptists consider check on women as pastors. *New York Times*, p. A16.

Niehoff, D. (1999). *The biology of violence.* New York: Free Press.

Nielsen Company. (2010). Television, internet and mobile usage in the U.S. *Three Screen Report, 8.* Retrieved September 14, 2010, http://en-us.nielsen.com/content/dam/nielsen/en_us/documents/pdf/White%20Papers%20and%20Reports/Nielsen_Three%20Screen%20Report_Q12010.pdf

Nielsen Company. (2011). *State of the media: TV usage trends: Q3 and Q4 2010.* Retrieved from: http://www.nielsen.com/content/dam/corporate/us/en/reports-downloads/2011-Reports/State%20of%20the%20Media%20TV%20Q3%20Q4%202010.pdf

Nieves-Squires, S. (1991). *Hispanic women: Making their presence on campus less tenuous.* Washington, DC: Association of American Colleges and Universities.

Nigro, S. A. (2001). Why homosexuality is a disorder. *Social Justice Review, 29*, 70–76.

Nikolic-Ristanovic, V. (1999). Living without democracy and peace: Violence against women in the former Yugoslavia. *Violence Against Women, 5*, 63–80.

Nilsen, A. P. (1991). Sexism in English: A 1990s update. In E. Ashton-Jones & G. A. Olson (Eds.), *The gender reader* (pp. 259–270). Boston: Allyn and Bacon.

Nishikawa, K. A., Towner, T. L., Clawson, R. A., & Waltenberg, E. N. (2009). Interviewing the interviewers: Journalistic norms and racial diversity in the newsroom. *Howard Journal of Communications, 20*, 242–259.

Niven, D. (1998). *The missing majority: The recruitment of women as state legislative candidates.* Westport, CT: Praeger.

Noble, K. D. (1989). Counseling gifted women: Becoming the heroes of our own stories. *Journal for the Education of the Gifted, 12*, 131–141.

Nonnemaker, L. (2000). Women physicians in academic medicine: New insights from cohort studies. *New England Journal of Medicine, 342*, 399–305.

Nordbo, R., et al. (2008). Expanding the concept of motivation to change: The content of patients' wish to recover from anorexia nervosa. *International Journal of Eating Disorders, 41*, 635–642.

Norris, J., & Kerr, K. L. (1991). *Hypermasculinity and violent pornography: Does alcohol consumption affect macho men's judgments?* Paper presented at the annual meeting of the American Society of Criminology, San Francisco, CA.

Norton, A. (2005). *Transplant living: Women less likely to survive heart bypass surgery.* Retrieved from http://www.transplantliving.org/community/news.aspx?id=481

Norton, M. B. (1997). *Founding mothers and fathers.* New York: Alfred A. Knopf.

Nosek, M. A., Howland, C., Rintala, D. H., Young, M. E., & Chanpong, G. F. (2001). National study of women with physical disabilities: Final report. *Sexuality and Disability, 19*(1), 5–39.

NPR. (2010, September 30). Student's suicide highlights bullying over sexuality. Retrieved from: http://www.NPR.org

O'Brien, N. (2011). Embryonic stem cell research immoral, unnecessary, bishops say. Retrieved from: http://www.americancatholic.org/news/stemcell/

O'Connor, S. D. (2002). *Lazy B: Growing up on a cattle ranch in the American Southwest*. New York: Random House.

O'Farrell, T., Harrison, R., & Cutter, H. (2006). Marital stability among wives of alcoholics: An evaluation of three explanations. *British Journal of Addiction, 76*(2), 175–189.

O'Kelly, C. G., & Carney, L. S. (1986). *Women and men in society: Cross-cultural perspectives on gender stratification*. Belmont, CA: Wadsworth.

O'Loan, S., McMillan, F., Motherwell, S., Bell, A., & Arshad, R. (2006). *Promoting equal opportunities in Education Project Two: Guidance on dealing with homophobic incidents*. Edinburgh: LGBT Scotland.

O'Neill, W. L. (1969). *Everyone was brave*. New York: Quadrangle.

O'Reilly, J., & Cahn, S. (2007). *Women and sports in the United States: A documentary reader*. Boston: Northeaster University Press.

O'Shea, K. A. (1999). *Women and the death penalty in the United States, 1990–1998*. New York: Praeger.

Oakley, A. (1980). *Becoming a mother*. New York: Schocken.

Oaxaca, R. I., & Dickinson, D. L. (2006). Statistical discrimination in labor markets: An experimental analysis. IZA Discussion Paper #2305. Retrieved from: http://ftp.iza.org/dp2305.pdf

Odean, K. (1997). *Great books for girls*. Mew York: Ballantine Books.

Odegaard, L. (2005). *The Goddess and the God: A synthesis*. Victoria, Canada: Trafford Publishing.

Odutolu, O., Adedimeji, A., Odutolu, O., Baruwa, O., & Olatidoye, F. (2003). Economic empowerment and reproductive behavior of young women in Osun State, Nigeria. *African Journal of Reproductive Health, 7*, 92–100.

Offen, K. (1988). Defining feminism: A comparative historical approach. *Signs, 14*, 119–157.

Offen, K. (2000). *European feminism, 1700–1950: A political history*. Palo Alto, CA: Stanford University Press.

Office of Juvenile Justice and Delinquency Prevention (OJJDP). (2006). *Census of Juveniles in Residential Placement 2006*. Washington, DC: OJJDP.

Office of Waste Management. (2005). Household hazardous waste. Retrieved from: http://www.extension.missouri.edu/owm/hhw.htm

Ogden, A. S. (1986). *The great American housewife*. Westport, CT: Greenwood.

Oldham, J. T. (2008). Changes in the economic consequences of divorces, 1958–2008. Family Law Quarterly, 42(3), 419–447.

Oliver, A. (2009). The search for the 'gay gene' and the medicalization of same-sex desire. *Journal of Sexual Diversity Studies*, (2), 61–69.

Olson, T. B. (2010). The conservative case for gay marriage. *Newsweek, 155*(3), 48–54.

Onishi, N. (1997, February 16). Reading Torah, women's group tests tradition. *New York Times*, pp. 43, 49.

Onishi, N. (2001, February 12). On the scale of beauty, weight weighs heavily. *New York Times*, p. A4.

Oorwijn, M. B., Boekaerts, M., Vedder, P., & Fortuin, J. (2008). The impact of a cooperative learning experience on pupils' popularity, non-cooperativeness, and interethnic bias in multiethnic elementary schools. *Educational Psychology, 28*, 211–221.

Oransky, M., & Marecek. (2009). "I'm not going to be a girl!" Masculinity and emotions in boys' friendships and peer groups. *Journal of Adolescent Research, 24*, 218–241.

Orenstein, P. (1994). *Schoolgirls: Young women, self-esteem and the confidence gap*. New York: Anchor/Doubleday.

Orenstein, P., & Van Straalen, A. (2001). *Flux: Women on sex, work, love, kids, and life in a half-changed world*. New York: Knopf.

Orrange, S. (2011). *Why are women still not receiving treatment for heart attack as fast as men?* Retrieved from http://www.dailystrength.org/health_blogs/dr-orrange/article/women-still-not-receiving-treatment-for-heart-attack-as-fast-as-men

Osborne, C., & McLanahan, S. (2007). Partnership instability and child well-being. *Journal of Marriage and Family, 69*(4), 1065–1083.

Osmond, M. W., Wambach, K. G., Harrison, D. F., Byers, J., Levine P., Imershein, A., &. Quadagno, D. M. (1993). The multiple jeopardy of race, class, and gender for AIDS risk among women. *Gender & Society, 7*, 99–120.

Ovens, H. J., & Permaul-Woods, J. A. (1997). Emergency room physicians and sexual involvement with patients: An Ontario study. *Canadian Medical Association Journal, 157*, 663–684.

Owen, B. (2001). Perspectives on women in prison. In C. M. Renzetti & L. Goodstein (Eds.), *Women, crime and criminal justice* (pp. 243–254). Los Angeles: Roxbury.

Ozgun, O., & Honig, A. (2005). Parental involvement and spousal satisfaction with division of early childcare in Turkish families with normal children and children with special needs. *Early Child Development and Care, 175*, 259–270.

Padevic, I., & Orcutt, J. D. (1997). Perceptions of sexual harassment in the Florida legal system: A comparison of dominance and spillover explanations. *Gender & Society, 11*, 682–698.

Page, A. D. (2008). Judging women and defining crime: Police officers' attitudes toward women and rape. *Sociological Spectrum, 28*, 389–411.

Page, D. C., Fisher, E. M. C., McGillivray, B., & Brown, L. G. (1990). Additional deletion in sex-determining region of human Y chromosome resolves paradox of X,t(Y;22) female. *Nature, 346*, 279–281.

Page, T. (2008). *The problem of the land is the problem of the woman: A genealogy of ecofeminism in Grailville*. Cambridge, MA: Harvard University Press.

Pagelow, M. D. (1981). Secondary battering and alternatives of female victims to spouse abuse. In L. H. Bowker (Ed.), *Women and crime in America* (pp. 277–298). New York: Macmillan.

Pagels, E. (1979). What became of God the mother? In C. P. Christ & J. Plakow (Eds.), *Womanspirit rising* (pp. 107–119). San Francisco: Harper and Row.

Pager, D., & Karafin, D. (2009). Bayesian bigot? Statistical discrimination, stereotypes, and employer decision making. *Annals of the American Academy of Political and Social Sciences, 621*, 70–93.

Pager, D., Western, B., & Bonikowski, B. (2007). *Discrimination in low-wage labor markets*. Working paper. Princeton, NJ: Office of Population Research, Princeton University.

Pale Reflections. (2011). *The eating disorders support community*. Retrieved from: http://www.pale-reflections.com/ed_stats.asp

Palepu, A., Carr, P. L., Friedman, R. H., Amos, H., Ash, A. S., & Moskowitz, M. A. (1998). Minority faculty and academic rank in medicine. *Journal of the American Medical Association, 280*, 767–771.

Palmer, L. (1993, November 7). The nurses of Vietnam, still wounded. *New York Times Magazine*, pp. 36–43, 68, 72–73.

Palmore, E., Branch, L., & Harris, D. (2005). *Encyclopedia of Ageism*. London: Psychology Press.

Papa, D., Moore Simas, T., Reynolds, M., & Melintsky, H. (2009). Assessing the role of education in women's knowledge and acceptance of adjunct high-risk human papillomavirus testing for cervical cancer screening. *Journal of Lower Genital Tract Diseases, 13*(2), 66–71.

Papper, B. (2007). Women and minorities in the newsroom: African Americans have gained ground in radio and TV while other minority groups have slipped. *Communicator*, July/August, 20–25.

Papper, B. (2008). The face of the workforce. *Communicator*, July/August, 9–12.

Paranjape, A., Corbie-Smith, G., Thompson, N., & Kaslow, N. J. (2009a). When older African American women are affected by violence in the home: A qualitative investigation of risk and protective factors. *Violence Against Women, 15*, 977–990.

Paranjape, A., Sprauve-Holmes, N. E., Gaughan, J., Kaslow, N. J. (2009b). Lifetime exposure to family violence: Implications for the health status of older African American women. *Journal of Women's Health, 18*, 171–175.

Paranjape, S., Turankar, A., Wakode, S., & Dakhale, G. (2005). Estrogen protection against coronary heart disease: Are the relevant effects of estrogen mediated through its effects on uterus—such as the induction of menstruation, increased bleeding, and the facilitation of pregnancy? *Med Hypotheses, 65*, 725–727.

"Parents and abortion." (2008, January 8). *State Legislatures, 34*(1), 10.

Park, A. (2010). *Are you a Type D personality? Your heart may be at risk*. Retrieved from http://health-land.time.com/2010/09/14/a-new-risk-factor-for-heart-disease-type-d-personality/

Parks, K. A., & Fals-Stewart, W. (2004). The temporal relationship between college women's alcohol consumption and victimization experiences. *Alcoholism, 28*, 625–629.

Parks-Stamm, E. J., Heilman, M. E., & Hearns, K. A. (2008). Motivated to penalize: Women's strategic rejection of successful women. *Personality and Social Psychology Bulletin, 34*(2), 237–247.

Parlee, M. B. (1982, September). New findings: Menstrual cycles and behavior. *Ms.*, pp. 126–128.

Parlee, M. B. (1983). Changes in moods and activation levels during the menstrual cycle in experimentally naive subjects. *Psychology of Women Quarterly, 7*, 119–131.

Parma, L. W. (2006). Sex differences in faculty tenure and promotion: The contribution of family ties. *Research in Higher Education, 46*(3), 277–307.

Parramore, L. (2008). *Reading the Sphinx: Ancient Egypt in nineteenth century literature.* New York: Macmillan.

Parsons, T. (1955). The American family: Its relations to personality and to the social structure. In T. Parsons & R. F. Bales (Eds.), *Family, socialization and interaction process* (pp. 3–33). Glencoe, IL: Free Press.

Pascoe, C. J. (2007). *Dude, you're a fag: Masculinity and sexuality in high school.* Berkeley: University of California Press.

Patchin, J. W., & Hinduja, S. (2006). Bullies move beyond the schoolyard. *Youth Violence and Juvenile Justice, 4,* 148–169.

Pattavina, A., Hirschel, D., Buzawa, E., Faggiani, D., & Bentley, H. (2007). A comparison of the police response to heterosexual versus same-sex intimate partner violence. *Violence Against Women, 13,* 4, 374–394.

Patterson, C. J. (2000). Family relationships of lesbians and gay men. *Journal of Marriage and the Family, 62,* 1052–1069.

Patterson, M. (2007, June 22). Finding "herstory": Pilgrims in Rome examine women's leadership in the early Christian church. *National Catholic Reporter,* pp. 10–13.

Patterson, P. (1996). Rambos and himbos: Stereotypical images of men in advertising. In P. M. Lester (Ed.), *Images that injure* (pp. 93–96). Westport, CT: Praeger.

Patton, L. D. (2009). My sister's keeper: A qualitative examination of mentoring experiences among African American women in graduate and professional schools. *Journal of Higher Education, 80*(5), 510–537.

Patton, L. D., & Harper, S. R. (2003). Mentoring relationships among African American women in graduate and professional schools. In M. F..Howard-Hamilton (Ed.), Meeting the needs of African American women. *New Directions for Student Services, 104,* 67–78.

Patton-Owens, T. (2001). "Ally McBeal" and Her Homies: The Reification of White Stereotypes of the Other. *Journal of Black Studies, 32,* 229–260.

Paul, B., & Shim, J. W. (2008). Gender, sexual affect, and motivations for Internet pornography use. *International Journal of Sexual Health, 20*(3), 187–199.

Paul, M., Daniels, C., & Rosofsky, R. (1989). Corporate response to reproductive hazards in the workplace: Results of the family, work, and health survey. *American Journal of Industrial Medicine, 16,* 267–280.

Pawelski, J. G., Perrin, E. C., Foy, J. M., Allen, C. E., Crawford, J. E., Del Monte, M., et al. (2006). The effects of marriage, civil union, and domestic partnership laws on the health and well-being of children. *Pediatrics, 118,* 349–364.

Pay Scale (2010). *Bona Fide Occupational Qualification Standards, Compensation Today.* Retrieved February 28, 2011, http://blogs.payscale.com/compensation/2010/07/bona-fide-occupational-qualification-standards.html

Pear, R. (2002, January 24). House Democrats propose making the '96 welfare law an antipoverty weapon. *New York Times,* p. A24.

Pear, R. (2008). *Gap in life expectancy widens for the nation.* Retrieved from http://www.nytimes.com/2008/03/23/us/23health.html

Pearlman, S. F. (1987). The saga of continuing clash in the lesbian community, or will an army of exlovers fail? In Boston Lesbian Psychologies Collective (Eds.), *Lesbian psychologies* (pp. 313–326). Urbana: University of Illinois Press.

Pearson, J., & Thoennes, N. (1996). What happens to pregnant substance abusers and their babies? *Juvenile and Family Court Journal,* pp. 15–28.

Peck, S. (1985). *Halls of jade, walls of stone: Women in China today.* New York: Franklin Watts.

Pelkey, W. L., & DeGrange, M. L. (1996). Gender bias in field training evaluation programs: An exploratory analysis. *Women and Criminal Justice, 8,* 79–90.

Peltola, P., Milkie, M. A., & Presser, S. (2004). The "feminist" mystique: Feminist identity in three generations of women. *Gender & Society, 18,* 122–144.

Peplau, L. A. (1986). What homosexuals want. In L. Simkins (Ed.), *Alternative sexual lifestyles* (pp. 118–123). Acton, MA: Copley Publishing Group.

Peplau, L. A., & Fingerhut, A. W. (2007). The close relationships of lesbians and gay men. *Annual Review of Psychology, 58,* 405–424.

Perkins R., Kleiner, B., Roey, S., & Brown, J. (2004). *The high school transcript study: A decade of change in curricula and achievement, 1990–2000.* Washington, DC: National Center Education Statistics.

Perrett, D. I., May, K. A., & Yoshikawa, S. (1994). Facial shape and judgments of female attractiveness. *Nature, 368,* 239–242.

Perry, B. (2001). *In the name of hate: Understanding hate crimes.* New York: Routledge.

Perry-Jenkins, M., Repetti, R., & Crouter, A. (2000). Work and family in the 1990s. *Journal of Marriage and Family, 62*, 4, 981–998.

Persell, C. H. (2010). Social class and educational equality. In Banks, J. A. & Banks, C.A.M. (Eds.) *Multicultural Education: Issues and Perspectives* (7/e), (pp. 85–106). Hoboken, NJ: John Wiley & Sons, Inc.

Persell, C. H., James, C., Kang, T., & Synder, K. (1999). Gender and education in global perspective. In J. S. Chafetz (Ed.), *Handbook of the sociology of gender* (pp. 407–440). New York: Kluwer.

Peter, T. (2009). Exploring taboos: Comparing male- and female-perpetrated child sexual abuse. *Journal of Interpersonal Violence, 24*(7), 1111–1128.

Peterman, L. M., & Dixon, C. G. (2003). Intimate partner abuse between same-sex partners: Implications for counseling. *Journal of Counseling and Development, 81*, 40–59.

Peters, A. et al. (2007). Causes of obesity: Looking beyond the hypothalamus. *Progress in Neurobiology, 81*(2), 61–88.

Petre, J., & MacFarlane, J. (2008). Depression in girls "linked to female sex." *Mail on Sunday*, p. 107.

Petroll, A., & Mosack, K. (2011). Physician awareness of sexual orientation and preventive health recommendation to men who have sex with men. *Sexually Transmitted Diseases, 38*, 63–67.

Pew Forum on Religion and Public Life. (2009). *U.S. Religious Landscape Survey*. Retrieved from: http://religions.pewforum.org/reports

Pew Research Center. (2006). *Less opposition to gay marriage, adoption, and military service*. Retrieved December 14, 2009 from http://people-press.org/reports/pdf/273.pdf

Pew Research Center. (2008). *Where men and women differ in following the news*. Retrieved October 20, 2010, www.pewresearch.org/pubs/722/men-women-follow-new/

Pew Research Center. (2010). *Ideological news sources: Who watches and why*. Retrieved September 27, 2010, http://people-press.org/reports/pdf/652.pdf

Philips, R. D., & Gilroy, F. D. (1985). Sex-role stereotypes and clinical judgments of mental health: The Brovermans' findings reexamined. *Sex Roles, 12*, 179–193.

Phillips, P. (1998). *Censored, 1998*. New York: Seven Stories Press.

Phillips, S. P., & Schneider, M. S. (1993). Sexual harassment of female doctors by patients. *New England Journal of Medicine, 329*, 1936–1939.

Philpot, T. S., & Walton, H. (2007). One of our own: Black female candidates and the voters who support them. *American Journal of Political Science, 51*, 49–62.

Philpott, H., & Christie, M. (2008). Coping in male partners of female problem drinkers. *Journal of Substance Abuse, 13*, 193–203.

Piechura-Couture, K., Tichenor, M., & Heins, E. D. (2007). *A study of elementary school students' achievement in single-gender versus mixed-gender classrooms*. Unpublished manuscript.

Pike, D. L. (1992). Women in police academy training: Some aspects of organizational response. In I. L. Moyer (Ed.), *The changing roles of women in the criminal justice system* (pp. 261–280). Prospect Heights, IL: Waveland.

Pike, J. J., & Jennings, N. A. (2005). The effects of commercials on children's perceptions of gender appropriate toy use. *Sex Roles, 52*(1/2), 83–91.

Pike, K. M., Dohm, F. A., Striegel-Moore, R. H., Wilfley, D. E., Fairburn, C. G. (2001). A comparison of Black and White women with eating disorders. *American Journal of Psychiatry, 158*, 1455–1460.

Pillemer, K., & Finkelhor, D. (1988). The prevalence of elder abuse: A random sample survey. *Gerontologist, 28*, 51–57.

Pillemer, K., & Suitor, J. J. (1998). Violence and violent feelings: What causes them among family caregivers. In R. K. Bergen (Ed.), *Issues in intimate violence* (pp. 255–266). Thousand Oaks, CA: Sage.

Pinel, J. P. J. (1997). *Biopsychology*. Boston: Allyn and Bacon.

Pizza, M., & Lewis, J. (2009). *Handbook of contemporary paganism*. Boston: Brill Publishers.

Plant, E. A., Hyde, J. S., Keltner, D., & Devine, P. G. (2000). The gender stereotyping of emotions. *Psychology of Women Quarterly, 24*, 81–92.

Pleming, S. (2001, March 7). Abuse of women inmates seen rampant. Misconduct found in all but one state, Amnesty USA states. *Boston Globe*, p. 7.

Pliner, P., Chaiken, S., & Flett, G. L. (1990). Gender differences in concern with body weight and physical appearance over the life span. *Personality and Social Psychology Bulletin, 16*, 263–273.

Poe-Yamagata, E., & Butts, J. A. (1996). *Female offenders in the juvenile justice system*. Washington, DC: U.S. Department of Justice.

Pogrebin, L. C. (1992). *Deborah, Golda, and me: Being female and Jewish in America*. New York: Crown Publishers.

Pogrebin, M. R., & Poole, E. D. (1997). The sexualized work environment: A look at women jail officers. *Prison Journal, 77,* 41–57.

Pollack, W. S. (2006). The "war" for boys: Hearing "real boys" voices, hearing their pain. *Professional Psychology: Research and Practice, 37,* 190–195.

Pollack, W.S. (2006). The "war" for boys: Hearing "real boys" voices, hearing their pain. *Professional Psychology, 37,* 190–195.

Pollard, D. S. (1990). Black women, interpersonal support, and institutional change. In J. Antler & S. K. Bilken (Eds.), *Changing education: Women as radicals and conservators* (pp. 257–276). New York: State University of New York Press.

Pollard, D. S. (1999, October). Single-sex education. *Women's Education Equity Act (WEAA) Digest,* pp. 1–2, 8–9.

Pollitt, K. (2005, October 17). Desperate housewives of the ivy league? *Nation,* p. 14.

Pollock-Byrne, J. M. (1990). *Women, prison and crime.* Pacific Grove, CA: Brooks/Cole.

Polyakov, S. (2010). *Oh no, the return of the Lolita syndrome: The fashionable housewife.* Retrieved from http://www.thefashionable-housewife.com/02/2010/oh-no-the-return-of-the-lolita-syndrome/

Ponterotto, J. G., Casas, J. M., Suzzuki, L. A., & Alexander, C. M. (Eds.) (2001). *Handbook of multicultural counseling.* Thousand Oaks, CA: Sage.

Poorman, P. B. (2001). Forging community links to address abuse in lesbian relationships. In E. Kaschak (Ed.) *Intimate betrayal: Intimate partner abuse in lesbian relationships* (pp. 7–24). New York: Haworth Press.

Pope, J. H. (1999). Missed diagnoses of acute cardiac ischemia in the emergency department. *New England Journal of Medicine, 342,* 1163–1170.

Pope, K. S., Levenson, H., & Schover, L. R. (2001). Sexual intimacy in psychology training: Results and implications of a national survey. *American Psychologist, 34,* 682–689.

Pope, K. S., Sonne, J. L., & Holroyd, J. (1993). *Sexual feelings in psychotherapy.* Washington, DC: American Psychological Association.

Popenoe, D. (1993). American family decline, 1960–1990. *Journal of Marriage and the Family, 55,* 527–541.

Popkin, B. M., Siega-Riz, A. M., & Haines, P. S. (1996). A comparison of dietary trends among racial and socioeconomic groups in the United States. *New England Journal of Medicine, 335,* 716–720.

Population Reference Bureau. (2011). *Smoking-related deaths keep U. S. life expectancy below other wealthy countries.* Retrieved from http://www.prb.org/Articles/2010/ussmoking.aspx?p=1

Porter, E., LeClair, M., White, J., & Keeter, S. (2008). Three 19th-century women doctors: Elizabeth Blackwell, Mary Walker, and Sarah Loguen Fraser. *Journal of the American Medical Association, 305*(12), 1165–1256.

Porter, K. H., & Dupree, A. (2001). *Poverty trends for families headed by working single mothers, 1993 to 1999.* Washington, DC: Center on Budget and Policy Priorities.

Porterfield, E. (2006). *Rise in c-sections begets cost debate.* Retrieved from http://www.bizjournals.com/seattle/stories/2006/05/15/focus4.html

Porter-O'Grady, T. (2009). Reverse discrimination in nursingleadership: Hitting the concrete ceiling. In C. E. O'Lynn & R. E. Tranbarger (Eds.), *Men in nursing: History, challenges, and opportunities* (pp. 143–152). New York: Springer.

Portman, A. R., & Van der Lippe, T. (2009). Attitudes toward housework and childcare and the gendered division of labor. *Journal of Marriage and Family, 71,* 526–541.

Postman, N. (2005). *Amusing ourselves to death: Public discourse in the age of show business.* New York: Penguin.

Poteat, V., & Espelage, D. (2007). Predicting psychosocial consequences of homophobic victimization in middle school students. *Journal of Early Adolescence, 27,* 175–191.

Poussaint, A. F., & Comer, J. P. (1993). *Raising Black children.* New York: Plume.

Powell, B., & Skarbek, D. (2004). *Sweatshops and third world living standards: Are the jobs worth the sweat? Independent Institute Working Paper Number 53.* Oakland, California: Independent Institute.

Powers, L. E., Hughes, R. B., & Lund, E. M. (2009). Interpersonal violence and women with disabilities: A research update. Harrisburg, PA: VAWnet. Retrieved February 22, 2010, http://new.vawnet.org/category/main_doc.phd?docid=2077

Pratt, N. F. (1980). Transitions in Judaism: The Jewish American woman through the 1930s. In J. W. James (Ed.), *Women in American religion* (pp. 207–228). Philadelphia: University of Pennsylvania Press.

Prell, R., & Weinberg, D. (2007). *Women remaking American Judaism*. Detroit: Wayne State University Press.

Prentky, R. A., Knight, R. A., & Lee, A. F. S. (1997). *Child sexual molestation: Research issues*. Washington, DC: U.S. Department of Justice, National Institute of Justice.

President's Council on Physical Fitness and Sport. (1997). *Physical activity and sport in the lives of girls*. Washington, DC: U.S. Department of Health and Human Services.

Prestage, J. L. (1991). In quest of African American political woman. *Annals of the American Academy of Political and Social Science, 515*, 88–103.

Preston, J. (2008). Employers fight tough measures on immigration. *New York Times*. Retrieved from: http://www.fosterquan.com/news/EmployersFightToughMeasuresOnImmigration.pdf

Preston, J. A. (1995). Gender and the formation of a women's profession: The case of public school teaching. In J. A. Jacobs (Ed.), *Gender inequality at work* (pp. 379–407). Thousand Oaks, CA: Sage.

Preves, S. E. (2003). *Intersex and identity: The contested self*. New Brunswick, NJ: Rutgers University Press.

Price-Bonham, S., & Skeen, P. (1982). Black and White fathers' attitudes toward children's sex roles. *Psychological Reports, 50*, 1187–1190.

Priebe, G., & Svedin, C. G. (2008). Child sexual abuse is largely hidden from the adult society: An epidemiological study of adolescences' disclosure. *Child Abuse & Neglect, 32*, 1095–1108.

Princeton Religious Research Center. (1992, April–June). Emerging Trends. Princeton, NJ: Author.

Probert, B. (2005). "I just couldn't fit in": Gender and unequal outcomes in academic careers. *Gender, Work and Organization, 12*, 50–72.

Professor says Southern Baptist seminary fired her over gender. (2007, January 27). *New York Times*, p. A9.

Ptacek, J. (1999). *Battered women in the courtroom: The power of judicial responses*. Boston: Northeastern University Press.

Puhl, R. M., Andreyeva, T., & Brownell, K. D. (2008). Perceptions of weight discrimination: Prevalence and comparison to race and gender discrimination in America. *International Journal of Obesity, 32*, 992–1000.

Purdie, M. P., Abbey, A., & Jacques-Tiura, A. J. (2010). Perpetrators of intimate partner sexual violence: Are there unique characteristics associated with making partners have sex without a condom? *Violence Against Women, 16*, 1086–1097.

Purvis, J. (2004). Grrrls and women together in the third wave: Embracing the challenges of intergenerational feminism(s). *NWSA Journal, 16*(3), 93–123.

Putallaz, M., & Bierman, K. L. (Eds.) (2004). *Aggression, antisocial behavior, and violence among girls: A developmental perspective*. New York: Guilford Press.

Puzzanchera, C. (2009, April). *Juvenile arrests 2007*. Washington, DC: U.S. Department of Justice, Office of Juvenile Justice and Delinquency Prevention. Retrieved October 26, 2009, from http://www.ncjrs.gov/pdffiles1/ojjdp/225344.pdf

Pyke, K. D. (1994). Women's employment as gift or burden? *Gender & Society, 8*, 73–91.

Queens of the Gridiron. (2011). *The women and girls of tackle football*. Retrieved from http://www.angelfire.com/sports/womenfootball/

Quenqua, D. (2008, April 21). Sending in the Marines (to recruit women). *New York Times*, pp. C1, C6.

Quester, G. H. (1982). The problem. In N. L. Goldman (Ed.), *Female soldiers—combatants or noncombatants?* (pp. 217–236). Westport, CT: Greenwood Press.

Quigley, D., Simmons, F., Whyte, H., Robertson, J., & Freshwater, D. (2009). Variations in reproductive and developmental toxicant identification. *Journal of Chemical Health and Safety, 17*(1), 29–53.

Quit, S. A. (2008). *Men, women & smoking: information sheet*. Retrieved from http://www.quitsa.org.au/cms_resources/documents/infosheet_men_women_smoking.pdf

Ra Mer Christiansen, H., & Sjorup, L. (2009). *Pieties and gender*. Boston: Brill Publishers.

Rabbi group OKs gay unions. (1996, March 28). Philadelphia: Associated Press. (Internet).

Rader, N. E. (2005). Surrendering solidarity: Considering the relationships among female correctional officers. *Women and Criminal Justice, 16*, 27–42.

Radio Television Digital News Association. (2008). *Media Report to Women: covering all the issues concerning women and media, Media Report to Women*. Retrieved from http://www.mediareporttowomen.com/statistics.htm

Raevuori, A. et al. (2008). Lifetime anorexia nervosa in young men in the community: Five cases and their co-twins. *International Journal of Eating Disorders, 41*, 458–463.

Raffaelli, M., & Ontai, L. L. (2004). Gender socialization in Latino/a families: Results from two retrospective studies. *Sex Roles, 50,* 287–299.

Ragins, B. R., & Scandura, T. A. (1995). Antecedents and work-related correlates of reported sexual harassment: An empirical investigation of competing hypotheses. *Sex Roles, 32,* 429–455.

Raiborn, M. H. (1990). *Revenues and expenses of intercollegiate athletics programs.* Overland Park, KS: National Collegiate Athletic Association.

Raines, H. (1983, November 27). Poll shows support for political gains by women in U.S. *New York Times,* pp. 1, 40.

Rajagopal, I., & Gales, J. (2002) It's the image that is imperfect: Advertising and its impact on women. *Economic and Political Weekly, 37*(32), 3333–33337.

Rajan, D. (2004). *Violence against women with disabilities* (No. H72-22/9-2004E). Ottawa. ON: Family Violence Prevention Unit. Health Canada.

Rajan, M., & McCloskey, K. A. (2007). Victims of intimate partner violence: Arrest rates across recent studies. *Journal of Aggression, Maltreatment, & Trauma, 15*(3/4), 27–52.

Raley, S. B., Mattingly, M. J., & Bianchi, S. M. (2006). How dual are dual-income couples? Documenting change from 1970 to 2001. *Journal of Marriage and Family, 68,* 11–28.

Ramaswami, A., Dreher, G., Bretz, R., & Wietloff, C. (2010). The interaction effects of gender and mentoring on career attainment: Making the case for female lawyers. *Journal of Career Development, 37,* 692–716.

Ramesh, B., Moses, S., Washtington, R., Isac, S., Mohapatra, B., Mahagaonkar, S., Adhikary, R., Brahmam, G., Paranjape, R., Subramanian, T., Blanchard, J. (2008). Determinants of HIV prevalence among female sex workers in four south Indian states: Analysis of cross-sectional surveys in twenty-three districts. *AIDS, 22* s35–s44.

Ramos, I., & Lambating, J. (1996). Risk taking: Gender differences and educational opportunity. *School Science and Mathematics, 96,* 94–98.

Rampell, C. (2009). As layoffs surge, women may pass men in the job force. *New York Times,* p. A1. Retrieved February 18, 2010, http://www.nytimes.com/2009/02/06/business/06women.html

Rampell, C. (2010). Women now a majority in U.S. workplace. *New York Times,* p. A10. Retrieved February 18, 2010, http://www.nytimes.com/2010/02/06/business/economy/06women.html

Ramsey-Klawsnik, H., Teaster, P. B., Mendiondo, M. S., Marcum, J. L., & Abner, E. L. (2008). Sexual predators who target elders: Findings from the first national study of sexual abuse in care facilities. *Journal of Elder Abuse & Neglect, 20*(4), 353–376.

Rand, M. R. (2009). *Criminal victimization, 2008.* Washington, DC: U.S. Department of Justice, Bureau of Justice Statistics.

Rand, M. R. (2008). *Criminal victimization, 2007.* Washington, DC: U.S. Department of Justice, Bureau of Justice Statistics.

Rankin, D. (1987, May 31). Living together as a way of life. *New York Times,* p. F11.

Rape as a war crime. (2009). *Contemporary Sexuality, 43*(1), 7.

Raphael, J. (2004). *Listening to Olivia: Violence, poverty, and prostitution.* Boston: Northeastern University Press.

Raphael, J. (2007). *Freeing Tammy: Women, drugs and incarceration.* Boston: Northeastern University Press.

Raskin, P. A., & Israel, A. C. (1981). Sex-role imitation in children: Effects of sex of child, sex of model, and sex-role appropriateness of modeled behavior. *Sex Roles, 7,* 1067–1077.

Rasmussen, S. (2003). Gendered discourses and mediated modernities: Urban and rural performances of Tuareg smith women. *Journal of Anthropological Research, 59,* 487–509.

Rathore, S. S., Berger, A. K., Weinfurt, K. P., Feinleib, M., Oetgen, W. J., Gersh, B. J., & Schulman, K. A. (2000a). Race, sex, poverty, and the medical treatment of myocardial infarction in the elderly. *Ciculation, 102,* 642–648.

Rathore, S. S., Lenert, L. A., Weinfurt, K. P., Tinoco, A., Taleghanic, C. K., Harlen, W., & Schulman, K. A. (2000b). The effects of patient sex and race on medical students' ratings of quality of life. *American Journal of Medicine, 108,* 561–566.

Räty, H., Vänskä, J., Kasanen, K,, & Kärkkäinen, R. (2002), Parents' explanations of their child's performance in mathematics and reading: A replication and extension of Yee and Eccles, *Sex Roles, 46,* 121–128.

Rautman, A. E. (Ed.) (2000). *Reading the body: Representations and remains in the archeological record.* Philadelphia: University of Pennsylvania Press.

Ray, R. (2006). Is the revolution missing or are we looking in the wrong places? *Social Problems, 53,* 459–465.

Ray, R., Gornick, J. C., & Schmitt, J. (2010). Who cares? Assessing generosity and gender equality in parental leave policy designs in 21 countries. *Journal of European Social Policy, 19*(5), 196–14.

Raymond, J. G. (1990). Fetalists and feminists: They are not the same. In S. Ruth (Ed.), *Issues in feminism* (pp. 257–261). Mountain View, CA: Mayfield.

Raymond, J. G. (2004). Prostitution on demand. *Violence Against Women, 10*, 1156–1186.

Rayner, B. (1997, August 10). Stamping out scourge of genital mutilation aid worker educates men, women about dangers of female circumcision. *Ottawa Sun*.

Raynor, O., & Hayward, K. (2009). Breaking into the business: Experiences of actors with disabilities in the entertainment industry. *Journal of Research in Special Education Needs, 9*(1), 39–47.

Read, J. G., & Bartowski, J. P. (2000). To veil or not to veil? A case study of identity negotiation among Muslim women in Austin, Texas. *Gender & Society, 14*, 395–417.

Real, T. (1997). *I don't want to talk about it*. New York: Scribner.

ReavEn, G. M., Fox, B., & Strom, T. K. (2000). *Syndrome X*. New York: Simon and Schuster.

Reczek, C., Elliott, S., & Umberson, D. (2009). Commitment without marriage: Union formation among long-term same-sex couples. *Journal of Family Issues, 30*(6), 738–756.

Reddy, A. (2001, September 2). Little women. *Washington Post*, pp. H1, H3.

Regan, L., & Petrie, T. A. (1998). Physical, psychological, and societal correlates of bulimic symptomatology among African American college women. *Journal of Counseling Psychology, 45*, 315–321.

Rehm, J., Mathers, C., Popova, S., Thavorncharoensap, M., Teerawattananon, Y., & Patra, J. (2009). Global burden of disease and injury and economic cost attributable to alcohol use and alcohol-use disorders. *The Lancet, 373*, 2223–2233.

Reichert, M., & Hawley, R. (2006). Confronting the "boy problem": A self-study approach to deepen schools' moral stance. *Teacher College Record*. ID Number 12813. Retrieved from: https://www.uwsp.edu/education/pshaw/ConfrontingtheBoyIssue.htm

Reid, G. M. (1994). Maternal sex-stereotyping of newborns. *Psychological Reports, 75*, 1443–1450.

Reid, P. T., & Trotter, K. H. (1993). Children's self-presentations with infants: Gender and ethnic comparisons. *Sex Roles, 29*, 171–181.

Reid, S. T. (1987). *Criminal justice*. St. Paul, MN: West.

Reid-Bowen, P. (2007). *Goddess as nature: Towards a philosophical theology*. Aldershot, UK: Ashgate.

Reinardy, S. (2009). Female journalists more likely to leave newspapers. *Newspaper Research Journal, 30*(3), 42–56.

Reinberg, S. (2008). *HIV infection rate for young black men 'alarming': CDC*. Retrieved from http://www.preventionman.com/PM/HOME_files/HIV-AIDS-Rate-Black-Men.pdf

Reinharz, S. (1992). *Feminist methods in social research*. New York: Oxford University Press.

Reiss, I. L. (1986). *Journey into sexuality: An exploratory voyage*. Englewood Cliffs, NJ: Prentice-Hall.

Rennison, C. M. (2001c). *Intimate partner violence and age of victim, 1993–99*. U.S. Department of Justice, Bureau of Justice Statistics.

Rennison, C. M. (2009). A new look at the gender gap in offending. *Women & Criminal Justice, 19*, 171–190.

Rennison, C. M., & Welchans, S. (2000). *Intimate partner violence*. Washington, DC: U.S. Department of Justice, Bureau of Justice Statistics.

Renold, E., & Allan, A. (2006). Bright and beautiful: High achieving girls, ambivalent femininities, and the feminisation of success in the primary school. *Discourse, 27*, 457–473.

Renzetti, C. M. (1987). New wave or second stage? Attitudes of college women toward feminism. *Sex Roles, 16*, 265–277.

Renzetti, C. M. (1992). *Violent betrayal: Partner abuse in lesbian relationships*. Newbury Park, CA: Sage.

Renzetti, C. M. (1996). The poverty of services for battered lesbians. *Journal of Gay and Lesbian Social Services, 4*, 61–68.

Renzetti, C. M. (2009). Intimate partner violence and economic disadvantage. In E. Stark and E. Buzawa (Eds.), *Violence against women in families and relationships*. Santa Barbara, CA: Praeger.

Renzetti, C. M., & Larkin, V. M. (2009). Economic stress and domestic violence. VAWnet: National online resource center on violence against women. Retrieved February 19, 2010, http://new.vawnet.org/Assoc_Files_VAWnet/AR_EconomicStress.pdf

Renzetti, C. M., Edleson, J. L., & Bergen, R. K. (Eds.) (2011). *Sourcebook on violence against women*. Thousand Oaks, CA: Sage.

Reskin, B. (1993). Sex segregation in the workplace. *Annual Review of Sociology, 19*, 241–270.

Reskin, B. (2000). Getting it right: Sex and race inequality in work organizations. *Annual Review of Sociology, 26*, 707–709.

Reskin, B. A., &. Hartmann, H. I. (Eds.) (1986). *Women's work, men's work: Sex segregation on the job*. Washington, DC: National Academy Press.

Reskin, B. F., & Padevic, I. (1999). Sex, race and ethnic inequality in United States workplace. In J. S. Chafetz (Ed.), *Handbook of the sociology of gender* (pp. 343–374). New York: Kluwer.

Reskin, B. F., & Roos, P. A. (1990). *Job queues, gender queues: Explaining women's inroads into male occupations*. Philadelphia: Temple University Press.

Rex, J., & Chadwell, D. (2009). Single-gender classrooms. *Administrator, 66*(8), 28–33.

Rheingold, H. L., & Cook, K. V. (1975). The content of boys' and girls' rooms as an index of parents' behavior. *Child Development, 46*, 459–463.

Rhode, D. L. (1997). *Speaking of sex*. Cambridge, MA: Harvard University Press.

Rich, J., & Palaz, S. (2008). Why has occupational sex segregation in Turkey increased since 1975? *Labour, 22*(1), 185–218.

Rickert, V. I., Hassed, S. J., Hendon, A. E., & Cunniff, C. (1996). The effects of peer ridicule on depression and self-image among adolescent females with Turner syndrome. *Journal of Adolescent Health, 19*, 34–38.

Rideout, V. J., Vandewater, E. A., & Wartella, E. A. (2003). *Zero to six: Electronic media in the lives of infants, toddlers and preschoolers*. Menlo Park, CA: Henry J. Kaiser Family Foundation. Retrieved from: http://www.kff.org/entmedia/upload/Zero-to-Six-Electronic-Media-in-the-Lives-of-Infants-Toddlers-and-Preschoolers-PDF.pdf

Ridgeway, C. L., & Smith-Lovin, L. (1999). Gender and interaction. In J. S. Chafetz (Ed.), *Handbook of the sociology of gender* (pp. 247–274). New York: Kluwer.

Ridgeway, C. L., & Correll, S. J. (2004). Unpacking the gender system: A theoretical perspective on gender beliefs and social relations. *Gender & Society, 18*, 510–531.

Riding, A. (1992, November 17). New catechism for Catholics defines sins of the modern world. *New York Times*, pp. A1, A17.

Riding, A. (1993, January 9). European inquiry says Serbs' forces have raped 20,000. *New York Times*, pp. 1, 4.

Riger, S. (1988). Comment on "Women's History Goes to Trial: EEOC v. Sears, Roebuck and Company." *Signs, 13*, 897–903.

Rimer, S. (1996, October 23). Blacks urged to act to increase awareness of the AIDS epidemic. *New York Times*, pp. A1, 16.

Rind, B. (2001). Gay and bisexual adolescent boys' sexual experiences with men: An empirical examination of psychological correlates in a non-clincal sample. *Archives of Sexual Behavior, 30*, 345–368.

Ripper, M. (1991). A comparison of the effect of the menstrual cycle and the social week on mood, sexual interest, and self-assessed performance. In D. L. Taylor & N. F. Woods (Eds.), *Menstruation, health, and illness* (pp. 19–33). New York: Hemisphere.

Risch, N., Wheeler, E. S., and Keats, B.J.B. (1993). Male sexual orientation and genetic evidence. *Science, 262*, 2063–2065.

Risen, J., & Thomas, J. L. (1998). *Wrath of angels*. New York: Basic Books.

Risman, B. J. (2003). From the SWS president: Valuing all flavors of feminist sociology. *Gender & Society, 17*, 659–663.

Risman, B. J. (2004). Gender as social structure: Theory wrestling with activism. *Gender & Society, 18*, 429–450.

Ritzer, G. (1980). *Sociology: A multi-paradigm science*. Boston: Allyn and Bacon.

Rivers, I. (2006). Bullying and homophobia in UK schools: A perspective on factors affecting resilience and recovery. *Journal of Gay & Lesbian Issues in Education, 4*(1), 11–43.

Roach, R. (2008). Monitoring the graduation rate gap. *Diverse: Issues in Higher Education, 25*(11), 16–17.

Roald, A. (2001). *Women in Islam: The western experience*. London: Psychology Press.

Robbins, C. A., Martin, S. S., & Surratt, H. L. (2009). Substance abuse treatment, anticipated maternal roles, and reentry success of drug-involved women prisoners. *Crime & Delinquency, 55*(3), 388–411.

Roberts, C. (2007). *Creation and covenant: The significance of sexual difference in the moral theology of marriage*. Retrieved from: http://jts.oxfordjournals.org/content/59/1/439.short

Roberts, T. A., Auinger, P., & Klein, J. D. (2005). Intimate partner abuse and the reproductive health of sexually active female adolescents. *Journal of Adolescent Health, 36*, 380–385.

Robertson, C., Dyer, C. E., & Campbell, D. (1988). Campus harassment: Sexual harassment policies and procedures at institutions of higher learning. *Signs, 13*, 792–812.

Robertson, J., & Fitzgerald, L. F. (1990). The (mis)treatment of men: Effects of client gender role and life-style on diagnosis and attribution of pathology. *Journal of Counseling Psychology, 37*, 3–9.

Robinson, L. S. (1992). A good man is hard to find: Reflections on men's studies. In C. Kramarae & D. Spender (Eds.), *The knowledge explosion* (pp. 438–447). New York: Teachers College Press.

Robinson, T., & Anderson, C. (2006). Older characters in children's animated television programs: A content analysis of their portrayal. *Journal of Broadcasting & Electronic Media, 50*, 287–304.

Robinson, T., Gustafson, B., & Popovich, M. (2008). Perceptions of negative stereotypes of older people in magazine advertisements. *Ageing and Society, 28*, 233–251.

Robinson, W. V., & Gosselin, P. G. (1998, January 29). Many workplaces ban certain relationships. *Boston Globe*, p. A1.

Robson, R. (1992). *Lesbian (out)law*. Ithaca, NY: Firebrand Books.

Rogers, J. K., & Henson, K. D. (1997). "Hey, why don't you wear a shorter skirt?": Structural vulnerability and the organization of sexual harassment in temporary clerical employment. *Gender & Society, 11*, 215–237.

Rogers, L., & Walsh, J. (1982). Shortcomings of the psychomedical research of John Money and co-workers into sex differences in behavior: Social and political implications. *Sex Roles, 8*, 269–281.

Rogers, S. C. (1978). Woman's place: A critical review of anthropological theory. *Comparative Studies in Society and History, 20*, 123–162.

Roiphe, K. (1993). *The morning after*. Boston: Little, Brown.

Rojek, J., & Decker, S. H. (2009). Examining racial disparity in the police discipline process. *Police Quarterly, 12*(4), 388–407.

Romero, M. (1992). *Maid in America*. New York: Routledge.

Rooks, N. M. (1996). *Hair raising: Beauty, culture and African American women*. New Brunswick, NJ: Rutgers University Press.

Roopnarine, J. L. (1984). Sex-typed socialization in mixed-age preschool classrooms. *Child Development, 55*, 1078–1084.

Root, M. P. P. (1990). Disordered eating in women of color. *Sex Roles, 22*, 525–536.

Roscoe, W. (1991). *The Zuni man-woman*. Albuquerque: University of New Mexico Press.

Rose, A. J., & Rudolph, K. D. (2006). A review of sex differences in peer relationship processes: Potential trade-offs for the emotional and behavioral development of girls and boys. *Psychological Bulletin, 132*, 98–131.

Rose, T. (2010). *High power jobs don't come without consequences*. Retrieved from http://www.resume-resource.com/resumeblog/high-power-jobs-dont-come-without-consequences/1013/

Rosen, L. W., Shafer, C. L., Dummer, G. M., Cross, L. K., Deuman, G. W., & Malmberg, S. R. (1988). Prevalence of athogenic weight-control behaviors among Native American women and girls. *International Journal of Eating Disorders, 7*, 807–811.

Rosen, L. N., Dragiewicz, M., & Gibbs, J. (2009). Fathers' rights groups: Demographic correlates and impact on custody policy. *Violence Against Women, 15*, 513–531.

Rosen, R. (2000). *The world split open: How the modern women's movement changed America*. New York: Viking.

Rosenberg, H. G. (1984). The home is the workplace: Hazards, stress, and pollutants in the household. In W. Chavkin (Ed.), *Double exposure* (pp. 219–245). New York: Monthly Review Press.

Rosenhan, D. L. (1973). On being sane in insane places. *Science, 179*, 250–258.

Rosenthal, D., Mallett, S., & Myers, P. (2006). Why do homeless young people leave home? *Australian and New Zealand Journal of Public Health, 30*, 281–285.

Roseth, C. J., et al. (2007). Preschoolers' aggression, affiliation, and social dominance relationships: An observational, longitudinal study. *Journal of School Psychology, 45* 479–497.

Rosin, O. (2008). The economic causes of obesity: A survey. *Journal of Economic Surveys, 22*, 617–647.

Roskies, J. (2010). *Missing from the map: Feminist theory and the omission of Jewish women*. Retrieved from: http://ww.yale.edu/yiisa/jenniferroskiesworkingpaper52010.pdf

Rospenda, K. M., Richman, J. A., & Nawyn, S. J. (1998). Doing power: The confluence of gender, race, and class in contrapower sexual harassment. *Gender & Society, 12*, 40–60.

Ross, C. E., & Bird, C. E. (1994). Sex stratification and health lifestyle: Consequences for men's and women's perceived health. *Journal of Health and Social Behavior, 35*, 161–178.

Ross, J., Zinn, A., & McCauley, E. (2000). Neurodevelopmental and psychosocial aspects of Turner syndrome. *Mental Retardation and Developmental Disabilities Research Review, 6*, 135–141.

Ross, L. (2000). Imprisoned Native women and the importance of Native traditions. In J. James (Ed.), *States of confinement: Policing detention, and prisons* (pp. 132–144). New York: St. Martin's Press.

Rossi, A. S. (1973). *The feminist papers*. New York: Bantam.

Rossi, A. S., & Rossi, P. E. (1977). Body time and social time: Mood patterns by menstrual cycle phase and day of the week. *Social Science Research, 6*, 273–308.

Rossi, P. (1989). *Down and out in America: The origins of homelessness*. Chicago: University of Chicago Press.

Roth, A. (2004). *Separate roads to feminism: Black, Chicana, White feminist movements in America's second wave*. New York: Cambridge University Press.

Roth, B. (2006). Gender inequality and feminist activism in institutions: Challenges of marginalization and feminist "fading." In L.A. Chapppell & L. Hill (Eds.), *The politics of women's interests: New comparative perspectives* (pp. 157–174). New York: Routledge.

Roth, L. M. (2009). Woman-hating and the LA Fitness massacre: Hate crimes against women. *Huffington Post*. Retrieved February 24, 2010, http://www.huffingtonpost.com/louise-marie-roth/woman-hating-and-the-la-f_b_254020.html

Roth, L., & Kroll, J. (2007). Risky business: Assessing risk preference explanations for gender differences in religiosity. *American Sociological Review, 72*, 205–220.

Rothblum, E. D. (1982). Women's socialization and the prevalence of depression: The feminine mistake. *Women and Therapy, 1*, 5–13.

Rothblum, E. D. (2000). Sexual orientation and sex in women's lives: Conceptual and methodological issues. *Journal of Social Issues, 56*, 193–204.

Rothman, B. K. (1984). Women, health and medicine. In J. Freeman (Ed.), *Women: A feminist perspective* (pp. 70–80). Palo Alto, CA: Mayfield.

Rothman, B. K. (1992). *Now available in the freezer section: Packaging the frozen embryo*. Paper presented at the annual meeting of the American Sociological Association, Pittsburgh, PA.

Rothman, E., & Silverman, J. (2007). The effects of a college sexual assault prevention program on first-year students' victimization rates. *Journal of American College Health, 55*, 283–290.

Roughgarden, J. (2004). *Evolution's rainbow: Diversity, gender, and sexuality in nature and people*. Berkeley: University of California Press.

Rowbotham, S. (1997). *A century of women in Britain and the United States*. New York: Viking.

Rowland, C. (2007). *The Cambridge companion to lberation theology*. Cambridge, UK: Cambridge University Press.

Roxburgh, S. (1997). The effect of children on the mental health of women in the paid labor force. *Journal of Family Issues, 18*, 270–289.

Rubin, J. Z., Provenzano, F. J., & Luria, Z. (1974). The eye of the beholder: Parents' views on sex of newborns. *American Journal of Orthopsychiatry, 44*, 512–519.

Rubin, K. H., & Coplan, R. J. (2004). Paying attention to and not neglecting social withdrawal and social isolation. *Merrill-Palmer Quarterly, 50*, 506–534.

Rubin, R. (2001, April 18). Teen birth rates drop to new low. *USA Today*, p. 1.

Rubin, R. T., Reinisch, J. M., & Haskett, R. F. (1981). Postnatal gonadal steroid effects on human behavior. *Science, 211*, 1318–1324.

Ruble D. N., Lurye L. E., & Zosuls K. M. (2007). Pink frilly dresses (PFD) and early gender identity. Princeton Report on Knowledge. Retrieved from http://prok.princeton.edu/2–2/inventions/pink_frilly

Ruble, D. N. (1977). Menstrual symptoms: A reinterpretation. *Science, 197*, 291–292.

Ruble, D. N., Martin, C. L., & Berenbaum, S. A. (2006). Gender development, In W. Damon (Series Ed.) & N. Eisenberg (Vol. Ed.), *Handbook of child psychology: Vol. 3, Social, emotional, and personality development* (6th ed.), (pp. 858–932). Hoboken, NJ: Wiley.

Ruble, D. N., Taylor, L. J., Cyphers, L., Greulich, F. K., Lurye, L. E., & Shrout, P. E. (2007). The role of gender constancy in early gender development. *Child Development, 78*, 4, 1121–1136.

Rudolph, K., & Hammen, C. (1999). Age and gender as determinants of stress exposure, generation, and reactions in youngsters: A transactional perspective. *Child Development, 70*, 660–677.

Ruether, R. R. (1988). *Women-church*. San Francisco: Harper and Row.

Ruether, R. R. (2010a). *Goddesses and witches: Liberation and countercultural feminism*.

Retrieved from: http://www.religion-online.org/showarticle.asp?title=1754

Ruether, R. R. (2010b). *The church as liberation community from patriarchy: The praxis of ministry as discipleship of equals*. Retrieved from: http://www.women-churchconvergence.org/WOW%20anniversary%20addresses/The%20Church%20as%20Liberation%20Community%20by%20Rosemary%20RR.pdf

Ruhlman, M. (1997). *Boys themselves: A return to single-sex education*. New York: Henry Holt and Company.

Ruitenberg, C. (2006). *How to do things with headscarves: A discursive and meta-discursive analysis*. Retrieved from: http://ojs.ed.uiuc.edu/index.php/pes/article/viewArticle/1554

Rumney, A. (2009). *Dying to please: Anorexia, treatment, and recovery*. Jefferson, NC: McFarland & Company.

Runfola, R. (1980). The Black athlete as super-machismo symbol, In D. S. Sabo & R. Runfola (Eds.), *Jock: Sports and male identity* (pp. 79–88). Englewood Cliffs, NJ: Prentice-Hall.

Runtz, M. G., & O'Donnell, C. W. (2006). Students' perceptions of sexual harassment: Is it harassment only if the offender is a man and the victim is a woman? *Journal of Applied Social Psychology, 31*(5), 963–982.

Rupp, L. J., & Taylor, V. (1999). Forging feminist identity in an international movement: A collective identity approach to twentieth-century feminism. *Signs, 24*, 363–386.

Rushton, J. P., & Ankney, C. D. (1996). Brain size and cognitive ability: Correlations with age, sex, social class and race. *Psychonomic Bulletin and Review, 3*, 21–36.

Russell, B. L., & Trigg, K. Y. (2004). Tolerance of sexual harassment: An examination of gender differences, ambivalent sexism, social dominance, and gender roles. *Sex Roles, 50*(7/8), 565–573.

Russell, D. E. H. (1993). Introduction. In D. E. H. Russell (Ed.), *Making violence sexy*, (pp. 1–20). New York: Teachers College Press.

Russell, R. (2008). United Methodists uphold homosexuality stance. Retrieved from: http://www.umc.org/site/apps/nlnet/content3.aspx?c=1wL4KnN1LtH&b=3082929&content_id={45E5D40C-0D18-46F7-B40B-BD2F0B9F528F}.

Rust, P. C. R. (2000). Bisexuality: A contemporary paradox for women. *Journal of Social Issues, 56*, 205–221.

Rustad, M. (1982). *Women in khaki*. New York: Praeger.

Rutenberg, J. (2009, June 18). Gay and lesbian leaders say federal same-sex benefits don't go far enough. *The New York Times*, p. 18.

Rutledge, T., et al. (2001). Psychosocial variables are associated with atherosclerosis risk factors among women with chest pains: The WISE study. *Psychosomatic Medicine, 63*, 282–288.

Rutter, M., et al. (2004). Sex differences in developmental reading ability: New findings from four epidemiological studies. *Journal of the American Medical Association, 291*, 2007–2012.

Rutter, P., & Leech, N. (2006). Sexual minority youth perspectives on the school environment and suicide risk interventions: A qualitative study. *Journal of Gay and Lesbian Issues in Education, 4*(1), 77–91.

Ruzek, S. (1987). Feminist visions of health: An international perspective. In J. Mitchell & A. Oakley (Eds.), *What is feminism? A re-examination* (pp. 184–207). New York: Pantheon.

Ryan, E. L (2010). Dora the Explorer: Empowering preschoolers, girls, and Latinas. *Journal of Broadcasting & Electronic Media, 54*(1), 54–68.

Ryan, K. M., & Mapaye, J. C. (2010). Beyond "Anchorman" A comparative analysis of race, gender, and correspondent roles in network news. *Electronic News, 4*(2), 97–117.

Ryan, L. T. (1994, February 20). Swimsuit model or victim stories, who will cover for me? *New York Times*, p. S11.

Rynbrandt, L. J., & Kramer, R. C. (1995). Hybrid nonwomen and corporate violence: The silicone breast implant case. *Violence Against Women, 1*, 206–227.

Ryu, M. (2008). *Minorities in Higher Education 2008: Twenty-third status report*. Washington, DC: American Council on Education.

Sabina, C., Wolak, J., & Finkelhor, D. (2008). The nature and dynamics of Internet pornography exposure for youth. *CyberPsychology & Behavior, 11*(6), 691–693.

Sabol, W. J., West, H. C., & Cooper, M. (2009). *Prisoners in 2008*. U.S. Department of Justice, Bureau of Justice Statistics. NCJ 228417.

Sachs, A., & Wilson, J. H. (1978). *Sexism and the law*. New York: Free Press.

Sachs, S. (2000a, December 5). Saudi mall-crawlers shop till their veils drop. *New York Times*, p. A4.

Sachs, S. (2000b, March 1). Egypt's women win equal rights to divorce. *New York Times*, pp. A1, A5.

Sack, K. (2001, April 5). Pressed against a "race ceiling." *New York Times*, p. A12.

Sacks, K. (1979). *Sisters and wives*. Westport, CT: Greenwood Press.

Sadker, D., & Zittleman, K. R. (2009). *Still failing at fairness: How gender bias cheats girls and boys in school and what we can do about it*. New York: Charles Scribner.

Sadker, M., & Sadker, D. (1994). *Failing at fairness*. New York: Charles Scribner's Sons.

Sadler, A. G., Booth, B. M., Nielson, D., & Doebbling, B. N. (2000). Health-related consequences of physical and sexual violence: Women in the military. *Obstetrics and Gynecology, 96*, 473–480.

Salazar, L. F., Crosby, R. A., & DiClemente, R. J. (2009). Exploring the mediating mechanism between gender-based violence and biologically confirmed Chlamydia among detained adolescent girls. *Violence Against Women, 15*, 258–275.

Salisbury, E. J., Van Voorhis, P., & Spiropoulos, G. V., (2009). The predictive validity of a gender-responsive needs assessment: An exploratory study. *Crime & Delinquency, 55*, 550–585.

Saltzman, A. (1996a, July 8). A look at the research: Lots on girls, little on boys. *U.S. News and World Report*, pp. 52–53.

Saltzman, A. (1996b, August 19). Life after the lawsuit. *U.S. News and World Report*, pp. 57–61.

Samble, J. N. (2008). Female faculty: Challenges and choices in the United States and beyond. *New Directions for Higher Education, 143*, 55–62.

Samborn, H. V. (2002). *Gender bias in the courts: Working toward change*. Chicago, IL: American Bar Association Commission on Women in the Profession. Retrieved February 24, 2010, http://www.abanet.org/women/perspectives/PSPGenderBias2.pdf

Samuels, A. (2010). The ugly roots of the light skin/dark skin divide. Retrieved from: http://www.newsweek.com/blogs/the-gaggle/2010/01/11/the-ugly-roots-of-the-light-skin-dark-skin-divide.html

Samuels, S. U. (1995). *Fetal rights, women's rights: Gender equality in the workplace*. Madison: University of Wisconsin Press.

Sanchez, L. (2001). Gender troubles: The entanglement of agency, violence, and law in the lives of women in prostitution. In C. M. Renzetti & L. Goodstein (Eds.), *Women, crime and criminal justice* (pp. 60–76). Los Angeles: Roxbury.

Sanday, P. R. (1981). *Female power and male dominance: On the origins of sexual inequality*. New York: Cambridge University Press.

Sanday, P. R. (1996a). Rape-prone versus rape-free campus cultures. *Violence Against Women, 2*, 191–208.

Sanday, P. R. (2002). *Women at the center: Life in modern day matriarchy*. Ithaca, NY: Cornell University Press.

Sanders, J. (2005, June 23). How to defuse "girl on girl" violence. *Christian Science Monitor*. Retrieved from http://www.csmonitor.com/2005/0623/p09s01-coop.html

Sandler, B. R., & Hall, R. M. (1986). *The campus climate revisited: Chilly for women faculty administrators, and graduate students*. Washington, DC: Project on the Status and Education of Women.

Sandler, K. (1992). *A question of color*. Film distributed by California Newsreel.

Sandmair, M. (1980). *The invisible alcoholics*. New York: McGraw Hill.

Sanneh, K. (2001). Black in the box: In defense of African American television. *Transition, 88*(4), 38–65.

Sapiro, V. (1986). *Women in American society*. Palo Alto, CA: Mayfield.

Sarbin, T. R., & Miller, J. E. (1970). Demonism revisited: The XYY chromosomal anomaly. *Issues in Criminology, 5*, 170–195.

Sargent, J. D., & Blanchflower, D. G. (1994). Obesity and stature in adolescence and earnings in young adulthood: Analysis of a British birth cohort. *Archives of Pediatric and Adolescent Medicine, 148*, 681–687.

Satcher, D. (2001). *Mental health, culture, race, and ethnicity*. Washington, DC: U.S. Department of Health and Human Services.

Saussy, C. (1991). *God images and self esteem*. Louisville, KY: Westminster/John Knox.

Savitt, T. (2001). Entering a white profession: African-American physicians. *Ethics and Health Care 4*(1), 1–4.

Sax, L. (2005). The promise and peril of single-sex public education: Mr. Chips meets Snoop Dogg. *Education Week*. Retrieved March, 26 2010, from http://www.singlesexschools.org/edweek.html

Sax, L. J. (2008). Her college experience is not his. *Chronicle of Higher Education, 55*(5), A32.

Sax, L. J. (2009). Gender matters: The variable effect of gender on the student experience. *About Campus*, 2–10.

Sax, L. J., & Harper, C. (2007). Origins of the gender gap: Pre-college and college influences on difference between men and women. *Research in Higher Education, 48*, 669–694.

Sax, L. J., Bryant, A. N., & Gilmartin, S. K. (2004). A longitudinal investigation of emotional health among male and female first-year college students. *Journal of the First Year Experience and Students in Transition, 16*(2), 39–65.

Sayer, S. (1996). "Out of the blue": Lesbian studies in Aotearoa/New Zealand. In B. Zimmerman & T. A. H. McNaron (Eds.), *The new lesbian studies* (pp. 240–243). New York: Feminist Press.

Sayers, J. (1987). Science, sexual difference, and feminism. In B. B. Hess & M. M. Ferree (Eds.), *Analyzing gender* (pp. 68–91). Newbury Park, CA: Sage.

Schacht, S., & Ewing, D. (2007). *Feminism with men: Bridging the gender gap*. New York: Rowman & Littlefield.

Schaffner, B., & Senic, N. (2006). Rights or benefits? Explaining the sexual identity gap in American political behavior. *Political Research Quarterly, 59*, 123–132.

Schecter, E., Tracy, A. J., Page, K. V., Luong, G. (2008). Shall we marry? Legal marriage as a commitment event in same-sex relationships. *Journal of Homosexuality, 54*(4), 400–422.

Schemo, D. J. (2000, December 28). Sex education with just one lesson: No sex. *New York Times*, pp. A1, A21.

Scherer, M. (2010). The new sheriffs of Wall Street. *Time Magazine*. Retrieved from: http://www.time.com/time/magazine/article/0,9171,1989144,00.html.

Schimelpfening, N. (2008). *5% of U.S. population is depressed*. Retrieved from http://depression.about.com/b/2008/09/16/5-of-us-population-is-depressed.htm

Schimelpfening, N. (2009). *Are there gender differences in suicide methods*. Retrieved from http://depression.about.com/od/suicid1/f/suicide.htm

Schinke, S., Cole, K., & Fang, L. (2009). Gender-specific intervention to reduce underage drinking among early adolescent girls: A test of a computer-mediated, mother-daughter program. *Journal of Studies on Alcohol and Drugs, 70*(1) 70–77.

Schmid, M. M., Cronauer, C. K., & Cousin, G. (2011). Perceived dominance in physicians: Are female physicians under scrutiny? *Patient Education and Counseling, 83*, 174–179.

Schmitt, E. (1994a, January 14). Aspin moves to open many military jobs to women. *New York Times*, p. A22.

Schmitt, E. (2001, May 15). For first time, nuclear families drop below 25% of households. *New York Times*, pp. A1, A20.

Schmitt, J. (2009). *Unions and upward mobility for service-sector workers*. Washington, DC: Center for Economic and Policy Research.

Schneider, F., Gur, R. C., Gur, R. E., & Muenz, L. R. (1994). Standardized mood induction with happy and sad facial expressions. *Psychiatry Research, 51*, 19–31.

Schoen, R., Landale, N. S., & Daniels, K. (2007). Family transitions in young adulthood. *Demography, 44*, 807–820.

Schofield, J. W. (2010). The colorblind perspective in school: Causes and consequences. In Banks, J. A. & Banks, C.A.M. (Eds.) (2010). *Multicultural Education: Issues and Perspectives* (7/e) (pp. 259–283). Hoboken, NJ: John Wiley & Sons, Inc.

Schooler, D., Ward, M., Merriwether, A., & Caruthers, A. (2004). Who's that girl: Television's role in the body image development of youth white and black women. *Psychology of Women Quarterly, 28*, 38–47.

Schreiber, R. (2010). Who speaks for women? Print media portrayals of feminist and conservative women's advocacy. *Political Communication, 27*, 432–452.

Schrock, D., & Schwalbe, M. (2009). Men, masculinity, and manhood acts. *Annual Review of Sociology, 35*, 277–295.

Schroering, J. (2003). *Gender bias among mental health professionals*. Retrieved from http://www.marshall.edu/etd/masters/schroering-joan-2003-ms.pdf

Schrott, H. G., Bittner, V., Vittinghoff, E., Herrington, D. M., & Hulley, S. (1997). Adherence to National Cholesterol Education Program treatment goals in postmenopausal women with heart disease: The Heart and Estrogen/Progestin Replacement Study (HERS). *Journal of the American Medical Association, 277*, 1281–1286.

Schuck, A. M., & Rabe-Hemp, C. (2005). Women police: The use of force by and against women officers. *Women and Criminal Justice, 16*(4), 91–117.

Schuler, S. R., Bates, L. M., Islam, F. (2008). Women's rights, domestic violence, and recourse seeking in rural Bangladesh. *Violence Against Women, 14*, 326–345.

Schulze, E., & Tomal, A. (2006). The chilly classroom: Beyond gender. *College Teaching, 54*, 263–269.

Schuppel, R., Buchele, G., & Koenig, W. (1998). Sex differences in selection of pacemakers: A retrospective observational study. *British Medical Journal, 316,* 1492–1495.

Schur, E. M. (1984). *Labeling women deviant.* New York: Random House.

Schussler Fiorenza, E. (1979). Women in the early Christian movement. In C. P. Christ & J. Plaskow (Eds.), *Womanspirit rising* (pp. 84–92). San Francisco: Harper and Row.

Schussler Fiorenza, E. (1983). *In memory of her: A feminist theological reconstruction of Christian origins.* New York: Crossroad.

Schwager, S. (1987). Educating women in America. *Signs, 12,* 333–372.

Schwartz, J., Steffensmeier, D., Zhong, H., & Ackerman, J. (2009). Trends in the gender gap in violence: Reevaluating NCVS and other evidence. *Criminology, 47,* 401–425.

Schwartz, L. M., Fisher, E. S., & Wright, B. (1997). Treatment and health outcomes of women and men in a cohort with coronary artery disease. *Archives of Internal Medicine, 157,* 1545–1552.

Schwartz, M. D., & DeKeseredy, W. S. (1997). *Sexual assault on the college campus.* Thousand Oaks, CA: Sage.

Schwartz, M. D., & Leggett, M. S. (1999). Bad dates or emotional trauma? The aftermath of campus sexual assault. *Violence Against Women, 5,* 251–270.

Schweder, R. A. (1997, March 9). It's called poor health for a reason. *New York Times,* p. E5.

Sciame-Giesecke, S., Roden, D., & Parkison, K. (2009). Infusing diversity into the curriculum: What are faculty members actually doing? *Journal of Diversity in Higher Education, 2*(3) 156–165.

Sciolino, E. (1990, January 25). Battle lines are shifting on women in war. *New York Times,* pp. A1, D23.

Sciolino, E. (1996, October 5). Political battle of the sexes is sharper than ever: For many White men Clinton's the reason to vote for Dole. *New York Times,* pp. 1, 24.

Sciolino, E. (1997, May 4). The Chanel under the chador. *New York Times Magazine,* pp. 46–51.

Sciolino, E. (2002, January 25). Servicewomen win, doffing their veils in Saudi Arabia. *New York Times,* p. A6.

Scott, D. (1994). *The power of connections in corporate-government affairs: A gendered perspective.* Paper presented at the annual meeting of the American Sociological Association, Los Angeles, CA.

Scott, D. B. (1996). Shattering the instrumental-expressive myth: The power of women's networks in corporate-government affairs. *Gender & Society, 10,* 232–247.

Scott, J. W. (1993). African American daughter-mother relations and teenage pregnancy: Two faces of premarital teenage pregnancy. *Western Journal of Black Studies, 17,* 73–81.

Scott, K., & Schau, C. (1985). Sex equity and sex bias in instructional materials. In S. Klein (Ed.), *Handbook for achieving sex equity through education* (pp. 218–260). Baltimore, MD: Johns Hopkins University Press.

Scranton, S., & Flintoff, A. (2002). *Gender and sport: A reader.* Chapter six: "Denial of power in televised women's sports." London: Psychology Press.

Scully, D., & Marolla, J. (1985). Riding the bull at Gilley's: Convicted rapists describe the rewards of rape. *Social Problems, 32,* 251–263.

Scully, J. L., Shakespeare, T., & Banks, S. (2006). Gift not commodity? Lay people deliberating social sex selection. *Sociology of Health & Illness, 28*(6), 749–767.

Sears, J. T. (1992). Educators, homosexuality, and homosexual students: Are personal feelings related to professional beliefs? In K. M. Harbeck (Ed.), *Coming out of the classroom closet: Gay and lesbian students, teachers, and curricula* (pp. 29–79). New York: Haworth Press.

Seavy, A. A., Katz, P. A., & Zalk, S. R. (1975). Baby X: The effect of gender labels on adult responses to infants. *Sex Roles, 1,* 103–109.

Seccombe, K. (2000). Families in poverty in the 1990s: Trends, causes, consequences, and lessons learned. *Journal of Marriage and the Family, 62,* 1094–1113.

Seefeldt, K. S. (2008). *Working after welfare: How women balance jobs and family in the wake of welfare reform.* Kalamazoo, MI: W.E. Upjohn Institute for Employment Research.

Seeking Corp. PAC money. (1986, Spring). *Women's Political Times,* p. 6.

Seelau, E. P., Seelau, S. M., & Poorman, P. B. (2003). Gender and role-based perceptions of domestic abuse: Does sexual orientation matter? *Behavioral Sciences and the Law, 21,* 199–214.

Seelye, K. Q. (2000, September 20). Marital status is shaping women's leanings, surveys find. *New York Times,* p. A23.

Seelye, K. Q., & Bosman, J. (2008, June 13). Critics and news executives split over sexism in Clinton coverage. *New York Times,* pp. A1, A22.

Seelye, K. Q., & Connelly, M. (2004, August 29). Delegates leaning to right of G.O.P. and the nation. *New York Times,* pp. DR1, DR13.

Segal, L. (1990). *Slow motion*. New Brunswick, NJ: Rutgers University Press.

Segura, D. A., & Pierce, J. L. (1993). Chcana/o family structure and gender personality: Chodorow, familism, and psychoanalytic sociology revisited. *Signs, 19*, 62–91.

Sehulster, J. (2006). Things we talk about, how frequently, and to whom: Frequency of topics in everyday conversation as a function of gender, age, and marital status. *The American Journal of Sociology, 119*(3), 407–432.

Seidler, V. J. (2009). *Recreating sexual politics*. London: Routledge.

Seklecki, R., & Paynich, R. (2007). A national survey of female police officers: An overview of findings. *Police Practice and Research, 8*(1), 17–30.

Selig Center. (2003). *Gay market advertising information*. Retrieved from http://www.mygayweb.com/info/advertising/

Seltzer, J. A. (2000). Families formed outside of marriage. *Journal of Marriage and the Family, 62*, 1247–1268.

Sentencing Project. (2008). *Reducing racial disparity in the criminal justice system*. Washington, DC: Sentencing Project. Available online: http://www.sentencingproject.org/doc/publications/rd_reducingracialdisparity.pdf

Serbin, L. A., Moller, L., Powlishta, K., & Gulko, J. (1991). *The emergence of gender segregation and behavioral compatibility in toddlers' peer preferences*. Paper presented at the annual meeting of the Society for Research in Child Development, Seattle, WA.

Sered, S. S. (1994). *Priestess, mother, sacred sister: Religions dominated by women*. New York: Oxford University Press.

Seto, M. C., Maric, A., & Barbaree, H. E. (2001). The role pornography in the etiology of sexual aggression. *Aggression and Violent Behavior, 6*, 35–53.

Sev'er, A., & Yurdakul, G. (2001). Culture of honor, culture of change: A feminist analysis of honor killings in rural Turkey. *Violence Against Women, 7*, 964–998.

Sex Abuse. (2009, November 16). *Gold Coast Bulletin*, p. 13.

Sex offender MDs still practicing. (1997, June 4). Washington, DC: Associated Press. (Internet).

Shakin, M., Shakin, D. & Sternglanz, S. H. (1985). Infant clothing: Sex labeling for strangers. *Sex Roles, 12*, 955–964.

Shanahan, L., McHale, S. M., Crouter, A. C., & Osgood, D. W. (2007). Warmth with mothers and fathers from middle childhood to late adolescence: Within- and between-families comparisons. *Developmental Psychology, 43*, 551–563.

Shanley, M. L. (1993). "Surrogate mothering" and women's freedom: A critique of contracts for human reproduction. *Signs, 18*, 618–639.

Shannon, K., Kerr, T., Bright, V., Gibson, K., & Tyndall, M. W. (2008). Drug sharing with clients as a risk marker for increased violence and sexual and drug-related harms among survival sex workers. *AIDS Care, 20*, 235–241.

Shanok, A. F., & Miller, L. (2007). Stepping up to motherhood among inner-city teens. *Psychology of Women Quarterly, 31*, 252–261.

Shapiro, A. (2010). The flight of Lilith: Modern Jewish American feminist literature. *Studies in American Jewish Literature, 29*, 68–79.

Shapiro, H. (1997, December 12). Western Wall posters warn women against "inviting" harassment. *Jerusalem Post*.

Shapiro, L. (1990, May 28). Guns and dolls. *Newsweek*, pp. 56–65.

Shariff, S. (2008). *Cyberbullying: Issues and solutions for the school, the classroom, and the home*. New York: Routledge.

Sharma, R. M. (2007). The ethics of birth and death: Gender infanticide in India. *Journal of Bioethical Inquiry, 4*(3), 181–192.

Sharp, S. F. (2002). *The incarcerated woman: Rehabilitative programming in women's prisons*. Upper Saddle River, NJ: Prentice Hall.

Shaywitz, B. A., Shaywitz, S. E., Pugh, K. R., Constable, R. T., Skudlarski, P., Fulbright, R. K., Bronen, R. A., Fletcher, J. M., Shakweiler, D. P., Katz, L., & Gore, J. C. (1995). Sex differences in the functional organization of the brain for language. *Nature, 373*, 607–608.

Shea, J. (2003). *The moral status of in vitro fertilization (IVF) biology and method*. Retrieved from: http://www.catholicinsight.com/online/church/vatican/article_475.shtml

Shears, J. K. (2007). Understanding differences in fathering activities across race and ethnicity. *Journal of Early Childhood Research, 5*(3), 245–261.

Sheldon, A. (1990). Pickle fights: Gendered talk in preschool disputes. *Discourse Processes, 13*, 5–31.

Shelton, B. A. (1992). *Women, men and time: Gender differences in paid work, housework, and leisure*. Westport, CT: Greenwood.

Shelton, D. E., Barak, G., & Kim, Y. S. (2007). A study of juror expectations and demands concerning scientific evidence: Does the "CSI effect" exist? *Vnderbilt Journal of Entertainment and Technology Law, 9,* 331–368.

Shem, S., & Surrey, J. (1998). *We have to talk: Healing dialogues between women and men.* New York: Basic Books.

Shenon, P. (1994, August 16). China's mania for baby boys creates surplus of bachelors. *New York Times,* pp. A1, A8.

Sherkat, D. E., De Vries, K. M., & Creek, S. (2010). Race, religion, and opposition to same-sex marriage. *Social Science Quarterly, 91,* 80–98.

Sherman, J. A. (1971). *On the psychology of women: A survey of empirical studies.* Springfield, IL: C. C. Thomas.

Sherman, J. A. (1982). Mathematics the critical filter: A look at some residues. *Psychology of Women Quarterly, 6,* 428–444.

Sherman, M. (2009, May). Supreme stats: 106 white males among 111 justices. Associated Press.

Shostak, M. (1981). *Nisa: The life and words of a !Kung woman.* Cambridge, MA: Harvard University Press.

Shrikhande, V. (2003). *Stereotyping of women in television advertisements,* Retrieved from http://etd.lsu.edu/docs/available/etd-0516103-141609/unrestricted/Shrikhande_thesis.pdf

Shulman, A. K. (1980). Sex and power: Sexual biases of radical feminism. *Signs, 5,* 590–604.

Shute, R., Owens, L., & Slee, P. (2008). Everyday victimization of adolescent girls by boys: Sexual harassment, bullying or aggression? *Sex Roles, 58*(7/8), 477–489.

Shutts, K, Banaji, M. R., & Spelke, E. S. (2009). Social categories guide young children's preferences for novel objects. *Developmental Science.* Published online.

Side effects of hormone replacement therapy (2011). *Estrogen replacement side effects.* Retrieved from http://www.estrogen-replacement-side-effects.com/html/about.html

Sidel, R. (1986). *Women and children last.* New York: Penguin Books.

Siegel, J. A., & Williams, L. M. (2003). The relationship between child sexual abuse and female delinquency and crime: A prospective study. *Journal of Research in Crime and Delinquency, 40,* 71–94.

Siegler, R. S., DeLoache, J. S., & Eisenberg, N. (2010). *How children develop.* New York: Worth.

Sigle-Rushton, W., & Waldfogel, J. (2007). The incomes of families with children: A cross-national comparison. Journal of European Social Policy, 17, 299–318.

Signorielli, N. (2009a). Minorities' representation in prime time: 2000 to 2008. *Communication Research Reports, 26,* 323–336.

Signorielli, N. (2009b). Race and sex in prime time: A look at occupations and occupational prestige. *Mass Communications and Study, 12,* 332–352.

Silveira, J. (1980). Generic masculine words and thinking. *Women's Studies International Quarterly, 3,* 165–178.

Silverstein, B., Perdue, L., Peterson, B., & Kelly, E. (1986). The role of the mass media in promoting a thin standard of bodily attractiveness for women. *Sex Roles, 14,* 519–532.

Silverstein, L. B., & Auerbach, C. F. (1999). Deconstructing the essential father. *American Psychologist, 54,* 397–407.

Simon, R. (1975). *Women and crime.* Washington, DC: U.S. Government Printing Office.

Simon, R. J., & Danzinger, G. (1991). *Women's movements in America.* New York: Praeger.

Simon, R. J., & Landis, J. (1991). *The crimes women commit, the punishments they receive.* Lexington, MA: Lexington Books.

Simons, M. (1997, December 31). Child care sacred as France cuts back the welfare state. *New York Times,* pp. A1, 8.

Simpkins, S. D., Davis-Kean, P. E., & Eccles, J. S. (2005). Parents' socializing behavior and children's participation in math, science, and computer out-of-school activities. *Applied Developmental Science, 9,* 14–30.

Simpson, R. (2005). Men in non-traditional occupations: Career entry, career orientation, and experiences of role strain. *Gender, Work and Organizations, 12,* 363–380

Sinclair, A. H., Berta, P., Palmer, M. S., Hawkins, J. R., Griffiths, B. L., Smith, M. J., Foster, J. W., Frischauf, A., Lovell-Badge, R., & Goodfellow, P. N. (1990). A gene from the human sex-determining region encodes a protein with homology to a conserved DNA-binding motif. *Nature, 346,* 240–244.

Singh, R. N., & Unnithan, N. P. (1999). Wife burning: Cultural cues for lethal violence against women among Asian Indians in the United States. *Violence Against Women, 5,* 641–653.

Sivakumaran, S. (2005). Male/male rape and the taint of homosexuality. *Human Rights Quarterly, 27,* 1274–1306.

Skarderud, F. (2007). Shame and pride in anorexia nervosa: A qualitative descriptive study. *European Eating Disorders Review, 15*(2), 81–97.

Skelton, C., Francis, B., & Read, B. (2010). Brains before 'beauty'? High achieving girls, school and gender identities. *Educational Studies, 36*, 185–194.

Skitka, L. J., & Maslach, C. (1990). Gender roles and the categorization of gender-relevant behavior. *Sex Roles, 22*, 133–150.

Slijper, F. M., Van der Kamp, H. J., Brandenberg, H., & de Muinck Keizer-Schrama, S. M., et al. (1992). Evaluation of psychosocial development of young women with congenital adrenal hyperplasia. *Journal of Sex Education and Therapy, 18*, 200–207.

Slocum, S. (1975). Woman the gatherer: Male bias in anthropology. In R. R. Reiter (Ed.), *Toward an anthropology of women* (pp. 36–50). New York: Monthly Review Press.

Smart, C. (1982). The new female offender: Reality or myth? In B. R. Price & N. J. Sokoloff (Eds.), *The criminal justice system and women* (pp. 105–116). New York: Clark Boardman.

Smitbers, A., & Robinson, P. (2006). *The paradox of single-sex and co-educational schooling.* University of Buckingham, Center for Education and Employment Research. Retrieved April 25, 2010, http://www.buckingham.ac.uk/education/research/ceer/pdfs/hmcsscd.pdf

Smith, B. (2007). *The psychology of sex and gender.* Boston: Pearson Education, Inc.

Smith, C. (Ed.) (1996). *Disruptive religion: The force of faith in social movement activism.* New York: Routledge.

Smith, D. E. (1993). The standard North American family. *Journal of Family Issues, 14*, 50–65.

Smith, D., & Wolf-Wendal, L. (2005). *The challenge of diversity: Involvement or alienation in the academy?* San Francisco: Jossey-Bass.

Smith, D. L. (2008). Disability, gender and intimate partner violence: Relationships from the Behavioral Risk Factor Surveillance System. *Sexuality and Disability, 26*, 15–28.

Smith, E. (1982). The Black female adolescent. *Psychology of Women Quarterly, 6*, 261–288.

Smith, E. (2000). How the other half read: Advertising, working-class readers and pulp magazines. *Book History, 3*, 204–230.

Smith, J. (1987). Transforming households: Working-class women and economic crisis. *Social Problems, 34*, 416–436.

Smith, K. A., Fairburn, C. G., & Cowen, P. J. (1999). Symptomatic relapse in bulimia nervosa following acute trytophan depletion. *Archives of General Psychiatry, 56*, 171–177.

Smith, K., & Christakis, N. (2008). Social networks and health. *Annual Review of Sociology 34*, 405–429.

Smith, L., & Foxcraft, D. (2009). The effect of alcohol advertising, marketing and portrayal on drinking behavior in young people: Systematic review of prospective cohort studies. *Biomedical Central Public Health, 51*(9) 1–11.

Smith, P. M. (1985). *Language, society, and the sexes.* New York: Basil Blackwell.

Smith, P. H., Thornton, G. E., DeVellis, R., Erp, J., & Coker, A. L. (2002). A population-based study of the prevalence and distinctiveness of battering, physical assault, and sexual assault in intimate relationships. *Violence Against Women, 8*, 1208–1232.

Smith, R., & Weber-Gale, G. (2008). *No pain, no gain: Investigating college athletes' sick role expectations.* Retrieved from http://convention3.allacademic.com/meta/p_mla_apa_research_citation/2/2/9/7/2/p229721_index.html

Snarey, J. (1993). *How fathers care for the next generation.* Cambridge: Harvard University Press.

Snell, W. E., Jr., Belk, S. S., & Hawkins, R. C. II (1987). Alcohol and drug use in stressful times: The influence of the masculine role and sex-related personality traits. *Sex Roles, 16*, 359–374.

Snipes, R. L., Oswald, S. L., & Caudill, S. B. (1998). Sex-role stereotyping, gender biases, and job selection: The use of ordinal logit in analyzing Likert scale data. *Employee Responsibilities and Rights Journal, 42*, 427–437.

Snow, J. T., & Harris, M. B. (1989). Disordered eating in southwestern Pueblo Indians and Hispanics. *Journal of Adolescence, 12*, 329–336.

Snow, M. E., Jacklin, C. N., & Maccoby, E. E. (1983). Sex-of-child differences in father-child interaction at one year of age. *Child Development, 54*, 227–232.

Snyder, G. (1997). *Children's television commercials and gender-stereotyped messages.* Paper presented at the Annual Meeting of the Association for Education in Journalism and Mass Communication, Chicago, IL.

Snyder, H. N., & Sickmund, M. (2006). *Juvenile offenders and victim: 2006 national report.* Washington, DC: U.S. Department of Justice, Office of Justice Programs, Office of Juvenile Justice and Delinquency Prevention.

Snyder, K. A., & Green, A. I. (2008). Revisiting the glass escalator: The case of gender segregation in a female-dominated occupation. *Social Problems, 55*, 271–299.

Snyder, T. D., & Dillow, S. A. (2007). *Digest of education statistics 2006*. Washington, DC: U.S. Department of Education, National Center of Education Statistics.

Snyder, T. D., Dillow, S. A., & Hoffman, C. M. (2008). *Digest of education statistics 2007*. Washington, DC: U.S. Department of Education, National Center of Education Statistics, Institute of Education Sciences.

Snyder-Joy, Z. K., & Carlo, T. A. (1998). Parenting through prison walls: Incarcerated mothers and children's visitation programs. In S. L. Miller (Ed.), *Crime control and women* (pp. 130–150). Thousand Oaks, CA: Sage.

Soares, R., et al. (2010). *2010 Catalyst Census: Fortune 500 women executive officers and top earners*. Retrieved from: http://www.catalyst. org/file/412/2010_us_census_women_executive_officers_and_top_ earners_final.pdf

Social Issues Research Centre. (2011). Mirror, mirror, mirror: Why we look in the mirror. Retrieved from: http://www.sirc.org/publik/mirror.html

Sokoloff, N. J. (1992). *Black women and White women in the professions: Occupational segregation by race and gender, 1960–1980*. New York: Routledge, Chapman and Hall.

Solomon, S. et al. (2009). Domestic violence and forced sex among the urban poor in South India: Implications for HIV prevention. *Violence Against Women, 15*, 753–773.

Sommer, B. (1983). How does menstruation affect cognitive competence and psychophysiological response. In S. Golub (Ed.), *Lifting the curse of menstruation* (pp. 53–90). New York: Haworth Press.

Sommers, C. H. (2008). Gender equity in math and Science. *USA Today*, 58–62.

Sommers, C. H. (2000). *The war against boys: How misguided feminism is harming our young men*. New York: Simon & Schuster.

Sonfield, A., Alrich, C., & Benson Gold, R. (2008). *Public funding for family planning, sterilization and abortion services*. Retrieved from http:// sparky.guttmacher.org/pubs/2008/01/28/or38.pdf

Song, Y. I. (1991). Single Asian American women as a result of divorce: Depression affect and changes in social support. In S. S. Volgy (Ed.), *Women and divorce, men and divorce* (pp. 219–230). New York: Haworth.

Sonne, J. L., & Pope, K. S. (1991). Treating victims of therapist-patient sexual involvement. *Psychotherapy, 28*, 174–187.

Sontag, D. (2001, April 11). Women seize counseling role on "family purity." *New York Times*, p. A4.

South Carolina Department of Mental Health. (2011). Eating disorder statistics. Retrieved from: http://www.state.sc.us/dmh/anorexia/statistics.htm

Spanier, B. (1995). Biological determinism and homosexuality. *NWSA Journal, 7*, 54–71.

Spector, J. D. (1991). What this awl means: Toward a feminist archeology. In J. M. Gero & M. W. Conkey (Eds.), *Engendering archeology*, (pp. 388–406). New York: Basil Blackwell.

Spencer, M., & Nichols, S. (2010). Exploring environmental education through ecofeminism: Narratives of embodiment of science. *Humanities, Social Sciences and Law, 2*, 255–266.

Spender, D. (1981). The gatekeepers: A feminist critique of academic publishing. In H. Roberts (Ed.), *Doing feminist research* (pp. 186–202). London: Routledge and Kegan Paul.

Sperry, R. (1982). Some effects of disconnecting the cerebral hemispheres. *Science, 217*, 1223–1226.

Spohn, C. (1990). *An analysis of the "jury trial penalty" and its effects on Black and White defendants*. Paper presented at the annual meeting of the American Society of Criminology, Baltimore, MD.

Spohn, C. (1998). Gender and sentencing of drug offender: Is chivalry dead? *Criminal Justice Policy Review, 9*, 365–399.

Spohn, C., & Brennan, P. (forthcoming). Sentencing and punishment. In C.M. Renzetti, S.L. Miller, & A. Gover (Eds.), *Handbook of gender and crime studies*. London: Routledge.

Spohn, C., & Holleran, D. (2000). The imprisonment penalty paid by young, unemployed Black and Hispanic male offenders. *Criminology, 38*, 281–306.

Sprinkle, J. E. (2009). Students perceptions of education effectiveness: A follow-up study. *College Student Journal, 43*, 1341–1358.

Stacey, A. M., & Spohn, C. (2006). Gender and the social costs of sentencing: An analysis of sentences imposed on male and female offenders in three U.S. district courts. *Berkeley Journal of Criminal Law, 11*, 43–76.

Stacey, J. (1986). Are feminists afraid to leave home? The challenge of conservative pro-family feminism. In J. Mitchell & A. Oakley (Eds.), *What is feminism? A re-examination* (pp. 208–237). New York: Pantheon.

Stacey, J. (1990). *Brave new families*. New York: Basic Books.

Stacey, J., & Biblarz, T. J. (2001). (How) does the sexual orientation of parents matter? *American Sociological Review, 66*, 159–183.

Stacey, J., & Thorne, B. (1985). The missing feminist revolution in sociology. *Social Problems, 32*, 301–316.

Stake, J. E. (2006). Pedagogy and student change in the women's and gender studies classroom. *Gender and Education, 18*(2), 199–212.

Stanczak, G. C. (2006). *Engaged spirituality: Social change and American religion*. New Brunswick, NJ: Rutgers University Press.

Stankiewicz, J. M., & Rosselli, F. (2008). Women as sex objects and victims in print advertisements. *Sex Roles, 58*, 579–589.

Stanko, E. A. (1985). *Intimate intrusions*. London: Routledge and Kegan Paul.

Stanko, E. A. (1992). Intimidating education: Sexual harassment in criminology. *Journal of Criminal Justice Education, 3*, 331–340.

Stanko, E. A. (1996). Warnings to women: Police advice and women's safety in Britain. *Violence against Women, 2*, 5–24.

Stanko, E. A. (2001). Women, danger, and criminology. In C. M. Renzetti & L. Goodstein (Eds.), *Women, crime and criminal justice* (13–26). Los Angeles: Roxbury.

Stanley, J., Bartholomew, K., Taylor, T., Oram, D., & Landolt, M. (2006). Intimate violence in male same-sex relationships. *Journal of Family Violence, 21*, 31–41.

Stanley, L. (1992). The impact of feminism on sociology in the last 20 years. In C. Kramarae & D. Spender (Eds.), *The knowledge explosion: Generations of feminist scholarship* (pp. 254–269). New York: Teachers College Press.

Stanley, S. (2004). *Holy boldness: Women preachers' autobiographies*. Knoxville: University of Tennessee Press.

Stansell, C. (1986). *City of women*. New York: Alfred A. Knopf.

Staples, R. (1995). Health among African American males. In D. Sabo & D. F. Gordon (Eds.), *Men's health and illness* (pp. 121–138). Thousand Oaks, CA: Sage.

Starhawk (1979). Witchcraft and women's culture. In C. P. Christ & J. Plaskow (Eds.), *Womanspirit rising* (pp. 259–268). San Francisco: Harper and Row.

Starr, P. (1982). *The social transformation of American medicine*. New York: Basic Books.

Statham, A., Richardson, L., & Cook, J. A. (1991). *Gender and university teaching: A negotiated difference*. Albany: State University of New York Press.

Steffens, M. C., & Wagner, C. (2004). Attitudes toward lesbians, gay men, bisexual women, and bisexual men in Germany. *Journal of Sex Research, 41*, 137–149.

Steffensmeier, D. (2001). Female crime trends, 1960–1995. In C. M. Renzetti & L. Goodstein (Eds.), *Women, crime and criminal justice* (pp. 191–211). Los Angeles: Roxbury.

Steffensmeier, D. J. (1982). Trends in female crime: It's still a man's world. In B. R. Price & N. J. Sokoloff (Eds.), *The criminal justice system and women* (pp. 117–130). New York: Clark Boardman.

Steffensmeier, D., & Demuth, S. (2006). Does gender modify the effects of race-ethnicity on criminal sanctioning? Sentences for male and female white, black and Hispanic defendants. *Journal of Quantitative Criminology, 22*, 41–261.

Steffensmeier, D., Kramer, J., & Streifel, C. (1993). Gender and imprisonment decisions. *Criminology, 31*, 411–446.

Steffensmeier, D., Schwartz, J., Zhong, S. H., & Ackerman, J. (2005). An assessment of recent trends in girls' violence using diverse longitudinal sources: Is the gender gap closing? *Criminology, 43*, 355–405.

Steffensmeier, D., Ulmer, J., & Kramer, J. (1998). The interaction of race, gender, and age in criminal sentencing: The punishment cost of being young, Black, and male. *Criminology, 36*, 763–797.

Steil, J. M., & Turetsky, B. A. (1987). Marital influence levels and symptomatology among wives. In F. J. Crosby (Ed.), *Spouse, parent, worker: On gender and multiple roles* (pp. 74–90). New Haven: Yale University Press.

Stein, D. (2004). *The women's book of healing*. New York: Random House.

Stein, D. K. (1978). Women to burn: Suttee as a normative institution. *Signs, 4*, 253–268.

Stein, M. B., Yehuda, R., Koverola, C., & Hanna, R. (1997). Enhanced dexamethasone suppression of plasma cortisol in adult women traumatized by childhood sexual abuse. *Biological Psychiatry, 42*, 680–686.

Stein, N. (2003). Bullying or sexual harassment? The missing discourse of rights in an era of zero tolerance. *Arizona Law Review, 45*, 783–799.

Stein, R. (2008). As abortion rate drops, use of RU-486 is on rise. *Washington Post*. Retrieved

February 17, 2010, http://www.washington-post.com/wp-dyn/content/article/2008/01/21/AR2008012102075.html

Steinbacher, R., & Gilroy, F. D. (1985). Preference for sex of child among primiparous women. *Journal of Psychology, 119*, 541–547.

Steinberg, J. (2000, December 17). Defending affirmative action with social science. *New York Times*, p. 41.

Steinberg, J. (2009). Harvard to endow chair in gay studies. *New York Times*, p. 1.

Steinberg, R. J., & Cook, A. (1988). Policies affecting women's employment in industrial countries. In A. H. Stromberg & S. Harkess (Eds.), *Women working* (pp. 307–328). Mountain View, CA: Mayfield.

Steinem, G. (1978, November). Erotica and pornography: A clear and present difference. *Ms.*, pp. 53–54, 75–78.

Steinfels, P. (1992, July 19). Vatican condones some discrimination against homosexuals. *New York Times*, p. 7.

Steinfels, P. (1994, May 14). Female concept of God is shaking Protestants. *New York Times*, p. 8.

Steinfels, P. (1995a, November 19). Vatican says the ban on women as priests is "infallible" doctrine. *New York Times*, pp. 1, 13.

Steinfels, P. (1995b, November 14). Women wary about aiming to be priests. *New York Times*, p. A17.

Steinfels, P. (1996, May 12). New York to hear Mass in Latin, language of Catholic discontent. *New York Times*, pp. 1, 16.

Steinke, J., Long, M., Johnson, M. J., & Ghosh, S. (2008). *Gender stereotypes of scientist characters in television programs popular among middle school-aged children*. Paper presented to the Science Communication Interest Group (SCIGroup) for the annual meeting of the Association for Education in Journalism and Mass Communication (AEJMC) Chicago, IL, August 2008.

Steinmetz, S. K. (1993). The abused elderly are dependent: Abuse is caused by the perception of stress associated with providing care. In R. J. Gelles & D. R. Loseke (Eds.), *Current controversies on family violence* (pp. 222–236). Newbury Park, CA: Sage.

Stenvinkel, P., Barany, P., Hee Chung, S., Lindholm & Olof Heimburger. (2002). A comparative analysis of nutritional parameters as predictors of outcome in male and female ESRD patients. *Nephrology Dialysis Transplantation, 17*, 1266–1274.

Sterk, C., Elifson, K., & German, D. (2000). Female crack users and their sexual relationships: The role of sex-for-crack exchanges. *Journal of Sex Research, 37*, 354–360.

Stermac, L., Del Bove, G., & Addison, M. (2001). Violence, injury, and presentation patterns in spousal sexual assaults. *Violence Against Women, 7*, 1218–1233.

Stern, S. (2001, October 16). New worry: Kids with both parents in combat. *Christian Science Monitor*. Available online: http://www.csmonitor.com

Stevens, P. E. (1998). The experiences of lesbians of color in health care encounters: Narrative insights for improving access and quality. *Journal of Lesbian Studies, 2*.

Stewart, K. (2011). *Everyday health: The health benefits of marriage*. Retrieved from http://www.everydayhealth.com/family-health/understanding/benefits-of-tying-the-knot.aspx

Stewart, M., Schiavo, R., Herzog, D., & Franko, D. (2008). Stereotypes, prejudice, and discrimination of women with anorexia nervosa. *European Eating Disorders Review, 16*, 311–318.

Stice, E., & Whitenton, K. (2002). Risk factors for body dissatisfaction in adolescent girls: A longitudinal study. *Developmental Psychology, 38*, 669–678.

Stichman, A. J., Hassell, K. D., & Archbold, C. A. (2010). Strength in numbers? A test of Kanter's theory of tokenism. *Journal of Criminal Justice, 38*, 633–639.

Stiehm, J. H. (1985). The generations of U.S. enlisted women. *Signs, 11*, 155–175.

Stillion, J. M. (1995). Premature death among males. In D. Sabo & D. F. Gordon (Eds.), *Men's health and illness* (pp. 46–67). Thousand Oaks, CA: Sage.

Stirling, K., & Aldrich, T. (2008). Child support: Who bears the burden? *Family Relations, 57*, 376–389.

Stockdale, M. S. (2005). The sexual harassment of men: Articulating the approach-rejection theory of sexual harassment. In J.E. Gruber & P. Morgan (Eds.), *In the company of men: Male dominance and sexual harassment* (pp. 117–142). Boston: Northeastern University Press.

Stoddart, T., & Turiel, E. (1985). Children's concepts of cross-gender activities. *Child Development, 56*, 1241–1252.

Stolberg, S. G. (2001, February 25). A new way to have children: The adoption of frozen embryos. *New York Times*, pp. 1, 20.

Stolberg, S. G. (2003, June 7). Working mothers swaying senate debate, as senators. *New York Times*, p. A1, A11.

Stombler, M., & Martin, P. Y. (1994). Bringing women in, keeping women down: Fraternity "little sister" organizations. *Journal of Contemporary Ethnography, 23*, 150–185.

Stombler, M., & Padevic, I. (1994). *Getting a man or getting ahead: A comparative analysis of African American and Euro-American fraternity little sister programs on college campuses*. Paper presented at the annual meeting of the American Sociological Association, Los Angeles, CA.

Stone, B. (2007). *Evangelism after Christendom: The theology and practice of Christian witness*. Grand Rapids, MI: Brazos Press.

Stone, L., & James, C. (1995). Dowry, bride-burning, and female power in India. *Women's Studies International Forum, 18*, 125–134.

Stone, M. (1976). *When God was a woman*. New York: Harcourt Brace Jovanovich.

Stone, P. (2007). *Opting out: Why women really quit careers and head home*. Berkeley: University of California Press.

Stoneman, Z., Brody, G. H., & MacKinnon, C. E. (1986). Same-sex and cross-sex siblings: Activity choices, roles, behavior, and gender stereotypes. *Sex Roles, 15*, 495–511.

Stone-Mediatore, S. (2007). Challenging academic norms: An epistemology for feminist and multicultural classrooms. NWSA Journal, 19(2), 55–78.

Stout, C. T., & Kline, R. (2011). I'm not voting for her: Polling discrepancies and female candidates. Political Behavior, 33, 479–503.

Straka, S., & Montminy, L. (2006). Responding to the needs of older women experiencing domestic violence. *Violence Against Women, 12*, 251–267.

Strange, H. (2010). Non-medical sex selection: Ethical issues. *British Medical Bulletin*. Available online.

Strate, L. (1992). Beer commercials. In S. Craig (Ed.), *Men, masculinity and media* (pp. 78–92). Newbury Park, CA: Sage.

Stratton, T., McLaughlin, M., Witte, F., Fosson, F., MA, S., & Margaret, N. (2005). Does students' exposure to gender discrimination and sexual harassment in medical school affect specialty choice and residency program selection? *Academic Medicine, 80*, 400–408.

Straus, M. A. (2007). Processes explaining the concealment and distortion of evidence on gender symmetry in partner violence. *European Journal on Criminal Policy & Research, 13*, 227–232.

Straus, M. A., & Gelles, R. J. (1990). How violent are American families? Estimates from the National Family Violence Resurvey and other studies. In M. A. Straus & R. J. Gelles (Eds.), *Physical violence in American families* (pp. 95–132). New Brunswick, NJ: Transaction Publishers.

Straus, M. A., & Smith, C. (1990). Family patterns and child abuse. In M. A. Straus & R. J. Gelles (Eds.), *Physical violence in American families* (pp. 245–262). New Brunswick, NJ: Transaction Publishers.

Strauss, R. S. (1999). Self-reported weight status and dieting in a cross-sectional sample of young adolescents: National Health and Nutrition Examination Survey III. *Archives of Pediatric and Adolescent Medicine, 153*, 741–747.

Strauss-Noll, M. (1984). An illustration of sex bias in English. *Women's Studies Quarterly, 12*, 36–37.

Strazdins, L., & Broom, D. (2004). Acts of love (and work): Gender imbalance in emotional work and women's psychological distress. *Journal of Family Issues, 23*(3), 356–378.

Streufert, M. (2010). *Transformative Lutheran theologies: Feminist, womanist, and mujerista perspectives*. Minneapolis: Fortress Press.

Strickland, B. R. (2000). Misassumptions, misadventures, and the misuse of psychology. *American Psychologist, 55*, 331–338.

Striegel-Moore, R. H., Silberstein, L. R., & Rodin, J. (1986). Toward an understanding of the risk factors in bulimia. *American Psychologist, 41*, 246–263.

Strober, M. H., & Lanford, A. G. (1986). The feminization of public school teaching: Cross-sectional analysis, 1850–1880. *Signs, 11*, 212–235.

Strober, M. H., & Tyack, D. (1980). Why do women teach and men manage? A report on research on schools. *Signs, 5*, 494–503.

Stromquist, N. P. (2006). Gender, education and the possibility of transformative knowledge. *Compare: A Journal of Comparative Education, 36*, 145–161.

Strough, J., & Diriwächter, R. (2000). Dyad gender differences in preadolescents' creative stories. *Sex Roles, 43*, 43–59.

Structure of Women's Soccer Leagues (2011). *List of United States soccer teams*. Retrieved from http://simple.wikipedia.org/wiki/List_of_United_States_soccer_teams

Students Against Drunk Driving (SADD) (2011). *Statistics*. Retrieved from http://www.sadd.org/stats.htm

Study on adoption and foster care by lesbians and gay men. (2009). *Gay Parent Magazine, 12*(57), 16–18.

Substance Abuse and Mental Health Services Administration (2010). *Results from the 2009 National Survey on Drug Use and Health: Volume I. Summary of National Findings.* Retrieved from http://oas.samhsa.gov/NSDUH/2k9NSDUH/2k9Results.htm#2.5

Sudderth, L. K. (1998). It'll come right back at me: The interactional context of discussing rape with others. *Violence Against Women, 4,* 572–594.

Suffragette's racial remark haunts college. (1996, May 5). *New York Times*, p. 30.

Suftin, E. L., Fulcher, M. Bowles, R. P., & Patterson, C. J. (2007). How lesbian and heterosexual parents convey attitudes about gender to their children: The role of gendered environments. *Sex Roles, 58,* 501–513.

Suit unfairly attacks effort to boost women's sports. (2002, January 21). *USA Today*, p. 10A.

Sullins, D. P. (2006). Gender and religion: Deconstructing universality, constructing complexity. *American Journal of Sociology, 112,* 838–880.

Sullivan, A. (2006). Students as rational decision-makers: The question of beliefs and attitudes, *London Review of Education, 4,* 271–290.

Sullivan, A., Joshi, H., & Leonard, D. (2010). Single-sex schooling and academic attainment at school and through the lifecourse. *American Education Research Journal, 47*(1), 6–36.

Sullivan, E., & Cameron, J. (2009). A rapidly occurring compensatory decrease in physical activity counteracts diet-induced weight loss in female monkeys. *American Journal of Physiology, 298,* R1068–R1074.

Sullivan, R. (2005). *Visual habits: Nuns, feminism, and American postwar popular culture.* Ontario, Canada: University of Toronto Press.

Surbeck, M., & Hohmann, G. (2008). Primate hunting by bonobos at LuiKotale Salonga National Park. *Current Biology, 18,* R906-R907.

Surgery that's painful—and popular in China. (2002, April 20). *National Post* (Vancouver, BC), p. B5.

Surprises in a study of life expectancies. (1997, December 4). *New York Times*, p. A24.

Survey finds bias on the front page. (1996, April 17). *New York Times*, p. A17.

Sussman, A. S. (2008). Peace must include tough rape laws. *Herizons, 21*(3), 9.

Sussman, T., & Ahmed, C. (2009). In Iraq, a story of rape, shame and "honor killing." *Los Angeles Times*. Retireved from: http://articles.latimes.com/2009/apr/23/world/fg-iraq-woman23.

Sutlive, V. H. (1991). *Female and male in Borneo.* Williamsburg, VA: Borneo Research Council.

Svallfors, S. (2006). *The moral economy of class: Class and attitudes in comparative perspective.* Stanford, CA: Stanford University Press.

Swarns, R. L. (2008, June 30). In quiet ascent, commanding a new role for women in the military. *New York Times*, p. A17.

Syme, S. L., & Berkman, L. F. (1997). Social class, susceptibility, and sickness. In P. Conrad (Ed.), *The sociology of health and illness* (pp. 29–35). New York: St. Martin's Press.

Taeuber, C. M., & Valdisera, V. (1986). *Women in the American economy.* Current Population Reports. Washington, DC: U.S. Government Printing Office.

Tahmincioglu, E. (2006). *From the sandbox to the corner office: Lessons learned on the journey to the top.* Hoboken, NJ: John Wiley & Sons.

Talbot, M. (2006). "Little hotties": Barbie's new rivals. *New Yorker*, p. 74.

Tallichet, S. E. (2006). *Daughters of the mountain: Women coal miners in Central Appalachia.* University Park: the Pennsylvania State University.

Tannen, D. (1990). *You just don't understand.* New York: William Morrow.

Tannen, D. (1994a). *Gender and discourse.* New York: Oxford University Press.

Tannen, D. (1994b). *Talking from 9 to 5.* New York: William Morrow and Company.

Tannen, D. (2010). He said, she said. *Scientific American Mind, 21*(2), 55–59.

Tanner, N., & Zihlman, A. (1976). Women in evolution. Part I: Innovation and selection in human origins. *Signs, 1,* 585–608.

Tauriac, J. J., & Scruggs, N. (2006). Elder abuse among African Americans. *Educational Gerontology, 32*(1), 37–48.

Tausch. N. et al. (2007). Cross-community contact, perceived status differences, and intergroup attitudes in Northern Ireland: The mediating roles of individual-level versus group-level threats and the moderating role of social identification. *Political Psychology, 28,* 53–68.

Tavernise, S. (2009, February 16). In quest for equal rights, Muslim women's meeting turns to Islam's tenets. *New York Times*, p. A8.

Tavris, C. (1992). *The mismeasure of woman.* New York: Simon and Schuster.

Taylor, F. (2003). Content analysis and gender stereotypes in children's books. *Teaching Sociology, 31*, 300–311.

Taylor, H. (2003, October 16). Most Americans believe in God but there is no consensus on His/Her gender, form or degree of control over events. *Harris Interactive Poll Research*. Retrieved from: http://www.harrisinteractive.com

Taylor, S. E., Cousino Klein, L., Lewis, B. P., Gruenwald, T. C., Guruny, R. A. R., & Updegraff, J. A. (2000). Biobehavioral responses to stress in females: Tend-and-befriend, not fight-or-flight. *Psychological Review, 107*, 411–429.

Taylor, V. (1990). The continuity of the American women's movement: An elite-sustained stage. In G. West & R. L. Blumberg (Eds.), *Women and social protest* (pp. 277–301). New York: Oxford University Press.

Teachman, Jay D., Tedrow, L. M., & Crowder, K. D. (2000). The changing demograpy of America's families. *Journal of Marriage and the Family, 62*, 1234–1246.

Teaster, P. B., Dugar, T. A., Mendiondo, M. S., Abner, E. L., & Cecil, K. A. (2006). *The 2004 Survey of State Adult Protective Services: Abuse of adults 60 Years of age and older*. Washington, DC: National Center on Elder Abuse.

Teilmann, K. S., & Landry, P. H., Jr. (1981). Gender bias in juvenile justice. *Journal of Research in Crime and Delinquency, 18*, 47–80.

Teltsch, K. (1992, July 22). As more people need care, more men help. *New York Times*, pp. B1, B4.

Temkin, L. (2004). Thinking about the needy, justice, and international organizations. *Journal of Ethics, 8*(4), 349–395.

Temple, J. R. (2005). "People who are different from you." Heterosexism in Quebec high school textbooks. *Canadian Journal of Education, 28*(3), 271–294.

Tenny, D., & Zahradnik, B. (2001). *The poverty despite work handbook*. Washington, DC: Center on Budget and Policy Priorities.

Terry, R. M. (1978). *Trends in female crime: A comparison of Adler, Simon, and Steffensmeier*. Paper presented at the annual meeting of the Society for the Study of Social Problems, San Francisco, CA.

Tewksbury, R., & Collins, S. C. (2006). Aggression levels among correctional officers: Reassessing sex differences. *The Prison Journal, 86*, 327–343.

Tews, M. J., Stafford, K., & Tracey, J. B. (2011). What matters most? The perceived importance of ability and personality for hiring decisions. *Cornell Hospital Quarterly, 52*, 94–101.

Texas A & M University. (2002). *Anderson retailing, projects*, Retrieved from http://digital.library.tamu.edu/Projects/AndersonRetailing/vol4/92Vol4No6P2.htm

The missing male teacher. (2009, September). *USA Today Magazine*, 138, 2772, p. 6.

Theberge, N. (1993). The construction of gender in sport: Women, coaching, and the naturalization of difference. *Social Problems, 40*, 301–313.

Theberge, N. (2000). *Higher goals: Women's ice hockey and the politics of gender*. Albany: State University of New York Press.

Thi, M., Brickley, D., Vinh, D., Colby, D., Sohn, A., Trung, N., Giang, L., & Mandel, J. (2008). A qualitative study of stigma and discrimination against people living with HIV in Ho Chi Minh City, Vietnam. *AIDS and Behavior, 12*(1), 63–70.

Thoits, P. A. (1987). Negotiating roles. In F. J. Crosby (Ed.), *Spouse, parent, worker: On gender and multiple roles* (pp. 11–22). New Haven: Yale University Press.

Thomas, S., Herrick, R., & Braunstein, M. (2002). Legislative careers: The personal and the political. In C.S. Rosenthal (Ed.),*Women transforming Congress* (pp. 397–421). Norman: Oklahoma State University.

Thompson, B. W. (1994). *A hunger so wide and so deep: American women speak out on eating problems*. Minneapolis: University of Minnesota Press.

Thompson, B. W. (1996). "A way outa no way": Eating problems among African American, Latina, and White women. In E. N. Chow & D. Wilkinson (Eds.), *Race, class, and gender: Common bonds, different voices* (pp. 52–69). Thousand Oaks, CA: Sage.

Thompson, C. (1964). *Interpersonal psychoanalysis: The selected papers of Clara M. Thompson*. New York: Basic.

Thompson, E. H. (1991). Beneath the status characteristic: Gender variations in religiousness. *Journal for the Scientific Study of Religion, 30*, 381–394.

Thompson, G. L., Warren, S., & Carter, L. (2004). It's not my fault: Predicting high school teachers who blame parents and students fo students' low achievement. *High School Journal, 87*(3), 5–14.

Thompson, L., & Walker, A. J. (1989). Women and men in marriage, work, and parenthood. *Journal of Marriage and the Family, 51*, 845–872.

Thompson, M. I. (1990). *Ida B. Wells-Barnett: An exploratory study of an American Black woman, 1893–1930*. Brooklyn, NY: Carlson Publications.

Thompson, R. A. (2006). Black skin-brass shields: Assessing the presumed marginalization of Black law enforcement executives. *American Journal of Criminal Justice, 30*(2), 163–175.

Thomson, R., Murachver, T., & Green, J. (2001). Where is the gender in gendered language? *Psychological Science, 12*, 171–175.

Thorne, B. (1992). Feminism and the family: Two decades of thought. In B. Thorne (Ed.), *Rethinking the family: Some feminist questions* (pp. 3–30). Boston: Northeastern University Press.

Thorne, B. (1993). *Gender play: Girls and boys in school*. New Brunswick, NJ: Rutgers University Press.

Thornhill, R., & Palmer, C. (2000). *A natural history of rape: Biological bases of sexual coercion*. Boston: MIT Press.

Thorson, E., & Mendelson, A. (1996). *Perceptions of news stories and news photos of Hillary Rodham Clinton*. Paper presented at the annual meeting of the Association for Education in Journalism and Mass Communication, Anaheim, CA.

Thun, M. J., Day-Lally, C. A., Calle, E. E., Flanders, W. D., & Heath, C. W., Jr. (1995). Excess mortality among cigarette smokers: Changes in a 20-year interval. *American Journal of Public Health, 85*, 1223–1230.

Thun, M., Henley, S., Burns, D., Jemal, A., Shanks, T., & Calle, E. (2006). Lung cancer death rates in lifelong nonsmokers. *Journal of the National Cancer Institute, 98*, 691–699.

Thys-Jacobs, S., Alvir, J. M. J., & Frataracangelo, P. (1995). Comparative analysis of three PMS assessment instruments—The identification of premenstrual syndrome with core symptoms. *Psychopharmacology Bulletin, 31*, 389–396.

Tidball, M. E. (1980). Women's colleges and women achievers revisited. *Signs, 5*, 504–517.

Tiemann, K. A., Kennedy, S. A., & Haga, M. P. (1998). Rural lesbians' strategies for coming out to health care professionals. *Journal of Lesbian Studies, 2*.

Tietz, W. M. (2007). Women and men in accounting textbooks: Exploring the hidden curriculum. *Issues in Accounting Education, 22*(3), 459–480.

Tiger, L., & Fox, R. (1971). *The imperial animal*. New York: Oxford University Press.

Till, C., Koren, G., & Rovet, J. (2008). Workplace standards for exposure to toxicants during pregnancy. *Canadian Journal of Public Health, 99*(6), 472–474.

Tille, J. E., & Rose, J. C. (2007). Emotional and behavioral problems of 13-to-18 year-old incarcerated female first-time offenders and recidivists. *Youth Violence and Juvenile Justice, 5*(4), 426–435.

Tisak, M. S., Holub, S. C., & Tisak, J. (2007). What nice things do boys and girls do? Preschoolers' perspectives of peers' behaviors at school and at home. *Early Education and Development, 18*(2), 183–199.

Tjaden, P. G., & Thoennes, N. (1998). *Prevalence, incidence, and consequences of violence against women*. Washington, DC: National Institute of Justice.

Tjaden, P., & Thoennes, N. (2000). Prevalence and consequences of male-to-female and female-to-male intimate partner violence as measured by the National Violence Against Women Survey. *Violence Against Women, 6*, 142–161.

Tjaden, P., & Thoennes, N. (2006). *Extent, nature, and consequences of rape victimization: Findings from the National Violence Against Women Survey* (No. 210346). Washington, DC: U.S. Department of Justice.

Todahl, J. L., Linville, D., Bustin, A., Wheeler, J., & Gau, J. (2009). Sexual assault support services and community systems: Understanding critical issues and needs in the LGBTQ community. *Violence Against Women, 15*, 952–976.

Tolman, R. M. (1999). Guest editor's introduction. *Violence Against Women, 5*, 355–369.

Tolman, R. M., & Raphael, J. (Eds.) (2001). Special issue: Welfare, poverty, and domestic violence. *Violence Against Women, 7*(2).

Tomaskovic-Devey, D., Zimmer, C., Stainback, K., Robinson, C., Taylor, T., & McTague, T. (2006). Documenting desegregation: Segregation in American workplaces by race, ethnicity, and sex, 1966–2003. *American Sociological Review, 71*, 565–588.

Toutkoushian, R. K., Bellas, M. L., & Moore, J. V. (2007). The interaction effects of gender, race, and marital status of faculty salaries. *Journal of Higher Education, 78*(5), 572–601.

Toutkoushian, R., & Conley, V. (2005). Progress for women in academe, yet inequalities persist. Evidence form NSOPF:99. *Research in Higher Education, 46*(1), 1–28.

Tracy, P. E., Kempf-Leonard, K., & Abramoske-James, S. (2009). Gender differences in delinquency and juvenile justice processing: Evidence from national data. *Crime & Delinquency, 55*(2), 171–215.

Traub, J. (2005). Lawrence Summers, Provocateur. *New York Times*. Retrieved June 9, 2010, http://www.nytimes.com/2005/01/23/weekinreview/23trau.html?oref=lo

Travis, C. B. (Ed.) (2003). *Evolution, gender, and rape*. Cambridge, MA: MIT Press.

Treichler, P. A., & Frank, F. W. (1989a). Introduction: Scholarship, feminism, and language change. In F. W. Frank & P. A. Treichler (Eds.), *Language, gender, and professional writing: Theoretical approaches and guidelines for nonsexist usage* (pp. 1–32). New York: The Modern Language Association of America.

Treichler, P. A., & Frank, F. W. (1989b). Guidelines for nonsexist usage. In F. W. Frank & P. A. Treichler (Eds.), *Language, gender, and professional writing: Theoretical approaches and guidelines for nonsexist usage* (pp. 137–278). New York: The Modern Language Association of America.

Trials rare after charges of sex assault at Annapolis. (2006, March 19). *New York Times*, p. 20.

Tripp, A. M. (2000). Rethinking difference: Comparative perspectives from Africa. *Signs, 25*, 649–675.

Trocki, K., & Drabble, L. (2008). Bar patronage and motivational predictors of drinking in the San Francisco Bay area: Gender and sexual identity differences. *Journal of Psychoactive Drugs, 5*, 345–356.

Trolley, B., Hanel, C., & Shields, L. (2006). *Demystifying and deescalating cyber bullying in the schools: A resource guide for counselors, educators and parents*. Booklocker.com, Inc.

Trotter, J. (2006). "Violent crimes? Young people's experiences of homophobia and misogyny in secondary schools. *Practice, 18*(4), 291–302.

Trotter, J. (2009). Ambiguities around sexuality: An approach to understanding harassment and bullying of young people in British schools. *Journal of LGBT Youth, 6*, 7–23.

Truman, J. L. (2011). *Criminal victimization, 2010*. Washington, DC: U.S. Department of Justice, Bureau of Justice Statistics.

Truscott, A. (2008). Congo ceasefire brings little relief to women. *Canadian Medical Association Journal, 179*(2), 133–134.

Tuchman, G. (1979). Women's depiction by the mass media. *Signs, 4*, 528–542.

Tuchman, G., Daniels, A. K., & Benet, J. (Eds.) (1978). *Hearth and home: Images of women in the mass media*. New York: Oxford University Press.

Tucker, M. B., & Mitchell-Kernan, C. (Eds.) (1995). *The decline in marriage among African Americans: Causes, consequences and policy implications*. New York: Russell Sage.

Turner, C. S. V., & Thompson, J. R. (1993). Socializing women doctoral students: Minority and majority experiences. *Review of Higher Education, 16*, 355–370.

Turner, H. A., Pearlin, L. I., & Mullan, J. T. (1998). Sources and determinants of social support of caregivers of persons with AIDS. *Journal of Health and Social Behavior, 39*, 137–151.

Turner, K. B., Giacopassi, D., & Vandiver, M. (2006). Ignoring the past: Coverage of slavery and slave patrols in Criminal Justice texts. *Journal of Criminal Justice Education, 17*(1), 181–195.

Turner, L. H., & Sterk, H. M. (1994). Introduction: Examining "difference." In L. H. Turner & H. M. Sterk (Eds.), *Differences that make a difference* (pp. xi–xvi). Westport, CT: Bergin and Garvey.

Turner, S. S. (1999). Intersex identities: Locating new intersections of sex and gender. *Gender & Society, 13*, 457–479.

Tyack, D., & Hansot, E. (1990). *Learning together: A history of coeducation in American public schools*. New Haven, CT: Yale University Press.

U.S Conference of Catholic Bishops. (2004, January 15). Report on implementation of the "Charter for the Protection of Children and Young People." *Origins, 33*(31), 522–540.

U.S. Bureau of Labor Statistics. (2009). *Employment characteristics of families in 2008*. Washington, DC: U.S. Department of Labor. Retrieved from: http://www.bls.gov/news.release/famee.nr0.htm

U.S. Bureau of Prisons agrees to reforms in settlement of sex suit. (1998, March 4). San Francisco, CA: Associated Press (Internet).

U.S. Conference of Catholic Bishops. (2010). *Always our children: A pastoral message to parents of homosexual children and suggestions for pastoral ministers*. Retrieved from: http://www.nccbuscc.org/laity/always.shtml

U.S. Department of Commerce, Bureau of the Census (2009d). *American community survey, 2006–2008 American Community Survey 3-Year Estimates, Table S1201*. Retrieved from: http://factfinder.census.gov/servlet/STTable?_bm=y&geo_id=01000US&-qr_name=ACS_2008_3YR_G00_S1201&-ds_name=ACS_2008_3YR_G00_&redoLog=false

U.S. Department of Commerce, Bureau of the Census (2009e). *Income, Poverty and Health*

Insurance Coverage in the United States: 2008. Retrieved from: http://www.census.gov/newsroom/releases/archives/income_wealth/cb09-141.html

U.S. Department of Commerce, Bureau of the Census (2010). Table 637. Workers paid hourly rates by selected characteristics:2008. Retrieved from: http://www.census.gov/compendia/statab/2010/tables/10s0637.xls

U.S. Department of Commerce, Bureau of the Census. (1976). *Historical statistics of the United States, Colonial Times to 1970, Part I*. Washington, DC: U.S. Government Printing Office.

U.S. Department of Commerce, Bureau of the Census. (1985). *Statistical abstract of the United States, 1985*. Washington, DC: U.S. Government Printing Office.

U.S. Department of Commerce, Bureau of the Census. (1991). *Statistical abstract of the United States, 1991*. Washington, DC: U.S. Government Printing Office.

U.S. Department of Commerce, Bureau of the Census. (1997). *Statistical abstract of the United States, 1997*. Washington, DC: U.S. Government Printing Office.

U.S. Department of Commerce, Bureau of the Census. (2000). *Statistical abstract of the United States*. Washington, DC: U.S. Government Printing Office.

U.S. Department of Commerce, Bureau of the Census. (2006). *Facts for features: Father's Day*. Retrieved from: http://www.census.gov Press-Release/www/releases/archives/facts_for_features_special_editions/006794.html

U.S. Department of Commerce, Bureau of the Census. (2007). *Living arrangements of children under 18 and marital status of parents by age, sex, race, and Hispanic origin*. Retrieved from: http://www.census.gov/population/socdemo/hh-fam/cps2007/tabC3-all.xls

U.S. Department of Commerce, Bureau of the Census. (2007, March). Single-parent households showed little variation since 1994, Census Bureau Reports. Retrieved from: http://www.census.gov/Press-Release/www/releases/archives/families_households/009842.html

U.S. Department of Commerce, Bureau of the Census. (2008). School enrollment in the United States: 2006. Washington, DC: U.S. Bureau of the Census.

U.S. Department of Commerce, Bureau of the Census. (2008g). Nearly half of preschoolers receive childcare from relatives. Retrieved from: http://www.census.gov/Press-Release/www/releases/archives/children/011574.html

U.S. Department of Commerce, Bureau of the Census. (2009b). As baby boomers age, fewer families have children under 18 at home. Retrieved from: http://www.census.gov/Press-Release/www/releases/archives/families_households/013378

U.S. Department of Commerce, Bureau of the Census. (2009c). *Statistical Abstracts of the United States 2009, Table 578*. Retrieved from: http://www.census.gov/compendia/statab/tables/09s0578.pdf

U.S. Department of Commerce, Bureau of the Census. (2011). *Statistical Abstract of the United States, 2011*. Retrieved from: http://www.census.gov/compendia/statab/

U.S. Department of Commerce, s Bureau of the Census. (2000). *Summary population and housing characteristics*. Retrieved from http://www.census.gov

U.S. Department of Defense. (2011). Active duty military personnel by rank/grade. Female active duty military personnel by rank/grade. Retrieved from: http://www.defense.gov

U.S. Department of Education, National Center for Education Statistics. (2007b). Schools and Staffing Survey (SASS), "Public School Teacher Data File" and "Private School Teacher Data File," 1993–94, 1999–2000, and 2003–04 and "Charter School Teacher Data File," 1999–2000. from: http://www.nces.ed.gov/programs/coe/2007/section4/table.asp?tableID=721

U.S. Department of Education, National Center for Education Statistics. (2008a). Bachelor's degrees conferred by degree-granting institutions, by race/ethnicity and sex of student: Selected years, 1976–77 through 2006–07. Table 284. Retrieved from: http://www.nces.ed.gov/programs/digest/d08/tables/dt08_284.asp

U.S. Department of Education, National Center for Education Statistics. (2008b). Employees in degree-granting institutions, by sex, employment status, control and type of institution, and primary occupation: Selected years, fall 1987 through fall 2007. Table 243. *Digest of Education Statistics: 2008*. Retrieved from: http://nces.ed.gov/programs/digest/d08/tables/dt08_243.asp?referrer=list

U.S. Department of Education, National Center for Education Statistics. (2008c). Employees in degree-granting institutions, by race/ethnicity, sex, employment status, control and type of institution, and primary occupation: Fall 2007. Table 246. *Digest of Education Statistics: 2008*. Retrieved from:http://nces.ed.gov/programs/digest/d08/tables/dt08_246.asp?referrer=list

U.S. Department of Education, National Center for Education Statistics. (2008d). Degrees in engineering and engineering technologies conferred by degree-granting institutions, by level of degree and sex of student: Selected years, 1949–50 through 2006–07. Table 304. *Digest of Education Statistics: 2008*. Retrieved from: http://www.nces.ed.gov/programs/digest/d08/tables/dt08_304.asp

U.S. Department of Education, National Center for Education Statistics. (2009d). *Condition of Education 2009*. NCES 2009-081. Washington, DC: Author.

U.S. Department of Education, National Center for Education Statistics. (2010). National Center for Education Statistics, College Navigator. Available online at: http://nces.ed.gov/collegenavigator/?s=all&ct=2+3&sp=2

U.S. Department of Education, National Center of Education Statistics. (2009e). Full-time and part-time instructional faculty and staff in degree-granting institutions, by field and faculty characteristics: Fall 1992, fall 1998, and fall 2003. Table 255. from: http://nces.ed.gov/programs/digest/d09/tables/dt09_255.asp

U.S. Department of Health and Human Services. (1998). *Child maltreatment 1996. Reports from the states to the National Child Abuse and Neglect Data System*. Washington, DC: Author.

U.S. Department of Justice, Bureau of Justice Statistics (2006). *Sourcebook of criminal justice statistics, 2006*. Retrieved February 23, 2010, http://www.albany.edu/sourcebook/pdf/t3322006.pdf

U.S. Department of Justice, Bureau of Justice Statistics. (2006). *Drug use and dependence, state and federal prisoners, 2004*. Washington, DC: U.S. Department of Justice, Office of Justice Programs.

U.S. Department of Justice, Bureau of Justice Statistics. (2007). *Homicide trends in the United States, 1976–2005*. Washington, DC: U.S. Department of Justice, Office of Justice Programs.

U.S. Department of Justice, Bureau of Justice Statistics. (2008). *Adult correctional populations, 1980–2008*. http://www.ojp.usdoj.gov/bjs/correct.htm#findings

U.S. Department of Justice, Bureau of Justice Statistics. (2008a). *Prisoners in 2007*. Washington, DC: U.S. Department of Justice.

U.S. Department of Justice, Bureau of Justice Statistics. (2008b). *Probationers in 2007*. Washington, DC: U.S. Department of Justice.

U.S. Department of Justice, Bureau of Justice Statistics. (2009). *Sourcebook of criminal justice statistics, 2008*. Available online: http://www.albany.edu/sourcebook

U.S. Department of Justice, Bureau of Justice Statistics. (2010). *Sourcebook of criminal justice statistics, 2010*. Available online: http://www.albany.edu/sourcebook

U.S. Department of Justice. (1994). *Violence against women*. Washington, DC: U.S. Department of Justice.

U.S. Department of Labor (2005). *Bureau of Labor Statistics, census of fatal occupational injuries*. Retrieved from http://www.bls.gov/iif/oshwc/cfoi/cfch0004.pdf

U.S. Department of Labor, Bureau of Labor Statistics. (2010). *The employment status- January 2010*. USDL-10-0141. Retrieved from: http://www.bls.gov/news.release/pdf/empsit.pdf

U.S. Department of Labor, U.S. Bureau of Labor Statistics. (2009a). *Employed persons by detailed occupation, sex, race, and Hispanic or Latino ethnicity*.from: http://www.bls.gov/cps/cpsaat11.pdf

U.S. Department of Labor, U.S. Bureau of Labor Statistics. (2009b). *Women in the labor force: A databook*. Washington, DC: Author.

U.S. Department of Labor, U.S. Bureau of Labor Statistics. (2010b). *The unemployment situation– August 2010*. Retrieved from: http://www.bls.gov/news.release/pdf/empsit.pdf

U.S. Department of Labor. (1997a). *The glass ceiling initiative: Are there cracks in the ceiling?* Washington, DC: Author.

U.S. Department of Labor. (1997b). *National census of fatal occupational injuries, 1996*. Washington, DC: Author.

U.S. Department of Labor. (2001). *National census of fatal occupational injuries in 2000*. Washington, DC: Author.

U.S. Department of Labor. (2002a). *Employment status of the civilian population by sex and age, January, 2001*. Available online: http://www.dol.gov

U.S. Department of Labor. (2002b). *Current population survey, 2001: Employed persons by detailed occupation, sex, race, and Hispanic origin.* Available online: http://www.dol.gov

U.S. National Center for Education Statistics. (2008). *Projections of education statistics to 2017.* NCES 2008-060. Retrieved from: http://nces.ed.gov/pubs2008/2008078.pdf

Uchitelle, L. (2001, June 26). Women forced to delay retirement. *New York Times.*

Uecker, J. E. (2008). Religion, pledging, and the premarital sexual behavior of married young adults. *Journal of Marriage and Family, 70,* 728–744.

Ullman, S. E., Filipas, H. H., Townsend, S. M., & Starzynski, L. (2007). Psychological correlates of PTSD symptoms severity in sexual assault survivors. *Journal of Traumatic Stress, 20,* 821–831.

Ullman, S. E., Starzynski, L. L., Long, S. M., Mason, G. E., & Long, L. M. (2008). Exploring the relationships of women's sexual assault disclosure, social reactions, and problem drinking. *Journal of Interpersonal Violence, 23*(9), 1235–1257.

Ulmer, J. T., & Bradley, M. S. (2006). Variation in trial penalties among serious violent offenses. *Criminology, 44*(3), 631–670.

Umansky, E. M. (1985). Feminism and the reevaluation of women's roles within American Jewish life. In Y. Y. Haddad & E. B. Findly (Eds.), *Women, religion and social change* (pp. 477–494). Albany: State University of New York Press.

UNESCO. (2003). *Education for all global monitoring report 2003/4.* Paris: UNESCO.

UNESCO. (2008). *Gender parity in education: Not there yet.*

UNICEF. (2006). *Gender achievements and prospects in education: The GAP report, Part 1.* http://www.ungei.org/gap/pdfs/unicef_gap_low_res.pdf

UNICEF. (2009a). *All children, everywhere: A strategy for basic education and gender equality.* http://www.unicef.org/publications/files/All_Children_Everywhere_EN_072409.pdf

UNICEF. (2009b). *The state of the world's children, 2009.* New York: UNICEF.

UNIFEM. (2008). *Who answers to women? Gender and accountability.* Available online: http://www.unifem.org/progress/2008

Union of Concerned Scientists, (2002). *Publications, Chapter 1, Union of Concerned Scientists,* Retrieved from http://www.ucsusa.org/publications/

United Nations. (2000). *The world's women, 2000.* New York: Author.

USA Today (2008, October 23). Women more pessimistic on economy's direction. p. A1.

USA Today. (2005, July 26). *U.S. stands part from other nations on maternity leave.* Retrieved from: http://www.usatoday.com/news/health/2005–07–26-maternity-leave_x.htm

Usher, D. R. (2005). *U.S. Senate reauthorizes feminist man hating bill* (also posted on other sites as: *U.S. Senate reauthorizes organized robbery and child abuse*). Retrieved February 19, 2010, from http://www.newswithviews.com/Usher/david5.htm

Ussher, J. (1989). *The psychology of the female body.* London: Routledge.

Vaishalli, C. (2009). Noose is no solution to bride burning. *Daily News & Analysis* (India), p. 1.

Valian, V. (1999). *Why so slow? The advancement of women.* Boston: MIT Press.

Van Anders, S. M. (2004). Whey the academic pipeline leaks: Fewer men than women perceive barriers to becoming professors. *Sex Roles, 51*(9/10), 511–521.

Van Dam, R. (2008). Christianization and communication in late antiquity: John Chrysostom and his congregation in Antioch. *Journal of Early Christian Studies, 16,* 267–268.

Van Goozen, S., Frijda, N., & Van De Poll, N. (1994). Anger and aggression in women: Influence of sports choice and testosterone administration. *Aggressive Behavior, 20,* 213–222.

Van Zeijl, F. (2007). War against women. *New Internationalist, 401,* 10–12.

Vandenbergh, J. G. (2003). Prenatal hormone exposure and sexual variation. *American Scientist, 91,* 218–225.

Vanderstaay, S. (1992). *Street lives.* Philadelphia: New Society Publishers.

Vatuk, S. (2008). Islamic feminism in India: Indian Muslim women activists and the reform of Muslim personal law. *Modern Asian Studies, 42,* 489–518.

Vaught, S. E., & Castagno, A. E. (2008). I don't think I'm racist. *Race, Ethnicity, & Education, 11*(2), 95–113.

Vega, V., & Malamuth, N. (2007). The role of pornography in the context of general and specific risk factors. *Aggressive Behavior, 33,* 104–117.

Ventura, S. J. (2009, May). *Changing patterns of nonmarital childbearing in the United States.* NCHS Data Brief, 28. Hyattsville, MD: National Center for Health Statistics.

Vianna, C., & Unbehaum, S. (2006). La inclusión de la perspectiva de género en las políticas públicas de la educación en Brasil. In N. P. Stromquist

(Ed.), *La construcción del género en las políticas públicas:_Perspectivas comparadas desde América Latina*. Lima, Peru: IEP, Instituto de Estudios Peruanos

Vickers, K. (2007). Aging and the media: Yesterday, today and tomorrow. *California Journal of Health Promotion, 5*(3), 100–105.

Villarosa, L. (2001, August 7). Women now look beyond HIV to children and grandchildren. *New York Times*, p. F7.

Vindhya, U. (2000). "Dowery deaths" in Andhra Pradesh, India: Response of the criminal justice system. *Violence Against Women, 6*, 1085–1108.

Violanti, J. M., Fekedulegn, D., Charles, L. E., Andrew, M. E., Hartley, T. A., Mnatsakanova, A., et al. (2009). Suicide in police work: Exploring potential contributing influences. *American Journal of Criminal Justice, 34*, 41–53.

Vision 2020. (2011). *Equality: Are we there yet?* Retrieved from: http://equalityinsight.wordpress.com/page/2/

Vitals (2010). *Dr. David Livingston, sex offender, still able to practice in Tennessee*. Retrieved from http://spotlight.vitals.com/2010/02/dr-david-livingston-sex-offender-able-to-practice-in-tennessee/

Vivian, J. (1993). *The media of mass communication*. Boston: Allyn and Bacon.

Vlahov, D., Des Jarlais, D., Hollinger, P., Lurie, P., Shriver, M., & Strathdae, S. (2001). Needle exchange programs for the prevention of human immunodeficiency virus infection: Epidemiology and policy, *American Journal of Epidemiology, 154*(12), s70–s77.

Volscho, T. (2010). Sterilization racism: A quantitative study of pan-ethnic and other ethnic disparities in sterilization, sterilization regret, and long-acting contraceptive use. *University of Connecticut*, 1–169.

Voss, L. S. (1997). Teasing, disputing, and playing: Cross-gender interactions and space utilization among first and third graders. *Gender & Society, 11*, 238–256.

Voyles, M. M., Haller, S. M., & Fossum, T. V. (2007). Teacher responses to student gender differences. *ACM SIGCSE Bulletin, 39*(3), 226–230.

Wadden, T. A., et al. (1997). Exercise in the treatment of obesity: Effects of four interventions on body composition, resting energy expenditure, appetite, and mood. *Journal of Clinical and Consulting Psychology, 65*, 269–275.

Wade, L. (2010). The Smurfette Principle. *Sociological images: Inspiring sociological imaginations everywhere*. Retrieved from http://thesocietypages.org/socimages/2010/02/28/lindsay-ellis-on-the-smurfette-principle/

Wahl, E. (1999, October). Acting on what we know. *Women's Education Equity Act (WEEA) Digest*, pp. 12, 10.

Waldfogel, J. (1997). The effects of children on women's wages. *American Sociological Review, 62*, 209–217.

Waldron, I. (1995). Contributions of changing gender differences in behavior and social roles to changing gender differences in mortality. In D. Sabo & D. F. Gordon (Eds.), *Men's health and illness* (pp. 22–45). Thousand Oaks, CA: Sage.

Walker, A., & Parmar, P. (1993). *Warrior marks: Female genital mutilation and the sexual blinding of women*. New York: Harcourt Brace.

Walker, G. S. (2010). The evolution and limits of Title IX doctrine on peer sexual assault. *Harvard Civil Rights—Civil Liberties Law Review, 45*, 95–133.

Wallace, R. A. (1992). *They call her pastor*. Albany: State University of New York Press.

Wallace, S. L., & Allen, M. D. (2008). Survey of African American portrayal in introductory textbooks in American government/politics: A report of the APSA standing committee on the status of Blacks in the profession. PS: *Political Science & Politics*, 153–160.

Wallerstein, J., Lewis, J., & Blakeslee, S. (2000). *The unexpected legacy of divorce*. New York: Hyperion.

Walsh, M. (2009). Sex-bias remedies upheld: High court to hear cases on student search, IDEA. *Education Week, 28*(19), 18–19.

Walzer, S. (1996). Thinking about the baby: Gender and divisions of infant care. *Social Problems, 43*, 219–234.

Wanderlich, S. A., Crosby, R. D., Mitchel, J. E., Roberts, J. A., Haseltine, B., DeMuth, G. & Thompson, K. M. (2000). Relationship of childhood sexual abuse and eating disturbance in children. *Journal of the American Academy of Child and Adolescent Psychiatry, 39*, 1277–1283.

Wang, Y., & Beydoun, M. (2007). The obesity epidemic in the United States: Gender, age, socioeconomic, racial/ethnic, and geographic characteristics: A systematic review and meta-regression analysis. *Epidemiological Reviews, 32*(1) 6–28.

Want, S. C. (2009). Meta-analytic moderators of experimental exposure to media portrayals of women on female appearance satisfaction: Social comparisons as automatic processes. *Body Image, 6,* 257–269.

Ward, E., Halpern, M., Schrag, N., Cokkinides, V., DeSantis, C., Bandi, P., Siegel, R., Stewart, A., & Jemal, A. (2008). Association of insurance with cancer care utilization and outcomes. *A Cancer Journal for Clinicians, 58*(1), 9–31.

Ward, M. C. (1996). *A world full of women.* Boston: Allyn and Bacon.

Ward, M. C., & Edelstein, M. (2006). *A world full of women.* Boston: Allyn and Bacon.

Warner, J. (2006). What girls ought to learn from boys in "crisis." *New York Times.* Retrieved from: http://select.nytimes.com/2006/07/12/opinion/12warner.html?_r=1

Warr, M. (1985). Fear of rape among urban women. *Social Problems, 32,* 238–250.

Warren, M. A. (1985). *Gendercide: The implications of sex selection.* London: Rowman and Allanheld Publishers.

Washington, P. A. (2001). Disclosure patterns of Black female sexual assault survivors. *Violence Against Women, 7,* 1254–1283.

Wasley, P. (2007). U. of Wisconsin settles with vice chancellor. *Chronicle of Higher Education, 53,* 43.

Waters, A. B. (1999). Domestic dangers: Approaches to women's suicide in contemporary Maharashstra, India. *Violence Against Women, 5,* 525–547.

Watkins, S., & Sherk, J. (2008). *Who serves in the U.S. military? The demographics of enlisted troops and officers.* Washington, DC: Heritage Foundation.

Watts, J. H. (2007). Porn, pride and pessimism: Experiences of women working in professional construction roles. *Work, Employment and Society, 21,* 299–316.

Waugh, I. M. (2010). Examining the sexual harassment experiences of Mexican immigrant farm-working women. *Violence Against Women, 16,* 237–261.

Weaver, J. (1992). The social science and psychological research evidence: Perceptual and behavioral consequences of exposure to pornography. In C. Itzen (Ed.), *Pornography: Women, violence, and civil liberties* (pp. 284–309). New York: Oxford University Press.

Weaver, M. J. (1995). *New Catholic women: A contemporary challenge to traditional religious authority.* Bloomington: Indiana University Press.

Webb, J. (2009). Gender and occupation in market economies: Change and restructuring since the 1980s. *Social Politics, 16*(1), 82–110.

Webber, J. (1983). Between law and custom: Women's experience of Judaism. In P. Holden (Ed.), *Women's religious experience: Cross-cultural perspectives* (pp. 143–162). London: Croom Helm.

Websdale, N. (2002). *Policing the poor: From slave plantation to public housing.* Boston: Northeastern University Press.

Wechsberg, W. M., Lam, W. K., et al. (2003). Violence, homelessness, and HIV-risk among crack-using African-American women. *Substance Use and Misuse, 38,* 669–700.

Wechsler, H., & Nelson, T. F. (2001). Binge drinking and American college students: What's five drinks? *Psychology of Addictive Behaviors, 15,* 287–291.

Wechsler, H., Dowdall, G. W., Davenport, A., & Castillo, S. (1995). Correlates of college student binge drinking. *American Journal of Public Health, 85,* 921–926.

Weeden, J., & Sabini, J. (2005). Physical attractiveness and health in western societies: A review. *Psychological Bulletin, 131,* 635–653.

Weidman, J. L. (Ed.) (1984). *Christian feminism.* San Francisco: Harper and Row.

Weidner, G., Kopp, M., & Kristenson, M. (2002). *Heart disease: Environment, stress and gender.* Amsterdam, The Netherlands: IOS Press.

Weinberger, C., & Kuhn, P. (2005). Leadership skills and wages. *Journal of Labor Economics, 23,* 395–436.

Weisman, D. (2010). Women and Judaism: New insights and scholarship. *Nashim: A Journal of Jewish Women's Studies, 20,* 164–166.

Weisner, T. S., Garnier, H., & Loucky, J. (1994). Domestic tasks, gender egalitarian values and children's gender typing in conventional and nonconventional families. *Sex Roles, 30,* 23–54.

Weiss, K. G. (2009). "Boys will be boys" and other gendered accounts: An exploration of victims' excuses and justifications for unwanted sexual contact and coercion. *Violence Against Women, 15,* 7, 810–834.

Weissman, M. M. (1980). Depression. In A. M. Brodsky & R. Hare-Mustin (Eds.), *Women and psychotherapy* (pp. 97–112). New York: Guilford Press.

Weitz, R. (1991). *Life with AIDS.* New Brunswick, NJ: Rutgers University Press.

Weitzman, L. J., Eifler, D., Hokada, E., & Ross, C. (1972). Sex-role socialization in picture books for pre-school children. *American Journal of Sociology, 77,* 1125–1150.

Weitzman, L., & Rizzo, D. (1976). *Images of males and females in elementary school textbooks.* Washington, DC: Resource Center on Sex Roles in Education.

Weitzman, N., Birns, B., & Friend, R. (1985). Traditional and nontraditional mothers' communication with their daughters and sons. *Child Development, 56,* 894–896.

Welch, S. D. (1985). *Communities of resistance and solidarity: A feminist theology of liberation.* Maryknoll, NY: Orbis Books.

Wennards, C., & Wold, A. (1997). Nepotism and sexism in peer review. *Nature, 307,* 341.

Werthheimer, B. M. (1979). "Union is power": Sketches from women's labor history. In J. Freeman (Ed.), *Woman: A feminist perspective* (pp. 339–358). Palo Alto, CA: Mayfield.

Wertz, R. W., & Wertz, D. C. (1986). Notes on the decline of midwives and the rise of medical obstetrics. In P. Conrad & R. Kern (Eds.), *The sociology of health and illness* (pp. 134–146). New York: St. Martin's Press.

West, C., & Zimmerman, D. H. (1987). Doing gender. *Gender & Society, 1,* 135–151.

West, H. C., & Sabol, W. J. (2008). *Prisoners in 2007.* U.S. Department of Justice, Bureau of Justice Statistics. NCJ 224280.

West, M. S., & Curtis, J. W. (2006). Organizing around gender equity. In J. W. Curtis and M. S. West (Eds.), *AAUP Faculty Gender Equity Indicators 2006.* Washington, DC: American Association of University Professors.

Westergren, S. (2004). Gender effects in the court of appeals revisited: The data since 1994. *Georgetown Law Review, 92.*

Weston, K. (1991). *Families we choose: Lesbians, gays, kinship.* New York: Columbia University Press.

Wetzstein, C. (2009). Porn common in college dorms. *Washington Times,* p. 17.

Wharton, A. S. (Ed.) (2006). Symposium: "The missing feminist revolution in sociology" twenty years later: Looking back, looking ahead. *Social Problems, 53,* 443–482.

What you can do about the war in Congo. (2009). *Nation, 288*(4), 8.

Whatley, M. A. (2005). The effect of participant sex, victim dress, and traditional attitudes on causal judgments for marital rape victims. *Journal of Family Violence, 20,* 191–200.

Wheeler, L., Pumfrey, P., Wakefield, P., & Quill, W. (2008). ADHD in schools: prevalence, multi-professional involvements and school training needs in an LEA. *Emotional and Behavioural Difficulties, 13,* 163–177.

Whipp, B. J., & Ward, S. A. (1992). Will women soon outrun men? *Nature, 355,* 25.

Whitaker, A., Johnson, J., Shaffer, D., Rapoport, J. L., Kalikow, K., Walsh, B. T., Davies, M., Braiman, S., & Dolinsky, A. (1990). Common troubles in young people: Prevalence disorders in a nonreferred adolescent population. *Archives of General Psychiatry, 47,* 487–496.

White, A. M. (1999). Talking feminist, talking black: Micromobilization processes in a collective protest against rape. *Gender & Society, 13,* 77–100.

White, J. C., & Dull, V. T. (1998). Room for improvement: Communication between lesbians and primary care providers. *Journal of Lesbian Studies, 2.*

White, M. J., & White, G. B. (2006). Implicit and explicit occupational gender stereotypes. *Sex Roles, 55,* 259–266.

White, P. G., Young, K., & McTeer, W. G. (1995). Sport, masculinity, and the injured body. In D. Sabo & D. F. Gordon (Eds.), *Men's health and illness* (pp. 158–182). Thousand Oaks, CA: Sage.

Whitehead, H. (1981). The bow and the burden strap: A new look at institutionalized homosexuality in Native North America. In S. B. Ortner & H. Whitehead (Eds.), *Sexual meanings* (pp. 31–79). New York: Cambridge University Press.

Whitton, G. (2001). *Review: Masculinities and Men's Health, Agenda, No. 47.* Retrieved from http://www.ngkok.co.za/Artikels/JSvdWatt_DTh_Masculanities.pdf

Who voted: A portrait of American politics, 1976–2000. (2000, November 12). *New York Times,* p. 4WK.

Widom, C. S., & Ames, A. (1988). Biology and female crime. In T. E. Moffitt & S. A. Mednick (Eds.), *Biological contributions to crime causation* (pp. 308–331). Dordrecht: Martinus Nijhoff Publishers.

Widom, C. S., Czaja, S. J., & Dutton, M. A. (2008). Childhood victimization and lifetime revictimization. *Child Abuse & Neglect, 32,* 785–796.

Widom, C. S., & Maxfield, M. C. (2001). *An update on the "cycle of violence."* Washington, DC: U.S. Department of Justice, National Institute of Justice.

Wienke, C., & Hill, G. J. (2009). Does the "marriage benefit" extend to partners in gay and lesbian relationships? Evidence from a random sample of sexually active adults. *Journal of Family Issues, 30*(2), 259–289.

Wikan, U. (1984). Shame and honour: A contestable pair. *Man, 19*, 635–652.

Wilkerson, I. (1991b, January 25). Blacks wary of their big role in military. *New York Times*, pp. A1, A2.

Wilkes, M. (2008). Conscience clauses revisitied. Retrieved from: http://www.fitnews.com/2008/08/19/conscience-clauses-revisited/

Wilkie, J. R. (1993). Changes in U.S. men's attitudes toward the family provider role, 1972–1989. *Gender & Society 7*, 261–279.

Wilkinson, D. L., Magora, A., Garcia, M., & Khurana, A. (2009). Fathering at the margins of society: Reflections from young, minority, crime-involved fathers. *Journal of Family Issues, 30*, 945–967.

Willard, N. (2007). *Cybersafe kids, cyber-savvy teens: Helping young people learn to use the Internet safely and responsibly*. San Francisco: Jossey-Bass.

Willcut, E. G., & Pennington, B. F. (2000). Comoribidity of reading disability and attention-deficit/hyperactivity disorder: Differences by gender and subtype. *Journal of Learning Disabilities, 33*, 179–191.

Willentz, J. A. (1991). Invisible segment of a veterans population: Women veterans, past omissions and current corrections. In M. L. Kendrigan (Ed.), *Gender differences: Their impact on public policy* (pp. 173–188). New York: Greenwood Press.

Williams, B. (1987). Homosexuality: The new Vatican statement. *Theological Studies, 48*, 259–277.

Williams, C. L. (1992). The glass escalator: Hidden advantages for men in the "female" professions. *Social Problems, 39*, 253–267.

Williams, C. L. (1995). *Still a man's world: Men who do women's work*. Berkeley: University of California Press.

Williams, C., Giuffre, P., & Dellinger, K. (2009). The gay-friendly closet. *Sexuality Research & Social Policy, 6*, 29–45.

Williams, J. A., Jr., Vernon, J. A., Williams, M. C., & Malecha, K. (1987). Sex role socialization in picture books: An update. *Social Science Quarterly, 68*, 148–156.

Williams, J. C. (2006). Hitting the maternal wall. *Academe, 90*(6), 16–20.

Williams, J. E., Paton, C. C., Siegler, I. C., Eigenbrodt, M. L., Nieto, F. J., & Tyrolen, H. A. (2000). Anger proneness predicts coronary heart disease risk: Prospective analysis from the Atherosclerosis Risk in Communities (ARIC) study. *Circulation, 101*, 2034–2039.

Williams, L. A. (1988). Toxic exposure in the workplace: Balancing job opportunity with reproductive health. In E. Boneparth & E. Stroper (Eds.), *Women, power and policy: Toward the year 2000* (pp. 113–130). New York: Pergamon.

Williams, M. R., Demuth, S., & Holcomb, J. E. (2007). Understanding the influence of victim gender in death penalty cases: The importance of victim race, sex-related victimization, and jury decision making. *Criminology, 45*, 865–891.

Williams, T., Connolly, J., Pepler, D., & Craig, W. (2005). Peer victimization, social support, and psychosocial adjustment of sexual minority adolescents. *Journal of Youth and Adolescence, 34*, 471–482.

Williams, W. L. (1986). *The spirit and the flesh*. Boston: Beacon.

Williamson, N. E. (1976). *Sons or daughters*. Beverly Hills, CA: Sage.

Willon, P. (2011, October 17). "Don't ask, don't tell" repeal means new challenges. *Los Angeles Times*. Retrieved from: http://articles.latimes.com/2011/oct/17/local/la-me-gay-military-20111017

Wilson, E. (2010). Beyond dualism: Expanded understandings of religion and global justice. *International Studies Quarterly, 54*, 733–754.

Wilson, E., & Ng, S. H. (1988). Sex bias in visual images evoked by generics: A New Zealand study. *Sex Roles, 18*, 159–168.

Wilson, G. (2010). Eating disorders, obesity and addiction. *European Eating Disorders Review, 18*, 341–351.

Wilson, T. D. (2002). Pharonic circumcision under patriarchy and breast augmentation under phallocentric capitalism: Similarities and differences. *Violence Against Women, 8*, 495–521.

Wilson, W. J. (1987). *The truly disadvantaged*. Chicago: University of Chicago Press.

Wilson-Jones, L., & Caston, M. C. (2004). Cooperative learning on academic achievement in elementary African American males. *Journal of Instructional Psychology, 31*(4), 280–283.

Wines, M. (2000, December 28). For all Russia, biological clock is running out. *New York Times*, pp. A1, A10.

Winslow-Bowe, S. (2009). Husband and wives' relative earnings: Exploring variation by race, human capital, labor supply, ad life stage. *Journal of Family Issues, 30*, 1405–1432.

Wise, E., & Rafferty, J. (1982). Sex bias and language. *Sex Roles, 8*, 1189–1196.

Wise, M. (1997, October 29). It's official: Two women are referees. *New York Times*, pp. C1, 2.

Withorn, A. (1986). Helping ourselves. In P. Conrad & R. Kern (Eds.), *The sociology of health and illness* (pp. 416–424). New York: St. Martin's Press.

Witkin, H. A., Mednick, S. A., Schulsinger, F., Bakkestrm, E., Christiansen, K. O., Goodenough, D. R., Hirschhorn, K., Lundsteen, C., Owen, D. R., Philip, J., Rubin, D. B., and Stocking, M. (1976). Criminality in XYY and XXY men. *Science, 193*, 547–555.

Witt, H. (2007). School discipline tougher on African Americans. *Chicago Tribune*. Retrieved from: http://www.chicagotribune.com/services/newspaper/eedition/chi-070924discipline,0,7975055.story

Witt, L., Paget, K. M., & Matthews, G. (1994). *Running as a woman: Gender and power in American politics*. New York: Free Press.

Wolf, N. (1991). *The beauty myth*. New York: William Morrow.

Wolf, R. (2010). Welfare rolls up in '09, more enroll in assistance programs. *USA Today*. Retrieved from: http://www.usatoday.com/news/nation/2010-01-25-welfare-rolls_N.htm

Women in INS custody. (2001, January 19). *Miami Herald*, p. A20.

Women's Heart Foundation. (2010). *Women and heart disease facts*. Retrieved from http://www.womensheart.org/content/HeartDisease/heart_disease_facts.asp

Women's Prison Association. (2009). *Mothers, infants and imprisonment: A national look at prison nurseries and community-based alternatives*. New York: Author. Available http://www.wpaonline.org/pdf/Mothers%20Infants%20and%20Imprisonment%202009.pdf

Women's Sports Foundation. (2011). *27 year study shows progression of women in college athletics*. Retrieved from http://www.womenssportsfoundation.org/Content/Articles/Issues/Participation/123/27%20Year%20Study%20Shows%20Progression%20of%20Women%20in%20College%20Athletics.aspx

Wong, M. S., McElwain, N. L., & Halberstadt, A. G. (2009). Parent, family, and child characteristics: Associations with mother and father-reported emotion socialization practices. *Journal of Family Psychology, 23*(4), 452–463.

Wood, D., Kaplan, R., & McLoyd, V.C. (2007). Low-income African American youth: The role of parents and the school. *Journal of Youth & Adolescence, 36*, 417–427.

Wood, E., Stoltz, J., Zhang, R., Strathdee, S., Montaner, J., & Kerr, T. (2008). Circumstances of first crystal methamphetamine use and initiation of injection drug use among high-risk youth. *Drug and Alcohol Review 27*, 270–276.

Wood, J. C. (1999). *When men are women: Manhood among Gabra nomads of East Africa*. Madison: University of Wisconsin Press.

Wood, S. (2005). *Cardiovascular disease on a global scale: No longer a disease of the rich*. Retrieved from http://www.theheart.org/article/453811.do

Woodruff, T., Carlson, A., Schwartz, J., & Giudice, L. (2008). Proceedings of the summit on environmental challenges to reproductive health and fertility: executive summary, *Fertility and Sterility, 89*(2), 281–300.

Woods, K. C., Buchanan, N. T., & Settles, I. H. (2009). Sexual harassment across the color line: Experiences and outcomes of cross- versus intraracial sexual harassment among Black women. *Cultural Diversity and Ethnic Minority Psychology, 15*(1), 67–76.

Woods, N. F., Dery, G. K., Most, A. (1982). Stressful life events and perimenstrual symptoms. *Journal of Human Stress, 8*(2), 23–31.

Woog, D. (1995). *School's out*. Los Angeles: Alyson Publications.

Wooley, S. C., & Wooley, O. W. (1980). Eating disorders: Obesity and anorexia. In A. M. Brodsky & R. Hare-Mustin (Eds.), *Women and psychotherapy* (pp. 135–158). New York: Guilford Press.

Woollett, A., White, D., & Lyon, L. (1982). Fathers' involvement with their infants: The role of holding. In N. Beail & J. McGuire (Eds.), *Fathers: Psychological perspectives* (pp. 72–91). London: Junction.

Worden, A. P. (1993). The attitudes of women and men in policing: Testing conventional and contemporary wisdom. *Criminology, 31*, 203–237.

Worell, J. (2001). *Encyclopedia of women and gender: Sex similarities and differences and the impact of society on gender*. Elsevier: Amsterdam.

World Bank (2007). *Genderstats*. Retrieved from: http://web.worldbank.org/WBSITE/EXTERNAL/TOPICS/EXTGENDER/EXTANATOOLS/EXTSTATINDDATA/EXTGENDERSTATS/0,contentMDK:21438836~menuPK:4080912~pagePK:64168445~piPK:64168309~theSitePK:3237336,00.html

World Bank. (2009). *Gender in agriculture sourcebook*. Washington, DC: Author. World Christian Database. (2009). Fastest growing religion. Retrieved from: http://fastestgrowingreligion.com/numbers.html

World Factbook, Central Intelligence Agency. (2009). Retrieved from: https://www.cia.gov/library/publications/the-world-factbook/geos/countrytemplate_ct.html

World Health Organization (2011). *Mental health: Gender and women's mental health*. Retrieved from http://www.who.int/mental_health/prevention/genderwomen/en/

World Health Organization. (1960). *Constitution*. Geneva: Palais des Nations.

World Health Organization. (2005). *The world health report 2005: Make every mother and child count*. Geneva, Switzerland: WHO. Retrieved from: www.who.int/whr/2005/whr2005-en.pdf

World Health Organization. (2008). *Female genital mutilation, fact sheet 241*. Geneva, Switzerland: WHO.

World Health Organization. (2011). South Dakota life expectancy: Live longer, live better. Retrieved from: http://www.worldlifeexpectancy.com/usa.south-dakota-life-expectancy

Wragg, P. (2005). *Improving sex and relationships education*. London: Terrence Higgins Trust.

Wright, J. C., Huston, A. C., Truglio, R., Fitch, M., Smith, E. & Piemyat, S. (1995). Occupational portrayals on television: Children's role schemata, career aspirations, and perceptions of reality. *Child Development, 66*, 1706–1718.

Wright, P. C. (1993). Variations in male-female dominance and offspring care in non-human primates. In B. D. Miller (Ed.), *Sex and gender hierarchies* (pp. 127–145). New York: Cambridge University Press.

Wright, R. (1996). The occupational masculinity of computing. In C. Cheng (Ed.), *Masculinities in organizations* (pp. 77–96). Thousand Oaks, CA: Sage.

Wright, R., & Jacobs, J. A. (1995). Male flight from computer work: A new look at occupational resegregation and ghettoization. In J. A. Jacobs (Ed.), *Gender inequality at work* (pp. 334–376). Thousand Oaks, CA: Sage.

Wu, J., & Spohn, C. (2009). Does an offender's age have an effect on sentence length?: A meta-analytic review. *Criminal Justice Policy Review, 20*, 379–341.

Wylie, A. (1991). Gender theory and the archeological record: Why is there no archeology of gender? In J. M. Gero & M. W. Conkey (Eds.), *Engendering archeology* (pp. 31–56). New York: Basil Blackwell.

Wynn, T. (2005). How can nuns survive in America? The new pope may be unable to stem decline in sisterhood. Retrieved from: http://www.msnbc.msn.com/id/7463291/ns/world_news_one_year_later_remembering_pope_john_paul_ii/

Yang, Y., & Lee, L. C. (2009). Sex and race disparities in health: Cohort variations in life course patterns. *Social Forces, 87*, 2093–2124.

Ybarra, M., & Mitchell, K. (2007). Prevalence and frequency of Internet harassment instigation: Implications for adolescent health. *Journal of Adolescent Health, 41*, 189–195.

Ybarra, M., Diener-West, M., & Leaf, P. J. (2007). Examining the overlap in Internet harassment and school bullying: Implications for school intervention. *Journal of Adolescent Health, 41*, S42–S50.

Ybarra, M., Espelage, D. L., & Mitchell, K. J. (2007). The co-occurrence of Internet harassment and unwanted sexual solicitation victimization and perpetration: Associations with psychosocial indicators. *Journal of Adolescent Health, 41*, S31–S41.

Ybarra, M., Mitchell, K., Wolak, J., & Finkelhor, D. (2006). Examining characteristics and associated distress related to Internet harassment: Findings from the Second Youth Internet Safety Survey. *Pediatrics, 118*, 1169–1177.

Yee, S. J. (1992). *Black women abolitionists*. Knoxville: University of Tennessee Press.

Yellin, E. (2004). *Our mothers' war: American women at home and at the front during World War II*. New York: Free Press.

Yescavage, K. (1999). Teaching women a lesson: Sexually aggressive and sexually nonaggressive men's perceptions of acquaintance and date rape. *Violence Against Women, 5*, 796–814.

Yoon, E., Funk, R. S., & Kropf, N. P. (2010). Sexual harassment experiences and their psychological correlates among a diverse sample of college women. *Affilia, 25*, 8–18.

York, E. A. (2008). Gender differences in the college and career aspirations of high school valedictorians. *Journal of Advanced Academics, 19*, 578–600.

Younai, S. (2011). Beautifulfigure. Retrieved from: http://beautifulfigure111.blogsopt.com/2009/01/plastic-surgery-for-african-americans.html

Young, I. (2005). *On female body experience: "Throwing like a girl" and other essays. Studies in Feminist Philosophy*. New York: Oxford University Press.

Yount, K. M. (2005). Women's family power and gender preference in Minya, Egypt. *Journal of Marriage and Family, 67*, 410–428.

Zaeske, S. (2000). Unveiling Esther as a pragmatic radical rhetoric. *Philosophy and Rhetoric, 33*, 193–220.

Zandian, M., Loakimidis, L., Bergh, C., & Sodersten, P. (2007). Cause and treatment of anorexia nervosa. *Physiology and Behavior, 92*, 283–290.

Zappone, K. (1991). *The hope for wholeness.* Mystic, CT: Twenty Third Publications.

Zavella, P. (1987). *Women's work and Chicano families.* Ithaca, NY: Cornell University Press.

Zerbe, K. J. (1993). *The body betrayed: Women, eating disorders, and treatment.* Washington, DC: American Psychiatric Press.

Zerbisias, A. (2008, January 26). Packaging abuse of women as entertainment for adults: Cruel, degrading scenes "normalized" for generation brought up in dot.com world. *Toronto Star*, p. L3.

Zicklin, G. (1992, August). *Re-biologizing sexual orientation: A critique.* Paper presented at the annual meeting of the Society for the Study of Social Problems, Pittsburgh, PA.

Zihlman, A. L. (1993). Sex differences and gender hierarchies among primates: An evolutionary perspective. In B. D. Miller (Ed.), *Sex and gender hierarchies* (pp. 32–56). New York: Cambridge University Press.

Zimbio. (2011). *Hot female news anchors, Zimbio.* Retrieved from http://www.zimbio.com/Hot+Female+News+Anchors

Zimmer, B. (2009). *Hunting the elusive first "Ms.", Visual Theatres.* Retrieved from http://www.visualthesaurus.com/cm/wordroutes/1895/

Zimmer, L. E. (1987). How women reshape the prison guard role. *Gender & Society, 1*, 415–431.

Zimmer, L. E. (1988). Tokenism and women in the workplace: The limits of gender-neutral theory. *Social Problems, 35*, 64–77.

Zimmerman, B., & McNaron, T.A.H. (Eds.) (1996). *The new lesbian studies: Into the twenty-first century.* New York: Feminist Press.

Zimmerman, M. K., & Hill, S. A. (1999). Health care as a gendered system. In J. S. Chafetz (Ed.), *Handbook of the sociology of gender* (pp. 483–518). New York: Kluwer.

Zink, T., Jacobson, C., Regan, S., Fisher, B., & Pabst, S. (2006). Older women's descriptions and understandings of their abusers. *Violence Against Women*, 12(9), 851–865.

Zittleman, K. (2007). Gender perceptions of middle schoolers: The good and the bad. *Middle Grades Research Journal, 2*(2), 65–97.

Zittleman, K., & Sadker, D. (2002). Gender bias in teacher education texts: New (and old) lessons. *Journal of Teacher Education, 53*, 168–180

Zoba, W. M., & Lee, H. (1996, April 8). Ministering women. *Christianity Today*, pp. 14–21.

Zoch, L. M. (1997). *Women as sources: Gender patterns in framing the news.* Paper presented at the annual meeting of the Association for Education in Journalism and Mass Communication, Chicago, IL.

Zoepf, K. (2006, August 29). Women lead and Islamic revival in Syria, testing its secularism. *New York Times*, pp. A1, A10.

Zoepf, K. (2008, May 13). Love on girls' side of the Saudi divide: Separate but accepting. *New York Times*, pp. A1, A12.

Zosuls, K. M., Ruble, D. N., Tamis-LeMonda, C. S., Shrout, P. E., Bornstein, M. H., Greulich, F. K. (2009). The acquisition of gender labels in infancy: Implications for gender-typed play. *Developmental Psychology, 45*, 688–701.

Zucker, K. J., Bradley, S. J., Oliver, G., & Blake, J. (1996). Psychosexual development of women with congenital adrenal hyperplasia. *Hormones and Behavior, 30*, 300–318.

Zuckerman, D. (2005). Breast implants: A woman's choice, but a safe choice? Retrieved from: http://www.foxnews.com/story/0.2933.154086.00.html

Zupan, L. L. (1992). The progress of women correctional officers. In I. L. Moyer (Ed.), *The changing roles of women in the criminal justice system* (pp. 323–343). Prospect Heights, IL: Waveland Press.

Zweig, J. M., & Burt, M. R. (2003). Effects of interactions among community agencies on legal system responses to domestic violence and sexual assault in STOP-funded communities. *Criminal Justice Policy Review, 14*, 249–272.

Zweig, J. M., Schlichter, K. A., & Burt, M. R. (2002). Assisting women victims of violence who experience multiple barriers to service. *Violence Against Women, 8*, 162–180.

NAME INDEX

SUBJECT INDEX

CREDITS